BUSINESS ENVIRONMENT FOR STRATEGIC MANAGEMENT

K. Aswathappa
M.Com., Ph. D.
Dean, Academics
Acharya Institute of Management and Sciences,
Bangalore
Former Director,
Canara Bank School of Management Studies
Bangalore University,
Bangalore

G. Sudarsana Reddy
M.B.A., M.Com., M.F.M., Ph. D.
Professor of Management
Acharya Institute of Management and Sciences,
Bangalore

ISO 9001 : 2015 CERTIFIED

First Edition : 1996
Second Revised and Enlarged Edition : 2007
Edition : 2008
Reprint September : 2008
Edition : 2009 to 2011
Edition : 2013
Edition : 2018
Edition : 2022
Edition : 2025

Published by : Mrs. Meena Pandey
for **HIMALAYA PUBLISHING HOUSE PVT. LTD.,**
"Ramdoot", Dr. Bhalerao Marg, Girgaon, Mumbai - 400 004.
Phone: 022-23860170, 23863863; **Fax:** 022-23877178
E-mail: himpub@bharatmail.co.in; **Website:** www.himpub.com

Branch Offices :

New Delhi : "Pooja Apartments", 4-B, Murari Lal Street, Ansari Road, Darya Ganj, New Delhi - 110 002.
Phone: 011-23270392, 23278631; Fax: 011-23256286

Nagpur : Kundanlal Chandak Industrial Estate, Ghat Road, Nagpur - 440 018.
Mobile: 09325409992, 09325908881

Bengaluru : Plot No. 91-33, 2nd Main Road, Seshadripuram, Behind Nataraja Theatre,
Bengaluru - 560 020. Phone: 080-41138821; Mobile: 09379847017, 09379847005

Hyderabad : No. 3-4-184, Lingampally, Besides Raghavendra Swamy Matham, Kachiguda,
Hyderabad - 500 027. Phone: 040-27560041, 27550139

Chennai : No. 34/44, Motilal Street, T. Nagar, Chennai - 600 017. Mobile: 09380460419

Pune : "Laksha" Apartment, First Floor, No. 527, Mehunpura,
Shaniwarpeth (Near Prabhat Theatre), Pune - 411 030.
Phone: 020-24496323, 24496333; Mobile: 09370579333

Cuttack : Plot No. 5F-755/4, Sector-9, CDA Markat Nagar, Cuttack - 753 014,
Odisha. Mobile: 09338746007

Kolkata : 3, S.M. Bose Road, Near Gate No. 5, Agarpara Railway Station,
North 24 Parganas, West Bengal - 700 109. Mobile: 09674536325

Printed at : Infinity Imaging System, New Delhi. On behalf of HPH.

Preface to the Second Edition

It took quite some time for us before we came out with the second edition of **Business Environment for Strategic Management**. More pressing other engagements have caused the delay. However, the book was made available on the market through several reprints.

We have made several changes in the second edition.

- The following four new chapters have been added:

  Chapter 32 — Business Environment

  Chapter 31 — External Sector

  Chapter 36 — Business Ethics

  Chapter 37 — Corporate Governance
- At the end of each environmental factor is included a section on its analysis and integration in the corporate strategic management.
- **Assignment** – a new feature is added at the end of each chapter. These assignments, if taken up by the students seriously, will help them bridge the gap between what is being practised in the industry and what is being read in the book.
- The book has become richer with new tables, exhibits and additional inputs to the text.
- The book is rich with pedagogic aids such as chapter outline, learning objectives and review questions. Margin notes in each page is a value add to the book.

We thank the esteemed readers for their patronage to the book. We also thank Mr. Niraj Pandey and Mr. Vijay Pandey of Himalaya Publishing House for their constant and sustained interest in the book. Our thanks are due to Mr. Madhu of Sri Siddhi Softtek for his excellent typesetting work.

We welcome readers to offer their comments on the book.

K.Aswathappa
dr_k_aswathappa@yahoo.com

G.Sudarsana Reddy
dr.ssreddy1973@gmail.com

Contents

Chapter 1 **Nature of Business** **1 – 16**

Scope of Business
Characteristics of Contemporary Business
Business Objectives
Critics of Business
Questions
Assignments
References

Chapter 2 **Business Environment** **17 – 28**

Nature of Environment
Analysis of Environment
Benefits of Analysis
Limitations of Analysis
Questions
Assignment
References

Chapter 3 **Meaning and Rationale for Globalisation** **29 – 52**

Nature of Globalisation
Drivers of Globalisation
Players in International Business
Challenges of International Business
Questions
Assignments
References

Chapter 4 **Strategies for Going Global** **53 – 74**

Strategies in Globalisation
Flow of FDI
Assignment
Questions
References

Chapter 5 **From Domestic Market to Global Markets** **75 – 92**

Historical Perspective
Investment Flows
Attracting Foreign Capital
Implications for Indian Industry
Destination India
Assignment
Questions
References

Chapter 6 India, WTO and the Trading Blocks 93 – 116

Basic Principles of WTO
Functions of WTO
GATT and WTO
WTO Structure
The Final Act
Implications for India
Trading Blocks
Analysis of Global Environment
Assignment
Questions
References

Chapter 7 Technological Environment 117 – 146

Main Features of Technology
Impact of Technology
Management of Technology
Status of Technology in India
Analysis of Technological Environment
Assignment
Questions
References

Chapter 8 Political Institutions 147 – 160

Three Political Institutions
Judiciary
Judicial Activism
Assignment
Questions
References

Chapter 9 The Constitution of India 161 – 170

The Preamble
The Fundamental Rights
Directive Principles of State Policy
Time for Change
Assignment
Questions
References

Chapter 10 Rationale and Extent of State Intervention 171 – 182

Reasons for State Intervention
Types of Intervention
Extent of Intervention
Consequences of Controls
Features of a Good Control System
Government-Business Interface–Historical Evolution
Assignment
Questions
References

Chapter 11 End of Government in Business? 183 – 192

Why should the Government Continue its Interventionist Policy?
What Should be the Form of State Intervention?
Analysis of Political Environment
Assignment
Questions
References

Chapter 12 Economic Environment **193 – 212**

Nature of Economic Environment
Economic Factors
Claims and Counter claims
Agenda for the Future
Assignment
Questions
References

Chapter 13 Industrial Policy **213 –224**

Rationale for Industrial Policy
Industrial Policy Resolution, 1948
Industrial Policy, 1956
Industrial Policy, 1991
Assignment
Questions
References

Chapter 14 Industrial Licensing **225 – 230**

Licensing and its Objectives
Legislative Framework for Licensing
Criticisms of Licensing
Assignment
Questions
References

Chapter 15 From the MRTP Act, 1969 to the Competition Act, 2003 **231 – 240**

Objectives of the MRTP Act
Regulation of Trade Practices
Objectives of the Competition Act
Provisions of the Act
Assignment
Questions
References

Chapter 16 From Foreign Exchange Regulation Act, to Foreign Exchange Management Act **241 – 256**

Objectives of the Act
Provisions of the Act
Some Reflections on the Act
Do We Need FERA?
Amendments to the Act
From FERA to FEMA
FEMA, 1999
Questions

Chapter 17 The Companies Act, 1956 **257 – 272**

Evolution of the Company
Meaning and Definition
Classification of Companies
Company Formation
Company Law
Company Law Administration
Observations on the Act
Companies Amendment Bill
Questions
Assignment
References

Chapter 18 Public Sector Enterprises 273 – 300

Definition and Objectives
Evolution of the Public Sector
Growth and Role
Performance
What Needs to be Done?
Reforms in Public Sector Enterprises
Bureau of Public Enterprises
Ownership Pattern of PSUs
Industrial Policy Statement 1991 on Public Sector
Questions
Assignment
References

Chapter 19 Privatisation 301 – 314

History of Privatisation
Nature and Objectives
Privatisation Routes
Record to Date
Disinvestment in India
Arguments Against Privatisation
Ranga Rajan Committee on Privatisation
Disinvestment Commission
Questions
References

Chapter 20 Small Scale Industries 315 – 334

Meaning of SSI Units
Growth of SSIs
Significance of SSIs
The Case for SSIs
Facilities
Problems and Remedials
Small Sector Industrial Policy
Recommendations of the Abid Hussain Committee
SIDBI Survey
Questions
Assignment
References

Chapter 21 Industrial Labour 335 – 350

Extent of Labour
Changes in Labour Force
Trade Union Movement
Industrial Disputes
Wage Policy
Social Security in India
Questions
Assignment
References

Chapter 22 Industrial Sickness 351 – 364

Definition of a Sick Unit
Extent of Sickness
Causes for Sickness
Effect of Sickness
Remedies
Omkar Swami Committee on Sickness
Questions
Assignment

Chapter 23 Exit Policy 365 – 370

Arguments for Exit Policy
Arguments against Exit Policy
National Renewal Fund
Questions
Assignment

Chapter 24 Infrastructure 371 – 390

Growth of Infrastructure
Concluding Remarks
Questions
Assignment

Chapter 25 Development Banks 391 – 404

Operations and Trends
Critical Assessment
Narasimham Committee on FDIs
The Road Ahead
Questions
Assignment
References

Chapter 26 Stock Exchanges 405 – 422

Nature of Stock Exchanges
Functions of Stock Markets
Benefits of Share Markets
Growth of Stock Exchanges
Dealings in Share Markets
Organisation of Stock Markets
The Securities Contracts Act
Positive Features
Negative Features
Reforms
Questions
Assignment
References

Chapter 27 Monetary and Fiscal Policies 423 – 446

Monetary Policy
Money Market
Fiscal Policy
Union Budget 2006-2007
Questions
Assignment
References

Chapter 28 Agriculture 447 – 458

Role of Agriculture
Extent of Farm Output
Problems
Agenda for Action
Questions
Assignment
References

Chapter 29 Balanced Regional Development 459 – 470

Criteria for Backwardness
Causes for Backwardness and Regional Imbalances
The Problem
Measures to Remove Regional Imbalances
Failure of Regional Planning
Suggestions to Remove Regional Imbalances
Questions
Assignment
References

Chapter 30 Price Distribution Controls 471 – 482

Objectives of Price and Distribution Controls
Control of Prices
Public Distribution System
The Essential Commodities Act, 1955
Questions
Assignment
References

Chapter 31 External Sector 483 – 504

Foreign Trade
Trade-in Services
Balance of Payments
Exchange Rate Management
Questions
Assignment
References

Chapter 32 New Economic Policy 505 – 520

Background to the New Policy
The New Policy
The Second Generation Reforms
Analysis of Economic Environment
Questions
Assignment
References

Chapter 33 Cultural Environment 521 – 548

Nature of Culture
Impact of Culture on Business
Business Participation in Cultural Affairs
Questions
Assignments
References

Chapter 34 Social Responsibility of Business 549 – 580

Nature and Models of Social Responsibility
Arguments for Social Responsibility
Arguments Against Social Responsibility
Barriers to Social Responsibility
Social Responsibility Strategies
Social Responsibility Implementation
Limits of Social Responsibility
Common Characteristics
Evolving Idea of Social Responsibility
Indian Scenario
Questions
Assignment
References

Chapter 35 Business and Society 581 – 618

Nature and Models of Social Responsibility
Ecology and Business
Women and Business Opportunities
Child Labour
Consumerism
Rural Development
Projects and People
Physically Handicapped
Fighting AIDS
Questions
Assignment
References

Chapter 36 Business Ethics 619 – 638

Nature of Ethics
Sources of Ethics
Why is Ethics Important?
Are Businessmen Ethical?
Ethical Dilemmas
Managing Ethics
Corporate Culture and Ethical Climate
Improving Ethical Decision Making
Questions
Assignment
References

Chapter 37 Corporate Governance 639 – 654

Nature of Corporate Governance
The Context
Factors Influencing Corporate Governance
Mechanisms of Corporate Governance
The Future
Government Report
Analysis of Social and Cultural Environment
Questions
Assignment
References

Chapter 38 Natural Environment 655 – 664

Nature of Physical Environment
Impact on Business
Analysis of Physical Environment
Questions
Assignment
References

Chapter 39 Integrating Environment and Strategic Management 665 – 679

Integration of Segments
Environmental Analysis Forming Part of Strategic Management
Political Strategy
Questions
References

Index 680 – 691

CHAPTER OUTLINE

What is Business?

- Scope of Business
- Characteristics of Today's Business
- Business Goals
- Critics of Business

LEARNING OBJECTIVES

After reading this Chapter, you should be able to:

1. Understand the nature and scope of business
2. Shortlist characteristics of contemporary business
3. Define vision, mission and goals of business
4. Describe criticisms of business

1 Nature of Business

This is an exciting and challenging time to study business environment. Never before the business environment has been so volatile and dynamic as it is today. Never before the challenges of managing a business successfully as daunting as they are now. Never before there were as many opportunities to strike and prosper as they are seen now. And never before, reading of this book was more appropriate and galvanising than it is now. Welcome to the ever green field of business environment. We will explain to you the nature of business first followed by other perspectives of business environment later.

NATURE OF BUSINESS

Business may be understood as the organised efforts of enterprises to supply consumers with goods and services for a profit.

Businesses vary in size, as measured by the number of employees or by sales volume. Large organisations such as Steel Authority of India Limited (SAIL) and Tata and Iron and Steel Company Limited (TISCO) count their employees in the hundred thousands and their sales revenues in thousands of crores. But most business units in our country are small units-independently owned and managed and employing fewer than twenty employees each.

> Business may be understood as the organised efforts of enterprises to earn profit. Business may be small or big in size, but all of them aim at making profit

Whether a business unit has one or two people working at home, 10 operating in a retail store, 1000 employed in a factory, or 100,000 operating in multiple units spread across the country, all businesses share the same purpose: ***to earn profits***.

The purpose of business goes beyond earning profit. It is an important institution in society. Be it for the supply of goods and services; creation of job opportunities; offer of better quality of life; or contributing to the economic growth of the country and putting it on the global map; the role of business is crucial. Society cannot do without business. It needs no emphasis that business needs society as much.

SCOPE OF BUSINESS

The scope of business is indeed vast. Let us assume that you have decided to buy an automobile. Behind your purchase, there is the supplier of raw materials; there is the manufacturer who converts these raw materials and other inputs into usable vehicles; there is the dealer who makes the vehicles available at places convenient to you; there is the transport agent who assists in moving materials to the manufacturing plant and vehicles from plant to the market; there is the banker to finance various activities; there is the advertising agency which tells you about the vehicles, where and how they can be procured; there is the insurance agent who assumes risks on your behalf; and a host of other activities. Not only an automobile, even a simple item such as a ball pen necessitates a long chain of activities so as to make your purchase possible.

> The scope of business is vast. The various different activities that bring raw materials to the factory and the end product from there to the market constitute business

The multitudinous activities involved in bringing raw materials to the factory and the end product from there to the market constitute a business.In other words, business includes all activities connected with production, trade, banking, insurance, finance, agency, advertising, packaging and numerous other related activities. Business also includes all efforts to comply with legal restrictions and government requirements and discharging obligations to consumers, employees, owners and to other interest groups which have stakes in business directly or indirectly.

What is important and what needs emphasis in the term '*business*' is that all the above activities are being organised and carried on with an important purpose, viz., earn profit by supplying goods and services to consumers to satisfy their felt needs. Thus, people occupy a central place around whom, by whom and for whom business is run. Business is people.

No wonder the principles and practices of managing a business are finding their place in non-business organisations too. Take an NGO, a hospital, or a B-School, you find designations of individuals like Vice-President, executive, and corporate and business practices like TQM and re-engineering being replicated. These and similar other organisations do not claim to work for profit but what all they do, do reflect business functions. They are justified in doing so. Competition among them is so severe, that they need to professionalise their practices if they were to survive and prosper.

CHARACTERISTICS OF CONTEMPORARY BUSINESS

When we describe the characteristics of today is business, we keep in our mind the Indian business. The Indian business has some interesting and unique features such as - transition, competition, opportunities, globalisation, technology and information (See Fig.1.1).

> A typical business person is sandwiteched between the compulsions of the new business environment and of the old parcties of doing business.

Business in Transition: For a long time, business in India was conducted in sheltered markets covering up inefficiencies, low productivity and high cost. Then came 1990s which lifted all protectionist measures. This followed by increased globalisation, changed the scenario altogether. The Indian business leaders find totally a new environment characterised by competition, both from within and from foreign businesses. Those who are competent are able to survive and those who are not are perishing. A typical business leader finds himself sandwiched between the compulsions of the new business environment and of the old practices of doing business. But there is no escape for him-he should shift himself from the left of the following continuum and move to the other end.

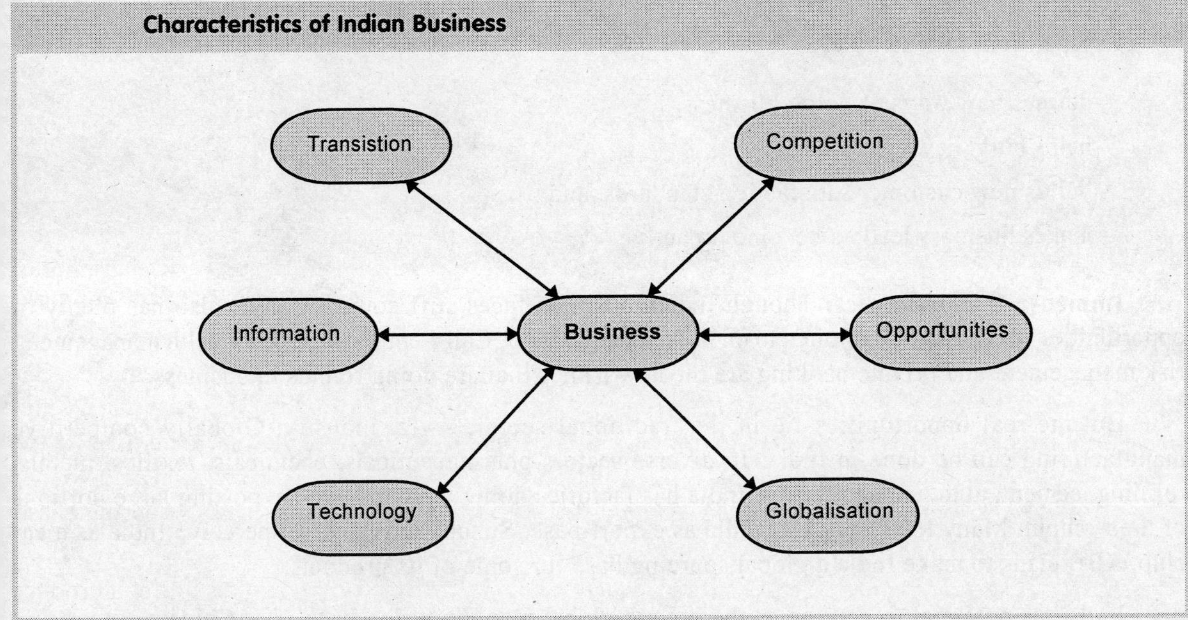

Characteristics of Indian Business

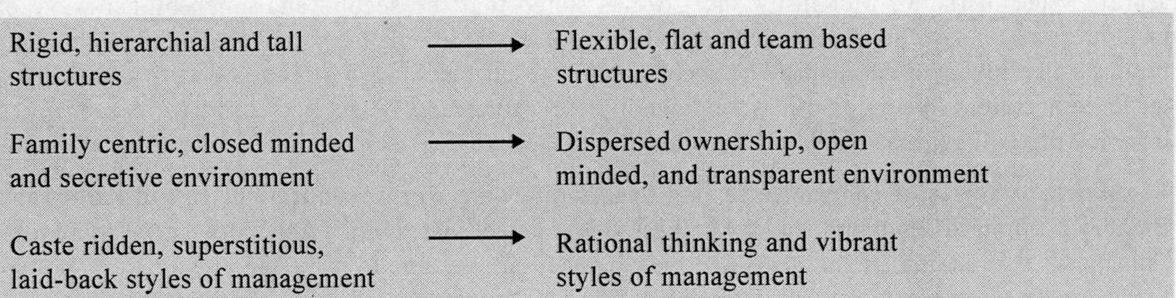

From		To
Rigid, hierarchial and tall structures	⟶	Flexible, flat and team based structures
Family centric, closed minded and secretive environment	⟶	Dispersed ownership, open minded, and transparent environment
Caste ridden, superstitious, laid-back styles of management	⟶	Rational thinking and vibrant styles of management

Pressure of Competition: As stated above, Indian businesses are competing among themselves and are exposed to competition from foreign firms. Competition though unwelcome to managers, is a boon to customers. Look at the experience of buyers and users in India. Recollect the scenario about 20 years back. Businesses enjoyed visual monopoly and this advantage they used to squeeze customers. Scarcities, high prices and low quality were the order of the day. One had to wait for 6 to 7 years to get a phone connection, 3 to 4 years to have a cooking gas connection, 8 to 10 years to get a new two-wheeler released and the list goes on.

The scenario is a contrast today. The customer has a choice. He or she can pick and choose. 'Customer is the king' was a mere slogan earlier. Now it is being practised. For the first time, the officer at the counter of an office of LIC greets you with a smiling face, the clerk in a bank addresses you politely as Sir or Madam, and for your surprise the cashier at the counter of a water supply board greets you politely and for your shock and disbelief, the conductor in a local transport bus is now the embodiment of politeness and cooperation.

Competition benefits the consumer as has been proved in our country. Government of India should have realised this fact longback and instead of enacting numerous consumer legislations in the name of protecting consumer interests could have allowed competition to play its free role.

Not that competition benefits only consumers. If benefits even the rival firms. Competing firms benefit from having strong domestic and foreign rivals.

Competition, for example,

—defines new ways of doing business,

—helps build new capabilities,

—builds new customer satisfaction standards, and

—makes business leaders become proactive.

Competition benefits rival firms by defining new ways of doing business, helping build new capabilities, building new customer satisfaction standards, making business executives become proactive

Immense Opportunities: Though Indian business faces stiff competition, it also has plenty of opportunities which can be exploited to one's advantage. BPO, Call Centres, IT, ITEs, wealth management, risk management and private banking are the new names that are doing rounds in business.

But the real opportunities lie in the traditional sector, - viz. industry. Globally competitive manufacturing can be done in India. In diverse sectors-pharmaceuticals, chemicals, textiles, metals, refining, cement, auto and ancillaries, India has factories doing well and even exporting large portions of their output. Many MNCs look at India as export-base. Suzuki and Huyndai perceive India as a car club. ABB plans to make India a global sourcing base for some of its products.

India has potential to emerge as the second global manufacturing base after China. In its recent report 'Made in India', McKinsey and Co. has stated that the second and much bigger wave of manufacturing outsourcing is yet to come. The first wave was $460 billion and consisted of low technology products like toys and garments. The second wave would reach $1.6 trillion and will include high technology sectors like automotives, engineering and chemicals. When the second wave comes, the beneficiaries will be India or China, or both.

Some examples of companies seizing opportunities are worth recollecting. Toyota Kirloskar's Bidadi's plant, near Bangalore, has the highest yield of steel plates in the Asian operations of Toyota. This means that the Indian engineers and their innovations are able to make more money out of steel than elsewhere in the vast Toyota world. Ford's Sriperambadur plant, near Chennai, is at the top among all Ford's plants worldwide, in terms of production efficiency. The plant now exports engines and panels to South Africa among others. Bajaj Auto's new plant at Chakan is world class. Tata Motor's Indica is perhaps the cheapest new car in world in terms of developmental expenditure. Tata Steel has emerged as one of the lowest-cost manufacturers of steel in the world. Jindal Stainless recently bagged an order to supply coin blanks to Monnaire De Paris - the French national mint. This means that some 7.5 bn Euro coins will use Indian stainless steel.[(1)]

Commodity business is another area where Indian companies are in a stronger position. L.N. Mittal in Steel, Ambanis in polyester, K.M.Brila in viscose fibre, and Bhart Forge in forgings are only some names that come to one's mind while we talk about the commodities stage (see Tables 1.1 and 1.2).

What makes Tatas, Mittal, Birla, Ambanis and the others command such enviable positions? Three reasons explain their commanding positions. *First* the low cost production. *Second* is the confidence these entreprenues love – confidence derived from their increased competitiveness and global outlook. *Third,* countries that were traditionally centres of manufacturing are finding their competitiveness eroded by other low cost countries, and are therefore opting out of the race. In Europe, for example, a number of small auto-component manufactures are selling out and are being taken over by the likes of Bharat Forge.

Globalisation: Going international is yet another trend followed by modern business houses. Political boundaries are no barriers to business. Production facilities are being set-up in different countries and products are being sold through a global network. Gradually, business houses are exposed to global competition which augurs well for consumers.

Commodity Czars

Company	*Product*	*Annual Capacity*	*Rank*
Mittal Steel	Steel	70 million tonnes	1
Birla Viscose	Viscose fibre	251,850 tonnes	1
Basell (Chatterjee/Access)*	Polypropylene	8 million tonnes	1
Reliance Industries	Polyester	1.8 million tonnes	1
Hero Cycles	Cycles	5.2 million units	1
Essel Propack	Laminated Packaging	4 billion units	1
Bharat Forge	Forgings	102,900 tonnes	2
Moser Baer	Optical media storage	2.5 billion units	3
Hero Honda	Two-wheelers	2.6 million units	1
Jubilant Organosys	Pyridine	22,500 tonnes	2
Orchid Chemicals	Cephalosporin	1,100 tonnes	5

*Deal yet to be concluded

(**Source**: *Business Today*, June 5, 2005)

Table 1.2 **Indian Heavyweights**

Tata Steel (after acquisition of Corus)	*World's fifth largest producer of steel*
Hindalco (after takeover of Novelis)	*One of the largest producers of aluminum globally*
UB	*Second largest liquor company in the world*
Hero Honda	*Largest two-wheeler company in the world*
Hero Cycles	*Largest producer of bicycles in the world*
Essel Propack	*World's largest producer of laminated tapes*
Bharat Forge	*World's second largest forging company*
Sundaram Fasteners	*World's third largest manufacturer of fasteners and radio caper*
Tata Tea	*Second largest branded tea portfolio in the world*
Moser Baer	*One of the top 3 optical storage media manufactures in the world*

Infact, internationalisation or globalisation is fast becoming imperative for modern business due to technological innovations; crumbling trade barriers; global flow of capital and technology; information explosion; intensity of market competition; changing life styles and the demand for new products. The success achieved by Japan and other Asian countries has demonstrated that imaginative and supportive economic and trade policies — domestic and external, accent on technological innovation, product design, quality, price, marketing strategy and infrastructure back-up play a vital role in carving a niche in the international business arena. Internationalisation of business is a means of sustaining a strong domestic base in terms of technology, product, market and the capital over a longer period. Globalisation will be discussed in greater detail in subsequent chapters.

> Modern business necessitates globalisation. Technological innovation, crumbling trade barriers, FDI, information explosion, influsing of market competition, changing life styles and demand for new products are the triggers of globalisation

Technology: Business is characterised by increasing use of technology. The impact of technology on business is pervasive. The way production function is organised; the way products are marketed; the way employees are hired and motivated; the way finance function is carried on; and the way managers and subordinates communicate with each other-all are influenced by technology. Because of its significance, we have devoted a full section to discuss the various dimensions of technology.

Information: Another characteristic of contemporary business is the recognition of and the need for information. The whole area of retrieving and extending information, including data processing, information systems analysis and preparation of effective records and reports, has achieved a major status. The complexities of modern business and government requirements have spearheaded this growth. But the vital reason for progress in this area is the availability of the computer and electronic devices that have made feasible the quick and accurate gathering, processing and distributing information. Man is now free from the drudgery of much detailed paperwork. He can further enhance progress by feeding proper information to proper people.

Meanwhile, Information Technology (IT) itself is subject to revolutionary changes. From a handwritten sheet of paper to typing to stencil cutting to photocopying to floppies to cyberspace, the advancement in information technology is commendable. As business gets globalised, online communication across the world would be highly useful. This can be seen in all spheres of human endeavour to succeed.

BUSINESS OBJECTIVES

Before we describe business objectives, it is desirable to be clear about related concepts, viz., vision, mission and objectives.

Vision: A vision is a broad explanation of why the firm exists and where it is trying to lead. The vision provides the point of reference on the horizon-a beacon of light. The vision seeks to answer the following questions:

Where do we go from here?

What changes lie ahead in the business landscape?

What differences will these changes make to the company's present business?

> Vision is a broad and hazy explanation of why the firm exists and where it is trying to march ahead. Vision is a beacon of light.

The vision gives the organisation a sense of purpose and a set of values that unite employees in a common destiny. The most effective vision is the one that inspires, and this inspiration often takes the form of asking for the best, the most or the greatest. It may be the best service, the most rugged product, or the greatest sense of achievement, but it must be inspirational. The vision of Infosys is-

"To be a globally respected corporation that provides best-of-breed business solutions, leveraging technology, vendors and society at large."

Mission: A mission statement outlines the fundamental purpose of the organisation. A vision becomes tangible as a mission statement. If the vision statement answers the question "where do we go from here?", the mission statement answers "What is our business?"

A mission statement typically gives the organisation its own unique identity, business emphasis, and path for development. A mission statement incorporates four elements:

> Mission statement seeks to give a difinite meaning to vision. If vision seeks to answer the question "where do we go from here", mission answers "what business we are in right now?"

1. Customer needs, or **what** is being satisfied.
2. Customer groups, or **who** is being satisfied.
3. The company's activities, technologies, and competencies, or **how** the firm goes about creating and delivering value to customers and satisfying their needs.[2]
4. The company's concern for survival, its philosophy, its self-concept and its concern for public image.

As stated above, mission statements are highly personalised-unique to the organisation for which they are developed. It is, therefore, normal that different firms in the same industry shall have different mission statements. The mission statement of Tata Motors is different from the mission statement of Toyota Kirloskar.

The mission statements of some companies are as follows:

"To achieve our objectives in an environment of fairness, honesty, and courtesy towards our clients, employees, vendors and society at large" (Infosys).

"Ford Motor Company is a world leader in automotive and automotive-related products and services as well as in newer industries, such as aerospace, communications, and financial services. Our mission is to improve continually our products and services to meet our customers' needs, allowing us to prosper as a business and to provide a reasonable return for our stockholders, the owners of our business."

Though mission statements are the hallmarks of successful organisations, not all Indian firms do have them as shown in Table 1.3.

Written Mission Statements

	Present	*Absent*	*Under preparation*
Manufacturing Sector	80%	17%	3%
Services Sector	69%	19%	12%
Infrastructure	50%	33%	17%
Overall	72%	18%	10%

(**Source**: *Business Today*, Feb 22-March 6, 1998).

Objectives

Mission statements are more specific than vision statements, but are not to be taken as concrete directions for action. Objectives render mission statements more concrete. In other words, mission statements seek to make a vision more specific and objectives are attempts to make mission statements more concrete. In short, they are compatible to each other. Objectives, therefore, represent the operational side of an organisation. (Read box 1.1 for a jinxed case of failed objectives and forgotten mission). We focus on objectives here.

It may be stated that a typical business unit seeks to achieve more than one objective and there are always restraints to the attainment of some objectives. Objectives vary with the passage of time. Objectives common to most contemporary businesses are explained here (Also see Fig.1.2).

1. Profit: Making profit is the primary goal of any business enterprise. Profit is the excess of income over expense. Profit is the main incentive, motivator, strong sustainer, judicious allocator of resources, objective indicator of productivity and a solid basis for growth, expansion and survival. Profit enables a businessman to realise his other objectives too.

Not all enterprises are interested in making profits. For example, hospitals, schools, charitable institutions and government agencies are not basically concerned with the acquisition of profits. The non-profit enterprises customarily rely on gifts, endowments, receipts from money raising projects, subsidies or taxes for sustenance. The basic objective of these establishments is the provision of a service which is socially desirable and useful (See also Box 1.2).

Box 1.1 **Failed Objectives and Forgotten Mission**

ET & T was set up in 1974 with a very small capital base of Rs.50 lakh only. This was raised in 1985 to Rs.5 crore, which was also not a very substantial amount in relative terms. The activities were being funded mainly by borrowing from other public-sector undertakings and the Government of India. The number of employees is less than 500.

Objectives and performance

To understand the true nature and large dimensions of ET&T's intended role in India's nascent electronics industry in the past two decades, one must look at its Memorandum of Association, which had spelt out the following objectives among others:

-to import and distribute in India electronic goods in short supply;

-to promote exports of all types of electronic products, and to explore and develop new markets abroad;

-to undertake techno-commercial negotiations with foreign organisations, in order to identify, locate, modify and standardise electronic plant and equipment for use in India;

-to locate proper technical know-how for production and development of electronic goods and infrastructure, and import these from abroad; and

-to promote joint production ventures with foreign enterprises.

The CAG sums up ET&T's performance vis-a-vis these basic purposes (read mission) as follows:

....The corporation has confined itself primarily to trading activities, by importing certain electronic equipment (mainly television picture tubes), selling kits of electronic items like TV sets, and undertaking limited exports of Indian electronic goods....

'Very little was done for achieving objectives like development of the Indian electronics industry through import of technical know-how, techno-commercial negotiations with organisations abroad, joint production ventures, and diversification of exports of Indian electronic goods'.

Figure 1.2 **Business Objectives**

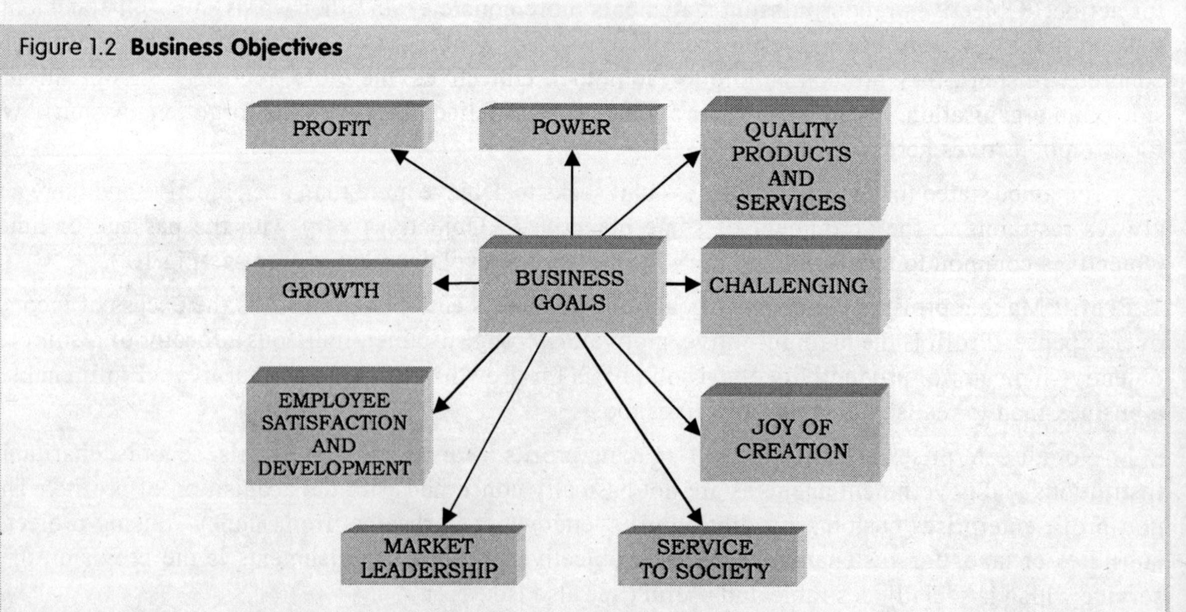

Box 1.2 **Institute of Excellence**

The Indian Institute of Management, Ahmedabad (IIMA), was set up in 1962 to pioneer professional management education in the country. It was set up with the support of the Government of India, the Government of Gujarat and industrialists of the city of Ahmedabad. By 1990 IIMA was widely regarded as one of the foremost institutions of its kind in the Third World. It had trained nearly 19,000 Indian managers, and nearly 4,000 doctoral and MBA students had graduated from it. Its faculty had written some 2,000 Indian management cases, nearly 3,000 technical notes and papers, and 600 books and research monographs. Very early in its history, IIMA decided that it was going to be a school of management, not just of business management. In other words, it was committed to bring professional management not just to the Indian corporate sector but also to such nationally important sectors as agriculture, rural development, health, education, energy, transportation and banking. In the nineties, it was committed to making contributions to such areas of management as strategic sick industries and their rehabilitation, pioneering and innovative entrepreneurship, the globalisation of Indian corporate management and the formulation and implementation of industrial policy. A national poll in 1991 indicated it to be the most highly regarded of all management institutions in India. And it is too well known that IIMA is a non-profit organisation.

In profit-making enterprises, profit should not be the end in itself. Profit should be the beginning — acting as seed money for more products, more plants, more dividends, more tax payments, more jobs and more opportunities. Profits should promote the well-being of all... the rich and the poor; privileged and less privileged; consumers and producers and investors and non-investors. Ignoring this and over-emphasizing profit may bring early death to an enterprise. For instance, wrote George R.Terry, "*promoting only products with high margins (to earn profits), ignoring research, and failing to provide working conditions satisfactory to employees, may in the ultimate, bring about the demise of an enterprise*."[3]

2. Growth: Growth is another primary objective of business. Business should grow in all directions over a period of time. An enterprise which remains stagnant for long is presumed to suffer from an organic defect.

The strategies adopted to achieve growth are:

(a) add more products/markets;

(b) diversify into new areas;

(c) integration—forward or backward;

(d) increase market share;

(e) mergers and acquisitions;

(f) expand markets or

(g) cut down costs and increase productivity.

> Business confers enormous power on owner and endows them with vast resources. Business executives make and unmarke political parties and political leaders.

3. Power: Business houses have vast resources (in the form of money, materials, men and know-how) at its command. These resources confer enormous economic and political power on owners and managers of business ventures. Next to the Prime Minister and Chief Ministers, perhaps, it is the business people who enjoy considerable clout in our country. Some businessmen mince no words in expressing the desire that they want more power. The late Aditya Birla used to assert that he built his empire to get more power.

Several enlightened businessmen have used their power for the good of society. One such illustration in our country was J.N.Tata, who passed away in 1904. He was a pioneer in industry, research, health care, art, literature and in many other areas. His name inspires awe and respect. It is hard to imagine what would have happened to the industrial map of our country if J.N.Tata had not been born in 1839 in a family of Parsi priests in Gujarat. "*He was above all a patriot*", wrote *The Times of India* (April 13, 1912) "*who made no public speeches. To his mind, wealth and the industry which led to wealth, were not ends in themselves, but means to an end, the stimulation of the latent resources of the country and its elevation in the scale of nations.*"

4. Employee Satisfaction and Development: "*If you want to plan for a year, plant corn. If you want to plan for 30 years, plant a tree. But if you want to plan for 100 years, plant men*"-so goes a Chinese proverb. Business is people, said we, in the beginning of this chapter. Caring for employee satisfaction and providing for their development has been one of the objectives of enlightened business enterprises.

Concern for employees continues to be an important aspect of management, contrary to the expectation that human element will lose its significance thanks to automation. In fact, quality of personnel is considered to be one of the hallmarks of best managed and highly respected companies.

The Tatas are a legend in pursuing this objective. Either in implementing labour welfare measures, constituting safety and security measures, or in providing training and development facilities, the name of Tatas should be mentioned first.

5. Quality Products and Services: Providing quality products and services is yet another objective of business. Those who insisted on and persisted in quality survived competition and stayed ahead of others in the market. Persistent quality of products earns brand loyalty, a vital ingredient of success. Hindustan Lever is flourishing mainly because of the quality of its products. Some of its products like Liril, Vim, Lifebuoy, Surf, Rin, Sunlight, Signal, Close-up, Lux, Rexona, Pears and others have become household names throughout the country. These products are accepted by buyers as safe, of high quality and reasonably priced. Behind its quality products, Hindustan Lever has an excellent Research and Development (R&D) set-up and a high degree of professional management. The company is sitting pretty and is almost invincible.

There are other business people who believe in quick money. Quick money comes through short-cuts. These are the people who give us razor blades which fail to give us one smooth and neat shave, bulbs that do not give at least 100 light hours of service, leaky taps and adulterated goods. Such enterprises will not survive for long.

6. Market Leadership: To earn market leadership is yet another objective of business. To earn a niche for oneself in the market, innovation is the key factor. Innovation may be in product, advertising, distribution, finance or in any other field. Blow Plast retains its market leadership by introducing soft luggage bags and totes. Hindustan Lever earned leadership in tooth paste by introducing mouth-washer in its 'Close-up.' Asian Paints adopted unconventional channels for the sale of its paints, which has pushed them ahead of their competitors. Ambani of Reliance Textiles introduced convertible debentures which have become attractive. This and other financial wizardies enabled Reliance to receive unprecedented response from investing public to any of its issues of securities.

7. Challenging: Business offers vast scope and poses formidable challenges. Success in a business venture smacks of the abilities of individuals who own and failure betrays their inability and incompetence. The worth of an individual is tested more in business than in any other profession.

For Ratan Tata running business has been a challenge. Confessed Tata is an interview thus: "I have asked myself this quite often. I don't have monetary ownership in the company in which I work and I am not given to propagating the position I am in. I ask myself why I am doing this and I think it is perhaps the challenge. If I had an ideological choice, I would probably want to do something more for the uplift of the people of India. I have a strong desire not to make money but to see happiness created in a place where there isn't".[4]

8. Joy of Creation: It is through business strategies new ideas and innovations are given a shape and are converted into useful products and services for the benefit of customers. (See Box 1.3)

Box 1.3 **Story of Xerox**

The story of Xerox has an old-fashioned, even a 19th century ring-the lonely inventor in his crude laboratory, the small, family-oriented company, the initial setbacks, the eventual triumph, gloriously vindicating the free-enterprise system.

The story flashes back to 1938 and a second-floor kitchen above in a bar in Astroia, Queens, which was being used as a makeshift laboratory by an obscure 32 year old inventor, named Chester F.Carlson. The son of a barber of Swedish extraction, and a graduate in physics of the California Institute of Technology, Carlson was employed in New York in the patent department of P.R.Mallory and Co. In quest of fame, fortune and independence, Carlson was devoting his spare time, trying to invent an office copying machine, and to help him in this endeavour, he had hired Otto Kornei, a German refugee physicist. The fruit of their experiments was a process by which, on October 22, 1938, after using a good deal of clumsy equipment and producing considerable smoke and starch, they were able to transfer from one piece of paper to another the unheroic message "10-22-38 Astoria." Thus, photocopying was born.

The idea of photocopying was then taken over by one Mr.Joseph C.Wilson of the Haloid Company which was manufacturing photographic papers. Overshadowed by the giant in the field, namely, Eastman Kodak, and dispirited by the Great Depression, Haloid Company was desperately looking for a new product which would bail the firm out of trouble. The idea of photocopying inherited by Carlson was a godsent opportunity to Haloid Company. Not that the company could reap fortunes out of the idea immediately. For several years, sleepless nights were spent and millions of dollars were poured in to further improvise the idea of Carlson. Only in 1950's, the real breakthrough was achieved and from then onwards, it was smiles all the way to the bank for everyone associated with the Haloid Company, which was subsequently named as Xerox Corporation. It was indeed joy of creation for both Carlson, the inventor as well as for Joseph Wilson, the developer. (See **Business Adventures** by John Brooks.)

Although it may be too difficult to list all the products and services that business houses have provided us till now, it is interesting to mention that in the coming two or three decades, the following will receive considerable attention from researchers and business people:

- Readily available artificial human organs, except the brain.
- A means of transportation without an automobile, perhaps an individual flying machine.
- Drugs to cure or prevent cancer and the common cold.
- A personal telephone, no larger than a cigarette pack, that can be used from any location.
- A pocket sized personal/business computer- i.e., a laptop or palm computers.
- Clothing that can be cleaned by placing it in a 'cleaning chamber' for one minute.
- A synthetic material to replace wood.
- A simple injection to determine the sex of an unborn child.

Will there be a greater joy to a businessman coming out with a drug which can cure cancer? Its availability in the market will be of benefit to those who need it.

9. Service to Society: Business is a part of society and has several obligations towards it. Some of them are:

(i) providing safe and quality goods at reasonable prices;
(ii) providing employment;
(iii) patronising cultural and religious activities;
(iv) maintaining and protecting ecology and
(v) supporting less privileged sections of people in society like Scheduled Castes and Scheduled Tribes, the physically handicapped, women and children.

Services of society is the main objective of a non-profit-making enterprise. Profit-making enterprises cannot afford to have service as the primary objective. It will be a secondary objective.

10. Good Corporate Citizenship: Good corporate citizenship implies that the business unit complies with the rules of the land, pays taxes to the government regularly, discharges its obligations to society and cares for its employees and customers. (See Box 1.4)

Box 1.4 **Corporate Citizenship**

Indian industry, for many years, has been doing community-related work such as medical centres, rural development, educational activities and several other areas. But, this is more an exception than the rule.

More recently, efforts have been made by the Indian industry to extend the frontiers of its involvement in such key issues as environment protection, population management, AIDS prevention etc. Gone are the days when industry could merely concern itself with production and profit and industry has realised that 'Corporate Citizenship' is an important character and responsibility, to be fulfilled wholeheartedly, as a current and future responsibility.

In shaping India's future, the integration of the corporate sector into community development in all its aspects is a reality and the managerial expertise of industry will help to build a stronger community at the micro level in a rural area and at the macro level in nation-building.

(***Source***: Issued by the CII on the eve of its National Convention on 26th April, 1993.)

Bending rules of the land, evading tax payments by under-invoicing exports and dubious tax-planning; cornering licences at the cost of others; adulteration of quality products; and indulging in other unethical practices may earn money. But such practices hardly speak highly of corporate citizenship. The Tatas are a contrast to the general trend. Unethical practices are anathema to the Tatas. The best way to substantiate this claim is to quote J.R.D. Tata. "*This factor has also worked against our growth. What would have happened if our philosophy was like that of some other companies which do not stop at any means to attain their ends. I have often thought of that and I have come to the conclusion that if we were like these other groups, we would be twice as big as we are today. What we have sacrificed is a 100 per cent growth.*"[5]

Strategies help realise vision and mission of business. Strategy seeks to answer 'how' of every dimenision

Crafting a Strategy

Till now we have described vision, mission and objectives which every business will define and formulate with great care. But these are mere statements on paper. To translate these into action, business needs to craft strategies. Strategies represent management's answers to **how** to achieve objectives and **how** to pursue the organisation's mission and vision. Strategy making is all about **how**-how to achieve performance targets, how to outcompete rivals and how to achieve sustainable competitive advantage. A strategy is needed for the company as a whole, for each business the company is in, and for each functional area of each business.

CRITICS OF BUSINESS

The discussion till now has reflected the positive side of business. There is also the negative side to it and the critics are not lagging behind in pointing out the shortcomings. The criticisms are many, but all are based on one idea, viz., people in business place profits before enduring values such as honesty, truth, justice, love, devoutness, aesthetic merit and respect for nature. Specific criticisms are the following:

1. Business activity has a corrosive effect on a range of cherished cultural values.
2. Business dehumanises and exploits workers.
3. Business harms interests of consumers.
4. Business degrades nature and the environment.
5. Business has destroyed handicraft and rendered artisans jobless.
6. Business causes scams and scandals.
7. Business multiplies needs and makes people greedy and avaricious.
8. Business leaders bend rules, cut corners, bribe officials and challenge existing authority.

Is business that bad? Has not business benefited society? Has it not built factories, provided jobs, saved lives and invented new things to the needy? Has not business promoted positive cultural values such as imagination, innovation, organised co-operation, hard work and orderly life? Has business not improved the standard of living of people? Has it not lifted millions of people from poverty, ignorance, squalor and disease? Has business not brought the entire globe closer? Answers to all these and other questions are on the affirmative.

Business is being criticised for several reasons such as – dehumanisation and exploitation of workers, denting cultural fabric of a society, scams and scandals, degradation of natural environment and the like.

A wide range of critics differ in the nature of their attacks and their prescriptions to eliminate perceived ills. For our purpose, there are five groups of critics.[6] (see Fig 1.3).

Figure 1.3 **Business Critics**

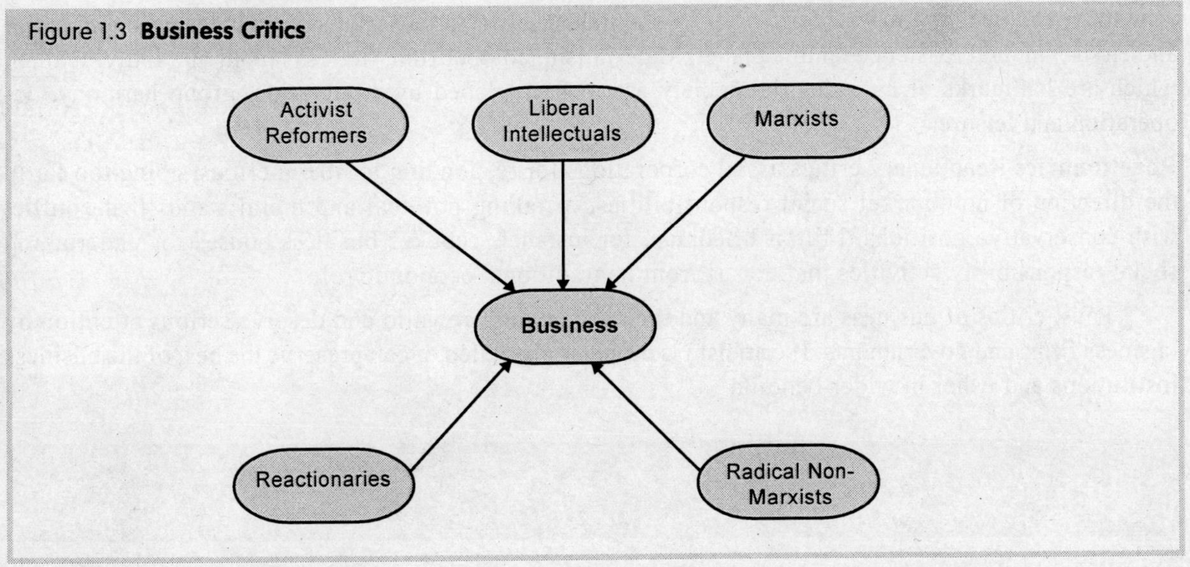

Activist Reformers This group comprises individuals and groups who accept and respect the basic legitimacy of the business system, but find flaws and try to rectify them. The philosophy of the activist reformer is exemplified by consumer Gandhi-Ralph Nader, who accepts American capitalism in its democratic setting but sees an imbalance of power between the people and the plutocracy. For 30 years, Nader has worked to redress this imbalance by building an organisation of public interest groups through which he and his followers pressure business houses and the government to accomplish reforms.

Activist reformers use a variety of tactics to make business houses follow fair business practices. Common tactics include negotiation, letter writing, speeches, lobbying legislatures and regulatory agencies, research and editorial writing. Labour unions frequently picket companies.

Liberal Intellectuals This group is comprised of thinkers who share a broad approach to social problems which they express with their pen rather than with the sword of criticism. This group believes that *(i)* human rights should be protected and enhanced, *(ii)* there is need to restrict corporate power, *(iii)* social arrangements can be improved through reforms, and *(iv)* government should be used to correct problems in society. Liberal intellectuals have a basic faith in democratic capitalism, but they find blemishes and suggest remedies consonant with their ideology. The writings of intellectuals with these broad beliefs have, over the years, been a source of great insight and timely ideas for reform.

Several great thinkers belong to the liberal intellectuals group. Galbraith, for instance, has written numerous books over 40 years advocating greater government control of business to reverse the loss of consumer sovereignty that results from the growth of large corporations. Similarly, in his 1956 book, *The Organisation Man*, sociologist, William H.Whyte, Jr., argued that big organisations produced undesirable conformity in employees.

Marxists These critics reject current institutional structures and demand replacement with a collective state. Unlike reform-oriented critics, this group believes that the faults of capitalism cannot be ameliorated through gradual reforms. Basic institutions such as free market and private capital must be swept away.

Inspired by their intellectual progenitor, Karl Marx, these critics held sway over the world for a long time. But today, their influence is waning. The overthrow of Marxist governments in Eastern Europe in 1989 and 1990 and the deteriorated economies of the former Soviet republics have blunted the appeal of their critique. Though the movement is moribund, to dismiss it now might be premature.

Radical Non-Marxists The great economist E.F.Schumacher, who wrote *Small is Beautiful*, is one of the radical non-marxist critics. Schumacher believes in restructuring the economy by limiting or ending growth. The radical non-marxist critics argue that industrialisation is seriously endangering stable social and environmental existence on this planet. Materialism, competition, tireless labour and individualism which are hallmarks of an industrial society are to be replaced by moderation, group harmony, co-operation and leisure.

Reactionaries Reactionary critics assail corporations for responding to liberal critics, going too far in the direction of non-market social responsibilities, or taking political and moral stands that conflict with conservative positions. Milton Friedman, for instance, rebukes business houses for undertaking social responsibility activities that depart from its traditional economic role.

Thus, critics of business are many and their arguments are valid and deserve serious attention by business firms and governments. If criticism is properly chanelled, it can preserve the best of the business institutions and usher in wider benefits.

QUESTIONS

1. What is business? How does business of today differ from that of four to five decades ago?
2. What are business objectives?

3. "Profit making is the primary goal of any business enterprise." Yes or no—discuss.
4. What do you understand by Vision, Mission and Objectives? How are they interrelated? Illustrate your answer.
5. Why are business houses criticised?

ASSIGNMENTS

1. Divide the class into two batches - one to argue in favour of business and the other against it. Arguments (for and against) shall take place in the class.
2. Study any family owned firm. Describe how it has transformed itself from traditional orientation to contemporary one.
3. Study the vision and mission statements of atleast five companies. Which according to you is the best? Why?

REFERENCES

1. *The Economic Times,* Nov 5, 2004.
2. Arthur A. Thompson and A.J.Strickland, *Strategic Management,* Tata McGraw-Hill, 2003, p.34.
3. George R.Terry, *Principles of Management*, p.100.
4. Gita Piramal, *Business Maharajas*, New Delhi, Viking, 1996, p.372.
5. R.M.Lala, *Creation of Wealth*, p.194.
6. George A.Stenier and John F.Steiner, *Business, Government and Society*, McGraw-Hill, 2000, pp.85-86.

CHAPTER OUTLINE

Nature of Environment
Analysis of Environment
Benefits of Analysis
Limitations of Analysis

LEARNING OBJECTIVES

After reading this Chapter, you should be able to:

1. Understand the nature of environment
2. Describe the stages in environmental analysis
3. List the benefits and limitation of analysis

2 Business Environment

The last chapter focused on the nature of business. This chapter deals with the nature of environment.

NATURE OF ENVIRONMENT

Environment refers to all external forces which have a bearing on the functioning of business. These forces are almost "givens" within which firms and their managements must operate in a specific country and they vary from country to country, increasing globalisation notwithstanding.

The environmental forces include political-legal, global, economic, technological, cultural and physical. Together, these forces make up the 'macroenvironment' of business. Not all these forces impact a firm simultaneously and with same intensity. Strictly speaking, a firm's macroenvironment includes all **relevant** factors and influences outside the company's gates; by relevant, we mean important enough to have a bearing on the decisions the company ultimately makes about its direction, objectives, strategy, and business model.

> Environment refers to all external forces that influence business. These factors are "givers" within which firms must operate.

Environment also includes certain internal factors such as suppliers, rival firms, buyers, new entrants, substitute products and the like. Popularly called the **internal environment**, these forces determine the company's resources strengths and weaknesses; the way the present strategy is working; competitiveness of the company's prices and costs; and what managerial interventions are needed.[1]

Fig.2.1 outlines the macro and microenvironments of business. A brief description of each factor follows.

The outer ring in the Fig.2.1 contains external forces: political-legal, economic, technological, global, social-cultural and natural.

Technological environment exercises considerable influence on business. Technology is understood as the systematic application of scientific or other organised knowledge to practical tasks. It is through

Figure 2.1 **Environment of a Firm**

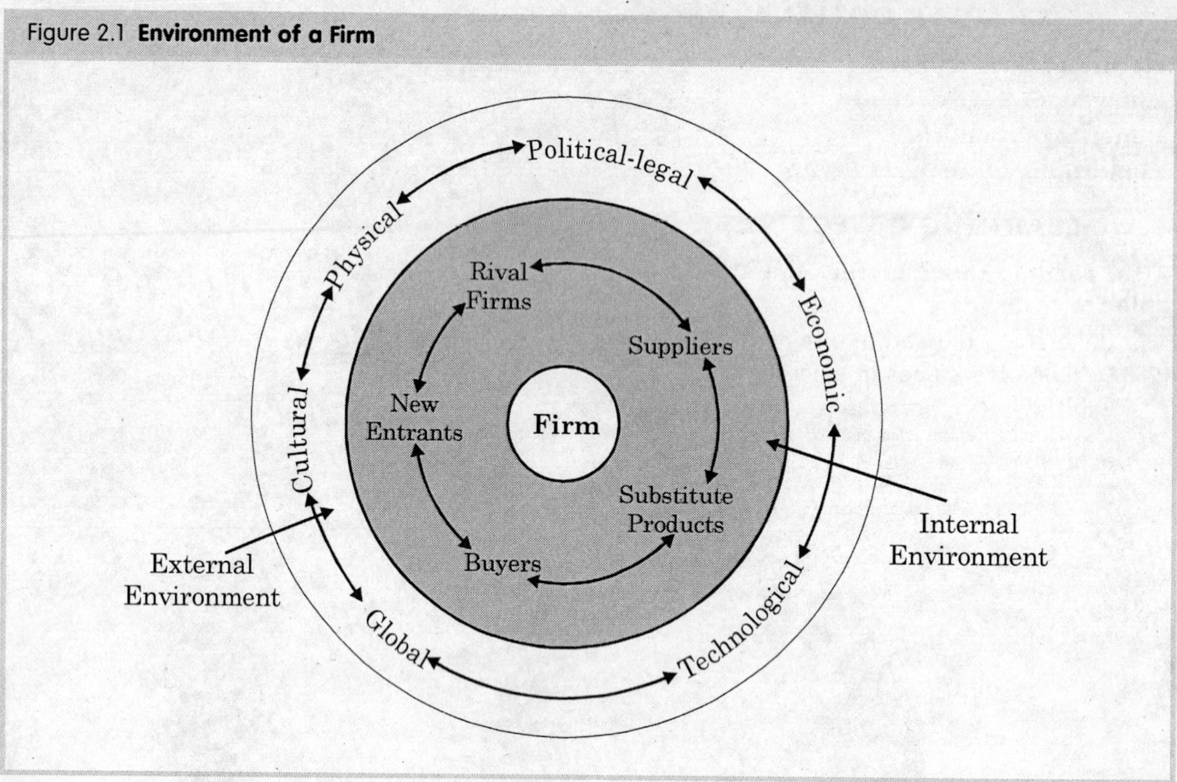

business that technology reaches people. Technology changes fast and to keep pace with it, businessmen should be ever alert to adopt changed technology in their businesses.

Economic environment refers to all forces which have an economic impact on business. Industrial production, agriculture, planning, basic economic philosophy, infrastructure, national income, per capita income, money supply, price level, population, savings, stages in the economic development and trade cycles are major factors which make up the total economic environment. There is close relationship between business and its economic environment. Business obtains all its needed inputs from the economic environment and it absorbs the output of business units.

Political environment refers to the influence exerted by the three political institutions, *viz.*, legislature, executive and the judiciary in shaping, directing, developing and controlling business activities. The legislature decides on a particular course of action; the executive, also called the government, implements whatever was decided by the Parliament and the judiciary functions as the watchdog in order to ensure that both the legislature and the executive function in public interest and within the boundaries of the Constitution. A stable and dynamic political environment is indispensable for business growth.

Notwithstanding spectacular advancements made in science and technology, man's attempt to conquer nature has not met with total success. He has no answer, for example, for the flourishing affluence co-existing with stark poverty; severe droughts and devastating floods occurring in sickening regularity; and some other such phenomena. Man still finds himself helpless before mighty nature. Business, an economic pursuit of man, continues to be dictated by nature. To what extent business depends on nature and what is the relationship between the two constitutes an interesting study.

Yet another environmental factor which is fast emerging as the force to reckon with is the global or international environment. Thanks to liberalisation, Indian companies are forced to view business issues from a global perspective. Business responses and managerial practices must be fine-tuned to survive in the global environment. A manager must understand that safe and protected markets are no more there; that the world is becoming small in size thanks to advanced means of transport and communication facilities; that learning of foreign languages is a necessity; that acquiring familiarity with strange and changing currencies is a must; that facing political and legal uncertainties is inevitable; and that adapting their products to different customer needs and tastes would only help companies survive amidst intense competition. Implications of the global environment are elaborated later in one of the subsequent sections.

Social and cultural environment refers to the influence exercised by certain factors which are beyond the company's gate. Such factors include people's attitude to work and wealth; role of family, marriage, religion and education; ethical issues and social responsiveness of business. Social and cultural environment is highly relevant for a business unit as the variety of goods it produces, the type of employees it gets and its obligation to society depend on the cultural milieu in which the firm operates.

Table 2.1 contains important variables of each environmental factor.

An analysis of these environmental forces helps a manager answer the following questions:

- What are the dominant economic features of the industry in which his company operates?
- What kinds of competitive forces are other managers facing, and how strong is each force?
- What forces are driving changes in the industry, and what impact will these changes have on competitive intensity and industry profitability?
- What market positions do industry rivals occupy-who is strongly positioned and who is not?
- What strategic moves are rivals likely to make next?
- What are the key factors for future competitive success?
- Does the outlook for the industry present the company with sufficiently attractive prospects for profitability?

Obviously, any manager needs clear answers for all these questions if he were to be successful in his business.

The inner ring comprises factors internal to the business. The internal factors determine the competitive strength of the firm. The five forces framework, as proposed by Michael Porter, is highly useful to analyse the competitive strength of the company (see Fig.2.2).

> The five forces framework of Porter is useful to analyse the competitive strength of a firm.

Competitive rivalry: The strongest of the five forces is the rivalry among competing sellers which reflects the market maneuvering and jockeying for buyer patronage that goes on among rival sellers of a product or service.[2] Several factors affect competitive rivalry.

(i) The extent to which competitors are **imbalanced.** Competition becomes intense when rivals are more or less of equal size and strength. When there is imbalance, dominant player will pull all the strings to gain market share. Obviously, rivalry is less intense.

(ii) Market **growth rates** may affect rivalry. Where the market is growing, every player will get a share. There may not be need for maneuring or jockeying for market share. Competition may not be intense. Competition becomes severe under conditions of stagnant growth or matured market conditions. Under the circumstances, what one firm gains will be loss for another resulting in severe fight and rivalry.[3]

(iii) Where there are **high exit barriers** to an industry, there is again likely to be the persistence of excess capacity and, obviously, increased competition. Exit barriers might be high for a variety of reasons. For example, high investment in fixed costs or high redundancy costs.

(iv) Rivalry becomes more volatile and unpredictable as the **diversity of rivals** increases in terms of visions, strategic intents, objectives, strategies, resources, and countries of origin.

Entry threats: The second among the five forces competitive analysis is the threat of new entries. Entry threats may be stronger or weaker. Threats become stronger when:

Table 2.1 **Environmental Factors and their Features**

Global Environment	*Technological Environment*	*Economic Environment*	*Political Environment*	*Social-Cultural Environment*	*Natural Environment*
• Increasing opportunity as world has become one market • Improving quality • Competition from MNCs • Capital and technology transfers • Deciding which markets to enter and how to enter • Adjusting the management process • India and WTO	• Technology reaches people through business • Increased productivity • Need to spend on R&D • Fast changing technology • Rise and decline of products and organisations • High expectations of consumers • Problem of technostructure • System complexity • Increased regulation and stiff opposition • Demand for capital • Social change	• Growth strategy • Economic system • Industry • Agriculture • Infrastructure • Money and capital markets • Per capita and national income • Population • New Economic policy	• Role of legislature • Role of executive • Role of judiciary • Constitution of India • New direction for government's role	• Culture creates people • Culture and globalisation • Culture determines goods and services • People's attitude to business and work • Caste system • Spirit of collectivism and individualisation • Education • Family and marriage • Authority • Scientific spirit • Ethics in business • Social responsibility • Social audit • Corporate governance	• Manufacturing depends on physical inputs • Mining and drilling depend on natural deposits • Agriculture depends on Nature • Trade between two regions depends on geographical factors. • Transport and communication depend on geographical factors

Figure 2.2 **The Five Forces Framework**

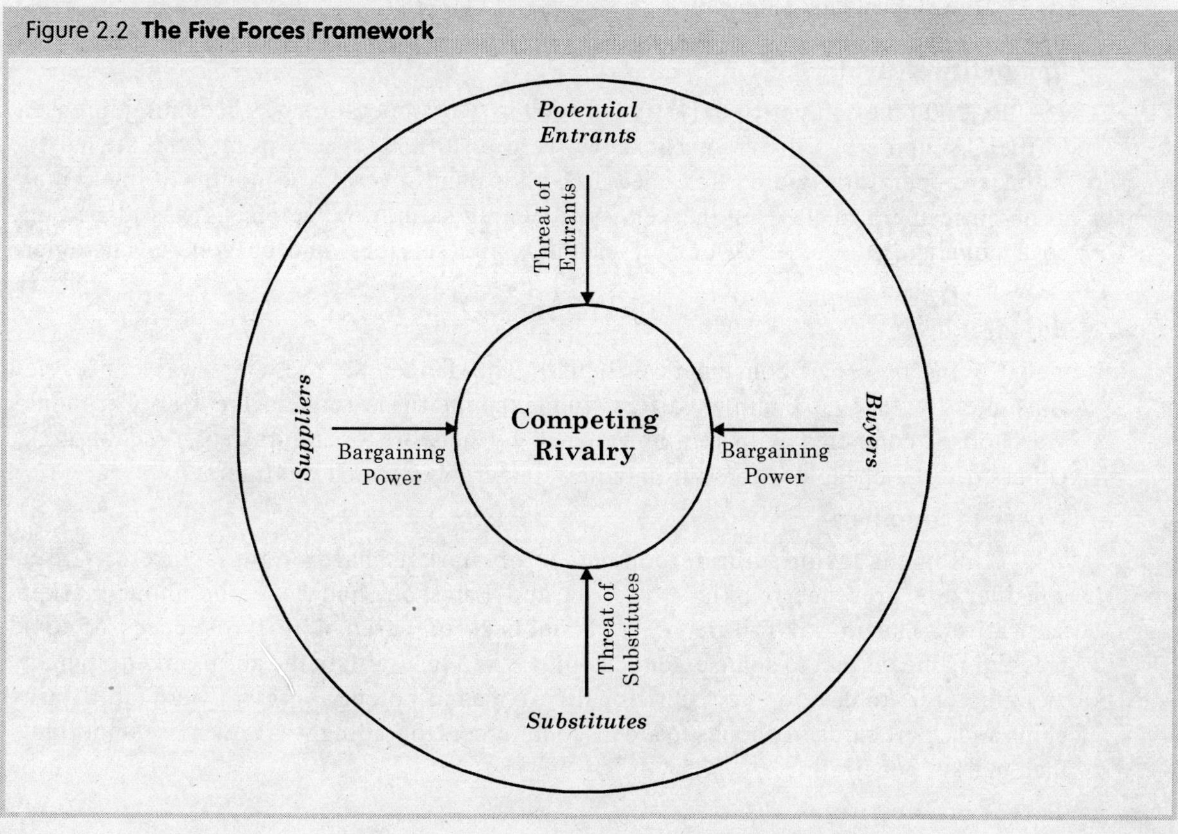

(a) The pool of entry candidates is large and some of the candidates have resources that would make them formidable market contenders.

(b) Entry barriers are low or can be readily hurdled by the likely entry candidates.

(c) When existing industry captains are looking to expand their market reach by entering product segments or geographic areas when they currently do not have a presence.

(d) Newcomers can expect to earn attractive profits.

(e) Industry captains are unable (or unwilling) to strongly contest the entry of new comers.

Entry barriers are weaker when:

(a) The pool of entrants is small.

(b) Entry barriers are high.

(c) Existing competitors are struggling to earn healthy profits.

(d) The industry's outlook is risky or uncertain.

(e) Buyer demand is growing slowly or is stagnant.

(f) Industry captains strongly contest the efforts of new entrants to gain a market foothold.

What are the barriers to new entrants in the first place? Several obstacles present themselves. For example, economies of scale, capital requirement of entry, access to distribution channels, experience, expected retaliation by existing players and government policies are the major barriers (See Exhibit 2.1 for a typical example of an industry and its five forces).

Box 2.1 **The Mobile Phone Industry**

Competitive Rivalry

By 2000 the competitive rivalry between network operators was becoming intense. In the UK numerous different packages were on offer. If a customer threatened to withdraw, operators would offer a new free phone and several free months of line rental as an enticement to stay. In markets approaching saturation, emphasis was placed on cost, coverage, the offering of new products and services, and on general customer services.

Buying Power

Buying power of consumers was high. The danger for providers was confusing consumers with over-complex offers. Independent firms (e.g. in the UK, Carphone Warehouse) competed with retailers owned by network operators (e.g. Vodaphone). Others offered cheapter deals through newspaper adverts and the Internet.

Power of Suppliers

Equipment manufacturers competed for market share. Manufacturers with a considerable presence, Nokia, Motorola and Ericsson, had concerns about market saturation. The initial failure of WAP phones compared with the success of text messaging meant that to some extent customers had lost faith in the ability of equipment manufacturers to develop new functionality. Areas of potential growth were multi-task chips and smart cards in phones to aid m-commerce. Upgrading was now more important than market penetration.

Threat of Substitutes

In the 1990s the main threat of substitution was 'technological regression' where customers returned to fixed line telephony because of high mobile call charges. By 2000, price decreases and the 'need' for everyone to have a mobile phone reduced this threat. More threatening was the convergence of mobile telephony with PDAs (personal digital asssitants) and with the Internet. This was threatening because of the difficulty in predicting how these new technologies would be accepted in the market. The other threat was location technology in mobile phones, making you easy to find. An opportunity for marketers, in emergencies and personal safety if lost, but bringing big brother cons as well.

Threat of Entrants

The threat of entrants was low because of the enormous cost in both licences (£ 22 billion in the UK alone) and in the general investment needed to be a player in new 3G (broadband) technology. Power was a function of who was ahead of the game in 3G. Future power struggles were likely to be a function of deregulation, upgrading and the uptake of new functionality.

(**Source**: Gerry Johnson and Kevan Scholes, *Exploring Strategy*, Pearson, 2002, P. 154)

Threat of Substitutes: Substitution reduces demand for a particular **class** of products as customers switch to the alternatives. Newspapers, for example, are feeling the threat of the general public turning to cable news channels for late-breaking news and using Internet sources to get information about sports results, stock prices and job opportunities.

Substitution tends to take different forms:

Product to product substitution: This is a head on substitute, as for example, e-mail substituting for a postal service and computers annihilating manual typewriters.

Substitution of need by a new product: This is exemplified by the more reliable and cheaper domestic appliances reducing the need for maintenance and repair services.

Genetic substitution: This occurs when products and services compete for disposal income, as for example, furniture manufacturers competing for household expenditure with suppliers of videos, cookers, cars and holidays.

How strong is the threat of substitutes depends on atleast three factors: (i) whether substitutes are readily available and attractively priced; (ii) whether buyers view the substitutes as being comparable or better in terms of quality, performance, and other relevant attributes, and (iii) how much it costs end users to switch to substitute.[4]

Power of buyers and suppliers: The power of buyers and suppliers can be combined as the two are linked. The relationship with buyers and sellers can have similar effects on the strategic freedom of a firm and influencing its margins.

Buyer power tends to be high under the following conditions:[5]

- There is a concentration of buyers, particularly when their volumes of purchases are high.
- The supplying industry comprises a large number of small operators.
- The component or material cost is a high percentage of total cost, since buyers will be likely to "shop around" to get the best price and therefore 'squeeze' suppliers.
- The cost of switching a supplier is lower, involves little risk, as for example, no long-term contracts exist or supplier approval requirements are not required.
- There is a threat of backward integration by the buyer (e.g., by acquiring supplier) if satisfactory prices or quality from suppliers cannot be obtained.

Supplier power tends to be stronger when:

- There is a concentration of suppliers or when there exist cartels.
- The 'switching costs' from one supplier to another are high, as for example in aerospace industry, where manufacturers' production processes depend on suppliers' products.
- The supplier's brand is powerful for example, a retailer cannot do without a particular brand.
- There is the possibility of the supplier integrating forwards if it does not obtain the prices, and hence the margins, it seeks.
- The suppliers' customers are highly fragmented.

It is not that companies are mere pawns sandwiched between buyers and suppliers. They play their games to balance the power between suppliers and buyers. For example -

- Many manufacturers, faced with competitive demands for lower prices and hence the need to reduce costs, have reduced the number of suppliers of components. The remaining suppliers gained in volume orders but have had to prove themselves against strict terms like price, quality and delivery.
- In the light of this trend, some suppliers might attempt to seek out market segments with less powerful buyers or to differentiate products so that buyers become more dependent on that product.
- A growing trend is to view the supplier/buyer relationship as a collaborative-one of mutual interest-effort. This collaboration is often described as **co-production** since the buyer increasingly takes on activities previously undertaken by the supplier.

We have examined each of the five forces of competitive strength. What would happen when combined strength of all the five forces is strong? The answer is obvious. Strong combined strength will reduce margins of businessmen considerably, even exiting some companies. But a business can be competitively unattractive without all five competitive forces being strong. Intense competitive pressures from just two or three of the five forces may suffice to destroy the conditions for good profitability and prompt some firms to exit the business. The manufacture of disk drives, for example, is brutally competitive. UBM recently announced the sale of its disk drive business to Hitachi, incurring a loss of over $2 billion on its exit from the business.[6]

ANALYSIS OF ENVIRONMENT

As Fig.2.1 shows, a firm's environment comprises both inner ring and outer ring. The outer ring consists of macro-factors and the micro-factors constitute internal environment of the company. Now, the manager needs to understand the environment (internal and external) so that he or she is in a position to formulate appropriate strategies that would help his or her company gain competitive advantage.

Understanding of one's environment involves at least four steps as shown in Fig.2.3.

Figure 2.3 **Steps in Environmental Analysis**

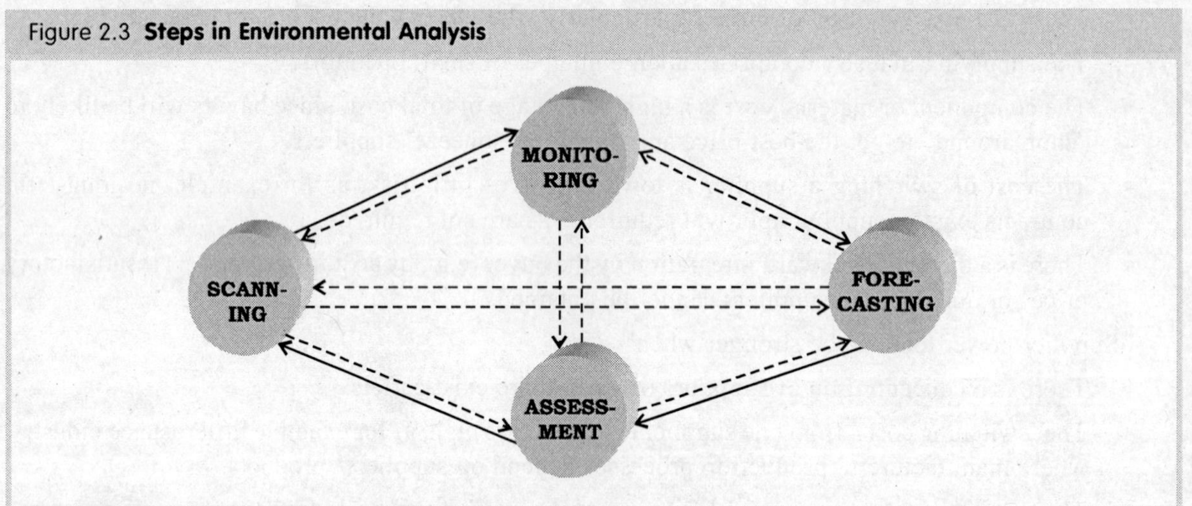

Scanning is general surveillance of all environment forces

Scanning - Being the first step in the process of environmental analysis, scanning involves general surveillance of all environmental factors and their interactions in order to (a) identify early signals of possible environmental change, and (b) detect environmental change already under way. The data collected are often vague and imprecise.

Scanning is ill-structured and ambiguous environmental analysis activity. The potentially relevant data for scanning are unlimited but are scattered, vague, and imprecise. The fundamental challenge for analysis in scanning is, therefore, to make sense out of vague, ambiguous, and unconnected data.

Monitoring refers to tracking of envrionmental trends, events or streams of activities

Monitoring - Monitoring involves tracking the environmental trends, sequences of events, or streams of ctivities. It frequently involves following signals or indicators unearthed during environmental scanning. The purpose of monitoring is to assemble sufficient data to discern whether certain trends and patterns are emerging. Thus, as monitoring progresses, the data turn frequently from imprecise to precise.

Three outcomes emerge out of monitoring: (a) a specific description of environmental trends and patterns to be forecast; (b) the identification of trends for further monitoring, and (c) the identification of areas for further scanning. These outputs (particularly the first) become inputs for forecasting. They will also cause for further scanning and monitoring.

Forecasting - Scanning and monitoring provide a picture of what has already taken place and what is happening. Strategic decision-making, however, requires a future orientation. Naturally, forecasting is an essential element in environmental analysis.

Forecasting is concerned with developing plansible projectors of the environment change

Forecasting is concerned with developing plausible projections of the direction, scope, and intensity of environmental change. It tries layout the evolutionary path of anticipated change. For example, how long will it take the new technology to reach the market place? Are current life-style trends likely to continue? These kinds of questions provide the grist for forecasting efforts.

Unlike scanning and monitoring, forecasting is well focussed and is much more deductive and complex activity. This is so because the focus, scope and goals of forecasting are more specific than the earlier two stages of environmental analysis.

Assessment - Scanning, monitoring and forecasting are not ends in themselves. Unless their outputs are assessed to determine implications for the organisation's current and potential strategies, scanning, monitoring and forecsting simply provide 'nice-to-know' information. Assessment involves identifying and evaluating how and why current and projected environmental changes affect or will affect strategic management of the organisation.

Assessment involves identifying and evaluating how projected environmental changes affect strategic management.

In assessment, the frame of reference moves from understanding the environment - the focus of scanning, monitoring and forecasting - to identifying what the understanding means for the organisation. Assessment, therefore, tries to answer questions such as what are the key issues presented by the environment, and what are the implications of such issues for the organisation?

Linkages Among Stages

Though conceptually scanning, monitoring, forecasting and assessment are seperate activities, they are inextricably intertwined as shown in Fig. 2.3.

For example, upon unearthing an emerging trend through scanning, one might quickly jump to potential implications for the organisation (assessment) by implicitly forecasting the future path of the trend. If warranted by the potential impact, one may then continue scanning and monitoring. Also, forecasting often proves difficult, if not impossible, because of insufficient knowledge and data about the topic or trends being forecast, thus forcing a return to scanning and monitoring efforts. Deriving implications (assessment) often allots the organisation to the need to conduct further scanning, monitoring and forecasting. Thus, environmental analysis is not as simple and as linear as moving from scanning to monitoring to forecasting to assessment.

BENEFITS OF ENVIRONMENTAL ANALYSIS

Environment analysis, brings several benefits to the company. It makes management to be more **proactive** than reactive in shaping its own future, it allows the firm to initiate and shape the activities and thus control its own destiny. It is not just that large business enterprises are practising the analysis. Small businesses, government undertakings and non-profit organisations too have realised the usefulness of such an analysis.

Secondly, environmental analysis **empowers** employees. At the stage of the analysis of environment, formulation of strategies, and implementation of strategies, employees are involved in decision making.

Managers and employees become surprisingly creative and innovative when they understand and support the firm's mission, objectives and strategies. An important benefit from environmental analysis is the opportunity that it provides to empower individuals.

Third, it has been clearly proved that firms which indulge in environmental analysis are more successful than those that do not. Businesses using concepts relating to analysis show significant improvement in sales, profitability, and productivity compared to firms without systematic planning activities.

It is estimated that more than 100,000 businesses in the U.S. fail annually. Business failures include bankruptcies, foreclosures, liquidations and court-mandated receiverships. Although, several other factors contribute to the large scale failure of businesses, the absence of systematic planning based on proper understanding of environment becomes conspicuous.[9]

Fourth, environmental analysis ensures to the firm such intangible benefits as enhanced awareness of external threats, an improved understanding of competitors' strategies, increased employee productivity, reduced resistance to change, and a clear understanding of performance - reward relationships. Analysis enhances the problem-preventor capabilities of organisations because it promotes interaction among managers at all divisional and functional levels.

In addition to empowering managers and employees, environmental analysis often brings order and discipline to an otherwise floundering firm. It can be the beginning of an effective and efficient management system. The analysis may renew confidence in the current business strategy or point to the need for corrective actions. The analysis provides a basis for identifying and rationalising the need for change to all managers and employees of a firm, it helps them view change as an opportunity rather than as a threat.[10]

Generally stated, the benefits of environmental analysis are on the following lines:[11]

1. It allows for identification, prioritisation, and exploitation of opportunites.
2. It provides an objective view of management problems.
3. It minimizes the effects of adverse conditions and changes.
4. It allows major decisions to better support established objectives.
5. It allows more effective allocation of time and resources to identified opportunities.
6. It allows fewer resources and less time to be devoted to correcting erroneous or ad hoc decisions.
7. It helps integrate the behaviour of individuals into a total effort.
8. It encourages forward thinking.
9. It provides a cooperative, integrated, and enthusiastic approach to tackling problems and opportunities.
10. It encourages a favourable attitude towards change.
11. It gives degree of discipline and formality to the management of a business.

LIMITATIONS OF ENVIRONMENTAL ANALYSIS

Environmental analysis, as with any other analysis, has certain limitations. These limitations are:

1. Environmental analysis does not foretell the future, nor does it eliminate uncertainty for any organisation. Thus, organisation that practises environmental analysis sometimes confront

unexpected events — events not anticipated during environmental analysis. Environmental analysis, however, should reduce the frequency and extent of surprises that may confront the company.

2. Environmental analysis in and of itself is not a sufficient guarantor of organisational effectiveness. It is only one of the inputs in strategy development and testing.
3. The potential of environmental analysis is often not realised because of how it is practised. It is sometimes used as a crutch for post hoc reflections. At times managers place uncritical faith in the data without thinking about the data's verifiability or accuracy.
4. Too much reliance is often placed on the information collected through environmental scanning. When there is overloading of information, one is likely to get lost and become inactive-typical of 'paralysis through analysis syndrome'.

Take the case of Norton Company, an industrial abrasives manufacturer and a competitor of 3M in the U.S.. Norton faithfully studied environment and fallowed all management models, systems and procedures. Inspite of all Norton's state-of-the-art management systems, its performance remained disappointing. Persistently poor results left the company vulnerable and, in 1990, it was absorbed into the French giant, Compagnie de Saint-Gobain.

Meanwhile, 3M achieved success but following a different path. The company did not get caught by the paralysis syndrome. Leaders here placed little emphasis on top-down planning and control. Instead, they nurtured the innovative ideas of sales engineers and sales representatives, thereby building an entrepreneurial engine that generated a stream of profitable new products and promising new technologies. Going into post-war boon, 3M and Norton were roughly the same size. By the mid-1980's, 3M was reporting sales eight times those of its old competitor. Ironically, just as Norton was swallowed up by Saint Gobain, 3M was named for the fifth time in six years to *Fortune's* list of the Ten Most Admired Corporations.[11]

QUESTIONS

1. What is environment? What are the benefits of the analysis of environment?
2. Bring out the limitations of environmental analysis.
3. State and explain the steps in environmental analysis.
4. What is five-forces model of analysing competitive strength of a company?

ASSIGNMENT

Divide the class into batches of five students. Each batch should pick up any Indian company and describe which of them is adopting environmental analysis and why? Batches should take one week for preparation. Presentations in the class to follow on an appointed day.

REFERENCES

1. Arthur A.Thomson, *et al*, *Crafting and Executing Strategy*, TMH, 2005, p.87.
2. *Ibid*, p.50.
3. Gerry Johnson and Kevan Scholes, *Exploring Corporate Strategy*, Pearson, 2005, p.156.

4. Arthur A.Thomson, *et al*, p.59.
5. Gerry Johnson and Kevan Scholes, *op.cit*, pp.155.156.
6. Arthur A.Thomson, *et al*, *op.cit*, p.67.
7. Fred R.David, *Strategic Management*, Pearson, 2003, p.200.
8. *Ibid*, p.201.
9. *Ibid*, p.16.
10. *Ibid*.
11. *Ibid*, p.17

CHAPTER OUTLINE

Nature of Globalisation
Drivers of Globalisation
Players in International Business
Challenges of International Business

LEARNING OBJECTIVES

After reading this Chapter, you should be able to:

1. Understand the nature of globalisation
2. Identify the triggers of globalisation
3. Describe the players in international business
4. Bring out the challenges of international business

3 Meaning and Rationale of Globalisation

Thanks to the economic reforms, Indian businessmen are now expanding their horizons and seeing beyond the physical boundaries of the country. Consequently, the captains of industries need to think and act, both actions being guided by international perspective. This section is devoted to a brief discussion of global environment and its implications for our businessmen.

The need to think and act from a global perspective is not peculiar to our businessmen alone. The need is universal. For a long time, businessmen everywhere believed that home markets were adequate and safe. They never felt the need to explore the overseas markets in a big way. If they could pick up some extra sales through exporting, these businessmen were more than satisfied. The scenario is different now. *'Globalise or perish'* is the slogan now-a-days.

NATURE OF GLOBALISATION

Globalisation, also called internationalisation, means several things to several people. For some it is a new paradigm - a set of fresh beliefs, working methods and economic, political and socio-cultural realities in which the previous assumptions are no longer valid. For developing countries, it means integration with the world economy. In simple economic terms, globalisation refers to the process of integration of the world into one huge market.[1] Such unification calls for the removal of all trade barriers among countries. Even political and geographical barriers become irrelevant (See Box 3.1).

At the company level, globalisation means two things: (a) the company commits itself heavily with several manufacturing locations around the world and offers products in several diversified industries and (b) it also means the ability to compete in domestic markets with foreign competitors.[2] In the popular sense, globalisation refers mainly to multi-plant operations.

Irrelevance of Nation-States

Nearly 30 years later, a new theory of cross-border affinities, of analyses that try to demolish the reality of nation-states has emerged. Kenichi Ohmae, an internationally renowned consultant, has authored **The End of the Nation State: The Rise of Regional Economies**.

In it, the author attempts to show that two major phenomena of the 1990s have highlighted forces at work that are knocking down borders, creating, as it were, a truly global market place with its agents governed by pure self-interest and not ideology or culture. These two events are the collapse of the Soviet Union and its satellites into so many republics, and the phenomenal rise of the South-East Asian economies. Both of them vindicate the strength of four 'I's, as Ohmae calls them: industry, investment, information technology and individual consumers. The interplay of these elements, at work for the past two decades, has rendered the nation-state redundant. As Ohmae points out in his preface: "The forces now at work have raised troubling questions about the relevance and effectiveness of nation-states as meaningful aggregates in terms of which to think about, much less manage, economic activity."

Ohmae asks crucial questions about the relevance of nation-states in the global economy. Are they the primary actors, notwithstanding their role in world affairs? The most critical and rather oversimplified question he asks is: in a world where economic borders are progressively disappearing, are there arbitrary, historically accidental boundaries geniunely meaningful in economic terms? The key assumption that he makes in asking this question are fundamental to his vision of the new world: economic borders are disappearing, and the nation-state has been a historical accident. In a sense, Ohmae distances the global economy, which he visualises as the consequences of deliberate rational human behaviour, from the nation-state which he dismisses as aberrations in today's world.

(**Source**: Cited in *Business India*, Oct.23-Nov.5, 1995).

A company which has gone global is called a multinational corporation (MNC). An MNC is, therefore, one that, by operating in more than one country, gains through research and development (R&D), leading to substantial production, marketing and financial advantages in its costs and reputation that are not available to purely domestic competitors. The global company views the world as one market, minimises the importance of national boundaries, raises capital and markets wherever it can do the job best.[3]

To be specific, a global company has six characteristics:

(i) It is a conglomerate of multiple units (located in different parts of the globe) but all linked by common ownership.

(ii) Multiple units draw on a common pool of resources such as money, credit, information, patents, trade names and control systems.

(iii) The units respond to some common strategy.

(iv) Product presence in different markets of the world.

(v) Human resource contains high diversity.

(vi) Transactions involving intellectual properties such as copyrights, patents, trade marks, and process technology across the globle.

Specifically, globalisation can be viewed as a four-dimensional construct based on the premise that an enterprise can be more or less global along each of four major characteristics: internationalisation of market presence, globalisation of supply chain, globalisation of capital base, and globalisation of corporate mindset[4] (See Fig.3.1).

Figure 3.1 **Assessing Corporate Globality**

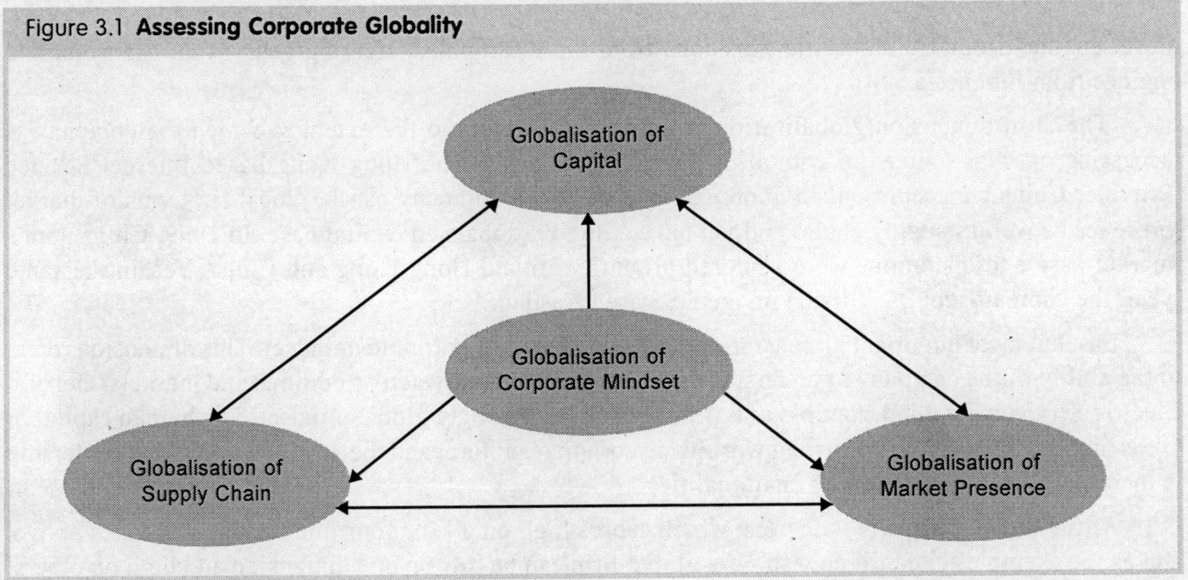

The first dimension-globalisation of market presense-refers to the extent to which company targets customers in all major markets within its industry throughout the world. On this count the presences of companies vary from low to high. For example, in 1993, NTT of Japan had no presence at all either in N.America or in Europe. In comparison, IBM, Sun Microsystems and Cannon were the most globalised firms (See Table 3.1).

Globalisation of market presence refers to the extent to which company targets customers in all major markets across the global

Table 3.1 **Percentage Regional Distribution of IT Sales for Selected Companies in 1993**

	N.America	*Europe*	*Asia*
IBM	41	33	16
Fujitsu	6	26	65
HP	51	34	9
NEC	6	4	88
Compaq	45	38	5
Canon	30	29	37
Sun Microsystems	51	24	25
NTT	0	0	100
Microsoft	56	30	9

(***Source:*** *The Economic Times*, December 26, 2003)

Internationalisation of supply chain (second dimension) refers to the extent to which the company is accessing the most optimal locations for the performance of various activities in its supply chain. It may be possible for a firm to have a fairly local or regional market presence and yet have a highly globalised supply chain, or vice-versa. For example, Toyota has a good supply chain. In 1995, Toyota produced about two-thirds of all its cars in Japan; the remaining one-third were produced in its affiliates spread over 25 countries in Americas, Europe and Asia. Furthermore, the company exported 38 per cent of its domestic production to foreign markets. Aside from this flow of capital, goods and know-how between Japan and overseas affiliates, Toyota also engaged in considerable intra-firm flows among the affiliates. For example, within its Southeast Asian regional network, it exported

Globalisation of supply chain refers to the extent to which the company is accessig the optimal locations for the performance of various activities in its supply chain

diesel engines from Thailand, transmissions from the Philippines, steering gears from Malaysia and engines from Indonesia.

Globalisation of capital base refers to the extent to which the company is accessing capital markets for financial resources

The third dimension-globalisation of capital base-refers to the extent to which the company is accessing optimal sources of capital on a worldwide basis. The Hong Kong based Internet Service Provider China.com represents a good example of how a company can be 'local' in terms of market presence as well as supply chain, and yet have a highly globalised capital base. In 1999, China.com's market base and operations were centered primarily around Hong Kong and China. Yet, in the same year, the company got itself listed on the US based Nasdaq.

Last but most important dimension is the globalisation of corporate mindset. This dimension refers to the ability of the company to understand and integrate diversity across cultures and markets. General Electric Services is a good example of a firm with an increasingly global mindset. The human capital of GE is highly globalised, it has strong worldwide corporate culture; and the composition of the leadership is increasingly diverse in terms of nationalities.

A true global company is the one which scores high on all the four dimensions discussed above. But as the examples cited till now show, a global firm can be low on one dimension and high on others.

A further development, perhaps, will be the *supranational enterprise*. It is a worldwide enterprise chartered by a substantially non-political international body such as International Monitory Fund or the World Bank. It operates as a private business without direct obligations. Its function is international business service, and it remains viable only by performing that service adequately for nations which permit its entry. With its integrative view, it should be able to draw the economic world closer together. It could serve all nations without being especially attached to any one of them. Because of its independence of any nation and its universal outlook, it is also called the extra-national enterprise, the '*geocorp*' and the '*cosmocorp*'. Somewhat related supranational organisations outside the business are the International Red Cross, religious bodies and scientific associations.

DRIVERS OF GLOBALISATION

Globalisation is not a new phenomenon. Trade across the countries is as old as business itself. However, the volume of international business and the number of players in it have increased dramatically over the last decade. Today every nation and an increasing number of companies buy and sell goods and services in the international market places. A number of developments around the world have helped fuel this activity.

Companies seek to take advantage by expanding their operations into foreign markets in a number of ways. First, rapidly developing economies have huge markets. For companies, mostly in developed countries, which have been operating below capacities, the emerging markets offer immense opportunities to increase their sales and profits. Second, many multinational corporations (MNCs) are locating their subsidiaries in low wage and low cost countries.

Third, changing demographics also adds to increasing globalisation. Demographic changes are more visible in India. The country has the largest number of young people in the world today. India has nearly 65 million children below 15 years of age, and as many as 400 million youngsters below the age of 23 years. These young people will join the ranks of working people in the next few years, thus creating a huge surge of productivity, incomes and savings. India's young people can be an asset to the global economy because while India's population will be getting younger in the coming decade, the population of all the developed countries will be getting older. The richest countries will face shortage of working age people while India will have surplus of them.

It is not just the number of people that India has quality of the people also is on the country's side. India has large low-cost and skilled workforce. This large labour pool will limit increases in wage rates for the next 20 years. In addition, India has a high availability of engineers, producing over 400,000 every year, next only to China's 490,000 and nearly 25 times Thailand's 17,000. In addition to engineers, India produces 850,000 graduates every year and over 70,000 diploma holders.

What do all these mean? Multinational corporations increasingly use India as destination for contracting out their functions. In addition, large number of Indians are available and are prepared to take up overseas assignments.

Fourth, regional trading blocks are adding to the pace of globalisation. WTO, EU, NAFTA, MERCOSUR and FTAA are the major alliances among countries. Trading blocks seek to promote international business by removing trade and investment barriers. Integration among countries results in efficient allocation of resources throughout the trading area, promoting the growth of some businesses and the decline of others, the development of new technology and products, and the elimination of old. This process is creating a large scale restructuring of industries and firms in the EU, with relocation of industry and many cross border mergers and alliances.[5]

But there are potential problems associated with the alliances. It is said that trading blocks might compete against each other. If this happens, free trade will exist within each bloc and each bloc will protect its market from outside competition with high tariffs. The possibility of the EU and NAFTA turning into "economic fortresses" that shut out foreign producers with high tariff barriers is not ruled out.

However, trading blocks generate more job opportunities. For example, between 90,000 to 160,000 jobs of various sorts were created in the US because of greater exports to Mexico (in the wake of the creation of NAFTA). There will also be easy movement of people among alliance partnering countries and replication of best HR practices. But there is also the possibility of jobs being shifted to low wage and low cost countries within or outside a trading block.

Fifth, declining trade and investment barriers have vastly contributed to globalisation. The early period of 20th century witnessed high levels of barriers on trade and investment. The aim of such restrictions was to protect domestic industries from foreign competition. Underlying the argument for protection of domestic industries is the infant industry argument. Tariff protection against the imported commodity is needed, so the infant industry argument goes, in order to allow the now higher-priced domestic producers enough time to learn the business and to achieve the economies of scale in production and the external economies of learning by that are necessary to lower unit costs and prices. With enough time and sufficient protection, the infant will eventually grow up, be directly competitive with developed country producers, and no longer need this protection. Ultimately, many domestic producers will be able to produce not only for the domestic market without a tariff wall or government subsidies but also to export their now lower-cost goods to the rest of the world.[6]

The infant industry argument had several takers. Each country started imposing tariffs on the goods of other countries. This led to the cumulative curtailment of demand resulting in the Great Depression of 1930s.

The Depression was characterised by a vicious circle - no income - no demand - no supply - no jobs - no income. In order to break this circle, free-flow of goods and services and capital across the globe was thought necessary. In otherwords, barriers were required to be dismounted. Thus, came the free trade regime resulting in the WTO.

Thanks to free trade regime, business across the globe has grown considerably. Goods, services, capital and technology are moving across the nations significantly. The volume of world trade has grown over 20 fold between 1950 and 2002. The average yearly outflow of FDI increased from about $25 billion in 1975 to a record $13 trillion in 2000.

Internalisation of business is being accompanied by outsourcing and off-shoring of activities. While outsourcing benefited India, Chinese are the gainers from off-shoring business processes.

Free trade also meant movement of labour across the globe, though not as freely as goods, services and capital. There is dichotomy here. Though all nations expect goods, services and capital to move freely, they place several conditional when it comes to the movement of people across countries. Nevertheless, globalisation has benefited people in terms of increased jobs and enhanced salaries.

Sixth, the most powerful instrument that triggered globalisation is technology. Revolution is probably the right word which can best describe the pace at which technology has changed in the recent past and is continuing to change. Significant developments are witnessed in communication, transportation, information processing, including the emergence of the Internet and the world wide web. It is said that the cost of a three-minute telephone call from New York to London in current prices dropped from about $250 in 1930 to a few cents today. In more recent years, the number of voice paths across the Atlantic has sky rocketed from 100,000 in 1986 to more than 2 million today. The number of Internet hosts has risen from 5000 in 1986 to more than 700 million now.[7]

Thanks to these developments in technology, MNCs are able to locate production facilities anywhere in the world to take advantage of low cost production. This trends helps create job opportunities in countries like Philippines, Mexico, China and India.

The Boston Consultancy Group has identified five currents of globalisation. These currents are:[8]

- the growth of rapidly growing developing economies (RDEs)
- the continuing cost and capital advantages of RDEs
- the development of talent and capabilities in RDEs
- the migration of customers to RDEs
- the emergence of RDE-based global competitors.

The RDEs identified are China, India, Brazil, Mexico, South East Asia and Central and Eastern Europe. The absolute growth in economic activity in the key RDEs over the next several years is expected to come close to that of the three leading developed regions. While the US, Western Europe and Japan are expected to grow by $3 trillion in collective GDP from 2004 to 2010, the key RDEs will grow by more than $2 trillion. Specifically, China's GDP is expected to expand by $750 billion, Central and Eastern Europe's by $450 billion, South East Asia's by $350 billion, and Brazil's by $200 billion. This growth will mean substantial consumption of consumer and industrial goods.

Many MNCs are strategising to generate a large portion of their global sales from RDEs. ABB, Emerson, Schneider Electric and Siemens have seen their China sales grow substantially - 5 per cent of their total sales.

RDEs offer immense opportunities to minimise operating costs and capital investments. Companies that globalise their cost structures to include RDEs can realise savings of 20 to 40 per cent in the landed costs of their products while reducing capital requirements by similar amounts. A major saving in operating costs stems from labour rates. A factory worker in the US or Europe costs $15 to $30 or more per hour, depending on where the factory is located, unionised or not, and the extent of benefits it provides. In contrast, a Chinese factory worker earns approximately $1 per hour, offering a cost advantage of fifteen fold or more. With regard to lower capital investment, two fundamental factors reduce the need for capital in RDEs: first, less expensive plant infrastructure, machinery, and equipment, and second, the opportunity to make use of labour in the place of costly technology.

RDEs offer not just cost advantage - they provide skill advantage too. The number of engineers in these countries is multiplying. China, for example, will have added 380,000 science and engineering graduates to its talent pool in 2004. India is rich by 360,000, and Russia by 240,000. By 2010, China, India and Russia will likely provide more than 2 million new scientists and engineers a year, compared with about 400,000 in the US. These graduates are not just adding to the numbers. Their competence, particularly those of Indians, is exceptionally good. The seven IITs and six IIMs in India are indeed centres of excellence. "The IIts became islands of excellence by not allowing the general debasement of the Indian system to lower their exacting stands," wrote a reputed journal. "You couldn't bribe your way to get into an IIT... Candidates are accepted only if they pass a grueling entrance examination. The government does not interfere with the curriculum, and the work load is demanding... Arguably, it is harder to get into an IIT than into Harvard or the MIT."[9] Obviously, in both blue and white collar labour pools, RDE workforces have demonstrated that they are talented, trainable and eager to move up the skill ladder.

Triggered by the first three currents - growth of RDE markets, the continuing cost and capital advantages and the development of talent and capabilities in RDEs - more and more manufacturing companies are moving their production to RDEs. This migration has major implications for their suppliers. While the current penetration of RDE - sourced industrial goods into US and European markets is still relatively small, it is clearly gaining momentum. In some sectors, RDE imports are growing at rates as high as 30 per cent per year.

The relocation of major industrial sectors has serious implications for the supplier base in the home markets. If these suppliers do not act quickly their businesses will shrink. Most companies need to evolve a two-fold strategic plan: to fill market gaps at home and also to follow selected customers to their new locations.

The emergence of RDE-based global competitors is the last dimension delianated by the BCG. As economies of RDEs grew at breakneck speed, large-scale global competitors emerge from these countries. India's Bharat Forge is one example of a company which is emerging as a strong global competitor. It recently made big news by acquiring a well-established $150 million German engineered-components company. Haier Group of China is another example.

Companies everywhere are required to monitor the emergence of RDE competitors in their industries, understand the extent and timing of a possible threat or opportunity, assess their own vulnerabilities as well as the advantages they may have over the new competitors and have action plans ready for various contingencies.

PLAYERS IN INTERNATIONAL BUSINESS

Every firm which conducts business across borders is a player in international business. Viewing from this perspective, an individual, a proprietary firm, a co-operative society, or limited company is a player in global business. But one special type of organisation engaged in global business is the Multi National Corporation(MNC.) An MNC is an organisation that engages in production or service activities through its own affiliates in several countries, maintains control over the policies of those affiliates, and manages from a global perspective. With a global perspective, top managers allocate resources and coordinate activities to take the best possible advantage of favourable business conditions throughout the world. Table 3.2 shows the world's most popular MNCs.

Some other expressions are also coined to name enterprises engaged in global business. United Nations agencies call these firms as transnational corporations (TNCs), and others prefer the term multinational enterprises (MNEs). But there is no common agreement about the choice of any of these expressions. However, there is a trend-Americans use the term MNC, Europeans call them MNEs and Indians go by what Americans use, viz., MNC (See also Box 3.2).

Table 3.3 shows Indian MNCs. There are no Indian MNCs in the strict sense of the term. Unlike a GM or a Siemens there is not even one company which has its operations spread around the world. But some of the Indian companies have acquired or strategising to acquire foreign based firms. From this narrow perspective, some Indian companies (shown in Table 3.3) are MNCs.

Colossal is the right word to describe the pre-eminent position of MNCs in the world of business. There are about 35,000 MNCs around the world today, controlling over 170,000 foreign affiliates. It is estimated that roughly half of all cross-border corporate assets are accounted for just by the top 100 MNCs.

Corporations that do business across national boundaries are so large that their annual revenues from worldwide operations exceed the value of goods and services (GDP) of entire nations. For example,

Table 3.2 **The Top 10 Global MNCs Ranked by Market Value, Sales, Profits, and Share-Price Gain, 2003**

Market Value Billions of U.S. Dollars		*Sales Billions of U.S. Dollars*		*Profits Billions of U.S. Dollars*		*Share-Price Gain*	
1 General Electric	$328.11	1 Wal-Mart Stores	$258.68	1 ExxonMobil	$20.96	1 Mizuho Financial	636%
2 Microsoft	284.43	2 BP	232.57	2 Citigroup	17.85	2 Research in Motion	550
3 Exxon Mobil	283.61	3 ExxonMobil	222.88	3 General Electric	15.00	3 UFJ Holding	420
4 Pfizer	269.66	4 Royal Dutch/ Shell	201.93	4 HSBC Holding	11.65	4 SK	383
5 Wal-Mart Stores	241.19	5 General Motors	183.24	5 Roayl Dutch/ Shell	11.41	5 Rakuten	381
6 Citigroup	239.43	6 Daimler Chrysler	166.61	6 Vodafone Group	11.36	6 Sumitomo Mitsui Fin.	331
7 BP	193.05	7 Ford Motors	164.20	7 Bank of America	10.81	7 Elan	311
8 AIG	191.18	8 Toyota Motor	156.48	8 Toyota Motor	10.51	8 Bharti Tele-Ventures	276
9 Intel	184.66	9 Mitsubishi	137.32	9 Microsoft	9.99	9 Yahoo! Japan	241
10 Royal Dutch/ Shell	174.33	10 General Electric	134.19	10 BP	9.54	10 Mitsui Trust Hldgs.	229

(**Source:** Richard M. Hodgetts, *et.al., International Management,* Tata McGraw-Hill, 2005, p.6).

Box 3.2 **What's in a Name?**

There is a debate about what to call a company whose business ranges across national borders, tying together home and host countries through corporate policies and practices. Here are some of the terms used to describe these companies.

Transnational Corporation (TNC)

Because companies "transcend" or operate across national borders, some experts prefer the term transnational corporation, or TNC. The United Nations favours this term and has created a Research Centre for the Study of Transnational Corporations.

Multinational Corporation (MNC)

The fact that companies operate in multiple countries has led some experts to adopt the term multinational Corporation, or MNC. This term is very popular in the business press and in textbooks. It seems to be the most generic name to describe corporations operating around the world.

Multinational Enterprise (MNE)

Because some of the international giants are state-owned enterprises, rather than corporations, the term multinational enterprise, or MNE, has entered the vocabulary of international trade.

Global Corporation

This term became very popular in the 1990s. The term seems to have first been used to describe a small number of companies whose business was conducted in dozens of-perhaps more than 100-nations. Hence, Nestle has long been described as truly global because the scope of its operations extends to more than 150 nations around the globe. The term is often applied to companies doing business in several areas of the world (e.g., Europe, Latin America, Asia-Pacific, and North America).

(***Source:*** James E.Post, *et al., Business and Society*, p.157)

Table 3.3 **Indian MNCs**

- Tata Motors to take over Daewoo in South Korea for $118 million
- Ambanis to take over Flag International for $211 million
- Ranbaxy took over RPG Aventis, France based firm
- Wockhardt acquired CP Pharmaceuticals and Wallis Laboratories-both of Britain
- Hindalco took over Mount Gardon and Nifty-Copper mines in Australia
- Sundaram Fasteners has acquired Dana Spicer Europe, the British arm of an MNC
- Sundaram Fasteners is setting up a greenfield project in China
- Amtek Auto has acquired the GWK group in the UK
- Kirloskar Brothers took over SPP Pumps, UK

General Motors had revenues of $164 billion in 1996, more than the entire GDP of Norway ($114 billion) or Thailand ($130 billion) and nearly equal to that of Indonesia ($167 billion). Other companies of comparable size in 1996 include Toyota, with worldwide revenues of $118 billion, General Electric ($79 billion) and Exxon ($116 billion). Obviously, the chief executives of General Motors, Toyota, IBM, and Exxon are responsible for economic activities equal to or greater than those managed by the political leaders of some of the world's most significant economies.

It is argued that the MNCs reign as the pre-eminent vehicle of international trade is nearing its end. It is slowly being displaced by firms that represent a new type of international enterprise, which is called the global corporation. The MNC operates in a number of countries and adjusts its products and services to each. The global corporation, on the other hand, operates as if the entire world were a single entity. Global corporations essentially sell the same things in the same way every where. Thus, a global corporation, such as Sony, sells a standardised product-Walkman-throughout the world, components of which may be made or designed in different countries.[10]

ABB is a typical MNC. ABB is a federation of national companies with a global coordination culture. It is a Swiss company having headquarters in Zurich, but only 100 professionals work at the headquarters. Only two of the eight board members are Swedish. Financial data are reported in US dollars and English is ABB's official language.

Although multinational companies tend to be rather large and engage in a substantial amount of cross-border transactions, an increasing number of medium and small business enterprises are also involved in international business. More than 75 per cent of Indian's total export earnings, for instance, come from small-scale units.

Benefits from MNCs

Benefits from MNCs can be studied under two broad heads:

(i) Benefits to the host countries; and

(ii) Benefits to the home countries.

Benefits to the host countries: To the host countries, MNCs are likely to bring the following benefits:

- Transfer of technology, capital and entrepreneurship to the host country.
- Improvement of the host country's balance of payments.
- Creation of local job and career opportunities.

MNCs confor several benefits to host countries, most prominent among them being creation of jobs opportunities, improvement in balance of payments position, and transter of technology. Home country's benefits include inflow of income from overseas profits, acquisition of materials from abroad, etc

- Improved competition in the local economy and better utilisation of available resources.
- Greater availability of products for local consumers.
- Greater access to high quality managerial talent that tends to be scarce in host countries, particularly the developing ones.
- Encouragement to world economic unity and through that, political and economic integration-all resulting in world harmony.[11]

It may be noted that in each of the above benefits, the opposite may occur. For example, an MNC may use local financing, thereby absorbing capital that might have financed indigenuous companies. Or a few well-advertised, standardised consumer products may drive many locally produced products from the market, thereby reducing consumer choice.

Benefits to home countries: The following benefits are likely to accrue to the home countries:

- Acquisition of raw materials from abroad, often from a steadier supply and at lower prices than can be found domestically.
- Technology and management expertise acquired from competing in global markets.
- Export of components and finished goods for assembly or distribution in foreign markets.
- Inflow of income from overseas profits, royalties, licensing fees and management contracts.
- Job and career opportunities at home and abroad in connection with overseas operations.[12]

Box 3.3 shows company-specific benefits of globalisation to India and to the countries of origin.

Problems Brought by MNCs

As is the case with many activities, there are potentially disadvantageous by-products that may accompany the benefits brought to both the host and home countries by MNCs.

A major fall-out of the MNCs is that the host country is likely to lose its economic sovereignty, since it is not able to control all that an MNC does. It is said that a large multinational company negotiates with a host government more like another sovereign state than of a resident business in the state.

The track record of the International Telephones and Telegraphs (ITT) of the US is worth recollecting here. The ITT regards itself as above governments, above controls and above morals. It presents itself as an American company in America, British in Britain, German in Germany; but it owes loyalty to none of them and regards each government as an unnecessary obstruction. The most heinous of its deeds is the overthrow of the marxist President of Chile, Salvador Allende, in the Seventies. Ideologies which divided the world during the cold war between the US and the Soviet Union made no difference to the ITT and it could target the communist regimes and achieve its objectives.

The host nation may also experience some loss of control over its own economy. The MNC's actions are guided partly by worldwide needs than internal needs of the host nation. Thus, some actions may not be consistent with what is desired by the host nation (See Box 3.4). For example, dislocations may occur in the host country's balance of payments, particularly when an MNC imports materials or transfers funds.

Benefits of MNCs

Transnational Links	*How the Indian Company benefits*	*How the Parent Company benefits*
P&G World-wide USA-P&G India	Infusion of funds will shore up sagging bottomline. Plans to launch more P&G brands, like Head & Shoulders shampoo will get a fillip. And five-fold growth in turnover will becomes feasible.	A lucrative foothold in the world's second largest, and fastergrowing, cleaning products, cleaning products market.
The Gillette company, USA-India Shaving Products	Access to Gillette brand name, both for existing products like blades and new products like swivel-head razors. Diversification into male deodorants and writing products takes on new meaning.	A chance to finally try to become the biggest player in the world's largest shaving products market.
Asea Brown Boveri, Switzerland - ABB Ltd.	Will obtain state-of-the-art technology to produce bigger range of power generation equipment. Can also diversify into locomotives and pollution control equipment, with Rs.700 crore investment.	A stronger presence in Asia, where the demand for capital goods will grow faster than in Europe in the 1990s.
Singer Corporation USA - The Indian Sewing Machine Company	Will produce the all-new series 900 range of sewing systems, possibly for the world market. Probable diversification into washing machines and audio and video systems.	Domination of a sewing machine market growing by 30 per cent annum, and the possibility of using it as a global production base.
Group Bull, France-PSI Data Systems	Immediate financial problems taken care of. A chance to market systems solutions with a full range of hardware, including large and medium-range IBM systems.	Apart from selling hardware, could use India as a software development base for global customers.
Digital Equipment Corporation, USA-DEIL	The firm will be able to offer more hardware products locally, in tandem with global releases.	Since it is moving rapidly into the software market, developing solutions in India could prove profitable.
Carrier Corporation, USA-Carrier Aircon	Access to technology to produce new products like air cooled chillers and high-end chilling systems. And all-out marketing support to break into the Far East and West Asian markets.	A chance to justify its investment in the Indian market, especially by using the Indian Co. as an Asian production centre.
C.P.C.International, USA-Corn Products	Running a Rs.2.27 crore loss between September 1991 and March 1992, the company's future looks bleak. Now, the equity expansion might just allow it to survive.	Strategic advantage of keeping its flag flying in a market attracting global processed food giants.
Leader A.G., Switzerland-Bata India	Will finally be able to invest in expanding and modernising all its shoe manufacturing units. Can also hope to launch new Adidas products, and thus boost its retail ambitions.	Can tap one of the world's cheapest production bases for leather hides, shoe uppers and finished products.
E.Merck, Germany-E.Merck(India)	Shore up beleaguered bottomline. Even if Indian patent laws do not change, can hope for faster transfer of technology from parent company.	Can use India as a base for increasing exports to other South Asian countries.

(**Source**: *Business Today*, July 22-August 6, 1992).

Box 3.4 **Coke pours into Asia**

The biggest prize and challenge, is China. To woo the country of more than 1.2 billion people, the company has made unprecedented compromises.

In 1993, it entered a marriage of convenience with the Chinese government, gaining wide access to the market-but at a high cost. Coke pledged to keep its predatory instincts in check, promising to do everything from upgrading the local industry to providing cash income to farmers by starting a new line of fruit drinks.

Beijing is counting on Coke to provide its expertise in key areas from hygiene to packaging to distribution. In return, the Chinese have allowed Coke and its partners to invest $300 million to build 10 new bottling plants, giving it a total of 23 by the end of 1997.

The first fruits of the company's investment are in sight. Coke says it has grabbed 23% of the soft drink volume in China and figures on eventually topping 40%. A new study by McKinsey & Co. says Coca-Cola is one of a handful of consumer goods companies that has a chance to hit $1 billion in sales in China by 2000, thanks to its large, systematic investment in the country.

The problem is, China is so large that Coke can't rely on its usual methods to ensure that all is well. In more developed markets, Coke bottlers distribute all of the products directly, giving the company complete control over its goods. But that's not feasible in China, where some 75% of Coke products go through independent wholesalers. That means it's nearly impossible for the company to police such things as coolers, product display, and pricing. All Coke can do in most cases is ship its product out and hope for the best.

Moreover, Coke doesn't always succeed in staying out of the way of nationalist crosscurrents. In 1995, a group of National People's Congress legislators called for Beijing to restrict the expansion of Coke and Pepsi to protect local manufacturers. This legislative motion spurred an announcement last May that further approvals of soft-drink plants for joint ventures would be put on hold.

Coke takes the threat of a backlash seriously. It recently subsidized a study by Cambridge University Professor Peter Nolan to defuse criticism that it wasn't helping China's economy. Nolan estimated that every job at a Coca-Cola plant leads to six additional jobs elsewhere. The company is spending heavily to build rural schools and libraries. And it has launched the line of fruit drinks even though the premi-umpriced Tian yu di-'Heaven and Earth'-is a flop, say Coke's sales representatives. They say that it's too sweet and too expensive for Chinese tastes. Politically, though, it's a winner, since it provides cash for local fruit growers.

(**Source**: *The Economic Times*, 9th Feb, 1997).

Take our own case as an example. We invited MNCs with several objectives. One objective is to widen consumer choice. This has been fairly realised. Yet another objective is to improve the balance of payments. There has been a fair measure of success in this respect too. The net inflow of foreign direct investment which was just $150 millions in 1991-92 had increased to $1,982 millions in 1995-96. Three other objectives have been to encourage some MNCs to use India as an export base; to ask others to invest in high priority and infrastructural areas and to add to the existing manufacturing capacity. All these three objectives seem to have failed.

With regard to developing India as an export base, Table 3.4 shows the export-import ratio of India and other countries. The ratio of a country's exports to imports is one indication of the extent to which an economy's purchases are financed by what it earns by selling its goods in the world markets. India's export-import ratio was at a low of 66 per cent in 1990-91, before it increased substantially over the next few years. But lately, the ratio has been showing a declining trend. Exports paid for 95 per cent of imports in 1993-94, 85 per cent in 1994-95, and 82 per cent in 1995-96.

Table 3.4 **International Comparison**

(Export-Import ratio, perent, 1994)

Saudi Arabia	169	*Japan*	144
Nigeria	144	*Indonesia*	125
Brazil	121	*Germany*	119
Italy	113	*Canada*	107
South Africa	107	*China*	105
France	102	*Malaysia*	99
South Korea	94	*India*	93
U.K.	90	*Thailand*	83
Pakistan	83	*Mexico*	77
U.S.	74	*Argentina*	74
Philippines	59		

(**Source**: *The Hindu*, Sept 2, 1996)

Coming to the other objective, *viz*., developing India's infrastructure and core sector, Table 3.5 shows that a major portion of foreign investment has gone into consumer goods like colas, corn flakes and fried chicken. Surely, these were not the areas where foreign capital was needed.

Table 3.5 **Total Inflow of Direct Investment from 1991-96**

	Rs.crores	*Percentage of total*
Basic goods	1235.24	12.3
Capital goods	1928.21	19.2
Intermediate goods	1248.48	12.5
Consumer goods	2549.31	25.4
Service sector	2111.33	21.1
Miscellaneous	244.95	2.4
Automobile	711.06	7.1
Total	10,028.58	100.0

(**Source**: *The Hindu*, July 29, 1996)

MNCs were invited to set up new plants so that additional manufacturing capacity may be created. The experience has been disappointing. A very large amount of foreign capital has been used for acquiring local companies or merging with them, thus denying the country the benefit of new manufacturing capacity.

Besides, MNCs were invited to our country to set up greenfield projects so that additional manufacturing capacities may be created. But the experience till now has not been encouraging. A very large amount of foreign capital has been used for acquiring local companies or merging with them, thus denying the country the benefits of additional production capacities.

Thus, MNCs seem to have benefited little into a country like India.

The host country may also have a feeling that its labour is being exploited by the MNCs, higher wages paid by them, notwithstanding. Companies in the host nation have a grouse that they are forced to pay higher wages to the workers. They also resent the competition thrown in by the MNCs.

In the most serious cases, a host country might exert power of a possessive nature on the MNCs. In some nations, the host governments may insist on being partial owner of foreign businesses, especially a core industry. In situations of sudden social upheaval or changes in government control, a country may nationalise, or expropriate, the assets of a company or plant even without paying compensation. This can be very costly to the multinational. There are several extreme examples, such as Cuba's nationalisation of $1.5 billion of assets in 1960 and Iraq's seizure of all Kuwaiti assets in 1990.

Unable to cope with the hostile domestic public opinion, several companies quit Myanmar in the recent months. They include Pepsi, Apple, Walt Disney, Motorola, Hewlett-Packard, Eastman Kodak, Heineken, Carlsberg, Levi Strauss, Peregrine and others (Also read Box 3.5).

Box 3.5 **Multinationals-backlash**

But Myanmar is only one place where controversial investments are once again causing grief to big multinationals, especially to oil and mining companies:

* RTZ-CRA, which is Britain's (and the world's) biggest mining group, and Freeport-McMoRan, an American firm, are under attack from environmentalists for a copper and gold mine in Irian Jaya, Indonesia. RTZ-CRA last year made pre-tax profits of $2.46 billion, up 42 per cent on the year before. But when the firm held its annual meeting in London in May, journalists preferred to write about the tribes-people who turned upto protest about the company and about the environmental activist who tried to storm the podium.

* Royal Dutch/Shell has similar woes. Despite being in the throes of a far-reaching reorganisation, the oil giant has seen all the public's attention focus instead first on its aborted plants to dump the Brent Spar, an oil platform, at sea and then on its relations with the military regime in Nigeria. These provoked an international outcry last year when Nigeria executed nine dissidents.

* Two North American firms, Cambior and Golden Star Resources, came under fire following an accident last year at a Guyanan mine, which resulted in cyanide spilling into a river.

* In Malaysia, a $5.5 billion hydroelectric dam to be built by a consortium including Asea Brown Boveri, a Swiss-based multinational, is being attacked by local people and western environmental groups for destroying rain forests.

The average oil baron or mining boss might once have shrugged off such events as little local difficulties. Some even relished a brawl. Nowadays, they recognise that the stakes are higher. It is not only the prospect of consumer boycotts that worries them. In addition, staff morale can suffer (many Shell employees opposed the sinking of the Brent Spar), political contacts can be upset (Nelson Mandela denounced Shell's.

*(**Source**: The Economic Times, 28 Aug, 1996)*

Economic issues such as high interest rates, capital shortages, export obligations, and restrictions on repatriation of profits affect multinational businesses.

The social and cultural differences among nations present formidable challenges for the MNC, its managers and their families. Differences in language, physical surroundings and values of the population can create important business and human conflicts (See also Box 3.6). Business has discovered that social and cultural differences may pose difficult problems in its relations with the host country and in establishing a productive and capable workforce in its foreign affiliates.

Box 3.6 **Business Problems because of Cultural Differences**

A few years earlier, Japanese television audiences watched as a Japanese woman's husband walked into the bathroom as she was bathing. While she told him about the new beauty soap she was using, he stroked her shoulder and hinted that he was interested in more than her soap. Many Japanese viewers were offended, feeling that the man was displaying bad manners to intrude in his wife's bath. Procter & Gamble's efforts to sell its Camay soap to Japanese consumers were set back by this advertisement. P&G had similar troubles marketing its US brand of bulky disposable diapers to Japanese buyers, who preferred cloth diapers or Japanese brands that were better fitting for Japanese babies. When they advertised P&G laundry detergent as working in all temperatures of water, they discovered that many Japanese wash clothes in cold water and did not care about P&G's claim. Problems like these caused the company to lose $200 million in its first years of entering Japanese markets. In Europe, the company's liquid laundry detergent could not be used in European-made washing machines which were designed to take only powdered laundry detergent. In trying to design portable liquid dispensers to be included in P&G's detergent package, the company discovered that each brand of washing machine required a different design. Procter & Gamble's marketing staff eventually overcame these blunders encountered in entering foreign markets so well that the company expected over half of its total revenues to come from foreign sales in the 1990s. The lesson was clear. Successful marketing requires a thorough knowledge of differing cultural attitudes and practices.

(**Source**: W.C.Frederick, *et al*, *Business and Society*, p.130.)

The most serious threat faced by the host country citizens is the loss of their cultural moorings. In the name of globalisation, MNCs usher in their own dress and food habits which are simply grabbed by the youth of the host countries. The youth of today are more familiar with cornflakes, pizza and fried chicken than *idlis, dosas* and *chutney* (See also Box 3.7).

In general, it is difficult to allay the fears of citizens and politicians in a host nation. They know that an MNC is deriving some benefits from its activities, so they feel exploited because they cannot rationalise that the activities may be of mutual benefit to both the company and the host nation.

It is worth nothing that although MNCs are viewed with caution and suspicion by some host country government officials, they are actively courted by most countries rather than denied entry.

People in the home country of an MNC may have objections to its activity. They see jobs being created in another nation, denying the same benefit to the home country citizens. Citizens in the home country may also be less tolerant of the host nation's culture. For example, they may claim that the operations of the MNC in a host nation having a dictatorship are supporting dictatorship, or that operations where there is a racial discrimination are supporting that practice. The MNC argues that it must fit into the culture of the host nation in the same way it does in the home country, and also that it can help accomplish social improvements better by staying in a nation than by leaving it.

All things considered, it may be stated that the benefits of MNCs far outweigh the problems they create. It needs to be emphasised that MNCs are change agents and are welcome particularly to developing countries where improving the standard of living is a top priority. However, MNCs must operate in host countries in such a way that their economic sovereignty is not eroded. Besides, the activities of MNCs must fit into the long term development plans of host countries even if it means sacrificing immediate gains.

Box 3.7 **Globalisation and Culture**

The existing cultural common sense in India has evolved from its historical experience and is drawn from a variety of sources. It is heterogeneous in character and plural in manifestation. The social and cultural practices and behaviour which admit of diversity reflect these qualities. Unlike the capitalist West, there is no standardisation. Be it food, dress, entertainment or gestures-almost all aspects of daily life-the rich legacy of a vibrant culture is apparent. Through the new cultural infrastructure fabricated by global forces, the indigenous common sense is not only being marginalised but is also being projected as anachronistic. It is sought to be replaced by the common sense of advance capital which privileges practices and behaviour linked with the products of advanced capitalism. The rationale for this displacement is the universal character of the cultural common sense of advanced capital. The globalisation, it is argued, affords the opportunity to internalise the universal culture and is thus to become part of a large whole. This, to say the least, is a convenient pretext, which conceals the interest of the dominant.

The cultural infrastructure, the global forces are currently fabricating in India, would pave the way for the internalisation of "universal" culture. The active collaboration of the bourgeoise facilitates its realisation. They are helping not only the dissemination of the values and tastes of the dominant culture but also contributing to its legitimacy. So are the Indian middle classes. The cultural transformation they have undergone during the colonial period had opened up the possibilities of what the West could offer them. They were disappointed that Independence did not give them the necessary freedom to pursue the utopia. The opportunity they were yearning for has now been offered by globalisation and therefore they have welcomed not only the "universal" culture but also become conduits for its free flow.

The principle, the bourgeoisie and the middle class, often invoke is the freedom of choice. They hold that they are voluntarily striking out a new path for our society. It is necessary, as Gandhiji has said, to keep the windows open. It is equally necessary that we refuse to be blown off our feet. Today the option to close the windows, if we so desire, does not exist. The initiative does not rest with us. Rather than free cultural interaction, cultural hegemonisation based on power differential and economic disparities is the evolving scenario. The freedom of choice is an illusion, even if culture operates with an aura of neutrality, as global forces do not exercise direct political control. The marginalisation of indigenous cultural practices is an inevitable outcome. The cultural invasion represented by the rapid intrusion of the electronic media tends to create the impression that the global forces are only introducing a new cultural element. The opposition, therefore, is confined to the "new" which militates against values Indian. This is quite misleading, as the global forces are working through the Indian shell by appropriating indigenous cultural forms and practices.

*(**Source**: K.N.Panikkar, "Globalisation and Culture", The Hindu*, Oct 5, 1995).

In order to allay the fears of host countries, MNCs need to respond in the following ways:

- Provide employment
- Train managers
- Provide products and services that raise the standard of living
- Introduce and develop new technical skills
- Introduce new managerial and organisational practices
- Provide greater access to international markets
- Raise the GDP
- Increase productivity

- Help build up foreign exchange reserves
- Encourage the development and spin-off of new industries
- Assume investment risk that may not otherwise be undertaken
- Mobilise capital for productive purposes from less productive uses

CHALLENGES OF INTERNATIONAL BUSINESS

Globalisation is a fact of life. The newspapers on a daily basis report about the global focus of companies-big and small. It is being reported how American firms are making inroads in to Japanese markets and how Japanese companies seek to invade American markets. Indian businessmen are not sitting pretty. They are scouting around for new partners, suppliers and buyers.

Challenges befare MNCs include –
- creating and maintaining competitive advantage
- facing local government regulations
- developing international perspectives
- managing diversity
- corporate citizenship

It is not just large companies that have a global focus. Increasingly, small businesses are also going global. The SSI sector in our country accounts for 44 per cent of our total exports.

Increasing globalisation poses its own challenges to trading countries. There are five areas in which each country must excel in order to emerge as a strong global player. First, the country must maintain competitiveness. Secondly, it must influence trade regulators so that other countries open their doors for its goods and services, being willing to buy from as well as sell to the country. Thirdly, the country's businesses must develop a global outlook that allows them to operate as true MNCs, not just as local firms doing business overseas.[13] Fourth, an MNC should know how to manage diversity in the global business canvas. Finally, a global firm needs to maintain a good image — an honest and socially responsibile firm.

Maintaining Competitiveness

Many factors contribute to the competitiveness of a nation. It is being argued that labour costs, interest rates, exchange rates and economies of scale make a nation competitive. These traditional factors, no doubt, contribute to the competitiveness of a country but not to be ignored are other sources which make a nation enjoy competitive advantage over others.

It has been demonstrated that the best way for companies to achieve competitive advantage is with innovation. Michael Porter has emphasised that the key to gain competitive advantage is the ability to innovate continually. Most successful MNCs have proved this claim. For example, 3M generates 30 per cent of its annual incomes from products that were brought to market in the last four years, and the number of patents issued to the company keeps rising every year. In 1990, it received 350,000 patents and the figure shot upto 500,000 by 1994. At the same time, 3M has managed to accelerate the product cycle by reducing cost and waste and bringing their products to fruition in record time. Other factors that contribute to competitiveness comprise quality, cost and service, to state only a few.

Why are some countries strong while others are weak? Porter's thesis provides the answer.

According to Michael Porter, a renowned expert on competition, competitive advantage of a nation depends on factor conditions, demand conditions, related and supporting industries and the environment in which firms compete (see Fig.3.2). These four attributes individually and interactively determine national competitive advantage.

Figure 3.2 **Porter's Determinants of Competitve Advantage**

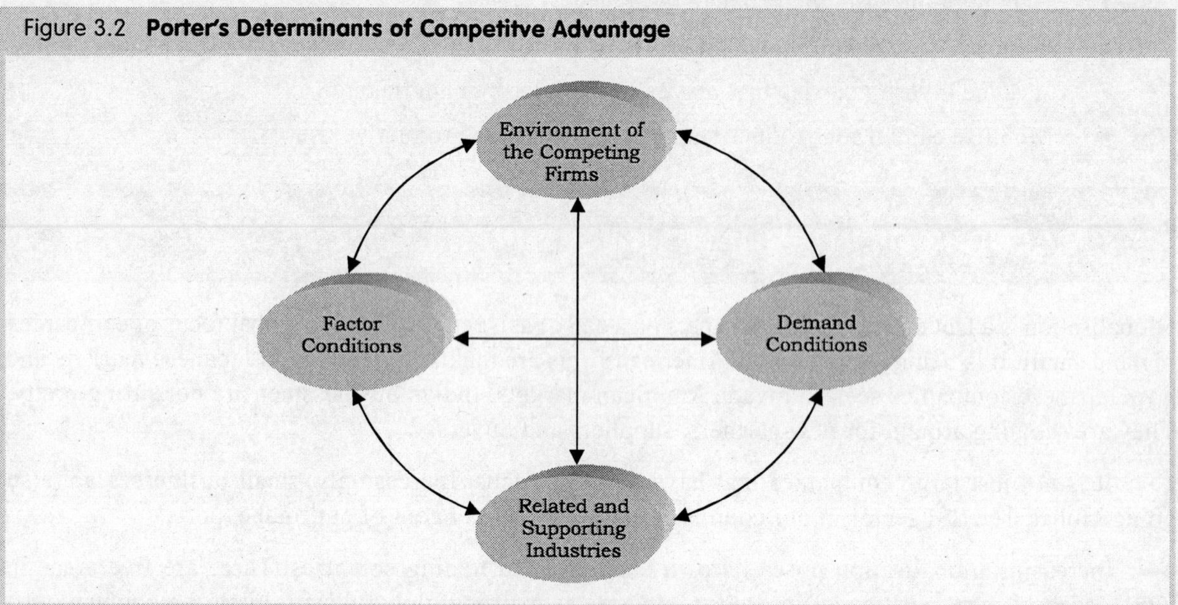

Factor Conditions According to basic international trade theory, a nation will export these goods that make best use of the factor conditions with which the country is relatively well endowed. These factor conditions include land, labour and capital. For example, if a country has large uneducated workforce, it will seek to export goods that are highly labour-intensive.

Sometimes, nations may develop factor conditions even if they are not endowed with. Japan, for example, has gained world market share in auto and consumer goods industries, though raw materials for these have been imported. To offset this disadvantage, Japanese manufacturers have improved productivity by using advanced production methods. High productivity has enabled Japan to gain advantage.

Demand Conditions A nation's competitive advantage, according to Porter, is strengthened if there is strong local demand for its goods and services. Denmark, for example, has gained leadership in the world market in water-pollution control equipment and windmills because of the high environmental concern of Danish people. Strong local market benefits sellers atleast in two ways. First, it helps the seller understand what buyers want. Secondly, if buyers want any change, local sellers can quickly respond before distant competitors can react.

Related and Supporting Industries Porter's third major determinant of national competitive advantage is the presence of related and supporting industries that are globally competitive. These are mainly service industries when suppliers are located near the producer, these firms often provide lower-cost inputs that are not available to the producers' distant competitors. In addition, suppliers typically know what is happening in the industrial environment and are in a position to both forecast and react to these changes. By sharing this information with the producer, they help the producer maintain its competitive position. The Italian shoe industry is an excellent example. Shoe producers interact on a regular basis with leather manufacturers, exchanging information that is useful to each in remaining competitive. This interaction is mutually beneficial to both the parties.

Environment Porter's fourth broad determinant of national advantage is the context in which the firms are created, organised and managed, as well the nature of domestic rivalry. Management practices vary across countries. Nations tend to do well in industries where the management practices match their industries' sources of competitive advantage. In Italy, for example, successful firms typically are small or medium sized enterprises serving small market niches and operate in fragmented industries such as lighting, furniture, footwear and packaging industries. In Japan, successful firms are often those that require unequal co-operation across functional lines and that demand the management of complex assembly operators.

National goals are equally important. Some nations expect quick results. Others tend to do well in industries where long-term development is expected.

Domestic rivalry is another determinant of a nation's competitive advantage. Nations which are leading world players tend to have strong local rivals. Switzerland enjoys competitive advantage in the pharmaceutical industry because of the rivalry among Hoffman, Ciba-Geigy and Sandoz. In Germany, BASF, Hoechst and Bayer help the country to keep ahead in chemicals.

Government and Trade Regulations

The government of any country can influence its international business significantly. For example, government intervention for the purpose of protecting domestic industries usually results in less movement of goods and services across borders.

A government's major role in global business may stem from its being a world trade negotiator. Many people believe that their government should limit competition from foreign goods in the interest of protecting local businesses and the jobs they offer. In the US, people question why the Japanese are allowed to set up auto plants in the US, while the country's farmers cannot sell rice in Japan even though imported rice would cost less than Japanese-produced rice.[14] In our country too, there is strong opposition to the import of anything. Infact, the controversy relating to *Videshi* (foreign) versus *Swadeshi* (domestic) was a major issue debated by political parties in the recently held general elections in our country.

Negotiations among countries to ease trade restrictions and prevent unfair trade practices are ongoing. The World Trade Organisation (WTO) is a major trade organisation that has been established to negotiate trade concessions among member countries. The members meet periodically and discuss the ways of minimising trade barriers.

Developing an International Perspective

Firms operating in cross border markets need to develop an international perspective. Three areas need special attention:experience, focus and attitude.[15]

Experience One way to acquire international perspective is to hire people with global exposure. A company cannot become a true MNC without having managers with an overseas perspective.

Focus The second way to develop an international orientation is by emphasising global orientation to human resource activities such as hiring, remunerating, performance appraisal, promotions and the like.

Attitude A third way to develop an international perspective is by changing the attitudes of managers towards their work. Companies should screen candidates carefully for overseas assignments and depute only individuals with the right attitudes.

Managing Diversity

Diversity is the outcome of globalisation. Workforce of any MNC comprises people from different countries. Within this diversity of national origins, there is even wider diversity of cultures, religions, languages and dialects, educational attainment, skills, values, ages, races, genders and other differentiating variables. Managing such a cosmopolitan workforce is a challenging task for any executive.

Before examining how to manage a multi-cultural workforce, it should be noted that diversity has both functional as well as dysfunctional consequences.

Among the potential problems associated with diversity is the likely absence of cohesion among workers. Where group lacks cohesion, members become less productive, and it becomes difficult to create a work environment that is conducive for efficiency and effectiveness. Another problem of diversity relates to inaccurate communication which may result from different meanings assigned to words; and different interpretations assigned to situations. Yet another problem resulting from diversity relates to sexual harassment. Many women are victims of sexual harassment in the workplaces. Sexual harassment consists of any unwanted sexual behaviour, including but not limited to suggestive looks, sexual jokes, touching, or pressure for sexual favours. Finally, earnings gaps exist in multi-cultural work groups. Earnings gaps refer to discrepancies between the earning power of workers of similar educational backgrounds but different races. An American or a German is paid much more in an MNC than his/her Indian counterpart.

While there are some potential problems associated with diversity, there are a host of benefits to be gained. Culturally diverse groups can enhance creativity, lead to better decisions and result in more effective and productive performance. A significant benefit from diversity relates to prevention of group think, which is a social conformity and pressures on individual members of a group to conform and reach consensus. Another benefit of diversity stems from the possibility of generating more and better ideas. Because group members come from a host of different cultures, they are able to create a greater number of creative and unique solutions and recommendations.

To reap the benefits listed above, managers must take steps to manage the issue of diversity. Steps depend upon the stage of group development: entry, work and action. In the *entry stage*, the focus should be on building trust and developing team cohesion. This can be a difficult task for diverse teams, whose members are accustomed to working in different ways. In the *work stage* of development, attention needs to be directed more towards describing and analysing the problem or task that has been assigned. This stage is often fairly easy for managers of multicultural teams, because they can draw on the diversity of the members in generating new ideas. In the *action stage*, the focus is to shift to decision making and implementation. This can be a difficult phase as it demands consensus building among members. In achieving this objective, experienced managers work to help the diverse group recognise and facilitate the creation of ideas with which anybody can agree.

Fig.3.3 outlines seven specific spheres of activity that together help manage diversity more effectively.

Need to Maintain Good Corporate Citizenship

An MNC will be successful if only it creates and sustains the image of a good corporate citizenship as reflected in honesty and social responsiveness

As MNCs disperse their activities worldwide, they become highly visible and are required to operate under diverse compulsions such as cultural, political, economic and legal factors of different host countries. An international business will be successful if only it creates and sustains the image of a good corporate citizenship-the two hall marks of which are honesty and social responsiveness. Quite often, MNCs confront issues and conflicts of the type described below.

It was on December 2, 1984 that disaster struck residents of Bhopal. Deadly methyl isocyanite (MIC) leaked from the pesticide plant of Union Carbide killing 4000 in the night of December 2, and crippling for life more than 100,000 people.

Figure 3.3 **Seven Spheres for Managing Diversity**

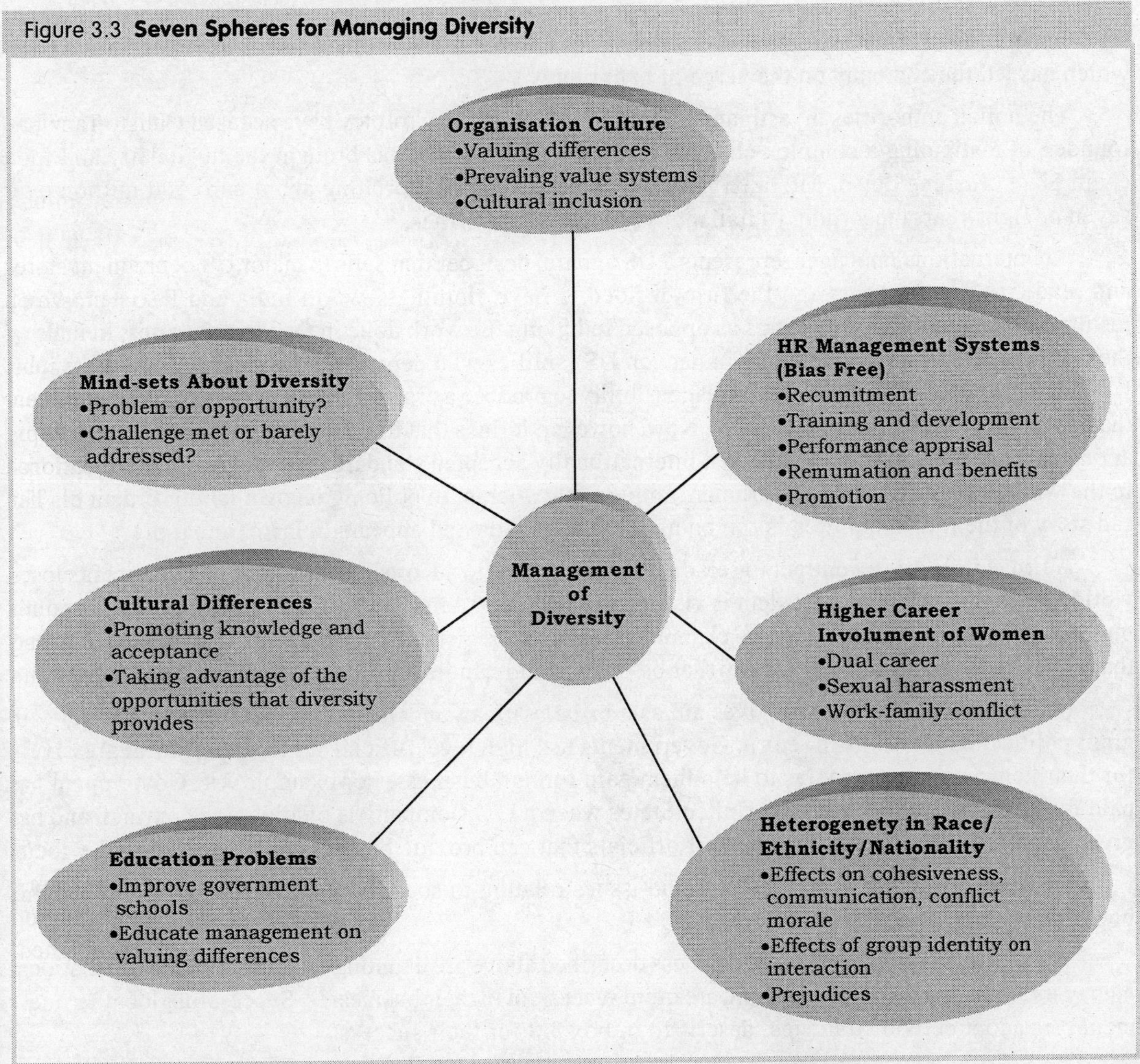

The people of Bhopal are yet to get an answer as to why the Union Carbide Corporation set up an outmoded plant in Bhopal when they had already developed an advanced computerised safety system for their West Virginia plant in the U.S. The refrigeration system was faulty; the valve lines and vent lines in the Bhopal plant were old and worn out. Parts that should have been replaced had not been changed for more than two years.

Though the accused in the criminal case linked to the Carbide disaster are facing the charge of "causing death not amounting to murder", citizens and activist groups continue to hold the multinational corporation guilty of "mass homicide" because, even though it was aware of the hazards of MIC and took safety precautions in its West Virginia plant, it did not take adequate steps here.

People here still want to know why the Government of India and the Government of Madhya Pradesh did not care to get adequate information about the hazardous nature of MIC and permitted Union Carbide to use such a deadly and lethal gas within city limits and store it in such huge quantities. At the time of the leak, more than 30,000 gallons of MIC had been stored. In contrast, the storage capacity in the West Virginia Plant was not more than 5000 gallons.

The Milan magistrates are now investigating Europe's 'biggest and spectacular' corporate scandal, where equivalent of some Rs.25,000 crores to Rs.50,000 crores cash assets in euros, have 'just vanished' from the company's Cayman Island (tax haven) accounts. According to the investigating Magistrates, the founder of the Parmalat Company, which employs about 39,000 staff, himself 'instigated fraud plan' which has led the company on the verge of bankruptcy.

The Italian authorities investigating Parmlat's slide into bankruptcy have accused Calisto Tanzi, its founder, of instigating a complex chain of financial schemes that has brought the huge dairy and food chain giant crushing down. Mr.Tanzi has now admitted misappropriating about euro 500 million over seven or eight years, according to Italian investigating authorities.

An international manager represents a US apparel designer that sells to major US department stores and retailers. Several years ago the firm decided to have clothing sewn in India and Pakistan, which resulted in tremendous cost savings as opposed to having the work done in the United States. In making the decision, the firm considered its impact on US families who depend on the income from these jobs. It opted for the cost savings, seeing its responsibility to produce a profit for shareholders as more important than providing jobs in the United States. Now, however, it finds that its contractor in India is overworking and abusing child labour in violation of internationally accepted standards for the treatment of children in the workplace. The Indian government shows little interest in policing its own labour practices. The sad story of the Indian children is run on national television and appears in the national press.

A firm enters into a contract to sell drilling equipment to a Korean company. The contract is closed while the Korean company president is visiting the US plant. After closing, the Korean executive points out that all imports to Korea must be channeled through a registered "local agent." He quickly suggests that a wholly owned trading company that be owns could handle all of the paperwork-for a fee.

US Government frequently gives aid as a bribe, with an understanding that the host country will grant political concessions in return. Governments use high level official visits and lobby aggressively for their home-based companies to help them gain foreign business. For example, US Government has paid for ministry heads to visit the United States when a U.S.Company is bidding or a contract, and has given scholarships to family members of officials that can provide business to US companies.

We will consider ethical dilemmas and issues relating to socially responsive actions later in this book.

The challenges of international business described above are daunting nodoubt. But the international managers are facing the challenges and are quite successful in their businesses. Successful global business managers adopt certain strategies, described in box 3.8 for their success.

Box 3.8 **Keys to Success**

Know the Customer: The successful manager has detailed knowledge of what different international customers want and ensures that the company is flexible enough to customize products to meet those needs.

Emphasize Global Awareness: Good global managers ensure that the company designs and builds products and services for export from the beginning, not as an afterthought following the conquest of domestic markets.

Market a World-Class Product: Successful managers insist on high-quality products; they know that customers everywhere demand reliability.

Give Workers a Stake in the Company: The best global companies provide special incentives for employees who perform well.

Know How to Analyze Problems: Successful managers rarely start out with solutions. Instead, they tackle problems one piece at a time by experimenting and taking risks as necessary.

Understand Technology: The best managers find ways to match technology with the customer's environment. They do not, for example, make changes out of love for technology but will build new product lines using new and cheaper material when it becomes available.

Keep an Eye on Exchange Rates: The increasing popularity of using exchange rates to control trade means that global managers must constantly deal with shifts in currency values. In short, they must understand how exchange rates function.

QUESTIONS

1. Bring out the nature and causes for globalisation of industry.
2. What is an MNC? Name some Indian MNCs.
3. Bring out the benefits and limitations of MNCs.
4. Why is there strong opposition to the entry of MNCs into our country?
5. Bring out the impact of globalisation on culture.
6. Why do companies go international?
7. Bring out the challenges of globalisation.

ASSIGNMENTS

1. In batches of 5-7 students, visit any mall on a Saturday and observe the patterns and buying behaviours of youth (who are invariably employees of new economy firms). Make a presentation of observations to the class.
2. Collect published statements of TCS, WIPRO and Infosys. Study how much of their revenues flow from foreign operations. Observe this trend over a five-year period.

REFERENCES

1. Arun Kumar Jain, *Managing Global Competition*, Competence Publishing Co., Dehradun, 1994, p.30.
2. *Ibid*, p.31.
3. Philip Kotler, *Principles of Marketing*, PHI, p.576.
4. Anil Gupta, "Global Elephants, *The Economic Types*, Dec.26, 2003.
5. Andrew Harrison, *et al*, *International Business*, Oxford, 2000, p.158.
6. Michael P.Todaro and Stephen C.Smith, *Economic Development*, Pearson, 2003, p.565.
7. Jagadish Bhagawati, *In Defense of Globalisation*, Oxford, 2004, p.11.
8. The Bostan Consultancy Group, 2005.
9. Supriya Roychowdury, "Globalisation and Labour," *Economic and Political Weekly*, Jan.3, 2004, p.106.
10. James A.F.Stoner and Edward Freeman, *Management*, PHI, 2000, p.773.
12. *Ibid*, p.774.
13. Rugman and Hodgetts, *International Business*, McGraw Hill, 1995, p.12.
14. *Ibid*, p.19.
15. *Ibid*, p.21.

CHAPTER OUTLINE

Strategies of Globalisation
Flow of FDI

LEARNING OBJECTIVES

After reading this Chapter, you should be able to:

1. Describe the various different strategies for going global
2. Understand theories of FDI
3. Describe organisational structures for MNCs
4. List the newer organisational models required for MNCs

4 Strategies for Going Global

The previous chapter provided the theoretical backdrop to globalisation. Globalisation has come to stay. The issue before any businessperson is not whether or not to global but how to go about it. This chapter is devoted to a brief discussion of the strategies for going global.

STRATEGIES OF GLOBALISATION

Globalisation involves decision-making on the following lines: (see also Fig. 4.1)

- Deciding whether to go global.
- Deciding which markets to enter.
- Deciding how to enter the market.
- Learning to handle differences.
- Adjusting the management process.
- Selecting a managerial approach.
- Deciding organization structure.

Deciding whether to go global

As stated above, globalisation has come to stay. Every manufacturer, whether producing tooth powder, herbal products, or software, is planning to take his products beyond the Indian shores. Open the newspaper or periodicals, you find profiles of companies fully illustrating joint venture deals with foreign companies or foreign investments flowing into power, roads and other infrastructural areas.

Figure 4.1 **Globalisation Strategies**

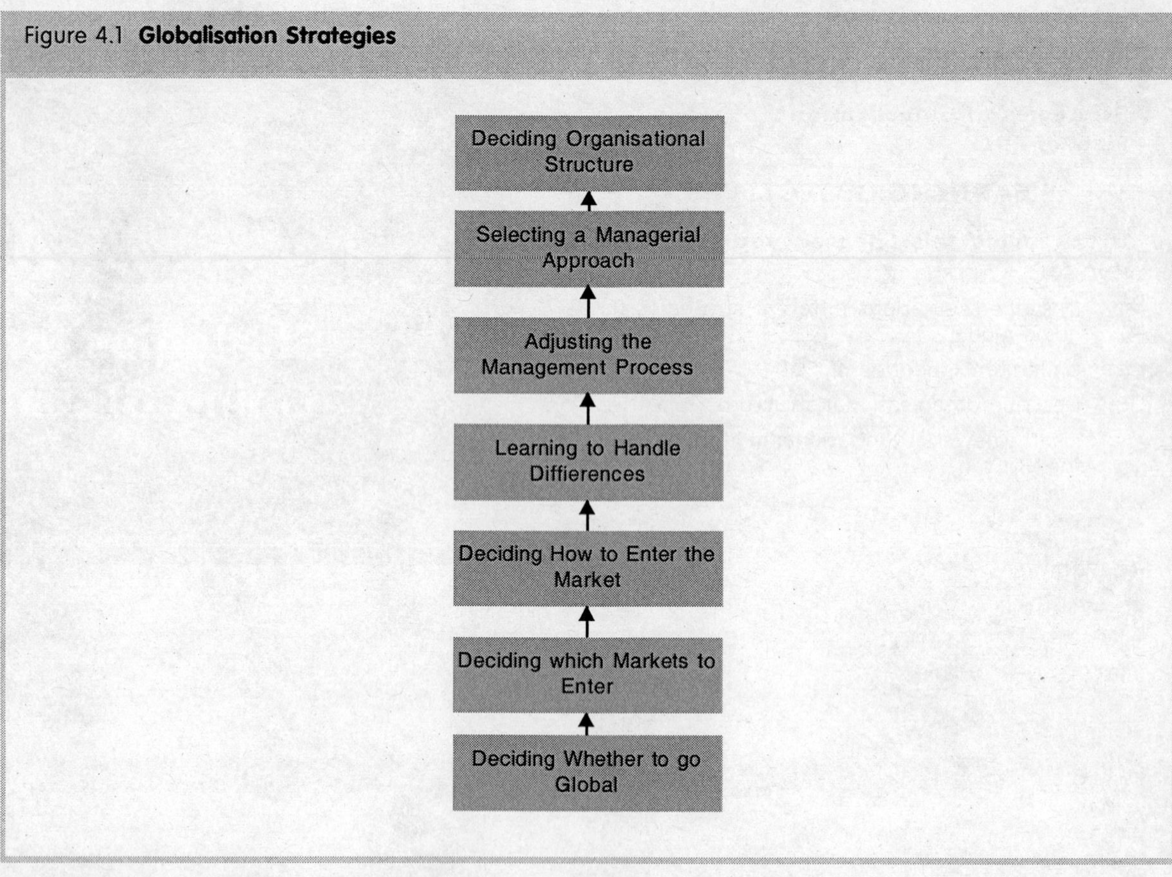

Local companies need to think about local markets.

However, theoretically, it may be argued that deciding whether or not to go global is a difficult job, particularly when domestic market is vast as it is the case with our country. For a long time, our businessperson enjoyed a sheltered and vast market where they could sell whatever they produced. But today's environment is different. Technological innovations, crumbling trade barriers, global flow of capital, revolution in the information technology, intensity of market competition, changing lifestyles and demand for new products are making internationalisation inevitable.

However, not all companies need to go global. Local businesses, for example, do well to concentrate on local markets. Companies that operate in global industries,* on the other hand, must think and act globally. Thus, IBM must organize globally if it is to gain purchasing, manufacturing, financial and marketing advantages. Companies in the global industry must compete on a worldwide basis if they should succeed.

Before going international, the company must weigh several risks and answer many questions about its ability to operate globally. Can the company learn to understand the preferences and buying behavior of consumers in other countries? Can it offer competitively with foreign nationals? Do the company's managers have the necessary international experience? Has the management considered the impact of foreign regulations and political environments?

Because of the risks and difficulties of entering foreign markets, most companies do not act until some situation or event thrusts them into the global scene. Someone - a domestic exporter, a foreign importer, a foreign government - asks the company to sell abroad and the company is saddled with overcapacity, then it becomes important that the former must find additional markets for its goods.[1]

*A global industry is one in which the strategic positions of competitors in given geographic or national markets are affected by their overall global positions.

Deciding which markets to enter

This involves deciding on-

(i) volume of foreign sales,

(ii) number of countries to market in, and

(iii) the types of countries to enter.

Most companies start small when they go abroad. Some plan to stay small, viewing foreign sales as a small part of their business. Other companies have bigger plans, seeing foreign business as equal or even more important than their home business.

There is temptation for a company to spread its wings in as many countries as possible, but it makes better sense to operate in a fewer countries with a deeper market penetration in each.

The types of countries to enter depend on the type of product, geographical factors, income and population, political climate and other related factors (see Fig.4.2). It is advisable to rank the countries on specific factors. The goal is to determine the potential of each country. It goes without saying that the country which assures long run returns on investments must be selected for entering its market.

Figure 4.2 **Indicators of Market Potential**

1. **Demographic Characteristics**
   Size of population
   Rate of population growth
   Degree of urbanization
   Population density
   Age structure and composition of the population
2. **Geographic Characteristics**
   Physical size of a country
   Topographical characteristics
   Climatic conditions
3. **Economic Factors**
   GNP per capita
   Income distribution
   Rate of growth of GNP
   Ratio of investment to GNP
4. **Technological Factors**
   Level of technological skill
   Existing production technology
   Existing consumption technology
   Education levels
5. **Socio-cultural Factors**
   Dominant values
   Life style patterns
   Ethnic groups
   Linguistic fragmentation
6. **National goals and plans**
   Industry priorities
   Infrastructure investment plans.

International businesses generally make political risk assessment before foraying into any foreign market.

Political risk is any governmental action or politically oriented event that could adversely affect fortunes of a company

Political Risk: Political risk is any governmental action or politically motivated event that could adversely affect the long-run profitability or value of a firm.[2] Political risk affects different firms in different ways. It can threaten the market of an exporter, the production facilities of a manufacturer, or the ability of a firm to repatriate its profits from a host country to its home country. Table 4.1 contains examples of political risks.

Table 4.1 **Examples of Political Risks and their Impact on International Business**

Risks	*Impact*
(A) Macro Risks	
(i) Expropriation of corporate assets without prompt and adequate compensation	Loss of future profits
(ii) Barriers to repatriation of profits	No motivation to improve efficiency
(iii) Confiscation of properties	Loss of assets and future profits
(iv) Loss of technology or other intellectual property	Loss of future profits
(v) Compaigns against foreign goods public relations	Loss of sales and increased costs of campaigns
(vi) Mandatory labour legislations	Increased operating costs
(vii) Civil wars	Destruction of property, loss of sales, increased security costs, disrupted production runs
(viii) Inflation	Increased operating costs
(ix) Currency devaluations	Reduced values of repatriated earnings
(B) Micro Risks	
(i) Kidnappings, terrorist threats, etc.	Disrupted production, higher security costs, reduced productivity
(ii) Increased taxation	Reduced after tax profits
(iii) Officials' dishonesty	Loss of business, increased operating costs.

Political risk varies from nation to nation. It is very high in countries like Yugoslavia, Afghanistan, Turkey, Iraq, Algeria, Sudan, Nigeria,Somalia, Congo, Angola, Myanmar and Indonesia. Political risk is almost non-existent in the US, Canada, Denmark, Australia and Western European countries.

Distinction is often made between macro and micro risks. A macro political risk affects all international businesses in the same way. Expropriation, the seizure of assets by government with little or no compensation to the owners, is a macropolitical risk. Communist governments in Eastern Europe and China expropriated private firms following World War II. Fidel Castro did the same in Quba from 1958 to 1959. Recently, governments in Angola, Chile, Ethiopia, Peru, and Zambia have expropriated private firms. In all these cases international businesses were hard hit.

Political boycotts also result in macropolitical risk. Since 1955, a number of Arab countries have boycotted firms with branches in Israel or companies that have allowed the use of their trade name there. Macropolitical risk can also come about because of indigenisation laws which bind international businesses accept equity participation by local citizens.[(3)]

Macro political risk has been changing in recent years. For example, Eastern European countries such as Poland, Hungary, and the Czech Republic are now inviting private investment, as does Russia. China's entry into WTO is a pointer to the changing environment in Asia. Vietnam's secret trade agreement with the US is another positive indicator. All these developments have certainly minimised the political risk but the risk continues to exist.

A micro political risk affects specific foreign businesses. Micro political risks include industry regulations, taxes, kidnapping and terrorist threats.

India's decision in 1975 to reduce foreign equity to 40 per cent and Peru's decision to nationalise its copper mines are examples of micro political risks. The US decision to tax textile imports is another instance. Yet another example is the bombing of Chinese embassy in Belgrade by NATO forces in 1997. In retaliation demonstrators in China trashed KFC stores but did not touch Pizza Hut stores though both were owned by a US based company. Chinese protestores did not attack Pizza Hut Stores thinking that it was Italian-owned.

India's decision in 1975 to reduce foreign equity to 40% is a micro political risk

Firms which have high visibility in host countries are targets of micro political risk. If agitation's cause is animosity between factories in the host country and the government of a foreign country, agitators may target only the most visible companies from that foreign country, like KFC.

Political Risk Assessment: International businesses must conduct some form of political risk assessment to manage risks. Typically, managers in host countries assess the potentially destabilising issues and evaluate their future impact on the firm, making suggestions for handling problems. Top management at head office then will establish guidelines for each host country managers to solve such problems.

Risk assessment by international businesses usually takes two forms. One is through the use of experts or consultants familiar with the host country or region under consideration. Such consultants, advisers, and committees usually monitor important indicators that may portend political change. They then assess the likelihood of political change and develop several scenarios to describe alternative political conditions in the future.

Political risk assessment is made either by developing inhouse capabilities or by retaining the services of consultants

A second and increasingly common means of political risk assessment used by international businesses is through the development of their internal staff and in-house capabilities. This type of assessment may be accomplished by having staff assigned to foreign subsidiaries or affiliates monitor local political activities or by hiring people with expertise in the political and economic conditions in regions critical to the firm's operations.

Whatever the method, timely information from the people on the front line should not be missed. Experts or consultants are no substitute for the line managers in the foreign subsidiaries, many of whom are host country nationals. These managers represent the most important resource for current information on the political environment and how it might affect their firm because they are uniquely situated at the meeting point of the firm and the host country. Prudent international businesses, however, weigh the subjectivity of these managers' assessments and also realise that similar events will have different effects from one country to another.[4]

Entry Strategies

Once the company has decided to go global, it must decide on the best mode of entry. The usual entry strategies are: (see also Fig. 4.3).

- Exports and imports
- Tourism and transportation
- Performance of services
- Use of assets
- Joint-ventures
- Wholly owned subsidiaries

As shown in Fig. 4.3, the entry strategies are arranged in the order of their degree of presence in global markets and the extent of foreign investment.

Figure 4.3 **Entry Strategies**

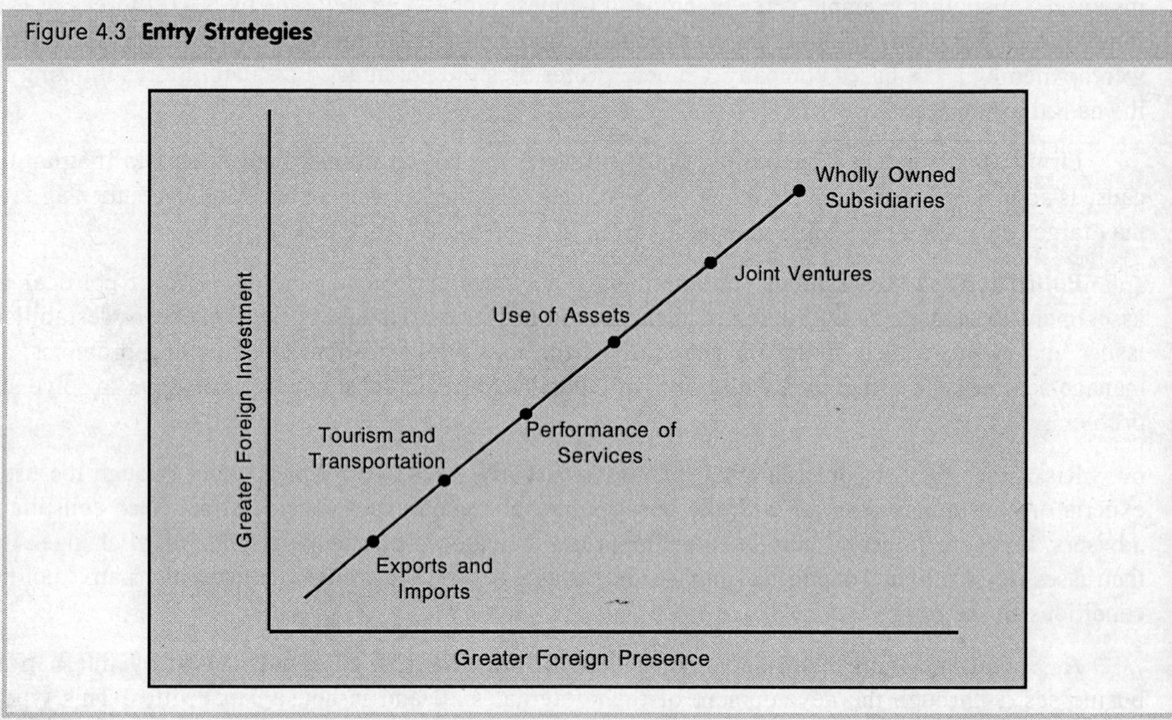

Exports or imports constitute the oldest mode of entry into a foreign market.

Exports and Imports: Exports are goods and services produced in one country but marketed in another country. Imports are goods and services produced in one country but bought by another country. Exports and imports do not take place only in tangible goods, but also include services such as those provided by international airlines, cruise lines, reservation agencies, and hotels. Infact, the trade in services is heavier than buying and selling of physical goods.

European Community (EC) is the world's single largest trading unit, followed by Asia and North America. The majority of this export and import activity is in the area of manufacturing such as industrial machinery, computers, cars, televisions, VCRs, and other electronic goods. But, as stated erlier, an increasing proportion of world trade is in services.

Though not a major player, India's presence in world business is steadily increasing. The exports from our country more than tripled from Rs.32,553 cr in 1990-91 to Rs.2,52,787 crore in 2002-2003. The country's imports also jumped from Rs.43,198 cr in 1990-91 to Rs.2,96,597 cr in 2002-2003. As a proportion of the GNP, foreign trade of India went up to 18.6 per cent as of today from 14.1 per cent from the beginning of 1990s.

Why do firms export? Reasons are not difficult to find. Expanding sales, gaining experience and building brand equity are the main reasons for firms selling goods and services in overseas markets.

Tourism and Transportation: Tourism and transportation are the routes of globalisation for such industries as shipping, airlines, hotel and travel agency. Some countries, Greece and Norway for example, depend on international tourism and transportation for employment, profits, and foreign exchange earnings. Earnings from foreign tourism are more important for the Bahamian economy than are earnings from export of merchandise. Similarly, in recent years the US has earned more from foreign tourism than from its exports of agricultural goods.

Performance of Services: International businesses earn money in the form of fees for services rendered. This is particularly true in banking, insurance, rentals, engineering, management service and the like. Turnkey operations are typical modes for earning such fees. Here, the company contracts with a foreign entity to design and build an entire operation. On completion, the operation is turned over to the owner who can use the facilities straight away. The Italian comnpany, Fiat, for example constructed a complete automobile plant in the erstwhile Soviet Union under this type of arrangement. Tata Consulting Engineers, India, are specialists in executing turnkey projects. Some of the major projects executed by them are: erection of 5x50 MW gas turbo-generators at Shuwaik Power Station, Kuwait, design and engineering of the 3XMW Derbendikhan hydro-electric project in Iran; installation of 50,000 spindle spinning mill in Tanzania; 180 room hotel project in the Yemen Arab Republic; and water supply augmentation scheme for Lilongwe, capital of Malawi.

Companies also earn fees through management contracts-arrangements in which one firm contracts with a foreign corporation or government to manage an entire project or undertaking for a specific period. Most management contracts provide for training of local personnel who will eventually take over the management responsibilities. An example of this was Bell Canda's contract with the government of Saudi Arabia to manage the installation of modern transmission and switching equipment in Saudi Arabia's Telephone System. Similarly, under a management contract, for a ten year period (1969-1979), Citibank had lent its managerial expertise to Grindlays Bank. Disney receives management fees from managing theme parks in France and Japan.

Turnkey projects and management contracts are examples of service mode of entry into foreign markets

Nearer at home, the late Aditya Birla was controlling his companies abroad through management contracts.

Use of Assets: Licensing and franchising are the modes which facilitate companies allow others to use their assets. Under a **license** agreement, one firm permits another to use its intellectual property for compensation called royalty. The firm that makes the offer is the licenser and the recipient firm is designated as the licensee. The property licensed generally includes such assets as patents, trade marks, copyrights, technology, technical knowhow, business skills, and the like. Licensing amounts to exporting intangibles.

Licensing and franchising are examples for use of assets – one of the entry modes into foreign marekts

Licensing has intutive appeal to many prospective global players. As a mode of globalisation, licensing requires neither capital investment nor detailed involvement with foreign customers. By generating royalty income, licensing provides an opportunity to exploit research and development already conducted. After initial costs, the licensee can reap benefits until the end of the license contract period. Licensing also reduces the risk of exproportion because the licensee is a local company that can provide leverage against government action. In recent years a number of host countries have demanded that MNCs license their assets rather than following only FDI routs.

The main disadvantage of licensing is that license fees are likely to be lower than FDI profits. Other disadvantages include:

- Possible loss of quality control
- Establishment of a potential competitor in third country markets
- Possible improvement of the technology by the local licensee, which then enters the licensor's home market
- Possible loss of opportunity to enter the licensee's market with FDI later
- Risk of technology being stolen
- High agency costs.

Multinational businesses do not typically use licensing of independent firms. On the contrary, most licensing arrangements have been with their own foreign subsidiaries or joint ventures. License fees are a way to spread the corporate research and development cost among all operating units and a means of repatriating profits in a form more acceptable to some host countries than dividends.

Another route of globalisation is **franchising**, which involves the granting of right by a parent company (the franchiser) to another (the franchisee) to do business in a prescribed manner. This right can take the form of selling the franchiser's products, using its name, production, and marketing techniques, or using its general business approach. Usually, franchising involves a combination of all these elements.

The major forms of franchising are manufacturer-retailer systems (such as a car dealership), manufacturer-wholesaler systems (such as soft drink companies) and service firm-retailer systems (such as lodging services, fast food outlets and hotel/motel industries).

Franchising is adaptable to the international arena, and with some minor adjustments for the local market, it can result in a highly profitable business. In fast foods, McDonald's Burger King, and Kentucky Fried Chicken have used franchise agreements to expand their markets from Paris to Tokyo and from Cairo to Carcas. In the hotel business, Le-Meridian among others has been very successful in gaining worldwide presence through the use of franchisees.

FDI allows the investors have a controlling interest in an overseas company.
FDI can be a joint venture or a wholly owned subsidiary

Franchise agreement typically requires the payment of a fee upfront and then a precentage on sales. In return, the franchiser provides assistance and, in some instances, may require the purchase of goods or supplies to ensure the same quality of goods or services worldwide.

Franchising can be beneficial to both the groups. It provides the franchiser with a new stream of income and the franchisee with a time proven concept and products that can be quickly brought to market.

Direct Investment: A direct investment is the one that allows the investor a controlling interest in a foreign company. Foreign direct investment (FDI) is another name for direct investment. FDI may take the form of a joint vernture or a wholly owned subsidiary.

A joint venture is a shared ownership in a foreign business. Generally, the venture is 50-50 ownership in which there are two parties, each of which holds a 50 per cent ownership stake and contributes a team of managers to share operating control. Fuji-Xerox is one of the most enduring and successful joint-ventures between two companies of different countries. The world famous company-Rolls Royce-has 25 joint ventures across all its business activities.

There are 868 Indian joint ventures abroad, out of which 286 ventures are in operation and 582 are under different stages of implementation. The approved equity of these ventures amounts to $1097.68 million.

Indian joint ventures are predominantly in other developing countries like Malaysia, Indonesia, Singapore, Sri Lanka, Nigeria, Kenya, UAE, and Thailand. Joint ventures have been set up both by private entrepreneurs and public sector undertakings.

Indian Joint Ventures are located mainly in developing countries

In a wholly owned subsidiary, the company owns 100 per cent of the equity. At present there are 733 wholly owned Indian subsidiaries abroad, out of which 216 are in operation and 517 are at various stages of implementation. The approved equity of these subsidiaries amount to $820.59 million.

A wholly owned subsidiary can be set up in a foreign market in either of two ways. The company can set up a totally new operation or can acquire an established firm and use the firm to promote its products. The subsidiary that is established starting from the ground up (i.e. from a greenfield) is called a **greenfield investment**. Compared to green field investment, a cross-border acquisition has a number of benefits. First, acquisition is quicker than establishing a firm. Greenfield investment requires extended periods of physical construction and organisational development. By acquiring an existing firm, an international business can shorten the time required to gain a presence and facilitate competitive entry into the market. Second, acquisition may be a cost-effective way gaining competitive advantages such as technology, brand names, and logistical and distribution advantages, while simultaneously eliminating a local competitor. Third, international economic, political, and foreign exchange conditions may result in market imperfections allowing target firms to be undervalued. Many firms throughout Asia have been the target of acquisition as a result of the Asian economic crisis impact on their financial health. Many companies were in dire need of capital injections for competitive survival.

Greenfield investment involves setting up of operations newly. Such an investment is heavy and risky too.

There is the flip side to cross-border acquisitions. There is the possibility of paying too high a price. Meshing different corporate cultures can be traumatic experience. Managing the post-acquisition process is characterised by downsizing to gain economies of scale and scope in overhead functions. This results in unhealthy impacts on the firm as individuals attempt to save their own jobs. There are also difficulties arising from host governments intervening in pricing, financing, employee hiring, and nationalism and favouritism.

FDI

Direct investment, (or FDI) through joint venture or wholly owned subsidiaries, is the most preferred way of entering into foreign markets.

Though expensive and risky, yet FDI is preferred because of
(i) transportation costs
(ii) market imperfections
(iii) competition
(iv) product life cycle
(v) location
(vi) developing countries

But, FDI is expensive and risky when compared to exporting and licensing. FDI is expensive because a firm must bear the costs of establishing production facilities in a foreign country or of acquiring a foreign enterprise. FDI is risky because of the problems associated with doing business in another culture where the "rules of the game" may be different. Yet, firms prefer to go all out to acquire enterprises abroad or establish subsidiaries in alien countries. Six factors explain such preference: (i) transportation costs, (ii) market imperfections, (iii) competition, (iv) product lifecycle, (5) location advantages, and (vi) developing countries.[5] (See Fig. 4.4)

Transportation Costs: From the transportation cost perspective, goods may be of low value to weight ratio type or the opposite, namely, high value to weight ratio type. In the former, (e.g. cement, soft drinks etc.) transportation cost is considerable and it is unprofitable to ship them over long distances. They can also be produced in almost any location. In products of this type, relative to either FDI or licensing, the attractiveness of exporting decreases. For products with a high value to weight ratio, however, transport costs are a minor component of total landed cost. Electronic components, personal computers, computer software, and the like belong to this category. In these products, transportation costs have little impact on the relative attractiveness of exporting, FDI, and licensing.

Market Imperfections: The market imperfections theory offers a major explanation why firms prefer FDI to exporting or licensing. Alternatively called *internationalisation theory* in the literature on

Figure 4.4 **Reasons for the Flow of FDI**

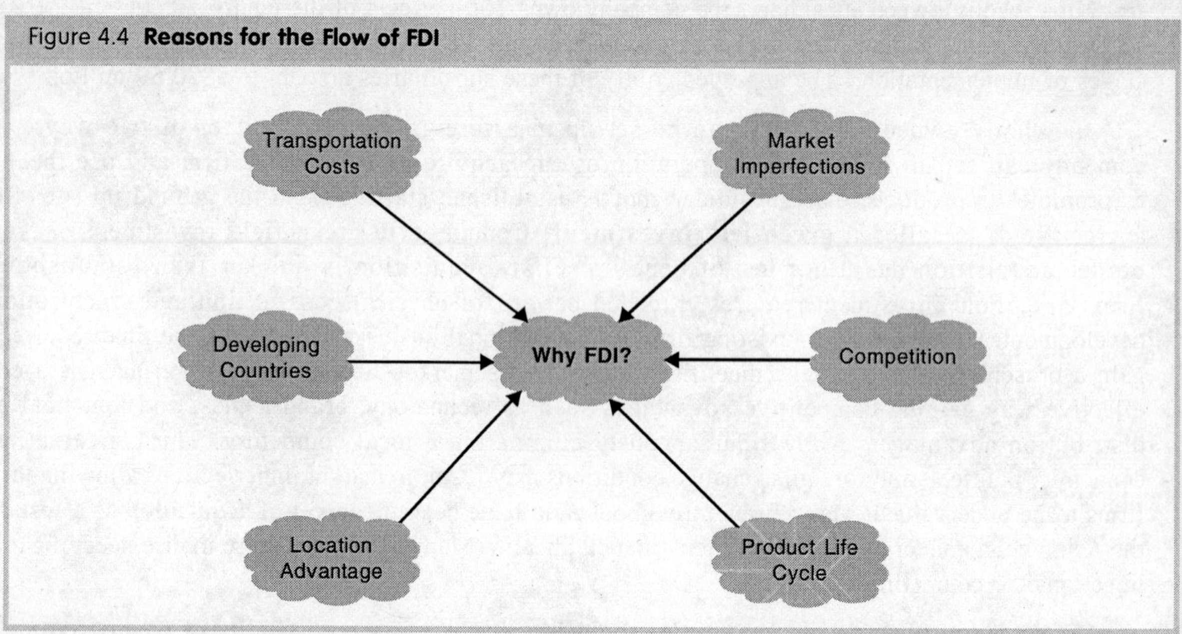

Barriers to exporting and barriers to the sale of knowhow prevent market perfections from happening

global business, this approach highlights two major *impediments:* barriers to exporting and barriers to the sale of know-how. These obstacles inhibit markets from working perfectly.

Impediments to the free flow of products between nations decrease the profitability of exporting, relative to FDI and licensing. Governments are the main source of impediments to the free flow of products between nations. By imposing tariffs on imported goods, governments can increase the cost of exporting relative to FDI and licensing. Similarly, by restricting imports through the imposition of quotas, governments increase the attractiveness of FDI and licensing.

Sale of know-how takes place through licensing. Impediments to the sale of know-how increase the profitability of FDI relative to licensing. Though licensing is less expensive and risky, firms do not prefer it because of three reasons. First, licensing may result in a firm giving away its know-how to a potential foreign competitor. For example, RCA Corporation licensed, in the 1960s, its leading-edge colour television technoilogy to a number of Japanese firms including Matsushita and Sony. At that time RCA saw licensing as a way to earn a good return from its technology in the Japanese market without the costs and risks associated with FDI. However, Matsushita and Sony quickly assimilated RCA's technology and used it to enter the US market to compete directly against RCA. As a result, RCA is now a minor player in its home market, while Matsushita and Sony have a much bigger market.

Secondly, licensing does not give a firm the right control over manufacturing, marketing, and strategy in a foreign country that may be required to profitably exploit its advantage in know-how. With licensing, control over production, marketing, and strategy is granted to a licensee in return for a royalty fee. However, for both strategic and operational reasons, a company may want to retain control over the functions. When tight control over a foreign entity is desirable, FDI is preferable to licensing.

Thirdly, a company's know-how itself may not be for licensing. This is particularly true of management and marketing know-how. It is one thing to license a foreign firm to manufacture a particular product, but quite another to license the way a firm does its business-how it manages its process and markets its product. Take Toyota, a company whose competitive advantage in the global auto industry is acknowledged to come from its superior ability to manage the overall process of designing, engineering, manufacturing, and selling automobiles; that is, from its management and organisational know-how. Toyota is credited with pioneering the development of a new production process, known as lean-production, that enables it to produce higher-quality automobiles at a lower cost than its global rivals.

Although Toyota has certain products that can be licensed, its real competitive advantage comes from its management and process know-how, which cannot be licensed. Toyota is increasingly pursuing a strategy of FDI; moving away from its traditional exporting route.

Thus, when one or more of the following conditions prevail, markets fail as a mechanism for selling know-how and FDI is more profitable than licensing: (1) when the firm has valuable know-how that cannot be adequately protected by a licensing contract, (2) when the firm needs tight control over a foreign entity to maximise its market share and earnings in that country, and (3) when a firm's skills and know-how are not amenable to licensing.

First entry into the US by Honda then followed by Toyota and Nissan typify how competition casuses inflow of FDI into any country. As per the competition theory, firms resort to FDI when competitors do it first.

Competition: FDI flows are often a reflection of rivalry among firms in the global market place. Assuming that three firms A, B and C dominate the market in the US (this situation is called oligopoly). Firm A established a subsidiary in France. Firms B and C reflect that if this investment is successful, it may affect adversely their export business to France and give firm A an advantage of early start. Furthermore, firm A might discover some competitive asset in France that, it could repatriate to its home country to harrow firms B and C in their native soil. Given these possibilities, firms B and C decide to follow firm A and establish operations in France.

Expounded by F.T.Knickerbockers in the early 1970s, the competitors theory for FDI flow has evidence for support. For example, Honda undertook FDI in the US and Europe during the 1980s. Toyota and Nissan followed suit.

The Product Lifecycle Theory: This theory has been propounded by Raymond Vernon. Vernon argued that often the same firms that pioneer a product in their home markets undertake to produce a product for consumption in foreign markets. Thus, Xerox introduced the photocopier in the US, and it was Xerox that set up production facilities in Japan (Fuji-Xerox) and Great Britain (Rank-Xerox) to serve those markets.

Vernon's view is that firms undertake FDI at particular stages in the lifecycle of a product they have pioneered. They invest in other advanced countries when local demand in those countries grows large enough to support local production (as Xerox did). They subsequently shift production to developing countries when product standardisation and market saturation give rise to price competition and cost pressures. Investments in developing countries, where labour costs are lower, is seen as the best way to reduce costs.

Apart from theories, strong reasons why FDI flows into any country are location-specific. Some regions are endowed with rich resources which attract FDI

Location Advantages: In addition to the various factors discussed till now, there are certain location-specific advantages that attract FDI. The location-specific advantages in particular, include natural resources such as oil and other minerals, which are by nature specific to certain locations. A firm must undertake FDI to exploit such endowments. This explains the FDI undertaken by many of the world's oil companies, which have to invest where oil is located. Another example is the valuable human resource, such as low-cost highly skilled labour force. The cost and skill of labour varies from country to country. A Canadian medium-sized plant is thinking in terms of renovating a plant near Warsaw in Poland as the price of labour in that country is fairly low. Other nearby countries have lower wage rates, but Warsaw, the company's specific choice, has a cadre of well trained factory workers who could be transferred to the renovated factory. Similarly, one major benefit of locating plants in Mexico is the highly skilled labour force that can be hired at fairly low wage rates. Additionally, manufacturing firms located in Mexico report high productivity growth rates and quality performance. France has been the target of much MNC activity. Daimler-Chrysler has recently built a new factory in France because of its faith in the workers' productivity and work ethic. Additionally, France's recent economic growth has impressed many MNCs.

Hyundai, the automobile giant from South Korea, has chosen Chennai in India for its new car manufacturing plant. Skilled labour at low wages; location of auto parts manufacturers such as Wheels

India, Brakes India, Sundaram Fasteners, Sundaram Brakes, Bimetal Bearings, Tafe, and India Pistons in and around Chennai; guaranteed power supply; cheap land and proximity to sea port have attracted the plant to the capital city of Tamil Nadu.

The argument that location-specific advantages attract FDI is propounded by the British economist John Dunning. Dunning believes that market imperfections make licensing and exporting difficult and thereby rendering FDI an obvious choice to globalisation.

FDI and Developing Countries: A developing country is characterised by low savings, low capital formation, and low investment. Such a country obviously looks for an external source to fill its resource gap.

In addition to the resource-gap, a developing country suffers from lack of advanced technology. As is well known, FDI brings, along with it, technology to the developing country. Besides, a developing country often needs to import rawmaterials that are not available domestically. The country needs foreign currency to pay for imports. FDI is of great help to the country in this respect.

FDI helps a developing country in another way also. When any MNC sets up its subsidiary in a developing country, along with capital and technology the parent company transfers its work culture, managerial concepts and skills, to the foreign affiliate (See Box 4.1 for an illustration). The recipient country benefits immensely from such transfer of managerial skills.

Box 4.1 **Toyota's 'Milk Run'**

For many years after it was founded in 1937, Toyota was derided as a company made up of "a bunch of farmers". Reason? It hired a lot of farmers to work its assembly lines and, in fact, the founding family's name Toyota meant "abundant rice field" in Japanese (the word Toyota, however, has no meaning in that language). Over the six decades, Toyota has come to acquire the most fearsome reputation in the industry for its exemplary manufacturing system, where costs and inefficiencies are pared not just every day, but every second.

Take a look at its low-fat Bidadi operations: the maximum amount of raw material at the factory at any point of time does not exceed two hour's production requirement; all finished cars leave the factory within 48 hours, and no dealer is sent more than 15 day's stock. So, just how does Toyota do it? The trick lies in its famous 'milk run', which involves picking up small quantities of supplies from vendors throughout the day. This is how it works: every morning small trucks leave a central stocking point (there is one each in Pune, Delhi, and Chennai), picking up supplies from the local vendors. These trucks then return to the hub, where the supplies are transferred to a bigger truck, which leaves for Toyota Plant at Bidadi every day. For vendors based in and around Bangalore, the milk runs are straight from the plant to the vendor and back.

(***Source:*** *Business Today*, October 28, 2001.)

Flow of FDI

FDI flows in all directions in the globe as Table 4.2 shows. Strictly speaking, developing countries should get major share of FDI inflow as these are the nations who are in need of foreign capital. But this is not happening as Table 4.2 shows. During 2002, for example, out of a total inflow of $651.2 billion, developed countries received 71 per cent ($460.3 billion) and the remaining 29 per cent ($162.1 billion) went to developing economies. India's share in the total inflow is negligible. The country received

Table 4.2 **FDI Inflows to Major Economies, 2001 and 2002**

(Billions of dollars)

Host Region/Economy	*2001*	*2002*
World	**823.8**	**651.2**
Developed countries	589.4	460.3
European Union	**389.4**	**374.4**
France	55.2	51.5
Germany	33.9	38.0
Luxembourg	..	125.6
United Kingdom	62.0	24.9
United States	144.0	30.0
Developing Economies	**209.4**	**162.1**
Africa	18.8	11.0
Algeria	1.2	1.1
Angola	2.1	1.3
Nigeria	1.1	1.3
South Africa	6.8	0.8
Latin America and the Caribbean	**83.7**	**56.0**
Argentina	3.2	1.0
Brazil	22.5	16.6
Mexico	25.3	13.6
Asia and the Pacific	**106.9**	**95.1**
China	46.8	52.7
Hong Kong, China	23.8	13.7
India	3.4	3.4
Korea, Republic of	3.5	2.0
Malaysia	0.6	3.2
Philippines	1.0	1.1
Singapore	10.9	7.7
Taiwan Province of China	4.1	1.4
Thailand	3.8	1.1
Central and Eastern Europe	**25.0**	**28.7**
Czech Republic	5.6	9.3
Poland	5.7	4.1
Russian Federation	2.5	2.4

(***Source:*** *World Investment Report,* 2003, p.7)

just $3.4 billion in 2002. The figure shot upto $5.6 billion in 2005-06. The next chapter throws more light on the reasons why India is a poor cousin in terms of the receipt of FDI.

Learning to handle differences

Another stage in evolving a global strategy is learning to handle differences that persist across countries. Differences are often difficult to perceive but careful observation yields dividends in the form of new opportunities and new ways of reducing risks.

Economists are being employed by Indian companies also. The Tata Group has six economists, Mahindra and Mahindra two, DHL one and Aditya Birla Group two

MNCs must forecast economic conditions in the countries they operate. Large companies have their own staff of economists; smaller ones tend to rely on the general knowledge of non-specialised line managers and on forecasts supplied by private companies, agencies, governments and banks.

One of the most important things an MNC must know about any country where it does business is the exchange rate between its currency and the currency of other nations. Fluctuations in exchange rates will benefit or affect the fortunes of the MNC.

Political environment varies across countries. Two distinct political environments exist in the world — democracy and totalitarianism. Democracies provide stable business environments through laws protecting individual property rights. Totalitarian or authoritaranian regimes are marked by corruption, coups and bloodbaths. The international manager needs to study the political environment obtaining in the host country and modify the strategies to shift the local needs.

More pronounced are the cultural differences existing across the globe. Food habits, buying habits, languages, communication systems, body languages, gift-giving and negotiation systems vary from country to country. No product can be sold in the standardised form to all the buyers; no ad can be designed and exhibited in the same way in all the media of the world; no good can be packaged with similar colours and displayed in the retail stores of all countries; and no international manager can use same body language, and nuanas while sitting across a table to negotiate with an Arab, a Japanese, a Korean, or an Indian businessman. In general, international managers are successful when they employ the following six strategies:[6]

1. Managers see themselves as citizens of the world and not belonging to one country.
2. Managers develop integrated and innovative strategies that make it difficult and costly for others to replicate.
3. Managers implement their strategies aggressively and effectively supported by huge investments from their eemployers.
4. Managers are aware of the fact that the developed countries alone are not the countries of excellence fit enough to come out with innovations in technologies. What is a poor country today can become a potential candidate to attract R&D establishments as has been recently proved in India.
5. Managers develop a system that keeps them informed about political changes around the world and implications of these changes on the firm.
6. Managers seek to achieve culture strategy fit while strategising their activities.

Adjusting the Management Process

Management process, as is well known, involves planning, organising, staffing and controlling. Now, this process needs to be different for an MNC operating in an international environment (see Table 4.3).

Management process at macro and micro levels needs to be oriented differently

Managerial actions both at the macro level and micro level need to be oriented differently. At the macro-level, issues generally involved are - What special steps are needed in the planning and control systems of MNCs? Should organisations be structured and co-ordinated differently in different countries? How to recruit people and compensate them adequately? Should the performance appraisal system differ from country to country?

Table 4.3 **Managing Domestic and International Businesses**

	Domestic enterprise (industrialized country)	*International enterprise*
Planning:		
Scanning the environment for threats and opportunities	National market	Worldwide market
Organising:		
1. Organisation sturcture	Structure for domestic operations	Global structure
2. View of authority	Similar	Different
Staffing:		
1. Sources of managerial talent	National labour pool	Worldwide labour pool
2. Manager orientation	Often ethnocentric	Geocentric
Leading:		
1. Leadership and motivation	Influenced by similar culture	Influenced by divergent cultures
2. Communication lines	Relatively short	Network with long distances
Controlling:		
Reporting system	Similar requirements	Many different requirements

(**Source**: Heinz Weihrich, et al, *Management-A Global Perspective*, McGraw-Hill, 1994, p.94).

At the micro-level, the decisions involved are: How should one individual interact with another from a different country? Should people in one country be managed differently from people in another country?

The thrust in adjusting the management process is to motivate people to think and act globally.

Selecting a Managerial Approach

What must be the appropriate managerial practices suitable for an MNC? For a long time, the popular belief was that the West European – American approach was ideal for any company, including a multinational. Then came the Japanese management about which no manager or consultant stopped talking about. Which of these approaches is suitable for an MNC? Before answering this question, it is useful to know what these approaches specifically mean.

William Ouchi has contrasted Japanese organizations with American ones as shown in Fig.4.5. The contrast is, however, based on human resource management practices.

As seen from Fig.4.5, the American approach is highly individualistic in spirit and action and this may not suit the less developed countries where collectivism and not individualism, is the main trait. Western managerial practices likewise have individualistic orientation.

Figure 4.5 **The Contrast**

Japanese Organizations	*Vs*	*American Organizations*
Life time employment		Short term employment
Slow evaluation and promotion		Rapid evaluation and promotion
Non-specialised career paths		Specialised career paths
Implicit control mechanisms		Explicit control mechanisms
Collective decision making		Individual decision making
Collective responsibility		Individual responsibility
Holistic concern		Segmented concern

(***Source***: William Ouchi, *"Theory Z"*, p.58)

What is needed for an MNC then is the synthesis of the American and Japanese approaches Infact, the most successful American and Japanese companies follow identical practices which are the result of fusion between the two approaches.

Fig 4.5 outlines management approaches unique to Japanese companies and American organisations Do Indian companies have an approach of their own?

The answer is in the affirmative. Following features are common to most Indian businesses.

- Most decisions are made not by professional managers, but by family members.
- Most executives are second generation entrepreneurs — sons of fathers — known for extravagance, and flamboyance. If their businesses have been successful, it is mainly because of the general environment prevailing in the country till 1990s. It is doubtful whether these abrasive individuals will be successful in the emerging environment.
- Siblings quarrel for shares in the fortunes. Personal ambitions are more important than the fortunes of the organisations built up by their parents.
- Most decisions are made by intution or on the advise of astrologers, palmists or *vastu* consultants.

Deciding an Organisation Structure

Efficient operation of an MNC requires an effective organisational structure. A successful organisation should maintain smooth operating internal communication and control, as well as sensitive and flexible interaction with the dynamics of the international business environment.

Several factors affect organisational design of an MNC. They can be classified as corporate objectives, management style, external constraints and internal constraints as shown in Fig. 4.6.

Figure 4.6 **Factors Affecting Organisational Structure**

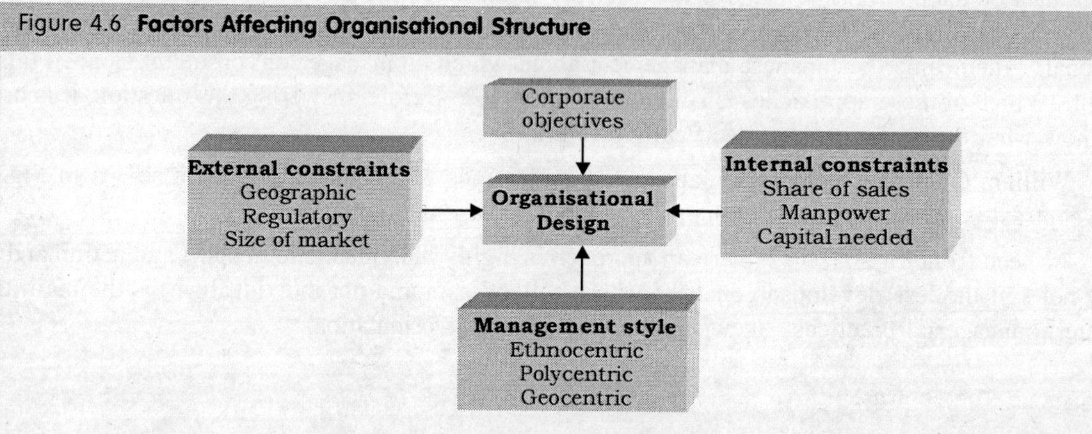

Ethnoculture management style expects centralisation in decision making. Polycentricism allows the opposite of ethnocentricsm. In geocentric organisations tend to become cosmopolitian

Management style can affect organisational design profoundly. The ethnocentric management style is characterised by strong control by the parent company. Its organisational structure reflects strong centralisation in decision making, and most of its managerial personnel are home country nationals. Polycentric management allows decentralisation of authority and decision making. Management personnel in foreign subsidiaries are largely of the host nationalities. In geocentric management, the organisational design is cosmopolitan, with little concentration of decision making and personnel in any particular nationality. The characteristics of these management styles are relevant not only in organisational design but also in marketing, production, finance, personnel, control and business strategy.[7]

An MNC can adopt any of the six fundamental structures. These are international division structure, worldwide functional organisation, geographic area organisation, product organisation, mixed organisation and matrix organisation.[8]

International Division Structure In the international division structure, the overseas unit is an adjunct to the domestic business. It handles all the international activities, which may be organized by function, product or geographic area. All of the overseas subsidiaries are under the authority of the international division Vice-President who coordinates the entire foreign operation. As the international activities are under one head, control and communication are easy. The structure can also respond quickly to changes in the international business environment. As overseas operations expand and deversifty, this structure fails to cope with the new demands. Fig.4.7 illustrates the international division structure.

Figure 4.7 **International Devision Structure**

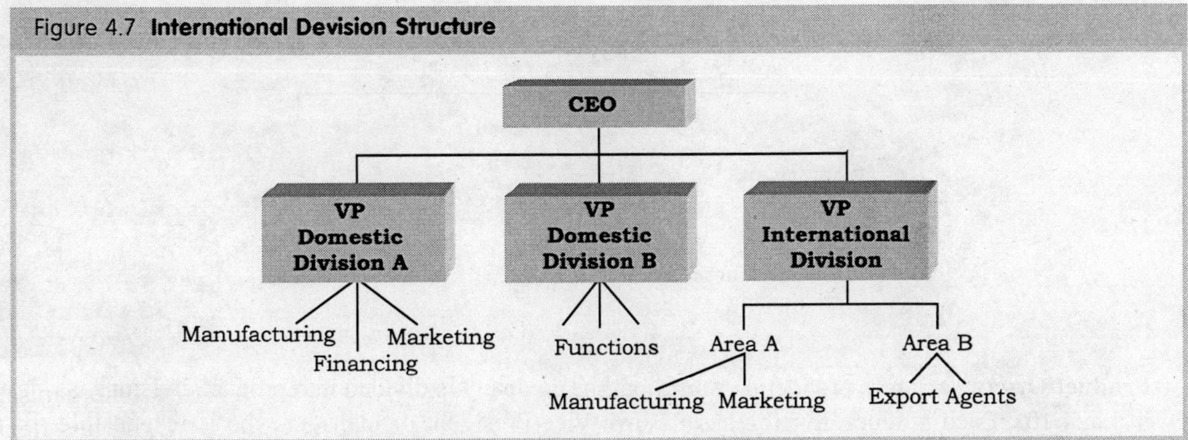

Worldwide Functional Structure In worldwide functional organisation, each functional department or division is responsible for its activities around the world. For example, the manufacturing department is responsible for world-wide manufacturing activities. It plans production activities according to the needs and capabilities of the firm's manufacturing locations. Since each functional area deals with the global market, specialisation and concentration of functional expertise can be taken advantage of. Control of various functions can be accomplished relatively easily (see Fig.4.8).

In worldwide functional structure, each department is responsible for its activities around the world.

Figure 4.8 **Worldwide Functional Organisation**

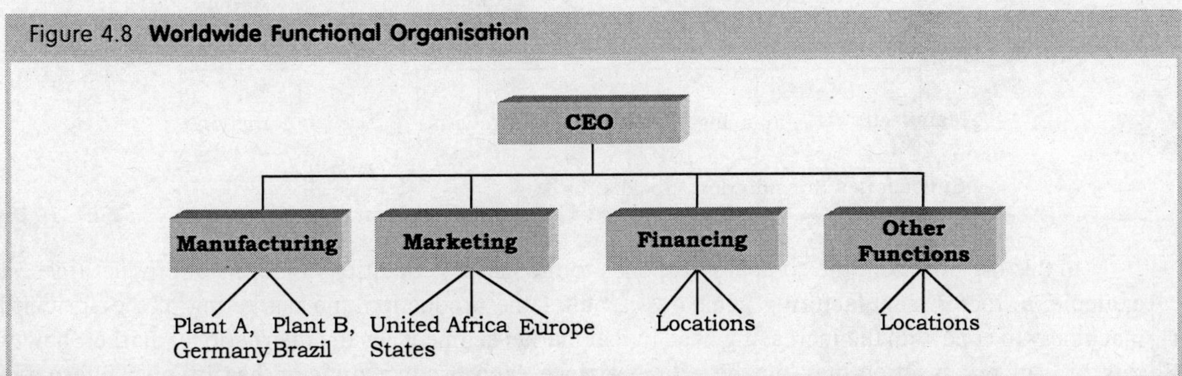

In this structure, each functional unit is responsible for its own worldwide operations and profitability. Communication among finance, marketing and manufacturing departments may become difficult since each department may have its operations in different foreign locations. Similarly, the mobility of expert managers or specialists within the company can be hindered because each of these people may be highly specialised only in the department or at one location.

Geographic area structure involves organisaiton of worldwide activities by spliting the globe into different geographic areas

Geographic Area Structure According to geographic area organisation, worldwide activities are organised by dividing the globe into different geographic areas. The regional manager or Vice-President of each area is responsible for all business activities within that geographical area (see Fig.4.9).

A geographic division can respond to the market conditions of a particular area much more efficiently than any other organisational structure. However, since there are different divisions covering different areas, there may be duplication of functions. There is also the problem or lack of communication among divisions. Since each division retains some degree of autonomy, each may abrogate its co-operation and co-ordination in production, marketing and other functions.

Figure 4.9 **Geographic Area Organisation**

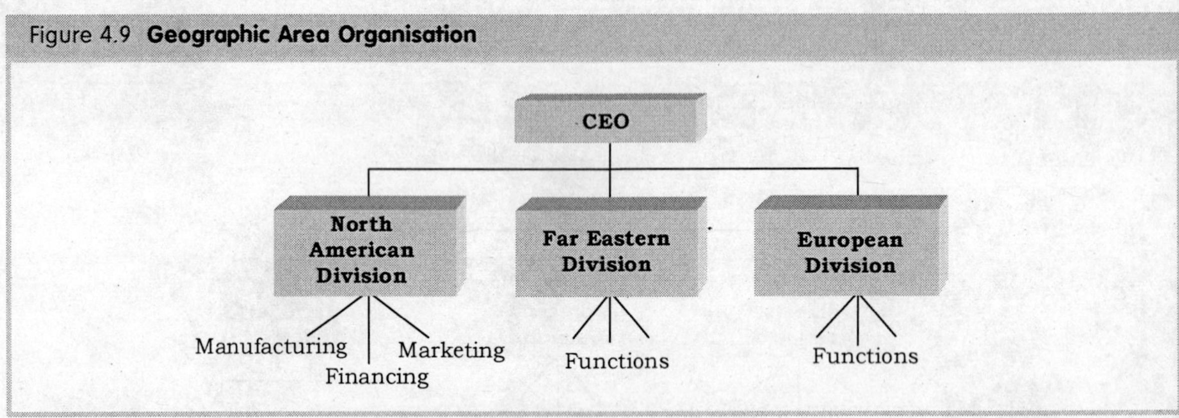

Product Organisation In product organisation, the company is divided into product divisions, as shown in Fig.4.10. Each product division has its own Vice-President or manager who is responsible for all functional departments, such as exporting, manufacturing, marketing and finance.

Figure 4.10 **Product Organisation**

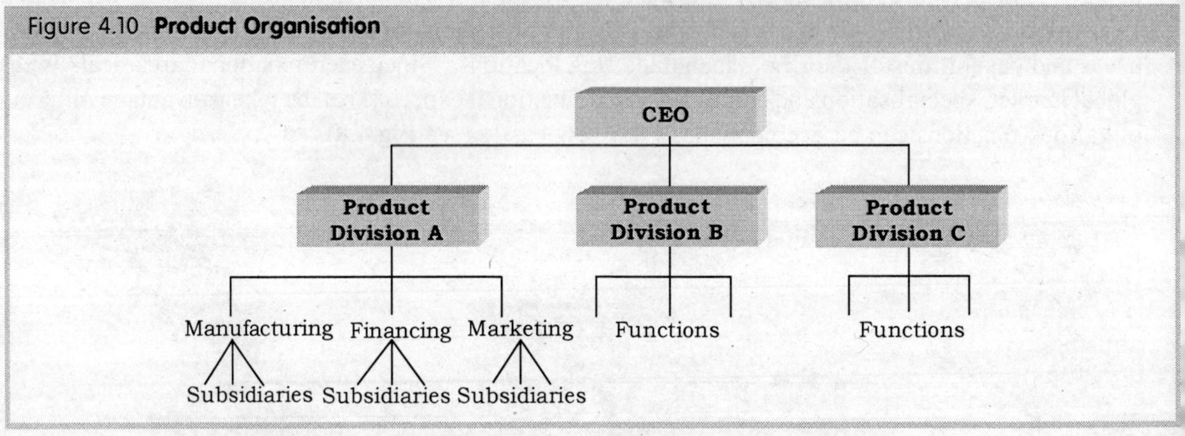

In product structure, the company is divided into product divisions. Each division is headed by a manager who is responsible for all functional departments

In this organisation, the company responds to the market conditions in terms of product lines. For example, a tractor manufacturing company can alter the production and marketing of the agricultural machinery to cope with the increasing need in that market segment. In the international market, however, this type of organisation may not be efficient since each product division has its own international subdivisions. By breaking production, marketing, sales, and other functional activities into different product divisions, international activities can be seriously disintegrated, especially in the areas of coordination and control. Another problem is that a product manager, although expert in technical and production aspects, may have insufficient knowledge of and experience with international structure. Air France, Pan American and other international airlines have diversified into passenger airlines divisions, cargo divisions, hotel divisions and so on. Large manufacturing firms such as Siemens and Westinghouse have successfully organised their activities into different product divisions, including industrial machinery, transport equipment, telecommunication equipment, electrical power generation equipment and household appliances.

Mixed Organisation A multinational business organisation can be composed of different organisational elements. A mixed organisation can combine the structures of function, product and geographic formats. Such an organisation allows geographic flexibility, quick response to market conditions and functional efficiency.

Mixed organisation combines structures of functions, product and geographic formats. Uniliver is one example of an MNC which uses mixed structure

A firm can combine product organisation and international divisions, as shown in Figure 4.11. For example, the tractor manufacturing company mentioned previously might have two domestic product divisions, a construction machinery division, an agricultural tractor division, an international division for all products with functional departments and a separate agricultural machinery division for each of two large geographic regions such as Europe and Asia. A multinational manufacturer of household appliances such as Phillips Electric and Sanyo, with subsidiaries in many foreign countries could use a mixed structure to meet the specific conditions of each of its foreign markets and to maximise the firm's operational and distribution capabilities.

Figure 4.11 **Mixed Organisation**

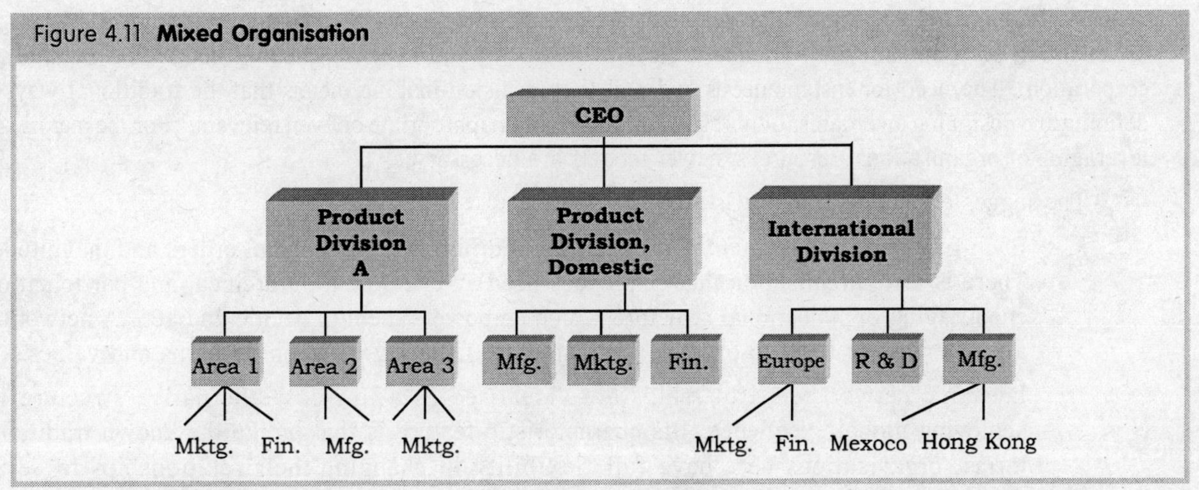

Indeed, Uniliver PLC, the consumer products giant uses mixed structures. It uses a classic regional structure with local managers in three areas of the world: Africa/Middle East, Latin America and East Asia/Pacific. But in Europe and North America, where consumer preferences are more similar, the structure is different. The President of Lever Brothers Co. in New York, for example, reports to the Uniliver worldwide detergents-products coordinator in London.

Martrix structure involves overlying one structure on another – a totally differentstructure. In matrix structure subordinates report to matrix bosses and matrix bosses share subordinates

Matrix Organisation A mixed organisation is just one form of matrix organisation. A matrix structure can be organised by combining regions, products and functions. In the organisation shown in Figure 4.12, for example, the product A division in geographic region 1 has different functions, such as manufacturing, marketing, financing and so on. The matrix structure is flexible and responsive to the changing market needs. Matrix organisations are often utilised by high technology firms, turnkey firms and construction firms, including TRW, Bechtel, NEC and Siemens.

Figure 4.12 **Matrix Organisation**

	Region 1	Region 2	Region 3
Project A	Functions	Functions	Functions
Project B			
Project C			

Need for Newer Models

The organisational structures discussed till now seem to fail to meet the requirements of contemporary global businesses. Thanks to advanced information technology, global managers sitting thousands of kilometers apart can interact and discuss face to face through effective communication networks. One of the biggest impacts of information technology is on the structural parameters of the corporation, as more and more areas of bureaucratic functions get automated and low-wage jobs get eliminated, and as the corporation becomes more skill-dominated and knowledge-oriented. The result of information technology is remarkable on the organisation of communication channels, flow of authority and decision-making inside and outside the corporation. The need for instantaneous and real-time decision-making means that the traditional ways of defining and designing an organisation's structure is no longer appropriate or even relevant.[9] For the maximized leveraging of organisational resources, newer models are necessary.

The suggested models for MNCs are:

- Each firm must create a *chain of networks* of different technological orders and magnitudes. There is also a realisation that employees need an open, non-hierarchical and participation-encouraging organisational structure which empowers them to decide and act. A network is a partnership of a group of firms (or employees) sharing common concerns and values.

  Dynamic networked partnerships are visualised as a low-cost alternative structure for achieving global excellence. Its characteristic feature is that unlike the known traditional terms, organisations here have full flexibility in changing their relationships to adjust themselves to the changes in the environment.
- Acquisition of smaller corporations/firms having an entrepreneurial spirit. The owner-manager may be allowed to function as an entrepreneur, creating, '*small-firm effects*' inside the big corporation.
- Allow the employees to leave the salaried jobs and work as '*extended hands*' of the organisation by helping them start their own small enterprises. The employees enjoy total freedom of running their own enterprises, while having the backing of a solid giant corporation. Reliance is understood to have embarked upon this strategy. So is the case with the Xerox Corporation.
- Alvin Toffler suggests a '*checkboard*' organisation. The concept emerges from Australia's political system after the Second World War. The two main political parties agreed that whoever won the elections would place a representative from the other party at the next post and so on for each alternate hierarchy. This type of structure can be profitably used in joint ventures, where at every second post, a manager from principal partners can be placed. This facilitates information dissemination and a remarkable degree of openness, leaving less scope for wariness of intentions between the partners.

Checkboard system, as suggested by Alvin Toffler, can be tried at joint venture

- Acquisitions are common among MNCs, as observed in the beginning of this book. For example, Siemens, the German electronics giant, purchased Nixdorf Computer of Great Britain, making Siemens the largest European-owned computer maker. When an acquisition takes place, the purchasing MNC needs to fashion a structural arrangement that promotes synergy while encouraging local initiative by the acquired company. The result is an organisation design that draws on the more traditional structures that have been examined earlier but still has a unique structure specifically addressing the needs of the acquirer and the acquired.
- Joint-ventures too are common among MNCs. In joint-venture agreements, each co-partner contributes to the undertaking but all co-ventures co-ordinate their efforts for the overall good of the enterprise. Samsung, the giant Korean MNC, has alliances with AT&T to create pen-based computers, with Toshiba to make 64-megabyte flash memory chips, with USA Video to create video file services, and with General Instruments to develop digital television.[10]

Any joint venture requires carefully formulated structure that allows each partner to contribute what it does best and facilitates efficient co-ordination of efforts of all co-ventures. In the case of Samsung, this calls for clearly spelling out the responsibilities of all parties and identifying the authority that each will have for meeting specific targets.

QUESTIONS

1. Discuss the issues involved in globalisation.
2. Describe the organisational structures suitable for an MNC.
3. Describe the entry strategies available to enter global markets.
4. Why are new models needed for multinational corporations?
5. Why has been the flow of direct investment uneven across the globe?
6. Why don't joint ventures last long?
7. How is a particular country selected for initial foraying?

ASSIGNMENT

Select a sample of 15 companies - cutting across different industries, domestic and foreign - and study their organisation structures. What similarities and dissimilarities do you come across them? Make presentations about your observations in the class.

REFERENCES

1. Philip Kotler, *Principles of Marketing*, New Delhi, PHI, 1991, p.583.
2. Helen Deresky, *International Management,* PHI, p.12.
3. Alan Rugman and Richard M.Hodgetts, *International Buisness,* Pearson, 2004, p.365.
4. Helen Derlskin *op.cit.,* p.13.
5. Charles W.L. Hill, *International Business,* Mcgraw Hill, 2000, p.183.
6. Richard M. Hodgetts and Fred Luthans, *International Management,* TMH, 2003, p.145.
7. Nanshi F.Matsuura, *International Business-A New Era*, San Diego, HBJ, 1991, p.455.
8. *Ibid*, p.456-458.
9. Arun Kumar Jain, *Managing Global Competition*, Competence Publishing Co., 1994, p.175.
10. Hodgetts and Luthans, *International Management*, McGraw-Hill, 1997, p.253.

CHAPTER OUTLINE

Historical Perspective
Investment Flows
Attracting Foreign Capital
Implications for Indian Industry
Destination India

LEARNING OBJECTIVES

After reading this Chapter, you should be able to:

1. Trace the history of global business
2. Bring out the reasons for poor FDI inflow
3. Suggests ways of making FDI attractive to India
4. Describe a new phenomenon - reverse FDI flow

5 From Domestic Market to Global Markets

The last two chapters provided theoretical backdrop to globalisation. This chapter deals with India's entry into the global markets and the challenges lying ahead.

Globalisation is a new phenomenon to us. We were for a long time content in serving the internal market which has been vast. Domestic production was insufficient to feed the vast market. We were compelled to import in order to supplement domestic production. We were also exporting to other countries. Our exports were composed of traditional commodities and the direction was mainly towards the erstwhile communist block. Globalisation, as it is understood now, did hardly exist during the past four and half decades.

> Globalisation is not new to our country. We were exporting to other countries and importing as well.

There are other reasons too which made us remain within the country's boundaries. For a long time, we did not have industries of the number and magnitude to think of globalisation. Vibrant economy filled with robust industries is a pre-requisite for internalisation. This was lacking in our country.

Secondly, for nearly four and half decades, we followed an economic policy which did not encourage competitive spirit among our industrialists. In the name of self-reliance, import substitution, *swadeshi* and economic sovereignty, we encouraged domestic industries to prosper, however inefficient they were. We gave them licences, fixed quotas, imposed tariffs and offered subsidies generously. We did not stop at this. We put several restrictions on foreign companies desiring to enter the Indian soil. This type of environment hardly promotes globalisation.

Finally, immediately after attaining Independence, we adopted the command economy of the erstwhile Soviet model to guide our economic development. While it is unnecessary to debate about the success or failure of centralised planning, it is sufficient to state that the world's greatest MNCs were born in the US, West Germany, Japan and the U.K. which incidentally did not have centralised planning.

Came 1990s. Dramatic developments took place across the globle. Soviet Russia collapsed and along with it the concept of centralised planning got discredited. Several countries, particularly Singapore, Thailand, South Korea, and China have achieved unprecedented economic prosperity through the integration of their economies with the global economy. Our country could not afford to remain isolated and poor any longer. Further, new technologies, information explosion, new materials, bio-energy, super fast micro-chips and other developments facilitated globalisation in a big way. Then came the Industrial Policy, 1991 which paved the way for globalisation in our economy.

HISTORICAL PERSPECTIVE

But our contacts with the world date back to the Buddha period itself. The main exports then from India to the West were spices, perfumes, jewels and fine textiles, but lesser luxuries such as sugar, rice and ghee were also exported, as well as ivory, both raw and worked. Indian iron was much esteemed for its purity and hardness, and dyestuffs such as lac and indigo were also in demand. Another requirement was live animals and birds; elephants, lions, tigers and buffaloes which were exported from India in appreciable numbers for the wild beast shows of Roman emperors and provincial governors, though these larger beasts went mainly overland through the desert trading city of Palmyra; smaller animals and birds, such as monkeys, parrots and peacocks, found their way to Rome in even larger quantities as pets of wealthy Roman ladies.

In return for her exports India, wanted little but gold. Pottery and glassware from the West found their way to India, and many sherds of Arretine and other wares, mass-produced in Western factories, have been found in the remains of a trading station at Arikamedu, near Pondicherry. There was some demand for wine, and the Western traders also brought tin, lead, coral and slave-girls. But the balance of trade was very unfavourable to the West, and resulted in a serious drain of gold from the Roman Empire.[1] (Also see box 5.1).

Box 5.1 **India's Early Global Trade**

The Yemerites, Nabataens, and Himyars had their share in Indian trade. Commercial relations existed between India, Rome and Greece, and the balance of trade was in favour of India from the very beginning, as a result of which Roman gold poured into India. The price of Indian goods was settled in Roman gold coins. The Romans also used Indian sesame oil in their food and indigo for colouring. Many kinds of Indian precious and semi-precious stones such as diamonds, onyx, sardonyx, agate, carnelian, crystal, amethyst, opal, cat's eye, ruby, turquoise and garnet were in great demand in Rome. India used to export at least three kinds of parrots to Rome, and Rome imported skins, pearls and coloured hides as well as wool for weaving shawls from India. Ivory from India and Africa was extensively used for inlay work. Indian ivory used to reach Rome by the land and sea routes and Indian made ivory figures also reached Rome (One such figure has been found in Pompeii). The Romans had a great liking for tortoise shells from the Indian Ocean and used to purchase pearls from the Gulf of Mannar, as the fashionable women of Rome were very keen to possess pearls. Rome also used to import silk and costly textiles by the silk routes. Shellac and some Indian herbs were used as medicines. But due to the difficulties of communication, the prices of these products were high. Black pepper had an important place in the trade between India and Rome. In addition to black pepper, India also exported ginger, cardamom, and cinnamon which the Romans used to use both as a spice and incense. The Greek traders imported the oils of lemon grass and ginger grass and the nard oil. The saffron costus produced in Kashmir was used in Rome for ointments and medicines and for perfuming the wings.

(**Source**: P.N.Agarwala, *A Comprehensive History of Business in India*, TMH, 2001, p.262.

While it is unnecessary to describe, in detail, what all has happened since the days when the Roman Empire became poorer because of the drain of gold, suffice it is to state that our country did have trade contacts with the rest of the world till the British invasion.

Even the so called MNC's in our country are not a sudden occurrence. They were there during the 18th century too. The first MNC that came to Indian shores was the East India Company. An aggressor in the most aggressive period of British empire-building process, it left a bad taste in the mouth for most Indians.

By the turn of the 19th century, managing agency systems was in full bloom and names like Bird and Hilgers, McKinnon McKenzie, Andrew Yule, Martin Burn Ltd. and Gallanders Arbuthnot became household names.

By the 1940s, many more MNCs joined the bandwagon. Be it Bata Shoes, Phillips Radio, Lever Brother's soaps, Huntley Palmer's biscuits or Reckitt and Colman's Dettol, MNCs were present in every household. The entire MNC culture received a major jolt in 1974 when the Foreign Exchange Regulation (FERA) was evoked.

International companies were forced to bring down their equity to below 40% in Indian companies and many an expert manager was replaced by Indians. This in fact, led to the creation of Indian companies with MNC linkages. The Indian Tobacco Company (ITC) being a classic case in point.

It was around this time that made-in-India brands started to show their aggressiveness in the market place. Nirma was taking on Surf, Godrej and Kelvinator were dominating the white goods market, the newly evolved IT industry is indigenous and the likes of Dabur, MTR Foods, Cavinkare, and Chandrika are showing the world that they are good in branding too.

Life, ofcourse, had come full circle with the liberalisation process, and MNCs back with a vengeance. While companies like Phillips, Levers, Siemens, P & G, Smithkline Beecham and Glaxo had always been keen on India and have indicated their deep commitment to be a part of India's economic development process, many more are coming to stay.

Coco Cola has forgotten the dark days of 1978 when they were made to leave the country and is back in strength as is IBM. Not to be left behind, Pepsi and Kelloggs are here to stay as is LeviStruss, McDonalds, Kentucky Fried Chicken, Heinz, Samsung, Sony and all the rest.

INVESTMENT FLOWS

Our businessmen have realized the need for integrating their activities with the world economy and hence, crossed Indian shores in search of new potential markets. They have chosen the joint venture route for globalising their activities.

The number of joint ventures at present is 868, out of which 286 are in operation and 582 are under various stages of operation. The approved equity of these joint-ventures amounts to $1097.68 million. In addition, there are 733 wholly owned subsidiaries abroad of which 216 are in operation and 517 are under implementation. The approved equity of these wholly owned subsidiaries amounts to $820.59 million.

> Our business houses have chosen joint venture routes to go global

Indian joint-ventures are found predominantly in developing countries like Nigeria, Sri Lanka, Thailand, Singapore, Kenya, Indonesia, Malaysia and the like. Joint-ventures owned by Indian companies are found in developed countries also but they belong to IT sector as Table 5.1 shows.

Table 5.1 **Top 15 IT Software and Service Providers and their Affiliates**

Rank	*Company*	*Selected locations of affiliates*
1	Tata Consultancy Services	Belgium, China, Germany, Japan, Netherlands, Singapore
2	Infosys Technologies Ltd.	Australia, Canada, China, Singapore, United States
3	Wipro Technologies	Japan, Sweden, United Kingdom, United States
4	Satyam Computer Services Ltd.	Germany, United Kingdom
5	HCL Technologies Ltd.	Bermuda, Ireland, Netherlands, United States
6	Patni Computer Systems Ltd.	United Kingdom, United States
7	Mahindra British Telecom Ltd.	United States
8	iFlex Solutions	United States
9	HCL Perot Systems Ltd.	Singapore, United Kingdom
10	NIIT Ltd.	Germany, Switzerland, United States
11	Polaris Software	Germany, United States
12	Birlasoft Ltd.	United Kingdom, United States
13	Mphasis BFL Ltd.	China
14	Pentasoft Technologies Ltd.	Indonesia, United States
15	Hexaware Technologies Ltd.	Germany, Singapore, United Kingdom, Untied States

(***Source:*** UNCTAD, based on National Association of Software and Service Companies, India and various media sources.)

Inward Flows

The flow of FDI into India is less compared to the size and need of the country. India's share in FDI inflow is much less when compared to other developing countries as Table 5.2 shows.

Table 5.2 **FDI Inflow into India**

(Billions of dollars)

	2001	*2002*	*2005*
Brazil	22.5	16.6	–
Mexico	25.3	13.6	–
China	46.8	52.7	–
HongKong-China	23.8	13.7	–
Singapore	10.9	7.7	–
Czech Republic	5.6	9.3	–
Poland	5.7	4.1	–
India	3.4	3.4	5.5

(**Source:** *World Investment Report,* 2003, p.7 and *Business Today,* November 6, 2005, p.141)

Inflow of FDI into India has been disappointing

Much smaller countries like Singapore (population 42 lakh) and Poland (400 lakh people) have received much higher share of FDI compared to India which has a population of ten thousand lakh. Reasons for poor inflow are many.

Reasons for Poor Flow

There are several barriers to foreign investment. And most of the barriers are the ones created with in the country. Among the factors hampering the flow of foreign investment is an increasingly visible distaste for democracy. As Indian democracy matures, it is throwing up situations and leaders that do not fit easily into old ideological patterns that the developed world is familiar with. The uncertainty of a political ethos that is not fully understood stands out in sharp contrast to the clarity of authoritarian regimes. Some investors even argue that since authoritarian regimes are more dependent on economic success to divert attention from political issues, they are more focused on the economy than democracies like India where other issues like religion, caste, language or even a Miss World Pageant take a major portion of a government's attention.

Democracy about which we are so proud of, is itself an impedement to the flow of FDI

Nothing can be more illustrative than the way the proposed project to put up an international airport at Bangalore is put on hold for decades. In contrast, in the past decade, China has built atleast 12 major international airports. Similarly, the Government of Karnataka has been dithering for years and has not been able to lay an express road between Bangalore and Mysore-a distance of 143 km. But the Chinese Government has laid in the last decade 29,000 km of high quality four-lane highways.

Table 5.3 shows India's inward FDI performance index from 1988 to 2000. The inward FDI performance index is the ratio of a country's share in global FDI inflow to its share in GDP.

Table 5.3 **India's Inward FDI Performance Index Compared**

	1988-90	*1998-2000*
India	0.1	0.2
Pakistan	0.6	0.2
Sri Lanka	0.5	0.4
Mongolia	0.8	0.5
Chinese Taipei	0.9	0.3
Brunei	0.0	0.1
Indonesia	0.8	-0.6
Malaysia	4.4	1.2
Myanmar	1.9	0.6
Philippines	1.7	0.6
Singapore	13.8	2.2
Thailand	2.6	1.3

(**Source:** *World Investment Report,* 2002, UNCTAD)

As shown in Table 5.3, India's performance index is very low-in fact it ranks 119th among the 140 countries listed in the *World Investment Report* 2002. However, India is the only country whose performance index shows an improvement in 1998-2000 over the decade 1988-90.

Apprehensions about investing in India have not been helped by the early record of joint ventures. American executives monitoring joint ventures in India believe that Indian partners are often not in a position to live up to their part of the deal. In some cases, this is the result of unrealistic expectations, in others it has to do with the liquidity crisis, making it difficult for smaller Indian partners to come up with their share of capital.

Foreign investores are not enthusiastic to invest in India

The sensitivity of foreign investors to these risks is heightened by the fact that India has less to offer than some other developing countries. The Indian market is proving to be smaller than investors may have believed. The earlier enthusiasm about a large middle class is tempered by the realisation that it does not have the purchasing power to absorb even items targeted at the lower middle class in the West. Western fast food chains, for instance, have become items of luxury consumption in India. The Indian market can be seen in perspective from one rather startling statistic. By 2001, the Indian demand for pagers was expected to grow rapidly to 1.7 million, but in that year, China's demand would be 73 million. Without the buffer of a large domestic market, the main attraction India can offer to foreign capital is its cheaper costs of production, particularly labour costs. But India is not the only country offering these advantages. Several smaller countries are already being preferred to India. Taken individually, each small country may not have the advantage of lower labour costs for long. A rush of foreign capital into each country will raise wages there and eat into its advantage in labour costs. But taken together foreign capital can move from one small country to another. Since some of the other countries like Indonesia are quite large, India would have a long wait before its competitors exhaust their low labour cost advantage. And other countries may also be able to offer advantages like less rigorous environmental standards.

We have not been able to integrate foreign capital into our economy

The ability to attract foreign investment can also be adversely affected if the inflow of foreign capital is not appropriately integrated into the economy. This could happen in different ways. Sometimes, the concessions offered to attract foreign capital can distort the local economy to such an extent that foreign capital no longer finds it worthwhile to invest. This has already happened in the stock markets. In the effort to woo foreign institutional investors, the small investor has been ignored. As a result, the kind of small investor participation that helped Reliance emerge as a major industrial house is no longer seen. Without the emergence of new giants with the help of the capital market, the number of companies that are actively traded remains small. This narrow base reduces the options that Foreign Institutional Investors (FIIs) have, dampening their enthusiasm to invest.

The tendency to ignore the consequences of the concessions that are being offered may soon become more visible in other sectors. In the eagerness to attract foreign investment in the infrastructure sector, the prices are being offered without sufficient attention being paid to whether the economy can absorb these higher prices. So when the project is completed, investors may find that they have overestimated the demand. The fast track power projects have tried to overcome this risk by getting guarantees of a fixed offtake of power. But such guarantees can hurt NTPC units, if in a relatively better power situation, they are asked to stop producing power so that the predetermined quantity of power can be evacuated from the foreign power plants. And if the government tries to avoid this situation by not offering guarantees, foreign investment in the power sector can also slow down.

The linkage between individual projects and the rest of the economy is often overlooked. The value of a modern expressway is lost if it takes a long time to reach a city

The ability to integrate foreign capital into the economy is also hampered by the project oriented approach to this task. With the focus being on individual projects, the linkage between individual projects and the rest of the economy is often not given sufficient attention. The value of a modern expressway, for instance, is eroded if the time saved on it is lost in going from the expressway to the city. Despite Bangalore's Electronic City being built on one such expressway, several computer firms are considering moving out of the city, citing poor infrastructure as the reason[2].

Policy guidelines lack clarity between central and state governments. Most policy guidelines are laid down by the central government but are left to the state governments for implementation. Delays take place at the implementation stage.

NRIs, who (numbering 22 million scattered across the globe and possessing collective wealth of Rs.200,000 crore) once accounted for 30% of the direct investment flow, have their own woes. They complain of bureaucratic red tape and demanding officials trying to extract money at every stage. Consequently, their interest in Indian companies declined as shown in Table 5.4.

Table 5.4 **NRIs Desert Indian Primary Market**

Year	*No. of issues offered to NRIs on preferential basis*	*No. of issues subscribed*	*Percent*
1991-92	32	25	78
1992-93	125	73	58
1993-94	406	109	27
1994-95	410	120	29
1995-96	701	30	4
1996-97 (Apr-Dec)	384	0	0

(**Source**: *The Hindu*, December 19, 1996)

We have innumerable labour laws which come in the way of improved labour productivity and the firm's profitability. Labour laws are so strange that even perennially sick units are made to work and workers are paid salaries even if they have no work to do. Payment of bonus is mandated even for a loss making unit. Dismissal of an errant worker or closure of a perennially sick unit is almost impossible. Labour laws need to be streamlined in tune with the demands of the competitive environment.

> Labour laws are highly rigid. Even sick units are made to pay regular wages and even bonus.

There are still caps on the percentage of equity holding in different industrial sectors. There are still two routes to setting up a project: an automatic route which requires no prior sanction and the FIPB (Foreign Investment Promotion Board) route. An investment exceeding US $120 million requires permission from no less than the Cabinet Committee on Foreign Investment. The route to take thus depends on the size of the investment, how much foreign equity is to be held and in which industrial sector.

The Confederation of Indian Industry (CII) estimated that a typical power project would require 43 clearances from the Central Government and 57 from provincial and municipal governments. The CII found that with such redtapeism and confusion, 55% of potential investors in 2000-2001 dropped out after obtaining the requisite FIPB approval.

India continues to be a mystery wrapped in an enigma in terms of business development to many foreign investors, particularly Japanese. To the Japanese, our country is a totally different world with communal riots, unhygienic conditions, severe poverty and many linguistic and caste conflicts unlike their own monoculture, single language country. Caste is something which they cannot grasp and religious conflicts frighten them as investors. And of course, India's last few decades of socialism have left their own negative impact.

Different political parties, wedded to their own ideologies, impede industrial progress particularly when they are voted to power. The case in point is repudiation of the Enron power project. Agreement to execute the power project was signed by the then ruling party in the State of Maharastra and the Enron Corporation. Later, a different party came to power in the state and it thought it fit, purely for political reasons though, to cancel the project. Such cancellations send wrong signals to foreign investors.

> The way Enron project was handled demonstates how political differences can hamper projects

ATTRACTING FOREIGN CAPITAL

The process of liberalisation that began in 1991 will continue and India, as a result, will experience more growth and within the next generation, will assume its rightful place as one of the premier economies of the world. It is not just its size, it is not just the fact that it is going to experience the growth it should have had 50 years ago. It is also a unique role that India will play as a model which its founders hoped it would do. But perhaps it is going to play this role in a way in which its founders did not anticipate and that is to demonstrate to the rest of the world that democracy is compatible with economic growth and change and that India can begin with democracy and still make the internal changes that make possible great economic growth. In many other parts of the world, the nations that have grown very fast, have been those that have had authoritarian regimes or only semi-democratic regimes. They allow individual freedoms in terms of economics and that in turn, made possible more democratic reforms. India will begin to show the world that she can do it in reverse, that she can begin with democracy and still set the stage for greater economic growth.[3]

In order to attract foreign investment on a large scale, the government has taken several steps to remove the barriers which have hindered the flow of investment on a large scale. (see box 5.2)

Box 5.2 **Measures to Attract FDI**

1992	Foreign firms obtained automatic rights over international brand names
1993	Requirement for industrial licensing in specified industries (white goods, entertainment electronics) abolished
	FIIs allowed to invest in new Mutual Fund schemes
1994	Banks allowed to set their own rates for lending
	Companies allowed to issue preferential equity to FIIs
1996	Overseas pension funds, charities, foundations qualify as FIIs
	FIIs allowed to invest in un-listed firms
	FIIs allowed to invest 100% of funds (previous 30%) in debt Instruments
1998	Further concessions to FIIs-now allowed to invest in Government securities, Treasury Bills, listed and un-listed debt securities
1999	FIIs allowed conditional forward foreign exchange cover
	FIIs could participate in open offers in accordance with take-over codes
2000	100% foreign equity allowed in infrastructure projects-ports, roads, highways
2002	Limited FDI in print media permitted
Recent Initiatives	• The number of products in which foreign investment is freely permitted has been considerably increased.
	• The foreign investors are now free to compete with the domestic producers in the Indian market.
	• In most cases, the foreign investor is free to own a majority share in equity.
	• Foreign Investment Implementation Authority (FIIA) is set up independent of the FIPB. FIIA is meant to simplify investment procedures.
	• Investment commission has been constituted to secure a certain level of investment every year.

Results Encouraging

The results of all these efforts are encouraging. As seen from Table 5.5, the inflow of foreign capital has been steadily rising from year to year, except in 1997-98.

Table 5.6 gives break-up of foreign direct investment approvals from August 1991 to June 1999.

Table 5.5 **Inflow of FDI**

Year	*Rs.crore*
1990-91	185
1991-92	326
1992-93	1,713
1993-94	13,026
1994-95	16,133
1995-96	16,327
1996-97	21,328
1997-98	18,520

(**Source**: *Handbook of Statistics on Indian Economy*, RBI [1998])

Table 5.6 **Foreign Collaboration Approvals**

	No.of Approvals	*Amt.Involved (Rs.million)*
Fuels(power, oil refinery and others)	581	6,18,479
Telecommunications	517	3,58,297
Transportation Ind.	993	1,41,972
Service Sector	670	1,20,308
Metallurgical Ind.	561	1,18,959
Chemicals (other than fertilisers)	1,423	1,14,770
Electrical Equipment	2,664	1,09,207
Food Processing(Ind.)	722	84,231
Hotel & Tourism	356	41,258
Textiles	578	29,999

(**Source**: *The Economic Times*, Nov 9, 1999).

Expectations and Concerns

At a recently concluded conference on FDI held in New Delhi sponsored by UNCTAD, a consensus seemed to emerge amongst Indian participants:

1. FDI into India was nowhere near its needs or potential. FDI levels would have to triple in the next 5 years if India was to attain its targeted growth rate of 8% p.a.
2. There still remained vestiges of resistance to FDI within the Indian establishment and the public at large. There was a need for effective advocacy groups to allay fears and permit more informed public opinion. Only civil society organisations can help dispel the complexes left behind by the East India Company.
3. The Government could play a much more positive role by being transparent and proactive in policy pronouncements. An atmosphere of secrecy and a Government which sporadically alters policy hardly promotes confidence.
4. Whilst FDI was eminently desirable, what was perhaps more important was a policy and regulatory framework which attracted investment and industrialisation as a whole, irrespective

of whether this was foreign or domestic. FDI tended to flow in where the industrial environment was favourable and where the economy was strong.

This is by no means comprehensive: several other measures, such as the repeal of the draconian Foreign Exchange Regulations Act in favour of FEMA (Foreign Exchange Management Act) served directly or indirectly as stimuli for foreign investment. The Government also periodically announced, by means of formal notifications, relaxations in the percentage of foreign equity permissible in different industries. The term 'relaxation' must be stressed: in no instance has there been a tightening or reversion.

Perhaps the most important of these relaxations from the foreign investor's viewpoint was the discontinuation in 2000 of the provision for 'dividend balancing' in 22 categories of industries (mainly consumer goods/consumer durables). Under this provision, dividends repatriated to the parent country had to be balanced by export earnings over a 7 year period, such exports being optionally from own production or merchant exports.

On occasion, external factors have forced relaxations in policy. In response to a U.S. complaint, the WTO ruled that the compulsion to raise the indigenous content of cars to prescribed levels was not permissible, and the Government of India had to withdraw this clause.

Over and above the inducements offered by the Central Government were the incentives offered by provincial governments. Land, for instance, was and still is offered at very low rates for foreign-owned factories. Waivers or concessions are routine: Ford obtained a 15 year holiday from local sales tax in Tamil Nadu. General Motors had a 30 Km stretch of road completely re-surfaced by the Government of Gujarat.

IMPLICATIONS FOR INDIAN INDUSTRY

Globalisation has some lessons for Indian industries:
- be quality conscious
- change attitudes
- keep customer satisfaction uppermost

Globalisation has serious implications for the Indian industry. For a long time, the Indian industry exhibited such characteristics as high cost, low productivity, junk machinery, outdated technology, inferior quality, high sickness and very low competitive spirit. With all these, industrialists were still making money because of the protected environment. Environment in future will not be the same thanks to economic reforms and globalisation. Catchwords from now onwards shall be competitiveness, efficiency, profitability, technology upgradation, foreign capital, safety net and golden handshake.

Specifically, globalisation shall herald the following challenges to our industry:

1. Customer satisfaction has been the greatest of the casualties in our country. This cannot continue. The manager must think of offering quality goods at reasonable prices to the customer.
2. Attitude of the Indian businessman must change. He must look beyond the boundaries of the country and set up his own enterprises or partnerships with other companies in overseas markets. What Socrates said centuries ago must come true in his case. "I am not an Athenian or a Greek", said Socrates, "but a citizen of the world."
3. Improve the quality of products to international standards. Global standards, quality certification and testing are a must.
4. In the advanced countries, total quality management (TQM) is almost by-word-the latest philosophy. Our industry must not lose time in achieving this goal. Having started late, we must move fast.

Any engineering industry goes through some distinct stages while attaining total quality. In the first stage, the organization aims at conformance to the product specification. This would need standards, technical ability to adhere to standards, an inspection and quality assurance department, and the right type of culture within the organisation. Such organizations will have solid quality assurance systems and with some effort, they can qualify for obtaining the ISO 9000 system accreditation. In this stage, the organisation tries to sell the products it can make.

In the second stage, an organisation moves beyond just adhering to its own product specifications. It tries to meet what the customer needs.

Engineering sector passes through four stages to attain total quality
- conforming product specification
- meet cunstomer needs
- compare with the best
- TQM

The marketing departments try to ascertain market needs and trends and the engineering and manufacturing departments fulfil this need. This is a feature of an organisation with substantial market orientation. This stage provides an enterprise with a competitive edge. Of course the source of feedback is one's own customer.

Beyond this is the third stage wherein an organisation is not just satisfied with customer satisfaction. It tries to measure and compare its performance in all aspects with those of better performers. This is known as *bench marking*. An organisation directs its focus outside its own walls. It studies competition, learns from the superior-competitors who have satisfied more demanding customers. In this process, it aims at identifying and beating the best proposition for its benefit.

Total quality management, the last stage, goes beyond beating the best. It is a process and a means for maintaining the leadership position through continuous change, adaptation and improvement. Total quality management is to improve the quality of work of all the people at all the functional areas of the organisation. It uses the fundamental ideas of group activity, participation of all, application of statistical and other QC tools, self-development and creativity. It imbibes the philosophy that there is always a better way of doing things.

World over, the best organisations are moving towards total quality management. A majority of them would have already gone through the earlier stages. In the race towards international competitiveness, organisations in India may have to pursue all these stages simultaneously. Pursuing them sequentially would take too long a time and we have to compress the time needed. This will make our task more strenuous. Industry must be prepared to make the effort.

5. Globalisation means more markets for our products. We must seize the opportunity and export our products on a large scale. Exports are necessary to earn foreign exchange. We cannot look to th government for its help in boosting exports. Government can only create a favourable environment and it is upto the Indian industry to use the environment to sell Indian products overseas on a massive scale.

Best companies around the world practise TQM

6. Nearly 96 per cent of the top 500 private sector companies in our country are family controlled and secretive. Holding small portions of equity capital, family members treat limited companies as their fiefdoms. They believe that they have right to inherit and control.

   While family inheritance and control may not be wrong, the brawls erupting between brothers or cousins send wrong signals to business community.

Majority of our private sector companies are privately held and are secretive

7. The eighties saw the development of global corporations and the global competitive arena. The earlier battles among the European and American companies were joined by the Japanese and Korean companies. Current developments in the Indian regulatory environments are opening the Indian gates for the expansion of the arena into India. Already some companies have taken positions through memberships in consortia, consulting projects, minority joint ventures, product-based technology transfer agreements, component supply arrangements, R&D agreements and the like. Some of the existing subsidiaries of the multinationals are looking for new strategic directions and strengthening their muscles to face the battle. The extension of the global competitive arena to India is a source of both a threat and an opportunity. There is the threat of mergers and acquisitions, and the elimination of medium and small companies from the market place. There is also the opportunity to forge strategic alliances and even test one's own strengths *vis-a-vis* multinational competition.

To be successful one should think global but act local

8. One of the requisites for success in globalisation is to think global but to act local. What this implies is that one must have an open mind to accept what is good but not to forget one's own moorings. This is what Mahatma Gandhi told us long back. 'I don't mind', said he, 'to keep windows open, but I don't want the wind to blow me off my feet'. This is also the lesson which Japanese teach to the rest of the world. Japanese have accepted foreign technology but never forgot their local culture.

DESTINATION INDIA

As was stated earlier, India is emerging as the most attractive country for foreigners to invest. There are several strong points why MNCs must invest their funds in our country.

We offer, to investors from abroad, a large market, a strong legal system (See Box 5.3), well developed capital markets, a class of private sector partners, and a rare commodity in the developing world - English speaking managers who can manage (not just operate) business.

Box 5.3 **Justice for All**

The troubles of Kentucky Fried Chicken in India have made foreign investors nervous about investing in India. But there is one aspect of the episode that should give them strong encouragement. It has proved that in India, the legal system offers swift and effective recourse to foreign investors against arbitrary acts of politicians and bureaucrats. This is in stark contrast with conditions in China, India's major rival in seeking foreign investment. When McDonald's lease in Beijing was abruptly terminated by the authorities there, the unfortunate company had no way of seeking any legal remedy. The authorities were, fundamentally, not challengeable. But in India, KFC was able to approach the courts, both in Bangalore and New Delhi, and get a reversal of acts of politicians and bureaucrats.

This point must not be stretched too far. The Indian legal system is in a terrible mess, and the courts take forever to convict anybody. No ordinary case is settled for years, may be decades. This is why many observers (including this newspaper) have often declared that the justice system is moribund. However, the KFC episode reminds us that the justice system can still deliver efficient remedies in respect of writ petitions, if not in normal litigation. This can be particularly important for foreign investors worried about political risk. It is often said that companies want an efficient legal system to enforce contracts, and this is unquestionably true. What is often forgotten is that companies also need protection against arbitrary action by the authorities which may have nothing to do with contracts. The closure of KFC outlets was not a violation of contract, it was administrative high-handedness, which happened to be even more damaging than contract violation. India has proved that it is capable of giving foreign investors a difficult time, but it has also proved that it is capable of giving investors some forms of recourse that would be unimaginable in China. However, we must add that this is not good enough, and that the judicial system needs a thorough overhaul to deliver reasonably speedy justice in ordinary cases. We need this for our own citizens, and we need to worry about their needs for justice far more than in the case of foreign investors.

(**Source**: Leader Comment, *The Economic Times*, Dec 8, 1995)

We also have well entrenched the democratic set-up and perhaps ours is the only country which has come out of the 40 year old socialist trap successfully. Most of Asia has done it at the cost of, or in the absence, of democracy. Most of Latin America is still to get there and Eastern Europe is still struggling (Also see Fig.5.1).

Figure 5.1 **Star Status of Countries**

General Approval Requirements	*China*	*India*	*Indonesia*	*Korea*	*Malaysia*	*Singapore*	*Taiwan*	*Thailand*
Foreign Investment	YES	Yes, automatic under certain conditions	YES	Yes, automatic in few cases	YES	NO	YES	No,except for restricted industries
Industrial Licensing	YES	No, except for few restricted industries	YES	YES	YES	No,except for few industries	YES	YES
Repatriation of Profit	YES	YES	YES	No,if in accordance with approved remittance schedule	NO	NO	NO	NO
Repatriation of Capital	YES	YES	Notification required	YES	NO	NO	YES	NO
Imports	NO	No, except for few restricted items	YES	YES	NO	NO	NO	NO
Foreign Loans	YES	YES	NO	YES	YES	NO	YES	NO
Domestic Loans	YES	NO	YES	NO	No,except above certain levels	NO	NO	NO
Technical Collaboration	YES	Yes,automatic within laid down parameters	NO	Notification required	YES	NO	YES	NO
Expatriate Employment	YES	YES	YES	YES	YES	YES	YES	YES
Incentives	YES	NO	YES	YES	NO	YES	YES	YES

India is also blessed with the exemplary characteristics associated with any booming economy - a huge and productive compliment of skilled manpower and excellent earnings growth providing attractive opportunities for international investors to diversify portfolio risks.

Our country's relatively good performance among Asian countries and the steady pace of economic reforms should attract more and more foreign capital. Box 5.4 contains Strengths and Weaknesses analysis of India.

Box 5.4 **India's Strengths & Weaknesses**

Strengths

- Consecutive GDP growth rate of 8 per cent per annum. The country is rated as the world's fastest growing free market democracy.
- Sensex soaring at higher and higher levels.
- Robust optimism among businessmen, as reflected in the aggressive and often hostle takeover of foreign firms.
- Narrowing space of the bottom of the income pyramid. At the foot of the pyramid, for a long time, was a large space denoting the widespread poverty in India. The space is now shrinking as more and more people are getting out of the poverty line.
- India is growing young. Fifty per cent of India's population is less than 25 years of age. Elsewhere, countries are growing old. Ten years from now, world will be looking at India for job takers.
- Excellent institutes of science, technology and management training thousands of youth every year. The country has 3 million graduates, 700,000 postgraduates, as against China's 1.5 million college students, out of a population of 1.3 billion.
- Judiciary is independent and is available for all Indians or foreigners. Judiciary is also fearless. Guilty are punished however powerful they are.
- Huge market. People have money and are willing to spend.
- By 2050 India, teaming with China, will account for nearly half of the world's GDP.
- India and China are named as the new tigers of Asia.
- Large number of home-grown entrepreneurs.
- India's growth model banks on its cultural experience and relaxed attitude towards the outside world, its cheap labour force, and its solid educational system.
- Vast pool of NRIs capable of converting India into world's technology lab.
- 25 per cent of Indian engineers possess the necessary skills to work in MNCs as compared to China's only 10 per cent of engineers.
- The country has moved upto 43 in the global competitiveness ranking in the World Economic Forum's Global Competitiveness Report 2005 (See Table 5.7).
- Proactive government that has a clear vision and capability and commitment to galvanise the country to reach the vision.

Weaknesses

- Regional political parties and politicians whip up parochial feelings among citizens and resort to regressive strategies like bundhs, agitations and hunger strikes.
- Terrorism with as many as 160 districts in the country declared as dangerous zones.
- Digital divide and division between urban and rural areas.
- Average infrastructure being less favourable than many developing countries.
- Extra payments connected with permits and licenses are common.

Table 5.7 **Rank Country/Economy Score-Scale 1 to 7**

Rank	Country/Economy	Score	Rank	Country/Economy	Score
1.	Switzerland	5.81	2.	Finland	5.76
3.	Sweden	5.74	4.	Denmark	5.70
5.	Singapore	5.63	6.	United States	5.61
7.	Japan	5.60	8.	Germany	5.58
9.	Netherlands	5.56	10.	United Kingdom	5.54
11.	Hong Kong SAR	5.46	12.	Norway	5.42
13.	Taiwan, China	5.41	14.	Iceland	5.40
15.	Israel	5.38	16.	Canada	5.37
17.	Austria	5.32	18.	France	5.31
19.	Australia	5.29	20.	Belgium	5.27
21.	Ireland	5.21	22.	Luxembourg	5.16
23.	New Zealand	5.15	24.	Korea, Rep.	5.13
25.	Estonia	5.12	26.	Malaysia	5.11
27.	Chile	4.85	28.	Spain	4.77
29.	Czech Republic	4.74	30.	Tunisia	4.71
31.	Barbados	4.70	32.	United Arab Emirates	4.66
33.	Slovenia	4.64	34.	Portugal	4.60
35.	Thailand	4.58	36.	Latvia	4.57
37.	Slovak Republic	4.55	38.	Qatar	4.55
39.	Malta	4.54	40.	Lithuania	4.53
41.	Hungary	4.52	42.	Italy	4.46
43.	India	4.44	44.	Kuwait	4.41
45.	South Africa	4.36	46.	Cyprus	4.36
47.	Greece	4.33	48.	Poland	4.30
49.	Bahrain	4.28	50.	Indonesia	4.26

Source: World Economic Forum.

Reverse Flow

Surprising thing is happening to India and to Indians. Concern is not any more of attracting FDI but its outflow. More and more Indian companies are investing abroad. True, during the last few years, India has been working hard to woo foreign investments in diverse sectors. Most of the state governments adopted several innovative methods to package themselves for potential foreign investors. Even Chief Ministers of some states participated in road shows abroad to attract MNCs.

Now it is the reverse flow - almost rewriting the investment theory. FDI need not necessarily flow from developed countries to the developing ones. It can flow the otherway also. During 2005-06, the FDI outflow from India reached $4.5 billion against an inflow of $5.6 billion.

Destinations for Indian investors are the US, UK, Belgium, Germany, Thailand, China, followed by other countries. Table 5.8 gives the top 20 destination countries for Indian investors.

Table 5.8 **Top 20 Destination Countries For Indian Investment**

(US $ Million)

Sl.No.	*Country*	*2005-06*	*Sl.No.*	*Country*	*2005-06*
1.	United States	1054.49	2.	United Kingdom	815.48
3.	Belgium	799.94	4.	Germany	657.79
5.	Thailand	486.74	6.	China	375.99
7.	Romania	343.5	8.	Singapore	192.34
9.	Australia	187.28	10.	Netherlands	171.33
11.	Canada	117.87	12.	Cyprus	89.1
13.	Mauritius	76.48	14.	South Africa	73.59
15.	Sweden	65.25	16.	Mexico	59.05
17.	Austria	56.44	18.	Korea	55.01
19.	Morocco	37.27	20.	Bermuda	35.56

Table 5.9 gives details about the top 10 investors. State Bank of India (SBI) stood first with an outflow of $1179.11 million, followed by Reddy Labs with $777.18 million.

Table 5.9 **Top 10 Overseas Investors**

(UA $ Million)

Investor	*Sector*	*2005-06*
State Bank of India	Bank	1179.11
Dr.Reddy's Laboratories Ltd.	Pharmaceuticals	777.18
Suzlon Energy	Energy	565.00
Tata Steel Ltd.	Metals	553.83
Ranbaxy Laboratories Ltd.	Pharmaceuticals	324.00
Videocon International Ltd.	Consumer durables	289.20
Videsh Sanchar Nigam Ltd.	Telecom	254.37
Matrix Laboratories	Pharmaceuticals	252.70
Tata Consultancy Services	Software	207.24
Wipro Ltd.	Software	154.08

(**Source:** Table 5.8 and Table 5.9 are based on *The Economic Times*, dated October 29, 2006).

The heightened FDI outflow means that the Indian corporate sector has now reached a state of maturity and confidence which allows them to look at opportunities on a global scale. Given the current business environment, it would appear that over the next three to five years, outbound investments would continue to outstrip inbound FDI.

QUESTIONS

1. Bring out the implications of globalisation to our businesses.
2. Point out the favourable and unfavourable factors about India as a market for foreign investment.
3. Why has been the flow of foreign capital into India poor?
4. Why should India be the destination for foreign investors?

ASSIGNMENT

1. Select five industries (two from old economy and three from new economy) and draw SWOT analysis for each of them.

REFERENCES

1. A.L.Basham, *The Wonder That Was India*, p.231.
2. *The Economic Times*, Oct, 3, 2004.
3. Malcolm S.Forbes.Jr., "India:The One Stop Shop", *The Economic Times*, April 11, 1995.

CHAPTER OUTLINE

Basic Principles of WTO
Functions of WTO
GATT and WTO
WTO Structure
The Final Act
Implications for India
Trading Blocks

LEARNING OBJECTIVES

After reading this Chapter, you should be able to:

1. Describe the principles, structure and main provisions of WTO
2. Bring out the benefits and apprehensions of India towards WTO
3. Bring out the major trading blocks
4. Describe the impact of the trading blocks

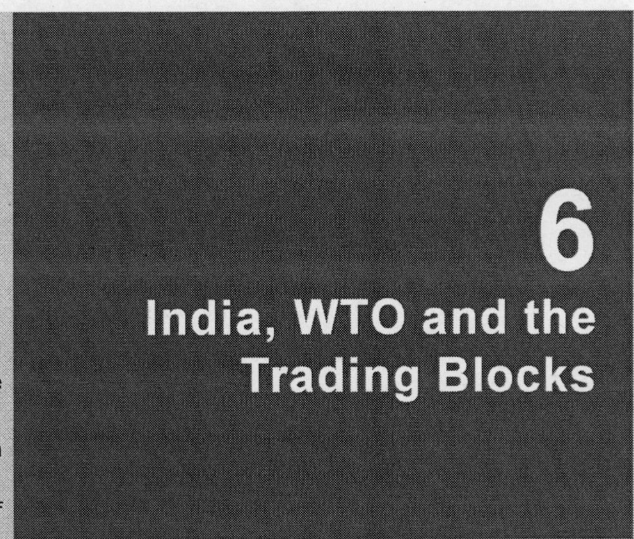

6 India, WTO and the Trading Blocks

The World Trade Organisation (WTO) was established on 1st January 1995. Governments had concluded the Uruguay Round negotiations on 15th December 1993 and Ministers had given their political backing to the results by signing the Final Act at a meeting in Marrakesh, Morocco in April 1994. The '*Marrakesh Declaration*' of 15th April 1994, affirmed that the results of the Uruguay Round would '*strengthen the world economy and lead to more trade, investment, employment, and income growth throughout the world.*' The WTO is the embodiment of the Uruguay Round results and the successor to the General Agreement on Tariffs and Trade (GATT).

The WTO administers the trade agreements negotiated by its members, in particular the GATT, the GATS (General Agreement on Trade in Services), and the TRIPS (Trade Related Aspects of Intellectual Property Rights). The WTO builds on the organisational structure that had developed under GATT auspices of the early 1990s.

The WTO has larger membership than GATT, the number of members stands at 150. India is one of the founder members of the WTO. How the membership benefits India is worth examining. This chapter is devoted for the purpose. Before this, it is useful to understand more about the WTO itself.

BASIC PRINCIPLES OF WTO

The WTO agreements are lengthy and complex as they are legal texts covering a wide range of activities. They deal with agriculture, textiles and clothing, industrial standards and product safety, food sanitation regulations, intellectual property and many more. Some basic principles run through all these documents. These principles are the foundation of the WTO. The fundamental principles are: non-discrimination, transparency, binding commitments, reciprocity and safety valves.[1]

WTO is founded on certain fundamental principles. They being: non-discrimination, transparency, binding commitments, reciprocity and safety valves.

Non-discrimination: This principle is based on the concept of **normal trade relations**-previously called the most-favoured-nation (MFN) rule. This rule requires that the WTO members extend the same favourable terms of trade to all members that they extend to any single member. For example, if Japan were to reduce its import tariff on German automobiles to five per cent, it must reduce the tariff it charges on imports from all other members to five per cent.

The normal trade relations principle applies unconditionally. Although exceptions are made for the formation of trading blocks (discussed latter in this chapter) and for preferential treatment of developing countries, the non-discrimination principle is basic pillar of the WTO. Because of this principle, importers and consumers will have the benefit of using low cost goods, irrespective of whichever country they are being produced.

The principle of non-discrimination has one more dimension: national treatment. National treatment enjoins all member countries to treat imported and locally produced goods equally. National treatment only applies only after a product, service or item of intellectual property has entered the market. Obviously, imposing customs duty on an import is not a violation of national treatment even if locally-produced products are not charged an equivalent tax.

Under transparency principles, member countries are required to publish their trade regulations.

Transparency: Transparency is a basic pillar of the WTO. WTO members are required to publish their trade regulations, to establish and maintain institutions allowing for the review of administrative decisions affecting trade, to respond to requests for information by other members, and to notify changes in trade policies to the WTO. The regular surveillance of national trade policies through the **Trade Policy Review Mechanism** provides a means of encouraging transparency both domestically and at the multilateral level.

Binding and Enforceable Commitments: In the WTO, when countries agree to open their markets for goods and services, they 'bind' their commitments. In the case of goods, these bindings amount to ceilings on customs tariff rates. Often countries, particularly the developing ones, tax imports at rates lower than the bound rates. But in developed countries, the rates actually charged and the bound rates tend to be the same.

A country can change its bindings, but only after negotiating with its trading partners, which can mean compensating them for loss of trade.

Reciprocity: Reciprocity operates during negotiations among countries when governments negotiate in WTO rounds, they do so with the objective of obtaining mutually beneficial arrangements through reciprocal reductions in tariff bindings. In particular, governments approach negotiators seeking a "balance of concessions", whereby the tariff reduction offered by one country is balanced against an "equivalent" concession from its trading partner.

When a country seeks to renegotiate and withdraws a previous concession, the WTO rules provide that the affected trading partner may retaliate in a reciprocal manner by withdrawing an equal concession.

The principle of safety value permits a member country to restrict its trade under special conditions.

Safety Valves: A final principle embodied in the WTO is that, in specific circumstances, governments should be able to restrict trade. Four types of provisions exist in this connection:[2]

1. Goods and services meant for noneconomic objectives such as public health and national security.

2. Industries likely to be injured by competition from imports.

3. Articles aimed at ensuring fair competition. Measures in this situation include the right to impose countervailing duties on imports that have been subsidised and anti-dumping duties on imports that have been dumped.

4. Provisions permitting intervention in trade for economic reasons. Economic reasons include measures to correct a serious unfavourable balance of trade or the desire to protect an infant industry.

FUNCTIONS

WTO is based in Geneva, Switzerland. Its functions are:

- administering and implementing the multilateral and plurilateral trade agreements which together make up the WTO;
- acting as a forum for multilateral trade negotiations;
- seeking to resolve trade disputes;
- overseeing national trade policies; and
- cooperating with other international institutions involved in global economic policy-making.

The main function of the WTO is to act as a forum for international cooperation on trade related policies-the creation of codes of conduct for member governments. These codes emerge from the exchange of trade policy commitments in periodic negotiations. The WTO can also be seen as a market in the sense that countries come together to exchange market access commitments on a reciprocal basis. It is, in fact, a barter market. In contrast to the markets one finds in any city or town, countries do not have access to a medium of exchange: they do not have money with which to buy; and against which to sell. Instead, they have to exchange apples for oranges; for example, tariff reductions on iron for foreign market access commitments regarding cloth. This makes the trade policy market less efficient than one in which money can be used, and this is one of the reasons that WTO negotiations can be tortuous and long-drawn process. One outcome of the market exchange is the development of the codes of conduct. The WTO contains a set of specific legal obligations regulating trade policies of member countries which are binding on them.(3)

The WTO is a 'member-driven' organisation, with decisions being made by consensus among all member governments. All decisions are made by the membership as a whole, either by ministers (who meet once in two years) or by their ambassadors or delegates (who meet regularly in Geneva).

The WTO is a member-driven organization, with decisions being made by consensus among all member nations.

In this respect, the WTO is different from other international organisations such as the World Bank and the International Monetary Fund. In the WTO, power is not delegated to a board of directors or to a Chief Executive Officer.

DIFFERENCES BETWEEN GATT AND THE WTO

The WTO is not a simple extension of GATT. On the contrary, it completely replaces its predecessor and has a very different character. The major differences between the two bodies are the following:

- The GATT was a set of rules, a multilateral agreement, with no institutional foundation, only a small associated secretariat which had its origins in the attempt to establish an International Trade Organisation in the 1940s. The WTO is a permanent institution with its own secretariat.
- The GATT was applied on a 'provisional basis' even if, after more than 40 years, governments chose to treat it as a permanent commitment. The WTO commitments are full and permanent.

- The GATT rules applied to trade in merchandise goods. In addition to goods, the WTO covers trade in services and trade-related aspects of intellectual property.
- While GATT was a multi-lateral instrument, by the 1980s, many new agreements had been added of a plurilateral, and therefore, selective nature. The agreements which constitute the WTO are almost all multilateral and thus, involve commitments for the entire membership.

  In contrast to the GATT, the WTO agreement is a "single undertaking"-all its provisions apply to all members. Under the GATT there was flexibility for countries to "optout" of new disciplines, and in practice many developing countries did not sign specific agreements on issues such as customs valuation or subsidies.
- The WTO dispute settlement system is faster, more automatic and thus much less susceptible to blockages, than the old GATT system. The implementation of WTO dispute findings will also be more easily assured.

'GATT 1947' continued to exist until the end of 1995, thereby allowing time for all GATT members to accede to the WTO and permitting an overlap of activity in areas like dispute settlement. Moreover, GATT lives on as 'GATT 1994', the amended and updated version of GATT 1947, which is an integral part of the WTO Agreement and which continues to provide the key disciplines affecting international trade in goods.

THE WTO STRUCTURE

The structure of the WTO is dominated by its highest authority-the Ministerial Conference. This body is composed of representatives of all WTO members. It meets atleast every two years and is empowered to make decisions on all matters under any of the multilateral trade agreements (see Fig.6.1).

Ministerial Conference, comprising all members, is the highest body to administer the provisions of WTO.

The day-to-day work of the WTO is entrusted to a number of subsidiary bodies; principally, the General Council, also composed of all WTO members, which is required to report to the Ministerial Conference. The General Council also convenes in two particular forms-as the Dispute Settlement Body and the Trade Policy Review Body. The former overseas the dispute settlement procedures and the latter conducts regular reviews of trade policies of individual WTO members.

The General Council delegates responsibility to three other bodies-namely the Councils for Trade in Goods, Trade in Services and Trade-Related Aspects of Intellectual Property Rights. The Council for Goods oversees the implementation and functioning of all the agreements covering trade in goods, though many such agreements have their own specific overseeing bodies. The latter two Councils have responsibility for their respective WTO agreements and may establish their own subsidiary bodies as deemed necessary.

Three other bodies are established by the Ministerial Conference who report to the General Council. The Committee on Trade and Development is concerned with issues relating to the developing countries and especially, to the 'least-developed' among them. The Committee on Balance of Payments is responsible for consultations among WTO members and countries which resort to trade restrictive measures in order to cope with their balance of payments difficulties. Finally, issues relating to WTO's financing and budget are dealt with by a Committee on Budget, Finance and Administration.

Each of the plurilateral agreements of the WTO-those on civil aircraft, government procurement, dairy products and bovine meat-establish their own management bodies which are required to report to the General Council.

Figure 6.1 **Structure of WTO**

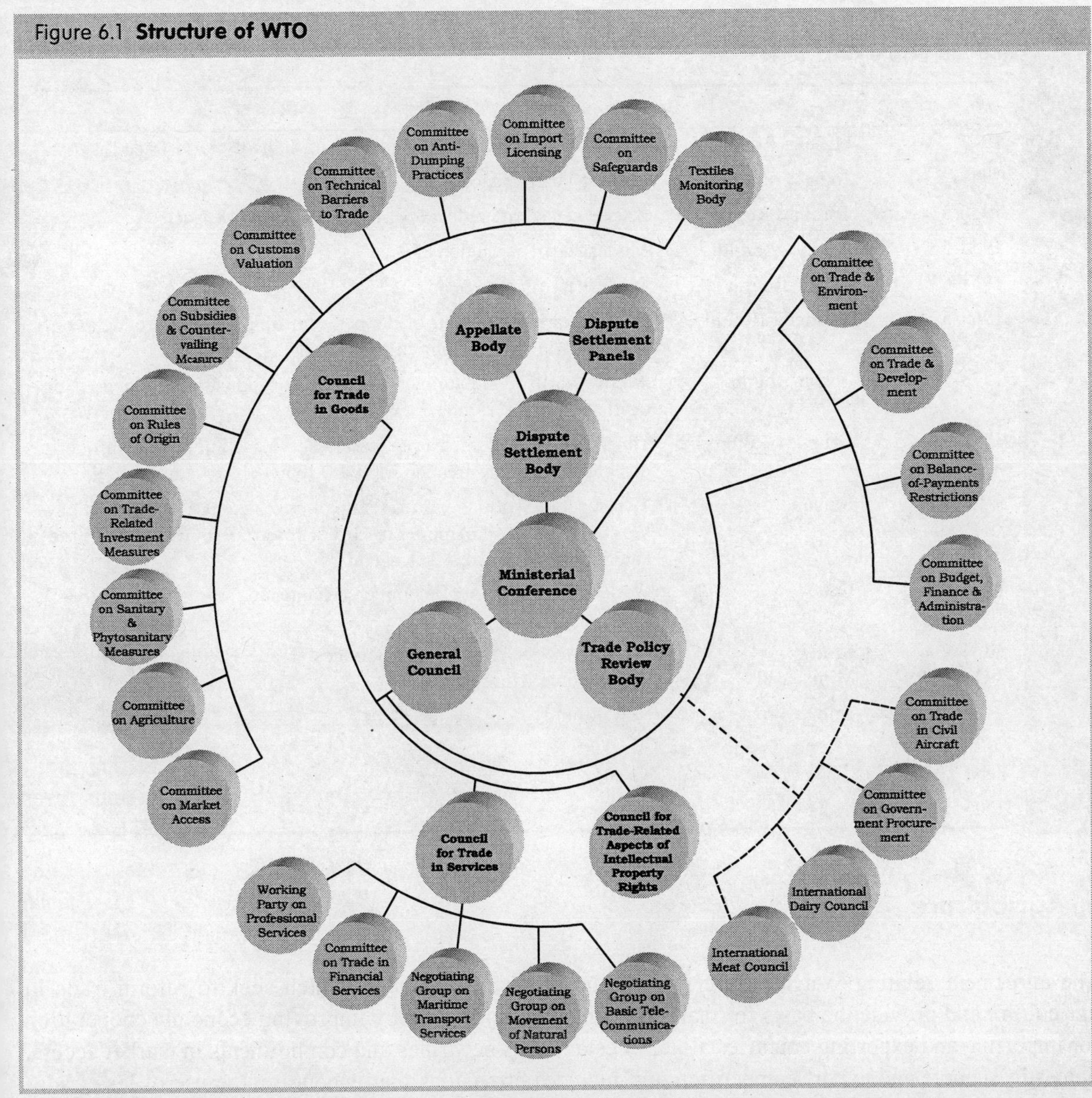

THE FINAL ACT

Ever since the GATT was established after the Second World War, it has been striving hard (along with the World Bank and the International Monetary Fund) to achieve international economic cooperation. Towards this objective, GATT has been conducting several trade rounds (see Box 6.1), the latest being the the Cancum round where no agreement was reached. The most expensive round was the Uruguay round which involved two thousand six hundred and thirty one days of negotiations and thousands of controversies and debates. Consensus was finally arrived and the agreement, called the Final Act, was signed in April, 1994 at Marrakesh, Morocco.

The major provisions of the Final Act (reportedly implemented by the WTO) relate to agriculture, sanitary measures, helping least developed countries, clothing, TRIPS, GATS and anti-dumping measures. A brief description of each of these follows is given below.

Box 6.1 **From GATT to WTO**

Date	*Name (Round)*	*Outcome*
1947	Geneva Round	45,000 tariff concessions representing half of world trade
1949	Annecy Round	Modest tariff reductions.
1950-51	Torquay Round	25 per cent tariff reductions in relation to 1948 level.
1955-56	Geneva Round	Modest tariff reductions.
1961-62	Dillon Round	Modest tariff reductions.
1963-67	Kennedy Round	Average tariff reduction of 35 per cent of industrial products, only modest reduction for agricultural products, anti-dumping code
1973-79	Tokyo Round	Average tariff reduction of 34 per cent for industrial products. Non-tariff trade barrier code.
1986-94	Uruguay Round	Tariffs, non-traiff measures, rules, services, intellectual property, dispute settlement, creation of WTO, etc.
9-13 Dec.	Singapore	Two separate working parties set up on investment, Competition Law. Working Group formed on Government Procurement, Trade Facilitation added to WTO agenda.
18-20 May 1998	Geneva Ministerial	Work, Programme on E-commerce launched
30 Nov. to 3 Dec 1999	Seattle Ministerial	Market Access, Agriculture, Services, Trade Facllitation, E-commerce, New Round
9-13 Nov. 2001	Doha Ministerial	New Round
Sept. 2003	Cancum	No agreement reached.
2006	Doha	No agreement reached.

Agriculture

The agreement relating to agriculture is made up of several elements which seek to reform trade in agriculture and provide the basis for market-oriented policies, thereby improving economic cooperation for importing and exporting countries alike. It establishes new rules and commitments in market access, domestic support and export competition and includes provisions that encourage the use of less trade-distorting domestic support policies to maintain the rural economy. It also allows actions to be taken to ease adjustment burdens and provides some flexibility in the implementation of the commitments. Specific concerns for developing countries are addressed including those of net-food importing developing countries and less developed economies.

Health and Safety Measures

The Agreement on the Application of Sanitary and Phytosanitary Measures concerns the application of food safety and animal and plant health regulations. It recognises government's rights to take sanitary and phytosanitary measures but stipulates that they must be based on science, should be applied only to the extent necessary to protect human, animal or plant life or health and should not arbitrarily or unjustifiably discriminate among members where identical or similar conditions prevail.

Helping Least Developed and Food Importing Countries

It is recognised that during the reform programme, least developed and net food-importing developing countries may experience negative effects with regard to giving food supplies on reasonable terms and conditions. Such countries need assistance. Therefore, a special ministerial decision calls for appropriate mechanisms related to the availability of food and the provision of basic foodstuffs in full grant form and aid for agriculture development. It also refers to the possibility of assistance from the International Monetary Fund (IMF) and the World Bank with respect to the short-term financing of commercial food imports. The Committee on Agriculture holds responsibility to monitor the follow up to the decision.

Textiles and Clothing

The objective of this agreement is to secure the integration of the textiles and the clothing sector-where much of the trade is currently subject to bilateral quota negotiations under the Multi-Fibre Agreement (MFA)-into the main stream of WTO. The integration, however, shall take place in stages (see box 6.2 for the stages). All MFA restrictions in force on 31st December 1994 would be carried over into the Final Act and maintained until such time as the restrictions are removed or the products integrated into WTO.

Box 6.2 **Textiles and Clothing-Integration Stages**

- On 1st January 1995, each party integrated from the specific list in the agreement products accounting for not less than 16% of its total value of textiles and clothing imports in 1990.
- On 1st January 1998, products accounting for not less than a further 17% of 1990 imports will be integrated.
- On 1st January 2002, products accounting for not less than a further 18% of 1990 imports will be integrated.
- On 1st January 2005, all remaining products will be integrated.

TRIPS

The WTO Agreement on Trade-Related Aspects of Intellectual Property Rights (TRIPS) recognises that widely varying standards in the protection and enforcement of intellec-tual property rights and the lack of multilateral disciplines dealing with international trade in counterfeit goods have been a growing source of tension in international economic relations. With this end in view, the agreement addresses the applicability of basic GATT principles and those of relevant international intellectual property agreements; the provision of adequate intellectual property rights; the provision of effective enforcement measures for those rights; multilateral dispute settlement and transitional implementation arrangements.

The TRIPS agreement contains three parts: Part 1 sets out the provisions and principles; Part 2 addresses different kinds of intellectual property rights and Part 3 concerns enforcement.

Trade Related Investment Measures (TRIMS)

Multinational firms are aware of the many restrictions on their investments in foreign countries. TRIMS are those restrictions a country places on foreign investment that adversely affect trade in goods and services. WTO members entered into the Agreement on Trade Related Investment Measures as a part of the Uruguay Round agreements.

The agreement does not set broad rules for investors in a member country. It simply prohibits laws or regulations that condition a country's right to import foreign goods on the volume of goods exported. For instance, Argentina may not say to a US MNC: "You may only import foreign raw materials on condition that you export an equal volume of finished goods from our country". Also prohibited are laws that condition the receipt of foreign exchange on the country's foreign exchange revenues. Thus, Argentina may not demand: "Our Central Bank will only permit you to transfer US dollars out of the country if you have brought into the country an equivalent amount this year in dollars, Yen, or other hard currency."[4]

GATS

The General Agreement on Trade in Services (GATS), negotiated during the Uruguay Round, is the first step of multilaterally-agreed and legally enforceable rules and disciplines ever negotiated to cover international trade in services. The agreement contains three elements: a framework of general rules and disciplines, annexes addressing special conditions relating to individual sectors (the sectors covered are: movement of natural persons, financial services, telecommunications and air transport services) and national schedules of market access commitments.

A Council for Trade in Services oversees the operation of the agreement.

Agreement on Subsidies and Countervailing Measures (SCM)

SCM is the outcome of negotiations during the Uruguay Round. Under the GATT agreement subsidies may be dealt within two ways. First, a WTO member country may appeal to the WTO for dispute resolution. The WTO may recommend that the subsidiary may be discontinued, its harmful effects be eliminated, or a countermeasure may be taken by the importing country. Second, an importing country may initiate its own administrative proceedings, similar to antidumping measures, to impose a countervailing duty on the subsidised products in order to eliminate their unfair price advantage.

A countervailing duty is a special tariff, in addition to the normal import tariff, levied on imports of subsidised goods in an amount equal to the amount of the counter-vailable subsidy. A countervailing duty may be brought at the same time as the WTO dispute settlement action.

Anti-dumping Measures

GATT allows members to apply anti-dumping measures. Such measures can be imposed on imports, if such dumped imports cause injury to a domestic industry in the territory of the importing members. More detailed rules governing the application of such measures-which take the form of either duties or undertakings on pricing by the exporter, were negotiated during the Tokyo Round and the same was revised in the Uruguay Round.

The WTO Agreement provides for greater clarity in the method of determining that a product is dumped. It sets out additional criteria for determining the injury caused to a domestic industry by the dumped product and the procedure to be followed in initiating and conducting anti-dumping investigations. Rules on implementation and duration of anti-dumping measures are also part of the agreement. In addition, it clarifies the role of dispute settlement panels in disputes relating to anti-dumping actions taken by the WTO members.

Dispute Settlement Procedure

One of the unique features of the WTO is its provision relating to dispute settlement mechanism. Infact, the power to settle trade disputes is what it makes the distinction between the WTO and the GATT. Under the GATT, nations could file a complaint against another member and a committee would investigate the matter. If appropriate, the GATT would identify the unfair trade practices and member countries would force the offender to change its ways. But in reality, rulings by the GATT (usually given after a prolonged investigative procedure) were more likely to be ignored than respected.

> What makes WTO distinct is its provisions relating to dispute settlement.

In contrast, the various agreements of the WTO are essentially contracts between member nations that commit them to maintaining fair and open trade policies. When a member files a complaint against another, the Dispute Settlement Body of the WTO steps in immediately. Decisions are to be made in less than one year-nine months if the case is urgent, 15 months if the case is appealed. The WTO dispute settlement system is faster and automatic and the decisions cannot be ignored or blocked by members. Offending countries must realign their trade policies according to the WTO guidelines or suffer financial penalties and even trade sanctions. Because of its ability to penalise offending member nations, the WTO dispute settlement system is the backbone of the global trading system.

Table 6.1 shows the number of dispute settlement cases between 1995 and 2000. As of September 2000, 207 complaints had been notified to the WTO. Industrial countries brought the most cases, and their share of total complaints (74 per cent) was greater than their share of world exports. Among the different categories of cases, those brought by industrial countries against developing countries have increased the most from 10 to 31 per cent. Over 40 per cent of industrial countries cases were against developing countries. The proportion of cases by developing countries against industrial countries was also higher (66 per cent of all developing country complaints). (See also box 6.3 for an illustration).

Table 6.1 **Number of Dispute Settlement Cases, 1995 through 2000**

	Complaint by			
	Industrialised countries	*Developing countries*	*Total complaints*	*Share of total cases (per cent)*
Complaint against:				
Industrialised countries	89	35	124	60
Developing countries	65	18	83	40
Total	154	53	207	100
Share of total cases (per cent)	74	26		
Memorandum:				
Share of cases under GATT (per cent)	84	16		

Note: Based on number of cases brought by each country. The European Union and its member countries are counted jointly.

(***Source:*** Bernard Hoekman, et al (ed.), *Development Trade and the WTO*, World Bank, 2002, p.76)

Box 6.3 **India Wins WTO Case Against EC**

India has won a case against the European Union at the World Trade Organisation (WTO) involving special tariff concessions on textiles being given to Pakistan.

The EU was given this speical treatment on the ground that Pakistan is a beneficiary of a scheme for countries involved in combating drug production and trafficking.

The WTO has ruled that the European Commission has violated its obligations to the international body by granting tariff preferences to 12 countries, including Pakistan, under this special Drug Arrangements program.

The program comes under the EC's Generalised System of Perferences (GSP) scheme, which provides lower traiffs on imports, largely from developing countries to the EU.

The decision will come as a big relief to textile exporters in India who are competing against Pakistan in the European market. The EC's decision to include Pakistan in the drug arrangement scheme since January 2002 had upset Indian exporters who were faced with a significant tariff reduction being provided to textile goods produced in the neighbouring country.

The WTO's decision provides relief to Indian exporters to the EC who are otherwise disadvantaged due to duty concessions to Pakistan under the Drug Arrangements.

The dispute, in the first place, arose primarily because the EC included Pakistan as beneficiary under its Special Traiff Arrangement for combating Drug Production and Trafficking within the GSP schemen for the years 2002-04. Such a scheme was in operation even earlier but the beneficiaries were restricted to Andean and Central American countries. While the scheme, India's view, was not compatible with WTO rules, even then it had not taken up the issue at the world body as it was not significantly affected. The inclusion of Pakistan, as a beneficiary country since January 2002, changed the situation since Indian exports were directly affected. There are a number of export sectors such as clothing where the two countries are close competitors in the EC market.

(**Source**: *The Hindu*, April 8, 2004)

Developing countries are not lodging complaints or others are not complaining against them. This is because of unwillingness on the part of developing countries or resource constraints they face.

Table 6.2 shows country-wise data in terms of appearances as complainants or respondents. From both perspectives, US tops the list. India appeared as complainant in eight cases and as respondent, the country appeared in 12 cases. Surprisingly least developed countries (sub-Saharan countries) had no complaints to lodge, nor any country lodged a complaint against them. This shows either unwillingness on the part of the least developed countries or resource constraints faced by them. The costs of dispute settlement procedure are disproportionately heavy for developing countries.

In general, developing countries do not enjoy a 'neutral' playing field. Although the dispute settlement procedure is not biased against any party in a dispute, developing countries are less well equipped to participate in the process: they have fewer people with necessary training, they are less experienced, and as noted above, they face resource constraints.

COMMON MISUNDERSTANDINGS ABOUT THE WTO

Table 6.3 brings out the common apprehensions held against the WTO and how each doubt has been cleared.[4(a)]

Table 6.2 **Participation in WTO Dispute Settlement Cases**

(April 1994 — March 1999)

No.of Appearances as Complainant		***No.of Appearances as Respondent***	
Member	*No.of Disputes*	*Member*	*No.of Disputes*
United States	54	United States	30
EC	43	EC	26
Canada	13	Japan	12
India	8	India	12
Mexico	7	Korea	10
Japan	7	Canada	9
Brazil	6	Brazil	8
Thailand	4	Argentina	8
New Zealand	4	Australia	6
Honduras	3	Indonesia	4
Guatemala	3	Turkey	4
Switzerland	3	Mexico	3
Argentina	2	Chile	3
Hungary	2	Ireland	3
Australia	2	Guatemala	2
Chile	2	Slovak Republic	2
Philippines	2	Belgium	2
Panama	2	Hungary	2
Korea	2	Greece	2
Uruguay	1	Pakistan	2
Sri Lanka	1	Philippines	2
Singapore	1	Sweden	1
Poland	1	Peru	1
Colombia	1	Thailand	1
Costa Rica	1	United Kingdom	1
Indonesia	1	Denmark	1
Ecuador	1	Czech Republic	1
Peru	1	Venezuela	1
Hong Kong	1	Poland	1
Pakistan	1	Portugal	1
Malaysia	1	Malaysia	1
Venezuela	1	Netherlands	1
Czech Republic	1	France	1
Memo items:			
G4	118	G4	90
Other OECD	22	Other OECD	27
Developing/Transition	43	Developing/Transition	47
Least Developed	0	Least Developed	0

Note: Excludes third parties.

(***Source:*** Bernard Hockman and Martin (Ed.), *Developing Countries and the WTO*, 2001, p.132)

Table 6.3 **Doubts and Clarifications**

Doubts	*Clarifications*
1. The WTO dictates policies	*Not true* The WTO does not tell the governments how to conduct their trade policies. Rather, it is a member-driven organisaiton. Decisions made at the WTO are based on consensus of members.
2. The WTO is for free trade at any cost.	*Not true* It is really a question of what countries are willing to bargain with each other. The role of the world body is to provide a forum for negotiating and implementing the tenets of liberalisation.
3. Commercial interests precede focus on environment	*Not true* Concern for environment is visible in many agreements reached at the WTO. Agreements also provide for efficient allocation of scarce resources. Sustainable development, protection of environment and efficient utilisation of resources are the primary objectives of the WTO
4. Commercial interests overtake the developmental needs	*Not true* The WTO believes that free trade promotes and not impedes economic development. Commerce and economic development supplement each other.
5. Interests of health and safety are compromised in favour of commercial interest	*Not true* Certain agreements (such as GATT Art. 20), allow governments to take actions to protect human animal or plant life and health. Some other agreements deal in greater detail with product standards, and with health and safety for food and other products made from animals and plants.
6. Jobs are destoryed and poverty worsened	*Not true* Trade helps promote economic ativities which in turn generate job opportunities which inturn reduce poverty. As a result of eight rounds of negotiations since 1948 (the year of origin of the world trade body), the average import tariff in the world came down from 40 per cent to 6 per cent. The annual value of goods and services traded across the globe is now 14 times more than what it was in 1948. These figures demonstrate the growth of trade and along with it jobs would have multiplied.
7. Small countries are becoming helpless	*Not true* Infact, small countries would become weaker without the WTO. The WTO has boosted their bargaining power. The fact that 75 per cent of the member countries are either poor or small nations shows how the WTO has been pro-small and pro-poor countries.
8. The WTO is the tool of power centres	*Not true* The WTO system offers govenments a means to reduce the influence of powerful lobbies. The 'round' type of negotiations and the decisions are the consequence of different interests being balanced.
9. Weaker countries are forced to join	*Not true* As told earlier, weaker counties would remain weaker by staying outside of the WTO. The principles of non-discrimination and transparency guarantee benefits to all member countries-small or large, poor or rich.
10. The WTO is undemocratic	*Not True* Decisions at the WTO are arrived on consensual basis. Consensus rule means every country has a voice, and every country needs to be pursuaded to join consensus.

IMPLICATIONS FOR INDIA

India was one of the 76 governments that became a member of the WTO on its first day. Divergent views have been expressed in support and against our country becoming a member of the WTO.

Arguments for Joining WTO

1. Ours is one of the few developing countries which has succeded in implementing liberalisation programmes. Over three-quarters of WTO members are developing countries in the process of economic reform from non-market systems. These countries have chosen to join WTO after careful deliberations in their respective countries. Obviously, they have perceived economic gains for themselves by becoming members. India should not be an exception.

   The criticism that the WTO exists only for industrialised countries is not all that valid. During the seven-year course of the Uruguay Round - between 1986 and 1993, over 60 developing countries implemented trade liberalisation programmes. Some did so as part of their accession negotiations to GATT while others acted on an autonomous basis. At the same time, developing countries and transition economies took a much more active and influential role in the Uruguay Round negotiations than in any previous round.

   Many developing countries have benefited by joining WTO. India is no exception.

   With the end of the Uruguay Round, developing countries showed themselves prepared to take on most of the obligations that are required of developed countries. They were, however, given transition periods to adjust to the more unfamiliar and difficult WTO provisions-particularly so far the poorest, 'least developed' countries. In addition, a ministerial decision on measures in favour of least-developed countries gives extra flexibility to those countries in implementing WTO agreements; calls for an acceleration in the implementation of market access concessions, affecting goods of export interest to those countries; and seeks increased technical assistance for them. Thus, the value to development of pursuing open market policies, based on WTO principles, is widely recognised and appreciated. So is the need for some flexibility with respect to the speed at which these policies are pursued.

2. The real importance of the WTO to India lies in the role that a dynamic export industry can play in the country's development. Both in terms of job creation, skill development and technological evolution, an opening up to the outside world is essential. The semi-autarkic earlier system resulted in a major leap forward in the development of indigenous industry and agriculture. But it lacked an internal dynamic. There were no incentives to improve technology and productivity. In short, it was a closed system that left no room for evolution. It is only by forcing industries to sell outside the country and compete for export markets that they will have an incentive to evolve.

   There is another reason why India needs to search for external markets. This is the crucial dependence on imports for survival. The country has for long believed that it is a self-sufficient, independent economy. But, infact, from petroleum and fertilizers to capital goods, raw materials and life saving drugs, the Indian economy is vitally dependent on imports. As long as it is dependent on imports, it needs to export to pay for these imports.

   As long as India needs to export and import, it makes far more sense to be part of the multilateral trading system than stay out of it. That is why even a country like China, despite its fiercely-guarded sovereignty and its status as the world's last major socialist power, has been desperatey trying to get into the WTO.

3. By being a member of the WTO, India can benefit from the International Trade Centre jointly operated by the WTO and the United Nations, the latter acting through UNCTAD (the UN Conference on Trade and Development). The International Trade Centre was earlier set up by GATT in 1964 at the request of the developing countries to help them promote their exports.

   WTO membership confers India the advantage of using International Trade Centre.

   The Centre responds to requests from developing countries for assistance in formulating and implementing export promotion programmes as well as import operations and techniques. It provides information and advice on export markets and marketing techniques, and assists in establishing export promotion and marketing services and training personnel required for these services. The Centre's help is freely available to the least-developed countries.

4. Estimates have been made by the World Bank, OECD and the GATT Secretariat, which show that the income effects of the implementation of the Uruguay Round package will add between 213 to 274 billion US dollars annually to world income. The GATT Secretariat's estimate of the overall trade impact is that the level of merchandise trade in goods will be higher by 745 billion US dollars in the year 2005, than it would otherwise have been. The GATT Secretariat further projects that the largest increases will be in the areas of clothing (60%), agriculture, forestry and fishery products (20%) and processed food and beverages (19%). Since India's existing and potential export competitiveness lies in these product groups, it is logical to believe that India will obtain large gains in these sectors. Assuming that India's market share in world exports improves from 0.5% to 1%, and that we are able to take advantage of the opportunities that are created, the trade gains may conservatively be placed at 2.7 billion US dollars extra exports per year. A more generous estimate will range from 3.5 to 7 billion US dollars worth of extra exports.

5. Another advantage of WTO membership stems from the fact that India (any member-country for that matter) is saved from entering into multiple bilateral trade negotiations with other countries. In the absence of WTO, India, for example, would be required to enter into as many bilateral agreements as the country desires to have trade links. With the WTO membership, our country has the advantage of having trade links with all other member countries without the need for bilateral agreements. The role of WTO is like that of a telephone exchange in this context.

   India is saved from entering into multiple bilateral, trade negotiations with other countries.

6. WTO provides for a multilateral set of rules which are beneficial to a country like ours. Such rules provide greater protection against bilateral pressures or against trade restrictions that cannot be justified under a multilaterally agreed framework. Further, the system of multilateral rules imparts greater predictability and stability to the international trading system. If the system of rules is not followed, the ensuring chaos and uncertainty will result in a trading system dominated by might rather than right[5].

7. There are several areas in the Uruguay Round package that relate to market access. The more important ones are tariffs, textiles and agriculture. India's position in all these sectors is advantageous to her and the provisions are favourable to the country.

Arguments Against Membership

Arguments against India's membership in WTO are equally strong. The major ones are stated below:

1. The claim that the world trade would increase substantially and that India's exports will expand considerably is not acceptable to many. The estimates relating to world trade (as shown above) may prove to be suspect. Flow of goods and services across the globe depends not much on trade restrictions but on factors like infrastructure, political environment,

technology, assured supply of exportable goods and quality consciousness of producing countries. It may, be observed that India is short, to some extent, in all these requisites. Removal of trade barriers will not guarantee expansion in world trade.

2. India and other developing countries have blindly walked into the trap laid by the developed countries. WTO, alongwith IMF and World Bank, represents the interests of developed countries. Rhetoric and platitudes notwithstanding, WTO will not ensure open trade for goods produced by developing countries. It ensures necessary climate for domination and hegemonisation by the consortium of the capitalist countries. Infact, the Uruguay Round negotiations were motivated by the needs of the United States and Western Europe to discover new markets for their industries, especially in sectors like services and finance.

3. It is claimed that there are several areas in the Uruguay Round package that relate to market access and India would, therefore, gain substantially in the long run because of the market access. Figures demonstrating the gains from market access are no doubt praiseworthy. But the gains, if any, in tariff concessions or removal of quotas could easily be lost because of the new rules and disciplines and potential for trade harassment.

4. The worst fears expressed about the WTO agreement relate to the steep hike in prices of drugs and agricultural inputs. Table 6.4 shows how select drug prices will be costlier across the globe.

Table 6.4 **International Comparison of Selecte Drugs Prices**

DRUG	INDIA	PAKISTAN	TIMES COST-LIER*	USA	TIMES COST-LIER*	UK	TIMES COST-LIER*
Anti-Bacterials							
Ofloxacin	73.03	151.26	2.07	192.39	2.63	178.77	2.45
Norfloxacin	33.61	161.94	4.82	613.77	18.26	290.88	8.65
Tobramycin	16.43	150.08	9.13	387.50	23.58	86.66	5.27
Anti-inflammatory							
Diclofenac	5.67	72.00	12.70	234.74	41.40	110.29	19.45
Anti-Ulcerants							
Ranitidine	30.03	336.00	11.57	729.93	25.14	553.88	19.08
Cardiovasculars							
Alenolol	7.86	111.78	14.22	223.85	28.48	118.78	15.11
Diltiazem	19.29	96.00	4.98	161.84	8.39	90.90	4.71
Anti-Viral/Fungal							
Ketaconazole	43.00	286.40	6.66	660.36	15.36	287.85	6.69
Anti-Histamine							
Aztemizole	6.00	156.00	26.00	427.74	71.29	115.14	19.19
Anti-Anxiolytics							
Buspirone	4.05	115.73	28.58	147.62	36.45	193.92	47.88
Anti-Cancer							
Mitoxantrone	446.25	N.A.	-	14876.65	33.34	9116.06	20.43
Vincristine	28.00	416.98	14.48	1047.26	36.36	624.79	21.69
Anti-Depressant							
Pluoxetine	29.00	798.40	27.53	507.60	17.50	647.21	22.32

Notes: 1.Prices are for 1991 and in rupees
2.*=Costlier over the Indian prices
3.Prices are for the same dosage and pack

(**Sources**: USA Prices-Annual Pharmacists Reference
UK Prices-UK Monthly Index for Medical Specialities (MIMS) December 1991
Pakistan Prices-Quarterly Index for Medical Pharmaceuticals (QIMP).)

Box 6.4 gives the balance sheet of the WTO for India. Also read Table 6.3

Box 6.4 **Balance Sheet for India**

Advantages

- Benefits from reduction of tariffs on the products of export interest to India.
- Improved prospects for agricultural exports as a result of likely increase in the world prices of agricultural products due to reduction in domestic subsidies and barriers to trade.
- Likely increase in the export of textiles and clothing due to the phasing out of the MFA by 2005.
- Advantages from greater security and predictability of the international trading system due to the revamped dispute settlement procedures, and the agreements on Safeguard, Subsidies and Anti-Dumping Measures.
- Compulsion imposed on us to be competitive in the world market.

Disadvantages

- Tariff reductions on goods of export interest to India are very small. On the other hand, there will be erosion of the preferences enjoyed by India and India will most probably be graduated out of the Generalised System of Preferences (GSP).
- Meagre prospects of increase in agricultural exports due to the very limited extent of agricultural liberalisation.
- There will be hardly any liberalisation of our textile exports during the next 10 years, with most of the liberalisation expected to come at the end of this period.
- We will be put under tremendous pressure to liberalise our services industries.
- There will be only marginal liberalisation to the movement of labour services in which we are competitive.
- We will lose policy options in several areas because of
  - The extensive bindings undertaken by us.
  - Prohibition of certain types of subsidies and making certain other types actionable.
  - Giving up the option of granting process patents only in some sectors.
  - Limitations put on our ability to apply restrictions on balance-of-payments ground.
- Increased outflow of foreign exchange due to commitments undertaken in the field of TRIPS, TRIMs and services.
- Technological dependence on foreign firms will increase as the R & D required to take advantage of the Uruguay Round may not be undertaken on an adequate scale due to paucity of resources.
- Concentration in market structure whereby only a few large firms or transnational corporations may benefit and smaller and tiny firms may disappear.
- Increasing intrusion in our sovereign domestic space in TRIPs, TRIMs, Services and Agriculture.
- The Uruguay Round has paved the way for similar other intrusions in future through linkages between trade and environment, trade and labour standards, and a new regime for the treatment of foreign capital.
- Trend towards neo-protectionism in developed countries against our exports.
- Possibility of cross-retaliation against our report of goods and services.

Conclusion

All things considered, it may be concluded that the WTO membership will prove advantageous to us in terms of the global market thrown open to our goods and servics. To take advantage of the world market, we must improve the quality of our goods and services, cut down costs and wastages, and improve our competitive strength. Only then we will be in a stronger position to sell our products abroad and survive in the competitive global market.

AGENDA FOR THE NEXT MILLENNIUM

The agenda for the next millennium before the World Body is on the following lines:

1. Agricultural products.
2. Services.
3. Tariffs on industrial products.
4. TRIPS, textiles, and anti-dumping duties and subsidies.
5. New issues-foreign investment, competition policies, transparency in government procurement, e-commerce.
6. Non-trade issues-linkage between trade and environment, linkage between trade and labour.
7. Technology transfer.
8. Non-tariff barriers.
9. The issue of commodity prices. Lack of stability in commodity prices has been causing economic instability among many developing countries.
10. Review of existing policies relating to subsidies, anti-dumping measures and countervailing duties.
11. Trading blocks (covered latter in this chapter) need to be reviewed as they are creating problems of trade diversion.

REVIEW OF PERFORMANCE

During the last decade of its existence, the WTO has proved to be totally different from its predecessor-GATT. GATT was toothless but WTO has been armed with adequate power by the way disputes between trading countries have been settled. It is to the credit of the WTO that even the mighty US was brought to book on more than one case. *Secondly*, GATT negotiating rounds took place once in a decade or so. But at Singapore, just two years after the conclusion of the Uruguay Round, the WTO virtually concluded an information technology agreement, and launched studies on investment, competition policy, transparency in government procurement and trade facilitation. *Thirdly*, the old leisurely pace of GATT is gone. Instead, there is enormous pressure to compress into the next few years what used to take decades to complete. *Fourthly*, the agenda of the WTO is expanding and the US is trying to push everything possible under the ambit of the WTO. This would facilitate smooth flow of trade across the globe. *Fifth*, the most favoured nation rule is advantageous to all member countries. This means that even when the US uses its muscle to take advantage of the Japanese market for beef and autoparts, the benefits are available not only to the US but for all members including India.

But at Singapore, just two years after the conclusion of the Uruguay Round WTO is a much improved organization than GATT. GATT had no teeth but WTO has.

Sixth, services trade is in place and many countries are opening their markets for trade and investment either unilaterally or through multilateral negotiations.

Finally, the Trade Policy Review Mechanism has created a process of continuous maintaining of trade policy developments thereby creating the process of liberalisation and reform.

WTO benefited, infact pro, developed countries.

There are shortfalls also which need to be taken note of. The WTO has benefited mainly the developed countries, leaving developing countries to fend for themselves. The multilateral trade policies are increasingly becoming a codification of the policies, perceptions, laws and regulations of the industrial countries. These are becoming norms and are made binding on developing countries. Consequently, the 'one-size-fits-all' approach is pushed down the throats of developing countries.

The gains to developing countries from the WTO did not match expectations. The implementation of some commitments was deliberately delayed and sidetracked. Many developing countries have confronted serious institutional and economic constraints in implementing some of the new WTO provisions. With the expansion of the agenda through the inclusion of very complex and slippery issues (such as services, intellectual property, technical barriers, and sanitary and phytosanitary standards), capacity of many developing countries to analyse and turn the analysis into sound negotiating positions is eroded. A proactive and constructive approach to new provisions is out of reach for developing countries because of resources and research capacity constraints.

Less said the better about the dispute settlement mechanism. Developing countries lack the expertise and resources to take advantage of the mechanism.

Experts talk highly about the dispute settlement procedure obtaining in the WTO. Though such a provision is an asset, it gives rise to a need to finance and develop expertise on international trade law in order to take full advantage of it. Given the level of technical expertise required, doubts have been raised about the capacity of developing countries to bring cases efficiently as complainants and to protect their interests as defendants. Even though some technical assistance is available from the WTO Secretariat, it is hardly available for developing countries.[6]

The agreement on GATS is regressive to say the least. It is argued that the rules of the agreement threaten public education, health, and environmental services, outlaw universal service obligations and subsidised supply; and undermine effective domestic regulation.[7]

Thus, there are appreciations for and criticisms against the WTO. In conclusion it may be stated that the world body is not an international organisation intended to govern the global economy or international trade relations. It is a member-driven organisation and does perform some functions such as providing a forum for trade rule-making; fostering transparency in the trading system and enforcing rules through a dispute settlement system. The WTO needs to be accepted and respected as such.

However, liberalism is ultimately about freedom of choice, and nobody can argue that such freedom is expanded by bringing new items onto the WTO agenda and forcing these down unwilling throats under the threat of trade retaliation. The US argues that a multilateral agreement on investment will be good for developing countries, even those opposed to it, since it will make them more attractive for foreign investors. But the logic of this argument itself is that countries which fail to liberalise foreign investment rules will suffer anyway, so why subject them to further penalties through trade sanctions? WTO serves a major purpose as a rule-making body for trade liberalisation. It should not be expanded into a sort of world government covering every economic subject under the sun, and then using the threat of trade sanctions to bring about a new world order.

TRADING BLOCKS

Discussion on globlisation is incomplete without a reference to trading blocks that are dotting the world map. Table 6.5 gives the trading blocks, names of member countries and years of establishment.

Table 6.5 **Trading Blocks**

Name of the trading block	*Member countries*	*Year of establishment*
1. EC (European Community)	Belgium, Denmark, France Italy, Luxumberg, Netherlands, Portugal, Spain and the UK	1957
2. EFTA (European Free Trade Association)	Australia, Finland, Iceland, Liechten-Stein, Norway, Swedem and Swithzerland	1960
3. NAFTA (North American Free Trade Agreement)	US, Canada and Mexico	1989
4. LAIA (Latin American Integration Association)	Mexico, Paraguay, Peru, Uruguay, Venezuela	1980
5. MERCOSUR (Southern Cone Common Market)	Argentina, Brazil, Paraguay, Uruguay	1991
6. ANCOM (Andean Common Market)	Bolivia, Colombia, Ecuador, Peru, Venezuela	1969
7. CACM (Central American Common Market)	Costa Rica, El Salvador, Guatemala, Honduras, Nicaragua	1960
8. CARICOM (Caribbean Common Market)	Antigua and Bermuda, Bahamas, Barbadas, Belize, Dominica, Geneda, Guyana, Jamaica, Montserrat, St.Kitts Nevis, St.Lucia, St.Vincent, Trinidad	1973
9. OECS (Organisation of Eastern Carribbean States)	Antigua and Bermuda, Dominica, Greneda, Montserrat, St.Kitts-Nevis, St.Lucia, St.Vincent, Grenadines and the Virgin Islands	1981
10. GCC (Gulf Co-operation Council)	Bahrain, Kuwait, Oman, Qatar, Saudi Arabia, UAE	1981
11. ACM (Arab Common Market)	Egypt, Iraq, Jordan, Lebanon, Libya, Mauritania, Syria	1964
12. AMU (Arab Maghreb Union)	Algeria, Libya, Mauritania, Morocco, Tunisia	1989
13. SACU (Southern African Customs Union)	Boputhatswana, Botswana, Ciskei, Legotho, Namibia, S.Africa, Swaziland, Transkei, Venda	1969
14. ECOWAS (Economic Community of West African States)	Benin, Burkina Faso, Cape Verde, Cote d'Ivorie, Gambia Ghana, Guinea-Bissau, Liberia, Mali, Mauritania, Niger, Nigeria, Senegal, Sierra Leone, Togo	1975
15. PTA (Preferential Trade Area for Eastern & Southern African States)	Burundi, Compros, Djibouti, Ethiopia, Kenya, Lesotho, Malawi, Mauritius, Mozambique, Rwanda, Somalia, Swaziland, Tanzania, Uganda, Zambia, Zimbabwe	1981
16. CEEAC (Economic Community of Central African States)	Burundi, Cameroon, Central African Republic, Chad, Congo, Equatorial Guinea, Gabon, Rwanda, Sao Tome, Zaire	1981

17. CEAO (West African Economic Community)	Benin, Burkina Faso, Cote d'Ivorie, Mali, Mauritania, Niger, Senegal	1959
18. UDEAC (Economic and Customs and Union of Central Africa)	Comeron, Central African Republic, Chad, Congo, Equatorial Guiena, Gabon	1964
19. MRU (Mano River Union)	Guinea, Liberia, Sierra Leone	1973
20. ASEAN or AFTA (Association of South East Asian Nations)	Brunei, Indonesia, Malaysia, Phillippines, Singapore, Thailand	1967
21. BA (Bangkok Agreement)	Bangladesh, India, Laos, S.Korea, Sri Lanka	1976
22. ANZCERT (Australia-Newzealand Closer Economic Relations and Trade Agreement)	Australia, Newzealand	1983
23. SAPTA (South Asian Preferential Trading Agreements)	SAARC countries	1993

Trading blocks emerged because of the erstwhile GATT's failure in establishing an open world trade. Surprisingly, GATT is reborn as WTO with renewed enthusiasm and wider membership. It is only hoped that the interests of WTO and the trading blocks do not clash.

Impact of Trading Blocks

There are potential gains for member countries from trading blocks (See Fig.6.2).

Figure 6.2 **Impact of Regional Groupings**

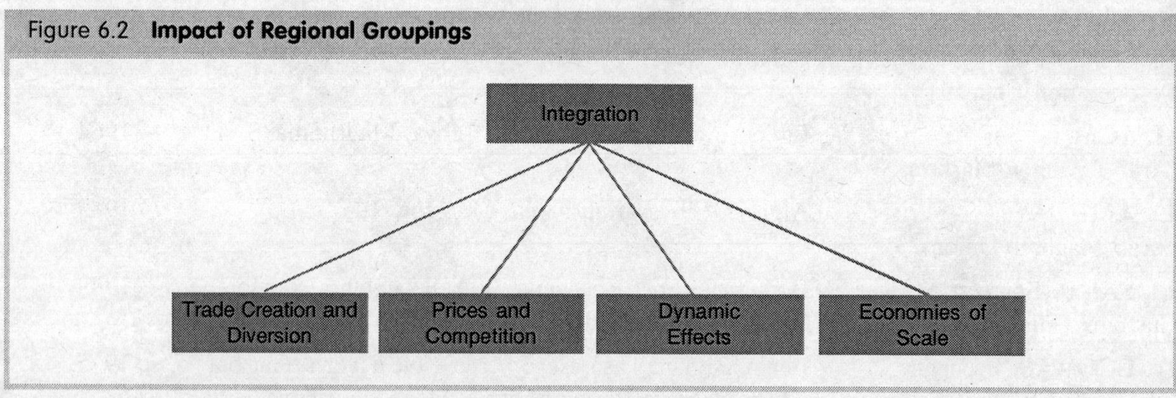

Trade Creation and Trade Diversion

When trade barriers between countries are removed, industries in respective countries will concentrate on the most efficient use of resources and produce those goods that they are most efficient in producing. The result is that all participants will gain from trade. In addition, when tariffs and other barriers are removed between the members of a trading area, new opportunities for trade are created. This is because exports can now be sold or imports bought at more reasonable rates inside the trading block. The efficient exporter can sell surplus goods abroad, and the importer, instead of producing the goods inefficiently at home, can reallocate resources to more efficient production.

Trade creation occurs when, because of free trade, industries produce more and more goods at lesser cost. This adds to the trade. Trade barriers being removed, new opportunities for trade are created.

Trade diversion occurs when trade is diverted from countries outside the trading area to countries inside. This results from the removal of tariffs and other barriers in the trading area, making it cheaper or easier to export to or import from these countries. External countries will find it especially difficult to retain their export markets if the common external tariff is higher than the previous importing country's tariff. In such a case, trade diversion may not be beneficial as trade may be diverted from a more efficient producer outside the trading area to a less efficient one inside. Generally, there will be gainers and losers from trade diversion-the net gain or loss will depend on the particular circumstances.[8]

Trade diversion occurs when trade is diverted from countries outside the trading area to countries inside.

The entry of Spain into the European Union provides an interesting example of trade creation and diversion.[9] In 1986, Spain formally entered the European Union (EU) as a member. Prior to membership, Spain-like all non-members such as the US, Canada, and Japan-traded with the EU and suffered from the common external tariff imposed by the EU. Imports of agricultural products from Spain or US had the same tariff applied to their products, for example, 20 per cent. During this period, the US was a lower-cost producer of wheat compared to Spain. US exports to UN members may have cost $3.00 per bushel, plus a 20 per cent tariff of $60, for a total of $3.60 per bushel. If Spain at the same time produced wheat at $3.20 per bushel, plus a 20 per cent tariff of $0.64 for a total cost to EU customers of $3.84 per bushel, Spain's wheat was more expensive and therefore less competitive.

But when Spain joined the EU as a member, its products were no longer subject to the common external tariffs; Spain had become a member of the "Club" and therefore enjoyed its benefits. Spain was the low-cost producer of wheat at $3.20 per bushel, compared to the price of $3.60 per bushel from the US. Trade flows changed as a result. The increased export of wheat and other products by Spain to the EU as a result of its membership is termed trade creation. The elimination of tariff literally created more trade between Spain and EU. At the same time, because the US is still outside the EU, its products suffer the higher price as a result of the tariff application. US exports to the EU fell. When the source of trading competitiveness is shifted in this manner from one country to another, it is termed trade diversion.

Prices and Competition

The removal of trade barriers has both consumption and production effects. The production effect of removal of trade barriers has been explained above. The consumption effects are noticed on prices and consumer choice. When trade barriers come down, consumers can buy goods more cheaply. This applies not just to tariffs, where price is directly affected, but also to non-tariff barriers like customs formalities which raise the cost of selling goods across the borders. Similar arguments apply to consumer choice. Trade creation increases the availability of goods enabling the consumers to pick and choose.

Trade barriers, when removed, will result in lower prices of products. Buyers can buy more at cheap rates.

The more relevant issue relates to competition. By removing barriers between national markets, trading blocks create competition. Generally speaking, the longer the trading area and the higher the level of integration, the more competition will be created. Competition benefits consumers immensely in the form of lower prices, wider choice, and better value for money. In addition, competition stimulates innovation, not only in the products themselves but also in the channels of distribution, methods of payment, customer areas, and so on.

Economies of Scale

Trading blocks necessitate huge volumes inuring in economies of scale.

Many industries, such as steel and automobiles, require large-scale production in order to obtain economies of scale in manufacturing. Obviously, industries of this type and others may not be economically viable in smaller, trade-protected countries. However, the formation of a trading block enlarges the market so that large-scale production is justified. The lower per unit cost resulting from scale economies may then be obtained. These lower production costs resulting from greater production for an enlarged market are called internal economies of scale.

In a common market, external economies of scale may also be present. Because a common market allows factors of production to flow freely across borders, the firm may now have access to cheaper capital, more skilled labour, or superior technology. These factors will improve the quality of the firm's product or service, or will lower costs, or both.[(10)]

Dynamic Effects of Integration

The term dynamic effects describes the continuous pressure for change that is a feature of an integrated competitive environment. Market forces act as a spur to improvements in efficiency, increase in investment, and continual innovation. A new product or process may create a competitive advantage for a time, but before long, a competitor will introduce something better. The search for success is ongoing. The need to innovate promotes investment in new technology, new methods of production and distribution, and product design. This investment has a multiplier effect on the level of economic activity generally and stimulates further increases in production, income, and demand. Competition also increases the necessity to be efficient. Not only do competitive firms try to minimise their costs of production, they also seek to maximise the effective use of resources.

Trading blocks promote integration which in turn results in efficient allocation of resources, promotion of some businesses and development of new technology.

In general, the dynamic effect of integration is that it brings about a more efficient allocation of resources throughout the trading block, promoting the growth of some businesses and the decline of others, the development of new technology and products, and the elimination of old.[(11)] This process is creating a large-scale restructuring of industries and firms in the EU, with the relocation of industry and many cross-border mergers and alliances. Obviously, it can be painful process, but it is one, which generally improves the competitiveness of European companies.

Meanwhile, India is a member of two trading blocks, viz., BA and SAPTA, in addition to being the founder member of WTO. India, as was stated earlier, stands to gain through multilateral trading systems as represented by the WTO. Trading blocks, on the other hand, negate multilateral trading and hence are not desirable. India has, therefore, done strategic thinking by shunning the membership of major trading blocks.

ANALYSIS OF GLOBAL ENVIRONMENT

Chapters 3 to 6 dealt with various dimensions of globalisation. How to analyse the international environment is more important than mere describing the different dimensions. As described in Chapter 2, environmental analysis comprises four steps: scanning, monitoring, forecasting and assessing. Before examining each environmental factor from scanning, monitoring, forecasting, and assessing perspectives, it is useful to remember that it may be highly difficult to analyse the whole environment as it is too complex and interconnected. The environment must therefore be decomposed into segments. Precisely for this reason, we have streamed the whole environment into different segments. How analysis of each environment is done is explained and towards the end, how the analyses of individual streams is integrated into strategic management is dealt with.

Scanning

Scanning of global environment demands answers to atleast three questions:

1. What are the current and emerging trends and patterns?
2. What are the indicators of these trends and patterns?
3. What is the degree of change within these patterns?

Scanning seeks to identify trends and patterns likely to have impact on the organisation. Identifying global trends may be relatively easy as publications, communication channels, intellectual and academic forums and world bodies are active in describing the likely trends and patterns. Only requisite is that the organisations should engage in certain activities. Organisational representatives need to attend seminars and conferences, subscribe to specialist journals and magazines and obtain reports from specialist bodies and government agencies. Scanning entails much reading and reflection.

The purpose of scanning is to detect current trends and patterns and also identify precursors of trends. The scanning, therefore, must go beyond mere collection of data relating to global environment. The data must be organised and interpreted so as to answer the three questions raised above.

Monitoring

Monitoring follows scanning. It involves tracking the global environmental trends, sequence of events, or streams of activities unearthed through scanning. The purpose of monitoring is to assemble sufficient data to discuss whether certain trends and patterns are emerging. Political risks inherent in some countries, destinations for FDI, antiglobalisation protests, future of WTO and digital divide are some of the issues which need monitoring as these are fertile grounds for emerging trends.

Forecasting

Scanning and monitoring provide a picture of what has already taken place and what is happening. Strategic decision making, however, requires a future orientation: it needs a picture of what is likely to take place. It helps develop plausible projections of the scope, speed and direction of environmental change. Thus, forecasting is an essential element in environmental analysis.[12]

Some of the issues relevant for forecasting are: will the antiglobalisation protests result in passing appropriate legislations in different countries? Will India lose its competitive advantage (blessed as she is with millions of engineers and technicians) in future, as more and more of today's youth are opting to work in call centres, after their plus two, instead of pursuing higher education in engineering? What stand the world would take towards 700 million Asians (representing two-thirds of the world's poorest people) remain trapped in extreme poverty? What trends would emerge from the attitude of leaders of poor countries who believe that the free trade is unfair and hypocritical?

Assessment

Scanning, monitoring and forecasting are not ends in themselves. Unless their outputs are assessed to determine implications for the organisation's current and potential strategies, scanning, monitoring, and forecasting merely provide "nice-to-know" information. Assessment involves identifying and evaluating how and why current and projected environmental changes affect or will affect strategic management of the firm.[13]

In assessment, the emphasis shifts from understanding the environment (the focus of scanning, monitoring, and forecasting) to identifying what that understanding means for the organisation. Assessment, obviously, answers two important questions: What are the key issues presented by the environment? What are the implications of the issues to the firm? Answers to these questions form inputs to strategy formulation both at the unit and functional levels.

QUESTIONS

1. Bring out the provisions of the Uruguay Final Act.
2. Bring out the arguments for and against India's membership of WTO.
3. Bring out the various trading blocks. Which benefits India most-bilateralism? Multilateralism? Discuss.
4. Discribe how is global environment analysed.

ASSIGNMENT

Now that globalisation is in place, study its impact on -

(i) Cart puller vending vegetables door-to-door.

(ii) Autorickshaw driver who is finding it difficult to make a living. A few years back, number of three-wheelers flying on the roads was less, but now it has trebled. Typically the situation was - 10 passengers were chasing one auto, now 10 autos chase one passenger.

(iii) Toy maker in a village who suddenly finds that there are no buyers for his wares.

REFERENCE

1. Bernard Hoekman, *et.al.,* (ed), *Development, Trade and the WTO,* The World Bank, 2002, p.42.
2. *Ibid,* p.44.
3. *Ibid,* p.42.
4. Richard Schaffer, *et.al., International Business Law & Its Ennvironment,* Thomson, 2002, p.353.

4(a).P.K. Vasudeva, *World Trade Organisaiton – Implications for Indian Economy,* Pearson, 2005, Pp.71.

5. Vijay L.Kelkar and V.V.Bhanoji Rao, *India-Development Policy Imperatives*, New Delhi, TMH, 1996, p.250.
6. World Development Report, 2004, p.105.
7. Bernard Hoekman, *et.al.,* p.486.
8. Andrew Harrison, *et.al., International Business,* Oxford, 1999, p.155.
9. Michad R. Czinkotia, *et.al., Global Business,* The Dryden Press, 1998, p.142.
10. *Ibid,* p.143.
11. Ardrew Harrison, *et.al., op.cit.,* p.158.
12. Lian Fahey and V.K.Narayaram, *Macro Environmental Analysis for Strategic Management,* West Pub. Co., 1986, p. 41.
13. *Ibid,* p.42.

7 Technological Environment

CHAPTER OUTLINE

Main Features of Technology

Impact of Technology

- Technology and Society
- Economic Effects of Technology
- Technology and Plant Level Changes

Management of Technology

Status of Technology in India

- Technology Policy
- Institutional and other Facilities to Promote Science and Technology

LEARNING OBJECTIVES

After reading this Chapter, you should be able to:

1. Describe the features of technology
2. Analyse the impact of technology on society, economy and on an individual plant
3. Discuss the problems in managing technology
4. Describe the status of technology in India
5. Understand our policy towards technology

Among all the segments of macro-environment, technological environment exerts considerable influence on business. This section is devoted to a detailed discussion of the interface between business and technology.

> J.K.Galbraith defines technology as a 'systematic application of scientific or other organised knowledge to practical tasks'.

During the last 150 years, technology has developed substantially. Science and technology(see Box 7.1 for the difference between the two terms) enabled man to conquer distances; control birth rate; save lives; generate, preserve and distribute energy; discover new materials and substitutes to existing ones; introduce machines to do the work of human beings; substitute mental work with computers; probe deep into the seas and space in search of new treasures; provide himself with lot of leisure and comfort *ad infinitum*.

Technology helps convert ideas into useful products.

As years roll by, new discoveries have been added. 1983 was particularly considered by scientists as the year of scientific success. In this year, scientists put a billion dollar technology into space; produced the world's first test-tube triplets and obtained evidence of another solar system. In the field of medicine, Japan marketed the much-awaited artificial blood system. A major breakthrough was achieved in the field of genetic engineering to cure dwarfism. The US physicists stripped off all the electrons from the uranium atom thus exposing the bare nucleus. It was also the year when the doctors were confronted with a baffling disease, *viz.*, AIDS (Acquired Immune Deficiency Syndrome) also named 'Gray Plague' that has taken a heavy toll of human lives.

The year 1998 belonged to nuclear scientists of India-they shook the world with serial underground nuclear blasts at Pokhran: resurrected a dead atomic rector in Rajasthan, and concluded negotiations with Russia on building a 2000-megawatt power station in Tamil Nadu.

Box 7.1 Science and Technology – The Semantics

It is useful to place the two words-science and technology-in their proper perspective. It may be noted that the word 'science' refers to a systematised body of knowledge and when this knowledge is put into practice, it becomes technology.

There are similarities and dissimilarities between the two terms. With regard to similarity, it may be stated that the two are inter-dependent. Advances in science help develop new technologies while at the same time, the need for new technologies and products provide the drive for new scientific discoveries. The difference between science and technology may be brought out as follows:

	Features	*Science*	*Technology*
1.	In pursuit of	Knowledge	Socio-economic gains
2.	People involved	Scientists	Engineers
3.	Agencies involved	Research institutions and universities	Industrial establishments
4.	Funding	Mostly government	Industry
5.	Motivation	To satisfy curiosity	To bring out need satisfying products
6.	Domain	Public	Private/secret
7.	Impact	Discontinuous	Continuous
8.	Time span	Uncertain	Evolutionary

Globally, the year witnessed an array of events: construction of an international space station, a lamb delivered by the world's first cloned sheep Dolly, the block-buster anti-impotency pill Viagra, teleportation and the discovery that a strange force is pushing the Universe apart.

We have left dusty footprints on the moon, created the Internet, and learnt how to read the human genome. The world of technology is not going to stop at this. The global economy could be on the cusp of an age of innovation equal to that of the past several decades. All the right factors are in place: Science is advancing rapidly, more countries are willing to devote resources to research and development and education. Table 7.1 contains some major innovations in the last couple of decades.

Table 7.1 Major Innovations

Business and Finance	*Information Technology*	*Health Care*
• Lean manufacturing	• Television	• Antibiotics
• Supply-chain management	• Transistors	• MRI and CT
• Big-box retailing	• Microprocessors	• Antidepressants
• Mutual funds	• Fiber optics and lasers	• Heart surgery and pacemakers
• Financial derivatives	• Internet	• Transplants
• Venture capital	• Cell phones	• Oral contraceptives
• Automated teller machines		• Minimally invasive surgery
• Credit cards		• Biotechnology

(***Source:*** *The Economic Times*, October 10, 2004)

Till now we have described the macro perspective of technology. At the micro level, technology refers to the level of sophistication with which a factory uses inputs such as labour, finance, machines and raw materials to produce output. Viewed from this perspective, technology may be compared to a black box (See Fig.7.1).[1] Several inputs enter the box on the one side and product Y comes out at the other side.

At the plant level technology refers to the set of machines, tools and other equipment used to convert inputs into outputs.

Figure 7.1 **Black Box**

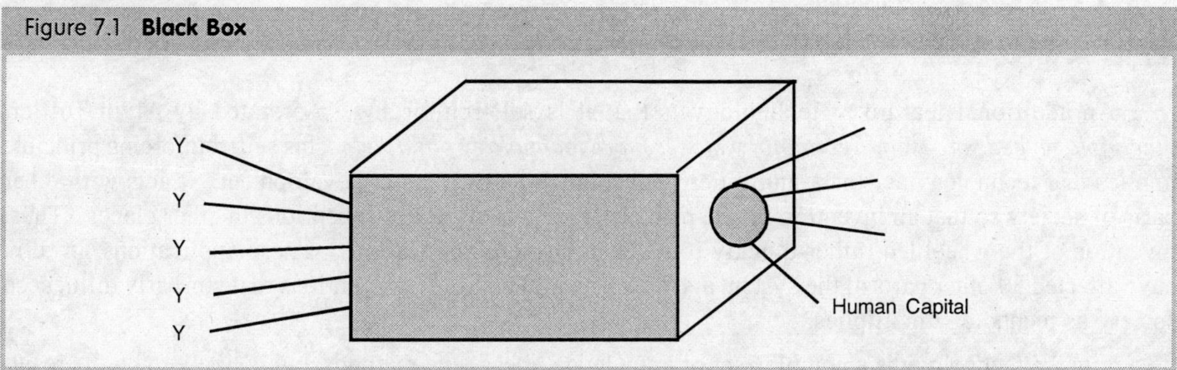

In this chapter, we understand technology from both its macro and micro perspectives.

Technology is the most dramatic force shaping the destiny of people all over the world. Some of the technological inventions the man feels, are wonders, some others are horrors, and yet others have mixed blessings. Automobiles and television, for example, have evoked mixed reactions. Hydrogen bomb, nerve gas and sub-marine guns have proved to be horrors. Penicillin, open heart surgery and birth control pills are wonders.

Whether one is enthralled or appalled by a technological invention depends on one's attitude towards it.

FEATURES OF TECHNOLOGY

Before we describe the impact of technology on business, we propose to bring out the salient features of technology. The first feature of technology is its change and then more change. Technology forces change on people whether they are prepared for it or not. In the modern society, it has brought so much change that it creates what is called *future shock*, which means that change comes so fast and furiously that it approaches the limits of human tolerance and people lose their ability to cope with it successfully.[2]

One feature of technology relates to its change.

More ideas are being worked on, the time gap between idea and implementation is falling rapidly and the time between introduction and peak production is shortening considerably (See Box 7.2). Experts have estimated that 80 to 90 of all the scientists who ever lived are still alive today. Business leaders must always watch out for changes and developments taking place around. New developments must be adopted and new ideas explored lest the business units would perish at the earliest.

Another feature of technology is that its effects are widespread, reaching far beyond the immediate point of technological impact. Technology ripples through society until every community is affected by it. The shock waves push their way into even the most isolated places. People cannot escape it. Even if they travel to remote places, as in Far East, technology is still represented by vapour trials from airplanes flying overhead, microwave communication signals from satellites moving at the speed of light and a haze from air pollution often preventing a view of the afar side.[3]

The second feature of technology is that its effects are widespread.

Box 7.2 **Innovation Time-from Idea to Successful Product**

Photography	112 Years
Telephone	85 Years
Steam engine	56 Years
Telegraphy	42 Years
Radar	18 Years
Transistor	5 Years
Fast logic	2 Years

Third feature of technology is that it feeds on itself.

An additional feature of technology is that it is self-reinforcing. As stated by Alvin Toffler, '*Technology feeds on itself. Technology makes more technology possible*'. This self-reinforcing principle implies that technology acts as a multiplier to encourage its own faster development. It acts with other parts of society so that an invention in one place leads to a sequence of inventions in other places. Thus, invention of the wheel led rather quickly to a dozen or more applications. These applications, in turn, have affected 50 other parts of the system and led to several additional inventions that similarly influenced society as technology multiplies.

Finally, technology is a complex set of knowledge, ideas, and methods and is likely to be the result of a variety of activities-both internal and external. Technological process, obviously tends to be a gradual process consisting of a sequence of small increments lying along a continuous path.

IMPACT OF TECHNOLOGY

We propose to discuss the impact of technology under three heads: (a) technology and social change, (b) economic effects of technology, and (c) technology and plant level changes (See Fig.7.2).

Figure 7.2 **Technological Environment of a Firm**

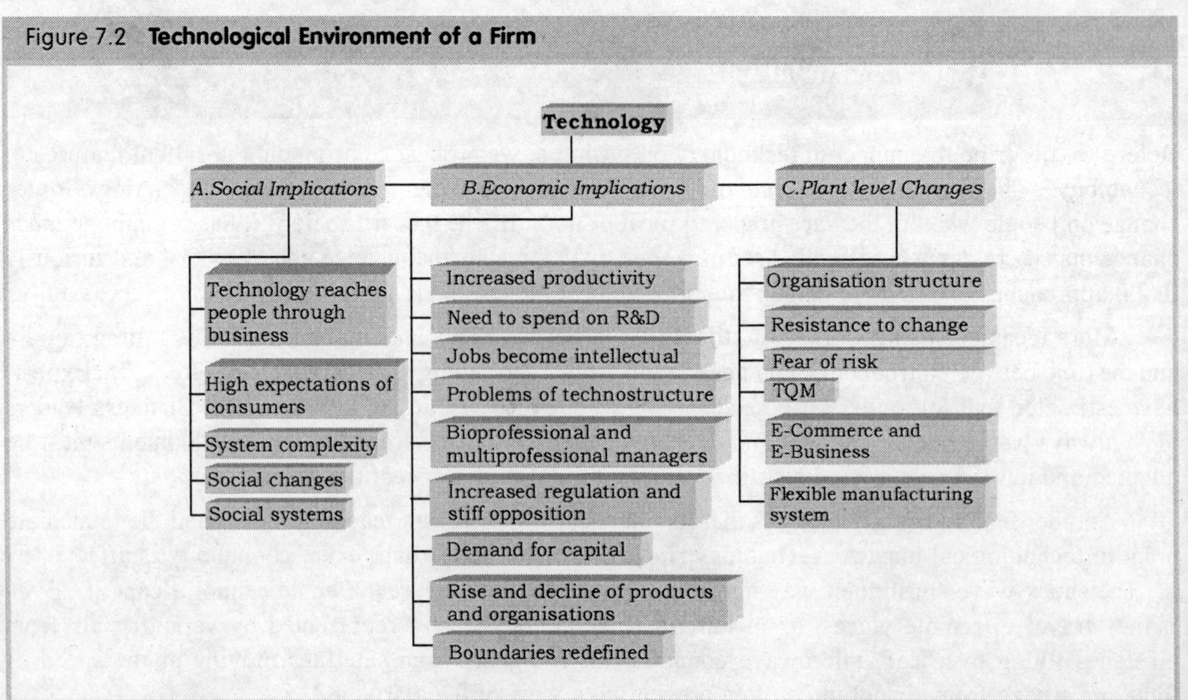

A. Technology and Society

Perhaps the most striking influence of technology is found on society. Practically every area of social life and the life of every individual has been, in some sense or the other, changed by the developments in technology.

• *Technology Reaches People Through Business*

Business is an institution through which man expects new discoveries to be converted into goods and services. Managers of business organisations pool the necessary resources and work on the new discoveries to convert them into useful products. New discoveries would remain mere ideas in mind, sketches on paper or mock models in laboratories but for business institutions.

People are using a great variety of goods and services thanks to technology.

Printing, housing, education and television are all dependent on business activities to make them work productively. Society depends on business to benefit from new discoveries flowing into useful goods and services for all mankind. Developing countries have learnt that scientific discoveries mean very little to them unless they have competent business units to produce for people what science has discovered. Developed countries have learnt that their progress stops unless they operate a business system which contributes to discovery and uses discovery to produce for their people.

That technology reaches people through business is only part of the story. The economic prosperity of a nation (of which business is a part) depends on technology. 50% of economic growth of USA, UK, Germany, France, and Japan has come from technical progress achieved in these countries.

• *High Expectations of Consumers*

Technology has contributed to the emergence of affluent societies. Affluent citizens want more of many things than more of same things. New varieties of products, superior in quality, free from pollution, more safe and more comfortable, are to be produced and supplied to the affluent sections. This calls for substantial investments in R & D. One important compulsion for investing in technological advances in Japan is its customer's high expectations regarding design sophistication, quality, delivery schedules and prices. Industry owners in Japan swear by the dictum-the customer is a god who is always right. High expectations of consumers pose a challenge and an opportunity to the owners of business institutions.

People have high expectations. They want not more of same things but newer things as well.

• *System Complexity*

Technology has resulted in complexity. Modern machines work better and faster, no doubt. But if they fail, they need services of experts to repair. They fail often because of their complexity (See Box 7.3). A machine or a system is composed of several hundred components. All parts must work in tandem to accomplish a desired task. Reliable performance of each part, therefore, assumes greater significance.

Also there is inter-dependence of systems. Failure of power supply, for example, will cause dry water taps, closed petrol bunks, suspended elevators between floors, dark streets, dark houses, no television and radio broadcasts, closed retail establishments and so on. A localised problem in a power house balloons into a regional problem affecting thousands of people. It is possible that technology might eventually lead to simplicity and small independent operational units. Such a possibility still

Technology creates complexity. As a result living becomes more complex.

Box 7.3 **Where Technology Failed**

Despite the remarkable organisation, discipline and technology of Japan, the havoc that nature wrought in just 20 seconds at dawn on Tuesday continues to exact heavy damage. By Wednesday evening 40 hours after the '1995 Southern Hyogo prefectural earthquake' struck Kobe and its environs, the overnight toll had risen to 2,585 with over a thousand still missing, in one degree centrigrade nights, and nearly 10,000 injured. And 2,40,000 people are to spend another night in shelters.

But in an extraordinary feat, almost all fires that were raging and spreading till last night were either put out or contained.

The Hyogo earthquake came exactly one year after the Los Angeles earthquake. Japanese engineers went to California and claimed that structural damage of that magnitude was never possible in Japan. Fortunately, no Tsunamis (tidal waves) have occurred.

As the newspapers and experts lambasted the city fathers, in the areas of heavy damage, for lack of foresight in employing better technology to protect the infrastructure, on the ground what shone was that one single quality that sets the Japanese people apart. The so-called group spirit and respect for authority. The Chief Cabinet Secretary, Mr.Kozo Igarashi, told reporters today that provision of food and water was the Government's main concern because of the inability to reach all affected people. Not a single case of burglary in evacuated homes or shops has been reported. Not one case of blackmarketing of food or medicines has taken place. Eight lakh homes are without gas supplies. Within eight hours, 80,000, people heeded a call to move out of the homes into shelters to avoid possible consequences of gas leaks. All this has freed law and order officials to focus on more important rescue measures. Above all, the highly-organised garbage collection system in normal times has ensured that there is no likelihood of any epidemic. This too frees medical personnel to concentrate on healing the injured and those affected by it.

Every few hours the round-the-clock television channels broadcast the names and details of those dead. Centres have opened in Tokyo, where even international calls can be received enquiring about missing people. These enquiries are broadcast over the Osaka radio channel.

But, all that said, the public is asking a lot of questions. Several times each year in most towns and cities an 'earthquake van' simulates various magnitudes of earthquakes for the public to experience. Nearly all homes are equipped with emergency kits for three-day self sustained survival. 'The rest of it,' says the Government, 'leave it to us.' But viewing the terrible damage to the Hanshin expressway, the collapsed railway stations and main infrastructure commentators have taken engineers and planners to task for making the excuse that upgrading of highways was not done because 'a quake here was not expected.' NHK TV said 'the myth of the invincibility of Japanese expressways has been shattered' as the highways have been uprooted from their foundations at several places, thus considerably reducing the efficiency of relief measures. Even bridges over which bullet trains pass have had pillars destroyed, severing the main national transport artery.

The entire planning and philosophy of Japan's anti-earthquake measures is under question. Annually, the country spends more than $100 million on damage prevention. In Japan, the focus is on heavy expenditure on building construction in the hope that there will be no damage while the Americans focus on relief. Japan has concentrated on earthquake early warnings and preventive measures, not so much on post-disaster relief and its efficiency. Whatever the reason, perhaps the lateral proximity of the epicentre area and the shallow epicentre of 20 km, the fact is that the transport infrastructure has failed.

Kobe has very large sections of land fill area. Engineers now say that in such places with weak foundations modern 'shock absorption' foundation constructions are not possible. But in this quake, as many as one-third of concrete buildings with such technology have fallen. Though libraries could not provide diagrams, the fundamental design implementation of these tall buildings has revolutionised technology.

(***Source***: *The Hindu*, Jan.19, 1995)

remains a distant dream. Meanwhile, more complexity in work and product systems is expected. Management is, therefore, under pressure to keep the whole system working all the time.

• *Social Change*

The role of technology on social change may be observed in more than one way. *First*, there is the change in social life which results from a change in a technological process. Thus, an invention may destroy the economic basis of a city; displace thousands of workers; yet the same invention may result in the creation of a new city somewhere else and create even more jobs than it originally destroyed. Technological changes of this sort create a constant turmoil in society, with socially uprooted, mobile populations drifting about in search of new centres of employment. Sometimes, this drifting may result in a new geographical distribution of population; an example is provided by the constant drift of population centres of electronic or aerospace industries.[4]

> Most dramatic effect of technology is felt on social life. Thousands of workers find that the jobs they have been engaged till now become irrelevant. They have to cope with new skills and new jobs.

Secondly, besides uprooting population, technology directly changes the patterns of their social life, for instance, the family, the sensitive recorder of all types of change, alters with technological development. An invention may open new employment opportunities to women, radically change hours spent at work and in the family, increase available leisure time, open jobs to youth, and deny them to middle aged or old workers. Technological development may basically change the stratificational system of a community. Skilled jobs, carrying great prestige, may be destroyed. Jobs maybe opened to members of discriminated and low-ranking or racial groups. Technological advancement tends to smoothen out social differences, if strategically targeted at the potential workforce. Industrial technology tends to iron out differences between the two sexes and between parents and children in a family.

Thirdly, though social differences tend to be ironed out, status differences are likely to be created by technological advancement in developing countries. Technology flows to less developed countries mainly through multinational companies. With vast resources at their command, multinational corporations (MNCs) have carved out places and images for themselves distinct from local companies. Along with the MNCs, people associated with them directly or indirectly behave like a class apart by themselves. Such people are better paid than their counterparts in local companies. With higher incomes, the standard of living enjoyed by these people is fairly high. They form exclusive clubs and are culturally more at home with the industrial West. Infact, the cultural integration of these neo-rich people with the industrial West is so complete that they read the same books, see the same films and TV programmes, have similar fashions, similar groups or organisations of family and social life, similar styles of decorating the home, building furniture and urban designs. Despite linguistic barriers, they have a far greater capacity for communication among themselves than is possible between illiterate and managerial persons in the same country speaking the same language. This international community, which has similar

> Technology helps iron out social differences but has created status differences instead.

patterns of consumption, must have similar patterns of income as well.[5] In India, the employees in foreign collaborations are paid much more than they are paid in other local Indian companies, though they do the same job in the same field.

Finally, the way we cook, communicate, use media and work are affected by technology. Even the language we use is changing: terms that until recently were not even part of our lexicon such as superconductivity, computer engineering, robotics, unmanned factories, miracle drugs, space communications, lasers, fibre optics, satellite networks, e-business, and electronic funds transfer have become common place. New terms continue to emerge as new products are introduced or improved-always with the anticipation that there will be a newer, faster, and better innovation in the market any day. Social changes are also reflected in our vocabularies. Words like *telecommunicating, house-husband, surrogate mother and domestic partner* all represent changes in society. It is, therefore, rightly said that the words are the bugles of social change. When our language changes, behavior will not be far behind.

• *Technological Phases and the Social Systems they Create*

Technology has brought, along with it, new words, new food, dress and food habits.

Commencing from the later part of the 17th century till the end of 20th century, five sages of technological development can be traced, as shown in Fig.7.3. Each stage leaves a distinct influence on work and on the social system. In history, nations have tended to move sequentially through each phase, beginning with the lowest technology and moving higher with each step, so that the five stages of technology roughly represent the progress of civilisation throughout history. Although one phase of technology tends to dominate a nation's activities at a particular time, other phases often will be practised at the same time.[6]

Figure 7.3 **Phases in Development of Technology**

Technology Level	*Phases in the Development of Technology*	*Approximate Period of Dominance*	*Activity*	*Primary Skill Used*
1	Nomadic-Agrarian	Until 1650	Harvests	Manual
2	Agrarian	1650-1900	Plants and harvests	Manual
3	Industrial	1900-1960	Builds material goods	Manual and machine
4	Service	1960-1975	Focuses on providing services	Manual and intellectual
5	Knowledge	1975-1990s	Abstractive work	Intellectual and electronic

Of particular interest is the knowledge level of technology. At this level, technology creates a distinct type of social system, *viz.*, knowledge society. In knowledge society, use and transfer of knowledge and information, rather than manual skill, dominates work and employs the largest portion of labour force.

In the knowledge society, the relationship between the knowledge worker and the organisation will be strange and amorphous, redefining itself all the time.The knowledge-worker will have to show why he should be retained, what benefit he can offer to the organisation, and how he can add value to whatever the organisation does. He will have to create new jobs in consultation with his employer. A job will then become a joint venture. When this happens, the worker can forget pension plans.

B.Technology and Economy

• *Increased Productivity*

Technology has contributed to increased productivity.

The most fundamental effect of technology is greater productivity in terms of both quality and quantity. This is the main reason why technology at all levels is adopted. In a hospital the objective may be qualitative, such as maintaining life with electronic monitoring equipment regardless of costs. In a factory, the objective may be quantitative in terms of more production at less cost.

Modern factories are now able to produce goods in a shorter period of time (to produce one car takes less than 10 seconds) and with fewer defects thanks to the introduction of "Six-Sigma" quality programmes. These programmes are designed to increase quality and to eliminate defects, thus enabling firms to compete in any international market. Six Sigma is a statistical term that means 3.5 errors per million, effectively eliminating performance problems and ensuring that products conform to standards. As a result of such programmes, Nokia has been able to dominate the international cellular telephone business and HP has become the world-leader in printers.

As a result of productivity improvements, real wages of employees tend to rise and prices of some products decline, which spreads the beneficial economic effects of technology throughout the whole social system. The result is that employees and citizens are motivated to want more technological advancement, thereby placing on business major responsibilities to introduce it with due concern for its social and environmental effects.

• *Need to Spend on R & D*

Research and Development (R&D) assumes considerable relevance in organisations as technology advances. In this context, firms are required to consider, decide and take action on atleast seven issues. *First,* is the allocation of resources to R & D. A company must make the required resources available for effective R & D. A company's R & D intensity (its spending on R & D as a percentage of sales revenue) is a principal means of gaining market share in global competition[7]. Besides, consistence in resource allocation to R & D across lines of business improves corporate performance by enabling the firm to better develop synergies among product lines and business units.

We spend very less on R & D. As percentage on GNP, our normal spending on R & D is less than one percent as shown in Table 7.2.

In contrast, UK spends more than 2%, Japan 1.96% and US 2.3%. In terms of absolute figures, these sums work out to be staggering because GNPs of these countries themselves run into astronomical figures.

Table 7.3 contains names of firms engaged in pharmaculticals. At the top is Dr.Reddy's Laboratories which spent 12 per cent of its net sales on R&D in 2003. This spending has been necessitated because

Table 7.2 **National Spending as Percentage on GNP**

1980-81	0.62
1985-86	0.89
1987-88	0.98
1989-90	0.94
1990-91	0.89
2002-03	1.00

Table 7.3 **Spending on R&D by Select Firms**

Sector Rank	*Company*	*%R&D Spend*
1	Dr.Reddy's Laboratories	12
2	Glenmark Pharmacuticals	10
3	Torrent Pharmacuticals	9
4	Sun Pharmacuticals Industries	7
5	Wockhardt	6
6	Panacea Biotech	6
7	Cadila Healthcare	6
8	Ranboxy Laborateries	5
9	Biocon	5
10	Pfizer	4

(**Source**: *The Economic Times 500*, Dec. 2004, p.36).

the company is focusing on research on new molecules. Glenmark, Torrent, Sun, Wockhardt, and others follow Reddy's Laboratories.

A noticeable trend is that the Indian arms of the multinationals have a much smaller R&D expenditure, compared to their Indian counterparts. This is because their parent companies do their research and the Indian subsidiary simply markets the products. Pfizer is the only exception, investing over 4% of its revenue on research in India. There have been quite a few successes in the Indian research labs. To date, India has already generated over 35 lead molecules, of which nine are undergoing clinical trials. Ranbaxy developed a superior delivery system for ciprofloxacin, which was licinsed to Bayer, the innovator, for global use.

This was not always so. Earlier, when only process patents were recognised, the R&D expenditure was virtually negligible. Indian companies were focussed on the domestic markets and could simply imitate the original innovator. They did not feel the need to spend on research.

Secondly, technology transfer, the process of taking new technology from the laboratory to the market place is equally important. This transfer takes larger time as organisations grow in size. The US based chemical giant Du Pont has long been known for its excellence in basic corporate research. In the early 1990s, for example, it led US chemical companies in patents applied for and granted. The company spent more than $13 billion on chemical and related research during the 1980s but the management admitted that the company failed to develop much in the way of major innovations.

Thirdly, time factor is important in R & D. The time between innovation and commercialisation is getting considerably reduced as shown in Box 7.2.

Companies can no longer assume that competitors will allow them the time needed to recoup their investment. Time to market, therefore, is an important consideration because 60% of successful potential innovations are imitated within four years at 65% of the cost of innovation. In the 1980s, Japanese auto manufacturers gained incredible competitive advantage over US manufacturers by reducing new products' time to market to only three years. US auto companies needed five years.

Fourthly, as new technology comes in, the old technology needs to be abandoned. The process of old replaced by new is called *technological discontinuity*. Such discontinuity occurs when a new technology cannot be used simply to enhance the current technology but actually substitutes for that technology to yield better performance. The R & D manager must determine when to abandon present technology and then to develop or adapt new technology.

Technological discontinuity-old replaced by new-is another dimension the businessman needs to keep in mind.

Fifthly, the firm must also decide on its own R & D or to outsource technology. The make or buy decision can be important to a company's R & D. Although in-house R & D has been traditionally an important source of technical knowledge for companies, firms can also tap the R & D capabilities of competitors, suppliers and other organisations through contractual agreements such as licensing, R & D agreements and joint ventures. When product life cycles were longer, a company was more likely to choose its own R & D, not only because it gave the firm a longer lead time before competitors imitated it, but also because it was more profitable in the long run. In today's world of shorter life cycles and global competition, a company may no longer have the luxury of waiting to reap a long-term profit. As a rule, it may be stated that a company should buy technologies that are commonly available but make (and protect) those that are rare, valuable, hard to imitate, and have no close substitutes. In addition, outsourcing technology may be appropriate when[8]—

Technology can either be outsourced or developed through in-house R&D.

- The technology is of little significance to competitive advantages;
- The supplier has proprietary technology;
- The supplier's technology is better and/or cheaper and reasonably easy to integrate into the current system;
- The technology development process requires special expertise; and
- The technology development process requires new people and new resources.

The *sixth* issue relates to the decision on product innovation or process innovation. In the early stages, product innovations are most important because the product's physical attributes and capabilities affect financial performance considerably. Later, process innovations such as improved manufacturing facilities, increasing product quality and faster distribution become important in maintaining the product's economic returns.German and Japanese firms have been most successful in process innovations as shown in Table 7.4.

Table 7.4 **Spending on Product and Process Innovations**

	Product	*Process*
Germany	50%	50%
Japan	30%	70%
US	70%	30%

(**Source**: M.Robert, "Market Fragmentation Versus Market Segmentation", *Journal of Business Strategy*, Oct, 1992, P.52)

Finally, in the days to come, organisations will be required to spend vast sums of money on R & D in the area of bio-technology. Japanese are ahead of other countries in this emerging area. In simple terms, bio-technology has been understood as the application of scientific and engineering principles to the processing of materials by biological agents to provide goods and services.

Organisations will be required to spend vast sums on R&D.

Though the amount required is enormous, bio-technology offers a wide range of opportunities to the industry as shown in Fig.7.4. It is upto the organisations to seize the opportunities and exploit them to their advantage.

Figure 7.4 **Industrial Opportunitites in Bio-Technology**

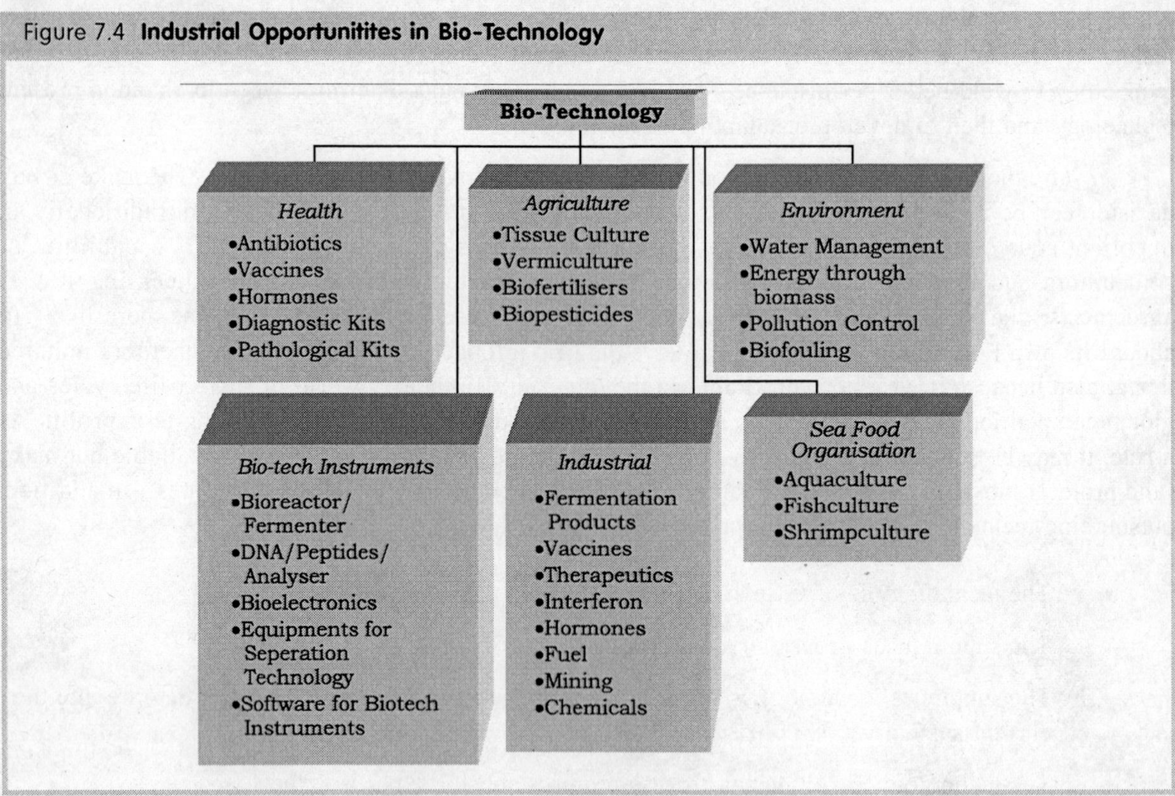

• *Jobs Tend to Become More Intellectual*

Advanced technology needs employees who are knowledgeable and skilled.

With the advent of technology, jobs tend to become more intellectual or upgraded. A job hitherto handled by an illiterate and unskilled worker now requires the services of an educated and competent worker. A clerical post in an office now demands the services of an expert in computers. Fig.7.5 demonstrates the change in the type of labour now required to work on machines.

Figure 7.5 **Changes in the Skill Distribution in Business Required by Advances in Technology**

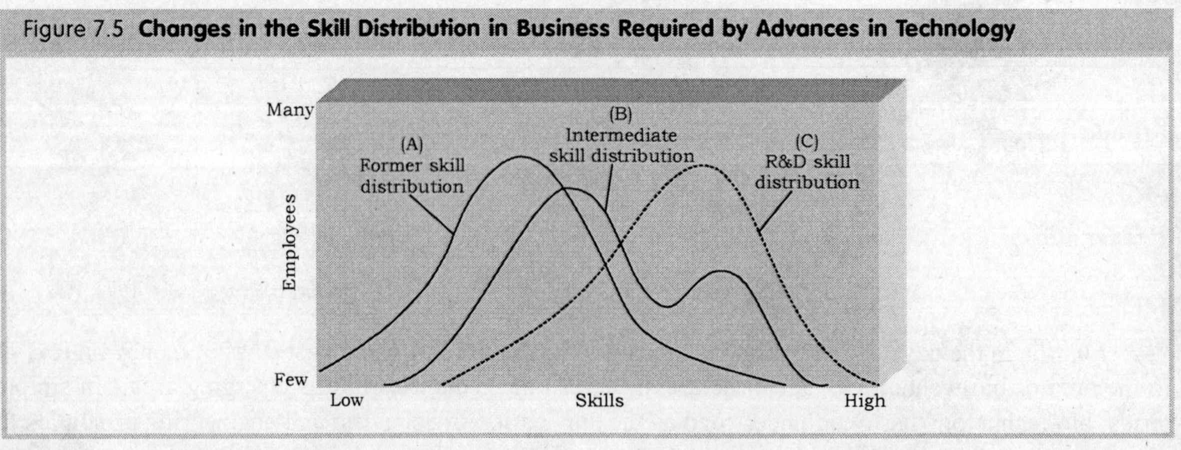

Decades ago, the typical factory had a range of skills resembling curve A. This curve was shaped like the normal curve of intelligence among people. Being matched to people, it suggested that an adequate supply of labour would be available at all levels of business in the long-run. In modern business, the curve has moved towards the right, higher in skill, as shown in curve B. And in many organisations, the skill distribution has become bi-model, as shown by the second top on the curve. Many scientific and professional people are required in research, development, planning and other specialised work, creating the secondary bulge towards the skills' end of the scale.

Curve C represents the skill distribution which is developing in firms oriented towards research and development. Though these firms manufacture products for sale, much of their effort is devoted to development and building prototypes. In some of these, the number of engineers, scientists, college graduates and specialists exceeds the total number of other employees.

Introduction of new technology dislocates some workers unless they are well-equipped to work on new machines. This makes it obligatory on the part of business houses to retrain its employees and to rehabilitate those displaced and untrainable. Equal is the responsibility of the government to provide training and educational facilities to its citizens. Government and businessmen should boldly demonstrate and convince the people that economic growth is more an insurance against unemployment than opposition to technological advancement.

But for those who pick up and acquaint themselves with the new technology, the job will be rewarding. The new job will be more challenging and rewarding. Working class, in general, stands to gain through increased productivity, reduced prices and increased real wages-all by-products of technological advancement.

Along with upgrading jobs, technology has its impact on human relations. Technology lays down the requirements for much of the human interaction in organisations. The arrangement of a production set-up determines who will be near whom. The work flow determines who needs to talk to whom. And since interaction and activity affect sentiments, technology indirectly determines what individuals in large groups will feel and think about one another and about their work situation.[9]

• *Problem of Technostructure*

> Technostructure creates new problems
> - traditional incentives fail to motivate
> - retention is a problem
> - difficulty in placing people in a pattern

Not only jobs become more intellectual, even the incumbents tend to become highly professional and knowledgeable. An organisation which has adopted the latest technology is flush with scientists, engineers, college graduates and highly skilled workers on its payroll. Though such an organisation can boast of a progressive and modern outlook of its personnel complement, the problems such an enterprise has to face on this account are serious, to say the least. Motivation of such employees, for instance, is a difficult task. Such mundane incentives as attractive remuneration, job security and just treatment, hardly inspire the enlightened employees to work more. They are instead motivated by opportunities which offer challenges or growth and achievement. *Secondly*, retaining such employees for long is a difficult job. Being cosmopolitan in their outlook, these professional employees are known for organisational rootlessness and job-hopping. Flighting and not sticking to one company is their culture. The company has to make several exceptions to discourage rootlessness of its professionalised employees. Regular attendance and punctuality have to be relaxed; dual promotion ladders have to be established so that distinguished technical people can rise in rank; profit-sharing to be provided to give creative persons a financial stake in the ideas they create; attendance at professional get-togethers has to be sponsored; writing professional articles has to be encouraged; and special assignments and part-time teaching may be allowed. *Thirdly*, scientific and professional workers constitute, what Galbraith calls, the *technostructure* of a modern organisation. The technostructure tries to control the organisation through influencing management's decision-making. While there may be nothing wrong in making decisions prompted by the technostructure, the problem lies in the social effect that is involved. People constituting technostructure are experts, no doubt. But they are more action-oriented and are yet to learn social problems of business decisions. Management is, therefore, in a tight position to balance the ruffled feelings of technocrats and the social consequences of business decisions.

The presence of technicians is not confined to the precincts of an industrial establishment, the influence goes beyond and covers the entire gamut of the society. The social values change to productivity, rationality and efficiency when the society gets dominated by technicians. Social institutions may be reconstructed or even eliminated. Family, for instance, might prove an anachronism as family loyalties might well interfere with rationality and job efficiency. Procreative functions might be according to the laws of eugenics, breaking the age-old barriers of inbreeding. Education could be made a purely pragmatic institution, devoted to scientific and technical disciplines. Most significant is the fact that scientists and technicians are and will continue to be the keymen in our civilisation.

• *Need for Bioprofessional and Multiprofessional Managers*

Technocrats, who assume reins of administration, need to be qualified in management education in addition to the proficiency they have acquired in the chosen fields of specialisation. Today's business needs bioprofessional and multiprofessional managers. To fill up a factory manager's post, for instance, the desired qualification stipulated is a degree in engineering and MBA from a recognised institution. The need for managers well-versed in different fields of knowledge is greatly felt now than ever before. Technological advancement has made the business more complex and its management more demanding.

Business and government must, therefore, spend more and more on spreading knowledge on know-how (technology) and do-how (management). Such a task is expensive but technology's greater productivity eases the burden of costly education and the training it requires.

• *Increased Regulation and Stiff Opposition*

Technology, no doubt, helps a lot but invites opposition and regulation.

A by-product of technological advancement is the ever-increasing regulation imposed on business by the government of the land and stiff opposition from the public. The Government has the powers to investigate and ban products that are directly harmful or hurt the sentiments of a section of society. Import of animal tallow has been banned by the Government of India because the alleged mixture of tallow with vanaspati oil hurt the feelings of Hindus. Continuous struggle launched by the FMRAI (Federation of Medical Representatives of India) produced gainful results like banning the sale of harmful drugs and banning of sales promotion and advertisement of infant formula through the mass media.

Technological advancement is inviting opposition from those who fear that new innovations are a threat to ecology, privacy, simplicity and even the human race. These people oppose the construction of high-rise buildings, location of industrial plants that eject harmful effluents, and setting up of hydroelectric plants. As the production process becomes more complex and products assume greater sophistication, public have to be assured of their (products) safety, their minimal propensity to cause pollution and their least threat to happiness and well-being of the human race.

The public must be enlightened that technology is not always uni-directional in its effects. It can be corrective as well as curative. Technology has created antibiotics which give rise to side effects. The same technology has also shown remedial measures for the side effects. Again, technology causes pollution, but it can also be used to check pollution caused by it and by human beings. Technology does contribute to urban blight, but it can also be used to beautify the city and make it more comfortable and enjoyable for the people to live in.

• *Insatiable Demand for Capital*

Today's technology necessitates massive investment of money on acquiring or discovering of new ideas and their adoption; educating, training and maintaining of the managers and the managed and on several other related areas. In fact, today's technology is characterised by its insatiable demand for capital. Business organisations should not only raise huge funds, exploiting all ways and means, but the mobilised funds must be judiciously employed for gainful purposes. This calls for honest and efficient financial management. Qualified and competent people must be appointed to assume responsibility for financial management and should be given due place in the hierarchy of an organisation.

Technology demands huge investment of capital.

• *Rise and Decline of Products and Organisations*

Change of technology, therefore, is a norm and not an exception. This poses another problem to business. A new technology may spawn a major industry but it may also destroy an existing one. Transitors, for example, hurt the vacuum-tube industry and xerography hurt the carbon-paper business. Television affected the business of radio broadcasting companies and movies and synthetic fibres reduced the demand for cotton fabrics. It is for this reason that Schumpeter saw technology as a force for '*creative destruction.*' And it is precisely for the same reason that the saying, '*Today's growth product is tomorrow's earthen pot*', becomes relevant. Products, like mortals, have life-cycles. A typical product, today, is subject to a cycle: introduction, growth, maturity, decline and abandonment.

Product has a life cycle of its own.

An organisation that is associated with a particular technology is influenced by it and will have the same life pattern as of the technology. Such an organisation will go in sequence through the introductory, growth, maturity and decline phases. The life of such an organisation may be composed of the following stages: (i) birth, (ii) growth, (iii) policy, (iv) procedure, (v) theory, (vi) religion, (vii) ritual, and (viii) last rites. In this eight-step sequence, an organisation is born and then has its growth. Policies are developed to guide decisions, and these are carried out through procedures. These procedures are refined and made more efficient with theories about efficiency. In time, the organisation may develop characteristics of a religion, it may worship the way it does things. Performance is by ritual; things are done by habit without questioning. The death and last rites of the organisation will ordinarily follow.[10]

So also an organization.

• *Business Boundaries Redefined*

- Technological change is a potent force in the reconfiguring of industry boundaries, it may broaden or narrow generally accepted industry boundaries. For example, advances in information technologies have rendered old conceptions of the financial services industry obsolete: insurance firms, banks and brokerage houses can now all be interconnected to provide new financial services, thus blurring long-held distinctions among the services offered by these industries.

- As a consequence of its impact on whole industries, technological change can have a significant impact on the prevailing business definition of individual companies. Companies may find themselves in a different business due to technological changes that they or others have effected. For example, Xerox (in the US) landed itself in such position in its copier business, thanks to the success of Japanese firms in miniaturising products. Because Japanese firms introduced smaller-sized copiers, Xerox found itself selling to different customers with different needs through different distribution channels and competing for different bases (price was much more important).

Definitions of individual businesses undergoes a change.

Product substitution and product differentiation are the by-products of technology.

- Technological change is one of the important factors giving rise to product substitution and product differentiation. For example, plastics have replaced many uses of steel, and microwave ovens are now frequently substituted for conventional ovens. Similarly in videotape recorders, companies have sought to differentiate their products through the introduction of technologically based features; longer recording time, longer recording time setting, sharper picture reproduction, clearer sound and so on.

  The above examples suggest that technological change is a dominant force in shaping competitive dynamics in many industries. It influences industry boundaries and structure, product substitution and differentiation, and the price and quality relationships between products.

- Technological change in the form of process (as opposed to product) and materials innovations may contribute to many of the impacts noted above. For example, process innovations such as automation, robotics and CAD/CAM have bestowed cost and quality advantages on many companies. Japanese automobile manufacturers have gained a significant competitive edge on their rivals elsewhere through the adroit use of this form of technological change.

- Finally, for multi-product companies (preceding discussion applies to single-business units), technological change may have multiple impacts. For example, technological change can create new synergies across businesses or obsolete existing ones. Advances in telecommunications and computer technologies have made new synergies possible across business dealing with computers, television sets and communications.[11]

C. Plant Level Implications

• *Technology and Organisation Structure*

Technology has considerable influence on organization structure.

Technology has considerable influence on organisation structure, length of the line of command, and span of control of the chief executive. Where companies use technology which is fast changing, *matrix structures* are more common. Some companies use a matrix even though the rate of technological change is not fast. Besides technology, other factors which have their influence on organisation structure are history and background of a company and the personalities of the people who founded the firm and managed it subsequently but the impact of technology is considerable.

In this context, three types of technology may be distinguished: small batch technology, mass production technology, and continuous-process technology. Each of these types has its impact on levels of hierarchy, span of control, ratio of managers to non-managers, shape of organisation, type of structure and cost of operation (See Fig.7.6).

Organisations that employ *small batch technology* make one-of-a-kind, customised products or small quantities of products. Furniture maker is an example for this type of technology. An organisation that uses small-batch technology needs to give people the freedom to make their own decisions quickly so that they can respond to customer's needs fast and produce what they want. For this reason, such an organisation has relatively flat structurise (three levels), and decision making is decentralised to small teams where managers have a relatively small span of control (23 employees). The most appropriate structure for small-batch technology is an organic structure in which managers and employees work closely to coordinate their activities to meet changing work demands. Small-batch technology is relatively expensive to operate because the work process is unpredictable and the production of made-to-order products makes production planning difficult.

Figure 7.6 **Technical Complexity and Organisational Structure**

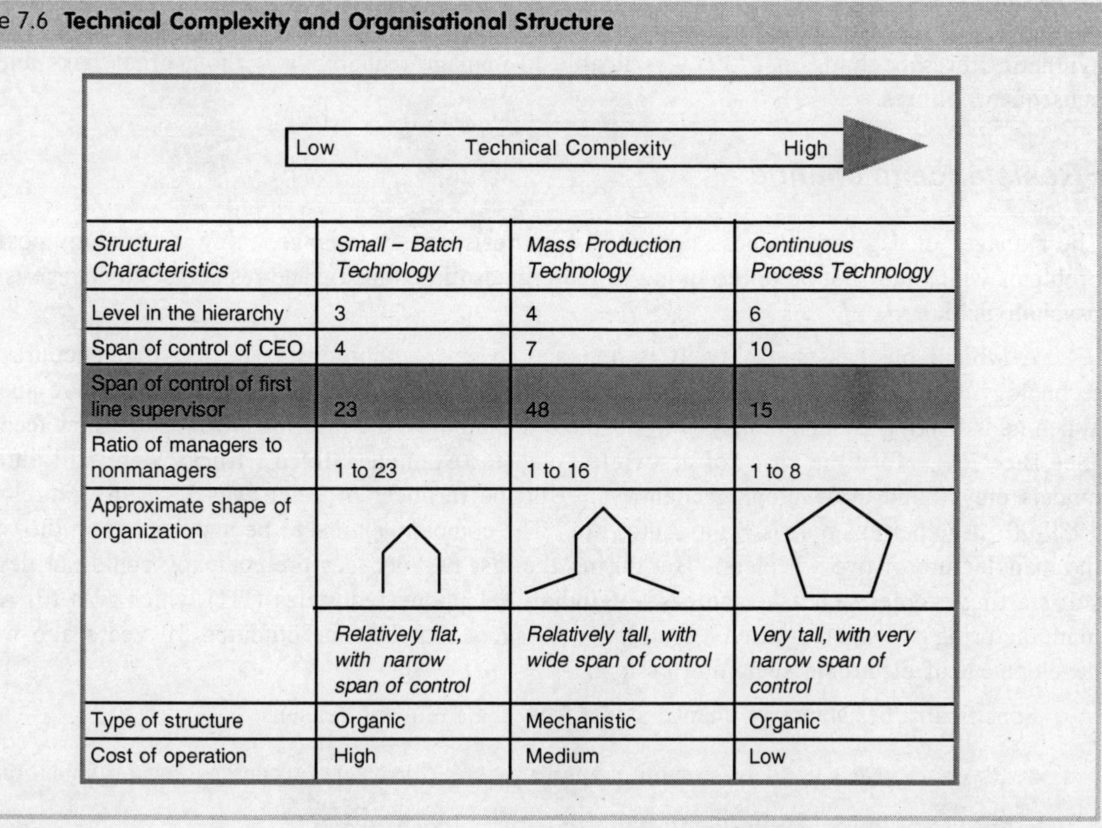

Low — Technical Complexity — High

Structural Characteristics	*Small – Batch Technology*	*Mass Production Technology*	*Continuous Process Technology*
Level in the hierarchy	3	4	6
Span of control of CEO	4	7	10
Span of control of first line supervisor	23	48	15
Ratio of managers to nonmanagers	1 to 23	1 to 16	1 to 8
Approximate shape of organization	*Relatively flat, with narrow span of control*	*Relatively tall, with wide span of control*	*Very tall, with very narrow span of control*
Type of structure	Organic	Mechanistic	Organic
Cost of operation	High	Medium	Low

(***Source:*** Gareth R.Jones, *Organisational Theory*, p.274)

Organisations with *mass production technology* produce large volumes of standardised products such as cars, razor blades, and soft drinks. Here machines control the work process. The use of machines allows tasks to be specified and programmed in advance. As a result, work activities are standardised, and the production process is highly controllable. Organisations with mass production technology have four levels of hierarchy, have span of control of seven each, have mechanistic structures and costs of operation are moderate.

Organisations with *continuous-process technology* produce continuously with little variation in output. In an oil refinery, for example, (an industry where continuous-process technology is employed) crude oil brought continuously to the refinery by tankers flows through pipes to cracking towers where its individual component chemicals are extracted and sent to other parts of the refinery for further refinement. Final products such as gasoline, fuel oil, benzene and tar leave the plant in tankers to be shipped to customers. Workers in a refinery or in a chemical plant rarely see what they are producing.

Organisations that employ continuous-process technology have six levels of hierarchy, have organic structures and costs of operation tend to be low.[12]

Technology has its impact on other areas of an organisation. Any technological advancement will result in (a) the expanded availability of a range of products and services; (b) substitution of capital for labour, leading to higher productivity and lower costs; (c) increases in sales or power for the innovating organisation relative to its competitors; (d) initiation of changes in behaviour among customers, suppliers, employees, or society; and (e) side effects on the quality of physical environment.

• *Fear of Risk*

There is always the fear of risk. Take the case of DuPont's Corfam, an intended substitute for the forecasted shortage of shoe leather. After an investment of $300 million, the company abandoned the project in 1971 because of quality and cost problems. Even a research-oriented company like DuPont, which was responsible for adding totally new dimensions to the textile industry with its introduction of synthetic fibres begining in 1939, was unable to manage technology without great risks and some subsequent failures.

• *Resistance to change*

The manager of a given business unit shall face resistance to change. New technology poses new problems which may not be to the liking of the organisational men. The resistance to change is purely psychological.

A typical businessman himself is opposed to new technology. He does not encourage new technology. Reasons are not purely psychological. Adopting new tecnology is expensive and risky. When he is making enough money with obsolete technology why must he worry about new tecnology? (See Box 7.4). Take the case of erstwhile Telco for example. Telco's trucks were still antiquated models only found in developing countries. But the turnover of Telco was Rs.1,969 crores during 1989-90. Another example is Bajaj Auto, Ltd. The company claims to be number two in the world in the manufacture of two wheelers. But during the last two decades the company could not develop a self-starting scooter. Or take the case of Indian Telephone Industries (ITI) which was till recently manufacturing strowger crossed switching equipment that became outdated 10 years ago with the development of electronic switching system.

Specifically, resistance to change stems from the following reasons:

1. Psychological and social commitments to existing products, processes and organisation,
2. Sizable capital investments in long-life single-use-facilities,
3. Low profits and reduced rate of growth,
4. Small size or fragmented activities,
5. Complacent top management,
6. Industry norms and associations or cartels which perpetuate industry-bound thinking,
7. Lack of successful entrepenurial models to emulate, and
8. Powerful labour resistance to changes in methods.[13]

• *Total Quality Management(TQM)*

Total Quality Management refers to deep commitment of an organisation to quality. Quality of product and service is an obsession and every step in the company's processes is subjected to intense and regular scrutiny for ways to improve it. Almost every issue is subject to exploration, and the process is a continuing one of long duration. Employers are provided withextensive training in problem solving, group decision making and statistical methods.

TQM replaces traditional beliefs about quality with a new set of principles. Traditional beliefs which are discarded include-

- High quality costs more.
- Quality can be improved by inspection.
- Defects cannot be eliminated completely.
- Quality is the job of the quality control personnel.

Box 7.4 **Thriving on Obsolescence**

Not a day passes without journals carrying advertisements proposing new investments running into crores of rupees. All of them explain how the latest equipment and machinery will be bought from abroad. Rarely does one hear of any proposal for investment in indigenous technology development.

Thus, as a rule, Indian industrialists have no interest in preserving the technology they have; no interest in acquiring top quality engineers; neither do they have plans for creating technology on their own. Evidently, in the Indian industrial scene, technology has no past that calls for preservation, no present that requires quality personnel and no future worth investing for.

There is a reason for this. The purpose of technology development is to generate super-normal profits-profits above what production and trading will normally yield. Unfortunately, in India, maximum profits are obtainable from tax evasion, smuggling, speculation and monopolisation, but not from superior production technology. So the technology that is patronised most is that of tax avoidance, customs evasion, speculative trading and, till recently, cornering of licences. When so much can be made in the innovative treatment of say, excise duties, there is understandably little interest in technology innovation. In any case, for the promoters, procuring technology from abroad is a most profitable exercise. Where, then, is the need to develop one's own technology?

Peter Drucker, the management guru, has emphasised that success depends on making obsolete one's own profitable technologies; and as quickly as possible. His logic is simple: however great your technology is, once a rival develops a better one, he will corner all super-normal profits, leaving you holding an unprofitable, even an unsaleable product. That is why in a competitive economy, entrepreneurs run like hell to remain where they are. Or else, as the experience of IBM and General Motors demonstrates, even the soundest operations are liable to be driven to the wall.

Indian industry has placed its faith in an exactly opposite philosophy: never let a technology depreciate. That is how we have Ambassador cars, Bajaj scooters and a host of other products continuing to stay on in the market place long after such products have been confined to the dust elsewhere. Singapore Airlines changes aircraft every three-four years; we operate the oldest Boeings. In fact, if anyone wants to set up a musuem of technology, the best place to look for is India.

Liberalisation, it was hoped, will force Indian entrepreneurs to look for indigenous technology development. Indications are that it is not going to be so; in the past, industrialists did not change their product till machinery crumbled down;instead, now, they will probably attempt a change as and when a new breed of second hand machinery becomes available. The culture remains the same; the dependence will continue to be on imported machinery.

Now it can be explained why Indian industrialists never ask for tax concessions on account of technology depreciation. Elsewhere, tecnology is embodied in ideas; in Indian industry, it is embodied in machinery. Hence, as technology depreciates, Indian industrialists look for new machinery, not for better ideas.

Also, ideas need innovative researchers; minding machines needs good mechanics. So, the Indian entrepreneur has little concern for technology depreciation, nor for high fliers in R&D.

In Aldous Huxley's Brave New World, there is a telling episode of how Beta type infants are conditioned; they are indoctrinated with the idea that they are happy and they are not alphas who have to struggle to remain ahead all the time. Indian industry is a self conditioned Beta type; happy and proud to be second rate, to borrow ideas from others; to make do with discarded technology.

This mental make-up gets deeply disturbed when anyone steps out of the line and tries to do something better, like for instance, what Sam Pitroda attempted to do. Every other country is greatly worried about external threats to technology; we need have no such fears. We know who the enemy is; it is us.

In his latest book, Drucker warns that the era of comparative advantage-which made competition important-is over; what we are facing is adversarial trade where the aim is the subjugation of others. Incidentally, the weapon for such subjugation is technology.

Isacc Asimov has a beautiful short story about how a brilliant and ambitious youngster is prevented from migrating to other far more glamorous worlds. In the denouement, he realises he can never leave this world because he has an A1 brain; the kind of brain which alone can produce better and better innovations. Emigration, he learns, is permissible only for inferior mortals.

Does any entrepreneur (or decision-maker) in this country understand what Asimov was driving at?

(***Source***: *The Economic Times*, Feb. 6, 1993)

The new principles of TQM are-

- Meet the customer's requirement on time, the first time, and 100% of the time.
- Strive to do error-free work.
- Manage by prevention, not by correction.
- Measure the cost of quality.

TQM has been introduced by almost all organisations. It has several implications for employees and organisations. Managers are required continuously to search for improved policies and activities. Employees can no longer rest on their past achievements. They too are required to search for newer and better ways of doing things. Some of them may experience stress from a work climate that no longer accepts complacency with the statusquo. Employees will be more and more involved in process improvement. Management will look at them as a source of improvement of ideas.

Some of our companies have excelled in quality and have won Deeming prize, a sort of Noble Prize for quality. Table 7.5 contains names of firms that have won the prestigious prize for excellence in quality.

• *E-Commerce and E-Business*

E-commerce through Internet is made possible through technology.

Technology has given birth to the Internet and the association world wide web which have made e-commerce possible. E-commerce is contributing to a growing number of transactions within a country and across nations. Viewed globally, the web is emerging as the great equiliser. It rolls back some of the constraints of location, distance, scale and time zones. The web allows, both small and large enterprises to expand their presence globally at a lower cost than ever before. The web makes it much easier for buyers and sellers to find each other, wherever they may be located, and whatever their size of operations.

While e-commerce focuses on marketing and sales process, e-business emphasises integration of systems, processes, organisations, value chains and markets. The integration operates through Internet and helps build new relationships between businesses and customers.

Table 7.5 **India's Deming Heroes***

Company	*Year*
Sundaram Clayton (Brakes Division)	1998
Sundaram Brake Linings	2001
TVS Motor	2002
Brakes India (Foundry Division)	2003
Mahindra & Mahindra (Farm Equipment)	2003
Rane Brake Linings	2003
Sona Koyo Steering Systems	2003
Lucas-TVS	2004

(***Source:*** *Business Today*, January 2, 2005, p.157)

*List includes only companies in the auto sector

The Internet and e-business provide a number of benefits to business in general including the following:

1. Convenience in conducting business worldwide; facilitating communication across borders which brings globe closer.
2. An electronic meeting and trading place, which adds efficiency in conducting business.
3. Power to consumers as they gain access to limitless options and price differentials.
4. Efficiency in distribution.

• *Flexible Manufacturing System(FMS)*

Flexible Manufacturing System (FMS) is another by-product of technology. Under FMS, machines are designed to produce batches of different products. Gone are the days of one machine producing multiple units of one component. It can now make dozens or even hundreds of different parts in any order management desires.

Under FMS, machines are designed to produce batches of different products.

The unique characteristic of FMS is that by integrating computer aided design, engineering and manufacturing, they can produce low-volume products for customers at a cost comparable to what had been previously possible through mass production. In effect, FMS is rewriting the laws of economies of scale. Management no longer has to produce on a massive scale to achieve low unit-cost of production. With flexible manufacturing, when management wants to produce a new part, it does not change machines-it needs to change the computer programming.

Under FMS, workers need more training and higher skills. Besides, employees in flexible plants are typically organised into teams and given considerable decision making discretion. Organisational structure needs to be so designed so as to facilitate decentralisation of authority into the hands of operating teams.

MANAGEMENT OF TECHNOLOGY

Technology is a high-risk, costly and uncertain activity. The world has entered an age in which many of the easy inventions and discoveries have already been produced. To achieve breakthroughs which have social significance and profit potentials for the originator, increasingly larger investments in research must be made. Quantum leaps forward in technological benefits require greater managerial and financial commitments. But while costs of discovery are increasing at an accelerating rate, the incremental pay-off results seem to be growing at a decreasing rate over the short-run.

To obtain cost-discovery effectiveness and justify research and development expenditures, firms need potentially high pay-offs. Pharmaceutical drug companies have been criticized for prices excessively higher than the cost of production and materials. But the uninformed public fails to consider the high research investment that preceded production of an effective and successful drug and all the dead ends and unsuccessful formulations that must be recovered from the successful ones.

There is the risk of a product being duplicated or closely imitated.

There is the added risk that a new product will quickly be duplicated or closely imitated, thereby reducing the market and profit potential for the original innovator. As the technology of any industry becomes easier to duplicate, the motivation for further innovation declines. Undifferentiated competitive advantage, whether in drugs, petro-chemicals, electronics, or building materials, ultimately leads to a slowdown in the rate of product improvements generated within the industry. In seeking more profitable potentials for future growth, management either turns more to manufacturing or distribution process improvements.

For a management which wants to import technology, there are problems. Basic infrastructural facilities like training of technicians and supervisors, testing facilities for raw materials, replacement parts, and the like are not easily available. A prestigious tool room located in Bangalore has a CNC mahine lying idle for the past two years. Reason-non-availability of a critical part which is worn out and a replacement is not available locally.

Developed countries do not easily lend technology to others.

Import of technology is also not easy because developed countries are not willing to lend it. Infact, these countries view India as a potential rival. The technology, the developed countries are willing to lend, is limited in scope and is mainly aimed at exploiting our dynamic competitive advantages in order to feed the markets they are interested in. They will not pass on their key technolgy, such as design know-how for manufacturing equipment, which could help us in challenging them in their own game.

If the East Asian Tigers, with hardly any natural resources, can be such wonders and prove a threat to Western MNCs, India with its rich resources-both natural and human-can become a greater threat to developed countries.

Even when a company is willing to transfer technology, finding a collaborator is a problem.

Assuming there are companies willing to transfer technology, there is the problem relating to choosing a right collaborator and obtaining clearance from the government. Despite the existence of several research establishments in our country, interaction between them and the industry is not encouraging. The management is forced to look for a collaborator for new technology. Getting a right collaborator is not an easy task. Similarly, any tall talk about streamlining and simplifyling the licensing procedure notwithstanding, it takes minimum one year for an enterpreneur to obtain final clearance from the government.

Three factors: pollution, depletion of resource base and social institutions impede technology.

Ability to absorb western technology is low in our firms. 'Bullet', India's once prized 350cc motorcycle manufactured by Enfield India, for example, could not for a long time, change the side of the foot brake-lever from left to right, thus putting the driver to considerable physical risk. The company could not adapt the design (supplied by an European company) for relatively minor changes to left-hand driving system. Bajaj Scooters, claiming to be the second largest scooter manufacturer in the world, took more than six months, after the promulgation of law to introduce direction blinkers on its scooters, and that too as crude protuberances. This was when the amendments in the Motor Vehicles Act were in offing for more than a year and all other leading scooter manufacturers in the world had already integrated blinking indicators in their models.

There are also constraints on the technological growth. Three constraints are significant: pollution, industrial resource base and social institutions (See Fig.7.7).

Figure 7.7 **Constraints on Technology**

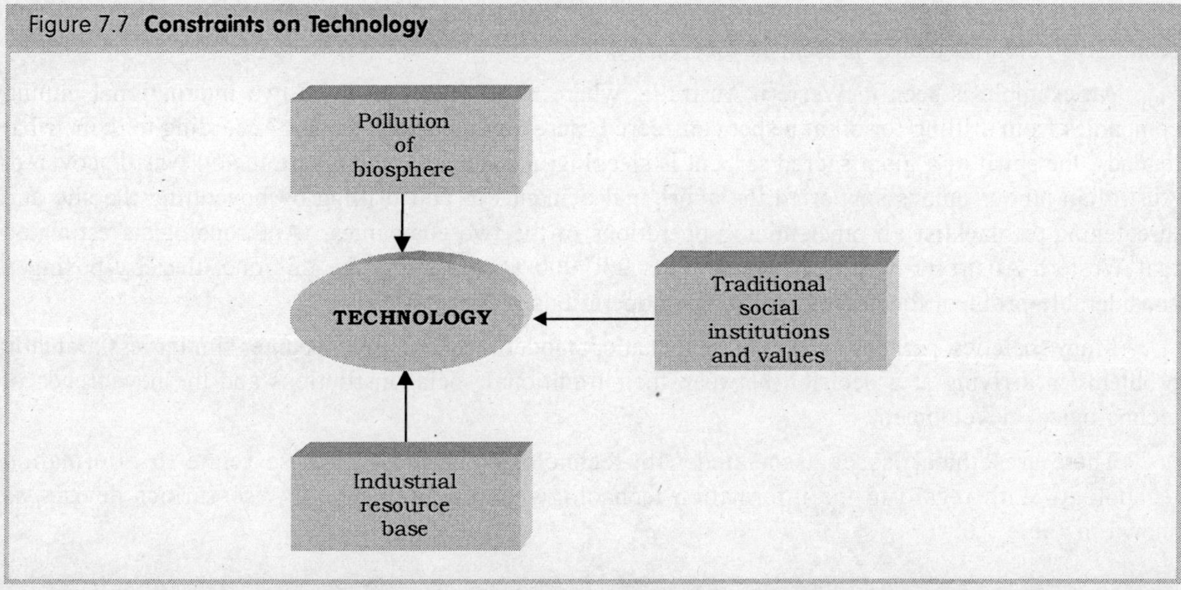

Pollution

Pollution is an unavoidable consequence of industrial production. Smoke, smell, noise, effluents and dust are generated by industrial establishments.

The biosphere-the land, air, water and natural conditions on which all life on earth depends- can absorb and break down many of these industrial pollutions without harm to people, animals or plants. But the biosphere is not all infinite sponge, and the build-up of harmful chemicals in the ecosystem poses a threat to life and the planet itself. The earth's absorptive capacity is especially limited when a single society concentrates its industrial technology and industrial products too densely in a single region. A critical issue today is society's capability to raise the standard of living everywhere as less-developed countries industrialise without causing irreparable damage to the earth's biosphere. Part of the answer to this potential obstacle to further technological development is to invent and use new and less polluting forms of technology and energy[14].

The Industrial Resource Base

Industrial resource base comprises minerals, different forms of energy, water supplies, skilled labour force, and human knowledge. There is limit to the availability of these and this limitation checks the advancement of technology.

But technology itself offers an answer to shortage of all resources. It has potential to discover new materials, substitutes for existing ones and new uses for existing materials. It also has potential to develop human knowledge and discover newer and newer forms of energy.

Technology need not be perceived as a threat to the resource base of society.

Social Institutions

A third factor limiting technology is social values and institutions that may be inconsistent with the full productive potential that is present in technology.

An example is seen in Western Australia, where aborigines prevented two international mining companies from drilling for oil at a spot considered sacred by the tribal group. According to their tribal legends, the spirit of a giant sacred serpent is sleeping under the ground where the oil was discovered. Australian labour unions supported the aboriginal demands to halt drilling by boycotting the site and threatening to blacklist all other mining operations of the two companies. Anthropologists estimated that Western Australia may have as many as 200,000 sacred sites like this one, thereby posing a considerable problem for mining and drilling operations there.

Many societies, perhaps most of those that adopt modern technology, encounter similar less dramatic problems in arriving at a decision between their traditional social institutions and the new trends of technological development.[15]

There are ethical issues associated with technology and most of these relate to information technology. With regard to the information technology, employees generally use various devises as shown in Table 7.6.

Table 7.6 **Unethical Activities Associated with New Technologies**

Unethical Activities Associated with New Technologies
Sabotage systems/data of current co-worker or employer
Sabotage systems/data of former employer
Access private computer files without permission
Listen to a private cellular phone conversation
Visit pornographic websites using office equipment
Use new technologies to unnecessarily intrude on co-workers' privacy (such as paging during dinner)
Copy the company's software for home use
Create a potentially dangerous situation by using new technology while driving
Use office equipment to network/search for another job
Wrongly blame an error you made on a technological glitch
Make multiple copies of software for office use
Use office equipment to shop on the Internet for personal reasons

(***Source:*** Laura P.Hartman, op.cit. p.660)

The above devises no doubt, have greatly contributed to increased productivity, expanded job-related knowledge, improved communication, improved time management, relieved job stress and balanced work and family needs. But the ethical issues created by the new technologies are challenging. The ethical issues of new technologies are shown in Table 7.7.

STATUS OF TECHNOLOGY IN INDIA

India, like any other third world country, attained political independence after prolonged colonial rule and exploitation. The country entered the modern world in a state of economic backwardness and poverty of a large section of its people. It is obvious that technology must attend to the basic problems of food, clothing, health and housing of people. At the same time, rapid industrial development through latest technology is necessary to catch up with the advanced countries.

With these objectives in mind, Government of India set-up Research and Development establishments, space research centres, medical research centres, agricultural research establishments, oil exploration centres, power development projects and the Council of Scientific and Industrial Research. Besides, several universities and institutes have been set up to provide higher education in science, technology and management. As of today, there are 4700 intermediate/junior colleges, 144 universities, and 44 deemed universities in the country. Also there are more than 500 science and technological institutions, and 1220 in-house research and development laboratories. There is also the Department of Science and Technology, an administrative wing of the government, to coordinate the activities of all research and technical activities in the country. (Also read the last section in this chapter).

With all these, our country ranks eighth among Asian Countries in the technology front (Read Box 7.5 and Table 7.7)

Box 7.5 **The Asian Technology Leaders**

Rank	*National orientation**	*Socio-economic infrastructure*	*Technological infrastructure*	*Productive capacity***
1	Singapore	Taiwan	Japan	Japan
2	Japan	Singapore	South Korea	Singapore
3	South Korea	Japan	Singapore	Malaysia
4	Malaysia and Taiwan	South Korea	China	South Korea
5	Hongkong	Hongkong	Taiwan	Taiwan
6	Indonesia	Malaysia	Malaysia	Hongkong
7	China	Indonesia	**India**	**India**
8	**India**	China	Indonesia	China and Indonesia

* Evidence that a nation is taking direct action to become competitive.

** Physical and human resources devoted to manufacturing products and the efficiency with which these are used.

Note:In socio-economic infrastructure, India's position is No.9

(**Source**: *Business World*, 16-31 March, 1997)

Table 7.7 **Status of Countries (1993-2003)**

	India	*China*	*Russia*	*Israel*	*Singapore*	*Taiwan*	*S.Korea*
US Patents obtained	30 354	60 366	62 268	306 1188	39 438	62 5300	764 3952
R&D Spending (% of GDP)	1	1.2	1.2	4.7	2.2	2.3	2.9
Science and Engineering Graduates ('000)	316	337	216	14	5.6	49	97

In 2003, US inventors secured 88,000 US Patents.

The US Spent 2.7% of GDP on R&D

(***Source:*** *The Economic Times*, October 10, 2004)

The Government also came out with a policy on scinece and technology spelling out its aims and the thrust areas. The salient features of the 2003 policy are mentioned below:

SCIENCE AND TECHNOLOGY POLICY 2003

Objectives of the Policy

- To ensure that the message of science (and technology) reaches every citizen of India.
- To ensure food, agriculture, nutritional, environmental, water, health and energy security of the people on a sustainable basis.
- To mount a direct and sustained effort on the alleviation of poverty, enhancing livelihood security, removal of hunger and malnutrition, reduction of drudgery and regional imbalances, and generation of employment.
- To vigorously foster scientific research in universities and other institutions.
- To promote the empowerment of women in all science and technology activities and ensure their full and equal participation.
- To provide necessary autonomy and freedom of functioning for all academic and R&D institutions.
- To use the full potential of modern science and technology to protect, preserve, evaluate, update, add value to, and utilise the extensive knowledge over the long civilisational experience of India.
- To accomplish national strategic and security-related objectives, by using the latest advances in science and technology.
- To encourage research and innovation in areas of relevance for the economy and society, particularly by promoting close and productive interaction between private and public institutions in science and technology.
- To substantially strengthen enabling mechanisms that relate to technology development, evaluation, absorption and upgradation from concept to utilisation.
- To establish an Intellectual Property Rights (IPR) regime which maximises the incentives for the generation and protection of intellectual property by all types of inventors.
- To ensure that all efforts are made to have high-=speed access to information at affordable costs.
- To encourage research and application for forecasting, prevention and mitigation of natural hazards, particularly, floods, cyclones, earthquakes, drought and landslides.
- To promote international science and technology cooperation towards achieving the goals of national development and security, and make it a key element of India's international relations.
- To integrate scientific knowledge with insights from other disciplines.

Strategies to Realise Objectives

In order to realise the above objectives, the policy spelt out several strategies. The strategies include:

1. To ensure science and technology governance and investments.
2. Optimal utilisation of existing infrastructure and competence.

3. Strengthening of the infrastructure for science and technology in academic institutions.
4. New funding mechanisms for basic research.
5. Human resource development.
6. Technology development, transfer and diffusion.
7. Promotion of innovation.
8. Interaction between industry and scientific laboratories.
9. Utilisation of indigenous resources and traditional knowledge.
10. Development of technologies for mitigation and management of natural hazards.
11. Generation and management of intellectual property.
12. Creation of awareness among public about science and technology.
13. Achieving international science and technology cooperation.
14. Build a new and resurgent India that continues to maintain its strong democratic institutions and traditions.

Institutional and Other Facilities to Promote Science and Technology

Government has established series of research establishments and granted recognition to in-house R&D centres run by private industries and educational institutions. The Government has been offering many monetary and fiscal sops for the purpose. The facilities available are as follows:

Institutional Arrangement

1. Apex Level Organisations

Department of Scientific and Industrial Research (DSIR)
National Research Development Corporation (NRDC)
Council of Scientific and Industrial Research (CSIR)
Department of Science and Technology (DST)
Department of Biotechnology (DBT)
Department of Space (DOS)
Department of Atomic Energy (DAE)
Department of Electronics (DOE)
Department of Defence R&D
Ministry of Non-Conventional Energy Sources
Ministry of Industry
Department of Mines
Department of Ocean Development
Venture Capital Companies for Technology Development

2. Research and Development by Industry

In-house R&D units recognised by the government. There are 1220 R&D units and the break-up is as follows:

Chemical and allied industries	425
Electrical and electronics industries	325
Mechanical engineering	240
Processing industries	180
Agro industries	50
Total	1220

Major Industry Associations such as FICCI, ASSOCHAM, CII, Indian Chemical Manufacturers Association and the like have also been active in promoting research.

3. Incentives

Income Tax relief on R&D expenditure
Weighted tax deduction for sponsored research
Accelerated depreciation allowance
Five year tax holiday to commercial R&D companies
Customs duty exemption on goods imported for R&D projects
Excise duty waiver on patented products
Excise duty waiver on non-commercial research institutions
Price control exemption on domestic R&D based bulk drugs

4. New Technological Initiatives

Technology parks
Joint R&D companies
Joint Industry-National Laboratory Programme
Joint Test/Evaluation Centres
Technology-Business Incubation Centres
Co-operative Research Associations for SSIs
Commercial R&D companies.

ANALYSIS OF THE TECHNOLOGICAL ENVIRONMENT

Scanning

Scanning of technological environment is a difficult task. Difficult because of three reasons.[16] First, technological developments take place simultaneously and at different lead times making it difficult to identify the developments, even to those who are engaged in them. Second, the data sources relating to technological developments are not in the public arena. They are shrouded in secrecy and deemed confidential. This is true even in governmental agencies where convenient excuse for not divulging data is national security. Third, even when data are available, people who are supposed to give information are experts. They tend to use technical terms which make communication more difficult than in other environmental segments.

Problems of data collection point out to the need for scanning to have investigative element. Data sources must be identified and primary sources need to be spoken to. Considerable time and resources may need to be devoted to this effort. Scanning cannot be devoted to only secondary sources unlike other environmental segments. In the technological arena, primary sources are critical because the appearance of technological developments as news often takes place at the innovation and diffusion stages, at which time a firm would have lost considerable lead time for strategic action.[17]

Data relating to technological arena are available both at the global and national levels. At the global level, macro level data (nation by nation) pertaining to R&D expenditures, level of scientific development, and level of scientific and educational efforts are available in advanced economies. Such data provide indicators of potential pockets of technological developments.

At the national level, many governmental agencies provide considerable data pertaining to their domain. Many non-governmental institutions too play major roles in shaping technological developments.

Monitoring

Scanning helps obtain data pertaining to technological developments. But unforeseen changes take place along the developments rendering scanning a tight-rope-walk. Monitoring assumes added significance as a result. Monitoring helps in two ways: tracking and describing technological changes more clearly and identifying areas requiring further scanning.

Forecasting

As stated earlier, forecasting gives future orientation to technological changes. These orientations become inputs for strategising. Before forecasting, the following questions deserve clean answers from forecasters:

What is the relevant technology?

In what stage is the technology's evolution?

What are the time spans over which the technology will unfold?

What forces are likely to impede or facilitate the technology's evolution?

What resources are available to those supporting or impeding the technological change?

How is the new technology superior to the old?

What forces will impact the adaption of the technological change?

Who bears the costs and benefits of the technological change?

Assessment

The final phase in the analysis of technological arena is the assessment. Scanning, monitoring and forecasting should result in sufficient inputs that become part of strategies. Assessment helps derive strategy relevant implications from technological environment.

Technological change has impact at two levels: (i) implications for other environmental segments; (ii) implications for firm's strategy formulation.

Technology lies at the heart of many environmental changes. These changes manifest in the form of new products, processes and materials. Economic and sociocultural patterns and structures are often derivatives of technological developments. Assessment should focus on these derivatives.

Technology impacts the competitive strength of a firm. As explained in Chapter 2, competitive strength of a company depends on five forces: competitive rivalry, threat of substitutes, threat from new entrants, suppliers' bargaining power, and bargaining power of buyers. Technology can have significant impact on these forces and this should influence how the firm crafts its strategies.

QUESTIONS

1. What is technology? What are its features?
2. Bring out the distinction between science and technology.
3. Explain the impact of technology on society.

4. Bring out the economic implications of technology.
5. Descuss the plant level impact of technology.
6. Bring out the forces that impact the growth of technology.
7. Bring out the salient features of our technology policy.

ASSIGNMENT

1. Identify five products that have faded out in the last ten years and five other products that have entered the market for the first time. Describe the impact of exit of the first five and entry of the other five on firms, and on society.

REFERENCES

1. Hendrik Van Den Berg, *Economic Growth and Development,* McGraw-Hill, 2001, p.191.
2. William C.Frederick, et al, *Business and Society*, New York, Mc Graw-Hill, 1992, p.434.
3. *Ibid*, p.435.
4. Eugene V.Schneider, *Industrial Sociology,* 4th Edition, New Delhi, p.548.
5. T.S.Mann, *Transfer of Technology*, Bombay, Himalaya Publishing House, p.255.
6. William C.Frederick, et al, op.cit,p.437.
7. Wheeler and Hunger, *Strategic Management and Business Policy* (5th edition), New York, Addison-Wesley, 1995, p.342.
8. *Ibid*, p.350.
9. William C.Frederick, et al, op.cit, p.443.
10. Hicks and Gullett, *The Management of Organisations*, p.565.
11. Fahey and Narayanan, *Macro Environmental Analysis For Strategic Management*, p.137.
12. Gareth R. Jones, *Organisational Theory,* Pearson, 2003, p.274.
13. Arun Kumar Jain, *Managing Global Competition*, p.154.
14. William C.Frederick, et al, op.cit, p.448.
15. *Ibid*, p.450.
16. Lian Fahey and V.K.Narayanan, *Macro Environmental Analysis for Strategic Management,* West Pub. Co., 1986, p.126.
17. *Ibid*.

CHAPTER OUTLINE

Three Political Institutions

— Legislature
— Executive
— Judiciary
— Judicial Activism

LEARNING OBJECTIVES

After reading this Chapter, you should be able to:

1. Understand that in our democratic set up, there are three political institutions.
2. Know that the role of Legislature on business is considerable
3. Appreciate that executive has responsibilities to business and business owes many obligations to government.
4. Understand that Judiciary is no more confined to its ivory towers and that its role in business is immense and is increasingly becoming activist.

8 Political Institutions

The influence of political environment on business is enormous. The political system prevailing in a country decides, promotes, fosters, encourages, shelters, directs and controls the business activities of that country. A political system which is stable, honest, efficient and dynamic and which ensures political participation of the people, and assures personal security to the citizens, is a primary factor for economic development.* The rich countries of today owed their success mainly to the political systems they richly enjoyed.

A stable, honest, efficient and dynamic political system is essential for economic growth.

'There is today', comments John Kenneth Galbraith, 'no country with a stable and honest Government that does not have or has not had a reasonably satisfactory state of economic progress.'[1] He further argues that 'In all these countries, the early emphasis was not on captital investment but on political and then on cultural development. In the United States, Western Europe, and more recently in Japan, a secure political context was stressed in both thought and action on economic development; it was considered the first requisite for economic progress.'[2]

Two basic political philosophies are in existence all over the world, *viz.*, democracy and totalitarianism. In its pure sense, democracy refers to a political arrangement in which supreme power is vested in the people. Democracy may manifest itself in any of the two fundamental manners. If each individual is given the right to rule and vote on every matter, the result is *pure democracy* which is not, however, workable in a complex society with a large constituency. Hence, the *republican* form of organisation follows whereby the public, in a democratic manner, elect their representatives who do the ruling.

---

* What is important is that the political system of the Government should be efficient and dynamic, besides being stable. Stability, though an important requirement, by itself will not guarantee economic prosperity as has happened to Tanzania. Nyerere ruled Tanzania for two decades and resigned in 1985 leaving a near-ruined country behind him. Similar is the story with Zaire under Mobutu and Zambia under Kenneth Kaunda.

Democracy comprises two types: pure and republican. Pure democracy requires every citizen to take part in governance. Republican democracy exists when leaders, elected by people, do the ruling.

In totalitarianism, also called authoritarianism, individual freedom is completely subordinated to the power of authority of the State and concentrated in the hands of one person or in a small group which is not constitutionally accountable to the people. Societies ruled by a pressure clique — political, economic or military — or by a dictator, plus most oligarchies and monarchies belong to this category.

During the First and Second World Wars, authoritarian governments began to appear in most mature economies. Even after the Second World War, the totalitarian system became most common in newly independent nations. Administrative effciency of the dictators was cited as an advantage for coping with the problems of new-born States. Surprisingly, nearly two-thirds of the nations are ruled by dictators or monarchies even today(see Box 8.1).

Box 8.1 **Face of the Third World**

The Third World is immensely varied. In 1983, the World Bank listed 73 countries with per capita annual incomes below $ 1700. Their combined population was just about 3000 million. They included colossal nations like China and India, as well as tiny nations. Infact, 45 poor nations had populations of less than 10 million. In religion, they ranged across all the major ones — Hinduism, Islam, Christianity and Buddhism. A few were ideologically right wing, a few left wing, but majority had mixed economies, with both public and private sectors. Most were authoritarian regimes but there were also a few geniune democracies. (See Pradip N. Khandwalla's Organisational Design for Excellence, p.27).

Three forms of totalitarianism are in place: theocratic, secular and tribal.

Totalitarianism, in itself, is of three types: theocratic, secular and tribal. When a country's religious leaders also act as its political leaders, its political system is called a **theocracy**. Religious leaders frame and enforce laws and regulations that are based on religious beliefs. A political system that is under the control of religious leaders is **theoretic totalitarianism**. Afghanistan, some Sheikdoms of the Middle East and Iran are the countries which have such political dispensation.

A political system in which political leaders are guided by military and buerocretic power is called secular **secular totalitarianism**. In this, the military controls the government and makes decisions which it deems to be in the best interest of the country. An example is Pakistan. Until the early 1980s, secular totalitarianisms were common throughout Latin America. They were also found in several Asian countries, particularly South Korea, Taiwan, Singapore, Indonesia and the Philippines. Since the early 1980s, however, this form of government has been losing its ground. The majority of Latin American countries are now genuine democracies, while significant political freedoms have been granted to the political opposition in countries such as South Korea, Taiwan, and the Philippines.

A third form of totalitarianism is the **tribal totalitarianism**. This exists principally in African countries such as Zimbabwe, Tanzania, Uganda, and Kenya. Tribal totalitarianism occurs when a political party that represents the interests of a particular tribe monopolises power.

As between democracy and totalitarianism, which political doctrine is ideal for business is a relevent question. The choice is apparently difficult because there are countries that represent the two political philosophies and both have achieved tremendous economic prosperity. America is a super power and it has achieved its position under democratic dispensation.

Similarly, former USSR attained its once super-power status but under communism. Economic development demands a political system which guarantees stability, dynamism, purposefulness, security to citizens and the involvement of people in developmental activities. Authoritarianism, no doubt, ensures stability but may fail in other respects. Democracy, in contrast, guarantees peoples' participation. The right leader being elected, democracy also can ensure stability, security, dynamism and purposefulness.

Between democracy and totalitarianism, democracy is preferable for economic growth.

It may be stated that democracy does not guarantee high rates of economic growth. Nor totalitarianism drives a country to slow economic growth. Rate of growth-the increase in the amount of goods and services produced by a nation-is influenced by many variables other than political and civil liberties. These include a country's tax system, policy towards foreign and domestic investment, political stability, judiciary, and the like.

THREE INSTITUTIONS

The political system under democratic dispensation, like ours, comprises three vital institutions, *viz.*, legislature, executive or government and judiciary.

Legislature

Democracy has three institutions: Legislature, Executive and Judiciary. Of the three, first is the most powerful one. But a typical business person interacts more with executive.

Of the three, the Legislature is the most powerful political institution vested with such powers as policy making, law-making, budget approving, executive control and acting as a mirror of public opinion.

The influence of the Legislature on business is considerable. It decides such vital aspects as the type of business activities the country should have, who should own them, what should be their size of operations, what should happen to their earnings and other related factors.

Executive or Government

Also called the 'State', the term Government refers to '... *the centre of political authority having the power to govern those it serves*.'[3] More or less a similar meaning is given by E.V.Schneider when he described government as '*that institution by which men everywhere seek to order society, that is, to control the structure and functioning of society*.'[4]

The founders of our Constitution provided for a federal set-up, with powers being divided between the national and the state governments. The powers and functions of the central and state governments are described in the Constitution. The emphasis throughout this section is on the role of national or central government in shaping, directing and controlling the business activities.

What are government's responsibilities to business? What are responsibilities of business houses to the government? Following paragraphs answer these questions.

Business Responsibilities to Government

Business firms have a number of responsibilities to the government (see Fig.8.1). Business firms must obey the laws of central, state and local governments. Such laws and regulations may pervade the entire gamut of a business enterprise. Business must go beyond obeying laws and regulations. It should look to the government for support, sustenance, encouragement and guidance. Business leaders must look

Figure 8.1 **Responsibilities of Business to Government and of Government to Business**

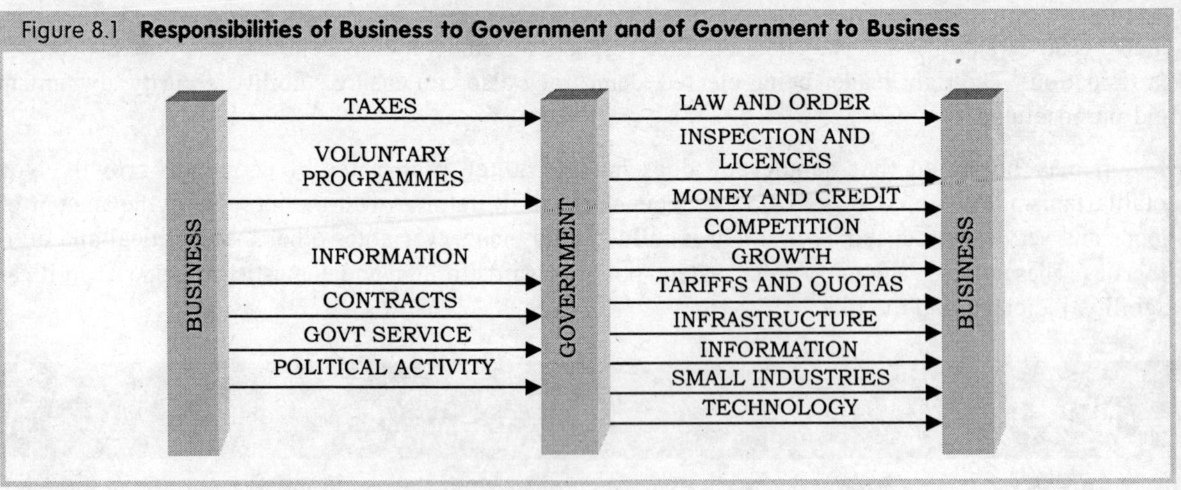

upon government as a big brother who is wiser, more matured, more mellowed and less impetous element in business. Business must also play a vital role in helping the government to develop its functioning capabilities. A few important responsibilities of business towards the government are explained below:

> Captains of business houses need to go beyond mundane things. They need to take government as a big brother who is wiser, more matured, more mellowed and less impetous element in business.

(a) *Tax Payment*: Taxes paid by business enterprises constitute a major source of revenue to the government. Firms themselves pay regular taxes on their sales, inputs and income and also deduct, at source, income taxes from salaries and wages of employees and remit the collections to the government.

(b) *Voluntary Programmes*: Business firms cooperate with government agencies on a voluntary basis in connection with various programmes such as withholding stated amounts from wages and salaries of employees for the purchase of National Savings Certificates, or giving special assistance to local governmental units in connection with drought relief, education, tree planting, sanitary works or recreational activities. In cooperation with the government, business firms train the unemployed and support non-descriminative recruitment of personnel and workmen. Business extends these facilities under the name of social responsibility.

(c) *Providing Information*: Political leaders, either because of inexperience or over enthusiasm, make certain decisions which may not be in the overall interest of business. The onus then lies with business leaders to place before the decision-makers the facts and problems, individually or through forums, and argue for the modification or change of decisions. Business leaders possess the necessary knowledge and experience to place their points of view before the political leaders.

(d) *Government Contracts*: Many business firms bid for government contracts and, if successful, carry out the resulting projects with the required specifications and standards. Housing projects, oil pipelines, turnkey projects and others are executed by private business houses for the government.

(e) *Government Service*: Business offers services of its leaders to the government. It is not unusual for business executives to lead or accompany delegations to foreign countries for exploring trade and industry prospects. Similarly, business leaders serve on various advisoy boards constituted by the government.

(f) *Political Activity*: Political participation is a much debated subject today. There are arguments for and against participation of business in political activities. Justifying business-politics nexus G.D.Birla once said, "*As the Bhagavad Gita says, every man must do his duty — which means if you are a wealthy man, you must do your duty by your wealth, and his dharma is to provide for general welfare. If political action is involved in this, I don't see why I should fight shy of if*". Edwin M.Epstein also support corporate involvement in politics. Involvement enhances the quality of pluralism and provides an additional safeguard against the authoritarian potential of a mass society.[5]

Business involvement in political activities generates varied arguments. Strong opinions are being expressed in favour and against involvement in politics. Arguments notwithstanding, captains of businesses do involve in political activities either by funding parties or by contesting elections.

Opposition to business involvement in politics is equally strong. J.R.D.Tata once wrote: "*I have never regretted my decisions to stay out of politics which I rationalised to myself by concluding that I could do more for my country in business and industry than in politics for which all my instincts in any case made me unfit*". More powerful argument came from Arnold Maremont. Stated he: "*It is my conviction that business ought, for its own good, to stay out of politics. I favour the widest possible participation in politics on an individual basis, for when it becomes the province of the elite few, our systems are in danger. It is when corporations begin running political classes, conducting political schools, and urging that their executives enter the political arena to expound the corporation's viewpoint that I become deeply fearful of the consequences*".[6]

Different viewpoints apart, business has been involved in political activities since long. Contrary to protestations of J.R.D.Tata, the Tatas did support political activities. They financed a number of organisations in Mumbai that are critical of what they call the Soviet model of development. They were also closely connected with the establishment of Swatantra Party in the 1960s. Birlas do much more. They run newspapers, finance political candidates and parties and even contest elections on their own. Infact, they have always played an active role in politics, and did so even before Independence, when it was much more hazardous to do so. Instances of this type are many. Nexus between business and politics is therefore, an established fact.

What are the ways of involvement is the next logical question. One way is to make monetary contributions to political parties, particularly at the time of elections. Corporate contributions to political parties have now been legalised in our country, merits and demerits notwithstanding. The other way of participation is for business leaders to contest elections as independents or on party labels. The third way of involvement is through lobbying which refers to behaviour after the elections and is concerned with securing legislation in the favour of business.

Government Responsibilities to Business

Responsibilities of government towards business are too clear. No business can function and survive without government's help.

Government responsibilities to business (see Fig 8.1) are much greater than the obligations of business to the government. Government has the power, will and resources to decide, shape, guide and control business activities. Being democratically elected and having accepted the mixed economy, our government is clear about the role it has to play and the responsibilities it has to discharge towards business houses. As promoter and regulator of business activities, the government has been discharging its obligations quite effectively, failures notwithstanding. Specifically, the government's responsibilities towards business are as follows:

Establishment and Enforcement of Laws: Government establishes and enforces laws and regulations under which the business fuctions. Laws and regulations covering all aspects of business are enacted by the government. Government is responsible for providing the 'rules of the game', which make the business systems function smoothly and which help maintian competition, or if monopolies develop, to regulate them or supplement them by government operations. It is the responsibility of government to enforce the laws and to provide a system of courts for adjudicating differences between business firms, individuals, or government agencies.

Maintenance of Order: Government has the responsibility of maintaining order and protecting persons and property. It would be impossible to carry on business in the absence of a peaceful atmosphere.

This is borne out by the decline in the number of industrial licences issued to Punjab during 1986. The total number of licences issued during 1986 was 618. Of these, Punjab accounted for only 37 as against 94 the state has bagged in 1984. "This is perhaps", remarks *Economics Times* of march 14,1987, "due to the disturbed conditions prevalent in the state". Read Box 8.2 for more details on the sordid state of lawlessness.

Box 8.2 **Saga of Mayhem, Killings and Extortions**

The state government's (Assam) ineffectiveness and the tea planters' money had created a Frankenstein's monster. No one really knew how to destroy it. ULFA hiked its demand on the tea majors to include a cess of Re.1 per Kg. As the kidnapping and killings increased, government was dismissed and President's rule imposed. That night (Nov 28, 1990), the army launched Operation Bajrang in the Brahmaputra Valley. Operation Rhino followed some months later, after state elections. In all, 3,500 ULFA members surrendered.

Four months later, ULFA demonstrated its muscle by kidnapping 13 senior government officials and a Soviet mining engineer. Two weeks later, the government was forced to release 400 ULFA detainees. Overjoyed by its success, ULFA went on a mad spree. During 1992-94, it gunned down police officers, Congress and BJP politicians, and five of Chief Minister's relatives. It also killed an ONGC engineer, kidnapped the head of Prag Bosimi Synthetics, murdered a manager of the Paul-run Assam Frontier, and drove out a French team of scientists. The toll rose rapidly to 400 executives.

ULFA's victories became a role model to a motley collection of terrorist organisations such as the Bodo Security Force(BSF). Like the ULFA, the BSF tapped tea managers for funds. One of its bigger successes was an attack on Subhir Roy, a manager of the Khaitan-owned Dimakuchi garden. On March 18, 1992, they stopped his car and abducted Roy and his driver. Khaitan was asked to pay a 'land tax' at the rate of Rs.20,000 per hectare to obtain his manager's release. During the negotiations, on April 3, the BSF gunned down a manager of the Kanoi-owned Panbari garden. Roy was released after 20 days of captivity. Like others before him, Khaitan vehemently denied that any ransom had been paid.

Today, the gardens are guarded night and day by Khaitan's private army. 2000 armed forces, 40 per garden, patrol its perimeters constantly. No manager is allowed to go outside the garden without some protection. If he does and he is kidnapped, it's his funeral. The management is not responsible for his ransom.

(**Source**: Gita Piramal, *Business Maharajas*, New Delhi, Viking, 1996, Pp.292-293)

Money and Credit: The government provides a system of money and credit by means of which transactions can be affected. It is also the responsibility of the government to regulate money and credit and protect the integrity of the rupee, that is, to guard against rapid fall in its value.

Orderly Growth: Orderly growth implies balanced regional development, distributive justice, full employment and protecting the economy against '*booms and busts*'. The Goverment has the resources and capabilities to ensure orderly growth.

Infrastructure: Business needs for its effective functioning such infrastructural facilities as transportation, power, finance, trained personnel and civic amenities. It is the responsibility of the government to provide these facilities.

Information: Government agencies publish and provide a large volume of information which is used extensively by business firms. Included are information services of the departments of commerce and industry, agriculture, labour, health, eduction, banking, atomic energy and host of others. These services carry on important activities in providing business firms and private citizens with objective and impartial information about economic and business activity in general, specific lines of business, scientific and technological developments and many other things of interest to business leaders.

Many state and local governments also provide information highly useful for business leaders in conducting their activities.

Assistance to Small industries: Small-size business establishments have special role to play in our economy. Being small in size, these firms face problems relating to finance, marketing, know-how and do-how and infrastructural facilities. It is again the responsibility of the government to provide the required facilities and encourage the small-scale sectors to grow.

Transfer of Technology: Government-owned research establishments transfer their discoveries to the private industry in order to put them to commercial production. The Indian Space Research Organisation (ISRO), a Central Government undertaking, has successfully spun off more than 130 products/processes from its labs to the Indian industry in the last decade. Of these, 110 are in active production. More striking success in the technology transfers is in the area of instruments for processing remote sensing data.

Government Competition: Government often competes with private business firms for the purpose of regulating competition, improving quality, or to supplement private activities with government programmes. In some cases, the government regulates the prices which may be charged for buyers.

Inspections and Licences: Government agencies conduct inspection activities-foods and drugs, for example, assuring quality products to consumers. Government issues licences to competent business establishments to carry on different activities.

Tariffs and Quotas: Tariffs and quotas are used by the government to protect business from foreign competition. One of the problems faced by exporting countries all around, particularly Japan, is the protectionist policies adopted by developed countries. Similarly, incentives and subsidies are granted by the government to encourage the development of home industries.

Many developed countries use protectionist measures like quotas and tariffs to protect domestic industries.

For many, the above obligations of the government may look irrelevant because of reforms introduced by the government in the recent past. While it is true that the reforms have resulted in the diminished role of the government, the role *per se* has not been abolished. Thus, industrial licensing continues though the list of industries subject to licensing has been pruned. Similarly, tariffs and quotas do exist though on a lesser scale.

Judiciary

The third political institution is the Judiciary. Judiciary determines the manner in which the work of the Executive has been fulfilled. It sees to it that the exercise of executive authority conforms to the general rules laid down by the legislature, it may declare that the particular order issued is, in fact, *ultra vires*. It also settles the relationship between private citizens, on the one hand, and between citizens and the government upon the other, where these give rise to problems which do not admit of solution by the government.[7]

The role of judiciary is to ensure that the executive authority conforms to the general rules laid down by the legislature.

Systems of Laws

There are four basic legal systems prevailing around the world: (1) Islamic law, derived from the interpretation of the Quran and found in countries where Muslims are in majority, (2) common law, derived from English law and found in countries which were under British influence, (3) Civil or code

Four systemsw law govern business everywhere. They are (i) Islamic law, (ii) Common law, (iii) Civil or Coded law, and (iv) Marxist law.

law, derived from Roman law found in Germany, Japan, France and non-Marxist and non-Islamic countries, and (4) Marxist legal system which has takers in communist countries.

The laws among these four systems and within each system vary considerably. Eventhough a country's laws may be based on the doctrine of one of the four legal systems, its individual interpretation may vary significantly-from a fundamentalist interpretation of Islamic law as found in Saudi Arabia to a combination of several legal systems found in the US, where both common law and civil law are reflected in the laws.

Islamic Law: Islamic law is derived from the interpretation of the Quran and the teachings of the Prophet Mohammed. The word "Islam" translates into English as 'submission' or 'surrender'. Muslims submit to the will of God, who decrees what is proper and what is improper. God's commandments, as revealed to Mohammed, provide a path, or **shari'a**, for true believers to follow. The **shari'a** is not a coded law. It provides ethical and moral precepts as well as the rules of public order.[(8)] Countries from Philippines to the former Soviet Union have substantial Muslims who follow Islamic cultural and legal traditions, and Islamic traditions dominate the legal and social environment of most Arab nations.

The idea of law in Islamic societies is quite different from that in most Western cultures. Where most Western nations perceive law as an expression of the will of the people acting through their legislatures, Islamic law is the product of divine revelation. It cannot be changed as the believers believe in the will of the God. The immutability of the law requires Islamic nations to look to other sources of law to resolve disputes and govern.

Receiving and paying interest is a taboo in Islamic law. Similarly, investments in alcohol, gambling and casinos are prohibited.

Among the unique aspects of Islamic law is the prohibition of paying or receiving interest. The Islamic law of contracts states that any given transaction should be devoid of **riba**, which is understood as unlawful gain by way of interest or usury. Prohibiting receipt and payment of interest is the nucleus of the Islamic system. Prohibition against interest affects banking and business practices severely. However, risk sharing, property rights, individual rights and duties and sanctity of contracts are advocated. Investments in alcohol, gambling and casinos are prohibited.

Islamic legal system places emphasis on the ethical, moral, social and religious values to enhance quality and fairness.

The business manager should have knowledge about the religion's tenets and understand the way the law may be interpreted in each region. Regional courts can interpret Islamic law from the viewpoint of fundamentalists or they may use a more liberal translation. The business manager should also know that the Islamic legal system places emphasis on the ethical, moral, social and religious dimensions to enhance equality and fairness for the good of society.

Socialist Law: This law comes from the Marxist socialist system and continues to influence regulations in former communist countries, particularly those from the former Soviet Union, as well as present day China, Vietnam, North Korea and Cuba.

Extensive codes are the main feature of socialist law. But ideology plays prominent role. Communist ideolism permeates socialist law.

Extensive codes are the primary sources of socialist law. From this perspective socialist law can be classified as civil law and the ideology thrust on the codes makes socialist law different from others. The legislature is the primary branch of government, and judiciary is next to the legislature. This structure owes its origin to the founding fathers of the socialist legal system who were trained as civil lawyers, and pre-revolutionary Russia was essentially a civil law country.

Ideology plays crucial role in Socialist law. Unlike a civil law code, which can be used by governments of widely differing political viewpoints, socialist legal codes are designed to achieve personal and societal transformation. The legal system is not just a set of institutions, but means to achieve a communist society, where each gives according to his or her abilities and takes according to his or her needs.

Communist ideology permeates socialist law. The legal environment provides for state ownership of the means of production and distribution, including most businesses. It also calls for state ownership of land, and in most cases collective use of land. There is little tolerance of private property rights. The codes support the centralised planning, allowing the Central Government to set national, and uniform standards for business practices.

At the centre of the socialist legal tradition is the Communist party. The party is the keeper of the ideology of the state, and through its powers to nominate officers, staff the bureaucracy, and monitor work places, it determines the norms that become law.

Russia and China are the two countries which come to one's mind while discussing socialist law. Each country has taken a different direction in its political economic growth. Russia is moving towards a democratic system, whereas China is attempting to activate private sector within a multicomponent or mixed economy in a socialist legal framework. Both the countries are busy with passing laws to suit charged political environments. China has implemented over 150 laws but most laws are vague. Russia's experience has been identical. Vaguely worded laws have been passed without mechanisms for implementation. These countries are struggling with universal issues such as states' rights, freedom, rights of property owners, taxation, and price control.

Common Law: Common law comes from English law and it is the foundation of the legal system in the US, Canada, England, Australia, New Zealand, India and other countries. Common law is based on the cumulative wisdom of judges' decisions on individual cases. In common law countries, vast areas of law, such as contracts, torts, and agency, are controlled by collections of principles deduced from specific disputes resolved in an adversary process.

> India follows common law. Common law is based on the cumulative wisdom of judges' decisions on individual cases. Tradition plays a major role in common law countries.

A key concept in the common law is that similar disputes should achieve similar legal results. Thus, parties to a dispute will look for similar, earlier cases with favourable decisions. These earlier cases have precedental value to a current dispute. If an earlier case is from a higher court in the same jurisdiction, a subsequent judge is expected to follow the earlier decision.

The practice of relying on past precedences provides stability required for business people to plan their future actions. But there is also the flip side. Laws affecting business practices vary somewhat in countries which follow common law, creating potential problems for the not so well informed international business manager. For example, manufacturers of defective products are more vulnerable to law suits in the US than in New Zealand as a result of evolutionary differences in the law of negligence in the two countries.

Legislation and its accompanying regulations are another major source of law in common law countries. Cases provide rules for individual, specific circumstances, whereas legislations offer blanket rules.

Finally, tradition is a major source of law in common law countries. The customary practices of an industry or of government institutions influence the way a judge will look at a particular case.

Civil Law: The civil law system, also called a codified legal system, is based on a detailed set of laws that make up a code. Rules for conducting business are a part of the code. Over 70 countries, including Germany, France and Japan follow civil law. The civil law system originated with the Romans in the ancient times, who spread it throughout the Western world.

The rules of judges and lawyers make civil law different from common law. In a common law system, the judge serves as a neutral referee, defining points of law and ruling on various motions put up by the opposing party's lawyers. These lawyers are responsible for developing their client's cases and choosing which evidence to submit on their client's behalf. In a civil law system, the judge takes on many of the tasks of the lawyers, as for example, determining the scope of evidence to be collected and presented to the court.

> Civil law system is based on a detailed set of laws that make up a code. Civil law is also called codified legal system.

The distinction between common law and code-law system becomes more pronounced in protecting intellectual property. Under common law, ownership is established by use; under code-law, ownership is determined by registration. In some countries where civil law prevails, certain agreements may not be enforceable unless properly notarised or registered; in a common law country, the same agreement may be binding so long as proof of the agreement can be established.

Judicial Powers

The judiciary in a country is influenced by its political system. The government of a country defines the legal framework within which firms do business-and often the laws that regulate business reflect the rulers' political ideology. Totalitarian states, for example, tend to enact laws that severely restrict private enterprise, while democratically elected governments pass laws that are pro-private enterprises and pro-consumer.

The legal system in a country does not change overnight. Laws change over a long period of time and may lag behind important cultural changes which are taking place in a country. In many cases, it is not culture change which invites changes in the law, but ambiguities in the law themselves which are challenged in the courts.

The powers of the judiciary are of the dual type:

(i) The authority of the courts to settle legal disputes; and

(ii) Judicial review-the authority of the courts to rule on the constitutionality of legislation.

As far as the second is concerned, the Judiciary gets activated when the legislature passes laws which are repugnant to the Constitution and when the executive implements the enactment approved by the legislature in a manner opposed to the requirements of the legislation. In other words, the courts of justice protect the citizens from unlawful acts passed by the legislature and arbitrary acts done by the Executive.

The power of the judiciary to settle legal disputes affects business considerably.

It is the power of the judiciary to settle legal disputes that affects business considerably. Disputes between employer and employer; employer and employees, employee and employee, employer and public and employer and the government are often referred to courts for settlement and their verdicts are sought.

The judicial pronouncements will have far-reaching consequences on business. The consequences will become more intense and severe because (i) judicial errors do occur, though infrequent; (ii) possibility of wrong assessment of penalty. Judges notoriously vary in the severity of punishment inflicted,[9] (see Box 8.3), (iii) judges are known for pronouncing conflicting verdicts on the same or similar disputes and (iv) there is a lot of confusion in labour laws themselves (Read Box 8.4).

Box 8.3 **All Pay and No Work at Mysore Tobacco**

All play and no work, for the last six years, seems to be the immense good fortune of the retrenched employees of the Mysore Tobacco Company Limited, a Karnataka state government public sector undertaking with an accumulated loss of Rs.6.32 crore at the end of March 1992. Mysore Tobacco Company Limited was established, nearly six decades ago, in 1937 with the objective of purchasing raw tobacco from farmers, processing, grading, redrying and packing it.

According to highly-placed sources, Mysore Tobacco Company Limited had been ordered into liquidation in 1983. The company had about 157 employees at that time. After a decision to liquidate the company was taken due to mounting losses, about 62 employees were absorbed in the various departments of the Karnataka government.

Subsequently, about 42 employees took voluntary retirement in 1986. However, what threw the spanner in the works was the fact that some of the employees went to the Labour Court in 1983. The Labour Court ordered the reinstatement of the employees with back wages. Subsequently, the state government appealed against this order to the Karnataka High Court in 1987.

In its order, according to the sources, the Court allowed the petition and ordered the Mysore Tobacco Company to pay these employees the last-drawn wages till the disposal of the case. The employees are being paid every month by cheque after the 20th of the next month. About 53 employees were retrenched in 1983 and of them about 36 continue to draw their salaries today. These employees are in the field staff category. In 1991-92, the company incurred an expenditure of Rs.4.61 lakh as salaries to the retrenched employees as per the High Court Order. In 1990-91, the figure was slightly higher at Rs.4.97 lakh. The figure for 1992-93 is expected to be the same as for 1991-92.

The current piquant situation at the company has been attributed by the sources to the fact that the case has been held up at the High Court for the last few years. "The state government is helpless and only the Court has to resolve it", the sources said. The decline in the fortunes of the company has been attributed to the problems on the export front and the setting up of the Tobacco Board, which became the sole agency for procurement of tobacco.

Box 8.4 **The Confusion in Labour Laws**

"......the sheer diversity of rules in the states. Consider the following. The states are allowed to set up labour courts. Some states have raised the upper age limit for labour court members from 65 to 67, and decreased the length of the prior judicial experience required for such appointments from five years to three or two years. Or consider the notice period that employers are required to provide state governments if they want to alter working conditions. The Industrial Disputes Act requires 21 days advance notice, but Andhra Pradesh and West Bengal have doubled the length of the notice period that employees are required to provide to 42 days.

Varying Wages*

State	*Minimum*	*Maximum*
Andhra	11.00	41.35
Assam	32.80	38.20
Bihar	23.00	39.70
Gujarat	15.00	48.00
Haryana	51.57	52.00
Maharastra	8.00	70.46

Lending a further dimension to this picture of confusion is the industrial relations position in the states. In West Bengal, trade unions affiliated to political parties are widespread. Maharastra has several independent enterprise-level unions. In Bangalore, several firms that operate in the new high-technology industries have no unions at all. And Gujurat has seen the rise of the so-called footpath unionism: briefless lawyers mobilise seven employees in an organisation, register a union, pursue their individual grievances in court, and pocket a sizeable share of any compensation that workers obtain.

What is more, minimum wages vary widely across different states. The Minimum Wages Act of 1948 was enacted by the Centre, but the states are responsible for setting up tripartite minimum wage advisory bodies- and they unilaterally declare minimum wage increases in the pursuit of populism. The outcome is predictable. In Maharastra alone, minimum wages for unskilled workers vary from Rs.8 to Rs.70 (See table)."

(**Source:***Business World*, April 1-15, 1997)

Particularly in the area of industrial relations, the role of judiciary has been more pronounced and unfortunately regressive. During the last decade and a half, in the name of 'Directive Principles', 'Social Justice', and 'activist law making', the Supreme Court, instead of having a balanced and reserved consideration of opposing interests, has entirely vitiated the industrial relations fabric by making wholesale dogmatic assertions in undermining discipline. To borrow a simile from G.K.Chesterton, while dealing with discipline cases, the Court lost not only the path but also the map and the compass. It has gone to the extent to say that even an 'illegal strike is justified.' By those whose horizons are limited, trifles are easily confused with technicalities. The result is that indiscipline in industry has spread like wildfire and sapped the national production and productivity. The classic case is the textile industry which has been wrecked by indiscipline. The conflagration is continuing to engulf various industries one by one.[10]

The role of judiciary in industrial relations has been regressive. Judiciary has gone to the extent of declaring an illegal strike as valid.

The problem is more compounded because the judiciary itself has landed in an unenviable pass. "Today, litigative justice has come to a grinding halt", wrote Justice V.R.Krishna Iyer, the judiciary has caricatured itself into a dinosaur and both the Bench and the Bar, alas, have become a law unto themselves, Indian humanity having come to discard the judiciary as barred by limitation of time except as a pantomime. If it is not to be regarded as a case of survival after death, a new clan is needed now. The cult of the robed process has short mileage! If all the judges and lawyers of India pull down the shutters of their law shops nationwide, injustice may not any more escalate. If at all, litigative waste of human and material resources may be obviated. What an obituary!

"Many superficial diagnosis, charlatan recipes and myopic prognosis have been offered which are as potent therapeutically as painkillers for terminal cancer. Esoteric jurists have interpreted the decadent judicial disorder in various ways. Our statesmanly task is to transform this imbroglio into an opportunity for overhaul which by performance, restores order and confidence not only in the lowly, the lost and the last. Business management must come to court! I am convinced that democracy will die soon if an independent, alert and quick-to-act judiciary-not a functioning anarchy-does not come alive as a sentinel on the ***qui vive***"![11]

Judicial Activism

Judicial activism is very much in the news in our country these days. This is so because the gentlemen wearing grey robes started moving out of their ivory towers and began interfering in areas which, it was thought, were not theirs.

Consider the following

Judiciary punishes officials and demoralises bureaucracy; pulls up and injects the Election Commission; monitors the quantum of rainfall and irrigation waters; checks and regulates admissions to professional colleges by issuing memoranda on capital deregulation; orders the closure of fume-emitting factories and measures up pollution levels; calls up data on deforestation; decrees CBI enquiry into scandals, crimes and custodial deaths; enquires into temple administrators; grants promotions as well as increments to officials; restrains and censures human rights violations and so forth. Common man understands this activist role as *judicial activism*.

Judiciary is no more passive. In the sense, the court is not waiting for some one to petition. Judiciary is acting suo moto.

In its real sense, judicial activism refers to the review power vested with the courts and its scope varies with the width of power conferred on courts. The scope is wider where the power of judicial review extends not only over executive action, as in the UK; but also other legislative action, as in the US and even over constitutional amendments as in India[12].

The term judicial activism was first used in the USA. It was in 1954 that the US Supreme Court, in the historic *Brown Vs Board of Education* case, declared that separate, segregated schools for blacks and whites were unconstitutional. The Court did something which Congress and the President feared to do because of the dangerous political fall-outs it would produce.

In our country, judicial activism is just 18 years old. It represents a sustained effort on the part of the highest judiciary to provide access to justice for the deprived sections of Indian humanity. With a legal architecture designed for a colonial administration and a jurisprudence structured around a free market economy, the Indian judiciary could not accomplish much in fulfilling the constitutional aspirations of the vast masses of underprivileged people during the first three decades of freedom. During the last 18 years, however, judicial activism has opened up a dimension of the judiciary process, and this new dimension is a direct emulation from the basic objectives and values underlying the Indian Constitution[13].

There are arguments for and against judicial activism. The proponents of judicial activism argue that it is an essential part of judicial process in a democracy like ours. Judicial activism is felt necessary to ensure distributive justice, to restore faith in the people towards social and political institutions and to check declining values in our society.

Judicial activism is opposed on several counts. It is said that judicial activism gives rise to much anxiety in the executive and the legislature, especially about the continuing prospect of our over-reaching judicial entry into the traditional areas of executive power. It is also said that judicial activism leads to a government by judiciary which is not supported by any popular mandate. Further, most of the judicial review cases cause enormous financial strain on the Exchequer.

The former Chief Justice of India, Dr. A. S. Anand, in his Millennium Law Lectures (October 1999) at the Kerala High Court Advocate's Association, while defending judicial activism emphasised the need for caustion to ensure that activism does not become "judicial adventurism." Otherwise, he warned, it might "lead to chaos and people would not know which organ of the state to look for to stop abuse or misuse of power." He reiterated the principle that "...the role of the judge is that of a referee. I can blow my judicial whistle when the ball goes out of play; but when the game restarts I must neither take part in it nor tell the players how to play." Dr. Anand added that the "judicial whistle needs to be blown for a purpose and with caution. It needs to be remembered that Court cannot run the Government. The Courts have the duty of implementing the constitutional safeguards that protect individual rights but they cannot push back the limits of the Constitution to accommodate the challenged violation."

Judicial activism should not result in judicial adventurism.

Inspite of the criticisms, it may be stated that the Indian judicial review today is an area of great promise. The world of law acclaims that some of the recent steps of the apex court certainly enhanced its status.

QUESTIONS

1. "Between democracy and totalitarianism, democracy is preferable for business growth." Discuss.
2. Discuss the impact of (a) Legislature, (b) Executive, and (c) Judiciary on business.
3. Describe the legal systems prevaling in the world.
4. What is Government? What are its responsibilities to business?
5. What is judicial activism? Is it necessary in our society.

ASSIGNMENT

Take two countries - one representing democratic system and another typifying authoritarian dispensation. Point out the roles played by both towards their respective businesses. Also point out what roles should they play.

REFERENCES

1. John Kenneth Galbriath, *Essays From the Poor to the Rich*, p.13.
2. *Ibid*, p.11.
3. V.A.Musselman and E.H.Hughes, *Introduction to Business: Issues and Environment*, p.533.
4. E.V.Schneider, *Industrial Psychology*, p.514.
5. Edwin M.Epstein, *Business and Society:Environment and Responsibility*, p.207.
6. Arnold Maremont, *Business and Society:Environment and Responsibility*, p.207.
7. Harold J.Laski, *A Grammar of Politics*, p.295.
8. Carolyn Hotchkirs, *International Law for Business*, Mcgraw-Hill, 1994, p.73.
9. *Ibid*, p.301.
10. S.C.Jain, *Productivity and Discipline-Victims of Misdirected Social Justice*, p.VII.
11. *The Week*, Dec.27, 1992.
12. P.N.Bhagavati, *Judicial Activision and Public Interest Litigation*, Dharwad, Jagrut Bharat, 1983, p.3.
13. *Ibid*, p.11.

CHAPTER OUTLINE

The Preamble

The Fundamental Rights

Directive Principles of State Policy

Time for Change

LEARNING OBJECTIVES

After reading this Chapter, you should be able to:

1. Understand the contents of Preamble and their impact on business.
2. List the Fundamental Rights and outline their economic implications.
3. Point out the Directive Principles of State Policy that have economic significance.
4. Analyse the reasons for and directions of changes desired in the Constitution.

9 The Constitution of India

The Constitution of India is the most significant document which is fundamental to the governance of the State. It has economic significance of far-reaching implications. This chapter is devoted to a brief discussion of the economic provisions of the Constitution.

The Constitution of the Indian Republic is the product not of political revolution but of the research and deliberations of a body of eminent representatives of the people who sought to improve upon the then existing system.

In order to understand and appreciate the philosophy underlying the Indian Constitution, one must look back into the resolution which was passed at the Karachi session of the Indian National Congress in 1931. The Resolution stated that "*in order to end the exploitation of the masses, political freedom must include the real economic freedom of the starving millions*." The State was to safeguard "*the interest of industrial workers*," ensuring that "*suitable legislation*" should secure them a living wage, healthy conditions, limited hours of labour, and protection from "*the economic consequences of old age, sickness and unemployment*." The State was to "*own or control key industries and services, mineral resources, railways, waterways, shipping and other means of public transport*."

The historic Objectives Resolution which was moved by Pandit Jawaharlal Nehru on 9 December 1946 and which was subsequently adopted by the Constituent Assembly on 22 January 1947, inspired the shaping of the Constitution through all its subsequent stages.

The Constitution has three parts, *viz*., the Preamble, the Fundamental Rights, and the Directive Principles of State Policy.

THE PREAMBLE

The Preamble is an introduction to the Constitution and contains its basic philosophy. The Preamble to the Indian Constitution states that

Preamble contains the philosophy for which the Constitution stands. Terms like sovereignity, secular, socialist and democracy have wider implications.

"We the people of India having solemnly resolved to constitute ourselves into a Sovereign, Socialist, Secular, Democratic Republic and to secure to all citizens:

"Justice, social, economic and political;

Liberty of thought, expression, belief, faith and worship;

Equality of status and opportunity; and to promote among them all fraternity assuring the dignity of the individual and the unity and integrity of the Nation.

In our Constituent Assembly this 26th day of November 1949 Do Hereby Adopt, Enact and give to Ourselves this Constitution."

The words- "We, the people of India...adopt, enact and give to ourselves this Constitution",-declare the ultimate sovereignty of the people of India and that the Constitution rests on their authority.

Thus, the goal envisaged by the Constitution is that of a "*Welfare State*" and the establishment of a socialistic pattern of society.

The Preamble recognises the truth of the proposition that political freedom is not an end by itself; it is a means to secure to all citizens social, economic and political justice. In other words, the Preamble commits India to the ideal of converting political democracy established by the Constitution into a social and economic democracy and that too in a democratic way, under the rule of law.

Certain key words in the Preamble need elaboration.

Sovereign

With the passing of the Indian Independence Act, 1947, India ceased to be a dependency of the British Empire. From 15th August, 1947, to 26th January, 1950, her political status was that of a Dominion in the British Commonwealth of Nations. But with the writing of the Constitution, India became a 'Sovereign Republic' like the United States of America or the Swiss Republic. However, India still remains a member of the Commonwealth of Nations. This peculiar position is the result of an agreement reached at the Commonwealth Prime Ministers' Conference held in London in April 1949.[1]

Socialist

The Word 'socialist' was added to the Preamble by the 42nd Amendment of the Constitution in 1976. Socialism implies State ownership and management of tools of production with the benefits to inure to the public. It also advocates agrarian reforms, a strong public sector, control over private investment and wealth and national self-reliance.

Socialism does not involve the equal division of existing wealth among the people but advocates an egalitarian principle. It believes in providing employment to all employable people and emphasizes suitable rewards to the efforts put in by every worker.

The word socialist in the preamble committed India to go by socialist ideology.

The Government of India has adopted socialism as the goal of its economic and social policy which the country shall pursue. This concept is used by the ruling party in different ways at different times. In the beginning, 'the socialist pattern of society' was emphasised. More recently, 'social justice with economic growth' is referred to. There are several political parties in the country which also proclaim socialism as their goal, though the meaning attached to the phrase by these parties is not clear. The word 'socialism', therefore, connotes different things to different parties and different individuals, and this is often reflected in the pronouncements of individual politicians as well as in the manifestoes of different political parties.[2]

The concept of 'socialism' is vague, as no one has defined it in concrete terms. Nationalisation of industries and other economic activities are adopted as the method to usher in socialism in our country. The result is that the urge to greater production has disappeared and the availability of goods is not enough to remove poverty. It has not been realised that the effort to make the few rich poor, will not make the many poor, rich. The question is whether nationalisation or '*takeover*' of existing units is not adopted in order to obtain more power and patronage to the politicians.[3]

Secular

The word 'secular' like the word 'socialism' was inserted in the Preamble by the 42nd Amendment to the Constitution in 1976. The real spirit of secularism is to make religion purely a private affair and to manage the affairs of the State free from any religious influence. In practice, secularism is understood to mean according equal encouragement to all religions. It is here that the national leaders seem to have erred on the wrong side, and it is because of this that the minorities in our country feel unsafe and insecure.

Secularism means confining religion to private life and manage the affairs of the state free from any religious orientation.

Democratic

The term 'democratic' is comprehensive. In a narrow political sense, it refers only to the form of government, a representative and responsible system under which those who administer the affairs of the State are chosen by the electorate and accountable to them. But, in its broadest sense, it embraces, in addition to political democracy, also social and economic democracy. The term 'democratic' is used in this sense in the Preamble.[4]

Republic

The term 'republic' implies an elected Head of State. A democratic state may have an elected or hereditary head. Britain is the best example of the latter type, where the monarch, the hereditary head, is not an hindrance to the democratic government as the real power of the State is in the hands of the elected representatives. Under the republican form of government, on the other hand, the head of State is always elected for a fixed term. Ours is a republican form of government and for every five-year period, we elect our President who is the head of State.

The Preamble proceeds further to define the objectives of the Indian Republic. These objectives are four in number: justice, liberty, equality, and fraternity. Justice implies a harmonious reconcilement of individual conduct with the general welfare of society. The essence of justice is the attainment of the common good. It embraces, as the Preamble proclaims, the entire social, economic and political spheres of human activity.[5]

Liberty

The term 'liberty' signifies the absence of any arbitrary restraint on the freedom of individual action and the creation of conditions conducive to the fullest development of the personality of the individual.

Since the society is composed of individuals, social progress depends on the development of the individual. Hence, it is in the interest of society to ensure the maximum liberty of thought and action of the individual, commensurate with the social conditions and circumstances.

Liberty and equality are complementary. Equality does not mean that all human beings are equal, mentally and physically. It signifies equality of status, the status of free individuals and equality of opportunity. Equality of opportunity implies the availability of opportunity to everyone to develop his or her potential capacities.

Fraternity

Fraternity demands the spirit of brotherhood. This spirit is essential in our society known for its diversity.

The term 'fraternity' implies the spirit of brotherhood. In a country like India with many disruptive social forces, communal and caste, sectional and denominational, local and regional, linguistic and cultural, the unity of the nation can be preserved only through a spirit of brotherhood that pervades the entire country, among all its citizens, irrespective of their differences. Through the establishment of a new nation based upon justice, liberty and equality, all must feel that they are the children of the same soil, of the same motherland and members of the same fraternity.[6]

The key words and the objectives mentioned in the Preamble have great economic significance. They indicate the need and scope of State intervention in economic activities.

Preamble does not have legal validity. But in times of doubt court may refer to the preamble for elucidation of the vague provisions of the Constitution.

The Preamble does not have any legal value, yet in cases of doubt, the Supreme Court often refers to the Preamble to elucidate some of the vague provisions of the Constitution. The real value of the Preamble lies in its psychological appeal to the citizens through words surcharged with emotion-justice, liberty, equality and fraternity. As Justice Hidayatulla has rightly said, "*The Preamble is more than a mere declaration. It is the soul of our Constitution and lays down the pattern of our political society. It contains a solemn resolve which nothing but a revolution can alter*."

THE FUNDAMENTAL RIGHTS

The Constitution has eight Fundamental Rights as mentioned below:

1. Right to equality;
2. Right to six freedoms, *viz.*,
   - (a) freedom of speech and expression;
   - (b) freedom to assemble peacefully and without arms;
   - (c) freedom to form associations or unions;
   - (d) freedom to move freely throughout the territory of India;
   - (e) freedom to reside and settle in any part of the territory of India; and
   - (f) freedom to practise any profession or to carry on any occupation, trade or business.
3. Right to life and personal property;
4. Right to freedom of religion;
5. Right to cultural and educational freedom;
6. Right against exploitation;
7. Right to Constitutional remedies.

Some of the Fundamental Rights have economic significance. The right to equality, for example, prohibits discrimination against any citizen on grounds of religion, race, caste, sex or place of birth. Implied in the right to equality is the concept of protective discrimination which assures protection to Scheduled Castes who have suffered discrimination for centuries. Special efforts are to be made for the development of the socially and economically backward sections of society.

Fundamental Rights such as right to equality, right against exploitation, right to practice any profession and the like carry economic implications.

Right to freedom is an important and the most valuable fundamental right guaranteed by the Constitution. As Nani Palkhivala has said, "*The Constitution is a part of the great heritage of every Indian. Its founding fathers wanted to ensure that even while India remained poor in per capita income, it should be rich in individual freedom*."[7]

Particularly, the right to practise any profession or to carry on any occupation, trade or business has great economic significance. The Constitution guarantees to citizens the fundamental right of freedom to take up any job or carry on any trade or business. The freedom of profession is however, exceptional in three cases, *viz*., (a) public interest, (b) requiring technical or professional qualifications, and (c) when a State itself decides to engage in any trade or occupation, the individual freedom is restricted.

The right to life has implications. The right to life includes-

(a) right not to be subjected to bonded labour

(b) right to decent environment

(c) right to privacy

(d) right to pure drinking water

(e) right to good roads.

The fundamental right against exploitation prohibits the exploitation of the weaker sections of society by individuals as well as by the State. Article 23 prohibits traffic in human beings and forced labour. Article 23 reads thus: "*Traffic in human beings and other similar forms of forced labour are prohibited and any contravention of this provision shall be an offence punishable in accordance with the law*." Article 24 provides special protection to children. It reads thus: "*No child below the age of fourteen years shall be employed to work in any factory, mine or engaged in any other hazardous employment*."

Thus, the fundamentals rights enshrined in the Constitution guarantee several economic rights to the citizens. At the same time, the State is empowered to impose reasonable restrictions on such economic rights in public interest. It is this power that has enabled the government to impose a series of statutory controls over business.

DIRECTIVE PRINCIPLES OF STATE POLICY

The Directive Principles of State Policy are a unique feature of our Constitution. Speaking on the Directive Principles, Dr.Ambedkar observed: "The Directive Principles are like the instruments of instructions which were issued to the Governor-General and the Governors of colonies, and to those of India by the British Government under the 1935 Government of India Act. What is called 'Directive Principles' is merely another name for the instruments of instructions. The only difference is that they are instructions to the legislature and the executive. Whoever captures power will not be free to do what he likes with it. In the exercise of it, he will have to respect these Instruments of Instructions which are called Directive Principles. He cannot ignore them."

The Directive principles are the directives to various states and agencies for governance.

The Directive Principles are the directives to the various governments and government agencies and are fundamental in the governance of the country. As Pylee observed, "The Directive Principles enshrine the fundamentals for the realisation of which the State in India stands. They guide the path which will lead the people of India to achieve the noble ideals which the Preamble of the Constitution proclaims: Justice-social, economic and political, liberty, equality and fraternity."

There are 17 Directive Principles and they may be classified, for convenience, under four heads as shown below:

1. Provisions dealing with Welfare (Art. 38, 42, 45, 47).
2. Provisions dealing with Social Justice (Art. 39, 41, 43, 46).
3. Provisions promoting Democracy (Art. 40, 44, 45).
4. Miscellaneous Provisions (Art. 48, 49, 50, 51).

The first two categories of provisions have economic significance.

Article 38(1) lays down that the State shall promote the welfare of the people by securing a social order in which justice - social, economic and political - shall inform all the institutions of national life. Justice and welfare are the twin objectives of our Constitution.

Article 38(2) lays down that the State shall strive to minimise the inequalities in income, and eliminate inequalities in status, facilities and opportunities, not only among individuals but also among groups of people.

Article 39 emphasises that the State shall direct its policy towards securing: (a) adequate means of livelihood to all citizens; (b) a proper distribution of the material resources of the community to the common good; (c) the prevention of concentration of wealth to the common detriment; (d) equal pay for equal work for both men and women; (e) the protection of the strength and health of workers and avoiding circumstances which force citizens to enter avocations unsuited to their age or strength; and (f) the protection of childhood and youth against exploitation or moral and material abandonment.

Article 41 lays down that the State shall, within the limits of its economic capacity and development, make provision for securing the right to work, to education and to public assistance in cases of unemployment, old age, sickness and disablement.

Article 42 states that the State shall make provision for securing just and humane conditions of work and for maternity relief.

Article 43 emphasises the necessity of an adequate or living wage in all sectors of economic activity. The Article enjoins that healthy conditions of work should be provided and a decent standard of living should be guaranteed. It also stresses the right to leisure for all working people. The cottage industries in rural areas should be promoted either through individual or cooperative efforts.

Article 43(A) states that the State shall take steps to secure the participation of workers in the management of undertakings, establishments or other organisations engaged in any industry.

The State shall promote, with special care, the educational and economic interests of the weaker sections of the people, and in particular, of the Scheduled Castes, Scheduled Tribes and shall protect them from social injustice and all forms of exploitation (Article 46).

The State shall endeavour to protect and improve the environment and to safeguard the forests and wildlife of the country [Article 48(A)].

Thus, the Directive Principles of State Policy enjoin upon the State varied responsibilities and provide vast scope for State intervention in the economy.

Distinction between Fundamental Rights and Directive Principles

There is a difference between the Fundamental Rights and the Directive Principles and it is useful to know the distinction. The Fundamental Rights are justiciable. If a fundamental right is violated, a legal remedy is provided for that. But the Directive Principles are non justiciable and if they are violated, there is no provision for legal remedy. Article 38 says that the 'State shall strive.' It does not mean that the State must fulfil these principles. If, for example, the State does not make provisions for compulsory free education for children under the age of 14 or if the judiciary is not separated from the executive, nobody can challenge it in a court of law. However, one thing should be kept in mind that the Directive Principles have been declared as fundamental in the governance of the country. This means that these principles are not to be lightly taken and the legislature and the government must make sincere efforts to fulfil these principles. In the words of Dr.Ambedkar, "the word 'strive' was purposely used because their intention was that, however adverse the circumstances that stand in the way for a government in giving effect to these principles and however unpropitious the time may be, they should always strive for the fulfilment of the principles. Otherwise, it would be open to the government to say that the circumstances were not good and the finances were so bad that they could not implement them."

Fundamental Rights are justifiable but Directive. Principles are not. Directive Principles are subsidiary to Fundamental Rights.

The Directive Principles are subsidiary to the Fundamental Rights and in case of conflict with Fundamental Rights, the former shall be declared unconstitutional. In the case of *State of Madras Vs.Champakan Dorairajan*, the Supreme Court observed, "The Directive Principles of State Policy which are expressly made unenforceable by a Court cannot override the provisions in Part III which...are made enforceable by appropriate writs, orders or directions under Article 32." Thus, the Directive Principles must have to conform to and run subsidiary to the chapter on Fundamental Rights. The State can act in accordance with the Directive Principles if that does not amount to the infringement of the Fundamental Rights conferred by the Constitution. The legal superiority of the Fundamental Rights over the Directive Principles has been established by the decisions of the Supreme Court of India.

Another difference between the Fundamental Rights and the Directive Principles is that the former are negative in character whereas the latter are positive. The Fundamental Rights are in the nature of injunctions requiring the State not to do certain acts and are prohibitive in character. The Directive Principles, on the other hand, are positive directions to the State to perform certain things for the good of the citizens. They urge that it is the duty of the State to implement the social and economic policy as embodied in the directives for the attainment of economic democracy and social justice. In the words of Gledhill: "Fundamental Rights are injections to prohibit the government from doing certain things; the Directive Principles are affirmative instructions to the government to do certain things."

Fundamental Rights are negative-specifying "don'ts". Directive Principles are positive. They contain "dos".

TIME FOR CHANGE

For more than four decades, the Constitution has been guiding the destiny of our country. It is said that the Constitution has put several roadblocks which checked the pace of the country's economic development, roadblocks manifesting through sporadic communal clashes, moral disintegration, growing regional and parochial tendencies, corrupt bureaucracy, umpteen regulatory legislations and their implementing agencies, and topping all, the helplessness of the government in attacking the roots of the menacing problems.

Partly, the problem lies with the background against which the Constitution was drafted and adopted. "It is of importance", wrote B.K.Nehru, "that we should remember how the Constituent Assembly was composed. The electorate was confined to a fraction of the total adult population, the qualifications for the vote being property, education and the payment of tax. The mass of the people, the great have-nots, were totally unrepresented on the body that framed the system which still governs us. Virtually, all the members of the Constituent Assembly were men of reasonable affluence and education. They were primarily concerned not with economic problems or hunger of the people but with the absence of civil liberties, particularly those liberties such as freedom of speech or of association, which had been lacking in British India and whose absence they had keenly felt. This is the explanation for the great stress in the Constitution on the Fundamental Rights of the individuals as practised in Western democratic society and the elaborate safeguards for their preservation.

"Furthermore, the Constituent Assembly was dominated by lawyers, trained solely in the British tradition and in the British system of law, who constituted a substantial proportion of membership of the Assembly. Their knowledge of constitutional law was largely confined within the horizon of the British constitution. That, like all British institutions and all British customs, no matter how unsuitable for our country, had been held up to us as a perfect model to be emulated by subject societies.

Constitution was adopted at a time when attaining political freedom was a dominant force. With the changed environment that exists today, the document needs relook.

"*...We should recognise that the Indian Constitution...is not helping the country to attain the goals it was meant to achieve. It is no use saying that the Constitution is perfect but it is the men who have failed.*"[8]

Further, the founding fathers failed to visualise the society and polity that would emerge in the decades to follow. The freedom movement was fought in a different milieu. The objective before the masses was clear and divisive factors like caste and religion were not a constraint. People from all walks of life forgot their differences and fought shoulder-to-shoulder with one aim in mind-freedom at any cost.

But their behaviour, particularly of the leaders, once freedom was acquired could not be predicted. The presumption that people will continue to be motivated by the same fire proved wrong. The dream of a prosperous and free society did not come true. The consequence: the country in 1996 is entirely different from what it was in 1947. Naturally, the Constitution of the early years cannot be relevant for 1990s.

The founding fathers gave greater role to State with an objective of ushering socialism in the country. But socialism has not been realised. On the other hand, it is capitalism which has been promoted.

The various reform measures which the State took in the following years strengthened capitalism, and not socialism. The impact of planned economic development of the country resulted in the emergence of capitalism in agriculture in selected areas, while it has also accelerated the growth of the manufacturing sector in the industry and the national market in India. Besides, a few more facts may be mentioned to understand the role of the State in building capitalism in India.

(a) The State is the chief mobilizer of resources and saving in the country for investment. Public-controlled institutions like the development banks and the nationalised commercial banks, have centralised resources in the hands of the State to be invested in the State capitalist sector and the private corporate sector.

(b) The State has actively supported science and technology and Research and Development efforts for building capitalism.

(c) The State has the responsibility to develop infrastructure like power, transport and irrigation for the development of capitalism.

(d) During the last forty years, the State has consciously developed and is trying to strengthen private property by encouraging small-scale and medium industries, and at the apex, it has harmonised the interests of big business, political leaders and public bureaucracy, who have common stakes in capitalism as investors and profit-seekers.

Thus, despite socialistic preventions, the State and the political parties, never accepted the philosophy of 'welfarism' either in economy or in polity.

Socialism which the Constitution seeks to promote itself has become irrelevant.

India has come a long way since 1950 when the centralised planning system was adopted for economic development. For a full forty years, the entire life, economic and political, was conditioned by a system in which everything was controlled by the government, which in reality meant, the politician. With the passage of time, the government became personified in an individual. The functioning of the government became such that development became sluggish and the country was out of alignment with global trends. Even when the Soviet system and the Eastern European block was crumbling and was changing to the new world order, the Indian system remained rigid. Whatever little changes were made were either not implemented or implemented half-heartedly.

From 1991 onwards, there has been a restructuring of the economy from the command to a market oriented one. Now the changes in the economic system have to be incorporated in the political system also, if a new order is to be established in the country. This necessitates a change in the Indian Constitution.

Eversince liberalization has been introduced, there has been considerable restructuring of the economy pushing it towards market orientation. These changes need to0 be integrated into Indian polity. Hence the document needs amendments.

With increasing globalization, the concept of nation-state is losing its relevance. Countries are gradually losing their identities. They are getting integrated into a global village. Against this background, the Constitution which seeks to protect country's identity, appears to be out of context.

Required Changes

A relevant question here is: What should the Constitution look like? Infact, a Constitution should give clear directions to the polity and the economy. The US Constitution directs the State to form a society based on freedom, liberty and general welfare. The social, political and economic development during the last two centuries has brought a system based on free market economy.

The British Constitution which, over the last few centuries, developed along with British thinking, is based on the rule of law. The entire edifice of the British polity and economy is based on this concept. The Indian Constitution has no direction in the beginning. But the rulers wanted to establish a socialist society. Since we have decided to say goodbye to it, the Constitution should be modified keeping in view the requirements of the changed economy.

The first need is to change the Preamble. The Preamble, as was pointed out earlier, determines the general purpose behind a Constitution and is never regarded as a source of power. Since the Preamble is meant to explain certain facts which are necessary to be explained before the enactments contained in the Act can be understood, it should not have too many such concepts. The original Preamble did not have too many confusing concepts. The original Preamble did not contain the words 'socialist, secular'. Moreover, the condition of the economy and the relationship between various religious communities have deteriorated since these two words were inserted by the Constitution (42nd) Amendment Act of 1976 by a Parliament whose credibility was doubtful. Juxtaposing it with the recent metamorphosis in the government policy, it is time to restore the original position of 1950 and declare India as only 'Sovereign Democratic Republic'.

The second change needed is to remove the Directive Principles. Directive Principles are not legally enforceable in the courts and the State cannot be held responsible for not formulating public policies in conformity with the Directive Principles.

Almost all the Directive Principles, like equal right to an adequate means of living, distribution to subserve the common good, checking concentration of economic power, equal pay for equal work and stopping entry to hazardous vocations are vague and confused. However, most of the developed countries have adopted these principles in their system by enacting legislations and strictly enforcing them.

The third need is to restore the right to property which was guaranteed by Article 31 of the Constitution. The 44th Amendment Act of 1978, again by a superannuated Parliament, omitted Article 31. Now, the legislature is free to take away a person's property without payment of any compensation. The person has no remedy before a court of law and the courts cannot challenge the validity of such a law. The need of the changing times is to restore Article 31.[9]

Whether or not these and other related issues will be taken up by the recently constituted panel to review Constitution, is to be seen.

QUESTIONS

1. State and elaborate the terms in Preamble to the Constitution which have economic significance.
2. What are Fundamental Rights? Which of them have economic significance and how.
3. State th Directive Principles of State Policy which have impact on business functioning.
4. "Constitution has put several road blocks which have checked the pace of the country's economic development." Elucidate.

ASSIGNMENT

Pick up 4th question as the topic for discussion. Have two batches of 5 students - one batch to debate in support of the statement and another to oppose it. The instructor shall summarise the proceedings towards the end.

REFERENCES

1. M.V.Pylee, *India's Constitution*, P.52.
2. C.N.Vakil, *Industrial Development-Policy and Problems*, p.450.
3. *Ibid*, p.xvi.
4. M.V.Pylee, *op.cit.*, p.52.
5. *Ibid*, p.53.
6. *Ibid*, p.54.
7. Nani Palkhivala, *We the People*,p.207.
8. *Indian Express,* Feb. 15, 1987.
9. *Financial Express,* July 12, 1992.

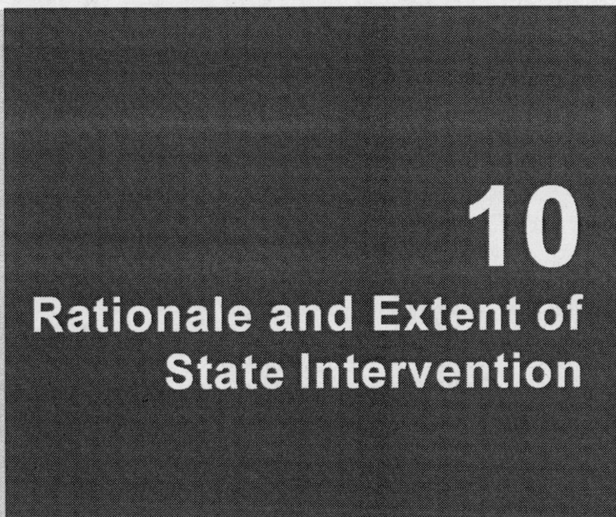

10

Rationale and Extent of State Intervention

CHAPTER OUTLINE

Reasons for State Intervention
Types of Intervention
Extent of Intervention
Consequences of Controls
Features of a Good Control System
Government-Business Interface
Historical Perspective

LEARNING OBJECTIVES

After reading this Chapter, you should be able to:

1. Understand reasons why government should intervene in business
2. Describe the various types of state intervention
3. Describe the extent and consequences of state controls
4. Bring out the qualities of a good control system
5. Trace the history of interface between government and business

One of the features of modern business is the increasing involvement of the government in business activities. As of today, there is no country in the world where the government of the land does not interfere, in one form or the other, in its economic activities (also read Box 10.1 and Table 10.1). Involvement is all the more pervasive in our economy which till recently was a planned and regulated one.

Box 10.1 **Government Intervention in the US**

If you own or manage a business in the US, government is your not-so-silent partner. When you hire workers, the hours they can work and the wages you can pay will be affected by law. Other laws will compel you to insure them against injury and unemploy-ment and may require you to bargain with them collectively. If you raise capital by selling stock, a government agency will control the offering. Your pricing and marketing practices will be affected by federal and state antitrust statutes. Depending on what you sell, you may be required to modify the design of your product or have it tested for safety and efficiency before you can bring it to the market. The truthfulness of your advertising claims will be scrutinised. Even your product's label will be affected by government regulations. You may be required to invest in equipment that the government deems the 'best available' for controlling pollution or safety hazards, or you may have to otherwise modify your production process to conform to environmental or safety guidelines. You will be required to obtain numerous licences, and government mandated paperwork will seem to never end. And even if you cheerfully comply with all these requirements, you may be sued if anyone comes to harm by either purchasing or consuming your product.

(**Source:**Stephen J.K.Walters, *Enterprise, Government and the Public*, New York, Mc Graw-Hill International, 1993, P.3)

Table 10.1 **Government Intervention in Asian Region**

(In Percentage)

	Too Much	*Just Enough*	*Too Little*	*None*
South Korea	94.9	5.1	-	-
Japan	75.5	15.6	8.9	-
Indonesia	75.0	17.5	7.5	-
Taiwan	61.9	26.2	11.9	-
Malaysia	60.8	39.2	-	-
Phillippines	51.2	48.8	-	-
Singapore	50.0	46.2	-	3.8
Thailand	46.3	36.6	17.1	-
Australia	38.5	61.5	-	-
Hong Kong	10.0	80.0	5.0	5.0

Note: Views expressed by business leaders across Asian countries.
(**Source**: *Economic Times*, 27th May, 1997)

REASONS FOR STATE INTERVENTION

Why the government should interfere in business activities is a relevant question. The following constitute the answer.

1. Economic historians have noted that the later a country moves towards economic development, the greater has to be the role of the State. Delayed growth has to be sponsored growth, and the government has to be the sponsor.[1]

Modern economy should be a planned economy. Government is the only agency which can plan and execute.

2. It is argued that the modern economy must be a planned economy. The need for planning becomes clear if we examine the dangers of non-planning. In the absence of planning, there is no proper direction to the economy, wrong priorities are chosen, scarce resources are wasted, and booms and depressions occur regularly. In order to check these and some other evils, and to ensure speedy and balanced development of the economy with the least wastage of resources, planning becomes necessary. Who else except the State should assume responsibility for planning and implementing the plans?

3. Ours being a socialist society, the government is compelled to enter directly into industrial and commercial activities. Our Constitution binds the government to take an active part in economic activities. The State's role is clearly underlined in the Preamble, the Fundamental Rights and the Directive Principles of State policy. Articles 38 to 48 of the Directive Principles; the Right to Equality, the Right to Freedom and the Right Against Exploitation of the Fundamental Rights and Justice, Liberty and Equality for all in the Preamble make it mandatory for the State to participate in economic activities.

What the people and the country need can only be understood and provided by government and not by private sector.

4. The considerations which apply in deciding what undertaking is to be established, how it should be run, where it should be established, how its products will be priced and distributed, all these and other considerations are influenced by the policy to which the government is committed. For instance, the government must consider not so much what the likely demand is going to be according to market projections, but may infact have to decide what the demand should be, and take steps to influence the demand, either to build it up or to pare it down or to vary it. If the country is to achieve a certain pace of development, if certain standards of living are to be attained, certain demands must be created. Otherwise the whole pace of development will slow down, and not be adequate to attain the targets which the nation has set before itself.

This is a feature which private enterprises cannot cope with. For example, the standard of living of a people can be statistically related to the power and to the steel per capita consumed in the country. There are several such indicators. A government politically committed to certain social objectives may then well decide that in order to achieve these per capita ratios, it may be necessary to setup, to evolve and to operate a pattern of prices, subsidies, incentives or disincentives of different kinds in order to influence the consumption pattern.[2]

5. The functions of the government which were originally limited to the maintenance of law and order have considerably expanded. In our country, the government has assumed the responsibility of social and economic well-being of the people. In this changed context, taxation can no longer be solely depended upon, and infact has proved inadequate, for the task of raising the total revenues, the State now needs for its multifarious activities. By active participation in business, the State has sought to tap the gold mines of industry and commerce for the funds needed to discharge the new and heavier burdens it now shoulders.[3]

6. State participation is necessary to lay a strong base for the future development of industry and commerce. The Government must assume responsibility for the development of core industries and facilities such as power, fuel, iron and steel, transport, atomic energy, machine building, machine tools, transportation and communication.

Markets generally fail. Where markets fail, state should intervene.

7. Finally, the failure of markets invites government intervention in an economy. As is too well known, markets may be monopolistic or competitive. Monopoly leads to the wastage of resources and exploitation of consumers. Clearly, avoidance of these evils is the main reason for State intervention. Infact, protection of consumers against trade practices harmful to public interest is the main objective of the Competition Act, 2002.

If monopolies fail, it does not imply that competitive markets succeed. Infact, competitive markets often fail because of atleast three reasons: (i) externalities, (ii) public goods, and (iii) information problems.

Externalities: Externalities are costs or benefits that the market transactor imposes or confers on third parties (those external to a transaction) without their consent. Externalities are also referred to as neighbourhood or spillover effects.

The most frequently used example of a negative externality is pollution, resulting from either the manufacturer or use of some product, which imposes costs on individuals who neither produce nor consume the product in question. In general, when production involves such negative externalities, competitive markets fail.

Public goods: Public goods are those having atleast two properties: (i) consumption of the goods by one person leaves no less of the goods available for anyone, and (ii) the costs of excluding those who do not pay for the public good are extremely high (i.e., the good is non-excludable). Obviously, many goods that we commonly describe as public are not truly public goods. However, markets fail to deal with a product which is purely or partly public in nature. Government financing or even production is required.

Information problems: Embedded in most discussions of competitive markets is an assumption that consumers are well informed about various sellers and the prices and attributes of their products. Obviously, the real world never conforms to this idealised assumption.

Even competitive markets, therefore, left to themselves impose serious welfare losses on the society. Hence, the relevance and need for State intervention.[4]

TYPES OF INTERVENTION

Also called as controls or regulations, government intervention assumes several forms. Thus, we may distinguish between formal and informal controls, between inducive and coercive controls, between direct and indirect controls, controls in relations to competition and promotional and regulatory controls (See Fig.10.1).

Figure 10.1 **Classification of Controls**

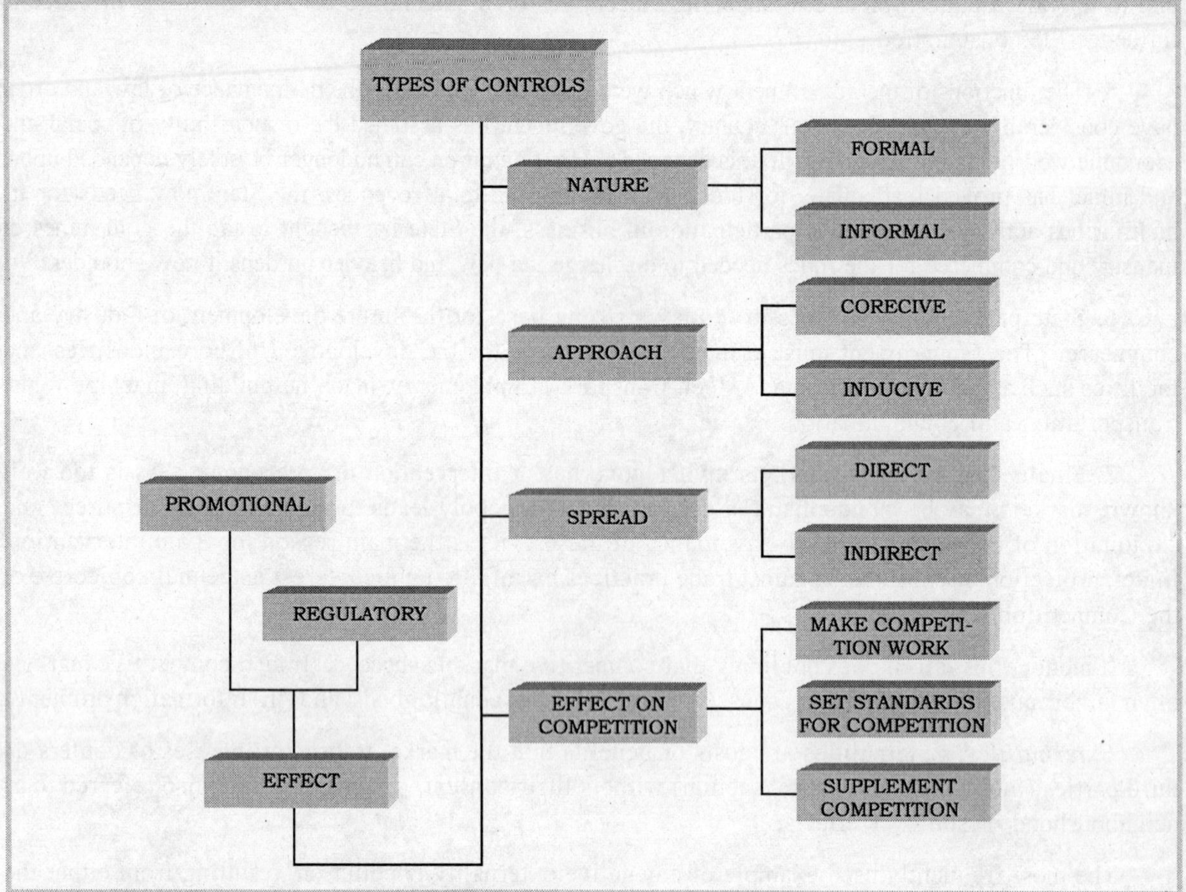

Formal and Informal Controls: Formal controls are usually those emanating from legislation, as for, example, the FEMA, the Companies Act, 1956 and the Competition Act 2002. Formal controls are very powerful and when we think of government control over business, we generally mean *formal* controls. Informal controls refer to the controls which various groups impose upon themselves out of need and custom. Business firms in various lines of activity develop conventions, informal agreements and accepted ways of doing things that have important regulative implications.

Coercive and Inducive Controls: Coercive regulations require performance of certain actions or refraining from others in order to avoid penalties. For instance, taxes must be paid or fine or imprisonment may result. In contrast, inducive controls hold out a promise of reward for compliance with the desired line of action. For example, subsidies may be granted to stimulate certain activities.

Businessmen prefer indirect controls as they are less cumbersome and severe.

Direct and Indirect Controls: When the government fixes prices of certain products or services, it is an example of direct control. The administered price policy of the Government of India is a direct control measure. The variation of corporate income tax to influence economic activity is an indirect control measure. Businessmen prefer indirect controls to direct regulations.

Effect on Competition: Depending on the relationship to competition, regulations may be:

(a) government regulations designed to make competition work, the Competition Act, for example;

(b) government competition with business firms as a means of setting standards of competition, or

(c) direct government ownership and operation to supplement competition.

Promotional and Regulatory Controls: Promotional measures are of a positive nature, and include such activities as expansion of public sector establishment and operation of development banks, revival of sick units, encouragement to small-scale units, removal of regional imbalances, provision of incentives and subsidies and export promotion.

Regulatory measures ensure orderly development of industries with the least wastage of resources. Regulatory measures include direct controls like the Industries (Development and Regulation) Act, the Competition Act, the Companies Act, the Foreign Exchange Management Act and price and distribution controls, labour laws and indirect controls like monetary policy and fiscal policy.

EXTENT OF INTERVENTION

Ours being a regulatory economy, government intervention is enormous and all pervasive. State intervention is noticed in all aspects of a business establishment. In Figure 10.2, an attempt is made to bring out the various regulations.

For a long time, state intervention was all pervasive in our economy.

The figure contains only important measures which apply to a large-size manufacturing unit. Regulatory measures that apply to small units are different and are equally powerful and numerous.

After years of liberalisation, State intervention in business has come down considerably as shown in Figures 10.3 and 10.4. It may be stated that both the figures show State regulation as it applies to foreign collaboration. Figure 10.3 obviously shows the procedure for foreign collaboration before liberalisation. Figure 10.4 shows changed procedure as it exists today. Even with regard to domestic business, state regulation has come down considerably as box 10.2 shows.

Box 10.2 **e-Governance and Unshackled Bureaucracy**

Then, early last year, an e-governance project speeded up the process by bringing the whole process online. It allows an entrepreneur to deal with the registrar of companies (RoC), the approving authority, online.

The results are glaring. The incorporation of a company now takes less than five days against 15 days that was the norm before. And company name is approved in a day, compared to a week earlier. Procedures regarding filing of annual returns, balance sheet, change of directors, registered office and increase in authorised capital now take just three days to be notified compared to two months earlier. The Ministry of Corporate Affairs, which implemented the project, aims to deliver all such services within 48 hours by the end of this fiscal.

The latest statistics show that the initial hurdles in giving wings to one's entrepreneurial skills have almost disappeared. As on July 31, 2007, about 65,000 companies were born online, some of them in less than an hour, after the e-governance was introduced in February, 2006. The elimination of the personal interface between the entrepreneur and the regulator was complete when all the 20 RoCs went online. Now, 92% filings with the regulator take place either from the entrepreneur's office or home.

However, incorporating the company is only the first hurdle for a business. As for the rest of its journey, India is not yet an ideal place. Agencies like the World Bank that studies international business environment ranks India 134th – 41 positions after China — "which is reforming at a faster pace". In its report 'Doing business in South Asia, 2007,' the World Bank says that policies of various Indian states differ significantly and if all adopt the best practices of others, the country would move up to the 79th position.

(***Source:*** Gireesh Chandra Prasad, "Archaive Laws, Licence Raj and Web of Charge", *The Economic Times*, Aug. 15, 2007)

Figure 10.2 **Various Controls**

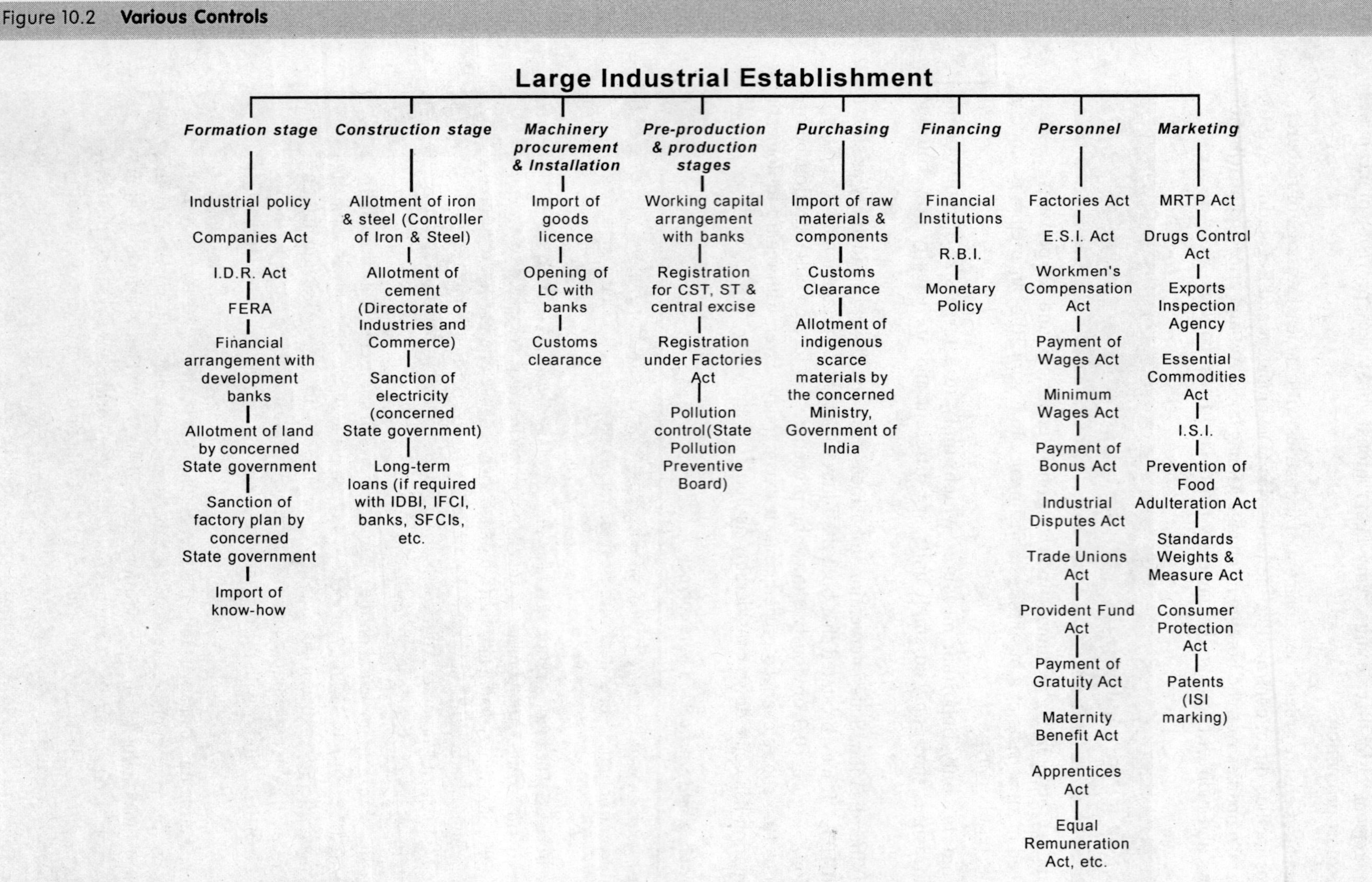

Figure 10.3

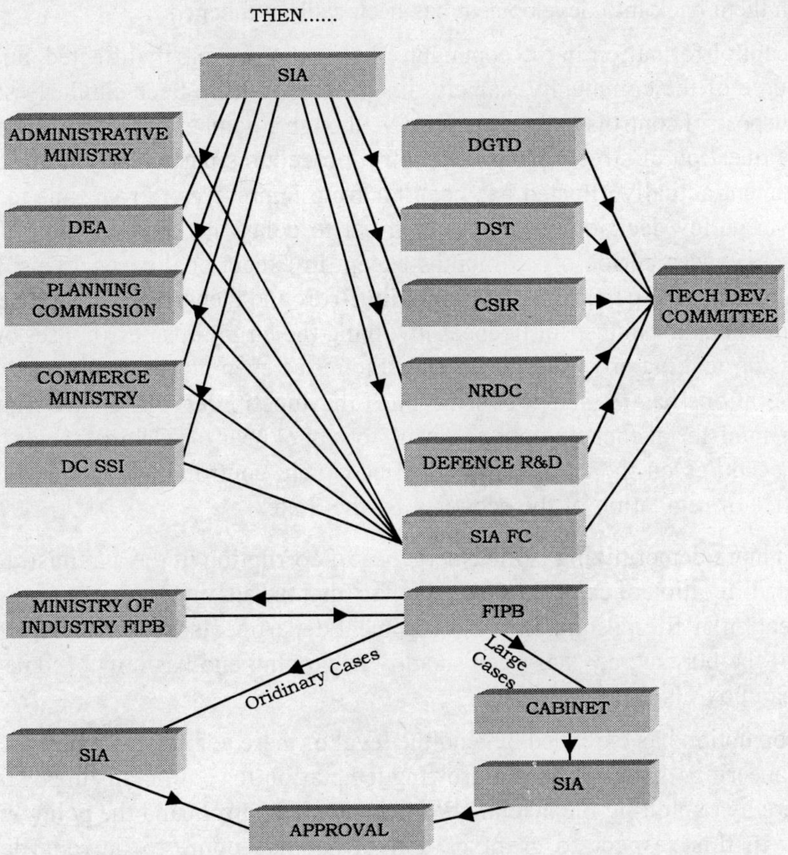

THEN......

SIA

ADMINISTRATIVE MINISTRY

DEA

PLANNING COMMISSION

COMMERCE MINISTRY

DC SSI

DGTD

DST

CSIR

NRDC

DEFENCE R&D

SIA FC

TECH DEV. COMMITTEE

MINISTRY OF INDUSTRY FIPB

FIPB

Oridinary Cases

Large Cases

CABINET

SIA

SIA

APPROVAL

Figure 10.4

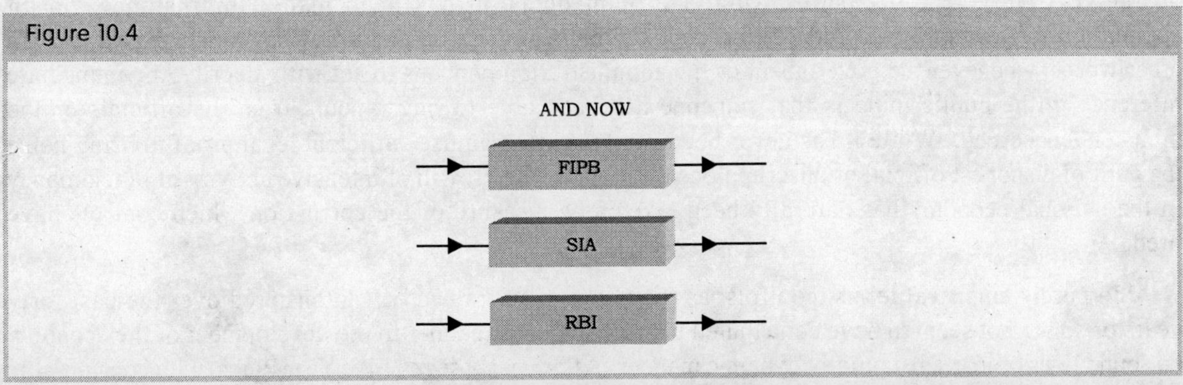

CONSEQUENCES OF CONTROLS

Controls have resulted in wastage of national resources.

Controls have negative consequences. Certain weaknesses and defects as have developed over the years in the framing or administration of policies of controls have become quite obvious. There has been, to start with, a considerable waste of national resources in an essentially negative manner. It has been pointed out that, although the ratio of tax revenue to national income has gone up from less than 6% in 1951 to about 15% now, there has been no corresponding increase in the government's current outlay on development. Almost the whole of the potential savings of increased taxation has been eaten up by the current expenditures of the Central and State Governments. This has been largely because the administration of various economic controls has involved an ever-increasing expansion of the bureaucracy at all levels throughout the country. As a result, the capacity of the fiscal machinery of the government to mobilise public savings and plough them back into development has been sadly weakened.

Wastage of time is another consequence of controls.

Controls have bred corruption at various levels.

Apart from capital formation in the community being thus adversely affected, an equally precious development resource of the community, namely time, seems to have been similarly squandered on the largely negative purpose of controls and regulations. Although a number of committees of the government have gone into the question of streamlining the control procedures particularly in the area of industrial licensing, improvement actually effected has been far from impressive. From time to time, it has been declared that a firm policy decision has been taken not to delay the consideration of applications for industrial licences beyond a period of six months except in exceptional cases. This, however, has not prevented the accumulation of pending business in Ministries and Departments much beyond six months. In the case of applications for industrial licences involving the larger business houses or foreign firms or investors, the decision-making processes have tended to move even more slowly, partly because a spate of political considerations has regularly overwhelmed the functioning of the government by elaborate procedures of inter-ministerial consultations or discussions at or near the Cabinet levels. The stranglehold of policies and procedures on the administration of economic controls has thus become an oppressive factor in the practice of regulation of the economy by the State.

Perhaps even more demoralizing is the emergence of corruption in the administration of politics as a corollary to the proliferation of controls. Given the fact that the administration is becoming increasingly a matter of file creation or file-pushing in the government departments, scope for bribery and corruption at various levels of the bureaucracy has been steadily expanding and has now become a major national industry. (Also read box 10.3).

Inevitably, corruption has extended beyond the level of mere administration. Partly because of the high cost of electioneering, there has been a growing temptation for politicians in power to collect funds for the party coffers by exploiting the machinery of economic controls and the policy-making powers of the government, in this respect to grant or deny what has come to be regarded as favours to individual businessmen or even whole industries. This drastic situation is fully reflected in the fact that, on the relatively rare occasions when a prompt decision has been made, for instance, on an application for an industrial licence, the popular feeling is that money must have changed hands. In other words, whenever the government or the administration happens to act with alacrity, the immediate inference in the public mind is that someone has been able to buy favours from the officials or the ministers concerned. While it has never been very easy to organise sufficient legal proof to bring home the guilt of dishonest official or unscrupulous politicians, the growth of intensive activity of black money in the national economy has naturally been taken as a measure of the corruption which controls have bred.

In purely empirical terms, controls, as they have been framed or administered over the past forty years or so, do not seem to have contributed in a conspicuous manner to the development of the economy on sound lines or in a substantially dynamic manner. After nearly seven Five Year Plans, with considerable dislocation of planning thrown in between, the country is now in a plight, where it is hampered by the population problem all along the line. The irony is that very few of the professed economic or largely social objectives of economic controls have been achieved to a substantial extent in practice. Precisely for these reasons, the economic reforms were initiated in 1991 and are continuing even today. The results of these reforms are quite encouraging as will be explained in subsequent chapters in this book.

Box 10.3 **Some Problems of Government Intervention in Developing Countries**

1. Individuals may know more about their own preferences and circumstances than the government.
2. Government planning may increase risk by pointing everyone in the same direction — governments may make bigger mistakes than markets.
3. Government planning may be more rigid and inflexible than private decision making because complex decision-making machinery may be involved in government.
4. Governments may be incapable of administering detailed plans.
5. Government controls may block private-sector individual initiative if there are many bureaucratic obstacles.
6. Organisations and individuals require incentives to work, innovate, control costs, and allocate efficiently, and the discipline and rewards of the market cannot easily be replicated within public enterprises and organisations. Public enterprises are often inefficient and wasteful.
7. Different levels and parts of government may be poorly coordinated in the absence of the equilibriating signals provided by the market, particularly where groups or regions with different interests are involved.
8. Markets place constraints on what can be achieved by government; for example, resale of commodities on block markets and activities in the informal sector can disrupt rationing or other nonlinear pricing or taxation schemes. This is the general problem of "incentive compatibility."
9. Controls create resource-using activities to influence those controls through lobbying and corruption—often called rent seeking or directly unproductive activities.
10. Planning may be manipulated by privileged and powerful groups that act in their own interests, and planning creates groups with a vested interest in planning, for example, bureaucrats or industrialists who obtain protected positions.
11. Governments may be dominanted by narrow interest groups interested in their own welfare and sometimes actively hostile to large sections of the population, Planning may Intensify their power.

(**Source**:Michacl P.Todaro and Stephen, C.Smit, *Economic Development*, P.698)

A GOOD CONTROL SYSTEM

A good system of control, if it were to avoid negative consequences, should have the following qualities:

(i) It must be democratic. This means that it must be exercised in the interest of the governed as they see their interests.

(ii) It should know what it wants.

(iii) It must be powerful - powerful enough to make an unwilling minority obey the will of the majority.

(iv) It must be efficient, and at the same time, it must not destroy the efficiency of the thing it is regulating.

(v) It must 'economise coercion'.

(vi) It must utilise all the strongest and most persistent motives of human nature, both generous and selfish hopes of reward, fear of punishment and those loyalties, persuasions and suggestions which rest upon the deeper fact that the individual is essentially a part of the community.

(vii) The duties imposed must be simple enough to be understood; and this means, among other things, that social control must follow precedent a great deal of the time.

(viii) Control must be guided by experience or by wise experiment.

(ix) It must be adaptable.

(x) It must have a wider vision and canvas to develop. It must look beyond the immediate effect of doing a given thing to the further results of leading people to expect it in the future.

(xi) And lastly, social control must be capable of progressively raising the level of mankind. In a democracy, where the mass of mankind does the ultimate controlling, this amounts to saying that social control must continue somehow, to rise higher than its source.[5]

GOVERNMENT INVOLVEMENT IN BUSINESS - HISTORICAL PERSPECTIVE

The laissez-faire policy ignored the fact that industrialization had always operated in an economy whose orderliness was guaranteed by the government.

State intervention in business seems to be as old as business itself. Even in the days of *laissez faire*, which apparently shunned State intervention, the government's role in the economy was almost inescapable. "There is a grave doubt", wrote Eugene V.Schneider, "as to whether this doctrine (*laissez faire*) gave an accurate picture of the relationship between the industry and the government even in the early days of industrialism. The *laissez faire* doctrine ignored the fact that industrialisation had always operated in an economy whose orderliness was guaranteed by the government. An aura of sanctity may have surrounded the contract, but in the last analysis, it was only the State which could enforce the contract. Similarly, the entrepreneur may have considered his property as belonging to him by virtue of divine right, or as a reward for his virtue, or as the outcome of a natural economic law, but it was only the government which could guarantee him continued possession and use of his property. Furthermore, even in the early days of industrialisation, the entrepreneur looked to the government for, and received from the government, many special favours. Tariffs protected him from foreign competition. His labour supply was ensured by the destruction, through governmental acts, of feudal ties between man and land, between the peasant and the nobleman. Later, the judicial machinery of the government would protect him against the 'conspiratorial' efforts of his working men to form unions. Franchises, grants of land, outright subsidies - all these special privileges and many others besides attested to the existence of a strong relationship between industry and the government".[6]

As years went by, State intervention became a historical necessity, particularly after the Industrial Revolution of the late 18th and early 19th centuries. The Industrial Revolution albeit revolutionised the methods of production, brought in its trail, social evils of a very bitter type. The era of Industrial Revolution witnessed the inhumanity of man to man and brutalisation of human nature in those very countries and in those very societies where the greatest advances were being made in the fields of science, technology and organisations.[7] Affluence and poverty, distress and luxury, and exploitation and helplessness become so juxtaposed that the need for State intervention began to be felt much more than ever before.

The factory laws of the 19th century marked the first normal and active State involvement. The establishment of trade unions compelled the State to intervene.

Then came the First World War, which confirmed the inevitability of State intervention in economic activities. War required that all economic activities be geared towards meeting its requirements and it was the State alone which ensured this. The Second World War only confirmed the trend.

Nearer at home, State intervention became forceful since 1939 when India become a participant in the War. India did not become a military base in the true sense of the word until the entry of Japan into the War in December 1941, more than two years after the War began. But even before that event, India was major supplier of goods and materials were needed to sustain the War effort of the Allies. Her economy was placed on a war footing and geared to cater to the needs of the War. It was when this happened that its inadequacies and shortcomings became forcefully apparent to those whose safety depended upon it. A period of controls and regulations began and lasted, in the case of India, till long after most similar controls had been lifted elsewhere. Plans began to be formulated and for the first time the concept of planning at government level was heard.[8]

India's participation in the first war triggered state intervention.

In 1944, when the War was still in progress, the Department of Planning and Development was setup. A new Industrial Policy was announced by the government and the then Viceroy, Lord Wavell, declared in 1945 : "Government has decided to take positive steps to encourage and promote industrialisation of the country to the fullest extent possible".[9]

Positive steps were taken and industries such as iron and steel, heavy engineering, machine tools, heavy chemicals and the like, which would lay the foundation for future economic development, were setup.

Even after the War, distortions in the economy continued, some of them in new dimensions, and many of the war-time regulations could not be removed or even relaxed.

The coming of Independence in 1947 did not bring any change in the role of State. On the other hand, the government's role in removing the poverty of millions of people and improving their living standards was realised by all concerned. Resources being limited and priorities being several, economic planning became a dire necessity which would usher in faster economic prosperity in a phased manner. Thus, the First Five Year Plan was launched, heralding a greater role for the State in the economic development of the country. As we went through Seven Five Year Plans, the role became deeply entrenched.

India's political independence reiterated the need for state intervention.

Then come 1990s when heralded launding of privatisation and liberalisation policies with these policies inplace, state's role in business is gradually reading should the government withdraw completely is argued in the next chapter.

State intervention in our economy is not peculiar to the present century. It was there during the Mauryan times and later. "*Thus, in Mauryan times*", observed A.L.Basham, "*every aspect of life of the individual was watched over, and as far as possible controlled, by the government. Though no later, the State developed the same degree of control as did the Mauryas, the ideas of the Arthasastra did not wholly disapprove. The government not only regulated the economic life of the country, but also took an important part in it. All mines, which term for the ancient India included pearl fisheries and salt pans, were owned by the State, and were either worked directly with the labour of criminals or serfs, or let out to entrepreneurs, from whom the King claimed a percentage of their output as royalty. The produce of the forests, from elephants to firewood, was the property of the State. There were large State farms, cultivated either by direct labour or on a share-cropping basis the products of which went to the State granaries. The State owned factories for spinning and weaving, which were staffed by indigent women, rather like the houses of industry under the Elizabethan Poor-Law. Munitions of war were made in State arsenals,. and ships were built in State shipyards, to be let out to fishermen and merchants. In fact, there was no question of laissez faire in ancient India*".[10]

QUESTIONS

1. "As on today there is no country in the world where government of the land does not interfere in its economic activities". Do you agree? Discuss.
2. Write a note on Fig 10.1.
3. Do you think that Fig 10.2 is complete in its content? If not, strengthen it.
4. What are the consequences of state control?
5. How to make controls effective?

ASSIGNMENT

The following five countries are under different political dispensations:

India

Pakistan

Russia

Cuba

Nepal

Study the roles of respective governments in these countries. Make a report offering your observations and recommendations.

REFERENCES

1. C.N.Vakil, *Industrial Development of India - Policy and Problems*, p.16.
2. *Ibid*.,p.248.
3. *Ibid*.,Pp.245-247.
4. Stephen J.K.Walters, *Enterprise, Government and the Public*,Pp.55-78.
5. J.M.Clark, *Social Control of Business*,p.10.
6. Eugene V.Schneider, *Industrial Sociology*,p.515.
7. S.S.Khera, *Government in Business*,p.7.
8. *Ibid.*
9. *Ibid.*
10. A.L.Basham, *The Wonder That Was India*,p.103.

11 End of Government in Business?

CHAPTER OUTLINE

Why should the Government Continue its Interventionist Policy?

What Should be the Form of State Intervention?

- Analysis of political environment

LEARNING OBJECTIVES

After reading this Chapter, you should be able to:

1. Appreciate the reasons why the government should continue its interventionist policy.
2. Describe the form of state intervention.
3. Come to the conclusion that government intervention will continue but in a modified form.
4. Analyse the political environment

Section 3 in this book had focussed on the detailed discussion of the role of the State in shaping, directing, controlling and promoting business activities in our country. As was stated in Chapter 10, government's intervention in business was necessitated by historical, economic, political and social reasons. During the past five decades, the government has been acting as a regulator and promoter of business activities. If the country has achieved reasonably satisfactory progress on the economic front, credit must go to the dynamic role played by the State, contrary views expressed by the critics notwithstanding.

India has achieved satisfactory level of progress thanks to state intervention.

A new realisation has dawned on economists, policymakers and academicians these days. These people perceive the government as the main bottleneck in development. Getting governments out of the business of development has become an important element in the policy advice given by international institutions, economic experts, and donor agencies. Thatcherism in the UK and Reganism in the USA contributed to this changed mood. Another important contributory factor has been the increasing economic difficulties of many developing countries, and the failure of their governments to take timely corrective action. Partly in response to their own experience and partly in response to international pressure, several developing countries are questioning the role of the government in their economies.[1] Spain, Venezuela, Zambia and the Latin American and African countries come into focus in this context. Our country is no exception.

But the above argument is questioned by everyone now-a-days.

Is this changed mood justified? Is everything over with the State intervention? Has government's role ended? The answer to these questions is 'no'.

WHY THE GOVERNMENT SHOULD CONTINUE ITS INTERVENTIONIST POLICY?

If doubts are expressed about the efficacy of the State to act as a change agent, probably there is justification. Over the years, a sort of false picture about the omnipotence of the State was created. The solution to every problem was sought to be found in the expansion of government activity in that area, irrespective of costs or results. Soon the expansion of the government became an objective in itself, and every priority or failure in the economic field generates a response in the form of new regulatory law or a new public sector corporation. The expansion of the government was also assiduously promoted by coalitions of powerful interests, which benefited directly from the increased economic power of the State. Overtime, the scale of the government became so large that the quality of intervention, as well as the quality of service, provided by the State, deteriorated.[2]

Nevertheless, State's intervention in the business must continue for several reasons.

State intervention is necessary to eliminate poverty.

The State activism in economic activities is necessary to eliminate poverty. It must be admitted that poverty still exists inspite of the growth registered in the economy. One must visit a village or travel in a village bus to understand the magnitude of the poverty. For every one RCC house, there are 10 thatched huts and for every one individual who is fully clad, there are atleast five people who are half clad. There are victims of malnutrition and reports of even starvation deaths in the media. There is illiteracy, ignorance and helplessness.

World Development Report (WDR), 1991, states that no market economy has ever eradicated poverty so far. It is only State intervention that has helped fund programmes that have alleviated poverty. Today even in the US there is the growing concern about the need for the State to intervene in the provision of healthcare and education. The World Bank is now supportive of the role of the government in the provision of education, health care, development of infrastructure and fostering of the human capital.

When markets fail governments must intervene. But governments also fail.

WDR is categorical in its assertion about the need for continued State intervention. To quote the Report "many sorts of interventions are essential if economies are to achieve their full potential. (When) markets 'fail', the government must step in. But countless cases of unsuccessful intervention suggest the need for caution. Markets fail, but so do governments. To justify intervention it is not enough to know that the market is failing; it is also necessary to be confident that the government can do better".

What is important is the quality of intervention but not intervention, per se.

The "central question of this Report is", says WDR 1991, "why countries like Japan have succeeded so spectacularly while others have failed." The essence of the answer to that question is that Japan facilitated a judicious mix of State interventionism and the operation of a competitive market. Successful interventionists like Japan, "*preserved incentives for technological change by maintaining international and domestic competition and imposing performance requirements in return for any credit subsidies, import protection or restrictions on domestic entry*." In the new found wisdom of the Bank, State intervention, *per se*, is not the villain of the piece but it is the 'quality' and 'quantity' of intervention that matters.

World Development Report 2004 too reitorates the role of state, particularly providing health and education to the citizens.

We are tempted to quote Mr.Deepak N.Nayyar, the former economic adviser in the finance ministry in this context. In an exclusive interview to the *Economic Times* of Feb.25, 1992, Mr.Nayyar strongly defended Central planning and State intervention. To quote him:

"There is neither magic in the market place nor divinity in the invisible hands of the market. There is as much evidence of market failure as there is of failure in State intervention. In India, we are far more familiar with the latter than with the former. But instead of jumping to over-simplified conclusions, it is essential to recognise that markets can only serve those who are part of the market system. In rural India, 200 million people who eke out a bare subsistence, or live in absolute poverty, are not even remotely integrated with the markets. For an economy at our levels of income and development, there is vital role for the government. Planning is essential. So is State intervention, although there is a clear need for change in the nature of this intervention. Sukhamoy Chakravarty used to say that the market is a good servant but a bad master. We would do well to remember his wisdom, lest there be a confusion between means and ends."

Market is a good servant but a bad master. Market should not be allowed to rule, particularly in developing countries.

Developing countries cannot rely on markets as they are known to fail because of several imperfections.(3) One such imperfection relates to the absence of information and the presence of uncertainty faced by producers and consumers alike. In many developing countries, producers are unsure about the size of local markets, the presence of other producers, and the availability of inputs, both domestic and imported. Consumers may be unsure about the quality and availability of products and their substitutes. Moreover, in contrast to their counterparts in developed markets, producers and consumers usually lack the tools to collect information.

Another imperfection in markets of developing countries is the presence of substantial externalities. Many goods may have a high social value that is not reflected in their market price. Because such goods, such as education and health services, must be provided at a price below their cost or even free, the private sector has no incentive to produce them. The government must, therefore, be responsible for providing these goods in order to ensure a minimum of welfare (See Box 11.1).

Another argument for state intervention relates to income distribution. Market mechanisms no doubt ensure better allocation of resources, but they tend to produce unequal distribution of income.

Box 11.1 **A Public Responsibility**

Governments - and the societies they represent - often see improving outcomes in health and education as a public responsibility. They are supported in this by the international endorsement of the Millennium Development Goals which are eight in numbers:

1. Eradicate extreme poverty and hunger
2. Achieve universal primary education
3. Promote gender equality and empower women
4. Reduce child mortality
5. Improve maternal health
6. Combat HIV/AIDS, malaria and other diseases
7. Ensure environmental sustainability
8. Develop a global partnership for development

A variety of reasons lie behind this responsibility: classic welfare economics arguments for government intervention, political economy reasons for intervention in key social sectors, and appeals to fundamental human rights. Governments demonstrate their responsibility by financing, providing, or regulating the services that contribute to health and education outcomes. The services come in many shapes: building and staffing schools, subsiding hospitals, regulating water and electrical utility companies, building roads, providing cash transfers to individuals and households.

(**Source**:*World Development Report*, 2004, P.32)

Most developing countries have a very skewed pattern of income distribution. Excessive reliance on the market mechanism will not improve that distribution.

It has become a fashion on the part of critics of State intervention to quote success stories of Taiwan, South Korea and other 'Asian Tigers' to prove how only market economy can usher in economic prosperity. Little do these critics realise that in these countries, as in Japan, prosperity has been achieved *via* State intervention and not by distancing the government from economic activities. Look at Box 11.2 for what has happened in South Korea and Taiwan.

Box 11.2 **Myths Exploded**

The replacement of market forces by State control of the economy, referred to as 'command capitalism' is exemplified by South Korea. Between 1961-79, Major General Park Chung Hee's government employed access to credit, protectionism, tax incentives and control over foreign investment for rapid economic development.

In 1961, the Park government nation-alised the banking system and by 1970, the State controlled 96.4 per cent of the country's financial assets. By the 1980s, only 9.9 per cent of manufacturing was financed by retained earnings and, instead, relied on credit from government-owned or controlled financial institutions. Guaranteed access to the government-controlled credit enabled Korea's largest business groups, known as the **chaebol**, to undertake projects which were costly, risky or unprofitable in the short term.

In addition to providing secured credit, the government promoted exports through export subsidies, including low tax rates on income earned from exports, accelerated depreciation allowances and duty-free import of selected components. Exporters were allowed to sell in the domestic market at above-market prices.

Exporters were also exempted from indirect taxes on income earned from export sales. Between 1961-72, exporters enjoyed a 50 per cent reduction of corporate and income tax on export earnings. The government also provided infrastructural services such as electricity, water, transportation and communications at low rates. Export firms could also purchase industrial sites at a discount.

Korea's domestic market enjoyed substantial protection from import competition. The share of freely importable commodities in the total import volume fell from 55.6% in 1968 to 38.8% in 1979 before rising back to 61.6% 1968 to 38.8% in 1979 before rising back to 61.6% in 1980.

The Korean foreign investment code imposed stringent controls on foreign capital. Foreign equity participation remained less than 50% in over 75% of all firms involving foreign investments. Majority foreign equity ownership was allowed only in free trade zones, export-oriented sectors and in certain high-tech intensive projects.

The Korean State further interfered in labour markets to maintain wages below the market levels. In 1964, the Park government dissolved unions. The Labour Union Law prevented the formation of unions by authorising the State to render a union decision null and void. Collective bargaining was also banned beyond the local union.

State intervention in the economy also replaced the operation of market forces in Taiwan. The Taiwanese economy is dominated by State-owned and Kuomintang-owned enterprises. The State controls 92.5% of the top 50 financial institutions and owns all commercial banks, the State owned Central Bank of China controls industry's access to credit by setting interest rates.

In the 1950s, State enterprises accounted for 51% of industrial production. By the mid 1980s, 59 large state enterprises dominated the petroleum, steel, railways, electric power, tobacco and spirits, ship-building and telecommunications sectors. Furthermore, seven of the top ten enterprises are state-owned and over 50 enterprises are by the party (KMT).

However, in contrast to India, Taiwan shifted from an import-substitution strategy to export-led growth in the mid-1960s. Therefore, despite domination of the domestic market by the large industrial houses, small and medium businesses thrived on export production.

If these countries are examples of success achieved through aggressive and judiciously selective State intervention and if governments can prove results in other countries, why not in India?

In addition to exerting control over financial institutions and industrial capital, the State of Taiwan influenced exports through a tariff and tax rebate system. Exporters obtained refunds on customs duties and other taxes on imported inputs. Alternatively, domestic producers of such inputs could sell them to the exporter at the lower world market price and receive the amount of tariff duties and other taxes which the exporter would have paid had he imported instead.

Little also is realised by the critics that it is the responsiveness of the individual company to the competitive forces that matters in attaining efficiency and not whether the unit is in public sector or in the private sector. It is no secret that the most efficient car manufacturing company was still recently in the public sector and the most slothful one continues to be in the private sector. To cry hoarse against the government's role may not be correct.

It is the management that matters but not whether a unit is in private sector or government sector.

It is not that the private sector in our country has credited itself with glory so as to demand total withdrawal of the government's presence in the economy. Failures of the private sector need no detailing here but suffice it is to say that all the possible ills of an industry do exist in companies owned by private industrialists too.

The private sector has not done better than the public sector.

WHAT SHOULD BE THE FORM OF STATE INTERVENTION?

The arguments listed above prove that State intervention in business must continue, but not in the form we had during the past four decades. The intervention should be different.

One aspect of the intervention in future relates to the quality of intervention. As is too well known, intervention schemes in 'Asian Tigers' have worked closely with the market forces.

The governments in these countries had alertness to use signals emanating from the world markets to judge dynamic efficiency of individual firms. This alertness kept the firms always on their toes. Thus, both in South Korea and in Taiwan, the State has often energetically used the carrot of easy loans and other benefits and the stick of international competition to prod the firms on to the technological frontier. Fortunately, policy makers in New Delhi seem to have realised the need for such qualitative interventions. Hence the economic reforms.

Governments elsewhere used carrots of easy loans and other benefits and sticks of international competition to make firms gain competitive advantage.

The other aspect of the new intervention strategy that deserves careful attention is the selectivity of intervention (in terms of strategic sectors, products and processes in different stages of early industrialisation). Such selectivity in targeting, as opposed to indiscriminate and blanket controls and regulations, saves on scarce administrative skills and makes it easier to pinpoint social costs of policies and adjust them in response to changing technical and market conditions. World Development Report (1996) prescribes four target areas for government intervention (Read Box 11.3 for details)

Quality and selectivity of intervention is what is required in the days to come.

Box 11.3 **Rationale for Government Intervention**

- Pure public goods such as defense, law and order and environmental protection cannot be provided by private markets alone. Because everybody shares their benefits automatically, no one is willing to pay for them individually. But governments can provide them and impose their cost on tax payers.
- Goods with positive externalities, or spillover benefits, are worth more to society than to any one consumer. Public health and education, for example, reduce infection rates, add to society's knowledge base and raise productivity. Markets tend to undersupply these goods, and complimentary public funding or provision can therefore improve efficiency. Similarly markets ignore negative externalities, such as industrial pollution; regulation to curb or clean up the activity causing the pollution can improve social welfare.
- Natural monopolies such as gas pipelines, local transport networks and other infrastructure services are most efficiently provided by a single firm. Unconstrained, monopoly producers tend to overprice and undersupply these services. But the public provision or regulation can in principle be efficient.
- Imperfect information, on the part of either consumers or providers, may make markets fail. Private commercial insurance, for example, cannot efficiently insure against risks like unemployment, longevity and deteriorating health in old age, because these risks are influenced by characteristics and behaviours of the insured that the insurer cannot observe, along with the government policy and they affect large parts of the population equally and simultaneously. Governments can regulate private pensions and insurance and complement them with basic public pensions and insurance to improve efficiency and fill gaps in coverage. Governments also inspect food, set standards for airline safety, approve new drugs and regulate banks and securities markets to protect consumers who have insufficient information about the quality of these goods.

(**Source**: *World Development Report*, 1996, p.110)

The third aspect of the new intervention strategy relates to its primary orientation and goals. The East Asian State looked upon its role as that of a pioneer and promoter of industrial transformation in close collaboration and partnership with the private sector. This is very different from a State that regards the private sector at best as a necessary evil and is primarily interested in regulating and supplanting private capital, through capacity licensing and other controls and possible nationalisation. Over the years, the Indian political culture has fluctuated between these two different roles of the State, although in recent years, the emphasis has slowly shifted in reality, if not in rhetoric, towards accepting the State as a primary provider of infrastructure and enabling environment for private as well as public investments to flourish. This is particularly prominent in the role the State plays in some of the new industries. Take the Indian electronics industry. There has been remarkable transformation in nature of State involvement here. The days of preoccupation with mere turf-protection and bureaucratic licensing first under the defence ministry, and then under the department of electronics, are largely over, and the emphasis in the eighties has been more and more on State-sponsored promotional and entrepreneurial projects, providing basic infrastructure in the more liberalised and competitive environment. One of the best examples is provided by Computer Maintenance Corporation(CMC) which graduated from computer servicing to being a major systems engineering firm. Many of its large projects (including the assive railways reservation system) have been aimed at providing informational infrastructure for domestic investments often at costs below major international competitors and it is now successfully bidding for international contracts. This is the stuff dynamic comparative advantage is made of and it shows that even Indian public sector companies have the potential. Similar entrepreneurial stirrings have been noticed in recent years in the hitherto somnolent Indian telecommunications industry.

In this context, it is useful to quote the World Development Report 1996. Commenting on the need for fundamental change in the government, the Report states: *First*, the role of the government in producing and distributing goods and services must shrink dramatically. Public provision must become the exception rather than the rule. State intervention is justified only where markets fail in such areas as defense, primary education, rural roads, and some special insurance- and then only to the extent that it improves upon the market. *Secondly*, the government must stop restricting and directly controlling private commercial activity and extricate itself from intimate involvement in the financial sector, focusing instead on promoting macro-economic stability and providing a legal and institutional environment that supports private sector development and competition. *Finally*, instead of providing generous guarantees to secure adequate living standards for all, governments need to foster greater personal responsibility for income and welfare. Providing social protection is a key function of the government in all economies but in a market economy it should be mainly targeted at those vulnerable groups who need it most.[4]

State intervention is justified in areas such as defense, education, healthcare and rural roads. These are the areas where markets fail.

Conclusion

In conclusion, it maybe stated that the role of the government in future must be redefined but not ended. The redefinition must be in the direction of improving quality of intervention. This must be India's agenda in future.

We are also reminded of what John Maynard Keynes once said. "The important thing for government", said he, "is not to do things which individuals are doing already, and to do them a little better or a litter worse; but to do those things which at present are not done at all". What is not done till now is the improvement of the social sector: primary education, health, housing, nutrition and the like. Let the Government concentrate on these areas. (Also read Box 11.4.)

Box 11.4 **8th Plan on the Role of the Government**

The role of the government should be to facilitate the process of peoples' involvement in development activities by creating the right type of institutional infrastructure, particularly in rural areas. These institutions are very weak particularly in those States where they are needed the most for bringing about an improvement in the socio-demographic indicators. Encouraging voluntary agencies as well as schools, colleges and universities, to get them involved in social tasks and social mobilisation, strengthening of the Panchayat Raj Institutions, reorientation and participation of all the village-level programmes under the charge of the Panchayat Raj institutions, and helping the cooperatives to come up in the organisation and support of local economic activities, for example, are some of the steps which the government must earnestly initiate. A genuine push towards decentralisation and people's participation has become necessary.

ANALYSIS OF POLITICAL ENVIRONMENT

Chapters 8 to 11 have portrayed different dimensions of political environment. How to subject the political environment to scanning, monitoring, forecasting and assessing? This section seeks to address the question. We will touch upon two institutions: legislature and executive. Judiciary, the third political institution, is not considered here as the legal system is expected to be fairly stable and predictable thus distancing itself from the environmental analysis.

Scanning

The political environment (read legislature) is highly volatile. It throws up issues of concern very often but it takes several years before an topic crystalises and assumes a legislation. Reservation for women, for instance, has been debated for quite some time. But when it will become an act is not clear. However, scanning whatever happens inside and outside legislature is possible. Both primary and secondary sources are available for the purpose. Primary data sources include public opinion leaders, of retired judges, retired government officials, journalists, essayists, authors of books, environmental groups, NGOs, political leaders, future-oriented research establishments, academia and the like.

Secondary sources for scanning include journals, magazines, papers, specialist trade and industry publications, government documents, news channels and opinions polls conducted by different organisations.

Two points deserve special emphasis while scanning the happenings in and outside legislature. First, any political change occurs at an exponential rate; that is, change initially takes place at a slow pace and latter picks up speed as the concern of a few gains the attention of many. Thus, detecting signals of potential political change is both possible and essential. Second, the emphasis should be upon threshold signals or indicators of potential political change. The focus should be on events that may provide momentum to an emerging political change or become a catalyst for further significant change.[5]

With regard to executive or regulatory environment, scanning involves searching for recent and emerging change and for precursors of change that is going to take place - both in the long and short terms.

Scanning for short-term regulatory change involves focusing on such indicators as the adoption of new regulations, proposed modifications to existing regulations, deregulations and change in the area of application of regulations.

Scanning for long term regulatory change may involve searching for indications such as agency initiatives or investigations, parliamentary mandates, judicial directives, public petitions, other agencies' actions or initiatives and internal agency studies and activities.

The process of scanning of both short-term and long-term regulatory change is greatly facilitated by the existence of a large number of governmental and non-governmental services and organisations that specialise in tracking and analysing regulatory activities. Many of these organisations issue periodic reports and analyses of what is happening in the executive arena.

Monitoring

Monitoring of legislature is a ticklish task. The analyst is required to draw patterns out of unrelated precursors of political change. For example, in the early stages of an emerging political concern, the analyst may have only a few key indicators to suggest that a new pattern might be forming: the actions of a few unconnected local communities, the statements of a few social activists, or a visionary statements of a leading politician. As the analyst searches through the data sources noted earlier, and also through discussions with opinion makers, he or she is confronted with the task of identifying what trends are apparent, to which extent a pattern is evident, what the connections are that constitute the pattern, and what the alleged pattern signifies regarding likely further political change. These are acts of intuition on the part of the analyst. The data do not speak for themselves; the analyst must infuse them with meaning. The creation of this meaning is what allows the analyst to see beyond isolated and seemingly unrelated data points.[6]

Monitoring the changes relating to legislature, as stated earlier, is no easy job. Identifying and tracking indicators in the political arena requires a certain degree of creativity and innovativeness on the part of the analyst. He or she must always be alert as changes, which the analyst was not aware of, may suddenly crop up. For example, the opinion poll about the electoral prospects of a political party might indicate positive trend, but on the day of counting the votes polled, reversals may come true.

Monitoring of regulatory milieu is equally important. Monitoring regulatory change involves tracking the regulatory processes, also called rule-making processes. Rule making is mainly formal and tracking events relating to the process of making a rule may be relatively easy for the analyst.

Forecasting

Forecasting future political change needs to be preceded by solid understanding of the current political change. Answers to the following questions might make forecast relatively easy:

- What are the focal political trends or patterns?
- What are the trends of the political change?
- What groups are manifesting and propagating the change?
- What other groups might support or oppose the change?
- What forces are driving the political change?

Forecasting regulatory milieu may be relatively easy as it is heavily dependent upon the political environment. However, for forecasting regulatory environment, answers to the following questions are a great help:

- What is the nature of the regulatory change?
- Who supports or opposes the change?
- What key forces might propel the chance?
- What is the relevant agency';s position?[7]

Assessment

Implications of political environment for business strategies are significant because a business unit cannot operate amidst purely economic forces. It operates within political environment too. The firm, therefore, must evolve a political strategy - a set of actions designed to anticipate, respond to, and manage varied stakeholder demands. And this political strategy must be linked to the firm's market strategy.

Notwithstanding liberalisation of economics, firms are still under the influence of regulatory agencies as chapters 8 to 11 have made it amply clear. Regulatory change needs to be embedded with firm's strategy because:

- Regulatory change might affect entry barriers thus unsettling competitive strength.
- Regulatory change can influence product features and markets.
- Degree of certainty or uncertainty in the regulatory arena has a lot of influence on the general expectations about the industry and volatility in such expectations.

What happened to Coke and Pepsi in the recent past and how the two MNCs have successfully tackled the problem clearly demonstrates the linking between legislature and executive on the one end and business on the other end.

A non-government body came out with a news that cola drinks of both the companies contain excessive pesticides. Following this, there was a hue and cry across the country to ban the drink from India. Protests became so loud and clear that governments of Kerala and Karnataka issued directives to prohibit the sale of cola bottle near educational institutions.

The two cola giants unleased a blitz to counter the allegation. The companies worked out clear strategies on two fronts: to demonstrate that the drink is safe and even good for health and the other to endorse the product by popular personalities. The strategies worked. The allegation became a non-issue, protests died down and the cola bottles are back in the retail outlets.

QUESTIONS

1. Bring out the points for and against continued State intervention in business.
2. What should be the role of State *vis-a-vis* business in the years to come?

ASSIGNMENT

The popular belife is that the government should have only minimal role to play. But reality is different. We still depend on government for water and electricity. Why is this? Argue.

REFERENCES

1. Bimal Jalan, *India's Economic Crisis*, Pp. 61-62.
2. *Ibid*, p.64.
3. Michacl P. Todaro and Stephen C. Smith, *Economic Development,* 2003, Pearson, p.701.
4. *World Development Report*, 1996, p.110.
5. Lian Fahey and V.K.Narayanan, *Macroenvironmental Analysis for Strategic Management,* West Publi. Co., 1986, p. 145.
6. *Ibid*, p.146.
7. *Ibid*, p.169.

CHAPTER OUTLINE

Nature of Economic Environment

Economic Factors

— Growth Strategy
— Basic Economic System
— Economic Planning
— Industry
— National Income and Per Capita Income
— Human Resources

Claims and Counter Claims

Agenda for the Future

LEARNING OBJECTIVES

After reading this Chapter, you should be able to:

1. Describe the nature of economic environment.
2. Shortlist factors that constitute the total economic environment.
3. Argue for and against the prevailing economic environment.
4. List the areas which demand concern and action in the years to come.

12 Economic Environment

Next to the political environment, it is probably the economic environment which exerts considerable influence on business. This section is devoted to a detailed discussion of the economic environment of business.

NATURE OF ECONOMIC ENVIRONMENT

Economic environment refers to all those economic factors which have a bearing on the functioning of a business unit.

Business depends on the economic environment for all the needed inputs. It also depends on the economic environment to sell the finished goods. Naturally, the dependence of business on the economic environment is total and it is not surprising because, as it is rightly said, business is one unit of the total economy.

> Economic environment comprises variables (economic) that have a bearing on business.

The importance of an economic environment is reinforced by the fact that more and more economists (business economists to be precise) are finding place in industrial establishments. Dr.Pendse was the economic adviser to the Tatas for a long time. Richard Freeman is the Chief Economist of ICI, an American company. These two are not isolated instances. There is the Society of Business Economists in England, whose membership now is more than 600. All these members are employed in different industries, if not as economists, but in planning, marketing or finance areas. Thus, trained economists supplying macro-economic forecasts and research are found in major companies in manufacturing, commerce and finance departments.

ECONOMIC FACTORS

It is difficult to be precise about the factors which constitute the economic environment of a country. It is equally difficult to draw the lines of distinction between the political environment and the economic environment and the technological environment. The type of monetary policy, dear money policy or cheap money policy, that the government wants to pursue may be partly political and partly economic. Again, importing a particular technology may be political, economic or both. It was for this reason that we said in the beginning of this book that all these environmental factors of business are closely interdependent.

Coming to the economic environment, we list the following factors which for our purpose, constitute the economic environment of business. We are not confining ourselves to pure economic principles such as the law of demand and supply, marginal utility and the like. We include major macro and micro economic factors which have considerable influence on business. Such factors are:

- Growth strategy,
- Economic systems,
- Economic planning,
- Industry,
- Agriculture,
- Infrastructure,
- Financial and fiscal sectors,
- Removal of regional imbalances,
- Price and distribution controls,
- Economic reforms,
- Human resources, and
- Per capita and national income.

All these have been explained in greater detail in this and subsequent chapters in this section.

Growth Strategy

Growth strategy of India was based on Soviet model.

The economic environment which now prevails in our country is the result of the economic growth strategy relentlessly pursued during the past five decades by the Government of India. It is therefore advisable to recollect the growth strategy. It may be recalled that the growth strategy followed was based on the Soviet Planning model which gave central role to the government in the control and direction of economic activity. Following the Soviet experience, it was believed that the savings rate in the economy and the growth rate, could be increased if India invested heavily in the capital goods and heavy industry sectors at the expense of the consumer goods sector. Since the investments in these sectors were high, largely beyond the capability of the private sector and profitability was low, it followed that such investments would have to be undertaken by the State.

The Second Five Year Plan (1956) was quite clear that "*It cannot be emphasised too strongly that unless steps are taken to augment rapidly the output of the means of production and to build up the fuel and energy resources which are so vital to development, the scale and pace of advancement in the coming years will be inhibited.*" As for policies to achieve these objectives, the Plan went on to state that:

"*In some cases, fiscal or price incentives may have to be relied on; in others, a licensing system may be essential; in still others, fixation of profit margins, allocation of scarce raw materials or other regulatory devices may be necessary... If the targets of planned investment are to be achieved, means have to be found to secure that the necessary resources do in fact, become available and are not devoted to consumption.*"

Market is a good servant but a bad master. Market should not be allowed to rule, particularly in developing countries.

The State emerged both as the mobiliser of savings as well as an important investor and owner of capital. Since the State was to be the primary agent of economic change, it followed that private sector activities had to be strictly regulated and controlled to conform to the objectives of the State policy.

Under this policy, foreign trade had a relatively small role, partly because of the belief that trade was biased against developing countries and primary producers and partly because of the intellectual conviction that export prospects were severely limited. The First Five Year Plan (1951) was practically silent on exports. It only highlighted the limitations to the prospects of increasing export earnings since the "*prices obtainable for exports depend on world factors and may, therefore, be subject to large variations*." The Second Five Year Plan (1956) attempted a projection of balance of trade but concluded that no significant increase in export earnings in the short run could be expected. The intellectual basis for pessimism about exports which was widely shared by the development economists of the time, was broadly the same as that articulated by Nurkse in his '*Export Lag*' thesis. The theory postulated that the exports of a primary producing country tend to lag behind the rate of increase in the international trade.

The growth followed earlier resulted in the negligence of agriculture.

The growth strategy also meant, in the early years of planning, a relative neglect of public investment in agriculture. This negligence of agriculture was supported by the prevailing view that a growing labour force in the developing countries could only be absorbed in industry, and that in the early stages of industrialisation, it was necessary for agriculture to contribute to the building up of modern industry by providing cheap labour. A faster development of industry was the central objective of planning.

The above is a thumbnail sketch of the growth strategy followed by the planners in the past four decades. The strategy has been subject to severe criticism particularly during the late 80s when the era of liberalisation was set in motion. The criticisms are: the neglect of exports and trade opportunities, excessive protectionism and import substitution, undue reliance on physical controls, inefficiency of the public sector and total neglect of agriculture. Much of this criticism is however exaggerated.[1] The growth strategy did contribute to the overall growth of the economy as mentioned in the later part of this chapter and in other relevant portions of this section.

Basic Economic Systems

Just as there are two political philosophies, *viz*., democracy and totalitarianism, there are three distinct economic philosophies, *viz*., capitalism, socialism and communism. The system of ***capitalism*** stresses the philosophy of individualism believing in private ownership of all agents of production, in private sharing of distribution processes that determine the functional rewards of each participant, and in the individual expression of consumer choice through a free market place. In its political manifestation, capitalism may fall in a range between extreme individualism and no government (anarchism) and the acceptance of some State sanctions as mentioned by Adam Smith and the later philosophers of modern capitalism.

Mention should be made of the Welfare State concept which has developed in recent years. This is a modification of modern capitalism that provides for an increasing degree of State regulation when certain deficiencies appear in the economy. These limitations placed on the free market operations such as workmen's compensation law, provision for social security, laws regulating industrial relations, or direct State financial aid to housing and agriculture, to name but a few, are accepted as a result of the members of a democracy becoming dissatisfied with certain conditions that prevailed or might prevail without these measures. The Welfare State is short of State socialism, in that it does not sanction the public ownership of the activities that are regulated. Some, infact, argue that the acceptance of certain welfare state objectives is necessary to provide flexibility for capitalism, otherwise it might become static and be destroyed because of certain faults. Welfare actions then become modifications within the framework that constitute the basic postulates of capitalism.[2] USA is the best example for capitalism.

The concept of welfare state has become very common now. Welfare state is a modification of capitalism that provides for state intervention when certain deficiencies occur.

Under ***socialism***, the tools of production are to be organised, managed and owned by the government, with the benefits accruing to the public. A strong public sector, agrarian reforms, control over private wealth and investment and national self-reliance are the other planks of socialism.

Under socialism, the tools of production are to be organized, managed and owned by the government.

Socialism does not involve an equal division of existing wealth among the people but advocates the egalitarian principle. It believes in providing employment to all and emphasises suitable rewards to the efforts put in by every worker. Also called *Fabian* socialism, this philosophy is followed in our country and other social democratic countries in the world.

Communism goes beyond socialism to abolish private property and property rights to income.

Communism goes further to abolish all private property and property rights to income. The State would own and direct all instruments of production. Sharing in the distributive process would have no relationship to private property since this right would not exist.[3] Alternatively called *Marxism*, communism was followed in Russia, China and East European countries.

Table 12.1 draws a comparison among the three economic systems.

Each economic philosophy has its own strengths and weaknesses. Capitalism, for example, encourages individual initiative, allows the market forces to have free play, promotes a competitive spirit and directs the scarce resources to most profitable uses. The weakness of capitalism stems from the fact that it results in gross inequities of income, recurrence of trade cycles because of the free play of market forces, exploitation of the poor by the rich and the corrupt influence of vested interests over the State. Capitalism results in the wastage of resources. It has a devastating effect on the environment. Finally, people in capitalist societies earn more and consequently indulge in excessive and wasteful expenditure on consumer durables and luxuries.

In common parlance, the terms *socialism* and *communism* are used interchangeably. The East European countries are often called socialist countries though they follow Marxist ideologies.

The great October Revolution of 1917 saw, for the first time, the emergence of a State based on Marxist principles. It was Lenin who set up a communist state in Russia and from here, the ideology spread to Czechoslovakia, Poland, Hungary, Rumania, Yugoslavia and China. Firmly entrenched in these countries, communism appeared to have answers for all the ills associated with capitalism. But cracks developed within the edifice built over a period of more than six decades. The structure started crumbling all of a sudden. We recently witnessed country after country going back on communism and almost embracing capitalism. Several reasons have contributed to the reversal of the Marxist economy. These reasons incidentally testify to the inherent weakness of communism.

The major weakness of Marxism is the denial of individual freedom. One of the essential requirements of human organism is freedom - to work, to earn, to express, to choose and to indulge in the expenditure of one's choice. This freedom is denied to people. The followers of Marxism believed that the ideology would guarantee individual freedom. This expectation was belied as it became clear in the communist countries. No individual freedom existed in these countries, contrary to the theoretical claims made about it.

Major weakness of communism is the denial of individual freedom.

Secondly, communism assumes total commitment of people to work and to contribute to the country's welfare. This has not been forthcoming from people in the communist countries. People worked more or less as they work under capitalism, being driven by the twin forces of the carrot and the stick. Infact, there was more slackness and more pilfering on the part of the workers and probably more corruption on the part of the management than in the capitalist societies.

Table 12.1 **Capitalism, Socialism and Communism Compared**

Characteristics (1)	*Capitalism* (2)	*Socialism* (3)	*Communism* (4)
Economic Markets	Freedom to compete with the right to invest	Limited competition with State-owned industries	Absence of competition with State-owned markets and industries.
Individual Incentives	Profits and wages in relation to one's ability and willingness to work	Profits recognised. Wages fairly in relation to efforts	Profits not allowed. Workers urged to work for the glory of the State.
Capital Sources	Capital invested by owners who may also borrow on credit. Capital may be reinvested from profits. Depreciation is legal	Obtained from owners and from State-issued bonds for State-owned industries. Depreciation permitted	State provides all resources to start business owned by the State. No depreciation
Labour	Workers are free to select an employer and an occupation	Workers allowed to select occupation. State planning encourages employment	The State determines one's employer and employment.
Management	Managers are selected on the basis of ability. Managers have freedom to make decisions	Managers in State-owned industries are answerable to the State. Non-monetary rewards emphasised	Key managers must be party members. Absence of freedom to make decisions.
Business Ownership	Individuals have the right to own a business and to contract with others	State owns the basic industries. Other businesses may exist	State owns all productive capacity including communes.
Risk Assumption	Losses assumed by owners. May transfer business risks to other businesses through insurance	People assume risks of State-owned industries. Losses taken from taxes	Economic production owned by the State. Risks assumed by the State. Losses reduce standard of living.

(**Source**: Vernon A Musselman and Eugene H Hughes, *Introduction to Modern Business-Issues & Environment,* p.20).

Thirdly, the communist economies failed to achieve significant economic growth. The rate of growth of these economies has been markedly lower than that of the economies relying on market forces. One of the most striking failures of State or collective ownership has been in agriculture where a super-power like Soviet Union, possessing one-sixth of the land surface on earth, found itself unable to feed its people even after 70 years of revolution.

Fourthly, equality which was the main plank of Marxists, did no succeed in the communist countries. The basic principle that every organised society is subject to stratification very much applied to communist societies also. Years back, therefore, the communist motto of "*for each according to his ability to each according to his need*" was changed in the Soviet Union without fanfare and almost surreptitiously to "*from each according to his work*". The Stakhanovites made a big dent into the communist theory by

The communist ideology of "for each according to his ability, to each according to his need was changed to from each according to his work".

being given economic rewards for their work and the differentiation that has been subsequently introduced consists not so much in the money wage but payments in kind and in privilege to those who occupy higher positions in the hierarchy; this, if translated into money, would show a very substantial difference.

Communist leaders did not set themselves as good examples.

Fifthly, the rulers themselves did not set fine examples for the followers to emulate. Lenin lived, till the end of his life, in one room in Kremlin whereas Brezhnev lived in the equivalent of many palaces and owned a fleet of most expensive of the world's cars. Late Caucescu and his wife in Romania lived in style and led a pompous life. Public anger against the couple was so much that together they died being shot by prosecutors mercilessly. More than 300 bullets were found on the dead bodies of Caucescu and his wife. The number of bullets bear testimony to the public wrath against the leaders who proclaimed equality but did not practise it.

Public sector units have become private properties to enjoy and squander.

Sixthly, communism has been obsessed with the rights of workers. This obsession has lead to the tendency to strike work, often on unjustifiable grounds. Walk in the streets of Calcutta or Thiruvananthapuram, you will find red flags hoisted at every business or industrial establishment. Public sector units have been taken as private properties to enjoy and squander.

Seventhly, the followers of communism seem to have several contradictions. One such contradiction which is too conspicuous is the attitude towards religion. Seventy years of communist rule in the erstwhile USSR did not help eradicate religion. Same is true in West Bengal and Kerala.

Finally, communism collapsed because of its inherent weakness - lack of flexibility and the absence of resilience. Capitalism survives because of its flexibility. It abandons the market where the survival of people is at stake. Look at the way the government intervenes in chosen areas even in the US economy.

Socialism seems to fall between capitalism and communism, partaking the strong points of both the philosophies and avoiding their weaknesses at the same time. It is for this reason that several developing countries of Asia, Latin America and Africa have adopted socialistic philosophy.

But the experience of several countries, particularly the African bloc, belies the expectations pinned on socialism. As the *Economic Times* of July 6, 1986 commented, the "common error of African rulers was to stick with economic policies derived from the half-understood European socialism of 1950s and earlier. Governments, they seem to have thought, could create wealth by decree. People's untidy lives could be improved by government management. So they set up huge bureaucracies (which they could not afford to pay properly, and which, therefore, become corrupt as well as idle) to regulate every aspect of life. They paid for government projects from funds that were meant to pay for crops, and held down food prices so that farmers subsidised towns-people. They passed laws saying that foreign currency could be exchanged only at a rate far below what the market said it was worth".

We chose mixed economy, a midway between capitalism and communism, as our economic philosophy. Closely resembling socialism, the concept of mixed economy admits the existence of private enterprises along with public ownership. The economic set-up under this philosophy is split up into three parts:

We followed mixed economy-midway between capitalism and communism. The mixed economy is like the amber colour on a signal post which keeps the driver of a vehicle guessing about what his next move should be.

- Sectors in which both production and distribution are entirely managed and controlled by the State to the complete exclusion of private enterprise;
- Sectors in which the State and private enterprise jointly participate in production as well as in distribution and
- Sectors in which the private enterprise has complete access subject only to the general control and regulation of the State.

The Industrial Policy of 1956 has clearly demarcated the areas meant for each of these three sectors of the economy. The concept of mixed economy has guided our economy for the past three-and-a-half decades.

The mixed economy has its share of criticisms. It has, for example, not enabled its followers to become either Americans or Russians. The mixed economy has been approximately compared to the amber colour on a signal post which keeps the driver of a vehicle guessing about what his next move should be.

Economic Planning

A mixed economy is necessarily a planned economy. It does not mean simply a controlled economy in which, the government interferes in economic matters through fiscal and monetary policies, but it is an economy in which the government has a clear and definite economic plan. The public sector will have to operate according to certain priorities and to realise specific social and economic goals. Naturally, the public sector should have an economic plan. At the same time, the government cannot leave the private sector to function in its own unorganised way.

The government has to prepare and implement a comprehensive economic plan integrating the private sector with the public sector. It is for these reasons that we have been having economic planning since 1951 when the First Five Year Plan was launched.

We have had five decades of economic planning. All the five-year plans were designed to achieve four important long-term objectives, *viz.*,

- Increase production to the maximum possible extent so as to achieve a higher level of national and *per capita* income;
- Achieve full employment;
- Reduce inequalities of income and wealth and
- Set up a socialist society based on equality and justice and the absence of exploitation.

Massive investments were made in all the five-year plans to realise these objectives. Table 12.2 gives the allocations of the plans.

Table 12.2 **Pattern of Resource Allocation in India's Plans**

(Percentage)

Heads of Development	*I*	*II*	*III*	*IV*	*V*	*VI*	*VII*	*VIII*	*IX*	*X*
Agriculture & Irrigation	37.0	20.9	20.5	23.3	22.1	22.2	20.2	20.6	19.4	20.06
Power	7.6	9.7	14.6	18.6	18.8	16.7	17.4	18.7	25.4	26.47
Industry	4.9	24.1	22.9	19.7	24.3	26.5	23.7	18.8	8.2	4.00
Transport & Communication	26.4	27.0	24.6	19.5	17.4	16.0	17.1	18.7	19.8	21.30
Social Services	24.1	18.3	17.4	18.9	17.4	18.6	21.6	23.2	27.2	28.17
Total	100.0	100.0	100.0	100.0	100.0	100.0	100.0	100.0	100.0	100.0

(**Source**: *Economic Survey and Planning Commission Annual Reports*).

Industry

In the mid-1960s, India had a better industrial base and possessed more pre-requisites for industrial growth than South Korea, Malaysia, Taiwan, Thailand and Indonesia. Since then, the country has

During the mid-1960s, India was ahead of Asian Tigers in respect of industrial base.

succeeded in creating a virtually autarkic economy, where all outputs and factors were subject to rigid price and quantity controls; where investment was strictly rationed; where there were multiple barriers to entry, investment, foreign trade, and competition, and where the objective of the financial system was to supply subsidised development funds irrespective of returns.[4] Consequently, all the countries, mentioned above, have overtaken India and are far ahead in industrial growth.

But the administrative controls held the country behind the Tigers.

Various administrative controls have held the country back in its road towards industrialisation. Industrial licensing, product reservation for public sector and small scale industries, MRTP and asset classification of companies, foreign exchange regulation, tariffs and quotas, labour market rigidities are some such draconian measures which hampered the country's progress. Though some of them have been lifted with the advent of new economic policy, several of them are still in force.

One way of assessing industrial development is to classify industries (on the end-use basis) and measure their growth over a period of time. Table 12.3 shows the classification of industries and their respective production growth rates from 1999 to 2004.

As seen from the table, growth rate in basic goods (those used in further production process) reached a low during 2001-02 but picked up two years later. Growth rate in capital goods (plants and machinery) fluctuated violably touching negative rate in 2001-02 and jumping to 13 per cent after two years. More or less same pattern is witnessed in consumer durables but the rate has been steady in consumer non-durables. The overall industrial growth rate has been six per cent now, five per cent later,

Table 12.3 **Industrial Production Growth Rates (%)**

	1990-00	*2000-01*	*2001-02*	*2002-03*	*2003-04(P)*
Basic goods	5.5	3.7	2.6	4.9	5.4
Capital goods	6.9	1.8	-3.4	10.5	13.1
Intermediate goods	8.8	4.7	1.5	3.9	6.3
Consumer goods	5.7	8.0	6.0	7.1	7.1
Consumer durables	14.1	14.5	11.5	-6.3	11.5
Consumer non-durables	3.2	5.8	4.1	12.0	5.7
P=Provisional					

(**Source:** RBI, *Handbook of Statistics on The Indian Economy*, 2003-04)

rises to eight per cent and falls back to five per cent again (See Fig.12.1). A sustained double digit growth rate over a period of atleast one decade is essential if the country were to be bracketed along with industrialised countries in the world.

India has potential to become a global player in industrial sector.

Past need not blind us from realising the potential possessed by the country in terms of industrial growth. Stated differently, India is well-poised to become a global player in the industrial sector. Potential is vast and prospects are varied as the following points indicate.

1. As of now, industry contributes nearly 26 per cent of GDP as compared to 53 per cent in China and 41 per cent in Korea (See Table 12.4).

There is the talk about India unshackling itself from the eight per cent growth rate in GDP syndrome. But can country achieve this without manufacturing is the question often raised. The answer is negative considering some simple arithmetics.

Agriculture cannot grow at more than 2 to 3 per cent trend rate. If industry grows at 8 per cent, services need to grow at 12 per cent for India to cross 8 per cent growth rate in GDP. If manufacturing grows at 8 per cent, services will need to grow at 10 per cent. Eventhough services sector is India's

Figure 12.1 **Industrial Growth Through Plans (Annual %)**

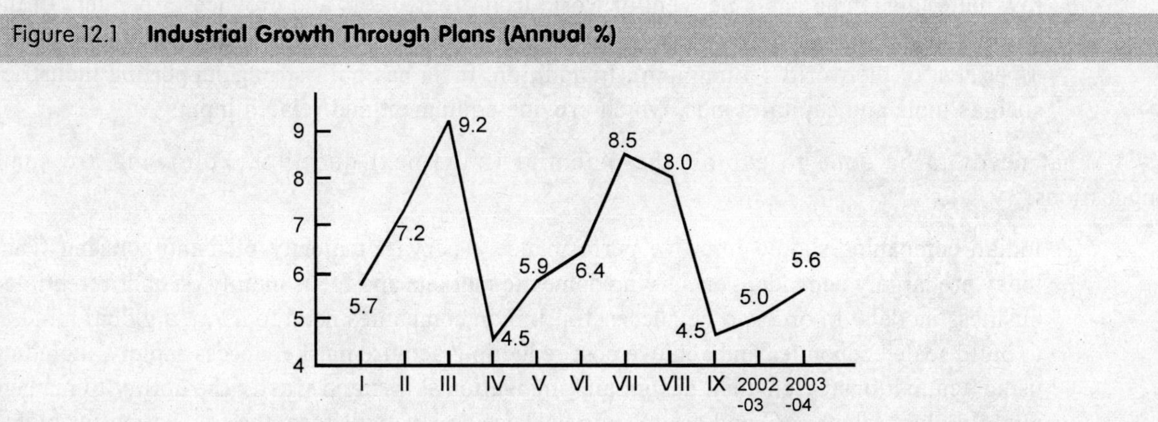

Table 12.4 **Economic Activities' Share in GDP (%)**

	China	*India*	*Korea*
Agriculture	14.8	22.7	4.4
Industry	52.9	25.7	41.4
Services	32.3	51.6	54.2

(***Source:*** "World Bank" as cited in *The Economic Times*, dated November 5, 2004)

strength (See Table 12.4), it has grown in double digits only once in the last 10 years. Obviously, India needs to lift the growth rate of manufacturing to double digits for GDP to grow at 8 per cent plus. In otherwords, industry should overtake services for the GDP to raise above 8 per cent. India cannot afford to ignore industries sector.[(5)]

Industrial sector should overtake services sector, if India were to attain 8 per cent growth in GDP.

2. There is enough scope for making globally competitive manufacturing carried out in India. In diverse sections-pharma, chemicals, textiles, metals, refining, cement, auto and ancillaries-Indian firms are performing competitively and are exporting major chunks of output. Any new plant coming up in any industry can be designed to become globally competitive. Several MNCs are willing to export out of India. Suzuki and Hyundai, for example, view India as a car club. ABB plans to make India a global sourcing base for some of its products which implies closing its European factories.

3. According to a study conducted by McKinsey and Co., a second and much bigger wave of manufacturing outsourcing is due to arrive. The first wave was $460 billion and consisted of low-tech items like toys and garments. The second wave could reach $1.6 trillion and will comprise high-tech areas like automotives, engineering and chemicals. When the second wave really emerges, two countries-India and China–will be the beneficiaries.[6]

McKinsey report says that a second a a much bigger wave of manufacturing outsourcing is due to arrive.

4. India has large low-cost and skilled workforce. The country has one of the world's largest labour pools (along with China). This large labour pool will limit increases in wage rates for the next 20 years. Besides, India has a high availability of engineers, producing over 400,000 every year, next only to China's 490,000 and nearly 25 times Thailand's 17,000. In addition to engineers, India produces 850,000 graduates every year and over 70,000 diploma-holders. As a result, the country has strong engineering capabilities whether in redesigning processes, products, or equipment, or in ensuring high quality production.[7]

India has large low-cost and skilled workforce. The country has one of the world's largest labour pools.

5. India has vast raw materials supply base. The country has abundant raw material, e.g., cotton (India is the third-largest producer of cotton accounting for 3 per cent of world output), ferrous

raw materials (India has 5 per cent of world iron-ore deposits and produces 3 per cent of the world's steel), and non-ferrous raw materials (She has 4 per cent banzite deposits and produces 3 per cent of the world's aluminum). In addition, India has built strong supporting industries such as tools and capital goods, which provide equipment and related inputs.

What needs to be done to exploit the potential is the next question. Following are some suggestions:

Indian firms must come out of the local-markets-enough mindset. They must build scale economies and achieve cost reduction.

(i) Indian companies should improve performance. The vast majority of manufacturing firms today are largely dependent on serving domestic markets and focus mainly on undifferentiated business models. In order to be successful, Indian companies need to adopt a global mindset to build scale economies and achieve cost reduction; acquire market access rapidly, including using acquisitions; strengthen design and innovation skills; and master the ability to manage a world-class talent pool and organisation. These actions will form the foundation for global growth and will require to be supported by a judicious choice of market segments and business models.

(ii) India's domestic market needs to be strengthened. China's success in industrial sector is build on a strong domestic market, achieved through the systematic reduction of indirect taxes from 32 per cent to 15 per cent of retail price in 1994. In India too the government should replace all indirect taxes on goods such as excise, sales tax (Central and State), octroi, and entry tax with a single nationwide VAT. It should also reduce tax levels from their current 25-30 per cent to 15 per cent of the retail price and duties on all imports to a single rate of 10 per cent by 2007.

Manufacturing clusters, on the lines of China's SEZ's, should be encouraged.

(iii) Manufacturing clusters need to be encouraged. Clusters in the form of special economic zones (SEZs) are a key feature in China's success at the industrial front. In India a lot more needs to be done before its SEZs can be considered world class.

Indian Labour laws need to reformed and made more flexible. Even the so called communist China's labour laws are more industry friendly than India's.

(iv) Labour laws need to be reformed. Many countries have created labour flexibility and attracted labour intensive industries (e.g. Thailand and Malaysia). Even a communist country such as China is much more flexible in its labour laws than India. To make Indian manufacturers globally competitive, the government should allow the use of contract labour for all activities (not just those of temporary nature), repeal S.5B of the Industrial Disputes Act and minimise the number of inspections.

Additionally, skill development should receive serious attention. To meet industry's need for technically qualified people (1.5 million trained technicians required every year till 2015-as compared to the current ITI output of 700,000-in order to meet the incremental requirement of 20 million skilled technicians by 2015), the government should set up a private-public-sector partnership to revamp the ITIs and encourage private sector investment in vocational training.[8]

National Income and Per Capita Income

Every sector of the economy employs natural, human and material resources and contributes to the aggregate flow of goods and services during a time period, usually specified as one year. This aggregate flow of goods and services represents the total income earned by factors of production employed during the year and is popularly called *national income* or national product. The rate of growth of the national income in an economy is an indication of the pace at which the economy has been growing. A high growth rate indicates that the economy is a developed one. Low growth rate signals that the economy is a developing or a poor one.

Furthermore, a high national income indicates that the economy is developed and the overall environment is favourable for business growth.

Table 12.5 gives details about national income and per capita income since 1980.

Table 12.5 **National Income and Per Capita Income at Current Prices**

	National Income (Rs.Crore)	*Per capita Income (Rs.)*
1980-81	1,10,685	1,630
1990-91	4,18,074	4,983
1991-92	4,79,612	5,602
1992-93	5,45,434	6,255
1993-94	6,26,957	7,060
1994-95	7,44,663	8,237
1995-96	8,56,663	9,473
1996-97	9,85,162	10,708
2000-01	17,02,454	16,701
2001-02	18,64,292	17,978
2002-03	11,61,902	11,013
2003-04	12,66,005	11,799
2004-05	13,27,627	12,263
2005-06	11,33,837	13,035

Note: Data from 2002-03 onwards are at constant (1993-94) prices.

Looking at the figures available in Table 12.5, it maybe stated that our performance compares favourably with that achieved by the currently high income countries when they were in their transformation phase. For example, our national income growth during 1950-1994 has been reported higher than that of the UK, France and Germany during the mid-19th to mid-20th countries, and about the same as the performance of the USA which was one of the most developing nations at that time.

Data relating to national and per capita incomes suggest that India is on par with currently high income countries when they were in their transformation phase.

However, it must be admitted that our growth rates have been less than the plan targets (see Table 12.6) and below the required growth rate of about 10% per annum. Reasons are obvious.

The primary reason for low growth levels in the national income is the deficiency in investment. This is followed by high capital-output ratio, low agricultural and industrial growth and population explosion. The last factor is mainly responsible for low per capita income, notwithstanding satisfactory growth in the national income.

Human Resource

Human resources constitute an important constituent of the total economic environment. There are several reasons which bring out the crucial role of people in an economy. In the first place, people provide ready market for goods produced and services rendered by business establishments. With more than 100 crore people, our country offers a vast market. This explains the reason why MNCs are keen in investing their funds in India. Secondly, people together constitute one of the factors of production. It is not enough if a country has land and capital, it needs labour (human resource) to put the other factors

Table 12.6 **Targets and Actuals in National Income**

(annual percentages)

	Targets	*Actuals*
I Plan	2.1	3.6
II Plan	4.5	4.0
III Plan	5.6	2.4
IV Plan	5.7	3.3
V Plan	4.4	5.0
VI Plan	5.2	5.4
VII Plan	5.0	5.7
VIII Plan	5.6	5.7

(**Source**: *Eighth Plan*, and *Economic Survey*).

Japan is an example of a nation which has prospered because of its people. Burma and Sri Lanka are the countries which are lagging behind because of people.

to proper use. Our country is endowed with a vast pool of scientists, technicians, administrators, managers, software experts, engineers, professors, doctors, civil servants, strategists, financial wizards and experts in marketing. All these professionals will help run organisations successfully. Thirdly, the degree of economic prosperity, for example, of a nation depends on the quality of its people. Japan's prosperity owes it to its people. The country has been able to reach its present status thanks to the motivated and hard working people. Lack of natural resources has not hindered the country's prosperity. Burma has all the ingredients to become rich-oil (first country in Asia to discover oil), foodgrains, timber, precious rubies, tungsten-but has failed to become one, thanks to its people who are generally not risk takers and majority of them are tribals. Same is the story with Sri Lanka. The country has rich potential to export natural rubber, tea, copra and precious stones. Thanks to the people who seem to believe more in violence and killings than in peace, Sri Lanka could not prosper economically. Fourthly, our economy has entered into a new and exiting phase thanks to the new economic policy measures initiated from the start of the 1990s. In order to sustain the momentum of growth, we need people with competence and motivation. Finally, people need economic growth just as prosperity demands the services of individuals. Whatever is produced should be used by people. It is only then that the economy will have served its purpose (Read Box 12.1).

Box 12.1 **Growth and Workers**

Economic growth is good for workers. This has long been true for those living in what are now the world's rich countries, and it has been spectacularly true for the newly industrialising economies of East Asia over the past few decades. Growth has reduced poverty through rising employment, increased labour productivity and higher real wages. Growth also tends to reduce poverty and inequality, including inequality between men and women. For today's low and middle income countries, the fear that growth will primarily benefit capital, create few jobs, and fail to raise wages is unfounded. Vietnam's workers are now some of the poorest in the world. If their country follows the path of other East Asian success, they could enjoy a doubling of their labour incomes in a decade or so.

(**Source**: *World Development Report 1995,* p.3)

India is the second largest populated country in the world with the total population being 102.7 cr according to 2001 census. This forms about 16 per cent of the world population. But in area wise, India has got only 2.4 per cent of the land area in the world. Comparisons are interesting. US maintains only 6 per cent of the world's population but has been gifted with 7 per cent of the total land area, Russia has 5 per cent and 12 per cent respectively.

India has 16 per cent of world's population but occupies only 2.4 per cent of the total land area.

Table 12.7 shows the population trend in India.

Table 12.7 **Population Trend**

(Crore)

Year	*Population*	*Year*	*Population*
1901	23.80	1951	36.10
1911	25.20	1961	43.92
1921	25.10	1971	54.81
1931	27.90	1991	84.63
1941	31.87	2001	102.70

(**Source**: *Eighth Five Year Plan*, Vol.1, and *Census of India 2001*).

There is another dimension to the problem of overpopulation. It is said that out of 185 nations in the world, we rank not first, second or 10th but 111th in population growth. It is also said that the population is growing more slowly than the world's two-thirds of the nations. Comparisons of this type have purely academic interest. The fact is, we have too many mouths to feed and this has been a drag on our development.

However, it goes to the credit of our country that it was the first in the world to adopt family panning as a State Policy. From the First Plan itself, the need to control population was recognised. During the Second Plan, though both these Plans indicated an official policy to control population, there was no effective implementation. The results of the 1961 Census confirmed the half-hearted efforts at population control and imparted a new urgency to the programme. The Third Plan recognised, for the first time, family planning which till then had relied heavily on the traditional clinical referral approach.

India deserves credit for its pioneering role in promoting family planning in the country.

The Fourth Plan described family planning as a programme deserving the highest priority. It introduced the time and target approach to family planning. The Fifth Plan continued to give this priority status to family planning. In April 1976, the population policy in India received a new impetus, when the government issued a statement in its national population policy. The statement contained several new measures and it reflected the government's realisation that the population explosion had reached a critical stage and was proving to be a major stumbling block in its efforts to raise the living standards of the masses. The programme underwent a change during the emergency, when it incorporated compulsory approach to family planning. In 1977, the nomenclature was changed to family welfare programme from family planning programme. During1977-79, the performance of the programme was extremely poor. The Sixth Plan listed limited population growth as one of its main objectives. The Seventh and Eighth plans too did emphasise the need for limited population growth.

All these efforts have not gone waste. The message of the red triangle has spread far and wide. It is gratifying to note that an illiterate villager now talks about the need for a small family and they accept family planning techniques with appreciation. A visit to a government hospital in a small town is a sight to be believed. The beds in the hospital are ever full with young mothers undergoing treatment after they have undergone tubectomies. There is no need to talk about the problem in cities. People are aware of the need for and advantage of spacing child births and stopping after the first two. Seeds for better tomorrow are sown and the fruits will be reaped in the years to come.

The years to come seem to hold bright future for India. The country has the largest number of young people in the world today. We have nearly 65 million children below 15 years of age, and as many as 400 million youngsters below the age of 23 years. These young people will join the ranks of working people in the next few years, thus creating a huge surge of productive activity, incomes and savings. India's young people can be an asset to the global economy because while India's population will be getting younger in the coming decade, the population of all the developed countries, including China and Russia, will be getting older. The richer countries will face shortage of working age people while India will have surplus of them. Obviously, India can bring in more than Rs.8.8 lakh crores of revenues every year from the richer countries and create 40 million additional jobs by providing a variety of services to the rest of the world.

CLAIMS AND COUNTER CLAIMS

What has been the result of all these developmental efforts? There have been claims and counter claims about the outcome. Official agencies claim that huge investments produced positive results. But these claims are not acceptable to the economists, intellectuals and politicians who do not see eye to eye with the government agencies. What these claims and counter claims are?

> The new government at the centre is serious about economic reforms, compulsions from the left parties notwithstanding. India is one of the fastest growing economies in the world. Domestic market is booming, jobs are multiplying and salaries are rising.

On the achievement side, the claims made relate to industry, agriculture, infrastructure, foreign trade, growth rate of the economy, control of inflation and the standard of living of the people. It is asserted that significant progress has been made in all these and many more during the last five decades of economic planning.

Of late, economy has been doing exceedingly well. The new government at the Centre has, despite the influence of the Communist parties, is serious about pursuing economic reforms. India is one of the countries in the category of fastest-growing economies in the world; the domestic market is booming; new jobs are being created and salaries are raising; and prospects of outsourcing are brighter.

The following developments, in particular, have made the Indian economy robust.[9]

1. Huge investments have been proposed in the near future. Between 2004-06, India will invest Rs.234,600 crore on infrastructure. Of this, 43 per cent will go to power sector, 20 per cent to roads and the rest to other sectors of the economy, with a consequent multiplier effect.

What is interesting is that bulk of this investments is being made by companies through internal accruals and motivated by the need to meet growing domestic and international demand.

Investments in the past were a contrast to those proposed now. The earlier investments were fueled by unrealistic hopes about the size of the domestic market and a desire to make quick money from a safe market created by high tariff walls. Investments in the past were financed through debt (now lying in the form of NPAs-non-performing assets in banks) or money raised from public issues.

Indian economy has obviously entered into an investment-led growth phase.

> In terms of business efficiency, India's rank has moved from 51 to 22, and in terms of economic performance from 22 to 12. Profitability of 500 companies has risen from 6.02 per cent in 2000-01 to 8.86 per cent in 2003-04.

2. Competitiveness of the India's economy is high, the country being ranked 34 in IMD's World Competitiveness Report 2004,, up from 50 in 2003. Additionally, in terms of business efficiency, India's rank has moved from 51 to 22, and in terms of economic performance from 22 to 12. The dismantling of industrial licensing system, rationalisation of tax regime, removal of competition-stifling tariffs and the like have boosted India's competitiveness. Profitability of *Business Today 500* companies has increased from 6.02 per cent in 2000-01 to 8.86 per cent in 2003-04.

3. The outsourcing boom has vastly contributed to India's richness. The country has emerged as hot spot for outsourcing IT, ITEs, pharmaceuticals, engineering design, R&D, clinical research, textiles, and auto components. Table 12.8 shows revenue accruing to India thanks to outsourcing. Outsourcing is going to be much more attractive in the days to come.

Table 12.8 **Outsourcing in Numbers**

(Figures in $ billion)

	2004	*2009*
IT & ITES	15.80	50.00
Pharma	0.61	3.00
Textiles	14.00	50.00*
Auto Components	0.80	2.60

**By 2010*

(***Source:*** *Business Today*, September 12, 2004)

4. Increasingly, Indian corporate sector is exploiting global opportunities. Companies are realising that a global presence can help insulate them from the vagaries of the domestic market. Take the example of Tata Motors which recently acquired Daewoo Commercial Vehicle Company of South Korea and is also investing Rs.9200 cr. in Bangladesh. Tata Steel has plans to acquire NetSteel (of Singapore) for Rs.1313 cr. The global foray of Tata Motors and Tata Steel is the culmination of the efforts of Indian firms to establish their presence outside India. In the 1990s, Indian manufacturing companies were considered not competitive enough to compete globally. Today, in areas as diverse as forgings, water pumps, commercial vehicles, and a range of auto components, Indian firms are catering to the global market. This is in addition to businesses such as IT and Pharma where Indian companies have already established themselves as lead players.

Indian companies have increasingly exploiting global opportunities by acquiring foreign firms.

5. Indian companies have become better pay masters. Salaries have risen by anything between 10 to 25 per cent. High-growth and high-attrition industries such as IT, ITES, telecom, banking and financial services have registered highest rise in remunerating employees (See Table 12.9).

Table 12.9 **Salary Hikes (%)**

	2003	*2004*
IT	15	17
ITES	23	25
Telecom (Services)	10	12
Insurance	23	25
Banking (Retail)	12	15

(***Source:*** *Business Today*, Sept., 12, 2004)

What is significant is an increase in salaries has resulted in a consequent increase in discreationary spending, thus, adding to the demand for goods and services.

6. Some other developments have also contributed to the growing demand. One billion people supported by high growth rates and a decrease in the number of the poor constitute a huge market. Since the 1990s the number of poor in India has declined from 35 percent of the population to 26 percent. The number of middle class stands between 200 and 250 million. Salaried incomes, as stated earlier, are raising - all these are pushing demand to higher levels.

7. The Central Government is pushing through economic reforms, notwithstanding opposition from Communist parties. The left parties are themselves in favour of liberalising the economy,

except on two contentions issues, viz, privatisation and labour laws. Economic reforms have thus become irreversible which augurs will for the country.

8. India's economy is the fastest growing in the world (with 8.2 percent rate in 2003-04). In 2003, the economy of US grew by 3.1 percent, Japan by 2.5 per cent, Brazil by a negative 0.2 per cent, and Asian Tiger Thailand by 7 per cent. IMF predicts that India's economy will grow by 6.8 per cent in 2004-05. Portion of this growth will translate into foreign investment and domestic demand.

9. Indians are becoming richer and richer. The number of billionares rose to 36 as Table 12.10 shows. This figure is more than Japanese tally of 24.

Table 12.10 **The Billionaire Club**

Rank	*Name*	*Age*	*Net Worth $bn*	*Rank*	*Name*	*Age*	*Net Worth $bn*
5	Lakshmi Mittal	56	32	390	Tulsi Tanti	49	2.4
14	Mukesh Ambani	49	20.1	390	Subhash Chandra	56	2.3
18	Anil Ambani	47	18.2	407	Uday Kotak	46	2.2
21	Azim Premji	61	17.1	432	Baba Kalyani	58	2.1
62	Kushal Pal Singh	75	10.0	488	Malvinder & Shivinder Singh	NA	2
69	Sunil Mittal*	49	9.5				
86	Kumar Birla	39	8.0	557	Narayana Murthy	60	1.8
88	Shashi & Ravi Ruia	NA	8.0	618	Anurag Dikshit	35	1.6
114	Ramesh Chandra	67	6.4	618	Venugopal Dhoot	55	1.6
137	Adi Godrej*	77	5.6	664	Vijay Mallya	51	1.5
210	Shiv Nadar	64	4.1	664	Jaiprakash Gaur	76	1.5
214	Dilip Shanghvi	61	4.0	717	Vikas Oberoi	36	1.4
279	Cyrus Poonawalla	51	3.1	754	Nandan Nilekani	51	1.3
287	Indu Jain	65	3.0	799	S. Gopalakrishnan	51	1.2
287	Kalanithi Maran	70	3.0	840	Pradeep Jain	41	1.1
349	Grandhi Rao	41	2.6	840	Kshub Mahindra	83	1.1
390	Savitri Jindal*	57	2.4	840	Rahul Bajaj	68	1.1

* & family

(***Source:*** *Economic Times,* March 14, 2007)

> With 8.2 per cent growth rate (2003-04) India's economy is the fastest growing one in the world. In 2003, US economy grew by 3.1 per cent, Japan by 2.5 per cent, and Brazil by a negative 0.2 per cent.

Counter-claims are equally forceful. It is alleged that all is not well with our industrial sector. The sector is facing too many problems as will be described later. Many industrial units are facing the threat of closure. About agriculture, it is alleged that the phenomenal increase in production of foodgrains is only in rice and wheat. Coarse cereals which are consumed by vast majority of villagers have not registered impressive increase in production. Besides, agriculture is highly dependent on monsoon, failure of which disrupts not only agriculture but the entire economy. The talk about achievements does not mean anything to the common man who still reels under poverty, illiteracy and ignorance. Then there is the ever increasing fiscal deficit.

The country has a huge unemployed population of 39 million(1995). China has little over five million. All other developing countries too have the problem of unemployment but not as much as India has.

The achievements of India stand nowhere near to those of China. In the past decade, China has built atleast 12 major international airport (we have been struggling to put up one at Bangalore), 29,000 kilometers of high quality four-line highways (we have not made any headway in laying expressway, a distance of 145 kilometers, between Bangalore and Mysore); renovated city centres, and built shopping districts. Its Guangzhou airport can handle 27 million passengers and one million tonnes of cargo a year. In comparison, all airports in India put together can handle barely three million visitors per year.

The achievements of India compare nowhere to those of China. In the past decade China has built atleast 12 major international airports and laid 29,000 km of high quality four lane national highways. Has India done any of these in a short span of time?

Thus, the debate can go on. But what should not be lost sight of is the fact that our economy has remarkable resilience. This is borne by the fact that it faced two wars, successive droughts and floods, enormous expenditure on defence and is sustaining more than 93 crore plus people. Whatever the critics may say, the truth remains that, over the years, the lifestyle and levels of living of the people have vastly improved. Population below the poverty line too has declined as is evident from Table 12.11. The late Prime Minister Indira Gandhi, was right when she said that wherever she went, she found smiles on the faces of people and this was the best indicator of economic prosperity that has taken place in our country. See also India Development Report, p.194.

Criticisms notwithstanding, it is a fact that Indian economy has resilience.

Table 12.11 **Population Below Poverty Line**

	%
1983-84	30.1
1987-88	25.5
1993-94	19.0

(**Source**: *Planning Commision,* New Delhi).

Let us also not forget the fact that we have failed in one important dimension of economic development, and it is the building of national character, strong integrity, staunch patriotic fervour and exquisite moral standards, especially among the youth as also in the rest of our countrymen. It is sad that we hardly find young men or women who can proudly say that this is our land and this is our country. It is equally sad that we hardly come across individuals who are inspired by fanatical commitment to their work and to the country. We have managers who do not manage, workers who do not work, teachers who do not teach and students who do not study.

AGENDA FOR FUTURE

Table 12.12 contains series of pressing questions which need satisfactory answers. These questions, incidentally, constitute the agenda for future.

Describing the various components of economic environment and leaving it at that serves no real purpose. What is important is to understand how the economic environment impacts an individual business firm. A chief executive should answer many questions as the following: How will my costs of operations change? Wage rates? Raw materials? Health and benefit costs of my employees? Interest rates on my borrowings? What new competition will I face in the global market? How will the unification of Europe affect my business? Will my competitors cut into my share of domestic market? How can I expand the demand for my products? How much should I spend on R&D? Answers to these and other related questions are available in the economic environment of business.

Table 12.12 Key Questions

Most of these topics have been discussed in detail at appropriate places in this book.

A. *Macro-economic scene*

1. What will be the likely growth of the economy?
2. What can be done to boost exports?
3. Can we achieve higher growth rate and sustain it?

B. *Inflation and Exchange Rates*

1. Why are interest rates high inspite of low inflation?

C. *Poverty and Public Policy*

1. What is the impact of reforms on poverty?
2. What has happened to anti-poverty measures?

D. *The Energy Scene*

1. Why is there power shortage?
2. Can private power plants help meet the shortage?
3. How can we bridge the gap between demand and supply?

E. *The Environment Scene*

1. What are the pressing environmental problems?
2. How can we deal with air, water and noise pollution?
3. How do we manage our forest cover?
4. What is happening to the Indian biodiversity?

F. *Agriculture and Rural Development*

1. What reforms are needed at the agricultural front?
2. What can be done with agricultural subsidies?
3. What have we done for rural development?

G. *Industry*

1. What can we do to accelerate industrial growth?
2. What can be done to improve efficiency of PSEs?
3. What can be done to contain growing sickness?
4. How about corporate governance?

H. *Labour Policy*

1. What kind of labour policy reforms are needed?

I. *Securities Markets*

1. What have reforms done to improve market efficiency?
2. What are the roles of primary and secondary markets?
3. Why has the stock market slumped?
4. What role do FIIs play?

J. *Banking Sector*

1. Have reforms improved the performance of public sector banks?
2. How should we improve the performance of the banking sector?

K. *Transport*

1. What are the problems of railways?
2. How should we improve railways' share of freight traffic?
3. What is the problem with roads and road transportation?
4. Has private entry benefited civil aviation?
5. How should we improve performance in ports and shipping?

L. *Telecommunication*

1. Why are our telecom services so poor?
2. How should DOT be regulated? What should be our telecom policy?

M. *Planning*

1. Why was planning undertaken in the first place?
2. Is delay on market mechanism justified?
3. What should be the role of planning?[10]

QUESTIONS

1. What is economic environment? How is it important for business?
2. Describe the economic environment as it prevails today in our country.
3. Do you think that the present economic environment is favourable to business? Discuss.
4. Bring out the unfinished agenda in the industrial sector.
5. State the key questions which need urgent answers.
6. Why is economic planning necessary? What has been our experience with planning?
7. Why has socialism failed?
8. Bring out the salient features of the basic economic systems.

ASSIGNMENT

Experts, policy makers and industry captains claim that the Indian economy is booming. To prove this claim they cite GDP growth rate, sensex, purchasing power and the like. What does all these mean-

(a) to a woman in a village who is forced to trek atleast one KM to fetch a potful of potable water?

(b) to a seriously sick person who cannot afford medical care?

(c) to a 7 year old boy who is taken off from his school and is made to work in a repair shop?

What are your answers for these questions?

REFERENCES

1. Bimal Jalan, *India's Economic Crisis-The Way Ahead*, Pp.21-23
2. John R.Beighline, *Business, Government and Public Policy*,p.7.
3. *Ibid.*
4. Vijay L.Kelkar and V.V.Bhanoji Rao, *Indian Development Policy Imperatives*, New Delhi, TMH, 1996, p.165.
5. *The Economic Times,* dated 5 Nov, 2005.
6. *Ibid.*
7. "Made in India" — Study conducted by McKinsey and Co. and excerpted in *Business India,* Oct, 11-24, 2004.
8. *Ibid.*
9. *Business Today,* Sept. 12, 2004, Pp. 41-52.
10. Some of the questions have been drawn from *Indian Development Report 1997*, Ed. by Kirit S.Parikh, New Delhi, Oxford University Press, Pp.1-25.

CHAPTER OUTLINE

Rationale for Industrial Policy
Industrial Policy Resolution, 1948
Industrial Policy, 1956
— Objectives
Industrial Policy, 1991
— Objectives
— Industrial Licensing Policy
— Foreign Investment
— Foreign Technology Agreements
— Public Sector Policy
— Monopolies & Restrictive Trade Practices Act
— Merits and Demerits of the Policy

13 Industrial Policy

LEARNING OBJECTIVES

After reading this Chapter, you should be able to:

1. Define industrial policy and explain its rationale
2. Explain Industrial Policy, 1948
3. Describe Industrial Policy, 1956 and make critical evaluation of it
4. Explain Industrial Policy, 1991 and describe its major components
5. Make a critical evaluation of the Industrial Policy, 1991.

One of the components of an economic environment is the industrial sector. As the economic environment is largely influenced by industrial production, it is useful to discuss all its related aspects. The aspects covered here are industrial policy, industrial licensing, regulation of trade practices harmful to public interest, regulation of foreign exchange, regulation of companies, industrial labour, public sector enterprises, SSI sector, industrial sickness, privatisation and the like. This and the next couple of chapters are devoted for a detailed discussion of all these.

Industrial policy is an important document which lays a wide canvas and sets the tone for implementing promotional and regulatory roles of the government. A discussion of the industrial policy is desirable before describing economic environment. This chapter is devoted for the purpose.

> Industrial policy is an important document. It lays a wide canvas and sets the tone for implementation of government's regulatory and promotional roles.

The term 'industrial policy' refers to the government's policy towards industries - their establishment, functioning, growth and management. The policy will indicate the respective areas of the large, medium and small-scale sectors. It will also spell out government's policy towards foreign capital, labour, tariff, and other related aspects. Naturally, the industrial development of a country will be shaped, guided, fostered, regulated and controlled by its industrial policy.

Industrial policy is probably the most important document which indicates the relationship between government and business. The document is helpful to planners and administrators in the government, in as much as it gives clear guidelines for promoting and regulating industries. It is equally helpful to industrialists and others for deciding areas and priorities of their investments.

> The industrial policy has no legal sanction and as such its violation cannot be challenged in a court. But it has justification for existence.

The industrial policy has no legal sanction and as such its violation cannot be challenged in a court as is possible in the case of Fundamental Rights guaranteed by the Constitution. However, it has certain broad guidelines for the government's administrative action and deals with only the qualitative aspects thereof. There are no physical targets to be fulfilled, no time-span, no financial commitment as in the case of an industrial plan. There is only a moral commitment on the part of the government to implement the policy in word and spirit.[1]

RATIONALE

Yet, industrial policy has strong justification for its existence. For example, it can:

- Correct the imbalances in the development of industries and help bring about a desirable balance and diversification in them.
- Direct the flow of scarce resources in the most desirable areas of investment in accordance with national priorities.
- Prevent the wasteful use of scarce resources and ensure their conservation and judicious utilisation.
- Empower the government to regulate the establishment and expansion of private industry in accordance with the planned objectives.
- Demarcate areas among the public, private and joint sectors of the economy, as well as large, medium and small-scale industries.
- Prevent, through fiscal and monetary policies, the formation of monopolies and concentration of wealth in a few hands so that the evils associated with monopolies can be effectively curbed.
- Give guidelines for importing foreign capital and the conditions on which such capital should be permitted to operate.

INDUSTRIAL POLICY RESOLUTION OF 1948

The first important industrial policy resolution was issued by the Government of India on April 6, 1948. Following were the main features of the 1948 industrial policy:

1. Acceptance of the importance of both private and public sectors. The industrial policy resolution accepted the importance of both public and private sectors in the industrial economy of India. It assigned a progressively active role to the State.

> Industrial Policy 1948 has four important features:
> (i) acceptance of the dual sectors:public and private,
> (ii) division of industries,
> (iii) small and cottage industries,
> (iv) role of foreign capital.

2. Division of the industrial sector. The Resolution divided industries into four categories. These categories were as under: *(i) Industries where State had a monopoly:* In this category *three* fields of activity were specified - arms and ammunition, atomic energy and rail transport, *(ii) Mixed sector:* In this category, 6 industries were specified - coal, iron and steel, aircraft manufacture, ship building, manufacture of telephone, telegraph and wireless apparatus (excluding radio sets) and mineral oils. However, existing private undertakings in this field were allowed to continue for ten years after which the government would review the situation and acquire any existing undertaking after paying compensation on a "fair and equitable basis". *(iii) The field of government control:* The government did not undertake the responsibility of developing these industries but considered them of such importance that their regulation and direction was necessary. Some of the industries included were - automobiles, heavy chemicals, heavy machinery, machine tools, fertilizers, electrical engineering, sugar, paper, cement, cotton and woollen textiles. *(iv) The field of private enterprise:* All other industries (not included in the above three categories) were left open to the private sector. However, the State could take over any industry in this sector also if its progress was unsatisfactory.

3. Role of small and cottage industries. The 1948 Resolution accepted the importance of small and cottage industries in industrial development. These industries are particularly suited for the utilization of local resources and for creation of employment opportunities.

4. Other important features of the industrial policy. The role of foreign capital in industrial development of the economy was recognized but the need for regulating and controlling it according to the needs of the domestic economy was deemed essential. Therefore, it was stated that in those industries where foreign investment was to be done, Indians should have a major say in the ownership and management. The Resolution called for harmonious relations between the management and labour since this was necessary for industrial development. For this purpose, the Resolution enunciated a policy of just labour conditions wherein workers would be given fair wages. For purposes of maintaining industrial peace, labour participation in mangement was also stressed.

INDUSTRIAL POLICY, 1956

The setting was favourable for the Industrial Policy, 1956. The country gave itself a Constitution which set out certain Directive Principles*. Planning began to be implemented on an organised basis and the First Five Year Plan was already completed. Parliament accepted the socialist pattern of society as the objective of social and economic policy. The country's resources also increased and the government's drive in expanding the public sector as a means for rapid economic development to countervail economic concentration and removal of regional economic disparities gained momentum.[2] These changes and developments necessitated a policy and then it was announced on 30th April, 1956.

Four developments set the tone for Industrial Policy 1956:
(i) adoption of Constitution,
(ii) planning began to be implemented,
(iii) socialist policy was accepted,
(iv) government was rich enough to invest in public sector.

Objectives of 1956 Policy

- To accelerate the rate of economic growth and to speed up industrialisation.
- To expand the public sector, develop heavy and machine making industry.
- To increase employment opportunities and improvement of living standards and working conditions of people.
- To prevent creation of monopolies and concentration of economic power.
- To reduce existing disparities of income and wealth.
- To build up a large and growing private sector.
- To expand the cottage, village and small-scale industries.
- To achieve balanced industrial development and other socio-economic objectives.

In the 1956 Policy, industries were classified into three categories (Fig.13.1). The first category included industries, the future development of which will be the exclusive responsibility of the State. The second category will consist of industries which will be progressively state-owned and in which the State will generally take the initiative in establishing new undertakings, but in which private enterprise will also be expected to supplement the effort of the State. The third category will include all the remaining industries, and their future development will be left to the initiative and enterprise of the private sector.

---

* Read Chapter 8 in this book for details.

Figure 13.1 **Categorisation of Industries – 1956 Policy**

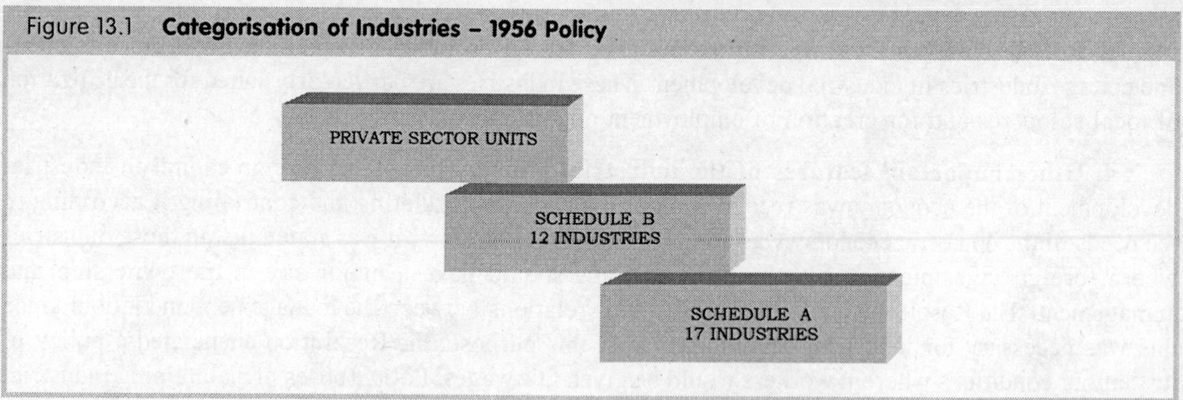

Schedule A of the policy contained 17 industries, 12 were listed under Schedule B and the rest were thrown open to private sector.

Industries in the first category were listed in Schedule A of the 1956 Resolution and included arms and ammunition and allied items of defence equipments; atomic energy; iron and steel; heavy castings and forging of iron and steel; heavy plant and machinery; heavy electrical plant, including large hydraulic and steam turbines; coal and lignite; mineral oils; mining of iron ore, manganese, chrome ore, gypsum, sulphur, gold and diamond, mining and procuring of copper, lead and zinc; aircraft, air transport; railway transport; ship-building; telephones and telephone cables and the generation and distribution of electricity.

Thus, the first category included as many as 17 industries. The expansion of exclusive monopolies was understandable in as much as the State's resources improved, and it was also realised that the government should play progressively a greater role in the industrial development of the country.

The second category industries were listed in Schedule B and included all other minerals except those defined in Section 3 of the Minerals Concession Rules, 1949; aluminum and other non-ferrous metals not included in Schedule A; machine tools, ferro-alloys and tools; drugs; fertilizers; synthetic rubber; carbonisation of coal; chemical pulp; road transport, and sea transport. With a view to accelerating their development, the State will increasingly establish new undertakings in these industries. At the same time, private enterprise will also have the opportunity to develop in this field either on its own or with State participation. Schedule B contains 12 industries.

The rest of the industries were thrown open to the private sector but this did not prevent the State from starting any new undertaking. State will facilitate and encourage the development of these industries in the private sector by providing infrastructural facilities.

The division of industries into separate categories did not imply that they were being placed in watertight compartments. There could be overlapping and dovetailing between industries in the private and public sectors. It would be open to the State to start any industry not included in Schedule A and Schedule B when the needs of planning so required or there were other reasons for it. Similarly, privately-owned units might be permitted to produce an item falling in Schedule A for meeting their own requirements or as by-products.

The 1956 Policy reiterated the government's determination to provide all sorts of assistance for the rapid development of small and cottage industries in view of the distinct advantages they possess in respect of the generation of employment opportunities, wider dispersal of industries and the equitable distribution of income and wealth.

The 1956 Policy came in for appreciation and criticism. The emphasis laid on certain socio-economic objectives was indeed laudable. The policy stressed the need for balanced regional development of the country, prevention of concentration of economic power, building up of a strong co-operative sector,

The 1956 Policy was hailed as the economic Constitution of India.

expansion of opportunities for gainful employment and improvement of living standards and working conditions of people. The public sector was to be expanded and encouragement to the small-scale sector was to be intensified. The virtue of mixed economy was further reaffirmed. The policy also emphasised that industrial development must be governed by the Directive Principles of State Policy enunciated in the Constitution and the more precise direction given to them by the Parliament through its acceptance of the socialist pattern of society. No wonder that the 1956 policy has been hailed as the '*economic constitution*' of India. The 1980 Policy Statement paid the highest tribute when it stated that "*the industrial policy announcement of 1956 in fact reflects the value system of our country and has shown conclusively the merit of constructive flexibility*."

The 1956 Policy was vehemently criticised on the role assigned to the public sector. It was said that a public enterprise in an impersonal industrial venture and an impersonal attitude towards an enterprise is hardly conducive to its growth. Further, it was contended that the State was unduly straining its already overburdened and overstrained financial and administrative resources. Some critics went so far as to suggest that it would bring about State capitalism and that the government will be well-advised to reconsider its policy.

The 1956 Policy no doubt set out some of the principles of Nehru's philosophy but retained sufficient ambivalence to placate the uncommitted elements. As latter developments proved, loopholes and exceptions were more readily availed of by the administrators and industrialists. In industries like coal, oil, etc., which were reserved for public expansion, licences were issued to the private sector. Similarly, three Western oil companies were allowed to establish refineries in the country. Besides, the government signed a deal with STANVAC (later ESSO) for oil exploration with minority participation by the Government of India.

Merits and demerits apart, the 1956 Policy continued to constitute the basic economic policy for a long time. This fact has been confirmed in all the Five Year Plans.

INDUSTRIAL POLICY, 1991

On 24th July 1991, the government headed by Mr.P.V.Narasimha Rao, announced a new industrial policy which sought to drastically alter the industrial scenario in our country. There are several fundamental departures in the new policy. The most important initiatives are with respect to the virtual scrapping of industrial licensing and registration policies, an end to the monopoly law and a more welcoming approach to foreign investments, apart from redefining the role of the public sector. These measures, long overdue, are welcome as they would free the industry from regulations, most of which have outlived their utility.

Objectives

Succinctly, the objectives of the New Industrial Policy are:

(i) Self-reliance to build on the many sided gains already made.

(ii) Encouragement to Indian entrepreneurship, promotion of productivity and employment generation.

(iii) Development of indigenous technology through greater investment in R & D and bringing in new technology to help Indian manufacturing units attain world standards.

(iv) Removing the regulatory system and other weaknesses.
(v) Increasing the competitiveness of industries for the benefit of the common man.
(vi) Incentives for the industrialisation of backward areas.
(vii) Enhanced support to the small-scale sector.
(viii) Ensure running of public sector undertakings (PSUs) on business lines and cut their losses.
(xi) Protect the interests of workers.
(x) Abolish the monopoly of any sector in any field of manufacture except on strategic or security grounds.
(xi) To link Indian economy to the global market so that we acquire the ability to pay for imports, and to make us less dependent on aid.

In pursuit of the above objectives, the Government has decided to take a series of initiatives in respect of the policies relating to the following areas:

The 1991 Policy comprised five dimensions:
(i) licensing
(ii) foreign investment
(iii) technology agreements
(iv) public sector
(v) MRTP Act.

A. Industrial Licensing
B. Foreign Investment
C. Foreign Technology Agreements
D. Public Sector Policy
E. MRTP Act

A package for the small and tiny sectors of industry is being announced separately. This policy will be discussed later in this book.

A. Industrial Licensing Policy

Industrial licensing is governed by the Industries (Development & Regulation) Act, 1951. Over the years, keeping in view the changing industrial scene in the country, the policy has undergone modifications. Industrial licensing policy and procedures have also been liberalised from time to time. A full realisation of the industrial potential of the country calls for a continuation of this process of change.

In order to achieve the objectives of the strategy for the industrial sector for 1990 and beyond, it is necessary to make a number of changes in the system of industrial approvals. Major policy initiatives and procedural reforms are called for in order to actively encourage and assist Indian entrepreneurs to exploit and meet the emerging domestic and global opportunities and challenges. The bedrock of any such package of measures must be to let the entrepreneurs make investment decisions on the basis of their own commercial judgement. The attainment of technological dynamism and international competitiveness requires that enterprises must be enabled to swiftly respond to fast changing external conditions that have become characteristic of today's industrial world. Government policy and procedures must be geared to assisting entrepreneurs in their efforts. This can be done only if the role played by the Government were to be changed from that of only exercising control to one of providing help and guidance by making essential procedures fully transparent and by eliminating delays.

The winds of change have been with us for some time. The industrial licensing system has been gradually moving away from the concept of capacity licensing. The system of reservations for public sector undertakings has been evolving to the ethos of greater flexibility and private sector enterprise has been gradually allowed to enter into many of these areas on a case by case basis. Further impetus must be provided to these changes which alone can push this country towards the attainment of its entrepreneurial and industrial potential. This calls for bold and imaginative decisions designed to remove restraints on capacity creation, while at the same time, ensuring that over-riding national interests are not jeopardised.

In the above context, industrial licensing will henceforth be abolished for all industries, except those specified, irrespective of the levels of investment. These specified industries will continue to be subject to compulsory licensing for reasons related to security and strategic concerns, social reasons, problems related to safety and overriding environmental issues, manufacture of products of hazardous nature and articles of elitist consumption. The exemption from licensing will be particularly helpful to the many dynamic small and medium enterprerneurs who have been unnecessarily hampered by the licensing system. As a whole, the Indian economy will benefit by becoming more competitive, more efficient and modern and will take its rightful place in the world of industrial progress.

B. Foreign Investment

While freeing the Indian industry from official controls, opportunities for promoting foreign investments in India should also be fully exploited. In view of the significant development of India's industrial economy in the last 40 years, the general resilience, size and level of sophistication achieved, and the significant changes that have also taken place in the world industrial economy, the relationship between domestic and foreign industry needs to be much more dynamic than it has been in the past in terms of both technology and investment. Foreign investment would bring attendant advantages of technology transfer, marketing expertise, introduction of modern managerial techniques and new possibilities for the promotion of exports. This is particularly necessary in the changing global scenario of industrial and economic cooperation marked by mobility of capital. The government will therefore welcome foreign investment which is in the interest of the country's industrial development.

In order to invite foreign investment in high priority industries, requiring large investments and advanced technology, it has been decided to provide approval for direct foreign investment upto 51% foreign equity in such industries. There shall be no bottlenecks of any kind in this process. This group of industries has generally been known as the 'Appendix I industries' and are areas in which FERA companies have already been allowed to invest on a discretionary basis. This change will go a long way in making the Indian policy on foreign investment transparent. Such a framework will make it attractive for companies abroad to invest in India.

Promotion of exports of Indian products calls for a systematic exploration of world markets possible only through intensive and highly professional marketing activities. To the extent that expertise of this nature is not well developed so far in India, Government will encourage foreign trading companies to assist us in our export activities. Attraction of substantial investment and access to high technology, often closely held, and to world markets, involve interaction with some of the world's largest international manufacturing and marketing firms. The Government will appoint a special board to negotiate with such firms so that we can engage in purposive negotiation with such large firms, and provide the avenues for large investments in the development of industries and technology in the national interest.

C. Foreign Technology Agreements

There is a great need for promoting an industrial environment where the acquisition of technological capability receives priority. In the fast changing world of technology, the relationship between the suppliers and the users of technology must be a continuous one. Such a relationship becomes difficult to achieve when the approval process includes unnecessary governmental interference on a case to case basis involving endemic delays and fostering uncertainty. The Indian entrepreneur has now come of age so that he no longer needs such bureaucratic clearances for his commercial technology relationships with foreign technology suppliers. Indian industry can scarcely be competitive with the rest of the world if it is to operate within such a regulatory environment.

With a view to injecting the desired level of technological dynamism in the Indian industry, the Government will provide automatic approval for technological agreements related to high priority industries within specified parameters. Similar facilities will be available for other industries as well if such agreements do not require the expenditure of free foreign exchange. Indian companies will be free to negotiate the terms to technology transfer with their foreign counterparts according to their own commercial judgement. The predictability and independence of action that this measure is providing to the Indian industry will induce them to develop indigenous competence for the efficient absorption of foreign technology. Greater competitive pressure will also induce our industry to invest much more in research and development than they have been doing in the past. In order to help this process, the hiring of foreign technicians and foreign testing of endogenously developed technologies, will also not require prior clearance as prescribed so far, individually or as a part of industrial or investment approvals.

D. Public Sector Policy

The public sector has been central to our philosophy of development. In the pursuit of our development objectives, public ownership and control in critical sectors of the economy has played an important role in preventing the concentration of economic power, reducing regional disparities and ensuring that planned development serves the common good.

The Industrial Policy Resolution of 1956 gave the public sector a strategic role in the economy. Massive investments have been made over the past four decades to build a public sector which has a commanding role in the economy. Today key sectors of the economy are dominated by mature public enterprises that have successfully expanded production, opened up new areas of technology and built up a reserve of technical competence in a number of areas.

After the initial exuberance of the public sector entering new areas of industrial and technical competence, a number of problems have begun to manifest themselves in many of the public enterprises. Serious problems are observed in the insufficient growth in productivity, poor project management, overmanning, lack of continuous technological upgradation, and inadequate attention to R & D and human resource development. In addition, public enterprises have shown a very low rate of return on the capital invested. This has inhibited their ability to regenerate themselves in terms of new investments as well as in technology development. The result is that many of the public enterprises have become a burden rather than being an asset to the Government. The original concept of the public sector has also undergone considerable dilutions. The most striking example is the take over of sick units from the private sector. This category of public sector units accounts for almost one-third of the total losses of central public enterprises. Another category of public enterprises, which does not fit into the original idea of the public sector being at the commanding heights of the economy, is the plethora of public enterprises which are in the consumer goods and services sectors.

It is time therefore that the Government shall adopt a new approach to public enterprises. There must be a greater commitment to the support of public enterprises which are essential for the operation of the industrial economy. Measures must be taken to make these enterprises more growth oriented and technically dynamic. Units which may be faltering at present but are potentially viable must be restructured and given a new lease of life. The priority areas for the growth of public enterprises in the future will be the following:

Essential infrastructure goods and services.

Exploration and exploitation of oil and mineral resources.

Technology development and building of manufacturing capabilities in areas which are crucial in the long term development of the economy and where private sector investment is inadequate.

Manufacture of products where strategic considerations predominate such as defence equipment.

At the same time, the public sector will not be barred from entering areas not specifically reserved for it.

In view of these considerations, government will review the existing portfolio of public investments with greater realism. This review will be in respect of industries based on low technology, small-scale and non-strategic areas, inefficient and unproductive areas, areas with low or nil social considerations or public purpose, and areas where the private sector has developed sufficient expertise and resources.

The government will strengthen those public enterprises which fall in the reserved areas of operation or are in high priority areas or are generating good or reasonable profits. Such enterprises will be provided a much greater degree of management autonomy through the system of memoranda of understanding. Competition will also be induced in these areas by inviting private sector participation. In the case of selected enterprises, part of government holdings in the equity share capital of these enterprises will be disinvested in order to provide further market discipline to the performance of public enterprises. There are a large number of chronically sick public enterprises incurring heavy losses, operating in a competitive market and serve little or no public purpose. These need to be attended to. The country must be proud of the public sector that it owns and it must operate in the public interest.

E. Monopolies and Restrictive Trade Practices Act (MRTP ACT)

With the growing complexity of the industrial structure and the need for achieving economies of scale for ensuring high productivity and competitive advantage in the international market, the interference of the government through the MRTP Act in investment decisions of large companies has become deleterious in its effect on India's industrial growth. The pre-entry scrutiny of investment decisions by the so called MRTP companies will no longer be required. Instead, emphasis will be on controlling and regulating monopoly houses to obtain prior approval of the Central government for expansion, establishment of new undertakings, mergers, amalgamation and take over and the appointment of certain directors. The thrust of policy will be more on controlling unfair or restrictive business practices. The MRTP Act will be restructured by eliminating the legal requirement for prior governmental approval for expansion of present undertakings and the establishment of new undertakings. The provisions relating to merger, amalgamation, and takeover will also be repealed. Similarly, the provisions regarding restrictions on the acquisition of and the transfer of shares will be appropriately incorporated in the Companies Act.

Simultaneously, provisions of the MRTP Act will be strengthened in order to enable the MRTP Commission to take appropriate action in respect of the monopolistic, restrictive and unfair trade practices. The newly empowered MRTP Commission will be encouraged to require investigation *suo moto* or complaints received from individual consumers or classes of consumers.

In view of the considerations outlined above the government has decided to take a series of measures to protect the Indian industrial economy from the cobwebs of unnecessary bureaucratic controls. These measures will be covered in appropriate places in subsequent chapters. (MRTP Act is now replaced by the Competition Act. Read Chapter 15 for details).

Merits of the 1991 Policy Statement

- The 1991 Policy Statement is truly historic, whether it is the result of IMF pressure or our own realisation that the time has come to open up the economy.
- The changes, long overdue, need to be welcomed as a bold initiative aimed at making Indian industry more competitive internally as well as internationally, and at freeing the industry from needless and irksome controls, most of which have outlived their utility.
- The delicensing of a host of industries and the abolition of all registration schemes will free Indian entrepreneurs from the need to make endless trips to New Delhi. They can now concentrate on their business and move quickly to seize business opportunities.
- The scrapping of any asset threshold or market share prescription for the definition of an MRTP company and a dominant undertaking allows companies to go ahead with investment programmes without delay.
- The liberalisation of the rules relating to direct foreign investment, permitting 51 per cent equity in a wide range of industries, the easier facilitation of foreign technology agreements and other related measures go a long way in attracting foreign investment and technology.
- Reforms relating to the public sector like privatisation and transferring sick units to BIFR will help improve the performance of the government undertakings.
- Finally, the new Policy Statement is a most welcome package. There is a greater reliance on the market, a bold attempt at deregulation, a desire to integrate with the world economy, and to modernise.

Limitations of 1991 Policy

- Virtual scrapping of licensing means absence of a mechanism to determine priorities and to develop backward areas.
- The policy is silent about tackling the growing industrial sickness. The government has not announced a clear exit policy for sick units. Clearly government seems to have yielded to the pressure of trade union lobby.
- Off-loading of 20 per cent equity in profit making public sector units to mutual funds is a revenue raising exercise than genuine attempt at privatisation.
- Even with the scrapping of all regulations, the expected foreign investment may not come through. Infrastructural deficiencies will deter foreign investment.
- The policy is drafted at the behest of IMF which means virtual surrender of economic sovereignty of the country to a foreign agency.

QUESTIONS

1. What is Industrial Policy? What are its objectives?
2. Why is the Industrial Policy, 1956 hailed as the Economic Constitution of India?
3. Comment on the 1991 Policy.
4. Explain the Industrial Policy 1948.

ASSIGNMENT

"One needs to be reminded that there is a document called industrial policy. In these days of globalisation, declining government role in business, SEZs, private sector dominance, and increasing flow of FDI, industrial policy and its regulatory provisions have lost their relevance." Do you agree or disagree with this statement?

REFERENCES

1. D.Amarchand, *Government and Business*, p.9.
2. *Ibid*, p.14.

CHAPTER OUTLINE

Licensing and its Objectives

Legislative Framework for Licensing

— Industrial (Development and Regulation) Act, 1951

Criticisms of Licensing

LEARNING OBJECTIVES

After reading this Chapter, you should be able to:

1. Define industrial licensing and state its objectives
2. Describe the provisions of the Industrial Act classifying the sections into preventive, curative and creative
3. Bring out the criticisms of licensing

14 Industrial Licensing

Ours is one of the few countries in the world where an entrepreneur is required to obtain an industrial licence from the government before venturing into a new business. This chapter is devoted to a brief description of the objectives, the recent changes announced by the government and other related matters relating to licensing.

Objectives of Licensing

A *licence* is a written permission issued by the Central Government to an industrial undertaking stating such details as the location, the article to be manufactured, production capacity and other relevant particulars.

> Licence is a written permission issued by the Central Government to an industrial enterprise to locate itself, and produce a stated product.

It is also subject to a validity period within which the licensed capacity should be implemented.

The main objectives of licensing are:

- to limit industrial capacity within the targets set by the plans;
- to direct investment in industries according to plan priorities;
- to regulate the location of industrial units so as to secure a balanced regional development;
- to prevent both monopoly and concentration of wealth;
- to protect small-scale industries against undue competition from large-scale industries;
- to foster technology and economic improvements in industries by ensuring units of economic size and adopting modern processes; and
- to encourage new entrepreneurs to start industrial units, thus broadening the entrepreneurial base.

The major objective of licensing is to give effect to the industrial policy of the Government. Any change in the industrial policy, therefore, will have its repurcussions on the licensing system.

LEGISLATIVE FRAMEWORK FOR LICENSING

The legislative framework for industrial licensing is provided in the Industrial(Development and Regulation) Act, 1951, MRTP Act, and FEMA.

Industrial(Development And Regulation) Act, 1951

Legislative framework for licensing is through Industries Act, MRTP Act and FEMA.

The Act seeks to secure planned industrial development of the country by regulating, controlling and developing industries that are included in the First Schedule to the Act. Regulation of industries is sought to be achieved by means of registration of existing industrial undertakings, licensing of substantial expansion, production of new articles, change of location of existing undertakings, etc. Control over these industries is sought to be achieved by causing investigation into the working of these industries and taking over of their management and control. Development of these industries, on the other hand, is sought to be secured primarily through the agencies of Central Advisory Council and Development Councils and by offering certain facilities as the government may think fit to be necessary for the development of the Scheduled industries.

Objectives of the Act

The Act has three important objectives, *viz.*,

The Industries Act has three objectives:
(i) implementation of Industrial policy
(ii) regulation and development of industries
(iii) development of new undertakings.

- *Implementation of the Industrial Policy*: The Act provides necessary means to the Central Government in order to implement its industrial policy.
- *Regulation and Development of Important Industries*: The Act brings under the control of the Central Government the development and regulation of a number of important industries listed in the First Schedule attached to the Act as the activities of such industries will affect the country as a whole and, therefore, the development of such important industries must be governed by the economic factors of all-India importance.
- *Planning and Future Development of New Undertakings*: A system of licensing is introduced under the Act to regulate planning and future development of new undertakings on sound and balanced lines as may be deemed expedient in the opinion of the Central Government. The Act confers on the Central Government power to make rules for the registration of existing undertakings for regulating the production and development of the industries specified in the Schedule attached to the Act. The Act also provides for the constitution of Central Advisory Council and Development Council.

The following excerpt from "*The Industrial Development of India:Policy and Problems*" adds a new dimension to the objectives of the Act:

"*Bringing industry within the purview of this Act has the effect of transferring from the States to the Central Government the responsibility and power of legislation for its regulation, control and development. Since most industries were brought under this Act, something like a constitutional revolution took place in 1952 by virtually making industry a Central subject rather than a State subject as envisaged in the Constitution. This change, however, is of vital and fundamental importance to the building up and the preservation of the economic unity of the country.*"[1]

Scope of the Act

The Act applies to the whole of India including the State of Jammu & Kashmir. The provisions of the Act apply to industrial undertakings manufacturing any of the articles mentioned in the First Schedule. An industrial undertaking (also called a factory) for the purpose of the Act is the one where the manufacturing process is being carried on:

(a) with the aid of power, provided that fifty or more workers are working or were working on any day of the preceding twelve months; or

(b) without the aid of power, provided that one hundred or more workers are working or were working on any day of the preceding twelve months.

(c) the Act applies only to industrial undertakings. Trading houses and financial institutions are outside the purview of the Act.

Provisions of the Act

The Act has thirty one sections and all of them can be classified into three broad categories, depending upon the purposes they seek to serve.(See Fig.14.1).

Figure 14.1 **Provisions of I(D&R) Act**

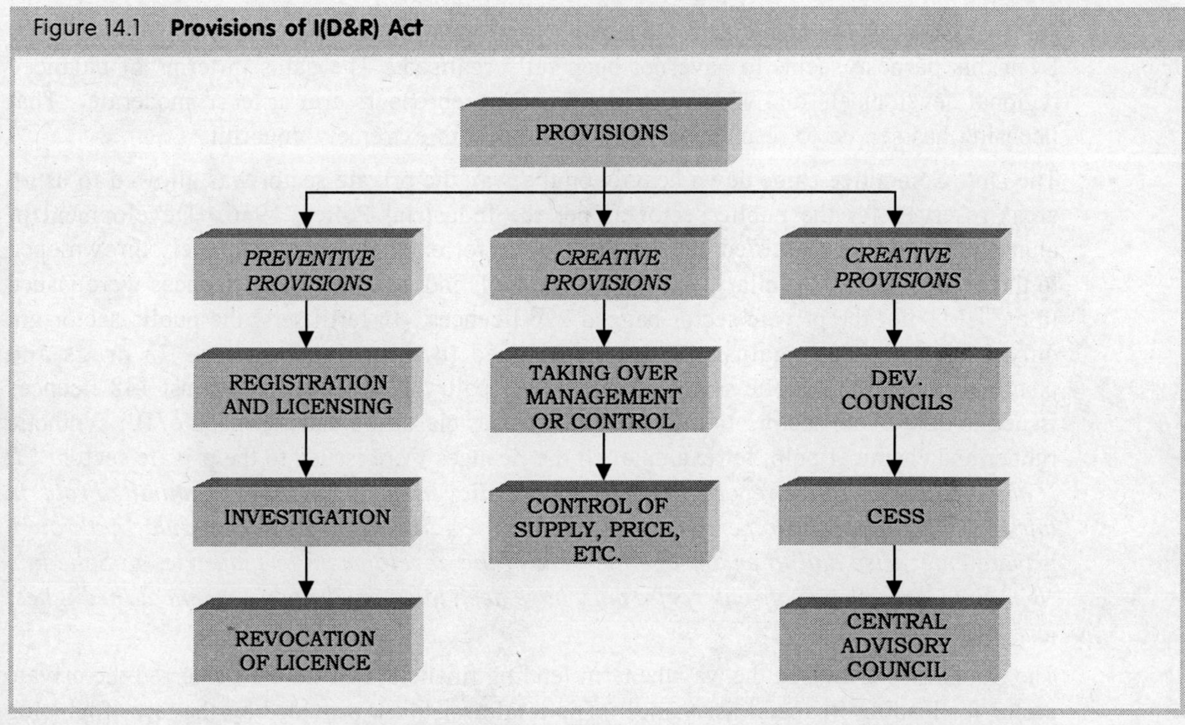

CRITICISMS OF LICENSING

No other regulatory measure of the government was subject to such criticism as licensing.

Licensing was introduced to serve useful purposes which were listed in the beginning of this chapter. However, in its implementation the system ran into disrepute. We state some serious criticisms against licensing with a note that the criticisms have historical value since licensing itself has almost become irrelevant today.

The following defects have been highly conspicuous:

- The issue of licences tends to give an exaggerated picture of industrial capacity which sometimes scares away genuine entrepreneurs who might be chronologically late, at the same time, as it encourages foreclosure of licensed capacity by influential groups and sitting tight on unimplemented licences.
- Licences are normally, in most cases, issued for a capacity 10 to 25 per cent above the target for the end-plan year and that too, mostly around the begining of the plan period. An excessive-though quantitatively unvariable-perssure is thus exerted on the available foreign exchange and possible collaborators and also on domestic suppliers. This leads to bottlenecks and delays, apart from adversely affecting the terms of negotiation with foreign and domestic suppliers and creditors.
- The process of consideration of applications at various levels and at various times contributes to delays and higher costs, without improving the feasibility of the project concerned.
- There is very little follow-up of licensing to see that the approved projects fructify in a satisfactory phased schedule. Even the authorities concerned are not fully aware of the total investment and foreign exchange commitments of licences issued or those under implementation at any particular period of time.[2]

The other criticisms against licensing policy are:

One of the purposes of industrial licensing is to achieve regional dispersal of industries. Even this purpose seems to have not been fully realised. The gains in terms of balanced regional development and wider distribution of entrepreneurs are, at least, moderate. That licensing has served to channelise investment appears extremely doubtful.[3]

- The Dutt Committee came down heavily on the way the private sector was allowed to usurp areas reserved for the public sector as per the Industrial Policy, 1956. Development of aluminium which is classified under Schedule 'A' for example, was completely thrown open to the private sector. Similary, in the machine tools industry, only nine licences were issued to the HMT but the private sector bagged 226 licences. In fertilisers, the public sector got only 12 licences as against 42 licences issued to the private sector. In drugs and pharmaceuticals, the public sector's share was a paltry 12 licences as against 148 licences issued to the private sector. In the case of industries classified under Schedule 'B', synthetic rubber and chemical pulp, for example, all the licences were issued to the private sector. "*It is obvious*", asserted the report, "*that licensing policy as such can play but a limited role in this respect. Decisions to permit development of certain industries in Schedule 'A' through private enterprise and to encourage the bulk of the development of industries in Schedule 'B' mainly through private enterprise must have been taken by the government at the highest level*" (p.107).
- The Committee criticised the way the term-lending financial institutions perferred the private sector for leading financial assistance. The total assistance provided by the term financing institutions during the period 1955 to 1966 was Rs.498 crores. Out of this, the public sector companies received as assistance of just over 10 per cent but private sector secured a massive 54.2 per cent.

- The provisions of the Industries (Development & Regulation) Act relating to licensing have been, over the years, observed more in its breach than in principle. A letter of intent, for example, is issued for a period of one year. If effective steps are not taken by the grantee to implement the letter of intent within the period of 2 years, it should lapse. Statistics, however, tell a different story. By the end of 1983, 805 letters of intent issued during 1974-79 remained unimplemented. Again between end October 1980 to end October 1986, out of 7,442 letters of intent issued, 2,234 have been converted into licences, 3,884 are yet to be implemented and the remaining 1,324 have lapsed.[4]

Further, "companies licensed to produce a specified quantity have produced 10 to 20 times that amount, the government's reaction invariably being a sightless stare. The big industrial houses and multinational subsidiaries have been the biggest offenders, freely creating unlicensed capacities and producting far in excess of the quantity permitted.

"...Crompton Greaves has a licensed capacity for producing 18,000 sets of metal-cased plugs and sockets. Production in 1979 was-hold your breath-224,207 sets. Hindustan Lever has a licensed capacity of 70,018 tonnes of soap, but has recorded a production of 162,278 tonnes. Similarly, J.L.Morrison's licensed capacity for medicated toothpaste is 31,250 kg. but production has been 67,196 kg. Yet, in over 30 years, there has not been a single case of any company being prosecuted for such acts of commission".[5]

- That industrial licensing is required to control waste of resources is one of those hoary chestnuts that the planners pass around when they have no other argument to fall back upon. Nothing could be more wasteful that the massive bulk of public sector which eats up more resources, monetary as well as physical, than the entire private sector put together. Yet the public sector expansion is a direct result of the licensing system and the commanding heights syndrome. The planners seem to be more worried about some young men getting together and putting up a small plant to make dairy machinery without a licence than the heavy engineering corporation gulping taxpayers' rupee after rupee with a proper licence, without coming anywhere near making both the needs meet.[6]

- "...neither IDRA nor MRTP has enabled it (the government) to put any of its declared social objectives into practice. In fact, going again by the official figures, the two Acts have worked in a perverse manner. Take the case of the textile industry, the oldest and the most rigorously regulated industry in the country. In a country which is said to have nearly 50 per cent of its population below the poverty line, there should be considerable demand for cheap cloth.

"But it is precisely the mills which make the cheap cloth that are in serious trouble - over a hundred of them are sick and have been taken over by a State *Pinjrapole* known as the National Textile Corporation - and those which make expensive cloth like synthetic fabrics are busy minting money. A company like Reliance Textiles which did not own a shed of its own 15 years ago is now the country's biggest textile company. Reliance also had to go through the same licensing churner but has apparently managed to emerge not only unscathed but done very well for itself and its shareholders in the bargain. This is also true of companies like Bombay Dyeing, Gwalior Rayon and Century which have gained enormously over the years, despite the fact that they all belong to large business houses and have had to cross not only the ordinary licensing hurdle but also the MRTP bar.... The fact is that an aggressive industrial society will assert itself no matter what the policy books might say, and the natural laws of supply and demand will make mincemeat of the best laid plans of mice and men, even if some of them are masquerading as planners with 'social objectives".[7]

- The government says that the large industry will not be allowed to expand into areas reserved for small-scale industry. But the truth is that in many cases, large industry owns small industry....J.K.Helene Curtis, a small-scale unit, is owned by the Singhania group; Dental Products of India Ltd., another small unit, belongs to Shaw Wallace, as does Vitro-Pharma Products Ltd., Indian National Diesel Co.Ltd., is owned by Mahindra, Ewac Alloys by L&T, Garment Enterprises Ltd., by Finlay and so on.[8]

The impact of licensing on the industrial sector had been a topic of considerable interest. A number of government committees had also been set up since the mid-sixties to examine the working of the licensing system (Government of India, 1964, 1965, 1967, 1969, 1978 and 1979). As a result of these studies and reports, the licensing system had been considerably liberalised since 1973. The reforms had included simplifications in procedure and removal of restriction on capacity expansion. Finally, the scope of licensing has been drastically curtailed and it is now made applicable to only six industries.

Not that the licensing system was an exercise in futility. It played its useful role during the 60s and 70s when our economy faced acute shortage of resources. Whatever resources we possessed had to be rationed across different industries through physical controls. Now that the economy has grown in all directions and has become fairly vibrant, licensing and other controls need to be removed. Our entrepreneurs need freedom to set up units of their choice and exploit the opportunities thrown open to them by the world economy which is becoming increasingly integrated. The delicensing phase initiated by the government, therefore, needs to be appreciated.

The economic reforms introduced from 1990s have made licensing almost irrelevant. As on today, licensing is required only for six specific groups for reasons as safety and overriding environmental issues and manufacture of products of hazardous nature.

The other legislations providing for licensing will be discussed in the next two chapters.

QUESTIONS

1. What is an industrial licence? What are the objectives of licensing?
2. "Licensing has laudable objectives. But in its implementation the system ran into disrepute". Comment.
3. Bring out the objectives and provisions of the Industries (Development and Regulation) Act, 1951.

ASSIGNMENT

Study the procedural compliances required to set up -

1. a retail mall.
2. a subsidiary of an MNC.
3. an industrial establishment involving Rs.1,000 cr. investment.
4. a food processing unit in any SEZ.

REFERENCES

1. R.K.Hazari, *Essays on Industrial Policy*, p.91
2. *Ibid*, p.346
3. R.K.Hazari, *Industrial Planning and Licensing Policy*, Final Report (1967), p.17.
4. *India Today*, March 15, 1987.
5. *Ibid*, Feb. 15,1982.
6. *Ibid.*
7. *Ibid.*
8. *Ibid.*

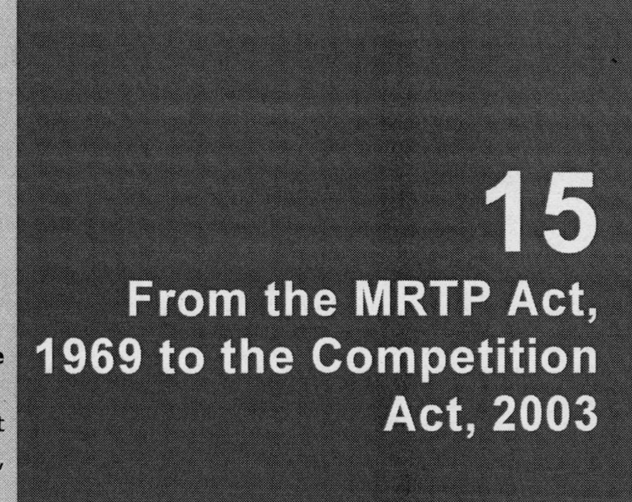

15
From the MRTP Act, 1969 to the Competition Act, 2003

CHAPTER OUTLINE

Objectives of the MRTP Act
Regulation of Trade Practices
— Monopolistic Trade Practices
— Restrictive Trade Practices
— Unfair Trade Practices
Objectives of the Competition Act
Provisions of the Act

LEARNING OBJECTIVES

After reading this Chapter, you should be able to:

1. Understand the objectives of the MRTP Act
2. Explain how the Act seeks to regulate MTPs, RTPs and UTPs
3. Understand the objectives of the Competition Act 2003
4. List the prevision of the Act

The Monopolies and Restrictive Trade Practices Act, 1969 (MRTP) is an important piece of economic legislation designed to ensure that the operation of the economic system does not result in the concentration of economic power to the common detriment. The authority for this is derived from the Directive Principles of State Policy contained in Article 39 of the Constitution of India, which enjoins upon the State to secure that

"the operation of the economic system does not result in the concentration of wealth and means of production to the common detriment".

The Act was promulgated on the patterns of Nehruvian-Mahalanobis model leaning towards the establishment of a socialistic pattern of society. Monopoly law in India as in any other country was based on the presumption that big business is not only harmful to distributive justice, but also results in monopolistic tendencies which could be misused to the detriment of the public at large and consumers in particular.

MRTP Act had a tinge with it-ushering in socialism.

The Act came into force from 1st June, 1970, and has been amended in 1974, 1980, 1982, 1984 and 1991. The Act applies to the whole of India except the State of Jammu & Kashmir.

Amendments made in 1991, is significant in as much as the philosophy of the Act underwent a total change. With the growing complexity of industrial structure and the need for achieving economies of scale for ensuring high productivity and competitive advantage in the international market, the thrust of the industrial policy of Central Government (announced in Parliament on 24th July 1991) has shifted to controlling and regulating the monopolistic, restrictive and unfair trade practices rather than making it necessary for certain undertakings to obtain prior approval of the Central Government for expansion, establishment of new undertakings, mergers, amalgamations and takeovers.

OBJECTIVES

Being a consumer legislation, MRTP Act seeks to regulate monopolies, in addition to regulating trade practices harmful to public interest.

The Act had two objectives before the amendment in 1991, *viz.*

- Regulation of monopolies and prevention of concentration of economic power, and
- Prohibit monopolistic, restrictive and unfair trade practices.

After the amendment, the first objective has become irrelevant as the relevant provisions to achieve the objective have been deleted. The objectives now are:

- Controlling monopolistic trade practices, and
- Regulating restrictive and unfair trade practices.

REGULATION OF TRADE PRACTICES

The main objective of the MRTP Act, that is, the regulation of monopolistic, restrictive and unfair trade practices, is sought to be achieved through the instrumentality of the MRTP Commission, a quasi-judicial body, set up by the government for the purpose of the Act. The Commission is empowered to inquire into any monopolistic, restrictive or unfair trade practices. In matters relating to monopolistic trade practices, the Central Government can pass an appropriate order after the Commission, on inquiry, came to the conclusion that the practice operates against the public interest. In matters relating to restrictive and unfair trade practices, the Commission is empowered to pass a *cease and desist* order, where it is of the opinion that the practice is against public interest.

Thus, the concept of public interest, which includes consumer interest, permeates the entire regulatory framework provided for the prevention of concentration of economic power, control of monopolies and regulation of monopolistic, restrictive and unfair trade practices. Public interest and consumer protection serve as the goal as well as the touchstone for evaluating the consequences of monopolies and trade practices.[1]

Monopolistic Trade Practices (MTPs)

In order to maximise profits and to increase market power, certain business firms tend to charge unreasonably high prices and prevent competition in the production and distribution of goods, by adopting unfair trade methods or deceptive practices. They tend to lower the quality of goods supplied, limit the capital investment or technical development for the production purposes; or increase the cost of production of goods or the charges for the provision of services and increase their profit unreasonably.[2]

These business practices tend to create monopoly and often harm the public interest through the exploitation of consumers and bring about economic imbalance in the country. Monopolistic trade practice is an aspect of monopolisation, and the effective control of monopoly should be the first priority of any effective economic legislation. Monopoly occurs when a dominant undertaking raises prices or excludes competitors. In order to bring about a balanced economic growth coupled with consumer welfare, it is necessary to curb these practices.

The statutory provisions relating to monopolistic trade practices and their regulations are contained in the MRTP Act. While Section 2(i), 10(b), 31, 32 and 37(4) of the Act are exclusively devoted to monopolistic trade practices, many other sections of the Act and the Rules and Regulations framed thereunder, contain measures pertaining to the regulations of these practices. They include Sections 12A, 12B, 12C, 14, 15, 27, 50, 55 and 61.

Meaning of MTP

A monopolistic trade practice is essentially a trade practice which represents the abuse of the market power in the production or marketing of goods, or in the provision of services, by charging unreasonably high prices, preventing or reducing competition, limiting technical development, deteriorating product quality or by adopting unfair or deceptive practices.

The concept of monopolistic trade practice, as used in the MRTP Act, is very wide and complex. The 1984 amendment to the Act has further widened the concept of monopolistic trade practices. Monopolistic trade practices have been defined under Section 2(i) of the amended MRTP Act as follows:

Any trade practice which has, or is likely to have, the effect of:

> Any trade practice which seeks to prevent competition and which results in high prices is an MTP.

- maintaining the prices of goods or the charges for services at an unreasonable level by limiting, reducing or otherwise controlling the production, supply or distribution of goods of any description or the supply of any services or in any other manner;
- unreasonably preventing or lessening competition in the production, supply or distribution of any goods or in the supply of any services;
- limiting technical development or capital investment to the common detriment or allowing the quality of any goods produced, supplied or distributed or any services rendered in India to deteriorate;
- increasing unreasonably:
  - — the prices at which goods are, or may be sold or re-sold or the charges at which the services are, or maybe provided or
  - — the profits which are, or may be derived from the production, supply or distribution (including the sale or purchase) of any goods or by the provision of services:
- preventing or lessening competition in the production, supply or distribution of any goods or in the provision or maintenance of any service by the adoption of unfair methods or unfair or deceptive practices.

Two tests will determine whether a trade practice is an MTP or not: abuse of market power and unreasonableness in any practice.

Thus, following are the MTPs:

- maintaining the prices of goods or charges for any services at an unreasonable level.
- limiting technical development or capital investment to the common detriment.
- unreasonably preventing or lessening competition.
- allowing quality of goods produced, supplied or distributed or any service rendered to deteriorate.
- increasing unreasonably the cost of production of any goods or charges for provision or maintenance of services.
- increasing unreasonably the selling price of goods or charges at which the services may be provided.

- increasing unreasonably the profits that are derived from the production, supply or distribution of any goods or the provision of any services and
- preventing or lessening competition in the production, supply or distribution of any goods or in the provision or maintenance of any services by adopting unfair methods or unfair practices.

Regulation of MTPs

As per Section 31 of the MRTP Act, where it appears to the Central Government that the owners of one or more undertakings are indulging in any monopolistic trade practice, the Central Government may refer the matter to the MRTP Commission for enquiry and report thereon. Such an enquiry may be conducted by the MRTP Commission on its own initiative or on information available to it. On the basis of the report, the Central Government may pass an appropriate order for:

- regulation of production and fixing the terms of sale(including prices);
- prohibiting any action that restricts competition and
- fixing standards for goods produced.

Restrictive Trade Practices (RTPs)

In order to maximise their profit and gain more market power, traders are often tempted to indulge in certain trade practices which restrict, reduce or prevent competition in the market and thereby harm the consumer interest. Such practices are referred to as restrictive trade practices. Because of their adverse effect on the consumer and public interest, they are sought to be regulated in almost every country of the world. In our country, such regulation is sought to be exercised through the MRTP Act.

A restrictive trade practice has the effect of preventing, distorting or restricting competition.

Broadly speaking, a trade practice which restricts or reduces competition may be termed as a restrictive trade practice.[3] As defined under the MRTP Act [Section 2(0)], a restrictive trade practice means, a trade practice which has or may have, the effect of preventing, distorting or restricting competition in any manner, and in particular, (i) which tends to disrupt the flow of capital or resources into the stream of production or (ii) which tends to bring about the manipulation of prices, or condition of delivery, or to affect the flow of supplies in the market relating to goods or services in such manner as to impose on the consumers unjustified costs or restrictions.

It may be stated that, the terms trade and trade practice are quite wide. The term *trade* is understood to include any trade, business, industry, profession or occupation relating to the production, supply, distribution of goods and includes the provision of any services. Trade practice is understood as any practice relating to the carrying on of any trade and includes (i) anything done by any person which controls or affects the price charged by or the method of trading of any trade or any class of trades and (ii) a single or isolated action of any person in relation to any trade.

Thus, a restrictive trade practice is not limited to trade alone. It would cover a practice followed in the production, distribution or supply of goods or in the provision of services. A restrictive trade practice can be adopted by a manufacturer, distributor, dealer, supplier of goods, or by one who provides any services or carries on any profession or occupation.

The following are the RTPs as described by Section 33(1) of the MRTP Act:

- *Refusal to deal with persons or classes of persons* - Any agreement which restricts or is likely to restrict by any methods, the persons or classes of persons to whom goods are sold or from whom goods are bought.
- *Tie-in sales or full-line forcing* - Any agreement requiring the purchaser of goods, as a condition of such purchase, to purchase some other goods.
- *Exclusive dealing agreement* - Any agreement restricting in any manner the purchaser in the course of his trade from acquiring or otherwise dealing in any goods other than those of the seller or any other goods.
- *Collective price fixation and tendering* - Any agreement to purchase or sell goods or take out tenders for the sale or purchase of goods only at prices or terms and conditions agreed upon between the sellers or purchasers.
- *Discriminatory dealings* - Any agreement to grant or allow concessions or benefits including allowances, discounts, rebate, or credit, in connection with or by reason of dealings.
- *Re-sale price maintenance* - Any agreement to sell goods on condition that the prices to be charged on re-sale by the purchaser shall be the prices stipulated by the seller unless it is clearly stated that prices lower than those prices may be charged.
- *Restriction on output or supply of goods* - Exclusive distributorship, territorial restriction and market-sharing.
- *Control of manufacturing* process.
- *Boycott* - Any agreement for the exclusion from any trade association or any person carrying on or intending to carry on, in good faith, the trade in relation to which the trade association is formed.
- *Price control* arrangements.
- *Governmental recognition* of practice as restrictive.
- *Residual restrictive trade practice* - Any agreement to enforce the carrying out of any such agreement as is referred to in the foregoing classes.

Under the Act, restrictive agreement must be submitted to the Registrar for registration within 60 days from the date of entering these agreements. Here the onus is on the company or the undertaking.

Regulation of RTPs

The MRTP Commission is empowered, under Section 37 of the Act, to conduct an enquiry into any RTP. If after the enquiry, the Commission is of the opinion that the practice is really restrictive and is prejudicial to public interest, it (the Commission) may, by order, direct that:

- the practice shall be dicountinued or shall not be repeated. This is called the cease-and-desist order and
- the agreement shall be void and shall stand modified in such a manner as may be specified in the order.

Division of Undertakings

Section 27 of the MRTP Act provides that if the Central Government is of the opinion that the working of a registered undertaking is prejudicial to public interest or has led, or is leading, or is likely to lead to the adoption of any monopolistic or restrictive trade practices, it can refer the matter to the MRTP Commission for an enquiry.

Further, if in the opinion of the Central Government, the continuance of inter-connection of an undertaking is detrimental to:

- the interest of the principal undertaking;
- the future development of the principal undertaking;
- the steady growth of the industry to which the principal undertaking belongs or
- the public interest,

it may refer the matter to the MRTP Commission for further enquiry.

The MRTP Commission shall conduct the necessary enquiry and recommend divisions, if necessary, subsequent to which the government may order the splitting of the concerned undertaking.

Unfair Trade Practices (UTPs)

It is said that the consumer needs no special protection and everything can be left to the market forces. The perfectly competitive market is an economist's dream and consumer sovereignty is a myth. In real life, products are of great variety, many of them being complex and the consumer has imperfect product-knowledge. Moreover, the supplier often has a dominant position against the buyer who has less bargaining power in the market. There has been a growing realisation for not depending on the old doctrine of *caveat emptor* - let the buyer beware. The consumer, therefore, needs legal protection against certain trade practices and business methods.

It is not the consumer alone who needs protection. Even an honest businessman needs legal protection from unscrupulous and dishonest competitors.

Several countries across the globe have adopted statutory measures for the control of unfair trade practices to protect the consumers. Names which come to one's memory in this context are UK, Australia, Canada and the USA.

In our country, the need for the protection of consumers is all the more great because the large majority of consumers are illiterate, ill-informed and possessing limited purchasing power, where there is a perennial shortage of many goods and where growth with social justice is the guiding principle. MRTP Act seeks to provide protection in this case.

Before the 1984 amendment, the MRTP Act contained no provisions for the protection of consumers from unfair trade practices, such as deceptive and misleading advertising, hoarding of goods and the supply of unsafe and hazardous products. The Act was directed against restrictive and monopolistic trade practices and the consumers' interest was sought to be protected by promoting competition and curbing of anti-competitive activities of manufacturers and dealers. However, the consumer needs protection not only from restrictive and monopolistic trade practices but also from unfair and unethical practices which are adopted by unscrupulous businessmen to maximise their profit and sales at the expense of the consumer.

The major provisions are contained in Sections 36A, 36B, 36C, 36D and 36E which have been inserted in the MRTP Act by the 1984 amendment, which became effective from August 1, 1984. Other provisions relevant to the regulation of unfair trade practices are contained in certain other sections of the Act, which include Sections 12A, 12B, 12C, 14 and 61.

Concept of Unfair Trade Practice

Broadly speaking, any trade practice which is considered unfair and harmful to the consumer is an unfair trade practice.

The genesis of unfair trade practice is human greed which leads to the exploitation of the consumer by the trader. Mahatma Gandhi said that the rich must act as the trustee of the poor for their wealth and that all must have bread before some have cake. It is breach of this dictum that initiates unfair trade practices.

Any trade practice which results in loss or injury to consumer becomes an unfair trade practice.

As defined under the MRTP Act, unfair trade practice refers to any of the five trade practices specified under clauses (1) to (5) of Section 36A, which are adopted for the purpose of any services, and which cause loss or injury to the consumer. Briefly stated, these trade practices are:

- Misleading advertisement and false representation;
- Advertising of bargain price (or bait advertising) and switch selling;
- Offering of pseudo gifts or prizes and conducting of promotional contests, lottery and games of chance or skill;
- Supplying of unsafe or hazardous products, and
- Hoarding or destroying of goods, or refusal to sell goods, resulting in a price increase.

The loss or injury to the consumer may arise by eliminating or restricting competition or otherwise.

Thus, the definition of unfair trade practice is not a general definition but is confined to the above mentioned five trade practices. While the definitions of a monopolistic trade practice and a restrictive trade practice, as given in the Act, are general in nature and any trade practice falling within the respective criterion may amount to the monopolistic trade practices, is a specific one in the sense that no practice other than the five practices specified for the purpose can be taken to be an unfair trade practice. Neither the MRTP Commission nor any other authority is empowered to include any other trade practice within the definition of an unfair trade practice.

Any trade practice would, therefore, amount to an unfair trade practice under the following conditions:

- The practice falls within one or more of the five trade practices mentioned above.
- The practice is adopted for any of the following purpose:
  - — promoting the sale, use or supply of any goods or
  - — provision of any services.
- The practice causes loss or injury to the consumers of the relevant goods or service.
- The loss or injury to the consumers may be caused by eliminating or restricting competition or otherwise.

To be specific, the following are the UTPs:

- The practice of making any statement, whether orally or in writing or by visible representation which:
  - — falsely represents that the goods are of a particular standard, quality, grade, composition, style or model.
  - — falsely represents any re-built, second-hand, renovated, reconditioned or old goods as new goods.
  - — falsely represents that the services are of a particular standard, quality or grade.

- represents that the goods or services have sponsorship, approval, performance, characteristics, accessories, uses or benefits which such goods or services do not have.
  - represents that the seller or the supplier has sponsorship, approval or affiliation which such a seller or supplier does not have.
  - makes a false or misleading representation concerning the need for or the usefulness of any goods or services.
  - gives to the public any warranty or guarantee of the performance, efficacy or length of life of a product or of any goods that is not based on an adequate or proper test thereof.
  - makes to the public representation in a form that purports to warranty or guarantee of a product or of any goods or service or a promise to replace, maintain or repair an article or any part thereof or to repeat or continue a service until it has achieved a specified result. If such purported warranty, guarantee or promise is materially misleading or if there is no responsible prospect that such warranty, guarantee or promise will be carried out.
  - materially misleads the public concerning the price at which a product or like products or goods or services have been or are ordinarily sold or provided and for this purpose, a representation as to the price shall be deemed to refer to the price at which the product or goods or services has or have been sold by sellers or provided by the supplier generally in the relevant market unless it is clearly specified to be the price at which the product has been sold or services have been provided by the person by whom or on whose behalf the representation is made.
  - gives false or misleading facts disparaging the goods, services or trade of another person.
- Permits the publication of any advertisement, whether in any newspaper or otherwise, for the sale or supply at a bargain price of goods or services that are not intended to be offered for sale or supply at the bargain price, or for a period that is and in quantities that are reasonable, having regard to the nature of the market in which the business is carried on, the nature and size of business and the nature of the advertisement.
- Permits: (a) the offering of gifts, prizes or other items with the intention of not providing them as offered or creating the impression that something is being given or offered free of charge when it is fully or partly covered by the amount charged in the transaction as a whole, (b) the conduct of any contest, lottery, game of chance or skill, for the purpose of promoting, directly or indirectly, the sale, use or supply of any product or any business interest.
- Permits the sale or supply of goods intended to be used or are of a kind likely to be used by consumers, knowing or having reasons to believe that the goods do not comply with the standards, prescribed by a competent authority relating to performance, composition, contents, design, construction, finishing or packing as are necessary to prevent or reduce the risk of injury to the person using the goods.
- Permits the hoarding or destruction of goods or refusal to sell the goods or make them available for sale, or to provide any service, if such hoarding, destruction or refusal raises or tends to raise or is intended to raise the cost of these or other similar goods or services.

Regulation of UTPs

The MRTP Commission may enquire into any UTP:

- Upon receiving a complaint from any trade or consumers' association with a membership of 25 or more;
- Upon a reference made to it by the Central or State Government;
- Upon an application made to it by the Director-General;
- Upon its own knowledge or information and
- With the latest amendment to the MRTP Act, upon a application from any member of public.

If the enquiry proves that the UTP does exist and it is prejudicial to the public interest the Commission may direct that:

- the practice shall be discontinued or shall not be repeated and
- any agreement relating to such an UTP shall be void or shall stand modified in such a manner as may be directed by the Commission.

THE COMPETITION ACT, 2002

Like its counterpart (discussed in the previous chapter), the MRTP Act also came into sharp criticisms. The MRTP Act, for example, was disparaged for having come in the way of industrial progress. It was also criticised for having failed to protect interests of consumers, though the Act was supposed to be a consumer legislation.

One by-product of economic reforms is the shift in focus from regulating monopolies to promoting competition.

The economic reforms initiated from the beginning of 1990 necessitated a shift in the focus from regulating monopolies to promoting competition. Competition, if encouraged, would improve productivity, increase quality and reduce quality-all benefiting consumers. The Competition Act precisely seeks to achieve this.

The Competition Act seeks to promote and sustain competition to protect the interests of consumers and to ensure freedom of trade.

Objective of the Act: The preamble to the Act says that the Competition Act seeks to provide, in view of the economic development of the country, for the establishment of a Commission to prevent practices having adverse impact on competition, to promote and sustain competition in markets, to protect the interests of consumers and to ensure freedom of trade. In short, this is an Act designed to promote and sustain competition and thereby protect the interests of consumers.

The Act runs into 66 sections, divided into nine chapters. It extends to the whole of India except Jammu and Kashmir.

Provisions

The Act seeks to establish Competition Commission of India. The Act also provides for the appointment of Director General (and additional, joint, deputy and assistant directors), advisers, consultants and officers to assist the Commission in conducting enquiry into any offences. The Act empowers the Commission to appoint a Registrar and other staff for the efficient performance of its functions.

Any person, consumer, consumers association, trade association, statutory authority, a state government or central government may lodge a complaint with the Commission. The Commission is empowered to act suo moto.

Any of the sources, stated above, can lodge a complaint with the Commission (the Commission can also act on its own) on the knowledge of anticompetitive agreements being entered into. It is unlawful, under the act, for any enterprise or persons to enter into an agreement in respect of production, supply, storage, distribution, acquisition or control of goods or provision of service, which causes adverse effect on competition.

Complaint can also be lodged when an enterprise indulges in the abuse of dominant position. An organisation has dominant position when it can operate independently of competitive forces prevailing in the market, or it can affect its competitors or consumers in its favour.

On receipt of a complaint (or on its own knowledge), the Commission shall conduct an enquiry.

After enquiry, if the Commission finds that there exists an agreement which is detrimental to competition or there exists an enterprise which is abusing its dominant position in the market, it may pass all or any of the following orders, namely:

(a) direct the enterprises or persons involved in such agreement, or abuse of dominant position to discontinue and not to repeat such activities;

(b) impose penalty on the offending parties. The fine shall not exceed 10 per cent of the average of the turnover for the previous three financial years.

The Commission has also power to regulate mergers, provided such conditions are likely to be detrimental to the growth of competition.

The Act empowers the Commission to award compensation for an individual who has suffered damage or loss from the use of a good or service. The compensation to be paid by an organisation that has caused loss or damage.

QUESTIONS

1. What are RTPs? How are they sought to be regulated?
2. What are UTPs? How are they sought to be regulated?
3. Why is MRTP Act criticised?
4. Give the objectives of the Competition Act. What are its main provisions?

ASSIGNMENT

Take 2006 as one year period as the base. Find out how many complaints have been lodged with the Competition Commission of India. Also find out how many of the complaints have been disposed of. Compare the functioning of the Competition Commission with its predecessor - MRTP Commission.

REFERENCES

1. D.P.S.Verma, *Monopolies, Trade Regulation and Consumer Protection*, p.12.
2. *Ibid*, p.181.
3. *The Hindu*, July 8, 1989.

CHAPTER OUTLINE

Objectives of the Act
Provisions of the Act
Some Reflections on the Act
Do We Need FERA?
Amendments to the Act
From FERA to FEMA
FEMA, 1999

LEARNING OBJECTIVES

After reading this Chapter, you should be able to:

1. Understand the objectives of FERA
2. Detail main provisions of FERA
3. Comment on FERA
4. Doubt about the relevance of FERA
5. List the various amendments to FERA
6. Detail main provisions of FEMA

16 From Foreign Exchange Regulation Act, to Foreign Exchange Management Act

OBJECTIVES

The principal objective of the Foreign Exchange Regulation Act (FERA) is to prevent the outflow of Indian currency and to see that the foreign exchange legitimately due to India should be received.

In detail, the objectives of the Act are as follows:

- To regulate certain payments.
- To regulate dealings in foreign exchange and securities.
- To regulate the transactions indirectly affecting foreign exchange.
- To regulate import and export of currency and bullion.
- To conserve the foreign exchange resources of the country and to utilise the same in the interests of the economic development of the country.
- To regulate holding of immovable property outside India.
- To regulate employment of foreign nationals.
- To regulate acquisition, holding, etc. of immovable property in India by non-residents.
- To regulate foreign companies.

The Act applies to the whole of India, to citizens of India outside India and to branches and agencies outside India of companies or corporate bodies registered in India. The Act came into force with effect from 1st January, 1974.

The objectives of the Act are sought to be achieved through certain provisions contained in its 50 plus sections. The important provisions are discussed below.

PROVISIONS

A. Regulation of Dealings in Foreign Exchange

FERA authorises only RBI to deal with foreign exchange transactions.

Under the Act, the Reserve Bank of India (RBI) is the only authority to regulate foreign exchange transactions. Section 8 provides that except with the previous permission of the Reserve Bank, no person, other than an authorised dealer, shall conduct a foreign exchange business with any other person who is not an authorised dealer. However, the sale and purchase of foreign exchange between any person and a money-changer in India will not be hit by restrictions imposed in the section. The section further provides that except with the previous permission of the Reserve Bank, no person shall enter into any transaction which provides for the conversion of the Indian currency into foreign or *vice versa* at rates of exchange other than the rates authorised by the Reserve Bank.

B. Restrictions on Payments

Section 8 of the Act also lays down restrictions on certain payments. It provides that unless authorised by the Reserve Bank, no person in India or no person resident in India shall:

(a) make any payment to or for the credit of any person resident outside India;

(b) receive, otherwise than through an authorised dealer, any payment by order or on behalf of any person resident outside India;

(c) draw, issue or negotiate any bill of exchange or promissory note or acknowledge any debt so that a right, actual or contingent, to receive a payment is created or transferred in favour of a person resident outside India;

(d) make any payment to or for the credit of any person by order or on behalf of any person resident outside India;

(e) place any sum to the credit of any person resident outside India;

(f) make any payment to or for the credit of any person or receive any payment for or by order or on behalf of any person as consideration for or in association with the receipt by any person of a payment or the acquisition by any person of property outside India and the creation and transfer in favour of any person any right, actual or contingent, to receive payment or acquire property outside India and

(g) draw, issue or negotiate any bill of exchange or promissory note, transfer any security or acknowledge any debt, so that a right, actual or contingent, to receive a payment is credited or transferred in favour of any person as consideration for or in association with any matter.

C. Restrictions Regarding Assets Held by Non Residents and Import and Export of Certain Currency and Bullion

Restrictions on Import-Export of Currency: Section 13 provides that no person shall, except with the permission of the Reserve Bank, bring or send into India any gold, silver, foreign exchange or Indian currency. Similarly, no person shall, without the permission from the Reserve Bank, take or send out of India any gold, jewellery, precious stones, Indian currency or foreign exchange other than foreign exchange obtained by him from an authorised dealer or money-changer.

D. Duty of Persons Entitled to Receive Foreign Exchange and Payment for Exported Goods

(i) *Persons Entitled Receive Foreign Exchange*: Section 16 lays down that no person who has a right to receive foreign exchange shall delay receipt of such foreign exchange without prior permission from the Reserve Bank.

(ii) *Restrictions on Export of Goods*: Section 18 lays down that the Central Government may, by notification, prohibit export of any goods unless the exporter furnishes to the prescribed authority particulars relating to the full export value of goods. The Central Government may also, by notification, specify that the goods shall not be sold at less than the declared value except with the permission of the Reserve Bank.

Sub-Section 3 of Section 18 provides that if the exporter does not receive payment for export within the prescribed period, the exporter is presumed to contravene the provisions of Section 18 of the Act.

Sub-Section 4 of Section 18 further lays down that if the prescribed period expires and the export proceeds have not been received by the exporter, the Reserve Bank may issue directions for receiving payments if goods have been sold or re-import of goods into India, if the exported goods have not been sold. The Reserve Bank may also authorise and issue necessary direction to the effect that the unsold goods or the right to receive payments in respect of the same if the goods are sold shall be transferred or assigned to the Central Government.

E. Restrictions on Appointment of Certain Persons and Companies as Agents or Technical or Management Advisers in India

Section 28 lays down that a person resident outside India, whether a citizen of India or not, or a person who is not a citizen of India but is resident in India or a company other than a banking company which is not incorporated under any law in force in India shall not, except with the general or special permission of the Reserve Bank,

- act or accept appointment, as agent in India, of any person or company, in the trading or commercial transactions of such person or company;
- act or accept appointment as technical or management adviser in India of any person or company and
- permit any trademark which he or she is entitled to use or to be used by any person or company for any direct or indirect consideration.

It is provided in the section that where any person or company as aforesaid acts or accepts appointment of such agent, technical or management adviser, or permits the use of trademark without the permission of the Reserve Bank, then such acting, appointment or permission shall be void.

F. Restriction on Establishment of Place of Business in India

Section 29 provides that a person resident outside India, whether a citizen of India or not or a person who is not a citizen of India but is resident in India or a company other than a banking company which is not incorporated under any law in force in India shall not, except with the general or special permission of the Reserve Bank,

- carry on in India or establish in India a branch office or other place of business for carrying on any activity of a trading, commercial or industrial nature other than an activity for the carrying on of which permission of the Reserve Bank has been obtained under the provisions of this section of the Act or
- acquire the whole or any part of any undertaking in India of any person or company carrying on any trade, commerce or industry or purchase the shares in India of any such company.

The section further provides that where any person or company carries on any activity as aforesaid at the commencement of the Act or has established a branch office or other place of business for the carrying on of such activity, then such person or company may within a period of six months from such commencement, make an application to the Reserve Bank for the permission to continue to carry on such activity or to continue the establishment of a branch office or other place of business for the carrying on of such activity. Whereas the first part of this section relates to the fresh permissions, the latter part of the section relates to the permissions and licences known as '*carry on business licences*' under the Foreign Exchange Regulations Act.

G. Prior Permission of Reserve Bank Required for Taking up Employment in India by Nationals of Foreign State

Section 30 lays down that no national of a foreign state shall without the prior permission of the Reserve Bank, practice any profession or carry on any occupation, trade or business in India, in a case where such a foreign national desires to acquire any foreign exchange being intended for remittance outside India out of any money(s) received by him in India by reason of such employment or the practising of such profession or the carrying on of such occupation, trade or business, as the case may be.

H. Restrictions on Immovable Property

Property in India cannot be gifted to an unknown person because such a holding enables the holder to sell it and insist on taking away currency. However, partition and other transactions of existing rights are protected. It may be noticed that a foreigner can buy and hold any property in India but such an investment by non-residents of any nationality have to be approved by the Reserve Bank of India.

The FERA is also a penal law, as it provides for the punishment for various offences of the Act, most of it for the misuse of foreign currency.

SOME REFLECTIONS ON FERA

1. The Foreign Exchange Regulation Act (FERA) is directly and primarily concerned with the flow of currency which to a great extent, is regulated by the Reserve Bank Act. It is highly

desirable that the provisions in FERA should be incorporated as one chapter in the RBI Act itself, because the bane of our country has been prolific and *ad hoc* legislation so that a comprehensive knowledge of the existing laws is not directly available and may lead to distortion in perception. There will be no conflict between the provisions of FERA and the Reserve Bank and it will contribute towards lessening the number of pieces of legislation.

2. While it is understandable that a country should attempt to protect its reserves of hard currency and prevent demands from other countries consequent upon the flight of currency of India, FERA appears to be not drafted with precision and appears also to be an attempt to string up certain ideas of principles of economics. When we look at Section 27, we find an absolute bar upon an Indian citizen or any other legal entity from associating himself, or itself, with any other person in any other country with a view to do business or to collaborate in potential business ventures. But the actual words used do not indicate any stage of the negotiations and even an exchange of letters or visits without the prior permission of the Reserve Bank of India appears to come within the mischief of the section so that even harmless, even preliminary enquiries, without the permission of the Reserve Bank of India, are considered to be offending the law. This is a very vague provision and in fact an infringement of the basic rights of citizens relating to personal freedom. The provision has failed to specify that any arrangement or understanding involving the expenditure of Indian currency would have to be entered into with the prior permission of the Reserve Bank of India. The section makes it an offence even to have a dialogue before a valid contract is entered into. This observation, however, is irrelevant as the section itself has been deleted.

3. One other provision, namely, Section 18, sub-clause 4, may be looked into to appreciate the nature of the drafting of FERA. That is a provision where if a person in India has not been able to recover money due to him from outside India, on account of sale etc., the right to recover money is legally deemed to have been assigned to the Government of India so that it can take steps to recover the same.

What is the *modus-operandi*? There is no simple legal forum or a court to recover the same and one must have recourse to International Commercial Arbitration which is worthwhile only if enormous amounts are involved and perhaps it would have been desirable that the Government should have applied at the diplomatic level and at the level of International Law to have a simplified procedure for recovery of dues.

4. It is pertinent to note that substantial changes are purported to be made by FERA in regard to property law. The principal enactment which covers the core of property law is the Transfer of Property Act, 1882. That Act completely defines transfers and encumbrances that could be validly created over property and one wishes that these provisions of FERA, namely, Section 24, 25 and 31, which deal with the acquisition, holding and settlement of properties, had been incorporated in that major Act, because it is natural that persons are seeking accurate information or advice on:

   (a) the capacity of foreigners to hold property in India;

   (b) the transfer of property by an Indian to a foreigner or to a non-resident Indian; and

   (c) the capacity of an Indian to acquire property abroad would automatically look into that Act for guidance. They would justifiably think that the Foreign Exchange Regulation Act would not deal with immovable property in India.

5. Government agencies have created the impression that foreign exchange is something precious and must be protected at all cost. So, we have the FERA which contains stringent provisions. FERA violators are treated as criminals; the frenzy is so much that an entrepreneur was once arrested for being in possession of Rs.450 in foreign exchange even though it was what was

left over from a journey abroad, undertaken with exchange money properly sanctioned by the Government.

Paradoxically, the same government agencies waste vast sums in foreign exchange in the name of 'policy.' A case in point is paraxylene, an input in the manufacture of DMT. Paraxylene was imported at a cost of more than $700 a tonne. Bombay Dyeing applied, way back in 1979 itself, to the government for permission to manufacture paraxylene. Permission was denied to the applicant on the grounds that paraxylene was reserved for the public sector.

6. There have been repeated demands of late, that FERA should be abolished, more particularly, after the corporates find themselves confronted by serious allegations of violation of the Act. Some people are of the opinion that since India has almost an 18 billion dollar foreign exchange reserve position and as there is no scarcity of foreign exchange, the Act must be done away with. Yet another school of thought prevails, which opines that the Act is outdated, draconian and needs to be either re-written completely or totally overhauled so as to keep in tune with the Government's avowed policy of de-regulation and economic globalisation.

Generally speaking, after the 1991 Industrial Policy was announced, the aim of which was to decontrol industrial activity in general (excepting a few) and de-bureaucratise the working of economic legislation in particular, it appears that much needs to be done to bring the FERA in tune with the current thinking, both in governmental and corporate sectors and the need of the economy as it stands today. Many experts state that since India has qualified for Article VIII under the articles of association of IMF, the rupee is deemed to be convertible on current account and hence FERA must be further liberalised. Corporate sector is generally of the opinion that restrictions on current account transactions imposed under the FERA virtually preclude transactions in foreign exchange by residence without the permission of the RBI. They are also of the view that international trade and cross border operations are impossible without free foreign exchange availability and freedom to utilise the available exchange for promoting legitimate business interests.

7. It is felt that piecemeal reforms of the FERA which have been attempted time and again, through the issuance of notifications by the Government and RBI, may not serve the purpose. Further, there is no harmony between FERA and direct tax laws in many respects. For example, the basic definition of 'resident/non-resident' in both legislations are dichotomous and totally different. It has also been the experience of the Government that FERA violations are driven by exchange rate and tax distortions. Hence it is imperative that the only effective check would be capital account convertibility. As one of the industrialists is reported to have said: '*A crime involving foreign exchange is treated as akin to murder*.'

For the foregoing reasons, it appears that the time has come to usher in a new policy and legislation to manage foreign exchange resources rather than control foreign exchange transactions through a maze of regulations.

Precisely for these reasons, the Finance Minister in his 1997-98 budget speech announced that FERA would be replaced by a more progressive and growth friendly legislation which might be called Foreign Exchange Management Act (FERA).

DO WE NEED FERA?

Box 16.1 seeks to answer this relevant question.

Box 16.1 **Running out of Steam**

In the light of the reforms introduced, do we need the Foreign Exchange Regulation Act (FERA) of 1973? After all, the precursor to FERA was originally introduced by the British during World War II. Consequently, the logic behind the introduction of the legislation is perhaps no longer valid now.

To a large extent, the Preamble to an Act describes the scope of the Act and the problems that the legislation is designed to handle. The Preamble to FERA is the following: "An Act to consolidate and amend the law regulating certain payments, dealings in foreign exchange and securities, transactions indirectly affecting foreign exchange and the import and export of currency and bullion, for the conservation of foreign exchange resources of the country and the proper utilisation thereof in the interests of economic development of the country." The focus is therefore on conserving foreign exchange and controlling its use, a demand management sort of exercise. Surely, this logic has very limited validity now.

Let us consider some example of FERA violations, instances where there have been prosecutions under FERA. The question to ask is would we like such instances to be violations of the law in the future as well? Or are these cases instances where norms of natural justice require the law to be otherwise? It is important to emphasise this, as law and natural justice are distinct entities. Legal justice may try to attain the ideal of natural justice, but the purpose of law is to ensure that the legislation is observed, not that justice is necessarily done. Oliver Wendell Holmes once remarked, "This is a court of law, young man, not a court of justice!"

Let us consider some instances.

Ajmer Singh, migrated to Malaysia in 1946 and became a Malaysian citizen. His wife and son joined him there in 1953-54. In 1968, the son returned to study in India and the father paid him Rs.27,000 towards the expenses of studying. Since the son was a resident of Malaysia, proceedings were initiated against Ajmer Singh under Section 9(1)(1) of FERA (Ajmer Singh vs. Union of India). This section stipulates that, without the approval of the RBI, no resident of India (Ajmer Singh) shall make any payments to a person who is a resident outside India (his son).

E.V.Marakkar had relatives who lived in Malaysia. These relatives used to send him money for the maintenance of their families. The families lived in Tamil Nadu. Section 9(1)(b) of FERA prohibits an Indian resident (Marakkar) from receiving payments from a non-resident (the relatives), except through an authorised dealer. Marakkar was, therefore, prosecuted (E.V.Marakkar vs F.E.R.Appelate Board).

A British resident, employed in India, asked the Indian acquantance to send a Sterling cheque to London. Since this was done without the permission of the RBI, and since the cheque was not obtained from an authorised dealer, there was a prosecution under Section 13(2) of FERA (G.Subramanyam vs H.D.Mundhra). Under Section 13(2), no one can send foreign exchange out of India without the permission of the RBI.

Kartar Singh and his wife spent some time in the United States. On their return to India, Kartar Singh was found to be in possession of foreign exchange, although he was not an authorised dealer. This was held to be a violation of Section 8(1) of FERA (Kartar Singh vs. Director of Enforcement). Kartar Singh maintained that this money was legally obtained through his and his wife's earnings while they were in the United States.

Due to ignorance of the law, Kartar Singh did not declare the foreign exchange to customs on returning to India. The documents produced showed that Kartar Singh and his wife had indeed earned foreign exchange in the United States. But no documentation could be produced to show that they had made savings out of these earnings. Section 71(3) of FERA stipulates that the burden of proving that foreign exchange has come into one's possession legally, is on the possessor. Since Kartar Singh had failed to do this satisfactorily, he was judged to be guilty.

A son who lived abroad, had various debts contracted in India. The son sent drafts to an individual in India in foreign currency and this individual gave Indian currency to the father (Syed Fareed) against these receipts. Fareed used this money to repay the son's debts. This was held to be a contravention of Section 9(1)(d) of FERA. This section stipulates that no payments can be made to anyone by order or on behalf of a person resident outside India (Syed Fareed vs. F.E.R.Appellate Board).

Most people would probably agree that, after liberalisation, we no longer need cases of this type. This is not to imply that there have been no changes in FERA after June 1991. Sections 11, 12, 15, 17, 20, 21, 23, 27 and 32 have been dropped.

Several other sections have been drastically amended. But, these changes have not really questioned whether FERA is at all necessary now.

Under Section 6 and 7 of FERA, only authorised dealers and money changers are allowed to deal in, or possess, foreign exchange. Quite often, violations take place because there is an ignorance about this requirement.

Do we really need this stipulation? Can ex-post facto approval from the RBI not suffice? Sometimes, exported goods are not lifted by the importer. Under Section 18(4)(ii), the exporter is not free to dispose off these goods. They have to be brought back to India and this greatly adds to the costs.

Under Sections 22 and 23, is there any need to have restrictions on the issue of bearer securities or provisions for governmental acquisitions of foreign securities? Do the powers of search and arrest (Sections 33 through 40) have to be as stringent as they are now? Should technical violations continue to be as important as they now are under Sections. 68 and 69? Under Section 69, for technical violations, is there any need to publish the names and places of business of companies convicted?

Naturally enough, no simplistic answer is possible to these questions. But, FERA essentially reflects a mindset where foreign exchange was perceived to be at a premium. Its use therefore, needed to be controlled and monitored.

With the unified exchange rate, the circumstances have changed. Why should legislation that reflects the mindset of an earlier era be accepted unquestioningly now?

Many years ago, the Dagli Committee had gone into the question of controls and subsidies in India. One of the basic tenets of the Dagli Committee's recommendations was that all dysfunctional pieces of legislation should be removed. A second tenet was that all legislations should be simplified. Under both these criteria, there is certainly a case for a hard look at FERA.

AMENDMENTS TO THE ACT

The need for a comprehensive review of the Foreign Exchange Regulation Act, 1973, has been evident for some time. The Act, 1973 reflected the requirements of a highly regulatory system. The recent changes in economic policy, especially the liberalistion of the industrial sector and the moves to open up the economy through changes in trade policy and the encouragement of foreign investments, have made it necessary to modify several provisions of the Act to bring them in line with the current economic realities. Accordingly, it was announced in the budget speech for 1992-93 that the government proposed to introduce comprehensive amendments to the Foreign Exchange Regulation Act.

In pursuit of these objectives and pending legislative changes, some important steps were taken about a year ago to reduce the rigours of FERA through certain notifications issued by the Reserve Bank of India. Various facilities were extended to foreign/FERA companies on the appointment of technical and management advisors, opening of branches, acquisition of immovable property, borrowing of money or acceptance of deposits etc. Facilities were also extended to NRIs, Indian companies and residents for the opening of foreign currency accounts in India, following the introduction of partial convertibility of the current account since 1st March, 1992. Notifications were also issued exempting NRIs returning to the country from making declarations on their arrival in India, regarding their assets abroad and from the requirement of prior approval for the acquisition of immovable property in India.

While the above changes in FERA were introduced by issue of notifications by the Reserve Bank of India or the Central Government, it was also felt that comprehensive amendments to the Act were necessary with a view to:

(a) incorporate into the law all the changes which have been made by the issue of notifications by the RBI/Central Government in order to give assurance of their permanence;

(b) delete sections which have lost their relevance over time and

(c) rationalise other sections which are considered necessary but should be amended to do away with the rigours or irrationalities experienced while administering the Act.

The important changes are summarised below:

Section 11: Restrictions regarding assets held by non-residents.

This Section was introduced in the 1973 Act to provide statutory backing to the RBI's practice of blocking the securities of persons who had migrated abroad as well as to block the bank accounts and securities of prospective emigrants. RBI no longer blocks such bank accounts. The accounts of such persons are treated as non-resident accounts on their becoming non-residents. Section 11 has now lost its relevance and is, therefore, deleted.

Section 12: Special accounts under which the Central Government can direct certain payments to be made into a special account

This Section has never been operated upon and hence is deleted.

Section 13: Restrictions on import and export of certain currency and bullion.

From now onwards, trade in gold and silver will be regulated by the Exim Policy while export and import of foreign exchange and Indian currency will continue to be regulated under this section. Only trade in gold or silver coins will continue to be regulated under the Act. All other trade in gold and silver will be covered by this Policy.

Section 15: Power of the Central Government to direct payment in foreign currency in certain cases.

This Section regulates the payment by non-residents in foreign currency while on a visit to India. As RBI has already granted general permission to firms/companies or other organisations to offer hospitality to non-residents on visits to India, this section has been deleted.

Section 17: Power to regulate uses etc. of imported gold and silver.

This Section has become redundant because of the change in Section 13 and it has, therefore, been deleted.

Section 18A:Payment for exported goods.

A new Section, 18A has been introduced, permitting the take out of goods on rental, lease, hire or on any other arrangement which does not amount to the disposal of such goods. This is an important relaxation which has been demanded by exporters and others.

Section 19: Export and transfer of securities.

Sub-clause (c) of Section 19(1) deals with the transfer of any security from a register in India to a register outside India. Since this was intended to take care of erstwhile sterling companies which had dual registers, this sub-section and sub-clause (c) of Section 19(4) stand deleted.

Under Section 19(5), three types of transfer of shares were regulated: (a) transfer by a non-resident to another non-resident, (b) transfer by a non-resident to a resident and (c) transfer by a foreign national resident in India to another resident. Under the changes, transfer of shares under category (a) will not to be regulated. Under (b) & (c), the questions of valuation of shares and permission for remittances outside India arise and, therefore, these are retained. The scope of 19(5) is widened by the inclusion of bonds and debentures.

Under Section 19(6), the Central Government is empowered to issue notifications exempting any transfer from the operation of the provisions of sub-section (5). These powers will be transferred to the RBI.

Section 20: Restrictions on payment in respect of government securities created or issued for raising public loans before the Independence of the country.

This provision has lost its relevance and stands deleted.

Section 21: Custody of securities by a depository or any other person.

With sub-sections of Section 19(1) on the acquisition, holding and disposing off of any foreign security being deleted, this section which relates to the custody of securities acquired under Section 19 is deleted.

Section 22: Restriction on issue of bearer securities

This section will have to continue but the powers of the Central Government have been given to the RBI.

Section 23: Acquisition by Central Government of foreign securities for purpose of strengthening foreign exchange position.

This section has never been invoked by the Central Government and is unlikely to be invoked and stands deleted.

Section 25: Restrictions on the holding of immovable property outside India.

This section has been amended suitably to enable RBI to grant general permission subject to certain conditions, as may be notified by the RBI from time to time.

Section 26: Certain provisions as to companies.

Until recently, there were restrictions on FERA companies, *inter alia,* in the matter of borrowing funds or raising deposits by them in India as well as taking over or creating any interest in business by way of transfer from a person resident in India in their favour under this Act. These restrictions are now done away with by deleting sub sections (1) to (5) and sub section (7) along with explanations (I), (II) and (III). Under this section, only sub section (6) has been retained, which regulates giving of guarantee by a person resident in India in respect of any debt or other obligation or liability in favour of a person resident outside India.

Section 27: Restriction on persons resident in India associating themselves with or participating in concerns outside India.

This section, as it was originally worded, covered apart from joint ventures, the acceptance of directorship in overseas companies by Indian nationals staying in India and required all applications to be made to the Government of India for specific permission in individual cases. Moreover, there was scope for interpretation that even association with overseas concerns for carrying on certain activities in India fell within its purview. There had been a large number of representations for deleting this section as it was very restrictive and had not served much purpose. Hence, it has been deleted.

Section 28: Restrictions on the appointment of certain persons and companies as agents or technical or management advisers in India.

It has been decided to take FERA companies outside the purview of this section in regard to the acceptance of appointment as an agent or technical management adviser or for the use of trademarks to which they were entitled. Restrictions on appointment as technical or management adviser and for the use of trademark with respect to other categories of persons or companies covered under this section have also been done away with. Therefore, restrictions under this section would henceforth, apply only to foreign companies, foreign citizens and non-residents with regard to their acceptance of appointment as an agent in India, of any person or company.

Section 29: Restrictions on establishment of places of business in India.

This section has been amended, exempting FERA companies from the prohibition imposed under clause (a) and (b) of sub-section (1) on the establishment of a branch office or a liaison office even when the non-resident interest in such company exceeds 40%. Such companies will also be allowed to acquire whole or part of any undertaking in India, of any person or company carrying on trade, commerce and industry, excepting agriculture and plantation activity. It is also clarified that restriction with regard to activities of companies registered outside India and foreigners would continue to be regulated under this section.

Section 30: Prior permission for foreign nationals before taking up employment in India.

Since the RBI or the Department of Economic Affairs do not wish to regulate the employment of foreign nationals any more after the employer had decided upon it, this Section has been amended accordingly. Ministry of Home Affairs will, however, continue its control through the grant of visas.

Section 31; Restriction on the acquisition, holding etc. of immovable property in India.

Henceforth, FERA companies do not need to take the permission of RBI for acquiring, holding, transferring or disposing of by sale, mortgage, deed, lease, gift, etc., any immovable property situated in India. However, restrictions on foreign companies and citizens will continue as at present.

Section 32: Regulation of booking of passages outside India and restrictions on foreign travel.

Airlines and shipping companies, travel agencies etc. will no longer be required to obtain a licence from the apex bank for carrying on the business of booking passages for travel abroad. Besides, 'P' form restrictions, most of which had already been done away with, have been completely removed. This section under FERA thus stands deleted.

Possession of foreign currencies

Under Section 71, the burden of proof for keeping foreign currency in excess of the equivalent value of Rs.250 was with the individual. This limit now stands raised to Rs.15,000 which is equal to $500 approximately.

Submission of returns/statement by ADs

A new Section 73A in the Act will be added to give enabling powers to the Reserve Bank of India to impose a penalty not exceeding Rs.10,000 and recurring penalty upto Rs.2,000 per day against authorised dealers etc. to ensure strict compliance with the directions given to them, particularly on the submission of periodical returns. Promotional and regular submission of returns has become imperative with large-scale delegation of powers. Earlier ADs/money changers were required to submit such returns under executive instructions.

Apart from the above changes, the Foreign Exchange Manual will be updated by the RBI and all the changes made in the FERA either through this ordinance or the notification/circulars issued earlier, will be incorporated in the new Manual. It is also intended that the powers of enforcement under FERA will be delegated to somewhat higher levels. The notifications on this will be issued by the Department of Revenue.

Major changes effected between the years 1991 to 1996 in the FERA and in Reserve Bank regulations:

1. Restructuring policy guidelines regarding foreign and NRI investment and investments by overseas corporate bodies (OCBs - i.e. companies incorporated abroad, wherein non-resident Indians have more than 60% stake in the beneficial interest and voting pattern of the company).
2. Removal of entry barriers for foreign capital in high-tech areas including hotels and tourism related industry, export oriented industries, computers, import substitution sectors, shipping etc.
3. Re-defining the restrictions for activity with respect to real estate development for NRIs and OCBs.
4. Permitting returning Indians including those of Indian origin (NRIs) to hold assets abroad without restrictions apart from permitting them to make fresh investments abroad out of their savings retained overseas.
5. Permitting foreign companies to have branches in India, where that would mean developmental assistance to Indian industries and assist in infra-structural development.
6. Permitting NRI and OCB investment on non-repatriation without the RBI approval.
7. Opening up of the financial sector of the economy for FIIs (foreign Institutional Investors).
8. Permitting foreign technicians to visit India for turnkey and start-up operations.
9. Permitting certain well defined categories of persons to own and hold exchange earners' foreign currency account, exporter's foreign currency account and under a scheme called resident foreign currency account, for returning Indians.
10. Liberalising regulations *w.r.t.* import of gold and silver subject to certain conditions which included amendment of Section 13 of the FERA.
11. Removal of several restrictions on export and transfer of securities.
12. Opening up areas for overseas joint ventures and wholly owned subsidiaries abroad by removal of major barriers for domestic industry to enter foreign markets as investors and collaborators.
13. Removal of ban on foreign brand name usage.
14. Introducing full convertibility on current account in transactions of foreign exchange through authorised dealers.
15. Providing for access by domestic industries to foreign currency loans in the form of external commercial borrowings (ECBs), where foreign lenders are prepared to advance finance to Indian business.
16. Opening up housing and real estate development activity to NRIs and OCBs.,
17. Permitting NRIs to promote companies in India.

It may however be noted that no foreign investment is permitted in agricultural land or activity related thereto. NRI and OCB investment in the said line of business is not permitted. NRIs are also not permitted to own agricultural land, or plantations or form houses. Also Indian companies with more than 40% non-resident equity holding, cannot engage directly or indirectly in agricultural or plantation activity or purchase shares in companies engaged in such activity.

FROM FERA TO FEMA

On August 4, 1998, finance minister introduced the Foreign Exchange Management Bill (FEMA) in the Lok Sabha. FEMA seeks to repeal the Foreign Exchange Regulation Act, 1973 (FERA).

The statement of objectives and reasons for FEMA states that FERA has outlived its utility on account of significant developments since 1993 such as substantial increase in foreign exchange resources, growth in foreign trade, rationalisation of tariffs, current account convertibility, liberalisation of Indian investments abroad, increased access to external commercial borrowings by Indian corporates and participation of foreign institutional investors in the stock markets. Keeping in view of the changed environment, FEMA aims at simplifying, consolidating and amending the law relating to foreign exchange with the objective of facilitating external trade and payments, and for promoting the orderly development and maintenance of foreign exchange markets in India.

FEMA, in a radical departure from FERA, has not only simplified the definition of a person resident in India but has also delinked it from the citizenship aspect to denote a person residing in India for more than 182 days during the course of a period of 365 days immediately preceding the date on which such a period is reckoned; any person or body corporate registered or incorporated in India; an office, branch or agency in India owned or controlled by a person resident in India/outside India.

Sections 8 to 31 of FERA reveal a labyrinth of regulations and restrictions ensnaring multifarious foreign exchange transactions to the point of stifling economic growth. FEMA, in contrast, seeks to establish a more liberal and orderly regulatory framework conducive to economic growth by limiting its ambit to:

(i) Current account transactions, such as payments due in connection with foreign trade, other current business, services and short-term banking and credit facilities in the ordinary course of business; payments due as interest on loans and as net income from investments; remittances for living expenses of parents, spouse and children residing abroad and expenses in connection with foreign travel, education and medical care of parents, spouse and children.

(ii) Capital account transactions, i.e., a transaction which alters the assets or liabilities, including contingent liabilities outside India, of persons resident in India or assets or liabilities in India of persons resident outside India.

(iii) Export of goods and services.

(iv) Realisation and repatriation of foreign exchange.

(v) Exemption from realisation and repatriation in cases like possession of foreign currency or foreign coins by any person upto such limit as the Reserve Bank of India (RBI) may specify; foreign currency account held or operated by such person or class of persons upto the limit the RBI may specify; foreign exchange acquired or received before 8 July, 1947 or any income arising or accruing thereon which is held outside India by any person in pursuance of a general or special permission granted by the RBI.

There is no gainsaying that FEMA, on enactment, would usher in a more liberal, transparent and orderly regulatory framework, conforming to the postulates of justice and fairness-essential pre-requisites for promoting further economic liberalisation and growth.

FEMA ACT, 1999

The FEMA Bill became an Act

The main objective of FEMA is to consolidate and amend the law relating to foreign exchange with a view to facilitate external trade.

The main objective of this Act is to consolidate and amend the law relating to foreign exchange with a view to facilitate external trade and payments and for promoting the orderly development and maintenance of the foreign exchange market in India.

The Act extends to the whole of India. The main provisions of the Act are as follows:

Section 3 Dealing in Foreign Exchange

No person shall deal in or transfer any foreign exchange or foreign security to any person; make any payment to or to the credit of any person resident outside India in any manner; receive any payments by order or on behalf of any person resident outside India in any manner; and enter into any financial transaction in India as consideration for or in association with acquisition, creation or transfer of the right to acquire any asset outside India by any person, without permission from the Reserve Bank.

Section 4 Holding of Foreign Exchange

No person, resident in India, shall acquire, hold, own, possess or transfer any foreign exchange, foreign security or any immovable property situated outside India, without permission from the Reserve Bank.

Section 5 Current Account Transactions

Any person may sell or draw foreign exchange to or from an authorised person if such sale or drawal is a current account transaction.

Section 6 Capital Account Transaction

Any person may sell or draw foreign exchange to or from an authorised person for a capital account transaction.

The Reserve Bank may, in consultation with the Central Government, specify any class or classes of capital account transactions which are permissible and limit upto which foreign exchange shall be admissible for such transactions.

Section 7 Export of Goods and Services

Every exporter of goods or services shall furnish to the Reserve Bank details regarding the export value of such goods or services.

Section 8 Realisation and Repatriation of Foreign Exchange

Where any amount of foreign exchange is due or accrued to any person resident in India, such a person shall take steps to realise and repatriate to India, such foreign exchange within a specified period of time.

Section 9 Exemption from Realisation and Repatriation

The following are exempted from the operation of Section 4 and Section 8:

(a) possession of foreign currency or foreign coins by any person upto such limit as the Reserve Bank may specify;

(b) foreign currency account held or opted by such person or class of persons and the limit upto which the Reserve Bank may specify;

(c) foreign exchange acquired or received before the 8th day of July, 1947 or any income arising or accruing thereon which is held outside India by any person in pursuance of a general or special permission granted by the Reserve Bank;

(d) foreign exchange held by a person resident in India upto such limit as the Reserve Bank may specify, if such foreign exchange was acquired by way of gift or inheritance from a person referred to in clause (c) including any income arising therefrom;

(e) foreign exchange acquired from employment, business, trade, vocation, services, honorarium, gifts, inheritance or any other legitimate means upto such limits as the Reserve Bank may specify and

(f) such other receipts in foreign exchange as the Reserve Bank may specify.

QUESTIONS

1. What are the objectives of FERA?
2. Bring out the provisions of FERA.
3. Comment on the operation of FERA.
4. Explain the major provisions of FEMA.

CHAPTER OUTLINE

- Evolution of the Company
- Meaning and Definition
- Classification of Companies
- Company Formation
- Company Law
- Company Law Administration
- Observations on the Act
- Companies Amendment Bills

LEARNING OBJECTIVES

After reading this Chapter, you should be able to:

1. Trace the evolution of the company form of ownership
2. Give the meaning of the company
3. Classify companies into different types
4. Bring out the main provisions of the Companies Act and describe how the Act is administered
5. Comment on the operation of the Act
6. Point out the salient features of the Amendment Bills, 1993 and 1997.

17 The Companies Act, 1956

The Companies Act, 1956, is a control measure used by the Government to regulate the functioning of the corporate sector in India. This chapter is devoted to a brief description of the provisions of the Act and their shortcomings. The discussion is preceded by a brief explanation of the nature of company and its types.

Company is not mere pattern of ownership of business enterprises but an institution vested with the responsibility of transforming the socio-economic fabric of a country.

Company is an important form of ownership. Also called a corporation, a company is not a mere form of ownership, but it is considered to be an institution vested with the responsibility of transforming the socioeconomic environment of our country. Writing about corporations, John Kenneth Galbraith asserted thus:

> "The institution that most changes our lives we least understand or more correctly seek most elaborately to misunderstand. That is the modern corporation. The modern, corporation lives in suspension between fiction and truth".[1]

EVOLUTION OF THE COMPANY

Company form of ownership dates back to Roman Empire.

The company form of ownership existed as early as the days of the Roman empire. In England, it was formed prior to 1600. In our country, a form of joint-stock company had come into existence in the middle of the 17th century in South India, understandably, as it was here the Indians first came into contact with the European merchants. During the 17th century, there was a considerable expansion of trade between India and Europe and European companies were competing with each other in South India to buy Indian merchandise of which cotton textiles constituted a very important part. So far, the European companies had followed the practice of procuring supplies through individual Indian merchants who were paid advances. The Indian merchants in turn advanced money to weavers to secure the output.

In a period of expanding trade, it was natural that the European companies had to deal more and more with a greater number of smaller merchants to procure supplies. This necessarily increased the cost of supplies as well as created uncertainty with regard to the quality and quantity of the goods supplied. Recovery of debts became a great problem. It was primarily to overcome these difficulties that the European companies seem to have fostered among the Indian merchants the idea of organising joint-stock companies. The small merchants of the Coromandal coast who were often badly hit by their own competition, eagerly accepted the idea, but the wealthy Surat merchants did not really favour it and secretly competed with their own joint-stock companies in buying goods from the market.

Generally, a joint-stock company consisted of between five and ten merchants who together subscribed an amount varying from 10,000 to 1,50,000 pagodas (gold coins current in South India at that time). From the 1660s, many such companies are mentioned in the records of the English and the Dutch East India Companies. Their number began to decline after about 1720, until they disappeared almost completely by the end of the 18th century.[2]

Then came the East India Company in the latter part of the 18th century. From then onwards, there was no going back and as times went by, numerous companies with huge capital investments came to be registered.

MEANING AND DEFINITION

A company may be understood as an association of individuals united for some common purpose, permitted by law to use a common name, and to change its members without winding up the association.

Chief Justice John Marshall of the US Supreme Court defined a corporation as '*an artificial being, invisible and existing only in contemplation of the law*'.

A second reading of the above paragraph reveals some essential features of the company form of ownership. These are:

Company is an artificial and invisible being recognised by law and created to pursue business objectives.

(a) *Separate Legal Entity*: Unlike proprietorship and partnership, a company is legally separate from its owners. A company is considered to be a legal '*person*' and can continue to exist even though its ownership may change many times. Since it is a legal person, a company can own property, take legal action and enter into contracts. A company has a domicile but is not regarded as a citizen either under Article 19 of the Constitution of India or under the Citizenship Act. It cannot ask for the enforcement of those Fundamental Rights which are exclusively available to the citizens. In the words of Hidayatullah,J. (afterwards C.J.), "....if all of them (the members) are citizens of India, the company does not become a citizen of India and more than that, if all are married, the company would be a married person". (*State Trading Corporation of India Ltd. v.* C.T.O.A.I.R. 1963 S.C.) (Also See Box 17.1).

The concept of legal entity cannot be used by the members of a company to defeat public convenience, justify wrong deeds or defend crime.

(b) *Limited Liability*: Another feature of the company is that the liability of its members is limited to the extent of the nominal value of shares held by them. A member cannot be held personally liable for the debts of the company except when provided by the statutes, e.g., when false and fraudulent representation is given in the prospectus, misdescription of the name of the company, etc. Courts can hold the members personally liable for debts arising out of such practices.

(c) *Transferability of Shares*: The shares of a company are transferable unless it is a private or a government company. If a member is unwilling to continue or is in the need of money, he/she can

Box 17.1 Supreme Court on Company's Personality

About separate juristic personality of a limited company, the Supreme Court has observed (AIR 1970 SC p.82) as under:

"...that obviously cannot be said of a company incorporated under the Companies Act whose constitution, powers and functions are provided for and regulated by its memorandum of association and the articles of association. An incorporated company, as is well known, has a separate existence and the law recognises it as a juristic person, separate and distinct from its members. This new personality emerges from the moment of its incorporation and from that date the persons subscribing to its memorandum of association and others joining it as members are regarded as a body incorporate or a corporation aggregate and the new person begins to function as an entity. (cf.Saloman Vs.Saloman and Co., 1897 AC 22). Its rights and obligations are different from those of its shareholders. Action taken against it does not directly affect its shareholders. The company in holding its property and carrying on its business is not the agent of its shareholders. An infringement of its rights does not give a cause of action to its shareholders. Consequently, it has been said that if a man trusts a corporation, he trusts that legal person and must look to its assets for payment; he can call upon the individual shareholders to contribute only if the Act or charter creating the corporation so provides. The liability of an individual member is not increased by the fact that the sole person is beneficially interested in the property of the corporation and that the other members have become members merely for the purpose of enabling the corporation to become incorporated, and possess only nominal interest in its property or hold it in trust for him. (cf. Halsbury's Law of England, 34d Ed. Vol. 9, p.9). Such a company even possesses that nationality of the country under the law of which it is incorporated, irrespective of the nationality of its members. The company so incorporated derives its powers and functions from and by virtue of its memorandum of association and its articles of association. Therefore, the mere fact that the entire share capital of the respondent company was contributed by the Central Government and the fact that all its shares are held by the President and certain officers of the Central Government does not make any difference. The company and the shareholders being, as aforesaid, distinct entities, the fact that the President of India and certain officers hold all its shares does not make the company an agent either of the President or the Central Government. A notice to the President of India and the said officers of the Central Government, who hold between them all the shares of the company would not be a notice to the company; nor can a suit maintainable by and in the name of the company be sustained by or in the name of the President and the said officers".

transfer the shares for a consideration to others. Such transfers can be affected without taking consent of other members or without causing a closure of the company.

(d) *Continued Existence*: A company enjoys relative permanence. If a shareholder sells his/her shares or the chairman of the company resigns, it will probably continue. It is the relatively stable existence that attracts the confidence of shareholders, goodwill of customers and the loyalty of employees.

CLASSIFICATION OF COMPANIES

Companies are of different classes as explained below:

- Public company;
- Private company;

- Foreign company;
- Company with liability limited by guarantee;
- Government company;
- Unlimited company; and
- Holding and subsidiary companies.

1. *Public Company*: The meaning of a company as given earlier relates to a public company. In other words, in a public company members are at liberty to transfer their shares without affecting its continuity. Liability of members is limited. Company has relative permanence. This company is called public or open company because it invites the public to subscribe to its share capital.
2. *Private Company*: A private company has some distinct features which make it different from a public company. Table 17.1 brings out the difference between the two. Incidentally, the meaning of private company can be made out from the table itself.

Table 17.1 **Difference between Public and Private Companies**

Factors	*Public Company*	*Private Company*
1. *How many members?*	Minimum seven and no limit to maximum	Minimum two and maximum 50
2. *Is transferability of shares allowed?*	Allowed	Not allowed
3. *Who can become members*	Public	Members of a family or friends
4. *How many directors*	Minimum three	Minimum two
5. *What should be in name?*	Word 'Limited'	Words 'Private Limited'
6. *When to start business?*	After obtaining certificate to commence business	After obtaining incorporation certificate
7. *Whether listed on the stock exchanges?*	Yes	No

3. *Foreign Company*: A foreign company is one which is registered outside India but has a place of business in India.
4. *Companies Limited by Guarantee*: Here members agree to pay a sum, in addition to the amount of shares held by them, if the need arises, to pay off the creditors of the company. The additional amount to be paid is laid down in the memorandum or articles of association. A guaranteed company maybe with share capital or without share capital. Where the company is without share capital, it raises the needed funds through entrance fees and subscriptions. Where the company has a share capital, liability of the members extends to the additional sum guaranteed when the company is wound up. A company limited by guarantee is generally formed to promote art, science, religion or charity.
5. *Government Company*: An enterprise becomes a government company when it has the following major characteristics:
   - It has most of the features of a private limited company;
   - The whole of the capital or 51 per cent or over if it is owned by the government;
   - All the directors or majority of them are appointed by the government;

- It is created under the provisions of the Companies Act, 1956; and
- Its funds are obtained from government and in some cases, from private shareholders and through revenues derived from the sale of its goods and services.

6. *Unlimited Companies*: A company not having any limit on the liability of its members is called an unlimited company. The members of an unlimited company are like a sole proprietor or partners of a firm, liable for its debts without any limit.

The concept of unlimited liability does not conform to the corporate concept which necessarily postulates limited liability. Hence, unlimited companies are rare but not extinct.

The concept of unlimited liability is not in tune with the nature of a company. Obviously, unlimited companies are rare but not extinct.

7. *Holding and Subsidiary Companies*: Any company that buys a sufficient number of shares in another is called a holding company and the acquired one is called the *subsidiary*. The acquiring company is known as the *parent* company. Some holding companies own all the shares of their subsidiaries. But owning of not less than half of the shares is enough to call the owing company a parent company.

Table 17.2 reveals the number of companies and their amounts of paid-up capital for a period of four decades.

Table 17.2 **Number of Companies and their paid-up Capital: 1950-51 to 1991-92**

	Number of Companies			*Paid-up Capital (Rs.Cr.)*	
Year	*Govt.*	*Private Indian*	*Foreign*	*Govt.Cos.*	*Non-Govt. Cos.*
1950-51	36	28496		26	749
1960-61	142	25438	569	547	1272
1970-71	314	29465	543	2064	2439
1980-81	851	64406	300	11443	4914
1988-89	1134	178774	420	42572	15131
1989-90	1160	200499	469	47451	17193
1990-91	1167	222796	489	54485	20313
1991-92	1180	248674	507	56482	22415

COMPANY FORMATION

Company formation is an elaborate, time-consuming and an expensive affair. A typical formation involves three stages, *viz*.: (a) registration; (b) capital raising and (c) commencement of business.

Formation of a company is an elaborate, time consuming, frustrating and expensive affair.

Registration: The Registrar of Companies is the appropriate official to register companies. Before registration, the Registrar expects the promoters to submit a list of names of the proposed company, memorandum of association, articles of association and a list of directors.

The memorandum of association, as is well-known, is an important document. It contains such details as the name of the company (earlier approved by the Registrar of Companies from a list submitted to him), the purpose of the company, the place of its registered office, the fact that the members' liability is limited and the capital of the company. The memorandum should be printed, be divided into suitable paragraphs and be affixed with stamps worth Rs.120.

The articles of association contain details about the way in which the internal affairs of the company are to be carried out. To be specific, it contains such details as types of shares; procedure for conducting meetings; powers, duties, rights and qualifications of directors; procedure for the declaration of dividends and capitalisation of reserves; maintenance of accounts and their audit; and winding up of the company. A private company and a company with liability limited by guarantee must have their own articles. A public company may or may not file its own articles. If it does not do so, it is understood that the public company follows the articles as given in Table A of the Companies Act, 1956. It is advisable to follow Table A as the articles provided therein are beyond all doubt.

As in the memorandum of association, articles of association should be printed and must be submitted to the Registrar after affixing stamps worth Rs.250.

The Registrar will scrutinise all documents submitted to him and will ensure that all formalities are complied with. The Registrar will then enter the name of the company in the register maintained by him for the purpose and will issue a certificate of incorporation. On registration, the company becomes an independent person in the eyes of law. For registration, the Registrar will charge a fee which depends on the authorised capital of the company. For an authorised capital of Rs.1 lakh, the registration fee is Rs.750. For a capital of Rs.3 lakh, the fee is Rs.1,750 and for a capital of Rs.1 crore, the fee is Rs.18,500.

B. *Raising of Capital*: The next step in company formation is the raising of capital. A public company raises its capital by inviting the public to subscribe to its share capital. The steps involved in raising capital are:

(a) Obtaining SEBI clearance.

(b) Entering into an agreement with the underwriter.

(c) Applying to the stock exchange for listing of its shares.

(d) Inviting the public to subscribe to its share capital through a prospectus.

(e) Allotment of shares.

> A public company should wait for a certificate to commence the business but a private company can do so immediately after it is formed.

C. *Commencement of Business*: A private company can commence its business immediately after it is incorporated. But a public company cannot commence its business unless it obtains a certificate for the purpose. To obtain a certificate, the following statement must be submitted to the Registrar:

- A declaration that a copy of the prospectus is filed with him.
- A declaration that minimum subscription has been received.
- A declaration that the directors have taken up the qualification shares and have paid for them.
- A certificate issued by a director or secretary to the effect that all conditions for the commencement of business have been fulfilled.

The Registrar then issues a certificate to commence business, following which a public company can now commence its chosen activity. The stage of formation of a company apparently comes to an end. What has been described so far is only a part but not the whole of the formalities to be observed in forming a company. It is said that as many as 21 clearances are required before setting up a company.

Before the new company commences its business, a team of people who can manage the company must be constituted. It is one of the characteristic features of the company that its owners do not manage its affairs. Management is entrusted to directors, who are collectively called the Board of Directors (BoD)or simply the Board. The first directors are appointed by the promoters. In their, absence, signatories to the memorandum of association will act as directors. The first directors, whether appointed by promoters or signatories to the memorandum acting as such, shall hold office till the first general body meeting, after which all of them must retire. The directors will then be elected by the shareholders.

COMPANY LAW

Companies in our country are governed by the Companies Act, 1956, as amended up-to-date. The Companies Act is one of the biggest legislations with 658 sections, 13 schedules, 32 rules and 107 forms with several guidelines and hundreds of clarifications issued by the government from time to time.

The Companies Act is one of the biggest legislations. Recently, the Irani Committee recommended pruning of the Act substantially.

The Act extends to the whole of India and applies to all classes of companies, i.e., public companies, private companies and associations not trading for profit. It also contains certain provisions relating to companies incorporated outside India, but which have an established place of business in India.

Objectives of the Act

While moving the Bill in the Parliament, C.D.Deshmukh, the then Finance Minister, declared the following as the main objectives of the Act:

- Minimum standard of business integrity and conduct in promotion and management of companies;
- Full and fair disclosure of all reasonable information relating to the affairs of the company;
- Effective participation and control by the shareholders and the protection of their legitimate interests;
- Enforcement of proper performance of their duties by the company management and
- Powers of intervention and investigation into the affairs of the companies where they are managed in a manner prejudicial to the interest of shareholders or to the interest of the public.

Speaking on behalf of the Supreme Court in *Delhi Cloth and General Mills Co.Ltd. vs. Union of India and Others (1983),* Justice D.A.Desai observed thus:

"The Companies Act of 1956, to some extent, also attempts to translate into action Arts.38 and 39 in Part IV of the Constitution, by which the State was directed that the ownership and control of the material resources of the community are so distributed as to subserve the common good and the operation of the economic system does not result in concentration of wealth and means of production to the common detriment. Further, Art.46 mandates the State to promote economic interest of weaker sections of the people from all forms of exploitation. A *fortiori*, every provision of the Companies Act must receive such interpretation as to suppress the mischief and advance the object for which it was enacted; as also to achieve and translate into action, the underlying intendment of the enactment for the realisation of the constitutional goals as set out in Part IV of the Constitution."

The arm of the Companies Act is quite long and touches every aspect of a company's existence. While it is unnecessary to describe the provisions of all its 658 sections, it is enough to say that they cover all aspects of the company's life, from its cradle to its grave. Be it the formation of the company, its management, holding meetings, maintaining accounts, declaring dividends, any action that is contemplated must be strictly in accordance with the provisions of the Act.

COMPANY LAW ADMINISTRATION

The provisions of the Companies Act are administered through a three-layer administrative machinery. At the top is the Company Law Board, charged with the overall responsibility for company law

The Company Law Board is the statutory authority which administers the provisions of the Act.

administration. The board facilitates administrative coordination with other related statutes concerning corporate enterprises.

The Board has the following powers:

(a) Alteration in the memorandum of the company;

(b) Power to authorise issue of shares at a discount;

(c) Power to order a general meeting and

(d) Power to accord approval wherever it is required under the provisions of the Act.

Next to the Company Law Board are four Regional Directors at Calcutta, Mumbai, Chennai and Kanpur. The Regional Directors form a link between the Registrars and the Central Government as well as between the Central Government and the State Governments and they keep the Company Law Board informed of all relevant matters.

Below the Regional Directors are the Registrars. In each State capital, there is a Registrar with whom companies can be registered. The functions of a Registrar are as follows:

(a) Collect and preserve vital documents relating to all companies in the respective States. These documents are available for inspection by members of a company and general public;

(b) Ensure proper functioning of the company by insisting on the prompt submission of reports and returns and

(c) Scrutinise the contents of the returns to determine whether they have complied with the law. If the Registrar suspects anything wrong with the affairs of the company, he can call for further explanation from the company, consult Regional Directors, or refer the matter to the Company Law Board for the purpose of investigation by inspectors.

SOME OBSERVATIONS ON THE ACT

The Companies Act deserves credit for its comprehensiveness, lucidity and endurance. The Act preaches discipline to the managers.

The Companies Act deserves full credit for its lucidity, comprehensiveness and endurance. "*The discipline of the company law is a good thing for managements*," wrote S.S.Khera, in his outstanding book *Government in Business*. "*It is a statutory discipline imposed by the law directly...A large number of articles, a large number of sections, well over a hundred sections of the Companies Act, prescribe disciplines, breach of any of which exposes the director to penal action under the law...These disciplines are very healthy. These are disciplines prescribed for all people who handle other people's resources, whether they be in the private sector or public sector*" (p.118).

However, certain flaws in the Act deserve serious consideration by the concerned authorities. The following are the major deficiencies:

1. It has all along been held that the workers or their trade unions have no right to be heard in the liquidation proceedings of a company. The Companies Act does not provide for any such right. Then came the landmark judgement delivered by the Supreme Court in the *National Textile Workers' Union vs. P.R.Ramakrishna, 1983, which read:* "It is not only the shareholders who have supplied capital who are interested in the enterprise, which is run by a company, but the workers who supply labour are also equally, if not more, interested because what is produced by the enterprise is the result of labour as well as capital, while the shareholders invest only a part of their money(s), the workers invest their sweat and toil, infact their life itself. The workers, therefore, have a special place in a socialist pattern of society. They are not mere vendors of toil, they are not a marketable commodity to be purchased by the owners of capital. They are producers of wealth as much as capital, nay, very much more. In view of the Preamble, the Directive Principles of State Policy and particularly the introduction of

Article 43-A, it is idle to contend that the workers should have no voice in the determination of the question whether the enterprise should continue to run or be shut down under an order of the court.

The Act has been criticised as it contains no provision for allowing representatives of employees to be heard in a legal dispute over the closure of a company.

The *audi alteram partem* rule which mandates that no one shall be condemned unheard is one of the basic principles of natural justice and if administrative proceeding involving adverse civil consequences, it would a *fortiori* applied in a judicial proceeding such as the petition for winding up of a company. (AIR, Supreme Court, 1983).

The provisions of the Companies Act show that only the company, the official liquidator, creditors, contributories and the Registrar have statutory rights to participate in the winding up of proceedings. The workers or their trade unions have not been given any such right. In the light of the Supreme Court Judgement, it is necessary that a provision for conferring the right of participation on the workers or their trade unions is incorporated in the Act.

2. There is an acknowledged concept of law, namely, the ability of the courts to lift or pierce the corporate veil of entity in order to understand the true nature, identity and composition of a company as first declared by the House of Lords in the UK in *Daimler vs. Continental Tyre Company*. This concept has been borrowed by the Indian courts and frequently utilised to prevent evasion of taxes as in the case of Meenakshi Mills, etc. It is suggested that this concept adopted by the courts appears to have developed on an ad hoc basis and requires to be clarified by the legislation itself about its applicability and limits.

The applicability and limits of the principle of "piercing or lifting the corporate viel" needs to be clarified.

3. One of the characteristics of the companies is that their shares are freely transferable. The Companies Act explicitly makes provision for transfer and registration of transfers also. In practice, transfers and their registration are effected at the sweet will of the directors. This practice is a clear discrimination of the worst and pernicious kind.

Transfer of shares is often done at the sweet will of directors.

A share is like any other property and when a person buys it, it should be registered in his name. Registration should not be made depending on the person who has bought it.

Share transfers are not registered by the directors, if they suspect that the purchaser would pose inconvenient and embarrassing questions at appropriate forums.

Though there is a power vested in the purchaser of shares and whose registration has been refused to seek remedy in a court of law, it is generally illusory. This is because the courts in the exercise of their jurisdiction have very limited authority which is supervisory only and not all-embracing.

It is time that provision is made for compulsory registration of transfer of shares.

4. The Act mandates companies to maintain proper records and books of account which should disclose full information about the business affairs. In practice, though records and books of account are maintained, they fail to disclose full information. For example, the corporate annual reports published in accordance with Schedule VI of the Act only mention the total profit the companies have made. Division-wise profit is not made available. Naturally, information provided is utterly incomplete, even misleading, if the division-wise position is not disclosed. "The aggregation of financial information", says S.K.Bhattacharya, Chief Executive of Management Structures and Systems, "in one balance sheet and profit and loss account, when the organisation is multi-product, multi-location, multi-technology company operating in many sectors of the company, transforms financial analysis into almost a make-believe game. How does one make any sense out of this *pot-pourri* which passes off as an appetising dish when it is entirely possible that the windfall profit in one product group is sustaining major inefficiencies in others? How does one interpret 'net' profit which is an amalgam which turns into

Accopunts and statements do not disclose required information adequately.

gross? How does one derive any insight regarding funds required for generating future profits from the disparate 'business' reported in one balance sheet?"[3]

"....Only one has to glance at the balance sheet of any American company to see the difference. The Federal Accountancy Standards Boards (FASB) in the USA prescribes exhaustive guidelines on disclosure, which companies have to scrupulously follow. This is essential, considering the dominant presence of conglomerates in the USA involved in diverse activities. Unless division-wise profitability is disclosed, it is next to impossible to gauge the performance of a company. The Board of Directors are expected to disclose their stake in the company and inside trading is a criminal offence".

"None of these provisions is applicable in India. As one chartered accountant admits, Indian balance sheets are great works of fiction. The good news is presented in the Chairman's statement upfront and the bad news is pushed into the footnotes."[4]

That a company should hold its annual general body meetings regularly is flouted with impunity.

5. Section 166 of the Act lays down that the companies should hold annual general meetings every year and the period between two such successive meetings should not exceed 15 months. In practice, this provision is often violated and the punishments for infringement are mild, involving a fine of a few hundred rupees. During 1984-85, in all about 442 companies did not bother to hold annual general body meetings.

Where such meetings are held, they turn out to be big pompous shows not serving any real purpose.

6. Where annual general body meetings are held, they turn out to be big pompous shows not serving any real purpose. Theoretically, an annual general body meeting is supposed to be a platform where shareholders can question their directors about the way the company's affairs have been managed. Practice is far from theory. In the first place, shareholders seldom attend general body meetings. They are mainly interested in ensuring that cheques for dividends come regularly and share prices zoom in the share market every day. Secondly, shareholders who care to attend such meetings evince more interest in receiving gifts, discount coupons, and relishing a sumptuous lunch and snacks. Thirdly, when a well-informed shareholder puts embarrassing and inconvenient questions, his voice is silenced by evasive replies and mayhem.

Thus, cynics are not wrong when they say that the annual general meetings are a big farce. This malady is not peculiar to our country. It is so everywhere. About annual meetings held in the USA, Galbraith wrote thus: "As stock-holders cease to have influence, however, efforts are made to disguise their nullity. Their convenience is considered in selecting the place of the meeting. They are presented with handsomely printed reports, the preparation of which is now a specialised business. Products and even plants are inspected. During the proceedings, as in the report, there are repetitive references to '*your company.*' Officers listen with every evidence of attention to the highly irrelevant suggestions of wholly uniformed participants and assure them that these will be considered with greatest care. Votes of thanks from women stockholders, in print dresses, owning ten shares, for the excellent skill with which you run your company-are received by the management with well simulated gratitude. All present show stern disapproval of the critics. No important stockholders are present. No decisions are taken. The annual general meetings of a large American Corporation is, perhaps, the most elaborate exercise in popular illusion."

There are however, exceptions. Annual general body meetings of some companies turn out to be stormy scenes wherein the directors are grilled by the enlightened shareholders for disappointing performance. Peico Electronics and Electrical Ltd. is one such example. In its annual general body meeting held in Calcutta on May 13, 1987, the management of the company was subjected to heavy criticism by its shareholders following slump in the company's profits to Rs.47.19 lakh (before tax) for the year 1986 from Rs.4.8 crore in the previous year. Dividend declined from 15% in 1985 to 10% in 1986.

7. Tribunals are a trend in every sphere of organised economic activity. Before 1976 there were tribunals to which an aggrieved party, be it a shareholder, director, employee or consumer, could make an appeal seeking redressal. But the tribunals were abolished under the Companies Tribunal (Abolition) Act, 1976. It is time the tribunals are revived.

True, there is the Company Law Board to which appeals can be made. But like any other government agency, the Company Law Board is known for red-tapism and delays.

8. Many people feel that the maximum number of shareholders in a private limited company should be increased by at least five times. There seems to be no justification for granting exemptions from the provisions of the Companies Act to a private company only for the sake of fifty shareholders. Perhaps, the rationale for putting a ceiling at fifty was to confine the private company to the members of a family. This has lost its relevance because large families have now become extinct. Therefore, private companies are now being formed by a homogeneous group of people cutting across families. Besides, today's business demands huge investment and it may be difficult for just fifty people to mobilise the required funds. Hence, the need for increasing the maximum number at least by five times.

There is an urgent need to lift the ceiling of 50 membership imposed on a private company.

COMPANIES (AMENDMENT) BILL, 1993

On May 14, 1993, the Minister of State for Company Affairs introduced in the Parliament the large, delayed and long-deferred Companies Bill, 1993.

The Bill clearly reflects the emerging trends in corporate law in the Commonwealth countries, particularly UK and the public awareness of the need for transparency in the dealings of the companies by the management, and the protection of investors, creditors and the members of the public at large are the guiding stars for the new enactment. At the same time, commendable efforts are made to liberate those in charge of company management from government regulations and bureaucratic delays, in the process throwing into the dustbin time-consuming and irritating paperwork.

The changes sought to be made in the Bill may tempt other countries to emulate the example of India.

The arrangements of the sections and the schedules have undergone a tremendous change which may for a short time cause confusion. Those dealing with company law, knowing by rote the numbers of important sections of the Act of 1956, may have to struggle for a while to clear their transitory cobwebs but by and large, such regrouping has logic and clarity.

The provisions of the Bill are as follows:

(1) The procedure for incorporating a company has been simplified. Some of the 'inherent powers' of a company are set out in a schedule (Schedule II), so that these may not be set out at length in the memorandum of association. It will be open to a company to modify these 'powers' in its memorandum-the result will be that now the companies, instead of elaborately setting out the normal and routing powers, adopt the provisions of Schedule II with such modifications to suit the company's particular requirements. This approach is similar to a company adopting Table-A of the Schedule (with modifications, if so desired) to avoid having to print lengthy articles of association.

(2) If a company wishes to alter its clause of the memorandum, all that is required to do is pass a special resolution, at a meeting of the members and not seek the approval of the Company Law Board. This change recognises the rights of the owners of the company, *viz*., the members, under the Act of 1956. The Company Law Board, while granting approval, stipulates

conditions or cuts down the effect of the alternation without sometimes appreciating the effect thereof. This will also enable the companies to diversify without interference of the Company Law Board.

(3) Now the Debenture Trust Deeds will be uniform, according to the prescribed format. The company will be under an obligation to ensure the execution thereof within the statutory period. It will also spell out the functions and duties of the debenture trustees. Very often, depositors do not receive interest from companies in time, either because of postal delays, or the companies deliberately delaying posting of interest. To overcome this situation, it is suggested that along with the deposit receipt, companies must be asked to send post-dated interest as in case of IDBI bonds.

(4) The companies which have defaulted in the repayment of deposits and interest thereon, will no longer be allowed to accept fresh deposits or to renew the existing ones and moreover, they will not be able to lend monies to other companies.

(5) The depositors will now be able to nominate a person of their choice to receive the repayment of deposits in case of death, thus avoiding the need for obtaining legal representation to the estate of the deceased.

(6) The unclaimed dividends remaining unpaid for seven years will be transferred to an 'investors protection fund' to be untilised for payment to investors who have lost their deposits due to inability of the company to repay their deposits. This change appears to be more a populist move rather than a measure of genuine relief. What is needed is some kind of insurance cover to be available to the small depositors, say upto Rs.10,000. The premium for such insurance can be collected from the companies receiving deposits. A small percentage of the amount of deposits collected by the companies cannot prove an enormous burden on the resources of the companies.

(7) The rights of companies to refuse transfer of shares and debentures are restricted to only specified grounds.

(8) Private companies will not become 'deemed public companies' only on the ground of turnover.

(9) Under the new dispensation a 'relative' of a director cannot be appointed auditor of the company, nor should an auditor be indebted to the company. This is to ensure independence of the auditors.

(10) Some of the provisions of the prospectus are made more stringent to ensure transparency and to give a fair deal to intending investors in shares and debentures of a company, and a format of 'abridged prospectus' is being prescribed to ensure all material disclosure.

(11) The companies will be required to disclose in their annual account, significant accounting policies and to make a statement that the published accounts are in conformity with the established accounting standards.

(12) The procedures for liquidation of companies is being simplified, and instead of the court liquidator, professionals (such as lawyers, auditors) can be appointed as liquidators. This will expedite the conclusion of liquidation proceedings, which at present ran into years and years, and in the meantime, the creditors may forget that they have any claim to recover.

(13) The companies will now be liberated from the cumbersome procedure of filing various (and sometimes, meaningless) returns with the Registrar of Companies. Instead of over 80 returns now required to be filed, only two or three returns will now be filed (See Box 17.2 for merits and demerits).

The Companies Bill 1997 and the recently promulgated Ordinance on Companies (Amendment) Bill 1997 have amended several provisions of the Act and introduced new provisions incorporating

Box 17.2 **Plus and Minus of the Bill 1993**

Plus Points

1. Companies can now change the objects clause of the memorandum of assoc-iation without the prior permission of the Companies Law Board.
2. Endorsement by government authorised agencies is not required for share transactions of nominal value.
3. Cost auditors no longer to be appointed by the Union government. This power has been given to shareholders, in the same manner in which statutory auditors are appointed.
4. Prior approval of the government not necessary for the payment of minimum remuneration to managers in the event of a company not making adequate profits.
5. Prior approval of the government not required for the payment of remuneration to the managers of loss-making companies.
6. Government approval necessary only if the strength of a company's board of directors exceeds 15, and not 12 as at present.
7. Liquidation proceedings can be conducted by professionals like lawyers and auditors. Court-appointed liquidators are no longer mandatory.
8. Voluntary liquidators now allowed to file misfeasance proceedings against directors of companies, without seeking prior permission of the Registrar of Companies.
9. Credit rating mandatory for companies intending to issue debentures or invite fixed deposits.
10. Shareholders approval now required for fixing rights issue premia. Earlier this was confined to public issue premia.
11. Unclaimed dividends, which earlier went into the government exchequer, will now go into an investor fund.
12. Stringent norms have been set for investor protection, accompanied by stiff fines and jail terms for those who dupe investors.
13. Greater transparency and uniformity in balance sheets.

Negative Developments, Controls Retained

1. The ceiling on managerial remuneration has been retained.
2. Restrictions on inter-corporate loans and investments to continue.
3. Industry's pleas that non-voting shares carrying higher rates of return be created have not been accepted.

   The bill is voluminous. No real attempt has been made to substantially reduce the size.
4. The sections imposing restrictions on dominant undertakings, which are transferred from the Companies Act to the MRTP, have been reintroduced in the bill - although chapter 3 of the MRTP Act, which dealt with the concentration of economic power, was deleted in 1991.
5. The section in the Companies Act which provides for the conversion of government loans into equity has been retained, even though the financial institutions have given up the practice of convertibility. Moreover, it will come into force even before the bill becomes law, and regardless of whether loan agreements include such a provision.
6. The minimum qualifying age for appointment as managing directors or wholetime directors has been in creased from 25 years to 30 years, while the upper limit has been reduced from 70 to 65 years.
7. There are contradictions between some provisions of the bill and certain other laws already in force:

(a) SEBI required debenture trust deeds to be completed in three months, but the Bill says this can be done in 18 months.

(b) SEBI says that merchant banks can underwrite issues upto the extent of five times their net worth, while the restrictions on inter-corporate investments (clause 389 of the Bill) stipulate that one company can sub scribe to another's equity only to the extent of 30 per cent of its paid up capital. In the event of development, there will be conflict between the two.

(c) SEBI guidelines specify that if a new company is being set up by existing companies, it will be free to price its issue on its own only if the promoters hold at least 50 per cent of the new company's equity. However, Clause 389 of the bill imposes a limit of 25 per cent.

internationally accepted corporate governance practices aimed at strengthening corporate democracy, protecting the interests of minority shareholders, and providing increasing flexibility to the companies in responding to the market needs. Among these, the amendments that have made headlines are permitting companies to buy back shares and the liberalisation of inter-corporate investments.

Simplifying the Company Law

Many of the suggestions in the recently submitted report of the Expert Committee on company law under J.J.Irani are welcome. They include a major pruning of the provisions and making them more contemporary. There can be no argument that the existing law derived from the Companies Act 1956, with its 658 sections and 15 schedules has become unwieldy. Besides, some of its provisions became dated long ago. The Irani report pitches for a more compact legislation with just 300 sections.

The major recommendation of the Committee are:

- Greater stress on corporate governance.
- One-third of board to consist of independent directors, instead of the current requirement of 50 per cent.
- Companies to self-regulate themselves instead of being administered by Central agencies.
- Provision for One Person Company (OPC) as against the current requirement of atleast two persons to form a company.
- Mergers to be consummated much faster.
- "Ornamental directors" (those who join a company's board just before a public issue to resign soon after) liable for their acts upto a period of two years.
- Liquidation/rehabilitation process to be time bound.
- Annual reports to contain information relating to criminal breaches of the Act.
- CEO, CFO and Company Secretary to be accountable to all stakeholders.

QUESTIONS

1. Define a company. What are the various classes of companies?
2. Describe the stages in the formation of a company.
3. Critically examine the operation of the Companies Act, 1956.

ASSIGNMENT

We have mentioned briefly the recommendations made by the Irani Committee. Study the report in detail and make a list of its pluses and minuses.

REFERENCES

1. John Kenneth Galbraith, *The Age of Uncertainty*, p.257.
2. Radhe Shyam Rungta, *The Rise of Business Corporations in India*, pp.1-2.
3. *Business India*, January 31-February 13,1983.
4. *Business India*, June 30-July 13,1986.

18 Public Sector Enterprises

CHAPTER OUTLINE

Definition and Objectives
Evolution of the Public Sector
Growth and Role
Performance
What Needs to be Done?
Reforms in Public Sector Enterprises
Bureau of Public Enterprises
Ownership Pattern of PSUs
Industrial Policy Statement 1991 on Public Sector

LEARNING OBJECTIVES

After reading this Chapter, you should be able to:

1. Define a public sector unit and list out its objectives
2. Trace the evolution of public sector
3. Explain the growth and performance of central government undertakings
4. Suggest ways of improving PSUs
5. Bring out the PSU reforms initiated by the government
6. Detail the functions of Bureau of Public Enterprises
7. Explain the ownership pattern of public sector enterprises
8. State the implications of 1991 policy on public sector

Also called state enterprises or government enterprise, public sector undertakings constitute a major segment of the industrial activity in our country. Born as the outcome of the conscious policy of the government to speed up the industrialisation of the country with a view to giving added impetus to economic growth as well as to achieve certain socio-economic goals as enunciated in Industrial Policy Resolutions of the government, these undertakings today cover a wide spectrum of activities in basic and strategic industries like steel, coal, minerals and metals, petroleum, heavy engineering, chemicals, pharmaceuticals and fertilizers on the one hand, and consumer goods, trading and marketing activities, transportation services, contract and consultancy service, tourist services, financial services and development of small-scale industries, on the other. While some of these enterprises are operating under monopoly/near-monopoly conditions, there are others working under competitive conditions. There is yet another segment of the public enterprises, *viz.*, sick units taken over from the private sector in order to protect employment. Thus, public enterprises comprise units engaged in different spheres of industrial and commercial activities, some capital-intensive-long gestation, low-profitability enterprises; while some others are low-risk and high-profitability enterprises. Added to this basic diversity in the composition of units is the multi-dimensional objectives of public enterprises which should be considered in appreciating the role these units have played in our economy.

DEFINITION

In simple terms, a public sector enterprise is an industrial, commercial or other economic activity owned and managed by the Central or State Government or jointly by both. A comprehensive definition of a public sector unit is given by experts at the International Centre for Public Enterprises (ICPE), Yugoslavia. To quote the Centre:

A public sector enterprise is an undertaking owned and managed by government.

"*A public enterprise is an organisation* which is:

- owned by public authorities including Central, State or local authorities, to the extent of 50 per cent or more;
- is under the top mangerial control of the owning public authorities, such public control including *inter-alia*, the right to appoint top management and to formulate critical policy decisions;
- is established for the achievement of a definet set of public purpose, which may be multi-dimensional in character;
- and is consequently placed under a system of public accountability;
- is engaged in activities of a business character;
- involves the basic idea of investment and returns
- and which markets its outputs in the shape of goods and services".

OBJECTIVES

The following are the objectives of public enterprises:

(i) Help in the rapid economic growth and industrialisation of the country and create the necessary infrastructure for economic development;

(ii) Earn returns on investment and thus generate resources for development;

(iii) Promote redistribution of income and wealth;

(iv) Create employment opportunities;

(v) Promote balanced regional development;

(iv) Assist the development of small-scale and ancillary industries;

(vii) Promote import substitution, save and earn foreign exchange for the economy;

(viii) Act as a countervailing force and put up an effective competition to undertakings in the private sector and

(ix) Gain control over the commanding heights of the economy.

EVOLUTION OF THE PUBLIC SECTOR

Public sector undertakings date back to 11th and 12th centuries.

Though the public sector was started with greater vigour only after 1947, the idea of State-owned undertakings was there long before. In South India, great dams and anicuts were built across the river Cauvery by the Chola Kings of the 11th and 12th centuries. They are magnificent testimonials to the wisdom and foresight of the Cholas. That is repeated in very many parts of the country. India was not merely a country of temples. There was a good deal of economic development by the State, directed towards sustaining the life of the community. And these dams and anicuts which were set-up by the State for the benefit of the people are testimony enough to acknowledge the evolution of the public sector.[1] Started by the great Chola Kings, the public sector went through periods of steady expansion until our country became a free nation. After 1947, the public sector became inevitable as the government realised that rapid economic development could be achieved only through State intervention in economic activities. The Industrial Policy Resolutions of 1948 and 1956 clearly reflect the need for expanding the public sector. The public sector has now grown tremendously and has become a leading light of our economy.

Rationale for State Owned Enterprises

There are several reasons for the creation and maintenance of public sector enterprises. First, there is persistence of monopoly power in many developing countries. Direct government control may be required to ensure that prices are not set above the marginal costs of producing the output. Moreover, certain goods that have a high social benefit are usually provided at a price below their costs or even free; hence the private sector has no incentive to produce such goods, and the government must be responsible for their provision.

Government control is necessary to produce certain goods which private sector will not do and to fix prices of goods and services at cheaper rates.

The second rationale for creation of state undertakings is capital formation, which is particularly important at the early stages of development, when private savings are very low. Investment in infrastructure at this point is critical to lay the foundation for further investment. Public sector undertakings remain important at later stages in industries that require massive funds. (1(a))

The lack of private incentive to engage in promising economic activities because of factors such as uncertainty about the size of local markets, unreliable sources of supply, and the absence of technology and skilled labour is a third major motivation for creating public enterprises. Governments of developing countries may also seek to expand employment and facilitate training of their labour force by engaging in public production. They may desire to increase export earnings by creating export industries, particularly those that might otherwise be unable to compete. For reasons of income distribution, the government may seek to locate enterprises in certain regions, particularly in backward regions and areas where there is no private incentive for creating such economic activity.

Other reasons for the creation of PSUs include the desire of some governments of developing countries to gain national control over strategic sectors of the economy such as defense, over MNCs whose interests may not coincide with those of the country, or over key sectors for planning purposes. Finally, ideological motivations may be a factor in the creation of government undertakings.

Government undertakings have justification to exist because of
(i) private sector does not come forward to invest in certain areas
(ii) government wants to retain control over sensitive areas.

Growth and Role

Government undertakings have, over the years, proliferated in terms of number, turnover, number of people employed, investments involved, and areas of activities covered. Table 18.1 reveals the phenomenal growth of these enterprises.

Table 18.1 contains data relating to manufacturing and non- manufacturing enterprises owned and managed by the Central Government. Banks and departmental undertakings such as railways, post office and telecommunication systems are excluded from the data. The figures are indeed awesome.

The table includes undertakings owned by the Central Government. If the figures relating to undertakings owned by various State Governments are added, the figures will be staggering.

These undertakings account for one-fourth of our GDP (Gross Domestic Product). They account for one-third of our exports. They have made significant contributions to import substitution. Industries like steel, aluminium and other non-ferrous metals, fertilizers, heavy engineering and oil have helped us save substantially on imports. Government undertakings account for more than 70% of the workers employed in the organised sector. They have greatly reduced imbalances in regional development and have laid a strong base for the rapid development of our economy. Together with the undertakings in the private sector, government enterprises have greatly contributed to the transformation of our so called poor and traditional economy into a fast developing and fairly industrialised (we now rank among the

Table 18.1 **Growth of Public Sector Undertakings**

Period	*Total Investment (Rs.Cr)*	*No.of Enterprises*
I Plan	29	5
II Plan	81	21
III Plan	948	47
Three annual plans	2410	73
IV Plan	3897	84
V Plan	6237	122
VI Plan	18150	179
VII Plan	42673	215
VIII Plan	135445	246
IX Plan	193121	242
X Plan	274114	233

top 20 industrialised countries in the world) country. Not to be ignored is the fact that some of our government undertakings have earned reputation for excellence at the international level. Some names to be quoted in this context are Bharat Heavy Electricals Ltd. (BHEL), Oil & Natural Gas Commission (ONGC) and Air-India. And some giants among public sector units, i.e., Indian Oil Corporation (IOC), Steel Authority of India Ltd. (SAIL) and ONGC figured in *Fortune International's* 500 large companies in 1998 (See Box 18.1). Over the years, the public sector undertakings have built up a huge reservoir of managerial talent in our country.

Box 18.1 **Large PSUs**

Six Indian Public Sector companies figure in the latest list of the 500 biggest industrial corporations, released by Fortune International. They are:

Name of company	*Ranking (Out of 500)*
Indian Oil Corporation	144
ONGC	278
SAIL	332
HPCL	371
Coal India Ltd.	371
Bharat Petroleum Corp.Ltd.	474

Of the Central PSUs, 161 are engaged in manufacturing while 75 are in the services sector including the financial sector. Four PSUs are in the construction sector. Together, the Central PSUs have a combined capital base of over Rs.2,74,114 crore as on March 31, 2001. Despite debilitating controls, contradictions and the imminent threat of privatisation, quite a few PSUs have emerged as islands of excellence. The public sector oil, telecom and power companies have consistently excelled in their performance and generated surpluses.

The following points highlight the role played by the PSEs in developing our economy:

1. Share in National Income

As stated above, Public Sector Enterprises (PSEs) account for one-fourth of our GDP. During the period of 42 years (1960-61 to 2001-02), these units together have practically doubled their share in the GDP.

2. Commanding Heights of the Economy

More than their share in the GDP, the versatility of PSEs is amazing. The sector is in command in almost all the strategic sectors of the economy like coal, oil-refining, electricity, telecommunications, iron and steel, paper, newsprint and the like, where it controls more than 80 percent of the total installed capacity. In all, it holds a dominating position in the production of 50 types of industrial commodities and services which are of decisive significance for the economy[2]. Only agriculture, wholesale and retail trade and small scale units have remained in the private sector.

3. Share in Capital Formation

Another important role of PSEs has been in respect of capital formation as revealed in Table 18.2. After having reached the peak during the Fourth Plan, the share of PSEs in total investment in each of the plans has, however, been on the decline.

Table 18.2 **Share of Public Sector in Total Investment (%)**

Plan	*Public Sector*	*Private Sector*
I	46.40	53.60
II	54.60	45.40
III	63.70	36.30
IV	60.30	39.70
V	57.60	32.40
VI	52.90	47.10
VII	47.80	52.20
VIII	36.50	63.50
IX	34.70	65.30

Another angle to study capital formation is to consider market capitalisation of companies. Table 18.3 shows the data of five of the public sector undertakings.

An important point to remember in this context is the types of capital which are being formed and the use of which they are being put. Investment in the private sector producing luxury goods should be evaluated lower than the similar type of investment in the public sector which makes basic infrastructure available to the economy as a whole. This is true even though profitability of the private sector is rated high. Viewed from this perspective, it may be stated that capital formation in the public sector is highly significant[3].

Table 18.3 **Companies and their Market Capitalisation**

Company	*Market Capitalisation in Dec.2004 (Rs.cr)*
Oil and Natural Gas Corporation	1,13,680
Indian Oil Corporation	50,177
SAIL	19,766
GAIL (India)	16,606
BHEL	15,453

(**Source**: *ET500*, Dec, 2004)

4. PSEs and Employment

Public sector has vastly contributed to the growth of employment in the country.

One of the evils of our economy has been growing unemployment. It goes to the credit of the PSEs that they have gone a long way in minimising this problem. As is well known, the organised sector contributes to 10 percent of total employment and 90 percent is accounted for by the organised sector. Out of the contribution of the organised segment, PSUs account for a lion share of 78.08 (in 1995) and the private sector's share is 21.92 percent. This trend is also evident from the compound rates of employment during a period of 20 years, i.e., from 1961-80. The average annual compound rate of employment growth in the public sector was 4.3 percent, whereas it was two percent in the private sector. During the eighties, the growth rates were: public sector two percent and zero in the private sector. However, during the first half of nineties, the trend was reversed. Growth rate of the public sector during 1990-95 was just 0.89 percent, whereas in the private sector, it was 2.89 percent. But, both public as well as private sectors have made equal contribution to the employment generation during this period. (see also Table 18.4).

Table 18.4 **Growth Rate of Employment in Organised Sector during 1999-2001**

(in %)

Year	*Public Sector*	*Private Sector*	*Total*
1990	1.71	1.83	1.78
1991	1.52	1.24	1.44
1992	0.80	2.21	1.21
1993	0.60	0.06	0.44
1994	0.62	1.01	0.73
1995	0.11	1.63	0.73
1996	-0.19	5.62	1.51
1997	0.67	2.04	1.09
1998	-0.09	1.74	0.46
1999	-0.02	-0.57	-0.19
2000	-0.68	0.97	-0.17
2001	-0.90	0.10	0.60

(**Source:** *Economic Survey*, 2002-03)

As seen from Table 18.4, the growth rate of employment in public sector slowed down considerably and became negative since 1996. But growth rate accelerated in private sector during 1990s. Table 18.5 gives details about actual number of jobs generated both in public sector as well as in private sector. Data in Table 18.5 tell the same story as told by Table 18.4.

Table 18.5 **Employment in Public Sector and Organised Private Sector**

(in millions)

	Public Sector	*Private Sector*
1990-91	19.06	7.68
1991-92	19.21	7.85
1992-93	19.33	7.85
1993-94	19.45	7.93
1994-95	19.47	8.06
1995-96	19.43	8.51
1996-97	19.56	8.69
1997-98	19.42	8.75
1998-99	19.41	8.70
1999-00	19.31	8.65
2000-01	19.14	8.65
2001-02	18.77	8.43

(**Source**: *RBI, Handbook of Statistics on the Indian Economy*, 2003-04, p.28)

Public enterprises have done remarkably well in acting as a model employer. In a country, where millions of employable people are without jobs, the role of government undertakings in providing jobs and ensuring decent level of living to those employed, is really commendable.

There are over two million employees in government undertakings and the average emoluments per annum amount to more than Rs.50,000 each. Besides paying higher salaries, public enterprises assure job security, good working conditions, attractive incentive schemes, participative management, high degree of safety and adequate training facilities.

The public sector undertakings are good pay masters as Table 18.6 indicates. Six of the top 10 spenders are owned by the Central Government. It is true that banks are not covered in this Chapter, but the fact that State Bank of India and Punjab National Bank are owned and managed by the Government of India cannot be denied.

Public sector undertakings are known as model employers.

Besides the in-plant facilities, public enterprises provide infrastructural facilities like housing, medical, educational and transport facilities to their employees. Conservative estimates show that SAIL has spent over Rs.1,500 crore on setting up huge infrastructural facilities at its plants from the time of its inception. During 1985-86 alone, SAIL spent Rs.120 crore on these facilities. The present thinking of the steel monolith is gradually to farm out these functions to other agencies without sacrificing the quality of services so as to concentrate on the primary business of producing steel.

Large-scale employment generation by PSUs has, infact, over the years, led to a situation where some of the enterprises are saddled with over-employment or excess manpower resulting in low-level of manpower productivity. Government has initiated a voluntary retirement scheme (VRS) to shed excess manpower and to improve the age-mix and the skill-mix. Simultaneously, training and retraining programmes have been undertaken to bring about overall improvement in manpower productivity.

Table 18.6 **Top 10 Paymasters**

Rank by Staff Cost	*Company*	*Staff Cost (Rs.Crore)*
1	State Bank of India	6,093
2	TCS	5,138
3	SAIL	4,758
4	Infosys Technologies	2,366
5	Punjab National Bank	1,654
6	BHEL	1,640
7	MTNL	1,619
8	IOC	1,589
9	TISCO	1,350
10	Satyam Computer Services	1,338

(**Source:** *ET500*, Dec.2004, p.21)

Even with regard to the employment of people belonging to reserved categories, the PSUs have done an excellent job.

5. Export Earnings

PSEs have been contributing greatly to the export earnings of our country.

What is more interesting is that most of these earnings come from firms which are engaged in highly competitive fields. Exports earnings have favourable impact on India's balance of payments condition.

Left parties are right when they argue that PSUs should continue to function as PSUs, economic reforms notwithstanding.

The Left parties in the country are right when they argue that PSUs should continue to function, economic reforms notwithstanding. PSUs did play crucial role in the past in the development of the economy and there is no reason to doubt their potential to continue to play such a role in future.

Following are some of the measures to improve performance of PSUs:

- Looking at the government for budgetary help is no more possible, for, such support has been withdrawn. Other privileges like purchase preferences and price preferences for purchase by government or other PSUs are also not available.
- PSUs need to face competition both from domestic competition and MNCs.
- Mindset of managers and employees needs to undergo significant change. Laidback style of managers should give place for dynamism and combative mood. The attitude of lethargy and laziness on the part of employees should change into one of eagerness to cooperate and work for production, productivity and profit.
- Capital base needs to be restructured. Huge loans to be converted into equity and PSUs should access capital markets for additional funds.
- Globalisation should not be taken as a threat but as an opportunity to access foreign markets, learn new managerial skills and practices, and raise cheaper offshore funds.
- Cost control and cost reduction to be achieved at every level.

- All the old rhetoric for PSEs- infant industry, a heavy industry based development strategy, lack of resources and low level of technical competence in the private sector, absence of developed regional development, employment promotion and protection, social obligation- have lost relevance in these days of market economy and globalisation. Public sector restructuring and disinvestment is currently taking place in a large number of developing countries including former socialist countries. We cannot remain isolated from this trend.

6. Balanced Regional Development

India is a vast country with wide variations in climate, demography' resource availability, fertility and topography. At a given time, some parts of the country will be reeling under floods, at the same time there will be severe draughts in other parts. One can also witness vast barren lands with sparce inhabitation by people, juxtaposed with thickly populated areas. Industrialisation has high potential in levelling such differences. The severe draughts being faced by Orissa, Rajasthan, Maharashtra and Madhya Pradesh are a case in consideration.

Public sector enterprises, by locating themselves in backward areas, help remove regional imbalances in development.

Recognising the existence of disparities in economic development of different regions, the Industrial Policy Resolutions of 1956, 1977 and 1980, emphasised the need for accelerated rate of growth in the economy and speedy industrialisation and removal of the regional imbalances. In this context, PSUs have a vital role to play since the setting up of large industries in public sector help eliminate regional disparities through such spin-offs as employment opportunities, growth of small and ancillary industries and development of infrastructural facilities. While deciding the location of PSUs, due considerations are given to the backwardness of various regions, subject to the over-riding consideration of techno-economic feasibility.

7. Industrialisation and Economic Development

Industrialisation, as is well known, is a *sine qua non* for economic development. The role of the public sector in achieving industrialisation is considerable. The role is particularly significant when one takes a look at the background against which the country started its industrial progress. "The position in 1947, when we became independent", wrote H.V.R.Iyengar, in a different context "was that we had the rudiments of an industrial apparatus, but we were almost completely dependent for the running of this apparatus on imported equipment and technology. This was the case even after the First Five Year Plan was started. I recall that when I became Secretary of the Ministry of Commerce and Industry in Delhi in 1952, the first thing that I did was to send for the Chief Industrial Adviser to the Government and ask him to look around in my room and tell me what were the items that could be produced in India but were imported. I asked, for instance, whether the ceiling fan which was whirling above our heads had been made in India. The Chief Industrial Adviser said, "Yes, it has been put together in India, but the varnish for the blade is made from the imported chemicals; the ball-bearings inside the fan are imported; the wire is of imported metal; the insulation above the wire is also imported." I asked about the table against which we were leaning. He said the timber was probably Indian, but the saw which cut the timber was imported and a good part of transport equipment used in hauling the timber was also imported such as the trucks and a good part of the railway equipment. The varnish used for the timber was also imported. I looked at the carpet which was spread on the floor in my office-room. He said the wool was probably Indian although he was not certain that the wool-top had not been imported, but the dyes used for colouring the carpet were certainly imported. In desperation, I asked about the paper and the pins and the clips on my table. He said the paper was undoubtedly Indian but the machinery used for manufacturing the paper had been imported and certainly the clips and pins were imported."[4]

Private sector shunned investment in critical areas. Public sector was conceived to fill the gap.

Such was the position with which the country started its industrialisation. The task of achieving industrialisation was naturally gigantic and the time available was short. The private sector could not be relied upon to achieve faster industrial development. Historically, the private sector was controlled by the British managing agency houses with overriding consideration of serving the interests of British industries at the cost of Indian industries. To expect an overnight change in the culture and orientation of private undertaking was unrealistic. Moreover, the private sector units had the problem of resources. Infact, the two private steel companies, *viz.* the Tata Iron and Steel Company (TISCO) and the Indian Iron and Steel Company, were each given a loan of Rs.10 crore by the government for modernisation. Besides, industrialisation demands a heavy investment in critical projects which involve low profitability, long gestation periods and massive resources. The private sector, whose primary consideration is quick returns and high capital appreciation, shuns the critical projects.

The public sector was conceived to fill the gap which it did ably. The phenomenal growth in investment indicates the way the government undertakings stood up to the challenge. From a mere Rs.29 crore investment in just five enterprises in 1950-51, the investment quantum jumped to Rs.2,74,114 crore, spread over 233 undertakings at the begining of the 10th plan.

In the successive Five Year Plans, preference was shown to the public sector units in outlays as shown in Table 18.2.

The products portfolio of public sector enterprises had both depth and width.

Such massive investments have yielded results. The products portfolio of public enterprises reveals both width and depth. The products produced include aircraft, ships, rail wagons, rail coaches, teleprinters, computers, sophisticated electronic equipment, telephone cables, earthmoving equipment, turbo-sets, transformers, power boilers, industrial motors, road rollers, diesel engines, steam and water turbines, two, three and four-wheelers, tanks and vessels, equipment for fertilizers, petrochemicals and other industries, water treatment plants, cranes, machine tools, crude oil, gas, petroleum products, synthetic drugs, antibiotics, surgical instruments, medical X-ray film, printing presses, agricultural tractors, equipment for steel and mining industries, equipment for fertilizer and petrochemicals, iron-ore, gold ore, zinc ingots, lead ingots, refractories, diamond, newsprint, cement, chemicals, additives, etc. What is heartening is the majority of these products are manufactured on indigenous scientific know-how and technical do-how.

PSUs enabled the country to achieve several breakthroughs.

Our country has attained several breakthroughs, thanks to the public sector enterprises. The Fertilizer Corporation of India (FCI), for instance, is one of the few organisations in the world to develop and produce a complete range of fertilizer catalysts. Similarly, the quality control laboratories of Hindustan Antibiotics are equipped with full-fledged units for all chemical, pharmacological, bacteriological and toxicity tests. Discoveries of new antibiotics in the laboratories have attracted international interest.

The massive expansion of public sector enterprises has its ripple effects on the economy in the form of increased export earnings; upgraded technology; higher contributions to the exchequer and increased internal resource generation; greater employment opportunities; opening up of backwards areas; and an overall increase in the style and level of living of the people.

Whatever the critics point out, the fact remains that public undertakings have, as mentioned above, vastly contributed to India being ranked as one of the fast developing countries. Nor should anybody deny the fact that public sector units are singularly responsible for laying a strong foundation for the further development of our economy.

8. Encouragement to Ancillary Industries

Small and ancillary industries occupy a position of importance in our economy. It has been the policy of the government to encourage the development of small and ancillary industries, as a part of overall strategy for industrial growth in the country. The Industrial Policy Resolutions and the successive Five Year Plan documents have spelt out various measures for their development. The approach to the Seventh Five Year Plan document lays down that ancillarisation should be given special emphasis and the necessary push at the licensing stage itself and encourage maximum number of ancillary units with each industrial licence.

The Bureau of Public Enterprises has been monitoring the progress of ancillary development in the Central public enterprises. To give a proper direction to ancillary growth and the needed thrust, the Bureau, initially in 1971 and later in 1974, issued guidelines to the public enterprises on the growth of ancillaries. In the light of the experience gained in their operation, comprehensive guidelines were issued in 1978 which hold validity today. These guidelines earmark the role of different promotional agencies so that better institutional cooperation could be achieved *vis-a-vis* the role of existing public enterprises, new enterprises and those effecting substantial expansion. The guidelines also provide an in-built mechanism for reviewing and monitoring the progress of ancillaries.

As a result of these efforts, there has been a significant progress both in terms of numbers as well as services rendered by the ancillary sector to the public sector enterprises.

Specifically, PSUs help ancillary units in the following ways:

(a) They take responsibility for providing technical know-how, managerial expertise, equipment selection and layout and production aids such as production design, tooling, blueprints, manpower planning, quality control, inventory management and the like.

(b) They guide ancillaries on sources of finance and procedures for obtaining them and

(c) They offer ready demand for the produce turned out by the ancillaries.

However, the obligation to promote ancillarisation is often misused by the executives of government undertakings who indulge in nepotism. In several cases, the kith and kin of the highly-placed executives, are encouraged to set up ancillary units and out-of-turn favours are shown to them. Adherence to rigid quality specifications is not insisted upon or shortage in weight or quantity of supply is conveniently overlooked. An altogether different treatment is meted out to the owners of ancillary units who have no connection of any sort with the executives of government undertakings.

> Obligation to ancilliarise production was often misused by PSUs.

Barring instances of nepotism and harassment, the role of public enterprises in promoting ancillarisation is noteworthy.

9. Resource Mobilisation

PSUs have contributed enormously to the resources of the Central Government through dividends, interest payments on loans, income tax, and excise and other duties.

In addition, PSEs have generated internal resources for themselves in the form of depreciation provision and retained profits including deferred revenue expenditure written off during the year. It may be stated that only commercial enterprises are allowed to generate internal resources. Enterprises engaged in development and promotional activities are not expected to build up sizable surpluses.

> PSUs have generated vast internal resources.

Thus, PSUs have occupied the commanding heights of the economy and have been regarded as the temples of modern India. Without them, India could not have stood in the comity of nations with the self-assurance that has characterised its stature. PSUs have been in the vanguard of the industrialisation process, supplying infrastructure, steel and capital goods essential for a rapidly evolving economy.

PSUs have demonstrated their competitiveness even in international markets.

In recent times, with the liberalisation of the economy, PSUs have demonstrated their competitiveness in the domestic and international arenas. Consider the case of the power utilities, which despite a decade of liberalisation remain in the public sector. The private sector played coy and quibbled over incentives and guarantees even as the National Thermal Power Corporation (NTPC) commissioned projects and added substantially to the thermal generation capacity year after year and experimented with new fuels and revamped old plans.

The public sector is the foundation on which the edifice of modern India has been built. Self-reliance in key infrastructure sectors-the *mantra* of the 1950s, 1960s and 1970s - helped build impressive capacities of petroleum, power, steel, fertilizers and railway and road networks. Even as public investments took care of long-gestation, capital-intensive infrastructure sectors, the private sector was free to provide other goods and services. The uniquely Indian concept of a mixed economy served the country well, but if there is a perception that its time is past, it is not because of the inherent weaknesses in the model itself but because of the distortions imposed by governments which tried to meet a multiplicity of objectives.

Performance

Assessment of performance of PSUs is rather difficult because they seek to fulfill multiple objectives.

Assessment of performance of PSEs is rather difficult because of the multiple objectives they seek to pursue and because some of the objectives conflict with one another. For example, profitability conflicts with employment generation or positive externalities. However, Table 18.7 gives indictions of profitability of PSUs.

Thus, poor performance and even losses have become a way of life with the Central Government owned undertakings. Read the financial statements of PSUs, every second enterprise reveals losses accumulated into hundreds of crores of rupees.

Table 18.7 **Profitability of PSUs**

	1990-91	*1991-92*	*1992-93*	*1993-94*	*1994-95*	*1995-96*	*1996-97*
No. of profitable enterprises	123	133	131	121	130	-	-
No. of loss making units	111	102	106	117	-	-	-
ROI (%)	4.50	2.80	2.3	2.0	2.2	4.5	-
Gross profit to capital employed(%)	10.9	11.6	11.4	11.6	-	15.1	14.5
Gross margin to capital(%)	17.9	18.8	18.0	17.3	-	-	-
Net profit to capital (%)	2.2	2.0	2.3	2.8	-	5.5	5.1

The performance of government undertakings is probably the lowest in the steel sector. The following figures tell their own story for the year 1998-99:

(Rs.in crore)

	Profit	*Losses*
Bhilai Steel Plant	457	-
Durgapur Steel Plant	-	489
Rourkela Steel Plant	-	591
Bokaro Steel Plant	-	160
Alloy Steel Plant	-	112
Salem Steel Plant	-	138
		1490

With the exception of Bhilai Plant, all the others have been piling up heavy losses over the years.

The scene in the entire public sector is even more chilling. According to the figures up to March 1999, the losses incurred by 29 PSEs trebled within one year from 1996-97 to 1997-98 from Rs.1040.29 crore to Rs.3655.38 crores.

As many as 66 (out of 117 loss making units) PSUs have been referred to BIFR. The major ones among these include Richardson & Cruddas, Bharat Pumps & Compressors, Triveni Structurals, Tannery & Footwear Corporation of India, Cycle Corporation of India, Mining & Allied Machinery Corporation, Heavy Engineering Corporation, Bharat Gold Mines and Nagaland Pulp & Paper Company.

However, as many as 120 enterprises have been earning surplus and these belong mainly to petroleum,power, service enterprises and agro-based enterprises.

With half of the units incurring losses and with meager ROI of 4.47 percent , PSUs seem to have no justification to exist. This argument gets reinforced when one compares profitability of public sector with private sector (see Table 18.8).

Table 18.8 **Comparing PSEs with Private Sector**

Profit after tax as a % of network	*1980-81*	*1990-91*	*1991-92*	*1992-93*	*1994-95*
PSEs including petroleum	-1.6	3.0	2.8	3.5	4.1
PSEs excluding petroleum	-3.8	-0.1	0.9	1.5	0.6
Private sector	13.7	15.9	14.2	11.4	13.5

(**Source**: Vijay Kelkar & V.V.Bhanoji Rao, *India-Development Policy Imperatives* (Ed,) New Delhi, Tata McGraw-Hill, 1996, P.200)

If the Central Government undertakings have been presenting poor performance, reasons can be found, not at their doors but elsewhere.

1. Political Interference

Political interference is a problem faced by public sector units. Be it the location of the enterprise, appointment of chief executives or workers, or any other factor, interference by political leaders is coming in the way of effective functioning of government undertakings.

Business India of Nov. 19,1984, writes that "*Last year, during an earlier strike (in Singareni Coal Co.), N.T.Rama Rao was enraged that it has been resolved in his absence, and as expected, the then Chairman and Managing Director was transferred in no time at all*". The same periodical also reveals how NTR stalled the proposed merger of Singareni with Coal Company, Ltd.

A senior public sector executive even put in his papers unable to cope with the steel minister's demands. This happened in 1991. The affected PSEs drift towards industrial sickness often beyond recognition. The Ranchi-based Heavy Engineering Corporation is one of the many examples.

It is not only the politicians who interfere. A public sector enterprise is subject to multiple masters (naturally, interference) - the Minister, the Secretary-in-charge of the Ministry, the Finance Ministry, Bureau of Public Enterprises, Public Investment Board, Planning Commission and their contradictory directives (Read box 18.2 for more details on intereference).

Box 18.2 **All Tied Up in Knots**

One of the main reasons why PSU managements move about like robots is because of the fact that the CMDs are governed by Article 12 of the Constitution, which makes them civil servants and not chief executives, which is what they are supposed to be if they are expected to run a commercial enterprise. "This accountability is killing us; we spend most of our time answering bureaucrats, ministers, different vigilance committees and finally, we have to regularly report to Parliament. Where is the time to run the company?" asks the chief of a public sector company.

As if that's not enough, major capital investments of public sector units have to be cleared by the public investment board (PIB). PIB meetings are a bit of a joke; there are enough instances of a PSU project being cleared by the board of directors, and then gathering dust at the PIB stage. Just as the PSU management heaves a sigh of relief when a date for a PIB meeting is set, the problems begin. The ministry secretary is suddenly out of town and the meeting is cancelled or the minister himself is busy visting his constituency and the meeting is put off.

"The biggest problem with the PIB aproach is that the law requires specific bureaucrats like the expenditure secretary, and the concerned minister and secretary to be present at once, otherwise the meeting cannot take place" says the frustrated project manager of a fertiliser company. According to him, a simple PIB clearance for one of his expansion projects took an amazing two years. As many as 12 PIB meetings were scheduled and promptly cancelled at the last minute.

"When I was informed on the telephone that the project was finally cleared, I didn't believe it. I actually sent somebody to the ministry to get the minutes of the PIB meeting," recalls the project manager.

Indeed so ubiquitous is red tape that at a recent seminar, economist Onkar Goswami launched a frontal attack on its impact on Indian PSUs. "Just look at the way public sector boards are being filled; board decisions are being emasculated by ministers," he said, citing the example of SAIL. The company has actually turned in a better operational performance than the private sector TISCO, yet it was the minister who decided on its advertising budget!

Goswami also came down heavily on the practice of PSUs signing MoUs with the government. "These MoUs are total nonsense; the targets are deliberately kept low so that in the end, when they are exceeded, everybody is happy," he said. Talk of number jugglery.

(***Source :*** *Economic Times*, 9th Feb.1997)

2. High Cost of Delay

Cost over-runs have eaten away the competitiveness of PSUs.

No public sector unit (with the honourable exception of Kudremukh which has the distinction of being the only government undertaking to be completed ahead of schedule) is completed as per schedule. *Economic Times* of March 12, 1986, reported that "Twenty-one power projects costing more than Rs.100 crores each with a total anticipated investment of Rs.8,865 crores had been delayed for reasons such as delay in the acquisition of land, supply of critical equipment and materials, approval procedure of foreign aid agencies, law and order disturbances, forest clearance and difficult geological conditions. Some of these reasons together with the problems of power supply had delayed 11 Central coal projects. The total anticipated investment in the coal projects was Rs.3,213 crore. These and other reasons, including slow construction and inadequate funding, had delayed the completion of four Central steel projects, each costing more than Rs.100 crore. The total anticipated investment in these steel projects was Rs.11,870 crore". What are the consequences of delay?

The project costs double and even more. Besides the increase in project costs, the other consequences of delay are the costs of output and employment foregone during the period of delay, the cost of inter-sectoral imbalances which strained production and investment, the cost of foreign exchange spent on making up shortfalls in the physical availability of goods, and above all, the impact of inflation triggered by cost escalation and its financing.[5] (See also Box 18.3). Roll of honour must go to the Metro Rail Project, Calculta. It took 20 years for completion and the cost shot up from Rs.140 cr to Rs.1600 cr.

3. Fear of Scams

Executives of PSUs are averse to take risks.

The all pervasive fear of the investigating agencies in the wake of scams involving senior public sector bank officials has deterred many PSE executives from using their discretion in making vital commercial decisions at a time when the market is becoming increasingly competitive. When budgetary support was withdrawn to the PSEs, they were asked to compete in the market. Competition implies "*risk taking*". No PSE executive is prepared to take risks.

4. Headless Plants

There has been considerable delay in filling vacant positions at the top of PSEs. Many undertakings, therefore, remain without chief executives for months.

By end of March 1988, as many as 24 chief executive positions and 52 director posts were lying vacant. Table 18.9 shows delays in filling the top positions. Also see Table 18.10.

Box 18.3 **Costs of Delay**

The chronic tardiness in implementing and completing government projects has been quantified yet again. From a sample of 307 projects monitored by the programme implementation department, it has emerged that delays have led to a cost escalation of 34.5 per cent. The consequent increase in costs has been Rs.25,468 crore on approved costs of Rs.70,0433 crore. The single biggest factor for the cost overrun has been slippages in project implementation, due to which 80 per cent of the increased cost outlay was incurred. Of the 307 projects reviewed, as many as 177 were behind schedule. The slippages and cost overruns have all been incurred in the industrial infrastructure sectors such as power, coal, steel, railways, telecom, natural gas etc., all of which are vital inputs for industry. Consequently, the total costs to the economy arising out of the delay in the 177 delayed projects will be a multiplier of the Rs.24,468 crore which has been revealed in the study. Again, this figure is by no means an indication of the total cost overruns in the country since it profiles only a fraction of projects under various stages of implementation.

Cost overruns are a drag on any economy, but especially so in a developing economy such as India, where capital is scarce and development needs are prioritised. Though cost escalation and project delays are not unknown in the private sector, the bare fact is that the commanding heights of such tardy practices are the preserve of the public sector, as revealed in this study. Though the issuance of such reports is an annual exercise, the one glimmer of hope this time around is that the incidence of such wasteful expenditures may decline in the future. This may happen not because one can expect better managerial practices from the public sector behemoths, but because private enterprise has been allowed an entry in many of the sectors hitherto the domain of public sector. Some will argue that private enterprise is not much better. Perhaps, but it at least recognises the value of money.

Table 18.9 **Growth of Public Sector Undertakings**

Name of post pending with the Cabinet	*Vacancy date*	*Date of PSEB recommendation*	*Delay (in Months)*
Chairman, MMTC	18.09.87	27.11.87	6
CMD, NPTC	03.11.87	05.02.88	5
Director, HEC	24.04.86	26.06.87	23
Pending with the Ministers			
MD, Scooters India Ltd.	26.12.86	24.04.87	16
Chairman, STC	08.10.87	27.11.87	6
CMD, Engineering Projects India	25.09.87	27.11.87	6
CMD, BHEL	12.11.87	18.09.87	5
MD, ITDC	18.03.87	24.03.88	12
Member(Finance)IAA	22.08.86	23.10.86	19
MD(Design)HAL	01.11.86	31.10.86	17

(**Source**:*India Today*, April 30, 1988.)

There are also reasons for poor performance of PSEs-reasons which are triggered by management failure. It is pertinent to recollect some of them.

Table 18.10 **PSUs Vacancies at the Top**

Units	*Turnover (Rs.crore)*	*Headless for Months*
State Trading Corp.	1043	5
National Airports Authority	293	2
Indian Airlines	1500	10
National Hydroelectric Power Corp.	250	18
State Farms corp.	24	17
Indian Oil Corp.	24000	9
Gas Authority of India	3500	27

(**Source**: *Business World*, Feb. 23,1994)

A. Ineffective Management

Management of Central Government undertakings is generally ineffective. This is so because (i) bureaucrats, with neither leadership qualities nor business acumen, are made chief executives; (ii) executives are not allowed to make decisions purely on commercial considerations and (iii) there is considerable delay in appointing executives and even after appointment, there is the uncertainty of tenure.

Management ineffectiveness has reflected on the poor performance of the organisation.

B. Huge Inventories

Stock-piling of inventories speaks volumes about inefficiency of management. SAIL carries a large inventory of over a million tonnes worth about Rs.1500 crore. The Visakhapatnam Steel Plant of Rashtriya Ispat Nigam Ltd., also has similar inventory. As many as 73 PSEs carry inventories equal to seven months cost of production. In the private sector, the corresponding figure is three months. Inventory management seems to be lacking or ineffective in most PSEs.

PSUs had piled up huge inventories.

C. Trade Unionism

Many of the public sector units are plagued with the multiplicity of trade unions and intra-union and inter-union rivalries. Union rivalries results in industrial disputes. Singareni Collieries must be remembered in this context. The company has 87,000 employees on its payroll. In 1993, its 19 trade unions went on strike 460 times resulting in a loss of 14 lakh mandays and production loss of 15 lakh tonnes. The sad part of the story is that one union or the other is always on strike and often the demands of rival unions are conflicting on the same issue.

D. Unimaginative Production and Unfavourable Pricing Policies

The products produced by many public sector units are unrelated to market demand. Yet products are being sold because their producers enjoy virtual monopoly. SAIL is an example to be quoted. For a long time, SAIL was producing thicker gauge steel instead of the thinner variety which the buyers want. Only now has SAIL changed its production pattern.

Another instance of unimaginative production policy is the Surgical Instruments Plant set up near Madras. For a long time, this unit could not work well because many of the instruments produced were too big to be used on Indians; the sizes were appropriate for Russians who are much bigger made. Still the unit was set up because technology and machinery were offered on easy terms by the then USSR.

As is well known, the Bureau of Public Enterprises has suggested two norms for pricing in the public enterprises. Accordingly, the enterprises in competition with domestic producers should fix their prices on the basis of the normal market forces of demand and supply and the enterprises in other market conditions should fix the prices of their products within the normal ceiling of the price level set by the '*landed cost*' of comparable imported goods. In case the exports of such goods are subsidised appreciably, the normal price of such goods in the country of their origin should be taken into account while calculating the 'landed costs'.

The pricing practice naturally reveals a lot of variations depending on the nature of the activities carried on by public enterprises. But the sad part of the story is that, irrespective of the practice, the product pricing is leaving only a meagre surplus in the form of excess of sales revenue over the cost of goods sold. This surplus before the provision for depreciation, interest and corporate tax has declined to 8.4 per cent of the total sales revenue during 1980-81 which subsequently increased to 11.0 per cent and continued to increase up to 13.5 per cent during 1984-85, revealing a change in the pricing policy since 1981-82. The gross profit obtained, after deducting the depreciation on the net block from the gross margin, has also declined to 4.9 per cent of the sales revenue during 1980-81, but subsequently it increased up to 8.5 per cent during 1984-85.

On account of heavy reliance on debt financing, an amount ranging from 3.1 to 4.8 per cent of the sales revenue has been paid as interest on loans which left only a meagre sum as pre-tax profit. It has been a mere 0.1 per cent of the sales revenue during 1980-81, but increased later on upto 3.9 per cent during 1984-85. The profit-earning public enterprises are also required to pay corporate tax which has reduced their aggregate net even to a negative value in certain years up to 1980-81. However, subsequently, there emerged a positive net profit but that could go up to 1.7 per cent of the sales revenue during 1984-85.

Most of the public enterprises engaged in producing and selling goods are capital-intensive and require a heavy provision for depreciation. Similarly, most of the enterprises rely on borrowings from the Central Government, State Government, foreign parties, financial institutions and individuals for financing their operations which drain off sufficient surplus in the form of interest on loans. Considering the inevitable high depreciation and interest charge, the gross margin, as per the present pricing practices, seems meagre, which necessarily requires some improvement.

E. Unutilised Capacities

Plant capacities of PSUs were never fully utilized.

Many PSEs have excess plant capacities. These capacities are never fully utilised. While plants operate at below full capacities, costs will be adversely affected because of overheads and wage bills. A study conducted in 1981 found that over the previous 20 years, each rupee of additional annual output had necessitated 7.4 rupees if the public sector was producing the goods, but only 3.6 rupees if the private sector did it.

During 1990-91, four percent of the units recorded capacity utilisation of less than 75 percent. Only 54 percent registered capacity utilisation of more than 75 percent (see Table 18.11).

Table 18.11 **Capacity Utilisation in Public Enterprises**

	1990-91	*1989-90*	*1988-89*
Units under production surveyed:	229	257	212
(a) Units which have recorded capacity utilisation of more than 75%	123 (54%)	136 (53%)	126 (60%)
(b) Units where capacity utilisation has been between 50-75%	59 (26%)	58 (23%)	43 (20%)
(c) Units where capacity utilisation was less than 50%	47 (20%)	63 (24%)	43 (20%)
Total	229	257	212

F. Others

Wrong choice of locations, uncertainty of financial allocations, poor quality products, high cost, higher social costs and nepotism and corruption have also contributed to the low performance of PSEs.

At the workers' level, absence of right attitude is the main problem. It is unfortunate that a majority of employees have taken the public sector enterprises as a milch cow meant for squeezing, little realising that the cow must be fed well if it is to hold sufficient milk. Employees have long forgotten the basic and simple philosophy that they have to serve the organisations they are employed in before expecting the organisations to help them (the workers). Dedication to work, commitment to serve and professionalism are woefully absent.

SIL epitomizes all the evils of a jinxed PSU.

Scooters India Ltd. (SIL) epitomises all the evils of a jinxed public sector undertaking. Read Box 8.4 for the saga of a misconceived, wrongly executed and badly managed undertaking.

In the recent past, the government withdrew budgetary support abruptly. Infact, the ushering in of competition in spheres hitherto reserved for the public sector happened simultaneously with the abrupt withdrawal of budgetary support. Yet the government was rather slow in phasing out the market-distorting administered price mechanism. Left to fend for themselves in the face of mounting competition from multinationals with deep pockets, lean structures and predatory practices, many PSUs find themselves at the crossroads today.

WHAT NEEDS TO BE DONE?

After reading through the chapter, it may be concluded that, except on the profit and profitability counts, public sector units have done fairly well in other areas. But it is the profit that matters and it is here that their performance is thoroughly disappointing.

Except in profit and profitability, PSUs have done well in all other areas.

Thus, there is urgent need to improve their performance. As public enterprises have come to occupy a dominant position in our economy, and as they collectively represent a colossal investment by the people of India for a better future for themselves and for the country, the task of improving their performance is a matter of national urgency. There is a clear admission of this in the approach document relating to the First Plan. In the Planning Commission's view, 'inefficiencies can be found in both public and private sectors, and the national task is to remove them'.[6]

How to improve performance in terms of profit is a big question. The answer lies in efficient management. There are instances where sick units have been turned around and made profitable units,

Box 18.4 **How not to Organise an Enterprise**

A brief recapitulation of the history of the SIL will be instructive. The government had decided in 1969 that a public sector unit for the manufacture of scooters should be set up. This decision was apparently taken because the demand for scooters had been rapidly increasing and, with the production by the two main producers, Bajaj Auto and Automobile Products India (API), being limited by their licensed capacity, there were long waiting lists and a flourishing black market. As developing an indigenous design was difficult, offers were invited from foreign concerns for collaboration. Piaggio of Italy, which had earlier collaborated with Bajaj Auto in the production of scooters, had made an offer which was initially considered good.

Innocenti Plant

But, in the meantime, the government came to learn that the other major Italian scooter manufacturing concern, Innocenti, was closing down its manufacture of scooters. This company had earlier collaborated with API in the production of scooters in India. The government then decided to explore the possibility of buying the plant that was being closed down in Italy. Apparently, the chairman of API, Mr.M.A.Chidambaram, played an important mediatory role in the negotiations. After an inspecting team of technical and financial experts of the government visited Italy in October, 1971, and after considering the report prepared by an appraiser from London, the government decided in 1972 to enter into an agreement with Innocenti and API. The Scooters India Ltd. was set up in September, 1972. The initial idea was that this would be a joint sector project with the government holding 51 per cent equity, and API and Innocenti together holding 49 per cent.

Among the reasons which were supposed to justify the government's preferring the proposal to by the Innocenti plant instead of a new plant as earlier suggested by Piaggio, the important ones were the equipment offered was in a reasonable good condition; the special purpose machines could last over eight years and the general purpose machines over four years, and these could be used for the production of five lakh scooters over a period of seven or eight years. This would ensure an initial saving in capital cost of about Rs.five crore.

Moreover, as production would commence earlier by about two years, that itself would provide a source of saving and generate additional resources which could help replacement of machinery, modernisation and expansion. Foreign exchange was also expected to be saved as well as, out of the price of $2 million to be paid to Innocenti, a part was to be adjusted towards the payment of equity capital by that company and the balance was to be paid out of export earnings over a period of seven years. As Innocenti was closing down its production of stooters, the trade name Lambretta and the worldwide market which it had already established was to be available to the new company, thus facilitating exports which were expected to start after a period of two years.

Irony of Fate

Incidentally, it may be mentioned that an important reason why the proposal of Bajaj Auto to increase its scooter production capacity from 24,000 to 100,000 was not supported by the MRTP Commission was that the government was investing a large amount in this new public sector scooter project and, therefore, it was said, that it would be against public interest if a large capacity was sanctioned to private producers. Acting on this recommendation, the government limited the additional capacity of Bajaj Auto as well as API at that stage (in

1972) to 48,000. It is also interesting to note that, SIL was sanctioned a capacity of 100,000 scooters in the beginning itself, in 1972.

The subsequent history shows that the project was badly handled right from the beginning. API was asked to prepare a detailed projected report; but this was never finalised and submitted. The government decided to go ahead with the purchase of the plant from Italy without a detailed examination of the machinery, even though appraisers had indicated that almost half the plant could only work for about four years. The plant was received in India, brought to Lucknow, and-it was claimed- 'overhauled, erected, tested and brought into use within a span of 14 to 18 months.' Even at this stage, no immediate steps for the replacement of machinery appear to have been taken. There was no technical collaboration or assistance available to the unit nor was there any arrangement for importing critical components from a collaborator.

Moreover, Innocenti soon went into liquidation. The idea, therefore, of the two private concerns joining as partners, had to be given up. The assumption that the purchase price would not have to be paid in foreign exchange had also to be given up as no equity could be contributed by Innocenti, and a guarantee for export commitment was found to be impracticable. Even the name 'Lambretta', which was supposed to be an useful asset, was not used because it was later felt by the management that the Lambretta Scooter-marketed by API in India had not made a good name for itself in the Indian market, and there was little opportunity for developing exports on a really significant scale.

Decline in Output

Another advantage expected from buying an old plant was that production could commence much sooner; but, in practice, it commenced only in February 1975. Within a few months, the defects in the plant and machinery began to be obvious; and inadequacies in the product and the resulting complaints gave the product bad publicity in the very initial stages. While originally it was thought that the imported plant was capable of producing an output of 100,000, the capacity was soon downrated to 60,000 on a more realistic basis. The production of vehicles slowly picked up to reach 30,000 in 1982 after which it went on declining to reach 15,000 in 1986. Sales were usually much less than the output despite there being a shortage of scooters and a flourishing black market in the country.

A peculiarity on the approach adopted by the management was that, even before the production of the basic item could be properly and fully established, a number of other developments were taken up instead of focussing all attention on making the basic line successful. Not only was the production of three-wheelers taken up on the basis of a similar old plant obtained from Innocenti, but it was also decided to produce power-packs of scooters to be sent to scooter units established by various state governments which were expected to assemble the vehicles and sell them.

It should be noted that the government itself appeared to have little idea about the importance of economies of scale in a product of this kind. It had licensed a number of state units. As it was found, these units were languishing and there was agitation about the employees who had been recruited, it appears that SIL had to enter into such arrangements under pressure. Many of the units faced marketing problems because of the poor quality of their products, and even had difficulties in ensuring regular supply of components. In turn, these units complained that SIL did not supply the power-packs as agreed upon.

Production Delay

The management also seems to have decided to organise its own sales outlets in an innovative manner through young graduates, but in premises hired by the company. It also took up the production of a moped supposedly based on its own R & D, in premises at Delhi which were acquired in 1976. Later, it was decided that the plant for mopeds should be set up in Lucknow itself. Even though prototypes were developed and the licence for the manufacture granted by the government in 1979, regular production could not be taken up as the product faced many difficulties. Attempts were then made to obtain established designs from abroad.

The premises obtained in Delhi were those of a sick electrical unit. It was decided to manufacture electric fans as the equipment was suitable and the employees had also been taken over. This obviously the government itself forced on SIL, mainly to prevent unemployment of the employees concerned. It is interesting to note that the Ganesh fan produced by SIL is the only item whose output has been steadily increasing so that production in 1986-87 was four times what it was in 1977-78!.

The lack of a sense of priorities in management can be further seen in Scooters India Ltd.'s decision in 1976 to organise a 'Farm Fuel Centre' to assist the rural population in the surrounding areas in meeting their essential requirements, at fair prices, for cycle tyres and tubes, fertilizers, seeds, tractor spare parts, drugs, controlled cloth, kerosene, oil, etc.

The Centre which had nothing to do with the business of the company and was not even a welfare facility for its own employees were taken up with much fanfare, probably at the instance of a senior union minister. With the idea of carrying out its social obligations, the company also organised a trucking scheme for the transport of its scooters which would employ ex-servicemen, with a nationalised bank giving credit to meet 85% of the cost of the truck, SIL 10% and the owner only five per cent.

The company also thought, even before establishing its production soundly, of securing export orders. An initial batch of 50 scooters was planned to be sent abroad in 1975. In 1978, it was claimed that the scooters were being well received in Europe, the Company participated in trade fairs abroad and secured an order for the supply of scooters and mopeds worth $6.50 million in 1978-79 - a period when the production of scooters was only getting established, and that for mopeds was quite uncertain. The company also became a joint partner in two state government units engaged in the production of certain ancillary requirements, another capital investment which gave little return, financial or otherwise.

Number of Changes

As usually happens in many public sector products, there have been a number of changes even in the critical managerial positions in the company. The first chairman lasted only for three years. The first managing director appears to have remained in charge for a longer span. But the other directors and also the main executive went on changing, especially from 1978 onwards. The Public Undertaking Committee of Parliament itself commented adversely in its Report (1983) on these changing appointments. The concern has remained without a regular chairman/managing director for quite some time. With such a lack of stability at the top, and all important decisions concentrated in the hands of the government, no wonder that there has been a lack of direction. The result has been that no one was responsible to put matters right, or at least to stop the continuous drift and waste.

One of the difficulties of all public sector enterprises appears to be that, under pressure from all sides, they tend to employ far too many persons. Even though production had reached nowhere near even the revised capacity, by 1980-81, the number of employees was 3600 as against 2200, the strength originally envisaged. It is also interesting that the excess was the largest in the clerical staff (245 employees instead of 25), when it was only plus nine per cent in the case of semiskilled labour, and in the case of skilled labour, the number employed was actually less than one-third of that originally envisaged.

No wonder that the costs of production went on escalating. The PUC had pointed out that the loss per two-wheeler had varied from Rs.997 to Rs.2,381 between 1975 and 1982, while for three-wheelers it had varied between Rs.6,893 and Rs.26,929. The net result of all this is that, according to the industries minister, SIL has accumulated losses up to January 1988 of Rs.128 crore against the total book assets of Rs.30 crore.

thanks to effective management. There is virtually no other way to explain how the Damodar Valley Corporation could increase its plant load factor by 50 per cent in just one year after its management was changed, or how Hindustan Photo Films and Burn and Standard, losing a rupee for every Rs.three of sales, could break even in four years under the new management or how Bharat heavy Plate and Vessels, which had never made any profit after the plant was commissioned and which was losing heavily, could break even in just one year after a new chief executive was brought in. It is also well known that the most efficient car manufacturing company was till recently a public sector undertaking and the most slothful one is in the privatesector.

A number of suggestions have been made and steps initiated to improve the performance of the public sector units.

The Arjun Sen Gupta Report, for example, has recommended several measures. Similarly, the report of the Economic Advisory Council on the public sector, has suggested many ways for improving the autonomy and accountability of these undertakings. The main theme of these reports is that the government should '*distance*' itself from the public sector, and there must be a '*balance*' between autonomy and accountability of the government units.

Forming '*holding companies*' for groups of public sector enterprises and entrusting the management of those enterprises to apex organisations is yet another suggestion offered to improve the performance of government undertakings. The government's job must be: appointment of key people, set targets for them and leave the management to holding companies. This would minimise the government's interference in the day-to-day operations of the public sector units.

It has also been suggested that the chronically loss making units must be allowed to die a natural death. Bharat Gold Mines and Scooters India Ltd., immediately come to mind. There are a few more undertakings in this category (see Table 18.12) which can be wound up.

It is also suggested that the public sector units must be allowed in areas where they enjoy a competitive edge over others. Clearly, soaps, scooters and hotels are not the areas meant for the public sector.

In order to improve the performance of the public sector, the government took a policy initiative by introducing the concept of *memoranda of understanding (MoU),* also called *performance contracting.* MoU is an instrument which defines clearly the relationship of the PSUs with the government and clarifies the respective roles of the PSUs as well the government in order to achieve better performance. The MoU is also an attempt to bring a proper balance between accountability and autonomy. The emphasis is on achieving the negotiated and agreed objectives rather than interfering in the day-to-day affairs.[7]

MoU system has been extended to cover 108 enterprises (Read Box 18.5 for full list of MoU enterprises). In 1993-94, of the 101 PSEs rated through the MoU process, 44 were rated as 'excellent', 29 as 'very good', 13 as 'good', seven as 'fair', and only six as 'poor'. However, majority of the units rated as good and above subsequently did badly financially, which means that the MoU system has not been very effective in improving performance of PSUs. This is to be expected, since the major players

Table 18.12 **Top 20 PSUs with Accumulated Losses (Rs. Cr.)**

PSU	Accumulated Losses
Fertiliser Corporation	6,853
Hindustan Fertiliser Corporation	6,150
Rashtriya Ispat Nigam	4,907
Bharat Coking Coal	4,066
Indian Bank	3,883
Eastern Coalfields	3,846
National Jute Manufacturer	2,763
Indian Drugs & Pharma	1,675
Hindustan Photo Films	1,475
National Textile Corp.(Mah North)	1,430
Cement Corporation of India	1,422
United Bank of India	1,359
Heavy Engineering Corporation	1,342
Konkan Railway Corporation	1,302
Mining & Allied Machinery Corporation	1,285
National Textile Corporation (South Mah)	1,271
National Textile Corporation (WB, Ass,Orr)	1,166
National Textile Corporation (UP)	1,158
Hindustan Shipyard	1,090
National Textile Corporation (Gujarat)	1,021

(**Source**: *The Economic Times*, dated Sept.6, 2002)

in defining yardsticks-the PSE manages and bureaucrats from the concerned administrative ministries-have a common interest to show '*success*'. More significantly, MoUs have no credible threats for non-performance and no corporate rewards for achievement. Yet, they are talked of as the alternative to privatisation: the magic wand with which all ministerial interference will cease forthwith, where demoralised or politically appointed manages will suddenly become paragons of corporate efficiency, and where shoddy goods and services will be automatically replaced by high quality output[8].

The Industrial Policy Statement announced by the Government in July 1991 envisaged disinvestment of a part of government holdings in the share capital of selected enterprises in order to provide market discipline and to improve the performance of public enterprises. A total amount of Rs.15,547 crore has already been disinvested to the public sector financial institutions, mutual funds and general public till 2003-04.

National Renewal Fund was set up in 1992 to protect interests of workers in PSUs.

To protect the interests of public sector workers, a National Renewal Fund (NRF) was set up in February 1992 and schemes have been proposed to assist the employees in re-training, redeployment and counselling. Provision of funds through NRF also exists for cases where workers retire voluntarily or are declared surplus. To implement the NRF schemes, an empowered authority has been created and a provision of Rs. 700 crore has been made in the current year's budget. A major portion of the amount has been utilised in the textiles sector.

In order to establish a system of rehabilitation and restructuring of PSUs without having the government to bear the whole financial burden, the provisions of the Sick Industrial Companies Act

Box 18.5 **List of MoU Enterprises**

1. Air India
2. Airports Authority of India
3. Andrew Yule & Company Ltd
4. Artificial Limbs Mfg. Corp. Ltd
5. Balmer Lawrie & Co. Ltd
6. Bharat Aluminium Co. Ltd
7. Bharat Bhari Udyog Ltd
8. Bharat Earth Movers
9. Bharat Petroleum Corp Ltd
10. Bharat Yantra Nigam
11. Bharat Heavy Electricals Limited
12. Bharat Electrical Limited
13. Bharat Dynamics Limited
14. Bonaiagon Refineries Ltd
15. Central Warehousing Corp
16. Central Cottage Industries Corp
17. Central Electronics Ltd
18. CMC Ltd
19. Coal India Ltd
20. Cochin Shipyard Ltd
21. Cochin Refinery Ltd
22. Container Corporation of India Ltd
23. Cotton Crop of India Ltd
24. Dredging Corp of India Ltd
25. Educational Consultants India Ltd
26. ECIL
27. Engineering Projects (India) Ltd
28. ET & T Corp Ltd
29. Export Credit & Container Corp
30. Ferro Scarp Nigam Ltd
31. Fertilizers & Chemical Trans. Ltd
32. Garden Reach Ship Build. & Eng.
33. GAIL
34. Goa Shipyard Ltd
35. Hindustan Latex Ltd
36. Hindustan Copper Ltd
37. Hindustan Zinc Ltd
38. Hindustan Aeronautics Ltd
39. Hindustan Insecticide Ltd
40. Hindustan Vegetable Oil
41. Hindustan Antibiotics Ltd
42. HPCL
43. Hindustan Organic Chemical Ltd
44. Hindustan Steel Works Cons. Ltd
45. Hindustan Cables Ltd
46. HMT Ltd
47. Hospital Services Consultancy Corp
48. Housing & Urban Dev. Corp
49. Hindustan Teleprinters Ltd
50. IBP Co.
51. Indian Tourism Dev. Corp
52. Indian Trade Promotion Org.
53. IREDA.
54. IOC
55. Indian Railways Finance Corp
56. Indian Airlines Ltd
57. Indian Rare Earth's Ltd
58. IPCL
59. IRCON International Ltd
60. ITI Ltd
61. Karnataka Antibiotics & Pharmaceutical Ltd
62. Kudremukh Iron Ore India Ltd
63. Lubrizol India Ltd
64. Madras Refineries Ltd
65. Madras Fertilizers Ltd
66. Manganese Ore India Ltd
67. Mazagon Docks Limited
68. Met. & Eng. Consult Corp
69. Mineral Exploration Corp
70. Mishra Dhatu Nigam Ltd
71. Mineral & Metal Trading Corp
72. Modern Food Industries India Ltd
73. Metal Scarp Trading Corp
74. National Building Cons. Corp Ltd
75. National Film Development Corp
76. National Handloom Dev. Corp
77. National Research Dev. Corp
78. NMDC
79. National Seeds Corp Ltd
80. National Small Scale Indus. Ltd
81. National Hydroelectric Power Corp.
82. NTPC
83. National Fertilizers Ltd
84. National Aluminium Co. Ltd
85. National Industrial Dev. Corp
86. NLC
87. North-Eastern Elec. Power Corp Ltd
88. NE Regional Agriculture Mark. Corp.
89. NE Power Grid Corp.
90. OIL
91. Paradeep Phosphates Ltd
92. Power Finance Corp
93. Projects Equipment Corp Ltd
94. Pyrite Phosphates & Chem. Ltd
95. Rail India Tech & Eco. Services
96. Rashtriya Ispat Nigam Ltd
97. Rashtriya Pariyojana Nirman Nigam Ltd
98. Rashtriya Chemicals & Fert. Ltd
99. Rural Electrification Corp.
100. Shipping Corp of India Ltd
101. Sponge Iron Ore India Ltd
102. State Farms Corp of India Ltd
103. Sate Trading Corp of India Ltd
104. SAIL
105. Telecom Consultants of India Ltd
106. Uranium Corp of India Ltd
107. VSNL
108. Water & Power Cons. Services Ltd.

(SICA) have been amended to bring PSUs under its purview. Several PSUs have been registered with Board of Industrial and Financial Reconstruction (BIFR). BIFR has so far issued orders for revival of IDPL and Biecco Lawrie Ltd. It has also so far recommended the winding up of National Bicycle Corporation Ltd., Cawnpore Textiles Ltd., Elgin Mills Ltd. and British India CorporationLtd.

Withdrawal of 696 Department of Public Enterprise Guidelines and the introduction of stock option schemes are other reform measures.

OWNERSHIP PATTERN OF PSUS

Though owned by the government, public sector units are organised differently for purposes of management and control. The following are the usual ways:

1. Ministry

In this, an undertaking is managed by a whole ministry of the government as is the case in the Indian Railways. Railways are run by the Ministry of Railways which is accountable to the Parliament. The Ministry has its own budget which is debated and approved by Parliament. The Ministry has a Ministry for Railways and its management vests with the Railway Board headed by a Chairman. Besides the Chairman, the Board has three members and a Financial Commissioner. These five persons enjoy the status of secretary to the Government of India.

2. Departmental Undertakings

These undertakings are directly subordinate to a ministry. Yet these units are self-contained, and each has a management responsible for its activities. The need for secrecy, strategic importance and similar conditions make the departmental form the most suitable organisation in certain areas, defence being one example. Chittaranjan Locomotive Works, Integral Coach Factory, Post and Telegraphs and Defence Production Units are run as departmental undertakings.

3. Statutory Corporations

The Life Insurance Corporation of India (LIC), Air-India, Industrial Finance Corporation, Reserve Bank of India, Employee's State Insurance Corporation, Oil and Natural Gas Commission and National Textile Corporation are examples of statutory corporations, also called public corporations.

A corporation is a body corporate created by a separate law, independently financed and vested with autonomy in managing its affairs. The corporation is answerable to the Parliament which has created it.

4. Central Boards

These are common in river valley projects which involve huge capital investments. Set- up jointly by the Central and concerned State Governments, the central boards are charged with the responsibility of executing big projects. Such boards were set up for Bhakra Nangal, Hirakud and Nagarjuna Sagar.

5. Companies

Companies are more common and are particularly preferable for commercial and industrial activities.

An enterprise becomes a government company when it has the following characteristics:

(a) It has most of the features of a private limited company.

(b) The whole of the capital or 51 per cent or over is owned by the government.

(c) All the directors or a majority of them are appointed by the government.

(d) It is created under the provisions of the Companies Act, 1956.

(e) Its funds are obtained from the government and in some cases, from private shareholders and through revenues derived from the sale of its goods or services.

If a part of the share capital is held by private investors, the enterprise is said to come under the joint sector.

A distinguished author, Professor W.A.Robson, has castigated the company form. Long before that, a former Auditor-General of India had commented that the company form was a fraud on the Constitution. Nevertheless, it seems to be the accepted pattern and is the pattern which is likely to prevail, unless something unexpected happens.[7]

That the companies are the accepted patterns stems from the following reasons:

1. A company provides for a great deal of flexibility and freedom of management.
2. Makes the government undertaking carrying on a commercial activity constitute itself into, and be seen to be, a separate business entity.
3. Being a separate entity, a company enables and stimulates the management to adhere and adopt sound commercial policies.
4. A company enables, legally, a very large formal delegation of functions and assignment of resources.
5. The Companies Act, 1956, which governs companies is beneficial for the management. It is a statutory discipline imposed by the law directly.

1991 INDUSTRIAL POLICY STATEMENT ON PUBLIC SECTOR

The Industrial Policy Statement (1991) identifies the following priority areas for the growth of public enterprises in future:

- Essential infrastructure goods and services.
- Exploration and exploitation of oil and mineral resources.
- Technology development and building of manufacturing capabilities in areas which are crucial in the long-term development of the economy and where private sector investment is inadequate.
- Manufacture of products where strategic considerations predominate such as defence equipment.

The following specific industries are reserved for public sector:

1. Arms and ammunition and allied items of defence equipment, defence aircraft and warships.
2. Atomic energy.
3. Coal and lignite.
4. Mineral oils.
5. Mining of iron-ore, manganese ore, chrome ore, gypsum, sulphur, gold and diamond.
6. Mining of copper, lead, zinc, tin, molybdenum and wolfram.
7. Minerals specified in the Schedule to the Atomic Energy (Control of Production and Use) Order, 1953.
8. Railway transport.

The Policy Statement also underlines that the public sector will not be barred from entering areas not specifically reserved for it.

In 1993, items 5 and 6 were deleted from the reserved list. Therefore, now only six items are reserved for the public sector.

QUESTIONS

1. What do you understand by Public Sector Enterprises? State their objectives.
2. Review the performance of PSUs.
3. Mention the reasons for poor performance of PSEs.
4. Explain the reasons for heavy losses in PSEs.
5. Suggest ways of improving the performance of PSUs.

ASSIGNMENT

The popular perception prevailing in the country is that Central Government owned and managed enterprises are performing much better than those run by State Governments. Take a sample of any two Central enterprises and any two from those run by Government of Karnataka. Make comparison and prepare a report.

REFERENCES

1. S.S.Khera, *Government in Business*,p.12.

1(a). Michael P.Todaro and Stephen C.Smith, *Economic Development,* Pearson, 2003, Pp.759-760.

2. Ishwar C.Dhingra, *The Indian Economy*, New Delhi, Sultan Chand and Sons, 1997, p.409

3. *Ibid.*

4. C.N.Vakil(ed.), *Industrial Development of India-Policy and Problems*, Pp.30-31.

5. *Economic Times*, March 12,1986.

6. C.N.Vakil(ed.), *op.cit.*,p.180.

7. *Economic Times*, May 26,1987.

8. Vijay L.Kelkar and V.V.Bhanoji Rao, *India Development Policy Imperatives,* New Delhi, TMH, 1996, p.206.

19 Privatisation

CHAPTER OUTLINE

History of Privatisation
Nature and Objectives
Privatisation Routes
- *Sale to Outsiders*
- *Management Employee Buyout*
- *Equal-access Voucher Privatisation*
- *Spontaneous Privatisation*

Record to Date
Disinvestment in India
Arguments Against Privatisation
Ranga Rajan Committee on Privatisation
Disinvestment Commission

LEARNING OBJECTIVES

After reading this Chapter, you should be able to:

1. Define privatisation and trace the history of privatisation
2. Explain the different routes of privatisation stressing that the 'sale to outsiders' route is more effective
3. Detail the extent of privatisation in India and outside
4. Argue against hasty privatisation
5. Recollect the recommendations of an expert committee on the subject.
6. Point out the task of Disinvestment Commission

In the previous chapter, it was stated that privatisation is one of the ways of improving the efficiency of PSUs. This chapter focusses on a detailed discussion of privatisation.

The word '*privatisation*' has been receiving much attention in business, government and academic circles on a global platform. Infact, the language and programmes of privatisation have disseminated so rapidly throughout the world that the phenomenon can be likened to a revolution or a boon.[1] Privatisation techniques have already been tried in countries like Great Britain, China, the US, Turkey, Brazil, Mexico and Japan. In our country too, a beginning towards privatisation has been made with the sale upto 20 per cent of the equity capital of 30 plus select public sector units (PSUs), first to mutual funds and financial institutions and later to the investing public. While the experience of disinvestment of PSUs has been a mix of encouragement and disheartenment, it is advisable to go slow in the direction. This chapter tries to justify the need for going slow in the process of privatisation. First, it is useful to know history, nature, objectives and the extent of privatisation in our country and elsewhere.

> Privatisation can be likened to a revolution or a boon.

HISTORY

The history of privatisation is very short-just 10 to 15 years old to be precise. Though real disinvestment started only in the 1980s, the word 'privatisation' first made its appearance way back in the late '60s. The credit for inventing the word goes to Peter F.Drucker, who used the term first in his famous book, ***The Age of Discontinuity*** in 1969.[2] Ten years later, Margaret Thatcher became Prime Minister of Great Britain and it was she who gave practical shape to privatisation. Later, country after country fell in line with Great Britain in the move towards privatisation.

NATURE AND OBJECTIVES

Privatisation is the process whereby activities or enterprises that were once owned and operated by government are now transferred to private hands.

Privatisation may be understood as the process whereby activities or enterprises that were once performed or operated by the Government and it employees are now performed, managed or owned by private business and individuals, often with much better results in terms of cost and quality of service. Privatisation achieves these results by replacing government monopolies with the competitive pressures of the marketplace to encourage efficiency, quality and innovation in the delivery of goods and services.[3]

Replacement of government monopolies by the market forces is often effected by the sale-full or partial-of ongoing PSUs or by the sale of their assets following liquidation.[4] Sale of the business or of its assets has been the most widely employed and debated form of privatisation and this is the option that is stressed in this chapter. The other techniques of privatisation are *contracts, leases* and *concessions*. In these three techniques of disinvestment, only the management of PSUs is privatised but not their ownership.

The basic objective of privatisation everywhere is to improve the performance of PSUs so as to lessen the financial burden on tax payers. The other objectives aim at increasing the size and dynamism of the private sector, distributing ownership more widely in the population at large; encouraging and facilitating private sector investments, from both domestic and foreign sources; generating revenues for the state; reducing the administrative burden on the state; and in the case of the former socialist countries-launching and sustaining the transformation of the economy from a command to a market model.[5] Popularisation of the private sector too is an objective of privatisation.

PRIVATISATION ROUTES

Privatisation is sought to be achieved through any or more of the four important routes: sale to outside owners, management-employee buy-out, equal-access voucher privatisation, and spontaneous privatisation.[6]

1. Sale to Outsiders

Disinvestment is one of the routes of privatisation.

This involves the sale of state enterprises, case by case, as going concerns to outsiders. Popularly called disinvestment of shares, this has been the best-known model, which had been very successful in established market economies like the UK and in developing countries like Chile. Sale to outsiders has been favoured as it fetches revenue and turn the firm to the real owners who possess the expertise and incentives to govern the company efficiently.

Sale to outsiders has largely fulfilled expectations about performance improvements. But the route is costly and slow and far more difficult to implement.

Lack of adequate domestic capital, resistance from managers and employees and difficulty of evaluating and negotiating deals make this route difficult to follow.

2. Management-Employee Buy-out

Management-employee buy-out is a widely used alternative to sale, notably in Croatia, Poland, Romania, and Slovenia. Buy-out is relatively fast and easy to implement, both politically and technically. The route may lead to better corporate governance as insiders have better access than outsiders to information needed to monitor managers.

There are disadvantages however. One disadvantage is that the benefits are unevenly distributed: employees in good firms get valuable assets while those in money-losers get little or nothing of value. Another disadvantage is that the governments typically charge low prices to insiders and thus realise little revenue. Insiders do not bring in new skills and new capital. There could be managerial and worker entrenchment that might block further reforms.

3. Equal-access Voucher Privatisation

A third form of privatisation distributes vouchers across the population and attempts to allocate assets approximately evenly among voucher holders. Such programmes excel in speed and fairness. But they raise no revenue for government and they have unclear implications for corporate governance. Mongolia, Lithuania and the former Czechoslovakia were the first to implement this route to privatisation.

4. Spontaneous Privatisation

This route to privatisation is easy, obstacle -free, with no revenue generation for the government and has doubtful impact on corporate governance. Small firms lend themselves to this type of privatisation. Russia has divested most of its small units through this route. So is the case with Czechoslovakia, Hungary and Poland.

Table 19.1 brings out the comparative picture of the four routes of privatisation.

Table 19.1 **Four Routes of Privatisation**

	Objectives				
Method	*Better corporate governance*	*Speed and feasibility*	*Better access to capital and skills*	*More government revenue*	*Greater fairness*
Sale to outside owners	+	—	+	+	—
Management employee buyout	—	+	—	—	—
Equal-access voucher privatisation	?	+	?	—	+
Spontaneous privatisation	?	?	—	—	+

(***Source:*** *World Development Report 1996*, p.52)

RECORD TO DATE

Privatisation, as was pointed earlier, is a global phenomenon. As many as 6,832 sales have taken place all over the world during 1980-91. Region-wise distribution of divestiture is shown in Table 19.2.

Table 19.2 **Number of PSUs Privatised World-wide by Region 1980-91**

Region	*No.of Sales*	*% of total*
1 *Former GDR*	4500	66%
2 *Latin America and Caribbean*	804	12%
3 *Eastern Europe(Other than GDR)*	805	12%
4 *Sub-Saharan Africa*	373	5%
5 *OECD*	170	2%
6 *Asia*	122	2%
7 *Middle East & N.Africa*	58	1%
	6832	100

(**Source**: *Privatisation-Lessons of Experience* by Sunita Kikeri, et al. p.22).

It is interesting to note that approximately 70 per cent of the 6,800 plus sales has taken place in industrial countries. The developing countries (see Table 19.3) have accounted for 2000 plus sales. Of these, a major share is accounted for by Eastern Europe, Latin America and Caribbean. Table 19.4 shows that India ranked ninth among developing countries in realisation of disinvestment proceeds between 1990 and 1998.

Table 19.3 **Number of PSUs Privatised in Developing Countries, by Region 1980-91**

Region	*No.of Sales*	*% of total*
1 *Eastern Europe*	805	37%
2 *Latin America and Caribbean*	804	37%
3 *Sub-Saharan Africa*	373	17%
4 *Asia*	122	6%
5 *Middle East & N.Africa*	58	3%
	2162	100

(**Source**: *Privatisation-Lessons of Experience* by Sunita Kikeri, et al. p.23).

DISINVESTMENT IN INDIA

Initiated a couple of years back, the Government till now has disinvested several PSUs (see Table 19.5) varying degrees of their equity. In 1997-98, a little over Rs.900 crore was raised, whereas only Rs.15,547 crore was realised in 2003-2004. (See Table 19.6). By the year end 2005-06, the Government could hire off 2 per cent of its investments in the public sector, raising Rs. 49, 214 crores in the process. Out of the 72 companies disinvested since 1991, 26 have been loss-making.

Table 19.4 **International Comparison of Disinvestments 1990-98 ($ million)**

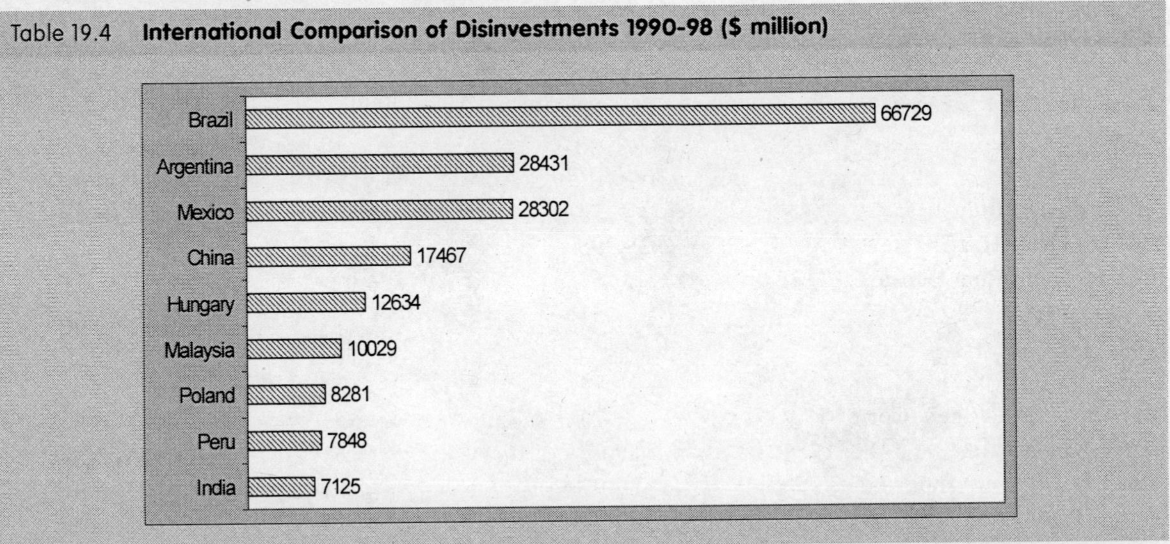

ARGUMENTS AGAINST PRIVATISATION

Privatisation, to be successful, requires certain pre-requisites. The way the disinvestment is pushed through clearly reveals that no adequate homework was done before the process was set in motion. This explains the reason why the Government failed to mop up the targeted amount of resources (see Table 19.6). Besides, privatisation has become an obsession with several people. The way it is sought to be implemented smacks of a motive which is not just disinvestment of a few PSUs but to dismantle the public sector itself. This is an unfortunate trend and hence needs to be checked. In short, there is the need for exercising caution and restraint while privatising PSUs. Any hasty move in this respect is going to result in avoidable negative consequences. Several reasons may be advanced in support of this argument.

1. The primary reason for privatisation must be to improve the efficiency of PSUs. It is believed that once the units are handed over to the private sector, they will be debureaucratised, will have professional management and will improve performance in all respects. Whether this claim holds any water can be seen if one were to dig for reasons which contributed to the sickness in the public sector in the first place.

In the *first* place, enterprises, irrespective of the sectors, would run profitablyy or otherwise by people. It is the people who matter and not the sector. If the enterprises are sick, it is because the people who man them are sick. Unfortunately, all the loss-making PSUs are manned by such people. These elite few have considered PSUs to be their private properties meant for personal use. *Secondly*, where there are bright spots, bosses in the government and political parties do not leave the bright men and women to run the enterprises on profitable lines. *Thirdly*, some of the PSUs are born with serious defects, locational aspects, for example. As is well known, many undertakings were set up in backward areas for political reasons. But inadequate infrastructure which had to be built up, haulage of raw materials from long distances and transport of finished goods to faraway markets hiked up both project and operational costs. Often, the labour available in the backward areas was not well trained to handle technology of the undertaking, with the result that sub-standard products were dished out which were promptly rejected by buyers. *Fourthly*, extraneous reasons often killed the PSUs even before they were born. Many factories, for example, were set up just because technology and machinery were offered on easy terms by countries like the erstwhile USSR. The Surgical Instruments plant near Chennai is a glaring example. For a

Table 19.5 **The Strategy So Far**

Realisation through strategic sale during 1999-2000 to 2004-05			
Name	*% of Govt. Equity sold*	*Realisation Rs.in Cr.*	*Profit/Loss during Disinvestment*
Modern Food Industries	74	105.45	Loss Making
(MFIL) Phase II	25.995	44.07	
Bharat Aluminium Co.Ltd.	51	826.92^	Profit Making
CMC Ltd.	51	152	Profit Making
CMC Ltd.*		6.07	
HTL	74	55	Profit Making
Lagan Jute Machinery Corp	74	2.53	Loss Making
Hotel Agra Ashok	89.97	3.61	Loss Making
Hotel Bodhgaya Ashok	89.97	1.81	Loss Making
Hotel Hassan Ashok	89.97	2.27	Loss Making
TBABR Mamallapuram	89.97	6.13	Loss Making
Hotel Madurai Ashok	89.97	4.97	Loss Making
Hotel Ashok Bangalore*	89.97	39.41	Loss Making
Qutab Hotel, New Delhi	89.97	34.46	Loss Making
Lodhi Hotel, New Delhi	89.97	71.93	Loss Making
LVPH, Udaipur	89.97	6.77	Loss Making
Hotel Manali Ashok	89.97	3.65	Loss Making
KABR, Kovalam	89.97	40.39	Loss Making
Hotel Aurangabad Ashok	89.97	16.5	Loss Making
Hotel Airport Ashok, Kolkata	89.97	19.39	Loss Making
Hotel Khajuraho Ashok	89.97	2.,19	Loss Making
Hotel Varanasi Ashoik	89.97	8.38	Loss Making
Hotel Kanishka, New Delhi	89.97	92.37	Loss Making
Hotel Indraprastha, N.Delhi	89.97	43.39	Loss Making
Chandigarh Hotel Project	89.97	17.27	Loss Making
Hotel Ranjit, New Delhi	89.97	29.28	Loss Making
HCI-Centaur Hotel, Juhu	100	153	Loss Making
HCI-Centaur Rajgir	100	6.51	Loss Making
HCI-Centaur Hotel, Airport	100	83	Profit Making
IBP Co.Ltd.	33.58	1153.68	Profit Making
Videsh Sanchar Nigam Ltd.	25	3689	Profit Making
Paradeep Phosphates Ltd.	74	151.7	Loss Making
Hindustan Zinc Ltd.	26	445	Profit Making
Hindustan Zinc Ltd.*		6.19	
Hindustan Zinc Ltd.**	18.92	323.88	
Maruti Udyog Ltd.	4.2	1000	Profit Making
IPCL	26	1490.84	Profit Making
STCI		40	
MMTC Ltd.		60	
Jessop & Co.Ltd.	72	18.18	Loss Making
Grand Total		**10257.19**	

* Including NPV of future earnings on MGAP and lease rentals including dividend and divi.Tax Copmpanies at Sr.No.5,23,25,26,27,36 are subsidiaries. The receipt is on account of transfer of cash reserves. Disinvestment in favour of employees.

** Realisation from call option shares also given to VSNL employees, the amount of which is not included.

(**Source:** Department of Disinvestment, GOI)

Table 19.6 **Disinvestment of Equity in PSEs**

Year	*Target*	*Proceeds*
1997-98	4,800	902
1998-99	5,000	5,371
1999-00	10,000	1,860
2000-01	10,000	1,871
2001-02	12,000	5,632
2002-03	12,000	3,348
2003-04	14,500	15,547

(**Source**: *Privatisation-Lessons of Experience* by Sunita Kikeri, et al. p.23).

long time, this unit could not run well because many of the instruments produced were too big to be used on Indians. The sizes were more appropriate for Russians. *Fifthly*, it is a historical irony that many of today's sick PSUs are earlier sick private sector units and got nationalised subsequently. National Textile Corporation Units, Cycle Corporation of India, Burn and Co. and Jessops and Braithwaite are but a few examples. *Sixthly*, nationalised banks have a different story. It is estimated that more than Rs.25,000 crore are locked up in '*non-performing*' assets with the nationalised banks. This amount, perhaps, represents the default of many private sector units. In other words, these are loans advanced to the private sector companies that have been neither repaid nor serviced.

One of the arguments for privatisation is to improve efficiency. Efficiency depends on people but not on the sector.

Thus, the reasons for the sickness of PSUs appears to be *ad infinitum* and most of them lie outside the public sector (Also read Chapter 18). The sad part of the story is that till now no serious efforts have been made to cure sickness in the PSUs. All efforts have been *adhoc* in nature, providing solutions such as constituting committees, injection of fresh finances or scattered price increases which were temporary. Now, privatisation is conceived to be a magic wand to cure sickness, little realising the fact that what disinvestment results in is mere change of hands.

2. A study made by Dr.Nagaraj (*Economic and Political Weekly*, Januaryy 16-23, 1993) adds a new dimension to the myth of the sickness of PSUs and strengthens our argument that there is need to go slow in privatisation. As is well known, one of the arguments toted for privatisation is that the PSUs are mainly responsible for fiscal imbalances in the recent years. His study reveals that the problem of growing fiscal imbalance is not on account of the declining savings rate of PSUs but due to administrative departments.

Another argument in favour of privatisation is that the PSUs are causing fiscal imbalances. But fiscal imbalances are caused not so much by PSUs but by administrative departments.

His study reveals that although overall deficit of PSUs, defined as net of all financial flows between PSUs and the Government as a proportion of GDP-increased marginally over the three decades since 1960-91, it is insignificant compared to the sharp deterioration in the gross fiscal deficit witnessed since the mid 70s. The widening gap between the two suggests that the increase in gross fiscal deficit is not on account of PSUs' overall deficits.

According to him, the two measures of budgetary burden estimated are (i) the sum of governments equity, loans and capital grants to PSUs as a proportion of the current GDP at market prices, and of (ii) PSUs' gross expenditure (defined as the sum of intermediate consumption, compensation to employees and gross investments). While the first measure of budgetary burden has nearly halved to two per cent of GDP since the mid 80s, the second measure of burden witnesses a fairly steady decline since the early 60s, from around 35 per cent in 1861-62 to about seven per cent in 1989-90.

Thus, the argument that PSUs are responsible for a major share of fiscal imbalance holds no water.

3. Privatisation presupposes the prevalence of country conditions-a composite factor that takes into account the extent to which macro-economic policy framework is or is not market friendly and the effectiveness of regulatory and supervisory institutions. Favourable macro-economic milieu helps attract private investors and makes the process feasible. It also ensures that privatisation will expand competition and produce efficiency rather than simply transfer rents from PSUs to new private owners. Successful privatisation such as seen in Chile and Mexico began macro-economic reforms well before privatisation.

Macro economic reforms-resulting in favourable country conditions should precede privatisation. This was what was done in Chile and Mexico.

It goes to the credit of the present government that it has partly succeeded in creating a favourable macro-economic environment which is market friendly (partly because, bureaucratic hassles are still there) and the so called reforms have not percolated down to the State's level. What any economist or finance minister advocates has no meaning to an official in an electricity board or water supply board.

A well-defined legal framework is especially important to successful privatisation. Creating such a framework entails developing important aspects of business legislation (property law, competition law, corporate dispute settlement, environmental legislation and so on), defining property rights, modifying the legislation of PSUs to be divested and developing laws for organising the privatisation process.

Favourable legal framework, by amending several existing legislations, should also precede privatisation.

Workers in PSUs, for example, are treated as government servants. Being government employees, they cannot be legally transferred to the private sector and transfer is however inevitable in any privatisation programme.

Similarly, there is also the fear of violation of constitutional provision which needs to be set right first. The present practice of off-loading equity to a handful of mutual funds and financial institutions has a consequence of benefitting a few and denying others of an opportunity to buy a part of national prosperity.

Privatisation should not tamper with constitutional provisions.

Legal hurdles of the type mentioned above are several. It is therefore, necessary to clear these barriers to make privatisation meaningful.

4. Yet another reason in support of the need for going slow stems from the fact that privatisation requires (i) adequacy of capital market to absorb new securities, (ii) availability of financial expertise to evaluate the work of PSUs' assets and (iii) possibility of undertaking financial and organisational restructuring to make PSUs' attractive to private investors. It is doubtful how we score on these three counts.

5. It may be stated that poorly planned privatisation will do more harm than any good. According to the Adam Smith Institute, London, many governments in Eastern Europe and in the former Soviet Union have committed the classic error of selling state monopolies intact into the private sector, without either breaking them up or creating mechanisms to regulate their prices. Privatisation programme ran into disrepute in these countries and has been, therefore, slowed down considerably.

Poorly planned privatisation will cause more harm than good.

6. One of the principles of privatisation is that revenue maximisation must not be the main objective of disinvestments of PSU equity. The objective, instead, should be to improve efficiency of these units. It is too well known that the objective of disinvestments to the tune of Rs.11,000 crore is more for revenue maximisation and not to improve the efficiency of PSUs.

7. Further, privatisation must not result in greater concentration of assets. Rather the process of disinvestment should ensure greater competition through more dispersed ownership. Though the process of disinvestment was set in motion sometime back, still no concrete efforts have

been made to disperse sales widely. What has happened till now is the divested equity-between five and twenty per cent of the 30 odd PSUs-has merely changed hands within the Government, i.e., from the Government to mutual funds and financial institutions which are again owned by the Government. Only a handful of scrips are listed and trading volumes in them are thin. Having secured these equities at throwaway prices, mutual funds and financial institutions are sitting tight on the scrips.

Cooperation from labour is a pre-requisite for successful privatisation. Such cooperation may not come forward easily.

8. Successful privatisation requires the cooperation of labour force which may not come forward for obvious reasons. Privatisation may involve the reduction of work force, retraining, change of technology or a combination of all which will not be acceptable to the employees of PSUs. This was demonstrated by the protest launched by the workers of the Dalla factory of the UP Cement Corporation. The agitation against the privatisation move of the factory turned violent resulting in the death of nearly 30 workers due to police firing.

9. Another principle of privatisation is that every transaction of sale must be transparent. Transparency can be ensured through clear and simple selection criteria for evaluating bids, clearly defined competitive bidding procedures, disclosure of purchase price and buyer, well defined institutional responsibilities and adequate monitoring and supervision of the programme. Lack of transparency can lead to a political backlog and is often associated with poorly and very costly sales. There may be a perception of unfair dealing and an outcry that can threaten not only privatisation but also reforms in general.

That there were irregulatiries in the disinvestment of PSUs was brought out clearly by the Janakiraman Committee. The question that is being increasingly asked is whether the Government went about the PSU disinvestment in the right manner and what were the ultimate gains out of it?

Sheer size of PSUs defers any privatisation efforts.

10. Another compelling reason why there is need to go slow in disinvestment is the sheer size of the public sector as a whole. There are 233 PSUs with a capital employed standing at a whopping Rs.274,114 crore employing 22.17 lakh people. It maybe stated that the entire organised private sector employs only less than half of this number. Who will absorb these employees as and when they are displaced?

11. It is stated that the privatisation of enterprises that produce tradables in competitive or potentially competitive sectors such as industry, airlines, agriculture and repair operations is easier than privatisation in the non-competitive sectors and is likely to yield solid and rapid economic benefits as long as there are no economy-wide distortions that hinder competition. As a rule, a government activity can work only if there is monopoly. It cannot function if there are other ways to do the job-if there is competition. As is clear from Table 18.4, many units which operate in the monopoly environment are put up for sale. This reinforces the argument that the sale of PSUs is designed to generate revenues and not to improve efficiency.

12. Privatisation to be successful needs strong will on the part of the government and consensus across political parties. To be fair to the Government, there is strong commitment to privatise PSUs and to usher in other economic reforms. But dependence on the Left parties for support makes the government vulnerable when the chips are down. Nor is there consensus among political parties about economic reforms. Opposition parties vie with one another in accusing the government of yielding to the International Monetary Fund (IMF) dictates and of subjugating economic sovereignty. Clearly this type of environment is hardly helpful to carry on the privatisation programme.

Public sector helped, shielded, and encouraged private sector. With privatisation, private sector is likely to become orphaned.

13. It is generally not realised that the dominance of the public sector has in fact admirably suited the private sector, saving it from the responsibilities and the criticisms it would have been exposed had it handled the enterprises now run by the former. The farming out of the supply of components, plant and machinery which the public sector undertakings needed to the private sector enabled it to strike it rich with earnings which would never have been otherwise possible. While the public sector enterprises themselves were incurring huge losses, the private sector firms which were meeting their requirements were having a good time with a steady flow of cash. If the disinvestment programme could change this scenario, it would pin down the private sector to the exacting tasks from which it had been kept free for decades by the pursuit of a policy aimed at raising the public sector to the "*commanding heights*" of the economy. It is doubtful whether the private sector is prepared to face the challenges (Also read Box 19.1).

Box 19.1 **Seven Sins of Privatisation**

Privatisation, conceived as one element of a total package, can stimulate private enterprise. Unfortunately, the process in many countries has been very different from this-more a 'garage sale' of public enterprises to favoured people than an integral part of a coherent strategy to encourage private investments.

Privatisation in developing countries has, therefore, had very mixed results. In some cases, as in Maxico, it has been part of a process of fundamentally altering the organisation of production-with benefits for consumers and the economy as a whole. In too many cases, however, privatisation has taken place in the wrong way. Many countries seem to have been committing one or more of the seven deadly sins of privatisation.

1. **For the wrong reason**-Many privatisation strategies have aimed at maximising short-term revenue rather than building competitive markets for the long-term. For example, the sale of a telecommunications company as a monopoly would probably get a better price from a buyer who thought the company's activities would not be closely regulated. Short-term revenue for the government but long-term losses for consumers and the efficiency of the economy as a whole is one of the reasons. As the World Bank cautioned in its latest review of privatisation experience: Maximis-ing short-term revenues should not be the primary consideration. So, it could be better to create a competitive environment than to maximise revenue from sales into protected markets.
2. **In the wrong environment**-Privatisation makes sense only if enterprises are released in an environment that allows them to become competitive and efficient. Where the market functions poorly and enterprises are still vulnerable to arbitrary government edicts, transferring ownership to the private sector is unlikely to achieve much.
3. **With non-transparent procedures**-Privatisation has sometimes been accompanied by allegations of corruption and claims that the process has enriched a few privileged cronies of the government. The disposal of assets should be so open and public that such allegations cannot arise. It should start with a publicity campaign explaining the rationale for the privatisation and the method of selling and then proceed through competitive bidding, preferably through the stock exchange.

The entire process of transferring ownership should be kept open to external scrutiny and should clearly state the national objectives that privatisation hopes to accomplish.

4. **Only to finance budget deficits**-Harassed finance ministers are often tempted to sell state assets to cover their current budget deficits. The sale of public assets should be

seen instead as a way of reducing the national debt-since these debts were often incurred in the first place for the establishment of such enterprises. Selling assets to meet current liabilities is mortgaging the options of future generations.

5. **With a poor financial strategy**-The best way to dispose off assets is through the capital markets selling shares to the public, difficult in many developing countries where capital markets are undeveloped. Rather than take into account that stock exchanges are narrow and monopolised by a privileged minority, the financial strategies of many governments often make matters worse. A surprising number of governments have actually tried to privatise while at the same time issue high-yield, low-risk, tax-free government bonds. Many governments have further narrowed their options by restricting sales of shares to foreigners. The aim instead should be a widespread distribution of shares to nationals and foreigners alike-with a proper timing and distribution of shares that both maximise revenue and protect national interest.

6. **With unrealistic labour strategies**- Some governments have been so nervous about labour agitation in the privatised industries that they have demanded guarantees from prospective buyers that no workers will subsequently be laid off. Others have 'bought' labour cooperations by offering handshakes so golden that they exceed the asset's sale value. Employment is one of the most sensitive areas of privatisation. But experience shows that it is better to have an open and free dialogue in advance. This should cover the possibilities of workers' ownership and retraining schemes, as well as the inevitable job losses.

7. **With no political consensus**-Privatisation is not merely a technocratic exercise. It is also a political process. A hasty privati-sation forced through executive orders, risks immediate conflict-and reversal after a change in governments. Should still attempt to build as broad a consensus as possible and to use democratic parliamentary procedures to minimise violent lurches in policy.

The enumeration of these sins is a caution not against privatisation, but against privatising within the wrong framework and without a human development purpose in mind.

(**Source**: *Human Development Report*, 1993(UNDP).

14. There is no advantage in transferring a public sector monopoly, no matter how inefficient, into the private sector, where it would become a private sector monopoly. It cannot improve further the performance of any undertaking. Inefficiencies in production units are more closely associated with their being monopolies, rather than with the type of ownership, public or private.

15. There is not a great deal that the government can do to ward off foreign competition, given its WTO obligations, nor can it favour particular firms in the private sector. Under the circumstances, some of our public sector enterprises are our best hope for emerging as globally competitive firms.[7]

Conclusion

The foregoing arguments do not in anyway constitute uncritical support for our PSUs. Undeniably, there is an urgent need to restructure them to improve their performance. But privatisation is not the only way to put the PSEs on the right track because the private sector is not rosy and glory. There is inefficiency, sickness, nepotism and corruption even among private sector units.

The exercise till now seems to be one of revenue generation rather than a genuine interest in transferring ownership of PSUs.

Further, with the government determined to hold on to atleast 51 percent equity in its PSEs, the question of privatisation does not arise. What has happened till now is to offload equity upto 20 percent of the selected PSUs. This exercise has been more in the nature of revenue- generation than handing over PSEs to private hands.

But the 66 PSEs which have been referred to BIF can be privatised through any of the first three routes discussed earlier. Here again there are three major 'ifs': (a) *if* the BIFR invites take-over bids for any of these companies as a part of a rehabilitation plan under S.18(4) of SICA, (b) *if* there are bonafide bidders whose offer prices are acceptable to BIFR, the banks and the FIs and (c) *if* such takeover is not stymied by labour unions through the High Court and Supreme Court appeals.[8]

RANGA RAJAN COMMITTEE ON PRIVATISATION, 1993

The Government appointed a Committee under the Chairmanship of Sri.C.Ranga Rajan to study and recommend new measures to make privatisation more effective. The Committee submitted its report in 1993.

The major recommendations of the Committee are as follows:

1. Units to be disinvested need to be identified.
2. There is need for the government to retain majority holding in the equity of undertakings in areas like defence and atomic energy. In others, disinvestment can be upto any level.
3. Disinvestment shall be in stages and the sales are to be staggered so as to fetch the best possible price from the bidders.
4. Workers' interests need to be protected. Employees of the privatised units are to be allowed to buy shares.
5. Disinvestment must be transparent.
6. An autonomous body needs to be set up to monitor the process of disinvestment.

DISINVESTMENT COMMISSION

The five-member Disinvestment Commission was set up on August 7, 1996. Its major tasks have been spelled out as follows:

i. To prepare long-term disinvestment programme.
ii. To determine extent of disinvestment in each PSU.
iii. To decide on instrument, pricing and time.
iv. To supervise sales process.
v. To monitor disinvestment process.

Among the guidelines provided to the Commission, important ones have been:

(i) Financial advisors for specified PSUs to be selected.
(ii) Substantial number of shares to be offered to workers.
(iii) Clawback mechanism and instalment purchases of shares to be introduced.
(iv) A chain of share shops to be encouraged.

The Commission plans to work on a four-point recipe for reforming PSUs:

— *Power to Hive Off Assets*: The board of directors of a PSU should be empowered to hive off a portion of its assets, either as an independent subsidiary or as a joint venture entity without being subjected to vetting by a government's decision-making process.

— *Powers to Form Joint Ventures*: No permission should be required for a PSU to form joint ventures, with Indian or foreign companies, in which the partner holds less than or equal stakes.

— *Power to Fix Salaries of Top Management*.

— *Introducing Accountability*: Salary structures and bonuses of the top management will be linked to performance parameters of a PSU. Performance assessment will be carried out at routine intervals.

NATIONAL INVESTMENT FUND

On November 30, 2005, the Government set up the National Investment Fund into which proceeds from the sale of PSUs will be credited. The major objectives of the fund are (i) to invest the proceeds in social sectors like education, health and employment generation, and (ii) to finance the captial projects in the potentially profitable PSUs.

With the Investment Fund being set up, proceeds from the sale of PSUs will be spent only on capital projects.

QUESTIONS

1. What do you understand by privatisation? What are its objectives?
2. Justify the need for the slow pace of privatisation.

REFERENCES

1. Ronald D.Utt, *Economic Impact, Privatisation:Shifting the Balance Towards Growth*, Number 69, 1989.
2. *Ibid*
3. *Ibid*
4. *Ibid*
5. Bimal Jalan, *India's Economic Crisis: The Way Ahead*, New Delhi, Oxford University Press, 1991, p.77.
6. *World Development Report,* 1996, p.51.
7. Ishwar C. Dhingra, *The Indian Economy – Environment and Policy,* Sultan Chand & Sons, 2004, p.429.
8. Vijay L.Kelkar and V.V.Bhanoji Rao, *Indian Development Policy Imperatives,* 1996, TMH, p.205.

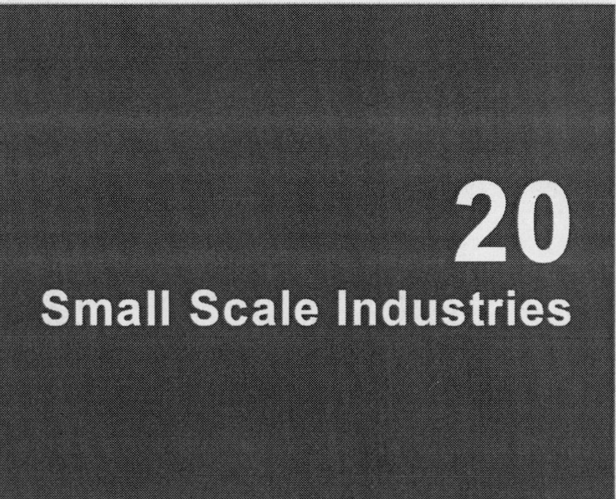

20 Small Scale Industries

CHAPTER OUTLINE

Meaning of SSI Units
Growth of SSIs
Significance of SSIs
The Case for SSIs
Facilities
- *Policy Initiatives*
- *Institutional Support*
- *Credit Dispensation*

Problems and Remedials
Small Sector Industrial Policy
Recommendations of the Abid Hussain Committee

LEARNING OBJECTIVES

After reading this Chapter, you should be able to:

1. Understand the meaning of an SSI unit
2. Trace the growth of SSI sector
3. Explain the significance of SSI sector
4. Describe the various facilities available for the growth of SSI sector
5. Bring out the problems faced and offer remedial actions to overcome the shortcomings
6. Bring out the salient features of SSI sector policy

The Small-Scale Industries (SSIs) have a place of pride in our economy. They have a high potential, among others, for generating employment, dispersal to semi-urban and rural areas, promoting entrepreneurship and earning foreign exchange. Aware of this, the SSIs have been accorded a strategic position in the successive five year plans towards fulfilment of the socio-economic objectives, particularly in achieving growth with equity. The importance of the small industries sector has been highlighted by its inclusion in the new 20-Point Programme which has reiterated the need for giving all facilities to the SSIs.

MEANING

The term 'small-scale industries' has been defined in three ways. The conventional definition includes cottage and handicraft industries which employ traditional labour-intensive methods to produce traditional products, largely in village households. They employ none or almost a few hired hands. The handloom textile industry is an example. Though once famous, this sector has been steadily declining.

The operational definition of SSI unit relates to the investment in fixed assets.

The operational definition for policy purposes includes all those undertakings having an investment in fixed assets in plant and machinery, whether held on ownership terms or by lease or by hire-purchase, not exceeding Rs.60 lakh. A tiny unit is one whose investment in fixed assets in plant and machinery does not exceed Rs.five lakh. An ancillary undertaking is one whose investment in plant and machinery does not exceed Rs.75 lakh and is engaged in (a) the manufacture of parts, components, sub-assemblies, toolings or intermediate; or (b) rendering of services or supplying 1/3 per cent of their total service or production, as the case maybe, to other units for production of other articles. The investment ceiling has been raised recently to Rs.3 crore for SSI units and to Rs.25 lakh for tiny units. (The government has decided to lower the ceiling from Rs.3 crore to Rs.1 crore). The operational definition is considered relevant for discussion in academic circles as well as policy decisions (See Box.20.1 for changing definitions).

The third definition of small-scale industries relates to national income accounting. This includes all manufacturing and processing activities, including maintenance and repair services, undertaken by both household and non-household small-scale manufacturing units, which are not registered under the Factories Act, 1948.

Box 20.1 **Changes in the Definitions of SSIs and Ancillaries**

Year	Units	Investment
The Industries(Development and Regulation)Act, 1951	SS	Rs.5 lakhs and employing less than 50 persons with power and less than 100 persons without power
1966	SS	Not exceeding Rs.7.5 lakh
1975	SS	Rs.10 lakh
	Au	Rs.10 lakh
1980	SS	Rs.20 lakh
	Au	Rs.25 lakh
1985	SS	Rs.35 lakh
	Au	Rs.45 lakh
1990	SS	Rs.60 lakh and Rs.75 lakh for EOU
1991	Au	Rs.75 lakh
1997	SS	Rs.3 Crore – but later reduced to Rs.1 cr
	Tiny	25 lakh

GROWTH OF SSIs

Table 20.1 reveals the growth of the small-scale units during 1991-92 to 2002-03.

The number of small-scale units, the volume and range of products manufactured, the employment provided and the value of exports by these industries have grown substantially during the last decade. During 1997-98, the production of SSIs was estimated to be around Rs.500,000 crore at current prices, providing employment to about 167 lakh persons. The small-scale sector accounts for 44 per cent of the total exports of our country.

The phenomenal growth in the small-scale industries sector is partly due to the encouragement, support and guidance given by the government. What the government has done to promote the decentralised sector and what are its problems are issues worth examining.

SIGNIFICANCE OF SMALL-SCALE INDUSTRIES

As we said in the beginning of this chapter, the small-scale sector has a high potential for providing employment, dispersal of industries, promoting entrepreneurship and earning foreign exchange to the country. The following points further demonstrate the importance of small-scale industries.

Table 20.1 **Growth of SSI Sector**

Year	*No.of units (in lakhs)*	*Output at current prices*	*Employment (lakh Nos.) (Rs.cr)*	*Export Earnings (Rs.cr)*
1991-92	20.82	1,78,699	129.80	13,883
1992-93	22.46	2,09,300	134.06	17,785
1993-94	23.90	2,41,648	139.40	25,307
1994-95	25.71	2,96,886	146.56	29,068
1995-96	26.60	3,62,656	152.61	36,470
1996-97	28.00	4,11,858	160.00	39,249
1997-98	29.40	4,62,641	167.20	43,946
1998-99	30.80	5,20,650	171.50	48,979
1999-00	32.10	5,72,887	178.50	53,975
2000-01	33.12	6,39,024	185.60	59,978
2001-02	34.42	6,90,316	192.23	N.A.
2002-03	35.72	7,42,021	199.65	N.A.

1. *Small is Beautiful*: 'Small is beautiful', said E.F.Schumacher. He maintains that man's current pursuit of profit and progress, which promotes giant organisations and increased specialisation, has infact resulted in gross inefficiency, environmental pollution and inhuman working conditions. Schumacher emphasises on small working units, communal ownership and regional work places utilising local labour and resources. For him, emphasis should be on the person and not on the product.

2. *Innovative and Productive*: It is the small units which are highly innovative, though they do not maintain their own research and development wings. "*...a disproportionate share of innovation and success in business seems to come from 'skunk works', tiny groups that tend to outperform the much larger labs that often have a cast of hundreds. We have now, several score examples of effective skunk works.*"[1]

3. *Individual Tastes, Fashions and Personalised Service*: Small firms are quick in studying changes in tastes and the fashion of consumers and in adjusting the production process and production accordingly.

Small firms seem to have an edge in industries that call for personalised service, attention to detail and the flexibility to adapt quickly to changes in the business or technological environment. For instance, in the garments and electronic fields, the small units have ruled the roost, a chorus of garment and TV industry voices says that big companies delegate responsibility down the line and cannot swiftly change the trace when necessary. Says a garment exporter: "*...the garment business is personalised, oriented to changing fashions and has to be tightly controlled. Professional managers do not have the motivation for all this. And most people in the electronic business agree that big firms have so far had limited success because of their lack of flexibility.*"[2]

Small units score better in areas requiring personalised service.

4. *Symbols of National Identity*: Small enterprises are almost always locally owned and controlled, and they can strengthen rather than destroy the extended family and other social systems and cultural traditions that are perceived as valuable in their own right as well as symbols of national identity.[3]

5. *Happier in Work*: People who work in small enterprises are happier in their work than those who work in large ones inspite of lower wages and poor standards of safety, comfort and welfare facilities.[4]

6. *Always Winners of the Game*: Small companies and new entrepreneurs were at the forefront of practically every business boom of the last decade, whether it was computers, television sets, consumer electronics, garments, diamond exports or advertising. And they frequently put the established large industrial houses in the shade with the quality of their performance, their ability to seize business opportunities and their aggressive feeding of burgeoning markets. Remarkably enough, the giants of the corporate sector fell flat on their faces in precisely these areas. With losses piling up, the JK group had to pull out of manufacturing television sets, while the Sarabhai's Telegrad limped along. In garments, virtually all the big firms, including the cigarette behemoth, the Indian Tobacco Company (ITC), tested the waters to call it quits or retain a small presence in the field.[5]

Small business owners are always winners of the game.

7. *Dispersal Over Wide Areas*: It is only small-scale units which have a tendency to disperse over wider areas. According to the second All-India Census of small-scale units, 62.19 per cent of the units are located in backward areas. (Also See box 20.2).

Box 20.2 **Growing Interest in SSI Sector**

Following are some of the reasons for the increased interest in small industry sector:

- The number of small businesses is growing (see Table 20.1)
- Small firms generate more employment opportunities (see Table 20.1)
- Public favours small business. Public supports small industries because of their propensity to disperse, are relatively pollution-free, test skills and abilities of owners; and turn youngsters into innovators and entrepreneurs
- There is increasing interest in small business entrepreneurship at MBA and other courses. The Bangalore University offers a specialisation stream of papers in small business management at its MBA course. And the Bangalore University is no exception
- Entrepreneurship is attractive to youth. Many women are taking interest in this area and there are exclusive programmes to train women entrepreneurs and facilities to help them run small businesses.

THE CASE FOR SMALL-SCALE ENTERPRISES

Small-scale enterprises have been the subject of controversy in the past and the controversy continues even to this day. Some are ardent supporters of small enterprises, while others vehemently oppose them. It would be worthwhile to examine the arguments favouring the growth of small enterprises. All these arguments have been briefly summarised in the Industrial Policy Resolution of 1956 which while emphasising the role of cottage and small-scale industries states:

"*They provide immediate large-scale employment; they offer a method of ensuring a more equitable distribution of the national income and they facilitate an effective mobilisation of resources of capital and skill which might otherwise remain unutilised. Some of the problems that unplanned urbanisation tends to create will be avoided by the establishment of small centres of industrial production all over the country.*" The Industrial Policy Resolution, therefore, puts forth four arguments in favour of small enterprises:

1. The Employment Argument Emphasizing the employment argument, Karve Committee 1955 stated: "*The principle of self employment is at least as important to a successful democracy as that of self-government.*" The argument is based on the assumption that small enterprises are labour-intensive and thus create more employment per unit of capital employed. It is also assumed that the low cost on

Small enterprises being labour intensive, are creaters of jobs.

overheads in such enterprises partly compensates for the otherwise high cost *vis-a-vis* large enterprises. Thus, it is argued that, let alone capital goods industries and the building up of social and economic infrastructure where capital intensive projects are a necessity, in other spheres of production in a developing economy, small enterprises which help to enlarge the volume of employment with scarce capital should be encouraged.

2. The Equality Argument The equality argument suggests that the income generated in a large number of small enterprises is dispersed more widely in the community than income generated in a few large enterprises. In other words, the income benefit of small enterprises is derived by a large population while large enterprises encourage more concentration of economic power. In this way, small enterprises bring about greater equality of income distribution. It is also held by some that as most of the small enterprises are either proprietary or partnership concerns, the relations between the workers and the employers are more harmonious in small enterprises than in large enterprises.

Income generated in SSI sector gets dispersed widely.

3. The Latent Resources Argument This argument suggests that small enterprises are able to tap latest resources like hoarded wealth. To the extent small enterprises encourage dishoarding, there is definite gain to the community. Secondly, small enterprises encourage the growth of a class of small entrepreneurs which introduces a dynamic element in the economy. There is no evidence of an overall shortage of small entrepreneurs in India. But the assertion does not appear to be very sound. If the small entrepreneurs were present in abundance, then what obstructed the growth of small enterprises? The growth of an entrepreneurial class requires an environment. Small enterprises provide that the environment which encourages a growing network of feeder and complementary relations among plants and firms. It is in this environment that latent talents of individual entrepreneurs find self-expression in localised innovations and cost-saving measures. The growth of a very large number of small firms in the post independence period only highlights the fact that given the basic conditions such as supply of power and credit facilities, the latent resources of entrepreneurship can be tapped by the growth of small enterprises only.

Dishoarding is encouraged by SSI units. Economy gains thereby.

4. The Decentralisation Argument This argument impresses the necessity of regional dispersal of industries. Large enterprises are mostly concentrated in metropolitan cities. The smaller towns and the countryside, in order to benefit from modern industrialism, must encourage small enterprises. Industrialisation of the country can become complete only if it penetrates into the remote corners of the country. It may not be possible to start small enterprises in every village, but it is quite possible to select a group of villages, and start small enterprises to cater to the needs of the small area from the local centre. The International Perspective Planning Team rightly pointed out-A policy of trying to implant large amount of industry in the most backward areas as directly in villages is doomed to fail and cannot be justified economically. The focus for industrial development under a dispersal policy should be neither the metropolis nor the village, but rather the large range of potentially attractive cities and towns between these two extremes. Decentralisation of industrial enterprises also helps to tap local resources-such as raw materials, idle savings, local talents and also improves the standard of living in backward regions. Moreover, decentralisation helps to solve the problems of congestion in the few industrial towns by enlarging the area of employment.

Small units disperse widely thus removing regional imbalances.

To sum up, small enterprises need to be developed along with large enterprises. This is also the accepted policy of the government. No doubt that the employment argument has a substantial weight in it, but it would be suicidal to encourage inefficient small enterprises in the long run. From a long period point of view, the capacity of small manufacturers to become technically progressive and efficient and develop competitive strength shall be the only justification for the continuance. In the intervening period, it would be fair to protect them, and the government should help to create conditions which facilitate their growth.[6]

From economic reasoning too there are strong justifications for SSI sector. Per-unit investment, employment-investment ratio, and output-labour ratio are positive indicators of small sector units.

FACILITIES

Realising the unique place of small-scale industries in our economy, the Central and the respective State Governments have been providing a variety of facilities for the growth and development of SSIs. (See Fig. 20.1).

Figure 20.1 **Facilities for SSI Sector**

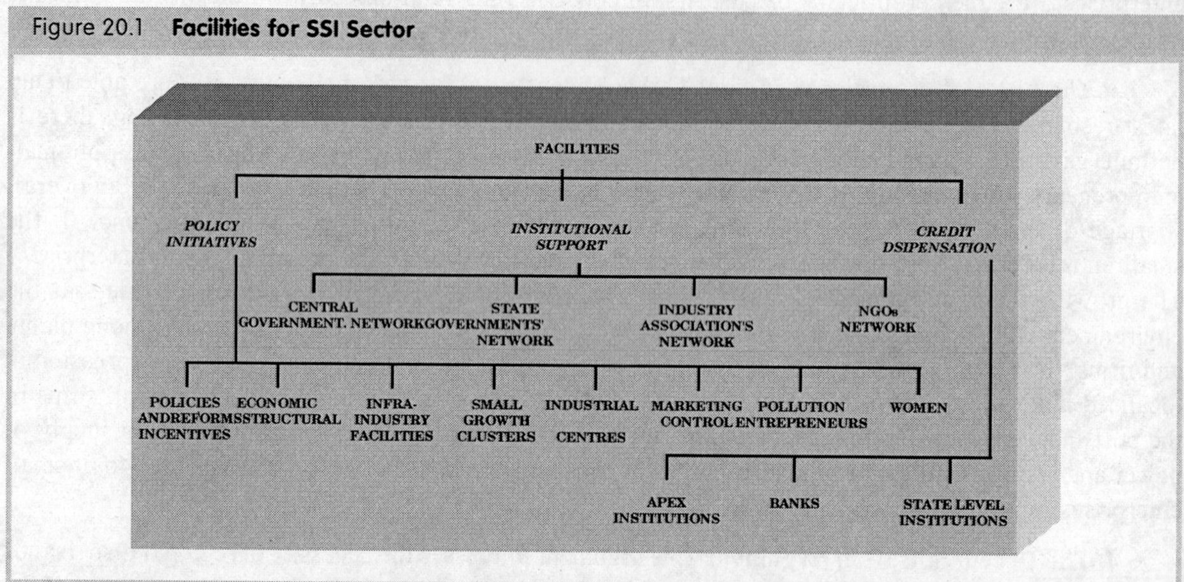

A. Policy Initiatives

(i) Small Industry Policies and Incentives

Starting from the Industrial Policy Resolution, 1948, the Central Government has come out with a total of six resolutions and statements. All the policies gave a thrust to the promotion of small units through various incentives. These incentives pertained to financial, fiscal, and infrastructure-related measures targeted at achieving the growth of the SSI sector.

Every state government or government of an union territory evolves its own industrial policy which shall be complementary to the policies of the Central Government. The state governments also design suitable incentives to encourage the growth of the SSI sector.

There is the policy of reservation of items for exclusive manufacture by small units. This policy has been made applicable only to those product lines which are techno-economically suitable for manufacture by SSIs. As on March 1, 2003, the number is reduced to 674.

There is also the Preferential Purchase Policy designed to help SSIs to market their produce better. The Director General of Supplies and Disposal (DGS&D) is responsible to buy stores from small units and supply them (the former) to different ministries.

Topping all these is the Small and Medium Enterprises Devlopment Bill 2005 (soon to became an Act). The Bill focuses on the growth contribution of small industry.

(ii) Economic Reforms and SSI Policy

Economic reforms initiated since 1991 facilitate the growth of the SSI sector. For example, foreign direct investment is allowed upto 24% in the equity of an SSI unit. This inflow of funds results in better financial strength, the upgradation of technology and promotion of exports.

(iii) Infrastructural Facilities

The Central as well as the State Governments have devised various schemes for the development of suitable infrastructure to encourage the growth of the SSI sector. The main schemes of the Central Government include the Industrial Estates Programme, Integrated Infrastructural Development Scheme and the Growth Centres Scheme.

(iv) Small Industry Clusters

A cluster is a sectoral and geographical concentration of enterprises. It may be a local agglomeration of enterprises, which produce and sell a range of related and complimentary products and services. Examples of clusters are found in items like sports goods (Meerut), glass products (Firozabad) and foundry (Agra).

SSIs operating in clusters derive their strength through a unique sense of togetherness. They also benefit from backward and forward economic linkages since such units have similar cultural and social backgrounds.

Clusters provide an active base for business and social interaction. The economies of agglomeration ensures a network of suppliers that provide raw materials, equipment, machinery, spares, repair and other services. Clusters encourage specialisation in manufacturing processes, inter-firm relationships in production, division of labour, and sharing of information.

The Government of India has evolved unique schemes for the development of clusters.

(v) Industrial Growth Centres

Growth centres were envisaged, way back in 1988, for the promotion of industries in backward areas. Once a growth centre has been identified, government provides to it the best of infrastructure. So far, 66 centres have been taken up and funds for them have been released by the Government of India to the respective State Governments.

(vi) Marketing

Marketing of products is a serious problem faced by small units. The marketing infrastructure, as available for SSIs, consists of a combination of agencies and incentives as shown below:

- National Small Industries Corporation (NSIC) to promote the marketing of SSI products to government departments under the preferential purchasing policy.
- 16 sub-contracting exchanges to identify items for ancillarisation from various public sector undertakings.
- Marketing Development Assistance (MDA) to reimburse expenses incurred by SSI delegations that visit foreign countries with a view to promote exports.
- Training programmes for export packaging.
- Organising exhibitions and international trade fairs.
- Export Promotion Councils.
- Quality certification by the Bureau of Indian Standards.

(vii) Pollution Control

The Water Act, 1974, the Air Act, 1981 and the Environment Protection Act, 1986 are the three legislations mainly concerned with ecology in our country. Provisions of these Acts do not apply to SSI units. However, certain highly polluting industries are required to obtain no objection certificates to establish units, even in the SSI sector.

Subsequently, the Government of India has notified 17 industries, wherein an SSI unit needs to obtain clearance from the Central Pollution Control Board.

For industries other than the 17, a mere acknowledgement by the State Pollution Control Board of the application form would serve as consent for an SSI Unit.

(viii) Women Entrepreneurs

The term 'Woman entrepreneur' signifies that section of the female population who venture out into industrial activities. With the passage of time, awareness has motivated women to start their own enterprises and contribute to the family income. According to the *Survey of Manufacturing Enterprises 1994-95*, there were more than two million women-owned proprietary units in our country. The activities covered by these units include food products, beverages, textiles, jute, wood, leather, chemicals, metals, transport equipment, printing, hosiery and several others.

In order to promote and develop units owned by women, a number of exclusive facilities have been provided. The Small Industries Development Organisation (SIDO) has been conducting development programmes for the women entrepreneurs.

In view of the changing outlook for the promotion of women enterpreneurs, the SSI Board in 1991 revised the definition of women entrepreneurs by omitting the condition of employing 50 per cent of women workers. This provided a boost to women entrepreneurs to take up businesses and avail of facilities as are applicable to all SSIs.

SIDBI too has been encouraging women entrepreneurs. The Bank has designed programmes, with a focus on women, *viz*., Mahila Vikas Nidhi, Mahila Udyam Nidhi, Micro Credit Scheme and Women Entrepreneurship Development Programmes.

Special recognition has been given to encourage women entrepreneurs in Andhra Pradesh. The State has set up an exclusive industrial estate for women in Ranga Reddy District.

B. Institutional Support

Series of institutions have been set up by the Central Government, State Governments, industry associations and non-government organisations.

Central Government Network

Institutions set up by the Central Government include Small Scale Industries (SSI) Board, Small Industries Development Bank of India (SIDBI), Small Industries Development Organisation (SIDO), Small Industries Service Institutes (SISIs), Product-cum-Process Development Centres (PPDCs), Regional Testing Centres (RTCs), Central Footwear Training Institutes (CFTIs), National Small Industries Corporation Ltd. (NSIC), Technology Transfer Centre (TTC) and National Productivity Council (NPC).

Institutes established by respective state governments include District Industries Centres (DICs), State Financial Corporations (SFCs), Small Industrial Development/Investment Corporations (SIDCs/ SIICs), State Small Industries Development Corporations (SSIDCs) and Technical Consultancy Organisations (TCOs).

Institutional support network made available by industry associations include the Confederation of Indian Industry (CII), Federation of Indian Chamber of Commerce and Industry (FICCI), Consortium of Women Entrepreneurs of India (CWEI), Indian Council of Small Industries (ICSI) and the like.

Beside the Central and State Governments and industry associations, there have been set up NGOs in different states to provide financial assistance, information, training, marketing support and legal advice to SSIs.

(C) Credit Dispensation

Availability of timely and adequate financial assistance is vital for the growth of SSI units. A multi-agency credit structure to fill the financial needs of small scale units has evolved over the years (See Box 20.3). The structure available for credit dispensation is as follows:

Box 20.3 **Milestones in Institutional Credit Facility**

- Setting up of National Industrial Credit (Long Term Operations) Fund as per the RBI Act, 1934
- Passing of State Financial Corporations (SFCs) Act, 1951 and establishment of SFCs
- Establishment of NSIC, 1955
- Establishment of SIDCs/SIICs/SSIDCs, 1956
- Establishment of KVIC, 1956
- Establishment of IDBI, 1964
- Nationalisation of 14 commercial banks in 1969 and six others in 1980
- Passing of SIDBI Act, 1989 and establishment of SIDBI in 1990

Apex Level Institutions

- Small Industries Development Bank of India (SIDBI)

Banks

- Commercial Banks (CBs)
- Regional Rural Banks (RRBs)
- Co-operative Bank (State, Central and Primary)

State Level Institutions

- State Financial Corporations (SFCs)
- State Industrial Development Corporations (SIDCs)/State Industrial Investment Corporations (SIICs)
- State Small Industries Development Corporations (SSIDCs)

PROBLEMS AND REMEDIALS

Thus, the facilities available to small industrial owner/manager are varied. Right from the stage of inception, all aspects of the small unit, *viz.*, production, marketing, finance, training, export, modernisation, turning around in case of sickness and others are taken care of by the government. It looks as though you should only make up your mind to start a small unit, you will be automatically raised to the status of an industrialist, just as you are pushed to the other end of the road by a huge and thick crowd, provided you allow yourself to be jostled.

But it is ironic that there are not many takers, though several facilities are available. One is tempted to question the educated youths why they should not grab the facilities thrown open by the government and start small-scale units instead of lining up before the employment exchanges for jobs.

If there are not many takers, there are supporting reasons. In other words, problems of the SSI sector are many and serious as explained below.

1. The expansion of the SSI sector till now has been policy-driven. Raising the assets limit, increasing the reservation net and providing concessions and subsidies have contributed to the enormous increase in the number of small scale units, many of them turning sick subsequently. If some units have prospered, it is because of the dynamism of the owners-managers. Successful entrepreneurs do not know what a small unit means. Nor are they aware of the reservation net (It is estimated that only 22 per cent of units have benefited from reservation). It is time that the policy-driven measures are replaced by more forward-looking and entrepreneurial-oriented measures like : (a) favouring the growth-oriented and viable units and the units satisfying the socio-economic norms; (b) fostering more of the clustered units to reinforce backward and forward linkages; (c) relying exclusively on assistance related to raw materials, marketing, machinery, technical advice etc., sparingly and (d) offering timely and adequate assistance.

2. In today's environment, it is performance and not protection that is at the top of agenda of any SSI unit. In order to achieve performance, small scale units require efficient and willing human resources. Since small scale units cannot offer the kind of packages that large companies can, they lose personnel. Remedial measures are needed to check high employee turnover in small units.

3. Sickness is a perennial problem afflicting the SSI sector. Table 20.2 shows the extent of sickness among small scale units. (See Table 20.3 for different causes).

Table 20.2 **Sickness in SSI Units**

Year	*No.of Units*	*Amount outstanding (Rs.cr)*
1999	3,06,221	4,313.48
2000	3,04,235	4,608.43
2001	2,49,630	4,505.54
2002	1,77,336	4,818.95
2003	1,67,980	5,706.35

(**Source**: Reserve Bank of India, *Handbook of Statistics on the Indian Economy*, 2003-04)

The causes for sickness are several as Table 20.3 shows. There are other causes for sickness which Table 10.3 fails to capture. Lack of exit route for a small industrialist often deters others from entering the field. A limited company has well defined exit route. In times of liquidation, promoters of the company lose only to the extent of their share amounts. Their personal properties are not attached. But in our

Table 20.3 **Closed Shop: Plagued with Problems**

Reasons	*No.of units*	*% of total (in '000)*
Labour problems	7	2.3
Disputes among owners	11	3.7
Rawmaterials problem	17	5.6
Finance problem	105	34.9
Marketing problem	43	14.3
Natural	10	3.3
More than one reason	50	16.6
Others	58	19.3
	301	100.0

(**Source**: Second Census of Small Industries Report).

country, banks attach the living homes of small industry owners when their units are woundup. Entrepreneurship is a rare trait and is protected elsewhere but not in India.

Economic reforms and globalisation have postulated competitive efficiency as the critical determinant factor in business. In order to re-emerge as organic parts of a globally competitive industrial economy, Indian small industries need adequate political and appropriate beauracratic support. The letter and spirit of RBI guidelines on credit delivery mechanism, aspects of collateral and term lending advances are often violated by banks. There is no accountability and control mechanism from the RBI to enforce its guidelines on commercial banks. The SSI ministries at the Centre and in the States are mute observers of this anomaly.

The issue of non-performing assets (NPAs) has engaged continual attention of banks, financial institutions and all others concerned. The NPA level in India, as shown by a study by Ernst and Young, is only 5 per cent of the GDP compared to 44 per cent in China, 41 per cent in Malaysia, 26 per cent in Japan and 25 per cent in South Korea. The governments in those countries still continue to support their banks. When there is growth, it is bound to face some failures also. The Indian banking sector should understand this basic factor and support the SSI units. Though the banks cite the high NPA as the reason for their stance, the fact is that they have become risk-averse because of the stringent accountability norms for bank officials.

It is a revelation that the amount locked up in sick small industries has gradually gone up from around Rs.2,792 crore in 1991 to over Rs.4,506 crore in 2001 out of the total outstanding amount of Rs.23,556 crore as on March 31, 2001 for both SSI and large industries. An interesting feature of this aspect is that in terms of percentage, the small industries account for 98.74 per cent out of a total of 2.53 lakh sick units in the country. On the other hand, in terms of outstanding amount, they represent just 19.12 per cent out of the total outstandings. The average amount blocked per SSI unit is only Rs.1.8 lakh whereas it is Rs.6 crore blocked per large unit.

The RBI has now directed stringent NPA norms for SSI units as part of the initiatives to achieve international banking norms. Earlier an account became NPA only when the interest repayment was due for three quarters (nine months). This period was reduced to two quarters (six months) and now it is one quarter (three months). Steps are under way for a further reduction to one month to classify an account as NPA. Many government undertakings like State electricity boards, PWD and other corporations make payments to SSI units after 120-180 days. Even the Delayed Payment Act has lost its validity to benefit the SSI units.

Instead of understanding the real problems of the SSI units, commercial banks aver that they are only regulated by the RBI guidelines for NPA norms. Once an account becomes NPA, the entrepreneur is deprived of credit facilities. This leads to a situation where the unit in distress cannot sustain for long and is forced to become sick. What is worrying more is that some banks are appointing private agencies to collect the dues from NPA account holders. The attitude of these agencies who work for a commission is well known through their behaviour at the entrepreneur's residence. Further, this will demoralise small entrepreneurs and their families and have a negative impact on the promotion of entrepreneurial activity. This move must be stopped immediately by the RBI.

The RBI has formulated norms for identifying sickness and devised a rehabilitation package for nursing sick SSI units. These are periodically reviewed to improve the mechanism of implementation. State level inter-institutional committees are set up in all the States by the RBI. The State government, banks and SSI associations are members of the committee which review and recommend rehabilitation measures for sick SSI units. However, the effectiveness of the SLIIC has not percolated down the stream as the RBI often takes sides with bankers and disallows the Association representations made in the right spirit.[7]

4. Finance has been a bugbear. Commercial banks have been fulfilling only partially their commitment to the SSI sector. Even while assessing small units, banks play safe by using conventional, objective yardsticks without appreciating the owner-entrepreneur-his enthusiasm, dynamism and innovative ability.

State Finance Corporations (SFCs), which lend long-term funds, have also become strict about lending particularly since many are deeply troubled by their own profitability concerns.

Nor small units can access capital market because of their size and costs involved. The Over the Counter Exchange of India (OTCEI), promoted as the small company's option, still excludes most of the small sector.

Lending agencies need relax their evaluation methods and be generous in extending credit to the worthy units (See Box 20.4 for expert committee recommendations).

5. The other problem is marketing. Small firms often do not have the resources for serious marketing efforts. A market development fund may be set up by the government to solve the marketing problem. Alternatively, the government could itself market products of small units under a common brand name. Government need not shy away from intervention although the present trend is non-intervention in economic activities.

6. Technology modernisation has become a problem particularly because of the asset limit being fixed at Rs.60 lakh for definitional purpose. To circumvent this problem, several entrepreneurs set up new units with modern technology leaving the old ones to languish.

In order to meet a long-standing demand, the government is now considering twin packages for the reserved and non-reserved sectors. First, the investment limit is likely to be raised to Rs.1.5 crore for units falling under the reserved net and Rs.5 crore for those falling outside. The logic is that since excise concessions stop after a unit reaches the Rs.two crore turnover limit, the revenue loss will not be high. Units will be able to start with modern technology, or upgrade the existing one. Small units might also choose to consolidate multiple units.[8]

7. There are endless hassles from the government and other agencies, who are otherwise meant for encouraging the development of the small scale sector. There are 30 to 40 inspectors from various departments visiting an average unit. The entrepreneurs are also confronted with cumbersome procedures. To the credit of the governments, both Central as well as State, are trying to minimise inspectors and reduce procedures.

8. There are a plethora of agencies (see Fig.20.1) offering advice, training, expertise and other support systems for small units. Unfortunately, most small units are unaware of what is available to

Box 20.4 **Naik's Committee Recommendations on SSI Financing**

1. Banks should give preference to village industries, tiny industries and other small scale units in that order, while meeting the credit requirement of the small scale sector.
2. Henceforth, for the credit requirement of village, tiny industries and other SSI units having aggregate fund-based working capital credit limits upto Rs.50 lakhs from the banking system, the norms for inventory and receivables as also the first method of lending will not apply. Instead, such units may be provided working capital limits computed on the basis of a minimum of 20% of their projected annual turnover for new as well as existing units.
3. The banks should step up the credit flow to meet the legitimate requirements of the SSI sector in full during the 8th Five Year Plan. For this purpose, the banks should draw up Annual Credit Budget for the SSI sector on a bottom-up basis.
4. An effective grievance redressal machinery within each bank which can be approached by the SSI in case of difficulties has to be set up.
5. Procedure and time-frame laid down for the disposal of loan applications received from SSI borrowers should be strictly enforced. Whenever an application for fresh limits/enhancement of existing limits was not considered favourably by the sanctioning official or where the limits applied for are proposed to be curtailed, the same should be referred to the next higher authority with all relevant particulars, to ensure scrutiny by an independent authority and the latter should confirm the decision of the sanctioning official or otherwise dispose off the same, within a time-bound manner.
6. Banks should adopt the single window scheme of SIDBI for meeting the credit requirements of small units.
7. Banks should take immediate steps to ensure full adherence in letter and spirit by all their branches and controlling offices to the RBI guidelines in the matter of financing the working capital requirements of small scale units, rehabilitation of sick small scale units, coordination between commercial banks and State Financial Corporations (SFCs) in meeting the credit requirements of these units and other related aspects.
8. Training to the bank staff to develop right aptitude, skills and orientation in regard to finance to the small scale sector. Training input may also consist of awareness of the importance of the small scale sector from the point of view of creation of additional employment opportunities, exports, etc. and a smooth loan recovery in respect of healthy small scale units. Banks may also consider awarding trophies to branches for outstanding performance in financing SSI units as a mark of public recognition.
9. Banks should desist insistence on compulsory deposit mobilisation as a '**quid pro quo**' for the sanction of credit facilities to the units.
10. State Financial Corporations (SFCs) to act as the principal financing agency for SSIs in 40 out of the 85 districts, each having more than 2000 registered SSI units, to take care of both term loan and working capital requirements of all new SSI units which can be financed under the Single Window Scheme (SWS) of SIDBI. Commercial banks should act as the principal financing agency under the SWS in the remaining 45 districts as well as in the rest of the country. It has also been decided that in order to effectively discharge their responsibility, commercial banks should open specialised branches to cater to the SSI clientele in the 45 districts where they will be acting as the principal financing agency as also in the 119 districts, each having between 1000 and 2000 registered SSI units.

them. Further, the agencies are content with providing existing infrastructure to the small units. The bodies must become more aggressive, mobilise resources and assist the growth of the small units.

9. Economic reforms will affect the fortunes of small units badly. This will be particularly true of the units which are engaged in the production of consumer goods without the benefit of any brand advantage. The new product launches of giant corporations will sooner or later encroach severely on the small segments of consumer markets which have hitherto been the sheltered domain of the SSI units.

10. The organisational base of many of the SSI units has remained weak in terms of what the emerging competitive conditions will warrant. The recent transformation of the Indian capital market has not benefited the SSI sector which continues to operate as proprietory concerns. If they are to access capital markets, small units must restructure their ownership forms into corporate outfits. This also implies that the SSI units must grow in size to become corporate entities.

11. Much of the current crisis faced by the SSI sector is the lack of clarity with regard to the nature of an SSI unit. There has been a proliferation of definitions of SSIs (See box 20.1) and consequently, many small entrepreneurs are not sure whether they fit into the government's definitions.

Ancillary units (with the stipulation that they should not be subsidiaries of other industrial units) hardly number 8,000 out of the nearly 24 lakh SSI units. Infact, it is this sub-sector which holds much promise for the emergence of sub-contracting as a major strategy for competitive positioning of our industry. Unfortunately, these units are likely to be lumped with other loosely-defined units for the purpose of benefits.[9] This problem needs to be tackled immediately.

Above are the remedies which are external to SSI units. What is more important is that the owner/manager himself or herself is the person who should manage the unit successfully. Many a time sickness is caused by the owner/manager himself or herself. Often, an individual not endowed with entrepreneurial qualities (see Box 20.5 for some such traits) starts a unit – may be to enjoy the benefits and incentives offered by the government or the person has no other avocation to engage himself or herself in. There are instances where the owner/manager siphoned off funds for personal use such as buying vehicles, jewelry, or celebrating marriages. Units become sick in the meanwhile.

Box 20.5 **Skills Needed to Run Small Businesses Successfully**

Technical Skills

- Writing
- Technical business management
- Ability to organize
- Management style
- Being a team player
- Monitoring environment
- Technology
- Network building
- Coaching

Business Management Skills

- Planning and goal setting
- Communication
- Marketing
- Accounting
- Control
- Venture launch
- Decision making
- Human relations
- Finance
- Management
- Negotiation
- Managing growth

Personal Entrepreneurial Skills

- Inner control/disciplined
- Innovative
- Persistent
- Ability to manage change
- Risk taker
- Change oriented
- Visionary leader

Conclusion

Because of the significant place the SSI sector occupies in our economy, an appropriate environment needs to be created for the growth and sustenance of the small scale units. This calls for steps to build on the strengths of small units; overcome their weaknesses; exploit their opportunities and ward off against their threats (See Box 20.6 for the SWOT of SSIs).

Box 20.6 **Small Sector: The SWOT**

Strengths
- Flexibility in production volumes and design changes
- Faster decision making
- Lower labour costs
- Lower overheads

Weaknesses
- Often lack of management, marketing or financial skills
- Technological obsolescence
- Poor financing
- Lack of marketing strength

Opportunities
- Large companies are outsourcing more to reduce their own costs
- Promising export markets
- Higher investment limits mean companies can expand and modernise
- Big companies can take a larger equity stake in small ones

Threats
- With concessions disappearing, inefficient units will die
- With dereservation, competition will come from large companies
- With import liberalisation, competition will come from MNCs and cheap inputs.
- Smaller, less aggressive companies will suffer

(**Source**: *Business India*, June 15, 1995).

SMALL SECTOR INDUSTRIAL POLICY

The government announced its policy towards the small sector on 6th August 1991. The main features of the policy are: (See Box 20.7 for highlights).

The primary objective of the new policy during the nineties would be to impart more vitality and growth impetus to the sector to enable it to contribute its mite fully to the economy, particularly in terms of growth of output, employment and exports.

Tiny Enterprises

The Government has already announced an increase in the investment limits in plant and machinery of small-scale industries, ancillary units and export-oriented units to Rs.60 lakh and 75 lakh respectively. Such limits in respect of 'tiny' enterprises would now be increased from the present Rs.2 lakh to Rs.5 lakh, irrespective of locations of the unit.

Box 20.7 **Salient Features of New Policy**

- Equity participation up to 24 per cent by other industrial undertakings including foreign companies.
- Legislation to limit financial liability of new and non-active partners/entrepreneurs to the capital invested.
- Hike in investment limit for tiny sector up from Rs.2 lakh to Rs.5 lakh.
- Services sector to be recognised as a tiny sector.
- Support from National Equity Fund for projects upto Rs.10 lakh.
- Single Window Loans to cover projects up to Rs.20 lakh. Banks too to be involved.
- Relaxation of certain provisions of labour laws.
- Subcontracting Exchanges to be set up by industry associations.
- Easier access to institutional finance.
- Factoring services through SIDBI to overcome the problem of delayed payments. Also, legislation to ensure payment of bills.
- Women enterprises redefined.
- Package for handloom and handicraft sector.
- Export development centre in SIDO.
- Marketing of mass consumption items by National Small Industries Corporation under a common brandname.

Service sub-sector is a fast growing area and there is need to provide support to it in view of its recognised potential for generating employment. Hence, all industry related service and business enterprises, irrespective of their location, would be recognised as small-scale industries and their investment ceilings would correspond to those of any enterprises.

It has also been decided to widen the scope of the National Equity Fund Scheme to cover projects upto Rs.10 lakh for equity support (upto 15 per cent). Single Window Loan Scheme has been enlarged to cover projects upto Rs.20 lakh with working capital margin upto Rs.10 lakh. Composite loans under Single Window Scheme, now available only through State Financial Corporation (SFCs) and State Small Industries Development Corporation (SSIDCs) would also be chanelised through commercial banks. This would facilitate access to a larger number of entrepreneurs.

Financial Support Measures

Inadequate access to credit-both short term and long term, remains a perennial problem facing the small-scale sector. Emphasis would henceforth shift from subsidised/cheap credit, except for specified target groups, and efforts would be made to ensure both adequate flow of credit on a normative basis and the quality of its delivery for viable operations of this sector.

To provide access to the capital market and to encourage modernisation and technological upgradation it has been decided to allow equity participation by other industrial undertakings in the SSI, not exceeding 24 per cent of the total shareholding. This would also provide a powerful boost to ancillarisation and sub-contracting, leading to the expansion of employment opportunities.

A beginning has been made towards solving the problem of delayed payments to small industries by setting up of 'factoring' services through Small Industries Development Bank of India (SIDBI).

Network of such services would be set up throughout the country and operated through commercial banks. A suitable legislation will be introduced to ensure prompt payment of small industries bills.

Infrastructural Facilities

A Technology Development Cell (TDC) would be set up in the Small Industries Development Organisation (SIDO) which would provide technology inputs to improve productivity and competitiveness of the products of the small-scale sector. The TDC would coordinate the activities of the Tool Rooms, Process-cum-Product Development Centres (PPDs), existing as well as to be established under SIDO, and would also interact with the other industrial research and development organisations to achieve its objectives.

Adequacy and equitable distribution of indigenous and imported raw materials would be ensured to the small-scale sector, particularly the tiny sub-sector.

Marketing and Exports

National Small Industries Corporation (NSIC) would concentrate on the marketing of mass consumption items under a common brand name and organic links between NSIC and SSIDs would be established.

Though the SSI sector is making significant contribution to total exports, both direct and indirect, a large potential remains untapped. The SIDO has been recognised as the nodal agency to support the small scale industries in export promotion.

Modernisation, Technology and Quality Upgradation

Industry associations would be encouraged and supported to establish quality counselling and common testing facilities. Technology and markets would be established.

A reoriented programme of modernisation and technological upgradation aimed at improving productivity, efficiency and cost effectiveness in the small-scale sector would be pursued.

Indian Institutes of Technology (IITs) and selected regional/other engineering colleges will serve as technological information, design and development centres in their respective command areas.

Promotion of Entrepreneurship

The Government will continue to support the first generation entrepreneurs through training and will support their efforts. Large number of EDP trainers and motivators will be trained to significantly expand the Entrepreneurship Development Programmes (EDP). Women entrepreneurs will receive support through special training programmes.

Village Industries

Handloom Sector Handloom sector contributes about 30 per cent of the total textile production in the country. It is the policy of the government to promote handloom to sustain employment in rural areas and to improve the quality of life for handloom weavers.

The Janata cloth scheme, which sustains weavers often on a minimum level of livelihood will be phased out by the terminal year of the VIII Plan and replaced by the omnibus project package scheme, under which substantial funds will be provided for the modernisation of tools, training, provision of better designs, provision of better dyes and the chemicals and marketing assistance.

Handicraft Sector

The key areas in handicrafts that could contribute towards a faster pace of rural industrialisation are production and marketing. Scheme for training and design development and for production and marketing assistance will be given encouragement.

Other Village Industries

The government recognises the need to enhance the spread of rural and cottage industries towards stepping up non-farm employment opportunities.

The activities of the Khadi and Village Industries Commission and the State Khadi and Village Industries Boards will be expanded and the organisations strengthened to discharge their responsibilities more effectively.

The programmes of intensive development of KVI through area approach with tie-up with DRDA, TRYSEM and ongoing development programmes relating to weaker sections like Scheduled Castes, Scheduled Tribes and women would be extended throughout the country.

RECOMMENDATIONS OF THE ABID HUSSAIN COMMITTEE

Following are the major recommendations made by the Abid Hussain Committee:

- Abolition of the reserved items
- Hiking the investment limit for SSI units.
- Scrapping the foreign investment ceiling of 24 per cent.
- New law to cover business practices.
- Special incentives to clusters of units.
- Inclusion of services sector under SSI units.
- National Research Institution for SSI units.
- Sanctioning of composite loans and credit rating of SSI units.
- Liberalising excise benefits for manufacturing brand name items.

QUESTIONS

1. Define a small industry. What is the role of small industries in our economy?
2. Explain the facilities available for the promotion of small-scale units.
3. Bring out the problems faced and remedials available for small units.
4. Bring out the salient feature of the SSI new policy.

ASSIGNMENT

A visit to an industrial estate will convince you that out of every five units located there atleast three of them have closed their shutters. Pick up atleast 25 such units and findout the reasons why they have been closed. You will get to know more reasons for sickness than the books have told you.

REFERENCES

1. Peters and Waterman Jr., *In Search of Excellence*, p.276.
2. *India Today*, December 21, 1985.
3. Malcolm Harper, *Small Business in the Third World.*
4. *Ibid.*
5. *India Today*, December 31, 1985.
6. Ruddar Datt and K.P.M.Sundaram, *Indian Economy*, p.569.
7. Selvaraj. A, "SSIs Deserve A Better Deal", *The Hindu,* June 20, 2005.
8. *Business India*, Jan 2-15, 1995.
9. S.Swaminathan, "Tall Talk on Small Industry", *The Hindu*, Feb 22, 2005.

CHAPTER OUTLINE

Extent of Labour
Changes in Labour Force
Trade Union Movement
Industrial Disputes
- *Causes for Disputes*
- *Dispute Settlement Methods*

Wage Policy
- *Concepts of Wages*

Social Security in India

LEARNING OBJECTIVES

After reading this Chapter, you should be able to:

1. Understand the changes that have taken place in labour front
2. Understand the role of trade unions and the changing profile of trade union movement
3. Understand the meaning of industrial disputes, and point out their causes
4. Describe the disputes settlement machinery
5. Understand the nature and relevance of wage policy and describe the various concepts of wages
6. Describe the social security in India

21 Industrial Labour

Labour is an important input in industrial production. Mechanisation and automation have not diminished the role of human element in industrial establishments. Infact, the role of the workforce has become highly critical in an automated plant. Nor have the economic reforms belittled the significance of labour. Liberalisation of economy has brought labour to centre stage. Human resource is taken to be an important factor to increase productivity, improve quality and reduce costs-all necessary to survive in the competitive world.

There are several issues related to labour. They are: trade union movement, wage policy and industrial relations. This chapter is devoted for a detailed discussion of these and other aspects.

EXTENT OF LABOUR

In 1900, the number of workers in our factories stood at just 5 lakh. By 1988, the figure went upto 26 million, an increase of more than sixty times over a period of nine decades. The annual growth rate of workforce, particularly in 80s, has been an average of two per cent. Table 21.1 gives data relating to employment in both public sector as well as in private sector. Table 21.1 gives details relating to employment in the organised sector (Public and Private Sectors combined)

Over the years the number of workers has risen considerably.

CHANGES IN LABOUR FORCE

Industrial labour in the organised sector has undergone the following important changes over the years:

1. Commitment to industry Labour is now committed to the industrial setting, thus contributing to the stable workforce. True, the worker might have his moorings in villages. But it is unlikely that he

Table 21.1 **Employment in Public and Organised Private Sector**

(in millions)

	Public Sector (end March)	*Private Sector (end March)*
1990-91	19.06	7.68
1991-92	19.21	7.85
1992-93	19.33	7.85
1993-94	19.45	7.93
1994-95	19.47	8.06
1995-96	19.43	8.51
1996-97	19.56	8.69
1997-98	19.42	8.75
1998-99	19.41	8.70
1999-00	19.31	8.65
2000-01	19.14	8.65
2001-02	18.77	8.43

(**Source**: Reserve Bank of India, *Handbook of Statistics on the Indian Economy*, 2003-04)

would go back to his village. He is settled in the city, his children are put into schools in city and, except himself, no one else in his family has an inkling of going back to the village. Besides, the present generation of young workers is mostly born and brought up in urban areas and has accepted industrial employment as a way of life.

But the sad part of the picture is that though labour is committed to the industry, it is not committed to work. This is the reason for the low productivity of our industrial labour.

India is probably the only country which is highly labour legislated country in the world.

2. Protective legislation From time to time, the government has been enacting a variety of labour legislations. Perhaps, ours is the only country in the world which has enacted so many legislations to protect the interests of workers. Distinction apart, there is no gainsaying the fact that working conditions in factories, payment of wages and other benefits, and general welfare of workers have improved over the years. This improvement has been mainly due to the protective legislation, though there were enlightened employers who were ahead of their times in providing amenities to the workers voluntarily. Such enlightened employees were few and far between.

There has been a social amalgam-status of the worker has improved.

3. Status of the worker The economic and social status of today's workers is vastly improved. Industrial employment is no longer the undesirable alternative left for those driven out from the villages. Improved skill contents of the jobs and increased emoluments have made industrial employment the first attraction of young job aspirants. Industrial employment is not now restricted to the socially low castes; the dynamic changes in the industrial sphere have, as the National Commission on Labour has observed, brought about a '*social amalgam*.' The status of the industrial worker of today is enhanced as a result of the readjustment in the value system in favour of industrial employment, which in turn, has the aggregate effect on his improved skills and his enlarged pay-packet. The stigma attached to the factory employment has gradually disappeared.[1]

4. Employment pattern Another feature noticed in the industrial labour is the change that has come about in the employment pattern of labour, due to changes in industrial activity, which has tremendously expanded and diversified and has undergone a technical transformation. In the early years, unskilled work predominated in industrial employment, so long as traditional industries like textiles and mining were in the forefront. In the process of expansion and diversification, new avenues of industrial enterprises in engineering, chemicals, pharmaceuticals, etc. have assumed importance and changed the composition of industrial employment. The improved technology of these new industries created new jobs with greater skill content, raising the minimum standard of education required. Industrial employment, inspite of being blue-collared in nature, is no more looked down upon as an inferior mode of earning a living. The employment pattern has further changed in the service industries like air transport and in newer industries like petro-chemicals, wherein the employment has become more and more white-collared and sophisticated.[2]

5. Growth of trade unionism Industrial labour is organised today, primarily to protect and promote its own economic interest. Industrial workers in the early days, being mostly ignorant and illiterate, were led by outside sympathisers and their organisations had close links with political activities. These legacies have proved to be serious hurdles in the path of building up strong trade unions even today. The trade unions are multiple in number and weak in strength. No doubt, strong trade unions are an essential prerequisite for the success of collective bargaining. In the absence of such unions, the government intervenes increasingly in the sphere of industrial relations, thereby leaving the trade unions weak and reducing bilateral relations, to a mere formality. There has been in the field of industrial relations in India a perennial controversy between the voluntary approach based on relatively free collective bargaining and the legal approach, providing for considerable State intervention for want of a sole and strong bargaining agent. However, the industrial worker today is better organised than before. With a higher level education, the workers have become more conscious and vocal. As leadership is gradually coming up from within, a tendency towards independent trade unions is growing.[3]

Number of trade unions has multiplied over the years.

TRADE UNION MOVEMENT

Started during the first quarter of the 20th century in India, the trade union movement has travelled a long way. As of toda, there are 59,968 registered unions and most of them are affiliated to one or the other central union. Table 21.2 gives details about the number of unions and their membership. Table 21.3 reveals figures of membership as on today.

As Table 21.2 shows, there has been a steady increase in the number of registered unions but their membership fluctuated from year to year. The figure slipped to all time low in 1993, but increased in the years that followed.

Table 21.2 **National Income and Per Capita Income at Current Prices**

Year	*No.of Unions Registered*	*Membership ('000)*
1990	52,016	7,019
1991	53,535	6,100
1992	55,680	5,746
1993	55,784	3,134
1994	56,872	4,094
1995	57,952	6,538
1996	58,805	5,613
1997	59,968	7,408

(**Source**: Various Issues of Labour Year Book)

Table 21.3 **Union Membership and March, 1996**

Trade Union	*(in lakhs Membership)*
BMS	31.1
INTUC	26.9
CITU	17.7
HMS	14.8
AITUC	9.4
UTUC(LS)	8.4
UTUC	5.8
Others	9.4
Total	123.6

Trends in Trade Union Movement

1. A major trend witnessed these days is the change in the attitude of unions towards the management, industry, government and the economy. The change is reflected in–
   - Unions are becoming substantially matured, responsive and realistic in their thinking and actions. Gone are the days of cat-call strikes, *bandhs, gheraoes* and violence.
   - Unions are reconciled to the economic reforms. Their accent is on opposing the adverse impact of reforms and not the reforms *per se*.
   - Discussion among trade union circles nowadays is on issues like productivity, Total Quality Management (TQM), technology, competition, MNCs, exports, and the like. Major unions of the telecom employees, for example, are online with the corporatisation of plans of the department. They are now talking about issues like gearing up for competition and inculcating a customer-friendly approach.
   - Unions have accepted that there is surplus labour everywhere and the organisation needs to be trimmed. Unions are, therefore, extending cooperation to schemes like voluntary retirement and the golden handshake. 35,000 workers of National Textile Corporation alone have retired voluntarily.

Attitude of the unions towards management has changed.

2. Depoliticisation of unions is another trend witnessed these days. It is too well known that the federations of the unions are affiliated to one political party or the other (Refer to Table 21.1). No surprise that the prominent national leaders in the post independent India were incidentally popular union leaders. Being affiliated to one or the other political party, the unions were more busy toeing the lines of their political bosses than protecting workers' interests. Unions have realised the futility of such affiliations and are now insulating themselves against political influence. In many leading companies such as Telco, Philips, Voltas, Siemens, Hindustan Lever, Blue Star, Pfizer, Tomco, and Hoechst, there are unions unions but not affected by political parties. The trend towards depoliticisation started in the 1960s and received further boost in the post-liberalisation era.

There has been depoliticisation in trade union movement.

3. Nature abhors vacuum, so goes the saying. Unions seem to relish affiliations. They are now formed on the basis of religion and caste. This is indicative of the socio-political realities after the Mandalisation of the polity and the heightened sectarian consciousness after the demolition of the disputed structure at Ayodhya.[4]

Unions now are being formed on the bases of religion and caste.

4. Workers' associations in our country are highly fragmented and the consequence has been the multiplicity of unions. Multiplicity is caused by ideological rifts, personal ambitions of leaders, craft divisions among workers and the management's own myopia. The number of unions in some organisations is truly mindboggling. The Bokaro Steel Plant is blessed with 68 of them. Calcutta Corporation has the unique distinction of having about 100 unions. The Singareni Collieries has 36 unions. The Collieries is gripped by labour problems almost everyday, the trouble started by one union or the other. Steel Authority of India Ltd. (SAIL) has 240 units and Delhi Transport Corporation has 50.

Multiplicity of unions weakens the bargaining strength of employees. Management's position is no better. For example, the management of the Calcutta-based Dolphin Laboratories which had raised money in the capital market on May 1994, to start a second manufacturing base in Gujarat, was forced to think two months later to shift completely from West Bengal because of intra-union rivalry over the duration of wage agreements.

The futility of multiple unions is being realised by the government and workers. Government proposes to amend the Trade Unions Act, 1926 to prescribe minimum strength for the formation of a union at 100 per cent or 10 per cent of the total staff, whichever is less.

Union leaders too are conscious about the need for single union plants. Of late, unions have presented a common front on issues like industrial sickness and the National Renewal Fund. At the 31st session of the Indian Labour Conference held in 1995, unions of varying status and affinities demanded better utilisation of the fund and felt that the amount should not be used merely for financing voluntary retirement schemes.

5. One of the effects of the trade union movement in our country has been the phenomenon of external leadership. Individuals who were not connected with a factory would assume the leadership mantle of the union. A Bangalore-based electrical company is an example to be quoted in this context. For a long time Mr.X, a communist leader, was the president of the worker's union, but he was neither a worker nor a supervisor in the company. Eight years back, workers decided against the practice and in the election held Mr.X and his coterie were defeated and the insiders became office bearers of the Union. Employees of a neighbouring plant too drew inspiration from the electrical company and re-enacted the coup and got the same Mr.X defeated in another election.

External leadership of the unions is unique to Indian trade unions.

Partly the fault for outsider leadership lies with the Trade Unions Act, 1926 itself. The Act permitted external participation to the extent of 50 per cent of the strength of office bearers in a Union. The government proposes to bring this down to one-third or two, whichever is less.

6. The clout of the central trade unions, which peaked during the post-nationalisation years, has started waning. For example, the membership of Indian National Trade Union Congress (INTUC), which claimed to have enjoyed a strength of 54.35 lakh in 1989, had slipped to 54.05 lakh in 1993, a fall by 30,000. Same is the fate of the Centre of Indian Trade Unions (CITU).

One of the reasons for this trend is the gradual realisation on the part of the workers, who are young and well educated, and that independent unions are more advantageous than being affiliated to all India federations.

7. The future is likely to witness a major battle between labour unions and the small and medium enterprise owners; though the unionisation of the workforce in the unorganised sector will prove to be arduous and difficult to deal with. The labour movement in India, despite its broad sweep and deep roots, has largely concentrated its energies in the organised sector, which provides employment to less than 10 per cent of the labour force. It has not been able to make any significant headway in the unorganised sector and the rural sector. Not surprisingly, while the employment generation in the organised sector has remained more or

Independent unions are better than affiliated ones.

less static, or grown slowly, there has been a veritable boom in the employment opportunities in the unorganised sector.

New types of employment opportunities may weaken unions further.

8. The other major trend that has already manifested itself, and will gather momentum in the new century, is the rise of new types of employment opportunities - especially in knowledge-based industries-where unionisation will have no role to play. Professionalisation of the service sector is also likely to weaken the need for collective bargaining. The manifold diversification of the process of industrialisation will also hamper the growth of a mass-based labour movement. Intensive unionisation in a few industrial and service sectors was possible in India because of the absence of diversification of business activity, thanks mainly to the fact that India missed the industrial revolution. But as diversification of businesses occurs, employment opportunities will increase, and the need for old-style unions will end up being obsolete.
9. There is a comprehensive change in the mindset of the country's working class. The individual has replaced the collective. In an economy that is increasingly becoming globalised, it is not dearness allowance that matters, it is the dollar earnings that do. Annually-renewable contracts will become the order of the day, as wage agreements become redundant.
10. Faced with the problem of declining membership and the fear of losing their relevance, trade unions are taking initiatives to fight unitedly. Many unions, including those affiliated to Left Parties, have joined together to fight for such causes as disinvestment, closure and modernisation. The merger between AICTU and HMS is on the cards. Union after union, in their respective annual conventions, is calling for united movement.

Unions are getting highly professionalised.

11. Professionalisation of trade union movement is yet another trend witnessed these days. To counter criticisms and also to fight organised forces of employers, trade unions, through various institutions such as Ambedkar Institute of Labour Studies, Maniben Kara Institute and National Labour Institute are trying to upgrade the quality leadership, personnel, as well as the services rendered. Topics like IT, strategic planning, diversity, networking, OD techniques, productivity and the like now form inputs in training programmes organised for union leaders.

There will be no more leaders who can drive the working classes into a frenzy by the sheer force of their personality and charisma. Tommorrow's labour leaders will match the managements in both style and content. Negotiation and not oratorial skills will determine how many followers a leader will have. The Datta Samants of the world have become history. In this brave new world, which is already upon us, George Fernandes has become a conformist joke. The man who brought the entire country to a standstill in 1974 when he led the railway strike, is used to sit in treasury benches and advising unions law to be more industry – friendly.

Thus, the trade unions are at the crossroads. Their membership is declining, their political support is waning, public sympathy is receding and their relevance itself is at stake. Management is, on the other hand, on the offensive. They are able to force unions to accept terms and conditions and sign on the dotted lines.

Unions should come out with innovative ideas to regain their lost grounds. One possible way is to extend unionism to non-traditional groups such as white collar and professional workers. Another way is to give up their obsession with strike and start serving the members.

INDUSTRIAL DISPUTES

Disputes are common in industries. They manifest in the form of strikes, *bandhs* and lock-outs. Consequences are loss of production, loss of profit, loss of market and even the closure of plants.

Table 21.4 gives details about the workdays lost due to strikes and lock-outs since 2000.

Table 21.4 **Mandays Lost**

Year	Mandays Lost
2000	28.8
2001	23.8
2002	26.6
2003	30.3
2004	23.9
2005 (Jan-Sept)	7.3

(**Source**: *Economic Survey 2005-06*)

According to the Industrial Disputes Act, 1947, an industrial dispute means any dispute or difference between employers and employers, or between employers and workmen, or between workmen and workmen, which is connected with the employment or non-employment or terms of employment or with the conditions of labour of any person [S.2(k)].

Causes for Disputes

The causes for industrial disputes are many and varied. The major ones relate to wages, union rivalry, political interference, unfair labour practices, multiplicity of laws and others.

Disputes arise out of wages, union rivalry, unfair labour practices, multiplicity of laws and others.

Wage Demands

By far, the most important cause for disputes relates to wages. The demand for wages has never been fully met because of high inflation and equally high cost of living. Wage agreement reached in one company will inspire unions in other plants in the locality and prompt them to pitch tents demanding similar rise in wages.

Union-rivalry

Most organisations have multiple unions. Multiplicity of unions leads to inter-union rivalries. If one Union agrees to a wage settlement, another Union will oppose it. Often, opposition is merely for the sake of it. The consequence is never ending disputes, as has been happening in the Singareni Collieries. The company had 445 strikes in 1990-91, resulting in a loss of production of 3.12 m.tons and 34.19 lakh mandays.

Multiplicity of unions pose additional problems to managers. One such problem relates to the authenticity of membership. Unions put up respective numbers of members in such a way that together the figure shall exceed the total number of workers in the organisation. Another problem relates to the selection of a bargaining agent for collective bargaining process to settle a dispute.

Political Interference

Major trade unions, as was stated earlier, are affiliated to political parties. Political affiliation is not peculiar to our country alone. Even a cursory look at the labour movement around the world would show that trade unions are, by their nature, political, and that the participation of labour is the rule rather than the exception. This is so much the case that Flanders, an acknowledged British expert on industrial relations, remarked, "Everywhere, trade unions have been compelled to engage in political action to obtain enough freedom from legal restraint to exercise their main industrial functions. Freedom of association, the right to strike and to picket, the prevention of undue influence in their internal affairs, are familiar objectives which have demanded the use of political methods. Unions have also fought for legislation that would assist them in collective bargaining and the like. Much more could be said about this, but these indications should suffice to show that, as a minimum, trade unions must be involved in politics in order to establish and maintain the legal and economic conditions in which they can flourish.... It makes the term '*non-political union*', taken literally, a nonsensical description, there is no such animal."[5]

What happens when unions get politicised? In the *first* place, distant ideological issues divide and fragment unions on party lines. When unions multiply, inter-union rivalry erupts and the consequences are too obvious. *Secondly*, inspired by their political ideologies, certain unions refuse to sign an agreement even if it is favourable to all the workers, thus the ever dissenters manage to keep the issue alive. The communist led CITU is an example to be quoted. "The CITU follows a pristine model of trade unionism drawn from the theory of class conflict... The communists love to fight, but hate to win. Victory for them appears to be defeat... The General Secretary, CITU, had an answer to the accusation that they never signed a settlement: 'When we start discussions, we know what is a fair settlement. Others may be willing to accept unfair terms, but we cannot. We are also opposed to long-term settlements. Many settlements here are for four years. Anything can happen during this time. The cost of living could triple. Our position is that no settlement should be for more than three years.'... In point of fact, the communists had managed to maintain their lily-white image by refusing to sign any settlement for fifteen long years."[6]

> Communists love to fight but hate to win.

Thirdly, every political party somehow engineers strikes, *gheraos* and *bandhs* to demonstrate its political strength. Invariably, the political party which is in power, favours a union which is affiliated to it, and the result is endless disputes.

Unfair Labour Practices

Majority of the disputes are management inspired. The following points[7] justify the assertion:

(i) Management generally is not willing to talk over any dispute with the employees or their representatives or refer it to '*arbitration*' even when trade unions want it to do so. This enrages the workers.

(ii) A management's unwillingness to recognise a particular trade union and the dilatory tactics to which it resorts to while verifying the representative character of any trade union have been initiating industrial strike.

(iii) Even when representative trade unions have been recognised by employers, they do not, in a number of cases, delegate enough authority to their officials to negotiate with their workers, even though the representatives of the labour are willing to commit themselves to a particular settlement.

(iv) When, during negotiations for the settlement of a dispute, the representatives of employers unnecessarily and unjustifiably take the side of the management, tensions are created, which often lead to strikes, go-slow or lock-outs.

(v) The management's insistence that it alone is responsible for recruitment, promotion, transfer, merit awards etc. and that it need not consult employees in regard to any of these matters, generally annoys workers, who become unco-operative and unhelpful and often resort to strikes.

(vi) The services and benefits offered by the management to its employees promote harmonious employer-worker relations. But a large number of managements have not taken any steps to provide these benefits and services for their workers.

Too Many Laws

Labour laws in our country, as in several other countries, have been enacted to create conditions for the protection of labour from unfair employment practices and to provide a legal framework within which industrial relations are to be regulated.

Labour legislation is regarded as the most dynamic institution. From a simple restraint on child labour in 1881, labour legislation in our country has become an important agency of the State for the regulation of working and living conditions of workers, as indicated by the rising number and variety of Labour Acts. This rapid development of labour legislation is an integral part of the modern social organisation.

> Labour legislation is conceived as an important agency for regulation of working and living conditions of workers.

There are about 108 Acts, both Central and State, earning our country the dubious distinction of being one of the few highly labour legislated countries in the world. What has been the outcome of all these?

Surely, the result has been endless industrial strife, loss of production and the exploitation of labour by the management and of the management by labour.

What is strange is that in developed countries of the Western world, labour legislation followed the emergence of industrialisation and in response to a demand for economic and social betterment of the workers. In India, the emergence of labour laws preceded industrial growth, as a result, the persons who benefited by such laws represent only a small percentage of the total workforce. We neither experienced an industrial revolution, in the true sense of the term, leading to gradual emergence of a welfare state, nor a socialist revolution which steels the public sector with a sense of performance. Yet we have evolved the most advanced industrial Jurisprudence in the world.[8]

Judiciary has not played a positive role either. During the last decade and a half, in the name of 'directive principles,' 'social justice' and 'activist law making,' the Supreme Court, instead of having a balanced and reasoned consideration of opposing interests, has entirely vitiated the industrial relations fabric by making wholesale dogmatic assertions in undermining discipline. To borrow a simile from G.K.Chesteron, while dealing with discipline cases, the court lost not only the path but also the map and the compass. It has gone to the extent to say that even an 'illegal strike is justified.' By those whose horizons are limited, trifles are easily confused with technicalities. The result is that indiscipline in the industry has spread like wildfire and sapped the national production and productivity. The classic case is that of the textile industry which has been wrecked by indiscipline. The conflagration is continuing to engulf various industries one by one.[9]

> While dealing with discipline cases, the Supreme Court has not only the path but also the map and the compass. It has gone to the extent to say that an illegal strike is justified.

Others

The Industrial Relations (IR) managers, who have the responsibility of promoting cordial relations among employers and employees, themselves stoke the fire and then extinguish it-all to justify their own existence in organisations.

The intellectual background of IR managers may have much to do with the way the function has evolved. Predominantly, they have been trained in either social work or law, and sometimes in both. Social work as a discipline is strongly oriented towards welfare, which is not the best intellectual equipment for a man who has to face the fire and brimstone of trade unionism. Law trains the manager in methods of punishing the errant, not of motivating the average.

Neither discipline teaches the pupil to regard trade unionism as anything more than a necessary evil. Industrial relations itself has not developed as an academic discipline, and there is just one university in this country which has a separate department for that subject. Sociology, political science and economics, which have far greater relevance, have never been major inputs.

With such meagre intellectual equipment, it is but natural that there should be a striking absence of conceptual clarity in the industrial relations managers. Managers assert that they have engaged in collective bargaining whereas they have only got the labour department to intercede. The mere existence of a settlement is often presumed to imply a bargain. They claim to practise participative management after setting up a few committees which discuss the strength of the canteen brew. Not a few wonder why they are steeped in conflict even after the union president has been nominated to the board.

Then there is much obfuscation about the social purpose of trade unionism itself. Everybody has his own idea of what the unions ought to be doing. Managers find it convenient to shrug off responsibility for discipline and productive efficiency, arguing that this is really a union function. With a better conceptual orientation, they would have known that trade unions are formed not to unburden them, but indeed to force them to cope with greater burdens. Conceptual knowledge would also have helped them to look inward instead of seeking scapegoats.

Trade unions are known to be responding much of the time to what the management does or fails to do, rarely ever taking the initiative to set the pace themselves. They are like opposition parties whose entire existence is built around the failings of the ruling party. It is really the managerial system which supplies the powder for the union armoury. What business would unions be left with, especially between settlements, if managers refrained from playing favourites, sharpened their sensitivity to the everyday problems of their subordinates and operated an effective grievance procedure? The best way to cope with the Union is not to smash it but to starve it of business.[10]

Dispute Settlement Methods

Several methods are available to settle industrial disputes. The well known methods are-

- Collective bargaining
- Code of discipline
- Grievance procedure
- Arbitration
- Conciliation
- Adjudication

Table 21.5 gives details about the disputes referred to various settlement methods.

Table 21.5 **Disputes Referred for Resolution**

Year	*No.of disputes referred to IR machinery*	*No.of failure reports received*	*Cases referred to adjudication*	*Cases referred to conciliation*	*Cases referred to arbitration*	*No.of disputes for which awards were available*
1975	58,575	15,168	10,581	197	10,778	5,480
1978	73,355	20,067	13,043	263	14,206	8,826
1979	62,821	17,931	10,360	346	10,706	8,044
1981	24,775	681	5,829	61	5,890	2,026
1983	68,887	26,796	16,094	141	16,235	7,879
1985	47,436	19,306	15,914	29	15,943	5,878

(**Source**: *Indian Labour Year Book*)

Collective bargaining is probably the most effective method of resolving disputes. It occurs when representatives of a labour union meet with the management representative to determine employee's wages and benefits, to create or revise work rules, and to resolve disputes or violations of the labour contract.

Collective bargaining is the most effective method of settling disputes.

The bargaining is collective in the sense that the chosen representative of the employees act as a bargaining agent for all the employees in carrying out negotiations and dealings with the management. The process may also be considered collective in the case of the corporation in which the paid professional managers represent the interests of the shareholders and the board of directors in bargaining with union leaders.

Collective bargaining is most effective because it creates a system of industrial jurisprudence. It also establishes rules which both the management as well as employees must observe.

Code of discipline defines duties and responsibilities of employers and workers. It is effective because (i) it ensures that employers and employees recognise each other's rights and obligations, and (ii) promotes constructive cooperation between the parties concerned at all levels.

Code of discipline determines responsibilities of employers and employees.

Grievance procedure is another method of resolving disputes. All labour agreements contain some form of grievance procedure. And if the procedure is followed strictly, any dispute can be easily solved.

When an employee feels aggrieved, he or she files a grievance which is resolved through a set procedure, *viz.*-

(a) Section head shall try to resolve, and if this fails;

(b) Departmental head shall intervene to resolve, and if this fails;

(c) Division head intervenes, and if this too fails;

(d) Complaint is referred to the union.

Arbitration is a procedure in which a neutral third party studies the bargaining situation, listens to both the parties and gathers information, and then makes recommendations that are binding on both the parties. Arbitration is effective because it is (a) established by the parties themselves and the decision is acceptable to them; and (b) it is relatively expeditious when compared to other methods.

Conciliation is a process by which representatives of workers and employers are brought together before a third party with a view to persuading them to arrive at an agreement by mutual discussions between them. The third party may be one individual or group of people.

It maybe stated that the conciliator has no power to force a settlement but can work with the parties seperately to determine their respective positions, explain a position more fully to the opposition, point out bases for agreement that may not have been apparent previously, help in the search for solutions, and generally facilitate the reaching of an agreement. Hence, conciliation can be effective in resolving disputes, but much depends on the third party.

Adjudication refers to a mandatory settlement of an industrial dispute by a labour court or a tribunal. Generally, the government refers a dispute for adjudication on the failure of conciliation proceedings.

Structural Adjustment Programme and Industrial Relations

In the context of the ongoing Structural Adjustment Programme (SAP) in the Indian economy, the industrial relations system now constitutes a major bottleneck which must be substantially removed if India's pursuit of industrialisation is to be renewed. The main problem is that industrialisation must be sustained through technological renewal accompanied by the scrapping of established organisational charts, deskilling of labour and the consequent redundancy and retrenchment. Coming in the way, the existing provisions of the I.D. Act have rendered either work reorganisation or sustained technological renewal and the resulting de-manning and the remanning of organisations too costly in money and time, if not altogether impossible. This has compelled entrepreneurs to opt for extensive automation with minimum manpower, instead of equally good labour-intensive machinery. Domestic entrepreneurs are shy of employing more labour, even in pressing needs and the interested foreign investors have kept away. In principle, this difficulty can be totally overcome through a law which will provide social insurance cover to those already employed in the designated industries. If this can be done, the Indian industry will be liberated from organisational overload of manpower cost which it can easily do without. Then, it can move forward to face boldly the challenge posed by the SAP.

WAGE POLICY

Wage policy refers to all systematic efforts of the government in relation to a national wage and salary system.

Wage policy refers to all systematic efforts of the government in relation to a national wage and salary system. It includes orders, legislators, etc. to regulate the levels or structures of wages and salaries with a view to achieving economic and social objectives of the government. Specifically, objectives of wage policy are:

- To obtain to the workers a just share in the fruits of economic development;
- To set minimum wages for workers whose bargaining position is weak;
- To bring about a more efficient allocation and utilisation of human resources through wage and salary differentials and
- To abolish malpractices and abuses in wage and salary payments.

The first step in the evolution of a wage policy was the enactment of the Payment of Wages Act, 1937. The main objective of the Act was to prohibit any delay or withholding of wages legitimately due to the employees. The next step was the passing of the Industrial Disputes Act, 1947, authorising all State governments to set up industrial tribunals which would look into all disputes relating to remuneration. Another notable development in the evolution of the wage policy was the enactment of the Minimum Wages Act, 1948. The purpose of the Act is the fixation of minimum rates of wages to workers in sweated industries such as woollen, carpet-making, flour mills, tobacco manufacturing, plantations, oil mills, quarrying, mica, agriculture and the like. The Act has been amended several times, making it applicable to more and more industries. Then came the Equal Remuneration Act, 1976, which prohibits discrimination in matters relating to remuneration on the basis of religion, region or sex.

The Constitution of India committed the government to evolve a wage policy. Successive five year plan documents have also devoted necessary attention to the need for a Wage Policy. Following the recommendations of the First and Second plans, the Government of India constituted Wage Boards for important industries in the country. A Wage Board is a tripartite body comprising representatives of the government, owners and employees. Technically speaking, a Wage Board can only make recommendations and they are normally implemented through persuasion.

Inspite of the legislations, tribunals and boards, disparities in wages and salaries still persist. Some of the disparities are:

- Employees of MNCs are paid much more than their counterparts in host countries for identical work.
- Different industries have different wage and salary structures resulting in disparities in remuneration for identical work.
- Wide gaps exist between wages and salaries of employees of the organised sector and of those in the unorganised sector, the latter earning much less than the former.
- Differences exist between the earnings of employees in the government sector and those in the private sector.
- Within the government sector, salary differences exist among employees of different departments.

Wage disparities are several. For example employees of MNCs are paid more than those working in host country industries.

Disparities are glaring. If an illiterate supervisor in a leather processing unit can earn Rs.12,000 plus per month and a hefty yearly bonus, how much a University Professor should earn? Rs.10,000 and no bonus? If an autodriver can earn Rs.3000 per month, how much a temporary lecturer in a college should earn? Rs.1200 per month? And remain temporary for ever? A sweeper in L&T is an income-tax assessee but a boy or a girl with B.E. or MBBS works for Rs.800 per month in a small scale unit or Rs.1200 per month in a private nursing home.

An illiterate supervisor in a leather processing unit earns Rs.12,000 plus per month and a hefty annual bonus. A University Professor does not earn that much.

Actually, there are clerks in Mumbai who get nearly twice as much as a labour tribunal judge-the man who arbitrates on everyone's wages and salaries. And a head clerk in the LIC gets, at the maximum of his grade, more than half of the salary of a High Court Judge, not less. An average worker in a government owned unit hardly soils his or her hand, yet clears a four figure salary every month.

In order to correct such disparities, the Government of India appointed a committee, headed by Mr.Bhootalingam in 1979. The brief given to the committee was to suggest a rational and integrated wage policy covering all sectors of the economy. Soon after the committee submitted its report, there was hue and cry raised against the recommendations. The report was criticised as anti-labour and impracticable. It was promptly and predictably shot down.

Concepts of Wages

While evolving a wage policy, three concepts of wages, namely, (i) minimum wages, (ii) fair wages and (iii) living wages are generally considered. These are broadly based on the needs of the workers, capacity of the employers to pay and the general economic conditions prevailing in a country.

Minimum wage

Minimum wage provides for the base sustenance of life but also for the preservation of the efficiency of the worker.

Minimum wage is the one which provides not merely for the base sustenance of life but also for the preservation of the efficiency of the worker. For this purpose, the minimum wage must also provide for some measure of education, medical requirements and amenities. Minimum wage may be tied by an agreement between the management and the workers, but is usually determined through the legislation. This is more so in the unorganised sector where labour is not unionised. In the fixation of minimum wages, besides the needs of workers, other factors like the ability of the concern to pay, contents of jobs, etc. are also considered.

Fair wage

Fair wage compares well with the going rate in some other trade.

Fair wage is understood in two ways. In the narrow sense, a wage is fair if it is equal to the rate prevailing in the same trade and in the neighbourhood for similar work. In the wider sense, it will be fair if it is equal to the predominant rate for similar work throughout the country and in the generacity of traders. Irrespective of the way the fair wage is understood, it can be fixed only by comparing with an accepted standard wage. Such a standard can be determined with reference to those industries where labour is well organised and has been able to bargain well with the employers.

Living wage

Living wage is a step higher than the fair wage. Living wage may be described as the one which should enable the wage earner to provide for himself and his family not merely the base essentials of food, clothing and shelter, but a measure of frugal comfort including education for children, protection against ill health, requirements of essential social needs and a measure of insurance against the more important misfortunes including old age. Living wage must be fixed considering the general economic conditions of the country. The concept of living wage, therefore, varies from country to country. In the more advanced countries, living wage itself forms the basis for the minimum wage.

Living wage is higher than the fair wage. It provides for basic sustenance and for other comforts in life.

In India, minimum wage is determined mainly for sweated industries under the provisions of the Minimum Wages Act, 1948. Fair wage is fixed for other industries considering prevailing rates of wages, productivity of labour, capacity of the employer to pay, level of national income and other related factors.

Tribunals, awards and wage boards play a main role in fair wage fixation. Many people are of the opinion that living wage is a luxury for a developing country like India and can, therefore, be deferred.

SOCIAL SECURITY IN INDIA

Social security is an essential aspect of economic development. It covers certain risks an individual is exposed to. Social security covers the entire population, but we are concerned with only industrial labour.

The government has come out with a series of legislative measures for the benefit of workers in our country. Such measures are:

- The Workmen's Compensation Act, 1926
- The Maternity Benefit Act, 1961
- The Employees State Insurance Act, 1948
- The Employers Provident Fund Act, 1952

- The Factories Act, 1948
- The Payment of Wages Act, 1936
- The Minimum Wages Act, 1948
- The Payment of Gratuity Act, 1972
- The Payment of Bonus Act, 1965

Regrettably, provisions of these and other acts and the benefits flowing from them go only to the workers in the organised sector. A large chunk of labour, specially in the agricultural sector and the unorganised sector, estimated at about 87 percent of the labour force, is outside the preview of the protective legislation. Even for the workers in the organised sector, benefits hardly reach. One should visit an ESI hospital to see the plight of an average worker seeking medicine and relief from the doctors. Experience of workers is no better in the provident fund offices. In many cases, managements fail to remit their and worker's contributions to the P.F. Commissioner regularly. For majority of the owners, social security is a charity and is treated as a burden to be avoided at the slightest pretext.

QUESTIONS

1. Bring out the important changes that have taken place at the labour front.
2. Outline the trends in the trade union movement.
3. Bring out the causes for industrial disputes. How are they resolved.

ASSIGNMENT

It is too well known that employees in IT firms, MNCs, call centres and BPO businesses are not unionised. Why is it so? Conduct a survey and prepare a report thereafter.

REFERENCES

1. C.N.Vakil, *Industrial Development of India-Policy and Problems*, p.367.
2. *Ibid.*
3. *Ibid*, p.368.
4. *The Economic Times*, April 9, 1995.
5. Cited in E.A.Ramaswamy, "Trade Union and Politics," *Business India*, Oct.7-20, 1985.
6. E.A.Ramaswamy, *The Rayon Spinners*, New Delhi, Oxford University Press, 1994, p.57.
7. Kudchedkar,L.S., *Aspects of Personnel Management and Industrial Relations*, p.105.
8. S.C.Jain, *Productivity and Discipline*, Allied, 1988, p.(XXIV).
9. *Ibid*, p.VII.
10. E.A.Ramaswamy, "From IR to HRD," *Business India*, April 21-May 4, 1986.

CHAPTER OUTLINE

Definition of a Sick Unit
Extent of Sickness
Causes for Sickness
Effect of Sickness
Remedies
- *Preventive Measures*
- *Curative Measures*

Omkar Swami Committee on Sickness

LEARNING OBJECTIVES

After reading this Chapter, you should be able to:

1. Define a sick unit, analyse causes for sickness and detail effects of sickness
2. Outline the extent of sickness in Indian industries
3. Suggest remedies to cure sickness
4. Detail recommendations of expert committee on sickness.

22 Industrial Sickness

Industrial sickness* is a natural concomitant of the market economy. In the UK, over 10,000 units fall sick every year. In the USA, the figure may be much higher. A study indicates that during the decade 1967-1976, one in four companies listed on the US stock exchanges had turned sick. In our country too, the problem of sickness is serious and is likely to grow worse in the years to come. This chapter is devoted to a detailed discussion of the nature, extent and causes of industrial sickness. Towards the end, reference is made to the remedial measures available to revive sick units.

DEFINITION OF A SICK UNIT

According to Reserve Bank of India (RBI), a sick unit is that which has incurred a cash loss for one year and is likely to continue incurring losses for the current year as well as in the following year and the unit has an imbalance in its financial structure, such as current ratio is less than 1:1 and there is a worsening trend in the debt equity ratio.

An appropriate definition of a sick unit is given by the Sick Industrial Companies Act, 1985 (SICA). According to the Act, a sick industrial company is an industrial company (being a company registered for not less than seven years) which has at the end of any financial year accumulated losses equal to or exceeding its entire net worth and has also suffered cash losses in that financial year and in the financial year immediately preceding it.

> A sick unit has accumulated losses equal to or more than its net worth.

The definition of sickness has been widened by the Companies (Second Amendment) Act 2002. As per the amended Act, a company becomes sick when it fails to repay debts within any three consecutive quarters on demand made by creditors.

Distinction is made between actual sickness and potential or incipient sickness.

* The usage *industrial sickness* came into being during 1970s when large units were facing closure in West Bengal.

Actual Sickness

(i) Erosion of net worth by 50 per cent or more.
(ii) Units being closed for a total period of six months and more during the last year, and
(iii) Default in payment of loan instalment.

Incipient Sickness

Capacity utilisation is less than 50 per cent of the highest achieved during the preceding five years.

According to State Financial Corporations (SFCs), any unit which fails to pay three consecutive instalments (half-yearly) of interest and/or principal is sick.

In the small-scale sector, a unit is treated as sick (according to the RBI), if it has:

(a) incurred cash loss in the previous accounting year, is likely to continue to incur cash loss in the current accounting year and has an erosion in its networth to the extent of 50 per cent or more and/or
(b) has defaulted on any interest payment for consecutive four quarters/instalments of principal for consecutive two quarters, with persistent irregularity in the operation of its cash credit limit.

Extent of Sickness

About 90 units fall sick every day. Every third or fourth small unit is sick and the ratio is 10th unit in medium and large categories.

Industrial sickness is growing at an annual rate of about 28 per cent and 13 per cent respectively in terms of the number of units and outstanding amount of bank credit. It is reckoned that as of today, there are more than three lakh sick units with an outstanding bank credit of over Rs.46,000 crore. Nearly 29,000 units are added to the sicklist every year, i.e., about 90 units fall sick every working day. Almost every third or fourth small sector unit and every tenth unit in the medium and large sectors are sick or dying. Table 22.1 shows more details about sickness among large, medium and small units.

Table 22.1 **Industrial Sickness**

(Rs. Billion)

As at end-March	*No. of Sick/Weak Units*			*SSI Units as Percentage of Total Units*	*Outstanding Amount*		
	Total	*SSI*	*Non-SSI*		*Total*	*SSI*	*Non-SSI*
1991	2,23,809	2,21,472	2,337	98.95	107.68	27.92	79.76
1992	2,47,924	2,45,575	2,349	99.05	115.33	31.01	84.32
1993	2,40,700	2,38,176	2,524	98.95	131.34	34.43	96.91
1994	2,58,952	2,56,452	2,500	99.03	136.96	36.80	100.16
1995	2,71,206	2,68,815	2,391	99.11	137.39	35.47	101.92
1996	2,64,750	2,62,376	2,374	99.10	137.48	37.22	100.26
1997	2,37,400	2,35,032	2,368	99.00	137.87	36.09	101.78
1998	2,24,012	2,21,536	2,476	98.89	156.82	38.57	118.25
1999	3,09,013	3,06,221	2,792	99.09	194.63	43.13	151.50
2000	3,07,399	3,04,235	3,164	98.97	236.55	46.08	190.47

(**Source**: *SIDBI*, 2002)

Not that any data are needed to prove the extent of sickness. A casual drive through an industrial estate or the suburbs of a city is enough to understand the magnitude. It is not uncommon to see that if about five units are working successfully, equal or probably more number of units are either closed or under indefinite lock-out.

CAUSES FOR SICKNESS

Causes for industrial sickness may broadly be classified into two categories: (a) internal; and (b) external. *Internal factors* mainly relate to the poor quality of the top management. Poor quality of top management may take one of several forms: excessive conservatism, excessive complacency, growth-mania, poor financial control, excessive centralisation and authoritarianism, weak board and a weak watchdog function, excessive commitment to policies that worked well once but no longer appropriate, poor financial or marketing management and the like.

There are external as well as internal causes why units fall sick.

External causes can be further classified into:

- industry-specific factors;
- government-related factors;
- financial institutions-related factors and
- others.

Industry-Specific Factors These relate to stagnation or recession in the industry (e.g., the textile industry), competition faced by the unit (e.g., small units, rayon grade, pulp units) and excess capacity in the industry (e.g., the type of industry).

Industry specific factors include stagnation, recession, competition, excess capacity and the like.

Entry of MNCs and strict qualtity and hygiene specifications prescribed and enforced by them have contributed to the sickness of several firms, particularly in the SSI sector. Take the case of metal cap industry. 16 out of 20 SSI units (supplying metal caps to bottlers of soft drinks) have gone sick as they failed to meet the specifications for metal caps prescribed by Coke and Pepsi. Similar is the story with several mango pulp processors in the Chittoor district of Andhra Pradesh. Here too, high qualtiy and house-keeping specifications prescribed by MNC's are beyond the reach of the traditional pulp processors.

Government-Related Factors These include tax burden on the unit, especially import duties, excise duties and sales tax; legal restrictions on the units; expansion/diversification (as with erstwhile FERA and MRTP companies); frequent changes in government policies affecting the unit; liberal imports that compete with the unit's products; the government or its agencies going back on its promises made to the unit (such as promised price performance to the joint sector units); poor law and order situation (as in parts of North and Eastern India) political interference in the unit's affairs (as in the public sector units and agro-based industry); unhelpful government machinery (e.g., in supplying power or in clearing a project) and the like.

That government provides incentives and other facilities for promotion of industries, itself is one of the contributing factors causing sickness.

Financial Institutions-Related Factors These include harshness in dealing with the unit; delay in providing finance to the unit; inadequate working and/or long-term capital provided by them and their inexpert assessment of the client's finance proposal. (See also Box 22.1).

Others Other external factors include customer resistance to the unit's products; erratic availability of raw materials/components/power/fuel to the unit (e.g., paper and sugar industries, aluminum units); inadequate transport facilities available to the unit (e.g., for transporting coal) and the like.

Box 22.1 **Interesting Findings on Sickness**

In a study on industrial sickness in textiles and engineering industries during a period of 20 years (from 1970-90), the following findings were drawn:

- Sickness has a long history. Today's BIFR companies have shown very different attributes from currently healthy firms, not just in recent years but over two decades. There is also a high degree of persis-tence...poor financial performance in the past increases the probability of sickness in future.
- The major difference between BIFR and healthy companies throughout the last two decades has been in interest cost and wage cost per rupee sale, i.e., in fixed costs. Both are statistically significant determinants of industrial sickness. Moreover, even small hikes in interest rates substantially increase a firm's risk of being sick and, in the case of a BIFR company, significantly reduces the probability of successful turn-around.
- Today's BIFR companies have always had higher debt-equity and total liability-equity ratios compared to the non-BIFR firms. Consequently, the BIFR firms were always poorly insured against the prospect of bad sales than the less leveraged non-BIFR companies.
- In the two decades, there has been no major difference in unit variable costs between the BIFR and non-BIFR firms. Indeed, there are many financially healthy firms in textiles and engineering that have higher variable costs (and lower variable profits) compared to the industry average, and even some of the sick firms.

It is the internal factors which contribute to major sickness. In an American study, it was found that external factors may have been mainly responsible for only about 10 per cent of corporate decline. Internal causes of decline, on the other hand, accounted for about 70 per cent of decline (The remaining 20 per cent declines were caused by a mix of external and internal factors). An RBI study estimated that nearly two-thirds of cases of sickness arise from inappropriate management, including faulty choice of product, technology/scale.

Specifically, internal factors contributing to sickness include shortage of working capital, managerial ineffectiveness, siphoning of funds for non-productive purposes, lack of proper planning, and the like.

Signals of Sickness The following actions of a unit indicate that the unit is sick or going to be sick:

There are several signals of sickness. For example:
- irregularities in clearing dues
- low capacity utilisation
- high rate of rejection of goods.

- Continuous irregularity in cash credit accounts;
- Low capacity utilisation;
- Profit fluctuations, downward trend in sales and stagnation or fall in profits followed by contraction in the share of the market;
- High rate of rejection of goods manufactured;
- Reduction in credit summations-whenever the companies are in financial difficulty, they open a separate account with another bank and deposit all collections therein;
- Failure to pay statutory liabilities;
- Larger and longer outstandings in the bills accounts;
- Longer period of credit allowed on sale documents negotiated through the bank and frequent returns by customers of the same;

- Constant utilisation of cash credit facilities to the hilt and failure to pay timely instalment of principal and interest on the loans and instalment credit;
- Non-submission of periodical financial data/stock statement etc. in time;
- Financing capital expenditure out of funds provided for working capital purposes;
- Decrease in working capital on account of:
  - (i) increase in debtors and particularly dues from selling agents;
  - (ii) increase in creditors;
  - (iii) increase in inventories which may include a large number of slow or non-moving items;
- A general decline in that particular industry combined with many failures;
- Rapid turnover of key personnel;
- Existence of a large number of law suits against a company;
- Rapid expansion and too much diversification within a short time;
- Sudden/frequent changes in management-whether professional or otherwise and/or dominated by one man/few individuals;
- Diversion of funds for purposes other than running the units;
- Any major change in the share holdings.

EFFECT OF SICKNESS

A sick industrial unit is like a patient at home. A patient, in addition to suffering from the ailment himself, causes inconvenience to others and often, spells ruin to the family, particularly when the treatment is prolonged and expensive. A sick unit too will have serious repercussions on the economy as a whole, besides adversely affecting the interests of people directly connected with it.

Sick unit is like a patient at home.

Impact of sickness on the economy is easy to guess. In the first place, sickness contributes to high-cost economy. This, in turn, will affect the competitiveness of the economy at home and abroad.

Secondly, industrial sickness is mainly the problem of 88 per cent terminally sick units, investment in which is completely dead. Dead investment is a burden on both banks and budget and ultimately consumers have to pay the high cost.

Thirdly, persistent nature of industrial sickness, especially when policies do not allow flexibility for exit and other forms of adjustment, not only tends to restrict new employment opportunities but also constrict technological innovation, thus keeping the employment stagnant. Unviable units remain closed and employment in these units, in effect, is disguised unemployment.

Finally, industrial sickness worsens the problem of stringency of financial resources in the economy. Money locked up in sick units gives no returns and affects the availability of resources to other viable units. The continued operations of chronic loss-making firms snatches markets from more efficient producers and acts as a drain on the financial system. Besides, the huge amount of capital, running into many thousands of crores, which is invested in sick units is being wasted which a capital scarce country like ours can ill-afford.

Sickness drains resources of the economy.

REMEDIES

Happily, a majority of the sick units are retrievable (See Table 22.2). An RBI study indicates that 84 per cent of the large sick firms for which viability studies were conducted were considered to be potentially viable, though only 10 per cent of the small units were so considered. These figures provide some idea about the potential for reducing sickness. The potential may be even greater. If effective steps can be taken to prevent sickness in the first place, the incidence of sickness could be potentially lowered even more. For the next decade, it may not be an impossible goal to cut down the incidence of sickness to half of what it may otherwise be: (a) by devising steps to prevent sickness in the first place, and (b) by strengthening the machinery to turn around expeditiously those units that do fall sick but are salvageable.

In order to tackle the problem of sickness from the two angles, *viz.*, preventing sickness from occurring and curing it if it has taken place but remediable, the role of three agencies assumes significance: (a) the government, (b) the financial institutions and (c) the industry associations.

Preventative Measures

Role of the Government If the number of industrial units in the country has increased some ten times since independence and if we have a diversified industrial structure with widespread entrepreneurship, the credit for this largely belongs to the government. Its efforts at creating infrastructural facilities, specialised industrial and financial institutions, package of incentives for entrepreneurs etc., have borne rich fruit. Equally, of course, the government's vacillating policies, incompetence in managing the core sector, excessive protection to domestic units and a Frankensteinian control structure that has mostly bred corruption and vitiated national objectives, are to blame for a good part of the structural sickness in the Indian economy.

Penalising managements that wilfully make units sick is the first thing that the government should do to prevent industrial sickness. Under the Sick Industrial Companies (Special Provisions) Act, 1985, the government has set-up a Board for Industrial and Financial Reconstruction (BIFR) which will have to be notified by the management of companies of their potential sickness. This early warning system may be supplemented by the government strengthening the monitoring role of the banks and the financial institutions. Not only in the public sector, but also in the private sector, the government can do much to mitigate the number one cause of sickness, namely, the ineffective management of the unit. The basic requirement for both sectors is to identify early the level of competence of the unit's management, help it upgrade itself if there is a potential for improvement, or otherwise replace it quickly and ruthlessly if the level is low and not much potential exists for improvement.

A second area where the government can be helpful is *vis-a-vis* industrial licensing. The very existence of licensing and monopoly regulation legislation implies that there is a stampede to '*get in*' whenever licensing is liberalised for an industry or the economy as a whole. The two-wheeler industry, the car industry and the television industry are recent examples of a stampede to get in which will inevitably lead to widespread sickness and a bad shake-out a few years from now.

Role of Financial Institutions The apex financial institutions like IDBI, IFCI, ICICI and nationalised commercial banks are in an extremely favourable position to prevent industrial sickness. After all, they are the direct and indirect purveyors of the bulk of the long-term and working capital needed to run private sector enterprises in India. They are the ones that by and large decide whether an enterprise will get stated or not, and once stated, whether it will run or not. Besides, they remain in constant touch with

Table 22.2 **Viability Status of Sick and Weak Units: End-March 1991**

	SSI		*Non-SSI*		*Total*	
	Number	*Outstanding bank credit (Rs.crore)*	*Number*	*Outstanding bank credit (Rs.crore)*	*Number*	*Outstanding bank credit (Rs.crore)*
1. *Viable units*	16140	693.10	941	3699.63	17081	4392.78
2. *Non-viable units*	202998	1997.13	974	2206.97	203972	4204.10
3. *Viability not assessed*	2334	101.81	422	2069.18	2756	2170.99
4. *TOTAL*	221472	2792.04	2337	7975.78	223809	10767.82
5. *(a) Units under nursing programme*	13224	550.08	578	2336.07	13802	2886.15
(b) per cent of viable units	81.93	79.37	61.42	63.14	80.80	65.70
			Composition			
1. *Viable units*	7.29	24.82	40.27	46.39	7.60	40.79
2. *Non-viable units*	91.66	71.53	41.68	27.67	91.20	39.04
3. *Viablility not assessed*	1.00	3.70	18.00	25.94	1.20	20.16
4. *TOTAL*	100.00	100.00	100.00	100.00	100.00	100.00

(**Source** : *Economic Survey*, 1992-93)

market conditions as well as funded units, and are in an excellent position for receiving an early warning of sickness.

The following are the ways by which sickness can be prevented by the financial institutions:

A. Continuous Monitoring of Unit

(i) Periodic financial reports.
(ii) Desk officer for client unit.
(iii) Institutional nominee(s) on the board.
(iv) Periodic inspections.
(v) Institutional adviser deputed to the unit, especially to monitor project implementation in risky ventures.
(vi) Inter-institutional reviews of unit.
(vii) Market intelligence and industry cells.

B. Careful Project Appraisal

(i) Independent verification of sales, profits etc., projections of the client.
(ii) Careful scrutiny of technology and plant size, choices of location, government-related contingencies and quality of management.
(iii) Use of external consultants for appraising large or risky projects.

C. Professional Institutional Response to Unit's Problems

(i) Training of desk officers and reputed advisers in professional management.
(ii) Discretionary authority to monitoring desk officers to commit the institutions (up to some limits) to immediate contingency reliefs.
(iii) Better coordination and faster response by financial institutions through a smaller consortium.
(iv) Lead agency concept.

D. Required Systems at Client Units

(i) Approval of financial institutions for appointing (or removing) internal and statutory auditors, etc.
(ii) Professional management training for promoters.

E. Incentives to Units to Remain Healthy

(i) Interest relief if there is no sickness.
(ii) Penal interest for avoidable project cost escalation, careless or false sales and profit projections.

Role of Industry Associations The industry associations in India have always played, albeit indirectly, some sort of a sickness prevention role. This has largely taken the form of lobbying the government for solving problems faced by or likely to be faced by the industry. A more explicit and direct role, however, may be feasible because of the intimate knowledge such associations can possess about industry-wise trends as well as the problems faced by their various member units. Besides, an alternative to bureaucratic and centralised regulation of the industry is industrial self-regulation in the light of national policies and a greater self-monitoring and sickness prevention role could strengthen the development of responsible industrial self-regulation. For this purpose, industry association should be broadened to include representatives from various stake holders-the government, labour, financial institutions, suppliers and customers.

How can industry associations play a concrete role in sickness prevention? A number of potentially useful steps are listed below.

A good practical review by each industry association of installed and usable capacity in the industry, capacity utilisation, growth trends, problems and opportunities etc., should be useful for the potential new entrants for deciding whether to enter the industry or not, and for existing firms for taking strategic diversification, expansion and project-mix decisions. This should also help the financial institutions to formulate industry-specific guidelines about funding project finance requests and the government to formulate industry-specific licensing guidelines.

The industry association could have some sort of a first aid cell. This could consist of professionals who could go to the aid of a unit that is beginning to fall, with the offer of managerial and technical help. These professionals would be particularly useful since they would be conversant with the nature of the industry and with practices that have effectively worked in the industry.

The industry association can perform a professionalising function by conducting training programmes for managers, technocrats etc. The programmes could be quite useful since they would be tailored to suit the needs of the industry. Suitable industry association periodicals could also disseminate case studies of effective practices.

The industry associations would facilitate acquisitions of weaker units by stronger units and other contractual arrangements to help out ailing units, such as loan of managers from stronger units, sharing of marketing or production facilities, sharing of import of technology, a fair sharing of imported inputs, collaboration in mounting export campaigns etc.

These suggestions do not necessarily go counter to a policy of fostering competition. On the contrary, by preventing ailing units from going sick and, indeed by strengthening them, they should promote a healthy competition, that is, competition for serving customers more effectively with better products at cheaper prices.

Curative Measures

Till now measures to prevent sickness were listed. Prevention is certainly better than cure. But with the best of preventive measures, sickness often creeps in. How to cure the sickness after it has crept in is a relevant question. The answer lies in the following paragraphs.

The preventive measures detailed above will, if extended, help cure industrial sickness. In addition, the existing machinery to rehabilitate sick units should be strengthened. The existing agencies are explained below.

There is the SICA . The Act was passed by the Parliament and received the assent of the President in January 1986. It was amended in December 1991 so as to bring government companies within the purview of the Act. The Act provides for the setting up of a Board for Industrial and Financial Reconstruction (BIFR). With the establishment of the BIFR, with effect from January 12, 1987, medium and large-scale companies whose networth has been eroded by 50 per cent or more, will be obliged to report this fact to the Board. The Board has been given wide-ranging powers in respect of the approval of rehabilitation packages for sick industrial companies, including their reconstruction and revival as well as the change of managements or amalgamation with any other company or sale or lease of a part or whole of the industrial undertaking or even winding up of the company.

Since inception upto December 31,2004, the BIFR received cases of 5147 of which 259 are under revival, 436 cases have been reviewed, winding up has been recommended in 1302 cases and 1377 have been dismissed (see Table 22.3).

Table 22.3 **Board for Industrial and Financial Reconstruction Yearwise Performance as on 31.12.2004**

Year	*Total Cases Regd. during the Year*	*Cases Disposed off during the year*			
		Cases under Revival	*Cases Revived*	*Winding up Recommended*	*Dismissed*
1	*2*	*3a*	*3b*	*3c*	*3d*
1987	311	0	0	0	8
1988	298	0	1	12	29
1989	202	0	1	31	78
1990	151	3	3	43	44
1991	155	3	4	47	28
1992	177	3	7	30	42
1993	152	6	13	64	59
1994	193	7	38	79	48
1995	115	13	25	63	29
1996	97	19	92	85	25
1997	233	5	35	85	21
1998	370	7	21	50	36
1999	413	7	10	64	69
2000	429	5	37	151	153
2001	463	28	47	129	114
2002	559	52	33	135	247
2003	430	54	40	145	260
2004	399	47	29	89	87
Total	5147	259	436	1302	1377

Since its inception upto June 30, 1996, the Board had reached a final decision on 1481 sick companies out of a total of 1802 companies referred to it. Of the total, rehabilitation packages had been approved or sanctioned for 493 companies; the Board also decided to wind up 446 units. Thus, of every three sick companies, two were approved for rehabilitation while one was wound up. The Board, by and large, has adopted a professional approach of being fair, just and pragmatic as far as possible. Within this framework, it has also tried to distribute sacrifices among the concerned parties in a fair and equitable manner and in the case of workers according to their ability to bear such sacrificers. The number of medium and large units revived against the total number of sick units is four out of 1534 in 1992, 11 out of 1867 in 1993, 16 out of 2000 in 1994, and 18 over 2000 in 1995.

As a result of the steps taken by BIFR to streamline internal procedures, it was possible to reduce the time taken between registration of a case and its first hearing. The average time taken during 1994 for the first hearing was 63 days, against an average of over 160 days in the first five years. The time taken for deciding cases was also considerably reduced from 700 days in the first five years of the functioning of the Board to 187 days in 1993.

The Board deals with only medium and large-scale sick industrial companies because it is in these companies that heavy amounts are sunk.

Further, there is the Industrial Reconstruction Bank of India (IRBI) which came into being on March 20, 1985 by converting the erstwhile Industrial Reconstruction Corporation of India. The IRBI is a principal reconstruction agency which provides assistance for the reconstruction and rehabilitation of sick industrial units. In addition to granting of loans and advances to industrial concerns, underwriting of shares and debentures, guarantee of loans and deferred payments, IRBI's wide spectrum of activities also include such developmental activities as providing infrastructural facilities, raw materials, consultancy, managerial and merchant banking services, machinery and other equipment on lease or hire-purchase basis for the purpose of reconstruction and the development of industrial concerns.

The IRBI itself came under sharp criticisms. For example, it was criticised for (1) inadequacy of resources at its disposal; (2) excess overdues; (3) majority of the loans were sanctioned but not disbursed; and (4) regional biases in the functioning.

A new bank, called Industrial Investment Bank of India, was set up in 1997 which took over the IRBI. Being more proactive and development focussed, the new bank would respond to changing needs of the industry better.

For sick units in the small-scale sector, separate facilities are available. State Finance Corporations and commercial banks will be asked to devise a scheme for the rehabilitation of sick units in the small-scale sector, and the assistance given by them for the revival of such units will be eligible for refinancing by the IRBI at a concessional rate of interest.

Mere strengthening of the existing machinery may often amount to taking an unwilling horse to the water. The horse should be made to drink. Here lies the importance of effective management. Ultimately, it is in the hands of the management to revive the sick unit and put it on the profitable track.

Growing evidence suggests that effective turnaround management can revive pretty hopeless cases, or at least drastically reduce the extent of sickness. There are several stunning examples of corporate turnaround. Sylvania and Laxman lost some 40 per cent on sales, and two years later, a turnaround of some 60 per cent on sales was achieved. In another four years, it quadrupled its sales. Similarly, Enfield India which lost over 25 per cent on sales in 1976-77 broke even in two years, and earned about seven per cent on sales three years later. What is significant is that both Sylvania and Laxman and Enfield operated in a fairly competitive market during their periods of turnaround. In both cases, there was a significant change in the style of the top management during this period.

Sylvania and Laxman and Enfield are two examples of dynamic turn around. It was the management that turned them around.

Even in the public sector where there is bureaucratic regulation of public enterprises and political interference in their operations, there are numerous examples of turnaround. For instance, Hindustan Copper lost some Rs.30 crore in 1982-83 but broke even next year, despite a fall in the price of copper in 1983-84. Bharat Aluminum Corporation (BALCO) reduced its losses from about Rs.528 million in 1982-83 to Rs.215 million next year without raising its prices. Burn Standard, which was losing some 30 per cent on sales until 1978, broke even four years later. Gujarat State Transport Corporation made a cash loss of about Rs.370 million in 1981-82 but reported zero cash loss in 1983-84.

The government and other buyers of the products of the small-scale industry will be directed to settle the dues of the small-scale units on a priority basis and commercial banks will be asked to ensure that the credit given to large-scale units for working capital is applied first towards meeting the dues of the small-scale suppliers.

In order to protect the investment of technical entrepreneurs in cases where the small-scale units promoted by them are forced to close down for reason beyond their control, the possibility of evolving a suitable scheme of risk insurance for safeguarding their interest may be examined.

Finally, if a unit is so sick that it is beyond redemption, it is advisable to allow the unit to die a natural death instead of clinging on to it on political or personal considerations. This should be so whether the unit is in public, private, joint, cooperative or in the small-scale sector.

OMKAR GOSWAMI COMMITTEE ON SICKNESS

A Committee was constituted in April 1993 to study and make recommendations on the question of industrial sickness and corporate restructuring. The Committee submitted its report under the chairmanship of Dr.Omkar Goswami on July 13, 1993.

The Committee observed that while there are sick companies, sick banks, ailing financial institutions and unpaid workers, there are hardly any sick promoters. 'There lies the heart of the matter,' it added.

The Committee has come out with a report recommending far reaching reforms to facilitate the end of non-viable firms.

Following are the highlights of the committee's recommendations:

- Five 'fast track' winding up tribunals in major cities for the closure of sick companies.
- Five recovery tribunals should be set up exclusively for recovering corporate debts to secured creditors and only cover cases exceeding Rs.50 lakh.
- The definition of sickness as mentioned in the Sick Industrial Companies Act (SICA) is '*backward*' looking. The BIFR should use the SICA's winding up provisions more frequently.
- A sick company's own reference to the BIFR should be voluntary, not mandatory.
- The selection of incipient sickness can be possible only if the scope of BIFR and SICA is fundamentally restricted to single-point facilitation and fast arbitration.
- There is a strong case for having SICA override the Foreign Exchange Regulation Act (FERA) to encourage foreign investors to take over potentially viable sick companies.
- The Reserve Bank of India's guidelines for rehabilitation should be altered and financial institutions should adjust the write-off against some equity of the sick company.
- The Central Board of Direct Taxes (CBDT) should remove all tax hurdles that prevent banks and financial institutions from converting debt to equity of sick companies.
- All financial institutions should create a common information pool about firms that have defaulted on term lending dues and list the names of the promoters of such firms.
- The Companies Act should be amended so that secured creditors can implement *defacto* changes in management and/or the board of directors in instances of repeated debt defaults.

The Government should amend the compensation for retrenchment and closure from 15 days wages to one month's/year of completed service.

The Omkar Goswami Committee's recommendation on industrial restructuring are a radical departure from earlier attempts at tackling this issue. In place of a piece meal approach, it has suggested a package of reforms addressing both industrial as well as financial sectors. If accepted, they will undoubtedly have far-reaching consequences for the industrial sector as well as the economy as a whole.

The Committee's recommendations led the Government to enact the Companies (Second Amendment) Act 2002. The amended Act provides for replacement of SICA and setting up of a National Company Law Tribunal (NCLT). The NCLT handles all the functions of SICA, BIFR, Company Law Board and High Courts.

QUESTIONS

1. Define industrial sickness. What are the causes for sickness?
2. What is the impact of sickness on the economy?
3. Suggest remedies to cure industrial sickness.
4. Bring out the impact of economic reforms on sickness.

ASSIGNMENT

We have described the causes for sickness in small units and of the large ones too. Make a comparison. What similarities and dissimilarities do you observe?

CHAPTER OUTLINE

Arguments for Exit Policy
Arguments against Exit Policy
National Renewal Fund

LEARNING OBJECTIVES

After reading this Chapter, you should be able to:

1. Advance arguments in favour of exit policy
2. Argue against exit policy
3. Describe the functioning and achievement of National Renewal Fund.

23 Exit Policy

One of the policies proposed by the government as a part of the total package of economic reforms relates to the exit of unretrievable sick industrial undertakings. Popularly called the Exit Policy, the new action plan entails closure of sick units, both in public and private sectors, via a well laid out route.

The proposed exit policy has evoked strong but varied response from all sections of society. While the idea is welcomed by some, it is equally condemned by others. It is useful to place the issue of exit policy in its proper perspective. This chapter is devoted for the purpose.

ARGUMENTS FOR EXIT POLICY

People who support exit policy offer the following views:

> The economy would be better off by closing sick units.

1. The economy would be better off than what it is today by closing sick units. This may sound paradoxical but a deeper analysis reveals the truth. As is well known, banks, financial institutions, State Governments and Central Government are asked to offer several concessions to keep the sick units going. Popularity called 'sacrifices,' these concessions include:

- Interest on terms loans can be reduced by two percentage points below the existing rate, and penalties for non-payment are waived.
- Liabilities on account of non-payment of workers, statutory dues and overdue creditors are shared between the participating banks and institutions on a fifty-fifty basis. The financial institutions also provide the margin money for additional working capital. The cost of rationalisation of labour is met by the financial institutions and banks on a fifty-fifty basis.
- Private promoters are expected to bring in 20 per cent of the additional long term funds requirements either as equity or non-interest bearing loan. This is reduced to 15 per cent if a firm is under new management.

- The State Governments must make many sacrifices: (i) sales tax loans at low or zero rate of interest; (ii) loan guarantees; (iii) preferential power supply, including not disconnecting for non-payment; (iv) exemption of sales tax and octroi; (v) waiver of all penal levies; and (vi) price preference to public sector suppliers.
- The Central Government's sacrifices are (i) exemption from central excise duties; (ii) income tax relief; (iii) preferential supply of canalised items; (iv) deferment of provident fund and ESI dues; and (v) exemption from paying the minimum bonus.

These sacrifices mean heavy subsidies offered to units which have become sick because of inefficient and inept managements. But none of these concessions is available to healthy units. Now, instead of maintaining the sick units through subsidies, it would be wise to divert the resources to healthy units and make them grow healthier.

2. There is a belief that workers would be thrown out of jobs if sick units are allowed to down their shutters. And in the absence of a safety net, these displaced workers would be put to sever hardship.

The belief that exit policy would displace workers is not correct.

The belief that the workers would be displaced permanently is unfounded. The truth is that usually the lenders to sick units do not recover their money and the shareholders lose all their equity. The new owners who buy the assets of the failed companies re-employ, usually an equal number of new workers, through terms that may not be as attractive as the earlier workers may have enjoyed. In fact, after an initial contraction employment expands. New jobs will be created through additional investments made in various sectors of the economy. Then there are MNCs which outsource of establish grantield projects in India.

Maintenance of sick units benefits managements and not workers.

3. Stressing the argument of workers' interests further, it may be stated that maintenance of sick units would, contrary to popular belief, benefit managements and State Governments and not workers. As is well known, labour accounts for only a fraction of total cost of production, in textiles it is 21 per cent and in engineering it is 20 per cent. Continued funding of sick units, therefore, implies that resources are not used to maintain labour alone but for other inputs; and in activities that result in negative nominal returns, chronic cash losses and negative net worth.

Chronically sick units die on their own-exit or no exit policy. Why not close down such units?

4. Continuing on the same subject, chronically sick units die their death, exit policy or no exit policy. In Gujarat alone, for example, 27 textile mills downed their shutters permanently between 1983 and 1988. An exit policy will ensure that at least the legitimate dues of displaced workers are paid to them satisfactorily. Without such a policy, these employees have to lose their dues, besides losing jobs. Precisely same thing happened to 45000 textile workers of Gujarat. Though the mills, where they were working, were closed nearly several years age, till to date not even one worker has been paid his/her dues. Same is true with the textile workers of Bombay where several mills were closed.

5. There is a belief that certain undertakings, particularly in public sector, must be maintained notwithstanding their losses. Textile industry, with hundreds of sick mills, is toted as an example in support of this view. It is stated that sick textile mills ought to remain in operation despite budgetary and other financial support because (i) these units produce subsidised *janata* cloth for the poor, and (ii) their output puts a downward pressure on textile prices. But these arguments also sound hollow.

That public sector units need to be maintained, losses notwithstanding is only bureaucratic mindset.

The so called poorer sections are increasingly buying synthetic textiles despite the fact that they are three to four times costlier than *janata* cloth. Thus, the first rationale for maintaining sick units, especially in the public sector, exists more in the minds of bureaucracy than in reality. Regarding the second, the downward pressure on prices is at the expense of budgetary support that maintains grossly inefficient units. If the objective is low prices, the same can be better achieved by giving a lumpsum subsidy to the efficient units. The same objective is met at a lower cost with probably better quality products.

6. Yet another argument relates to the infant industry theory. According to this, a sick unit shall remain so only in the short run and can be nurtured to efficiency in the long-run. But how long is really long-run is not clear. If one takes a look at the sick units referred to the BIFR, majority of them continued to remain sick for more than five years in spite of massive concessions given. To be specific, 18 to 24 sick textile mills (75 per cent) remained sick from 1982 to 1990 without showing any sign of rehabilitation. Similarly, of the 22 sick engineering firms 15 were chronically sick from 1985, and nine from 1982. It is difficult to find an economic canon that justifies continous injection of subsidised funds for a decade so that the long term considerations might finally prevail.

7. Many countries that have successfully carried out economic reforms have exit policies. Be it Singapore, Malaysia, Thailand or Indonesia, exit policy is implemented without resistance. The results of such policies are encouraging. Why not we try similar policy in our country too?

Countries with successful economic reforms have exit policies.

8. We are talking in terms of integrating our economy with the world economy. There is no point in trying to globalise Indian economy if a company can not do anything about its surplus labour or close a sick unit both of which any competing country can easily do. Indian companies will be at a competitive disadvantage as a result. If Indian companies cannot sell assets like surplus land while their competitors overseas can, this again will weaken the competitive strength of Indian corporate sector. If workers cannot be transferred in India but can be elsewhere, again our industry will be at a disadvantage. Overseas firms are allowed to 'exit' their sick units. Our corporate sector too must have the facility, so that captains of industry can operate on a level playing field.

Integrating India's economy with the world economy demands that an employer shall have freedom to handle labour in his own way.

ARGUMENTS AGAINST EXIT POLICY

People who oppose exit policy have equally strong arguments on their side. Place the above points on the flip side of the coin, we have arguments against exit policy. But there are some more arguments which need a mention here. The arguments against exit are as follows:

1. Why think of an exit policy as the only remedy available for tackling industrial sickness? Surely, closure is not the ideal solution for sickness even as death cannot be an answer to illness. Other strategies like merger, takeover, turnaround management, revamping management and the like may be tried before planning for exit of sick units.

Death cannot be an answer to illness. So also closure is no solution to sickness.

2. What should happen to workers who would be displaced thanks to exit of sick units? Where should they go? Do we have a safety net which would ensure that an unemployed worker is not a starving worker but merely a worker on the dole, that unemployment does not mean any loss of old age pension, nor the loss of house, nor the denial of health care, nor the dreaded thought that bright young kids have to be taken out of school because their fathers are jobless?

In the absence of safety net can we displace workers?

3. People who advocate exit policy have an ulterior motive, a motive to denounce and scrap Nehruvian socialism altogether. It has now become a fashion, symbol of progressivism on the part of intellectuals to criticise socialism, the opinion being emboldened by the fall of communism every where. What is not realised is that the socialism we have in our country is different from what it was in other parts of the globe. We have been having a mixed economy embodying both State enterprises and private ownership, a system where both sectors existed and functioned in the pursuit of shared goals.

People who advocate exit policy are hitting at Nehruvian Policy.

We never prevented private enterprises from growing. In fact, we gave them all facilities and encouragement but imposed some regulations to ensure that the private enterprises would sub-serve national goals. We defined the role of State in the economy and by and large the government confined itself to its role, stray excesses notwithstanding. But all of a sudden Nehruvian socialism has become untouchable and all its planks, including protected employment, has been reduced to total irrelevance.

How can a philosophy, i.e., (Nehruvian socialism) which has worked for 40 years and which has produced reasonably good results become untouchable overnight? Why talk of condemning the philosophy instead of correcting mistakes, if any?

The exit policy is obviously dictated by the World Bank and the IMF.

4. The exit policy is clearly dictated by the World Bank or the IMF. Why should we be guided by an agency which derives its strength and inspiration from Western World and which has no understanding of the problems peculiar to our country?

NATIONAL RENEWAL FUND (NRF)

The National Renewal Fund (NRF) was constituted on February 4, 1992, with an initial corpus of Rs. 200 crore. The size of the fund has since been raised to Rs.2.250 crores. The non-statutory fund, which will provide a safety net to the labour force, would cover both public and private sectors. The contributions to the fund will come from the Central Government, the State Governments, financial institutions, industrial units and the General Insurance Corporation of India (GICI).

The fund would mainly provide assistance to cover the costs of retraining and redeployment of labour arising as a result of modernisation and technology upgradation and also provide compensation to labour affected by restructuring of any industrial unit.

The NRF will be in operation for 10 years only. After that only the Insurance Fund for Employees (IFE), one of the three constituents of NRF, would remain operational and will be self-financing in nature. This means that there will be no open ended government liability for NRF beyond this period.

NRF is proposed to be divided into three parts. The first part of the fund, Employment Generation Fund (EGF), will provide resources for approved employment generation schemes. The second part, the National Renewal Grant Fund (NRGF), will deal with the immediate requirements of labour in sick units arising from revival or closure of such units. The funds will be disbursed as grants. The third part of the fund, IFE, will permit industries to prepare for future changes in their employment structures with changes in technology and modernisation.

Eligible Units

The following four categories of units have been identified which would be eligible for drawing money from the various funds under the NRF:

(i) Units which are potentially viable and require money for schemes like voluntary retirement;

(ii) Units which require money for technology upgradation urgently to survive competition;

(iii) Sick units which need to be closed down requiring money for compensating the retrenched workforce; and

(iv) Units requiring funds for training of workers and generating employment for weaker sections of the society.

Operation of the Fund

For the operation of the NRF, the Government has set out guidelines for identifying and categorising workers in all the unviable units on the basis of age, skill and family commitments. Based on this classification, every enterprise faced with closure is to formulate its action plan for counselling and guidance, or retraining and redeployment of workers. Five major centres for retraining and redeployment have been set up with the assistance of the ASSOCHAM (Kanpur), CII (Bombay), Gandhi Labour Institute (Ahmedabad), NSIC (Calcutta) and SISI (Indore). Twenty-one institutes-including 15 industrial training institutes-have also been authorised to run vocational courses for rationalised labour. Based on the current statistics of worker outflows, 48 locations in 16 states have been identified for setting up employee assistance centres spanning the unit, city and district levels which will assist actively in job searching, labour placement, skill-matching, and counselling. Skill, educational attainments, age, family responsibilities and also preferences will be taken into account. Those who so desire will be assisted to go back to farming, others, who are middle-aged or above will be helped to get self-employment. The younger lot will be retrained, and redeployed in the labour market.

Starting from 1991-92, when the NRF was announced, upto 1996-97, a total of Rs. 1,918 crore has been spent on NRF schemes.

Conclusion

Till now we have presented the views for and against the exit policy. In conclusion, we many state that it is advisable for a sick unit to have well laid out exit route both in the interest of workers and in the interest of the economy. Such a route can be via the BIFR. To its credit it may be stated that in all the units whose closure was ordered by the Board, it saw to it that the workers' interests were taken care of.

With the launch of the National Renewal Fund the much talked about criticism that there is no safety net for workers, will also be removed.

QUESTIONS

1. What is exit policy? Why is it necessary?
2. Enumerate arguments for and against exit policy.

ASSIGNMENT

Which paragraphs of this chapter did you like most? Explain.

24 Infrastructure

CHAPTER OUTLINE

Growth of Infrastructure

- *Energy*
- *Transport*
- *Communications*

Concluding Remarks

LEARNING OBJECTIVES

After reading this Chapter, you should be able to:

1. Understand the role of infrastructure in the development of our economy
2. Trace the growth of energy with its various components
3. Make a SWOT analysis of electricity
4. Trace the growth of transport agents and make SWOT analysis of railways, road and shipping
5. Trace the growth of communication facilities and make a SWOT analysis of this vital sector
6. Rank India among other countries in respect of infrastructural facilities

Adequate quantity, quality and reliability of infrastructure is key to the growth of any economy. Power is needed to turn the wheels of machines; vehicles are essential to transport goods and services and communication links are vital to talk to suppliers, customers and creditors. Economic growth is not possible if any of these facilities is lacking. This is precisely what has happened to our country. Due to the lack of infrastructure, India is losing a battle that could have placed it firmly in the midst of the most advanced nations in the world.

Adequate quantity, quality and reliability of infrastructure is key to the growth of Indian economy.

Infrastructure is a tiny word which encompasses the entirety of a nation. But for the purpose of this chapter, infrastructure shall include-

- *Energy*: Electricity, coal, oil and non-conventional sources.
- *Transport*: Railways, roads, shipping and civil aviation.
- *Communications*: Posts and telegraphs, telephones and telecommunications.

Infrastructural facilities are also called the *social overheads* and belong to the core sector of the economy.

GROWTH OF INFRASTRUCTURE

Most infrastructure services in India have until recently been provided by public monopolies and quasi-monopolies and have been beset by severe problems like the lack of accountability, low productivity, poor financial performance and over-employment. In order to meet the challenges of rapid economic growth and international competitiveness, there is an urgent need to achieve greater efficiency and accountability in these sectors, much greater prevalence of commercial principles and much more

Most infrastructural facilities till recently were provided by public and quasi monopolies.

competition in the provision and operation of infrastructure services. As the government's ability to undertake investments in the infrastructure is severely constrained, it is necessary to induce much more private sector investments and participation in the provision of social overheads. The entry of private suppliers can also encourage better risk sharing, accountability, monitoring and management in infrastructure sectors.

Coming to the growth of infrastructure, it maybe stated that massive allocations were made in successive five year plans towards infrastructure (See Table 24.1). As a result of huge investments, there has been phenomenal increase in the facilities over the years, as seen from Table 24.2.

Table 24.1

(Rs.Billion)

	1993-1994	*1994-1995*	*1995-1996*	*1996-1997*	*1997-1998*	*1998-1999*	*1999-2000*
Key Infrastructure Sectors	352.7	379.5	412.1	429.2	427.9	487.8	531.9
Energy	190.8	195.6	201.9	193.9	201.3	226.4	244.0
Power	53.9	59.6	62.8	55.1	64.3	71.3	76.3
Petroleum & Natural Gas	110.9	109.5	117.4	114.0	115.6	123.8	124.7
Non-Conventional Energy	0.1	0.4	2.3	3.8	3.7	4.0	5.9
Coal	26.0	26.0	19.5	21.0	17.8	27.3	37.2
Transport	97.2	108.6	111.9	134.5	115.2	126.5	139.0
Railways	66.0	68.9	75.0	83.0	84.0	87.6	89.7
Surface Transport	16.7	16.9	16.4	29.2	15.3	21.1	32.7
Civil Aviation	14.5	22.8	20.5	22.3	15.8	17.8	16.7
Communications	64.7	75.4	98.3	100.8	111.4	134.9	148.9
Other Sectors of which	86.2	106.3	109.7	113.2	121.7	90.2	85.7
Steel	27.6	36.5	36.5	32.5	25.9	48.4	12.9
Mines	2.9	1.9	3.4	3.4	5.3	4.4	12.1
Chemicals & Fertilisers	14.2	15.6	31.3	34.8	43.0	21.2	11.8
All Sectors	438.9	485.9	521.8	542.5	549.6	578.0	617.5
Memo:(% GDP)							
Key Infrastructure Sectors	4.5	4.1	3.8	3.5	3.1	3.1	3.0
All Sectors	5.6	5.3	4.9	4.4	4.0	3.6	3.5

(**Source:** Government of India, *Expenditure Budget*, Vol.I, various issues)

Table 24.2 **Infrastructure in India**

Year	*Railway Freight (million Tonns)*	*Railway Trarff (millions)*	*Road Length Surfaced (km)*	*Road Length Unsurfaced (km)*	*Direct Exchange Lines ('000)*	*Cargo handled by ports ('000 tonnes)*	*Coal Production ('000 tonnes)*	*Electricty generated (million units)*	*Crude Oil Production (million tonnes)*	*Natural Gas Production (million metric Metrs)*
1990-91	341	3,858	1,046	970	5,075	1,51,665	NA	NA	NA	NA
1991-92	360	4,049	1,071	1,059	5,810	1,51,665	NA	NA	NA	17,998
1992-93	371	3,749	NA	NA	6,797	1,66,575	238.26	NA	26.95	NA
1993-94	378	3,708	NA	NA	8,026	1,79,260	246.04	NA	27.08	NA
1994-95	381	3,935	NA	NA	9,795	1,97,262	NA	3,50,490	NA	NA
1995-96	391	4,158	NA	NA	11,978	2,15,263	NA	3,80,084	35,16	22,639
1996-97	NA	NA	NA	NA	14,882	NA	NA	NA	32.90	NA
2002-03	543	4,971	NA	NA	44,968	1,09,590	NA	5,32,430	33.06	31,390

(**Source:** *Economic Surveys*, Issues of *Infrastructure in India*, and *India Development Report*, 2004-05)

Energy

Energy is the most important determinant of a country's economic growth. Infact, per capita consumption of energy is taken as an indicator of a country's prosperity.

Energy is created through several sources. The sources are conventional and non-conventional (See Fig.24.1). The first category shall include commercial and non-commercial sources of energy.

Figure 24.1 **Sources of Energy**

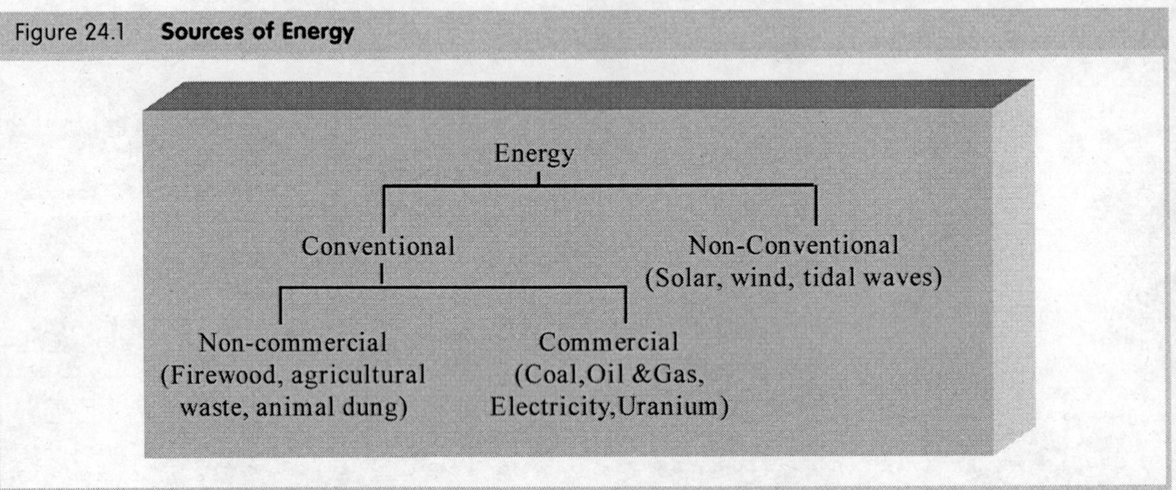

Commercial energy is so called as it commands a price.

Commercial energy is so called as it commands a price and the user is expected to pay it for its use. Non-commercial energy commands no price (theoretically, because a kg of firewood now costs Rs.five to six) and the user can take it as a free good gifted by nature. Non-conventional energy is a recent discovery and its use is confined to limited pockets in our country.

Coming to the commercial energy, it maybe stated that *coal* is the main source, accounting for 67 per cent of the total energy consumed in the country. Coal production stood at 246 m.tons in 1993-94, registering an increase of 3.3 per cent over the previous year. Low productivity and high ash content are the major constraints of coal.

The Government has initiated several steps to improve the supply of coal. Private sector participation is allowed in coal mining. Imports of cooking coal under the Open General Licence (OGL) are being allowed and the import tariff has been slashed from 85 per cent to 35 per cent.

Power generation in 2003-2004 stood at 55813.4 million units from 350490 million units during 1994-95. While thermal contributes 71 per cent, hydel power generation for 27 per cent and only 2 per cent is accounted for by nuclear power.

Power has been bugbear of our economy.

Power has been a bugbear of our economy. Lack of sufficient power supply has checked the growth of industries all over the country. Coming down to per capita consumption of power, we rank very poorly with 282 kwh. In contrast, Canada has 18,117 kwh, Sweden 16,655 kwh, and the US 12,160 kwh.

The Indian power sector is dominated by State Electricity Boards (SEBs). These boards have been traditionally monopolies controlling generation, transmission and distribution of power in the country. Almost 60 per cent of the total installed capacity is controlled by SEBs, 30 per cent by the central generators and around 10 per cent is in the private sector.

For a long time, the focus in the power sector was on generation. As expected, the power generated fell short of demand for it and it was felt that power sector would help fill the gap between demand and supply. In the early 1990s, the power sector was liberalised. Incentives such as guarantees, assured returns and duty cuts were offered to attract private developers. But transmission and distribution did not receive much attention. Much of the generated power was lost in transmission and distribution. Loss was only an euphemism used to describe theft of power. SEB's inefficiencies and corruption added to the woes in power sector.

> For a long time the focus in our country has been on generation, at the cost of transmission and distribution.

By the late 1990s, realisation dawned on the government that some drastic changes were needed if power sector were to be improved. Theft should be minimised and networks should be upgraded. This meant investments in transmission and distribution, neglected till now. More importantly, the SEBs should be restructured to make them accountable. There was also a need to establish independent regulators which could set commercial tariffs.

Action was initiated on all the fronts. 10 SEBs have been restructured (including in Karnataka) and are now made corporations. There are regulators in 19 states, apart from the central regulator. Power tariffs are being rationalised through tariff orders issued by these regulators.

> 10 SEBs have been corporatised. Spearheading the reforms is the Electricity Act 2003.

Spearheading the revival is the Electricity Act 2003, which contains provisions for power trading and open access, thus removing the monopoly of the SEBs and letting market forces come into play.

For a long time SEBs owed huge sums to the Central Government. In order to settle these dues, tripartite agreements were signed between state governments, central government and the Reserve Bank of India under which states were to issue tax-free bonds to securitise the outstanding dues of the SEBs.

The government has also launched an intensive programme called the Accelerated Power Development Reform Programme (APDRP) under which easy loans are provided to the states which undertake measures to plug the leaks and reform distribution systems. Greater the reduction in losses, the more loans and incentive a state earns. As a result of the APDRP incentives, several states have reduced losses and improved revenues.

Obviously, power sector in India is on the revival spree and hopefully, the country will have, in the days to come, uninterrupted supply of power to light the lamps, turn the wheels and run the pumps.

> Power sector in India is on the revival spree.

Read Box 24.1 for strengths, weaknesses and remedies for the power sector.

As with power sector, *oil* sector (crude oil and natural gas) was, for a long time fully in the hands of public sector undertakings. Until the late 1990s, the National Oil Companies (NOCs), Oil and Natural Gas Commission (ONGC) and Oil India Limited (OIL) were the only players in exploration and production while gas transmission and distribution was the domain of GAIL India Ltd.

On April 1, 2002 government announced deregulation. Following the deregulation, there has been an increasing participation by private and foreign players in exploration, refining and retailing oil and gas. Thus, we find Reliance, Essar Oil and Shell being busy in the oil and gas sector. Disinvestment is also in place. The disinvestment saga was initiated by the sale of IBP and IPCL.

> Since 2002, there has been an increasing participation by private and foreign players in exploration, refining and retailing oil and gas.

Coming to the production figures of crude oil, it may be stated that the output has witnessed ups and downs. For example, the production was 35.16 (m.tonnes) during 1995-96 but it came down to 31.95 (m.tonnes) during 1990-00. The output stood at 33.06 m.tons in 2002-03.

Domestic crude production is less than the demand for it, necessitating import of crude oil. Crude oil imports stood at 82.34 million tonnes during 2002-03, up from 27.34 million tonnes during 1995-96. Crude oil imports have witnessed a compounded annual growth of over 14 per cent since 1995-96.

Box 24.1 **Strengths, Weaknesses and Remedies (Electricity)**

A.Strengths

- Elaborate organisational framework for the growth of electricity has been provided by the Electricity (Supply) Act, 1948. Now, Electricity Act, 2003.
- Power and responsibilities neatly divided between centre and states. Former confines itself to planning, co-ordination and regulation. Latter looks after generation and distribution.
- Vast network of generation, transmission and distribution facilities spanning the length and breadth of the country
- Joint ventures among states in power generation.
- Numerous amendments to permit private participation in power generation.

B.Weaknesses

- Very low plant load factors.
- Declining share of hydro-power.
- Too much subsidy burden on state electricity boards.
- Incompetent and corrupt electricity boards
- Frequent and heavy load-shedding
- Capital intensive but starved of funds
- Heavy losses during transmission and distribution

C.Remedies

- Formulate unambiguous guidelines for private sector investment and ensure speedy clearance
- Expedite formulation of guidelines for private participation in transmission and distribution
- Create autonomous regulatary authorities at the central and state levels
- Corporatise SEBs, with separate generation, transmission, and distribution segments
- Set cost-based pricing for each consumer group, building in pre-determined tariff increases.

(**Source** : Remedies from *Business Today,* Oct. 22- Nov. 6, 1996)

With regard to natural gas, the output has been increasing steadily. The output was 22.64 (million metric metres) in 1995-96. It rose upto 31.39 (m.metric metres) in 2002-2003.

Started in 1844, Indian Railways have travelled long lines and as on today has a network of 63122 kms. IR runs about 14000 trains every day to ship 13 million tones of freight and 13 million passengers. IR is the second largest in the world

Transport

Transport sector includes railways, roads, shipping and civil aviation.

The *Indian Railways* (IR) have a long history as Box.24.2 tells. They consist of an extensive network spread over 63122 kms which is the second largest in the world. IR runs about 14000 trains every day to transport 13 million passengers and 1.3 million tonnes of freight.

IR has played an important role in defining the social and economic landscape of India. It contributes one per cent to the GDP and is the largest employer in the country with a workforce of about 1.6 million,

Box 24.2 **Tracks in Time**

1844-46: MacDonald Stephenson asks the Bengal government, administered by the East India Company (EIC), to build a railway line from Calcutta to the North West Frontier. Bombay businessmen ask for a line across the Western Ghats. Two companies, the East India Railways (EIR) and the Great Indian Peninsular Railways (GIPR) are formed and the directors of the EIC approve their proposals. Lord Hardinge, the governor general, argues that railways will facilitate, "the rapid concentration of infantry and artillery," and promote "the cheap prevention of insurrection, speedy termination of war and safety of the empire."

1850: The EIR and GIPR begin railway construction.

1853-1859: The first experimental railway line, running between Bombay and Thane, opens. Lord Dalhousie, the new governor general, sees this as a means to expand trade and writes in his famous Railway Minutes, "Great tracts are teeming with produce they cannot dispose of." The railways have the expected explosive impact on trade: imports of cotton and woollens grow over 100 per cent and machinery over 250 per cent from 1848 levels. Exports of raw cotton grow by 240 per cent, and that of foodgrains by a whopping 580 per cent in the same 10 years. India begins to globalise.

1860-1868: Over 4,000 miles of lines are built at a cost of Rs.89 crore by eight private sector companies. To promote infrastructure investment, the government issus guarantees: an assured rate of return of 4.5 to 5 per cent on capital, at a fixed exchange rate of 22 shillings to a rupee. By 1869, the flaws of these guarantees become apparent-goldplating imposes huge costs on the government. Costs, initially estimated at £9,000 to £15,000 per mile, shoot upto £20,000 per mile, with EIR building lines at £23,000 per mile. Reformers ask for guarantees to be scrapped.

1869: Though the old railway companies remain, the government decides to implement new projects by itself. This boosts efficiency: new lines cost 30 per cent less than the company lines, and 88 per cent new lines are added in 10 years. But company lines have higher returns than state lines.

1882-1900: Famines and war drain government finances. And stoke demand for bigger railways investment as well. The government decides to call back private investors. This time, guaranteed returns are lower at 3.5 per cent and the state and companies decide to split profits. Though operations on company lines are privately managed, the state retains notional ownership over lines. By 1900, railway tracks cover over 24,000 miles. However, administration-split between companies, the British government, princely states, native states and foreign governments-is chaotic.

1920: World War I takes a heavy toll on the railways. The cash strapped government neglects new investments for many years, and the quality of service drops dramatically. A committee chaired by Sir William Acworth, decides to separate the railway budget from the consolidated budget of the government. This, Sir William believes, will sever the railways' dependence on government funds. This is also why India continues to have a rail budget apart from the Budget of the Union government.

1947 to the present: At Independence, India gets 34,083 miles of railway tracks; about 7,000 miles go to Pakistan. India's early planners put great store by railway development and fund it generously. However, political interests, state ownership, controls and corruption in the railway bureaucracy turn it into a trundling dinosaur-vast but liked by nobody. Route kilometres expand by about 290 per cent in 50 years, a growth rate of a little more than two per cent per year.

constituting six per cent of the 27 million employed in the organised sector. IR operates three of the largest suburban services in the world - in Mumbai, Kolkotta and Chennai.

Compared to Chinese railways, IR is a poor cousin.

IR is managed by the Railway Board which in turn is supervised by the Ministry of Railways. The actual management of IRs operations is vested in nine zonal offices. Each zone is further subdivided into 60 divisions, each being headed by a divisional railway manager.

The Ministry of Railways has set up several public sector units to handle different areas of activities. These include Rail India Technical and Economic Services, which offers consultancy services in India and abroad; Ircon International Ltd., which is engaged in construction activities in India and abroad; the Indian Railways Finance Corporation, which helps monitor finance; the Container Corporation of India, which handles domestic and international container cargo; and RailTel Corporation of India which is spearheading IRs telecom sector.

IR has also developed two special purpose vehicles-Gujarat Pipavav Port Ltd., for improved rail connectivity to ports; and Rail Vikas Nigam Ltd., to implement projects such as the Golden Quadrilateral and port connectivity.

All these details are, no doubt impressive, but do not compare well with those of China for example, as Table 24.3 reveals. Over a period of 50 years, IR's progress in various dimensions has been almost stagnant while in the same period China's railways witnessed meteoric rise.

Table 24.3 **The Long and Short of it**

	*China Railways**		*Indian Railways***	
	1950	*2003*	*1950-51*	*2002-03*
Route km	22,161	73,002	53,596	63,122
No.of passengers (million)	157	973	973	4,971
Total passengers km (billion)	21	479	63	515
Average journey length (km)	135	492	52	104
Freight carried (million tonnes)	100	2,212	93	543
Freight tonne km (billion)	39	1,724	44	356
Average lead (km)	395	780	470	656

(**Source**: *Tiedao Zhishi, **Ministry of Railways, India)

With corporatisation of its organisation and structure, commercial autonomy, involvement of private sector and foreign investment, Chinese Railways (CR) has been steadily downsizing, hiving off non-core businesses, introducing fare and freight tariffs consistent with market economy tenets, and constantly improving freight and passenger services. Indian Railways, on the contrary, remains engrossed mostly with trivial issues.

The problem is, unlike Chinese railways, IR has been run on ideological grounds and not as a commercial enterprise.

IR has been run on ideological grounds and not as a commercial enterprise. It has been operating uneconomical routes, and cross-subsidising losses in passenger traffic through revenues from cargo movement. IR has excess staff and 50 per cent of revenue goes to employee remuneration and benefits. Ever increasing freight tariffs are forcing several customers to shift to roads. There has been considerable loss of traffic in cement, petroleum and iron and steel.

By and large, the railway journey is still a nightmarish experience as it was 100 years ago (See Box 24.3). Obviously, many passengers are shifting to road transport. Journey by trains is not safe too as a major accident occurs every three months (see also Box 24.4). By the turn of the millennium, a quarter of the tracks, 40,000 coaches and wagons, several hundred bridges and thousands of signals had outlived their service life.

Box 24.3 **Facilities in Railways 86 Years Ago**

(Letter written by a traveller in 1909)

Dear Sir,

I am arrive by passenger train Ahmedpur station and my belly is too much swelling with jackfruit.

I am therefore went to privy, just doing the nuisance that guard making whistle blew for train to off and I am running with lotah in one hand and dhoti in the next when I am fall over and expose all my shocking to man and female women on platform. I am got leaved at Ahmedpur station. This too much bad. If passenger go to make dung that dam guard not wait train five minutes for him. I am therefore pray your honour to make big fine on that guard for public sake. Otherwise I am making big reports to papers.

Your faithful servant
Okhil Ch.Sen.

Box 24.4 **OFF TRACK: The Railway Accident Roster**

	Brief Particulars	**Killed**	**Injured**
18 Apr' 89	Derailment of 927 Dn Karanataka Express between Lalitpur and Dailwara stations of Central Railway	69	216
1 Nov' 89	Derailment of 8 Dn Udyan Abha Toofan Express at Sakaldiha stations of Eastern Railway	50	60
16 Apr' 90	Fire in a coach of 383 passenger train near Gulzarbagh stations of Eastern Railway	75	47
21 Sep' 93	1593 Dn collied with 'N' SRE Up Goods between chhabra Gugur and Bhulon stations of Western Railway	78	88
14 May' 95	Head-on collision of 6019 Dn Madras kanya Kumari Express with Up Empty Super Jumbo goods train between Lokur and Danishpet stations on Palghat Division of Southern Railway	54	50
20 Aug' 95	Rear-end collision of 2801 Purshottam Express and 4023 Kalindi Express at Firozabad Station on Allahabad Division of Northern Railway	310	252
18 Apr' 96	Head-on collision between 583 Up Passenger and Dn GKP Tank Empty at Domingargh station of North Eastern Railway	54	84
14 Sep' 97	Derailment of 8033 Ahmedabad-Howrah Express between Naila and Champa stations on South Eastern Railway	88	369
5 Jan' 98	Rear end collision between 136 Dn passenger and 4258 Dn Kashi Vishwanath Express between Masit and Karna stations on Northern Railway	51	66
26 Nov' 98	Side collision between 3152 Dn Jammu Tawi-Sealdah Express and 2903 Up Golden Temple Mail between Khanna and Chawapil Stations on Northren Railway Ambala Division	209	140
21 Apl' 2005	Sabarmati Express rammed into goods train near Vadodara in Gujarat	18	114
20 Feb' 2007	Samjhauta Express Fire bombed near Panipat	68	50

It is argued that it is difficult to make IR accident-free because of its sheer size. One train is added nearly every day to its 63,000 km plus long network. Though most are freight trains, the addition of four express trains every month further burdens the staff who are already grappling with the task of transporting over 500 crore passengers every year.

IR has been initiating measures to improve its operations. Much attention is being focussed on upgradation of technology. Some of the high points have been the manufacture of thc state-of-the-art electronic locomotives (through technology transfer from ABB), diesel locomotives (technology transfer from GE) and light weight coaches with anticlimbing features.

Excess staff is the bone of contention with the IR.

The Special Railway Safety Fund (SRSF) amounting to Rs.170 billion has been set up for the replacement of overdue renewal assets by the end of 10th plan period.

One criticism against the IR relates to its excess staff strength. It has been limiting the hiring of additional staff. Between 1991-2001, the staff strength was cut by 2,62,000 reducing the number to 1.545 million. The target is to further trim the staff strength to 1.18 million by 2010 (Read also Box 24.5).

Box 24.5 **Strengths, Weaknesses and Remedies (Railways)**

A.Strengths

- Historical advantage- 85 percent of track being inherited from the British
- Largest in Asia and the third largest in the world
- Substantial electrified tracks
- Competitive advantage in project consultancy and construction
- Agenda for national integration

B.Weaknesses

- Ever increasing traffic load
- Inadequate finance
- Low productivity
- Low speed of goods as well as passenger trains
- Poor service to the passengers
- Absence of suitable transportation policy
- Too many social objectives
- Unslite Travel

C.Remedies

- Corporatise with detailed terms of reference approved by the Parliament
- Unbundle disparate operations like transportation of freight and passengers and equipment-manufacture
- Corporatise all manufacturing units and privatise them gradually
- Commercialise passenger services by abolishing all free travel, and privatise ticket-checking
- Phase out cross-subsidisation of passenger fares, through freight charges, so as to reflect real costs
- Make commercial use of railway property by selling or leasing it, to the private sector

(**Source**: Remedies from *Business Today,* October-November, 1996)

Roads occupy pivotal role in the economic development of any country. Road is the oldest and the most popular mode of transportation.

India has one of the largest road networks in the world (3.3 million km), comprising national highways (6556.9 km), state highways (131,899 km), district roads, rural roads, urban roads and special roads designed for defence purposes and for port connectivity. Together, Indian roads carry 85 per cent of passenger and 70 per cent of freight traffic.

India has one of the largest road networks in the world.

Organisational arrangements include the Ministry of Road Transport and Highways and the National Highways Authority of India to monitor and supervise national highways. State highways are managed by public works departments of respective state governments. Some states have specific road and building departments to develop and maintain state road networks.

The National Highways Authority of India has started the National Highways Development Programme (NHDP) aiming to four – laning of 13,146 km of national highways.

The NHDP involves three phases. The Golden Quadrilateral Project (in Phase 1) spans a length of 5,846 km of national highways and is designed to connect four metro cities - Delhi, Mumbai, Chennai and Kolkotta. The project is scheduled to be completed by December 2005. Phase 2 spans a length of 7,300 kms of national highways. This phase, also called North-South-East-West (NSEW), seeks to cut across the country diagonally, linking the northern tip at Srinagar to the southern tip at Kanyakumari and Porbandar in the west to Silchar in the east. Phase 3 involves the development of 10,000 km of roads.

The NHDP involves three stages-
Phase 1 – 5846 km
Phase 2 – 7300 kms
Phase 3 – 10000 kms

Road conditions in general are not good. Arterial roads suffer from severe capacity constraints. Most national highways are two-lane or single-lane. Only recently four-laning of national highways has started. Connectivity is another issue as 40 per cent of inhabitants are not connected by good roads. In addition, road safety is low. India has nine per cent of the world's road facilities while only 4.2 per cent of the world's vehicles fly on the Indian roads (Read also Box 24.6).

Shipping plays a crucial role in a nation's economy. Nearly 90 per cent of India's trade is handled by ships. India has 62.5 ships with gross registered tonnage of 69,44,206.

India has a rich maritime history, thanks to an extensive coastline and strategic location. During the 1970s and early 1980s, the Indian shipping industry flourished, achieving significant milestones. It had a well diversified fleet, soaring business and a well-developed shipping building and repairing industries. But today, Indian shipping is a miniscule component of the world's shipping industry.

India has a rich maritime history thanks to an extensive coastline, and strategic location.

Shipping is a central subject. The National Shipping Board advises the government on shipping matters. The industry is governed by three separate acts - the Merchant Shipping Act, 1958; the Inland Vessels Act, 1917; and the Coastal Vessels Act, 1838.

The state-owned Shipping Corporation of India dominates the industry. There is private sector participation also with Great Eastern Shipping, Essar Shipping, Varun Shipping and Shabi Shipping playing their due shares. In ship building, state owned Hindustan Shipyard based in Visakapatnam is the leader. India has seven public sector shipyards and about 20 small-to-medium sized shipyards in the private sector.

The present fleet of shipping companies is quite diversified as it has modern liner vessels, tankers, bulk carriers and semi-container ships as also ships catering to refrigerated cargos. But there are problems. The shipping industry was hit by severe recession, through since 2000 it has improved. Domination of foreign lines is another problem. Port facilities have not kept pace with the advancements made in shipping industry.

Box 24.6 **Strengths, Weaknesses and Remedies (Road Transport)**

A.Strengths

- One of the world's largest, stretching for almost 3.3 million across the country.
- Relatively low vehicle density per km.
- Ease the burden on railways.

B.Problems

- Only 1.6 percent of road strength is occupied by national highways, 5.86 percent by state highways and 92.54 percent by district and village roads. Except the national highways, the condition of other roads is pathetic.
- Several missing links, unbridged river crossings, weak culverts and inadequate road pavement enroute.
- Remote parts of the country are still not connected.
- Veritable death traps.
- Lack of adequate finance.
- Increasing pollution.

C.Remedies

- Allocate additional resources for upgrading and widening existing national and state highways.
- Create a highway development fund as an extra-budgetary development fund for funding highways.
- Set up a financing mechanism for funding road construction, using the toll system for cost recovery.
- Encourage private sector participation in highways by institutionalising build-operate-transfer schemes.
- Earmark a proportion of the state's levies on vehicles and fuels for road maintenance.
- Amend the loans to allow for Right of Way in land acquisition for laying roads.

(**Source**: Remedies from *Business Today,* Oct-Nov, 1996)

When we talk about shipping, ports cannot be left out. India has 160 odd ports along its coastline. But only a few of these are cargo handling installations. These include 12 major ports (controlled by the Union Government) and 40 minor ports in the private sector. 12 major ports handle three-fourths of the cargo traffic and the remaining carry one-fourth of the cargo.

Each major port is managed by a port trust, with a chairman appointed by the Central Government. The minor ports are under the administrative control of the respective state governments. Gujarat leads in minor ports having 20 of them.

Indian ports are governed by the Indian Ports Act, 1908, and the Major Port Trusts Act, 1963. All the major ports are under the regulatory authority of the Tariff Authority for Major Ports (TAMP), which determines tariff. Maritime boards oversee minor ports in Gujarat, Maharastra and Tamil Nadu.

Ports in general face several problems. Lack of modernisation, ineffective managerial practices, excess staffing, cumbersome operational procedures and absence of a multi-modal network are some of them.

The phenomenal growth of our merchant navy from a modest base of 0.2 m.GRT in 1947 to 6.3 m.GRT has placed our country 17th among the maritime nations of the world, realising the dream of

Jawaharlal Nehru, who was "*impatient to see Indian ships carrying the flag of India across the distant seas to far away countries*." Today, our shipping industry can boast of a modern versatile and technically superior fleet with an average of 13 years as against the world average of 17 years and is well equipped to compete in the international markets.

On the flip side, it needs to be stated that the nation is losing more than $10 billion because of the lack of efficient shipping services. China, which is keen on importing coal and chemicals from us and has recently signed air and shipping agreements is facing a unique predicament: *lack of direct shipping links*. This results in a loss of $1 billion. Other serious problems related to the congestion and poor turnaround time for ships. Around half the time at ports is used for unloading a ship (Read also Box 24.7).

The country is losing more than $10 billion because of the lack of efficient shipping services.

Box 24.7 **Strengths, Weaknesses and Remedies (Shipping)**

A.Strengths

- Long coastline of over 5700 kms and almost the whole of foreign trade passing across the seas.
- Largest merchant shipping fleet among the developing countries and 14th in the world in shipping tonnage.
- Skilled and competent managerial and ship board personnel.
- Huge potential in the wake of India becoming one of the signatories of the WTO. There will be considerable increase in sea-borne trade.

B.Weaknesses

- Limited cargo handling capacities of ports
- Challenge from containerisation which is highly prevalent in advanced countries.
- Fund starving.
- Undue hardships to ship owners due to conversion of FOB items into CIF which has been introduced because of decanalisation.

C.Remedies

- Amend the Major Port Trust Act, 1963, to allow private sector BOT projects at the 11 major ports.
- Raise the capital expenditure ceiling of the port trust boards from Rs.5 crore to Rs.200 crore.
- Abolish the need for PIB approvals for private projects that do not need port trust investment.
- Unbundle activities like cargo handling and warehousing into profit centres.
- Allow port-based businesses to create captive facilities for themselves under the BOT system.
- Initiate restraining programmes to reduce labour resistance to private sector participation.

(**Source**: Remedies from *Business Today, Oct 22-Nov 6, 1996*)

Civil Aviation has three functional sub sectors: operational, infrastructural and regulatory-cum-developmental. On the operational side, Indian Airlines Limited, Vayudoot (which functions as a separate identifiable division of Indian Airlines Limited) and private air lines (Scheduled and Non-Scheduled) provide domestic air services. Air India Limited and Indian Airlines Limited are domestic airlines which provide international air services. Pawan Hans Limited provides helicopter support services, primarily to the petroleum sector. Infrastructural facilities are provided by the International Airports Authority of India (IAAI) and the National Airports Authority (NAA). These two authorities are being merged to form a single authority *viz.* Airports Authority of India as a result of the enactment of the Airports Authority of India Act, 1994. The regulatory and developmental functions are looked after by the Ministry of Civil Aviation and the offices of the Directorate General of Civil Aviation.

The Air Corporation Act, 1953, was repealed on March 1, 1994, ending the monopoly of Indian Airlines, Air India and Vayudoot over scheduled air transport services. Six private operators, who were hitherto operating as air taxis, have since been granted scheduled airlines status.

With the policy of open skies, competition in the airline industry is heating up.

The competitive environment on domestic services has been, in effect, existent since April, 1993. By March 1994, 19 aircraft in the 120 plus category, belonging to private air taxis, were in operation. The natural consequence of creating a competitive environment in this sector was that, by March 1994, 25 per cent of the market was being catered to by private air taxis. The number of passengers carried by air taxi operators has increased from 15,000 in 1990 to 4.1 lakh in 1992, 29.2 lakh in 1993 and is expected to cross 35 lakh during 1994. Thus, Indian Airlines, on the one hand, had to share the market on its profitable trunk routes. On the other hand, it faced the threat of loss of critically skilled personnel to private operators who offered much higher emoluments. This affected its ability to optimally deploy its existing aircraft capacity. Indian Airlines has also geared itself since June, 1993 to the challenging task of adapting itself to a competitive environment. Several measures have been taken, mainly centred on making the organisation adopt a marketing approach to decision-making and considerably improve the quality of its product. It has improved its passenger facilities both on board and on the ground, on time performance, flight safety measures and has also increased employee participation to provide better services.

The Indian Airlines suffered a loss of Rs.235 crore during 1993-94, up by Rs.66 crore over the previous year. However, Air India earned a profit of Rs.200 crore in 1993-94 down by 40 per cent compared to the profit of the corresponding previous year.

Poor service, mediocre designs, poor maintenance, indifferent standards of operation and resource crunch are the major problems of civil aviation network.

There are problems at the aviation front. Poor service, mediocre designs, poor maintenance, indifferent standards of operation and resource crunch are the major problems beguiling our civil aviation network.

As on today there are five categories of air ports - international, joint venture, custom, domestic, and others. The total passenger traffic across all these five categories rose by 27.2 per cent during April-June 2004 as compared to April-June 2003. There was also an increase in the aircraft and cargo movements during this period. Aircraft traffic increased by 17.8 per cent in the same period and that of cargo traffic rose by 18.5 per cent.

Indian airports handled an all-time high of 59.3 million passengers in 2005. The figure, released by the Airport Authority of India, represents a 21.7% growth over the 48.7 million passengers handled in 2004. The huge growth places Indian airports among the fastest-growing in the world next only to China, where a few airports have reported higher growth.

The AAI manages 126 airports, which include 11 international and 89 domestic ones. Mumbai's Chhatrapati Shivaji Airport has historically been the top performer, with an 18% growth in traffic handling 15.7 million passengers in the year ended March 2005. Delhi airport grew faster at 23%, handling 12.8 million passengers. Domestic passenger numbers grew at a faster clip at 24.2%, while international passenger growth in 2005 was 16.7%.

Telecommunications

One infrastructural facility that has witnessed a revolutionary change is the telecom sector. This sector is witnessing technological advancements, greater competition, better service standards and lower prices. Consumers now have choices in any segment of any circle.

Basic services In the ongoing developments worst hit segment is the fixed line service. The subscriber base in this segment grew from 41.48 million on March 31, 2003 to 42.84 million on March 31, 2004, a growth of just three per cent. Experts believe that with this trend the fixed line service will be overtaken by mobile subscriber base in the immediate future.

Fixed line service is the worst hit.

The low growth in the fixed line segment is due to a combination of a low subscription rate and many subscribers surrendering their fixed line phones.

The talking point in the basic service segment has been the phenomenal growth achieved by CDMA-based WLL (M) operators. From a subscriber base of only 320,000 in March 2003, the industry added 7.25 million new subscribers by March 2004, thus registering an incredible growth rate of 2266 per cent. Reliance Infocom emerged as the largest WLL(M) operator with 6.47 million subscribers. The other key player is the Tata Teleservices Limited which had a subscriber base of 1.62 million by March 2004.

Cellular services By September 2004, the total number of cellular subscribers was 33.55 million. This sector has been attracting 1.4 million subscribers per month. The main reasons for this rapid expansion are aggressive marketing, and the falling prices of airtime and hand sets. The public perception of cellular phones has changed from that of a luxury item to an utilitarian device needed by even those in lower income groups.

Internet services The Internet subscriber base has grown from 3.32 million in 2003 to 4.92 million in 2004. There are about 189 Internet service providers operating across India. BSNL, VSNL and MTNL are the top players in Internet segment.

For a population of 1.08 billion, a subscriber base of 4.92 million is not encouraging. The main reason for low penetration of Internet is the high cost. Lack of accessibility is another reason for low subscriber base. However, realising the importance of information networking, the government has decided to give a major thrust to Internet connectivity and subscriber additions. It has announced a policy on accelerating Internet and broadband penetration in October 2004.

For a population of billion plus, an Internet subscriber base of 4.92 million is miniscule.

Private sector operators like Sify, Bharti, Reliance and TTSL are vigorously promoting Internet solutions like kiosks, cyber cafes, wireless broadband through mobile, and the like (Also read Box 24.8 and Box 24.9).

India has the largest network of *Post Offices* in the world. By the end of March 1994, the national postal network had over 1.5 lakh post offices. The long term objective was to locate a post office within 3 kms of every village. During 1993-94, a total of 637 additional extra-departmental branch post offices and 116 departmental sub-post offices were sanctioned. The department has also worked out plan to accelerate this effort by providing basic postal facilities on a contractual basis by utilising the existing infrastructure of Panchayats in these areas. The Panchayat Dak Sewa Scheme, formulated in this regard, has the twin advantage of reducing dependence on budgetary resources for expanding postal facilities to the needy areas and generating employment opportunities in such areas.

India has the largest network of post offices.

Box 24.8 **Milestones in India's Telecom**

1851	First telephones in India
1943	Government of India nationalised private telephone companies.
1984	Manufacture of subscriber equipment commences in private sector.
1985	Creation of Telecommunications Board and DoT within the Ministry of Communications.
1986	Creation of MTNL and VSNL
1989	Telecommunications Board replaced by Telecommunications Commission.
1991	Telecom equipment manufacture opened up to private sector. Major international players entered equipment manufacture.
1992	Value added services opened to private sector (subject to licence fees).
1993	Private networks allowed in industrial areas.
1994	Licences for paging in 27 cities issued.
May 1994	New Telecom Policy announced.
Sept 1994	Broad guidelines for private entry into basic services announced.
Nov 1994	Licences for cellular services in four metros issued.
Dec 1994	Tenders floated for bids in cellular services in 19 cities (other than four metros) on a duopoly business.
Jan 1995	Tenders floated for 2nd operator in basic services(in addition to DOT) on a circle basis.
July 1995	Cellular tender bid opened.
Aug 1995	Basic service tender bid opened amidst controversy. Most bids considered 'too low'. VSNL's Internet services commence.
Dec 1995	LoIs issued to some operators for cellular.
Jan 1996	Rebidding took place for basic services in 13 circles. The response was poor. TRAI formed.
March 1996	LoIs issued for basic service.

(**Source**: Rakesh Mohan Expert Group Report (1996) CMIE and other sources.)

Box 24.9 **Strengths, Weaknesses and Remedies (Telecommunications)**

A.Strengths

- Huge potential for expansion.
- Rapid growth in the last couple of years with annual growth of 13 percent between 1984 and 1994 and 20 percent thereafter.
- Relatively high density with 7.97 phones per 100 towns people ahead of China and Indonesia.
- High technology- 66 percent of exchanges are digital.

B.Weaknesses

- Waiting period of nearly two years to get new connections
- Poor maintenance- 218 faults for 100 lines every year.
- Privatisation efforts not successful.

C.Remedies

- Accelerate the clearance process for private sector entry into basic telecom services.
- Offer incentives to private telecom companies for meeting connection and low-fault targets.
- Resolve disputes between private operators and the DoT over long-distance connections immediately.
- Convert the DoT into a holding corporation, with its subsidiaries operating services in different circles.
- Replace the Indian Telegraph Act, 1885 with a new Act incorporating the impact of technology changes.

(**Source**: Remedies from *Business Today,* Oct 22-Nov 26, 1996)

CONCLUSION

Though the picture presented till now is impressive, there is no gainsaying the fact that our country lags behind in overall infrastructure development. Whether it is per capita energy consumption, number of telephone installations or percentage of good roads, we rank the lowest (See Table 24.4). Consequently, our country ranks very poorly in global competitiveness as Table 24.5 indicates. Obivously, this is not a good sign for a country which wants to invite foreign investments in a big way.

With regard to overall infrastructure development, India lags behind China.

Table 24.4 **Critical Comparisons**

	*Per capita energy used**	*Telephone lines per 1,000 persons*	*% of paved roads in good condition*
India	235	6	20
Pakistan	223	8	18
Brazil	681	63	30
Malaysia	1445	89	n.a.
Mexico	1525	66	85
S.Korea	2569	310	70
Indonesia	303	6	30
Thailand	614	24	50
USA	7662	545	85+

*Equivalent to kg oil

(**Source** : *World Development Report*, 1994)

Take a look at China, instead. In the past decade, China has built at least 12 major international airports, 29,000 kilometres of high quality four-lane highways and numerous renovated city centres and bustling shopping districts. It is using cutting technologies, including high-speed trains and newest telecommunication technologies. Its Guangzhou airport can handle 27 million passengers and one million tonnes of cargo a year. In comparison, all of India receives barely three million visitors a year.

In 2002, China made English a mandatory language starting from an early age and it is the top destination for foreign investment for three years running. Its Haier group (white goods), TCL Corp

Table 24.5 **India's Ranking in Global Competition**

(out of 48 countries)

Years	*Ranking*
1991	10
1992	13
1993	14
1994	41
1995	43

(**Source :** *World Competitiveness Report*, 2004)

(electronics and telecommunications), Bird International (mobile phones) and Lenovo group (computers) are expected to become global brands within 20 years. The Chinese are also very significant in oil, gas and energy, and heavy industries. No wonder, China is ahead of us in all respects.

But all is not lost. Better days are ahead of the country as Box 24.10 shows.

Box 24.10 **Better Days Ahead**

India's economic growth is intertwined with its infrastructure development and there is a strong positive association between the two. The infrastructure deficit continues to haunt India. Provision of quality infrastructure is vital for India to nudge its sustainable growth trajectory upwards.

A rapidly expanding telecom sector and intense competition amongst the various service providers have resulted in improvement in quality of the services and their affordability. Service providers have offered innovative and attractive value added packages in order to acquire, expand and retain their subscriber base. Increasingly, the mobile phone is being viewed as the instrument that will help bridge the digital divide. Competition and a growing economy will continue to raise the performance bar for the telecom sector in the medium term. The sector, however, would need to address and harness the challenges being posed to it by the Internet and the convergence architecture. The completion of substantial portions of the Golden Quadrilateral is fueling demand and facilitating the growth of productivity in the country. The model concession agreement (MCA), which has been finalised for the roads sector is expected to give a further impetus to the timely completion of the road projects.

MCAs are also being developed in the ports and airports sectors to facilitate PPPs. Privatisation of designated services will further improve the productivity of these sectors. Port connectivity is still the soft underbelly of the port sector and the current efforts to bolster it will improve freight movement in the medium term. The benefits of these new projects and initiatives would be visible after a time lag of a few years, as long gestation periods are usually associated with these projects. The power scenario in the country continues to be a matter of concern. Lack of reliable power supply dampens the growth impulses in different sectors of the economy.

With the ongoing reforms and better management of the coal and gas supplies to the thermal plants, the situation could improve.

Urban infrastructure is a crucial element of the Indian infrastructure scenario. The JNNURM is a significant step to address the important issue of urban infrastructure, but detailed planning will be required to implement this scheme successfully throughout the country.

(**Source:** *Economic Survey*, 2005-2006).

QUESTIONS

1. Outline the present status of infrastructual facilities in our country.
2. Point out the constraints which inhibit the rapid growth of infrastructual facilities.
3. Bring out the role of infrastructure in the economic growth of a country.
4. Bring out the strengths, weaknesses and remedies for different areas of infrastructure.
5. Comment on the new budget proposals for infrastructure development.

ASSIGNMENT

This chapter is full of statistical figures. Figures are really impressive. But why is that farmers in Andhra Pradesh are agitating? Why are roads are awful in several parts of the country? Make a study.

CHAPTER OUTLINE

Operations and Trends
Critical Assessment
- *Promotion of Small Scale Industries*
- *Promotion of Entrepreneurs*
- *Development of Backward Areas*
- *Industrial Development*
- *Other Features*

Narasimham Committee on FDIs
- *Appreciation*
- *Weaknesses of DFIs*
- *Recommendations*

The Road Ahead

LEARNING OBJECTIVES

After reading this Chapter, you should be able to:

1. Understand the meaning of development banks.
2. Analyse the operations and describe the trends of DFIs.
3. Make a critical evaluation of the role played by DFIs.
4. Recollect the findings of the expert committee on DFIs.
5. Carve the role of DFIs during the days ahead.

25 Development Banks

The financial sector is another segment of an economy, covering such areas as development banks, stock exchanges and monetary policy. Development banking is covered in this chapter. Stock exchanges and monetary policy will be discussed in the next two chapters.

Financial institutions, also called development banks or development financing institutions (DFIs), are owned and managed by the Central Government or the concerned State Government. This is so because, with the adoption of economic planning, building up an appropriate structure of financial institutions has become a necessity.

"It would be inconsistent," wrote E.Nevin, "with a general development programme if the financial mechanism by which the programme must be applied in practice is operating in a direction different from the priorities laid down by the government's economic policy."[1]

Development banks are owned and managed by the Central Government. There are 57 such banks in existence as on today.

Naturally, the government should make finance available to business, in an organised way, as an integral part of its broad strategy of planned development. The first step towards building up a structure of financial institutions was taken with the establishment of the Industrial Finance Corporation of India in 1948. Since then ,there was no going back. At regular intervals, either a new institution was setup or an existing unit in the private sector was taken over by the government. As of today, we have 57 DFIs in our country, catering to the different needs of industry. The break-up is as follows: (Also see Fig. 25.1)

A. All-India Financial Institutions (AFIs)

Industrial Development Bank of India (IDBI) (now merged with IDBI Bank).

Industrial Finance Corporation of India Ltd (IFCI).

Industrial Credit and Investment Corporation of India Ltd. (ICICI).

Life Insurance Corporation of India(LIC).

Figure 25.1 **All Financial Institutions**

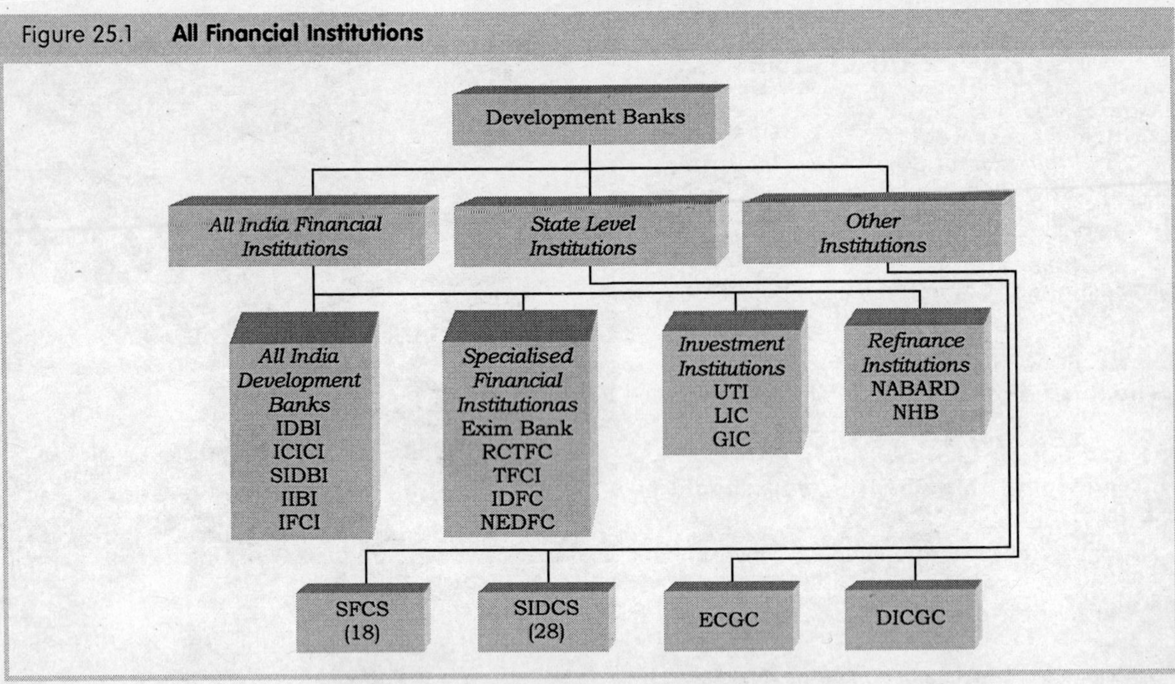

General Insurance Corporation of India(GIC).

Unit Trust of India(UTI).

Industrial Investment Bank of India Ltd.

National Housing Bank.

Infrastructure Development Finance Co. Ltd.

Export-Import Bank of India(EXIM Bank).

Small Industries Development Bank of India(SIDBI).

Risk Capital and Technology Finance Corporation Ltd. (RCTFC).

Technology Development and Information Company of India Ltd.(TDICI).

North-Eastern Development Finance Corporation.

Tourism Finance Corporation of India Ltd.(TFCI).

National Bank for Agriculture and Rural Development(NABARD).

B. State-Level Institutions

State Financial Corporations(SFCs)-there are 18 SFCs in operation.

State Industrial Development Corporation(SIDCs)-there are 28 SIDCs in operation.

Technical Consultancy Organisation(TCOs)-there are 17 TCOs in operation.

IDBI is the premier institution which coordinates the activities of all other DFIs at the national and state levels.

C. Other Institutions

Export Credit and Guarantee Corporation (ECGC).

Deposit Insurance and Credit Guarantee Corporation(DICGC).

IDBI is the premier institution which coordinates the activities of all other DFIs at national and state levels.

Among the all India institutions, IDBI, IFCI and ICICI provide financial assistance to medium and large industries, whereas SIDBI caters to the needs of small and tiny industries. These institutions also undertake promotional and developmental activities. RCTC, TDICI and TFCI are called the specialised financial institutions. RCTC and TDICI provide risk capital, venture capital and technology development finance. TFCI extends finance to hotels and tourism related projects. LIC, GIC and UTI are called the investment institutions. The first two deploy their funds in accordance with the priorities set for them. UTI mobilises the savings of the society through the sale of units and channelises them into corporate investments. The investment institutions are major players in the secondary market; they also extend assistance to the corporate sector by way of term loans/underwriting/direct subscription to equity and debentures. The SFCs provide finance mainly to small and medium enterprises, whereas SIDCs cater to the needs of medium and large industries in their respective states. Apart from providing financial assistance, the SFCs and SIDCs also play promotional and developmental roles. TCOs provide, under a single roof, a total package of consultancy services to small and medium enterprises at reasonable rates. TCOs render consultancy services to individual entrepreneurs, government departments and agencies, various state level developmental/ financial institutions, commercial banks and other institutions in their tasks relating to industrial development and financing.

IDBI, IFCI and ICICI cater to the needs of medium and large scale units. SIDBI finances small scale units.

The financial institutions have been providing term finances to the industry in the form of loans, underwriting/direct subscriptions to shares/debentures and guarantees for almost four decades. Over the years, the institutions have developed and introduced a variety of products and services to meet the growing needs of the corporate sector. Besides expanding the scope of their financing activity, the institutions have diversified into newer fee-based services offering an array of services such as merchant banking, debenture trusteeship and forex services.

Financial institutions lend term loans to business units in the form of loans, equity participation and guarantees.

In tandem with the emerging needs of industry in the liberalised environment, these institutions have reoriented their policies and assistance structure with much sharper customer focus, by developing and introducing a variety of products and services. In the post-reform period, AFIs set up several subsidiaries/associate concerns for offering a wide range of such newly developed products and services as also for capital market infrastructure development covering such areas as commercial banking, investment banking, non-banking finance, investor servicing, broking, venture capital financing, infrastructure financing, custodial services, electronic trading in stock exchanges, capital market regulation, registration and transfer services, credit rating and e-commerce.

In tune with the demands of liberalisations, these institutions have come out with new products and services.

OPERATIONS AND TRENDS

The aggregate sanctions and disbursements of all financial institutions are shown in Table 25.1.

As seen from Table 25.1, the cumulative sanctions and disbursements during 1999-2000 stood at Rs.10,43,408 million and Rs.684,804 million respectively. Certain trends can be observed from the assistance provided by the financial institutions.[2]

1. While the absolute amount of assistance provided has increased over the years, there has been a continuous decline in the share of assistance in the total cost of projects sanctioned. The decline has been mainly due to the increasing contribution made by the promoters of projects. Another factor has been the absence of large projects seeking assistance.
2. The development banks which concentrated largely on long-term finances have now widened their operations to medium term finance such as asset financing, deferred payment system and the like.

Table 25.1 **Assistance Sanctioned and Disbursements by All Financial Institutions**

(Rs.million)

Year	*Sanctions*	*Growth Rate %*	*Disbursements*	*Growth Rate %*
1990-91	191961.0	32.8	128101.0	32.9
1991-92	223148.0	16.2	162729.0	27.0
1992-93	331933.0	48.8	231525.0	42.3
1993-94	409870.0	23.5	266243.0	15.0
1994-95	578324.0	41.1	335772.0	26.1
1995-96	599363.6	3.6	386979.7	15.3
1996-97	501418.2	(-)16.3	429427.4	11.0
1997-98	749355.0	49.4	536560.1	24.9
1998-99	837943.5	11.8	583947.2	8.8
1999-00	1043407.6	24.5	684804.2	17.3
Cumulative upto end March 2000	6181747.2		4354065.1	

(**Source**: IDBI, *Report on Development Banking in India*, 1999-2000, p.6)

3. The repeal of the convertibility clause since 1992 has its impact on lending. Financial institutions are now demanding equity participation from borrowers at the time of loan negotiation. There is also some trade-off between equity participation and the rate of interest. The equity offering encourages institutions to consider charging lower rates of interest. The companies also prefer to raise the debt component of the project through the capital market either fully or to some extent.
4. The relative role of development banks is on the decline while that of the investment institutions- LIC, UTI and GIC is on the rise. With access to concessional funds being phased out, development banks have lost their competitive advantage. At the same time, much of their funds are tied up in long term loans, resulting in a shortage of lendable funds. They have to rely increasingly on capital markets to raise funds which are more expensive.

CRITICAL ASSESSMENT

The role of development banks has been praiseworthy in the following areas:

Promotion of Small Scale Industries

Financial institutions have done immense service to the cause of SSI sector.

Small-scale industries, as was stated in an earlier chapter, have a place of importance in achieving the national objectives of increased industrial production, generation of additional employment, more equitable distribution of income and reducing regional disparities.

Among the development finance institutions, SFCs operating at the state level promote and provide assistance to small industries. The National Small Industries Corporation at the state level assists small units in the procurement of raw materials and in marketing their products. They also operate hire-purchase schemes for the purchase of machinery and equipment.

With increasing support of DFIs, the small-scale industries have played a vital role in the economy. The contribution of small-scale industries to the net domestic product of the manufacturing sector as a whole is about 50 per cent at present. Nearly a fifth of the country's total export earnings is earned by the SSI sector.

Promotion of Entrepreneurs

Financial institutions have been promoting entrepreneurial activities.

The development finance institutions have taken a number of measures aimed at the identification and training of potential entrepreneurs. The IDBI along with other financial institutions and commercial banks has sponsored 17 technical consultancy organisations (TCOs) covering the entire country. The basic objective of TCOs is to provide to entrepreneurs a package of services such as preparation of feasibility studies and project reports, providing technical and management services for sorting out operational problems etc. Financial institutions have also been regularly sponsoring appropriate entrepreneur development programmes. They also extend assistance to new technicians and professional entrepreneurs who have the necessary ability to run and manage projects but lack the necessary financial resources. To supplement the efforts of such promoters to raise adequate equity capital, institutions have introduced special Seed Capital Schemes to provide assistance in the form of equity capital to new entrepreneurs. The IDBI operates its Seed Capital Scheme directly as well as through SIDCs and SFCs. Under the scheme, eligible new technical and professional entrepreneurs are extended seed capital assistance, subject to a maximum of Rs.55 lakh per project on very soft terms, to fill in the gap between the equity capital an entrepreneur can actually bring in and what is normally expected from him. The IFCI also provides seed capital in the form of interest-free loans to entrepreneurs. For this purpose, it has sponsored an institution - the Risk Capital Foundation.

Development of Backward Areas

The role of financial institution in the removal of imbalances is no less significant.

At the time of independence, the Indian economy had already acquired a modest industrial base. Whatever industrial development that had taken place, however, was in response to the emerging market conditions and as a result of planned effort. After independence, balanced regional growth became a major goal of the national economic policy. The financial institutions have been encouraging the flow of assistance to industrially-backward areas by offering concessional interest rates and liberal financing norms, such as lower promoter's contribution, higher debt-equity ratio and longer moratorium and amortisation period.

As seen in the Table 25.2, cumulatively upto March 31, 1994 sanctions to backward areas aggregated to Rs.26,286.3 crore.

Development of backward regions is a highly complex process. Even with the best of intentions and change in attitudes, financial incentives alone will not be adequate to ensure the setting up of projects in backward areas at the desired pace. Considerable preparatory and promotional work has to be done to instill an industrial culture. The promotional efforts should include identification of project ideas, preparation of feasibility studies and managerial and entrepreneurial talents, providing managerial and technical assistance, continuous follow-up and monitoring projects.

Table 25.2 **Assistance to Backward Areas**

(Rs.crore)

Sector	*1991-92*	*1992-93*	*1993-94*	*Cumulative upto end March, 1994**
Backward areas	2131.6	2958.0	3403.0	26286.3
Non-backward areas	4399.1	6240.1	9508.1	46825.8
	6530.7	9198.1	12911.1	73112.1

*Includes assistance to the small scale sector upto end March, 1990.

(**Source**: IDBI, *Development Banking*, 1993-94).

Industrial Development

The DFIs have come to occupy a place of importance in the planning and promotion of industries in the country. Responding to the emerging requirements of industrial and economic growth, they have not only continuously increased the flow of assistance, (Read Table 25.3 for lending to corporate sector by just one institution, viz., IDBI) but also developed a coordinated approach towards industrial financing. Within a span of 25 years or so, a wide network of DFIs has been established with some of them specialising in particular areas of development finance. At the same time, all DFIs have introduced important organisational changes, including decentralisation and delegation of powers to their branch offices. Lending procedures have undergone changes in response to the emerging requirements and as a result, the process of appraisal of project finance proposals as also sanctioning and the disbursal of assistance has become considerably simpler and quicker. Simultaneously, consistent with their role as catalysts in economic development, the financial institutions have been continuously enlarging the scope of theiroperations from providing financial assistance to the identification of industrial opportunities, identification and training of entrepreneurs, provision of techno-economic consultancy facilities, industrial research and other promotional activities.

Table 25.3 **IDBI's Financial Assistance**

(Rs.Crores)

	Sanctions	*Disbursements*
1990-91	6331	4501
1991-92	6339	5769
1992-93	9285	6737
1993-94	12153	8100
1994-95	18607	10648
1995-96	19469	10636

(**Source**: *Report on Development Banking in India,* 1995-96, IDBI)

Other Positive Features

- Long-term finance has been provided at fixed interest rates, thus doing away with considerable uncertainty to cash flow that a variable interest rate mechanism would have imparted;

- A substantial portion of equity of the new projects has been taken up by these institutions;
- These institutions have by and large, kept their financial position on sound lines; and
- They have promoted specialised financial institutions during the past decade[3].

The weaknesses of development banks are many. The prominent among them are:

1. The profitability of the financial institutions has been low for obvious reasons. In the first place, quality of their portfolio has been poor. Until recently, there was a system of industrial licensing and once a licence was granted to an industrial unit, the term lending institutions did not bother to follow the required standards of project evaluation for loan approval. Besides, sick units were financed for employment considerations. Asset quality has, therefore, been poor.

Profitability wise financial institutions have lost heavily.

Certain financial institutions have been specialising in unisectoral lending. This sectoral concentration does not permit the diversification of portfolio and the total risk, therefore, increases. This has also led to the poor quality of portfolio.

2. The financial institutions have been operating in a competition- free environment. Development banks join hands with investment institutions and operate on a consortium basis. They act like a cartel. This is an unhealthy practice, particularly when these institutions jointly own a large part of the corporate debt and equity. The borrowers, however, have found the consortium approach advantageous as they were assured of the required finance. But it is high time that a competitive environment is gradually introduced for the efficient functioning of these institutions, for better customer service at low cost and for safeguarding against scandals.

Development banks have joined hands with investment institutions to form cartels thus killing competition.

3. Government control and political influence are damaging the institutions to a considerable extent. The situation is much worse at the state level, where state financial institutions are treated like government departments by the political bosses. These institutions should be made autonomous in the true sense by appointing professional people, rather than politicians at the top management levels. Loan sanction should be based on proper financial and technical criteria of the project and not be guided by extraneous considerations[4].

4. Majority of the financial institutions have shown interest in the direct market purchase of shares than providing initial capital or underwriting issues. A close look at the activities of some of those development banks would reveal that they have mainly purchased shares of erstwhile FERA companies than financing new projects. The motive has been to earn more profits. Even where these institutions can underwrite the economically viable and socially necessary but smaller projects, they have preferred to invest their funds in subscribing to the new issues of the existing companies.

Several financial institutions are showing interest in purchase of shares than lending initial capital or underwriting issues.

This coupled with the latest trend of investing more in debenture stocks for a secured interest earning as well as limited-time liability and convertible bonds, diverts investible funds more to existing large companies than to the upcoming small and young entrepreneurs.[5]

5. The gap between sanctions and disbursements has been widening as shown in Table 25.4

This gap reflects laxity on the part of term-lending institutions in the area of resource mobilisation.

Claims notwithstanding, regional inbalances continue to persist.

6. Though tall claims are made about the role of development banks in removing regional imbalances, analysis of their lending reveals a totally different picture. For instance, during 1994-95, the four industrially advanced states like Gujarat, Maharastra, Tamil Nadu and West Bengal were sanctioned projects worth impressive sums of Rs.15,031 crore, Rs.10,492 crore,

Table 25.4 **Disbursement/Sanction Ratio**

(Percentage)

	1992-93	*1993-94*	*1994-95*	*1995-96*
IDBI	69.78	64.61	53.55	44.6
ICICI	57.44	51.97	45.66	38.9
SCICI	63.91	59.27	38.73	28.6
IFCI	73.83	57.75	49.63	33.1

(**Source**:*Business World*, 10-23, July 1996)

Rs.7,507 crore and 7,108 crore respectively, industrially backward states *viz.*, Uttar Pradesh, Rajasthan, Orissa and Madhya Pradesh could get sanctioned measly sums of Rs.2,303 crores, Rs.2,269 crores, Rs.2,197 crores and Rs.1,359 crores respectively. Development banks, as with captains of industry, have gone in search of green pastures to invest their funds.

Nor the role of development banks in removing sickness is noteworthy.

7. Development banks could not tackle the problem of growing sickness. The approach, to remedy sick units, till now has been on predictable lines-deferment of interest, funding of interest, rescheduling of loans, and provision of further finance- which has not made any dent. What is needed is pro-active approach to anticipate maladies early and to take steps in order to prevent their occurrence.

8. State Financial Corporations have their own weaknesses. There were times, not long ago, when commercial banks were envious of State Financial Corporations (SFCs), the main direct term lending institutions for small scale industries (SSIs) and other small businesses, on the ground that the SFCs were empowered by statute to seize assets in case of overdues, while banks and central financial institutions had to put up with inordinate judicial delays to lay their hands on collateralised assets.

Now, the position is reversed. Banks and central FIs have been empowered copiously by the new law on recovery of dues, while SFCs face an uncertain future. A working group appointed by the Reserve Bank of India (RBI) on development financial institutions (DFIs) has recommended the winding up of the SFCs, saying they have "outlived their utility". The group (headed by N.Sadasivan, Banking Ombudsman, Maharashtra) pointed out that the non-performing assets (NPAs) of the 18 SFCs varied from 38 per cent to 99 per cent, and that hardly four of them were viable. It blamed the "single product" (term loan) character of SFCs, lack of professional expertise, lack of clarity as to who was the statutory regulator of SFCs and emergence of universal banking practices by commercial banks for the present plight of SFIs.

The role of nominee directors in the boards of loanee firms has not been effective.

9. Development banks, over the years, have acquired majority stakes in several firms in the private sector as box 25.1 indicates. Their nominees are board members of these companies. But these directors have not been playing proactive roles in running the companies successfully. The directors are being accused of being indifferent and apathetic. Things have now changed for better. The nominee directors are now taking active interest in the affairs of the loanee companies.

NARASIMHAM COMMITTEE ON DFIS

The Narasimham Committee which submitted its report in 1991 has both appreciation and criticism on DFIs. Following are its views and recommendations:

Appreciation

The Committee feels that in the last 40 years or more, the DFIs have largely succeeded in meeting their primary objective of providing funds for industrial investment. They have also tried to channel increasing flow of assistance to industrially less developed states and backward areas. The corporate sector has come to rely increasingly on the DFIs. Over the years, the DFIs have been increasing their share in the equity of the private corporate sector, have representation in the boards of management of companies (see box 25.1) and played a major role in corporate mergers and acquisitions.

Box 25.1 **FIs in Drivers' Seats**

Name of Company	*Group Share(%)*	*Promoters*	*FIs Share (%)*
ACC	Tata	11.96	40.70
TISCO	Tata	10.85	44.93
TELCO	Tata	19.26	40.73
Mysore Cement	Birla	20.66	48.07
VXL	Birla	18.54	35.12
Mahindra & Mahindra	Mahindra	8.35	46.35
Mahindra Ugine	Mahindra	23.73	64.11
Kirloskar Pneumatic	Kirloskar	23.53	60.63
Best & Crompton	Mallya	18.38	55.78
Modi Rubber	Modi	26.49	51.08
Calcutta Electric	Goenka	12.19	48.94
Kamani Engineering	Goenka	32.00	41.00
Dunlop	Chabria	5.39	34.69
Ashok Leyland	Hinduja	3.46	38.68
Larsen & Toubro	-	-	41.04
S.I.Shipping	Essar	26.43	56.51
Usha Rectifier	Rai	24.63	66.30
SPIC	MA Chindambaram	14.36	46.81
Escorts	Nanda	14.39	44.54
Bharat Gears	Raunaq Singh	14.82	42.18
TVS Electronics	TVS	12.14	58.69
India Cements	Sankar	11.65	50.46
SRF	DCM	1.3	56.57
Lakshmi Machines	Lakshmi	20.75	44.49
Premier Tyres	Desai	19.34	51.73

(**Source**: *Economic Times,* June 19, 1992)

From the very beginning, DFIs have enjoyed a privileged and concessional access to resources through the SLR mechanism. Besides, they were able to raise funds from the market at the relatively low and stable rate because of the guarantee offered by the government. At the same time, the lending rates of the DFIs were also low and stable, but the spread between the borrowing and lending rates was reasonable and enabled the DFIs to earn a reasonable rate of return.

In recent years, however, these conditions have been changing. There has been increasing competition from other parts of the financial sector, there is pressure on the availability of privileged and concessional funds through banks, SLR investments and there is progressive deregulation of interest rates. All these points clearly indicate the need for DFIs to become more competitive, more efficient and more profitable.

Weaknesses of DFIs

According to the Committee, the DFIs have suffered some decline in profitability in recent years, even though the all-India institutions, by and large, have managed to retain their financial viability. This has been due to certain weaknesses in their loan operations.

In the first place, the Indian licensing system has been deficient in the sense that it has led to the promotion of several unviable projects by entrepreneurs without proven competence. The DFIs have been induced to finance them, often through considerable and unwanted relaxation in the appraisal standards.

Secondly, the government's policy regarding the nursing of sick units has forced DFIs to provide financial support to sick units against their better commercial judgment.

Thirdly, state level institutions have been working as wings of State Governments rather than as autonomous financial institutions.

Finally, there is a total absence of competition to DFIs' operations in the field of term finance.

DFIs have been operating almost like a cartel, since different institutions join together and offer consortium finance. Borrowers have a limited choice in the matter of selecting an institution for financing their projects. The advantage of the system of consortium finance is that the borrowers need not approach several institutions for arranging their finance, but the disadvantages as pointed out by the Committee are:

- if the consortium rejected an application of a borrower, he did not have any other option and
- it militates against the participating institutions developing a sense of accountability and responsibility for a large portion of their portfolio.

Recommendations

The recommendations of the Committee are based on its assumption that the DFIs are relevant in the Indian context, even though their promotional and developmental role can be expected to diminish as the Indian economy acquires greater sophistication with greater industrial development. At the same time, with the progressive deregulation of the industry and curtailment of the area of industrial licensing, the responsibility of developing on DFIs would be much greater. The major recommendations can be summarised as follows:

(i) The ownership pattern of DFIs should be broad-based, like that of ICICI.

(ii) The government should work out an action plan to be implemented in the next three years which would usher in a measure of autonomy of the DFIs in matters of internal administration.

(iii) The appointment of chief executives of DFIs (as in the case of banks) should be men of proven professional competence and should be selected on the recommendations of a panel of eminent persons.

(iv) The boards of DFIs should include representatives from the industrial sector.

(v) In the case of state-level financial institutions, the link with the State Governments should be broken and these institutions should be helped to work with improved efficiency, take up only that number of projects which they can efficiently follow up and recover their dues and approach the capital market for their funds.

(vi) The DFIs should raise their funds from the capital market at market-related rates. They should also mobilise the savings of the household sector through some schemes which do not conflict with the commercial banks.

(vii) As regards loan sanctions, each DFI should have the sole responsibility in loan sanctions. It should be guided by professional appraisal of the technical and economic aspects of the project evaluation of the promoters, competence and integrity. The DFIs should supervise their own loan implementation.

(viii) The present system of consortium funding should be given up. The cross-representation in each other's boards is no more necessary with the giving up of consortium funding.

(ix) The role and functions of IDBI should be changed. The IDBI should retain only its apex refinancing role and its direct lending function should be transferred to a separate institution which could be incorporated as a company.

(x) In the matter of corporate take-overs, DFIs should lend support to existing managements with proven record beneficial to all concerned, except in these cases where the new management can do better. In all cases, the DFIs should exercise their individual professional judgements free of any pressures.

The Committee has proposed that DFIs should adopt internationally accepted norms, restore capital adequacy, inject an element of competition in term lending finance with a view to providing greater choice to the borrowers. The Committee has also recommended that commercial banks should be encouraged to extend term finance while the DFIs should start extending loans for short periods for working capital requirements.

THE ROAD AHEAD

The days ahead offer the following new vistas for development banks:

1. As box 25.1 shows, development banks are holding majority stake in the equity of the borrowing companies. They are in a vantage position to bring about better corporate governance which will be the need during the coming days. Regretfully, role of the financial institutions till now has been passive as revealed by the recent happenings in ITC.
2. There is a need for gradual privatisation of the development banks in a phased manner. Ensuring true autonomy to these institutions will generate competitive spirit and will subject them to market discipline. Besides, privatisation will gve them the incentive to introduce financial innovation and improve their financial viability. The process of disinvestment can start with ICICI, which is the most successful institution.
3. As mentioned earlier, the approach of development banks towards project evaluation should be different in the post-liberalisation era. In the pre-reform days, any licensed unit could get loans without detailed evaluation. Infact, licence itself was enough to obtain loans. In the days ahead, any project must be subject to close scrutiny to determine its economic viability before sanctioning assistance.
4. Concessional funds have almost dried up and as a result, financial institutions are forced to mobilise their own resources from money and capital markets through innovative products. Securitisation of assets has a potential to resolve the resource crisis through the faster turnover of assets. Asset securitisation, which was widely used elsewhere, has not taken off in our

country, largely due to problems associated with stamp duty, income tax and accounting treatment.

5. Technology development financing would be another new direction in which institutional finance would flow in future. The objectives of this would be towards induction, absorption and development of the latest technologies into the country, in 'sunrise' industries like electronics, bio-technology, pharmaceuticals, engineering, plastics etc. Venture Capital Financing (VCF) introduced by the ICICI and other institutions would be a major instrument in this respect. Unlike traditional financing, the VCF would largely relate to high-technology projects in the small and medium scale selectors. VCF would also contribute to new entrepreneurial development. One distinguishing feature of VCF would, however, be the institutional right to share in the prosperity of the venture as a reward for the risks undertaken by them. VCF would, thus, be a blend of developmental and commercial approaches to project financing.

6. Concomitant with the maturing of the Indian economy and the rapid industrial development planned for the future, service sectors like transportation, communications, medicare, recreation and tourism, consultancy and computer software services, insurance and investment banking would assume greater importance in future. Institutions which have already made a beginning in this direction by financing hospitals, hotels, airlines and computer software houses would need to gear themselves to assist this sector in a larger way in future.

7. Turnaround finance or asset restructuring finance would be another major direction in which institutional finance would flow in future. Resulting from the extensive liberalisation measures introduced by the present government, the Indian corporate sector would have to move from the sheltered market of the past, and face the harsh but healthy winds of competition in future. This might necessitate companies to reorganise themselves to remain competitive by several means like disinvestments and acquisitions. An institutional portfolio is today burdened with non-performing loans, resulting predominantly from projects assisted because of developmental consideration. Considering the era of low spreads that is emerging for institutions, henceforth, a selective approach with a view to minimising non-performing loans would need to be followed in future. This could be achieved partly by mutual take-over, induction of new managements etc. Institutional support would need to be provided in future to the corporate section in the afore-mentioned efforts.

8. The shift in the flow of institutional finance covered till now relates mainly to the large and medium scale industries. However, the small sector assumes vital importance in the nation's efforts to achieve industrial pre-eminence by the turn of the century. Today's small-scale entrepreneurs are tomorrow's medium and large-scale industrialists. Hence, the need to focus institutional efforts in this direction. It is in recognition of this need that the government has formed the Small Industries Development Fund (SIDF) with a corpus of Rs.2,500 crore. This is expected to give a further boost to institutional assistance to the small-scale sector which has shown rapid growth during the last one decade. The small-scale sector has a tremendous potential, particularly in fields like ancillary units for automobile and engineering industries, textiles, garments, pharmaceuticals and pesticide formulations, food processing etc. In some of these fields, the small-scale sector cannot only produce for the domestic market, but with a conscious effort towards quality and cost, can also contribute substantially to the country's export drive. Besides, ensuring a growing flow of financial and non-financial assistance to the small-scale industry sector, the SIDF has the responsibility to provide a focal point for effectively coordinating the activities of the various organisations engaged in promoting the growth of this sector and also give a new thrust to their activities.

In line with the segmentation of the private sector investment in future into mega projects, large-scale projects, medium-scale projects and small projects, the future may witness a greater segmentation of the industrial sector, to service the needs of each of these sectors with greater efficiency.

9. The financial institutions recently have been instructed to monitor the end-use of funds raised by private sector units. This is an additional responsibility which the institutions must shoulder with competence in order to ensure that the funds raised by the companies are used for the purpose intended.

QUESTIONS

1. Review the performance of DFIs over a period of 10 years.
2. What are the new directions in which DFIs must proceed?
3. Bring out the recommendations of the Narasimham Committee.
4. Explain the challenges lying ahead of financial institutions.

ASSIGNMENT

Why is it that several premier development institutions have forayed into non-core activities? Study and make a report

REFERENCE

1. E.Nevin, *Capital Funds in Developed Countries*, p.56.
2. Ishwar C.Dhingra, *Indian Economy,* New Delhi, Sultan Chand and Sons, 1997, p.660.
3. *Ibid*, p.661.
4. Vijay L.Kelkar and V.V.BhanojiRao, *India-Development Policy Imperatives*, TMH, 1996, p.323.
5. Ishwar Dhingra, *op.cit*., p.662.

CHAPTER OUTLINE

Nature of Stock Exchanges
Functions of Stock Markets
Benefits of Share Markets
Growth of Stock Exchanges
Dealings in Share Markets
Organisation of Stock Markets
The Securities Contracts Act
– *Provisions of the Act*
Positive Features
Negative Features
Reforms

LEARNING OBJECTIVES

After reading this Chapter, you should be able to:

1. Define a stock exchange and describe its functions
2. Explain the benefits of share markets
3. Bring out the growth of stock markets
4. Describe the speculative dealings
5. Bring out the organisation structure of stock exchanges
6. List the provisions of the Securities Contracts Act
7. Evaluate functioning of all stock exchanges
8. Bring out the reforms of stock exchanges

Stock exchanges have attracted unusual public attention in the recent past. It all started with the unprecedented boom in share prices a couple of years back (BSE Sensitive Index touched a record 4,467 points from a base of 100 in 1978-79) followed by a series of setbacks. The downfall started with the unearthing of the securities scam. This is followed by free pricing of share issues with the repealing of the Capital Issues Control Act; strict enforcement of rules by SEBI and consequent skirmishes between SEBI and brokers; income tax raids; poor results revealed by companies and the absence of direct budget benefits to investors. The consequence of all these developments is that share prices got crashed and stock markets have become cool to new issues by companies.

For whatever the reason, share markets are in the news everyday. Unusual interest in the shares and stock exchanges has resulted in the addition of a few more words to the English language. For example, 'Big Bull', 'Scam', 'Bourse' and the like are readily used in conversation and writings on stock exchanges these days.

A time has, therefore, come to take a close look at the stock exchanges and the legislation which governs their functioning.

NATURE OF STOCK EXCHANGE

A stock exchange is a market where securities, i.e., shares, debentures and government securities are bought and sold. The Securities Contracts (Regulation) Act, 1956, defines a stock exchange as

> "an association, organisation, or body of individuals, whether incorporated or not, established for the purpose of assisting, regulating and controlling of business in buying, selling and dealing in securities."

A share market exists because certain owners of securities wish to sell them, others wish to buy them and the titles to the securities are transferable. A securities exchange does not itself engage in the purchase or sale of securities. Rather, its function is to make such trading as smooth and efficient as possible.

FUNCTIONS

The share market performs certain essential economic functions. It :

- Provides a ready market for buying and selling of securities;
- Performs an 'act of magic' as it enables long-term investments to be financed by funds provided by individuals who are otherwise interested in short-term or medium-term investment;
- Directs the flow of capital in the most profitable channels;
- Induces corporate enterprises to raise their standards of performance;
- Offers an easily understood evaluation of the financial conditions and prospects of listed firms;
- Facilitates speculation;
- Promotes the habit of saving and investment among the general public and thereby helps capital formation and
- Promotes industrial growth and economic development of the country by encouraging industrial investments rather than hoarding or investing in gold.

Because of its functions, the stock exchange is regarded as an essential concomitant of the capitalist system of economy. It is indispensable for the proper functioning of an corporate enterprise. It brings together large amounts of capital necessary for the economic progress of a country. It is the citadel of capital and the pivot of the money market. It provides necessary mobility to the capital and directs the flow of capital into profitable and successful enterprises. It is the barometer of general economic progress in a country and exercises a powerful and significant influence as a depressant or stimulant of business activity.[1]

BENEFITS

Speaking in the Lok Sabha in connection with his motion for reference of the Securities Contracts (Regulation) Bill to a joint committee of the Parliament in 1955, the then Finance Minister said; "The economic services, which a well-constituted and efficiently run securities market can render to a country with a large private sector, operating under the normal incentives and impulses of private enterprise, are considerable. In the first place, it is the only organised securities market which can provide sufficient marketability and price continuity for shares, so necessary for the needs of investors. Secondly, it is only such a market that can provide a reasonable measure of fair dealing in the buying and selling of securities. Thirdly, through the interplay of demand for and supply of securities, a properly organised stock exchange assists in a reasonably correct evaluation of securities in terms of their real worth. Lastly, through such an evaluation of securities, the stock exchange helps in the orderly flow and distribution of saving as between different types of competitive investments." Though the Finance Minister summed up the benefits of share markets succinctly, for the sake of greater clarity, its advantages can be analysed as follows:

Benefits to the Community

- Stock exchange encourages people to save and invest their savings in shares and debentures. The recent boom in share markets has created financial awareness among the middle class. The stock market has become a central factor in household financial planning.
- By encouraging people to save and invest, the stock exchange helps capital formation which is an essential ingredient for quicker industrial development.
- Through capital formation, the stock exchange enables companies to undertake expansion and modernisation schemes. Every company talks in terms of hundreds of crores of rupees of investments in new projects these days. The stock exchange is an Alibaba Cave from which business community can draw unlimited money.
- Stock exchanges encourage several closely-held companies to go public. This means that ownership is broad-based, management is diffused and more scrips are offered to the public for trading.
- Superior performance of companies is reflected through stock exchanges. Companies with a proven track record are considered to be blue chip companies and their shares and debentures are briskly traded in the share markets.

When an efficiently-run company issues shares or debentures the to public for subscription, there is a tremendous response from investors. A sort of record was established by Kinetic Honda when its issue was over subscribed by 150 times. Hero Honda Motors was offered Rs.46.8 crore for an offer of just Rs.4.46 crore. The role of share bazaars is no less in this unbelievable response.

- Stock exchanges provide a market for the government to sell its securities in order to raise funds for meeting developmental activities.
- Stock market acts as a mirror through which the general economic condition is clearly reflected.

Benefits to Investors

- Stock exchange is a money spinner-an El Dorado for millions of investors across the country. Investors become overnight rich, thanks to the stock exchange. "Bimal Jain, a New Delhi housewife", writes *India Today* (of July 31, 1985), "bought 500 debentures of Reliance Textiles a year ago at the then market price of Rs.92. The company then offered to convert these into shares, which are ruling at record levels. Jain's initial investment of Rs.46,000 is now worth Rs.1.56 lakh in barely a year."
- Stock exchange offers a ready market for buying and selling the securities. Share bazaar is the busiest market with crores of rupees being put at stake. The Bombay Stock Exchange, the premier share market, registers dealings worth several hundred crore a day.
- The interest of investors is safeguarded by the strict enforcement of rules and regulations. Every share market has its own by-laws besides complying with the provisions of the Securities Contracts (Regulation) Act, 1956. By-laws and provisions of the legislation protect the interests of investors, big or small.
- The stock exchange provides information about the scrips dealt therein and the prices at which they are quoted. All newspapers and periodicals carry columns on the stock markets. This enables investors in making a sound investment choice.
- More important is the fact that the stock exchange is a powerful hedge against inflation.

Benefits to Companies

- Wide market for shares and debentures.
- Image of the company goes up once the shares are listed on a stock exchange.

- Quicker response from the investors to the listed securities.
- The market rates of shares and debentures will be higher because of daily dealings on the stock markets. This enhances the bargaining position of a company in the event of its merger with some other company.

GROWTH

There has been a phenomenal increase in the number of stock exchanges, number of investors, the number of listed companies and market value of listed companies over a period of time. Between 1980 and today, the number of exchanges has gone up from nine to 23. The number of listed companies went up from 2265 from 1980 to 6480 in 1992, and the number of listed stocks increased from 3697 to 9642 (See Table 26.1 for more details).

Table 26.1 **Growth Pattern of Listed Stock**

(Rs.crore)

	1980	*1985*	*1991*	*1992*
No.of stock exchanges	9	14	20	21
No.of listed companies	2265	4344	6229	6480
No.of stock issues of listed companies	3697	6174	8967	9642
Market value of capital of listed companies (Rs.Crore)	6750	25302	110279	354106

(**Source**: Bombay Stock Exchange *Official Directory*, Vol.9)

DEALINGS

Stock exchange dealings are subject to the rules and regulations of the market and the provisions of the Securities Contracts (Regulation) Act, 1956. Dealings on the floor of any market are permitted only in the listed securities through the members and their authorised clerks during fixed working hours.

Membership is limited to Indian citizens. To become a member of a stock exchange, one should be above 21 years of age. Only an individual (not a firm or a company) can become a member. The application for membership should be sponsored at least by two existing members.

Two types of dealings are carried on the stock exchange: ready delivery contracts and forward delivery contracts; in two kinds of scrips, namely, 'A' group and 'B' group securities. Ready delivery contracts, also known as cash contracts or cash trading, are to be settled on the same day on which they are entered into, or within a period of seven days. Cash trading is allowed in 'B' group scrips. Forward transactions are settled on specified days which are fixed at fortnightly intervals. The buyer can carry transactions to another, sometimes for years together. Forward dealings are allowed in 'A' group scrips. 'A' group securities are also known as 'specified' securities and are big daddies of the market, like ACC, TISCO, Reliance and Century. It may be noted that forward dealings were banned by the government in 1969 and were reintroduced later.

Speculation

Transactions on a stock exchange are carried on either for investment or for speculation. Investment transactions are made with the intention of holding the investments more or less permanently. Ready delivery contracts, referred to above, are generally for investment purposes. Speculative transactions, on the other hand, are made with the intention of making quick money by selling securities when their prices shoot up. Forward transactions, described above, are generally carried on for speculative gains. Speculative transactions are more in number, and they keep stock exchanges active and busy.

Types of Speculators

Members of a stock market are of three types: bulls, bears and the stags. A bull, also known as the *tejiwala*, is a speculator who buys shares in the expectation of selling them later at higher prices. He makes money when the share prices are rising. When the share prices are rising, it is called a *bullish* trend. How does a bull ride the wave up? He buys low and waits. When the settlement day comes, he can take delivery of the shares, which means that he will now hold shares valued at higher than the prices he paid. If he does not have the money to take delivery or if he is very daring-nowadays the two go together-he can carry forward the transaction, paying another person contango charges (*badla* charges in the vernacular) to put the money on his behalf. These days, with hundreds of badlas every day, the badla financiers are making a packet. To cool the market down, the authorities impose margins, which means that a percentage of the money has to be paid to the stock exchange authorities.[2]

A bear, also known as *mandiwala*, is one who sells securities in the expectation of a fall in their prices in future. A bear rides the scrip on the way down by selling short, that is, selling a scrip at, say, Rs.100 and hoping to buy it back when it touches, say, Rs.80. His profit on a scrip which he may never have held in his hot little hands is the difference between the two prices.[3]

A stag neither buys nor sells but applies for subscription to the new issues expecting that he can sell them at a premium. The bulls, the bears and the stags are collectively known as *jobbers* or brokers. Brokers or their clerks, as mentioned earlier, alone can trade on a stock exchange.

ORGANISATION

There is no uniformity in the form or ownership of 23 stock exchanges that are functioning in the country today. Mumbai, Indore and Ahmedabad exchanges are organised as voluntary associations. Calcutta and Delhi Exchanges are limited companies and those of Chennai and Hyderabad are guaranteed companies. 14 exchanges are organised as limited companies six as companies limited by guarantee and three are voluntary non-profit agencies of the 23, only nine have permanent recognisation others seek renewal of recognition every year. Table 26.2 reveals the type of ownership of the first 15 stock exchanges.

Whatever the form of ownership, the stock exchange is managed by an executive committee/ council of management/governing body to which the government is empowered to nominate not more than three members. The rules and by-laws of the share market shall be in conformity with such conditions as may be prescribed by the government from time to time.

Table 26.2 **Types of Ownership**

Name of Exchange	*Type of Ownership*
1. *The Ahmedabad Stock Exchange*	Association
2. *The Stock Exchange, Bombay*	Ltd.Company
3. *Bangalore Stock Exchange*	Ltd.Company by shares
4. *The Calcutta Stock Exchange*	do
5. *Cochin Stock Exchange*	Ltd.Co.by guarantee
6. *Delhi Stock Exchange*	Ltd.Co. by shares
7. *Gauhati Stock Exchange*	do
8. *Hyderabad Stock Exchange*	Ltd.Co.by guarantee
9. *Kanara Stock Exchange*	Ltd.Co.by shares
10. *Ludhiana Stock Exchange*	do
11. *Madras Stock Exchange*	Ltd.Co.by guarantee
12. *Madhya Pradesh Stock Exchange*	Ltd.Co.by shares
13. *Pune Stock Exchange*	do
14. *The Uttar Pradesh Stock Exchange*	do
15. *Magadh Stock Exchange*	do

THE SECURITIES CONTRACTS (REGULATION) ACT, 1956

The Securities Contracts (Regulation) Act, 1956, is a legislation which empowers the government to regulate the functioning of stock exchanges in the country. The Act applies to the whole of India and has the following objectives:

(i) To prevent undesirable transactions in securities.
(ii) To regulate dealings in securities.
(iii) Regulation of stock exchanges.
(iv) Regulation of buying and selling of securities outside the limits of stock exchanges.

Provisions of the Act

The provisions of the Act provide for: (See Fig.26.1)

1. Grant of recognition to the stock exchanges.
2. Submission of periodical returns.
3. Power to direct rules to be made or to make rules.
4. Power to make or amend by-laws.
5. Power to supersede the governing body and suspend business.
6. Power to make listing of securities compulsory.
7. Power to impose penalties.

Figure 26.1 **Provisions of the Securities Contracts (Regulation Act)**

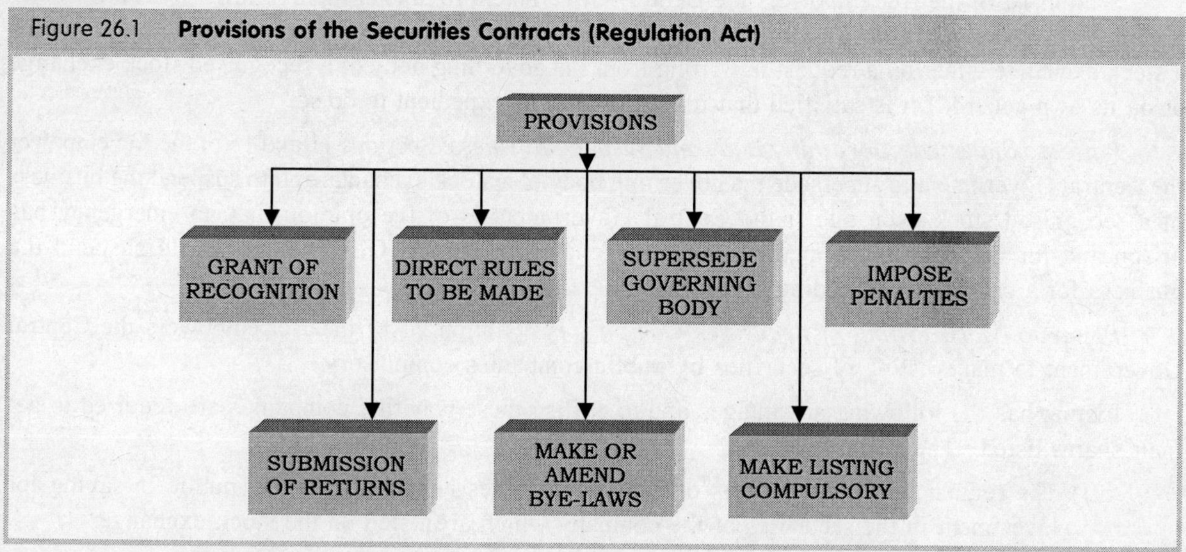

Grant of Recognition: The Act provides that only recognised stock exchanges can function in the country. As of today; all the 23 stock exchanges have been recognised by the government. Any exchange which is desirous of getting recognition should apply to the Central Government in a prescribed form, giving necessary details.

If the Central Government is satisfied that the information furnished is adequate, and the stock exchange concerned is willing to comply with the necessary conditions and it will be in the interest of trade and public to grant recognition to the stock exchange, then the Central Government shall grant recognition to the applicant stock exchange.

The grant of recognition of the stock exchange shall be published in the Gazette of India and will come into effect from the date of publication in the Gazette.

Submission of Returns: Sec.6 of the Act lays down that every stock exchange shall furnish to the Central Government such periodical returns as may be prescribed relating to its affairs. The periodical returns shall be filed by the recognised stock exchange before 31st January each year along with the detailed information as laid down in the Securities Contracts (Regulation) Rules, 1957.

Section 6 further provides that every stock exchange and every member thereof shall maintain and preserve for a period of five years such books of accounts and other documents as may be required by the Central Government.

Power to Direct Rules to be Made or to Make Rules: Section 8 of the Act empowers the Central Government to direct the stock exchange to frame rules or to amend rules already made in respect of the following:

(a) *Management of Stock Exchange*: Constitution of management of stock exchange and the manner in which the business of a recognised stock exchange will be transacted.

(b) *Duties and Powers of Office-Bearers*: The powers and duties of the office-bearers of the stock exchange; the admission of members into the stock exchange and their suspension, expulsion and re-admission.

(c) The procedure for the registration of partnerships as members in cases where the rules provide for such membership.

Power to Make or Amend Bye-Laws: Section 9 of the Act empowers the recognised stock exchange to make by-laws for the regulation and control of contracts with the previous approval of the Central Government.

Section 10 of the Act empowers the Central Government to amend the bye-laws as framed under Section 9 or to make bye-laws. The Central Government will exercise its power to make bye-laws for a stock exchange either on a request in writing from the governing body of a recognised stock exchange or on its own accord if it is satisfied that it is necessary or expedient to do so.

Power to Supersede Governing Body and Suspend Business: Sections 11 and 15 of the Act empower the Central Government to supersede the governing body of a stock exchange and to suspend the business of a recognised stock exchange if the Central Government is of the opinion that an emergency has arisen and for the purpose of meeting the emergency, the Central Government should suspend the business for a period not exceeding seven days.

Power to Make Listing of Securities Compulsory: Section 21 of the Act empowers the Central Government to make listing of securities by public companies compulsory.

Listing has the following advantages and to realise these benefits, companies are required to get their shares listed. The advantages are:

(i) The regular and latest reports on listed companies help the investing public in saving for investment in the securities of the company which are listed on the stock exchange;

(ii) The companies are under an obligation in terms of the listing agreement to inform its shareholders about the various corporate details and therefore, the listed companies keep approaching unintentionally to the investors, from time to time;

(iii) The transactions in listed securities are published widely in leading newspapers and journals and therefore, corporate details like working results, dividend announcements, expansion and diversification plans of the listed companies are also published.

(iv) On account of the liquidity, marketability and free transferability, which are conferred by the listing of the securities on a stock exchange, securities of the listed company qualify for preferential treatment for investment by institutional investors and foreign investors;

(v) An official quotation on the floor of the stock exchange is an important indicator to the company as well as to the investors as prices are arrived at publicly on the basis of demand and supply;

(vi) Listing of shares results in improved marketability as the confidence of the investors is enhanced due to regulation of the stock exchanges, trading procedures, greater liquidity, reduced risk etc. These, in turn, influence the price of a share;

(vii) Listing also adds to the prestige and importance of the listed companies;

(viii) Listed companies also enjoy certain concessions under the direct tax laws and official quotations are accepted by the tax authorities. If the shares are quoted on a stock exchange, the company will be treated as a company in which the public are substantially interested. Hence, there is benefit of lower tax rate and no compulsion to distribute profit.

(ix) Listing confers a collateral value for credit facilities for borrowing from banks; and

(x) Listing requirements provide for compulsory and timely disclosure of corporate information relating to dividend, bonus or rights issue, advance notice for closing the register of members etc., facilities for transfer, registration of rights and fair and equitable allotment.

Listing Requirements and Obligations

A company shall satisfy certain conditions for enlisting. Once listed, the company shall follow specific obligations. The following are the requirements and obligations:

(i) The memorandum and articles of association of the company must contain prescribed provisions;

(ii) The company must offer for public subscriptions through a prospectus at least the prescribed minimum percentage of its issued capital;

(iii) The company should inform the exchange authorities about the dividend distribution immediately after the board meeting;

(iv) The company should give an undertaking that it will comply with the provisions of the Companies Act and the Securities Contracts (Regulations) Act as well as the rules made thereunder;

(v) The company should notify to the stock exchange, without delay, of the date of meeting of its Board of Directors at which the recommendations or declaration of a dividend issue of right or bonus shares or convertible debentures or the passing over the dividend is due to be considered. Information must be given to the stock exchange in respect of the decision taken by the Board of Directors as referred to above;

(vi) Companies have to promptly forward to the stock exchange copies of the annual reports, notices, resolutions and circulars sent to the shareholders in order that those investors who are not shareholders of the company should also be informed of the affairs of the company;

(vii) The company should publish, in a form approved by the stock exchange, such periodical interim statements on its working and earning as it shall, from time to time, agree upon with stock exchange; and

(viii) The company shall keep the stock exchange informed of events like strikes, lockouts, closure on account of power cuts and so on, both at the time of occurrence of the events and subsequently, after the cessation of events in order to enable the shareholders and the public to appraise the position of the company.

Power to Impose Penalties

Section 23 of the Act lays down penalties for offence committed by individuals. Section 24 of the Act provides for the same but for offence committed by companies. The penalty may include imprisonment for a period of one year or fine or both.

Directorate of Stock Exchanges

The Directorate of Stock Exchanges is the implementing agency of the provision of the Act. The Directorate was set up in 1959 and is headquartered at Mumbai with branch offices in Delhi and Calcutta. The functions of the Directorate include the following:

(a) Acting as a link between stock exchanges and the Central Government;

(b) Keeping a close watch over the day-to-day operations of the stock exchanges and, in particular, checking over-trading or illegal transactions by brokers;

(c) Advising appropriate authorities in regard to untoward developments or expected crisis;

(d) Ensuring strict compliance with listing requirements on the part of companies and

(e) Issuing licence to dealers and brokers in securities in areas beyond the jurisdiction of recognised stock exchanges.

POSITIVE FEATURES

Stock exchanges in our country have grown in all directions overtime. Whether it is the volume of business transacted, mobilising resources for the corporate sector, promoting the habit of saving among people, or professionalising the management of the share markets themselves, the growth has been phenomenal. Particularly the eighties have been eventual in the history of the stock exchanges. A few important developments observed in the recent past in functioning of the stock exchanges are listed below:

1. The stock exchanges in our country have grown so sharply in the eighties that the decade itself has been christened as a decade of the capital market. The extent of growth can easily be measured by the fact that as against an annual average amount or just Rs.90 crore raised from the new issues market in the seventies, Rs.6,000 is being raised during 1989-90. The daily turnover in the Bombay Stock Exchange alone has shot up from about Rs.10 crore in 1979 to about Rs.300 crore in 1989-90. The turnover of National Stock Exchange now stands at Rs.1500 crore per day.
2. The number of shareholders has risen sharply from about a million in the beginning of the eighties to 12 million by the end of the decade. Shareholding population-wise, our country is the third largest in the world, next only to the US and Japan which have about 50 million and 25 million investors respectively. Along with the increase in the number of investors, the number of brokers has also gone up to about 3,000 active stock brokers as against about 1,250 a decade ago.
3. Yet another positive development relates to the broad basing of investing public. Contrary to popular belief that investors include only middle income groups from urban areas, peasants, peons, drivers and rickshaw pullers constitute a major chunk of investors. It is said that every eighth shareholder in our country today is a farmer.[4]
4. The share boom has resulted in several spin-offs. In addition to active brokers who number about 3000 as on date, there are about 30,000 sub-brokers and consultants spread all over country. Dailies and periodicals are being published exclusively to deal with financial and share movements.
5. The inauguration of Over The Counter Exchange of India (OTCEI) on August 14, 1990 signifies another landmark in the functioning of stock exchanges in our country. The Exchange is a Rs.10 crore venture set up jointly by financial institutions in order to provide easy and safe access to the capital market for companies.
6. Mega issues have become quite common nowadays. Rarely does a company come out with an issue of less than Rs.100 crore issue (see Table 26.3).
7. The final positive feature of our stock markets is the inflow of foreign portfolio investments. From 1993 onwards, roughly Rs.40,000 crore worth of securities have been picked up by foreign institutional investors. This accounts for seven per cent of the total market capitalisation.

NEGATIVE FEATURES

While the points listed above are positive, there are some negative features of our stock markets. Some of them are listed below:

Table 26.3 **Mega Issues between November 1995 to January 1996**

Company	*Issue size (Rs.crore)*	*Instrument*	*Issue*
SCICI	1311.00	Partly convertible debenture	Rights/Public
SPIC Petrochemicals	715.00	Equity	Public
Sanghi Cement	259.00	Fully convertible debenture	"
T.N.Newsprint	220.00	Equity	"
Lloyds Finance	200.00	Debentures	Rights/Public
Jindal Ferro Alloys	184.74	Convertible preference shares	"
Advance Radio Mast	180.00	Equity	"
Search Chem.Industries	141.30	Equity	Rights
Pitti Cement	114.77	Fully convertible debentures	Rights/Public
Subhagh Projects	109.58	Equity	Rights
Flex Engineering	100.00	Equity	Rights/Public

1. The first negative feature relates to poor liquidity. Barring a small proportion of scrips which are actively traded in stock exchanges and are highly liquid, most are traded infrequently and hence, lack liquidity. About 90 per cent of the total transactions in the stock markets are confined to 200 to 250 actively traded scrips (out of a total of 6480 listed companies).

Some more details are worth citing. There are nearly seven lakh companies in India, of which some 6,000 or so are listed in various exchanges. Though nearly 9,000 scrips are listed in exchanges, more than half were not quoted or traded during 2004. Another 25 per cent were quoted only a couple of times during 2004. The share of just the top 10 companies commanded nearly 45 per cent of the trade turnover during the year.[5]

2. The second negative feature of our stock exchanges is the absence of adequate instruments. Equities and equity-linked instruments such as convertible debentures are the only ones presently traded. Preference shares have virtually dried out of markets. Cumulative convertible preference shares, in respect of which the government had issued guidelines in 1984, have proved to be practically a non-starter.

3. Another disturbing feature is that our stock markets are virtually dominated by a few players. The stock markets are considerably influenced by the actions of a few financial institutions, particularly the Unit Trust of India and some speculative operations. Share prices, therefore, do not reflect the true demand and supply position of scrips.

4. Insider trading is yet another disturbing feature of our stock markets. Insider trading refers to the use of price sensitive corporate information by vested interests to make private gains or to avoid losses. This obnoxious practice is not peculiar to our county. It is there everywhere. But in other countries, there are suitable legislations to curb the evil practice. We are yet to evolve an appropriate legislation for the purpose though Sacvhar Committee (1978) and Patel Committee (1984) recommended the same.

The present provision contained in Section 307 of the Companies Act requiring shareholding and debenture holdings of directors to be recorded and kept open for inspection of any shareholder or debentureholder during the period of 14 days before and three days after the annual general meeting of a company has proved to be totally ineffective in controlling insider trading. Publication of half-yearly results by listed companies as required by Clause 41 of the listing agreement in operation since 1987 has also not minimised such trading (see also Box.26.1).

Box 26.1 **Insider Trading – Heavy Toll**

Different countries have legislation or a code of conduct to check the menace of insider trading. The US and UK have comprehensive legislation and monitoring bodies to ensure its strict enforcement. Countries like West Germany have a voluntary code of conduct to be followed by stock exchange dealers and banks to keep insider trading to the minimum.

The US Congress has strengthened the restrictions on insider trading by empowering the Securities Exchange Commission (SEC) to seek a triple penalty under the provisions of the Insider Trading Sanctions Act, 1984. Section 21 of the Act enables SEC to bring enforcement actions against violators of any provisions of the securities laws. Mr.Ivan F.Boesky, who made illicit profits of the tune of $203 million by insider trading, was convicted and sentenced for three years imprisonment in addition to a fine of $100 million.

In the UK, the Companies Act, the Company Securities (Insider Dealing) Act, 1985, and the Financial Services Act, 1986, contain comprehensive provisions to prevent insider trading. An individual is prohibited from dealing on a recognised stock exchange in the listed securities of a company with which he is, or at any time during the preceding six months has been, knowingly connected and by virtue of his connection possesses price sensitive information relating to the securities. A person is connected with a company for these purposes if he is a director of it or of a related company, or if he is an officer, employee or other person, standing in a professional or business relationship with a company, or its related company, whose relationship gives him access to the unpublished price sensitive information.

Recently a major toll of insider trading was the resignation of Mr.Geoffrey Collier, Securities Chief of Morgan Grenfell Merchant Bank, UK. Mr.Collier asked a stock broking firm to buy 50,000 shares of an engineering company, which was being taken over by another company, utilising the services of Morgan Grenfell as its corporate adviser. Mr.Collier, advising on the pricing and other details of the take-over, possessed full knowledge of the proposed bid. The stock broking firm informed Morgan Grenfell of the shares deal after the takeover bid was over. On inquiry, Mr.Collier admitted breach of conduct on his part and submitted his resignation. More recently, Mr.R.J.Brealey was arrested on the charge of insider trading on the London Stock Exchange under the Financial Services Act. It was reported that Mr.Brealey made a bid to acquire the controlling interest in shares of Titaghur Jute Factory (TJF) registered in Scotland, from Mr.Mehta and the Associates of Thomas Duff in Calcutta.

In Japan, three major insider trading scandals rocked its parliament and the business world. In Recruit Cosmos scandal, top politicians, civil servants and businessmen were involved. To buy favours from the government, 1,15,000 unlisted shares in Recruit Cosmos, a subsidiary of Recruit were offered under the table to politicians. They sold these in a month's time when the issue was made public in October 1986 and made profits of more than 250 million yen or $2 million. The Meidenko affair involved insider trading in shares of Sankyo Seiki. Nippon Steel secured a stake in Sankyo Seiki Manufacturing for 53 billion yen. An investigation by the Tokyo Stock Exchange found evidence that 30 to 40 employees of the two companies bought shares in Sankyo Seiki in the weeks before the public announcement of the deal in July 1988 and made unfair gains. In the third case, the Hanshin Sogo Bank, the lead bank to Tateho Chemical, sold its shares in Tateho, just a few hours before the company announced heavy losses.

5. Manipulation of share prices at the time of subsequent issues is a common occurrence. The process starts well before a company seeks permission from the concerned authorities for the issues of further capital. Not only an attempt to get a higher premium on the basis of prices manipulated is being made but attempts at manipulating prices continue thereafter to lure the investors to subscribe for these subsequent issues. Later when the allotments are made, it is quite a common spectacle to find these prices slide down to their natural levels, often below the offer price. While attempts to stabilise prices at the time of issues are understandable and also justifiable, the attempts to manipulate prices are reprehensible, to say the least. Equally reprehensible are the attempts by others, by the speculators or rival groups, to depress the prices. Unfortunately, we do not have a deterrent provision against price-manipulation in our stock markets.
6. Frequent entry into the market by some companies, particularly those involved in expansion, diversification and modernisation is truly indicative of the vibrancy of the Indian capital market. Unfortunately, the practice followed by some of them of delaying not only allotments but subsequently not returning shares lodged with them for sub-division, consolidation and transfer in time, thereby creating an artificial scarcity in the market with a view to manipulating the prices in the secondary market, has harmed the investors greatly. It is, therefore, essential to ensure that there is a time gap of at least one year between two consecutive issues or alternatively companies may be permitted to enter the market again only six months after the listing of the previous issues.
7. Permitting companies to offer convertible debentures with provision for conversion at two or three points, the latter towards the end, is indeed a welcome proposition as the market in these debentures continues to remain active because of the close linkage between equity and debentures. What, however, needs to be fixed right at the beginning are the terms of conversion, at all the points, including the last one. Leaving these terms open is tantamount to offering an open bait to the management to rig up the prices, which they can do more easily if the quantum of shares emanating after the initial issues is not significant to gain a higher premium.
8. There is the problem posed by the sub-brokers. There is a fairly good measure of protection to the investors from the stock brokers. While this has no doubt to be improved upon, the class of sub-brokers who have proliferated all over the country, both in the areas where recognised stock exchanges are situated and outside, pose a serious threat to investor protection. It is estimated that about 50 per cent of the complaints against the stockbrokers is because of the sub-brokers. On a rough reckoning, there are atleast 50,000 such sub-brokers not subject to any regulations, constantly posing serious threat to investors. Some of the sub-brokers in the jurisdictional areas of stock exchanges also commit the illegality of issuing contracts, bills, memos, etc. in their own names to lend authenticity to their operations and the gullible investors, who are not normally aware that these can legally be issued only by a member of a stock exchange in the jurisdictional areas covered by the stock exchange, fall prey to such gimmicks.

In order to overcome this serious lacuna in regulation, a working group set up by the Securities and Exchange Board of India (SEBI), has recommended a system of authorisation of these sub-brokers based on the criteria of professional competence, financial soundness and record of integrity and payment of suitable admission fee, security deposit and annual subscription. The group has also recommended creation of a customers' protection fund by earmarking 25 per cent of the sub-broker's annual subscription towards this fund. The group has further recommended that while the sub-broker would be primarily responsible to the client, the principal broker would ultimately be responsible to the client in case of a sub-broker's default. The group was also of the opinion that over a period of time, sub-brokers must be authorised to issue contracts in their own names to their clients.

9. Odd lots constitute a major bugbear for investors. Out of total market capitalisation of over Rs.60,000 crore, equities worth about Rs.15,000 crore are in odd lots. Investors normally receive 15 to 20 per cent less than the market price when they sell, and have to pay 15 to 20 per cent more than the market price when they buy odd lots. Schemes evolved by some of the agencies and companies to fetch a better price for the investors have not proved to be much of a success. Even the recent scheme launched by the Unit Trust of India for the barter of odd lots against units cannot be said to be attractive as capital appreciation of units is generally negligible compared to equities which are bartered.

10. An anomaly peculiar to our share bazars is that the members of the governing body of a stock exchange themselves are allowed to carry on business on a share market. In other words, President, Secretary, Treasurer or any officer bearer of a stock exchange can, like any other broker, buy and sell securities. In the event of a dispute, the same people have to sit on the judgement to resolve the dispute. This means that the offender himself becomes the arbitrator.

11. There is inordinate delay in admitting the securities for trading in stock exchanges. This delay is caused by the companies themselves. Collection of applications from different centres of the country, processing of application, issue of allotment letters/share certificates and the posting of these documents to the applicants by the issue houses take a long time and stretch beyond 70 days from the date of closure of the subscription list. Needless it is to emphasize that this affects liquidity of investments.

12. Take-overs have become common in our country. While the take-over of one company by another is not wrong, it would be desirable to ensure that energies of the entrepreneurial class do not get dissipated by engaging themselves in take-overs and a fair deal is meted out to the non-management shareholders. To achieve this objective, a new clause is incorporated in the listing agreement of stock exchanges pursuant to a directive issued by the government in April 1984. According to this clause, any acquisition company on securing the effective control of the management of a company by acquisition of the shares of the existing directors and others who effectively control or manage the company, irrespective of the percentage of their holding, should be preceded by the offer to the remaining members of the company to acquire their shares at a price not lower than the price at which the shares of the company are being acquired. This is, however subject to the public shareholding not being reduced to less than 20 per cent of the voting capital of the company.

There have been quite a few take-overs ever since this clause came into operation particularly during the last one year. Unfortunately, this clause has not proved to be effective in taking care of the interest of the non-management shareholders because of four major reasons. Firstly, acquisitions of shares is limited to 24.9 per cent of the voting capital of the company, thus conforming to the letter of the law while totally violating its spirit and brazen facedly arguing about the correctness of such a move. Secondly, the acquisition of shares would actually result in an effective change in the control of the management of the company but would not ostensibly look so, as for example, only four out of eight directors change and there is no foolproof way of deciding that there is an effective change in the control of the management of the company. Thirdly, while there would be no change in the pattern of shareholding of the parent company, holding shares in the company is important as a result of which, there would be change in the effective control of management of the company. Finally, acquisition of shares ostensibly takes place at a price much below the ruling market price but in actually at a much higher price, the difference being settled privately.

13. Service provided by brokers leaves much to be desired. The number of brokers (6500 from all stock exchanges) itself is inadequate. Consequently, a small number of brokers handles a large volume of turn-over. Service is obviously sacrificed.

14. The trading and settlement system continues to be archaic. The system is not in accordance with the internationally accepted standards. Settlement delays cause liquidity crunch.
15. There is no transparency in transactions. Lack of transparency will make the investor feel suspicious. The actual rate and date of the execution of the order are not made known to the client by the broker. It is often found that the brokers give to the investor only a statement of the net amount to pay in respect of purchases and the net to receive in respect of sales. Even the actual brokerage charged is not revealed by the brokers.
16. Mega issues, though are welcome, cause their own problems. Poor disclosure standards, misleading advertisements and price manipulations are some of the problems which persist, strict guidelines from SEBI not withstanding.
17. Finally, there is the problem of excess speculation. Speculation is necessary to keep the market vibrant. But excessive speculation will lead to broker-defaults which will kill the market. Most of our stock exchanges are speculative driven.

REFORMS

Realising the need for better investor protection and to overcome the inadequacies in the existing regulations, the Central Government and SEBI initiated several measures which will go a long way in ensuring healthy capital markets in our country. These measures are based on the recommendations made by several committees. The new measures are:

(1) Setting up of the Securities and Exchange Board of India (SEBI).
(2) Constituting OTC Exchange of India.
(3) Introducing Stock Invest Scheme.
(4) Safety net scheme to ensure buying back confidence.
(5) Three significant developments marked the period between 1994 and 1996. They are: (i) Open electronic limit order book market, (ii) nation wide integrated markets and clearing house that guarantees the trade. These three developments signal the healthy growth of stock markets in India. Demutulisationis yet another development that has taken place recently.

Open Electronic limit order Book Market (ELOB)

Till 1994, the physical organisation of markets in our country used 'open cry', which consisted of a pit in which traders shouted and hand-signalled in the process of trading. ELOB dispenses with the 'open cry' system. The system was first used by the National Stock Exchange (NSE), then followed by the Bombay Stock Exchange (BSE). In barely two years after it first appeared in out country, the ELOB has become the dominant technology underlying markets in the country. (Read also box 26.2)

Nationwide Integrated Markets

Prior to 1994, India's markets were dominated by the BSE. The financial industry in other locations was unable to have equal access to markets and participate in forming prices, as compared with market participants in Mumbai. Trading orders from outside Mumbai would generally be transmitted to a

Box 26.2 How Automation and Competition have Changed the BSE

As of 3 November 1994, India's market was dominated by the BSE, a monopoly market that did trading by open outcry. Seven months later, as of 2 June 1995, India's market was dominated by the competition between the BSE and the NSE, where both markets were open electronic limit order book markets. It should be noted that NSE was trading only around 1300 stocks, whereas there were around 4000 other stocks on the BSE where there is no competition for order flow. One related change which took place across these events was a sharp fall in the brokerage fees, following the large-scale entry into the brokerage business that accompanied the NSE.

In Shah and Thomas, this beautiful natural experiment is used to illuminate the consequences of automation and competition. The main findings here may be summarised as follows:

- Liquidity in the economy as a whole appears to have improved sharply across these changes. The improvement in liquidity on the BSE is made up of two parts: a positive effect attributed to automation and a negative effect attributed to competition.
- The gains in liquidity fed into gains in market efficiency, exactly as economic theory predicts. Two forms of market efficiency were explored. One direct form of market efficiency is that returns should not be forecastable based on historical data about returns or prices; i.e., that returns should be purely random. There is strong evidence that short-term correlations are much diminished after the introduction of automation and competition.

Another interesting idea about prices capturing information concerns good news vs bad news. Firms would generally advertise good news about themselves, but try to conceal bad news from the markets. In this case, bad news would gradually leak into prices through several small price drops, instead of one large drop. This would generate a skewness in returns, where large price drops are observed less often than ought to be the case. Improvements in the market efficiency should hence be associated with a reduction in the skewness of returns. Strong evidence for such reduction is found after the introduction of automation and competition.

- There is circumstantial evidence about reduction in mis-reported high and low prices, which were probably part of gala, the mechanism through which brokers reported a different trade price to the investor as compared with the truth.
- Volatility on BSE is elevated with automation, but is diminished with cross-listing on NSE. The volatility increase is likely to be consistent with the enhanced market efficiency. The cross-listing effect is likely to be associated with the market surveillance procedures on the NSE.

Mumbai broker who would carry them to the trading floor. The introduction of additional intermediaries would increase the transaction costs faced by the ultimate investor.

Nationwide integrated markets would help any trader anywhere in India to have equal access to the markets. This integration has been made possible through satellite communications. NSE was the first to launch such facilities and all its members have equal access to the market regardless of their location. As of October 31, 1996, NSE had 1,000 VSAT terminals located all over the country through which trading takes place. The BSE and the Delhi Stock Exchange also are in the process of establishing similar facilities.

Clearinghouse That Guarantees the Trade

There are always possibilities that parties to a contract default in their obligations and such breaches have a cascading effect, resulting in a major financial crisis. It happened in April 1995 in the context of M.S.Shoes, where a default involving a total exposure of Rs.18 crore led to a payments crisis on the BSE which halted the functioning the exchange for three days. To prevent such happenings in future, the National Securities Cleaning Corporation (NSCC) was set up on NSE, on 4 July, 1996. NSCC guarantees all trades on NSE. Thus, if A and B make a trade, NSCC interposes itself between them. If A was supposed to buy from B, then NSCC buys from B and NSCC sells to A. If either A or B defaults, then NSCC meets the obligations for the other leg of the trade. Thus, every trade that takes place is freed from any risk of default and its cascading effect.

Demutualisation

Recently the Securities Contract (Regulations) Act was amended to make demutualization of stock exchanges mandatory. The process of converting stock exchanges into corporate entities, with a wider ownership and the resulting oversight by regulatory bodies is called demutualization.

The amendment not only requires separation of ownership and trading rights, it also requires that the majority ownership rests with the public and those without any trading rights. Through these conditions, the Government has signaled a major shift in its earlier stand that stock exchanges should be self-regulating agencies of their members. It now desires that they should be externally regulated.

(Box 26.3 contains several other steps to make stock exchanges more effective).

Box 26.3 **Steps to Improve Efficiency of Stock Exchanges**

1. Introduce scripless trading.
2. Replace jobbing by market making.
3. Streamline settlement system.
4. Allow companies to buy back their own shares.
5. Integrate working of all exchanges.
6. Improve information dissemination system.
7. Allow multiple membership for brokers.
8. Increase the number of brokers. Give them better education and training.
9. Allow brokers to advertise their businesses.
10. Pool all the odd lot shares and convert them into marketable lots.
11. Remove one-year limitation of the validity period of the transfer deed.
12. Simplify transfer procedure.
13. Make rating of equities compulsory.
14. Reduce number of holidays.
15. Introduce two trading sessions in the place of the present one session trading.
16. Create investor awareness.
17. Make signature verification efficient.
18. Activise role of financial institutions.

QUESTIONS

1. Define a stock exchange. What are its functions?
2. What are the benefits of stock exchanges?
3. Describe the dealings in a stock exchange.
4. What is speculation? Do investors invest in shares for speculative gains always?
5. What are the recent trends of stock markets in our country?

ASSIGNMENT

It is an interesting phenomenon. Anything heppens anywhere gets relfected on stock prices. For example, a train accident somewhere, a minister sneezing elswhere, a statement made by a politician at some other place and the like do affect share prices. Why?

REFERENCES

1. S.C.Kuchal, *Corporation Finance - Principles and Problems*, p.261.
2. *Ibid*,p.262.
3. *Ibid*,p.263.
4. *India Today*, July 31, 1985.
5. *Business Line*, March 24, 2005.

CHAPTER OUTLINE

Monetary Policy
- Extent of Money
- Expansion of Money
- Contraction of Money
- Evaluation of Monetary Policy
- Structural Adjustments & Monetary Policy

Money Market
- Functions of Money Market
- Growth of Money Market
- Operations in Money Market
- Commercial Banks

Fiscal Policy
- The Budget
- The Union Budget
- Evaluation of Fiscal Policy
- Agenda for Future

LEARNING OBJECTIVES

After reading this Chapter, you should be able to:

1. Define monetary policy, understand techniques to measure the extent of money, and evaluate RBI's monetary policy
2. Understand the meaning and functions of money market, examine operations in money market and assess functioning of commercial banks
3. Define fiscal policy, know how budget operates and make critical assessment of fiscal policy

27 Monetary and Fiscal Policies

MONETARY POLICY

The monetary policy is assuming greater relevance nowadays because the government has now shifted from physical controls like control over output, capacity utilisation and licensing to non-physical controls like monetary policy in order to regulate business activities. Two reasons are quoted in support of this shift. One is that the changes in the quantum of saving and its characteristics are reasons enough for considering the Indian economy to be ready for indirect management through financial controls. It is argued that the physical management of the economy through controls and licences, which had been an unavoidable necessity during the earlier phase of the development of the Indian economy is no longer necessary and, indeed, may turn out to be counter-productive when the economy is poised for a higher level of performance and growth as shown by the high rate of saving (from 10 per cent of DGP in 1950-51 to 26 per cent in 1978-79 and 20.7 per cent during 1985-92).

Government nowadays relys more on measures like the monitory policy to regulate economy.

The second reason which is claimed to favour the indirect management of the economy through financial controls is the findings of the Planning Commission that in recent years, especially during the Sixth Plan period of high growth rate, there has been a perceptible fall in the incidence of poverty. (In 1983, the percentage of population below the poverty line declined from 48.3 to 37.4 and further came down to 26 per cent in 1999-2000). The Commission's reasoning is that reduction in the incidence of poverty is being brought about by the accelerated rate of growth of the economy and what the economy needs in the decade ahead is growth which can be achieved through appropriate macro-policies based primarily on fiscal, monetary and credit policies.

Nature of Monetary Policy

RBI uses the monitory policy to ensure price stability in the economy. The policy also provides norms for financial bodies.

Monetary policy is the policy statement, traditionally bi-annual, through which the Reserve Bank of India (RBI) targets a key set of indicators to ensure price stability in the economy. These factors include:

- Money supply, commonly referred to as M3.
- Interest rates.
- Inflation.

Besides, the policy also provides a platform for the apex bank to announce norms for financial bodies governed by the RBI such as banks, financial institutions, non-banking finance companies, residual non-banking companies, *nidhis*, primary dealers in the money markets and authorised dealers in the foreign exchange markets. It is also an opportunity for the RBI to spell out its overview on the economy, and an occasion for it to indicate deposit and advance targets for banks in the half-year.

Historically, the monetary policy has been announced twice a year-one for the slack season (April-September) and one for the busy season (October-March), in accordance with agricultural cycles. These cycles also coincide with the halves of the financial year. However, with the share of credit to agriculture coming down, the share of non-food credit in total credit has gone up. Since non-food or industrial credit is not seasonal, the RBI has, in 1998-99, experimented with one policy announcement in April, followed by a review in October. In 1999-2000, the RBI has decided that the policy will be an annual affair.

The RBI's monetary policy has been characterised as one of controlled expansion, i.e., adequate financing of economic growth and at the same time, ensuring reasonable price stability.

Extent of Money

RBI's monitory policy has been described as the controlled-expansion one.

Before initiating measures for the expansion or contraction of money supply, the RBI generally measures the extent of money and credit available in the economy at a given time. The following indices are generally used for the purpose.

M_1 This represents money supply with the public. M_1 has two components; (a) currency with the public and (b) deposits of the public with the banks.

M1 to M4 are the indices used by RBI to measure the supply of money at a given time.

Currency with the public is the sum total of notes in circulation and circulation of rupee coins and small coins minus the cash on hand with banks.

Deposits of the public with banks is the sum total of demand deposits with banks and 'other' deposits of the public with the RBI.

M_2 This represents the total of M_1 plus post office savings and bank deposits.

M_3 It is the sum total of M_2 and the time deposits with banks.

M_4 This represents M_3 plus total post office deposits.

M_1 is called 'narrow money' while M_3 is called 'broad money'. M_3 represents the aggregate monetary resources or the money stock of the entire banking sector.

What are the representative sources of M_3? These are: (a) the net bank credit to the government, (b) bank credit to the commercial sector; (c) net foreign exchange assets of the banking sector and (d) the government's currency liabilities to the public (Also read box 27.1).

Box 27.1 **Broadening the Meaning of Money**

A Committee constituted by the RBI (in its report submitted in June, 1998) recommended, among others, the following:

- Exclusion of the data on post office accounts. The argument is that these deposits were included in measures of money supply at a time when the banking network was under-developed in the rural areas. Since this is no longer the case and as post offices cannot be considered 'depositories', these deposits should be excluded. Accordingly, M_4 will disappear.
- In order to reflect recent monetary trends, it has been suggested that the monetary measures, M_2 and M_3, should be altered. M_2 should exclude fully repatriable bank deposits (of up to one year maturity) held by non-resident Indians. And M_3 should include what the banks borrow in the call market from 'non-depository' financial corporations.

But what of deposits with non-banking financial companies and development financial institutions that are increasing in magnitude? And while certificates of deposit with banks are already included in M_2, what about those CDs issued by development financial institutions? Shouldn't these two categories of deposits also be considered money?

The RBI Committee has chosen instead to devise three new measures, not of money supply but of liquidity. This is apparently what some other countries have done. While deposits with NBFCs are numerically large, the NBFCs do not provide services similar to banks, hence the exclusion of deposits with them from measures of money supply.

The three new aggregates of liquidity suggested are:

- L_1 which will be M_3 and all deposits with post office savings banks.
- L_2 which will be L_1 plus fixed deposits with development financial institutions and certificates of deposit of these institutions.
- L_3 which will be L_2 and deposits with the NBFCs.

The RBI is expected to compile estimates of these three liquidity aggregates, as it has been doing of M_1, M_2 and M_3. The objective is to track similar and as yet distinctive measures of money. The new liquidity aggregates encompass a much broader notion of money. But it would appear that M_3 will continue to be the focus of monetary policy. The RBI is to put out only monthly estimates of the three measures of liquidity while it will continue to make fortnightly compilations of M_1, M_2 and M_3.

Expansion of Money

Money is pumped into the economy through the issue of currency by the RBI, budgetary operations of the government and borrowings by the government from foreign countries.

Expansion of money has always been on the increase. Between 1970-71 and 1983-84, as against 3.7 per cent average annual growth in output, money supply registered an annual expansion of 17.2 per cent. This phenomenon is not unique to our country. It is universal. Particularly, 1986 has been a year of money expansion as is evident from Table 27.1.

Expansion in money supply is not wrong, nay it is desirable, in a developing economy as money is needed to match the growth of real national income. Infact, the growth in money supply must be higher than the growth in the real national income. This stems from two reasons: (a) as incomes grow, the

Table 27.1 **Money Expansion**

		Target	Actual
U.S.A.	M_1	3 p.c. to 8 p.c.	15 p.c.
	M_2	6 p.c. to 9 p.c.	8.9 p.c.
France	M_3	3 p.c. to 5 p.c.	4.8 p.c.
Britain	M_4	11 p.c. to 15 p.c.	18.6 p.c.

(**Source**: *Economic Times*, January 26, 1987.)

demand for money as one of the components of savings tends to increase. (b) an increase in money supply is also necessitated by the gradual reduction of the non-monetised sector of the economy. In our country, the rate of increase in money supply has been far in excess of the rate of growth in real national income. Hence the inflationary pressure is there on the economy.

Contraction of Money

Money supply is sought to be contracted through general and selective controls.

Unlimited expansion of money and credit results in hyper-inflation, which hits all sections of society, particularly the poor. The Reserve Bank has a responsibility to ensure that money supply is within manageable limits and inflation is not too harsh. For this purpose, the Reserve Bank has been using different control measures, popularly called '*credit control measures*'. These control measures can be broadly classified into two categories, *viz*., (a) general, (quantitative) controls and (b) selective (qualitative) controls.

General Credit Controls

The general controls affect the total quantity of credit and the economy generally. General controls include: (a) Bank Rate; (b) Open Market Operations; (c) Cash Reserve Requirements; (d) Statutory Liquidity Requirements and (e) Refinance Policy.

Bank rate is one of the general control measures. It is the rate at which RBI rediscounts or lends money to commercial banks.

Bank Rate: Also called the discount rate, bank rate refers to the rate at which the Central Bank rediscounts or lends money to commercial banks. During inflationary periods, the bank rate is hiked so as to increase the rates of interest on borrowings. This will have a dampening effect on the borrowers. The reverse course of action is taken during the periods of falling prices.

The RBI has changed the bank rate several times - from 4.5 per cent in 1963, the rate was raised to 5 per cent in 1964, to 6 per cent in 1965, to 7 per cent in 1973, to 9 per cent in 1974 and to 10 per cent in 1983. It was further raised to 11 per cent in 1991 and subsequently increased to 12 per cent. Since March 1, 1999, the rate has been reduced to 8 per cent and since April 1, 2000, it has been further cut to 7 per cent. The rate has been further cut to 6 per cent from April 2003.

(a) *Open Market Operations*: Open market operations refer to the purchase or sale of securities, foreign exchange and gold by the government. Purchase of securities and gold from public results in the expansion of money. Sale of securities and gold results in the contraction of money supply. It was with this objective that 13.5 tonnes of gold was auctioned during 1977-78. (see Table 27.2 for more details).

(b) *Special Facilities to Some Groups*: The Reserve Bank advises commercial banks to advance liberally to special groups or priority sectors like small-scale industries, cooperatives, small

Table 27.2 **Reserve Bank's Open Market Operations in Central Government Securities**

(Rs. Crore)

Year	*Purchase*	*Sales*	*Net Sales*
1988-89	2,403.5	3,888.7	1,485.2
1990-91	2,291.2	2,238.1	-53.1
1992-93	6,273.4	11,793.5	5,520.1
April-June			
1992-93	2,791.3	6,984.9	4,193.6
1993-94	446.3	568.2	121.9

transport operators, self employed and the like. This also results in the expansion of money supply.

(c) *Liberalisation of the Bill Market Scheme*: Under this, commercial banks get additional finance from the Reserve Bank. With additional funds at their disposal, commercial banks will be able to advance credit further.

(d) *Development Banks*: Since Independence, the RBI has setup a series of development banks like IFCI, IDBI, SFCs etc. through which funds are made available to finance economic activities.

CRR requires that every bank should keep certain minimum cash with RBI.

Cash Reserve Requirements (CRR): Under the RBI Act, 1935, every commercial bank has to keep a certain minimum cash reserve with the RBI. The RBI is empowered to vary the CRR between 3 per cent and 15 per cent of demand and time deposits. Like the bank rate, CRR was changed several times. In 1973, it was 7 per cent, in 1984, 9 per cent, increased by 0.5 per cent with effect from February 28, 1987, and subsequently hiked to 10 per cent. CRR was further hiked to 15 per cent in 1991 but brought down to 14 per cent from May 14, 1994 with a view to inject a measure of liquidity in the banking system, CRR was cut down to 10 per cent with effect from Jan, 1997. It is 4.5 per cent since June 2003. CRR is a powerful weapon. An increase in the CRR would reduce the available funds for bank credit and a reduction would have the opposite effect.

SLR mandates that every bank should deposit, in the form of liquid assets, a certain percentage of its total time and demand deposits.

Statutory Liquidity Ratio (SLR): In addition to CRR, every commercial bank should keep a certain percentage of its total demand and time deposits with the RBI in the form of liquid assets like cash, gold or unencumbered approved securities. Maintenance of adequate liquid assets is a basic principle of sound banking. Hence, commercial banks have been required by the Banking Regulation Act, 1949, to maintain a minimum ratio of liquid assets. The RBI has been empowered to change the ratio. Accordingly, it raised the SLR from 25 per cent to 30 per cent in 1972, to 32 per cent in 1973, to 35 per cent in 1981, to 36 per cent in 1984 and to 37.5 per cent in 1987. This was raised to 38.5 per cent in 1991 and subsequently reduced to 25 per cent.

The Narasimham Committee recommended a gradual reduction of SLR to 25 per cent over a period of five years. Consequently, the SLR was reduced to 30 per cent on incremental basis in April 1992, and a further reduction of 0.75 per cent was announced in October 1992. It has been reduced to 25 per cent with effect from October 16, 1993. Further reduction in SLR would be planned taking into account the evolving monetary situation.

It may be mentioned here that the effect of stepping up of CRR and SLR is the same, *viz.*, they reduce the capacity of commercial banks to expand credit to business and industry and thus are anti-inflationary.

Refinance Policy: The system of refinance provided by the RBI to commercial banks affects their credit. The system is changed periodically to allow or disallow certain flows by banks. The scope of refinance as an instrument of credit control depends on the liquidity position of the commercial banks. Over the years, the commercial banks' dependence on the RBI for refinance has come down except in the case of subsidised refinance of agricultural and rural credit. The effectiveness of refinance policy has, therefore, come down.

Selective Credit Controls

Selective controls are sector specific.

Selective credit controls affect particular sectors of the economy and include such measures as:

(i) insisting on minimum margins for lending against specific securities;

(ii) fixing a ceiling on the amounts of credit for certain purposes;

(iii) charging discriminatory rates of interest on certain types of advances;

(iv) moral suasion and

(v) direct action.

Under moral suasion, RBI appeals to the good sense of banks not to do or do certain things.

While the first three are self-explanatory, the latter two need clarification.

Under moral suasion, the RBI addresses periodical letters to banks urging them to exercise control over credit in general, or advances against particular commodities or unsecured advances. Periodic discussions are also held by the Governor of the Reserve Bank with the authorities of commercial banks urging them to restrain from lending liberally.

Direct action may involve refusal by the Reserve Bank to rediscount bills of a particular commercial bank which has failed to comply with the directives of the former. It may, in the extreme case, involve cancellation of licence of an erring bank. Direct action is too severe and is, therefore, rarely followed.

An Evaluation of Monetary Policy

RBI seems to have failed both in controlling or expanding money supply.

Monetary policy has become a target of severe criticism. As was mentioned in the beginning of this chapter, RBI's monetary policy has been characterised as one of controlled expansion. It is said that the RBI has failed both in expansion and control of money and credit in our economy. With regard to the expansion of credit, it is said that the major component of the increase in money supply was the Reserve Bank credit to the Central Government. The inability of the Reserve Bank to deny or regulate credit to the Central Government due to both legal and practical considerations has been interpreted by the Committee (Sukhamoy Chakravarty Committee) as an important factor in the Reserve Bank's helplessness in controlling the rise in money supply. Thus, money supply has expanded inspite of the Reserve Bank and not because of it.

With regard to the role of the RBI in controlling inflation, criticism is equally strong. It is said that the monetary policy operated by the RBI did not play any effective role in containing inflation in the economy. The growth of money supply in recent years was much higher than the growth in output. The average annual growth in output (net national product at factor cost at 1970-71 prices) between 1970-71 and 1983-84 was 3.7 per cent per annum. The increase in money supply on an average annual basis between March 1971 and March 1984 was as high as 17.2 per cent. You have a growth rate of 4 per cent per year and money supply of over 17 per cent. It is this divergence between the two key factors governing the health of the economy which led to the average annual rise of prices of nearly 10 per cent during this period.

The reasons for the failure to formulate an effective monetary policy should, perhaps, be found elsewhere and not with the RBI. The Sukhamoy Chakravarty Committee has strongly indicted the Central Government for living beyond its means and making the central banking authority impotent in discharging its responsibility in maintaining the value of the currency. The report has clearly shown that the indiscipline of the fiscal policy has made the monetary policy an exercise in futility. The Central Government has opened the flood-gates of monetary growth and asked the Reserve Bank to plug the small leaks. In simple words, the report conveys that the emperor of monetary policy has no clothes on.

Another argument to prove the Reserve Bank's helplessness is that the powers and weapons of the bank cover only the commercial banks. To the extent inflationary pressure is the result of bank finance, the Reserve Bank's general and selective credit controls will have effect. But if inflationary pressure is really brought about by deficit financing and shortage of goods, the Reserve Bank's control may not have any effect at all. Besides, the apex bank has no power over non-banking financial institutions and indigenous bankers who continue to play a considerable role in financing trade and industry.

Table 27.3 brings out the strengths and weaknesses of the RBI's monetary policy.

Table 27.3 **Monetary Policy**

Weaknesses	*Strengths*
– Higher proportion of non-banking credit – No check on price rise – High currency-deposit ratio rendering the RBI's role less effective – Selective application of credit constraints – Defective statistical and monitoring system. – Growing fiscal needs of the economy	– Decision making and implementation is faster than fiscal policy – More reliance on selective credit control measures and less on quantitative controls making RBI's pressure on commercial banks less severe – Has been responsive to the needs of the economy

Structural Adjustments and Monetary Policy

In tune with the ongoing structural adjustment programme, objectives and instruments of the monetary policy have been redefined. The major considerations which underline the monetary policy in recent years have been: (a) bringing about a deceleration in monetary expansion with a view to containing inflation without hampering the revival of economy; (b) reducing the monetised deficit, i.e., printing of new currency consistent with the government's objective of bringing down gross fiscal deficit and (c) boosting exports in order to alleviate the problem of external payments deficit.

To achieve these objectives, the following instruments of monetary policy have been employed:

1. The stipulation of a minimum lending rate for advances of over Rs.2 lakh has been discontinued and banks would be free to fix their own prime rates.
2. SLR has been reduced to 25 per cent, sharply shrinking the captive market for government securities.
3. State governments too would have to go to market for loans.

4. Automatic monetisation of the budget deficit would cease and has been replaced by a system of *ways and means advances* under which temporary accommodation provided to the Central Government would have to be liquidated by the end of the financial year.
5. The RBI would endeavour to develop an active market in securities for which it would undertake to develop institutions and instruments as well as an appropriate structure of market-determined rates of interest on securities.
6. A close linkage would be established between monetary policy and exchange rate policy.
7. The RBI is prepared to accept that the bank's choice of asset holdings would be determined not by statutory prescriptions but by risk-reward perceptions.
8. Guidelines have been issued for the promotion of market-makers in major stock exchanges and for the grant of bank advances for the purpose, without any ceiling and without applying the 50 per cent margin applicable to advances against shares.

MONEY MARKET

Meaning of Money Market

Money market is a mechanism through which short-term funds are borrowed or lent.

The *money market* is the market in which short-term funds are borrowed and lent. The Reserve Bank defines a money market as "*centre for dealings, mainly of a short-term character, in monetary assets; it meets the short-term requirements of the borrowers and provides liquidity or cash to lenders. It is the place where short-term surplus investible funds at the disposal of the financial and other institutions and individuals are bid by borrowers, again comprising institutions and individuals and also by the government*". The money market does not deal in cash or money, but in short-term financial assets like trade bills, promissory notes and treasury bills which are drawn for short periods. These short-term bills are known as *near-money*.

The money market may be distinguished from the capital market. Capital market refers to the market for long-term funds, while the money market refers to the market for short-term funds. "*The maturity boundary that divides the money and capital markets is rather arbitrary, ranging from one to five years, depending on who is doing the classifying*".[2]

Some authors use the term 'money market' to include capital market as well. No such synonymity is maintained in this section. In other words, the two are independently used, money market referring to short-term funds and capital market referring to long-term funds.

Functions of Money Market

Money market adds to the support of funds. It also avoids seasonal fluctuation of funds.

1. By providing various kinds of credit instruments suitable and attractive for different sections, a money market augments the supply of funds.
2. The efficient working of the money market helps minimise the gluts and stringencies in the money market due to the seasonal variations in the flow of and demand for funds.

3. A money market helps avoid seasonal fluctuations in interest rates.
4. A money market, by augmenting the supply of funds and making them readily available to the legitimate borrowers, helps in making funds available at cheaper rates.
5. A well-organised money market, through the quick transfer of funds from one place to another, helps avoid regional gluts and stringencies of funds.
6. It enhances the amount of liquidity available to the economy.
7. A money market, by providing profitable investment opportunities for short-term funds, helps increase the profit of financial institutions and individuals.

Growth of Money Market

For several years, turn-over in our money market was low because of a limited number of players and administered interest rate regime. As is well known, earlier only commercial banks were allowed to operate in the money market. As years went by, several other players were also allowed entry into the money market. The players now include all commercial banks, cooperative banks, development financial institutions, UTI, mutual funds and insurance corporations. Infact, any one having funds to lend is allowed access to the market. To be specific, the following banks and institutions are the big players in the money market:

* All Scheduled Commercial Banks
* Life Insurance Corporation of India
* General Insurance Corporation of India and its subsidiaries
* Industrial Credit and Investment Corporation of India Ltd.
* Unit Trust of India
* Industrial Reconstruction of Bank of India
* Export Credit Guarantee Corporation Ltd.
* Industrial Development Bank of India
* Industrial Finance Corporation of India
* National Bank of Agriculture and Rural Development
* Discount and Finance House of India Ltd.
* National Housing Bank
* Shipping Credit and Investment Company of India Ltd.
* Tourism Finance Corporation of India Ltd.
* Export Import Bank of India
* Small Industries Development Bank of India
* SBI Mutual Fund
* GIC Mutual Fund
* CANBANK Mutual Fund
* LIC Mutual Fund
* BOI Mutual Fund
* Indian Bank Mutual Fund

* PNB Mutual Fund
* Madhya Pradesh Rajya Sahakari Bank Maryadit
* Maharashtra State Cooperative Bank Ltd.
* Tamil Nadu State Apex Cooperative Bank Ltd.
* Urban Cooperative Banks as shown below:
    - Abhyudaya Cooperative Bank Ltd.
    - Bassein Catholic Cooperative Bank Ltd.
    - Bombay Mercantile Cooperative Bank Ltd.
    - Development Cooperative Bank Ltd.
    - Sangli Urban Cooperative Bank Ltd.
    - Shamrao Vithal Cooperative Bank Ltd.
    - Saraswat Cooperative Bank Ltd.
    - Janata Sahakari Bank Ltd.
    - Rupee Cooperative Bank Ltd.
    - New India Cooperative Bank Ltd.
    - Goa Urban Cooperative Bank Ltd.
    - Ahmedabad Mercantile Cooperative Bank Ltd.
    - Cooperative Bank of Ahmedabad Ltd.
    - Kalupur Commercial Cooperative Bank Ltd.
    - Madhavpura Mercantile Cooperative Bank Ltd.
    - Rajkot Nagarik Sahakari Bank Ltd.
    - Surat People's Cooperative Bank Ltd.

Note: 1. All the above banks/institutions are also permitted to participate in the call/notice money market. Other cooperative banks not included in the above list are participants in the call/notice/term money market.

2. Institutions in the above list participate as lenders only in the call/notice money market.

It maybe stated that out of all the above institutions, only commercial banks can operate both as lenders and borrowers. Financial institutions and mutual funds are allowed to operate only as lenders.

It may be also stated that the Reserve Bank of India is the regulatory authority controlling all the players and their operators in the money market.

In addition to the permission given to other players to operate in the money market, the Reserve Bank of India withdrew ceiling on interest rates in the money market with effect from May 1989. Furthermore, new instruments were introduced from time to time to cater to the needs of various investors.

Establishment of the Discount and Finance House of India Ltd. (DFHI) in April 1988 was a landmark in the development of the Indian money market.

Another measure contemplated towards the growth of the money market relates to the decision to permit scheduled commercial banks and their subsidiaries to set up Money Market Mutual Fund (MMMF). The measure would provide an additional short-term avenue to investors and bring money market instruments within the reach of individuals and small bodies.

The Indian money market has grown in maturity over a period of time.

Thus, the Indian money market has grown, over the years, in its stature and versatility. The inspiration behind this phenomenal growth has been the recommendations of the Chakraborthy Committee and the Vaghul Working Group.

Operations in the Money Market

Operations in the money market take place in different ways. The major ones are:

(i) Call (overnight) money
(ii) Notice money
(iii) Commercial Bills
(iv) Treasury Bills
(v) Certificates of Deposits
(vi) Commercial papers.

Table 27.4 shows the main features of these investment methods.

Table 27.4 **Features of Investment Methods**

Money Market instruments	*Minimum amount per transaction (Rs.in crore)*	*Period*	*Secured/ Unsecured*	*Liquidity*	*Participants*
1. *182 Days Treasury Bill*	0.25	1-182 Days	Secured	Easy	Open to all
2. *Commercial Bill*	0.50	1-90	Secured Days	Reasonable	Scheduled commercial banks, select cooperative banks, all-India financial institutions and mutual funds
3. *Certificates of Deposit*	0.25	46-365 Days	Secured	Moderate	Open to all
4. *Commercial papers*	0.25	90-180 Days	Unsecured	Moderate	Open to all
5. *Call Money*	1.00	1 Day	Unsecured	Easy	Commercial and cooperative banks, all-India financial Institutions and Mutual Funds
6. *Notice Money*	0.50	2-14 Days	Unsecured	Easy	-do-

Call/Notice Money

All categories of banks and financial institutions are allowed to participate in call/notice money market. The funds are lent for one day or from Saturday to Monday (call/overnight money) or for a period upto 14 days (notice money) in the call/notice market. In view of the short tenure of such transactions, it is desirable that both the borrowers and lenders have current account with the Reserve Bank of India. This will facilitate quick and timely debit and credit operations. The call market is taken recourse to by banks and institutions to even out their day-to-day deficits and surpluses of money and specially to bridge the shortfall in maintaining the requisite CRR/SLR levels to avoid punitive measures by the RBI. The interest rates in the call money market are highly elastic to the demand-supply position and are known to have moved from a low of 2-3 per cent to over 70 per cent per annum. Even on the same day, variation upto 10 percentage points has been observed. There is, therefore, high interest rate risk to both borrowers and lenders in operating in the call money market. The lenders having steady inflow of funds (e.g., LIC, UTI) look at the call market as a temporary parking place for funds as well as means for deploying funds on a short term basis.

Commercial Bills

Discounting commercial bills is one of the ways for banks to extend credit.

One of the ways banks extend credit to their customers is by discounting their commercial bills. Such credit-bill finance is repayable on maturity of the bills. During the usance period, banks have a recourse to the money market to rediscount the eligible bills and get ready money. The eligibility criteria prescribed by the Reserve Bank of India for rediscounting a bill stipulates *inter alia* that the bill should arise out of genuine trade or commercial transactions and the maturity date of the bill should fall within 90 days from the date of rediscounting. The individual bills can be substituted by derivative usance promissory note of equivalent aggregate amount and of maturity by the issuing bank to eliminate movement of papers and facilitate multiple rediscounting. The Government has exempted stamp duty on the discounting of such bills and on derivative usance promissory notes. The bill rediscounting rate is dictated by the market forces. There is less volatility in interest rates in bill rediscounting market than in the call market.

182 Days Treasury Bills

This is a short term government debt security introduced in November 1986. It has certain special features. The Treasury Bill is issued on auction by the Reserve Bank of India. It is issued at a discount and on maturity, the face value is paid to the holder. Every fortnight, Reserve Bank of India invites bids for sale of 182 Days Treasury Bills. The bidder has to specify (i) the price per rupees hundred nominal value and (ii) the face value of the proposed investment. Bids are opened and examined by a committee headed by a Deputy Governor of the RBI. The committee decides on a cut-off price and all bids quoting price equal to or higher than the cut-off level are accepted for full allotment. Others are rejected.

Applications in the prescribed form are to be tendered before 3.00 p.m. on the specified date at the Reserve Bank of India, Mumbai. Results of the auction are displayed at the Reserve Bank of India, Mumbai the next day, indicating the price upto which bids have been accepted. Successful bidders are required to collect the letter of acceptance and deposit the amount with the apex bank within 24 hours from the announcement of the results.

All banks, institutions, corporations and individuals can submit bids at the auction. These treasury bills are eligible assets for the purpose of maintenance of banks' SLR requirement. The discounting rate being based on bidders' quotes at the Reserve Bank of India auctions, gives expected returns to the investors. There is very active secondary market with both outright sale and '*repos*' (buy-back) facilities, providing full liquidity to the instrument. Banks having swing in their demand and time liabilities find this instrument very handy for conversion from cash to treasury bills and *vice versa*. Others like local bodies, corporations etc. which are flush with funds, may also find this instrument attractive.

Certificate of Deposit

The Reserve Bank of India introduced Certificates of Deposit(CD) in 1989. CD is a front-ended negotiable instrument, issued at a discount and the face value is payable at maturity by the issuing bank. In terms of the provisions of the CD Scheme, scheduled commercial banks are allowed to issue CDs to their customers. The CDs are short-term deposit instruments for a period ranging from three months to one year. Further, the minimum amount of a CD is fixed at Rs.25 lakh in the denomination of Rs.5 lakh. These instruments are subject to the payment of stamp duty like usance promissory notes. A CD is transferable by endorsement and delivery any time after 45 days of issue. The amount of a CD is included in the demand and time liabilities of the issuing bank for the purposes of reserve requirements (CRR and SLR).

> Certificate of deposit is a negotiable instrument issued at a discount but face value is payable at maturity by the issuing bank.

Being a negotiable instrument, it is traded in the secondary money market and can be rediscounted after 45 days of holding by the first holder. If a bank acquires, by rediscounting, a CD issued by another bank, it is treated as an inter-bank asset while working out the demand and time liabilities of the rediscounting bank, thereby giving it the benefit in working out its reserves requirements.

Since a CD is eligible for rediscounting in the money market only after 45 days of holding, the maturity period of CDs available on the market can be anywhere between one day to 320 days. A CD is therefore another step in filling the gap between Treasury Bills/Commercial Bills and dated securities.

The discount rates for the issue of CDs are market-determined. The banks can use the CD Scheme to increase their deposit base by offering higher discount rates. Anyone can take CDs issued by banks. Also, there is a fair degree of liquidity to the investments, though it is somewhat restricted due to the non-eligibility of transfer for 45 days after the issue. This is an ideal instrument when surplus cash is to be parked for three months to one year. Banks also find this instrument suitable to reward its big size depositors with a better rate of return than on household deposits.

Commercial Paper

The Reserve Bank of India introduced a scheme of Commercial Paper(CP) in January 1990. CP is a short-term negotiable money market instrument and is issued by companies in the form of a usance promissory note, redeemable at par to the holder on maturity. The period of CP is 15 days to 365 days from the date of issue and is issued at a discount. CP can be transferred by simple endorsement and delivery. Further, the maximum amount for which CP can be issued by a company is limited to 100 per cent of the working capital limit, sanctioned by the company's bank and after the issue of CP, the working capital credit limit is automatically reduced. However, the financing bank can give stand-by facility for meeting the redemption liability on maturity.

> Commercial paper is a short-term negotiable instrument issued by companies redeemable at par to the holder on maturity.

Reserve Bank of India has been continuously bringing about relaxations in the scheme and as per the April 1991 credit policy announcement, the conditions for the issue of CP have been relaxed as follows:

(i) The fund-based working capital limit of the issuing company should not be less than Rs.4.00 crore from the banking sector and the company can issue a CP upto 100 per cent of its working capital credit limit.

(ii) The tangible networth of the issuing company should not be less than Rs.4 crore.

(iii) A CP issue should be of a minimum size of Rs.25 lakh (face value) and can be issued in denominations of Rs.5 lakh or multiples thereof.

(iv) The condition of 'prior' clearance from Reserve Bank of India is dispensed with.

(v) The credit rating awarded by CRISIL to the issuing company should be P_2 or higher or A_2 by ICRA, PR_2 of CARE.

(vi) The shares of the company should be listed in one or more stock exchanges.

(vii) The borrowal account should be treated as a *standard asset* by the finanical bank.

(viii) The current ratio should be 1.33:1 minimum, as per the latest audited balance sheet.

The CPs are traded in the secondary money market and are therefore adequately liquid. These are good investment for entities having short term cash surplus.

Role of DFHI

As was stated earlier, the setting up of the Discount and Finance House of India Ltd. in 1988 was a landmark in the development of the Indian money market. During its short span of four years, the role played by the DFHI is noteworthy.

DFHI has been set up by the Reserve Bank of India jointly with public sector banks and all-India financial institutions to deal in short-term money market instruments. It started operations in April 1988. At present, DFHI participates in the inter-bank call/notice money market and term deposit market, both as lender and borrower. It also purchases and sells 182 Days Treasury Bills, commercial bills, CDs and CPs. DFHI has an authorised capital of Rs.250 crore of which Rs.150 crore has been paid up. Apart from its paid up capital, it has lines of refinance from the RBI and a line of credit from the consortium of public sector banks.

During 1990-91, DFHI opened branches at Delhi, Calcutta, Chennai, Ahmedabad, and Bangalore in order to decentralise its activities and provide money market facilities at the major market centres in the country.

The participation of DFHI in the money market has activised the secondary market specially for 182 Days Treasury Bills and commercial bills. RBI does not purchase 182 Days Treasury Bills before maturity nor does it sell these bills except through the fortnightly auctions. DFHI fulfils the role of provider of liquidity to the Treasury Bills. It quotes every day its bid and offers discount rates for different instruments. While the selling of Treasury Bills by DFHI at the 'offer' rate depends upon the availability of such bills in its assets portfolio, DFHI is willing to purchase Treasury Bills at its '*bid*' rate.

The DFHI also provides '*repos*' facility (buy-back and sell-back) to banks, select financial institutions and public sector undertakings, upto a period of 14 days at pre-determined interest rates.

In regard to commercial bills, the introduction of derivative usance promissory notes (DPN) for rediscounting bills has facilitated multiple rediscounting of this instrument in the secondary money market. DFHI purchases and sells DPN for a period upto 90 days at its bid and offer rediscount rates.

The call money operations of DFHI has enabled the pooling of borrowers' demand and lenders' supplies to the extent that both borrowers and lenders opt to avail of DFHI services for their operations.

The operations of the DFHI during the first three years of its existence are shown in Table 27.5.

Table 27.5 **Discount and Finance House of India Ltd., Operations at a Glance**

			(Rs. in crore)
	1988-89	*1989-90*	*1990-91*
Business Turnover			
* *Call and Notice Money*	20,362	88,577	2,02,792
* *182 Days Treasury Bills*	11,024	21,953	32,329
* *Commercial Bills*	2,866	10,682	12,675
* *Term Money*	-	244	3,532
* *Commercial Paper*	-	26	107
* *Certificates of Deposit*	-	3	8
Operating Results			
* *Profit before tax*	11.20	26.76	50.20
* *Profit after tax*	5.25	12.14	26.97
* *Dividend*			
Amount	4.23	10.81	17.25
Percent	5.00	10.00	11.50
* *Return on capital employed*	12.80%	24.78%	33.50%

Commercial Banks

The banking system consitutes the core of the financial sector and plays a critical role in transmitting monitory policy impulses to the economy.

Banking is more than 225 years old in the country.

Banking is more than 225 years old in our country. The first bank called the Bank of Hindoostan was established in 1770. Since then, there has never been any let up and as of today, there are 295 banks with 66,514 branches spread across the country.

The banking system in our country comprises three constituents: public sector banks, private sector banks and foreign banks (see Fig.27.1). There are 27 public sector banks accounting for 81 per cent of the total assets of all banks (as on March 31, 1999).

We have private sector banks, whose role has considerably narrowed down after two-step nationalisation. Private sector banking received a shot in arm with the announcement of the New Economic Policy. The number of private banks stand at 32 with 5624 branches (see Fig.27.1).

Foreign banks in the private sector are branches of banks incorporated outside India. There are 36 such banks with 204 branches on end March 1999.

The Indian commercial banks have played a significant role in the economic development of the country. Be it branch expansion, deposit mobilisation, credit expansion, minimising regional imbalances or promotion of new entrepreneurship, the role of commercial banks is considerable. There are shortcomings nevertheless. For example, the banking services have not reached all parts of the country, loan recovery has become a big problem for banks; inefficiency and customer complaints are common in banks and losses have become a way of life. Banks often find it difficult to strike a balance between their commercial compulsions and social obligations.

The Indian commercial banks have played a significant role in the economic development of the country.

Figure 27.1 **Structure and Assets Composition of Scheduled Commercial Banks**

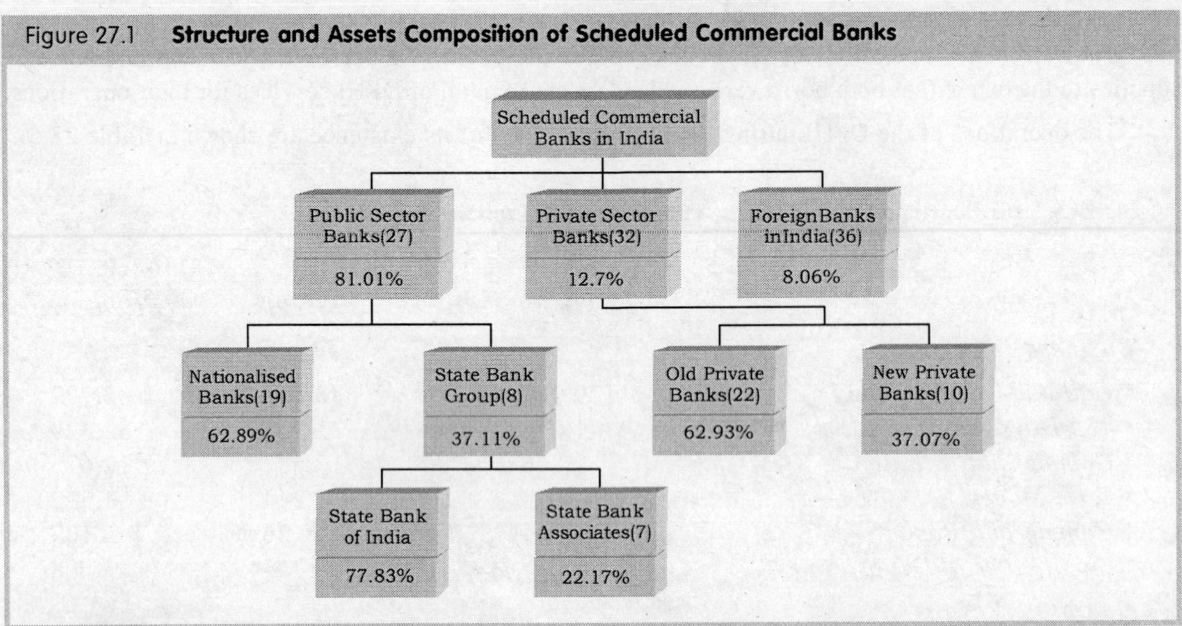

Factors Affecting Competitiveness and Efficiency in Banking

The financial sector plays a major role in the mobilisation and allocation of financial savings. Financial institutions, instruments and markets which constitute the financial sector act as a conduit for the transfer of financial resources from the net savers to net borrowers. The gains to the real sector of the economy, therefore, depend on how efficiently the financial sector performs this basic function of intermediation so that the transaction cost is kept at the minimum. The banks form the most important segment of the financial sector. However, till the seventies, government regulations in most of the countries shielded the banks from the forces of competition. This policy was advocated keeping the '*safety and soundness*' aspect of the banking institutions in mind. The market imperfection, however, led to operational inefficiency in the banks as under the administered interest regime, they could earn adequate spreads to cover their high operational costs. Consequent to various developments covering *inter alia* the tremendous growth in information technology which dismantled the geographical boundaries and the prolific growth of the non-bank financial companies which made a dent on the banks' assured clientele, the competitive environment in the banking industry has increased.

Changes in the banking policy further facilitated the creation of a competitive environment. Deregulation of the banking industry through the abolition of administered rates for deposits and loans gave the banks the freedom in fixing prices for their products. To compete effectively with non-bank intermediaries, the banks were permitted to undertake newer activities like investment banking, securities trading and insurance business though on a selective basis. The number of players in the market was increased by easing entry barriers. In this set up, margins on traditional banking business declined, prompting the banks to look for more fee-based services and simultaneously, the banks were forced to pay maximum attention to operational efficiency so that their transaction costs remained at the minimum. Increased competitiveness led to inevitable changes in the market. The weak players were either crowded out or they were amalgamated with the strong ones.

Till the eighties, banks were operating in a protected environment.

In India, till the eighties, the banks were operating in a protective environment characterised by administered interest rates, high levels of pre-emptions in the form of reserve requirements and directed credit. Banking sector reforms were initiated in India in 1992 against the backdrop of challenges faced by the Indian banks from within and outside the banking system in the country as well as forces of globalisation operating worldwide. The accent of the reform process was to improve productivity and efficiency of the financial system. The major policy initiatives taken under the financial sector reform included a planned reduction in the level of statutory pre-emptions and a gradual deregulation of interest rates. As part of the financial sector reforms, effective pre-emption level has been brought down from 54 per cent to less than 35 per cent. The structure of administered interest rates has been almost totally dismantled. Competition among the banks was sought to be fostered by two different policy measures. First, with the amendment of the Nationalisation Act, State owned banks were allowed to access the market to raise funds from the public. Having public as part of the ownership of the bank makes it more conscious of the need to run the institution efficiently and earn profits. Accountability in that sense increases. Secondly, new banks in the private sector were allowed to be set up and the entry of foreign banks was liberalised. The decision to allow the setting up of Local Area Banks was taken with the purpose of creating a more competitive environment in rural and semi-urban areas. Simultaneously with the deregulation measures, capital adequacy measures and prudential norms relating to income recognition, asset quality and provisioning requirements were introduced so as to strengthen the safety and soundness of the banking system.

Induction of information technology and communications networking system is set to change the operating environment of banks drastically. Technology has already enabled some of the banks to introduce innovative products to their customers in the form of ATM facility, telebanking, homebanking, '*anytime*' and '*anywhere*' banking. Technology can also be harnessed in automating and networking the branches that will ensure timely flow of information and aid decision making process. A proper Management Information System (MIS) can make a major impact on the pricing of deposits, loans and other services provided by banks. The Committee on Technology Upgradation in the Banking Sector, appointed by the Reserve Bank, in its Report submitted in July 1999, has provided a medium term road map for the absorption of technology by banks and financial institutions. The banks that can adopt and absorb the new technology faster will have a competitive edge over their rivals.

> Information technology and communication networks have changed the operating environment of banking.

While the enabling policy framework and the operating environment provide a platform for improving the efficiency of the banking sector, its ultimate success depends on how individual banks respond to the competitive environment, identify their core competencies and reposition themselves effectively. These issues have been adequately addressed by the Second Narasimham Committee (1998) and according to the Committee, will form part of the agenda of the second generation of reforms in the banking sector. One of the major factors affecting efficiency is the organisational structure of the banks. With a view to reaping full benefits of liberalisation, the organisational structures of the banks need to be studied carefully. In this context, the chain of command needs to be shortened with adequate authority delegated to the branches. This would also help to enhance efficiency. In addition to the organisational structure, the adoption of proper internal systems and methods can greatly help in the efficient functioning of the banks. Another issue that assumes importance in improving the efficiency of the banks is the human resource development. Recruiting the right people, training/retraining them on a continuous basis keeping in view the changing environment and increasing complexities, and having a remuneration/incentive structure conducive to keeping their morale high, are considered integral part of the process. Another significant factor determining competitiveness is the customer service. The realisation that customer satisfaction is essential for survival and growth has dawned on all the banks. The banks that will emerge as the winners in the impending era will be truly customer-centric banks.

> In tune with the liberalisation, organisation structure of the banks needs to be changed from chain of command to the delegated system.

The above description being general in nature, it is useful to take a look at each sector of the commercial banks.

Private sector banks no doubt have done well but they have neglected rural sector.

Private sector banks As shown in Fig.27.1, there are 32 banks in the private sector with 5624 branches spread across the country. The private sector banks received a shot in the arm thanks to two major recommendations made by Narasimham Committee. The recommendations are: (1) no more nationalisation of private banks, (2) there is no difference in the treatment between public sector and private sector banks. The acceptance of these two recommendations by the RBI and the resultant reforms in the financial sector helped private sector banks considerably.

The private sector banks seized the opportunities thrown open to them. They have outperformed their counterparts in the public sector on a number of indicators like loan growth, average yield on earning assets, new provisions and operating expenses. Many of these banks are approaching capital market to raise capital to meet capital adequacy requirements and also to comply with the provisions of the RBI/SEBI.

There are criticisms nevertheless. It is pointed out that the private sector banks have neglected rural sector. Out of their total deposits, only 4 per cent comes from rural areas and together these banks lend about 2 per cent of their money to rural areas. Even in urban areas, private sector banks try to reach out to plum account holders. These banks also practice client discrimination in favour of plum customers by extending customised products, free bank lockers, invitation to events, access to treasury instruments, personalised banking, and telebanking.

Foreign banks have brought in fresh air into the banking sector in India.

Foreign banks As the Fig.26.1 shows there are 36 foreign banks with 204 branches spread across major cities in the country. These are called foreign banks as they are incorporated outside India but have operations in India.

Foreign banks have brought in, along with them, a fresh air into the banking sector in India. Their new technology, professional management practices and innovative products have greatly helped Indian banking improve their functioning.

The flip-side of foreign banks should not be overlooked. They have created a hype around them claiming that they are the 'best' in the industry. Appearance of their buildings, their infrastructure, the dress their employees wear, the language the employees speak and the parties they attend seem to justify their claim.

Foreign banks have succeeded in creating a hype around them.

What does this hype mean to an ordinary account holder? Who can open an account in a foreign bank in the first place? An ordinary citizen having salaried income is not welcome to open an account. Only elite can do. Account being opened, one needs to keep a minimum balance which varies from Rs.25,000 to Rs.1,00,000.

The customers are not happy either. The personal touch which you receive when you go to a nationalised bank to draw or deposit money is lost in a foreign bank. For withdrawal, you need to stand in a que near ATM. You are not encouraged to go to the bank for withdrawing cash. You are harassed if you become a loanee. Service charges are too heavy. Still people prefer foreign banks as they carry snob value.

RBI permits foreign banks to open branches in cities, Indian banks are advised to open branches in rural areas.

Foreign banks have made huge profits. But these profits have come not from traditional banking but from treasury operations, portfolio management, ATMs and plastic money. The profits earned by foreign banks are seldom used for the development of Indian economy. If foreign banks are shining well, largely blame lies with the RBI. While giving licences to new branches, foreign banks are encouraged to establish branches in metropolises, but Indian banks are advised to disperse and locate new branches in rural areas. And rural branches are not that profitable ones.

FISCAL POLICY

Fiscal policy refers to the policy of the government regarding taxation, public expenditure and public debt. There is a general belief, from Keynes in the thirties, that the governments can influence business activities through fiscal measures. Inspired by this belief, governments all over the world have been using fiscal measures to regulate their economic and business activities in order to achieve such objectives as:(1) accelerating the rate of investment; (2) promoting socially desirable investment; (3) achieving rapid economic development; (4) achieving full employment; (5) promoting foreign trade; (6) reducing inequalities of income and (7) establishing a welfare state.

Fiscal policy refers to government's policy towards revenue, debt and expenditure.

The Budget

Fiscal policy operates through the budget. Infact, fiscal policy is also known as budgetary policy. The term 'budget' is derived from the French word '*Bougette*', which means a leather bag or a wallet used to carry financial papers. The Chancellor of the Exchequer in England used to carry his papers in a leather bag to the House of Commons. Thus, the word 'budget' has come to mean papers containing financial matters.

Fiscal policy operates through budget. Budget refers to a set of papers containing financial matters.

The budget simply means an estimate of revenue and expenditure. In its true sense, budget is not only "*a plan of revenue and expenditure but the entire condition of material finances as disclosed in the ministerial statement placed before the legislature and orderly administration of the financial affairs for the government*" (F.Shirras). A more comprehensive definition is given by Philip V. Taylor when he says that "*Budget is a master financial plan of the government. It brings estimates of anticipated revenues and proposed expenditures, employing schedule of activities to be undertaken towards the direction of national objectives. It is a device for consolidating various interests, objectives, desires and needs of the people into a programme whereby they provide for their safety, convenience and comforts*".

The Union Budget

Our Constitution provides that: (i) no tax can be levied or collected except by the authority of law; (ii) no expenditure can be incurred from public funds except in the manner provided in the Constitution, and (iii) the executive authorities must spend public money only in the manner sanctioned by the Parliament in the case of the Union and by the State legislature in a state.

Budget approval is a big exercise because without it (i) no tax can be levied, (ii) no expenditure can be incurred, and (iii) government can spend only on approved items.

In deference to the provisions of the Constitution, our government has been preparing annual budgets, placing them before Parliament, getting its approval and spending and raising revenues as stipulated in the yearly budgets.

The work of preparing the Union budget begins in the month of August every year and after finalisation, it is presented to the Parliament on the last day of February. The budget is generally presented by the Finance Minister in the name of the President of India. The budget speech of the Finance Minister is of great importance and is eagerly awaited by the finance and business circles as it contains information about fresh taxes and proposals relating to expenditure. No discussion is allowed on the date of presentation of the budget. Discussion follows on later dates and then the budget demands are put to a vote. When the budget is passed by the Parliament, it goes to the President for his assent.

The tax proposals of the budget are embodied in another Bill which is passed as the Finance Act of the year.

Occasionally, in times of financial crisis, an interim budget may be introduced later in the year to increase taxation and expenditure. Sometimes, there may be slight modifications of taxation and expenditure without the formality of introducing a revised budget.

The receipts and expenditure of the government are audited by the Comptroller and Auditor-General in order to ensure that the executive has spent the appropriated money in accordance with the wishes of the legislature. The office of the Comptroller and Auditor-General came into being in 1913. The Government of India Act, 1935, gave the office constitutional recognition (Article 141).

Two parts make up the union budget: (a) revenue, (b) capital. First deals with revenue receipts and expenses and the second covers capital receipts and expenses.

The budget is divided into two parts, *viz.*, (a) revenue budget and (b) capital budget. The revenue budget deals with revenue receipts, which include receipts from taxes, interest receipts and dividends and profits and revenue expenditure which is mainly on administration. The capital budget is the statement of all capital expenditure and capital receipts which include market loans, external aid, deposits and provident funds. Table 26.6 contains budgetary positions of the Government of India from 1969-70 to 1997-2000. The budgetary position includes both revenue budget and capital budget.

Trends in Revenue

It is useful to analyse the trends in resources and expenditure over the years. For simplicity sake, we take the Union budgets only.

Taking the resources first, it may be stated that the demand for them has been growing since the government is committed to realise the objectives of the fiscal policy stated above. In addition, there have been other demands on public authorities: (i) the demand for resources continues to grow with growth in population which in turn necessitates increased expenditure on education, health, family welfare and the like; (2) ever increasing inflation adds to the demand for resources and (3) increase in defence expenditure since early 1960s.

With such a large demand to be met, the fiscal authorities are forced to raise resources from varied channels - both internal as well as external. Over the years, dependence on external sources has been sought to be given up. The government is increasingly relying on domestic sources. Domestic sources include taxation, market borrowings, deficit financing, surpluses of PSEs, retained earnings of the RBI and balance from current revenue at the pre-plant tax rates. Of these, the first three have been principal sources, although deficit financing has not been favoured as a source of finance.

Taxation has been receiving increasing attention to raise resources. Authorities use taxation to realise certain socio-economic objectives such as: (i) to raise revenue to finance the public sector projects without severely affecting saving and investment of the private sector; (ii) to spread tax burden on different sections of the society so as to minimise inequalities in incomes and wealth; (iii) to discourage conspicuous consumption by sections of the society; (iv) to divert investment from capital-intensive and luxury goods industries to labour-intensive and essential goods industries and (v)to mop up excess profits[3].

In order to achieve the objectives stated above, both central and state governments have taxed the citizens extensively and intensively. The taxes cover *almost all tax bases*-income, wealth, property, comsumption, transfer of income and property, capital gains, intermediary transaction of goods, exports and imports. Table 27.6 shows sources of tax revenue. As to the *intensification* of taxation, a successful attempt has been made to make both direct and indirect taxation fairly progressive.

Table 27.6 **Growth and Composition of Total Union Budgetary Deficits**

(Rs. crores)

	IV Plan 1969-70 to 1973-74	*V Plan 1974-75 to 1978-79*	*VI Plan 1980-81 to 1984-85*	*VII Plan 1985-96 to 1889-90*	*1990-92*	*VIII Plan 1992-97*	*IX Plan 1997-2000*	*X Plan 2002-2007*
1. Deficit (-) or Surplus (+) under Revenue Account	+411.20	+2671.70	–9157.70	–46905	–31439	–145875	–387704	–217004
2. Deficit under Capital Account	–2433.90	6327.90	–1629.10	+9557	+12948	+107680	+387704	+217004
3. Total Budgetary Deficit	–2046.30	–3656.20	–10786.80	–37348	–18491	–38195		

The following features are observed in our tax system:

(i) The tax base is narrow both for direct as well as indirect taxes.

(ii) There has been a progressive increase in indirect taxation (see Table 27.7).

(iii) Tax structure has been fairly progressive.

(iv) The tax burden on non-agricultural sector is higher as compared to that of the agricultural sector.

(v) Tax burden has been heavy.

However, in the post-liberalisation era, significant changes took place in our tax system. More important of them are:[4]

Post liberalisation witnessed significant developments: (i) tax structure and tax lavies are simplified, (ii) better tax administration, and (iii) long term fiscal policy.

(i) Simplification of tax structure and tax laws;

(ii) Better tax administration and the rationalisation of the tax rates;

(iii) Long-term fiscal policy that removed uncertainty of tax changes;

(iv) Increased reliance on fiscal and monetary measures as opposed to physical controls and planning and

(v) Attempts to realise economies in government's current expenditures.

Trends in Expenditure

Expenditure of the government may be revenue expenditure and capital expenditure. Revenue expenditure includes expenditure on social and community services, economic services and grants-in-aid to the state governments. Capital expenditure includes expenditure on general services, social and community services, economic services and loans and advances.

Government expenditure may also be classified as developmental and non-developmental. The first includes expenditure on social and community services, economic services and grants-in-aid to state governments and union territories for developmental purposes. Non-developmental expenditure includes the amount spent on defence, interest payments etc.

Table 27.7 **Sources of Tax Revenue**

	1990-91		1991-92		1992-93		1993-94		1994-95		1995-96		1996-97		1997-98		1998-99	
	A	B	A	B	A	B	A	B	A	B	A	B	A	B	A	B	A	B
*Direct taxes**	19.1	2.1	22.6	2.5	24.3	2.6	26.8	2.5	28.4	2.7	29.2	2.9	29.4	3.2	29.8	3.6	30.8	2.9
Personal tax	9.3	1.0	10.0	1.1	10.6	1.1	12.0	1.1	12.2	1.2	13.0	1.3	13.8	1.5	14.4	2.0	13.8	1.3
Corporate tax	9.3	1.0	11.7	1.3	11.9	1.3	13.3	1.3	14.7	1.4	14.9	1.5	14.4	1.5	14.2	1.5	15.9	1.5
Indirect taxes	78.9	8.5	75.5	8.3	73.7	7.8	71.6	6.8	71.4	6.8	70.6	7.0	70.6	7.4	70.2	6.5	69.1	6.5
Customs	35.9	3.9	33.0	3.6	31.9	3.4	29.3	2.8	29.4	2.8	28.4	2.8	33.6	3.6	34.3	2.9	30.8	2.9
Excise	42.6	4.6	41.7	4.6	41.3	4.4	41.8	4.0	41.1	3.9	41.2	4.1	35.6	3.6	34.0	3.4	36.2	3.4
Gross tax revenue	100.0	10.8	100.0	10.9	100.0	10.6	100.0	9.5	100.0	9.5	100.0	9.9	100.0	10.6	100.0	10.1	100.0	9.4

* Includes expenditure, interest, gift tax and estate duties
A=as a percentage of gross tax revenue B=as a percentage of GDP.

Expenditure of the government has been increasing from year to year. The total expenditure during 1990-91 was Rs.105,298 crore. It went up to Rs.202,024 crore in the year 1996-97. As the percentage of GDP, the expenditure has gone up from 11.1 percent in 1950-51 to 32.5 percent in 1995-96.

Reasons for increase in public expenditure are too obvious. In the last couple of decades, government machinery expanded considerably because of the socialist philosophy sought to be pursued by the government. According to one research[5], the reasons for the growth of public expenditure are- ideology, bureaucratic controls, demographic changes, income elasticity of public goods, increasing cost of government production, foreign aids, etc.

Government expenditure may be developmental and non-developmental. Developmental expenditure includes spending on social and community services and non-developmental items include payments towards interest, spending on defence and the like.

Evaluation of Fiscal Policy

The effectiveness of our fiscal policy can be assessed from three angles: (a) fiscal policy and savings and capital formation, (b) fiscal policy and economic inequalities, and (c) fiscal policy and inflation control. With reference to the first item, it may be safely concluded that fiscal policy has failed to produce enough savings for public investment. Financial crunch has become a standard excuse to avoid or postpone project implementation. With regard to the impact of public revenue and public expenditure on minimising income inequalities, less said the better. Over the years, the chasm between the rich and the poor has widened. For example, in 1992, the top 20 per cent of the population accounted for more than two fifths of the total consumption expenditure, while the bottom 20 per cent had a share of just 8.5 per cent of the total consumption. In the same year, the top 10 per cent of our population spent eight times as much as the bottom 10 per cent. The tax system has, obviously failed to rob Peters and public expenditure has failed to pay Pauls. Finally, fiscal policy has been successful in controlling inflation. The rate of inflation during the last couple of years has been lovering around five percent – a good sign indeed.

Agenda for Future

Fiscal reforms were included as a part of economic reforms initiated since 1991.

The fiscal reforms must be an ongoing process. In the years to come, our approach to fiscal policy must be-

(i) Completion of the tax reform agenda

(ii) Curb wasteful expenditure

(iii) Minimise budgetary allocations to public sector undertakings

(iv) Adopt a new approach to administered prices

(v) Reduce and redirect subsidies

QUESTIONS

1. Define Monetary Policy. What are its objectives?
2. What are credit control measures of the RBI? Explain each in brief.
3. Critically examine the working of monetary system in our country.

4. What is fiscal policy? What are its objectives?
5. What is a budget? Why is it so important?
6. Bring out the nature and operations of money market.
7. Comment on the Union Budget 2000-2001.

ASSIGNMENT

Elaborate on each of the five dimensions of new agenda for future we have shown above.

REFERENCES

1. Ishwar C.Dhingra, *Indian Economy*, Sultan Chand, 2000 p.807.
2. James C.Van Horne, *Fundamentals of Financial Management*, Oxford, 1997, p.193.
3. Ishwar C.Dhingra, *Op.Cit.* p.768.
4. *Ibid*, p.800.

CHAPTER OUTLINE

Role of Agriculture
Extent of Farm Output
Problems
Agenda for Action

LEARNING OBJECTIVES

After reading this Chapter, you should be able to:

1. Appreciate the role agriculture has played in our country
2. Give data substantiating the production of foodgrains
3. Enumerate the problems confronted by the farm sector
4. Lay down a plan of action for policy makers with respect to agriculture

28 Agriculture

The agricultural sector is a major component of our economic environment. Hence, a discussion of the role of agriculture, its problems and the challenges is in order.

ROLE OF AGRICULTURE

For several reasons, agriculture is crucial for our national economy.

1. 24.5(2002-03) per cent of our GDP comes from agriculture alone. It was around 57 per cent in the beginning of 1950s. With gradual industrialisation, the share of agriculture has declined and it is what it should be. As an economy prospers, the share of agriculture in the GDP declines giving place for secondary and tertiary sectors (see Table 28.1).

> Agriculture contributes to a major chunk (24.5%) of India's GDP.

2. Agriculture is the backbone for any country's economic development. It is a popular belief that economic development takes place because of rapid industrialisation. But industrial development itself cannot take place without agriculture. Specifically, agriculture contributes to economic development in atleast four ways: (i) product contribution, i.e., making available food and raw materials; (ii) market contribution, i.e., providing the market for goods produced by other sectors; (iii) factor contribution, i.e., making available labour and capital to the non-agricultural sector and (iv) foreign exchange contribution.[1]

> Industrial production precedes economic growth. Agriculture precedes industrial growth.

3. Gunnar Myrdal pointed out emphatically that "it is in the agricultural sector that the battle for long-term economic development will be won or lost." Traditionally, the role of agriculture in economic development has been viewed as passive and supportive. Based on the historical experience of Western countries, economic development was seen as requiring a rapid structural

Table 28.1 **Sectoral Shares of GDP (In GDP at factor cost at 1980-81 prices)**

	Agriculture	*Industry*	*Services*
1980-81	38	26	36
1990-91	31	30	39
1992-93	30	29	41
1994-95	29	30	41
1996-97	26	31	43
1997-98	24	31	44

Gunnar Myrdal said that it is in the agricultural sector that the battle for long-term economic development will be won or lost.

transformation of the economy from one predominantly focussed on agriculture activities to a more complex modern industrial and service society. As a result, agriculture's primary role was to provide sufficient low priced food and manpower to the expanding industrial economy, which was thought to be the dynamic "leading sector" in any overall strategy of economic development.

But today economists are less sanguine about the desirability of placing such heavy emphasis on rapid industrialisation. They have come to realise that far from playing a passive, supporting role in the process of economic development, the agricultural sector must play an indispensable part in any overall strategy of economic progress, specially for the 61 low-income developing countries.[2] Such is the role of agriculture in economic development of a country.

In the last couple of decades, people should have got absorbed in industry. This did not happen people still depend on agriculture.

4. Agriculture has been a major source of livelihood for our people. A large percentage of the working population (more than 70% see Table 28.2) is engaged in agriculture. As the economy progresses, the dependence on agriculture for livelihood must decline and more and more people must get absorbed in secondary and tertiary sectors. This has not happened in our country as is evident from Table 28.2. This only shows how dependent people are on agriculture.

Table 28.2 **Distribution of Employment by Broad Economic Sectors**

Sectors	*Total*		*Male*		*Female*	
	1981	*1991*	*1981*	*1991*	*1981*	*1991*
Primary	69.4	67.3	66.2	63.4	81.5	81.0
Secondary	16.5	14.5	17.2	15.3	13.7	11.7
Tertiary	17.7	20.5	19.7	23.3	12.0	10.8

Agri exports amount to Rs.10000 crore per annum.

5. Agriculture plays an important role in our international trade too. The main agricultural commodities which are exported are tea, oil cakes, fruits and vegetables, spices, tobacco, cotton, coffee, cocoa, sugar and sugar products, hides and skins and other varieties of animal hair and vegetable oils. Agri exports now amount to Rs.10,000 crore per annum. The figure is expected to rise to Rs.15,000 crore in the near future.

6. Fluctuations in agricultural output play a key role in the state of the national economy. Rural consumption of industrial goods is nearly three times that of urban consumption. As a matter of fact, the current spurt in the rural consumption of durable goods has led to a redefinition of consumer demographics itself. Obviously, there is a direct relationship between agricultural

production and income and the demand for industrial goods. Similarly, performance in agriculture also influences total demand *via* government savings and public investments. For example, a rise in agricultural production results in increased government savings both as a result of the buoyancy of government revenues and reduction in expenditures like drought relief which might otherwise become necessary.[3]

Since agriculture is the main contributor to national income, this sector is also the primary source of savings, and hence capital formation. Rate of capital formation has a major impact on economic growth.

7. Agricultural sector has transformed itself dramatically during the last few decades. Throughout the past century, some of the most vivid images of India were drawn against the backdrop of its farm sector. Most of them were depressing. They depicted famines, relentlessly unchanging bullock-cart economies, undressed and under nourished humans - mostly bonded labour - parched lands fed partly by water - wheels, and a lazy unchanging haze of heat and dust. Such imagery acquired archival value in the second half of the 20th century, particularly the last 30 years, and Indian agriculture underwent a profound transformation.

As pointed out once by J.K. Galbrath, the most significant development that took place in our economy during the past four decades relates to the farm sector. From the position of a net importer of foodgrains, our country has now reached the stage of self-sufficiency. With an annual production of more than 190 million tonnes of foodgrains and overflowing buffer stocks, the problem now is one of storage and not of shortages.

Because of green revolutions we have surplus stocks of foodgrains. The problem now is one of storage and not shortages.

In the year 1960-61, we were depending heavily on PL-480 food and oil imports. We have come a long way since then, having made rapid strides in agriculture, both in the matter of inputs as well as output.

8. Going away from Indian economy, agriculture has its impact on work discipline, power structure and behaviour of peasants (see box 28.1).

Box 28.1 **Agriculture and Society**

Every society imposes its own distinct work discipline or 'regimen.' Workers are supposed to obey certain rules, often unspoken. Their performance on the job is maintained, polished and a structure of power is in place to enforce the rules.

In First Wave or agricultural societies, most peasants toiled endlessly, yet barely survived. This agrarian work force, organised into family production teams, followed a regimen set by the rhythms of season, sunrise and sunset.

If a peasant was absent or lazy, his own relatives disciplined him. They might ostracise him, or cut his food rations. The family itself was the dominant institution in society, and exceptions aside, it imposed the work regimen. Its dominance over the individual family member was reinforced by social pressures from the villagers.

Local elites might hold the power of life and death over the peasantry. Tradition might restrict social, sexual, and religious behaviour. Peasants often suffered the cruelest hunger and poverty. And yet in their daily work lives, they seemed less minutely restricted than those in the small but growing industrial labour force.

The agrarian work regimen had lasted for millennia, and until only a century or two ago, the vast majority of human beings knew no other and assumed it to be the only logical and eternal way of organising work.

(**Source**: Alvin Toffler, *Power Shift*, p.207).

EXTENT OF FARM OUTPUT

Indian agriculture has attained both stability and resilience. Output of foodgrains has been increasing from year to year as is evident from Table 28.3. and Fig 28.1.

Table 28.3 **Output of All Foodgrains**

	(million tonnes)
1992-93	179.5
1993-94	184.3
1994-95	191.5
1995-96	180.4
1996-97	199.3
1997-98	193.1

(**Source**: *The Hindu Survey of Indian Agriculture*, 1999)

Figure 28.1 **Foodgrains Production**

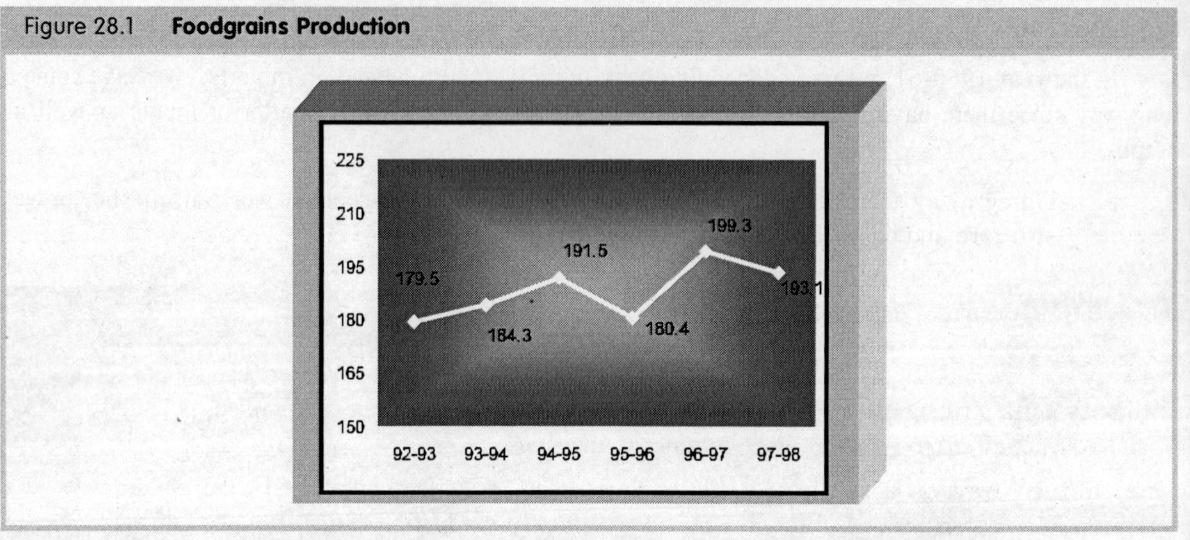

More than 75 per cent of the total output during 1994-95 is accounted for by two crops, *viz*., rice (43 per cent) and wheat (32 per cent). The remaining 25 per cent has been contributed by coarse cereals (17 per cent) and pulses (eight per cent).

The net availability, per capita per day, of foodgrains increased from 395 kg in 1951 to 470 kg in 1994-this was despite the rise in population. This growth has been achieved mainly from domestic production. We hardly depend on imports which, infact, came down from 2.6 m.tonnes per year during the Seventies and to 4.4 lakh tonnes during the Eighties. Droughts or floods need to be well managed without any panic or large scale imports. Something skategic needs to be done to combat the drought situation which is being faced in Gujarat, Orissa and Madhya Pradesh.

PROBLEMS

Agricultural sector is beset with serious problems. Some of them are stated here.

(i) Productivity in the primary sector is very low as shown in Tables 28.4, 28.5 and 28.6.

Many factors have contributed to low productivity in agriculture. More important of them are: (a) too many people depend on agriculture, (b) rural environment is not conducive for modernisation of agricultural activities, (c) small size holding, (d) poor techniques of production, and (e) inadequate irrigation facilities.

Farm productivity is very low.

Table 28.4 A View of Indian Agricultural Productivity

	World Rank	
	Output	*Yield*
Rice	2	54
Wheat	2	38
Groundnut	1	72
Rapeseed	2	33
Tobacco	3	42

(**Source**: Arun Kumar Jain, *Managing Global Competition*, 1994, p.156).

Table 28.5 Production of Rice, Paddy

Country	*Area (million hectares)*	*Output (million tones)*	*Yield (Kgs per hectare)*
India	42.30	122.24	2890
China	31.85	192.97	6059
Indonesia	11.20	46.29	4133
Vietnam	7.09	27.65	3899
Pakistan	2.33	6.59	2827
Japan	1.95	12.53	6416
U.S	1.29	8.18	6364

(Figures relate to 1998)

(**Source**: Food and Agriculture Organisation)

Table 28.6 Land Productivity in Developed and Developing Countries, 2000

Country	*Average grain yield (kgs per hectare)*	*Population (million)*
U.K.	6,975	60
Japan	5,971	127
U.S.	5,794	278
Indonesia	3,915	207
Bangladesh	2,786	128
Mexico	2,640	97
India	2,293	998
Pakistan	2,255	135
Nigeria	1,208	124
Congo	781	50

(**Source:** MiChael P.Todaro and Stephen C.Smith, *Economic Development*, p.425)

(ii) Though the total output has increased, the output of crops, other than rice and wheat, has stagnated. While pulses and coarse grains have registered no growth, the shortfall in oilseeds output *vis-a-vis* the demand has necessitated heavy import of edible oils.

The impact of green revolution has not evenly spread across the country.

(iii) The wide regional disparities in the impact of the green revolution and consequently in the output, still persist. While Punjab and Haryana have almost 90 per cent of the area of rice and wheat under HYV, it is less than 40 per cent in some of the Eastern states. A major portion of our agriculture is still operated under rainfall conditions which has also affected the consumption of fertilisers. Inspite of the heavy investment on irrigation and the tall talk about its achievement, 70 per cent of the cropped area still depends on rainfall and grows such important crops as coarse grains, pulses and bulk of cotton.

(iv) Over the years there has been a decline in public investment in agriculture. Resources for higher public investment can only become available if the current large subsidies on agricultural inputs can be scaled down. Cutting down subsidies tends to invite public wrath.

Since the early years of planning, primacy was accorded to capital accumulation by the state which also meant relative neglect of public investment in agriculture. This relative neglect of agriculture was supported by the prevailing view that a growing labour force in developing countries could only be absorbed in industry, and that in the early stages of the industrialisation, it was necessary for agriculture to contribute to the building up of modern industry by providing cheap labour. A faster development of the industrial sector was the central objective of planning.[4]

(v) Large increases in procurement and minimum support prices of foodgrains have undoubtedly strengthened production incentives for these crops. But they have also contributed to general inflation through large increases in the prices of wage goods and diversion of foodstocks from private trade to the Food Corporation of India (FCI), with its attendant high unit costs of storage, handling and distribution. Rising prices for foodgrains particularly have adverse consequences for the poorest segments of rural population, most of whom have very limited access to the Public Distribution System (PDS).

(vi) In the course of half a century of development during 1947-97, the share of agriculture in India's GDP fell from 59 per cent to 31 per cent. Yet, the share of India's population engaged in it has come down relatively marginally during the same period - from 71 per cent to 63 per cent. This implies that industry - led growth philosophies did not yield expected results. The notion that industrial growth will provide remunerative alternative work in the farm sector has been belied. Even at the threshold of the new millennium, the unchanging truism is that the vast majority of Indians are sustained entirely by the agricultural sector. Growth in Indian agriculture would have to develop several times to bring any reasonable well being to them.

There are large scale distortions in pricing of agricultural inputs.

(vii) Agriculture suffers from large scale distortions the in pricing of critical inputs such as power, water, fertilisers and credit. These are being provided to farmers at prices that are much below their cost of supplying or their opportunity costs. This leads to huge economic inefficiency in the use of resources on the one hand, and bankruptcy of input supplying agencies on the other, jeopardising further investments in those sectors. In the early 1990s, for instance, for every rupee of planned expenditure in agriculture, there was one and a quarter of a rupee that was being doled out as subsidies through underpricing of inputs. This clearly reveals that input subsidies are eating into the investments in agriculture.

(viii) Agriculture, right from the beginning, enjoyed high priority, but agriculture exports were discouraged or banned altogether, which had the effect of reducing farmers' income.[5]

The winds of globalisation have been deliberately kept away from touching the farm sector. Government frowns harshly at imports as well as the exports of most farm products. Foodgrains, which are the largest product segment of our agriculture, are the most regulated. Imports of these items are tightly controlled by canalising agencies, the only exception being pulses which can be freely brought into the country by anyone. Exports continue to be within the bounds of an archaic licence - the permit raj. Exports of edible oils (from oilseeds) have been virtually banned. Cotton imports were decanalised only recently, and their exports are strictly licensed. Tea and coffee can be freely exported but their imports are almost illegal.

Globalisation is kept away from agriculture.

(ix) Many agricultural reforms such as special support programmes for small farmers, strengthening of rural credit, revival of agricultural cooperatives, revitalisation of panchayats and other local bodies and the like remain only on paper. They are yet to be implemented.

(x) There are various inherent structural problems inhibiting agriculture. Numerically, agriculture is dominated by small and marginal farmers which account for 78 per cent of holdings but operate only 32 percent of the area. Land ceilings and tenancy laws promote the proliferation of small and marginal farms. Fragmented holdings do not encourage much investment on farms. They cannot reap economies of scale in marketing or in access to modern inputs or in the efficient utilisation of capital inputs.

(xi) There is very high wastage of foodgrains as shown in Table 28.7.

Table 28.7 **Wastemates**

Points of Wastage	*Waste in million tonne*	*Millions of people who could be fed for a month*
Transportation	0.30	20
Moisture in Storage	1.38	100
Birds' Pickings	1.73	130
Processing Losses	1.87	140
Thrashing Losses	3.41	250
Rodents in Field & Storage	5.08	380
Insects in Storage	5.18	380
Total	18.94	1400

(**Source**: Ministry for Food and Civil Supplies & *India Today* estimates)

Estimates of waste are based on foodgrain production of 203 million tonnes during 1998-99. The calculation of the number of people who could be fed is based on the assumption of net per capita cereal availability of 451 grams a day.

The figures Table 28.7 contains is staggering: the foodgrains India wasted in 1998-99 could have fed upto 117 million people for a year or the entire country for almost six weeks. Rodents and insects alone polished off the monthly food requirement of 760 million people.

A recent estimate by the Ministry of Food and Civil Supplies puts the total preventable (post-harvest) losses of foodgrains at 10 per cent of the total production-or about 20 million tonnes a year. That's roughly the amount of foodgrain Australia produces annually. India also wastes about 30 per cent of its fruits and vegetables worth Rs.28,810 crore annually-which is more than what the UK consumes in a year.

These revelations are grim because they exhibit an upward trend in foodgrain wastage which was between 6 per cent and 7 per cent of the production till the late 1970s. They also point to a fundamental flaw in the government's policy on foodgrains which remains focussed on enhancing production with scant attention to saving what has been produced.

(xii) There are problems relating to seeds and other farm inputs. Take seeds first. Often farmers are put to severe losses and hardships because of the poor quality of seeds supplied to them as Box 28.2 tells.

Box 28.2 **Monsanto Told to Compensate Farmers**

The district administration (Warangal in A.P.) has asked the Mahyco-Monsanto company to compensate farmers for the loss of yield due to the use of defective Bt Cotton seed supplied by the company.

The Mahyco-Monsanto sold 25,000 packets of MCH-12/MCH-162 and MCH-184 varieties of cottonseed. Each packet contained 400 gm. of seed, enough for an acre of land. Raasi company sold 26,000 packets of Bt Cotton seed. However, farmers who purchased the seed from Mahyco-Monsanto complained about poor growth and flowering and sarcospora and black arm diseases.

Following the complaints and protests by farmers from Mahabubabad division, the district administration constituted joint teams involving the mandal revenue officer, mandal agricultural officer, panchayat secretary and representatives of farmers and the company in October and collected samples from fields. The samples were then sent to agricultural research centres in Guntur and Jagitial in Karimnagar district.

The Joint Director (Agriculture), M.Laxman Rao, said scientists declared that the loss of crop was on account of soil variations, long dry spells and moisture stress and not on account of seed defect. Following disputes within the joint teams, the district administration again deputed a district-level MoU committee that inspected fields at random and collected samples.

The total yield loss was estimated between 30 per cent and 60 per cent and the average loss was placed at 45 per cent. The committee came to the conclusion that 50 per cent of the loss was due to seed defect and the rest due to natural reasons such as low rainfall, pests and diseases. The officials said on an average, the loss was 1.57 quintal per acre, of which 0.78 quintal of produce should be measured in terms of money and the same should be paid to farmers.

Accordingly, the officials concluded that the farmers lost the crop in an extent of 22,130 acres, the worth of which was Rs.3.3 crores. The committee said the company should pay the compensation.

(**Source**: *The Hindu*, March 6, 2005)

We fall short of targets with regard to the consumption of fertilisers. With regard to the pattern of consumption, there is disparity. In certain regions, a few crops and the rabi season account for the bulk of the fertiliser use at the cost of others.

Poor quality seeds supplied to the farmers has hit the farmers badly.

(xiii) Finally, there has been considerable loss of biodiversity. The spread of high-yielding varieties, developed through modern plant breeding and biotechnology have resulted in the loss of biodiversity in the country. There has been a drastic reduction both in the number of plant species chosen for cultivation and such genetic homogeneity enhances vulnerability to pests and diseases. Divergent gene pools are also the feed stock necessary for the modern genetic industry.[6]

AGENDA FOR ACTION

If agriculture is to record abundance; if poverty is to be abolished quickly and if the chasm between rural-urban divide is to be curtailed, agriculture must grow at the rate of about four percent. This needs action on the following lines[7]:

1. Building Institutions for People's Participation

People's participation at different levels of developmental activity is needed urgently. In particular, their due representation in the decision-making bodies of critical input supplying agencies/sectors such as irrigation, electricity, seeds and extension and in output marketing boards/committees can be a catalyst towards better resource use efficiency and higher profitability in agriculture. At present, all these bodies have a typical '*top-down*' approach for decision making and communication. They are known for inefficiency, delay and corruption.

People participation in the critical inputs-supply process is vital for agricultural growth.

The 73rd amendment to the Constitution is welcome as it has cleared decks for the empowerment of people through Panchayat Raj institutions.

2. Freeing up Agricultural Markets

Besides empowering farmers, another area needing immediate action relates to cleaning up all the mess that has accumulated in output and input markets over the years. First, a clean sweep is required in the domestic output markets. All controls on free movement, stocking limits, futures trading etc. must be abolished. Levies on rice and sugar should also be abolished.

Markets need to be freed from middlemen.

On the inputs side, many of the inputs (like land, irrigation, electricity, etc) are non-tradable in nature. They, therefore, should be tackled through institutional reforms. The main tradable inputs are seeds, fertilisers, farm machinery and pesticides. Successive governments have failed to introduce any drastic reforms in their areas for political reasons. It needs a strong political will to tackle the issue of subsidies.

On the external markets, it is advisable to take an appropriate approach while the long term objective should be to replace all physical controls on the export and import of agricultural commodities by tarification. In the short run, the export market must be thrown open to agricultural products.

3. Carving an Investment Policy

While building of institutions on the lines of the participatory development model is expected to attain higher efficiency in the use of existing resources, freeing up of agricultural markets would make Indian agriculture more remunerative, thus inviting greater levels of private investments for promoting higher growth rates in agriculture. In order to ensure that this growth remains sustainable, and even accelerates, the government should carve out a comprehensive investment policy, clearly defining the roles of public and private sector investments in agriculture. As is well known, one of the problems is declining/stagnating investment in agriculture since the early 1980s. If this trend is not reversed, the aggregate supply response of agriculture to institutional changes as also freeing up of markets will remain very limited. Therefore, from the long-term point of view, it is very essential that investments in agriculture are raised.

4. Restructuring Rural Credit

There is a need for restructuring rural credit. Agriculture, falling under the priority sector, deserves 18 per cent of the total lending by commercial banks. But the actual lending still remains lower than 15 per cent. If banks and other lending agencies are reluctant to extend specified rural credit, they have justifiable reasons *viz*;

- Concessional rates of interest for the priority sector and
- High default rates in agriculture.

Both are legitimate reasons, and appropriate policy changes would have to be made if agriculture is to be ensured larger credit availability from institutional sources.

The steps needed are-

- Withdraw concessional rates of interest for agriculture gradually within a period of two to three years.
- Resort to group lending approach to check defaults.
- Loans may be lent to women where defaults tend to be less.
- Local NGOs may be involved in the lending process to exercise moral pressure on borrowers.

5. Irrigation

Next to land, water is the scarciest resource among farmers. Through its proper use, even supply of cultivable area can be augmented. The country has an ultimate irrigation potential of about 153.5 million hectares. During 1951-90, India has added 55 million hectares to its irrigation, taking the total irrigated area from 23 to 78 million hectares. This means that there is still ample scope for tapping the remaining irrigation potential. Since crop yields on irrigated lands are much higher (about two and a half times in case of foodgrains) than the yields on unirrigated lands, there is ample scope for increasing agricultural production in the years to come. But this requires proper planning and proritisation of issues relevant for the growth and efficiency of the irrigation sector.

The following may be suggested in this direction:

- Improve maintenance of existing canal network.
- Involve farmers in maintaining the canal systems from distributory level onwards.
- Leave distribution of water and collection of dues thereof to farmers' organisations.
- Introduce volumetric pricing of electricity for ground water irrigation.

6. Dry Land Farming

Mr.Monsoon has been agriculture minister of India.

More than one-third of our cultivated area depends on monsoon and Mr.Monsoon is always the agriculture minister of India. The rainfed areas are characterised by cropping patterns, dominated by coarse cereals, pulses, oilseeds and cotton. The yields of these crops are generally low and fluctuate widely, revealing a high risk factor.

One way of overcoming the above problem is to provide high priority to water harvesting and soil conservation programmes in the rainfed areas. Atleast minimum moisture is needed to raise productivity of dry land crops. To give a boost to such water harvesting schemes, they may be tied with employment generating schemes such as the Jawahar Rojgar Yojana in rural areas. Thereafter, emphasis needs to be placed on the input delivery system and the development of markets such that farmers can be assured of reasonable returns on their investments. A policy of crop insurance can also be thought of to encourage private investments on dry land farms.

It is said that dry land areas are more suitable for horticultural crops, which require less water but more investments. Credit lines need to be strengthened for encouraging horticultural crops. Besides, live stock development holds a better future in these areas than the traditional crop husbandry. Thus, the strategy for dry land areas would comprise high priority to water harvesting, soil conservation schemes and diversification towards horticulture and livestock.

7. Revitalising Research

Research is vital to introduce cost reducing technology and better seeds for cultivation. This fact seems to have not been realised in our country. The status of research in agriculture, as of today, speaks about the general apathy:

Research outlay on agriculture is a pitiable low of 0.3 per cent of GDP.

- Expenditure on agriculture research is pitiably low accounting for just 0.3 percent to agricultural GDP. In the US, it is 2 per cent to 3 per cent, and 0.7 per cent in the group of developing countries.
- Not only the percentage is too low, from year to year, the investment on research has been declining. We have failed to realise the fact that investment on research has high returns.
- The imported technology in terms of HYV seeds remained restricted to primarily irrigated areas of the north-west for almost two decades, and travelled eastwards only in the late 1980s and early 1990s. Vast areas, particularly unirrigated ones, still do not have any access to better technology.

How to reverse the trend? The following needs to be done immediately:

- Invest more on research. Use private agri-based industry to fund research.
- Government research to focus on fundamental (say in breeder and foundation seeds) and private sector to take up the production of certified seeds.
- Streamline laws relating to intellectual property rights to ensure smooth and effective co-operation between the government and the industry.
- Government research must go beyond foodgrains and focus on sunrise areas like horticultural and animal husbandry.
- ICAR to give high priority to dry land crops. Its focus in the past has confined to irrigated regions contributing to regional disparities.
- The coming revolution will be in bio-technology which our country cannot afford to miss. Biotechnology requires huge investments but yields will be greater than under HYV technology. To ensure that we get into this at the right time, ICAR must give high priority to bio-tech research.

8. No More Discrimination

In addition to the action on the seven areas suggested above, there is the need to end discrimination meted out against agriculture till now. Our agriculture has been grossly discriminated against, through a subtle but powerful instrument of trade policy. High protection accorded to the industry, past the stage of infancy, acted as a deterrent to agriculture and prevented it from growing to its full potential. Agriculture has been hit in atleast two ways: (i)Excessive protection resulted in high prices of industrial products relative to agri-products, which hurt the rural poor as consumers of industrial production. (ii) Protectionist policy increased the profitability of industrial production as compared to agricultural activities, thus shifting investments away from agriculture.

Discrimination against agriculture is revealing. Investments, as stated above, went away from agriculture. Government resorted to large scale industrialisation through its public sector enterprises. Private sector industries secured liberal credit through several public and private financial institutions. Infrastructure in terms of roads, electricity, telecom facilities, railways, etc., had a strong bias in favour of industry and urban areas. In comparison agriculture and rural areas were neglected.

This discrimination against agriculture must end.

QUESTIONS

1. Bring out the role of agriculture in the Indian economy.
2. What are the problems faced by the agricultural sector?
3. Discuss the tasks lying ahead in the agricultural front.
4. Why has agriculture been discriminated against? What are the consequences?

ASSIGNMENT

How do agriculturalists benefit from the new retail revolution that is taking place now? Prepare a brief report.

REFERENCES

1. S.Kuznets, cited in the *Indian Economy* by Ishwar C.Dhingra, Sultan Chand & Sons, 1997, p.235.
2. Michael P. Todaro and Stephen C. Smith, *Economic Development,* Pearson, 2003, p.419.
3. Ishwar C.Dlingra, *Indian Economy*, Sultan Chand & Sons, 1997, p.238.
4. Bimal Jalan, *India's Economic Crisis*: *The Way Ahead*, Oxford University Press, 1991, p.23.
5. *Ibid*, p.10.
6. Iswar C. Dhirgra, *op.cit.,* p.261.
7. This section is based on *Indian Development Policy Imperatives*, ed. by Vijay Kelkar and Bhanoji Rao, TMH, 1996, Pp.141-156.

CHAPTER OUTLINE

Criteria for Backwardness
Causes for Backwardness and Regional Imbalances
The Problem
Measures to Remove Regional Imbalances
- Resources Transfer
- Special Area Development Programmes
- Disposal of Industries
- Growth Centres
- Nucleus Plants and Ancillaries
- Banking Policy

Failure of Regional Planning
Suggestions to Remove Regional Imbalances

LEARNING OBJECTIVES

After reading this Chapter, you should be able to:

1. Determine criteria for backwardness
2. Point out the reasons for regional imbalances
3. Appreciate the extent of regional imbalances
4. Suggest remedies to remove regional disparities
5. Understand why regional planning has failed and suggest ways of making it successful

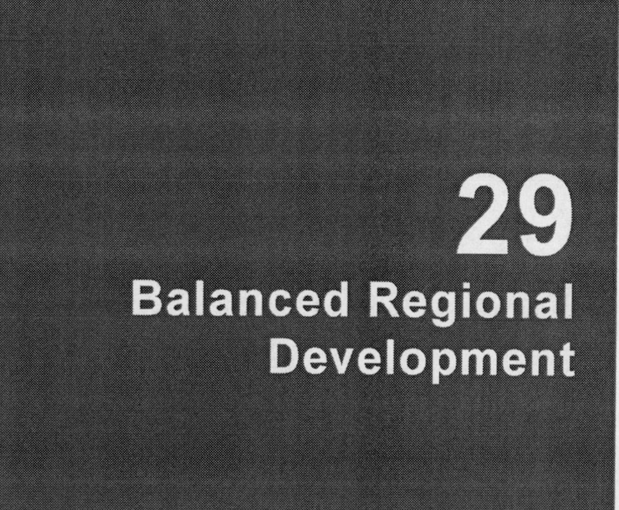

29 Balanced Regional Development

One of the planks of economic development in our country has been the removal of regional imbalances, or positively put, achieving balanced regional development. After four and a half decades of economic planning where we stand in realising this objective, and in the light of the past experiences, what could be done in future are the issues worth examining. We propose to discuss these in this chapter.

> Achieving balanced regional development has been one of the planks of India's economy.

Before discussing other aspects of balanced regional development, it is useful to know the meaning of the terms 'region' and 'balanced regional development'. Generally understood, a region means a state within the Union of India like Karnataka, Andhra Pradesh or another state. But for the purpose of planning, a region may be an area within a state, as for example, North Karnataka, Old Mysore and the like. It is an economic entity within a state.

Balanced regional development means the fullest development of the potentialities of an area according to its capacity so that the benefits of overall economic growth are shared by the inhabitants of all the regions. Balanced regional development does not mean self-sufficiency in each state or region. Neither does it mean equal level of industrialisation, nor a uniform economic pattern for each state. Rather, it means widespread diffusion of the industry to backward areas so far as it is economically feasible, the ultimate aim is to raise the living standards of the people in backward regions to those of the advanced. It may be through the development of agriculture, industry, trade or commerce.[1]

The idea of regional planning originated with Stalin. Stalin wanted to develop each region in the former Soviet Russia in such a way that in the event of an invasion, the occupation of any region by the capitalist powers might not cripple the economic power of the country. The first Western country to recognise the problem of regional disparities was Great Britain. The British Government took its first tentative action in the field of industrial location in the 1930s

> It was Stalin who conceived the idea of regional development.

when unemployment in the older specialised industrial regions of Northern England, Wales and Scotland rose to alarming levels. Two policy objectives were recognised: the alleviation of the short-run unemployment problem and the long-run need to strengthen the economic structure of the declining regions. It was assumed that both objectives could be achieved by the same policy - that of taking work to the workers, a proposition which is still largely adhered to despite strong arguments and much evidence to the contrary.[2]

In our country, efforts at removal of regional imbalances were first initiated during the Second Plan. The Second Plan admitted that in any comprehensive plan of development, it is axiomatic that special needs of the less developed areas should receive due attention. The pattern of investment must be so devised as to lead to balanced regional development. Originated during the Second Plan, the concept of regional development has been underlined by the planners in all subsequent plans.

CRITERIA FOR BACKWARDNESS

The Sixth Plan mentioned 17 criteria for determining the prevalence of backwardness. These were density of rural population, percentage of urban population to total population, percentage of Scheduled Castes and Scheduled Tribes, percentage of area irrigated, agricultural output per hectare, farm investment per cultivator household, rural unemployment rate, consumption standards of weaker sections in rural areas, percentage of debt owed by all households to landlords and moneylenders, surfaced road mileage, percentage of villages electrified, per capita industrial output, number of persons engerged in secondary and tertiary activities per lakh of population and the like. Going by the criteria, the Sixth Plan identified the following backward areas:

(a) *High Population Density Areas in the Gangetic Plains*: These areas have a high potential for agricultural production but the potential is not fully exploited with the result agricultural yield rate tends to be low. There is heavy pressure on land due to the high density of population. The debt bondage to lands and moneylenders is quite high.

(b) *Areas With Exceptionally Low Agricultural Productivity*: Mostly found in Central and Western India, these areas fall in the drought-prone belt. Many of these areas have a high density of population with limited opportunities for non-agricultural employment.

(c) *The North-East*: The problem of this region arises partly from its remoteness from the national market and partly from the socio-cultural base.

(d) *Tribal Areas*: These are generally found in two compact blocks, one in the North-Eastern part of the country and the other in Central and Eastern India. In the former case, the problems are largely locational and social. As regards the latter, small pockets of modern industry co-exist with backward rural areas with a high rate of unemployment.

(e) *Ecological Problem Areas*: These include desert and hill areas which have a limited scope for economic development.

CAUSES FOR BACKWARDNESS AND REGIONAL IMBALANCES

The causes for economic backwardness and regional imbalances may be historical, geographical, economic or political.

Historically, the existence of backward regions started from the British rule in India. The British helped the development of only those regions which possessed facilities for prosperous manufacturing and trading activities. Maharashtra and West Bengal were two states preferred by the British industrialists. Further, under the land system of the British, the rural areas were continuously pauperised and the farmers remained the most oppressed class, the zamindars and the moneylenders were, of course, the only prosperous persons on the rural scene. The absence of effective land reforms allowed the structure in most of rural India to remain inimical to economic growth. Again, the uneven investments in irrigation during the British period helped some areas to become prosperous under British rule.

Britishers developed some regions at the cost others, thus leading to imbalances.

Geographical or physical factors are still major causes having their bearing on wide disparities prevailing in the development of regions. The development of a particular region or country depends on a favourable climate for settlement of the people; availability of natural resources for their conversion into wealth; possibilities for carrying on agricultural operations; facilities for starting and developing industries and the convenience with which trade and commerce can be handled. Physical environment prescribes boundaries, and places hurdles in the path to progress of all these economic activities, notwithstanding the tremendous technological breakthrough achieved by man during the past 150 years.

Richness of factor endowments of a region is also a cause for regional imbalances.

Economic factors refer to locational advantages in terms of transport, labour market, technology, raw materials and other related factors enjoyed by certain regions. As is well known, not all the regions possess all the locational advantages in equal proportions. The areas which are right in materials possess a vast market, and enjoy a high degree of infrastructural facilities that attract new investments, particularly in the private sector.

Political factors play an important role in the location of business undertakings, particularly in the public sector; resource transfer or in special area development programmes. Political considerations are becoming more powerful these days. Local leaders are whipping up regional feelings among the public at the time of elections to state assemblies. Tall promises are made to the electrorate to catch votes and after gaining power, undue patronage is meted out to the areas or regions not realising the fact that such unequal favours are highly divisive in nature.

It is not just economic factors alone, even political factors contribute to regional imbalances.

Colin Clark, in his famous book *The Conditions of Economic Progress*, has stated that the levels of income are higher in those regions where a larger proportion of the working population is engaged in the manufacturing and tertiary sectors. Since these activities are not evenly spread, there are bound to be disparities in incomes.

The introduction of new technology in agriculture has added to the disparities among regions. There have been differences in the use of new technology and of improved variety of seeds.

Sanctions and disbursements by financial institutions and commercial banks have shown a distinct tendency towards the concentration of investments in the relatively more developed states. Subsidised lending by banks for financing priority credit and refinancing facilities given by financial institutions have helped the richer states to gain greater access to investible funds at subsidised rates.

Financial institutions and banks have played no less role. They preferred borrowers from developed regions.

There exists a glaring regional imbalance and disparity among different states in the provision of educational and training facilities, particularly technical education. According to a report by the All India Council for Technical Education (AICTE), four states of Karnataka, Andhra Pradesh, Tamil Nadu and Maharastra account for as many as 1056 technical institutions out of a total of 1818 in the country.

The operations of the system of public finance in the country have also added to regional imbalances. In the low income states, for example, the level of public investment, infrastructural growth and standard of administrative services are lower compared to those in the high income states, thus perpetuating disparities. Similarly, the prevailing system of sales taxation has facilitated the richer states to export a significant portion of their tax burden to the residents of poor states.

Fiscal policy, by favouring high income areas for public investment and spending, has also contributed to regional imbalances.

Regional disparities are caused by differences in resources, policies and institutions and the interaction among them. Ironically, pattern of income distribution shows that some of the well-endowed states such as Bihar, Orissa, Madhya Pradesh and Uttar Pradesh are the poorest. A recent study mapping the growth patterns of different districts with the system of land settlement showed that the areas under the zamindari system grew at much slower rates than those under the Ryotwari system underlining the importance of structure of incentives created by institutions. In places where land reforms were relatively successful, the growth has been faster. This underlines the importance of institutional reform. While the initial conditions created by the colonial interests were unfavourable, after liberalisation the investments have tended to gravitate towards states with better market access and institutions.

In a federal system, adoption of appropriate regional policies and intergovernmental transfers are used as instruments to redress regional disparities. The analysis shows that the distribution of Central government investments in public enterprises has been regressive. In 2002-03, the low-income states with a population share of 44.5% accounted for 28.7% share of GSDP. The stock of Central investment in public enterprises in these states was just 28.7% and they accounted for just 41.2% of employment. As regards Central transfers to states, although these are equalising, they have failed to offset the fiscal disabilities of poorer states from their low revenue raising capacity. While the Finance Commission transfers have the highest equalising element, the Centrally-sponsored schemes have little equalising component. Besides, controls over prices and output and origin-based tax system tend to create their own source of invisible transfers which are disequalising.

This is shown by the pattern of development spending. There are systematic variations in per capita expenditures on social and economic services among states. The coefficient of variation in development expenditures among states has increased from 0.28 in 1993-94 to 0.39 in 2004-05 and the correlation coefficient of per capita expenditures with per capita NSDP has been consistently over 0.8. This pattern of public spending will only contribute to further accentuation of disparities and unless immediate measures are taken, the situation will become explosive.

THE PROBLEM

In order to assess the extent of backwardness, the Centre for Monitoring Indian Economy (CMIE) has developed an aggregate index to show economic development using district-wise data on various aspects of development.

All India average has been taken at 100. The index numbers prepared for different states indicate a range from 1075 for the Union Territory of Delhi down to 10 for Manipur. Eight states are above the all India average, while 13 states and five union territories are below the average. The better developed parts of the country are Goa, Gujarat, Haryana, Karnataka, Kerala, Maharastra, Punjab, Tamil Nadu and West Bengal. Chandigarh and Pondicherry (both union territories) also fall under this category. Union territories and states which are below average and backward are Andhra Pradesh, Assam, Bihar, Dadar and Nagar Haveli, Himachal Pradesh, Lakshwadeep, Madhya Pradesh, Meghalaya, Mizoram, Nagaland, Manipur, Orissa, Rajasthan, Sikkim, Tripura and Uttar Pradesh. The data for there new states, viz., Jharkhard, Chattisgarh and Uttranchal are not available.

Another index-known as the index of disparity, is measured as a ratio of the per capita income of the most affluent state to that of the one at the bottom. This index which stood at 2.88 during the Sixth Plan, moved up marginally to 2.97 during the Seventh Plan before widening to 3.29 in the early nineties.

In 1992, the top 20 per cent of the population accounted for more than two-thirds of the total consumption expenditure, while the bottom 20 per cent had a share of just 8.5 per cent of the total consumption. In the same year, the top 10 per cent of India's population spent eight times as much as the bottom 10 per cent (Also see Fig.29.1).

Across the globe too, disparities are glaring. Disparities in Brazil are the widest in the world. During 1990s, the top 20 per cent of the Brazilian population had more than two-thirds of the national income while the bottom 20 per cent had a meagre 2.1 per cent share.

A summary measure of inequality is the Gini Index-closer the index is to 100, greater the inequality and a value of 0 indicates perfect equality. On this count as well, Brazil has the dubious distinction of a

Figure 29.1 **Inequality in India (Share of each Quintile in Consumption, 1992)**

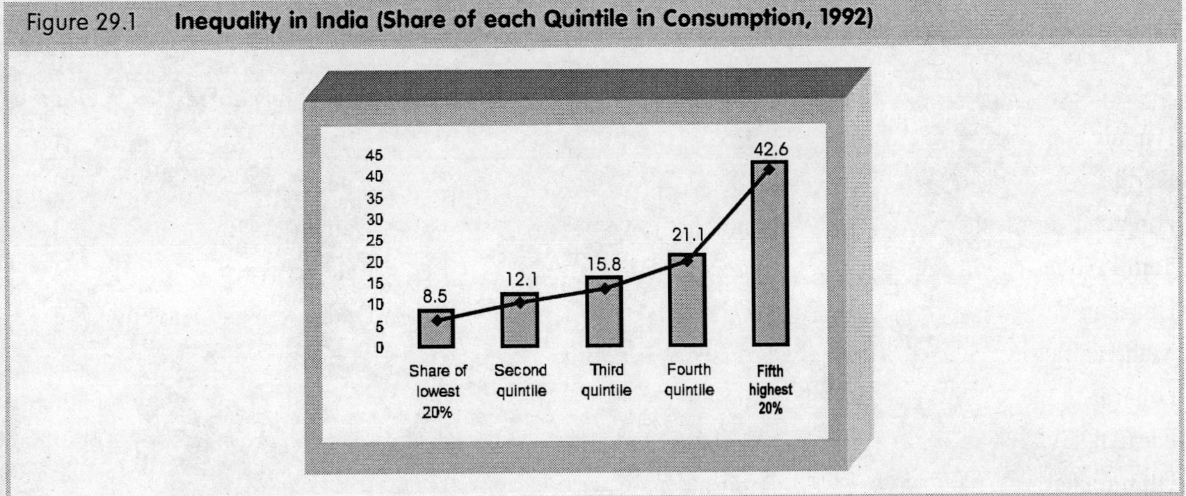

very high Gini Index. South Africa-just recovering from decades of apartheid, naturally has wide disparities.Surprisingly, inequality in China is worse than in India-perhaps because of unequal opportunities thrown up after the 1978 reforms.

Disparities in Russia too are wide. But in most former socialist economies, the gap between the rich and poor is less than elsewhere. Poland has the lowest inequality record. Generally, the Scandinavian countries (example, Sweden) enjoy a much less unequal distribution of income.In Japan too, disparities are less than in most other parts of the world.

Then there is the competitiveness index for rating the states. The ratings are[3]: Karnataka 56.19, Punjab 82.80, Gujarat 60.63, Kerala 67.71, Rajastan 39.80, Maharastra 48.77, Uttar Pradesh 25.27 and Bihar 22.36.

Table 29.1 gives more details about wide disparities prevailing among different parts of the country.

While Maharastra and West Bengal are flourishing, BOMARU states are languishing.

Economic boom witnessed during the post-reform period has only widened the disparities. For example, during 1980s, the slowest growing state had a growth rate of 0.9 per cent while the fastest growing one had a growth rate of 4.7 per cent. During the 1990s the respective growth rates were 0.7 per cent and 8.6 per cent. More glaring is the fact that two prosperous states-Maharastra and West Bengal-account for about one-fourth of NDP. But the BOMARU States (Bihar, Orissa, Madhya Pradesh, Assam, Rajasthan and Uttar Pradesh) are languishing.

India Today, the leading magazine in India, has ranked all the states and union territories on eight performance factors. The variables identified and employed are: agriculture, industrial environment, consumer market, health, education, law and order, infrastructure and budget and prosperity. Table 28.1 contains the ranking. Among the big States, Punjab tops the list, Goa occupies the top slot among the small states and Chandigarh sits on the top of the heap among union territories. The lowest ranking goes to Bihar, Meghalaya and Dadra and Nagar Haveli among the three categories respectively.

Intra-state Disparities

Imbalances exist not only among states but within a state, disparities are found among districts. The CMIE study (covering 172 districts in seven states in July 1996) reveals the following:

Table 29.1 **India's Best and Worst States**

Big States	*Rank*	*Small States*	*Rank*	*Union Territories*	*Rank*
Punjab	1	Goa	1	Chandigarh	1
Kerala	2	Delhi	2	Andaman & Nicobar	2
Himachal Pradesh	3	Pondichery	3	Daman & Diu	3
Tamil Nadu	4	Mizoram	4	Lakshadweep	4
Haryana	5	Sikkim	5	Dadra & Naga Haveli	5
Maharastra	6	Arunachal Pradesh	6		
Gujarat	7	Manipur	7		
Karnataka	8	Nagaland	8		
Uttaranchal	9	Tripura	9		
Jammu & Kashmir	10	Meghalaya	10		
Andhra Pradesh	11				
Rajasthan	12				
West Bengal	13				
Madhya Pradesh	14				
Chattisgarh	15				
Assam	16				
Uttar Pradesh	17				
Orissa	18				
Jharkhand	19				
Bihar	20				

(**Source:** *India Today*, August 15, 2005)

- The more developed the state, the more inequitous is the pattern of development in the state.
- Districts classified as backward by the state appear to have much higher per capita DDP than the so-called non-backward districts; and
- Relatively developed or under-developed districts tend to be spatially concentrated ignoring the intervening state boundaries.

We have villagers who have not boarded a train, not seen a movie in a theatre, take hours to visit an alopathic doctor and wait for floods, for in the wake of such events, relief materials pour in.

It is not that any figures are necessary to demonstrate the imbalances prevailing among different regions. The problem is there for anybody to see. Ours is a vast country supporting a huge population. We have villages where inhabitants have not seen a train yet; not gone to a movie; take hours to take a seriously ill patient to an allopathic doctor; and feel highly blessed when rivers overflow submerging villages, for devastating floods bring in their wake scores of relief measures which guarantee ration, blankets and utensils that would last at least one full year. There are tribals who offer you, with gratitude, a basketful of fruits just plucked from the trees very cheap. There are villages which are not electrified, have no good roads, no schools and no sanitation. There are villages where nearly 50 per cent of the inhabitants are infected with tuberculosis, the disease being mainly caused by the thick smoke which comes out of ovens, while cooking food and there being no openings in the thatched roofs for the smoke to go out. The streets of villages are narrow, often zigzag and are literally dirtied by beedi butts and enormous spits. Half-clad children in an unkempt condition play in the streets with gay abandon amidst themselves and admilst dirty dogs. All eyes will be focussed on you if you happen to pass through the streets as if you had come down from the city. If you go with a vehicle (even a two wheeler), the children surround you, touch the vehicle, feel it, sound the horn, touch the buttons and wonder how it would run and how you could ride.

MEASURES TO REMOVE REGIONAL IMBALANCES

The problem of regional imbalances is not peculiar to our country. The problem is universal. The successful planning of a regional economic development programme is one of the most difficult tasks facing the modern world. It is a problem shared by advanced industrial nations and those in the earlier stages of development, and it exists in both capitalist and socialist economic systems.[3]

The following measures have been taken to remove regional imbalances in our country. They are:

(a) Recognition of backwardness as a factor to be taken into account in the transfer of financial resources from the Centre to states;

(b) Special area development programmes directed at the development of backward areas;

(c) Dispersal of industries;

(d) Growth centres;

(e) Nucleus plants; and

(f) Banking policy.

Resources Transfer

Financial resources are transferred from the Centre to states. The main criterion for transfer is backwardness of states. Often, Central funds are transferred to fill state's revenue gaps, if any.

Funds are transferred based on the recommendations of Finance Commissions from time to time. Funds transferred from Fifth to Tenth Commissions are given in Table 29.2.

Table 29.2 **Transfers to States**

Commission	*Amount (Rs.Crore)*	*% of Central Revenue*
Fifth	5,421	27.90
Sixth	11,048	25.90
Seventh	22,880	26.09
Eighth	29,452	24.10
Ninth	1,06,062	22.74
Tenth	2,26,643	24.50

As seen from the Table 29.2, transfers were increasing in absolute terms, but declining percentage-wise.

Resource transfers, instead of minimising regional imbalances seem to have contributed to disparities as is evident from Table 29.3.

Table 29.3 **Per Capita Transfers**

States	*Ninth Commission (1981 Census)*	*Tenth Commission (1991 Census)*	*% increase*
		High Income States (Rs)	
Maharastra	961	1741	80%
Gujarat	996	2159	116%
Punjab	935	1785	90%
		Low Income States (Rs)	
Uttar Pradesh	1544	2606	68%
Rajasthan	1769	2402	36%
Orissa	2028	3081	50%

As is clear from this table, the percentage increase in per capita transfer is the highest in the most advanced state, *viz.*, Gujarat. Rajasthan, which is highly backward, registered the least increase in per capita transfer of central funds.

(Tables 29.2 and 29.3 are based on the *Economic Times* dated Jan.4, 1996).

Special Area Development Programmes

Special schemes have been evolved by the Central Government for the development of deserts, hill areas, tribal areas and drought prone areas.

Dispersal of Industries

The most effective way of achieving balanced regional development is to ensure dispersal of industries to backward areas. Backward areas, it is believed, will shed their backwardness once they are brought on the industrial map of the country.

There is reluctance on the part of private entrepreneurs to go to backward areas because of the absence or inadequacy of infrastructural facilities. The government should take the initiative and locate its industrial undertakings in backward areas. The government did take the initiative and established a number of undertakings in backward areas.*

Besides establishing its own undertakings in backward areas, the government has been encouraging private investors to go to backward areas for locating their industrial enterprises. Encouragement has been shown in the form of fiscal and monetary incentives given to entrepreneurs who select backward areas for locating plants. The government has identified 303 districts (see Table 29.4) as backward areas for awarding fiscal and monetary incentives.

Licensing of industries has been used as a weapon to ensure the dispersal of industries to backward areas. The share of backward areas in the total letters of intent issued has been steadily increasing. It was 33.2 per cent in 1978, 43.9 per cent in 1980 and shot up to 61.5 per cent in 1983.

* For more details, read chapter on 'Public Enterprises' in this book.

Table 29.4 **Statewise Division of Backward Districts**	
1. Andhra Pradesh (14 Districts)	16. Himachal Pradesh (Entire State)
2. Bihar (18 Districts)	17. Jammu & Kashmir(Entire State)
3. Gujarat (11 Districts)	18. Manipur (Entire State)
4. Haryana (4 Districts)	19. Meghalaya (Entire State)
5. Kerala (7 Districts)	20. Nagaland (Entire State)
6. Karnataka (11 Districts)	21. Sikkim (Entire State)
7. Madhya Pradesh (36 Districts)	22. Tripura (Entire State)
8. Maharashtra (14 Districts)	23. Arunachal Pradesh (Entire State)
9. Orissa (8 Districts)	24. Goa (Entire State)
10. Punjab (5 Districts)	25. Mizoram (Entire State)
11. Rajasthan (16 Districts)	26. A & N Islands (Entire Union Territory)
12. Tamil Nadu (9 Districts)	27. Dadra & Nagar Haveli (Entire Union Territory)
13. Uttar Pradesh (41 Districts)	28. Daman & Diu (Entire Union Territory)
14. West Bengal (13 Districts)	29. Pondichery (Entire Union Territory)
15. Assam (Entire State)	30. Lakshadweep(Entire Union Territory

But of late, there has been a decline in the number of licences issued to the backward areas. In 1986, a total of 618 licences were issued. Out of this, 278 were for the backward areas. In terms of percentage, this works out to be about 45 per cent. By 1988, the number of licences issued had come down to 360 and the share of backward areas to 42.5 per cent, or only 153 licences. By 1990, the number of licences stood at 387. The share of backward areas was about 43 per cent (See Table 29.5).

Table 29.5 **Share of Backward Areas in Total Licences Issued**

Year	*Total licences*	*Share of backward areas*	*% of backward areas*
1986	618	278	45.0
1987	472	192	40.7
1988	360	153	42.5
1989	418	175	41.9
1990	387	167	43.2

Further, financial institutions have been** directed by the government to give loans at concessional rates of interest to entrepreneurs who locate their enterprises in backward areas.

Growth Centres

One of the reasons for poor industrial activities in backward regions is the lack of good and adequate infrastructural facilities. For promoting industrial development in backward areas, it was announced, in

** The role played by the financial institutions in the development of backward areas is explained in the chapter on "Development Banking" in this book.

Growth centres, equipped with funds and infrastructural facilities, would promote industries in backward areas.

1988, that the focus would henceforth be on the development of growth centres that would attract industries. The growth centres would be endowed with infrastructural facilities at par with the best available in the country, particularly in respect of power, water, telecommunications and banking. It was decided to develop 70 such centres during the Eighth Plan. These would be allotted to different states. Each growth centre would be provided with funds ranging from Rs.25 crore to Rs.30 crore. So far, locations of 64 growth centres have been identified and notified.

Six years after the announcement, the scheme of growth centres seems to be destined to die a natural death for the want of funds. Although, land has been acquired in many cases, construction work is yet to begin, thanks to the paucity of funds.

Meanwhile, a new scheme of integrated infrastructural development, including technological back-up services, to facilitate location of industries in rural and backward areas and to promote stronger linkages between agriculture and industry is being finalised in consultation with concerned authorities.

Nucleus Plants and Ancillaries

Nucleus plants and ancillaries would also help remove imbalances.

A nucleus plant is one which is located in a backward area and which is expected to promote ancillary units around it. For this obligation, the nucleus plant will be entitled to central and state level incentives. The nucleus plant will be so called only after the Ministry of Industry certifies it to that effect. It is hoped that the concept of a nucleus plant will contribute to the development of backward areas.

Banking Policy

Expansion of banking facilities to rural areas is yet another way of development of backward regions. Geographical spread of the branches is emphasised by the Reserve Bank of India while permitting the opening of new branches. The extension of the monetary infrastructure to backward regions is expected to provide an impetus for the growth of these regions.

The setting up of Regional Rural Banks (RRBs) marked another step towards increasing the flow of monetary resources to the backward regions. Particular attention has been given to expand the RRBs in backward states-Orissa, Uttar Pradesh and Rajasthan.

FAILURE OF REGIONAL PLANNING

There are pockets of poverty in developed states and areas of affluence in underdeveloped regions.

Inspite of the measures undertaken by the government, the problem of regional imbalances, as was pointed out earlier, still persists. One peculiarity of the problem is that there are pockets of poverty in well-developed states and highly developed patches in the underdeveloped states. The reasons for this are not difficult to see. The most important reasons are as follows:

(i) One basic reason for the widening of disparities is that the richer states refuse to shoulder their part of the responsibility of transferring through the Central Government some of the resources to the poorer states. The advanced states like Punjab and Haryana have a per capita development expenditure of about two and a half times the level of the less developed states like Bihar. Naturally, the rate of economic development is faster in these states which leads to the accentuation of the existing regional imbalances.

(ii) At the same time, the poorer states rely too much on the flow of resources from the richer states through the Central Government and they do not believe in self-effort and self-help to promote their own development. These less developed states have developed an attitude of a lethargic reliance on whatever resources that can be got out of the Central Government by pathetic pleading or bland political pressures. Besides, the poor states attempt to waste their limited resources and accordingly, their development effort is chronically inadequate.

States refuse to transfer resources among them. Sharing of river water, for example, has been a contentious issue between Karnataka and Tamilnadu.

(iii) Most of the area development measures are specially meant to help the drought-prone areas or hilly areas or those inhabited by Scheduled Tribes. But these measures do not come under the above categories. Besides, the barriers to development in backward regions are such that an integrated approach is necessary. The First Plan ignored such an approach. The Sixth Plan strategy of integrated rural development attempts to remove this weakness.

(iv) The method of locating large central projects in the backward states has not paid off in any significant way in improving their economics.

(v) The benefits of Central Government subsidy for industrial investment in specified backward state areas are concentrated in a few districts/areas. Besides, the amounts given as subsidy are not related to employment but to capital investment. Moreover, the government has not so far made any discrimination in favour of those industries which could have a favourable effect on employment or on resources development of forward linkages. Because of the limited infrastructure facilities such as transport, power, communication etc. and inadequate monetary and fiscal incentives by the state governments, there has been no development of any ancillary, secondary and tertiary industries around these major Central industrial complexes.

There is however very little evidence to show that this investment has led to any noticeable progress in the regional development of the backward areas where these projects were located. In this connection, the Sixth Plan states: "Our experience with large industrial projects in backward areas shows that their spread effects are low and the surrounding areas continue to remain poor and undeveloped. Infact, such development by creating a dualistic economic structure may pose more problems than it solves. However, location of industries in some backward regions is very essential, particularly in those areas which are densely populated and which have natural resources for industrial development."

(vi) Only a few entrepreneurs have approached the public sector financial institutions for concessional finance even though sufficient publicity has been given to the facilities. Besides, as in the case of investment subsidy, the benefits have accrued to a small proportion of the districts covered.

(vii) The state governments alone can tackle the problem of intra-state imbalances and local planning is the main plank of any strategy for balanced spatial development within a state. The process of planning will have to be decentralised and priorities as well as sectoral proposals should be put forward as the district and regional levels to be later integrated into state plans. Punjab, Haryana and Tamil Nadu have encouraged private sector entrepreneurs to set up industrial ventures by offering them many incentives. But other states were lukewarm in attracting industrial units. In most cases, private entrepreneurs treated states like Orissa in a stepmotherly fashion and did not locate big projects in these states.

Private sector participation in setting up industries in backward areas has not been encouraging.

(viii) Not all states have earmarked separate outlays for the development of backward and special problem areas. It is absolutely necessary for the states to recognise the fact that without special efforts including the allocation of separate funds, disparities between different areas will not be eliminated.

(ix) The figures of utilisation of outlays in the First Five Year plan show that in four of the six backward states, the percentage utilisation of the outlays provided has been less than the overall utilisation factors. The same pattern is observed in the figures of loans and advances given by the public sector financial institutions to the various states.

SUGGESTIONS TO REMOVE REGIONAL IMBALANCES

The following might help remove regional disparities:

- The first and the major thing to be done is to develop infrastructure facilities like water supply, electricity and transport.
- Planning needs to be decentralised. Multi-level planning facilitates people's participation in the decision making.
- Centrally collected resources must be progressively allocated to states.

The suggestions are only indicative but not the only ones.

QUESTIONS

1. What is balanced regional development?
2. How is backwardness determined? What are the causes for backwardness?
3. Suggest measures to remove regional disparities.
4. Why have the efforts to remove regional imbalances not been successful?

ASSIGNMENT

The Chief Minister of West Bengal is of the opinion that real economic growth can take place through industrialisation. He is not the only person to entertain such an opinion. Do you agree with this perception?

REFERENCES

1. M.L.Jingham, *The Economies of Development and Planning*, p.592.
2. Ruddar Datt and K.P.M.Sundaram, *Indian Economy*, p.372.
3. D.M.Nanjundappa, "*Regional Imbalance in State Must Go*" *Deecan Herald*, March, 15, 1997.

CHAPTER OUTLINE

Objectives of Price and Distribution Controls
Control of Prices
- Demand Management
- Supply Management

Public Distribution System
- Rationale of PDS
- Supplies to the PDS
- Form of PDS
- Measures to Strengthen PDS
- Goods to be Included in the PDS
- Success of PDS
- Revamped PDS
- Problems of Controls

The Essential Commodities Act, 1955
- Objectives of the Act
- Essential Commodity
- Scope of the Act
- Provisions of the Act

LEARNING OBJECTIVES

After reading this Chapter, you should be able to:

1. Understand the purposes why price and distribution controls are imposed
2. Understand that demand management and supply management are the two ways of enforcing price controls
3. Describe the functioning, pitfalls, and measures to improve PDS
4. Describe the objectives and bring out the provisions of the Essential Commodities Act, 1955

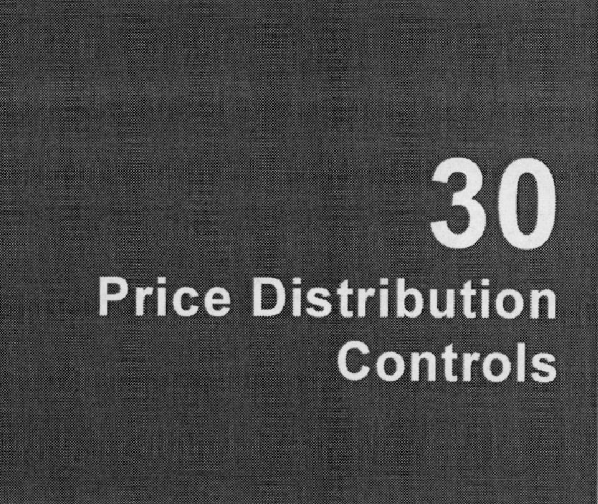

30 Price Distribution Controls

Control of prices and the distribution of essential commodities is yet another component of economic environment. This chapter is devoted to a brief discussion of price and distribution controls.

OBJECTIVES OF PRICE AND DISTRIBUTION CONTROLS

The following are the objectives of price and distribution controls:

- Supply of essential commodities at reasonable prices;
- Prevention of hoarding and black-marketing;
- Maintain quality of goods and services;
- Prevent monopolistic, restrictive and unfair trade practices;
- Ensure supply of inputs to priority sectors;
- Ensure price stability; and
- Ensure minimum returns to producers.

CONTROL OF PRICES

Till 1961, there was not much urgency in price policy as the rise in prices was gradual and there was no public agitation against rise in prices. Since then, inflationary pressure was so great, that anti-inflationary measures were given priority by the government. A wide range of measures were adopted to ensure stable conditions as well as to prevent speculators from taking an undue advantage of the conditions of scarcity. Since the price situation was the outcome of shortages in basic supplies and a rapid growth in money supply and bank credit, various types of measures relating to money supply, pricing and distribution of commodities were pressed into service.

Demand Management

Demand management has been sought to be achieved through monitory and fiscal measures.

The accent of price policy since 1973-74 has been mostly to rely on fiscal and monetary measures with a view to check the demand of the general public for goods and services.

(i) *Fiscal Measures*: In July 1974, the Government of India promulgated three ordinances to limit the disposable money incomes in the hands of consumers through freezing wages and salaries on one side and dividend incomes on the other. In January 1984, the Government of India announced a package of programmes to curtail public expenditure, to postpone fresh recruitment to government jobs, etc., and thus attempted to reduce government expenditure. Instead, the governments-both Central and State Governments-have been spending tax-payer's money recklessly and wastefully. Besides, they have always adopted a policy of deficit budgeting. Thus, instead of checking prices, the government policy has actually pushed up prices.

It was only in the last three or four years that the Government of India has appreciated the importance of reducing fiscal deficit and bringing inflation under control. Government has been taking all measures to bring down fiscal deficit to around four per cent.

(ii) *Monetary Measures*: The monetary policy of RBI consists of the extensive use of general and selective credit control measures. The main thrust has been to restrict bank-credit against inflation sensitive goods and to influence the cost and availability of commercial bank credit. The RBI relies heavily on selective credit controls on inflation sensitive commodities (such as foodgrains, cotton, oil-seeds and oils, sugar and textiles) so as to discourage speculative hoarding. The appx bank has frequently used the bank rate as an anti-inflationary weapon. Since July 1974, the RBI has frequently raised the bank rate from 7 to 12 per cent and has also raised the minimum lending rates on bank advances.

During the Sixth and Seventh Plan periods, monetary policy was essentially directed to prevent any excessive increase in liquidity and at the same time to ensure that the genuine credit requirements of the productive and the priority sectors are adequately met.

Reserve Bank took steps to tighten monetary and credit expansion in September 1981 when the cash reserve ratio (CRR) was raised from six to eight per cent in four stages. These steps resulted in a large measure, in mopping up excess liquidity in the economy, moderating monetary and credit expansion and consequently helped in bringing down the rate of inflation towards the end of 1981-82. Since 1990-91, money supply had accelerated considerably and there was continuous rise in inflationary pressure. Accordingly, RBI had to adopt monetary policies which would slow down money supply and reduce liquidity in the economy. When the inflationary pressure was reduced during subsequent years, RBI adjusted the monetary policy so as to stimulate production.

Supply Management

Supply management is related to the volume of supply and its distribution system.

Supply management is related to the volume of supply and its distribution system. On the commodity front, the government has generally focussed its attention in securing greater control over the prices of rice, wheat, sugar, oils and other commodities of mass consumption. Through increase in domestic supplies, large releases from official stocks and widening and streamlining of the network of public distribution, the government attempts to prevent an undue increase in the prices of essential commodities.

Let us touch some of the important aspects of this policy:

(a) *Fixation of Maximum Prices*: For eliminating the incentives for hoarding and speculative activity in foodgrains, the state governments have been asked to fix the wholesale and retail prices of foodgrains. Further, the government also fixes minimum procurement prices for major crops on the recommendation of the Agricultural Prices Commission (APC). Prices of other important goods like cloth, sugar and vanaspati are also controlled.

(b) *The System of Dual Prices*: The government has adopted a system of dual prices in the case of goods like sugar, cement, paper etc. Under this system, the weaker sections of the community are supplied these goods through fair price shops, at controlled prices and the rest are allowed to purchase their requirements at higher prices from the open market. Dual pricing generally failed to serve the purpose; it created confusion in the market and led to erratic price movements.

(c) *Increase in Supplies of Foodgrains*: The government attempts to increase supplies of foodgrains and other essential goods in times of internal shortage through larger imports. During 1970s and 1980s, the Central Government took advantage of the success of the green revolution and gradually built up large reserves of foodgrains; and at one time, reserves exceeded 30 million tonnes. It was strongly believed in government circles at one time that the intensive procurement drive, along with the fixation of wholesale and retail prices of foodgrains would compel hoarders to disgorge their stocks on the market, thereby releasing the pressure on prices.

(d) *Problem of Oilseeds and Edible Oils*: In recent years, the prices of oils along with those of pulses, tea and sugar have been responsible for rise in the general price level. The government has prepared medium and long-term plans to step up the production of oilseeds in the country. The Government has announced higher support prices for groundnut, soyabean and sunflower seeds-the last two crops offer the maximum scope for augmenting the supply of edible oils in the country. In the short period, the government has been relying on the imports of edible oils even though it has found out that imports do not necessarily bring down prices for the domestic consumers.

(e) *Public Distribution System and Consumer Protection*: An important aspect of the government's policy was the strengthening of the public distribution system. The government has set up a network of fair price shops numbering nearly 4,00,000 which cover a population of over 500 million and which distribute wheat, rice, sugar, imported edible oils (palm oil), kerosene, soft coke and controlled cloth. The public distribution system serves two purposes. Firstly, it helps to hold down prices. Secondly, it provides essential commodities to low income groups at relatively low prices. But whenever the public distribution is hard pressed due to inadequate supply, prices tend to rise.

(f) *Control over Private Trade in Foodgrains*: To check prices and to eliminate hoarding and speculative activity in foodgrains trade, wholesale dealers in foodgrains were licensed in many states. The government also enlisted the help of associations of foodgrains traders in regulating their activities and improving practices through voluntary sanctions. Steps were also taken to curb profiteering by traders by prescribing margins of profits. Limits were also fixed beyond which traders and producers could not hold stock without declaration. At the end of September 1977, Pulses and Edible Oils (Storage Control) Order was issued under the Essential Commodities Act to fix the maximum limits of stocks that could he held by wholesalers and retailers in respect of pulses, edible oils and vanaspati. The Food Corporation of India came in a big way to buy in surplus areas and sell in deficit areas and thus moderate the difference in prices.

(g) *Measures to Increase Agricultural Production*: Side by side with the measures for regulating prices and distribution, attention was also focussed on long-term measures to stimulate the production of agricultural commodities. Imports of fertilizers were increased substantially, measures were taken to increase output from indigenous fertilizer plants and also to set up new fertilizer plants. Pesticides and tractors are also of importance and attempts are being made to increase imports in the short run and establish additional capacity in the long run. Attention is being given to the multiplication and distribution of improved varieties of seed, speeding up the implementation of irrigation projects etc.[1]

PUBLIC DISTRIBUTION SYSTEM (PDS)

Rationale of PDS

PDS refers to the distribution of essential commodities through fair price shops.

The distribution of essential commodities through fair price shops at government-controlled prices has come to be known as the public distribution system. There are various reasons for the setting up of the public distribution system in India.

In order to maintain stable price conditions, an efficient management of the supplies of essential consumer goods is necessary. The demand for such commodities being largely inelastic, even a marginal fall in the production and supply often leads to a disproportionate increase in their prices. Moreover, as most of these commodities are agriculture-based, their prices are subject to large seasonal variations. Public distribution will, therefore, have to play a major role in ensuring supplies of essential consumer goods of mass consumption to people at reasonable prices, particularly to the weaker sections of the community.

As mentioned above, state trading and buffer stock operations on the one side, and public distribution on the other are essential in the case of agricultural products. A large proportion of agricultural products-both foodgrains and industrial raw materials-come to the market soon after the harvest when prices are depressed. It is necessary to devise a scheme to buy such commodities at prices which ensure a certain minimum profit to the producers. The Food Corporation of India (FCI) and other institutions have been set up to buy agricultural prices that also help in stabilising agricultural prices. At the same time, these goods would be supplied through public channels to consumers especially the weaker sections of the community-this would mean that in critical times, they would receive supplies of essential commodities at reasonable prices. The public distribution system has become a stable and permanent feature of India's strategy to control prices, reduce fluctuations in prices and achieve an equitable distribution of essential consumer goods.

The public distribution system is also required to operate the dual pricing system wherever it is applied. As explained above, a certain proportion of the output of the commodities involved is procured by public agencies for distribution through the public distribution system at reasonable prices to the vulnerable sections, and at the same time, the producers are allowed to sell the balance in the free market at higher prices and realise on the whole a fair price for their produce.

Goods to be Included in the Public Distribution System

Since distribution is a highly complex matter, only the most essential goods of mass consumption should be brought under the public distribution system, e.g., cereals, sugar, edible oils and vanaspati, kerosene, soft coke, controlled cloth, tea, toilet soap and washing soap, match boxes, exercise books for children etc. Even though all these goods are essential, there can be regional variations in preferences-rice in the South and West Bengal and wheat in North and Central India. Besides, different commodities may assume importance in the scheme of public distribution at different points of time. The main emphasis should be to cover the whole country and supply the essential goods through the public distribution system at reasonable prices only to the vulnerable sections of people in the country.

Most essential goods of mass consumption-cereals, sugar, kerosene, etc. are routed through PDS.

Supplies to the Public Distribution System

Both Central and state governments have made arrangements to procure essential commodities and supply them through the public distribution outlets. In the case of foodgrains, FCI undertakes the necessary operations. In regard to sugar, FCI undertakes the operations in some states and in others, civil supplies corporations or co-operatives undertake these operations. The State Trading Corporation(STC) has been entrusted with the responsibility of importing and distributing edible oils. The Department of Coal and Coal India Limited (CIL) handle soft coke. Kerosene is being handled by the public sector corporations like Indian Oil Corporation (IOC), Hindustan Petroleum and Bharat Petroleum. The production of controlled cloth has now been generally entrusted to the National Textile Corporation(NTC) and distributed through the National Consumers Co-operative Federation(NCCF). The NCCF also procures and distributes tea, while coffee is being supplied by the Coffee Board. In ordinary times, these arrangements have been functioning smoothly. But the government has to keep a continuous watch over these arrangements and strengthen the system and make changes as and when necessary.

Form of Public Distribution

At the state level, the distribution of essential commodities received from or through Central agencies is done through Food and Civil Supplies Departments, Civil Supplies Corporations and Essential Commodities Corporations. At the lowest level, there are fair price shops to sell essential goods ultimately to the consumers. The total number of fair price shops both co-operative and private, in the country was nearly 4.24 lakh as on 31 March 1994.[2]

Success of the Public Distribution System

For the success of the public distribution system, the maintenance of the supply line of commodities selected for distribution is of crucial importance. Even a temporary interruption in supplies would create great hardship to the people. This necessitates forward planning i.e., suitable programmes to increase the production of essential commodities of mass consumption and timely imports when domestic supplies are anticipated to be inadequate to match the internal demand.

Supply chain management is most crucial for the success of PDS.

Another factor for the success of the public distribution system is the necessary link between production, procurement, transportation, storage and distribution of the selected commodities. In the past, responsibilities for these were fragmented and this contributed to the weakness and inefficiency of the public distribution system. The Sixth and Seventh Plans had followed an integrated approach and paid attention not only to production and procurement, but also to storage and the transportation of the selected commodities.

For the public distribution system to be really useful, it is necessary to expand it quickly to cover all areas in the country, particularly the backward, remote and inaccessible areas. Special attention has to be given to rural areas as the system is relatively less developed in such areas. The public distribution system is extremely weak in inaccessible areas inhabited by the tribals and weaker sections of the community because of the non-viability of operations there.

In the states where a strong cooperative movement exists, the apex body of consumer co-operatives and marketing societies may take up the responsibility of procurement, storage, movement and the distribution of essential commodities. In other states, however, it would be necessary to set up Civil Supplies Corporation or Essential Commodities Corporations to undertake these operations.

Measures to Strengthen PDS

In recent years, the government has taken the following measures to strengthen public distribution and make it more effective and useful:

(a) Steps to reduce the cost of distribution by taking advantage of the economies of bulk handling and building up a network of rural godowns;

(b) Measures to strengthen co-ordination and linkage between the consumer and marketing co-operatives so that the former could procure farm products directly from farmers;

(c) Steps to expand the storage capacity of co-operatives to enable them to play a larger role in the public distribution systems;

(d) Measures to increase the usefulness of the public distribution system through horizontal linkages with the plan programmes, e.g., organisation of mobile fair price shops at centres where rural works were in progress and the setting up of regular fair price shops in areas where large-scale employment was being generated under the plan projects and programmes;

(e) Steps to supply production inputs to the tribals, besides supplying essential consumer goods to them and also arranging to procure the products of the tribals at reasonable prices so as to eliminate their exploitation by the middlemen;

(f) Launching a scheme from January 1992 to revamp the PDS in about 1,700 blocks falling in the drought prone, desert, integrated tribal development project areas and certain designated hill areas; in these areas, additional commodities like tea, soap, pulses and iodised salt are also to be distributed[3] ; and

Targeting is most crucial in PDS.

(g) Better targeting is another measure suggested for improving the PDS. Better targeting implies making the commodities available only to the needy. Right now rations are not explicitly targeted. The general belief is that, due to their characteristics, they will get implicitly targeted. However, when most of the population uses the system, there is a wastage associated with such subsidies in the sense that the non-targeted population also receives part of the subsidy due to the absence of direct targeting. On the other hand, a part of the deserving classes may be left out of the scheme due to various reasons, such as, the absence of a proper address (ration cards are issued only to households with registered residential addresses), lack of enough money at a single time (for workers on daily wages) to buy the rationed goods sold for a minimum period of a week, a fortnight or a month and the inability to make purchases on a regular basis (for migrant workers). Hence, explicit targeting assumes relevance.

Revamped Public Distribution System

From June 1992, a special scheme to revamp the PDS (RPDS) was introduced where additional items like tea, soap, pulses and iodised salt began to be supplied by state governments to serve tribal, hill and arid area populations in 1775 blocks located in backward and remote areas characterised by poor infrastructure. Additional quantities of 3.1 million tonnes of foodgrains (rice and wheat) for RPDS, over and above the normal allocations to states, are assured for distribution in these '*revamped*' FPSs at a price which is lower than the central issue price (CIP) by Rs.50 per quintal as compared to normal PDS elsewhere. The state governments are also advised to ensure that the retail prices at the '*revamped*' fair price shops are not higher than CIP more than 25 paise/kg. Besides, the existing 17.75 RPDS blocks, government has identified additional 409 blocks for inclusion under the RPDS scheme.

In 1997, the Government of India introduced the Targeted Public Distribution system. This is a system which makes a distinction between Below Poverty Line (BPL) and Above Poverty Line (APL) households. It also introduced a pricing system.

In his 2000-2001 budget, the Finance Minister has announced steep price increases for rice and wheat supplied through fair price shops. Specifically, Central issue prices will be set at half the 'economic cost' incurred by the Food Corporation of India (FCI) of BPL households and at the full 'economic cost' for APL households. The economic cost comprises the procurement price of grain, costs related to procurement price of grain, and costs of distribution. Wheat will now be available at Rs.8.40 (against Rs.6.82) a kg and rice at Rs.11.70 (against Rs.9.05) per kg for APL families. BPL families will be charged Rs.4.20 (against Rs.2.50) per kg of wheat and Rs.5.85 (against Rs.3.50) per kg of rice.

Problems of Controls

The problems associated with price and distribution controls are many. In the first place, it often happens that the controlled prices fixed by the government are above the free market level. For instance, when there is a glut in the market due to the heavy supply of a particular commodity, its price would crash, resulting in heavy losses to the producers. The losses may be too much for the producers to bear. The controlled prices fixed are above the market level to avoid such losses. But the controlled prices would result in waste, inefficiency and the misallocation of resources.

> Administered prices are often above market rates or below market prices.

Secondly, the controlled prices often will be fixed below the free market price. This happens when there is a short supply of a commodity. Being forced to sell below the market price, producers will be denied profits they would have earned had they sold their produce in the open market. This discourages fresh investments, expansion, modernisation and the setting up of new enterprises.

Thirdly, price control is inevitably followed by distribution control. In essence, rationing implements price control. Theoretically, distribution control ensures equitable distribution of essential commodities. But the success of rationing depends on civic consciousness and public trust in the system both of which are difficult to come by.

Fourthly, price and distribution controls, like any other control, leads to corruption, inefficiency, hoarding and blackmarketing. It is rightly said that the price control is '*the father of blackmarketing and carries with it an insidious threat to public morality...a means to expose every citizen, everyday of his life, of a temptation to break the law or the organised conventions of the society*.'[4]

> Price controls lead to corruption, inefficiency, hoarding and black marketing.

Fifthly, while fixing prices, authorities take into consideration the 'fair return' that the producers would get. A study of different reports made from time to time to fix a '*fair return*' and to decide a price will only show that the task is an extremely difficult one. First of all, the selection of representative units (when there are a large number of units); secondly, calculation of capital employed or other reasonable basis; thirdly, the expenditure that is to be covered by the '*fair*' rate of return; and fourthly, special allowances or problems typical to any industry, if any, are the issues to be tackled while deciding a price. Apart from covering the cost of raw material, labour, depreciation etc., cost of capital employed is also important and whether a particular cost (e.g., managerial remuneration or bonus to workers) is to come under the cost itself or to be covered by the '*fair rate of return*' is the problem that has been dealt with differently. Determination of a fair rate of return on capital depends on the definition of '*capital*' as well as on the judgement of what constitutes a fair or appropriate return in the context of the stage of economic development at a time.[5]

Sixthly, the system of price and distribution controls, the use of much manpower and other economic resources merely in working controls, and exposing the public services to a strain which may in the end prove unbearable.[6]

Seventhly, controls, particularly the PDS, have been a heavy drain on the nation's exchequer as shown in Table 30.1.

Table 30.1 **Drain on Exchequer**

	Foodgrains distributed (million tonnes)	*Subsidy paid to FCI (Rs.crore) Rs.*	*Subsidy per tonne of grains distributed Rs.*
1981-86	70.5	3,995	566.7
1986-91	96.0	10.326	1075.6
1991-95	77.5	18,900	2438.7

(**Source**: *The Hindu*, dated June 15, 1995).

Arguing that the subsidy is targeted to benefit the poor, our PDS seems to have failed in reaching the really poor. During 1992-93, UP, Bihar and Madhya Pradesh, which account for 34.5 per cent of total population and 42.2 per cent of the poor in the country were allocated only 13.7 per cent of the food grains distributed by the PDS all over the country. On the other hand, Andhra Pradesh, Kerala, and Delhi, which account for not more than 11.4 per cent of the total population and only 10.5 per cent of the poor in the country, had received 28.7 per cent of the total quantity of foodgrains distributed. Inequities in the distribution of foodgrains are most glaring in the cases of Delhi and Bihar. Delhi, which has a population of not more than one per cent of the total population of the country, and that too of the richest in the country, had received 5.3 per cent of foodgrains. Whereas Bihar, the poorest among all states and with population exceeding 10 per cent of the total, had received only 4.01 of the total foodgrains distributed.[7] (See also Table 30.2).

That PDS supports farmers is also not correct.

Finally, the claim that the PDS provides support to farmers is also not true. Hardly any coarse grain is ever purchased from farmers. For building up its rice stocks, the PDS mostly depends on levies realised from the rice mills. Even for wheat purchases there is a growing dependence on middlemen. In fact, support to farmers has transformed into support to rice millers and other middlemen. In any case, the minimum support prices take every factor into consideration, except the level of prices, which farmers have to pay for their own requirements (See also box 30.1).[8]

Whatever may be the problems, price and distribution controls have been resorted to and have come to stay in our country.

Box 30.1 **Indictments**

1985: Planning Commission Study

Beneficiary households were not drawing the ration even for one out of 11 commodities because of their irregular supply and poor quality.

1994: Kirit Parikh Report

In Punjab, Haryana, Uttar Pradesh, Bihar, Orissa and Madhya Pradesh, more than 90 per cent of the people do not buy any cereals from the PDS.

1995: Planning Commission Report

Out of the 64 villages sampled ration cards were not provided to all the selected households in 30 villages.

1997: World Bank Study

The impact of the PDS on poverty and the nutritional status was minimal. A sum of Rs.4.27 was spent to transfer one rupee of income to the poor.

1997: Radhakrishna & Rao

Access to PDS is very limited and it is particularly weak in the states with the highest incidence of poverty.

2000: CAG Report

The benefits of subsidized price have not reached BPL households and income transfer through the PDS is poor.

2005: Planning Commission Study

In 2003-04, 16 states were issued 14.07 mt of foodgrain of which only 5.93 mt reached BPL families. More than 5 mt leaked out in transit and over 3 mt was diverted from the system.

Measures of Improve PDS

1. It is essential that coarse grains are introduced into the PDS. Half of the food grains allocation under the PDS should be of coarse grains, and in states where the staple diet of the poor is coarse grains, no other grains should be distributed.
2. Sugar to be removed from the PDS. Instead gur (jaggery), which is a substitute for sugar in many places, may be introduced into the PDS. Most families in cities keep ration could and buy sugar and if this incentive is withdrawn, ABL households will not buy ration at all. This will make the PDS largely different for the rich and the middle class.
3. Government should open ration shops at the places where poor people live. Bihar, UP, MP, Orissa and Rajasthan have pockets of poverty and it is at these pockets that ration shops need to be opened. It is only then that the real purpose of PDS, *viz*, removing poverty, will be realised.
4. In order to discourage traders from diverting foodgrains from PDS stream to the open market, panchayats may be involved in the system of distribution. Services of panchayats may also be used to identify the rural poor.
5. It may also be stated that PDS alone will not solve the problem of food security. Apart from higher economic growth, a mix of policies such as effective implementation of anti-poverty programmes, including PDS, controlling inflation, improving health facilities is needed for increasing food security in the country.

Table 30.2 **Who Benefits from PDS?**

	Wheat lifted from FCI *% of country total, 1985-1996*	***Proportion of Poor*** *% of country '93-94*	*Proportion of poor who do not buy any ration*	
			Urban	*Rural*
Andhra Pradesh	1.86	4.90	40.30	48.60
Assam	3.91	3.00	75.40	57.00
Bihar	7.38	18.70	98.30	92.90
Gujarat	8.25	3.20	55.50	68.00
Haryana	1.37	1.30	96.90	92.90
Himachal Pradesh	1.52	0.50	71.80	74.70
Jammu & Kashmir	1.72	0.60	76.70	21.40
Karnataka	3.98	4.90	38.10	37.30
Kerala	4.24	2.50	12.30	13.00
Madhya Pradesh	4.34	6.50	90.60	82.60
Maharastra	14.43	9.30	52.30	56.20
Orissa	3.27	4.90	98.30	86.20
Punjab	0.37	0.70	99.90	95.40
Rajasthan	10.37	4.00	91.20	94.40
Tamil Nadu	2.74	6.50	46.50	44.60
Uttar Pradesh	6.06	18.70	97.90	*93.00*
West Bengal	13.74	7.90	73.10	40.20

(**Source**: *Indira Gandhi Institute of Development Studies*; Lakdawala Committee Estimates)

THE ESSENTIAL COMMODITIES ACT, 1955

Most of the controls over price and distribution of consumption goods have been resorted to under the provisions of the Essential Commodities Act, 1955. Hence, a brief discussion of the Act follows:

Objectives of the Act

The objectives of the Act are laid down in its Preamble. The following are the three important objectives:

- Control of production, supply and distribution of essential commodities;
- Check inflationary trend in prices and
- Ensure equitable distribution of essential commodities.

Scope of the Act

The Act extends to the whole of India. The Act came into force on 1st April, 1955, repealing the Essential Commodities Ordinance No.1 of 1955 which was promulgated by the President on 26th January, 1955.

Essential Commodity

Section 2(a) of the Act defines 'essential commodity,' meaning any of the following classes of commodities:

(a) Cattle fodder including oil cakes and other concentrates;
(b) Coal, including coke and other derivations;
(c) Components, parts and accessories of automobiles;
(d) Cotton and woollen textiles;
(e) Drugs;
(f) Foodstuffs, including edible oilseeds and oil;
(g) Iron and steel, including manufactured products of iron and steel;
(h) Paper, including newsprint, paperboard, strawboard;
(i) Petroleum and petroleum products;
(j) Raw cotton whether ginned or unginned and cotton seeds;
(k) Raw jute and
(l) Any other commodity which the Central Government may notify as an essential commodity.

Provisions of the Act

Section 3 of the Act is most crucial. Under this section, the Central Government, whenever it is of the opinion that it is necessary or expedient to do so for maintaining or increasing supplies of any essential commodity or for securing an equitable distribution and the availability at fair prices of the essential commodities and for securing an essential commodity for the defence of India or the efficient conduct of military operations, may by order, provide for regulating or prohibiting the production, supply, distribution and trade and commerce in essential commodities as maybe specified in the order.

The sub-sections of Section 3 are supplementaries to Section 3. Sub-section (1) empowers the Central Government to issue an order as mentioned above. Sub-section (2) enumerates various categories or orders which can be made in exercise of the powers conferred by sub-section (1). Sub-section (3) provides for the fixation of price to be paid to a person who sells any essential commodity to the government or any other person or authority specified by it under an order. Sub-section (3-A) enables the Central government to control the rise in prices and to prevent the hoarding of any foodstuff in any locality. Under sub-section (4), the government, if it is of the opinion that it is necessary for maintaining or increasing the production and supply of an essential commodity, may appoint an authorised controller to exercise powers of control with respect to any undertaking engaged in the production and supply of the essential commodity.

Other Provisions

The Act makes it obligatory on the part of the government to exercise powers conferred on it by Section 3 in the interest of the general public and not in the interest of dealers.

It is also provided in the Act that the powers conferred by Section 3 are generally exercised by the Central Government unless delegated to the state governments.

Section 6 of the Act declares the orders of the Central Government passed under Section 3 to be effective, notwithstanding the said orders being inconsistent with other enactment.

Section 7 of the Act provides for imprisonment and fine for the contravention of Section 3. Section 7 lays down that if any person contravenes any order made under Section 3, he shall be punishable with fine and imprisonment with a term which may extend to one year.

QUESTIONS

1. What are the objectives of price and distribution controls?
2. Bring out the mechanisms of price and distribution controls.
3. Enumerate the problems of price and distribution controls.
4. Bring out the provisions of the Essential Commodities Act.

ASSIGNMENT

List five products whose prices are determined by government and five others whose prices are market driven. Which of them are functioning well? Why?

REFERENCES

1. Ruddan Datt and K.P.M.Sundaram, *Indian Economy*, pp.380-382.
2. *Ibid.*, p.387.
3. *Ibid.*, p.388.
4. J.E.Meade, *Planning and the Price Mechanisms*, p.7.
5. D.Amanchand, *Government and Business*, p.147.
6. *Ibid.*, p.148.
7. Bhanu Pratap Singh, "PDS at Its Dead End", *The Hindu*, June 15, 1995.
8. *Ibid.*

CHAPTER OUTLINE

Foreign Trade
- Foreign Trade and Economic Development
- Extent of Foreign Trade
- Significance of Exports
- Export Strategy
- Imports
- Regulation of Foreign Trade

Trade-in Services
- Determinants of Service Exports
- Promoting Service Exports

Balance of Payments

Exchange Rate Management

LEARNING OBJECTIVES

After reading this Chapter, you should be able to:

1. Understand the significance of foreign trade in economic development
2. Assess the status of India's overseas trade
3. Suggest an export strategy to boost India's exports
4. Understand how India's foreign trade is sought to be regulated
5. Appreciate the role of invisible exports in India's foreign exchange earnings and suggest ways of promoting them further
6. Define the term 'balance of payments'
7. Understand the mechanism of exchange rate management

31 External Sector

The external sector comprises India's foreign trade, trade-in-services, foreign capital flows, balance of payments and exchange rate management. Of these, the flow of foreign capital was covered in Chapter 5. The remaining components of the external sector are discussed in this chapter.

The external sector has been posing a major challenge in recent years, particularly since September 1997. In 1998-99, the East Asian crisis cast its shadow. In addition, the crisis which affected Russia in 1998 and Brazil in 1999 had affected global economic prospects considerably. The economic prospects of Japan as well as the economies of Europe remained uncertain. In addition to the unfavourable external situation, India faced other problems, *viz.*, the economic sanctions imposed by several industrial countries, the suspension of fresh multilateral lending, the downgrading by international rating agencies and the reduction in investment by foreign institutional investors. It goes to the credit of the Reserve Bank of India that it has managed the external sector reasonably well through its monetary policy measures.

FOREIGN TRADE

Foreign trade, also called international trade, is as old as history. Trade among countries is normal and desirable. It exists for different reasons. The fact remains that the natural resources of the earth are not evenly distributed. One country possesses product X in surplus and lacks in respect of product Y. In another country, the reverse may be true. It is mutually advantageous for both the countries to exchange their surplus stocks. Then there is the advantage of comparative cost. One country produces a particular commodity at less cost than does another country. Economically, the lowest cost producer should produce and satisfy the demands for that product. There is also the prevalence of technological gaps which make foreign trade relevant and desirable. Developed countries spend substantially on research and development

Foreign trade is as old as history.

and as a result, develop new products keeping in mind the global customer profile. In the initial stages, these countries enjoy virtual monopoly in the manufacture of new products. Other countries, particularly less developed countries, are forced to buy new products from the developed countries.

Foreign Trade and Economic Development

Imports that help create new capacity or enlarge capacity in the other lines are called developmental imports.

Imports made in order to make full use of the developed capacity are called maintenance imports.

Whatever the reasons for the existence of foreign trade, there is no gain-saying the fact that foreign trade is significant for the economic development of countries, particularly the developing ones. It provides the urge to develop the knowledge and experience that makes development possible, and the means to accomplish it. An economy which has decided to embark on a programme of development is required to extend its productive capacity at a fast rate. For this, imports of machinery and equipment which cannot be produced in the initial stages at home are essential. Such imports which either help to create new capacity in some lines of production or enlarge capacity in the other lines of production are called *developmental imports*. For instance, imports required for the setting up of steel plants, locomotives and hydro-electric projects are developmental imports. Secondly, a developing country which sets in motion the process of industrialisation at home requires the imports of raw materials and intermediate goods so as to properly utilise the capacity created in the country. Imports which are made in order to make full use of the productive capacity are called '*maintenance imports*'. These imports are vital for a developing economy as many of the industrial projects are also held up for the lack of maintenance imports. For a developing economy, developmental and maintenance imports set limits to the extent of industrialisation which can be carried out in a given period. Besides these imports, a developing economy is also required to import consumer goods which are in supply at home during industrialisation. Such imports are anti-inflationary because they reduce the scarcity of consumer goods. One example of such imports is the foodgrains imports in India in the post-Independence period which helped to arrest the rise of prices at home.

It is, therefore, inevitable that during the early years of development, imports have to be increased at a very fast rate. It is natural that the balance of trade in such a situation will turn heavily against the developing countries. This necessitates the enlargement of exports. External assistance can help share the burden of growth in the short-run, but in the long period, the developing country has to bear the burden of development itself. To meet the growing foreign debt in view of inelastic imports, a developing country must increase its exports.

The influx of foreign goods into the country and along with them the flow of technology, the skills, speed and feed of production, the tastes and the experiences will have considerable influence on domestic production, marketing, lifestyles and the levels of living of people. In order to pay for imports and to service earlier borrowings, developing countries have to export their goods and services. This is a challenging task; a challenge in terms of upgrading technology, increasing productivity, reducing costs, and improving quality of goods and services to meet international challenges. The challenge compels these countries to shed their ennui, spruce up and develop fast to survive in the global business scenario. Thus, international trade sets in a chain of events which help transform the less developed economies into developed ones. This was the reason why G.Heberler remarked that "*My overall conclusion is that international trade has made a tremendous contribution to the development of less developed countries in the 19th and 20th centuries and can be expected to make an equally big contribution in the future*".

Extent of Foreign Trade

The value of foreign trade of our country has been rising from year to year. It rose from Rs.30,553 crore during 1985-86 to Rs.8,38,575 crore during 2004-05, representing an increase of six times.

The break-up of foreign trade in terms of exports and imports from 1985-86 onwards is shown in Table 31.1.

Table 31.1 **National Income and Per Capita Income at Current Prices**

(Rs.Crores)

Year	*Exports*	*Imports*	*Total Value of Trade*	*Balance of Trade*
1985-86	10,895	19,658	30,553	-8,763
1986-87	12,452	20,201	32,653	-7,749
1987-88	15,741	22,399	38,140	-6,658
1988-89	20,232	28,235	48,467	-8,003
1989-90	27,681	35,416	63,097	-7,735
1990-91	32,553	43,198	75,751	-10,645
1991-92	44,040	47,851	91,892	-3,810
1992-93	53,688	63,375	1,17,063	-9,687
1993-94	69,751	73,101	1,42,882	-335
1994-95	82,674	89,971	1,72,645	-7,297
1995-96	1,06,353	1,22,678	2,29,031	-16,325
1996-97	85,623	97,111	1,82,734	-1,488
1997-98	1,26,286	1,51,553	2,77,839	-25,267
1998-99	1,01,850	1,32,447	2,34,297	-30,597
2002-03	2,55,137	2,97,206	5,52,343	-42,069
2003-04	2,91,582	3,53,976	6,45,558	-62,394
2004-05	3,56,625	4,81,950	8,38,575	1,25,190

(**Source**:Govt.of India, *Economic Surveys*)

The volume of our foreign trade has been increasing, the trade to GDP ratio has gone up from 13 per cent in 1980 to about 20 per cent as of now. What is interesting to note is that there has been a sea change in the composition of our foreign trade. India is no longer exporter of primary commodities and importer of manufactured goods. It exports manufactured goods and imports raw materials, intermediate and capital goods. As far as the direction of trade is concerned, it may be stated that the USA and the UK continue to be our principal buyers. After the break-up of the erstwhile Soviet Union, our exports to Asia and Oceania markets have shown a sharp jump. Infact, the current boom in exports is sustained largely by an unexpected and healthy rise in exports to the Asian and Oceania countries, which include ESCAP countries like Australia, Iran, Japan, Korea, Malaysia, Singapore, Thailand, Hong Kong, Bangladesh and Nepal. The shift in favour of these countries is facilitated by lower freight costs. Further, the fact that India is honouring its commitment

Share of foreign trade has gone up from 13 per cent of GDP in 1980 to 20 per cent as of now.

and repay back a total debt of the value of Rs.30,000 crore in hard currencies over a period of 12 years, beginning with 1993, should once again initiate exports to Russia.

Oil producing countries import considerably from the US.

We continue to buy significantly from the US and the UK. But our imports from these two countries have declined in recent years. Our sellers now include Canada, Belgium, France, Germany and Japan. The EU as a group accounts for about 24 per cent of our imports. Russia and East European countries also export to us, but together, their share is around two per cent of our total imports. The oil producing countries have emerged as significant purchasing centres for us. This has been caused largely by sharp increase in the unit value of petroleum and its products. The OPEC alone accounts for about 22 per cent of our total imports.

Analytically, India's foreign trade is highly concentrated. In 1996-97, for example, 53.4 per cent of our exports found their distination in the EU, the USA and Japan. Likewise, about 41.5 per cent of our total imports originated from the EU, the USA and Japan.

It is because of the high stakes involved in foreign trade that the Government of India has assumed sweeping powers of control over our exports and imports.

The principle of sovereignty states that each country has complete control over her merchandise. But this principle is tempered by reciprocity.

It maybe stated that the relationship of the government to international trade is based on the concept of sovereignty, the concept which recognises that a nation has complete control over her international affairs as far as other nations are concerned. Accordingly, a nation becomes very much concerned about her nationals and their property once these have passed into the confines of another nation or are on the high seas. In a world of strict sovereignty, nations would probably have no relations with each other except to be at war. But sovereignty has been tempered by reciprocity; that is, there are treaties of friendship and commerce, and treaties covering many other situations and relationships that give the nationals of the signatories the right to travel, reside, trade, hold property and make investments in other countries. These treaties also provide for the interchange of diplomatic officials and consuls (representatives of business interests). Treaties also cover the treatment of ships, sailors, airplanes and cargo when in foreign jurisdictions.

Foreign trade policy may be either outward directed or inward oriented. In the former, the government encourages exports but it is the reverse in the latter.

It is also good to know that trade policies can be characterised as *outward-oriented* or *inward-oriented*. An *outward-oriented* strategy provides incentives which are natural between production for the domestic market and exports. Because international trade is not positively discouraged, this approach is often, although somewhat misleading, referred to as *export promotion*. In truth, the essence of an outward-oriented strategy is neither discrimination in favour of exports nor bias against import substitution. By contrast, in an inward-oriented strategy, trade and industrial incentives are biased in favour of domestic production and against foreign trade. This approach is often referred to as *import substitution* strategy. In some countries, the bias against foreign trade has been extreme.

An *inward-oriented* strategy, usually, means overt protection. What is less obvious is that sheltering domestic industries puts exports at a great disadvantage because it raises the costs of the foreign inputs used in their production. Moveover, an increase in the relative costs of domestic inputs may also occur through inflation or because of an appreciation of the exchange rate as import restrictions are introduced.

In practice, trade policy contains elements of both approaches. Differences arise as much from the choice of instruments as from the absence or presence of intervention. Outward-oriented policies favour tariff over qualitative restrictions. These tariffs are usually counterbalanced by other measures, including production subsidies and the provision of inputs at 'free trade' prices. Governments aim to keep the exchange rate at a level that provides equal incentives to produce exports and imports substitutes. Overall protection is lower under an outward strategy than under an inward strategy; equally important, the spread between the highest and lowest rates of protection is narrower.

Inward strategies typically prefer quantitative restrictions to tariffs, and they involve a higher overall level of protection, together with greater variation across activities. Exchange rates are generally overvalued because of high protection and the use of quantitative restrictions. Industrial incentives are administered by an elaborate and expensive bureaucracy.

A major component of foreign trade is exports. It is, therefore, desirable to know about the exports, their direction, composition and prospects.

Significance of Exports

Exports are crucial for our economy for several reasons:

1. We need export earnings to finance our imports. Imports would tend to grow as the economy grows further. We would be required to spend more foreign exchange earnings on the import of oil, investment-induced inputs and technology. This calls for massive export earnings.
2. It is not advisable to depend on external assistance to finance essential imports. It is necessary that we depend on our own feet, earn on our own, and use the same to buy essential items from the exporting countries.
3. We have huge debts and we need foreign exchange earnings to service the debts. It is bad policy to contract new loans to service old debts. Old debts must be liquidated hence we need more and more export earnings.
4. Exports would make our economy highly vibrant. Exports call for quality products produced at reasonable costs. Industrial establishments must be strong in fundamentals to achieve high productivity. Exposure to foreign markets would compel domestic industries to become more competitive.
5. Competitive firms would optimise resource utilisation. The consequence would be increased supply of goods and services. Added to this are the increased production capacities of plants resulting from upgraded technologies. As days go by, supply would outstrip domestic demand, leaving exportable surplus. Surplus would necessitate exports.

Exports help finance imports.

Export earnings help service external debt.

Our exports have increased by more than 200 times during the last 50 years, from Rs.606 crore in 1950-51 to over Rs.291,582 crore in 2003-04. The figures may look impressive, but what is essential is to study the relative position. Two approaches may be used to make a comparison: exports as a share of national income and India's exports as compared to the world exports.

The share of exports to GDP has increased over the years, from a mere 3.1 in 1965-66 to about 9.0 per cent in 2003-04 (see Table 31.2). This growth reflects the growing importance of exports to our economy.

But the percentage figures make poor comparison with those of high income countries whose exports account to 15 per cent of their aggregate GDP. Even low income economies show the figure at 18 per cent.

India's exports, as compared to the global exports, have been slow to grow. Infact, many developing countries have recorded export growth rates much higher than ours. Whereas our exports increased at an annual average rate of 5.9 per cent during 1980-92, the corresponding growth rates for other developing countries like China, South Korea, Malaysia and Pakistan, exceeds 11 per cent. Our ranking among the world's export-nation slipped from 16th in 1953 to 20th in 1983 and further to 30th as of now. This is inspite of our natural comparative advantages such as low wages, intelligent and educated workforce, raw cotton and preferential access to OECD countries.

Table 31.2 **Exports as a Percentage of National Income**

1960-61	6.8
1970-71	3.8
1980-81	5.4
1990-91	7.2
1996-97	9.6
1997-98	8.4
1998-99	8.0
1999-00	8.5
2000-01	8.8
2001-02	8.7
2002-03	9.0

Why are our exports lagging behind? Reasons are too many.

Shortage of supply hampers exports.

1. We face shortage of almost all products in the domestic market. When supply is not adequate to meet demanda of the home market, export becomes meaningless. Often, we curbed domestic consumption so as to have exportable surplus, just to earn foreign exchange. A classic example is sugar.

Besides, fast growing exportable goods now comprise new technology products. Our country has yet to make its mark as an exporter of such goods, except for some recent breakthrough in software exports.

2. There is the problem of quality of our goods and services. We have not been able to create an image as a supplier of quality products. Our tea, which holds a large market share, was found adulterated with cowdung.
3. Inadequate transportation and shipping facilities have stood in the way of export promotion. Though we have ports and ships, the average Indian port performs at one-third of the efficiency levels of ports in other Asian countries like Singapore and Hong Kong. We lose around $400 million every year on account of container delays, ship-waiting and poor feeder technology.
4. Lack competitive advantage when compared to other countries. The cost of production of our products is much higher than what it prevails in other countries. For example, the average cost of production in our country as a percentage of output value at world prices is 130 but it is 98 in Korea. The reason lies in the market conditions which prevailed before 1990s. Indian industries did not adequately feel the need for cost consciousness because of the sheltered market they enjoyed for a long time.

Lack of competitive advantage too impedes exports.

Further, the productivity of our industries is much lower than other countries. Lower productivity adds to the cost of production.

The industrial upgradation which should be taking place gradually, by learning from others' experiences made available through expanding trade relations with other countries, has not taken place due to limited foreign capital inflow.[1]

5. Our exports, like exports from other developing countries; are pitted against tariff and non-tariff barriers imposed by the developed countries.

Exports are also hampered by quotas under the Multi-Fibres Arrangement, ceilings under the generalised system of preferences, and '*administrative surveillance*', which enables the European side to initiate consultations followed by quantitative restrictions.[2]

Our sales to other countries are also saddled by emerging regional trading blocks like the EU, NAFTA and Asia Pacific Rim.

6. The so called export-promotion measures have failed in their objectives. Take the case of 100 per cent export-oriented units, for example. The scheme was launched with much fanfare in 1981 and bolstered time and again with the help of a variety of concessions. But the scheme failed to take off. Although, 569 units were given approvals since inception, only 99 have commenced production. In the five-year period (1981-85), the total foreign exchange earned by them was a meagre Rs.355 crore as against the target of Rs.5,000 crore. Those that were set up have virtually become 100 per cent import-oriented units, instead of functioning as 100 per cent export oriented units. And with regard to incentives offered to promoters, less said the better as Box 31.1 reveals.

Regional trading blocks are also coming in the way of India's exports.

Box 31.1 **Incentive Scams**

Starting with R.Chidambaram in 1991, a succession of commerce ministers has gone into over-drive to boost India's exports, offering generous incentives to exporters. With unscrupulous exporters only abusing such schemes, incentive schemes became incentive scams and have cost the exchequer Rs.10,000 crore between 1991 and 1999. A third of the losses may have been due to the controversial Value-Based Licensing (VABAL) Scheme alone.

Announced under the 1992-97 Exim Policy, and scrapped in April 1997, the VABAL Scheme allowed exporters to import inputs upto a specified value without restrictions. But the exporters gave wrong figures to the government and the latter had no mechanism to check the irregularities. Of the 10,758 licences allowing duty-free imports of Rs.5,380 crore, irregularities were noticed in 2,487 cases, entailing a loss of Rs.3,532.20 crore. Of these irregularities, 278 had not made any exports while they had imported inputs valued at Rs.292.49 crore. The scams came to light thanks to the audit (for the period 1992-98) done by the Comptroller and Auditor General of India.

(Reported in *Business Today,* April 7-21, 2000).

7. Exporters are subject to severe foreign exchange controls, reforms notwithstanding. Their travel abroad is limited to stipulated allowance in foreign exchange determined by the Reserve Bank of India (RBI). Exporters still need permission to spend foreign exchange in exhibitions and trade fairs. They still cannot retain their foreign exchange earnings in dollars indefinitely, and meet expenses out of their earnings.

8. Reform of export incentives shows a lack of clear direction and stability. International Price Reimbursement Scheme was abolished and then reintroduced. In every budget, there is a threat of abolition of 100 per cent exemption of export profits (80 HHC), which creates considerable uncertainty in the minds of exporters.

9. The process of trade liberalisation began in high gear-abolition of CCS in one stroke, introduction of the negative list for imports and partial convertibility of rupee. The pace then slackened somewhat and at present, there is again some tinkering with the finer points of export incentives:expansion of items under Special Import Licence, reduction of a few canalised items, reduction in minimum export price for rice, extension of items under Export Processing Zone schemes, extension of EPCG-Schemes for the service sector, expansion of EPCG schemes for merchant exporters and the expansion of the category of '*deemed exports*'. These changes bring back memories of liberalisation of the past through licensing.

10. There has been anti-export bias. For example, while import controls for raw materials and capital goods have been removed, they still have to go through the process of obtaining

Anti-export bias is another hindrance.

licences and fulfilling obligations monitored by officials (Advance Licence System and EPGC scheme which is also a licence). Duty drawback computations have been simplified but payments are not automatic and are still subject to delays as compared to international standards. Transport costs of exports, especially by air, are considerably higher than those charged by competitors. Other infrastructural problems are more acute than in the competitor countries. Indian exporters and importers face a series of complicated procedures and a large number of approvals while exporters and importers in other countries obtain approvals instantaneously with one signature. Further, there is a need to view the whole industrial sector in India as a potential export sector. Thus, while existing exporters get duty free imports of raw materials and machinery, the rest of the industrial sector still pays considerably higher duties. This acts as a *drag* in expanding the narrow export base.[3]

Efficient trade information system is non-existent.

11. An efficient trade information system is essential for success in the dynamic global market. But our marketing infrastructure as well as the marketing techniques are neither effective nor efficient. We do not have any machinery to keep prompt track of business information overseas, as is done by JETRO in Japan, KOTRA in Korea, CETDC in Hong Kong and STDB in Singapore with a wide network of offices abroad. These organisations have evolved an efficient system which helps them get information pertaining to tenders and the like much before these are released officially. In India, we get these details, at times, after the expiry date. India has, no doubt, a plethora of organisations - government, semi-government and non-government - engaged in this task in one way or another. Yet we do not have an easy access to market intelligence and information.[4]

12. By and large our exports comprise goods and services which do not represent technological advancements except some gains in software. Across the globe new technology goods formed about half of the world trade in 1980; two decades later these constitute more than two-thirds. India's technology intensive exports constitute just 3 per cent of her total exports as against 40 per cent in the case of Singapore.

Export Strategy

In the coming years, we need to step up our exports drastically. Need for increased export earnings stems from several reasons: (i) Imports will increase and to finance them, we need higher export earnings; (ii) it is not advisable to depend on external assistance to finance imports and (iii) debt-servicing burden is ever mounting, necessitating increased export earnings.

Coupled with the above stated causes for increased export earnings, there have developed, in the recent past, certain factors which are conducive to expand our exports. The favourable factors are-

- Emergence of China, Zimbabwe and Pakistan as new customers.
- Possible acceleration in world output and trade in the wake of economic growth picking up in most developed market-economy countries.
- Opulence of Gulf countries.
- Greater scope for exports of turn-key and construction projects and consultancy services in Asia and African countries.
- Multilateral trade negotiations.[5]

In order to encash on the above stated favourable factors and to promote our exports considerably, we need an appropriate strategy. Such a strategy shall proceed on the following lines:

a. Strategic planning for exports can be the key to achieve quantum jump in our exports. This has to be undertaken at the national level.

b. Separate administrative set up on the lines of JETRO of Japan and KETRO of South Korea maybe considered.

India has competitive edge in turnkey and construction projects, BPO, and consultancy services and there are several takers of these services in Asia and African countries. Most of the newly independent countries are also keen to launch such projects and are keen to use India's help. India should take advantage of these opportunities.

Export strategy should focus on key strengths of India's economy.

c. The debate on large-scale sector *vs*. small scale sector must go. We must take advantage of the synergy between the two.

d. Build up a viable and stable export production base and supportive infrastructural facilities.

e. Parallel to building up of production capacity, appropriate technology needs to be developed.

f. Olympic approach-picking up the best of our products, procedures and markets-needs to be considered immediately. Table 31.3 contains India's top export markets along with products. Such exports must be given all facilities to increase their exports.

Olympic approach is needed to identify products which can be exported.

g. A strong push should be given to free trade zones to bring about an expansion of export production.

h. Exporters must change their mindset. Exporters should get dedicated to 'marketing' which is the exchange of 'satisfaction' for money, as distinct from 'trading' which is the exchange of goods for money. The former can be described as *sadhana*, while the latter is *pooja*. Marketing needs perseverance.

Exporters should develop export-oriented mindset from trade oriented approach.

i. As national economies are getting integrated, the share of foreign components in manufactured products is increasing considerably. For example, of the $20,000 for General Motors automobile, $6,000 goes to South Korea for routine labour and assembly operations, $3,500 to Japan for advanced components and electronics, $1,500 to Germany for design engineering, $800 to Taiwan and Singapore for small components, $500 to UK for advertising and marketing seminars and $100 to Ireland and Barbados for data processing and about $800 to strategists in Detroit, banks and insurance in the US. India should carve a niche for herself in this emerging scenario.

j. Warehousing facilities need to be provided at important commercial centres abroad, particularly for fast-moving consumer goods. Importers are reluctant to keep heavy inventories. It is the responsibility of the exporters to maintain stocks at convenient locations to enable importers to buy even in small quantities.

k. A well-directed foreign trade policy should be based on accurate trade information supported by reliable data which are to a large extent lacking. Trade related data are new compiled on the basis of the information supplied by Export Promotion Councils. The information supplied by these councils is biased and inaccurate.

l. There are a large number of export promotion councils, commodity boards and other similar agencies-all in the name of promotion. Existence of multiple agencies has, instead of increasing exports, resulted in confusion and they seem to be working at cross purposes. In order to make them effective, they need to be reorganised with clearly defined roles and functions.

Table 31.3 **India's Top Export Markets**

Exports: Five Fastest Growing Sectors			
Items	*2003-2004($bn)*	*2004-2005 ($bn)*	*(%) Change*
Petroleum crude & products	3.57	6.79	90.34
Software	13.30	17.9	34.00
Gems and jewellery	10.57	13.71	29.62
Machinery and instruments	2.78	3.49	25.82
Drugs, pharmaceuticals, fine chemicals	3.31	3.71	12.14

Top Five Exports, Then and now			
1994-1995($bn)		*2004-2005($bn)*	
Gems and jewellery	4.50	Software	17.20
Readymede garments	3.28	Engineering goods	14.58
Cotton yarn, fabrics, made-ups	2.23	Gems and jewellery	13.70
Marine products	1.13	Chemicals & related products	12.67
Leather(excluding footware)	1.06	Textiles	12.01

Five Fastest Growing Export Destinations			
Country	*2003-2004($bn)*	*2004-2005 ($bn)*	*(%) Change*
Singapore	2.12	3.80	78.63
China	2.96	4.59	55.20
United Arab Emirates	5.13	7.10	38.48
US	11.49	13.27	15.45
Hong Kong	3.26	3.65	11.94

m. India should adopt a four-pronged approach to meet the joint challenge of a united Europe and opening up of East Europe. The approach should consist of four elements: (a) restructuring of the corporate sector; (b) better quality products; (c) revaluation of General System of Preferences (GSP), and (d) linkages in industrial products.

n. Standards and standardisation, quality systems, certification and inspections, measurement systems, testing laboratories, their accreditation and calibration services and production and supply of standard reference materials, are all important building blocks. Quality control through the agency of the Export Inspection Council leaves much to be desired. It is often alleged that the agency plays a retrograde role, albeit inadvertently. This needs to be rectified.

o. We need to realise that a healthy export sector can be built up only on a strong and efficient domestic economy. A strong economy is a must if we want to have a self-sustained buoyant export sector.

We must build up our own brands internationally and not depend upon artificial supports (provided in the form of permission to use internationally known brands, e.g., the use of UK brands).

We too have several agencies, bodies and departments exclusively meant to promote exports. Prominent among them are EOUs, and SEZs. An Export Orient Unit (EOU) can be located anywhere in the country and is entitled for duty-free import of capital goods, raw materials and components. The unit is exempt from paying excise duty on domestic purchases.

SEZ's would be treated as utilities and hence are free from strikes and disputes

Special Economic Zones (SEZs) are a recent convert from Export Processing Zones (EPZs). Each zone provides to the units located therein, basic infrastructural facilities like developed land, factory buildings, roads, power, telephone exchanges, water supply and drainage, in addition to a whole range of fiscal incentives. SEZs would be treated as public utilities and hence are saved form labour strikes.

There is also centrally sponsored Export Promotion Industrial Park Scheme (introduced in August 1994) under which state governments would be involved in the creation of infrastructural facilities for export oriented units.

Imports

As with exports, our imports too have been increasing from time to time. The value of imports has increased from Rs.608 crore in 1950-51 to Rs.3,53,976 crore in 2003-04. While exports have been mainly dependent on world demand and availability of exportable surplus, imports have largely been a matter of government policy.

In relation to national income, imports during the first 30 years of planning varied between 6.5 per cent and 8.5 per cent of the GDP, the variation being minimal. Again, since 1979-80, this percentage varied between eight and 12, signifying that the imports ratio to GDP has been fairly stable.

It may be observed that in planned economies, the development effort is likely to increase imports faster than national income, because investment as a proportion of GDP is stepped up and the import content of investment is high in the early stages of development.

Regulation of Foreign Trade

As was stated earlier, the government has enormous powers to regulate our foreign trade. The Foreign Trade (Development and Regulation) Act, 1992, empowers the government to regulate imports and augment exports. The act underlines the role of foreign trade in our economic development. Technology, investment and production are becoming increasingly interdependent upon each other, and foreign trade brings these elements together and sums economic growth.

The government announces its foreign trade policy once in five years. Popularly called the Exim Policy, the latest policy was announced in March, 2007 and is valid for five years - 2007. The principal objectives of the policy are-

Exim Policy 2002-2007

The Exim policy 2002-2007 has the following objectives:

- To accelerate the transition of economy to a globally integrated vibrant economy.
- To stimulate sustained economic growth by providing access to essential raw materials, intermediates, components, consumables and goods required for enhancing production.
- To improve the technological strength and efficiency of agriculture, industry and services, thereby improving their competitiveness, and encouragement of globally accepted quality standards.
- To provide consumers with good quality products at reasonable prices.

Highlights of Exim Policy 2002-07 (as amended upto 31.3.2003)

1. Service Exports

Duty free import facility for service sector having a minimum foreign exchange earning of Rs.10 lakhs.

The duty free entitlement shall be 10% of the average foreign exchange earned in the preceding three licensing years. However, for hotels, the same shall be 5% of the average foreign exchange earned in the preceding three licensing years. This entitlement can be used for import of office equipments, professional equipments, spares and consumables. However, imports of agriculture and dairy products shall not be allowed for imports against the entitlement. The entitlement and the goods imported against such entitlement shall be non-transferable.

2. Agro Exports

(a) Corporate sector with proven credential will be encouraged to sponsor Agri Export Zone for boosting agro exports. The corporates to provide services such as provision of pre/post harvest treatment and operations, plant protection, processing, packaging, storage and related R&D.

(b) DEPB rate for selected agro products to factor in the cost of pre-production inputs such as fertiliser, pesticides and seeds.

3. Status Holders

(a) Duty-free import entitlement for status holders having incremental growth of more than 25% in FOB value of exports (in free foreign exchange).

This facility shall however be available to status holders having a minimum export turnover of Rs.25 crore (in free foreign exchange). The duty free entitlement shall be 10% of the incremental growth in exports and can be used for import of capital goods, office equipment and inputs for their own factory or the factory of the associate/supporting manufacturer/job worker. The entitlement/goods shall not be transferable. This facility shall be available on the exports made from 1.4.2003.

(b) Annual Advance Licence facility for status holders to be introduced to enable them to plan for their imports of raw material and components on an annual basis and take advantage of bulk purchases.

(c) The Input-Output norms for status holders to be fixed on priority basis within a period of 60 days.

(d) Status holders in STPI shall be permitted free movement of professional equipments like laptop/computer.

4. Hardware/Software

(a) To give a boost to electronic hardware industry, supplies of all 217 ITA-1 items from EHTP units to DTA shall qualify for fulfillment of export obligation.

(b) To promote growth of exports in embedded software, hardware shall be admissible for duty free import for testing and development purposes. Hardware upto a value of US $10,000 shall be allowed to be disposed off subject to STPI certification.

(c) 100% depreciation to be available over a period of 3 years to computer and computer peripherals for units in EOU/EHTP/STP/SEZ.

5. Gem and Jewellery Sector

(a) Diamond and Jewellery Dollar Account for exporters dealing in purchase/sale of diamonds and diamond studded jewellery.

(b) Nominated agencies to accept payment in dollars for cost of import of precious metals from EEFC account of exporter.

(c) Gem and Jewellery units in SEZ and EOUs can receive precious metal i.e. Gold/Silver/Platinum prior to exports or post exports equivalent to value of jewellery exported. This means that they can bring export proceeds in kind against the present provision of bringing in cash only.

6. Export Clusters

(a) Upgradation of infrastructure in existing clusters/industrial locations under the Department of Industrial Policy and Promotion (DIPP) scheme to increase overall competitiveness of the export clusters.

(b) Supplemental efforts to be made under the ASIDE scheme and similar schemes of other Ministries to bridge technology and productivity gaps in identified clusters.

(c) 10 such clusters with high growth potential to be reinvigorated based on a participatory approach.

7. Rehabilitation of Sick Units

For revival of sick units, extension of export obligation period to be allowed to such units based on BIFR rehabilitation schemes. This facility shall also be available to units outside the purview of BIFR but operating under the State rehabilitation programme.

8. Removal of Quantitative Restrictions

(a) Import of 69 items covering animal products, vegetables and spices, antibiotics and films removed from restricted list.

(b) Export of 5 items namely paddy except basmati, cotton linters, rare earth, silk cocoons, family planning devices except condoms removed from restricted list.

9. Special Economic Zones Scheme

(a) Sales from Domestic Tariff Area (DTA) to SEZs to be treated as export. This would now entity domestic suppliers to Drawback/DEPB benefits, CST exemption and Service Tax exemption.

(b) Agriculture/Horticulture processing SEZ units will now be allowed to provide inputs and equipments to contract farmers in DTA to promote production of goods as per the requirement of importing countries. This is expected to integrate the production and processing and help in promoting SEZs specialising in agro exports.

(c) Foreign bound passengers will now be allowed to take goods from SEZs to promote trade, tourism and exports.

(d) Domestic sales by SEZ units will now be exempt from SAD.

(e) Restriction of one year period for remittance of export proceeds removed for SEZ units.

(f) Netting of export permitted for SEZ unit provided it is between same exporter and importer over a period of 12 months.

(g) SEZ units permitted to take jobwork abroad and exports goods from there only.

(h) SEZ units can capitalise import payables.

(i) Wastage for subcontracting/exchange by gem and jewellery units in transactions between SEZ and DTA will now be allowed.

(j) Export/import of all products through post parcel/courier by SEZ units will now be allowed.

(k) The value of capital goods imported by SEZ units will now be amortised uniformly over 10 years.

(l) SEZ units will now be allowed to sell all products including gems and jewellery through exhibitions and duty free shops or shops set up abroad.

(m) Goods required for operation and maintenance of SEZ units will now be allowed duty free.

10. EQU Scheme

(a) Agriculture/Horticulture processing EOUs will now be allowed to provide inputs and equipments to contract farmers in DTA to promote production of goods as per the requirement of importing countries. This is expected to integrate the production and processing and help in promoting agro exports.

(b) EOUs are now required to be only net positive foreign exchange earner and there will now be no export performance requirement.

(c) Foreign bound passengers will now be allowed to take goods from EOUs to promote trade, tourism and exports.

(d) The value of capital goods imported by EOUs will now be amortized uniformly over 10 years.

(e) Period of utilisation of raw materials prescribed for EOUs increased from 1 year to 3 years.

(f) Gems and jewellery EOUs are now being permitted sub-contracting in DTA.

(g) Wastage for subcontracting/exchange by gem and jewellery units in transactions between EOUs and DTA will now be allowed as per norms.

(h) Export/Import of all products through post parcel/courier by EOUs will now be allowed.

(i) EOUs will now be allowed to sell all products including gems and jewellery through exhibitions and duty free shops or shops set up abroad.

(j) Gems and jewellery EOUs will now be entitled to advance domestic sales.

11. EPCG Scheme

(a) The scheme shall now allow import of capital goods for pre-production and post-production facilities also.

(b) The Export Obligation under the scheme shall now be linked to the duty saved and shall be 8 times the duty saved.

(c) To facilitate upgradation of existing plant and machinery, import of spares shall also be allowed under the scheme.

(d) To promote higher value addition in exports, the existing condition of imposing an additional Export Obligation of 50% for products in the higher product chain to be done away with.

(e) Greater flexibility for fulfillment of export obligation under the scheme by allowing export of any other product manufactured by the exporter. This shall take care of the dynamics of international market.

(f) Capital goods upto 10 years old shall also be allowed under the scheme.

(g) To facilitate diversification into the software sector, existing manufacturer exporters will be allowed to fulfill export obligation arising out of import of capital goods under the scheme for setting up of software units through export of manufactured goods of the same company.

(h) Royalty payments received from abroad and testing charges received in free foreign exchange to be counted for discharge of export obligation under EPCG scheme.

12. DEPB Scheme

(a) Facility for provisional DEPB rate introduced to encourage diversification and promote export of new products.

(b) DEPB rates rationalised in line with general reduction in Customs duty.

13. Advance Licence

(a) Standard Input Output Norms for 403 new products notified.

(b) Anti-dumping and safeguard duty exemption to advance licence for deemed exports for supplies to EOU/SEZ/EHTP/STP.

14. DFRC Scheme

(a) Duty Free Replenishment Certificate scheme extended to deemed exports to provide a boost to domestic manufacturer.

(b) Value addition under DFRC scheme reduced from 33% to 25%.

15. Reduction of Transaction Cost

(a) High priority being accorded to the EDI implementation programme covering all major community partners in order to minimize transaction cost, time and discretion. We are now gearing ourselves to provide on line approvals to exporters where exports have been effected from 23 EDI ports.

(b) Online issuance of Importer-Exporter Code (IEC) number by linking the DGFT EDI network with the Income Tax PAN database is under progress.

(c) Applications filed electronically (through website www.nic.in/eximpol) shall have a 50% lower processing fee as compared to manual applications.

16. Miscellaneous

(a) Actual user condition for import of second hand capital goods upto 10 years old dispensed with.

(b) Reduction in penal interest rate from 24% to 15% for all old cases of default under Exim Policy.

(c) Restriction on export of warranty spares removed.

(d) IEC holder to furnish online return of imports/exports made on yearly basis.

Assessment

The Exim Policy has both strengths as well as weaknesses.

Strengths

1. The policy envisages a massive role for state governments to participate in export promotion.
2. Extension of export obligation period for sick units is a welcome step in as much as it helps them recover from sickness.
3. The policy helps increase India's share in the international trade of agricultural products.
4. The policy's focus on development of SEZs, export houses, industrial clusters and EOUs would help in propelling economic activity and promoting exports.
5. The move to allow setting up of overseas banking units within the SEZs would encourage lending to units in SEZs at internationally competitive rates.

Weaknesses

1. The policy is silent on critical labour laws and infrastructural bottlenecks.
2. There are too many export promotion schemes leading to duplication and confusion. The policy should have provided for a combination of all the schemes into one comprehensive policy.
3. The policy is also silent on dumping and what the government should do to curb it.

TRADE-IN-SERVICES

Services encompass telecommunications, transportation, tourism, banking, insurance, construction, computer-related-services and professional services. World trade in services stood at a whopping $1320 billion in 1998. The lion share went to the U.S. ($240 billion) followed by the U.K. ($101 billion), France ($85 billion) and the like. India showed $11 billion worth of services, registering 24 per cent rise over the previous year. This rise is significant because all other global players registered negative growth or marginal rise, as shown in Table 31.4. Another interesting development is that India's share in world's exports of services is more than the share of India's merchandise exports in the world's total merchandise exports.

Table 31.4 **Global Players in Trade-in-Services**

($ billion)

Country	*1997*	*1998*	*% change*
U.S.	235	240	2
U.K.	92	101	9
France	80	85	5
Germany	77	79	3
Japan	68	62	-9
Hong Kong	38	34	-10
China	25	24	-2
S.Korea	25	24	-2
India	9	11	24

(**Source**: *WTO Annual Report*, 1999)

It is surprising that for a long time, the role of the services sector was not realised and the potential was not exploited to the advantage of our country. As the Box 31.2 reveals, it is only since 1980s that the services sector started receiving attention from statisticians and policy makers.

Composition-wise, our service exports generally consist of business services, tourist services, software, and transportation services. Direction-wise, India's service exports are widely transacted across the globe.

Determinants of Service Exports

Following are the principal determinants of our service exports:[5]

Box 31.2 **Growth Locomotive but not Recognised**

At the beginning of the twentieth century, services were deeds performed by nameless hands in servitude or bondage. The end of this period has seen a redefinition of the term, giving it fresh economic potential.

Services are the latest group of knowledge-utilities that are deemed to be the core of the wealth of nations in the new age. This semantic evolution connotes the comprehensive transformation of an entire spectrum of economic mindsets, among thinkers as well as governments. Not so long ago, both regarded services to be insignificant. The guru of classical economics, Adam Smith, epitomised the archaic view. To him, the economic value of services was absolutely transient; something that would perish in the very instant of its performance. According to this viewpoint, services could never amount to anything much, and measured upto even less. This was no ancient myth; many national accounting systems till recently had no estimate for the services.

Accounting systems of the erstwhile Soviet Union mindfully attributed no value to services. Other communist countries too banished them from national economic assessments as being immaterial. Even today, data systems of China cannot give full measure to the value of its services sector. Official statistical systems in India started detailed accounting for this sector only in the mid-1970s.

Of course in the last 30-35 years of the past century, services came to acquire a vast range of positive economic attributes. Again, these were intellectual as well as statistical. Neo-classical economists drastically overhauled the tenets of Adam Smith and imbued services with the quality of transforming the economic capacity and capabilities of their recipients. Economic development was itself viewed as a linear evolution towards the dominance of services in value terms (over agriculture or manufacturing). By the mid-1970s, the national accounting systems of most industrialised nations gave prominence to presenting valuations of services. In these countries, the rise in the share of services in national income was associated with overall economic growth as well as improvement in the quality of life. By the beginning of the 1980s, Indian statisticians too were tracking the evolution of the organised services sector in detail.

- Receipts from travel depend on tourist facilities in the country.
- Transportation receipts depend on merchandise exports originating from the country.
- Insurance receipts depend upon exports of merchandise.
- Receipts of repatriation of international investment income depend mainly on the growth of world economy.
- Professional, technical and other services receipts depend on the development of expertise in the country.

Promoting Service Exports

World trade in services will expand considerably and it is in our interest that we must take advantage of booming exports, particularly because we have a competitive advantage in software. It should go to the credit of the Government that it has already initiated a number of steps to strengthen the infrastructure for electronic data interchange and electronic commerce in view of the changing mode of trade transactions (see Box 31.3 for details). Similarly, we have vast potential in tourism and business services. In order to

Box 31.3 **Electronic Commerce**

Electronic Commerce (EC), in a general sense, refers to all forms of commercial transactions that are based on electronic processing and data transmission. EC is likely to emerge as the major mode of commerce in view of lower information and transaction costs.

EC, which spurted in the mid-nineties essentially through non-proprietary networks such as the Internet, is expected to expand rapidly in the coming years. Estimates of EC turnover for the period 2000-02 range from US $10 billion to US $1.522 billion [OECD (1998)]. Currently, about 80 per cent of the EC transactions are intra- or inter-organisation type with about 80 per cent of the global EC transactions taking place in the United States. India remains one of the forerunners in EC development among the emerging markets with the Union Ministry of Commerce designated as the nodal agency for implementation of Electronic Data Interchange (EDI) and EC in India. The United Nations' standard (UN/EDIFACT) has been accepted as the national standard for EDI while four bodies - EDI/EC Council, India EDIFACT Committee, EDI Working Group and Message Development Group - have been formed in order to facilitate the development of EDI/EC in India. Special steps have been taken to introduce EDI/EC in areas such as ports, airlines, banks, tax administration, information exchange between organisations and interface of the authorities with the private sector. Electronic trading of financial instruments such as equity shares has been implemented by the National Stock Exchange.

The global nature of EC results in cross-border transactions often in intangibles with EC based payment mechanisms which pose new challenges for tax administration. The present taxation laws, based either on business connection or permanent establishment, are difficult to apply as the physical location of given transactions loses its importance, making it difficult to determine their revenue jurisdiction. Furthermore, e-commerce through internet, by and large, results in a distinct change in the pattern of intermediation by banks and other institutions limiting the ability of authorities to rely on them to collect withholding tax. Taxes could be source-based or destination-based. While source-based taxes applied to electronic commerce have clear compliance and administrative cost advantages over their destination-based counterparts, problems of evasion still remain. Special types of taxation such as the "bit tax" on data transmission have been proposed. However, tax administration would need to strike a balance between maximising the potential "efficiency gains" out of technology and protecting the revenue base.

Revenue implications of EC for India are limited at this stage as it is possible to identify most forms of cross-border EC transactions (including those involving intangibles) from the banking channel due to the existing reporting norms relating to foreign currency transactions.

References

1. Government of India, Annual Report, Ministry of Commerce, various issues, New Delhi.
2. OECD (1997), The Report of the Group of High-level Private Sector Experts on Electronic Commerce (Sacher Group Report), Paris.
3. OECD, (1998), The Economic and Social Impact of Electronic Commerce, Paris.

realise this potential, we should learn in terms of flexibility, customised operations, technologies and global strategies from the service providers of the North.

BALANCE OF PAYMENTS

Before proceeding further, it is useful to distinguish between '*balance of trade*' and '*balance of payments*'. The balance of trade refers to the difference between merchandise exports and imports during a period, which is usually one year. When the exports exceed imports, a country is said to enjoy a favourable balance of trade. Balance of trade of the country becomes unfavourable when it buys more from other countries than what it sells to them.

The balance of payments (BoP) is broader in its scope and include trade in merchandise and services. It is a systematic record of all international economic transactions, visible and invisible, of a country during a given period, the period generally being one year. BoP, therefore, presents a better picture of a country's financial transactions with the rest of the world than the balance of trade.

The analysis of BoP can be done in terms of two major sub-divisions - *current account* and *capital account*. Transactions relating to goods, services and income constitute the current account. A surplus on current account leads to an acquisition of assets or repayment of debt previously contracted; and a deficit involves the withdrawal of previously accumulated assets or is met by borrowings. The capital account presents transfers of money and other capital items and changes in the country's foreign assets and liabilities resulting from the transactions recorded in the current account. The deficit on the current account and on account of capital transactions can be financed by external assistance (loans and grants), drawings from the International Monetary Fund (IMF) and allocation of the Special Drawing Rights.

Most developing countries start as debtor economies, i.e., they start with deficit BoP. This is so because such countries need to import more visible and invisible items than they can export. As the economy progresses, a developing country's debtor position is likely to become a balanced one in terms of BoP and, finally, becomes a creditor economy, exporting more than it imports. Thus, from being a net debtor in the beginning, it becomes a net creditor in the end and, infact, begins to invest abroad rather than have others lending to and investing in it.[6]

India had faced pressures on BoP from time to time either due to certain domestic compulsions or due to external factors, as shown in Table 31.5. Factors responsible for BoP deficits are many. Ever increasing imports, gradual decline in net receipts from invisibles and reduction in flows of concessional assistance to India are the major causes for deficits in BoP.

The crisis reached its peak during 1990-91, when current account deficit touched 3.3 per cent of the GDP, as seen in Table 31.5. This crisis unleashed series of measures such as strict fiscal and monetary discipline to control aggregate demand; dual exchange rate system (introduced in the Budget for 1992-93); full convertibility on current account (introduced in the Budget for 1994-95); substantial deregulation of trade and industry, standby arrangement with the IMF; structural adjustment and social security net loans from World Bank and financial sector loan negotiated with the ADB.

Countries make use of their respective exchange rates while dealing with other countries.

The above measures yielded positive results. The BOP situation has undergone a dramatic change during the nineties. The foreign exchange reserves, which were just enough to pay for only a fortnight's imports in 1991, have grown ten times since then (from Rs.11,416 cr as on end March 1991 to Rs.125,446 cr as on 31st March 1999).

EXCHANGE RATE MANAGEMENT

Countries make use of their respective exchange rates while dealing with other countries. It is the endeavour of every country to maintain equilibrium exchange rate. An equilibrium exchange rate is the proper rate of exchange at which there are no disharmonies in the economic system and the demand for

Table 31.5 **Key Indicators of BoP**

(% of GDP)

Year	*Exports*	*Imports*	*Net Invisibles*	*Trade Balance*	*Current Account Balance*
1985-90 (Average)	5.10	8.30	0.90	-3.20	-2.30
1990-91	6.25	9.43	-0.08	-3.18	-3.26
1991-92	7.30	8.15	0.01	-0.85	-0.84
1992-93	7.80	9.80	-0.20	2.40	-1.80
1993-94	8.80	9.70	0.50	-0.90	-0.20
1994-95	8.90	10.50	0.80	-1.70	-0.80
1995-96	9.90	12.60	1.10	-2.70	-1.60
1996-97	9.50	13.00	2.50	-3.50	-1.00
1997-98	8.36	12.28	2.42	-3.94	-1.52
1998-99	8.20	11.40	2.20	-3.20	-1.00
1999-00	8.30	12.30	2.90	-4.00	-1.10
2000-01	9.40	12.40	2.50	-3.00	-0.50
2001-02	10.36	13.28	3.24	-2.92	0.32
2002-03	9.00	13.00	5.27	-4.00	1.27

(**Source**: *RBI*, Annual Report)

the currency is equal to its supply in the foreign exchange market. At this rate, the domestic currency is neither undervalued nor overvalued in terms of foreign currency and thus does not give stimulus either to export or to import. The main objectives of our exchange rate policy are:[7]

- Reduce excess volatility in exchange rates, while ensuring that the market correction of overvalued or undervalued exchange rate is orderly and calibrated.
- Maintain an adequate level of foreign exchange reserves.
- Eliminate market constraints with a view to the development of a healthy foreign exchange market.

As with other any other aspect of international trade, reforms were effected in our exchange rate over the years. Starting with a two-stage cumulative devaluation of the rupee by about 20 per cent in July 1991, there was the Liberalised Exchange Rate Management System (LERMS) introduced in March 1992, and there was also the United Exchange Rate System (UERS) brought into force in March 1992. The LERMS was characterised by the dual exchange rate system and this was replaced by the UERS which, as the term signifies, United Exchange Rate System. The result was an effective devaluation of the rupee by around 35 per cent in nominal terms and 25 per cent in real terms between July, 1991 and March 1993.

The UERS has the following features:

- The rates of exchange are determined in the market.
- The freely floating exchange rate regime continues to operate within the frame-work of exchange control.
- Current receipts are surrounded to the banking system, which in turn meets the demand for foreign exchange.

- RBI intervention in the market to modulate the volatility and sharp depreciation of the rupee.
- The US dollar is the principal currency for the RBI transactions.
- The RBI effects transactions at a rate of exchange which could change within a margin of five per cent of the prevailing market rate.
- The RBI also announces a Reference Rate based on the quotations of select banks in Mumbai at 12 noon every day. The Rate is applicable to SDR transactions and transactions routed through the Asian Clearing Union.

Thus, with the introduction of UERS, our rupee has matured to a regime of the floating exchange rate from the earlier versions of a 'managed float'.

Along with the UERS, the rupee became fully convertible on current account with effect from August 20, 1994. Accordingly, several provisions like remittances for services, education, basic travel, gift remittances and donation and provisions of the Exchange Earners Foreign Currency Account (EEFC) have been relayed. In a further move, as announced on January 9, 1997, the RBI liberalised the existing regulations with regard to the payments for various kinds of feasibility studies, legal services, postal imports and the purchase of designs and drawings. With this, India has acquired IFF Article VIII Status. Under the status, IMF members undertake to refrain from imposing restrictions on the making of payments and transfers for current international transactions and from engaging in discriminatory currency arrangements or multiple currency practices without the approval of the IMF.

The Article VII status instils confidence among the international investing community, paving the way for further inflow of foreign capital. India is now committed to allowing free outflow of current account payments like interest, even if there is a serious foreign exchange crisis.

With regard to the capital account convertibility, it maybe stated that foreign exchange can be brought into the country with little or no restrictions, but it can be taken out only under specified conditions. There are exceptions however. For example, foreign institutional investors can bring in dollars to invest in the stock markets and take them out at will. In addition, NRIs can deposit funds in our banks, earn high interest rates and withdraw funds whenever they want. RBI has also expanded the scope of borrowing or raising funds abroad for resident Indians.

The reforms described above do not indicate that forex traders can make a quick buck in our country. Our forex market is restricted and is dominated by the Reserve Bank.

QUESTIONS

1. Bring out the role of foreign trade in a country's economic development.
2. Why are exports lagging behind targets? What can be done to promote exports?
3. How is foreign trade sought to be regulated?
4. What are trade-in-services? What is their role in our export earnings?
5. What is exchange rate management? Bring out the reforms in our exchange rate management?
6. What do you understand by balance of payments? Describe our balance of payments position over the years.

ASSIGNMENT

We have huge forex reserves fo more than $170 billion. How can we use the amount?

REFERENCES

1. Ishwar C.Dhingra, *The Indian Economy-Environment and Policy*, Sultan Chand & Sons, 2000, p.687.
2. *Ibid*, p.688.
3. *Ibid*, 1996, p.558.
4. *Ibid*, pp.563-566.
5. P.C.Verma, "India's International Trade in Services", *The Indian Economic Journal*, January-March, 1997.
6. Ishwar C.Dhingra, *Op.Cit.*, p.695.
7. *Ibid*, p.719.

CHAPTER OUTLINE

Background to the New Policy

The New Policy

- Evaluation of the Policy

The Second Generation Reforms

LEARNING OBJECTIVES

After reading this Chapter, you should be able to:

1. Understand the reasons why the New Economic Policy became a necessity
2. Describe the new policy and make a critical evaluation of it
3. List the second generation reforms
4. Assess the effects of 10 years of reforms

32 New Economic Policy

Since July 1991, the government has initiated a series of radical changes in its policies relating to industry, trade, finance, foreign investments and fiscal aspects. The various changes, also called *structural* adjustments, when put together, constitute an economic policy which marks a total departure from the policy pursued earlier. This chapter is devoted to a brief discussion of the various aspects of the new policy.

BACKGROUND TO THE NEW POLICY

The new economic policy was necessitated by the worst economic crisis which was never witnessed by the country after Independence.

> The new economic policy was announced in 1991, following the worst economic crisis that ever occurred in the country.

The most visible sign of the country's economic crisis was its extremely low foreign exchange reserves of Rs.2400 crore, which was reached in early 1991. The reserves were just enough to buy, from abroad, only three weeks requirements. The situation became even more precarious when international agencies lowered the country's credit rating.

The second major aspect of the economic crisis was the rapidly increasing burden of national debt, which exceeded 60 per cent of GNP in 1991. The fiscal deficit of the previous five years forced the government to borrow increasingly to meet shortfall in the revenue account. Borrowing added to the already prevailing debt burden.

> Spirling prices, dwindled forex reserves and heavy debt burden triggered the economic crisis which in turn resulted in the new economic policy.

The third and the most damaging feature of the 1991 crisis was the high price level. During 1985-90, the GDP grew at an average rate of 5.7 per cent but money supply increased at 15.7 per cent per annum. This excess liquidity led to high price rise which touched 17 per cent. (See Table 32.1 for more details about the price rise).

Table 32.1 **Trends in Wholesale Price Index and Consumer Price Index**

	1989-90	*1990-91*
(A) WPI (1981-82 = 100)		
All Commodities	8.1%	13.5%
(a) Primary articles	3.6%	18.9%
(b) Fuel, power and light	2.3%	19.2%
(c) Manufactured products	11.8%	9.6%
(B) CPI (1982 = 100)		
For Industrial workers	5.4%	13.7%

THE NEW POLICY

As part of the budget of 1991-92, through the latest one and also outside of the budgets, the government announced a number of economic reform measures. (It does not mean that attempts were not made earlier to reform the regulatory, trade and taxation regimes. It is just that their pace and frequency were slow).

The main objectives of the policy initiatives were:

(a) Reducing the government deficit to 6.5 percent of GDP in 1991-92 and five percent in 1992-93, with further reduction thereafter leading to containment of inflation;

(b) Reduction of the current account deficit in the balance of payments to 2.7 percent of GDP in 1991-92 and to 1.5 percent by 1995-96 as a result of export-growth and

(c) Raising GDP growth to around six percent by the mid-1990s

The new economic policy has four components, *viz.* (a) liberalisation, (b) privatisation, (c) globalisation and (d) stabilisation.

Four dimensions form the chunks of the new economic policy: liberalization, privatization, globalization and stabilization.

Together called the structural adjustment programme (SAP), the new policy envisages the measures as shown in Table 32.2.

The SAP has been forced on the economy because of several reasons. They are : *(i)* excess of consumption and expenditure over the revenue, resulting in heavy government borrowing; *(ii)* growing inefficiency in the use of resources; *(iii)* over protection; *(iv)* mismanagement of the firms and the economy, *(v)* distortions such as poor technological development and a shortage of foreign exchange and *(vi)* imprudent borrowing from abroad and mishandling and mismanagement of foreign exchange reserves.

Evaluation of the Policy

Two questions are relevant in the context of critical assessment of the new economic policy. They are: (i) Is the policy unavoidable? (ii) What are the achievements and failures of the policy?

Table 32.2 **Model of Economic Management in India**

Pre-reform strategies	*Economic reform strategies*
Closed economy	Open economy
Self reliance	Integrate with world markets
State-led economic growth	Market determined economic growth
Import substitution strategies	Export oriented strategies
Licence dominated regime	Delicensing, deregulation,debureaucratisation
Frequent state interventions	Selective and effective state interventions.
Political administered prices	Market determined prices at large.
Not much concern for deficits	Contain all kinds of deficits
Development by inflationary process	Deflationary monetary and fiscal policies
PSUs as engines of growth	Private investment as growth engine
Dominance of PSUs	Withdrawal from the area of private interest
Philosophy of natural monopoly	Minimise gap between public and private sector.
Restrictions of FDI and MNCs	Inducement to FDI and MNCs
Restrictions on currency movement	Liberalisation of restrictions
State controlled interest rates	Deregulation of interest rates
State controlled credit	Credit policy reforms
Underdeveloped capital market	Reforms in capital market
Huge public sector budgetary resources (PSBR) liability on the government	Minimise PSBR
High tax rates	Tax reforms

With regard to the first question, the answer is in affirmative considering the mire in which our economy was caught during the late 1980s and the early 1990s. A lasting solution to the crisis was not possible without the restoration of fiscal balance, infusing dynamism and competition and an increase in outward orientation.

Economic policy should move towards free market. No reversal of the direction at all.

As to the second question, it maybe asserted that the results have been quite encouraging. There has been a remarkable surge in the growth rate of the economy. After the crisis induced low growth of 0.9 per cent in 1991-92, the economy has responded smartly to the economic reforms to record a growth of 6.8 per cent in 1996-97. Industrial growth has registered around 8 per cent per annum.

Exports have grown comfortably and foreign investment inflow has been exceedingly good. Consequently, foreign currency reserves have stock piled. Price level too has been brought down to less than 8 per cent. And contrary to what the critics might say, poverty has come down (See Box 32.1).

In general, economy has become vibrant. Captains of industry are buoyant and are not deterred by the entry of MNCs. There is an overall increase in productivity, quality and competitiveness of Indian goods and services. For an economy which was under the grip of controls for nearly four decades, the new economic policy has not been a big jolt. It has absorbed the shocks of the structural adjustment with remarkable resilience and is looking ahead for more reforms. This has been realised by all political parties and hence the talk about the irreversibility of economic reforms.

Thanks to new measures, economy has become vibrant.

There are problems nevertheless: (1) The pace of economic reforms, though fast during the first three years, slowed down from 1994 onwards. Reason is obvious. Elections to several state assembles

Box 32.1 **Encouraging News About Poverty**

For all those following the debate on poverty trends since the reforms of 1991, there is encouraging news from the National Council of Applied Economic Research (NCAER). It's latest consumer survey for 1993-94 shows that:

- The proportion of low income households has diminished after the economic reforms of 1991, a continuation of the declaiming trend evident since 1985-86 when it conducted its first survey. (See Table 32.3).

Table 32.3 **National Income and Per Capita Income at Current Prices**

(Low income group%)

	Rural	*Urban*	*Total*
1985-86	73	42	65
1987-88	69	40	61
1989-90	67	37	59
1992-93	65	38	58
1993-94	65	37	57

- Social mobility is substantial, and people are moving up the income ladder from the bottom to the middle, and from middle to the top. (See Table 32.4).

Table 32.4 **Up the Income Ladder**

(% of households)

	Low income		*Lower middle income*		*Middle/high income*	
	Overall	*Rural*	*Overall*	*Rural*	*Overall*	*Rural*
1985-86	65	73	25	22	10	5
1987-88	61	69	28	25	11	5
1989-90	59	67	27	24	14	9
1992-93	58	65	25	23	17	12
1993-94	57	65	26	23	17	12

(Low income is defined as upto Rs.12,500 per year per household; lower middle income is Rs.12,500 to Rs.25,000 per year; middle/high income is above Rs.25,000 per year. All figures are at 1989-90 prices)

were held in 1994. Two Rupees a kg of rice was the main promise in elections to the Andhra assembly. The promise was accepted by the electorate and the party which promised highly subsidised rice won the landslide majority. This opened the eyes of the rulers in the Central Government. Suddenly there was talk about subsidies and poverty and all attention was focussed on these issues. Economic reforms were sidelined and the trend continues till to date.

Economic reforms are announced by Central Government, but it is the state governments which need to implement them.

(2) Though economic reforms are announced by the Central Government, their implementation is in the hands of state governments. For example, industries have been freed from investment and production restrictions. But basic infrastructure such as land, power, water needs are to be provided by the state governments. And except Haryana, Kerala, Orissa, Punjab, Rajasthan, West Bengal and Maharashtra (See Box 32.2) other states have not responded favourably to the

Box 32.2 **Industrial Policy Reforms: Selected State Government Initiatives**

Haryana

- Several steps taken to simplify procedures and ensure time bound clearances.
- Industrial Assistance Group as a single window services further extended to district level to ensure effective coordination among various government organisations.
- Powers to allot, transfer, lease and rent industrial plots/sheds; sanction/disbursement of loans by Haryana Financial Corporation, sanction of electric load upto a certain limit-delegated to district level.
- Time bound clearance/sanctions encompassing all aspects - Project Approval (15 days), Registration as small unit (1 day), NOC (no objection certificate) by State Pollution Board (15 days), allotment of plots/shed (10 days) from receipt of application.
- All sales tax barriers through the state removed.
- High level coordination committee set up to ensure all clearances within the stipulated time. An Empowered Group (including representatives from various organisations) set up to revamp administration.
- High Powered Committee set up to take spot decisions on foreign investments, NRI projects and 100 per cent export oriented projects
- A state level grievance committee set up to address problems faced by entrepreneurs.
- Visits of inspectors has been streamlined and rationalised.

Kerala

- Several steps are proposed/have been undertaken for attracting more investments and for procedural/rules simplification.
- State Industrial Development Committee will be formed for ensuring speedy clearance of applications of new SSIs, within prescribed time limit, review and maintenance of good industrial relations and monitoring of industrial development activities.
- District Development Committee to be formed in each district
- Industrial Relations Committee to be extended to all existing and potential industrial areas.
- A new Green Channel Scheme will be introduced for expediting all clearances and all unneccesary licensing and clearances will be abolished.
- An Industrial Infrastructure Development Authority will be established.
- A special cell will be created to coordinate activities relating to central projects.
- New units will be exempted from all state taxes for the first seven years.
- Investment subsidy will be increased to 15 per cent, with certain ceilings.

Orissa

- A nodal committee constituted at the state government level of clearance of proposals for providing infrastructural facilities and government assistance, and to recommend measures for the rehabilitation of sick industrial units.
- The Foreign Investment Division in the Industrial Promotion and Investment Corporation of Orissa will act as a single window for investments by Non-Resident Indians and foreign investors.
- Nodal committees constituted at the district level to resolve local problems faced by entrepreneurs.

Punjab

- A new package of incentives to attract investments, avoid multiplicity of incentives and procedures, create new job opportunities and speedy clearance of new enterprises announced and made applicable from October, 1992. Steps undertaken/contemplated include:
- A committee constituted for providing land 'off the shell'
- Udyog Sahayaka acting as a single window service for clearing projects.
- State government signed MoUs with selected industrial units to upgrade Industrial Training Institutes.
- Privatisation of Public Sector Units to be undertaken.
- Develop selected industrial corridors as part of infrastructural development. Use private initiative for infrastructure development, specially power.
- Procedures for providing credit by State Financial Institutions to be simplified. For promoting exports, foreign bank branches to be set up in Ludhiana.
- The state is formulating a policy to ensure granting of clearances for setting up industries within 24 hours of receipt of request.

Rajasthan

- Several steps taken for expanding and strengthening infrastructure, simplifying rules and procedures, ensuring speedy availability of inputs/clearances, increasing role of private sector, enhancing employment and investment.
- Power generation, telecom services, tourism and hotelling in the private sector encouraged.
- Enabling legislation put in place to allow private parties to collect tolls from roads/bridges constructed by them.
- Amendments made in rules relating to the conversion and allotment of land for industrial purposes.
- 155 SSIs exempted from obtaining No Objection Certificate from State Pollution Control Boards. Power to grant NOCs decentralised.
- Industries to be inspected under Factories Act reduced from 15 to three. Common inspection in accordance with a checklist prepared for the purpose. Even simpler procedure for the SSIs.

West Bengal

- State, wherever appropriate, welcomes foreign technology and investments.
- State recognises the importance and the key role of the private sector in accelerating growth.
- An Empowered Committee at the State level, under the Chairmanship of the Chief Secretary, to take quick decisions on investment proposals.
- The Single Window Agency of the West Bengal Industrial Development Corporation Ltd. strengthened to provide effective 'Escort Service' to new projects.
- Committees in each district formed under the Chairmanship of District Magistrates to ensure quick decisions on land, employment and other related matters.
- Private sector investment in power generation encouraged to meet increased demand.

(**Source**: Govt. of India, *Economic Survey, 1994-95*).

economic reforms. Without active support from the state governments, it is difficult to carry out the reforms successfully.

(3) The Central Government's fiscal deficit continues to be high and this is reflected in continuing inflationary pressure. The borrowing requirements of a high fiscal deficit are a source of pressure on interest rates and adversely affect the availability of resources for productive investment, especially at a time when a strong industrial recovery has resuscitated private sector demand for investible funds.

(4) Foreign exchange front may not continue to be comfortable for all the days to come. Unless fiscal restraint is observed and reforms in tax and trade policies continued, the recent improvements in international competitiveness and export growth could falter and thus bring the balance of payments under renewed stress. Moreover, in today's increasingly open and competitive international environment, perceptions of weakness in macroeconomic policy of economic reforms could adversely affect the flow of foreign savings.

(5) Weakness in reforms is already visible. Not only the pace has slowed down, the process of reforms is not complete even though reforms are decade old. Many areas need policy changes. For example, phasing out subsidies, reducing the number of agencies which give clearance for new projects, amending the Companies Act, 1956 to allow amalgamations and inter-corporate investments, and the like await government's clearance.

Reforms have hit the labour hard.

(6) The reforms have hit the labour hard. Emboldened by the new economic policy, both public and private sector enterprises have resorted to voluntary retirement schemes to get rid off surplus labour. Surplus may be the labour force, but removal is not the ideal solution. Excess labour could be retrained and redeployed instead of being asked to go home for good.

The labour is hurt on the employment front too. As pointed out by the mid-term appraisal document of the eighth Plan, "although employment growth was better in 1992-95 than during 1985-92, when the average rate of growth was only 1.78 per cent (equivalent to a net annual addition of about five million per year), it has been substantially lower than the Plan's target of an average employment growth rate of 2.6 to 2.8 per cent.

"Consequently, the growth in employment opportunities of six million in each of the three years 1992-95 have fallen short of the target envisaged in the Plan by about 2.5 million each year. It has also been smaller than the estimated growth of the labour force during the period. Therefore, the level of unemployment in the economy which was estimated at 17 million in 1992, is likely to have increased to 19 million in 1994". Obviously, economic reforms seems to have failed in generating additional jobs.

Gains from economic reforms are grossly exaggerated.

(7) The success of reforms is highly exaggerated. If one were to look into the economy closely, nothing seems to have changed from pre-reform days. The share of manufacturing in GDP for example, was 27.5 percent in 1989-90. It was slightly less at 27.3 percent in 1994-95. The share of agriculture fell from 33.7 percent in 1989-90 to 31.5 percent in 1994-95. (See Table 32.5)

(8) Contrary to what the Table 32.3 and 32.4 indicate, poverty during the ninetees has worsened as shown in Table 32.6. As seen from the Table, the progress achieved during the eightees in poverty reduction got reversed or ground to a halt during the Nineties.

All things considered, it maybe stated that the reforms are inevitable. Our economy cannot remain isolated from what is happening in the global business scenario. However, the policy makers do well to realise the past mistakes and correct them on the way to further reforms.

Table 32.5 **Unchanging Face of Economy**

	1984-85	*1989-90*	*1994-95*
% share of agriculture in GDP	37.6	33.7	31.5
% share of manufactures in GDP	24.9	27.5	27.3
% share of banking,insurance and real estate	9.1	10.0	11.2
% composition of imports of crude oil, fertilizers, capital goods, iron and steel and chemicals	63.9 (1985-90)	–	-63.8
% composition of exports of gems and jewellary	16.0 (1990-91)	–	17.1
% cotton yarn	6.34	–	8.41
% transport equipment	2.21	–	2.91

(**Source**:*Economic Times*, Jan 21, 1997)

Table 32.6 **Percentage of People below Poverty Line**

Year	*Rural*	*Urban*	*All-India*	*Number (million)*
1983	45.6	40.8	44.5	322.8
1987-88	39.1	38.2	38.9	304.9
1989-90	33.7	36.0	34.3	276.0
1990-91	35.0	35.3	35.1	291.0
1992	41.7	37.8	40.7	348.0
1993-94	37.3	32.4	35.1	320.5
1994-95	38.0	34.2	37.0	329.5
1995-96	38.3	30.0	36.1	328.0
1997	38.5	34.0	37.2	348.8
1998	45.2	34.6	43.0	406.3
2007	45.2	34.6	43.0	300.0

THE SECOND GENERATION REFORMS

What has been accomplished till now through SAP is significant. Yet much more needs to be done to reap the full benefits of what has so far been done. This calls for the implementation of the *second generation reforms*. The second generation reforms should help our firms grow and become strong MNCs, and offer greater opportunities to our vast pool of educated youth to realise their potential and alleviate the sufferings of people still languishing below poverty line.

In brief, the second generation reforms comprise the following:

A. Exploiting the Knowledge-based Global Economy

(i) Revolutionising the telecom sector to help integrate India's economy into world economy.

(ii) Building institutes for higher education to turnout competent youth to take advantage of newer opportunities.

(iii) A system of intellectual property rights to reward innovations adequately.

(iv) Venture capital and 'private equity funds' to finance risk projects of the knowledge based economy.

Second generation reforms include:
(i) exploiting global economy,
(ii) growing Indian MNCs,
(iii) high growth in agriculture,
(iv) empowering the poor,
(v) human development,
(vi) clean environment,
(vii) better governance.

B. Growing Indian Transnational Corporations

(i) Indian firms to enjoy flexibility in entry and exit. Freedom to diversify and to close down unsuccessful units helps Indian companies compete successfully with MNCs.

(ii) Bring in more trade reforms so that resources could be put to more productive uses.

(iii) Liberalise domestic trade, besides freeing international trade.

(iv) Liberalise and move towards capital account convertibility.

C. High Growth of Agriculture

(i) Free farmers from all domestic restrictions on storage, transport and sale of agricultural products.

(ii) State to ensure that adequate investments are made in irrigation, agricultural research and infrastructure.

D. Empowering the Poor

(i) Integrate and consolidate anti-poverty measures.

(ii) Set up a system for old age income security.

E. Human Development

(i) Knowledge industries require educated people. Make primary education compulsory.

(ii) Involve private sector to provide better primary education.

F. Clean Environment

(i) Arrest damage to environment.

(ii) Promote clean and healthy environment.

G. Improvements to Governance

(i) Reform of public finance.

(ii) Rationalise electricity prices.

(iii) Bring in legal reforms that ensure inexpensive and speedy justice and at the same time facilitate economic growth.

DECADE PLUS YEARS OF REFORMS[1]

We are into nearly 15 years of economic reforms. It is time that we take a look at the effect of economic reforms initiated in 1991. The following questions and their answers give us an objective assessment of the reforms. The questions raised are -

1. How fast the economy is growing?
2. How sustainable is our growth performance?

3. What are the prospects of the economy?
4. What is the state of poverty?
5. What is the access to clean water, and sanitation in rural India?
6. What is the state of health in India?
7. What have we done for social sector?
8. What is the role of new and emerging technologies?
9. What can we expect from new agricultural varieties?

Growth of the Economy

India needs a sustained growth rate of 15 per cent to become a developed one.

So far as rate of economic growth is concerned, expectation during the early 1990's was that it would be in double digits. The growth rate was 5.5 per cent since 1997-98 (though it was 7.5 from 1991 to 1997). It went up to 8 per cent in 2003-04. Development experts are of the opinion that India should have a growth rate of atleast 15 per cent sustained over a period of 10 to 15 years, if it were to become a developed economy. We fall short of this expectation considerably.

How Sustainable?

With regard to sustainability, the Indian economy exhibited considerable resilience in the recent past, inspite of several shocks it has received - Est Asian crisis, global depression, border tension, Iraq war, earthquake, tsunami, oil price fluctuations, and draughts (See also Box 32.3). The growth rate of 5.5 per cent against this backdrop is commendable by any standard.

Given the stable economic environment and better prospects lying ahead, sustaining the growth rate may not be difficult.

Economic Prospects

Economy seems to have everything going in its favour.

The economy seems to have everything going in its favour. Some instances are:

- Rate of inflation is slow and stable
- Abundant liquidity at low interest rates
- Exchange rate is stable under managed float regime
- Huge forex reserves
- Short-term external debt is low
- Stocks of foodgrains are comfortable
- Industrial sector is passing through a process of restructuring, consolidation, adoption of cost cutting measures, foreign collaboration and technology upgradation
- Growing integration of the economy with the world economy
- Diversification of agriculture in favour of vegetables, horticulture, livestock, afforestation, and agro-processing

Box 32.3 **Shocks Hitting the Economy after the mid-1990s**

Incidents	Date	Details
Exchange rate Volatility	October 1995-March 1996	Sharp extended rise in interest rates and short-lived credit squeeze.
Asian currency crisis	1997	Heightened fear of volatility in currency markets and of capital flight.
India's bomb	11 May 1998	India conducts three nuclear explosions at its Pokhran nuclear test-site. These include a fission-device, a low-yield device, and a thermonuclear device.
	13 May 1998	India conducts tests of two sub-kiloton nuclear devices at Pokhran.
Sanction	13 May 1998	President Bill Clinton reported to Congress that he had imposed sanctions on India under Section 102 of the Arms Export Control Act, otherwise known as the Glenn Amendment.
Earthquake	29 March 1999	Chamoli UP.
War	31 May 1999-28 June 1999	Kargil war.
Cyclone	18-19 October 1999	Orissa, Andhra Pradesh, and West Bengal.
Global price shock	October 2000	Oil price hike.
US recession	Last quarter 2000-First quarter 2001	Triggers global slowdown.
Stock prices fall	Early 2001	Dotcom burst.
Scam	March 2001	SEBI restrains Anand Rathi from trading.
Earthquake	26 January 2001	Gujarat earthquake.
Scam	13 March 2001	Tehelka.com tapes released.
Scam	30 March 2001	Madhavpura Mercantile Cooperative Bank in trouble.
Enron dispute	May 2001	Work stops at Dabhol.
Financial crisis	May 2001	Software slowdown.
Scam	May 2001	Home trade CEO held for fraud.
Scam	August 2001	Arvind Johari, promoter of Lucknow-based Cyberspace Infosys Ltd. (CIL), held on the charge of misappropriating Rs.32.08 crores from Unit Trust of India (UTI).
International terrorism	11 September 2001	WTC bombing in New York.
War	November 2001	Afghan war.
Terrorism in India	13 December 2001	Bombing at the Parliament.
Price shocks	7 February 2002	Gold prices zoom to 5-year high.
Riot	27 February to 16 March 2002	Riots in Gujarat after Godhra Incident.
Tension	June 2002	Indo-Pak tension at the border.
Monsoon failure	June 2002	
Scam	July 2002	Worldcom scandal.
War	March 2003	Iraq war.
Epidemic	3 April 2003	SARS hits Asia.
Strike	3 April 2003	Truckers' strike.
Disaster	24 December 2004	Tsunami

— Exports and imports together account for 23 per cent of GDP as against just 15 per cent in 1990-01

— Stable and proactive government

State of Poverty

The growth achieved at the economic front has percolated down to the people. The proportion of the population below poverty line has fallen as Table 32.7 shows.

Table 32.7 **Decline in Poverty**

	(%)
1970s	50
1980s	39
1990s	26

Poverty rate has declined.

How has this decline been achieved? The reduction in poverty rate can be attributed to higher economic growth, improvement in real wages, and proliferation of poverty alleviation programmes. It is likely that the incidence of poverty continues to decline and will become residual by the end of this decade.

Access to Water and Sanitation

One needs to treck long distances to fetch a bucket of water.

Drinking water, basic to human beings, continues to be a major problem in India, both in villages as well as in cities. The latter is better in the sense that water trickles through taps atleast on alternate days. But it is nightmarish in rural areas. One has to trek kilometers to fetch a bucket of water or pay Re.0.50 per bucket if water is delivered at your doorstep. Urban or rural, full-pressure, "24-7" water supply remains a pipe dream.

Less said the better so far as sanitation is concerned. In rural India, about 71 million households fetch water from outside by spending some 102 billion hours in a year. Further, only 7 per cent of rural households are connected to the sewerage system and only 9 per cent households have in-house toilet facilities. The opportunity cost of the time thus spent is high, particularly in terms of schooling for girls and social and economic opportunities for women.

Status of Health

Poor people in most countries have the worst health services. They are pushed further into poverty due to ill health. Luckily, India has over the years, built up a vast health infrastructure and manpower at primary, secondary, and tertiary care in the government, voluntary, and private sectors. The expenditure on health accounts for 5.6 per cent of the total GDP while the public health expenditure is at 0.9 per cent. Technological advances have made deep inroads into health services. During 1951-96, the number of hospitals and dispensaries increased from 9209 to 43,322 and hospital beds from 1.17 to 8.70 million; and during 1951-99 nursing personnel rose from 0.18 to 8.7 lakh and alopathic doctors from 0.62 to 5.0 lakhs. Such massive expansion on the supply side has resulted in the eradication of leprosy, small pox, guineaworms, and in the near eradication of polio.

However, the country is far from realising the 1978 Alma Ata declaration of 'Health for All by 2000' incorporated as a goal in its National Health Policy, 1983. About 2.2 million children die every year because of malnutrition and inadequate supply of vaccines. Less than 20 per cent of the population utilise public health facilities. Preventable and treatable diseases take a huge toll among the poor. Disparities exist between poor and rich and between rural and urban so far as health care facilities are concerned.

The country is far from reaching the goal of reaching "health for all".

Social Sector

The poor lack access to safe drinking water, decent housing, adequate sanitation, and health care. They depend on public services for their needs. But public spending on the social sector is less than what is spent in other developing countries. This low spending has been further badly affected during the economic reforms period.

Emerging Techniques

The Indian economy has witnessed several technological advancement particularly in the fields of information and communication. New technologies promise great opportunities for Indians. It is estimated that, by 2008, exports by India's information technology (IT) industry will form 35 per cent of the country's total exports and 6 per cent of the total global IT exports. It is also estimated that IT industry will generate 2.2 million additional jobs in India by 2008.

By 2008, India's IT exports account for six per cent of global exports in the IT sector.

New technologies will have 'trickle down effect' on rural India and on disadvantaged sections of society. Information and communication technologies have been used to enhance effectiveness in the delivery of health services in rural and remote locations; in programmes to impart literacy among adults; and as a tool for improving efficiency in agriculture and traditional industries. These technologies have been used in governance to speed up the process of interaction between citizens and administration.

New technologies shall 'trickle down' and reach poor people. But lack of infrastructure may check the trickling down effect.

But there are hurdles which come in the way of technologies reaching out to the people. We lack infrastructure for the spread of digital technologies. Access to phones, computers, and internet is not widespread. Illiteracy and social inequalities also check the spread of technologies to vast majority of people. Investment in physical infrastructure and R&D is the urgent need if benefits of technologies were to spread across the country.

New Agricultural Varieties

A major development that has occurred in India's agricultural sector is the discovery of high yielding varieties. The high yielding varieties have played significant role in the economic development. Poverty ratios are lower in states such as Punjab, Haryana, Andhra Pradesh, and Tamil Nadu that have higher adoption rates of modern varieties of rice. Three related developments have taken place thanks to the new varieties. First, overall food supply has improved while real prices declined. This has improved consumer welfare. Second, more output has been produced with relatively less labour and thus facilitating development of the non-agricultural sector. Third, the surpluses generated because of increased farm production are reinvested in development of the non-agricultural sector and on improved human capital.

Adoption of modern varieties of rice has helped reduce poverty.

Thus, the Indian economy has travelled a long way. It needs to travel further and travel faster, as Box.32.4 shows. The economy has strengths as the description above indicates. It has weaknesses too. There is inequality, poverty and underemployment. Labour laws are regressive. SSI sector is languishing. Infrastructure is inadequate. But these are weaknesses which can be overcome.

Box 32.4 **India Vision 2020**

A report entitled 'India Vision 2020' (Planning Commission, 2004) has recently formulated a set of long-term economic goals for the nation realisable by proper utilisation of untapped potentials. Prepared by a committee of the Planning Commission, the report recognizes the changing environment and the wide range of new possibilities open before the nation-rapid rise in educational levels, technological advancement, cheaper and faster communication, quick availability of information, and access to world market due to globalization. Some salient features of the Indian economy as visualised in the report over the next two decades are:

- India could aspire to attain an average level of living of the current upper middle income countries such as Argentina, Malaysia, and South Africa.
- The nation would be able to produce food needed for the projected population of 1.3 billion and generate some exportable surplus. But this by itself would not ensure eradication of under-nutrition due to lack of purchasing power of the poor.
- A comprehensive national food security strategy must include security of livelihood. Labour force is expected to expand by 45 per cent and generation of about 200 million new jobs over the next 20 years would be a major challenge before the nation.
- A significant departure from earlier government statements is the report's advocacy of access to gainful employment as a constitutional right for the citizens to enable them 'to exercise their economic rights in a market economy.'
- Changing demographic composition would double the number of senior citizens necessitating adoption of special measures for them.
- The report describes the knowledge revolution as an uncommon opportunity and human resource as the most important determinant of future output and employment growth. It recommends school education as 'an essential prerequisite for citizens to adapt and succeed economically.'
- Further growth is likely to concentrate in big cities of one million or more population and urban population is expected to reach 40 per cent of the total. This would put more strain on urban infrastructure development calling for innovative solutions.
- Establishment of links among the major rivers could channel surplus water from flood-prone areas to drought-prone areas and help increase the irrigation potential.
- India has to meet the challenge of global competition and seize upon the global capital flows destinations by providing secure and attractive returns.

(**Source:** *India Development Report*, 2004-05, p.27)

ANALYSIS OF ECONOMIC ENVIRONMENT

As many as 21 chapters (from 12 to 32) have been devoted for a detailed discussion on various components of the economic environment. The huge space devoted is justified for the simple reason that the interface between business and its economic milieu is direct. After all, the firm is but one unit of the economic environment. It should import all its inputs from economic environment and export to it the finished goods. Analysis of economic environment, therefore, assumes special significance.

Scanning

Scanning economic environment is easier than in any of the other segments. A plethora of data on economic activity is readily available. Besides, several government and private organisations are active in scanning economic changes.

Table 32.8 shows sample economic indicators that can be used to scan the economic arena. The indicators listed in Table 32.8 are updated frequently.

Table 32.8 **Key Indicators**

	Absolute Values				*% Change Over Previous Period*			
Items	*2003-04*	*2004-05*	*2005-06*	*2006-07*	*2003-04*	*2004-05*	*2005-06*	*2006-07*
Gross domestic product (at factor cost) (Rs. Thousand crore)								
At current prices	2549.4	2855.9	3250.9Q	3717.5A	12.5	12.0	13.8Q	14.4A
At 1999-2000 prices	2222.6	2389.6	2604.5Q	2844.0A	8.5	7.5P	9.0Q	9.2A
GDP-Agriculture and allied sectors (Rs. Thousand crore) (at 1999-2000 prices)	2765.5	3126.6	3567.2Q	4100.6	12.5	13.1	14.1Q	15.0A
Gross national product (at factor cost) (Rs. Thousand crore)								
At current prices	2531.2	2833.6	3225.9Q	3693.4A	12.6	11.9	13.8Q	14.5A
At 1999-2000 prices	2204.7	2367.7	2580.7Q	2822.1A	8.7	7.4	9.0Q	9.4A
Index of agricultural production (1)	150.4	181	298.6P	–	–	20.3	-1.0P	–
Foodgrains production (mt)	213.2	198.4	208.6	209.2+	22.0	-6.9	5.1P	0.3+
Index of industrial production (2)	189.0	204.8	221.5	239.0^	7.0	8.4	8.2	10.8^
Electricity generated (bn kwh)	558.3	587.4	617.5	493.1^	5.0	5.2	5.1	7.5^
Wholesale price index (3)	180.3	189.5	197.2	209.2#	4.6	5.1	4.1	6.7#
Consumer price index for industrial workers (4)	504	525	551	588$	3.5	4.2	5.0	6.9$
Money supply (M3) (5) (Rs. Thousand crore)	2005.7	2251.4	2729.5	3071.7(6)	16.8	12.3	17.0@@	21.1(5)
Imports at current prices								
(in Rs. Crore)	359108	501065	660409	598287***	20.8	39.5	31.8	40.6^^
(in US $ million)	78150	111518	149166	131212***	27.3	42.7	33.8	36.3^^
Exports at current prices								
(in Rs. Crore)	293367	375340	456418	408394***	15.0	27.9	21.6	406^^
(in US $ million)	63843	83536	103091	89489***	21.1	30.8	23.4	36.3^^
Foreign currency assets (7)								
(in Rs. Crore)	466215	593121	647327	764501*	36.5	27.2	9.1	29.7*
(in US $ million)	107448	135571	145108	173081*	49.5	26.2	7.0	29.4*
Exchange rate (Re/US $) (8)	45.95	44.93	44.27	45.48@	5.3	2.3	1.5	-2.7@

Note: Gross domestic product and Gross national product figures are at factor cost (new series base 1999-2000). P-Provisional Q-Quick estimates; A-Advance estimates; * At the end of January, 2007 ** At the end of December, 2004 *** April-January, 2006-07 #As on February 3,2007 $ As on December, 2006 ^April-December, 2006 + 2nd advance estimates 2006-07

1. Index of agricultural production (of 46 crops, including plantations) with base triennium ending 1981-82=100 (revised) 2. Index of industrial production; (base 1993-94=100) 3. Index (with base 1993-94=100) at the end of fiscal year 4. Index (with base 1982=100) at the end of fiscal year 5. Outstanding at the end of financial year

6. As on January 19, 2007, year-on-year growth (net of conversion of a non-banking entity into

7. Outstanding at the end of financial year.

8. Percent change indicates the rate of appreciatin (+)/depreciation (–) of the Rupee vis-à-vis the US Dollar

(**Source:** *Economic Survey*, 2006-07)

The data for the economic segment are basically quantitative and are available in plenty from secondary sources. Nonetheless, making sense of the data is complicated: the forces driving the trends have to be derived, requiring a qualitative understanding of the shifts in the economy.[2]

Monitoring

Monitoring, like scanning, economic segment is relatively easy as many economic trends and patterns are readily available and tracking them is not difficult. Nevertheless, monitoring needs to be carefully done because many of the trends and patterns can come about quickly.

So much data and so many sources are available (see Table 32.8) that one problem in scanning and monitoring the economic arena is the abundance but not inadequacy of data sources. The analyst is likely to get lost amidst the vast data available. But he or she should track the changes and identify potential indications.

Forecasting

Forecasting gives future orientation to the changes currently happening. Economic forecasting helps identify changes likely to occur in future. Several models are available for forecasting. While it is outside the scope of this book to discuss all the models, suffice it is to state that the analyst needs to select an appropriate technique to foresee the likely changes that might take place in future.

Assessment

The forecasts thus made shall become part of firm's strategies. It may be stated that all strategies are anchored on economic forecasts. Three points deserve consideration in this context. First, economic forces affect different industries in different ways. Second economic factors affect strategy formulation at all levels: corporate, business and functional. Finally, the economic trends and patterns must be updated on a regular basis. All these must find their due places in strategy formulation.[3]

QUESTIONS

1. Bring out the various economic reforms. Why were these reforms necessary?
2. How far has the new economic policy succeeded? Failed? Discuss.
3. What are second generation reforms?
4. Describe how economic environment might be analysed.

ASSIGNMENT

Take Table 32.8 as the base. Which other data can you thinkof for using in analysing the economic environment. Collect those data.

REFERENCE

1. This section is based on *India Development Report, 2004-05.* (ed) by Kirit S. Parikh and R. Radhakrishna.
2. Liam Fahey and V.K.Narayanan, *Macroenvironmental Analysis For Strategic Management*, West Pub.Co., 1986, p.108.
3. *Ibid*, p.117.

CHAPTER OUTLINE

Nature of Culture
Impact of Culture on Business
- Culture Creates People
- Culture and Globalisation
- Culture Determines Goods and Services
- People's Attitude to Business
- Attitude to work
- Collectivism and Individualism
- Ambitious or Complacent
- Education
- Family
- Authority
- View of Scientific Method
- Ethics in Business
- Religion
- Marriage
- Time Dimension
- Cultural Resources

Business Participation in Cultural Affairs

LEARNING OBJECTIVES

After reading this Chapter, you should be able to:

1. Understand the nature of culture
2. Describe the interface between culture and business
3. Explain why business takes active part in culture

33 Cultural Environment

Cultural environment refers to the influence exercised by certain social factors which are '*beyond the company's gate*.' Such factors include, among others, attitude of people to work, attitude to wealth, family, marriage, religion, education and ethics. This and next five chapters deal with culture and related topics.

NATURE OF CULTURE

In its narrow sense, culture is understood to refer to such activities as dance, drama, music and festivals. In its true sense, culture is understood as that complex whole which includes knowledge, belief, art, morals, law, customs and other capabilities and habits acquired by an individual as a member of a society. "Culture consists of", writes Elbert W.Steward and James A.Glynn,

Culture include several behavioural influencing factors shared by members of a society and passed through generations.

> "The thought and behavioural patterns that members of a society learn through language and other forms of symbolic interaction-their customs, habits, beliefs, and values, the common viewpoints which bind them together as a social entity. Cultures change gradually, picking up new ideas and dropping old ones, but many of the cultures of the past have been so persistent and self-contained that the impact of any sudden change tears them apart, uprooting their people psychologically."[1]

The following characteristics of culture are worth knowing:

1. *Learned* - Culture is not inherited or biologically based, it is acquired by learning and experience.
2. *Shared* - People as members of a group, organisation, or society share culture; it is not specific individuals.

3. *Transgenerational* - Culture is passed on from one generation to the next.
4. *Symbolic* - Culture is based on the human capacity to symbolise or use one thing to represent another.
5. *Adaptive* - Culture is based on the human capacity to change or adapt, as opposed to the more genetically driven adaptive process of animals.

LEVELS OF CULTURE

There are three levels of culture, viz., national culture, business culture and the occupational and organisational cultures (See Fig.33.1).

Figure 33.1 **Levels of Culture**

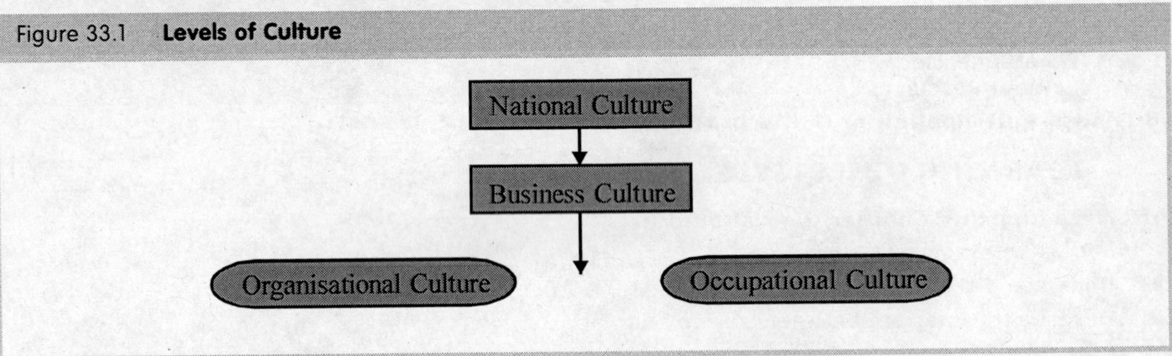

National Culture National culture is the dominant culture within the political boundaries of a country. Formal education is usually taught and business is generally conducted in the language of the dominant culture.

Business Culture Business culture guides everyday business transaction. What to wear to a meeting, when and how to use business cards, whether to shake hands or embrace - all are examples of business etiquette taught by business culture. It needs no mention that business culture is a part of the total national culture. In any society, business closely interweaves with the broader cultural values, norms and beliefs. Examples include the priorities given to age and seniority, the role expectations of women, and expectations concerning treatment of subordinates by bosses.

Organisational Culture

> Organisational culture is shared by members of an organization and are tied together by it.

Within national and business cultures, there develop organisation-specific and occupation-specific cultures. Organisational culture (or its sister-term corporate culture) refers to the philosophies, ideologies, values, assumptions, beliefs, expectations, attitudes, and norms that knit an organisation together and are shared by its employees.

Organisational members tend to internalise cultural nuances and like to internalise newcomers into such mores. Some of the practices are so thoroughly internalised that no one questions them-they are taken for granted, that is, they get institutionalised.

> Several joint ventures were wound up because of the clannish culture of Indian companies.

Besides institutionalization, deification or glorification tends to occur in organisational cultures. Heroes emerge, especially among the founding fathers of the firm, whose sacrifices, valorous deeds and ingenuity in the difficult initial years of the organisation or during later crises periods are embellished into stories and sagas. The firm itself may come to be regarded as a source of pride, and in some sense unique. Employees begin to feel a strong bond with it that transcends material returns given by the company, and they begin to identify with it. The organisation turns into a sort of clan and the organisational members become ethnocentric. Clannish organisations often pose problems to managers. Most Indian companies had developed the clan culture. The clan culture led to the collapse of several joint ventures between Indian companies and overseas firms. Mention may be made of the breaking up the marriage between Tatas and IBM and Daimler Benz, of Godrej with P&G and GE, of DCM with Toyota, of LML-Piaggio and of Mahindra with Ford.

Occupational Culture

Different occupational groups such as physicians, professors, lawyers, accountants, and crafts people have distinct cultures-called occupational cultures. Occupational cultures are the norms, beliefs, and expected ways of behaving of people in the same occupational groups, regardless of which organisations they work for.

IMPACT OF CULTURE ON BUSINESS

The interface between business and culture is brought out in the following paragraphs (also see Fig 33.2).

1. Culture Creates People

The concept of culture is of great significance to business because it is the culture which generally determines the ethos of the people. It trains people along particular lines, tending to put a personality stamp upon them. Thus, we have Indians, Japanese, Americans, Germans, Britisha and so on. It is not that all people are alike in a particular culture. There are sub-cultures within a culture. People have their own idiosyncrasies and are a blend of heredity, cultural experience, sub-cultural experience, family experience, and unique personal experience.[2]

When people with different cultural backgrounds promote, own and manage organisations, organisations themselves tend to acquire distinct cultures. Thus, the culture of the Tata group of companies is different from that of the enterprises owned by the Birlas.

Organisational culture has functional and dysfunctional consequences. Culture performs at least four functions. *First*, culture creates distinctions between one organisation and another. *Secondly*, it conveys a sense of identity for orgnisational members. *Thirdly*, it facilitates the generation of committment to something nobler than one's own self interest. *Finally*, it enhances the social system stability. Culture is the social glue that helps hold the organisation together by providing appropriate standards for the behaviour of organisational members.

Organisational culture has positives as well as negatives.

Culture becomes a liabiltiy where the shared values are not in agreement with those that will further organisation's effectiveness. This is most likely to happen where organisation's environment is dynamic. When the environment is changing fast, the organisation's entrenched culture may no longer be appropriate. So consistency of behaviour is an asset to an organisation when it faces a stable environment. It may, however, burden the organisation and make it difficult to respond to changes in the environment. This has what precisely happened to ITI. In the pre-economic reforms decades, the telephone company had stable environment. It had developed its own identity as a monopolist in

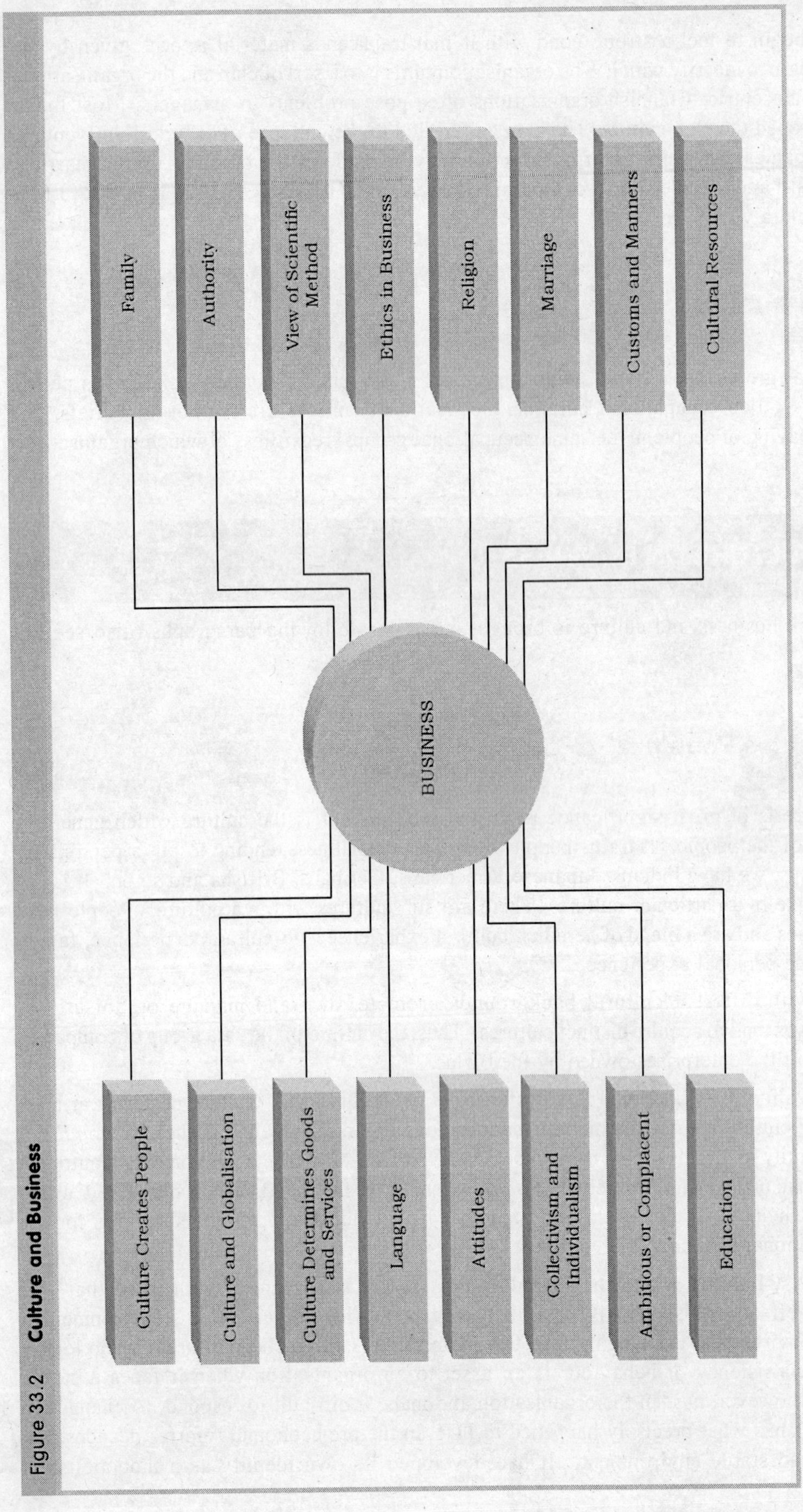

Figure 33.2 **Culture and Business**

telephones and thrived well sticking to old and outdated technology. In the changed environment of today, neither its culture, nor its old technology could save the ailing ITI.

2. Culture and Globalisation

As business units go international, the need for understanding and appreciating cultural differences across various countries is essential. Work motivation, profit motivation, business goals, negotiating styles, attitudes towards the development of business relationships, gift-giving customs, greetings, significance of body gestures, meaning of colours and numbers, and the like vary from country to country. Table 33.1 brings out a summary of how major management concepts are perceived by the Japanese and Americans.

Table 33.1 **Major Concepts in the Comparative Analysis of US and Japanese Management**

Management Concepts	*How Perceived in the United States*	*How Perceived in Japan*
Company	Team in sport	Family in village
Business goal	To win	To survive
Employees	Players in a team	Children in a family
Human relations	Functional	Emotional
Competition	Cut-throat	Cooperation or sin
Profit motivation	By all means	Means to an end
Sense of identification	Job pride	Group prestige
Work motivation	Individual income	Group atmosphere
Production	Productivity	Training and diligence
Personnel	Efficiency	Maintenance
Promotion	According to abilities	Length of service
Pay	Service and results	Award for patience and sacrifice

(**Source**: Adapted from M.Murayana, "A Comparative Analysis of U.S. and Japanese Management Systems", in Sang M.Lee and Gary Schwendiman(eds.) *Management by Japanese System*, p.237).

Table 33.2 reveals contrasting cultural factors between India and Japan.

When people from different cultures converge in a workplace, management will be required to manage *diversity*. Workforce diversity has important implications for management practice. Managers will be required to shift their philosophy from treating everyone alike to recognising differences and responding to those differences in ways that will ensure employee retention and greater productivity while, at the same time, not discriminating. Diversity, if positively managed, can increase creativity and innovation in organisations as well as improve decision making by providing different perspectives on problems. Where not managed properly, diversity is likely to result in increased turnover, reduced communication and heightened inter-personal conflict.

When people from different cultures converge in a workplace, the problem of managing diversity comes in.

If diversity is managed well, consequences will be high employee turnover, conflict and reduced communication.

Any move from one country to another will create a certain amount of confusion, disorientation and emotional upheaval. This is called *culture shock*. An executive transferred from India to Germany, for example, would require lot of adjustment to make. Language differs,

Table 33.2 **Contrasting Social and Cultural Factors-India vs Japan**

Social/Cultural Factors	*Japan*	*India*
Principles of government/ administration	Emphasis on government by the virtuous and abrogation of coercion, mutual trust between employer and employee and acceptance of basic goodness of human nature. Results in minimum control from above, high level of delegation, highly motivated workforce	Prevalence of impersonal bureaucratic social relations, mistrust of fellow beings based on the assumption of human nature as evil. Results in highly centralised administration, overemphasis of hierarchial status in decision-making, bureaucratic delays, low levels of delegation, dissatisfied workforce, and accentuation of apathy in individuals and groups
Attitude towards work and goals	Highly result-oriented and directed towards perfection and growth through dedicated effort	General and deep-seated apathy, dissociation of work from its results based on the belief that the results are pre-ordained. Tasks are performed without any interest, dedication or pride
Discipline and order	Highly disciplined, respect for superiors and respect for authority	Lack of discipline at all levels, basic mistrust of authority, poor superior-subordinate relationships
Group harmony	Very high based on informal affiliative pattern of behaviour	Assumption of inequality of human beings, nagging suspicion of fellow beings and highly self-centered behaviour resulting in a lack of cooperation and teamwork
Emphasis on education	Very high	Generally indifferent and highly ambivalent

(**Source**: *Vikalpa*, Oct.-Dec.1991, IIMA)

climate varies, food habits are different and the socialisation pattern will be totally new. Culture shock will be severe when the new environment is totally different from the old one. Organisations, particularly MNCs, must be prepared to cope with the culture shock.

3. Culture Determines Goods and Services

Culture broadly determines the type of goods and services a business should produce. The type of food people eat, the clothes they wear, the beverages they drink and the building materials they use to construct dwelling houses vary from culture to culture and from time to time within the same culture. Business should realise these cultural differences and bring out products accordingly.

The fact that culture determines the types of goods and services is not as important as its varied manifestations. Culture expresses itself through people's views of themselves, others, organisations, society, nature and cosmos (See Box 33.1 for varied expressions of culture).

Box 33.1 **Cultural Manifestations**

People's Views of Themselves: People vary in the relative emphasis they place on self-gratification versus serving others. The move towards self-gratification was especially strong during the 1960s and 1970s. Pleasure seekers sought fun, change and escape. Others sought self-realisation and joined therapeutic or religious groups. The marketing implications of a 'me society' were many. People bought products, brands and services as a means of self-expression. They bought 'dream cars' and 'dream vacations.' They spent more time in health activities (jogging, tennis), no introspection, and no arts and crafts. The leisure industry (camping, boating, arts and crafts, sports) benefited from the growing number of self-gratifiers.

People's Views of Others: Some observers have pointed to counter movement from a 'me society' to a 'we society.' They think that more people want serious and long-lasting relations with others. Some recent advertising features people in groups sharing things with others. A Doyle Dane Bernbacb survey showed a widespread concern among adults about social isolation and a strong desire for human contact. This portends a bright future for 'social support' products and services that promote direct relations between human beings, such as health clubs, vacations, and games. It also suggests a growing market for 'social surrogates', things that allow people who are alone to feel that they are not, such as television, home video games and computers.

People's Views of Organisations: People vary in their attitudes towards corporations, government agencies, trade unions, and other organisations. Most people are willing to work for these organisations, although they may be critical of particular ones. There appears to be decline in organisational loyalty. People are giving a little less to these organisations and trusting them less. The work ethic is eroding. Many see work not as a source of satisfaction but as a necessary pursuit to earn the means to enjoy their non-working hours.

Several marketing implications follow from this outlook. Companies need to find new ways to win consumer confidence. They need to review their advertising communications to make sure their messages are honest. They need to review their various activities to make sure they are being 'good corporate citizens.' More companies are turning to social audits and to public relations to improve their image with their publics.

People's Views of Society: People vary in their attitudes towards their society, from those who defend it (preservers) to those who run it (makers), those who take what they can from it (takers) to those who want to change it (changers), those who are looking for some thing deeper (seekers) those who want to leave it (escapers). Often peoples' consumption patterns will reflect their social attitude. Makers are high achievers, who eat, dress, and live well, while changers live more frugally by driving smaller cars, wearing simpler clothes, and so on. Escapers and seekers are a major market for movies, music, surfing, and camping.

People's Views of Nature: People vary in their attitude towards the natural world. Some feel subjugated by it, others feel harmony with it, and still others seek mastery over it. A long-term trend has been people's growing mastery over nature through technology and the attendant belief that nature is bountiful. More recently, however, people have awakened to nature's fragility and finite supplies. People recognise that nature can be spoiled and destroyed by human activities.

People's love of nature is leading to more camping, hiking, boating, and fishing. Business has responded with hiking boots, tent equipment and other gear for nature enthusiasts. Tour operators are packaging more tours to wilderness areas. Food producers have found growing markets for 'natural' products, such as natural cereals, natural ice cream and health foods. Marketing communications are using more scenic backgrounds in advertising their products.

People's Views of the Universe: People vary in their beliefs about the origin of the universe and their place in it. Most Americans are monotheistic, although their religious conviction and practices have been of waning through the years. Church attendance has fallen steadily, with the exception of certain evangelical movements that have not been lost but have been redirected into an interest in Eastern religions, mysticism, the occult and the human-potential movement.

As people lose their religious orientation, they seek more of the 'good life' here on earth. Self-fulfilment and immediate gratification are the emerging cultural values. At the same time, every trend seems to breed a counterforce. From time to time, a 'futurist' will announce a new list of trends that warrant attention.

4. Language and Culture

Language is the foundation of any culture. It is an abstract system of word meanings and symbols for all aspects of culture. Language includes speech, written characters, numerals, symbols, and gestures of non-verbal communication.

The interrelationship between language and culture is very strong and often the farmer determines the latter. Words provide the concepts for understanding the world. All languages (there are approximately three thousand of them) have limited sets of words. These restricted word sets in turn constrain the ability of the users to understand or conceptualise the world. Since language structures the way we think about what we see and behave, it determine cultural patterns.

The interface between languages and culture is strong. There are three thousand languages across the world.

The above hypothesis that language determines cultural patterns is not acceptable to several experts. Many social scientists argue that language does not determine human thought and behaviour patterns. For example, humans possess the physical ability to make millions of colour distinctions, yet languages differ in the number of colours that are recognised. The English language distinguishes between yellow and orange, but some other languages do not.[3] The word **punya** is popular in Indian languages but there is no equivalent of that in the English language.

There is no perfect equivalent in English for the word Punya.

Obviously, it is not that languages determine culture. It is the culture that comes first and requires the development of certain concepts and thus certain words. Notwithstanding the arguments, there is close interrelationship between language and culture.

High- and Low- Context Languages

The world's languages can be classified, based on whether the message conveyed is explicit or implicit, into two groups. Languages in which people state things directly and explicitly are called **low context**. The words provide the meaning. There is no need to interpret the situation to understand the import of the words. Languages in which people state things indirectly and implicitly are called **high context**. In the high context language, communications have multiple meanings that can be interpreted only by reading the situation in which they occur. So important are the ideas of high and low context that many people refer to the whole culture as being high or low context.

Language can be either low context or high context. Low context language is direct but high context language carries multiple meanings with it.

Most northern European languages, including German, English, and the Scandinavian languages, are low context. People use explicit words to communicate direct meaning. In contrast, Asian and Arabic languages are high context. In Asian languages, often what is left unsaid is just as important as what is said. Silent periods and the use of incomplete sentences require a person to interpret what the communicator does not say by reading the situation. Arabic introduces interpretation into the language with an opposite tack. Extensive imprecise verbal and nonverbal communication produces an interaction where reading the situation is essential for comprehending.

European languages are low context type. Asian languages are high context type.

Among all languages, Chinese is widely used across the globle (See Table 33.3). But in corporate world, it is English which is widely used. Naturally, countries go out of the way to promote teaching and learning of english among their citizens. Infact, one of the competitive strengths of India is the capabilities of her citizens to talk in English.

A clear understanding and effective use of language is essential for the success of any business particularly global business. It helps determine success in the following ways:

- It provides a clearer understanding of a given situation. Having the ability to communicate in the host language enables an international manager to conduct business directly with his/her hosts without the need for an interpreter. There is no need for a third person to explain the situation or what is being discussed. Thus, the manager is able to size up the situation instantly and act accordingly. This obviously saves time and adds spontaneity to social intercourse.
- Language establishes one of the most effective and flattering bridges to local people. To speak the host's language means having direct access to hosts who are more willing and delighted to communicate openly in their own language. In many instances, this is how friendships develop and prosper, as in most cultures speaking the host's language is one of the most flattering ways to pay compliments to the host culture and those who belong to it.
- Even the most competent interpreter could have difficulty conveying hidden, implied meanings of words and nuances, phrases, or slang. Speaking directly with the host in his/her language gives the speaker a feel for the emotions and significance with which the host communicates.
- Language properly and effectively learned and practised, provides one of the most practical means of understanding another culture. When learning a foreign language, one is not just acquiring a means of communication but also developing a deeper understanding and appreciation of the host's history, politics, social life, and other cultural aspects.
- Learning a language, understanding all the nuances and cliches, and enjoying ways of socializing with a host are some of the most practical and rewarding experiences for an international manager. It builds confidence and earns the respect and admiration of local people. In short, they help make a manager more effective.

Language plays an important role in making business a success by
(i) providing a clear understanding of the situation,
(ii) establishing a flattering bridge, and
(iii) making it easy to understand any culture.

Table 33.3 **Language Distribution of the World**

Rank	*Language*	*Primary country*	*[Population]*
1	Chinese, Mandarin	China	885,000,000
2	Spanish	Spain	332,000,000
3	English	United Kingdom	322,000,000
4	Bengali	Bangladesh	189,000,000
5	Hindi	India	182,000,000
6	Portuguese	Portugal	170,000,000
7	Russian	Russia	170,000,000
8	Japanese	Japan	125,000,000
9	German	Germany	98,000,000
10	Chinese, Wu	China	77,175,000
11	Javanese	Indonesia, Java, Bali	75,500,800
12	Korean	South Korea	75,000,000
13	French	France	72,000,000
14	Vietnamese	Vietnam	67,662,000
15	Telugu	India	66,350,000
16	Chinese, Yue	China	66,000,000
17	Marathi	India	64,783,000
18	Tamil	India	63,075,000
19	Turkish	Turkey	59,000,000
20	Urdu	Pakistan	58,000,000

(**Source:** Adapted from Barbara F.Games(ed)(1996) *Ethnologue Languages of the World*, 13th Edition)

5. Attitudes

Attitude are positive or negative evaluations that determine one's behaviour.

Attitudes are positive or negative evaluations, feelings and tendencies which make an individual behave in a particular way towards people or objects. Attitudes include many things including opinion about individual freedom, democracy, truth and honesty, role of sexes, justice, love, marriage, and sex. Of particular interest to us in this context are one's attitude towards work, attitude towards business, and attitude towards time and the future.[4]

Attitude **towards work** is important as it has significant impact on motivation, morale, job satisfaction, productivity and other aspects of human resource management. Positive attitude towards one's work, also called **work ethic**, makes a worker a more productive and a more satisfied employee. Compensation and reward system are critical elements in determining work attitudes. A business firm needs to devise a system of compensation and reward that would help promote work ethic.

Japanese worker is supposed to have a strong work ethic. On the other hand, Indian ethos such as detachment from work, **nirvana**, and renunciation are said to be inconsistent with the positive work attitudes of workers. This observation is not true, for, it is only in India that an average worker takes work as worship. For him or her work is everything. No worker touches his or her tools, wheel, mouse or button in the morning without closing his or her eyes for a few seconds, worshiping the almighty expressing gratitude for having bestowed his blessing in the form of work. The Indian worker has earned appreciation from everywhere for his or her sincerity, hard work, loyalty and honesty.

The culture of the land determines its people's **attitude towards business**. Business systems are a product of beliefs, mores, and customs of the society in which they exist. Infact, their very existence depends upon social philosophies which conduct and support various kinds of business functions. Business people must have some basic set of philosophies to guide their actions. Beliefs and value systems concerning what is right and what is wrong are basic to all business activities and serve as a justification for doing or not doing something in a particular value system by which actions of business persons and other groups are judged.

Culture determines people's attitude towards business.

In capitalist systems an individual perceives business basically as profit-seeking organisation producing goods and services in response to market demand. In Islamic social systems, business is an all-important institution based on personal relationship, trust and respect. Business firms are viewed not just providers of goods and services but as partners in progress and prosperity. Attitudes towards profit-making and business in general are an important part of the decision of an MNC to expand into a particular country.

French culture is known for its emphasis on elegance, elitism, and concern for form. Not only does this get reflected in its 1200 museums, its 5000 variety of wine (which are classified, like the French society, into from superior to ordinary table wine), more than 50,000 drama performance per year, but also in the fact that France has always been the capital of fashion industry.

French culture lays emphasis on elegance, eliticism and form. But Mexican culture is death oriented.

On the other hand, Mexican culture is known for its "pro-death" values: Mexicans celebrate The Day of the Deads, have folk art forms which feature skeletons, have museums of Mummies, adorn the graves as a work of art, and even have a popular magazine called La Calavera (meaning The Skeleton)!! Not surprisingly, life insurance industry is not a flourishing business in Mexico. In mid 90s, less than 20% of employed population had life insurance cover, and the insurance premium formed just about 1.5% of the GDP (as compared to 5.5% in Brazil, and close to 9% in US).

People's attitudes **towards time** depend on culture. Most western and capitalist societies believe that time is money. To waste time is to waste money. For most westerns punctuality is a must. Being late for a meeting or appointment is not only considered rude but also offensive. Every business activity is timed in terms of hours, minutes, days, months, and years. Long-term strategic plans are prepared to ensure targets are met in time. Time seems to control every aspect of human endeavour. Pay and productivity are measured in terms of the time it takes to complete a given task. But in some other societies time is viewed as something not to be taken seriously. Punctuality is observed rarely.

Another dimension of time is the people's perception of future. In some societies, the prevailing belief is that people can influence and even control the future. Educational systems offer a variety of training and self development courses to help individuals develop strong internal locus of control — the ability to carve out one's own future. In Islamic societies and in India the belief is that future is pre-ordained and no one can alter it. This attitude often manifests itself in an almost total absence of forward business planning, with each day taken as it comes. What is not finished today can be continued tomorrow.[5]

6. Collectivism and Individualism

The spirit of collectivism and individualism is related to such personnel aspects as employee morale, multiplicity of trade unions and inter and intra-union rivalries. It is said that our culture, unlike Christianity, stresses individual salvation and negation of the world. Behind a small charity or a good deed, it is pointed out, there is the motive of self, rather than society's welfare. This is the main reason for the low morale of our workers, multiple unions and the rivalries among them.

The feeling of collectivism or individualism has its influence on employee morale, multiplicity of unions and inter-union rivalry.

Contrary to popular belief, our culture did advocate collectivism and general welfare. As a proof of collectivism, we are told about guilds which played a major role in the economy of ancient India. "This was the guild (*Sreni*)", wrote A.L.Basham, 'a form of industrial and mercantile organisation which played a big part in the economy of ancient India as it did in that of most other ancient or medieval civilizations. There are faint and uncertain references to some sort of guild organisations even in vedic literature, and by the time of the composition of Buddhist scriptures, guilds certainly existed in every important Indian town, and embraced almost all trades and industries-we even read of a guild of thieves.'

"The guild united both the craftsmen's cooperatives and the individual workman of a given trade into a single corporate body. It fixed rules of work and wages and standards and prices for the commodities in which members dealt, and its regulations had the force of law and were upheld by the king and government. Over its own members, the guild had judicial rights, which were recognised by the state. A guild court could, like a caste council, expel a refractory member, a penalty which would virtually preclude him from practising his ancestral trade and reduce him to beggary. We read in Buddhist literature of guild courts settling quarrels between members and their wives, and the rules of Buddhist order lay down that a married woman may not be ordained a nun without the consent of her husband and his guild. Thus, the guild had the power not only over the economic, but also over the social life of its members. It acted as a guardian of their widows and orphans, and as their insurance against sickness. Its powers and functions in this respect were very similar to those of the caste councils in more recent times, and though some authorities would disagree with us, we cannot but conclude that the guilds played an important part in the evolution of trade castes."[6]

Primary importance of community welfare is stressed even by Manu. Charity and philanthropy have a high moral value in our tradition.

Collectivism is the hallmark of our society. Whether it is celebrating a marriage, a social function, inauguration of a business unit or installing a CNC machine in a factory, we believe in people and crowds. We have factories (particularly in Public Sector) which have thousands of employees and we have trade unions whose membership runs into lakhs.

7. Ambitious or Complacent

Culture makes a person to become ambitious or complacent.

An individual's ambition to grow or remain complacent depends on his cultural ethos. An ambitious individual is highly motivated, is wealth acquisitive, has a strong urge to excel, is prepared to change organisations and even take risks. Economy becomes vibrant if a large proportion of the population comprises ambitious people.

Majority of our people are known to be complacent. An average citizen will be happy to get into a government job (lower the order, the better) as it assures safety of tenure and demands no initiative, no skills and no hard work. He is not prepared to join the private sector as the job here demands hard work and high productivity. Complacency of citizens is attributed to be one of the reasons for the backwardness of our economy.

Contrary to popular belief, our society has been known for its ambition, particularly in wealth acquisition. Ours is probably the only society in the world where wealth is worshipped in the form of Goddess *Lakshmi* unlike in the West where wealth is merely respected.

Looking at the past, in most Indian literature, the world is viewed from the angle of well-to-do. Poverty, it is more than once said, is a living death; to serve another for one's keep is a dog's life, and not worthy of an Aryan. From the time of the RigVeda, which contains many prayers for riches, worldly wealth was looked as morally desirable for the ordinary man, and indeed essential to lead a full and civilized life. The ascetic who voluntarily abandoned his wealth performed an act of renunciation which entitled him to the utmost respect, though by such renunciation, he assured himself of spiritual advancement, as well as the way to salvation (*Moksha*). The fourth and ultimate aim of existence, the ascetic's life, was not that of an ordinary man, and the theoretical classification of the four stages* of life gave ample scope in the second stage to the householder, who was indeed encouraged to build up the family fortunes, and to spend part of them at least on the pleasures of the senses. Thus, the ideals of ancient India, while not perhaps the same as those of the West, by no means excluded money-making. India had not only a class of luxury-loving and pleasure-seeking dilettante but also one of wealth-seeking merchants and prosperous craftsmen, who, if less respected than the Brahmins and warriors, had an honourable place in society.[7]

8. Education

The close interface of business and higher education is a new development. Centuries ago, each had a somewhat hands-off attitude towards the other. A relatively small section of the intellectual elite maintained their seclusion in university halls, educating a few selected students to become intellectual and social leaders of their nation. Education was not for the masses who laboured in factories, fields and stores. University education had little interest in business and businessmen had little interest in education. Each lived in a different world. Many educators showed an *elitist* disdain for businessmen who were perceived as less nobly motivated than educators. Most businessmen admitted that the disdain was mutual since men in the ivory tower had little that was practical to offer to business.

> The inter-face between business and education, though a recent phenomenon, but is a significant one.

The separation of business from education gradually waned as higher education expanded in accordance with the democratic ideals of equal opportunity, but the real breakthrough came with the rapid trend towards a knowledge-oriented society.[8]

> For a long time there was a stand-off between business and higher education. Now they have become closer.

Industrial societies of today are knowledge-oriented and educated, and education is considered as one of the social overheads that has been accorded due priority among the developmental activities. But there are variations. A society without too many constraints on social mobility may accord prestige to the teaching profession and a large part of the national income will be spent on educational equipment than in a society which is more rigidly stratified. Educational institutions are sometimes resented in countries where children are regarded as a source of income. Other countries, by no means always the same ones, will be opposed to welfare support for adults.[9]

In our traditional society, education was a preserve of the Brahmins and it was unfortunate that people of other castes were denied the facility. The economic environment of the day also supported the prevailing system. Our economy was primitive, and occupations were based on heredity. No education was needed for a cobbler to stitch footwear, for a barber to shave, for an agriculturist to till land or for a goldsmith to make a piece of gold ornaments. All these and other crafts were passed down from one generation to the other.

Things changed over the passage of time. Economy gradually shed its primitiveness and almost turned into an industrialised one, demanding technical education at all levels and of all castes. Educational institutions sprang up in all corners of the country and it is estimated that we have more number of primary schools than the USSR and USA put together. Vast sums have been spent on education in successive plans.

---

* The four stages are: (1) Brahmacharya-student life, (2) Grihstha-married and householder, (3) Vanaprastha-hermit in a forest, and (4) Sanyasin-old man and a homeless wanderer with all earthly ties broken.

Education has considerable business implications. Economic progress of a country depends on the education of its citizens. This being a broad statement, specific economic implications are as follows:

Impact of education on business is basically three-fold: attract high wage industries, market potential is enhanced, type and quality of advertising and packaging.

1. Countries rich in educational facilities vastly attract high wage industries. By investing in education, a country can attract (nay, create) the kind of high-wage industries that are often called "brain power" industries.

2. The market potential of a country depends on education. Educationally advanced countries such as England, France and Germany are more likely to be markets for computers and high-tech equipment than are less educated countries such as Poland, the Czech Republic, and Romania. It is also likely that MNCs doing business in these countries will find it easier to hire and train local managers in Western Europe than in Eastern Europe.

3. The level of literacy and educational attainment determines the nature of advertising, packaging, quality of marketing research, and distribution system.

9. Family

Basic to all types of social organisations is the family, the institution which concerns itself with love, sexual relationship, marriage, reproduction, socialisation of the child and the various levels of status and roles involved in kinship organisation. Little wonder that the family is referred to as a remarkable institution.

Family is a remarkable institution vested with several significant contributions.

The family is recognised as the institution responsible for procreation and child-rearing. In civilised societies, especially, the process of child socialisation has come to have tremendous significance. Gone are the days when the children should be seen but not heard; on the contrary, the importance of childhood and the effects of home life on personality and character formation have been widely recognised. Infact, as the basic primary group, the family probably has more to do with the child's ultimate behavioural pattern than does any other single environment factor, and it is on this assumption, that a loose home life is so often associated with delinquency.

The family, through the husband-wife relationship, is also a recognised institution for the fulfilment of sexual needs. The sex urge is a powerful one and most societies have set-up rather elaborate safeguards to ensure that sexuality is kept within bounds. In a very real sense, the family is answer to man's sex problems.

The family is also one of the chief agencies of social life. This was not always so, and in some societies, it is not the case today. In different cultures, for example, men and women have tended to socialise in same sex-groupings. Yet over the years, wherever women have been accorded a relatively equal status, the husband-wife relationship has taken on an added meaning in terms of companionship, shared activities, satisfaction of emotional needs and other manifestations of primary group association.

The family is important for a variety of other reasons, such as those relating to protection, inheritance, property rights, morality, care of the sick and the aged, and the transmission of cultural values.[10]

Such is the role of the family in societies. Family ties have been very strong in our culture. The joint family, also called the extended family system, peculiar to our society, has flourished for centuries. A joint family is understood as a group of people who generally live under one roof, who eat food cooked at one hearth, who hold property in common and who participate in important family events, are related to each other and stand together in crisis.[11]

Like the European and Semitic family, the joint family was patriarchal and patrilinear. The father was the head of the house and the administrator of joint property and except in Kerala, the headship descended in the male line of hierarchy.

The joint family had its plus points. In times of distress, a man could rely on his sapindas, and the never-do-well cousin or the indolent good-for-nothing uncle, live in a corner of the family home in comparative comfort while adding little or nothing to the family fortunes.[12]

Secondly, in the joint family, affection as well as dependence is diffused among so many relatives that the loss of even an important member, such as a parent, is less critical than in the nuclear family system, which is so small that every member plays a decisive role. In reality, the joint family is a revolving system which provides a full complement of young and adult people at all times to carry out its various functions.[13]

Joint family had several benefits to offer but sadly it is waning.

Thirdly, safety and security needs of man, the second-level needs as per Maslow's need stage of hierarchy, are met through the joint family system. *Finally*, and the crucial point is the role of the joint family in entrepreneurial development. There are some who believe that the individual is constrained and held back by the group. On the other hand, there is some evidence that, atleast in the initial stages, the joint family may be a useful institution in capital accumulation. Birlas, for instance, manage what is virtually a joint family business, but the brothers and the sons and the nephews live separately and the companies they control are also separate entities. The Mafatlals in Mumbai live in the same building but the brothers have now separated and the companies have been parcelled out among the brothers.[14]

The joint family system had its blemishes. There was strain in the relationship among family members; life was not peaceful; women generally were forced to bear a larger share of family strains and as Basham put it, "*The deep sense of solidarity led, as might be expected, to nepotism and various other abuses, and today the joint family system is beginning to weigh heavily on the younger generations...*"[15]

The extended family system is almost on the wane, thanks to the spread of education, technological development, unmanageable size of families, the Mitakshara school of law which permits division of property even while the *paterfamilias* is alive and India's fight for Independence shook the older customary patterns of behaviour.

We do come across the existence of joint families here and there. One such instance is a family of 217 strong, living at Shimoga in Karnataka (Box 33.2 gives more details).

Nuclear families have now become common in our society replacing the traditional extended family system. Women now enjoy equal status with men and most of them supplement family income by their own earnings. People have money and are prepared to spend on children's education, household appliances and on vacations. Children have become spenders instead of earners-a position they held in joint families. With big families being broken up, family businesses are slowly turning into limited companies. All these developments are significant to business.

Joint families are now being replaced by nuclear families.

10. Authority

The exercise of authority varies according to the management styles, but different styles are likely to be present in different cultures. One research relevant to this has produced a measure of the cultural differences-the power distance measure. This is defined, '*as a measure of inter-personal power of influence*', between a boss and a subordinate, as perceived by the least powerful of the two, while the distance is seen as the extent to which either participant can influence the behaviour of the other. It is suggested that the distance is to a considerable extent determined by their national culture. The evidence

Different management styles prevail in different cultures

Box 33.2 **Strengthening Family Ties**

It is heartening to note that a family in Shimoga has been zealously trying to maintain its links, as a result of which it now is 217-strong. Financial and other constraints might have forced a division in the family, but all those coming under the family umbrella make it a point to meet or get together at least once a year only to strengthen family ties, deriving the pleasure and warmth of living in a joint family at least on that one day.

The descendants of three brothers, the late Davangere Halappa, Davangere Manjappa and Davangere Hanumanthappa, spread now over five generations, meet once a year, preferably in the first week of April or the last week of June depending on the convenience of the majority of the members and make it an exclusively family affair.

As the date and the venue for the family get-together are fixed three months in advance, various committees are formed for its preparations. It is not an easy job to arrange to feed 217 people. It is like organising a conference, says Mr.D.M.Ranganath.

The day invariably starts with a religious programme, a homam or yagna which is then followed by lunch. Quizzes and games are arranged in such a manner that all the members, regardless of age, participate in them. There is also an entertainment session. Besides, a separate game is devised for the newly-weds.

However, the most interesting part of the cultural programme is a competition in which prizes are given to those who can give the correct names, age and relationship of all the family members-the idea behind this contest being that everyone in the family is known to the others. It is interesting to note that no one in the family has yet won the first prize in this contest.

The atmosphere is joyous. A suggestion was made last time that a separate session be held for gossip and chatter.

Mrs.Seethamma, 80-year-old widow of Davangere Manjappa, is the sole survivor of the first generation. She is the oldest member of the family.

The yearly family meet, which was held for the third time in succession in May last year, was the fulfillment of a suggestion by Mr.N.Krishnappa. He addressed the family members on one such occasion, and highlighted the efficacy of the Hindu Joint Family system.

The three brothers, Halappa, Manjappa and Hanumanthappa, hailing from a well-known business family in Davangere, migrated to Shimoga some four generations ago. Though the brothers are no more, their children, grandchildren and great grandchildren spread over four generations have been making their presence felt in various activities in Shimoga. There is hardly any field where the family has not made its impact.

The family's contribution to politics in particular is noteworthy. Four members of the family were jailed for their active participation in the freedom struggle. Only one of them claimed a freedom-fighter's pension.

The family had lived in their ancestral house in Gandhi Bazaar till it was burnt down. The damaged house was rebuilt but the family did not stay there and shifted to another house. The total strength of the family was 70 in 1957 when it branched out.

The family has proposed to form a trust for the well-being of society.

(**Source:** *The Hindu*, Jan.17, 1995).

for this statement has been provided by research in 39 countries in which questions were asked on such subjects as the fear subordinates have of expressing disagreement with their bosses (answers expressed by 'I am afraid very frequently' through to 'I am afraid seldom'). The answers have been assembled in a series of tables showing power distance index values varying 94 ('very often afraid') for the Philippines to 11 ('very seldom afraid') for Austria.[16]

What applies to the Philippines applies to our country, too, where the boss is held almost as a *demigod*. It is for this reason that egalitarian concepts like participative management do not mean much to our managers and workers.

Traditionally, our society was known for authority and power being concentrated with the King. But the greatest merit of our society has been that the king or the boss is governed by the principle of *Dharma*, a concept which is unique to our culture.

11. The View of Scientific Method

It is said that, unlike Western society, our society is steeped in fatalism and the theory of *Karma*. The followers of our religion do not appreciate the logic of things-logic of wealth, rainfall, demand–supply mechanisation and related phenomena. It is also said that they believe in preserving traditional mores and are not adaptive to things modern.

Contrary to popular belief, our views did not conflict with science. A study of the Upanishads will show that Vedanta postulates that the universe is the result of a gradual unfolding of the creative power inherent in the primordial substance. Infact, it may be said that the philosophy of our religion anticipated the basic theories of biology and physics. The very approach to things in the Upanishads, the insistence on adherence to truth and on tireless investigation is remarkable in the nature of an anticipation of the methods of science.[17]

The followers of our culture are receptive and open. They have always absorbed new technology and adopted the latest methods of production. Most of our industrial establishments are highly mechanised and automated. Being scientific does not mean one should reject one's traditional culture. Traditional culture and modern science can go together as is proved in our country. Probably, it is only in our country that a manager performs *pooja* before installing a new machine in his factory. It is a tribute to our worker that he does not touch his tools on the shop floor in the morning without closing his eyes for a second in remembrance of god.

> Indians have absorbed new technology and adopted the latest methods of production.

Even in a village, a farmer is not averse to adopting new varieties of seeds, fertilisers or new methods of cultivation. The two green revolutions we had experienced so far would not have been possible if our farmers had stuck to the traditional methods of cultivation. The farmer should only be told about the possibilities and benefits of new varieties and methods, and then he would gladly adopt them. But never will he forget to break a coconut before sowing the seeds or harvesting the crop.

> The fact that green revolutions occurred in India is a proof that people are open to new technologies.

12. Ethics in Business

Ethics refers to the code of conduct that guides an individual in dealing with others. A formal definition of ethics is that it deals with personal conduct and moral duty and concerns human relations with respect to right and wrong. Ethics concerns morals and philosophy. It deals with the behaviour of individuals and the standards governing the interrelationship between individuals.[18]

Ethics is a science of morals. Ethics may be external or internal.

Ethical rules differ from legal rules inasmuch as the former are not enforced by public authority whereas the latter are. Legal rules become unnecessary when ethical rules are observed by businessmen. Society expects businessmen to act ethically.

Ethics maybe internal or external. As regards the former, a manager must be honest with oneself, since one's greatest asset is one's character. One should be honest and straightforward with others, treating them in the same manner in which one wishes to be treated. Fairness in dealings with co-workers and subordinates is mandatory; one should never discriminate by dispensing special favours or privileges, whether for remuneration or not. Information coming to one confidentially should neither be revealed nor used to the disadvantage of any co-worker. One should ensure one's employment right to privacy. With reference to external ethics, the same suggestions as stated above can be followed.[19]

Is it enough if the manager, as an individual, is ethical in his behaviour and dealings? Many people believe so. This is however, erroneous. Every individual has a responsibility of not only himself being ethical; he must make his group so. Ethical people doing nothing is the best way for moral decay to take over.

13. Religion

Religion refers to a specific and institutionalized set of beliefs and practices agreed upon by a number of persons.

Religion refers to a specific and institutionalised set of beliefs and practices generally agreed upon by a number of persons or sects. There are nearly 100,000 religions across the globe, but the major one's among them are Hinduism, Christianity, Islam, Buddhism and Confucianism. Each has its own distinct characteristics and followers.

Religion has considerable impact on one's life, irrespective of the country to which he or she belongs. People go to any extent and practice abnormal activities in the name of religion. Animals and human beings are scarified to propitiate god, heads are tonsured, cheeks and tongues are pierced, sex and food are given up for days, dip in rivers and roll over around places of worship-all in the name of religion. People are compelled to change their religious faiths, places of worship are destroyed and pillaged, people are beheaded and battles are fought over religious matters. In modern democracies, elections are fought on issues relating to religion.

People practice abnormal things in the name of religion.

Religion has its impact on the economy of a country. Take Hinduism for example with nearly 500 million adherents, Hinduism is found mainly in India. Critics argue that by emphasising **moksha, dharma,** renunciation and ascetic principles, Hinduism negates entrepreneurialism and wealth acquisitive nature of its followers.

This perception is not all that correct. India has produced hundreds of entrepreneurs who have made it big in India and abroad. India is, probably, the only country in the world where wealth is worshiped in the form of goddess **Lakshmi,** unlike in the west where richness is merely respected.

Major Religions of the World

Christianity is the most widely practised religion in the world. About one billion people, approximately 20 per cent of the world's population, identify themselves as Christians. The vast majority of Christians live in Europe, the Americas, although their number are growing in Africa.

Capitalism has grown out of protestianism.

Protestianism (one branch of Christianity, the other being Catholicism) has considerable implications for business. Capitalism, which is the most dominant economic philosophy today, has grown out of Protestianism. Protestatianism advocating hard work and encourages wealth acquisition. Hard work and wealth are essential requisites for capitalism to grow.

Islam is the second largest religion with followers being spread over more than 35 countries and inhabit a nearly continuous stretch of land from the North West Coast of Africa, through the Middle East, to China and Malaysia in the Far East.

Islam prohibits receipt or payment of interest which is considered usury. To the devout Muslim, receipt of interest is considered to be a grave sin. This principle has been codified in certain countries. In 1992, for example, Pakistan's Federal Shariat Court, the highest Islamic law-making body in the country, declared interest to be un-Islamic and therefore illegal.

Fearing that rigid adherence to the above principle could wreak havoc with a country's banking and financial system (thereby driving away international businesses), Islamic banks have been experimenting with profit-sharing system.

Though receipt and payment of interest are prohibited, profit sharing is allowed in Islam.

Under this system, when a bank lends money to a businessman, the lending bank takes a share in the profit earned by the business person, instead of demanding interest payment. Similarly, a depositor of money will not get interest from the accepting bank, but takes a share in the profit earned by it.

Some critics argue that Islam discourages profit. This is not true. The Quaran speaks appealingly of free enterprise and of earning legitimate profit through trade and commerce.

Islam also advocates marketing based systems. Given this proclivity, Muslim countries tend to attract international businesses so long as they behave in a manner that is consistent with Islamic ethics.

There has been an upsurge of fundamentalism in the Islamic countries. This fundamentalism is being associated in the media with militants, terrorists, and violent upheavals such as the bloody conflict occurring in Algeria or the killing of foreign tourists in Egypt. This characterisation is not true. Fundamentalism is not peculiar to Islam. It may be noticed in Hinduism or Christianity.

Buddhism has 250 million followers and is being practised in Central and Southeast Asia, China, Korea and Japan. Buddhists stress spiritual achievement and obviously wealth creation is not encouraged. In Buddhist societies, we do not see the same kind of cultural stress on entrepreneurial behaviour that we see in the Protestant west.

Creation of wealth is not encouraged in Buddhism.

Confucianism: Confucians numbering over 150 million, are found in China, Korea and Japan. The religion teaches the importance of attaining personal salvation through right action. Confucianism is built around a comprehensive ethical code that sets down guidelines for relationships with others. The need for high moral and ethical conduct and loyalty to others is central to Confucianism.

Confucianism has economic implications too. It teaches the followers to lower the costs of doing business and this has largely contributed to the success of Japan, South Korea, and Taiwan.

Three principles are central to Confusianism-loyalty, reciprocal obligations and honesty. Loyalty to one's boss is considered to be essential for salvation. This belief helps organisations maintain cordial employer and employee relations. Loyalty to one's superior brings the concept of reciprocal obligations to the centre-stage. The principle of reciprocal obligations enjoins the superior to bestow "blessings" on subordinates for their loyalty. The employees of a Japanese company are loyal to the leaders of the organisation, and in return the leaders bestow on them the "blessings" of life time employment. Honesty is the third principle of confuscianism. The religion points out that dishonest behaviour fetches only short run benefits. Ethical conduct is vital for long term benefits of organisations. Ethical conduct begets trust-trust eliminates expensive lawyers to resolve disputes and contractual obligations are discharged without hassles.

Honesty, loyalty and reciprocal obligations are central to Confucianism.

14. Marriage

Performance of household sacrifices, progeny and sexual gratification are the three objectives of marriage.

Traditionally marriage had three objectives: the promotion of religion by the performance of household sacrifices, progeny whereby the father and his ancestors were assured of a happy after-life and the line was continued and *rati* or sexual pleasure.

While the three objectives are relevant even today, what needs to be stressed is that the marriage is a social institution which results in the multiplication of people, settled life and systematised and organised activities. All these have economic significance.

Marriage also means several things to several people. A single marriage may spark off protest from women and approval from men. What is more, marriage may even revive a recession hit economy (see Box 33.3).

Box 33.3 **Superwoman in Shackled**

Japan has a severe case of royal fever. And the gloom of recession, last week's announcement that Crown Prince Naruthito, seemingly destined to a lonely life of bachelorhood, has finally found a bride, has provoked a range of emotions from tears of joy among shoppers to a forecast that the economy will grow by an extra 0.8 per cent this year.

There is a general sense that the crown prince, the 32-year-old heir to Japan's Chrysanthemum Throne, has chosen well. Miss Masako Owada, 29, a career diplomat, speaks English, French and German, shares his love of skiing and tennis and, after a stint at Harvard, studied, like the prince, at Oxford University.

But his choice has also provoked a debate about the role of women in Japan. Miss Owada, whose father is vice foreign minister, is on a fast track on her career. She has sat in negotiations with Mr.James Baker, the former US Secretary of State, and Mrs.Carla Hills, the US trade representative. She has also been responsible for policy formulation on semiconductors, one of the most sensitive trade issues between the US and Japan.

Her career will be sacrificed for the cloistered life of loyal wife to the crown prince, responsible for official tree planting and paper folding festivals. Miss Owada, likely to be wed in May, has already handed in her notice, and her decision has provoked dismay among some Japanese women, who are painfully making their way through the male dominated hierarchies of business and the government bureaucracy. "I can't believe she's giving up her job", said one career woman, expressing her shock over the resignation of Miss Owada, dubbed 'Superwoman' by the media.

By contrast, many Japanese men, who feel threatened by the emergence of stronger career women, are sure she has done the right thing. "Japanese women should follow her example, they've just not made for the workplace", says one male office worker.

But Miss Owada's acceptance of the imperial proposal has also inspired hope that she may be able to weaken the stifling influence of the Imperial Household Agency, the division of the civil service that is in charge of imperial matters and keeps the imperial family aloof from the public. Many Japanese want their royal family to become more accessible, and see the British royal family as a model.

The agency's determination to maintain its tight control over royal affairs and the mystique of the imperial family was shown in a recent controversy over Prince's Aki's hair.

The agency was outraged by an unauthorised snapshot of Prince Akishino, the younger brother of the crown prince, having a strand of hair swept from his forehead by Princess Kiko, his wife, moments before the wedding. The picture was banned by news agencies and the photographer was sacked.

Another sign of the agency's strong grip on royal affairs was its ability to impose a black-out on media coverage of Prince Naruhito's search for a bride. It blamed previous media reports for his difficulty in finding a match and said that, as the next emperor and spiritual head of the Shinto religion, Naruhito should be protected from press intrusion.

On a more worldly level, Japanese businessmen are hoping that the imperial marriage will stimulate the sluggish economy. Consumer spending revived before the wedding of Akihito, the current emperor, and empress Michiko in 1959. The research arm of Nippon Life, the country's largest life assurer, estimates that the royal engagement could add as much as Y3,300bn (sterling 17bn) in consumer spending this year through the sales of commemorative souvenirs and new housing demand triggered by an increase in the number of couples getting married.

Electronics manufacturers hope for a boost from a new "Michiboom-the sharp increase in sales of television sets to people wanting to watch the 1959 wedding. Most Japanese now have a television set, but that has not stopped profit-starved executives

from suggesting that a royal wedding could be just the thing for high-definition television, which has so far been an over-priced flop.

The imperial wedding will certainly be over-promoted, with the Japanese government suggesting recently that it would be made a national holiday, and media organisations already assigning squadrons of reporters to prepare programmes on every conceivable royal issue. But whether the imperial marriage is a flop depends on Prince Naruhito, who will either take Miss Owada by the hand and lead her into a new era of openness or ensure a life of frustrating, refined confinement.

The prince has expressed a desire for a more informal relationship between the imperial family and the people, and has complained about excess security precautions. Film footage of the prince's life behind the palace walls this week showed him jogging, apparently alone, until the camera panned to the right, showing a pack of security officials scurrying behind him.

Having observed the British royal family during his time as a graduate student at Oxford, the prince recently expressed his admiration for the Windsors' social profile. After their recent problems, however, the crown prince may well be hoping that his journey through married life proves somewhat smoother.

15. Cultural Resources

Cultural resources refer to the heritage which makes the country distinctive. Our country is vastly rich in cultural heritage. A look at our past is a pleasant and rejuvenating experience. It makes an individual feel proud that he is an Indian. It certainly makes him raise his head and look ahead with confidence and hope.

Ours is a beautiful country with vast, varied and rich mineral resources, splendid flora and fauna, varied animal life, beautiful rivers, huge mountains, dense forests, splendid architecture, innumerable temples and mosques and great thinkers and seers. It is on this land that Adishankara, Gautam Buddha and Swami Vivekananda were born and it was here that Mahatma Gandhi led the country to freedom from colonial rule through non-violence.

The whole of South East Asia and Central Asia received culture from India. Along with culture, India conferred many practical blessings on the world, notably rice, cotton, sugarcane, many spices, the domestic fowl, the game of chess and the most important of all, the decimal system of numeral notation-the invention of an unknown Indian mathematician early in the Christian era. India developed a grammatical system which is unparalleled in any other country. And Sankrit literature is one of the greatest contributions India has made to the culture of mankind.

Today, there are few Indians whatever their creed, who do not look back with pride on their ancient culture and there are few intelligent Indians who are not willing to abandon some of its effete elements that India may develop and progress. Politically and economically, India faces many problems, and no one can predict her future with any certainty. But it is to be hoped that whatever the future maybe, the Indians of the coming generations will not be unconvincing and self-conscious carbon copies of Europeans, but will be men rooted in their own soil and traditions and aware of the continuity of their culture. Already the extremes of national self-denigration and fanatical cultural chauvinism are disappearing. In the past, Hindu civilisation had received, adapted and digested elements of many different cultures-Aryan, European, Mesopotamian, Iranian, Greek, Roman, Scythian, Turkish, Persian, Mughal and the Arabs. With each new influence, it has somewhat changed. Now, it is well on the way to assimilating the culture of the West.

Bhagavad Gita inspires men of action and Upanishads men of thought.

Our civilisation will, we believe, retain its continuity. The *Bhagavad Gita* will not cease to inspire men of action, and the Upanishads men of thought. The charm and graciousness of the Indian way of life will continue, however much affected it may be, by the labour-saving devices of the West. People will still love the tales of the heroes of the *Mahabharatha* and the *Ramayana*, and of the loves of Dushyanta and Puruvas and Urvasi. The quiet and gentle happiness provided to Indian life, where oppression, disease and poverty have not overclouded it, will surely not vanish before the more hectic ways of the West.

Much that was useless in ancient Indian culture has already perished. The extravagant and barbarious hecatombs of the Vedic age have long since been forgotten, though animal sacrifice continues in some sects. Widows have long ceased to be burnt on their husbands' pyres. Girls may not by law be married in childhood, caste is vanishing and the old family system is adapting itself to the present day conditions. Infact, the whole face of India is altering, but the cultural tradition continues, and it will never be lost.[20]

Culture is a big business too. Countries export cultural products to and earn foreign exchange. US is making big money by selling culture-movies, music, T.V.programmes, and home video-to other countries. Pop culture is so popular that only the sale of aircraft and related equipment accounts for more US exports. American music industry earns about 70 per cent of its profits outside the US with sales of US TV programmes to Europe accounting for over $600 million a year. One of the most popular films of all time is **Titanic**, which grossed more than $ 1 billion.

Japan is earning vast sums through the exports of its cultural products. International embrace of Japan's pop culture, films, food, style and arts is second only to that of US. Revenues from royalty and sales of music, videogames, animation, art films and fashion had gone up to $12.5 billion in 2002, up 300 per cent a decade ago.

16. Customs and Manners

Customs are common or established practices. Manners are behaviours that are regarded as appropriate in a particular society. Customs dictate how things are to be done; manners are used in carrying them out. Further, manners are part of an individual's character whereas customs are what society collectively expects its members to do.

The businessman should understand manners and customs of his or her country citizens. Failure to understand and respect local customs and manners may land the manager in trouble, besides losing business.

Customs are established practices. Manners are behaviours that are regarded as appropriate in a particular society.

Customs and manners differ from country to country. In Arab countries, for example, it is considered bad manners to attempt to shake hands with a person of higher authority unless this individual makes the first gesture to do so, unlike in the US where a person would not hesitate to offer his or her hand regardless of the person's rank. Similarly, shaking hands with the opposite sex is not appreciated in India, though the practice is prevalent in rich countries. Table manners vary from culture to culture, ranging from precise placement of eating implements to using fingers instead. Understanding customs and manners is particularly important during discussions and negotiations. Bodily expressions may contradict what is being said or implied. Observing manners and respecting customs are essential ingredients of successful negotiations in Far and Near Eastern cultures.

BUSINESS PARTICIPATION IN CULTURAL AFFAIRS

Till now we described the various cultural factors which influence business generally. Specifically, business does four things in the name of culture: (a) support to cultural activities; (b) beauty in building design; (c) multicultural literacy, and (d) managing diversity.

Support to cultural activities include such activities as employing artists and musicians, organising exhibitions of contemporary paintings, sponsoring cultural programmes through TV, instituting awards for excellence, sponsoring Sangeet Sammelans and maintaining Sangeet Research Academy as is done by the Indian Tobacco Company(ITC) in Kolkotta.

Earlier beauty in the building was not considered in designing and constructing. Generally, factories and business buildings focussed mainly on utilitarian functions. The result was not just an absence of beauty, but distasteful; ugliness, sometimes called the '*nineteenth century ugly school of factory design*.' Things are different now. Factory buildings are now constructed keeping in mind aesthetic values. Many factory sites are now industrial parks, more beautiful than the surrounding residential houses.

Why should business participate in the cultural affairs? Business justifies its involvement because of the better quality of life in the community. In turn, this quality of life improves recruiting and the retention of employees. It also improves satisfaction of the employees with their community, provides a better place for their children to grow up, and encourages each employee's own cultural growth. The effects continue in many directions in the same way that a stone cast into the water extends its ripples to the limits of the lake. If, for example, the firm sells its products locally, a community with a better cultural life should have improved chances of growth, thus providing more customers. Further, culture should attract better quality of citizens thus improving the quality of the labour pool from which the firm recruits. Cultural opportunities also may challenge youth in the community to raise their achievement, drives and provide favourable outlets for their energies, thereby reducing tendencies towards delinquency. In turn, less crime and delinquency may reduce the tax burden. When a system's view as this is taken, it can be argued that an instrument in community cultures tends to improve the entire social system.[21]

Business participates in cultural activities for mutual advantage.

Cross-Cultural Literacy

As Indian businesses are increasingly getting integrated into world economies, managers need to become multiculturalists. They should initiate steps to remove multicultural illiteracy among themselves and employees.

One way to remove multicultural illiteracy is to appoint local citizens to do business in a particular culture. Firms should also ensure that home-country executives are cosmopolitan enough to understand how differences in cultures affect the ways of carrying on international business. Transferring executives overseas at regular intervals to expose them to different cultures will help build a cadre of cosmopolitan managers. Hitachi is now taking this approach as it transforms itself from a purely Japanese company into an MNC for a long time.

For a long time Hitachi was a typical Japanese company. With globalisation, along with many other enterprises, Japanese society also has realised that monoculture firms will not survive. In 1991, Hitachi set up a department to educate executives about other cultures. This department downplays the old notions of harmony and consensus decision-making. Hitachi is also sending increasing numbers of its executives for prolonged postings overseas, and it is starting to bring foreign managers back to Japan. The foreign experience has encouraged senior managers to seek firmer leadership in Japan – to shift away from the old consensus decision-making – and Hitachi's top executives have encouraged this trend.

An international business must also be constantly on guard against the dangers of ethnocentric behaviour. The ethnocentric person sees his or her own group as the center or defining point of culture and views all other cultures as deviations from what is normal. Hand-in-hand with ethnocentrism goes a disregard or contempt for the cultures of other countries.

It was ethnocentrism that led China's Emperor Chien Lung to dispatch the following message to Great Britain's George III in reply to the latter's request that the two nations establish trade ties.[22]

> Our Celestial Empire possesses all things in prolific abundance and lacks no produce within its own borders. There is, therefore, no need to import the manufactures of outside barbarians in exchange for our own produce. But as the tea, silk and porcelain, which the Celestial Empire produces, are absolute necessities to European nations and to yourselves, we have permitted, as a signal mark of favour, that foreign business houses (at Canton) be supplied and your country thus participate in our beneficence –. As your ambassador can see for himself, we possess all things. I set not value on objects strange or ingenious and I have no use for your country's manufactures –. I do not forget the lonely remoteness of your island, cut off from the world by intervening wastes of sea, and I overlook your excusable ignorance of the usages of our Celestial Empire, I have consequently commanded my minister to enlighten your ambassador on the subject.

Unfortunately, ethnocentrism is all too prevalent; many Indians are guilty of it, as are many Americans, French, Japanese, Britishers, and so on. Ugly as it is, ethnocentrism is a fact of life and the international businesses must be on continual guard against it.

How do international managers learn to live with other cultures? The first step is to realise that there are cultures different from their own. They must then go on to learn the characteristics of those cultures so that they may adapt to them.

Managing Diversity

Managing diversity means establishing a heterogeneous workforce to perform to its potential in an equitable work environment where no member (or groups of members) has an advantage or a disadvantage. Managing diversity is a challenge for any manager. The challenge is to create a work environment in which each person can perform to his or her full potential and therefore compete for promotions and other rewards on merit alone.

Both domestically and internationally, organisations find themselves leading workforces that have a variety of cultures (and sub-cultures) and consist of a largely diverse population of women, men, young and old people, blacks, whites, Indians, Latins, Asians, Arabs, lesbians, physically challenged, and even people who are significantly overweight. Days were when a typical Indian firm was manned with Shettys, Reddys, Nairs, Raos, Patels, Mehtas, or Singhs. A typical firm today is an amalgam of a diverse workforce in terms of gender, race, and ethnicity. One can find a Shastri rubbing shoulders with a Khan, both jostling with a Gowda, and all shaking hands with a Singh.

Interaction helps bring employees together, thus leading to diversity. Most companies encourage interaction and therefore go in for exchange programs. Wipro introduced exchange programs to that American Management System (AMS) employees could come to Bangalore and vice versa. HCL in its first three months sent 20 employees each on both sides for an exchange program so that the two sides could work together as a team. MphasiS encouraged its Chinese engineers to work alongside MphasiS engineers on its US accounts. Similarly, for a Japanese project, the development is co-located in Shanghai and Mumbai, involving travel, coordination and knowledge sharing across both locations. All this goes a long way in buildings a rapport between teams. WIPRO has come out with an interesting concept of 'buddies'. This means that for every five employees of AMS, there is one WIPRO employee as their buddy who would guide them on WIPRO rules and regulations.

Most Indian managers perceive diversity in its restricted meaning. For them, diversity means having women as employees. HLL's management team comprises 11 per cent women, up from six per cent four years earlier. At Kodak India, 70 per cent of the company's marketing staff and 85 per cent of the workforce at its Bangalore factory are women.

Infosys has gone beyond appointing women. 40 per cent of Infoscians are non-Indians. At HSBC, half the employees worldwide are women. In terms of race, 30 per cent are Asian and nearly 70 per cent are Latin American.[23]

Another important aspect of diversity is **generational diversity** – differences in values, aspirations, and beliefs that characterise the present generation. Today's youth measure success in terms of sales volume, quantifiable results, and swelling bank balances. For them, ends justify means. Older people have no tolerance for the youth.

Diversity – Advantages and Disadvantages: Diversity, though a challenging task to manage, carries with it certain advantages. One main benefit of diversity is the generation of more and better ideas. Because group members come from a host of different cultures, they are often able to create unique and creative solutions and recommendations. A second major benefit is that culturally diverse groups can prevent *groupthink*, which is social conformity and pressures on individual members of a group to conform and reach a consensus. When this occurs, group participants believe that their ideas and actions are correct and those who disagree with them are either uninformed or are deliberately trying to sabotage their efforts. Multicultural diverse groups are able to avoid this problem, because the members do not think similarly or feel the pressure to conform. As a result, they typically question each other, offer opinions and suggestions that are contrary to those held by others, and must be persuaded to change their minds. Therefore, unanimity is achieved only through a careful process of deliberation. Decision-making may be very slow, unlike in a homogeneous group, but the decisions reached tend to be very effective.

There are perceptual problem too. When culturally diverse groups come together, they often bring preconceived stereotypes with them. A related problem is inaccurate biases. Japanese firms, for example, depend on groups to make decisions. Entrepreneurial behaviour, individualism, and originality are downplayed.

Yet another potential problem with diverse groups is inaccurate communication, which could occur for a number of reasons. One is misunderstandings caused by words used by one but not clear to others. Another problem is the way in which situations are interpreted. Many Japanese nod their heads when others talk, but this does not necessarily imply their approval. They are merely being polite and attentive. Different uses of time may also lead to communication problems. For example, many Japanese will not agree to a course of action on-the-spot. They will not act until they have discussed the matter with their own people because they do not feel empowered to act alone. Many Latin managers refuse to be held to strict timetables, because they do not have the same time-urgency that US managers do.[24]

Managing Diversity-Some Practical Measures: Having discussed the diverse workforces, and their benefits and potential problems, it is appropriate to list out some practical steps that managers can take to manage diversity. Here are some such steps:

- Focus on bringing in the best talent, not on meeting numerical goals. Geocentric policy towards staffing should be the guiding principle.
- Hold managers accountable for meeting goals of diversity.
- Establish monitoring programmes among employees of same and different races.
- Develop career plans for employees as part of performance reviews.
- Develop an age, gender, and race/ethnic profile of the present workforce.
- Promote minorities and other disadvantaged sections to decision-making positions, not just to staff jobs.
- Diversify the company's board of directors.
- Provide extended leaves, flexible scheduling, flexitime, job sharing and opportunities to telecommunicate, particularly for disadvantaged workers.

QUESTIONS

1. Define culture. How does culture influence business?
2. In Table 33.1, provide one more column and list how all the concepts are understood in our country.
3. What is business ethics? What are ethical problems?
4. How do you make businessmen ethical?
5. Discuss why business should participate in cultural affairs?
6. What specific actions businesses take to promote culture?

ASSEIGNMENTS

1. Pick up five Indian companies and study their employee composition. How diversified are they? Prepare a report.
2. Observe the way your classmates speak. Whose language is high contextual and whose language is low contextual? Why is it so?

REFERENCES

1. Elbert W.Steward and James A.Glynn, *Introduction to Sociology*, p.53.
2. *Ibid.*
3. Richard T. Schacfer and Robert P. Lamn, *Sociology,* McGraw-Hill, 1998, p.73.
4. Andrew Harrison, *International Business,* Oxford, 2000, p.111.
5. Keith Davis and Robert L. Blamstron, *Buisness and Society – Environmnet and Responsibility,* McGraw-Hill 1998, p. 152.
6. C.Rajagopalachari, *Hinduism-Doctrine and Way of Life*, p.44.

7. A.L.Basham, *The Wonder That Was India*, p.219.
8. *Ibid*, pp.217-18.
9. Keith Davis and Robert L.Blomstrom, *op.cit,* p.391.
10. Michael Brooks and Hutchinson, *op.cit,* p.230.
11. William M.Kaphart, *The Family, Society and the Individual*, p.2.
12. Irawati Karve, *Kinship Organisation*, p.10.
13. A.L.Basham, *op.cit,* p.157.
14. Aileen D.Ross, *The Hindu Family in Its Urban Setting*, p.15.
15. *India Today*, dated July 15, 1983.
16. A.L.Basham, *op.cit,* p.157.
17. Michael Brooks and Hutchinson, *op.cit,* p.232.
18. C.Rajagopalachari, *op.cit,* p.32.
19. George R.Terry, *Principles of Management*, p.224.
20. *Ibid*, p.313.
21. Keith Davis and Robert L.Blomstrom, *op.cit,* p.407.
22. James W.V. *Sociology,* McGraw-Hill, 1996, p.40.
23. *The Economic Times,* dated August 15, 2003.
24. Hodgetts and Luthans, *International Management,* THM, 2003, p. 169.

34
Social Responsibility of Business

CHAPTER OUTLINE

Nature and Models of Social Responsibility
Arguments for Social Responsibility
Arguments Against Social Responsibility
Barriers to Social Responsibility
Social Responsibility Strategies
Social Responsibility Implementation
- Monitoring Social Demands and Expectations
- Internal Social Response Mechanisms
- Corporate Accountability

Limits of Social Responsibility
Common Characteristics
Evolving Idea of Social Responsibility
Indian Scenario

LEARNING OBJECTIVES

After reading this Chapter, you should be able to:

1. Define social responsibility and explain its models
2. Argue for and against social responsibility
3. Outline barriers to social responsibility
4. Point out social responsibility strategies
5. Explain how organisations implement social responsibility actions
6. Bring out the limiting factors of social responsibility
7. Point out the salient features of socially responsive firms
8. Trace the historical evaluation of social responsibility in India and abroad

Business depends on to society for the needed inputs like money, men and skills. Business also depends on the society for market where products may be sold to their buyers. Thus, business depends on society for existence, sustenance and encouragement. Dependence of business on society is so complete that as long as the latter wants the former, business has reason to exist. Once society ceases to have any use for business, it has no place and reason to live. Being so much dependent, business has definite responsibility towards society. Popularly called the social responsibility of business, the subject has become an important topic for discussion in business and academic circles.

Social responsibility, also known as corporate social responsibility (CSR), is understood as the obligation of decision-makers to take actions which protect and improve the welfare of society as a whole along with their own interests.

SR refers to the responsibility of decision-makers to take actions which help society and serve own interests.

Every decision the businessman takes and every action he contemplates have social implications. Be it deciding on diversification, expansion, opening of a new branch, closure of an existing branch or replacement of men by machines, the society is affected in one way or the other. Even routine matters like overtime and night shifts, subcontracting, and laying off employees due to load-shedding have a social impact. Whether the issue is significant or not, the businessman should keep his social obligation in mind before contemplating any action.

Social responsibility of business is not new to our country. In the olden days, whenever there was a famine, the leading businessmen of the area would literally throw open their godowns and their treasure chests to provide food and other assistance to the needy. The history of every region of this country is replete with stories of the magnificent manner in which businessmen rose to the occasion in times of calamity. Even in ordinary times, it was the businessmen who looked after the welfare of the destitute, the *goshalas*, wells and ponds wherever water was difficult to get, the *pathashalas* and so on. So to accept social responsibility is no more than rededicating ourselves to the cherished values of our ancestors in the field of business. Gandhiji reminded us of these values when he propounded the theory of trusteeship.[1] (Read Box 34.1 for trusteeship in action).

Box 34.1 **A Way of Thought**

India's largest and internationally best known group of companies with a turnover of approximately four billion dollars and an employee strength of about 240,000 was launched by its founder, Jamsetji Tata, over a century ago with a textile mill in Central India.

The enterprises promoted by Tatas were born at a time when India was no more than a geographical expression, in need of all the basic and vital necessities of life.

The key nation-building activities that Tatas promoted called for a spirit of adventure, the taking of great risks and a commitment to build castles on the clouds of intention. Over the years, not only did Tata enterprises develop and branch out into many diversified fields of commercial activity, but they came to represent a way of thought bringing the industrial revolution to a vast multilingual subcontinent, hitherto wedded exclusively to agricultural pursuits.

Started in 1907, Tata Steel, India's first integrated steel plant, and at one time the biggest in the then British Empire, came into being at a time when British experts laughed at the very idea of Indians wanting to produce steel to British specifications.

Nearly 40 years later, Tata Steel promoted The Tata Engineering and Locomotive Company Limited initially to produce locomotives for the Indian Railways, then diversifying to emerge as the country's largest and most modern commercial vehicle producer and consequently a major foreign exchange earner.

In 1939, Tata Chemicals, struggling hard for years, ultimately mastered the soda ash production technology which was until then a closely guarded secret of about six world giants.

Three years after Jamsetji Tata's death in 1904, saw one of his dreams came true, bringing hydro-electric power to Western India, making Bombay the first smoke free industrial city in the country. It was also in Bombay that Jamsetji Tata built another Taj Mahal, which today, some three quarters of a century later, is recognised as one of the finest hotels in the world.

To support and preserve the results of a growing green revolution, Tatas promoted Voltas, a leading enterprise in refrigeration and air-conditioning. The country's largest private sector Trading House, Tata Exports, was set up in the early 1960s. Simultaneously, a series of diversification activities took place ranging from the manufacture and processing of tea to genetic engineering, from cosmetics to management consultancy services, from oil rigging to telecommunications.

Through a pioneering concept of trusteeship in management, the benefits of the profits of many of these companies are channeled back to the people through major philanthropic trusts with nearly 80 per cent of the capital of the holding company, Tata Sons Limited, being held by these Trusts. As a result, great national institutions have come into being in the areas of science, medicine, atomic energy and the performing arts.

Once upon a time, Indian cottons and muslins were sold in the markets of Babylon and Indian pepper was weighed against gold in the Forum at Rome. Today, after hundreds of years of stagnation, Indian manufactures are travelling back into the market places of the world on a bridge built by Tata enterprises.

SOCIAL RESPONSIBILITY MODELS

There are two basic approaches to the concept of **corporate social responsibility**. Some theorists, focusing on the 'micro' level of analysis, try to show individual companies how they can be more socially responsive. Other researchers concern themselves with the 'macro' level of analysis, assuming that the government, not individual companies, should establish a country's social goals. Needless to say that it is the micro level of analysis which is significant.

Ackerman's Model: Micro-level theorist Robert Ackerman was among the earliest people to suggest that responsiveness (he prefers to use the term responsivness) should be the goal of corporate social endeavour. Ackerman described three phases through which companies commonly tend to pass in developing a response to social issues (see Table 34.1).

Table 34.1 **Ackerman's Three Stages of Social Responsibility**

ORGANIZATIONAL LEVEL	*PHASES OF ORGANIZATIONAL INVOLVEMENT*		
	Phase I	*Phase II*	*Phase III*
Chief Executive	**Issue**:Corporate obligation **Action**:Write and communicate policy **Outcome**:Enriched purpose, increased awareness	Obtain knowledge Add staff specialists	Obtain organisational commitment. Change performance expectations.
Staff Specialists		**Issue**:Technical problem **Action**:Design data system and interpret environment **Outcome**:Technical and informational groundwork	Provoke response from operating units. Apply data system to performance measurement
Division Management			**Issue**:Management problem **Action**:Commit resources and modify procedures **Outcome**:Increased responsiveness

In phase 1, A corporation's top managers learn of an existing social problem. At this stage, no one asks the company to deal with it. The chief executive officer merely acknowledges the problem by making a written or oral statement of the company's policy towards it.

In phase 2, the company hires staff specialists or engages external consultants to study the problem and to suggest ways of dealing with it. Upto this point, the company has limited itself to declaring its intentions and formulating its plans.

Phase 3 is implementation. The company now integrates the policy into its ongoing operations. Unfortunately, implementation often comes slowly-and often not until the government or public opinion

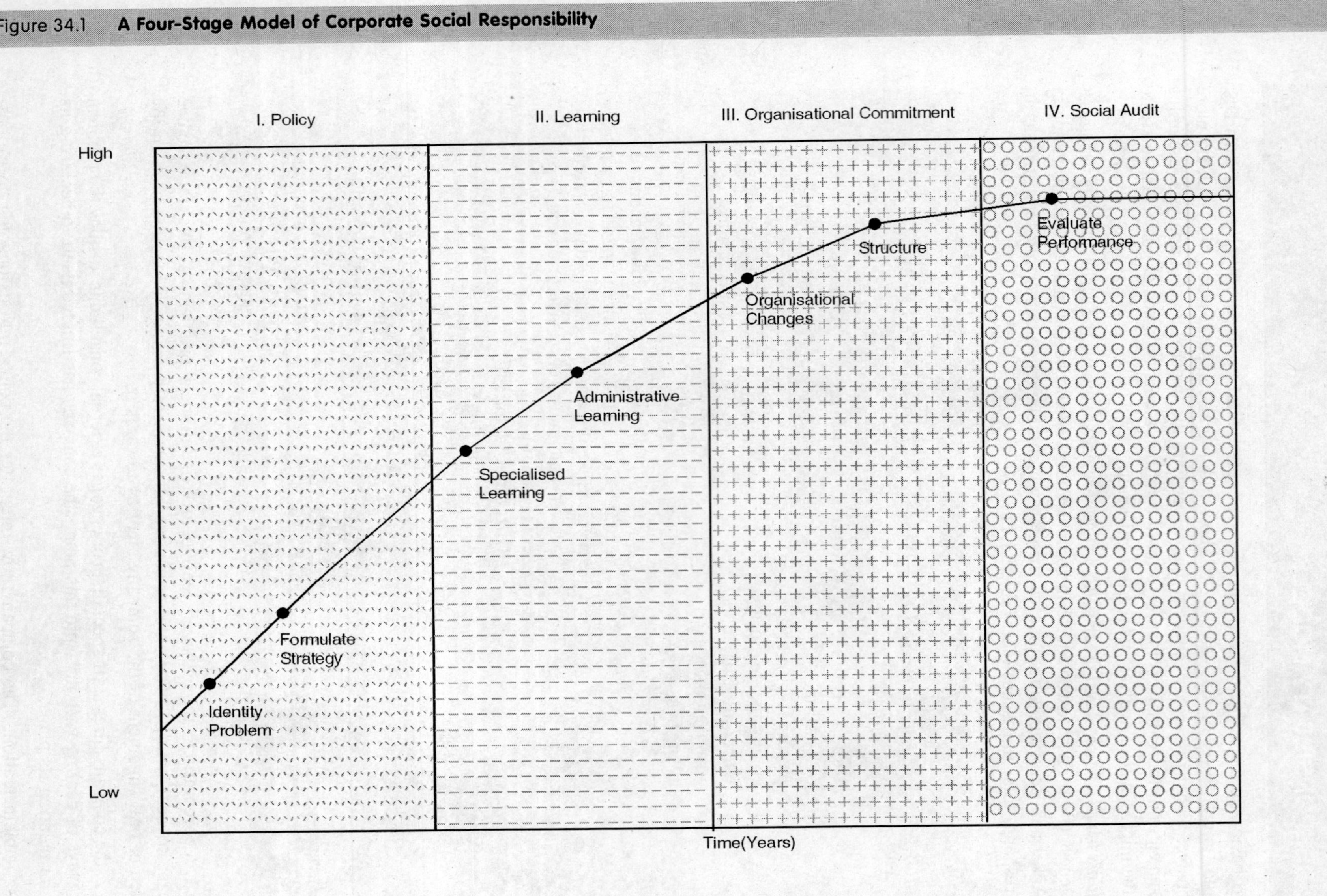

Figure 34.1 **A Four-Stage Model of Corporate Social Responsibility**

forces the company to act. By that time, the company has lost the initiative. Ackerman thus advises that managers should "*act early in the life cycle of any social issue in order to enjoy the largest amount of managerial discretion over the outcome*."

For example, it has recently been suggested that women who spend a great deal of time working at video display terminals, such as word processors or computer operators, stand a higher than average chance of having problem pregnancies. The research is preliminary, tentative and disputed by some investigators. Ackerman's point is that as this issue unfolds, as more actors and competing interests become involved in efforts to resolve it, managers could conceivably lose control over their ability to handle the issue at their own discretion. We can easily imagine several studies confirming these early indications and the resulting drama of congressional hearings, work stoppages, lawsuits, and bureaucratic regulations. Ackerman's model suggests developing options early in the life cycle of an issue. In this case, 'enlightened' companies could make the best information available to their employees, encourage them to ask questions, and even seek transfers or retraining if they believe it is warranted. Being responsive may well be the only responsible course of action.[2]

Women who spend a great deal of time before computers tend to have problem pregnancies.

Another model of social responsibility is shown in Fig.34.1.

In the **policy stage**, the firm becomes aware of those parts of the environment to which it needs to respond and act on. Awareness may occur after stakeholder's expectations change, or it may result from an analysis of environment. Whether or not stakeholder pressure exists, a firm's management may think, based on environmental analysis, that it should respond to emerging issues, concerns, or social needs. The firm needs to formulate an appropriate policy to respond to the society's needs. The policy provides a framework for shaping other aspects of the organisation's response. New production policies, for example, may result in better quality control, remove job hazards, and reduce water pollution.

Socially responsive strategy varies from rejection of the idea to take proactive steps towards socially responsive actions.

A firm must develop a socially responsive strategy. The strategy may vary from an outright rejection to a proactive approach (See Fig.34.2). Including these two, there are six strategies towards corporate social responsibility.

Figure 34.2 **Socially Responsive Strategies**

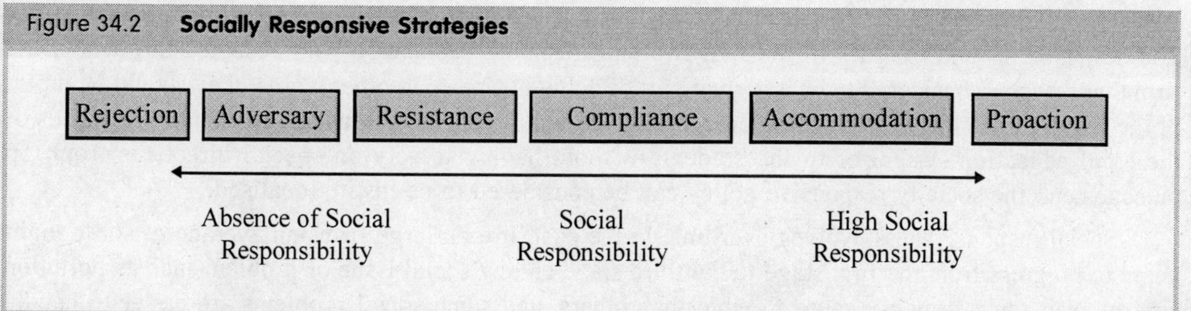

First is **rejection**, a strategy in which a firm denies any responsibility for taking action on a social issue. Strategy of rejection, though sounds harsh, is justified particularly when fringe groups make unreasonable demands on firms. At the same time, rejection and other defensive strategies invite more pressure and a fight in which the corporate image may be dented.

Second, is the **adversary** strategy, in which a firm fights to avoid having to take social actions but will, under severe pressure, cave in. In 1996, the U.S. government ordered the then Chrysler Corp to recall more than 91,000 Chryslers and Dodges because of unsafe seat belts. Chrysler refused to comply, as it believed the belts were safe. The result was continuing controversy between Chrysler and the government. In 1998, Chrysler was fined $8,00,000 for disobeying government's order.

Socially responsive strategies may vary from outright rejection to one of proaction.

The company said it would appeal this decision made by a US District Court Judge after two years litigation.[4]

Resistance strategy is the third approach in which a firm may make token moves or act slowly to satisfy demands that it considers are beyond its social responsibilities.

Fourth is **compliance** strategy. In this posture, the firm simply decides to abide by a government request or a reasonable demand of some stakeholder group.

Fifth is the **accommodation** strategy in which a firm takes actions designed to address potential future stakeholder demands or other pressures. Firms in this category do not oppose, strongly resist, or act reluctantly. They develop social programmes to meet the felt needs of committees. Hewlett-Packard, for example, is responsive to needs of universities for advanced computer equipment. Coca-Cola is responsible to civil rights causes.

Sixth is the **proaction** strategy in which a firm takes actions designed to address potential future stakeholder demands or other pressures. Polaroid, for example, has developed a programme that groups chemicals it uses into toxicity categories and develops plans to reduce or eliminate them. In this way, the firm may avoid future demands for such action.

In the **learning stage**, the firm must learn after it has identified a social problem, how to tackle the problem and make the new policy work. Two kinds of learning are needed here: specialised learning and administrative learning.

Specialised learning occurs when a socio-technical expert-for example, an educational expert who is thoroughly familiar with the culture, lifestyles, motivations and special problems of high school youth-is employed to advise firm's managers. The kind of specialised knowledge that the expert can provide is particularly helpful in the early stages of social responsiveness when the firm is unfamiliar with social problems, whether it is school dropouts, excessive pollution, or toxic chemical hazards.

Administrative learning occurs when a firm's managers become familiar with the new routines that are necessary to cope with a social problem. A technical expert can assist the firm in taking its first step to solve a problem but cannot do the whole job alone. Social responsiveness requires the full cooperation and knowledge of line managers and staff experts. Personal involvement is essential.

Organisational commitment refers to the institutionalization of the new social policy by the firm.

Organisational commitment refers to the institutionalisation of the new social policy by the firm. The new policies and routines in the first two stages should become so well accepted throughout the firm that they are considered to be a normal part of doing business. In other words, they should be a part of the firm and its standard operating procedures. For example, when managers respond to the needs of the local education system or to the students without having to rely on special directives from top management, the socially responsive policy can be considered to be institutionalised.

Social responsiveness evolves overtime. In the past, it took large firms an average of six to eight years to progress from the first stage to the third stage on any social issue or problem such as pollution control. Yet, some firms are more flexible than others, and some social problems are easier to handle than others, so the time involved may vary considerably. It is obvious, however, that a combination of internal factors, particularly management determination; and external factors, especially continued stakeholder action on the problem, is necessary for effective change to occur.

The next step in becoming a socially responsive firm is to change the organisational design to be more responsive to external social challenges and better able to implement socially responsive strategies. This structure evolves from the values and beliefs held by the company's top managers and is expressed through socially responsive business strategies. There are four basic design dimensions that help distinguish a socially responsive structure in a firm. They are breadth, depth, influence, and integration.

Breadth is the number of staff units that specialise in the socially responsive strategies undertaken by the firm. The breadth of the design must be sufficient to enable the firm to adequately monitor and respond to the demands made by stakeholders. Depth is the intensity of the organisational learning process in response to the potential for social challenges and is addressed by the socially responsive strategy process. Firms more vulnerable to social challenges require more developed social response functions, which provide a wide range of perspectives and responses.

Influence and integration are the two final dimensions of the socially responsive organisational design. They refer to the quality of relationships that exist among the firm's staff units. The absence of this influence and integration could undermine or bias the firm's socially responsive strategy process since it could lead to one staff unit, or a few, dominating the process at the cost of other units. The ultimate effectiveness often is due to the degree of integration achieved among the staff units.

Social audit: The last stage in the model is **social audit**. A social audit is a systematic study and evaluation of a firm's social performance. Social audit leads to a report on the social actions of a firm.

Social audit is a systematic study and evaluation of a firm's social performance.

FORCES PRESSURING SOCIAL RESPONSIVENESS

Not all firms are vulnerable to social group pressures and social regulations. Only some firms are pressured to undertake social responsibility actions. The forces that make firms become socially responsive are: government, community interests and demands, environmental concerns, competitive pressures, shareholder/investor pressures, philanthropic requests and initiatives and crises (See Fig.34.3).

Figure 34.3 **Pressures Leading to Social Responsibility**

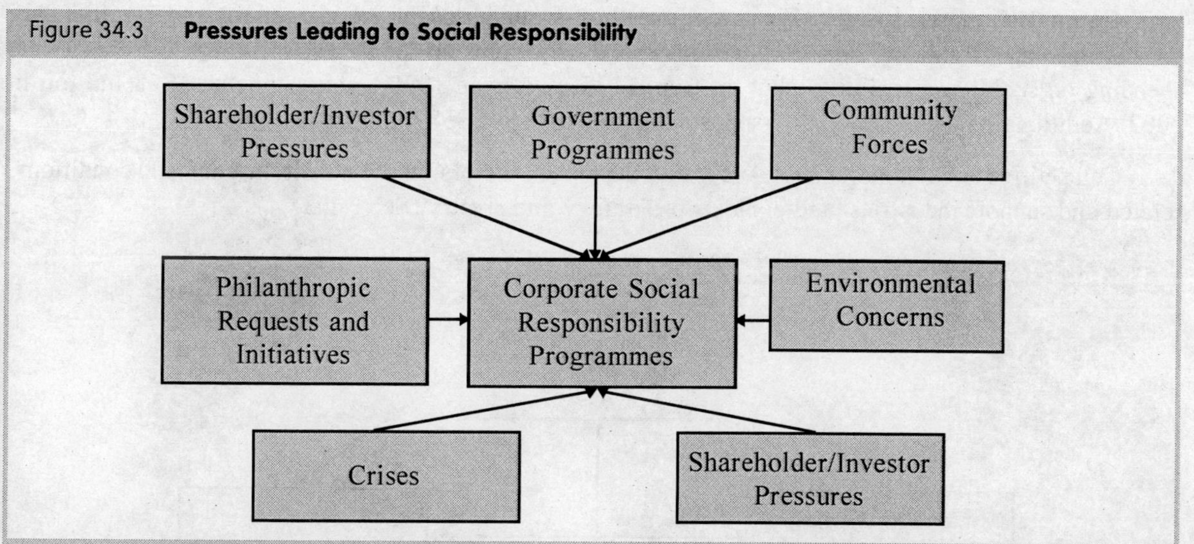

Government Programmes: Government (foreign and domestic) are the most significant forces pressuring firms for social actions. Most government pressures concern compliance with existing regulations. But governments are also major sources of potential rules, a fact which businesses need to take note of. Governments ask businesses to volunteer to help them solve their problems.

Government forces pressure social actions.

Governments mandating social actions are not new. In the 1300s, for example, Londoners who violated the city's smoke pollution ordinances were beheaded. In the US, laws that regulated the purity or quality of certain goods date from colonial times and state and federal efforts to control water pollution began in the late 1800s.

Londoners who violated the city's smoke pollution ordinances were beheaded.

Foreign governments exert pressures on international businesses to abide by codes of conduct that they and international organisations have drafted. These codes expect businesses to respect human rights and social justice, pay fair wages, protect the environment, ensure safety and health of workers, improve worker living conditions, and behave ethically.

Community Interest and Demands: Firms undertake many programmes that benefit society in general, not necessarily favouring stakeholders. Programmes can range widely, from helping rebuild disadvantaged sections to providing executive talents to run government undertakings.

MNCs from the US undertake a wide range of programmes in foreign countries, for example, creating scholarships for poor but deserving students from Korea, Malaysia, and Mexico, to pursue higher studies.

Environmental Concerns: Environmental programmes of firms mainly result from standards established by government agencies. The Government of India, for example, enacted the Environment Protection Act 1986. The main objective of the Act is to protect and improve the environment and the prevention of hazards to human beings, other living creatures, plant and property. Pollution Control Boards set up under the provisions of the Act, have laid down norms that firms are expected to comply with.

Human rights violation made the shareholders of Pepsi force the company withdraw from Myanmar.

Shareholders/Investors Pressures: Large shareholders such as pension funds have long-range interests in the financial success of their investments. Some of them, obviously, exert pressure on firms to respond appropriately to community social interests. For example, shareholders of Pepsi Co. launched a campaign to force the company to pull out of Myanmar because of the human rights violation of the military regime in that country. Pepsi Co. did oblige the shareholders.

Competitive advantage[5]: Firms believe that by undertaking social actions they would gain competitive edge. Realising this, corporations spend huge sums on social responsibility. U.S. corporate spending on social responsibility shot up from \$125 million in 1990 to an estimated \$828 million in 2002. Additionally, spending on arts sponsorship amounted to \$589 million in 2001.

Competitive advantage comprises four interdependent factors: factor conditions, demand conditions, related and support industries, and context for strategy and rivalry (See Fig.34.4).

Figure 34.4 **Four Elements of Competitive Strength**

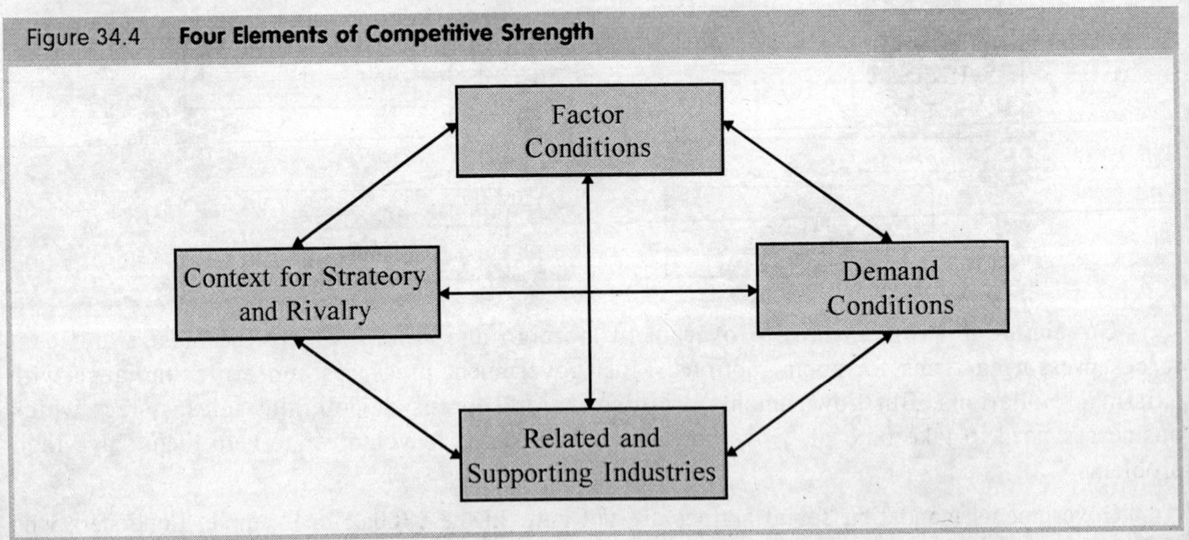

(**Source:** Adapted from Michael E.Porter and Mark R. Kramer, *op. cit., p.60*)

Factor Conditions: These include the availability of trained workers, high quality scientific and technological institutions, adequate physical infrastructure, transparent and efficient administrative processes and natural resources. All these are the areas that social responsibility actions can influence.

Demand Conditions: Demand conditions in a country or a region include the size of the local market, the appropriateness of product standards, and the sophistication of local markets. Sophisticated local customers enhance the regions competitiveness by providing firms with insight into emerging customer needs and applying pressure for innovation.

Social actions influence size and quality of local market.

Social actions can influence both the size and quality of the local market. Apple Computer has donated computers to schools as a means of introducing its products to young people. This provides a clear social benefit to the schools while expanding Apple's potential market and turning students and teachers into more sophisticated purchasers.

Related and Supporting Industries: Productivity of a firm can be greatly enhanced by having high quality industries and services close by. While outsourcing from distant suppliers is possible, it is not as efficient as using capable local suppliers of services, components, and machinery. Proximity enhances responsiveness, exchange of information and innovation, in addition to lowering cost on transportation and inventory.

Social responsibility can foster the development of clusters and strengthen supporting industries. American Express, for example, depends on travel related expenditure for a large share of its credit card and travel agency revenues. Hence, it is part of the travel cluster in each of the countries in which it operates, and it depends on the success of these clusters in improving the quality of tourism and attracting travellers.

Context for Strategy and Rivalry: The rules, incentives, and norms governing competition in a nation or region have a fundamental influence on productivity. Policies that encourage investment, protect intellectual property, open local markets to trade, break up or prevent the formation of cartels and monopolies, and reduce corruption make a location a more attractive place to do business. Social responsibility can have a strong influence on creating a more productive and transparent environment for competition. For example, 26 US corporations and 38 corporations from other countries have joined to support Transparency International in its work to disclose and deter corruption around the world. By measuring and focussing public attention on corruption, the organisation helps create an environment that rewards fair competition and enhances productivity. This benefits local citizens while providing sponsoring companies improved access to markets.

ARGUMENTS FOR CSR

There are many arguments in support of socially responsive actions. More important of them are explained below:

There are several arguments in favour of socially responsive actions of a firm.

1. Changed Public Expectations of Business One of the most potent arguments for social responsibility is that public expectations from business have changed. It is reasoned that the institution of business exists only because it satisfies the valuable needs of society. Society gave business its charter to exist, and the charter can be amended or revoked at any time that the business fails to live up to society's expectations. Therefore, if business wishes to remain viable in the long run, it must respond to society's needs and give the society what it wants.[3]

2. Better Environment for Business Another argument favouring social responsibility is that it creates a better environment for business. This concept rationalises that a better society produces environmental conditions more favourable for business operations. The firm which is most responsive to the improvement of community quality of life will as a result have a better community in which to conduct its business. Labour recruiting will be easier, and labour will be of a higher quality. Turnover and absenteeism will be reduced.

As a result of social improvements, crime will decrease with the consequence that less money will be spent to protect property, and less taxes have to be paid to support police forces.[4] The arguments can be extended in all directions to show that a better society produces a better environment for business.

3. Public Image Another argument in favour of social responsibility is that it improves public image. Each individual firm seeks an enhanced public image so that it may gain more customers, better employees, more responsive money markets and other benefits. A firm which seeks better public image should support social goals.

4. Avoidance of Government Regulation Government is a massive institution with long arms. It seeks to regulate business in the public interest. Government regulation is costly and denies the much needed freedom in decision making. Before the government stretches its long arms, business should discharge its obligation to society.

5. Balance of Responsibility with Power Another argument for social responsibility is that business's responsibility should be more related to its power. It is reasoned that businessmen have vast amounts of social power. They do affect the economy, minorities, and other social problems. In turn, an equal amount of social responsibility is required to match their social power. If each institution is to perform its social role in an orderly relationship with other institutions, then responsibility must be accepted whenever there is power. Any other arrangement invites irresponsible behaviour.[5]

6. Business has the Resources Another argument for social responsibility is that business has a vast pool of resources in terms of men, talents, functional expertise and money. Probably, business is without peers in respect of the resources it possesses. With these resources at its command, business is in a better position to work for social goals.

7. Let Business Try One interesting argument for business social responsibility is a sort of back-handed one. It is that many other institutions have failed in handling social problems, so why not turn to business. Many people are frustrated with the failures of other institutions, and in their frustration, they are turning to business.[6]

8. Prevention is Better Than Cure The last point is that prevention is better than cure. If business delays dealing with social problems now, it may find itself constantly occupied with putting out social fires so that is has no time to accomplish its goal of producing goods and services. Since these social problems must be dealt with at some time, it is actually more economical to deal with them before they develop into serious social breakdowns that consume most of the management's time.[7]

There is no gainsaying the fact that criticism of business is far reaching. The criticism is evidenced by protests at global meetings of WTO since Seattle in 1999 as well as actions targeting individual firms. In 2002, the accounting and governance scandals associated with Enron, WorldCom, and other major corporations have further contributed to the criticism.

Time it is for businesses to become socially more responsive and accountable.

Social responsibility has moral tinge also.

9. Moral Responsibility It is said that the acceptance of corporate social responsibility is the morally correct position. This notion suggests that our modern industrial society faces many serious social problems brought on, to a large extent, by large corporations. The corporations therefore have a moral responsibility to help solve or ameliorate these problems. A corollary to this notion is that because business firms control so many of the resources in our economy, they should devote some of these resources to the overall betterment of society.

10. Citizenship Argument Corporations are institutional members of society. If individual members of the society have an obligation to improve society-to leave the world better than they found it-corporations also have this responsibility. After all, corporations unlike citizens, are created by society. Corporations are citizens, and citizens have civic duties and responsibilities.

11. Duty of Gratitude Business units benefit from society. On the basis of the commonly accepted principle that one owes debts of gratitude towards those who benefit us, the corporation has certain debts that it owes to the society.

12. Globalisation: The recent globalisation of large corporations has led to firms increasingly operating in countries with very different and generally much lower standards of living than found in their respective home countries. More extensive media reach coupled with advances in information technology (e.g. NGO use of websites) has allowed rapid and widespread exposure of alleged corporate abuses even in the remote parts of the globe, as both Shell (oil spills in Nigeria exposed on television documentaries) and Nike (exposure of sweetshop labour conditions in its subcontractor operation in developing countries) have learnt to their cost. Such revelations compel global firms undertake social actions.

Failure to undertake social actions may dent the reputation and brand image of the firms. Infact, firms are likely to be penalised by consumers and other stakeholders, for actions that are not considered socially responsible.

ARGUMENTS AGAINST CSR

Arguments against social responsive actions are equally strong. Some arguments are as follows:

Economic efficiency should be the top priority of any business. Other things shall come later.

1. Profit Maximisation The first and the most forceful argument disfavouring social responsibility is that business has profit maximisation as its main objective. Infact, the business is most socially responsible when it attends to its interests and leaves other activities to other institutions. Since business operates in a world of poverty and hunger, the economic efficiency of business is a matter of top priority and should be the sole mission of business. Business's function is economic, not social and economic values should be the only criteria used to measure success. In this kind of system, managers are the agents of the stockholders, and all their decisions are controlled by their desire to maximise profits for the stockholders while reasonably complying with law and social custom.[8]

2. Society has to Pay the Cost Another argument is that the costs of social responsibility will be passed on to the society and it is the society which must bear them. Can the society afford these additional costs?

3. Lack of Social Skills Business managers are best at managing matters relating to business. They are not equally good at solving social problems. Their outlook is primarily economic and that their skills are the same. They really do not feel at home in social matters. If society is going to depend on someone to work with social problems, why choose a group which is so poorly qualified? Does society really want economic and technical people meddling in social affairs? Will they broaden their outlook and will their skills transfer? Can business really do the job? Is it better equipped than the government and other institutions?[9]

This problem is, however, sought to be overcome to a considerable extent. We have a number of fairly high calibre institutions, like the Xavier Institute of Social Sciences and Institute of Rural Management Anand (IRMA), which train students specifically for social work. Corporates like the Lalbhais, Mafatlals and Shroffs have already attempted to bring in management professionals into the social responsibility area.

4. Business has Enough Power Another argument is that business already has enough social power, therefore, society should not take any steps which give it more power. According to this line of reasoning, business is one of the two or three most powerful institutions in society at the present time. Business influence is felt throughout society. It is felt in education, in government, in the home and in the market-place. It moulds many social values. The process of combining social activities with the established economic activities of business would give business an excessive concentration of power. Business is an institution which is considered to be not so good and giving more power to it is not advisable.

5. Social Overhead Cost Cost on social responsibility is considered to be a social cost which will not immediately benefit the business. Why spend money on an object, the benefits of which will be realised only in the future? It is the heavy social overhead cost which is one of the reasons for the dismal performance of some of our government undertakings.

Businessmen have no direct accountability to people.

6. Lack of Accountability Another point of view is that the businessmen have no direct accountability to the people, therefore, it is unwise to give businessmen responsibility for areas where they are not accountable. Accountability should always go with responsibility, and it is poor social control to allow any other kind of arrangement. Until the society can develop mechanisms which establish direct lines of social accountability from business to the public, business must stand clear of social activities and pursue only its goal of profit where it is directly accountable through the market system.

7. Lack of Broad Support Another point is that business involvement in social goals lack support from all groups in society. If business does become socially involved, it will create so much friction among dissident parties that business cannot perform its social assignment. Although many persons desire business to become more socially involved, others oppose the idea. There is lack of agreement among the general public, among intellectuals, in the government and even among businessmen themselves.[10]

"If you find an executive who wants to take on social responsibility, fire him fast".

8. Drucker, Friedman and Levitt's Views The most cogent criticism has been voiced by the economist Milton Friedman. Friedman based his arguments on two principal contentions, one economic and one legal. From the economic perspective, he asserted that if managers spend corporate funds on projects not intended to maximise profits, the efficiency of the market mechanism will be undermined and resources will be misallocated within the economy. On the legal side, Friedman contended that because managers are legal agents of the stockholders, their sole duty is to maximise the financial return to the stockholders. Hence, if they spend corporate funds for social purposes, they are essentially stealing from the stockholders. Moreover, Friedman suggested that if the stockholders want money spent on social causes, they are free to do so individually with their dividends.

Peter Drucker opposed social responsibility bittaly. Said he,

"If you find an executive who wants to take on social responsibility, fire him fast."

Theodore Levitt argued against corporate social responsibility fearing that business values might come to dominate society. He posited that business, as an institution, would become the twentieth-century equivalent of the medieval church-the all-embracing institution in society. He suggested that this would not be healthy for society.

Nearer at home, we have the late Dhirubhai Ambani, of Reliance fame, who was opposed to corporate social responsibility.

The late Ambani was not a believer in social responsibility.

"As an industrialist my job is", declared he, "to produce goods to satisy the demand. Let us be very clear about it. Everyone has to do his job. My commitment is to produce at the cheapest price and the best quality. If you dabble in everything then you make a mess of things. If we cannot take care of our shareholders and employees and start worrying about the world, then that is hypocrisy"[11].

PROMINENCE OF CSR

Counter arguments notwithstanding, social responsibility has come to stay. In its **1981 Statement of Corporate Responsibility**, the Business Round Table, a group of 200 leaders of large corporations, said that the pursuit of profit and assumption of social responsibility were not incompatible. Social responsibility has been one of the leading topics at 2003 World Economic Forum (WEF) meetings. A report from the WEF observes that the three pressures of corporate competitiveness, corporate governance, and corporate citizenship, and the linkage among them, will play crucial role in shaping the agenda for business leaders in the coming decade. Similarly, the World Business Council for Sustainable Development (WBCSD), a coalition of 120 international businesses, refers to the increasing calls for firms to assume wider responsibilities in the social arena and claims that social responsibility is firmly on the global policy agenda. Among the many other organisations that are advocating greater attention to social responsibility are the Business for Social Responsibility (BSR), and Business in the Community (BITC).

The government of UK has appointed a minister for social responsibility. The European Commission adopted a new strategy on social responsibility in July 2002. The strategy reads thus: "Many businesses have already recognised that social responsibility can be profitable and social actions have mushroomed. However, the EU can add value in atleast two key ways: by helping stakeholders to make social responsibility more transparent and more credible, and by showing that social responsibility is not just for multinations - it can benefit smaller businesses too.

BARRIERS TO CSR

Efforts to achieve greater social responsibility encounter practical problems at every level of the organisation. Awareness of the problems is helpful to take steps to overcome them.

The Individual Manager The individual manager is the person who is ultimately responsible for the social action programmes of any organisation. The manager can initiate, advocate, and put programmes into effect. The manager can also balk, hinder, and prevent programmes from being planned or implemented. Almost all employees in business are employers. Their careers may be in jeopardy if they consistently advocate actions of which their superiors disapprove or if they make unprofitable trade-offs. For this reason, most managers are cautious about proposing significant changes in their organisation's behaviour.

> The manager who can initiate, advocate, and implement social actions himself or herself can be a barrier.

The Organisation At the organisation's level, the greatest barrier is the focus on profits. Social action projects must always be evaluated in terms of the net cost. Shareholders want profits distributed in dividends or invested to expand production. Employees want higher salaries and better working conditions. Against these competing claims, social programmes may have little chance.

> Focus on profit itself is an organizational barrier to social responsibility.

The Industry There may not be support from competitors in the same industry for social action programmes.

The Division Like the organisation of which it is part, a division must try to maintain itself as a profit centre. Any social responsibility decision that reduces the level of profit might threaten the division's viability. Thus, most divisions are slow to initiate socially responsible programmes until they receive clear instructions to do so from the top management.

CSR IMPLEMENTATION

Establishing methods of monitoring social expectations and responsiveness and developing internal social response mechanisms are the two requisites of social responsibility

Social responsibility has two facets: first, to whom the business is accountable and the second, business's responsibility to society. The first relates to accountability of business to its owners, employees, government and consumers. This accountability or responsibility is popularly called *corporate accountability* in the literature available on the subject. Corporate accountability is discussed in this chapter and the responsibility of business to society is dealt with in the next chapter.

Irrespective of the facet of social responsibility, two processes are essential in developing organisation's social responsiveness. First, it is necessary to establish methods of monitoring social demands and expectations in the external environment. Secondly, it is important to develop internal social response mechanisms.[12]

Monitoring Social Demands and Expectations

Important means of assessing social needs and expectations relative to organisations include social forecasting, opinion surveys, issues management, social scanning and social audit.

Social Forecasting This is the systematic process of identifying social trends, evaluating the organisational importance of those trends and integrating these assessments in the organisation's forecasting programme. One approach to social forecasting is the use of *futurists*, individuals who track significant trends in the environment and attempt to predict their impact on the organisation, usually 10 or more years hence. Some organisations use consultants and research institutes that specialise in social forecasting.

Opinion Surveys Associations and major business publications often conduct surveys of public opinion on various issues of social concern. These surveys often provide feedback to companies regarding the perceptions of social responsibility among various groups.

Issues Management This is the process of identifying a relatively small number of emerging social issues of particular relevance to the organisation, analysing their potential impact and preparing an effective response. Typically, 10 to 15 issues are identified, but the number can vary depending on organisational circumstances. Issues management attempts to minimise 'surprises' resulting from environmental forces and to facilitate a proactive stance towards environmental change. Issues management helps identity a definable social need, a potential source of serious stakeholder concern, or the likelihood of government action. Once identified, firms will try to resolve the issue before it reaches a critical stage.

Social Scanning Social scanning is the general surveillance of various elements in the environment to detect the evidence of impending changes that will affect the organisation's social responsibilities. Unlike issues management, social scanning is usually done on an informal and unsystematic basis. Executives frequently draw upon their own experiences of factors that are likely to have important organisational implications. They may also rely on data from more systematic assessments.

Social Audits This is a systematic study and evaluation of social actions of an organisation. It includes an assessment of the social impact of a firm's activities, an evaluation of programmes specifically aimed at achieving social goals, and a determination of areas in need of organisational action. Social audits are difficult to carry out because disagreements can arise regarding what should be included, results can be difficult to measure, and interpretations of what is adequate or good social performance are likely to vary. Nevertheless, companies are increasingly implementing social audits to assess their social action programmers.

Internal Social Response Mechanisms

The most common internal response mechanisms used by firms include executives, temporary task forces, departments or combinations of these.

In relatively small firms, *individual executives* are required to handle social issues, as and when they occur. In some companies, *temporary task forces* are constituted to deal with a critical social issue. When the issue is resolved, the taskforce is disbanded. Many companies will have *permanent departments* that coordinate various ongoing social responsibilities, identify and recommend policies for new social issues. Popularly called the *Public Affairs Department*, such a department may be responsible for coordinating government agencies, community relations and other external activities. In practice, organisations may use a *combination of mechanisms* to enhance social performance.

Corporate Accountability

Coming to the facets of social responsibility, business's responsibility is towards (i) employees, (ii) consumers, (iii) government and (iv) owners (see Fig.34.5).

Figure 34.5 **Corporate Accountability**

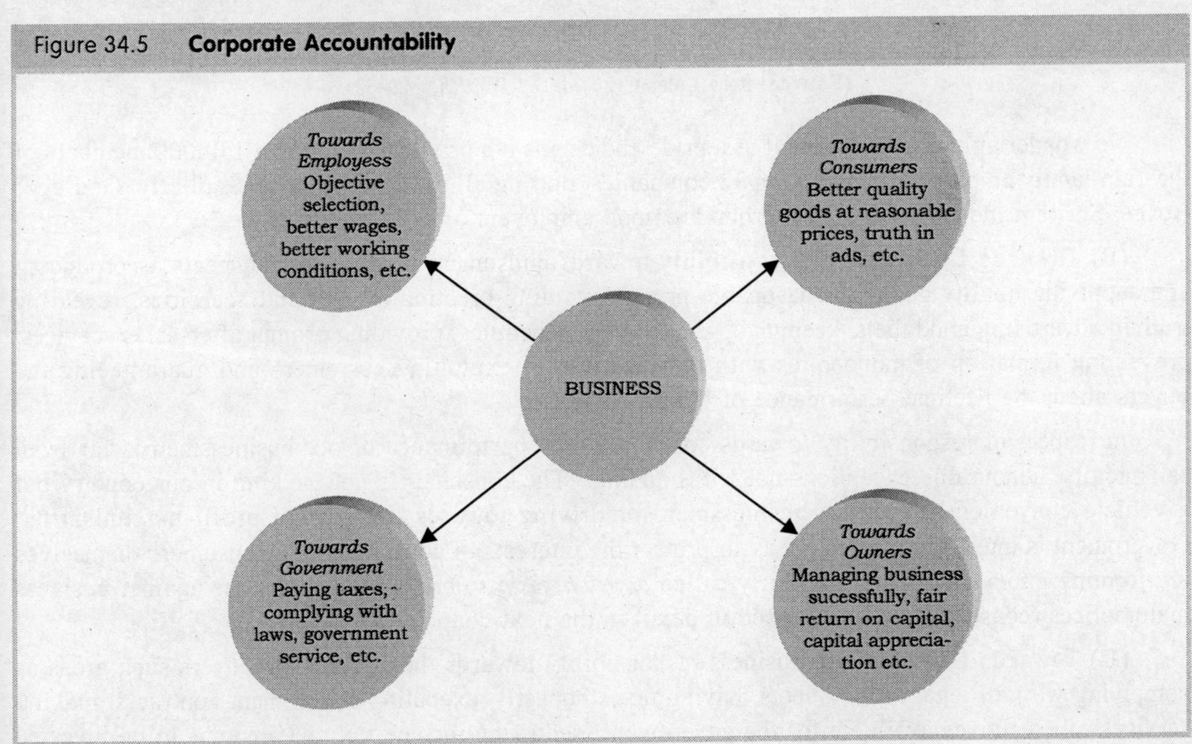

(A) Towards Employees Responsibility towards employees is in the form of just selection, training, promotion, fair wages, levelling out variations in employment, comfortable working conditions, safety and health, social measures, scope for initiation and advancement, participative management, workers' education and the like.

Business is primarily responsible for employees, consumers, government and owners.

It is heartening to note that most business establishments are fully aware of their responsibility towards their employees and are doing a lot for their improvement. The first name to be mentioned is the Tatas who have no peers in the pursuit of labour welfare. It was the Tatas who first introduced many welfare measures for the benefit of their employees and several years later,

Tatas had no peers in the pursuit of labour welfare.

the government made them compulsory for other business houses to follow. Table 34.2 gives the firsts to the credit of Tatas.

Table 34.2 **Firsts of Tatas Towards Employees**

	Tisco Introduction	*Enforced by Law*	*Legal Measures*
Five-Hour Working Day	1912	1948	Factories Act
Free Medical Aid	1915	1948	ESI Act
Welfare Dept.	1917	1948	Factories Act
Works Committees	1919	1947	Industrial Disputes Act
Leave with Pay	1920	1948	Factories Act
Provident Fund	1920	1952	Employees P.F.Act
Accident Compensation	1920	1924	Workmen's Compensation Act
Training of Apprentices	1921	1961	Apprentices Act
Maternity Benefit	1928	1961	Maternity Benefit Act
Profit-Sharing Bonus	1934	1965	Payment of Bonus Act
Gratuity	1937	1972	Gratuity Act

(**Source**: R.M.Lala, *Creation of Wealth*, p.203).

No wonder an individual takes it as a pride and deems it a privilege to join the 150,000 members of the Tata family employed in more than 32 companies, dotting all over the country. Similarly, Godrej & Boyce, Shriram Industries and TVS group are good employers.

(B) Towards Consumers Responsibility towards consumers includes such aspects as producing and supplying quality goods at reasonable prices, avoiding creation of artificial scarcities, revealing truth in advertising and labels, keeping up the delivery schedules, providing prompt after-sales services, preventing formation of monopolies with the intention of exploiting customers and guaranteeing the buyers about the lifetime performance of the products.

In respect of responsibility towards consumers, the performance of our businessmen is far from satisfactory, honourable exceptions not withstanding. The consumer is not the king in our country but a vehicle conveniently used by businessmen for driving towards the goal of profit maximisation. Government is interfering in a big way to protect the interests of consumers and consumers themselves are forming into a movement, popularly called *consumerism* to protect their interests against business malpractices (consumerism is discussed in detail in the next chapter).

(C) Towards Government Business responsibility towards the government covers such areas as complying with all legal requirements, paying taxes honestly, executing government contracts, making services of executives available for the government, deducting income-tax and amounts to be invested in national savings certificates from wages and salaries of employees and acting as a willing partner with the government in pursuit of public welfare.

In respect of responsibility to the government, our businessmen have come under dark clouds. The series of raids conducted on business houses and the reasons made known for the raids demonstrate clearly that businessmen have failed to discharge their responsibility towards the government.

(D) Towards Owners Corporate accountability towards owners covers such areas as managing the business profitably, ensuring fair and regular return on capital employed, guaranteeing capital appreciation and consolidating the financial position of the business so that it can withstand fluctuating fortunes so common in business.

LIMITS TO SOCIAL RESPONSIBILITY

The social responsibility actions of businesses are limited by cost, efficiency, relevance and scope. As a result of these constraints, actions fall short of public expectations.

Social responsibility actions are constrained by cost, efficiency, relevance and scope.

Cost: Social responsibility costs money. Whether a company desires to adopt a village, donate to a college or school, build a hospital, maintain parks or undertake relief operations in times of calamity, it costs money.

Efficiency: Social responsibility affects efficiency adversely. Being obliged to the employees, say a company runs its plant, even if it is incurring losses every year. Its efficiency goes down and its ability to compete is lost.

Relevance: According to several critics, business has no obligation to society. The only obligation is to run the business successfully. Social responsibility is irrelevant. According to Friedman, for example, "*There is one and only one social responsibility of business: to use its resources and energy in activities designed to increase its profits so long as it stays within the rules of the game*...(and) *engages in open and free competition, without deception and trend*...". Friedman contends that corporate officials are in no position to determine the relative urgency of social problems or the amount of organisational resources that should be committed to a given problem. He also insists that managers who devote corporate resources to pursue personal, and perhaps misguided notions of the social good, unfairly tax their own shareholders, employees and customers. In short, business should produce goods and services efficiently and leave the solution of social problems to the concerned individuals and government agencies.[13]

Often, social responsibility action is undertaken for wrong reasons rendering the exercise to irrelevance and ineffectiveness. Consider what has happened to Brij Mohan Khaitan, the tea giant. In the beginning of 1990s, Khaitan was under tremendous pressure from the Bodo Security Force (BSF). One of his executives was kidnapped and another was gunned down by the militants. BSF demanded hefty sums as a pre-condition for peace. It was at this time that Khaitan reflected and set up a school at a cost of Rs.22 crore. The school could not help Khaitan buy peace from the BSF[14].

Scope and Complexity: Society's problems are too massive, too complex, and too deep seated to be solved by even the most socially conscientious company or even by all companies acting together.

The problems such as environmental pollution-acid rain, ozone depletion, destruction of rain forests; health problems-AIDS, drug and tobacco use; racial discrimination; sex discrimination; ethnic and religious animosities and the like defy solutions however conscientious one might be.

Business has its own limitations. It should deliver quality goods at reasonable prices, earn profits for shareholders, pay taxes to the government and plan strategies to survive in the competitive world. Amidst such varied problems, how can business solve yet another complex problem, *viz*., social responsibility?

COMMON CHARACTERISTICS

As the 1990s wear on, more and more companies are realising that they can no more function or be judged solely on the basis of their thick bottom lines. A positive impact on employees, customers and

More and more companies are realizing that their actions can no longer be judged by their thick bottom lines.

the community at large has assumed an equal or even greater significance in the overall picture. This realisation has made them undertake socially responsive actions. All companies with social orientation exhibit 14 characteristics as shown in Table 34.3.

Table 34.3 **Common Characteristics of Socially Responsible Firms**

1. Initially founded by far-sighted people who visibly set the firm's moral tone.
2. Stuck to the basics and produced only high quality goods and services for specific market niches.
3. Developed a public image that emphasised their commitment to quality and often used non-traditional means to promote it.
4. Firmly practised the dual principles of self-management and decentralisation.
5. Brought in outside people to provide needed talent and additional perspectives.
6. Encouraged all employees to become part of the shared mission through full worker participation in decisions.
7. Paid fairly and usually offered benefit packages exceeding the competition.
8. Emphasised a democratic people orientation and did without executive perks.
9. Constantly solicited feedback from customers on all subjects from product direction to corporate donations.
10. Top managers possessed an extensive knowledge of current events and took a wide-ranging interest in affairs outside their business.
11. Offered donations in cash or services to people in need of help.
12. Took an active role in the operations of their local communities.
13. Deal with like-minded businesses and encourage their employees to do the same.
14. Constantly look to the future but always pay attention to the past.

THE EVOLVING IDEA OF SOCIAL RESPONSIBILITY

The social responsibility idea evolved over a period of time. Some major stages in the long history are outlined here.

Business Social Responsibilities in Classical Economic Theory[15]

The classical economic theory assigned profit making as the sole objective of business.

Throughout history, classical economic theory has been the fundamental inspiration of people in business. In the classical economic view, a business is acting in a socially responsible fashion if it utilizes resources as efficiently as possible to produce goods and services that society wants at prices consumers are willing to pay. The sole objective of business is to maximize profits while operating, of course, within the law. If this is done, say classical theorists, firms carry out their major responsibility.

This easily understood goal, derived from Adam Smith's *Wealth of Nations,* was never sought in business practice without reservations. Even Adam Smith voiced a surprising number of exceptions to his principles for social reasons. Throughout our history, business and business people have modified the strict profit maximization principle to address social concerns-not much at first, but more and more over time. Nevertheless, today, this fundamental classical ideology remains entrenched.

The Eighteenth and Nineteenth Centuries

In the colonial era, businesses were very small. Merchants practised thrift and frugality, which were dominant virtues then. But charity was a co-existing virtue and the owners of these small enterprises made contributions to schools, churches and the poor.

In the early nineteenth century, companies were not effusive in their social concerns. Charitable contributions continued and grew over time as great fortunes in business were made. In most cases, wealthy entrepreneurs who gave their fortunes to benefit society did so without any reference to the interests of the companies that were the fountainheads of their wealth.

For instance, John D. Rockefeller, who accumulated a fortune in the second half of the nineteenth century, gave in his lifetime, more than $550 million and endowed the Rockefeller Foundation, "*to promote the well-being of mankind throughout the world*." Andrew Carnegie gave away $350 million during his lifetime to social causes, built 2,811 public libraries and gave 7,689 organs to American churches.[16]

Changing Views of Social Responsibility in the Late Nineteenth and Early Twentieth Centuries

During the latter part of the nineteenth century and into the twentieth, a number of forces converged to lead business leaders, especially of the larger corporations, to address social problems out of self-interest. Vigorous industrial growth had many negative social impacts. Business feared new government regulations and sought to blunt their urgency. Business leaders, many of whom by this time were not the original entrepreneurs, but owned only a small part of the stock of the companies they managed, felt freer to use corporate assets for social action. Business sought and found arguments to circumvent the *ultra vires* doctrine.

By the 1920s, three inter-related themes had emerged to justify broader business social responsibility. *First*, managers were *trustees,* that is, agents whose corporate roles put them in positions of power where they could enhance the welfare of not only stockholders, but others such as customers, employees and communities. *Secondly*, managers believed they had an obligation to *balance* the interests of these groups. They were, in effect, coordinators who reconciled the competing claims of multiple stakeholders on their enterprises. And *thirdly*, many managers subscribed to the *service principle,* a principle with two distinct definitions. One definition was a near-spiritual belief that business, simply by operating for profit, had the power to redeem society by creating a broad general welfare. If individual managers served society by making a business economically successful; the aggregate business system would then work to eradicate social injustice, poverty and other ills. A second understanding of the service principle, however, was that although the capitalist system elevated humanity, individual companies and managers were still obligated to undertake social programmes to benefit or serve the public.

Three developments-trusteeship, balancing of interests, and service-gave boost to social responsibility.

These three inter-related ideas-trusteeship, balancing of interests and service-were accepted by more and more business and opinion leaders. Although uplifting, they did not foster lavish contributions for social programmes, nor did they divert most individual managers from their *laissez-faire* attitudes and dominant emphasis on profits.[17]

The Contemporary View of Social Responsibility

In the last forty years, the concept of business social responsibility has continued to evolve and expand. Today, the efficient use of resources to make a profit is still seen as the primary social responsibility of business. But added to economic performance are the ideas of previous eras about the meaning of social responsibility. The view that total social responsibilities are broader than simple economic responsibilities, has become more compelling, more accepted by managers and more widely put into practice than ever before.

The range of social programs assumed by business has continuously expanded since the early years of the century. Today, corporations carry out a wide array of social actions. The span includes programmes for education, public health, employee welfare, housing, urban renewal, environmental protection, resource conservation, day-care centres for working parents and many others. In each of these areas, the programmes that different corporations have implemented run into thousands.[17]

In a way, social responsiveness arises from the impacts of corporate actions on society.

The fundamental reason why the concept and range of social responsibilities have expanded is that accelerating industrial activity continuously changes society. In this situation, social responsibilities arise from the impacts of corporate actions on society. And we know more today about adverse consequences of some business activities. For example, early in this century, carcinogens in industrial effluents were unknown.

Social programmes also arise from the intractable social problems in the corporate's environment.

Corporate social programmes also arise from a second source-intractable social problems in the corporation's environment. "*A healthy business and a sick society are hardly compatible*," notes Peter Drucker. Racism, wars, violent crime, epidemics such as AIDS and failing schools are societal pathologies a corporation has not caused but may benefit from mitigating.

INDIAN SCENARIO[19]

The idea of social responsibility is very old in our country. The concept of parting with a portion of one's surplus wealth for the good of society is neither modern nor a Western import into India. The business community occupied a significant place in ancient Indian society. Merchants were treated with respect and civility and regarded as an instrument of social good, not least because of their philanthropy. Nourished by a social and religious ethic which put charitable giving high on its list of virtues, charity was an ingrained part of the life of most hereditary merchant communities that form the backbone of the modern business class.

The idea of corporate charity was unique to India.

Merchants provided relief in times of famine or epidemics by throwing open godowns of food and treasure chests to look after the needy; built and supported temples, *dharamshalas* (pilgrim rest houses), night shelters, bathing *ghats,* water tanks, wells and *panjrapoles* (animal refuges) and provided drinking water facilities. They donated for education in traditional schools and even for dowries for poor girls.

The practice of business giving continued through the ages, though as economic, political and social conditions changed, so did business response to social needs. This can be summed up as a shift from merchant charity to corporate citizenship. Four phases in the shift are distinct.

Four Phases of Modern Philanthropy 1850 - 1914

The first shift was from a more or less purely ameliorative charity for religious reasons and causes during the pre-industrial era (pre-1850), towards the more Western form of philanthropy in the period 1850-1914. The period saw the beginnings of industrialisation in India and like their counterparts in the West, the new rich business families began to set up trusts and endow a host of modern institutions such as schools, colleges, hospitals, orphanages and widows homes, art galleries and museums for the welfare of society and the preservation and propagation of Indian culture. At the same time, they continued to contribute to older forms of charity such as building and maintenance of temples, *dharamshalas* and water tanks so that there were elements of both charity and philanthropy in business giving. The Gujarati and Parsi business communities of Mumbai in particular, led by Jamsetji Jejeebhoy, Jamsetji Tata, Sir Dinshaw Petit and Premchand Roychand, spearheaded the new trend. The early pioneers of industry were leaders not only in the economic but also the social fields and took active interest and part in the religious and social reforms and in public life.

1914 - 1960

In the second phase (1914-1960), which was the golden period of both Indian capitalism and business philanthropy, there was a maturing of philanthropic practice. Apart from making political donations for the freedom struggle, business also contributed to many of the social and cultural causes associated with the movement such as revival of Indian art and culture, nationalist education and so on. Many of India's leading businessmen-GD Birla, Jamnalal Bajaj, Lala Shri Ram, Ambalal Sarabhai and others came under the spell of Mahatma Gandhi and his theory of trusteeship of wealth. They contributed liberally to his programmes for the removal of untouchability, women's emancipation and rural reconstruction, even as the earlier preoccupation with creating a physical and social institutional infrastructure continued, further honed by the vision of a free, progressive and modern India.

When India became free, the independent state looked to the business community to propel the country to a prosperous future and in the euphoria of Independence, the business class, confident of its capabilities, responded both by creating more wealth and utilising it for non-business purposes. Several business leaders like GD Birla, JRD Tata, Lala Shri Ram, Kasturbhai Lalbhai and others, endowed institutes of scientific and technical research as well as art academies and institutes for the study of Indian history and culture. Many of the best Indian institutions in several fields, such as the Tata Institute of Fundamental Research, the Birla Institutes of Technology at Pilani and Ranchi, the Calico Textile Museum, Ahmedabad to name but a few, owe their existence to private business munificence of the time.

1960 - 1980

The next shift came in the 1960s which ushered in an era of economic and political troubles and saw the business community operating under several constraints. The state also took on many of the obligations that were traditionally the responsibility of the society as a whole, such as education, care of the sick, relief in the wake of natural calamities and care of the destitute. It led to a corresponding decrease of interest in private philanthropy. Mistrust of business consequent to sharp and unethical practices by some, coupled with high taxes to finance state-led development, further contributed to the disinclination to part with private wealth for public benefit. Ironically, the high tax regime aided by a deterioration in business morality led to a large expansion in the establishment of charitable trusts for purposes of tax planning.

The disillusionment consequent to the failure of the government to remove poverty and bring about social change at the pace required to remove the ever widening gap between the rich and the poor and to provide a richer quality of life, led to a renewed interest in private initiative to spearhead change. It made individuals look to voluntarism as a solution and an alternative to official action, and made business more conscious of the need to contribute to approved national development goals.

The 1970s thus saw a renewed corporate interest in social concerns and a new element emerged on the philanthropic scene-corporate philanthropy, as distinct from family business philanthropy. Spurred partly by the realisation that supporting community development through philanthropic giving is in their own best business interests and partly by the use of the carrot and stick method by the government, several business leaders began to advocate more social responsibility on the part of business. Of this, philanthropic giving was only one aspect, the others being more ethical business practices and concern for the physical environment in which business operated. There was a diversification in the causes supported, such as afforestation, science education for the people, preservation of monuments, women's rights and consumer education.

1980 -

The post-1980 period saw an upswing in business fortunes due to economic reforms and other factors and with it, a re-emergence of self-confidence. It increased both business willingness and ability to give, as well as public and government expectations of business. This contemporary phase, characterised by corporate citizenship, has seen a further swing away from charity and traditional philanthropy towards more direct engagement in mainstream development concerns and in helping disadvantaged groups in the society.

In sum, the development of business and industry in India has been accompanied by a clear change in the attitudes of society and the business community itself about its obligations to society and how they need to be expressed. It may be stated that the shift from merchant charity to corporate citizenship is not complete and it is not unusual to find all the three-charity, philanthropy and corporate citizenship-being practised by the same business family or corporation.

Table 34.4 gives details about what corporate India has done in the name of social responsibility.

Table 34.4 **An Illustrative List of the Philanthropic Activities of Some Companies/Groups**

Company/ Groups	*Major Institutions Established*	*Company's Community Programme*	*Trusts/Foundations*	*Fields Supported*
Tatas	• Indian Institute of Science • Tata Institute of Social Sciences • Tata Memorial Rural Cancer Project • Tata Agriculture and Rural Training Centre for the Blind, Gujarat • Tata Memorial Centre for Cancer Research • Tata Institute of Fundamental Research • National Centre for Performing Arts • Tata Energy Research Institute • National Institute of Advanced Studies • Management Centre for Human Values	Through each individual company coordinated by Tata Council for Community Initiatives	• Lady Tata Memorial Trust • Lady Meherbai D Tata Trust • JRD Tata Trust • Jamsetji Tata Trust • Sir Dorabji Tata Trust • Sir Ratan Tata Trust • JN Tata Endowment Fund for Higher Education	Scientific research education, health and community services, education in social work, art and culture, medicine, energy research, rural development
Birlas(All Groups)	• Birla Institutes of Technology Pilani and Ranchi • Birla Institute of Scientific Research • Birla Eco. Research Foundation • Calcutta Medical Research Institute • BM Birla Heart Research Centre	Slum clearance scheme, Tenements for slum dwellers in Hyderabad	• Hindustan Charity Trust • BM Birla Foundation • KK Birla Foundation • MP Birla Foundation	Technical education, agricultural research, medicine, art and culture, scientific research, education, temple building, renovation and archaeology

Company/ Groups	*Major Institutions Established*	*Company's Community Programme*	*Trusts/Foundations*	*Fields Supported*
	• Birla Archaeological and Cultural Research Institute • Birla Academy of Arts and Culture • Planetariums in various cities • Temples-Venkateshwara, Lakshmi Narayan, Kali, Hanuman, Natraj, Govind Deoji • Sanskrit Kala Mandir, Varanasi • Sangeet Sagar, Calcutta. • JD Birla Institute of Home Science • Schools and Colleges, e.g. Modern High School, Rani Birla Girls College			
Videocon				Sports
Essar Group		Schools around plant		
Singhania	• Institute of Applied Physics and Technology, Allahabad • JK Institute of Sociology and Human Relations, Lucknow • Institute of Radiology and Cancer Research Centre • Institute of Cardiology • Lakshmipat Singhania Academy • Kamlapat Memorial Hospital, Kanpur • Sunitidevi Singhania Hospital and Medical Research Centre, Bombay • Pushpawati Singhania Research Institute for Liver and Renal and Digestive Diseases	Maintaining ambulances, blood banks, relief vans, laboratories	• Lala Kamalpat Primary School Building Trust • Lakshmipat Singhania Education Foundation • Lakshmipat Singhania Medical Foundation • Kailashpat Singhania Sports Foundation	Primary education, higher education, technical education, social sciences, medicine and health care, religion and values, sports activities, city beautification

Company/ Groups	*Major Institutions Established*	*Company's Community Programme*	*Trusts/Foundations*	*Fields Supported*
	• Laksmipat Singhania Auditorium • Shripati Singhania Auditorium • Temples			
Larsen and Toubro	• L&T Institute of Technology, Bombay • Polytechnics	Life Line Express (Train), Hospital on wheels, L&T Welfare Centre, Family planning, Mother and child care, TB and Leprosy, AIDS control, TB clinic, Skills for self-employment, Tree plantation		Health, community welfare, etc., in Mumbai at HQ and around plants
Thapar Group	• Thapar Institute of Engineering and Technology, Patiala • Football Academy, Punjab	Development of factory and neighbourhood		Technical education, sports, community welfare
Modis/All groups	• Shri Modi Eye Hospital and Ophthalmic Research Centre • MM Modi Degree College • Sanskrit Pathshala • Sainik Bhawan	• Adult Education Centre • Mahila Samaj Kalyan Parishad • Samaj Kalyan Vibhag	• RB Multianimal Modi Charitable Trust • Modi Science Foundation • Modi Foundation • Dayawati Modi Foundation	Medicine, scientific research, welfare of women, education, community welfare, religious and spiritual education
Godrej	• Dr BP Godrej Students Centre • SP Hakimji School • Foundation for Medical Research • Godrej Sailing Club	Family planning centres, well baby clinics, Godrej Ganga Ecology Panel	• Pirojsha Godrej Foundation • Soonabai Pirojsha Godrej Foundation	Education, health and medicine, sports, environment and wildlife, conservation of nature nature, family planning, arts

Company/ Groups	*Major Institutions Established*	*Company's Community Programme*	*Trusts/Foundations*	*Fields Supported*
	• Naoroj Pirojsha Godrej Boating Station • Godrej Technical Institute • Pirojsha Godrej Research Lab • Soonabai Godrej Dance Academy • Pirojsha Godrej National Conservation centre			
Hero Honda	• Bahadur Chand Munjal Arya Model Senior Secondary School	Mobile clinics, schools, mini ITI round company units		Education, environment, health, sports
Hindustan Levers		Reclamation of land at Etah, dairy development at Etah, adopted Etah for development work, rural schools programme		Community development, rural education
Mahindra & Mahindra			• Mahindra Foundation • KC Mahindra Education Trust	Education, health, environment
Usha Martin		Krishi Gram Vikas Kendra to implement rural development programmes		Community development
MRF	• MRF Football Academy		• MRF Pace Foundation	Sports
TVS		Community development work around factory units		Rural community development

Company/ Groups	*Major Institutions Established*	*Company's Community Programme*	*Trusts/Foundations*	*Fields Supported*
ACC		Restoration and rehabilitation of used up mining area forming water bodies of rain water, recontouring afforestation, landscaping parks, creating green belts & bird sanctuaries, pollution control equipments		Environment, community development
RAMCO	• PAC Ramaswamy Raja Polytechnic • PA Chinnaiha Raja Memorial High School • PACR Ammani Ammal's Girls Higher Secondary School • TAKM Tamammal Elementary School • Sri Ram Primary School • Chinmaya Vidyalaya • Ramaswamy Raja Matriculation Higher Secondary School • RAMCO Industrial Training Institute • PAC Ramaswamy Raja Hospital • Temples • Hall at Loyala College • Sri Sarda College for Women • Sri Sankara College	• Anti Polio Campaign • Vision Research Foundation • Anti Asthma Camps • Marriage Halls • Seminar Halls • Community Hall • Sri Meenakshi Sundershwar Temple	• Raja Charity Trust • PAC Ramaswamy Raja Education Charity Trust • PACR Sethurammal Charity Trust	Education, medical and health care, community welfare, culture, heritage and arts
Bajaj	• Institute of Gandhian Studies • Gandhi Centre for Science and Human Values • Jamnalal Bajaj Institute of		• Jamnalal Bajaj Foundation • Jamnalal Bajaj Seva Trust • Kamal Nayan	Community development, higher education, upliftment of widows/orphans,

Company/ Groups	*Major Institutions Established*	*Company's Community Programme*	*Trusts/Foundations*	*Fields Supported*
	Management Studies • Shiksha Mandal • Gita Pratishthan • Gandhi Gyan Mandir • Gitai Mandir		Bajaj Charitable Trust	scholarships, spiritual and cultural development, literacy
ITC	• ITC Sangeet Research Academy	Tree plantation in cities, parks		Indian culture and heritage, sports, environment, education wildlife, welfare of handicapped
Apeejay Surrendra	• Apeejay Schools • Kamala Memorial Society for the Handicapped • Medical Research Centre		• Apeejay Trust	Education, health, vocational training
Mafatlal (Arvind Mafatlal Group)	• Vidhyadham Higher Secondary School • Sri Ram Sanskrit Maha Vidyalaya • Shri Ram Mitra Mandal • Dr Manibhai Desai Management Training Centre		• Shri Sadguru Seva Sangha Trust	Community health care, family welfare, sports, education, livestock development, agriculture development, empowerment of women through education, self employment, famine relief
Magor-Macneill Williamson and Co Ltd	• Magor Football Academy • Sports Stadium, Tinsukhia • Prince of Wales Technical Institute • Dibrugarh Medical College • Assam Valley School • Assam Gallery and Arts Centre, Guwahati	Community health programmes through hospitals, Diagnostic Centre at Tea Estate, schemes of self-employment, tree plantation (trees for life), Assam Valley Sports, ecology	• Magor Education Trust	Literature and arts, education, community health and welfare programmes, self-employment, environment, higher education,

Company/ Groups	Major Institutions Established	Company's Community Programme	Trusts/Foundations	Fields Supported
		Wildlife Society, irrigation and flood control		
Murugappa Chettiar Group	• AMM Education Society • Vellayan Chettiar Higher Secondary School • Sri Ramaswamy Mudaliar Higher Secondary School • TI Matriculation School • AMM Matriculation School • Arunachalam Higher Secondary School • Murugappa Polytechnic, Avadi • AMM Medical Society • AMM Hospital • Valliammai Achi Hospital • Sir Ivan Steadforth Hospital, Ambattur • AMM Murugappa Chettiar Research Centre • Temples		• AMM Foundation • AMM Charities Trust	Education, medicine and health, scientific research, self-employment schemes, community welfare measures
TCI Bhorukia Group of Companies	• Bhoruramji Ram Das Public School • Indian Institute of Health Management Research, Jaipur	In Rajasthan villages	• Bhoruka Charitable Trust • PD Agarwal Foundation	Integrated community development programme, education, health education
Deepak Group of Companies		Health care, promotion of smokeless chulla, community bio gas, education and family planning	• Deepak Medical Foundation • Deepak Charitable Trust	Integrated community development, health and education
Chandaria Group			• Anarde Foundation	Integrated rural development

Company/ Groups	*Major Institutions Established*	*Company's Community Programme*	*Trusts/Foundations*	*Fields Supported*
Shri Ram (DCM Group)	• Shri Ram College of Commerce • Lady Shri Ram College for Women • Shri Ram Bharatiya Kala Kendra • Shri Ram Centre for Performing Arts • Shri Ram Institute of Industrial Research	• SIEL's Community Programme	• Shri Ram Education Trust	Education, technical and scientific research, art and culture

(**Source** : Pushpa Sundar, *Beyond Business,* TMH, New Delhi pp. 368-377)

QUESTIONS

1. Define social responsibility.
2. Why is social responsibility important for business?
3. What are your arguments against social responsibility?
4. What are the practical problems that confront social action programmes? How do you overcome them?
5. Trace the historical evolution of social responsibility.

ASSIGNMENT

Pick up five firms, which you feel are socially responsive. Study about their annual budget allocation for CSR and which are all the actions they undertake in the name of CSR. Prepare a report.

REFERENCES

1. C.N.Vakil(Ed.), *Industrial Development of India-Policy and Problems*, p.429.
2. Stoner and Freeman, *Management*, p.112.
3. James E. Post *et.al., Business and Society,* McGraw-Hill, 1999, p.85-86.
4. George A.Steiner and Jalin F. Stenier, *Business, Government and Society*, McGraw-Hill, 1997, p.165.
5. Michacl E.Porter and Mark R. Kramer, *The Competitive Advantage of Corporate Philanthropy,* HBR, Dec. 2002, p.57.
6. Gray and Smeltzer, *Management-The Competitive Edge*, p.87.
7. Keith Davis and Robert L.Blomstrom, *Business and Society-Environment and Responsibility*, p.24.
8. *Ibid*, p.25.
9. *Ibid*, p.27.
10. *Ibid*, p.28.
11. *Ibid*, p.30.
12. *Ibid*, p.30.
13. *Ibid*, p.33.
14. Gita Piramal, *Business Maharajas*, New Delhi, Penguin, 1996, p.15.
15. Kathryn M. Bartol and David C. Martin, *Management*, McGraw-Hill, 1998, p.113.
16. Cited in *Management* by Stoner and Freeman, p.98.
17. Gita Piramal, *Op.Cit.,* p.294.
18. George A. Steneir and John F. Steiner, *Business, Government and Society*, McGraw-Hill, 1997, p.106.
19. Pushpa Sundar, *Beyond Business*, New Delhi, TMH, 2000, Pp-10-13.

CHAPTER OUTLINE

Nature and Models of Social Responsibility
Ecology and Business
- Natural Pollution
- Population Explosion
- Standard of Living
- Deforestation
- Vehicular Traffic
- Heavy Irrigation
- Agriculture
- Industry the Scapegoat
- Ecology & Economic Development
- Sustainable Development

Women and Business Opportunities
- Women in Business
- Problem of Female Employment

Child Labour
- Why are Children Employed?
- Universal Phenomenon
- Remedies

Consumerism
- Cost of Consumer Protection

Rural Development
Projects and People
Physically Handicapped
Fighting AIDS

35 Business and Society

LEARNING OBJECTIVES

After reading this Chapter, you should be able to:

1. Understand how ecology is disrupted by different polluting agents
2. Understand that industry is only one of the agents causing pollution, and what the industry is doing to prevent pollution
3. Understand that ecology and development go together
4. Appreciate the obligations of business towards women
5. Understand that child labour is exploited everywhere and suggest ways of preventing abuse of child labour
6. Understand business obligations towards consumers, rural poor, disabled citizens and AIDS victims

The first aspect of social responsibility of business, namely, its immediate accountability to consumers, employees, owners and government was discussed in the previous chapter. In this chapter, it is proposed to discuss the second part of social responsibility, namely, business's responsibility to society.

Business's responsibility towards society goes beyond the interest of its stakeholders.

Responsibility of business towards society includes such broad areas as concern for ecology; consumerism; improving the lot of women; rural development; new projects; physically handicapped people and fighting AIDS.

(See Fig. 35.1) Business may or may not have direct or day-to-day interaction with these interest groups. But business has obligations towards women, child labour, ecology and village development which are a part of society. The well-being of society is the well-being of business.

ECOLOGY AND BUSINESS

Ecology is concerned with the relationships of living things and their environment. It provides a framework by which we can see that all living things are related to other living things, and they are likewise related to their physical environment.

The eminent humanist-biologist, Paul Ehrlich, in this book, *The Population Bomb* listed seven inalienable rights of mankind:

- The right to eat well,
- The right to drink pure water,

Figure 35.1 **Business and Society**

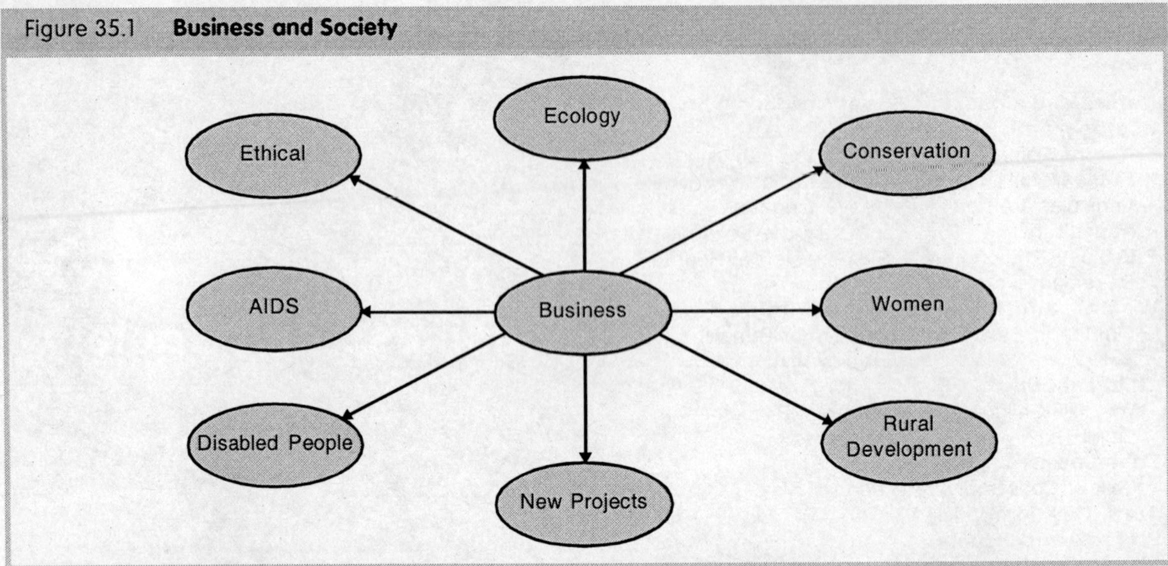

- The right to decent, uncrowded shelter,
- The right to enjoy natural beauty,
- The right to avoid pesticide poisoning,
- The right to freedom from thermo nuclear war and
- The right to limit families.[1]

The rights propounded by the eminent thinker have proved to be mere fantasises as day-by-day, the rights themselves are being alienated from the tchnology savvy human; thanks to the ever increasing environmental pollution which is disrupting the ecology.

Pollution of air, water and soil is caused by several agents. The main among them are:

- Natural pollution,
- Population explosion,
- High standard of living of people,
- Deforestation,
- Vehicular traffic,
- Agriculture,
- Dams and canals
- Industrial establishments.

Natural Pollution

Nature causes air pollution enormously. Duststorms, dirt and debris into the air, natural forest fires cast a pall of smoke over mountain valleys, and lightening creates certain chemical compounds. The pollution from volcanoes is phenomenal. The Director of the United States Geological Survey, states that only three eruptions in the last 150 years-Krakotoa in Java in 1883, Mt.Katmai in Alaska in 1912 and Hekla in Iceland in 1947 have produced more air pollution than mankind in all of history.[2]

Perhaps the most uncomfortable and irritating of all natural pollutants, as many victims of allergies can testify, is the pollen released everyday by trillions of plants. This pollution causes great human suffering.

Population Explosion

Population explosion, characteristically called, the population bomb, is probably the biggest source of pollution. It is estimated that world population is doubling every thirty-five years. If existing rates continue, population of over three billion will be over six billion by the year 2000.[3]

Population is the biggest pollutant.

What makes population explosion serious is that every additional person adds pollutants to land, air and water. It is rightly said that man is a dirty animal. He is poisoning his world. He has managed to make rivers rotten, converted green pastures into deserts, and has choked the air with chemicals and dust. He is a menace to himself and other species.[4]

Standard of Living

Industrialisation has raised the standard of living enormously. Increased standard of living acts as a source of pollution. As people consume more, their consumption tends to create more wastes. The more elegant their tastes for food become, the more garbage and other refuge they produce. The more they buy, the more paper and packaging are required, most of which become refuge.

Contrary to the popular perception, pollution is not caused by poor people alone. Poor and rich alike cause damage to the environment for different reasons, one for sheer survival and another for leading grand lifestyles.

Take the case of the rich. Rich constitutes just 25 per cent of the world's population but enjoy fruits of extremely uneven economic development. The rich consume disproportionately higher share of resources to maintain their lifestyle. For example, this 25 per cent uses 80% of commercial energy while the remaining 75 per cent in 128 countries use only 20 per cent energy. The per capita consumption of plywood, particle wood and veneer is 213 kgs as against 19 kgs for the poor. Per capita consumption of cereals among the rich is 716 kgs but in poor Africa it is just 130 kgs. The average annual per capita milk consumption of the rich is 320 kgs, as against 39 kgs for the poor. Similarly, the per capita consumption of paper and paper products is 148 kgs (11 kgs for the poor), of fertilisers 70 kgs (15 kgs) and concrete and concrete housing 451 kgs (130 kgs). While 80% of iron and steel is used by the rich, only 20 per cent is used by the poor. Nearly 85 per cent of metals, minerals, and chemicals, 70 per cent of fossil fuels, 90 per cent of automobiles, and 85 per cent chemical products are used by the rich.

Higher the consumption, greater the scope for causing pollution.

Poor also causes pollution, but for its sheer survival. They resort to woodcutting, wood being used both as firewood and as marketable product. Illiteracy and ignorance make them lead unhygienic and unhealthy life. Spitting and defecating in the open are common sites. The late Prime Minister Indira Gandhi had said that the poor are the greatest polluters.

Deforestation

Forests are an essential part of the environment. They check soil erosion, counter floods and landslides, shelter vast variety of flora and fauna and cause rainfalls. The Chipko slogan best sums up the importance of forests. The slogan reads thus:

Forests bear soil, water and air which are the essence of life.

> "What do the forests bear
> Soil, water and pure air.
> Soil, water and pure air
> Are the bases of life."

Man has systematically ravaged forests for his agricultural operations, cooking purposes and for lumbering. It is estimated that we are losing 1.3 million hectares of our forests every year due to deforestation. Inspite of having 15 per cent of the world's population and despite the 1952 forest policy statement laying down that at least one third of the land area must be under forests, we have less than one per cent of the productive forest area left (See Fig. 35.2 for more data).

Figure 35.2 **India's Forest Cover (State-wise as per 1995 Assessment)**

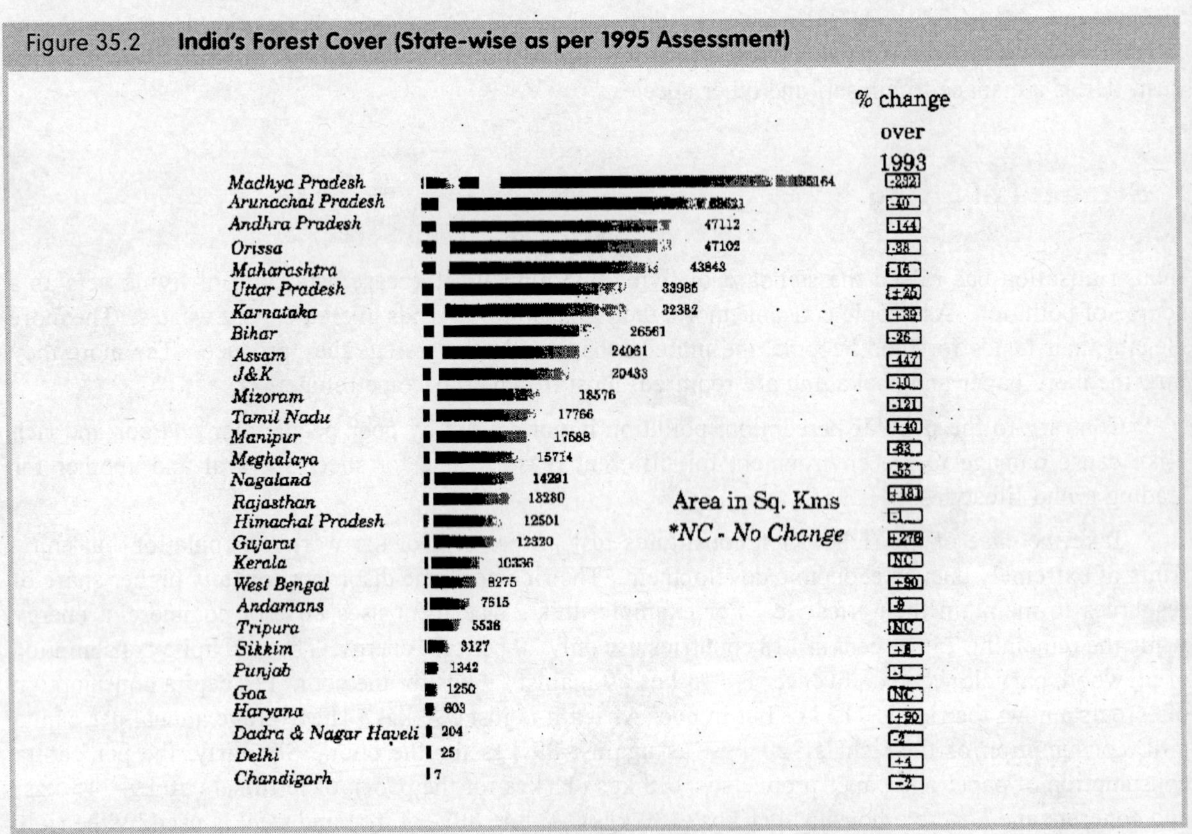

Besides destruction by man, danger to forests comes from acid rain which is common in the industrialised countries. In the Federal Republic of Germany (FRG), 34 per cent of the nation's forests were dead by 1981 due to acid precipitation.

In FRG, the problem is so serious that a new word, '*Waldsterben*' (forest death) has entered the vocabulary and the agenda of virtually all political parties. In Poland, 1,80,000 hectares of forests are reported to be dead or dying as a result.[5]

Vehicular Traffic

Damage to the environment caused by vehicular traffic is equally significant. Moving vehicles cause both air and noise pollution. Pollution of the air is the severest and there are agencies to monitor the magnitude of the problem.

As on today, there are more than 1.3 million registered vehicles plying on Delhi roads and about 1,20,000 are being added annually. These vehicles emit more than 800 tonnes of noxious gases into Delhi's atmosphere everyday. This constitutes more than 60 per cent of the air pollution of the city. During the peak traffic hours, emissions from vehicles amount to 1500 kg of carbon monoxide, 100 kg of hydrocarbon and 100 kg of nitrogen oxides. Two and three wheeler vehicles constitute about 63 per cent of the total vehicles and contribute 60 per cent of the total carbon monoxide and 83 per cent of the hydro carbon emissions. Heavy traffic, on the other hand, contributes to 55 per cent to 80 per cent of the nitrogen oxide emission. Thus, on an average, each vehicle emits approximately 2.5 kg of pollutants per day. Oxides of nitrogen and carbon monoxide are known as air pollutants, causing enormous damage to human health. Besides, the oxides of nitrogen react with rainwater to produce acid rain.[6]

Vehicular traffic destroys ecology considerably

Noise pollution caused by vehicles has reached such alarming proportions that sign boards with '*no horn please*' are seen near hospitals and schools in all cities. In fact, life has become traunatic in most of the cities, thanks to incessant blowing of horns, continuous ear-splitting noise from vehicles.

Heavy Irrigation

Heavy irrigation schemes like canals and dams are pollutants. Waterlogging and increased salinity and alkalinity of soil are the manifestations of this type of pollution.

The great Aswan Dam on the Nile River is often quoted to substantiate the charge that heavy irrigation schemes cause considerable damage to the environment. The dam was to offer countless benefits to Egyptians who needed flood protection, a more stable water supply and irrigation for parched desert farm lands. Predictions indicated that the entire lower Nile valley would be a better life area because of the dam.

Now that the dam has been built, unforeseen negative effects on the ecosystem are being discovered. The established water flow prevents the build-up of silt dunes at the end of the delta as the Nile enters the sea. These dunes formerly kept the sea away from rich delta farm lands, but now sea erosion is overcoming these dunes and flooding one million acres of a farmland with salt water. An additional problem is the spread of water hyacinths which evaporate large amounts of water lake above the dam. Another danger predicted is that a disease-carrying snail may spread through 500 miles of new irrigation canals below the dam. Peasants using the canals may catch the painful and normally incurable disease it carries.[7] Similar is the story with the Indira Gandhi Nahar Pariyojana (IGNP), the largest irrigation canal (See box 35.1 for more details).

Huge dams disrupt ecology.

Box 35.1 **Degraded Envrionment and Alienated Communities**

When it was planned a few decades ago, the canal was primarily intended as a strategic defence barrier along the Indo-Pak border and the Planning Commission put its stamp of approval on the Rs.66.43 crore project in 1957.

Thirty-four years and Rs.800 crore in expenditure later, only one-third of the total command area of 1.5 million hectares has been covered, and Stage II is still on. On the plus side, the canal has greened portions of the desert, checked the movement of sand dunes, provided drinking water to parched villages and attracted thousands of people to settle. But on the way, the canal has also run into numerous problems which threaten its very viability.

The warnings had been clear from the very beginning. In 1971, a decade or so after construction started, the Food and Agricultural Organisation (FAO) released a 10 volume survey of the canal command area and came up with a grim prediction:irrigation will be disastrous for the terrain's varying micro-ecosystems unless the government gave massive financial support for setting up expensive drip or sprinkler systems and drainage facilities. The warning was ignored. The consequence:a degraded environment and alienated communities.

In Stage I of the command area (0.5 million hectares), numerous villages have been submerged by waterlogging. And smaller patches all along the canal suffer from waterlogging, salinated soil and salinated groundwater supplies. According to a study financed by the government itself, the area affected by waterlogging/salinity accounts for about 34 per cent of the total irrigated area in Stage I. And according to a report of the Rajasthan Groundwater Department, over 50 per cent of the most fertile regions in both Stage I and Stage II will be waterlogged by the year 2000.

Some villages have had to be completely evacuated due to water logging and the rising groundwater level presages a similar fate for many others. The monitoring of the groundwater table in the command area between 1981 and 1989 revealed that it is rising at an average rate of one metre a year.

It is not environmental degradation alone that is the major ill effect of a dam. There are other side effects too such as breaking up of cultures, loss of fish, uprooting of forests and others as beautifully revealed in a ballad for ecology authored by Kenneth E.Boulding (see Box 35.2 for the ballad).

The realisation that canals and dams have serious negative consequences has made governments and funding agencies to slower the pace of construction, particularly the construction of dams. The slow-down process started since 1975. This process is justified on economic grounds and other reasons.

As is well known, governments that want to build dams make their public case on the basis of four benefits:irrigation, water, flood protection and electric power. Until recently, the costs were the focus of much less attention. More attention has been paid to the costs of building dams since the publication, in 1984, of *The Social and Environmental Effects of Large Dams* by Edward Goldsmith and Nicholas Hildyard. They argued that irrigation schemes often created no more new land than they destroyed; that resettling people caused huge economic and cultural disruption; that dams frequently failed to control floods; and that the profits from building them tended to end up in the pockets of multinationals, urban elite and the politicians. An end in the World Bank's assistance to the Sardar Sarovar project on Narmada river reflects this trend.

Nevertheless, funding and construction continue, though not at the same speed and enthusiasm witnessed before 1975. Any opposition to a dam from any quarter is sought to be met with equally well marshalled facts and figures that speak about the steps taken and benefits to be derived for the dam (See box 35.3 for the benefits of the Sardar Sarovar project and the efforts initiated to conserve ecological balances). Opposition notwithstanding, construction of dams and canals continues posing substantial damage to the environment.

Agriculture

Agriculture is also a pollutant.

Agriculture also causes pollution. Dust from fallow fields, increased turbidity of run-off water, nitrate pollution of surface and ground water, pesticide pollution and water-logging are some of the forms of pollution arising out of agriculture.[8]

Fertilisers cause immense damage to the environment.

Greatest damage to the environment comes from the use of fertilisers. While increased use of fertilisers has helped improve crop yields, their use has resulted in:

Box 35.2 **Ballad for Ecology**

The cost of building dams is always underestimated,
There's erosion of the delta that the river has created,
There's fertile soil below the dam that's likely to be looted,
And the tangled mat of forest that has got to be uprooted.

There's the breaking up of cultures with old haunts' and habits, loss,
There's the education programme that just doesn't come across,
And the wasted fruits of progress that are seldom much enjoyed
By expelled subsistence farmers who are urban unemployed.

There's disappointing yield of fish, beyond the first explosion;
There's silting up, and drawing down, and watershed erosion.
Above the dam the water's lost by sheer evaporation;
Below, the river scours, and suffers dangerous alteration.

For engineers, however good, are likely to be guilty,
Of quietly forgetting that a river can be silty,
While the irrigation people too are frequently forgetting,
That water poured upon the land is likely to be wetting.

Then the water in the lake, and what the lake releases,
Is crawling with infected snails and water borne diseases.
There's hideous locust breeding ground when water levels low,
And a million ecologic facts we really do not know.

There are benefits, of course, which may be countable, but which
Have a tendency to fall into the pockets of the rich,
While the costs are apt to fall upon the shoulders of the poor.
So cost-benefit analysis is nearly always sure
To justify the building of a solid concrete fact,
While the Ecologic Truth is left behind in the abstract.

- Improving the natural nitrogen-fixation process,
- Introducing toxic nitrates in water supplies and
- Contributing to air/land pollution besides having adverse effects on fish, wildlife and humans.

Industry the Scapegoat

Unfortunately, the industry is held the scapegoat for disrupting ecology, though other agencies, as explained earlier, cause equal if not more damage to the environment.

Every magazine and every newspaper which carries an article on environment links an industrial establishment with pollution. (Read box 35.4 for stories of heavy pollution).

If you are resident of any of our major cities, you do not need any example to demonstrate the pollution caused by our industries. It should be your own experience too. You should have seen the thick smoke emanating from factory chimneys engulfing your surroundings (it is for this reason that the factories are often called smoke stacks). If your house is located near a factory, small particles from it shall be seen settling on your window panes, garden plants, clothes, utensils and on the drinking water. You are sure to be disturbed every morning by loud sirens.

Box 35.3 **Sardar Sarovar Project Benefits-Major and Secondary**

Major Benefits

- Project will irrigate 1.8 million acres of land in Gujarat, 75,000 acres in Barmer and Jalore Districts of Rajasthan.
- 75% of command area is drought prone.
- Drinking water for 135 urban centres and 8215 villages, to serve 30 million people.
- 40 trees planted for every tree submerged.
- 1450 MW power generation.

Secondary Benefits

- Increase in vegetal cover in 24 million hectares.
- Prevention of loss of cattle during drought years.
- Prevention of large-scale migration during drought years.
- Arresting falling trend in groundwater tables, and contributing to its rise.
- Gains due to compensatory forest and tree plantations.
- Boost to agriculture related industries.
- Control of hygiene related diseases.
- Flood control.
- Development of fisheries.

Resettlement Package

(a) Each land based family gets two hectares of irrigable land.

(b) Every major son, above 18, treated as a separate family.

(c) Full compensation for existing houses; dismantled components transported free of cost.

(d) Subsistence allowance of Rs.15 per day, for 25 days in a month, for the first year of settlement.

(e) Resettlement grant of Rs.750 plus escalation at 8% from January 1980.

(f) Insurance cover.

(g) Free residential plot of 60 ft. x 90 ft. Assistance up to Rs.10,000 for plinth.

(h) Subsidy of Rs.5,000 for purchase of productive assets.

(i) Rs.600 as cultivation assistance.

(j) Vocational and technical training to PAPs and preference in appropriate categories of jobs in the project.

(k) Civic amenities like roads, electricity, water supply, health care, school, seed store, etc.

(l) Every PAP is consulted and given a choice of three alternative locations for resettlement.

(m) 5000 families have already been provided agricultural facilities.

Environmental Impact Studies

To plan environmental alleviation measures, the government initiated an environmental impact assessment in the early stages, to gather basic data at the grassroots level relating to the prevailing conditions. A multi-disciplinary group of scientists of the M.S.University studies a whole range of parametres including climate, geology, erosion patterns, vegetation health and so on.

Other studies carried out related to the safety of dams, seismic conditions, foundation and rim stability and fisheries. Outcome of the studies facilitated planning environmental protection progra-mmes. These related to:

(a) Forest Conservation.

(b) Development of Sanctuaries.

(c) Fisheries Development.

(d) Health Aspects.

(e) Archaeological Aspects.

Box 35.4 **Victims of Industrial Pollution**

1. The inhabitants of the village Navalagulu in Karnataka were the victims of the poisonous rubbish that was pumped into the air, dumped on the roadside and callously discharged into rivers (by the Harihar Polyfibres). The common symptoms were skin eruptions, boils, pockmarks as in small pox, dry skin and skin irrigation, cracked soles, burning sensation accompanied by cough, yellowing of the eyes as in jaundice and an unknown malady of the intestines. Dogs had deserted Navalagulu once the slow poisoning of the air they breathe, water they drink and the earth they tread was set in motion. Nevertheless, the Navalaguluans unlike their dogs stayed on to work on their daily chores with forlon hope and stoic patience.[9]

2. Effluents from a caustic soda manufacturing firm containing traces of deadly mercury are threatening to unleash Bhopal gas leak type tragedy on the local population along the state (Karnataka) West Coast. This has potential of creating a situation similar to the Minamata disease of Japan which claimed nearly 400 lives and affected many more persons with paralysis due to mercury poisoning.[10]

3. River Ganges has become a network of cesspools and drains thanks to constant discharge from industries located on the banks. The Hoogly estuary is chocked by the discharge from over 300 industries and most of its fish have been killed.[11]

4. Of course, there is the Bhopal gas tragedy which killed thousands and disfigured several thousands (the tragedy was unleased by the Union Carbide Corporation in December 1984) which is still green in one's memory.

If you pass by a sugar mill or a chemical plant, you will experience a stinking smell. You have to hold your breath and close your nostrils tight, otherwise your stomach will start squelching.

Do not stay close to a factory.

Carbon-dioxide emissions (CO_2) caused by burning of fossil fuels and discharged by cement plants are posing serious threat to the well being of people. Table 35.1 shows CO_2 emissions discharged in 1996.

Ironically, we all have learnt to live with pollution. We are all adopting to intense crowding, to deficient or excessively abundant or deficient diets, to monotonous, ugly and depressing environments. All over the world, the most polluted, crowded and traumatic cities are also the ones that have the greatest appeal and where population is increasing most rapidly. Furthermore, conditions that appear undesirable biologically do not necessarily constitute a handicap for economic growth. Great wealth is being produced by men working under high nervous tension in atmospheres containing chemical fumes, or in crowded offices polluted with tobacco smoke and bidi butts.

Table 35.1 **How much they Pollute**

(Million tonnes, 1996)

Country	*Total*	*Per Capita*
U.S.	5301	20.0
China	5364	2.8
Japan	1168	9.3
Russian Federation	1580	10.7
India	997	1.1
Germany	861	10.5
U.K.	557	9.5
Canada	409	13.7
S.Korea	408	9.0

(**Source**: *World Development Indicators*, 1999)

Fortunately, things are changing. There is increased realisation that man needs, not factories alone, but free and clean environment. Towards this end, several steps are being taken to protect ecology. Before listing the steps, it is advisable to know why the industry pollutes environment in the first place.

Why Cause Pollution?

It is cheaper to pollute environment than to preserve it.

If factories are held scapegoats for disrupting the ecology, there is some justification. Industrial establishments are more visible in the pollution than other agencies. It is easy to see black smoke oozing out of the chimney, scar on a green hill or dirty yard (see box 35.5) in a factory than other agencies. Hence, all fingers are raised at industrial establishments.

Industrial units pollute the environment for two reasons. First is the economic benefit available to them. It is simple common sense that causing pollution is cheaper than preventing it. For the management of a chemical factory, for example, it costs nothing to let effluents into a lake or stream untreated than installing a treatment plant for treating the discharges.

The second reason is that the environment has mostly been an economic free good for a businessman to use it as he wished. This reasoning especially applies to air and water, two of society's main areas of pollution.

The steel maker could use oxygen from the air for his blast furnace without spending a paise on it and use the same air as a common dumping ground for his wastes. Similarly, he could draw water from the river and discharge his wastes into it without paying for this service.[12]

Ways of Preventing Industrial Pollution

What is the way out? Can the pollution be stopped? Can ecology be saved? Answers to all these questions are in the affirmative.

There are basically two ways of preventing pollution:

Box 35.5 **A Dirty Business**

Even as the Supreme Court has sought to clean up the mess created by effluents and emissions from Indian factories, there are alarming reports that the country has become a dumping ground for the waste generated by industries in the 'developed' world. And this disturbing trend has drawn the attention of Greenpeace, the international organisation campaigning for a cleaner environment.

Greenpeace has pointed out that plastic waste, lead-ash and metal scraps are being regularly shipped to India, Pakistan and Bangladesh from the United States, Canada, United Kingdom, Australia and Germany.

The Baeal Convention, finalised on 5 March, 1994, has called for phasing out such waste exports and totally banning them by the end of 1997. However, some developed countries have been trying to bypass it through bilateral agreements with the 'weaker' nations.

The soft drinks multinational, Pepsi, is one of the biggest players in the toxic trade. In 1993, Pepsi had dumped about 4,500 tonnes of plastic waste in Madras in 23 shipments. Greenpeace has also objected to Pepsi setting up a joint-venture plastic recycling facility in Madras as it would be hazardous to the environment and public health.

Close on the heels of the Greenpeace move came revelations that Calcutta, too, has become a landing station for foreign waste.

(**Source**: *Sunday*, 26 March-1 April, 1995)

- Environmental movement, and
- Interference from the government. It is not any of these three and efforts should be made from all fronts if the environment were to be saved.

Environmental Movement: Environmental movement is a voluntary association formed to protect the environment from pollution. The movement took its birth in our country in 1968 and the genesis was setting the river Ganga ablaze by the effluents discharged into it by the Barauni Oil Refinery. Since then, the movement has grown in strength and as of today there are 54 voluntary organisations located in different parts of the country. The Chipko movement and Save Silent Valley are the two major successes of the voluntary bodies. The other projects opposed are the controversial Tehri dam in river Alkananda, the Koel Karo and Suvernerekha in Bihar, the Pollovaram in Andhra Pradesh, the upper Indravati project in Orissa and the Inchampalli and Bhopalpatnam dams on the borders of Maharashtra and Andhra Pradesh. The most important agitation against any developmental project seems to be the Sardar Sarovar Project across Narmada river.

With regard to industrial pollution, the associations make their presence felt whenever there is a disaster. The role played by Kalpavriksha, a Delhi-based organisation, is worth quoting in this context. Months before the acid leakage took place at the Sriram Food and Fertilizers Industries, Delhi (three people died and 700 injured as a result), Ashish Kothari of Kalpavrikesha had demonstrated outside the plant against the potential danger to the densely populated area. Kothari noticed minor leakages leading to the major one.[13] The management of the factory did not heed to the warning given by Kothari. Three people paid with their lives because of the negligence.

Violent agitation by villagers and environmental NGOs led to the shift of Thapar Dupont Nylon 6, 6 plant from Goa to Madras.

Government Interference: Instances of anti-pollution measures initiated voluntarily, or through pressure from environmentalists are few and far between. Government interference, therefore, becomes imperative.

Drawing inspiration form the Stockholm Conference of United Nations on Human Environment, which was held in 1972 and realising the need for its interference, the Government of India came out with a series of statutory provisions and fiscal incentives in order to protect the environment from industrial pollution.

Statutory Provisions: The Central Government enacted the Water (Prevention and Control of Pollution) Act, 1974. Under the Act, the Centre and States (majority) have constituted Centre and State Boards for the prevention and control of water pollution. Land pollution is also covered by the Act.

In 1977, the Water (Prevention and Control of Pollution) Cess Act was enacted with a view to enable the pollution control boards to levy cess on the consumption of water by specific industries and local bodies at the rates specified in the schedule to the Act. The amount thus collected will be used by the boards to discharge their functions effectively.

The Government of India enacted the Air (Prevention and Control of Pollution) Act, in 1981 in order to control air pollution. Latest in the series is the comprehensive legislation called the Environment(Protection) Act, 1986. The main objective of the Act is to protect and improve the environment and the prevention of hazards to human beings, other living creatures, plant and property.

Then there is the Department of Environment in Delhi, set up in 1980, where clearance is now made compulsory of any new industrial enterprise to be set up.

Environmental management reporting has now been made compulsory, specially in the case of public sector undertakings.

Fiscal and Financial Incentives : With a view to encourage industrial units to undertake pollution control measures and to foster a clean environment, the Government of India has offered several fiscal incentives. Accordingly, fiscal sops in the form of tax exemption, depreciation allowance at increased rates, reduction in water cess, etc. have been offered to industrial units which introduce pollution control devices.

The World Bank has earmarked in 1991, a line of credit amounting to $156 million to be used exclusively for funding pollution control. The Bank has appointed ICICI and IDBI as the disbursing agencies for Indian industries. The credit facility is available at an interest rate of 15.5 per cent. There are not many takers of this facility, though exceptions are found here and there (read box 35.6 for one such exception).

The Bank cleared, under Phase II, another line of credit of $330 million to be disbursed among Indian Industries.

Results Encouraging

Statutory provisions enforced and fiscal incentives offered by the Central and State governments have borne fruits. The Central and the State (Prevention and Control of Pollution) Boards have conducted a countrywide survey to identify water polluting large and medium scale industrial units, along with the availability of effluent treatment facilities. The study points out that as on 31st December 1984, out of the 4045 industrial units in th country; 1731 large and 2323 medium sized units which had been identified as relevant to water pollution, 2075 units (51 per cent) had taken approximate precautions to treat waste before discharge, 67 per cent units in the large scale sector and 39 per cent firms in the medium scale sector had adopted appropriate pollution control measures.

The State of Karnataka, Gujarat and Maharashtra led in the setting up of effluent treatment facilities with 95 per cent, 86 per cent and 80 per cent of the units in the respective states having such facilities.

Box 35.6 **Affluence from Effluents**

The Rashtriya Chemicals and Fertiliser's Chembur plant is one of Mumbai's most well known cases of industrial pollution. The company, in the face of sustained public pressure, is making attempts to reduce enviromental damage. When the World Bank instituted the Industrial Polluiton Control Project (IPCP), RCF was one of the first to approach IDBI. In January 1993, RCF entered into an agreement with the financial institution for a DM 12.5 million (approximately, Rs.45 crore) loan at 15.5 per cent.

RCF's problem was its two ammonia plants. These plants have been the sore spot for the company and have been shut down on more than one occasion. At the time the plants were set up, it was not mandatory to include cost of pollution control equipment in the project cost. But as local residents startd complaining about the pollution levels, RCF started looking for alternatives.

There were modifications going on in both plants. RCF had to wait till these were complete to be able to estimate the volume of pollutants that would require treatment. Finally, a Ministry of Environment notification in the late 1980s ordering them to clean up forced RCF into action.

In the process of manufacuturing ammonia, certain gases are accumulated which need to be removed by purging. Using cryogenic technology bought from a German firm, RCF decided to set up a purge gas recovery plant, which would, in the process of treating pollutants, help them to recover among other gases, argon and methane-rich fuel, both of which can be sold commercially, thereby making pollution control not just pay for itself but also generate additional resources. And at the end of the process, the plant produces no effluents.

RCF's choice of technology is determined by financial considerations. They had three options. In the first case, they could simply treat ammonia, which is all they are required to do under the regulations. Their internal rate of return (IRR) for just ammonia recovery was an uneconomical 10.7 per cent. Their second option was to choose ammonia and synthetic gas recovery, for which the IRR was 27 per cent. The final option, the one they chose, includes the recovery of liquid argon and gives them an IRR of 46.3 per cent. Payback period is a brisk 26 months.

The purge gas recovery plant is expected to generate Rs.28.32 crore annually, while outgoings on interest amount to Rs.1.67 crore and repayment of capital, Rs.4.62 crore per year.

Whether RCF will actually earn its projected income is doubtful. Since the time the plant has come up, argon prices have crashed due to excess capacity and intense competitors are mainly the steel and automobile industry, which use argon for welding. RCF officials, however, say they are safe, because even recovery to the synthetic gas stage gives them an IRR of 27 per cent, leaving RCF a comfortable profit margin.

Andhra Pradesh, West Bengal, Tamil Nadu, Haryana and Uttar Pradesh lagged behind though several polluting units were located in these states. (See Table 35.2)

The industry-wise analysis made by the study reveals that considerable progress was made between 1981 and 1984 in installing waste water treatment facilities. Eight industries were identified as priority areas under pollution prevention implementation Phase-1 (Sixth Plan period). These were sugar, distillery, caustic soda, fertilisers, oil refining, man-made fibres, iron and steel and textiles. While the growth in the number of units in these industries during the period of survey had been 48 per cent, the number of units having waste water treatment facilities had gone up by 60 per cent. In all, 51.4 per cent of the units had effluent treatment facilities at the end of 1984, as against 47.4 per cent in April 1981.

Table 35.2 **Status of Pollution Control**

	Units surveyed	*Units without pollution control devices*
Uttar Pradesh	224	100
Andhra Pradesh	173	66
Maharashtra	335	42
Gujarat	177	10
Bihar	60	24
Tamil Nadu	110	1
West Bengal	58	45
Karnataka	85	38
Delhi	5	3
Chandigarh	1	0
Pondicherry	6	3

(**Source**: *Survey by the Central Pollution Control Board*).

The industries, other than the eight listed above, are to be covered for water pollution control in Phase-2 of the programme (Seventh Plan period). The progress in these other industries has been even better with 51 per cent of the units having effluent treatment facilities by the end of 1984, as against 36 per cent but the number of units with effluent treatment facilities went up by 37.9 per cent.[14]

As government pressure has intensified, several companies all over the country are slowly starting to beef up their environment portfolios by increasing budgets, hiring or upgrading specialised staff and acquiring state-of-the-art technology.

TISCO has record for environment protection.

Tata Iron and Steel Company Ltd. (TISCO), for instance, spent Rs.27 crore on upgrading its pollution control plants between 1988 and 1991. For the next three years, it has more than doubled its budget for the purpose. The company also has a staff of 24 people in its environment department, including specialised environmental engineers and scientists, headed by a director.

Whether due to government fiat or self motivation, corporate India seems to slowly waking up to the need for better environmental management. A recent survey of 400 plants conducted by the Federation of Indian Chambers of Commerce and Industry (FICCI) is, perhaps, indicative of the current trend. According to the survey, 96.7 per cent of the units had already initiated some steps for pollution prevention and 86.1 per cent of the units have taken measures for treating effluent wastes.

Ecology is Inconsistent with Economic Development?

It is said that ecology is a word which is more appropriate to affluent countries. For a developing country like ours, ecology is least in priority. Our first priorities are elimination of malnutrition, disease, poverty, unemployment and illiteracy. These traditional ills can be removed through rapid economic development which is possible through massive industrialisation. In other words, we want more industries and not ecology.

What is unfortunately not understood is that ecology and development are not inconsistent. They can go together. Environmental quality, human health and social well being need not be sacrificed or unduly injured, let alone irreversibly altered as a result of the developmental activities.[15]

It is, infact, proved that economic growth promotes a clean environment. How does it happen? Growth raises expectations and creates demands for environmental improvement. As income levels and standards of living rise and people satisfy their basic needs for food, shelter and clothing, they can afford to pay attention to the quality of their lives and the condition of their habitat. Once the present seems relatively secure, people can focus on the future.

Ecology and economic development go together.

Within the developed countries, demand for better environmental protection (for example, tighter controls on land development and the creation of new parks) tend to come from property owners, often affluent ones. Homeowners want to guarantee the quality of their surroundings. On the other hand, environmental issues have never ranked high on the agenda of the economically disadvantaged. Even though the urban poor typically experience environmental degradation most directly, the debate proceeds for the most part without their active participation.

The correlation between rising income and environmental concern holds as true among nations as it does among social groups. The industrialised countries with strong economies and high average standards of living tend to spend more time and resources on environmental issues and thus to be better off environmentally. Between 1973 and 1984, when Japan emerged as a global economic power, it also took significant steps to clean up its historic legacy of pollution. In contrast, the developing nations, mired in poverty and struggling to stay one step ahead of mass starvation, have had little time and even less money to devote to environmental protection. Some of the world's worst and most intractable pollution problems are found in the developing world or in Eastern Europe-contaminated rivers, polluted cities, shrinking rain forests and encroaching deserts.

Economic growth can mitigate these resources and environmental pressures in the developing nations in two closely related ways: by reducing poverty and by helping to stabilise population growth. Many global environmental problems result less from the activities of those supposed villians, the profit-hungry multinational corporations than from the incremental, cumulative destruction of nature from the actions of many individuals-often the poor trying desperately to eke out a living. These actions range from the rural poor clearing land for title, for cattle or for subsistence farming; to gold miners, electroplates and small factories releasing toxic substances into the air and water; to farmers ruining fields and groundwater with the excessive application of pesticides.

In the developing nations especially, the population explosion of the past few decades (developing countries have more than doubled in population just since 1960) has greatly intensified accumulating pressures on the environment. Even though the rate of increase is starting to fall in most of the Third World, population growth in some countries has contributed and will continue to contribute to global degradation, to the loss of natural resources, to poverty and hunger. Continued rapid population growth will cancel all our environmental gains and offset environmental investments.

One widely acceptable strategy that can make an important contribution to lowering fertility rates is education. The World Bank has drawn attention to the close correlation between education of children-specifically bringing basic literacy to young girls and reduction in the birth rate. Economic growth also offers hope for some relief. As countries grow economically, their fertility rates tend to decline; in most developed nations, the birthrate has dropped below replacement levels, although it is creeping back in some countries. Stable populations coupled with economic growth mean rising per capita standards of living. Education and economic development are the surest paths to stabilising population growth.

The benefits of economic growth just described-higher expectation for environmental quality in the industrialised countries, and reduced resources use and environmental pressures in the developing nations-show up on the demand side of the prosperity/progress equation. But economic expansion contributes on the supply side as well by generating the financial resources that make environmental improvements possible.

Economic progress guarantees safe environment.

In the United States, for example, economic prosperity has contributed to substantial progress in environmental quality. The gains the country has made in reducing air and water pollution since 1970 are indisputable. Air emissions of particulates went down by 63 per cent between 1970 and 1988; the Environmental Protection Agency (EPA) estimates that without controls, particulate emissions would be 70 per cent higher than current levels. Sulfur dioxide emissions are down 27 per cent; without controls, they would be 42 per cent higher than they are now. And without controls on lead, particularly the phase-in of unleaded gasoline, lead emission to the air would be fully 97 per cent higher than they are today. Instead, atmospheric lead is down 96 per cent from the 1970 levels.

Similar, although more localised, gains can be cited with respect to water pollution. Twenty years ago, pollution in Lake Erie decimated commercial fishing; now, thanks to municipal sewage treatment programmes, Lake Erie is the largest commercial fishery in the Great Lakes. The Potomac River in Washington was so polluted that people who came into contact with it were advised to get an inoculation for tetanus. Now on a warm day, the Potomac belongs to the windsurfer.

It cost the American taxpayers, consumers and businessmen a great deal of money to realise these gains. The direct cost of compliance with federal environmental regulations is now estimated at more than $90,000 million a year-about 1.7 per cent of gross national product (GNP), the highest level among Western industrial nationals for which data are available. The United States achieved this progress during a period when GNP increased by more than 70 per cent.

We can learn two important lessons from the US experience of the past two decades. First, environmental commitments were compatible with economic advancement; the United States is now growing in a qualitatively better, healthier way, because those commitments were made. And secondly, it was not just good luck that substantial environmental progress occurred during a period of economic prosperity. The healthy economy paid for environmental gains; economic expansion creates the capital to finance superior environmental performance.

The contrast between the US experience and that of the former Soviet Union and Eastern Europe over the past two decades is both stark and illuminating. While the United States prospered and made a start on cleaning up, Poland, Hungary, Rumania, former East Germany, Czechoslovakia and the former Soviet Union were undergoing an environmental catastrophe that will take many years and thousands of millions of dollars to correct. In Eastern Europe, cities are blackened totally by thick dust. Chemicals make up a substantial percentage of river flows. Nearly two-thirds of the length of the Visual, Poland's longest river, is unfit even for industrial use. The Order River, which forms most of Poland's border with Eastern Germany, is useless over 80 per cent of its length. Parts of Poland, Eastern Germany, and Romania are literally uninhabitable; zones of ecological disaster cover more than a quarter of Poland's land area. Millions of people in the former Soviet Union live in cities with dangerously polluted air.

The former Soviet Union and most of the rest of Eastern Europe are plagued by premature deaths, high infant mortality rates, chronic lung disorders and other disabling illnesses. The economic drain from these environmental burdens, in terms of disability benefits, health care and lost productivity, is enormous-15 per cent or more of GNP, according to one Eastern European government minister.

Authoritarian and centrally planned societies pose a threat to environment.

The lifting of the Iron Curtain has revealed to the world that authoritarian, centrally planned societies pose much greater threats to the environment than capitalist democracies. Many environmental principles were undefendable in the absence of private property. Both the factory and the nearby farmland contaminated by its pollution were the property of the state. And the state, without elections, was not subject to populate restraints or reforms. Equally important, decisions to forego environmental controls altogether, in order to foster all-out, no-holds barred economic development, now can be seen to have done nothing for the economy. The same policies that ravaged the environment also wrecked the economy.

There is good reason that no economic benefits have been identified from all the pollution control costs these nations avoided. Healthy natural systems are a *sine qua non* for all human activity, including economic activity.

What has happened in the United States and Eastern Europe is convincing evidence that in the modern industrial world, prosperity is essential for environmental progress.[16]

Sustainable Development

Concern for environment has grown in its approach. Earlier, the approach was a mere control of pollutants and the punishment of guilty industries. Now the emphasis is on sustainable development. Sustainable development refers to development that meets the needs of the present without compromising the ability of future generations to meet their own needs. The concept of sustainable development goes much beyond environmental protection, it is based on a recognition that economic growth must be viewed as a process that provides fairness and opportunity for all the world's people, not just the privileged few, without further destroying the world's finite natural resources and without compromising the world's carrying capacity.

The Earth Summit held at Rio De Janeiro on June 15, 1992, addressed itself to the problem of sustainable development (see Box 35.7 for Rio declaration).

WOMEN AND BUSINESS OPPORTUNITIES

Historically, women have been discriminated against in the male dominated society. Most girls were married when they were in their teens; widow remarriages were considered to be a social taboo; education beyond the primary or at the most school level was rare; girls, especially in rural and small towns, were deliberately undernourished and denied access to the outside world; and women were considered to be fit to cook food but not to work in business establishments. Even the Constitution has not been free from bias against the fair sex. Throughout the Constitution, women are referred to only six times, and in five of them, they are clubbed together with men and children. Equality of gender has not been explicitly expounded as a specific constitutional value, though Articles 14 and 15 guarantee the quality of status, opportunity and social, political and economic justice.

The report of the National Committee on the Status of Women has made startling revelations. Major findings in the report are: a decline in the sex ratio due to excessive mortality among women and female children; disparity in access to healthcare and widening gap between women and men in literacy, education and training for employment (see Table 35.3 for more details). Daily newspapers publish reports about rape, bride burnings, dowry deaths and wives beaten to death. Women are afraid of going out alone after dark and cannot go for shopping without male escorts (Also read box 35.8).

Some statisties are worth recolleting in support of this assertion. Out of the 1.3 billion poor people in the world, 70 percent are women, the majority of whom are illiterate with no access to basic amenities like safe drinking water. Two-thirds of the 130 million children worldwide who are not in school are girls. Between 75 and 80 per cent of the world's 27 million refugees are women and childern. The majority of women earn on average about three-fourths of the pay of males for the same work. Worldwide 20 to 50 percent of women experience some degree of demostic violence during marriage. The primary victims today's armed conflicts are civilian women and children who are sexually abused by soldiers.

As we go into the future, discrimination against women will go and they will occupy equal status along with their male counterparts. Seeds for better tomorrow have already been sown. Today's girls

Box 35.7 **The Rio Declaration**

The following is the Rio declaration of principles on general rights and obligations on environment protection initiated by heads of governments at the United Nations Conference on Environment and Development.

Recognising the integral and interdependent nature of the earth, our home, we proclaim that:

Human beings are at the centre of concerns for sustainable development. They are entitled to a healthy and productive life in harmony with nature.

States have, in accordance with the charter of the United Nations and the principles of international law, the sovereign right to exploit their own resources pursuant to their own environment policies, and the responsibility to ensure that activities within their jurisdiction or control do not cause damage to the environment of other states or areas beyond the limits of national jurisdiction.

The right to development must be fulfilled so as to meet developmental and environmental needs of present and future generations.

In order to achieve sustainable development, environmental protection shall constitute an integral part of the development process and cannot be considered in isolation from it.

All states and all people shall corporate in the essential task of eradicating poverty as an indispensable requirement for sustainable development.

The special situation and needs of the developing countries, particularly the least developed and those most environmentally vulnerable, shall be given special priority. International actions in the field of environment and development should also address the interest and needs of all countries.

States shall co-operate in a spirit of global partnership to conserve, protect and restore the health and integrity of the earth's ecosystems. In view of the different contributions to global environment degradation, states have common but differentiated responsibilities. The developed countries acknowledge the responsibility that they bear in the international pursuit of sustainable development in view of the pressures their societies place on the global environment and of the technologies and financial resources they command.

To achieve sustainable development and a higher quality of life for all people, states should reduce and eliminate unsustainable patterns of production and consumption and promote appropriate demographic policies.

States should co-operate to strengthen indigenuous capacity building for sustainable development by improving scientific understanding through exchanges of scientific and technological knowledge, and by enhancing the development, adaptation, diffusion and transfer of technologies, including new and innovative technologies.

Environmental issues are best handled with the participation of all connected citizens, at the relevant level. At the national level, each individual shall have appropriate access to information concerning the environment that is held by public authorities, including information on hazardous materials and activities in their communities and the opportunity to participate in decision-making process. States shall facilitate and encourage public awareness and participation by making information widely available. Effective access to judicial and administrative proceedings, including redress and remedy, shall be provided.

States shall enact effective environmental legislation. Environmental standards, management objectives and priorities should reflect the environmental and developmental context to which they apply. Standards applied by some countries may be inappropriate and of unwarranted economic and social cost to other countries, in particular, developing countries.

States should co-operate to promote a supportive and open international economic system that would lead to economic growth and sustainable development in all countries, to redress in a better way the problems of environmental degradation. Trade policy measures for environmental purposes should not constitute a means of arbitrary or unjustifiable discrimination or a disguised restriction on international trade. Unilateral actions to deal with environmental challenges outside the jurisdiction of the importing country should be avoided. Environmental measures addressing transboundary or global environmental problems should, as far as possible, be based on an international consensus.

States shall develop national law regarding liability and compensation for the victims of pollution and other environmental damage. States shall also co-operate in an expeditious and more determined manner to develop further international law regarding liability and compensation for adverse effects of environmental damage caused by activities within their jurisdiction or control to areas beyond their jurisdiction.

States should effectively co-operate to discourage or prevent the relocation and transfer to other states of any activities and substances that cause severe environmental degradation or are found to be harmful to human health.

In order to protect the environment, the precautionary approach shall be widely applied by states according to their capabilities. Where there are threats of serious or irreversible damage, lack of full scientific certainty shall not be used as a reason for postponing cost-effective measures to prevent environmental degradation.

National authorities should endeavour to promote the internalisation of environmental costs and the use of economic instruments, taking into account the approach that the polluter should, in principle, bear the cost of pollution, with due regards to public interest and without distorting international trade and investments.

Environmental impact assessment, as a national instrument, shall be undertaken for proposed activities that are likely to have a significant adverse impact on the environment and are subject to a decision of a competent national authority.

States shall immediately notify other states of any natural disasters or other emergencies that are likely to produce sudden harmful effects on the environment of those states. Every effort shall be made by the international community to help states so afflicted.

States shall provide prior and timely notification and relevant information to potential affected states on activities that may have a significant adverse trans-boundary environmental effect and shall consult with those states at an early stage and in good faith.

Women have a vital role in environmental management and development. Their full participation is therefore essential to achieve sustainable development.

The creativity, ideals and courage of the youth of the world should be mobilised to forge a global partnership in order to achieve sustainable development and ensure a better future for all.

Indigenuous people and their communities, and other local communities have a chattel role in environmental management and development because of their knowledge and traditional practices. States should recognize and duly support their identity, culture and interests and enable their effective participation in the achievement of sustainable development.

The environment and natural resources of people under oppression, domination and occupation shall be protected.

Warfare is inherently destructive of sustainable development. States shall therefore respect international law providing protection for the environment in times of armed conflict and cooperate in its further development as necessary.

Peace, development and environmental protection are interdependent and indivisible.

States shall resolve all their environmental disputes peacefully and by appropriate means in accordance with the charter of the United Nations.

State and people shall co-operate in good faith and in a spirit of partnership in the fulfilment of the principles embodied in this declaration and in further development of international law in the field of sustainable development.

Table 35.3 **Gender Disparities (From 1991 Census Survey)**

Women		*Men*
933.11 (per 1,000 males)	*Sex ratio*	1000
58.1 Yrs	*Life expectan1cy at birth*	57.7Yrs
6.3%	*Population aged 60+Yrs*	5.7%
35.9%	*Population aged 0-14 Yrs*	36.5%
75	*Infant mortality rate (1993)*	73
54.16%	*Literacy (2001)*	75.85%
	School enrolment (1993-94)	
42.9%	*Primary*	47.1%
39.3%	*Middle*	60.7%
	Drop-out rate (1993-94)	
39.1%	*Primary*	36.1%
10.2%	*Women in polytechnic s and ITIs*	89.8%
22.27%	*Work participation rate*	51.61%
14.8%	*Organised sector*	85.2%
8.7%	*All India services*	91.3%
8%	*Parliament*	92%

Note: Data excerpted from Censes 1991, unless otherwise stated.

are better educated, more assertive and more bold. Added to this is the women's liberation movement, to protect and improve the lot of women. Business and other professional activities are multiplying, demanding the services of talented people, including women. The government is also keen on uplifting the status of women.

Women in Business

Participation of women in business as owners, managers and employees is less encouraging, considering the size of the population and the vast opportunities available. While women account for 48 per cent of

Box 35.8 **What Women's Day? She was denied even a Dignified Death**

Patna : She was a nubile young enthusiast of 17 years when she participated in the International Women's Day celebrations seeking empowerment of eves on March 8 this year.

Ironically, only two days later in the wee hours of March 11, she found herself writhing in pain helplessly as dogs savoured her intestine hanging out of her body after she was gan-graped and stabbed repeatedly by four felonies.

In fact, Poonam Kayam, daughter of a late Daroga, is now history, having breathed her last on March 13, while undergoing treatment in a Ranchi hospital.

Five days on, incidentally, the Ranchi police are yet to make any headway, that the gory incident figured in the Legislative Assembly proceedings on Wednesday notwithstanding.

"I wish they had killed me instead," wails Poonam's mother, Sukumati who is a constable with Bihar police and is posted in Jamshedpur.

She got the job on compassionate grounds after her husband's death and decided to leave her four offsprings back at their Saraitaand house in Ranchi so as not to disrupt their studies.

Poonam, an Intermediate Science student, was the eldest sibling and, as such, she looked after her younger sister and two brothers like a male member of the family.

That she was actually not a male, proved Poonam's nemesis, though. On March 11, when four criminals barged into her house and lay their hands on a box and Rs 1,400 in cash, young Poonam could not escape their villainous eyes.

Along with the box and cash, Poonam too became a part of their booty.

Only furlongs away on the banks of a river, the foursome ravaged the crying Poonam repeatedly and before leaving, inflicted several stabs on her nude body.

Sobbing Poonam was brought back to home only when people, including a relative of hers, went to the banks to attend Nature's call.

Part of her intestine was eaten by dogs, they recall while narrating the hair-raising sight of the blood-soaked Poonam lying almost lifelessly.

Who were the beasts? Poonam's mother suspects the hand of her brother-in-law (husband's brother), Santosh Kayam, who, she alleges, wanted to usurp the land bought long back by her husband.

At that time, theirs was a joint family and her husband, she claims, had made a small house and informally given it to Santosh.

Now Santosh wanted to capture the whole land, she adds, tearfully.

(**Source**: *Times of India,* 17th March, 2000)

the population, the 1991 Census put the female workforce at 20.85 per cent. Those that take up jobs are content with lower paid jobs. Women occupying top positions are few and far between. Reasons are not difficult to seek. The main reasons are:

- Women are known to have lower attachment to work and are, therefore, content with lower positions;
- They do not consider themselves as primary earners and withdraw from the labour force once family income reaches adequacy;

- They lack education and training commensurate with men as marriages and home-making take precedence; and
- They are less preferred to men in recruitment and selection because of legal and other problems mentioned below.

Problems of Female Employment

Though there is no legislation which binds employers to hire women in preference to men, a subtantial percentage of the fair sex is generally employed, partly because for certain jobs they are appropriate, and partly because suitable male candidates are not available. On being employed, women pose additional problems to the employers. Provisions of the Factories Act and the Maternity Benefit Act should be complied with. Then there is the defiant attitude of a male worker to work under a woman manager or an unwanted chivalrous attitude if the former is a boss. Further, women should be paid equal wages as their male counterparts, though the former are less prepared to take up duties involving more physical strain. Payment of equal pay has been made mandatory.

There is also the cost of employing women. It is said that the cost of employing women is greater than the cost of employing men. Career interruptions, plateauing and turnover are more common with women employees and all these traits are expensive. The money companies invest in recruitment, training and development is less likely to produce top executives among women than among men, and the invaluable company experience that developing executives acquire at every level as they move up through management ranks is more often lost.

Problems notwithstanding, owners of business establishments must encourage and prefer women while hiring people for different positions. Businessmen must generously contribute to the education and nourishment of women. Whatever is done by businessmen is little considering the primary place occupied by women as mothers, wives, sisters and nurses to all of us.

This has been realised and more and more women are taking up jobs as Table 35.4 shows.

Table 35.4 **Women Employees in IT Firms**

Company	*Employees*	*of Women Percentage*
WIPRO	43,880	24
TCS	43,681	21
INFOSYS	31,000	22
HCL Technologies	20,249	22
Satyam	20,000	20
Cognizant	13,000	28
Accenture	11,000	25
Patni	5,980	19
iFlex	4,688	20

(**Source:** *Business Today*, April 10, 2005, p.36)

CHILD LABOUR

The historic judgement delivered by a Division Bench of the Supreme Court on December 10, 1996 brought issue relating to the child labour to the centre stage. For a country, which has the shameful record of tolerating the exploitation of not less than 35 million children as workers in a wide range of industries and in the services sector, the judgement of the Supreme Court will go down as a triumph of human sensitivities over a mindset which is stuck to the myth that child labour is inevitable.

The Supreme Court has directed that in nine industries, already identified as 'hazardous' including the match industry in Sivakasi, the glass industry in Ferozabad and the carpet industry in Mirzapur, child workers are to be replaced by adult labour, while employers who have been engaging child labour in contravention of the Child Labour (Prohibition) and Regulation Act, 1986, would pay a compensation of Rs.20,000 for each such child, which would enable them setting up of a Child Labour Rehabiliation-cum-Welfare Fund. The fund will be augmented by a contribution of Rs.5,000 by the State Government concerned, for each child, incase the State is unable to provide a job to an adult member of the family in question. The income accruing from the corpus would be used to ensure the child's education in a suitable institution with a view to making the child in due course a better citizen.

The Apex Court has prohibited the employment of children below 14 years of age in hazardous occupations connected with the transport of passengers, goods or mail by railways, cinder-picking, clearing of an ash pit or building operations in railway premises, catering establishments in railway stations, work relating to selling of fireworks or crackers and abattoirs and slaughter houses.

The judgement also bars the employment of children in beedi-making, carpet weaving, cement manufacture, cloth printing, dyeing and weaving, manufacture of fireworks, matches and explosives, mica-cutting and splitting, binding and construction industry, soldering, processes in electronic industry, tanning, soap manufacture, wool cleaning, slate pencils, building and the construction industry.

Why are Children Employed?

There are several economic and social reasons why children are put on jobs. The most obvious reason is the poverty of parents which compels them to send their children to jobs than to schools. Even where schooling is free, children are still sent to work as without their income, parents and other members in the family become even poorer.

Child labour exists because there are people willing to use children for a profit. A child is paid much less, is obedient, does not join unions and a child can be moulded to perform repetitive jobs. All these are advantageous to the employer.

Economic and social causes justify use of child labour.

There was a strong belief among certain societies that the members were forbidden from pursuing education- it was a sin and if any member disobeyed and went to school, he would be punished by the divine powers. This belief prevented parents from putting their children to school. Fortunately, this superstitious belief has faded out now.

Universal Phenomenon

Child labour is not peculiar to our country alone. All developing countries use child labour and so is the case with the developed countries. Infact, some of the most exploitative forms of labour like child prostitution exists in US, Germany and France. (Read also Box 35.9)

Box 35.9 **Tortured Childhood**

Life can be harsh and cruel for a child. The world abuses a boy or a girl in a hundred ways without the slightest of remorse. While millions of children are forced into virtual slave labour in many developing countries, which are shameless enough to cite poverty as a reason for this, both in the industrial and the developing nations, the young are **pushed into** sex or the **pornographic industry**. Even more heartrending than these is what happens in Brazil, where gangs of 'cleaners' massacre street kids often in night-long operations. In other places little ones are kidnaped for ransom, and if the money does not come, they are killed in cold blood. But more often than not, they are abducted to be physically maimed and 'employed' as beggars. Again, instances of severe corporal punishment are not rare; there have been cases of a child being crippled by teachers, who believe in bullying their way through. The scars on the body may go away with time, but those on the mind, seldom ever. The feelings of our little men and women are trampled upon so causally by society that human rights not only seem like a big farce, but also appear to be the prerogative of adults.

The recent incident at Alwar in Rajasthan is a case in point. There was a reported move to initiate a 12-year-old boy from Amritsar into monkhood. Although the Rajasthan High Court intervened and granted a stay, it is said that Jain Munis of the Vardhman Sthankwasi Dhravak Sangh were determined to go ahead with the ceremony that would have pushed the lad into a life of renunciation and sacrifice. The district administration eventually rescued him and two other minors, who were also being forced to take to 'sanyas'. There was drama and tension in the town; charges and countercharges were traded as well. Some of the residents alleged that it was a matter of "forcible conversion to Jainism", but the head of the Sangha, Acharya Devendra Muni, said that the child's parents had agreed to this initiation. Be that as it may, a more pertinent issue here would be the 12-year-old's trauma of having been abandoned by his mother and the father, who were also merciless enough to rob him of just about every childhood pleasure.

Twelve-year-old Bilkis Khatun and 76 other young girls from West Bengal suffered even more, when they found themselves in Saudi Arabia, far away from their relatives and in utterly humiliating surroundings. They had to beg at Mecca and hand over their collections to an organised gang, which specialises in luring girls away from their poverty-stricken existence with the promise of a Haj trip to Islam's holy city. But once they are there, the children find themselves trapped in a degrading situation. Fortunately, these 77 girls, some barely old as four, were rescued and sent back home, but the fact remains that the parents of some knew that their daughters were being taken away for begging. It is said that such things should happen in the age, and in a country that never misses an opportunity to point out how progressive its thinking is. This certainly sounds hollow, if not absurd, in the face of an attitude, callous enough to perpetrate such misery on the child.

(**Source**: *The Hindu*, Feb. 27, 1997)

However, our country holds the dubious distinction of having the largest percentage of child labour. That the country has 35 million children working on petty jobs has already been told. Some more data are worth quoting. In the decade from 1983-94, 33 per cent of its children were born in the presence of trained health workers, the average for all developing nations is 63 per cent. Whereas seven out of every 100 infants die after birth on an average in these nations, a little more than eight such deaths occur here; by the age of five, 9.7 out of every 100 die on an average, but if they are Indians, 12 will perish. Even if they live, illiteracy, disease and malnutrition kill around half of the nation's children.

Read also box 35.10 for a story of Peter Smart which dates back to 1832. One comes across today several Peter Smarts everywhere in our country.

Box 35.10 **Children and the Factory System**

The following testimony was given by Peter Smart to a Parliamentary Committee investigating working conditions in 1832. Similar testimony was provided by numerous others.

Q. Where do you reside?

A. At Dundee.

Q. Have you worked in a mill from your youth?

A. Yes, since I was 5 years of age.

Q. Had you a father and mother in the country at the time?

A. My mother stopped in Perth, about eleven miles from the mill, and my father was in the army.

Q. Were you hired for any length of time when you went?

A. Yes, my mother got 15 shillings for six years, I having my meat and clothes.

Q. What were your hours of labor, as you recollect in the mill?

A. We began at 4 o'clock in the morning and worked till 10 or 11 at night; as long as we could stand on our feet.

Q. Were you kept on the premises constantly?

A. Constantly.

Q. Locked up?

A. Yes, locked up.

Q. Night and day?

A. Night and day; I never went home while I was at the mill.

Q. Do the children ever attempt to run away?

A. Very often.

Q. Were they pursued and brought back again?

A. Yes, the overseer pursued them and brought them back.

Q. Did you ever attempt to run away?

A. Yes, I ran away twice.

Q. And you were brought back?

A. Yes, and I was sent up to the master's loft, and thrashed with a whip for running away.

Q. Do you know whether the children were, in point of fact, compelled to stop during the whole time for which they were engaged?

A. Yes, they were.

Q. By law?

A. I cannot say by law; but they were compelled by the master; I never saw any law used there but the law of their own hands.

(**Source**: Quoted in *Human Socieities* by Gerhard Lenski, New York, McGraw-Hill, 1995, p.269.)

The Remedies

It is good to know that there are four main approaches to child labour policy. The first stresses the need for eliminating poverty as that is the main cause for child labour. This approach does not address the child labour directly. The second appraoch emphasises strategies to get more children to school, particularly incentives to induce parents to send their childern to school, such as free text books, uniform and midday meal scheme implemented in Karnataka. The third approach considers child labour ineviteable, atleast in the shortrun, and stresses pallative measures such as regulating it to prevent abuse and to provide support services for working childern. This approach is most commonly associated with UNICEF which has prepared a check list of regulatory and social appraoches that could meet the "best interest of the child". Workplace schooling, stricter law enforcement against illegal child labour trafficking and providing support services for parents and for childern working on the streets are some of the regulations contained in the UNICEF's agenda. The fourth approach advocated by the ILO, favours banning child labour altogether. If this is not possible, atleast child labour in its most abusive form should be banned. The most abusive practices include slavery, sale of trafficking of childern, debt bondage and serfdom. This modified approach has received much attention and in 1999 the ILOs "Worst Forms of Child Labour Convention" was adopted".[16a]

How to end the exploitation of child labour? Compulsory schooling is one answer to the problem. As Table 35.5 shows, a large number of children are outside schools. Mandating schooling for all children must be the top priority for all countries in the 21st century.

Table 35.5 **Children out of Schools**

Percentage of children of primary school age not attending school	
Sub-Sahara Africa	47%
Middle East and North Africa	16%
South Asia	34%
East Asia and Pacific	6%
Latin America and Carribean	12%
Central and East Europe, Common wealth of Independent States and Baltics	13%
World	20%
of which developing countries	23%
developed world	1%

(**Source**: UNICEF, 1996)

Stringent enforcement of labour laws is a must if the children were to be ensured of education, good food, clothing and health. In our country there is, as was stated earlier, the Child Labour (Prohibition) Regulation Act, 1986. Article 24 of the Constitution prohibits employment of children in hazardous occupations. Factories Act, 1948, also contains provisions relating to the employment of children on dangerous machines. The Act makes the occupier of the factory liable for prosecution if he violates the provision.

Enactments and orders seem to have little impact on the abolition of child labour. With all the hoopla witnessed in the recent past, no restaurant owner has stopped using children for cleaning tables and utensils, nor the owner of a garage has told the kids not to clean engines and inflate tubes and tyres from tomorrow. Exploitation seems to continue. What is needed is that the conscience of the exploiters must be pricked. All of us must realise that the tender age of children is not to be misused for a profit. Children must be fed well, clothed decently, schooled adequately so that they could grow into healthy citizens.

The UNICEF report recommends allocation of 20 per cent of government budgets to education and basic social services and exhorts donor governments to do the same with their official development assistance.

Countries like the US and Germany have begun to ban the import of the products of child labour. If such products are banned, it is believed, producers might stop producing and children would not be exploited. This argument holds good in the long-run but may fail to have any impact in the short-run. In the short-run, factories stop production, children lose their jobs and parents lose their additional incomes forcing them to abuse their children in a much more horrendous manner.

The most effective way of tackling the problem is realisation on the part of parents, governments, NGOs and all other sections of society that the innocent child should not be exploited for a profit.

CONSUMERISM

Consumerism is a movement to inform consumers and protect them from business malpractices. The movement focusses on inferior and dangerous merchandise, unfair business practices and false or misleading advertisements. Unfair practices by businessmen abound. Artificial scarcities are created; prices are unreasonably hiked; adulteration is unabashedly practised; under-measurement and under-weighing are rampant; money is accepted in advance, promising delivery of product in question within a specified time but seldom honoured and after-sales services are mostly an unkept promise. Ads and labels are misused and are full of sex, false claims and half truths.

Consumerism is a movement to inform consumers and protect them from unfair practices.

Businessmen should realise their moral responsibility and avoid indulging in practices that are harmful to consumers. Such enlightened self-realisation is unfortunately lacking. Government regulation becomes necessary to protect consumer interest.

The government has appropriately passed several legislations and issued notifications and orders to restrain businessmen from indulging in felonies. Consequently, we have around fifty laws which have been enacted to protect their interest. The Consumer Protection Act, 1986, is the latest to be enacted by the Central Government. This is the most powerful piece of legislation which provides effective protection against unfair trade practices, unsatisfactory services and defective goods. The Act provides for setting up of special forums at district, state and Central levels to deal exclusively with consumer complaints and issues. It provides for awarding compensation to the aggrieved consumer. The Act brings in its fold even public undertakings which were excluded by previous legislations.

The apex court, called the National Commission, functions in Delhi. Every state government has a State Commission. There are 543 (January 1999) district fora. All these courts have handled nearly 13 lakh cases of which about 10 lakh cases have been disposed off.

The Consumer Protection Act has been regarded as the most progressive, comprehensive and unique piece of legislation. In the last international conference on consumer protection held in Malaysia in 1997, the Act was hailed as one "*which has set in motion a revolution in the field of consumer rights, the parallel of which has not been seen anywhere else in the world*".

Besides enacting legislations, the government has taken other measurement to protect consumer interest. The government has included consumer protection as an item of the 20 Point Programme. A Consumer Advisory Council has been set up by agencies, including state governments, the Textile

Committee and the Department of Science and Technology. The media is giving coverage to the subject and AIR and Doordarshan have been organising programmes like Lok Samasyani Sansad and Janavani.

Apart from what the government does, the consumer should himself assert his rights and protect himself against business malpractices. This is the genesis of consumerism. Various consumer movements have come up in different parts of the country and as of today, there are 237 and odd consumer organisations working towards consumer protection. The consumer movement is still in its nascent stage. It is sure to grow and become more powerful as we go into the future (Read box 35.11 for the list of consumer groups).

Box 35.11 **Consumer Groups in India**

Sr.No.	Name	Year of Estbl.
1.	Passengers and Traffic Relief Association (PATRA)	1915
2.	Women Graduate Union (WGU)	1915
3.	Women's India Association (WIA)	1917
4.	Triplicane Urban Cooperative Stores (TUCS)	1949
5.	Indian Association of Consumer (IAC)	1956
6.	Fredric Naumann Foundation (FNF)	1960
7.	Gayatri Charitable Trust(GCT)	1960
8.	International Organisation of Consumers Union (IOCU)	1960
9.	Jyoti Sangh Grahak Suraksha Vibhag	1962
10.	Bombay Civil Trust (BCT)	1963
11.	Consumer Guidance Society of India (CGSI)	1966
12.	Baroda Citizen Council (BCC)	1966
13.	All-India Bank Depositors Association (AIBDA)	1968
14.	Surat Consumer Association (SCA)	1969
15.	Karnataka Consumer Services Society (KSCC)	1970
16.	Visaka Consumer Council (VCC)	1973
17.	Akhil Bharatiya Grahak Panchayat (AGBP)	1974
18.	Trichy District Consumer Council (TDCC)	1976
19.	Consumer Education and Research Centre (CERC)	1978
20.	Mumbai Grahak Panchayat (MGP)	1979
21.	Grahak Panchayat (GP)	1979
22.	Jagrut Panchayat (JP)	1980
23.	Consumer Forum (CF)	1980
24.	Consumer Education Centre (CEC)	1982
25.	Voluntary Organisation in the Interest of Consumer Education (VOICE)	1984
26.	Consumer Unity and Trust Society (CUTS)	1984
27.	National Centre For Human Settlements & Environment (NCHSE)	1984

28.	Consumer Guidance Society of Jamshedpur (CGSJ)	1984
29.	Consumer Action Group (CAG)	1985
30.	Common Cause (CC)	1985
31.	SMN Consumer Protection Council	1986
32.	Bombay Telephone Users' Association (BTUA)	1989
33.	Federation of Consumer Organisations of Tamil Nadu (FEDCOT)	1990
34.	Confederation of Indian Consumer Organisations (CICO)	1992
35.	Gujarat Federation of Consumer Organisations (GUSFECO)	1992
36.	Consumer Coordination Council (CCC)	1992

A powerful consumer movement bestows certain responsibilities on business. Understanding consumer needs and producing goods and services to satisfy the needs do not complete the businessmen's responsibilities. They have additional responsibilities such as:

Truth in Ads and Labels

Advertising is a vehicle through which the seller seeks to inform and guide the buyer to make intelligent buying decisions. In practice, advertising carries false claims, half-truths and sex pictures. Advertisement fails to help the buyer to make intelligent buying decisions.

It is heartening to note that the advertising profession has also realised the need for observing a certain code of conduct while advertising products. In April 1982, the Ad-Club of India (ACB) appointed a committee to formulate a regulatory code for the profession that includes advertisers, agencies and the media. The committee suggested the following code which has been accepted:

Advertising Code

- Make honest claims and do not mislead the consumer.
- Do not offend the generally accepted standards of public decency.
- Safeguard against the excessive promotion of products which are regarded as hazardous to society or individuals.
- Observe fairness in competition between different brands of the same product, or a product and its substitute.

The code seeks to ensure protection to consumers against spurious advertising and guarantee that generally accepted standards of morality are upheld.

With the formation of the code, the advertising profession has started working on establishing a body to implement advertising norms and standards. The body, a public limited company, is called the Advertising Standards Council of India (ASCI).

Closely related to truth in advertising is the question of truth in labelling. The label gives additional information about the product and the seller seeks to enable the buyer to know what the product will or will not do for him. Like ads, labels are also misused. To check such misuse, the government has passed the Central Packaged Commodities (Regulation) Order, 1975, which requires the disclosure of such information about the products as the name of manufactures, date of manufacture, date of expiry, net weight, and sale price on the containers and the packages.

Responsibility for Product Performance

Consumers have the right to expect the products they buy to be what their producers claim them to be and further they have a right to expect them to be safe. In the past when products were simple and familiar to consumers, it was reasonable to expect them to share responsibility for product performance. As the products become varied and complex and unfamiliar to the buyers, responsibility in performance should not be theirs. Businessmen should assume full responsibility. Such assurances as moneyback guarantee and guarantee for a said period are not enough. Responsibility for performance and safety throughout the life of the product should be assumed by businessmen. Luckily, for businessmen, product liability suits are not filed in law courts by consumers in India as is done in the US.

Cost of Consumer Protection

Consumer protection has cost implications.

Consumer no doubt needs protection against business malpractices. But too much protection is not advisable as it has cost implications. Consumer protection costs may be defined in three ways:

Economic Costs: Economic costs are connected with the defending charges of regulatory agencies and cost of manufacturing consumer safety devices such as safety belts, pollution control devices and built-in safety measures. The economic costs are passed on to the consumers through increased prices of goods and services.

Social Costs: More severe are the social costs which reflect themselves in at least three ways. First is the loss of freedom of choice to the buyer. Increased protection means that the consumer depends more on the system, thus depriving him of an opportunity of making a choice, no matter if mistakes are committed in the process. Mistakes, it is said, are a part of growth. Secondly, increased protection results in the proliferation of government agencies which upsets pluralistic balance. Finally, the fear of product liability discourages innovation.

Opportunity Costs: A third category of consumer protection cost is opportunity costs. These costs arise from the ordering of social priorities.

"Resources used for one purpose make them unavailable for other use." Observe Keith Davis and Blomstrom, "Disproportionate concern with consumer protection may divert attention and resources away from social problems which should have equal or perhaps greater priority."[17]

RURAL DEVELOPMENT

Majority of people in our country, as is well known, live in villages. The living conditions of villagers are far from satisfactory. Anything that is done in the direction of improving their living conditions is welcome. The Government of India is doing a yeoman service in this direction under its Integrated Rural Development Programme (IRDP). The efforts of the government need to be supplemented by business establishments, because the task of making living decent and comfortable for villagers is stupendous, considering the number of villages in our country and their geographical spread.

Rural development encompasses a wide variety of activities such as laying roads, providing drinking water, offering jobs and the like.

What specific activities can business undertake in the name of rural development? There are many urgent and important facilities to be provided such as good roads, drinking water, employment, medical aid, family planning, housing, schools and nutrition programmes.

Many progressive business houses have adopted certain villages for their all-round development. Particular mention may be made of the public sector giant Bharat Heavy Electricals Ltd.(BHEL) which has carved out a name for itself in this direction.

There are other instances also. An IMRB study conducted recently reveals that 83 per cent of the 150 sample companies are active in rural development. On top are the Tatas who had set up Tata Steel Rural Development Society, way back in 1979 itself. Mafatlals were also one of the first industrialists to set up a rural development organisation, *viz*., *Satguru Seva Sangh*. Many companies are active in playing a facilitative role in implementing World Bank sponsored projects or the government's Integrated Rural Development projects. Mangalore Chemicals and Fertilizers(MCF), a UB group company, has been involved in socio-economic development work for several years now. In 1975, the United Kingdom, under what is known as the Colombo Plan, granted aid for the overall growth of villages in the developing countries. As part of the aid, 2,700 million tonnes of fertiliser was supplied to MCF by the UK government to undertake overall development activities in the underdeveloped regions of Karnataka. MCF sold this and with the proceeds, created a corpus of Rs.40 lakh.

MCF surveyed several villages in the districts of Bellary and Raichur, keeping in view the irrigation potential, agricultural practices followed, adequate representation of small and medium land holding farmers as also rural artisans and selected Sangankal village of Bellary district and Herur village of Gangavathi taluk of Raichur district for implementation of the project. The project name is rather a mouthful: UK-MCF-TGB. Introduction of double cropping, use of balanced fertilisers, better water management etc. are a few of the achievements which have increased the income of farm families from Rs.4,000 to Rs.10,000 annually. From the interest accrual on the corpus fund of Rs.40 lakh, the trust has so far spent Rs.21.26 lakh towards various developmental activities.

Further down South, SPIC's agro-service centres (ASC) are yielding similar results. 10 ASCs were set up in Tamil Nadu. Today, there are 21 and extend to the neighbouring states of Andhra Pradesh, Karnataka and Pondicherry. Each ASC has 10 villages attached to it as satellite villages, located within a radius of 10-15 km from the main centre.

Apart from the ASCs, SPIC has rural development centres in Tamil Nadu and Andhra Pradesh for training in scientific farming and helping in integrated farming efforts, the agricultural and rural development programmes are conducted by technical assistants. Necessary tools like tractors with accessories, pre-fabricated buildings, agricultural implements and plant protection equipment are offered at subsidised rental rates.

PROJECTS AND PEOPLE

Citing a project in a particular area is not always welcome. The project once completed will result in, among other things, displacement or even death (see Box 35.12) of people who were hitherto inhabiting the area. It is the responsibility of the business to rehabilitate such displaced persons. Unfortunately, this responsibility is not realised by promoters-government or private. The Visakhapatnam Steel Plant provides a typical example. The project authorities had given an assurance that 5,000 displaced persons would be absorbed in the project subject to their suitability. So far, 1,339 of them have found jobs. Another 3,500 were to have been employed by the contractors. But it is not clear what happens to them once the contractor's job is over.[18] Another example is the Yeluru reservoir project in Andhra Pradesh which will displace 10,121 persons, including 3,000 from the Scheduled Castes and Tribes.[19] (see Box 35.13).

Huge projects displace people who need rehabilitation.

It is heartening to note that the late Mrs.Indira Gandhi took a firm stand on the conditions that should be fulfilled before a green field project can be considered for clearance... at least two schemes that the state governments must tie up before they can expect to secure approval for their industrial

Box 35.12 **Biju Patnaik Reveals a 30-year-old Secret**

Biju Patnaik is no stranger to making wacky statements. Residents of Orissa put it all down to his advancing years. But a recent admission shocked even those who had by now gotten used to his pronouncements.

Patnaik said that 200 children had been sacrificed at the altar of economic development. It all happened 30 years ago, when Biju Patnaik was overseeing the construction of the Paradip port. At the time, he was in his first term as Chief Minister. To get the project completed in record time came as a challenge, especially as the Congress government at the Centre-Biju was a Congressmen then-he had not favoured the project due to the area's adverse topography.

Paradip was completed in two years. But three decades later, it has been revealed by Patnaik himself-that his 'glorious success' was steeped in the blood of 200 children.

While addressing a gathering at a seminar on fiscal discipline organised by the Orissa Financial Service Association (OFSA) in Bhubaneswar, the 78-year-old ex-Chief Minister spoke of the lightening speed with which construction work at Paradip had been completed. In the same breath, he lamented today's slow pace in completing projects.

Patnaik recalled that he had entrusted the construction of the port project along with that of the Daitari-Paradip highway to an executive engineer, instructing him to complete the jobs in record time.

The engineer accepted on one condition:no action should be taken against drivers of the hundreds of trucks pressed into service if people were killed in road accidents caused by the lorries. Patnaik agreed.

The engineer had imported about 900 trucks and drivers from Punjab. The vehicles piled at breakneck speed in and out of villages around the projects. Although 200 children were run over by the fast-moving trucks, no driver was arrested in view of Patnaik's agreement with the executive engineer.

These revelations set off reactions of shock and anger. Patnaik baiters are now wondering how many children will be sacrificed for the Chief Minister's latest pet project, a steel plant at Daitari.

(**Source**: *Sunday* 13-19 June, 1993).

Box 35.13 **Narmada Dam Oustees' Condition Pathetic**

"When waters will come, rats and men will flee alike." This was the terse comment of an official of the Sardar Sarovar Narmada Nigam Limited (SSNNL), when asked about the delay in the rehabilitation and resettlement (R&R) of the tribals and villagers displaced by the Sardar Sarovar Project (SSP).

The flippancy showed the power of might over right. It also showed that R&R is low on priority in the scheme of SSNNL. Said Arjun, a tribal-oustee, "Once a leaf falls off the tree, can you implant it? Likewise, once we tribals are uprooted from our ancestral homes, can we be rehabilitated? We are as good as dead."

Two years after the swirling waters of the Narmada inundated their homes, the Vasava tribals of Makkerkheda are yet to be rehabilitated. Still living under tin sheds in their make shift accommodation at Vadaj, they are awaiting the permanent homes they were promised. This is the second rehabilitation site they've been put up at. The earlier site, at Taraswa, was so secluded that the oustees were frequently robbed off whatever belongings they had salvaged. Ultimately, they were shifted to Vadaj.

They have spent two seasons of summer and winter in discomfort and uncertainty. Being tribals, they sowed jowar, arhar and maize, but the land is so saline that despite two monsoons they've failed to reap a harvest. Many of them, the men particularly, go out to nearby towns and cities in search of daily labour. Nobody from this village has been given ownership rights (pattas) to the land promised.

Women in worse situation

Women are in a much worse situation. They have to walk additional two to three kilometres to fetch fuel wood. In addition, they have to arrange fodder for their cattle in the wilderness. This has increased their working hours. In desperation, most have started burning the 'balls' and other wood they had brought from their home in the forest to be used for constructing the new homes. Kapila, 26, thought the 'balls' would last them at least a year. She said most people from their village were feeling lost and rootless in their new surroundings. Many have gone back. The rehabilitation site is not electrified and the water is brackish.

The families of Birchi and Raman of Simalkhedi village in Maharashtra were among the 30 who literally fled their homes faced by submergence. They were shown lush green fields in Thuvava village near Baroda. They were promised fertile lands where they'd be given ownership rights and could farm. Their lives would be better off, they were told. As the waters rose and swamped their homes they decided to take the offer one year ago.

Today, they regret and yearn to go back. Said Birchi, "We have no hope here. We don't know what we will leave behind for our children. If only they give us back our land we would prefer to go back to Simalkhedi rather than live this rootless life in Gujarat."

Even though their rehabilitation site is barely 12 kilometres from Baroda, they still live in tin sheds. The promised Rs.10,000 per family to rebuild their houses has not yet been given. Worse still, the displaced persons live in fear of voicing their miseries. They fear being hounded out of the new sites, which will render them homeless and shelterless.

The World Bank withdrew its support to the project in 1993 under pressure from the Narmada Bachao Andolan which questioned the non-participatory development model imposed on a section of the people (tribals and villages) who have no lobby. However, the World Bank set R&R benchmarks, to which the Gujarat government gave its commitment. But a visit to the R&R sites in Thuvava, Vadaj and nearby villages showed that rehabilitation and resettlement is pathetic.

Significantly, the government of Madhya Pradesh, where the displacement of tribals is the largest-33,514 families-has publically expressed its inability to resettle such a large population. It said it has neither the land nor the resources.

(**Source**: *The Hindu*, Jan 19, 1995).

projects: one of them relates to afforestation and the other to rehabilitation of displaced persons. Both are aimed at safeguarding human interest.

PHYSICALLY HANDICAPPED

Yet another social action of business houses is the rehabilitation of physically handicapped people. We have 70 million disabled citizens in the country and the response of the corporate sector towards these

Physically handicapped people need protection and not sympathy.

hapless citizens has been lukewarm. The Disability Act, 1995, which mandates that every enterprise in the organised sector should reserve three per cent of its workforce for the physically handicapped, has not made any difference. According to a study conducted by the National Centre for Promotion of Employment for Disabled People (NCPEDP), the average percentage of physically handicapped in the total workforce of public sector enterprises is just 0.4 per cent. In the private sector, it is much less - 0.23 per cent. Table 35.6 gives more dctails about the number of disabled employees in select private and public sector enterprises.

ACQUIRED IMMUNE DEFICIENCY SYNDROME (AIDS)

The year 1983 goes down in history as the darkest year for it was in this year that scientists discovered a baffling disease called AIDS, also named 'Gray Plague', that has taken a heavy toll of human lives. Across the globe, 2.3 million people died in 1997 because of the dreadful disease. At the beginning of 1998, more than 30 million people, about 0.5% of the earth's population, have been infected with HIV- the AIDS-causing virus.

The African continent is the worst hit. In Zimbabwe and Botswana, for example, a quarter of the adult population is infected. Unless there is an unforeseen breakthrough in treatment, all those infected will die from AIDS. As a result, the life expectancy of the average Zimbabwean, having risen steadily until 1990, when it was 56, is likely to fall to only 49 by the end of the century and that of a Botswana, will fall by a decade.

The virus is also spreading into areas that were previously AIDS free. In some of the former communist countries of Europe, rates of HIV infection have risen several hundred-fold over the past three years. In China, where HIV was until recently confined to the south-west and the coast, every province has now registered people affected with the virus.

India also has fallen into the vortex. Nearly five million people have already become victims and the scourge is spreading across the country. (See Fig. 35.3 and 35.4).

Figure 35.3 **HIV Growth in India**

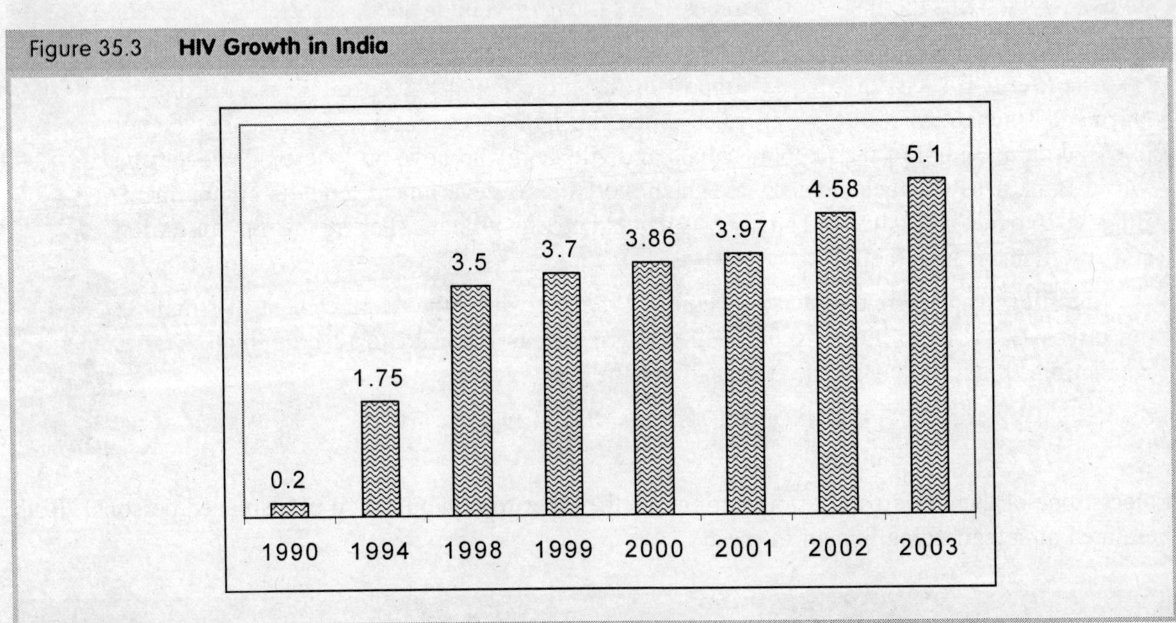

AIDS is likely to cause considerable confusion and disruption in the workforce. When employees realise that they are working with an infected worker, they demand that the hapless employee should be dismissed. If the management discharges the employee, the law is violated, particularly in the US

Figure 35.4 **Cases of AIDS in India**

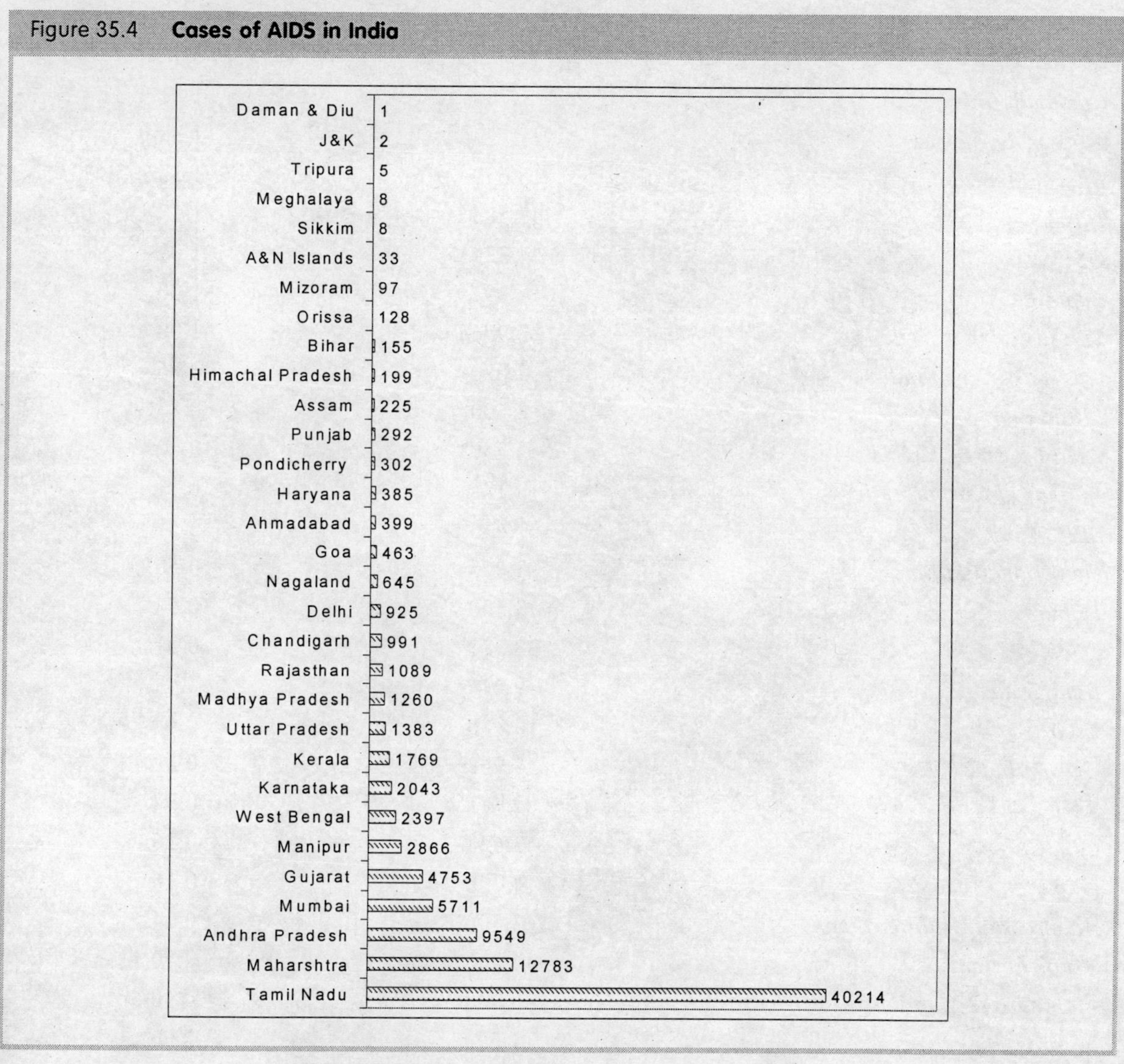

where individuals who have AIDS are protected by federal, state and local laws. This protection generally comes in the form of protection against discrimination and is based on the fact the virus cannot be spread by casual contact.

Organistions are hard hit by additional costs-direct and indirect-when their employees contact the disease. Direct costs are in the form of increased medical burden. Indirect costs result from the loss of productivity when employees refuse to work with an AIDS-infected worker.

Much of the problems relating to AIDS stems from the ignorance of people about the disease. They believe that the disease is highly infectious and there is no remedy for the victims. It is the responsibility of the government and business and non-governmental organisations to create better awareness about the disease in the minds of the people and extend appropriate medical help.

The government seems to be content with merely releasing advertisements, advising the public about the need to use AIDS preventive devices. An active government should go beyond this and take measures to control the epidemic.

Credit should go to the Central Government undertakings, particularly HMT and BHEL, for initiating measures to prevent AIDS. Teams of doctors from in-house Occupational Health Services

Table 35.6 **Disabled Employees**

Company	*No.of Employees*	*% of disabled*
Cochin Refineries	1,766	1.81
Madras Refineries	1,737	1.38
Bharat Electronics	15,639	1.37
HPCL	11,583	1.18
GSFC	4,329	1.02
Lupin Labs	897	1.00
Videsh Sanchar Nigam	2,976	1.00
Gas Authority of India	3,020	0.86
MRF	8,500	0.85
Asea Brown Boveri	250	0.80
Indian Oil Corporation	13,188	0.71
SPIC	2,635	0.57
Hero Honda Motors	3,055	0.56
Dabur	3,500	0.54
Telco	35,180	0.51
Bajaj Auto	9,611	0.48
Escorts	10,900	0.45
Grasim Industries	4,948	0.32
SAIL	2,02,781	0.32
ONGC	43,628	0.26
Glaxo	4,296	0.16
Andhra Valley Power Supply	3,500	0.14
Ashok Leyland	14,400	0.10
Mahindra & Mahindra	16,000	0.10
Madras Computers	1,600	0.06
Indian Hotels	13,000	0.02
TISCO	60,205	0.01
HLL	40,000	0.01
Bombay Dyeing	10,000	Nil
Castrol	1,300	Nil
Colgate-Palmolive	1,300	Nil
EID Parry	1,500	Nil
Essar Shipping	82	Nil
Indian Rayon	278	Nil
Ispat Industries	1,100	Nil
L&T	488	Nil
Nagarjuna Fertilisers	1,545	Nil
NOCIL	1,971	Nil
Tata Chemicals	389	Nil
Zurai Industries	1,005	Nil

visit plants and give lectures to employees on AIDS prevention. Lectures are held once or twice every year.

ASHA Foundation (Action Service Hope for AIDS) is a Bangalore-based voluntary organisation which is rendering yeoman service in creating awareness of AIDS infection and counselling to HIV-posivitive persons, their families and the community. There are similar organisations in other cities too.

What is needed most for the employers is to educate workers about AIDS. The following guidelines need to be followed to make the educational programme effective:

- Employees must be made a understand how AIDS is contacted. Understanding about the ways of contacting AIDS will ensure that the activities do not occur at the workplace.
- Presentations to employees must be handled by professionals, preferably from experts. This is necessary as the message presented is going to include sexual references which, if not handled properly, are likely to have a negative impact on employees.
- All employees must attend the sessions.

BE AN ETHICAL FIRM

Since ethics is an import requisite of any business a separate chapter (Chapter 36) is devoted for its discussion.

QUESTIONS

1. What is ecology? How is it disrupted?
2. What is the responsibility of business towards ecology?
3. Do you think that clean environment and economic development are inconsistent? Discuss.
4. What is consumerism? How does it affect business?
5. What are the obligations of business towards women?
6. Discuss the ways through which business can contribute to rural development.
7. Bring out the social responsibility towards disabled people and those afflicted with AIDS.

ASSIGNMENTS

1. Select five women executives. Go with questionnaires and seek answers from those executives. Questions to cover such areas as how the women are balancing work and life, how they are tackling workplace harassment and the like. Prepare a report based on the responses.
2. Select 25 families where small boys and girls have been taken off from schools and are converted into wage-earners. Find out the reasons and prepare a report.

REFERENCES

1. Cited in *Eco-Crisis*, Ed., Cecil E.Johnson, New York, John Wiley and Sons, 1970, p.2.
2. Keith Davis and Robert L. Blomstrom, *Business and Society-Environment and Responsibility*, p.431.

3. Sir Edmond Hillary, Ed., *Ecology 2000-The Changing Face of Earth*, p.21.
4. Cecil E.Johnson, Ed., *Eco-Crisis*, p.116.
5. Homi J.H. Taleyarkhan, *Environment and Forestry in Economic Development*, p.7.
6. AMBIDO, *A Journal of the Human Environment*, Sweden, Vol.17, No.6, 1988, p.412.
7. Keith Davis and Robert L.Blomstorm, *op. cit., p.427.*
8. A.D.Karve, "Does Intensive Agriculture Damage Environment", *Namma Parisara*, Journal by Karnataka State Pollution Control Board, Oct.1985, p.10.
9. *India Today*, Feb.1-15, 1981.
10. *State of India's Environment*, 1982, New Delhi.
11. *Deccan Herald*, Bangalore, Dec.12, 1982.
12. Keith Davis and Robert L.Blomstrom, *op. cit.*, p.437.
13. Bhupesh Mangala, "Environmental Challenges; More Government or Better Government or Better Governance", AMBIO, Vol.17 No.17, No.6, 1988, p.411.
14. P.L.Diwakar Rao, *Pollution Control Handbook, 1986*, Hyderabad Utility Publications Ltd. p.4.
15. Bengt Lundholm, *Ecology and the Less Developed Countries*, Swedish Natural Science Research Council, Sweden, 1971, p.92.
16. *Span*, April, 1992,
16(a). Michael P.Todaro and Stephen C.Smith, *Economic Development*, Pearson, 2003, Pp.375-376.
17. *Economic Times*, dated May 1, 1996.
18. *Ibid.*
19. *Ibid.*

CHAPTER OUTLINE

Nature of Ethics
Sources of Ethics
- Religion
- Cultural Experience
- Legal System

Why is Ethics Important?
Are Businessmen Ethical?
Ethical Dilemmas
- Face-to-Face Ethics
- Corporate Policy Ethics
- Functional Area Ethics

Managing Ethics
- Top Management
- Codes of Ethics
- Ethics Committees
- Ethics Hotlines
- Ethics Training Programme
- Ethics and Law

Corporate Culture and Ethical Climate
Improving Ethical Decision Making
- Difficulties in Decision Making
- Suggestions for Making Ethical Decisions

36 Business Ethics

LEARNING OBJECTIVES

After reading this Chapter, you should be able to:

1. Understand the nature and sources of business ethics
2. Appreciate the need for ethics and assess whether or not our businessmen are ethical
3. Outline ethical dilemmas and ways of resolving the conflicts
4. Suggest ways of managing ethics
5. Draw a matrix showing interaction between culture and ethical climate
6. Shortlist difficulties in ethical decision making and suggest ways of improving decision making

Till now we have discussed the various facets of business together with its environmental factors. What needs to be emphasised here is that the shape of business, the players in the field of business, their actions and motives and the role of regulatory agencies will be different in the days to come. We will have captains of business for whom volumes and bank balances alone matter. Social responsibility actions which inspired leaders of the past may cease to be motivators in future. Principles and policies which guided actions of business people in the past may look archaic and irrelevant.

Future captains of the industry will be in a great hurry to expand businesses and to swell bank balances. Any motive and any action which help achieve these will be accepted and respected. Ends will justify the means.

The most conspicuous causality in the emerging business scenario will be ethics-the moral values which will discriminate between what is desirable and what is undesirable and between what is acceptable and what is not acceptable. But ethics should never be compromised. Businessmen should be told that ethics and ethics alone will help them survive and succeed in their ventures.

The relevance of ethics is felt more now than ever before. Universities and institutes have made it a point to introduce one paper on ethics in any course relating to business. Any book or a journal on business management contains discussions on business ethics. This book is no exception.

This chapter is devoted to a detailed discussion of the nature of ethics and the need for ethics, ethical issues, managing business ethics and improving decision making on ethical issues.

NATURE OF ETHICS

Ethics refers to a system of moral principles-a sense of right and wrong and goodness and badness of actions and their motives and consequences. *Business ethics* refers to the application of ethics to business. To be more specific, business ethics is the study of good and evil, right and wrong and just and unjust actions of businessmen.[1]

Business ethics is an extension of values of personal life to business.

Business ethics does not differ from generally accepted norms of good or bad. If dishonesty is considered to be unethical and immoral in society, then any businessman who is dishonest with employees, customers, shareholders or competitors is acting unethically and immorally. If protecting others from any harm is considered to be ethical, then a company that recalls a defective and harmful product from the market is acting ethically. To be considered ethical, businessmen must draw their ideas about what is desirable behaviour from the same sources as anybody else. Businessmen should not try to evolve their own principles to justify what is right and wrong. Employees and employers may be tempted to apply special or weaker ethical rules to business situations. But society does not condone or permit such an exception. People who are in business are bound by the same ethical principles that apply to others.[2]

Two theories are pertinent when one talks about the nature of ethics.

Theory of amorality suggests that business actions should not be judged by general ethical standards. But the theory is not acceptable to many.

The *theory of moral unity* essentially advocates the principle that business actions should be judged by the general ethical standards of society. There exists only one ethical standard which applies to business and to non-business situations.

Opposed to the theory of moral unity is the *theory of amorality,* which argues that business can be amoral, and the actions of businessmen need not be guided by general ethical standards. Managers may act selfishly because the market mechanism distills their actions into benefits to shareholders and society at large. Adam Smith argued that the 'invisible hand' of the market assures that by

> "pursuing his own interest (a merchant) frequently promotes that of the society more effectively than when he really intends to promote it."

In this way, capitalism provides moral justification for the pursuit of profit through behaviour which is not purposefully ethical.[3]

However, the theory of amorality is not acceptable to anybody. Everyone agrees that business actions should be subject to the same ethical standards as the one applicable to the society in general.

SOURCES OF BUSINESS ETHICS

Managers in every society are influenced by three repositories of ethical values: religion, culture and law. These repositories contain unique systems of values that exert varying degrees of control over managers. A common thread, the idea of *reciprocity* or *mutual help,* runs through all the value systems. This idea reflects the central purpose of all ethics which is to bind the vast majority of individuals in society into a co-operative whole. Ethical values are a mechanism that controls behaviour in business and in the other walks of life. Ethical restraints are more effective than are cruder controls such as police, law suits or economic incentives. Ethical values channel individual energy into pursuits that are benign to others and beneficial to the society.

Religion

One of the oldest sources of ethical inspiration is religion. More than 100,000 different religions exist across the globe. But despite doctrinal differences, the major religions converge on the belief that ethics is an expression of divine will that reveals the nature of right and wrong in business and other areas of life. The world's great religions are also in agreement on fundamental principles which are similar to the building blocks of secular ethical doctrine. The principle of reciprocity towards one's fellow human beings is found in all major religions such as Hinduism, Buddhism, Christianity, Islam, Judaism and Confucianism. The great religions preach the necessity for an orderly social system and emphasise social responsibility in such a way so as to contribute to the general welfare. Built upon such verities are many other rules of conduct.[4]

Cultural Experience[5]

Culture, as was stated earlier, refers to a set of values, rules and standards transmitted among generations and acted upon to produce behaviours that fall within acceptable limits. These rules and standards always play an important part in determining values, because individuals anchor their conduct in the culture of the group. Civilisation itself is a cumulative cultural experience in which people have passed through three distinct phases of moral codification. These stages correspond to the changing economic and social arrangements in human history.

For millions of generations in the *hunting and gathering stage* of human development, ethics was adapted to conditions in which our ancestors had to be ready to fight, face brutal foes and suffer the hostile forces of nature. Under such circumstances, a premium was placed on pugnacity, appetite, greed and sexual readiness, since it was often the strongest who survived. Trade ethics in the early civilisations were frequently conducted by brute force and violence.

During hunting and gathering stage, premium was placed on pugnacity, appetite and greed.

Civilisation passed into an *agricultural stage* approximately 10,000 years ago, beginning a time when industriousness was more important than ferocity, thrift paid greater dividends than violence, monogamy became the prevailing sexual custom because of the relatively equal numbers of the sexes and peace came to be valued over wars, which destroyed crops and animals. These new values were codified into ethical systems which even guide the managers today.

Two centuries ago, society entered an *industrial stage* of cultural experience, and ethical systems once more began evolving to reflect the changing physical, cultural, institutional and intellectual environment. Large factories and corporations, population growth, capitalist and socialist economic doctrines and technologies have all assaulted the ethical standards of the agrarian stage. Industrialism has not created a distinct ethics, but it has created tensions with old ethical systems based on the values of agricultural societies. It does this by changing values related to what is good and bad. For example, the copious outpouring of material goods from factories has encouraged materialism and consumption at the expense of older virtues such as moderation and thrift. Managers run an industrial enterprise on the cutting edge of cultural experience. The tensions their actions create make business more ethically complex. For instance, the widespread use of computers for data storage and communication raises new issues of privacy and individual expression unlike those present in the agrarian societies.

The Legal System

Laws are rules of conduct, approved by legislatures, that guide human behaviour in any society. They codify ethical expectations and keep changing as new evils emerge. But laws cannot cover all ethical expectations of society. Law is reactive; new statutes and enforcement always lag behind the opportunity for corporate expediency.

Whatever ethics that law codifies, it is binding on business. Society expects business to abide by law and obeying law is presumed to be ethical behaviour.

Although society expects business to be law abiding, seldom does the business adhere to the rules. Law breaking in business is common. Taxes are evaded, hundreds of employees die because of occupational diseases, many die because of industrial accidents and million others receive disabling injuries on the job. The blame for these deaths and injuries can be shared by careless employees and by employers who fail to adhere to occupational health and safety laws.

Consumers suffer because of poor quality and high priced products supplied by businessmen. And business causes misery to the society by damaging the environment, disregarding environment protection laws.

WHY IS ETHICS IMPORTANT?[6]

Ethics is important to business for several reasons as stated below:

Ethics does not carry ethical ting only. It makes business sense too.

(i) *Ethics corresponds to basic human needs* It is a human trait that man desires to be ethical, not only in his private life but also in his business affairs where, being a manager, he knows his decisions may affect the lives of thousands of employees. Moreover, most people want to be part of an organisation which they can respect and be publicly proud of, because they perceive its purpose and activities to be honest and beneficial to the society. Most top managers would like to respond to this need of their employees; and they (managers) themselves feel an equal need to be genuinely proud of the company they are directing. These basic ethical needs compel the organisations to be ethically oriented.

(ii) *Values create credibility with the public* A company perceived by the public to be ethically and socially responsive will be honoured and respected even by those who have no intimate knowledge of its actual working. There will be an instinctive prejudice in favour of its products, since people believe that the company offers value for money. Its public issues will attract an immediate response.

(iii) *Values give management credibility with employees* Values are supposed to be a common language to bring leaderships and its people together. Organisational ethics, when perceived by employees as genuine, create common goals, values and language. The management has credibility with its employees precisely because it has credibility with the public. Neither sound business strategy, nor a generous compensation policy and fringe benefits can win employee credibility; and perceived moral and social uprightness can.

(iv) *Values help better decision making* Another point of great importance is that an ethical attitude helps the management make better decisions, i.e., decisions which are in the interest of the public, their employees and the company's own long term good, even though decision making is slower. This is so because respect for ethics will force a management to take various aspects-economic, social, and ethical- in making decisions.

(v) *Ethics and profit* Ethics and profit go together. A company which is inspired by ethical conduct is also profitable one. Value driven companies are sure to be successful in the long run, though in the short run, they may lose money.

(vi) *Law cannot protect society, ethics can* Ethics is important because the government, law and lawyers cannot do everything to protect society. Technology develops faster than the government can regulate. People in an industry often know the dangers in a particular technology better than the regulatory agencies. Further, government cannot always regulate all activities which are harmful to society. Where law fails, ethics can succeed. An ethical oriented management takes measures to prevent pollution and protect workers' health even before being mandated by law.

ARE BUSINESSMEN ETHICAL?

Are our businessmen ethical? The answer (with honorable exceptions) is in the negative (See Fig.36.1). As is too well known, most of our businessmen are lured by the fast-buck culture, i.e., to earn as much money and as fast as possible. Ends justify the means for our businessmen.

Figure 36.1 **Greasing the Palms**

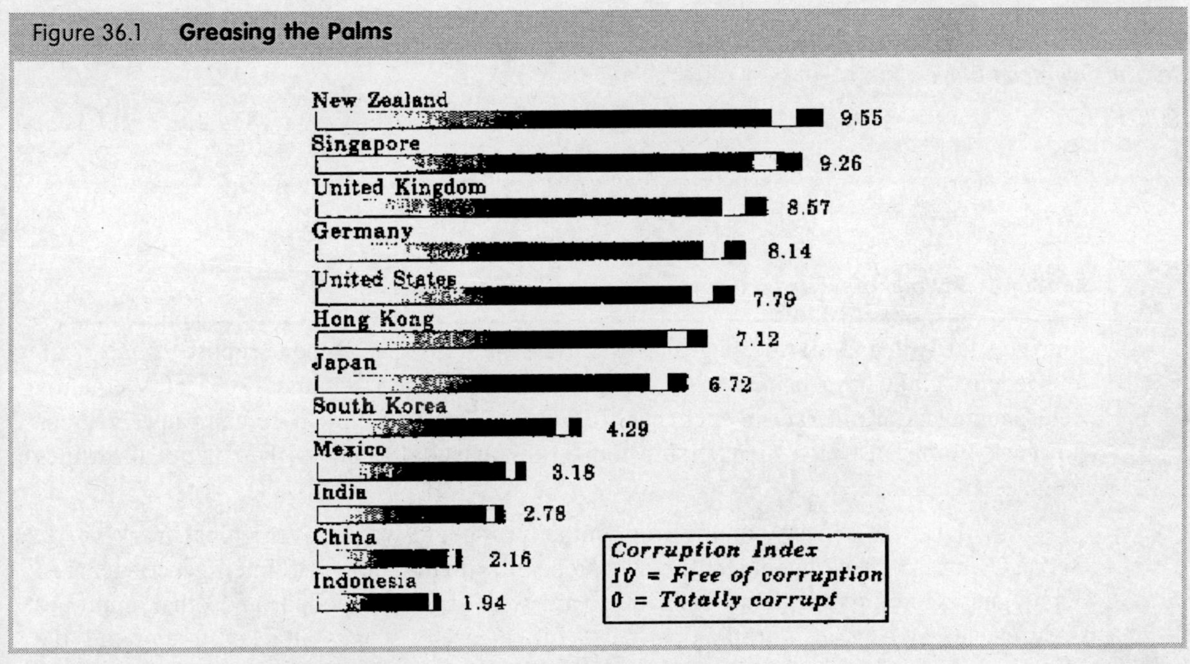

(**Source**: *Newsweek*).

(Ranking of businessmen's perceptions of the level of bribery and dishonesty in 41 nations)

Table 36.1 shows the number of frauds in public sector banks. These frauds reinforce the assertion that our bussinessmen are generally unethical. Corruption is not peculiar to our country. It is universal as Box 36.1 reveals.

Unethical practices were found even in our ancient culture. Not only rates of interest were exorbitant (60 per cent, 120 per cent and 240 per cent) but were charged differently to different castes. Manu and some other lawgivers laid down a sliding scale of interest for unsecured loans, according to the class of the debtor: Brahmins 24 per cent, Kshatriyas 36 per cent, Vaisyas 48 per cent, and Sudras 60 per cent per year.[7]

Manu recommended differential rates of interest depending on the castes.

Table 36.1 **Frauds in Public Sector Banks**

Bankwise frauds detected and amount involved in Rs. lakh during the year 1995 and 1996 (upto March)

Bank	*Number of fraud cases*	*Amount*
State Bank of India	657	2119.16
Canara Bank	216	1996.12
Bank of Maharashtra	39	1935.38
Bank of Baroda	147	1325.08
Syndicate Bank	131	805.11
Oriental Bank of Comm.	16	632.74
Bank of India	209	632.61
State Bank of Patiala	35	614.53
Andhra Bank	48	528.60
Punjab National Bank	83	403.75
UCO Bank	82	401.01
Union Bank of India	77	383.24
Indian Overseas Bank	53	332.31
Others	357	1814.20

(**Source:** *Ministry of Finance*)

Box 36.1 **A World of Greased Palms**

Intrigue fairly leaps off the pages of the classified US government report. A German electronics giant pays bribes to win export sales. France demands 20% of Vietnam's telecommunications market in exchange for aid. A European aerospace company threatens to block European Union membership for Turkey and Malta unless their national airlines purchase its planes.

It's all part of a nasty, multibillion-dollar war being waged over global markets. A secret Commerce Department study, newly prepared with the help of US intelligence agencies, catalogues scores of incidents of bribery, aid with strings attached, and other improper inducements by America's trading partners. In the case of strings-attached foreign aid, the deals may violate international trade pacts. And the cost of such practices to the US economy appears enormous. In 1994 alone, US intelligence tracked 100 deals worth a total of $45 billion in which overseas outfits used bribes to undercut US rivals, the study says. The result: Foreign companies won 80% of the deals.

Sanctimonious? Among the main culprits are some of America's staunchest political allies: France, Germany and Japan. The corporations involved aren't cited by name in the study, which have been in the works for months and key parts of which were reviewed by **Business Week**. But government sources identify premier European hightech companies - including Germany's Siemens, France's Alcatel Alsthom and the European airframe consortium Airbus Industries as among the major practitioners. Foreign governments and companies, of course, gripe that the Clinton Administration has been doing lots of aggressive advocacy of its own to win deals for US business. "Each time we win a deal, it's because of dirty tricks," says an Airbus official with bitter sarcasm. "Each time Boeing wins, it is because of a better product."

Indeed, many officials overseas view the US holier-than-thou attitude about shady business practices as naive and hypocritical. As word of the report's contents gradually leaks (some 50 copies recently were distributed to Congress and key agencies), US trading partners may be angered to learn how closely American spies are tracking their dealings. Indeed, the growing role of the CIA and its sister shops in commercial information-gathering already is controversial, with critics contending that the spies are inappropriately trying to justify a $28 billion budget in the post-cold-war era. But former CIA general counsel Elizabeth J Rindskopf says the CIA is simply responding to demands from other US government agencies for information to help level the global playing field.

There's more to it than that, "As the importance of geopolitical struggle has declined, conflict has found a new home," says Edward N Luttwak, senior fellow at the Centre for Strategic and International Studies.

Economic trends tell the tale: The US is more dependent than ever on exports to fuel its economic growth. Europe and Japan are saddled by slow growth. Heightened global competition adds to the temptation to seek advantages through questionable tactics - particularly in key sectors such as aerospace, where demand is weak. "Companies and governments are more willing to resort to unconventional methods to make a sale because any sale is precious," says Joel Johnson, international vice-president for the Aerospace Industries Association of America. During the next decade, the pervasiveness of such practices spells trouble for US companies girding to compete for an estimated $1 trillion worth of overseas infrastructure projects. American business already is handicapped by the US comparatively puny spending on export promotion. The Commerce report, which also reviews legitimate competitive practices such as trade missions and financial aid to exporters, reveals a stark gap.

Even so, Republican trade hawks on Capitol Hill want to slash funds for Commerce's trade programmes. Commerce officials hope the competitive-practice report will help derail those moves. It's certainly a timely showcase for Commerce Secretary Ronald H Brown to reemphasise his role as roving advocate for American business. "The findings are alarming," Brown told **Business Week**.

Wads of Cash. To some European executives, the Clinton administration doesn't shy away from questionable arm-twisting. An Airbus official calls President Clinton's 1993 phone call to King Fahd of Saudi Arabia to lobby for Boeing Co. and McDonnell Douglas Corp a 'blatant' disregard for the rules. "The power of the American government is far greater than any European government," the official says. Too bad, retorts one US official: "If we're going to provide a security umbrella for a country, it's reasonable to expect our companies to get treated fairly." Certainly, not all US companies have clean hands. In October, a former vice-president at Lockheed Martin Corp was sentenced to 18 months in prison and a $125,000 fine for bribing a member of the Egyptian Parliament to win an order for three C-130 cargo planes. The case is surprising because Lockheed was at the centre of a bribery scandal in Japan neraly 20 years ago and has signed a consent decree to refrain from such practices. That paved the way for the 1977 Foreign Corrupt Practices Act, which bars US companies from paying bribes to win business.

Some US companies find creative ways to skirt the law. To secure a mining venture in a developing nation, an American company recently flew officials from the country to the US, put them up in a fancy hotel for a week, and gave them a wad of cash for a shopping spree. A US intelligence source says the trip is problematic: "What's the difference between giving an official shopping money and handing him an envelope of cash in his office?"

But US and other trade experts have little doubt that overseas companies are more likely to offer bribes because their cultures and legal systems permit it. In Francc, foreign payments to middlemen are considcred legitimate business tax deductions. Germany has similar rules, though officials in Bonn say they might junk them if there were an international accord to outlaw bribery.

Even so, there's little US support for easing anti-bribery laws. Instead, many American executives are urging the administration to mount an aggressive campaign to get foreigners to play more by US rules.

US officials vow to fight for reform. And foreign trading partners may find that a good idea as long as everyone including the US-promises to play by the rules.

(**Source**: *The Economic Times*, Nov.19, 1995)

Debtors were imprisoned or enslaved by creditors until they had paid off their debts. There were instances of debtors committing suicide unable to bear the harassment by creditors. We read stories about the atrocities committed by *Sresti* or Setty, the trader in his village. These stories may be mere tales, but we are sure, they were inspired by real situations which existed centuries ago.

ETHICAL DILEMMAS

Several ethical dilemmas confront a manager. The ethical dilemmas stem from three sources: face-to-face ethics, corporate policy ethics and functional-area ethics.[8]

Face-to-Face Ethics These arise mainly because there is a human element in most business transactions. For example, a purchasing agent may develop personal relationship with the sales representative who sells supplies to a company; they frequently know one another on a first-name basis, have lunch together and talk often on the phone. A company's best customers may be well known to people in the production department; it helps to ensure that the company's products fit the customer needs.

Because business is composed of these human transactions, it should not be surprising that face-to-face ethical dilemmas arise often.

It is likely that the quality assurance man winks at minor defects and approves a lot delivered by a supplier because of the personal relationship the two enjoy between them. It is also not unlikely that the supervisor over-rates the performance of an employee because of the similar relationship that exists between the two.

Corporate Policy Ethics Companies are often faced with ethical dilemmas that affect their operations across all departments and divisions. Following conflicting situations are typical:

Corporate policies generate ethical dilemmas.

(a) Your R & D department has modernised one of your products. It is not really '*new and improved*' but you know printing this statement on the package and using it in the advertisement will increase sales. What would you do?

(b) You are interviewing a former product manager who just left a competitor's company. You are thinking of hiring him. He would be more than happy to tell you all the competitor's plans for the coming years. What would do you?

(c) You have a chance to win a big account that will mean a lot to you and our company. The purchasing agent hinted that he would be influenced by a gift. Your assistant recommends sending a fine colour television set to his home. What would you do?

(d) You produce an anti-dandruff shampoo that is effective with one application. Your assistant says that the product would turn over faster if the instructions on the label recommended two applications. What would you do?

(e) You work for a cigarette company and up to now have not been convinced that cigarettes cause cancer. A recent report has come across your desk that clearly establishes the connection between cigarette smoking and cancer. What would you do?[9]

Another issue relates to the consequences of employment contraction in labour intensive basic industries because of the improved methods of production. Modern technology replacing older methods of production results in hundreds being rendered jobless. The issue therefore is: global economic competitiveness or local social-psychological stability?

The ethical burden of deciding corporate policy matters normally rests upon a company's top management. The top managers and directors are responsible for making policies and implementing them too. The ethical content of their policies can have enormous impact throughout the company. It can set an ethical tone and send strong signals to all employees as well as to external stakeholders.

Functional Area Ethics Functional areas of business are likely to confront ethical issues. Accounting is a critical function of any business. Accounting statements reveal to the managers and owners about the financial soundness of a company. Managers, investors, regulating agencies, tax collectors and trade unions rely on accounting data to make key decisions. Honesty, integrity and accuracy are absolute requirements of the accounting function. Professional accounting organisations have evolved generally accepted accounting standards whose purpose is to establish uniform standards for reporting accounting data. When they are followed, these standards ensure a high level of honest and ethical accounting disclosures. Rarely are they followed in practice.

Ethical dilemmas crop up in purchasing departments where strong pressures are felt to obtain the lowest possible prices from suppliers and where suppliers too feel a similar need to bag lucrative contracts. Bribes, kickbacks and discriminatory pricing are temptations to both the parties.

Marketing is another area of the ethics issue. Pricing, promotions, advertising, product information, relations between ad agencies and their clients and marketing research are potential areas of ethical dilemmas.

Then there is the area of sophisticated communication technology which is grossly abused or misused to realise one's ambitions.

MANAGING ETHICS

In the past, it was assumed in most companies that ethics was a matter of individual conscience. But the scenario has changed. Today, many companies are using managerial techniques that are designed to encourage ethical behaviours. Some of the managerial interventions to ensure ethical conduct are explained below. (see Box 36.2).

Top Management

It is the chief executive officer who should take initiative in ensuring ethical standards in his organisation. The words of J.R.D. Tata are worth recollecting in this context.

> "..... has also worked against our growth. What would have happened if our philosophy was like that of some other companies which do not stop at any means to attain their ends. I have often thought of that and I have come to the conclusion that if we were like these other groups, we would be twice as big as we are today. What we have scarificed is a 100 per cent growth."[10]

Box 36.2 **Tata's Code of Conduct**

FOR THE COMPANY

* To supply goods and services of the highest quality standards to ensure the total satisfaction of customers.
* To engage only in activities beneficial to the national interest of the country they operate in.
* To be fully transparent in accounting and financial reporting standards.
* To fully strive for the establishment and support of a competitive open market economy and to abhor unfair trade practices.
* To neither give nor take any illegal payment, remuneration, gift, donation or comparable benefit to obtain business or favours.
* To comply with all regulations regarding the preservation of the environment.
* To be a good corporate citizen and to actively assist in the improvement of the quality of life of the community with the objective of making it self-reliant. These social activities are regarded as an integral part of their business plans and not as an optional part.
* To co-operate and share physical, human and management resources with other Tata companies so long as this does not adversely affect its business interests and shareholder value.

FOR THE EMPLOYEES

* Conduct themselves professionally with professionalism, honesty, integrity as well as high moral and ethical standards and to be fair and transparent and to be seen so by third parties.
* Not derive any benefit from any information about the Company or Group which constitutes inside information.
* Report to the management any actual or possible violation of the Code or an event that the employee becomes aware of, that could affect the business or reputation of the employee's company or any other Tata company.
* Permits employees to pursue an active role in civic or political affairs as long as it does not affect the business or interests of the company or the group.

In addition, management must avoid adopting business strategies, schedules and reward systems that place unreasonable pressure on employees.

Code of Ethics

Code of ethics have become popular. Codes vary from book-length formulations to succinct statements which in one or two pages, express a general philosophy for managing conflicts. Nearly 95 per cent of Fortune 500 companies have codes and the trend is visible in our corporate sector also. Read box 36.2 for a typical code of conduct.

Industry associations too have evolved codes of conduct of their own. For example, the Council for Fair Business Practices (CFBP) established in 1966, by leading private sector industrialists in Western India, adopted the following code of fair business practices:

- To charge only fair and reasonable prices and take every possible step to ensure that the prices to be charged to the consumer are brought to his notice.
- To take every possible step to ensure that the agents or dealers... do not charge prices higher than fixed.
- In times of scarcity, not to withhold or suppress stocks of goods with a view to hoarding or profiteering.
- Not to produce or trade in spurious goods of standards lower than specified.
- Not to adulterate goods supplied.
- Not to publish misleading advertisements.
- To invoice goods exported or imported at their correct prices.
- To maintain accuracy in weights and measures of goods offered for sale.
- Not to deal knowingly in smuggled goods.
- Providing after-sales service where necessary or possible.
- Honouring the fundamental rights of the consumers-Right of Safety, Right to Choose, Right to Information and Right to be Heard.
- Discharging social responsibilities and the responsibility to protect the environment and nature's infrastructure.
- Ensuring that the product-warranty is offered in simple, unambiguous and concise language, highlighting the rights of the consumer under it.

It is evident that the above recommendations constitute a primary-level, self-regulating charter for enlightened citizenship amongst business entities. The CFBP has instituted a set of prizes and awards called 'Jamnalal Bajaj Uchit Vyavahar Puraskar' (or Jamnalal Bajaj Prize For Fair Business Practices) to promote exemplary application of the above norms. The CFBP President claimed that sustained pressure from this Council had resulted in the creation of the Advertising Standards Council of India (ASOI) and in the promulgation of the Consumer Protection Act.

The Federation of Indian Chambers of Commerce and Industry (which excludes the MNCs) has recently issued a declaration on 'Norms of Business Ethics' consisting of ten points. The list is almost identical to that of the CFBP. The Punjab, Haryana and Delhi Chamber of Commerce has also lately formulated a 'Code of Ethics'. The code says:

- Business must maintain the highest standards of behavior...(for) the benefit of industry, employees, customers, shareholders and the society.
- Goods and services must conform to the commitment promised to customers. Business must be realistic and truthful in stating claims.
- Customers must be given best possible service and treated with respect and fairness.
- Business must understand and respect the needs, concerns and welfare of the community and society. It should use knowledge and experience for upgrading the quality of life. All business endeavours must combine the qualities of private excellence for public good.
- The best way of promoting high standards of business practices is through self-regulation. The Code has been designed as an instrument of self-regulation to serve as a voluntary guideline towards better quality of life and higher standards of business practice.

The Advertising Standards Council of India expects, among other things, that there will be:

(a) no offense to generally accepted norms of public decency;

(b) truthfulness and honesty in claims and representation and

(c) no indiscriminate advertising of products which are hazardous to society or individuals.

Whoever evolves the code, its purpose is to provide guidance to managers and employees when they encounter an ethical dilemma. The most effective codes are those drawn up with the co-operation and widespread participation of employees. An internal enforcement mechanism, including penalties for violating the code, adds teeth to the code.

Ethics Committees

Many companies have ethics committees to advise on ethical issues.

Such a committee can be a high-level one comprising the board of directors, chaired by the CEO of the company.

The committees field questions from employees, help the company establish policy in new or uncertain areas, advise the board of directors on ethical issues and over see the enforcement of the code of ethics.

Ethics Hot Lines

In some companies, when employees are troubled about some ethical issue but may be reluctant to raise it with their immediate supervisor, they can place a call on the company's 'ethics hot line.' A member of the ethics committee receives the confidential call and then quickly investigates the situation. Elaborate steps are taken to protect the identity of the caller, so as to encourage more employees to report any deviant behaviour. This technique is advantageous in as much as ethics hotlines encourage internal whistle-blowing, which is better for a company than to have disgruntled employees take their ethical complaints to the media.[11] (See Table 36.2).

Ethics Training Programmes

Nearly all companies which take ethics seriously provide training in ethics for their managers and employees. Such training programmes acquaint company personnel with the official company policy on ethical issues, and they show how those policies can be translated into the specifics of every day decision making. Often, simulated cases based on actual events in the company are used to illustrate how to apply ethical principles to on-the-job problems.

Generally speaking, ethics training is most effective when it is conducted by company managers, and is steered away from abstract philosophical discussions to focus on specifics from the work environment of those attending.

Table 36.2 **Whistleblowing in Action**

Sl No.	*Organisation*	*Whistleblower*	*Consequences*
1	Enron	Sherron Watkins	Liquidation of the company
2	Kellog India	Senior Executive (Name not known)	Sacking of two senior executives who were promoted for excellent performance a few months before
3	Director, FBI, US	Coleen Rowly	Attack on the World Trade Centre, US
4	Worldcom	Cynthia Cooper	Company gone bust
5	Xerox	Name not known	CFO made to pay $5.5 million in fines and banned by the SEC from practising accounting
6	Heinz India Jhonson and Johnson Bayer India	Installed Whistle-blowing system	No incident reported
7	LG India	Names not known but 10-12 cases have been reported to head office, South Korea	Not known
8	National Highway Authority of India	S.K.Dubey	S.K.Dubey murdered. Nothing happened to the organisation.
9	Hong Kong City Civil Service	Lo Pui-Laru	Guilty disciplined but Lo has been ostracised by fellow workers
10	Modern Food Industries Ltd.,	Gobind Yadav	Suspended and dismissed, however, Delhi High Court ordered his reinstatement

Ethics and Law

Law and ethics aim at one thing-defining proper and improper behaviour. But the two are not quite the same. Laws are a society's attempt to formalise-that is, to reduce to written rules-ideas about what is right and what is wrong in various walks of life. However, it is rarely possible for written rules to capture all the subtle shadings that people give to ethics. Ethical concepts are more complex than written rules. Ethics deals with human dilemmas that frequently go beyond the formal language of law and the meanings given to legal rules.

Similarities and differences apart, legal rules help promote ethical behaviours in organisations. Some of the Acts which seek to ensure fair business practices in our country are the following:

The Foreign Exchange Regulation Act, 1973 now replaced by FEMA

The Companies Act, 1956

The Monopolies and Restrictive Trade Practices Act, 1969, now replaced by the Competition Act, 2002.

The Consumer Protection Act, 1986

The Environment Protection Act, 1986

The Essential Commodities Act, 1955

CORPORATE CULTURE AND ETHICAL CLIMATE

Corporate culture is a blend of ideas, customs, traditional practices, company values and shared meanings that help define normal behaviour for everyone who works in a company. Every organisation has a culture and it exercises considerable influence on employee behaviour.

Hewlett-Packard is well known for a culture that stresses values and ethics. Called the 'HP Way' by employees, the most important values of the culture are confidence in and respect for people, open communication, sharing of benefits and responsibilities, concern for the individual employees and honesty and integrity.

In some companies, one can feel the blowing of ethical winds. People pick up subtle hints and clues that tell them what behaviour is approved and what is forbidden. This unarticulated understanding among employees is called an *ethical climate*. It is that part of corporate culture that sets the ethical tone in a company.

One way to view ethical climate is diagrammed in Fig.36.2. Three different types of ethical yardsticks are egoism (self-centredness), benevolence (concern for others), and principle (respect for one's own integrity, for group norms, and for society's laws). These ethical yardsticks can be applied to dilemmas concerning individuals, one's company or society at large. For example, if a manager approaches ethics issues with benevolence in mind, he would stress friendly relations with employees, emphasise the importance of team play and co-operation for the company's benefit and recommends socially responsible courses of action. However, if the manager used egoism to think about ethical problems, he would be more likely to think first of self-interest, promoting the company's profit and striving for efficient operations at all costs. A company's ethical climate depends on which combination it has of these nine possibilities.[12]

Corporate culture and ethical climate can put much pressure on people to channel their actions in certain directions desired by the company.

Figure 36.2 **The Components of Ethical Climate**

Ethical Criteria	*Focus of Ethical Concern*		
	Individual Person	*Company*	*Society*
Egoism	Self-interest	Company interest	Economic efficiency
Benevolence	Friendship	Team interest	Social responsibility
Principle	Personal morality	Company rules and procedures	Laws and professional codes

IMPROVING ETHICAL DECISION MAKING

Ethical decisions are difficult to make. They cannot be programmed like production and inventory decisions. But decisions need to be made in business. This section contains practical difficulties in decision making and guidelines which help a manager in making a choice.

Difficulties in Decision Making

There are atleast nine reasons why decision making becomes difficult.

First, managers face dilemmas in deciding on a course of action. These conflicts were elaborated earlier in this chapter.

Managers offen confront a distinction between facts and values. Facts are statements about what is and values are statements about what ought to do.

Second, managers confront a distinction between facts and values when making ethical decisions. Facts are statements about *what is* and values are statements about what *ought* to be. *What is* can never define what *ought* to be. For example, the cost of researching, developing and producing a life saving drug may necessitate fixing a high price, as far as the company is concerned. But the price may be perceived by users as exploitative.

Third, good and evil exist simultaneously, in tandem and interlocked. Nestle's sales of infant formula in Kenya and Zambia have led to infant deaths as mothers mixed the powdered food with contaminated local water and their babies died of dysentery. But evidence also shows that the same formula has saved lives of several other infants. Evil should be minimised, but it cannot be eliminated.

Fourth, knowledge about the consequences of an action is limited. One of the principles of decision making is utilitarian. This implies that if an act results in the greatest good of greatest numbers, it is taken as morally acceptable. This principle assumes that the consequences of the act are knowable. But in an uncertain business environment, consequences cannot be easily predicted.

Fifth, antagonistic interests frequently use incompatible ethical arguments to justify their intentions. Thus, the ethical stand of a corporation is often based on entirely different premises from the ethical stand of critics. Animal lovers may argue against slaughter on the ground that beasts are entitled to rights similar to those enjoyed by humans, including the right to life. Poultry growers, on the other hand, contend that raising food animals inure benefits to society.

Sixth, some ethical standards vary with the passage of time. Donations to political parties were forbidden earlier but it is allowed now. In addition, certain bribes and payments are accepted practices in Asian, African and Latin American countries but are not regarded as ethical in the US Doing business with close friends and family is a standard practice in the Arab world but is treated as nepotism in Western Europe.

Seventh, the ethical behaviour is moulded from the clay of human imperfection. Unethical practices abound everywhere (See Fig.36.3 for different crimes). An honest manager finds himself like a babe in the woods, not able to do anything, surrounded as he is, by dishonesty anywhere.

Eighth, the early 21st century presents managers with new and emerging ethical problems that are not solved easily with traditional ethical guidelines. For example, modern ethical theory has not yet developed an adequate principle for weighing human life against economic factors in a decision. Cancer studies may predict that workers exposed to chemicals will become ill in small numbers far in the future. How should this information be balanced against costs of regulation, capital investment or job loss?

Finally, the growth of large scale organisations in the 21st century gives new significance to ethical problems such as committee decision making that masks individual responsibility, organisational loyalty versus loyalty to the public interest and preferential hiring of disadvantaged sections of society. These are ethical problems peculiar to large organisations.

Practical Suggestions for Making Ethical Decisions

Individuals in business can take a number of steps to resolve ethical problems.

First, three well known principles to resolve an ethical issue are moral idealism, intutionism and utilitarianism.

Moral idealism postulates that certain acts are good and others are bad. Pursue those acts which are good and avoid the bad ones. Moral idealism gives definite answer to ethical issues.

> Moral idealism defines what is good and what is bad and prescribes definite do's and don'ts.

Intution leaves it to the individual concerned to sense the moral gravity of the situation. If he feels that his motives are good and that they do not intend to hurt any one, he is taking an intuitive approach to morally difficult situations.

Utilitarianism seeks to establish the moral locus not on the act or the motives but on the consequences. If the consequences represent a net increase in society's happiness, or atleast not a net decrease, the act is morally right.

Principles of the type described help a manager in making a decision in ethically difficult circumstances.

Second, consider some decision tactics that illuminate moral choices. One such device is to engage in imaginary conversations with a hypothetical opponent as an antidote for certitude. Have a conversation or debate with an intelligent person who takes a different view. Seek out a more experienced, ethically sensitive person in the organisation to be your adviser. Alternatively, write an essay in favour of a stand and then a second, opposed to it. Write a case study in the third person about your situation. Try to apply ethical principles in answers to questions raised by the case.

Third, write down pros and cons in the form of a balance sheet. The balance sheet approach helps decision making by presenting information in an organised way.

Fourth, sort out ethical priorities before problems arise. Prioritisation shall help consider alternatives when one is not under stress.

Fifth, one should commit oneself publicly on ethical issues. He should identity potential areas of ethical conflict and make clear his opposition to padding expense accounts, stealing supplies from the company, price fixing or damaging ecology. Once the stand is made clear, co-employees will be less tempted to approach with corrupt intentions.

Figure 36.3 **The Corporate Crimes**

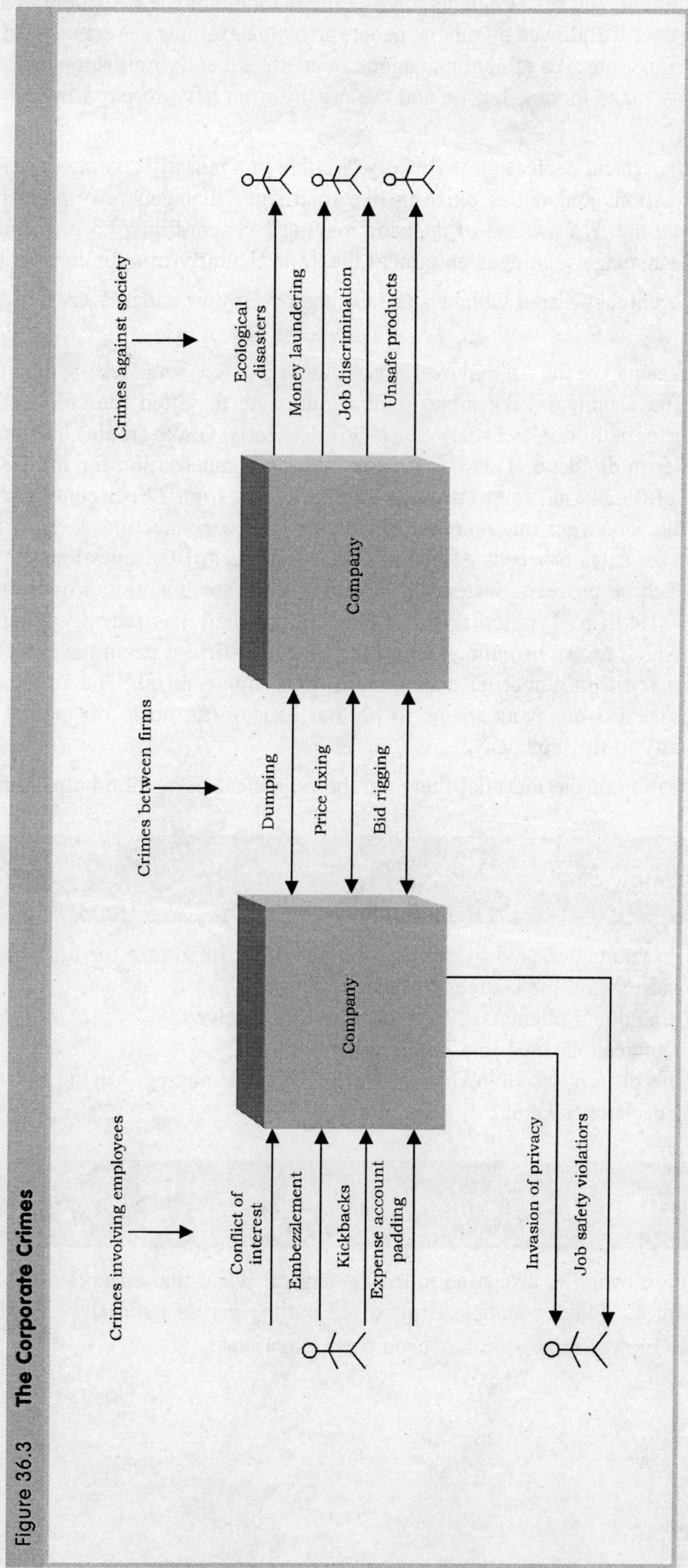

(**Source**: Adapted from *Business and Society* by Frederic, Post and Davis, *op.cit.*, p. 70)

Sixth, one should set a good personal example for employees. As the *Bhagavad Gita* says-'Whatever a great man does is followed by others; people go by the example he sets up'. This is one of the fundamental managerial functions. An ethical manager can create a merely uplifting work environment. An unethical manager may make money, but he and the organisation have to pay heavy price-and the price is one's integrity.

Finally, ethical perfection is illusory. We live in a morally complex civilisation with profuse rules, norms, obligations and duties existing like road signs that generally point in the same direction, but sometimes do not. No method of decision making ends conflicts, no principle penetrates unerringly to the good, no manager achieves an ethical ideal, particularly in situations as these:

"The Kentucky Fried Chicken (KFC) controversy provides a case of unethical, but very subtle practice.

A spokesman of the Animal Welfare Society revealed some telling details about the use of harmful hormones and chemicals like monosodium glutamate to fatten the chickens used by KFC (*Times of India*, letter to the Editor, February 29, 1996). Recently, Glaxo (India) had announced an incredible 175 per cent interim dividend. This is surmised to be a compensation for the UK-based parent company's investment of Rs.340 million to raise its equity holding from 32 per cent to 51 per cent. The declaration had come too soon after this increase to rule out such a connection. Even if this dividend were largely paid out of the sales proceeds of one of the divisions, still the question remains: why repatriate large sums out of these proceeds instead of investing them for business growth in India? (*Business Today*, January 22, 1996, p.51). Similarly, another US company has recently patented an oil-extracted from *neem* tree which grows in India. The medicinal properties of neem have been of household knowledge and used in India in numerous forms from times immemorial. The implication of the above patent secured by the US company seems to be that henceforth, neem oil cannot be used in India without paying royalty to this company."

Realisation of the fact that there can be no ethical perfection helps a manager considerably.

QUESTIONS

1. What do you understand by ethics? Why is ethics important for business?
2. State and explain the sources of business ethics.
3. What are ethical dilemmas? How can they be resolved?
4. How is ethics managed in a business unit?
5. State the difficulties involved in ethical decision making. Bring out the guidelines which help ethical decision making.

ASSIGNMENT

Whistle blowing is discussed much as magical wand that ensures ethical behaviour on the part of companies. Select a sample firms of 25 cutting across industries. Study how many of them have whistle blowers and what has been their experience.

REFERENCE

1. George A.Steiner and John F.Steiner, *Business, Government, and Society*, McGraw-Hill, 1997, p.180.
2. Frederick, Post & Davis, *Business and Society*, McGraw-Hill, 1992, pp.53-54.
3. George A.Steiner, *et al.*, *op.cit.*, p.182.
4. *Ibid.*, 185.
5. *Ibid*, pp.189 & 190.
6. The discussion here is based on *Corporate Ethics*, edited by Theophane A.Mathias, and Published by Allied.
7. Frederick, Post and Davis, *op.cit*, p.57.
8. R.M.Lala, *Creationof Wealth*, p.194.
9. Frederick, Post and Davis, *op.cit*, p.95.
10. *Ibid.*, p.85.
11. George A.Steiner and John Steiner, *op.cit.*, p.239.
12. *Ibid*, p.240.
13. *Ibid*, p.238.

CHAPTER OUTLINE

Nature of Corporate Governance
The Context
Factors Influencing Corporate Governance
- Ownership Structure
- Structure of Company Boards
- Financial Structure
- Institutional Environment

Mechanisms of Corporate Governance
- Companies Act
- Nominees on Company Boards
- Securities Law
- Statutory Audit
- Code of Conduct

The Future

LEARNING OBJECTIVES

After reading this Chapter, you should be able to:

1. Understand and define the term corporate governance
2. Justify the contemporary relevance of corporate governance
3. Describe the factors influencing corporate governance
4. State and explain the mechanisms of corporate governance
5. Look ahead and predict the shape of corporate governance far into future.

37 Corporate Governance

In the previous chapters we discussed, in detail, business ethics and corporate social responsibility. The central theme of all this discussion is that a business unit should operate in an ethical and socially responsive way. Who are the people to ensure such a behaviour from a company? What mechanism does exist to ensure that the people involved in running a business operate in the way that is expected of them? This chapter seeks to answer these and other related issues.

NATURE OF CORPORATE GOVERNANCE

Corporate governance is the overall control of activities in a corporation.

It is concerned with the formulation of long-term objectives and plans and the proper management structure (organisation, systems and people) to achieve them. At the same time, it entails making sure that the structure functions to maintain the corporation's integrity and responsibility to its various constituencies.[1] (Also see box 37.1).

Corporate governance is the overall control of activities in a company.

The structure to ensure corporate governance, for our purpose, includes the board of directors, top management, shareholders, creditors and others. Role of each of these stakeholders is crucial in guaranteeing responsible corporate performance. Before examining the role of each of these groups, it is useful to understand the relevance of corporate governance in the present context.

Box 37.1 **Good Governance**

Transparency

Well governed companies regularly disclose detailed infromation on their ownership and a mangement structure, latest operating and financial data, and transactions with their affiliates and subsidiaries. They also fully disclose executive compensation and any outside business ties to auditors.

Shareholder Rights

The golden rule is equal treatment of all shareholdes, regardless of stock class. In other words, one share, one vote. At a minimum, investors should have the right to vote on the election of directors, changes in the company's articles of incorporation, raising of a new capital, and major acquisitions or divestments.

Board Effectiveness

To successfully supervise management, board members must be accountable to all investors, not just majority shareholders. Boards should act indendently of management and third parties. Compensation, audit and nomination committees must be comprised of independent directors.

THE CONTEXT

Corporate governance has been an active subject of academic and policy debate for quite a long time in many of the advanced countries, particularly the US, UK, Germany, and Japan. The international competitiveness and successful functioning of companies in these countries has of late, alerted company owners and managers in the developing and transition economies to the fact that effective corporate governance is crucial for competitiveness and success in the long run. Infact, the importance of corporate governance has been highlighted by international agencies like the OECD and the World Bank. In particular, the World Bank has been in the process of formulating a draft code on corporate governance for developing countries that would review the principles of effective governance, built on international guidelines, assess governance practices in emerging markets, and distil the best practices from these and developed countries.

In our country, while several mechanisms of governance have formally been in place for much a longer time than in most of the developing countries, the issue of proper governance has assumed pertinence only recently. In fact, the lack of adequate governance of Indian companies has been highlighted in academic circles and other forums as one of the primary reasons for underperformance of industrial establishments.

At least three reasons have triggered off concern in corporate governance in our country.

First, since 1991, the country has moved into liberalised economy and one of the victims of the market-based economy is transparent fair business practices. In the survival of the fittest scenario, norms and principles are thrown to thee winds. Infact, a number of company failures have been reported in the recent past. Several instances of mismanagement have been alleged, with some well-known and senior executives being hauled up for non-performance and/or non-compliance with legal requirements. Some norms of behaviour to ensure responsive behaviour are of great help.

Second, both domestic as well as foreign investors are becoming more demanding in their approach towards the companies in which they have invested their funds. They seek information and want to influence decisions. Increasing integration with global markets calls for a correspondingly improving compliance with global practices in all spheres of corporate activity.

Third, interests of non-promoter shareholders and those of small investors are increasingly being undermined. Several MNCs, for example, have sought to set up 100 per cent subsidiaries and transfer their businesses (carried through Indian joint-venture partners) to them. In many cases, there was no thought of consultation with non-promoter shareholders whose interests would be affected.

Again, well known Indian companies, in recent years, raised funds in the GDR markets abroad and in India, for specific objectives. But these funds were diverted to investments elsewhere, without consulting the shareholders. Obviously, the sufferers are the minority shareholders.

FACTORS INFLUENCING CORPORATE GOVERNANCE

Four factors influence corporate governance, namely, (i) the ownership structure of a corporation, (ii) its financial structure, (iii) the structure and functioning of the company boards and (iv) the legal, political and regulatory environment within which the company operates.[2]

The Ownership Structure

The structure of ownership of a company determines, to a considerable extent, how a corporation is managed and controlled. The ownership structure can be either dispersed among individual and institutional shareholders as in the US and UK or can be concentrated in the hands of a few large shareholders as in Germany and Japan. But the pattern of shareholding is not as simple as the above statement seeks to convey. The pattern varies across the globe. According to a study on corporate ownership conducted in 1998, 36 per cent of the firms in the world are widely held, 30 per cent are family controlled, 18 per cent are state controlled and the remaining 15 per cent are in miscellaneous categories.[3]

Our corporate sector is characterised by the co-existence of state owned, private and multinational enterprises. The shares of these enterprises (except those belonging to the public sector) are held by institutional as well as small investors. Specifically, shares are held by (i) the term-lending institutions (ii) institutional investors, comprising government owned mutuals funds, Unit Trust of India and the government owned the insurance corporations (iii) corporate bodies (iv) directors and their relatives and (v) foreign investors. Apart from these block-holdings, there is a sizeable equity holding by small investors. Table 37.1 shows the shareholding pattern of select companies.

Which pattern of shareholding, dispersed or concentrated, is ideal for good corporate performance? Large shareholders tend to be active in corporate governance either through their representatives on company boards or through their active participation in annual general body meetings. This has been demonstrated by Reliance Industries Ltd. which has the highest number of equity shareholders spread across the country. Block-holding too has not proved to be a failure either. Dominant shareholders are better informed than the dispersed shareholders. Under the concentrated ownership structure, as has been demonstrated through the Bajaj Group, corporate performance tends to be better.

The Structure of Company Boards

Along with the structure of ownership, the structure of company boards has considerable influence on the way the companies are managed and controlled. The board of directors is responsible for establishing corporate objectives, developing broad policies and selecting top-level executives to carry out those

Table 37.1 **Pattern of Equity Ownership in Select Companies**

	Directors and relatives %	*Corporate bodies %*	*Foreign %*	*Financial institutions %*	*Institutional investors %*	*Public %*
Private companies owned by business houses	8.1	33.8	9.2	4.2	10.2	34.5
Private stand-alone companies	21.6	18.5	7.2	3.1	3.1	46.5
Foreign companies owned by business houses	0.8	18.3	42.0	4.3	12.2	22.4
Foreign stand-alone companies	2.8	13.8	43.3	1.7	8.4	30.0
All	15.7	23.8	9.9	3.5	6.1	41.0

Note: Data pertain to 1613 sample companies and relate to 1995-96.

(**Source**: *India Development Report, 1999-2000*, p.206)

objectives and policies. The board also reviews management's performance to ensure that the company is run well and shareholders' interests are protected.

Company boards are permitted to vary in size, composition and structure so as to best serve the interests of the corporation and the shareholders. Board membership may include both inside directors and outside directors. Again, boards can be single-tiered or two-tiered.

With regard to the size of board, opinions and practices vary. Some argue that the adequate size is to range from nine to fifteen. Some others put the figure at ten and yet others recommend a minimum of five and a maximum of ten. Company boards in the UK have, on an average, seven directors on their boards. Japanese companies have larger boards, the figure going upto sixty. A quick survey of the thirty companies actively traded on the Bombay Stock Exchange, and which form the basis for Sensex Index, reveals that as of 31st March, 1997, the median number of directors in these companies was 13.5, with 20 and five at the extremes. The corresponding numbers as of 31st March, 1994 were median 12, high 21, and low five.[4] It should be noted that it is the quality of the directors, the interests they take, and the roles that they assume which are more important than mere numbers or composition.

The Financial Structure

Along with the notion that the structure of ownership matters in corporate governance is the notion that the financial structure of the company, i.e. proportion between debt and equity, has implications for the quality of governance. Contrary to the Modigliani-Miller hypothesis that the financial structure of the firm has no relationship to the value of a firm, recent research has shown that the financial structure does matter. It is no secret that the lenders exercise significant influence on the way a company is managed and controlled. Banks as creditors, for example, can perform the important function of screening and monitoring companies as they (banks) are better informed than other investors. Further, banks can diminish short-term biases in managerial decision making by favouring investments that would generate higher benefits in the long run. Also, banks, because of the close financial relationships they foster with the companies to which they lend, and in some cases because of their nominees on company boards, are considered to play a more favourable role than other investors in reducing the costs of financial distress.[5]

The Institutional Environment

The legal, regulatory, and political environment within which a company operates determines in large measure the quality of corporate governance. Infact, corporate governance mechanisms are economic and legal institutions and often the outcome of political decisions. For example, the extent to which shareholders can control the management depends on their voting rights as defined in company law, the extent to which creditors will be able to exercise financial claims on a bankrupt unit will depend on bankruptcy laws and procedures; and the extent to which the market for corporate control efficiency operates to discipline underperforming management will depend on take-over regulations.[6]

MECHANISMS OF CORPORATE GOVERNANCE

The fundamental institutions of corporate governance in our country have been in existence for a long time. Compared to many developing countries, mechanisms of corporate governance in India are much more institutionalised. However, inspite of such institutions, corporate governance has not been a major issue until the announcement of the new economic policy in 1991. Since then, corporate governance has assumed greater relevance for reasons stated earlier.

In our country, there are six mechanisms to ensure corporate governance: (i) The Companies Act, 1956; (ii) The Securities and Exchange Board of India (SEBI) Act, 1992; (iii) a market for corporate control; (iv) participation of block shareholders in the governance of companies; (v) statutory audit; and (vi) Code of Conduct (see Fig. 37.1).

Companies Act

Companies in our country are regulated by the Companies Act, 1956, as amended upto-date. The Companies Act is one of the biggest legislations with 658 sections and 14 schedules. Through the consolidation of many successive amendments, and a large number of statutory rules and regulations, the Act aims at not only ensuring that the interests of all stakeholders are adequately protected but purports to go beyond. The Act, to some extent, seeks to translate into action Articles 38 and 39 in Part IV of the Constitution, by which the State was directed that the ownership and control of the material resources of the community are so distributed as to subserve the common good and the operation of the economic system does not result in the concentration of wealth and means of production to the common detriment.

The arms of the Act are quite long and touch every aspect of a company's existence. But to ensure corporate governance, the Act confers legal rights to shareholders to (a) vote on every resolution placed before an annual general meeting; (b) to elect directors who are responsible for specifying objectives

Figure 37.1 **Mechanisms for Corporate Governance**

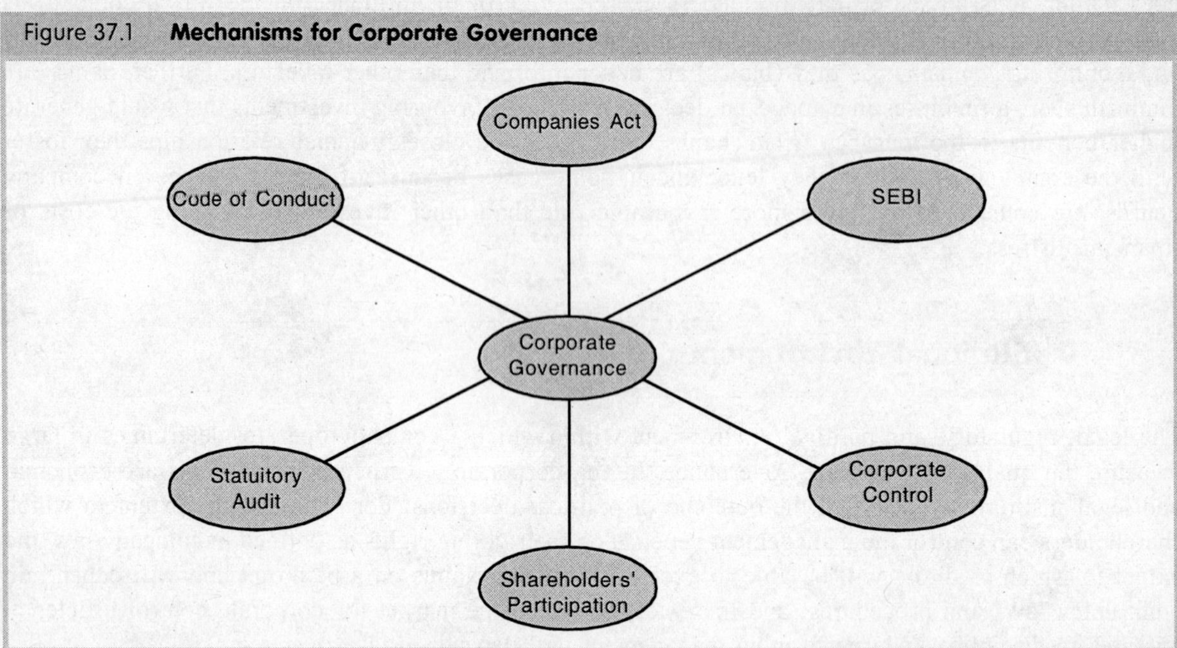

and laying down policies; (c) determine remuneration of directors and the CEO; (d) removal of directors and (e) take active part in the annual general meetings.

The Companies Bill, 1997 and the recently promulgated Ordinance on Companies (Amendment) Bill, 1997, have amended several provisions of the Act and introduced new provisions incorporating some internationally accepted corporate governance practices aimed at strengthening corporate democracy, protecting the interests of minority shareholders and providing maximum flexibility to the companies in responding to the market needs. Among these, the amendments that have made headlines are permitting companies to buy back shares and the liberalisation of inter-corporate investments.

Securities Law

The primary securities law in our country is the SEBI Act. Since its inception in 1992, the Board has taken a number of initiatives towards investor protection.

One such initiative is to mandate information disclosure both in prospectus and in annual accounts. While the Companies Act itself mandates certain standards of information disclosure, SEBI Act has added substantially to these requirements in an attempt to make these documents more meaningful. One of the most valuable is the information relating to the performance of other companies in the same group, particularly those companies which have accessed the capital market in the recent past.

Another aspect of the SEBI regulations is that in most public issues, the promoters (typically the dominant shareholders) are required to take a minimum stake of about 20 per cent in the capital of the company and to retain these shares for a minimum lock-in period of three years.

Yet another area in which SEBI has laid down guidelines, relates to prohibiting preferential allotments to dominant shareholders at a price lower than the average market price during the preceding six months.

Also, SEBI intervenes in corporate take-overs in order to protect the interests of minority shareholders. As per the securities law, the acquirer of a controlling block of shares must make an open offer to the public for atleast 20 per cent of the issued share capital of the target company at a price not below that was paid for the controlling block.

Finally, the Board constituted a Committee under the chairmanship of Kumaramangalam Birla to suggest ways to promote and raise the standards of corporate governance in listed companies. The Board, in its meeting held on January 25, 2000, considered the recommendations of the Committee and decided to make amendments to the listing agreements by adding a new clause, namely clause 49, to the listing agreement.

The clause 49 provides for the optimum composition of executive and non-executive directors; setting up of a qualified and independent audit committee; remuneration of directors; Management Discussion and Analysis Report to form part of annual report to the shareholders; a separate section on Corporate Governance in the annual reports of the company (See Box 37.2); for information to be furnished in the report on corporate governance; and auditor's compliance certificate to the effect that all the conditions of corporate governance have been complied with.

Box 37.2 **Suggested List of Items to be Included in the Report on Corporate Governance in the Annual Reports of Companies**

1. A brief statement on company's philosophy on code of governance.
2. Board of Directors
   - Composition and category of directors, for example promoter, executive, non-executive, independent non-executive, nominee director, which institution represented as lender or as equity investor.
   - Attendance of each director at the BoD meetings and the last AGM.
   - Number of other BoDs or Board Committees he/she is a member or Chairperson of.
   - Number of BoD meetings held, dates on which held.
3. Audit Committee
   - Brief description of terms of reference
   - Composition, names of members and Chairperson
   - Meetings and attendance during the year
4. Remuneration Committee
   - Brief description of terms of reference
   - Composition, names of members and Chairperson
   - Attendance during the year
   - Remuneration policy
   - Details of remuneration to all the directors, as per format in main report.
5. Shareholders Committee
   - Name of non-executive director heading the committee
   - Name and designation of compliance officer
   - Number of shareholders' complaints received so far
   - Number not solved to the satisfaction of shareholders
   - Number of pending share transfers
6. General Body Meetings
   - Location and time, where last three AGMs held.
   - Whether special resolutions were put through postal ballot last year, details of voting pattern

- Person who conducted the postal ballot exercise
- Procedure for postal ballot

7. Disclosures
   - Disclosures on materially significant related party transactions i.e. transactions of the company of material nature, with its promoters, the directors or the management, their subsidiaries or relatives, etc., that may have potential conflict with the interests of company at large.
   - Details of non-compliance by the company, penalties, strictures imposed on the company by the Stock Exchange or SEBI or any statutory authority, on any matter related to capital markets, during the last three years.
8. Means of Communication
   - Half-yearly report sent to each household of shareholders.
   - Quarterly results
   - Which website, where displayed
   - Whether it also displays official news releases
   - The presentations made to institutional investors or to the analysts.
   - Whether MD&A is a part of annual report or not
9. General Shareholder Information
   - AGM:Date, time and venue
   - Financial calendar
   - Date of book closure
   - Dividend payment date
   - Listing on stock exchanges
   - Stock Code
   - Market Price Data: High low during each month in last financial year
   - Performance in comparison to broad-based indices such as BSE Sensex, CRISIL Index, etc.
   - Registrar and Transfer Agents
   - Share Transfer System
   - Distribution of shareholding
   - Dematerialization of shares and liquidity
   - Outstanding GDRs/ADRs/Warrants or any convertible instruments, conversion date and likely impact on equity
   - Plant locations
   - Address for correspondence

Discipline of the Capital Market

Capital market itself has considerable impact on corporate governance. Herein lies the role the minority shareholders can play effectively. They can refuse to subscribe to the capital of a company in the primary market and in the secondary market, they can sell their shares, thus depressing the share prices. A depressed share price makes the company an attractive take-over target.

A debt-holder too has a role to play in disciplining a company's management. Unlike the shareholder who is a residual claimant, the creditor has contractual rights to reclaim his interest and principal; and this enables him to monitor the actions of the management. Most debt contracts involve covenants that make it less easy for the dominant shareholders to indulge in gross abuses. The ability of debtholders to monitor the company is quite high because typically, they are large institutions with high stakes.

In a well functioning capital market, there is a strong incentive for corporate managements themselves to voluntarily adopt transparent processes and subject themselves to external monitoring to reassure potential investors. An untested management group is likely to find that the market places a '*management discount*' on them that reflects what the market has come to expect of management groups in general. The management then has every incentive to take steps that will reduce this by making governance abuses more difficult. In the last few years, we have seen Indian companies voluntarily accepting international accounting standards though they are not legally binding. They have voluntarily gone for greater disclosures and more transparent governance practices than are mandated by law. They have sought to cultivate an image of being honest with their investors and of being concerned about shareholder value maximisation.

What makes capital market discipline so much more attractive than regulatory intervention is that unlike the regulator, the market is very good at micro level judgements and decisions. Infact, the market is taking micro-decisions all the time. It is its success in doing so that makes it such an efficient allocator of capital. Unlike the regulator, the market is not bound by broad rules and can exercise business judgement. It therefore makes sense for the regulator to pass on as much of the burden of ensuring corporate governance to the markets as possible. The regulator can then concentrate on making the markets more efficient at performing this function.[7]

Nominees on Company Boards

Development banks hold large blocks of shares in companies. They are equally big debtholders too. Being equity holders, these investors have their nominees in the boards of companies. These nominees can effectively block resolutions which may be detrimental to their interests. Unfortunately, the role of nominee directors has been passive, as has been pointed out by several committees including the Bhagavati Committee on Takeovers and the Omkar Goswami Committee on Corporate Governance. However, signs of active role by nominee directors are emerging as revealed in box 37.3.

Statutory Audit

Statutory audit is yet another mechanism directed to ensure good corporate governance. Auditors are the conscience-keepers of shareholders, lenders and others who have financial stakes in companies.

Auditing enhances the credibility of financial reports prepared by an enterprise. The auditing process ensures that financial statements are accurate and complete, thereby enhancing their reliability and usefulness for making investment decisions. Credible financial statements are essential for business enterprises to raise capital and for society to have trust in limited companies. Obviously, good corporate governance depends, in part, on good auditing. As the Cadbury Committee observed, "*The annual audit is one of the cornerstones of corporate governance. Given the separation of ownership from management, the directors are required to report on their stewardship by means of the annual report and financial statements sent to the shareholders. The audit provides an external and objective check*

Box 37.3

- FIs have been asked by the Finance Ministry to take 'full responsibility' for corporate governance in companies where they have substantial stakes. The objective is to boost investor confidence and pep up the capital market. The government has issued a four point directive to FIs asking them to insist on (i) making adequate disclosures, (ii) moving towards internationally accepted accounting standards, (iii) maintaining distance between the CEO and chairman where applicable, and (iv) holding regular board meetings with proper recording and dissemination of proceedings.
- FIs have in recent times pressed for change in management of under-performing and defaulting companies like those in Narmada Cement and Rajinder Steel.
- FIs have successfully opposed a move by the Associated Cement Company (ACC) to make a preferential issue to the Tata group that will enhance the latter's stake, citing as justification the need to protect the rights of minority shareholders of the ACC.
- FIs have implemented new norms for appointment of nominee directors, which have drastically cut down the total number of such directors on company boards. According to the new criteria for nomination, financial institutions are required to place their nominees only in companies where their combined exposure is above Rs.50 crore or their shareholding is above 26 per cent or in the event of the company showing signs of problems such as defaults on loans.
- FIs are in the process of revising guidelines for nominee directors. The IDBI is coordinating the process, and the norms will be drawn up in consultation with the Ministry of Finance and the RBI. Among the norms under consideration is one making it mandatory for FI nominee directors on boards of companies to attend specific board meetings, especially those related to finalization of accounts.
- FIs are insisting on setting up of audit sub-committees comprising 'adequate' number of non-executive independent directors of the company board in each and every large and medium corporate to strengthen internal control structures and safeguard shareholder interests. Constitution of an audit sub-committee, according to the FIs, would help bring in substantial financial discipline on the part of management and check against executive malpractice.
- The UTI is asking leading corporates where it has sizeable stakes to make presentations outlining their plans and expected performance after the declaration of half-yearly results. The objective of the exercise is more hands-on governance to give confidence to the unit holders. Several big corporates like Reliance have made presentations to the UTI, LIC, and GIC.

(**Source**: *India Development Report*, p.211).

on the way in which the financial statements have been prepared and presented, and it is an essential part of the checks and balances required."

In practice, this is not always true. Users of auditors' services are often disenchanted with the performance of auditors and seldom believe auditors live up to the solemn image presented by the Cadbury Committee. Auditing is often considered to be just an annual ritual. Caustic comments such as auditors being '*hand in glove*' with the management, or the financials being '*dressed up*' are often voiced by shareholders, employees and tax officers. So, what ails auditing? Auditor independence or the perceived lack of it, is a major issue. Other lacunae include problems concerning audit quality, the role of auditors in detecting frauds and reviewing internal controls and the record of the accounting profession in establishing accounting and auditing standards.

Codes of Conduct

The mechanisms discussed till now are regulatory in approach. They are mandated by law and violation of any provision invites penal action. But legal rules alone cannot ensure good corporate governance. What is needed is self regulation on the part of directors, besides of course, the mandatory provisions.

The famous '*Code of Best Practice*' was advocated by the Cadbury Committee in the UK. The committee was constituted by the London Stock Exchange in 1992, following the collapse of several British companies. The cause of anxiety then, was not so much that the companies had failed, as that their annual reports and financial statements - just prior their failure - gave no forewarning of the true state of their financial affairs. Subsequent scandals relating to '*excessive*' remuneration paid to directors, created the climate for business to establish more effective norms of corporate behaviour.

How did the Cadbury Committee address this situation? Basically, good governance issues were seen as relating to both the effectiveness and the accountability of the Board of Directors:

- Effectiveness was seen as a measure of the quality of the leadership of the directors, to be judged by the company's financial results and the resultant growth in shareholder value.
- Accountability was seen as largely a matter of disclosure of all relevant information-transparency in short-focussing on the subject of, to whom a company is answerable.

The Code is thus based on checks and balances, especially at the level of the board of directors and the chief executive, to guard against undue concentration of power, and, adequate disclosure to enable those entitled to have the information they need, in order to exercise their rights. It comprises four sections:

- *Role of the Board of Directors* It was proposed that the ('*inside*') executive directors be balanced by adequate number of ('*outside*') non-executive directors, with the posts of the board chairman and chief executive being separated.
- *Role of Non-executive Directors* It was emphasised that the majority of the Board should be '*independent*' (in the sense of being free of any business relation which could materially interfere with the exercise of independent judgement), that non-executive directors should be appointed only for a specific term and that there should be a formal process for their appointment involving the board as a whole.
- *Executive Directors* The main concern was with their remuneration-that there should be a full and clear disclosure of directors' emoluments, and that pay should be set by a Remuneration Committee, consisting mainly of non-executive directors.
- *Financial Reporting and Controls* It was recommended that properly constituted Audit Committees of the Board be appointed, and that non-executive directors report regularly on the effectiveness of systems and internal financial control.

In due course, the London Stock Exchange, while not mandating compliance with any element of the code, asked all listed companies to append to their Annual Reports, a declaration of the extent of their compliance with the Code. Shareholders were left to draw their own conclusions about the quality of governance in their companies.

The Confederation of Indian Industry (CII) issued a draft code of '*Desirable Corporate Governance*' for the Indian industry in April 1997, in response possibly to the Finance Ministry's veiled threats that soften the self-regulatory regime, greater the likelihood of harsher government regulations.

The CII Code, leaning heavily on the British model, is based on the explicit assumption that "good governance helps to maximise shareholder value, which will necessarily maximise corporate value and, thereby, satisfy the claims of creditors, employees and the State."

Whether the code will stimulate a change in corporate governance, only time will tell.

THE PRESENT

The corporate governance movement in India picked up momentum after the debacle of big companies such as Enron, Worldcom and BCCI Bank.Those were times when the confidence of the financial community, shareholders, and investors took a beating the world over. It was around that time that foreign financial institutions started investing money in Indian companies, which also triggered the need for greater accountability. Today, fund managers view firms such as Tata Motors, ITC, Ranbaxy, Infosys and Hero Honda Motors as having higher governing standards. Luckily many companies are exhibiting good governance standards.

The *Economic Times* did a survey of Indian Corporate Governance and published its findings in its issue dated August 19, 2005. Table 37.2 shows the ranking of Indian companies. The criteria used by the ET survey to identify the winners are:

Table 37.2 **Roll of Honour**

Rankings	
1	Infosys Technologies
2	Tata Steel
3	Wipro
4	HDFC Bank
5	HDFC
6	Tata Motors
7	Reliance Industries
8	ITC
9	Ranbaxy Laboratories
10	Hindustan Lever
11	Hero Honda Motors
12	Larsen & Toubro
13	State Bank of India
14	Bajaj Auto
15	ONGC
16	Gujarat Ambuja Cement
17	Hindalco Industries
18	Grasim Industries
19	Cipla
20	BPCL

(**Source:** *ET Corporate Governance Survey*, 2005)

- Accounting quality
- Value creation focus
- Fair policies and actions
- Communication
- Effective governing board
- Reliability

As the Table 37.2 shows, at the top of the heap is Infosys and the 20th place goes to BPCL.

THE FUTURE

As we go into the future, corporate governance will become more relevant and a more acceptable practice. Seeds are already sown towards honest business practices. More and more progressive companies are drawing and enforcing codes of conduct, are accepting tougher accounting standards and are following more stringent disclosure norms than are mandated by law. These tendencies would be further strengthened by a variety of forces that are acting today and would become stronger in years to come. Such forces are:

* *Deregulation* Economic reforms have not only increased growth prospects, but they have also made markets more competitive. This means that in order to survive, companies will need to invest continuously on a large scale.
* *Disintermediation* Meanwhile, financial sector reforms have made it imperative for firms to rely on capital markets to a greater degree for their needs of additional capital.
* *Institutionalisation* Simultaneously, the increasing institutionalisation of the capital markets has tremendously enhanced the disciplining power of the market.
* *Globalisation* Globalisation of financial markets has exposed issuers, investors and intermediaries to the higher standards of disclosure and corporate governance that prevail in more developed capital markets.
* *Tax reforms* Tax reforms coupled with deregulation and competition have tilted the balance away from black money transactions. This makes the worst forms of misgovernance less attractive than in the past[8].

ANALYSIS OF CULTURAL ENVIRONMENT

Chapters 33 to 37 have elaborated on the soft side of business. Culture, ethics, governance, and social responsibility constitute, for our purpose, the soft side of any company. How to analyse socio-cultural segment of business? The following paragraphs seek to answer this question.

Scanning

Scanning societal segment is extremely difficult as the number of strategic factors is very high. Cultural mores and values of people are not readily manifest, individuals are often unable to articulate their likes and dislikes. Besides, values that individuals espouse and the values that are operant are not congruent.[9]

This makes changes in social milieu difficult to detect and measure. Further, not many measurement scales exist unlike other environmental segments. Nevertheless, the following precursors of social change present themselves before the analyst:

Lifestyle changes

Consumer activism

Career expectations

Birth rates

Growth rate of population

Age distribution of population

Regional shifts in population

Life expectations

Attitude towards business

Religious festivals and beliefs.

Monitoring

The precursors of societal segment identified above need to be monitored. Such tracking of indicators will help discern whether certain trends and patterns emerge in the social milieu.

Forecasting

Unlike political, technological and economic segments, comparatively little attention has been devoted to assess and forecast societal segment. However, analyst needs to forecast socio-cultural environment to predict changes likely to take place in future. The following questions help the analyst greatly:

- What is the focal cultural trend or pattern?
- Who are the indicators of cultural change?
- What is the nature of the change?
- Who is manifesting the change?
- What forces are driving the change?

Assessment

Socio-cultural changes have important implications for the strategic context of the firm. The firm cannot function in isolation. Its strategies must align with the culture of the society in which the firm operates. The following deserve due consideration in this context.[10] First, social segment and its changes can impact the acceptance accorded to company's current and potential products in the market place. This is often evidenced in strong public support for or opposition to the products of entire industries or industry segments. Public reaction, for instance, to environmental pollution has caused many chemical firms to drop products and modify others. Second, changes in values contribute to industry structural change through their impact on customers' tastes and product attribute preferences. These changes frequently result in product substitutions. This is evidenced by the way diet forms have substituted many food and beverage categories. Third, value changes impact many industries and the strategies of companies within them through their effect on consumption patterns. For example, the increase in two-earner families has contributed to the increased demand for ready-to-eat packaged and convenience foods. Fourth, value changes cause more indirect implications for the strategic management of firms than other sources of environmental changes. In otherwords, the impact of value change is exerted through change in other environmental segments. These indirect implications are especially waged through the political-legal environment. For example, many industries or individual firms have found themselves confronted by demands from local, regional, or national interest groups to take their products off the market, to change how they compete, or to change their corporate policies.

QUESTIONS

1. Define corporate governance. Why is it assuming greater relevance nowadays?
2. What is corporate governance? Explain the factors influencing corporate governance.
3. State and explain the mechanisms of corporate governance.
4. Bring out the role of (a) board of directors, and (b) capital market in bringing out honest business practices.
5. Explain how you would analyse cultural environment.

ASSIGNMENT

Figure 37.2 contains top 20 companies ranked on the criterion of corporate governance. Make a study, why they have been ranked so. What is unique with them?

REFERENCES

1. George A.Steiner and John F.Steiner, *Business, Government and Society*, McGraw-Hill, 1997, p.624.
2. *India Development Report* 1999-2000, Edited by Kirit S.Parikh, p.203.
3. *Ibid*, p.203.
4. N.Balasubramanian (ed.), *Corporate Boards and Governance*, Sterling, 1998, p.222.
5. *India Development Report*, *op.cit.*, p.204.
6. *Ibid*, p.204.
7. N.Balasubramanian, *op.cit.*, pp.78-79.
8. *Ibid*, pp.80-81.
9. Liam Fahey and V.K.Narayanan, *Macroenvironmental Analysis For Strategic Management*, West Pub.Co., 1983, p.93.
10. *Ibid*, p.103.

CHAPTER OUTLINE

Nature of Physical Environment

Impact on Business

Analysis of Physical Envrionment

LEARNING OBJECTIVES

After reading this Chapter, you should be able to:

1. Understand the nature of physical environment
2. Describe how physical environment influences functioning of a firm
3. Explain how natural environment can be analysed

38 Natural Environment

NATURE OF PHYSICAL ENVIRONMENT

Equally significant, but sadly ignored, are factors like climate, minerals, soil, landform, rivers and oceans, coastlines, natural resource, and flora and fauna which have considerable influence on the functioning of a business.

These and other related factors constitute natural environment or physical environment, a discussion of which is highly relevant in a book on the environment of business.

Physical environment, though significant, is sadly ignored.

Many dispute the validity of the statement that natural environment does exert significant influence on business activities. They have reasons to do so. Man's ingenuity, over the years, has enabled him to be almost independent of Nature. Climate, once considered as a decisive factor in plant location, has receded in significance as man has acquired technology for creating artificial climate. Uneven landform, rivers, oceans, forests and deserts have not restrained him from laying roads and constructing factories, as he now knows how to bulldoze land, dig tunnels, fell trees and construct bridges. Infertile soil and erosion of soil no more handicap him from undertaking agricultural practices as he knows the preservation and treatment of soil. Failure of rains may not worry him as much as it did to his forebearers, as he knows how to pump out ground water from fathoms deep and divert water from rivers and streams for irrigating crops. Schumacher's famous dictum-*Small is Beautiful*-seems to have no effect on today's man. His search for new areas of mineral deposits and substitutes and new uses for resources under exploitation have given him courage and confidence to launch giant manufacturing plants, consuming resources on an unprecedented scale. Mountains, deserts, forests, oceans and distances are no barriers to him to reach any part of the globe to sell his products. Thus, man's technological progress during the last 150 years has been so great, his insight into nature so deep that his ingenuity has finally given him the whiphand and that the natural environment is something of secondary importance, something essentially passive, existing to serve him as he sees fit.

It is this belief that has prompted several universities and professional bodies to drop the subject of Economic Geography from their curricula. Natural environment hardly finds a mention in literature on economic development or development planning. Sometime back, thousands of development economists from different parts of the world met in New Delhi for the World Congress of the International Economic Association. The subject of the Congress was the appropriate balance between industry and agriculture in economic development. There were in all 16 sessions at the Congress. Of these, none was on the basis of resources development activity. Clearly, natural resources have not entered the agenda of analysis in development economics and national planning. We do not know of any Indian Masters syllabus in economics which contains resources economics as a topic. And this despite the fact that over the past decade and a half, there has grown a large body of work on both analytical and applied resource economics published in books, economic journals and in some half-a-dozen international journals specialising in the economics of natural resources. Development economics, in general, and development planning in particular, have with rare exceptions passed resource economics by, rather like ships in the night.[1]

Is this negligence justified? Put another way, has man learnt to be completely independent of Nature? Has he conquered Nature? The answer to all these questions is a firm 'no'. Despite tremendous advancement in science and technology, today's man is not able to control floods, droughts, earthquakes, storms, heat and cold waves, volcanoes and of rapidly silting reservoirs. Similarly, he has no answers to such paradoxes as the existence of beauty with ugliness and poverty with affluence. It is amazing to him why people of different parts of the world talk differently, dress differently and adopt different cultures. Further, modern man is not able to explain why we are not able to produce everything everywhere at the same cost, grow every crop everywhere with ease, and fish or mine in any place of our choice. The *tsunami* which hit several parts of Asia (including India) on Dec 26, 2004, further demonstrates the supremacy of Nature.

Thus, modern man has not become completely independent of Nature. His activities are directly or indirectly guided by his natural or physical environment. This is particularly true in the case of his business activities.

IMPACT ON BUSINESS

Manufacturing is impacted by natural environment.

Manufacturing, which is one of the aspects of business, depends on physical environment for inputs. Take, for instance, the manufacture of a tractor. A tractor requires for its manufacture, iron and steel, rubber, plastics, non-ferrous metals, labour of various skills, factory machinery, materials, water and so on. Of these, to take for example, steel, for its production requires iron, coal, furnaces, water, labour, materials and so forth. The furnaces, in turn, require for their manufacture, among many things, iron ore, brickworks and labour. One can thus break down any produced good into inputs involved in its manufacture and one can, if one has sufficient patience, trace them ultimately to a combination of labour and natural resources.

It is tempting to stop at this point in the natural history of a produced commodity. But one should not. For, of course, labour too is a produced good. Even raw labour is produced, manufactured by those natural resources which sustain life, resources such as the multitude of nutrients we consume, the air we breath and the water we drink.[2]

Besides, much manufacturing is carried on in or very close to areas of considerable population density rather than in sparsely populated regions far from major markets, and most of these more heavily populated areas were originally developed because they were favourable to other economic activities, more directly dependent upon suitable conditions of the physical environment. Also, although the location of a particular industry or a particular plant may be the result of the initiative of one man or a small group of men, many types of industries, especially heavy, cannot be located too far from the source of raw materials or from a place to which raw materials can be brought easily and inexpensively.[3]

Mining of coal and ores, drilling of oil, and the quarrying of stone, clay or other materials are extractive industries, which depend on the availability of minerals for which nature is the repository. Minerals are scattered widely over the earth. Exploitation of mineral resources, therefore, shows a pattern of irregular design which is characterised by small pockets of intensive activity and concentrated population separated by large areas of little mineral activity and comparatively sparse population. It is generally believed that economic prosperity of a nation and the well-being of its people depend on the type and the extent of mineral deposits the country is gifted with. However, mere existence of deposits does not guarantee prosperity. What is required is exploitation of the physical resources for general well-being. Oil-rich countries of today were merely sandy deserts fifty years ago, despite the fact that the Arabian countries were gifted with rich deposits of oil. Oil is now pumped out and is supplied to the rest of the world. In the process, affluence of the Arabs has increased enormously. Though exploitation fetches wealth, indiscriminate extraction is not advisable as most of the minerals are not inexhaustible. It is, however heartening to note that all over the world, continuous search is made for new area of deposits and new substitutes for minerals under exploitation.

Mining, drilling, and quarrying are affected by physical environment.

Of all the economic activities of man, it is agriculture which depends most on Nature. The term *agriculture* in its broadest sense refers to all of man's activities related to the cultivation of the soil and to those activities that are directly dependent upon the soil, such as the raising of livestock. The production of vegetable food and meat made man less dependent upon the luck of the chase and therefore, less subject to periods of famine following periods of feast. Nevertheless, the influence of nature upon agricultural activities was great and has remained so to this day. The types of crops that can be grown in an area depend first upon climate and soil and there is little that man has ever been able to do against the vagaries of weather, such as unseasonal frosts, unexpected droughts, or periods of super-abundant rainfall. Differences in the physical background have resulted in many types of agriculture throughout the world, and the number of types of agriculture has been further increased by varying economic conditions.[4]

Agricultural operations are significantly influenced by nature.

Trade between two regions of a nation or between two nations is the result of geographical factors. Because of the natural factors, certain areas are more suitable for production of certain goods. Apples and saffron, for example, are grown in Kashmir, coffee in Coorg, tea in Assam, cotton in Maharashtra and jute in West Bengal. On the international level, instances of specialisation are plenty, but one that should not be missed is the superiority of Denmark which can economically provide eggs, butter and bacon. Specialisation of production is the order of the day. Goods produced in some areas must be transferred to other areas which are not so well suited to produce the same. This is the genesis of trade and this explains why the massive movement of oil, iron ore, grains, fruits, vegetables and electronic goods takes place across borders of various countries.

Transportation and communication, the main prop of business, depend to a larger extent on geographical factors. Uneven landform, deserts, oceans, forests and rivers are barriers to develop this vital infrastructure. True, today's man has learnt to cut across these natural barriers but he has to pay heavily for overcoming these physical obstacles in the form of higher rates necessitated by initial high cost of construction and subsequent maintenance. This explains the reason why vast areas of the globe in the form of oceans, deserts, dense forests, mountains and ice caps exist even today, bereft of transportation and communication. Such areas hardly can sustain any business activities.

The natural environment is particularly important to man in two respects: (i) it is a storehouse of certain ***source materials*** that will be consumed by him ultimately and (ii) it provides certain ***physical and biological conditions*** within and on which man's production, exchange, consumption and happiness depend (Read also Box 38.1).

Box 38.1 **Saga of Fire and Ice on an Isolated Island**

It's official. In a poll of 18 nations, the Gallup Organisation discovered that icelanders are the happiest people alive. All 266,786 of them. Subtract the percentage of malcontents from the percentage of contents and Gallup found 82% of all Icelanders were satisfied with their personal life. The US ranked fifth at 72%, Japan was at 42%. Deeply unhappy are Mexicans and Hungarians, as here the number of malcontented far exceeds the number of the contented.

Some people would say that happy Iceland is just a statistical fluke. This is a country so small, any one can make an appointment to see the President. And it is a homogeneous society, a freckled, watery-eyed nation. What could Iceland possibly teach America, with its big, big problems?

Yet, this is the second study that has highlighted the happy Icelander. Something good must be going on.

Utopia? No. Iceland is no utopia. In downtown Reykjavik, sailors collapse on curbsides, swig the local firewater, brennivin, and sing just to hear themselves shout. Icelanders are great boozers-not as heavy as Finns or Danes, but Icelanders have a fisherman's history of bingeing. Nor are the nation's morals in such hot shape:Almost a third of the children are born out of wedlock.

But that's precisely what makes the Gallup study so interesting. Icelanders have problems just as the rest of us do, but they still say they are happy. This, though they dwell on an isolated, windswept island condemned by nature to just three or four hours of daylight in the winter.

I have some clues as to what makes Icelanders so contented with their lot. For the past 19 years, I have fished there annually. I have come to know some of the people well.

Let me start by introducing Thorir Hlynur Thorisson, age 28. This summer Hlynur spent a month working 16-hour days, seven days a week, as a fishing guide on the Nordlingafljot River in Iceland.

Without a break, he bagged salmon, drove jeeps, washed dishes. No, he was not working this hard just for money. This was his vacation. It was how he chose to spend his time off. It was "heaven on earth," he said of that month.

In late July, after a single night off in Reykjavik, Hlynur was back at his regular job at sea, on a large fishing boat. For the next 24 days in a row, he worked six hours on, six hours off, around the clock. I guess we would call Hlynur a workaholic, but so are most of his fellow countrymen.

This hard work does pay off in material ways. With a per capita gross domestic product of $26,400 (the US figure is $25,617), Icelanders are among the wealthiest people on earth. Their tax dollars buy them excellent education and medical care.

Iceland has the lowest infant mortality rate in the world and almost the highest longevity.

But the dour Swiss have a well-run state, too, and all their material needs met, yet no one could accuse them of a cheerful outlook.

Thorolfur Thorlindsson, professor of sociology at the University of Iceland, believes the secret of Iceland's happiness lies not in its comforts, but in its age-old discomforts. It has taught Icelanders to be grateful for what they get. Isolated in the cold North Atlantic, buffeted by a hostile sea, the people have for centuries lived with the vagaries of volatile fish catches.

"Our culture is coloured by the harshness of nature," says Thorlindsson. "That's why Icelanders have a more tolerant attitude to the problems of life. They don't expect the same sort of stability often expected in other nations."

And so it seems. By any measures, Americans, average Americans, are considerably better on by material standards than they were a couple of generations ago. We spend increasing amounts on education, on pensions, on medical care, on taking care of the unemployed. But we seem less happy, less content with our lot.

Like Icelanders, Americans are individualists. Where the latter seem to differ is in their respective senses of community. Iceland-known as the land of "fire and ice"-is about living with opposing forces. It is one of the most active volcanic countries on earth; but its 4,536 square miles of glacier include Europe's largest ice flow-heat and cold, coexisting. No surprise then, that its society reconciles so well to another set of powerfully opposing forces: individualism and the needs of the collective community.

Anyone who thinks Americans invented rugged individualism has only to visit Iceland. This nation has an ancient respect for freedom and independence. Way back in the 10th century, Iceland was a republic that established a parliament called the Althing, some 300 years before Britain's "Mother of Parliaments" was created. In their love for freedom, Icelanders resist being put into slots. You meet sailors planning to become actors; accountants, against the odds, passionately building salmon rivers. "Icelanders place high value on individualism," says Thorlindsson.

But here's the seeming paradox: This individualism coexists with a praiseworthy sense of community. For years I have known a wholesome, middleclass Icelandic family that matter-of-fact embraces and includes a family drunk and an illegitimate child. The wife treats her husband's illegitimate son as her own.

This family impresses me for having dealt responsibly with the downside of individualism. It never abandoned its offbeat souls. It never let them drift anonymously through the community, human flotsam to be beached at some state institution. "Studies show, in comparison to other nations, Icelanders have strong systems of support and interpersonal relationships," says Thorlindsson.

A small country, but not small-minded. The Japanese are as rich as the Icelanders. They also have a homogeneous society stretch-ing back generations. But Japanese score low on the contentment geiger counter. Both Japan and America could learn from Icelanders.

Tolerance is not just a hollow phrase in Iceland. The word for "stupid" in Iceland is **heimskur**, which roughly means "comes from home", -or as we would say, "provincial" or "narrowminded". Icelanders believe only a dolt is unable to see the other fellow's position. In this sense, they find some of what passes for political debate in the US, absolutely **heimskur**.

Most Icelanders travel out into the world as young adults. It's an ancient tradition to look for the world beyond their own narrow borders: Iceland's Leifur the Lucky touched the New World 500 years before Christopher Columbus. That tradition of looking beyond the horizon has survived into the age of jets and Internets. Early on, young Icelanders learn that theirs is not the only way of doing things. Yet this worldliness never translates into contempt for their own small island and its history.

The 12th centruy Icelandic sagas are studied at universities the world over and are much revered at home. For many, the myths are still vibrant. Catch your first salmon here, and you're pressured to join in the age-old custom of chewing off its fin. Turn on the radio, and on tip of the charts is Bubbi Morthens, a real troubadour.

This summer in the lava fields of Icesland's interior, a small experience told me a lot about Iceland. Accountant Sigmar Bjornssor pointed out a cave where notorious thieves had hidden. He showed me where they stored their weapons, where the villagers attacked, told me how one of the thieves hopped with an amputated leg to the glacier on the horizon.

When had these characters holed up in this cave? I asked, expecting it was something quite recent. About 900 years ago, was the answer. Nearly a millennium and the myth is still alive. How many Americans today have that kind of familiarity with their nation's past, its myths, its history? How many even care?

I wish America's multiculturalists, its deconstructionists, its historical revisionists would grasp what the Icelanders understand: that trashing your nations myths is the wrong way to go about creating a better society.

Maybe I'm wrong, but I suspect that this loss of "centre" is what makes so many affluent Westerners unhappy amidst their homes full of consumer goods.

(**Source**: Reproduced from *Forbes* in the *The Economic Times* supplement dated Dec. 2, 1995).

As a storehouse of materials, it may be stated that the earth is a gigantic repository of materials that man, through the ages, has learnt and is learning to utilise to his advantage. Nearly every commodity that man has produced and consumed existed originally in the natural environment. In addition, nearly all the energy used in production and distribution comes from nature.

Besides being the origin of needed materials, the natural environment provides certain physical and biological conditions within which man lives and works. These conditions may be positive or negative, favourable or unfavourable with respect to man's livelihood. For example, the flat lands of plains normally may be a decisive asset and undulating and hilly land may be the distinct liability to the production and transportation of most commodities. Conversely, in times of flood, the flat land may be a liability and the undulating and hilly land an asset.

Though every country in the world is spending millions of rupees on the development of its own technology, the physical environment of each nation determines its stage of progress in the field of technology. Obviously, there are wide differences in progress attained in this sector. Technological advancement and in its wake, the levels of income and standard of life enjoyed in the United States and in other industrial nations have not yet come to many other parts of the world. To a person born and bred in a large city like New York, London, Tokyo, Delhi or Mumbai, and accustomed to the amenities of modern life, it would be extremely difficult indeed to really understand the way of life and thinking of a group such as the Halakki Vokkaligas of N.Kanara numbering around 50,000 or the Bindibu of Central Australia, who have no huts, practically no clothing, no agriculture, but only a flint and a few wood implements. People living in such conditions are becoming rare. Nevertheless, there are still many regions wherein, compared to those in modern countries, life is fairly primitive; where people carry on their economic activities much the same way as they had done in past centuries; where they perform the same tasks, think on parallel lines; are spurred to the same types of action and have the same hopes and fears as their forebearers (Also read Box 38.2).

Thus, natural environment exerts a profound influence on man and his economic activities. Every law that is enacted to regulate his personal life and every legislation framed to control his business activities have one overriding consideration, *viz., public interest or natural justice*. The expression 'natural justice' or 'public interest' is derived from the natural environment.

Character and attitudes of people are shaped by physical environment.

Besides, it has been said that the scale of natural phenomena in India, and her total dependence on the monsoon, have helped to form the character of her people. Even today major disasters such as floods, famine and plague are hard to check, and in older times, their control was almost impossible. Many other ancient civilisations, such as those of the Greeks, Romans and Chinese, had to contend with

Box 38.2 **As Wet as Cherrapunjee**

To rain cats and dogs, seems to be true as far as Cherrapunjee is concerned. Geography books describe this small town as one of the regions receiving the highest amount of rainfall in the world. Situated 1,300 metres above sea level, surrounded by green hills and deep gorges, Cherrapunjee is the rainiest rainbelt in the world.

According to geographers, the main reason for the torrential rainfall in the entire South East Asiatic region is the South-West monsoon wind which comes during the summer season. The wind originates in the Bay of Bengal, and starts flowing in the north east direction. On its way, the moisture-laden wind gets obstructed in the Meghalaya plateau and falls in a downpour as a result of the orographic factor. Cherrapunjee which is situated immediately in the windward side of the area, gets the direct effect of this wind and gains the greatest amount of rainfall averaging more than 1,000 cm a year. According to estimates, the town received 905 inches (approx 2,264 cm) in 1861, 503 inches of which was recorded in June and July.

Nature has had considerable influence on the beliefs, ideas and attitudes of the Khasi people (Khasis are the indigenous tribe of Meghalaya). They revere the mountains in the region. Diengiel and Sohpethneng are two such mountains, worshipped by the Khasis and described as the primeval cradle of the Khasi tribe.

The weather here is as unpredictable as it is famed to be-all of a sudden the skies turn cloudy and there is a drizzle. You are enveloped by a thick fog unawares, and driving in zero visibility can be exciting. The fog clears as swiftly, to reveal the scenic beauty once again.

hard winters, which encouraged sturdiness and courage. India, on the other hand, was blessed by the bountiful nature which demanded little of man in return for sustenance, but in her terrible anger, could not be appeased by any human effort. Hence, it has been suggested that the Indian character has tended to fatalism and quietism, accepting fortune and misfortune alike without complaint.[5]

As a nation, we are passing through the most critical period with fundamentalism, communalism and linguistic and regional differences assuming ugly and pernicious proportions. At this criticl juncture, let us look to nature for solace.

Nature is around us with its subline beauty and splenderous joy. It never deceives us: the rocks, the mountains, the streams, always speak the same language. A shower of snow may hide the verdant woods in spring. A thunderstorm may render the blue limpid and make the rivers turbulent. But in a little while, all the sources of beauty are revivewd and revitalised. Nature's fruits are all balmy and sweet.[6]

It must never be forgotten that man and nature have a deep symbiotic link. As in the concept of the ancient Vedas, we must realise that this planet of ours is the earth mother-*Bhawani Vasundhara* in the Hindu tradition, *Gaia* in the Greek.

Five thousand years ago, the seers of the Vedas composed the famous *Bhumi Suktam* (Hymn to the earth). Its 63 verses are a magniticent paean to our mother planet, from which we can still derive deep inspiration. Indeed, these should be required reading for all those involved in trying to protect the fragile environment of our earth.

ANALYSIS OF NATURAL ENVIRONMENT

Among all the environmental segments, analysis of physical environment is relatively easy for two reasons. First, changes in the physical environment are few and far between. In otherwords, natural environment is relatively stable and predictable, though calamities like *Tsunami* takes any person off the guard. But calamities are not too frequent, though their occurrence cannot be ruled out. Second, as stated in the beginning of this chapter, scientific breakthroughs and technological advancements have enabled today's man to be fairly independent of nature.

But physical environment should not be taken for granted. Business needs to evolve strategies with provisions for protecting ecology and proactive measures to combat emergencies being embedded.

Physical environment has several strategic implications.[7] It is the duty of the analyst to scan, track, forecast and assess these implications so that they form part of firm's strategies.

First, may it be understood that both employees as well as consumers are resentful of firms taking more than giving to the natural environment. Similarly, people are appreciative of businesses that conduct operations in a way that mends rather than harm the environment. No surprise that businesses of today are purchasing their own independent, nonpolluting power source. This strategy is in contrast to continuing to purchase electricity from large, polluting, coal-burning activities.

Second, environmental issues that are of concern to businesses are ozone depletion, global warming, depletion of rain forests, destruction of animal habitats, protecting endangred species, developing biodegradable products and packages, waste management, clean air, clean water, destruction of natural resources, and pollution control. These issues need to be embedded in the firm's strategies. For example, firms are increasingly developing green product lines that are biodegradable and are made from recycled products-Green products sell well.

Third, managing environmental affairs should not be taken as incidental or secondary function of a firm. Product design, manufacturing, and final disposal should not only have orientation towards environmental protection, but also be driven by it. Firms that manage environmental affairs will enhance relations with consumers, regulators, regulations, vendors and other industry players – substantially improving their prospects of success.

Fourth, managing environmental affairs can no longer be a simple a technical function performed by specialists in a company; more emphasis should be placed on developing an environmental perspective among all executives and other employees of the firm.

Many companies are becoming proactive. They are making environmental protection a line function (hither to considered as a staff function), thus making the chief executive personally superwise the activities of the management of environmental affairs.

Fifth, environment has brought in a new category of people — environmentalists or activists. These are the individuals who are affluent and live mainly in cities. These people engage in activities such as not buying products from companies known for insensitivity towards environment, avoiding aerosol products, recycling paper and bottles and using biodegradable products. These details should help the firm formulate strategies for product development and market penetration.

Finally, firms should formulate and implement strategies from an environmental perspective. Environmental strategies should include developing or acquiring green businesses, diversting or altering environment – damaging businesses, striving to become low-cost produces through waste minimisation and energy conservation and pursing a differentiation strategy through green-product features. In addition to crafting strategies, company should include an environmental activist on the board of directors, conduct periodic environmental audits, implement bonuses for favourable environmental results, become involved in environmental issues and programmes, incorporate environmental values in mission statements, acquire environmental skills, and provide training programmes for company managers and employees.

QUESTIONS

1. What is natural environment?
2. How does natural environment affect business? Discuss.
3. How do you analyse physical environment?

ASSIGNMENT

Pick up any five eco-friendly firms. Identify their green - oriental activities. Critically evaluate whether or not these firms have geniune concern towards ecology.

REFERENCES

1. *Economic Times*, dated March 17, 1987.
2. *Ibid.*
3. Van Royen and Bengtson, *Fundamentals of Economic Geography*, p.7.
4. *Ibid*, p.3.
5. A.L.Basham, *The Wonder That Was India*, p.3.
6. Homi,J.H. Talayarkhan, *Environment of Forestry in Economic Development*, p.3.

CHAPTER OUTLINE

Integration of Segments

Environmental Analysis Forming Part of Strategic Management

Political Strategy

LEARNING OBJECTIVES

After reading this Chapter, you should be able to:

1. Explain how environmental analysis becomes part of strategic management
2. Describe the impact of environmental inputs on each phase of strategic management
3. Explain the political strategies

39 Integrating Environment and Strategic Management

In all the previous chapters, we have described global, economic, political, socio-cultural and natural segments in greater detail. We have also described, at the end of each segment, how the environmental analyst scans, monitors, forecasts and assesses each environmental factor. Now, the analyst has before him or her, bundle of indications of change which should become part of strategy formulation and implementation. This chapter seeks to address two issues: (i) how the analyst integrates the indicators identified from each segment, and (ii) how these indicators are considered at each stage of strategic management process.

INTEGRATION OF SEGMENTS

Integration of different segments serves atleast three objectives: (i) to identify issues generated by the trends and patterns in each segment; (ii) to discover relationships among trends and patterns across the environmental segments; and (iii) to keep environmental analysis manageable, since an organisation's capacity to identify and assess issues is constrained by its available resources.

Steps involved in Integration

Before describing the steps it is essential to understand the sequence of actions that precedes identification of issues that have strategic implications. The general process is:

Trends → Patterns → Issues

Trends are disjointed events that occur. These events, if repeated and become regular, constitute patterns. And the patterns generate issues that will become inputs for strategy formulation and implementation (See Fig.39.1).

Figure 39.1 **Patterns Generate inputs for Strategy Formulation and Implementation**

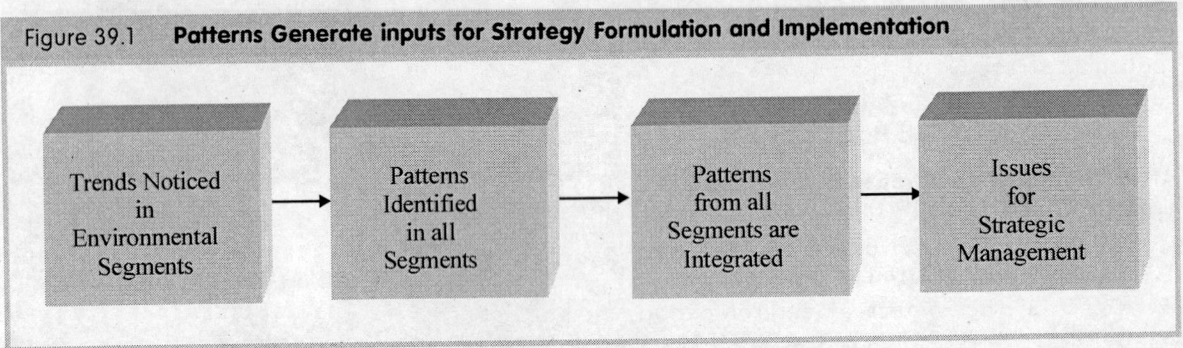

As shown in Fig.39.1, three sequential steps emerge in the integration of segment analysis: (i) discern of meaningful patterns across environmental segments, (ii) identification of interrelationships among patterns, and (iii) choice of strategic issues.

Patterns within and Across Segments: Analysis of each segment unearths some discrete trends and patterns. These trends and patterns should be identified and aggregated. The aggregation of trends and patterns emerging from all segments helps the analyst have a holistic picture about the macroenvironment. Inferring a meaning from segment-specific trend, taken each in isolation, is often difficult and if pursued the analysts is likely to miss the forest for trees, as it were.

Interrelationships among Patterns: The second step in the integration is to consider the interrelationships among patterns identified in the political, global, economic and social segments. What needs to be emphasised at this stage is that patterns in one segment may reinforce, conflict with, or be unrelated to patterns in other segments. For example, increasing health consciousness may cause health care cost to add up further, jointly may increase regulatory pressures in the health field, and may accelerate commitment to research to prevent/cure diseases such as cancer. Obviously, there is need to consider the mutual impacts among patterns.

Choice of Strategic Issues: The analyst need not be unduly concerned by all the patterns and issues triggered by scanning and monitoring the environmental segments. In order to integrate patterns and issues into strategic management, care should be taken to pick up only such issues that have positive or negative impacts on the firm.

Emphasis should be placed upon the judgement required to identify issues, that are affecting or will affect the organisation. Judgement involves assessing and prioritising patterns against atleast four criteria:

- How might the pattern impact the firm?
- What is the likely evolution of the pattern?
- How great will be eventual impact on the company?
- When is the issue likely to peek?

ENVIRONMENTAL ANALYSIS BECOMING PART OF STRATEGIC MANAGEMENT

As pointed out by us at several places, environmental analysis provides intelligence out of which strategy is formulated. Obviously, analysis should precede strategy formulation. Fig.39.2 depicts the sequence of steps.

Figure 39.2 **Linkage to Strategic Management**

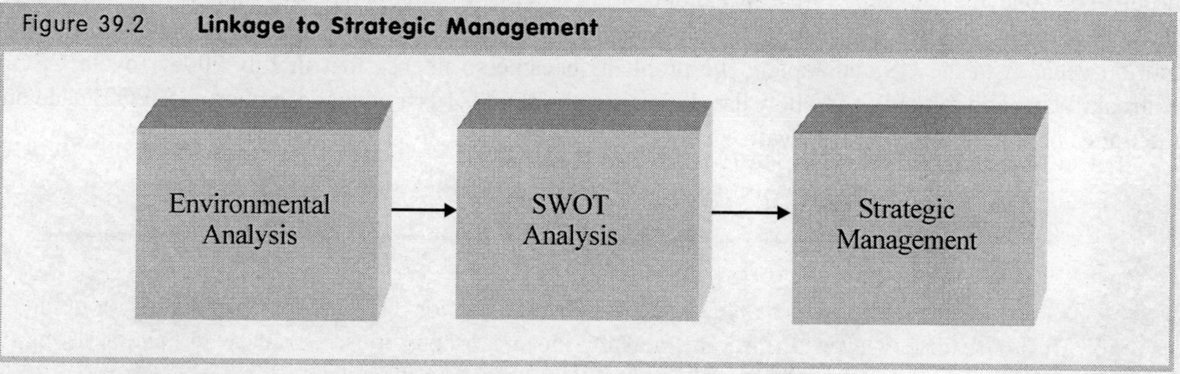

SWOT Analysis

SWOT is the acronym for strengths, weaknesses, opportunities and threats that are strategic factors for a firm. Analysis of internal environment helps identify strengths and weaknesses, whereas opportunities and threats are revealed by the understanding of macroenvironment.

Analysis of internal environment helps identify strengths and weaknesses, whereas opportunities and threats are revealed through the understanding of external environment.

Strengths are positive internal characteristics that the firm can exploit to achieve its goals. **Weaknesses** are internal traits that might inhibit or restrict the firm's performance. Fir.39.3 gives a checklist that can help identify strengths and weaknesses of an organisation. The details sought relate to specific functions such as marketing, human resource, finance, production and R&D. Internal analysis also examines such areas as organisation structure, centralisation of decision making, quality of staff and competence of managerial personnel (Also see Fig.39.3). Based on the information thus collected managers draw their company's strengths and weaknesses vis-a-vis their competing firms. Toyota's strength is that it is built on details. After decades of study and refinement, the company has developed thousands of pages of guidelines that lay out exactly what

Figure 39.3 **Checklist for Analysing Strengths and Weaknesses**

Management & Organisation	*Marketing*	*Human Resources*
• Management quality	• Distribution channels	• Employee experience, education
• Staff quality	• Market share	• Union status
• Degree of centralisation	• Advertising efficiency	• Turnover, absenteeism
• Organisation charts	• Customer satisfaction	• Work satisfaction
• Planning, Information,	• Product quality	• Grievances
	• Service reputation	• Morale
	• Sales force turnover	
Finance	*Manufacturing*	*R&D*
• Profit margin	• Plant location	• Basic applied research
• Debt-equity ratio	• Machinery obsolescence	• laboratory capabilities
• Inventory ratio	• Purchasing system	• Research programmes
• Return on investment	• Quality control	• New product innovations
• Credit rating	• Productivity/efficiency	• Technology innovations

(**Source:** Richard L.Daft, *Management*, Thomson, 2003, p.249)

needs to be done at every step of the car manufacturing process. But its weakness is that growing number of flaws have started to surface tarnishing the image of Toyota. Since 2004, the automaker has had to recall 9.3 million vehicles in the US and Japan. The problems became so intense that in July 2006, Toyota CEO-Katruaki Watanabo-felt obliged to bow deeply in apology. Box.39.1 is a typical depiction of SWOT made on the Bangalore based electric car-Reva.

Box 39.1 **SWOT Analysis of Reva**

Strengths

- India's first and only battery operated electric car for city drive, ideal for those looking for second or even a third car, and for those eco-conscious citizens who have a strong desire to save blue planet.
- Cheapest among electric operated cars in the world with unbeatable running costs as low as 40p per km.
- Slim look, comfortable driving, small turning radius and easy parking-ideal for Bangalore roads, notorious for traffic congestion.
- Fresh infusion of $20 million by international venture capital firms. Along with funds, two experienced executives from the funding firms are on the Board of Directors of Reva.
- Eyeing on global market, already 600 Revas sold in London and looking for markets in other geographic areas in Europe.
- Plans to expand production capacity, release new models and undertake promotional activities.
- Developed, in 2005, a prototype of a two-seat roadster called Reva-NXG. Reva-NXG uses sodium nickel chronide batteries instead of the conventional lead acid batteries.

Weaknesses

- Top speed of 60 km per hour and the distance it cant ravel on a single charge is only 80 km.
- Reva is underpowered when compared to a regular car.
- Reva is overpriced at Rs.2.5 lakhs particularly because Maruti 800 with AC is cheaper.
- Scores low on comforts, interiors, motor and performance. Can carry 2 adults and 2 kids but Maruti 800 can carry 4 adults with kids being stuffed in.
- At intervals of 80 km, Reva needs charging and charging points are not available on all roads. Charging is less convenient (takes 7 hours) than getting your tank filled up in a petrol bunk.
- Initially, time and money was spent on technology and getting the product right. Initial investment of $25 million mainly went into developing prototypes. No funds were left for publicity and brand building activities.
- In the last four years till end 2005, Reva sold only 1800 numbers against a target of 6000 per annum.
- Solely dependent on electric car unlike major global players like GM, Toyota and Ford.

Opportunities

- Lots of scope in a new world where volts, amps and watts replace bhp, rpm and exhaust times.
- Market is growing, Freedonia group estimates that this segment has grown from a $650 million market in 1999 to an estimated $16 billion in 2004 and is expected to reach $45

billion in 2009. Dwindling oil resources, rising oil prices, increasing congestion and environmental concerns and stricter governmental regulations add to the growing market.

- Tremendous potential for exports and to ramp up production volumes as Reva's competitors' price is 2-3 times higher in Europe and North America.
- Elsewhere several subsidies and concessions have been extended to this segment. In UK sales and road taxes are exempted so also parking and congestion fees are waived. In the US $4000 subsidy is offered per vehicle. Reva did enjoy a Rs.1 lakh subsidy initially but was discontinued later. Reva still enjoys benefits like a lower excise duty of 8 per cent, against 16 per cent applicable to petrol and diesel cars. Governments everywhere are bound to extend more attractive sops to electric car segment boosting demand for the eco-friendly cars.

Threats

- Several big players have already launched or have plans to launch electric cars, posing entry barriers to penetrate overseas markets. Daimler Chrysler has recently launched the electric version of its city car called SMART. The French auto major AXIOM has also launched its version of similar car. GM, Nissan and Mitsubishi have announced that they would be launching electric vehicles.
- Reva's target market - housewives, professionals and college going youth - are not impressed by the car and are vulnerable to be targeted by rivals.

(**Source:** Based on inputs from *Business India*, Dec.31, 2006, *Business World*, Jan.15, 2007, and *Autocar*, Jan, 2007).

Analysis of external environment helps identify threats and opportunities. **Threats** are the characteristics of the external environment that impede the growth of the firm. **Opportunities** are the indicators of the external environment that have the potential to help the firm achieve its goals. Managers evaluate the external environment on the lines described at different places in this book. Analysis of regulatory, global, economic, technical, social and physical segments throws enough light on the company's opportunities and threats. Indian Bank has discovered the prevalence of huge unbanked populace, particularly in villages and slums around cities. Seizing this segment, the once declared as no-hope bank has opened 1.64 lakh no-frills accounts in 677 villages. The bank has extended 15,772 O.D. facilities involving Rs.2.62 cr. It has opened a branch at Dharuvi in Mumbai exclusively for slumdwellers. The bank has threat of being overshadowed by aggressive foreign and private Indian banks. Indian Bank has the tradition of being a south based that too having roots in Tamil Nadu.

Threats are the characteristics of the external environment that impede the growth of the firm. Opportunities are the indicators of the external environment that have to potential to help the firm achieve its goals.

STRATEGIC MANAGEMENT

Integration of all environmental segments help draw SWOT analysis of the firm. Environmental analysis earmarked strategic factors. SWOT analysis helped place the company in proper perspective vis-a-vis its competing firms. Now the stage is set for formulating strategies. An understanding of strategic management process is in order.

Strategic management refers to a set of decisions and actions resulting the formulation and implementation of strategies designed to achieve the objectives of a firm (See Fig.39.4).

Figure 39.4 **Strategic Management Process**

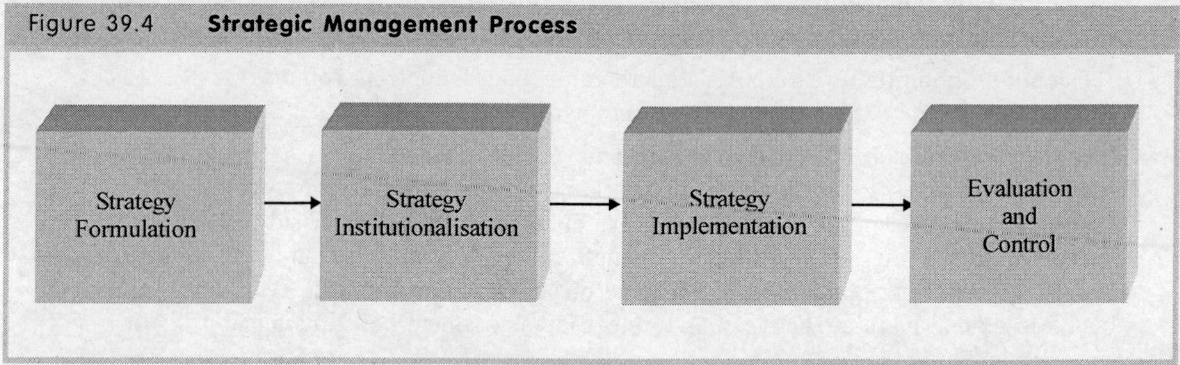

Benefits of Strategic Management

Strategic management offers immense benefits to a firm. In addition to a healthy bottomline, strategic management contributes to behaviourally based effects on a company. Such behavioural effects that can be expected are:[1]

1. Strategy formulation activities should enhance the problem prevention capabilities of the firm. As a consequence of encouraging and rewarding subordinate attention to planning considerations, managers are aided in their monitoring and forecasting responsibilities by workers who are alerted to the needs of strategic planning.
2. Group-based strategic decisions are most likely to reflect the best available alternatives. Better decisions are possible outcomes of the process for two reasons: First, generating alternative strategies is facilitated by group interaction; Second, screening of options is improved because group members offer forecasts based on their specialised perspectives.
3. Employee motivation should improve as employees better appreciate the productivity-reward relationships inherent in every strategic plan. When employees or their representatives participate in strategy formulation process, a better understanding of the priorities and operations of the organisation's reward system is achieved, thus adding incentives for goal directed behvaviour.
4. Gaps and overlaps in activities among diverse individuals and groups should be reduced as participation in strategy formulation leads to a clarification of role differentiation. The group meeting format, which is characteristic of several stages of a strategy formulation process, promotes an understanding of the delineations of individual and sub-group responsibilities.
5. Resistance to change should be reduced. The required participation helps eliminate the uncertainty associated with change, which is at the root of most resistance. While participants may no more be pleased with their own choices than they would be with authoritarian decisions, their acceptance of new plans is more likely if employees are aware of the parameters that limit the available options.

Strategy Formulation: The first step in strategic management is strategy formulation (see Fig.39.4). A strategy is a comprehensive master plan of a firm stating how it achieves its objectives. A company has strategies at three levels: corporate, business and functional levels (see Fig.39.5).

Figure 39.5 **Three Levels of Strategy**

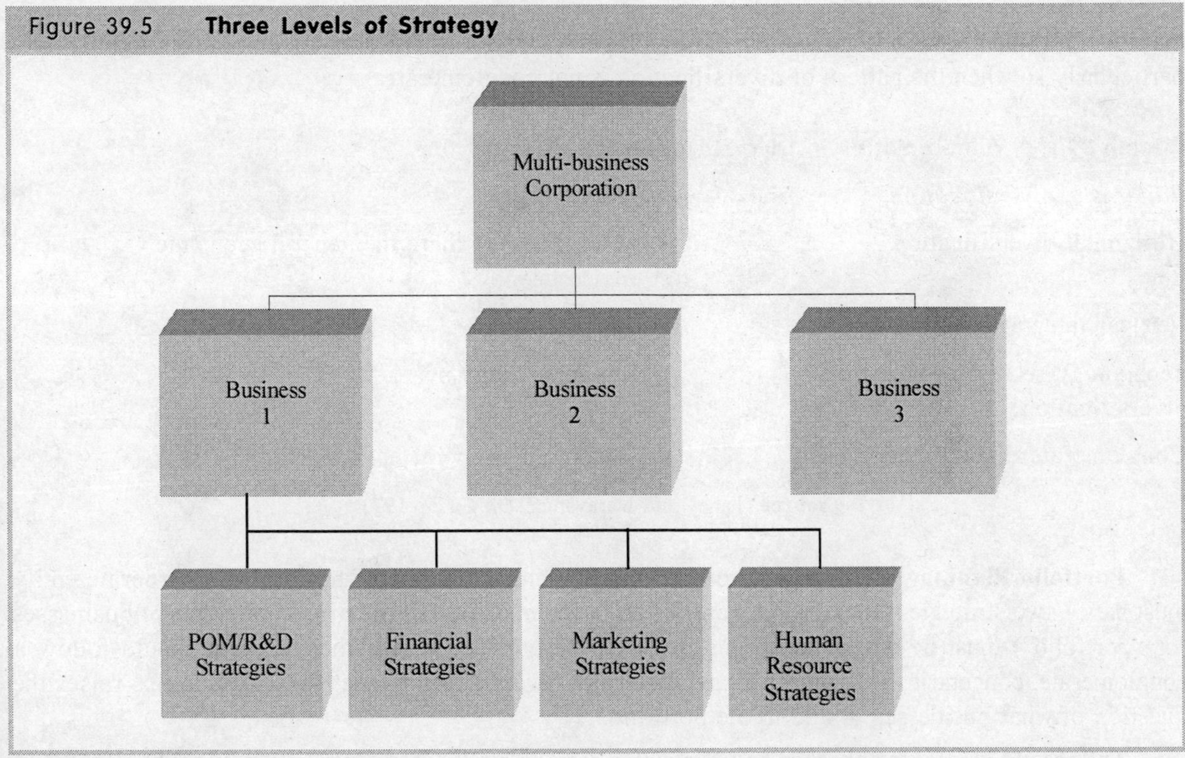

Corporate Level Strategy

This strategy is formulated by top management to oversee the interests and operations of an organisation made up of more than one line of business. The major questions at this level are: What kinds of business should the company be engaged in? What are the goals and expectations for each business? How should resources be allocated to reach these goals?

In formulating corporate-level strategy, Peter Drucker suggests, corporations need to decide where they want to be in eight areas: market standing, innovation, productivity, physical and financial resources, profitability, managerial performance and development, worker performance and attitudes, and public responsibility.[2]

Environmental Impact on Corporate Level Strategy

At the corporate level strategy, environmental impact on three key issues are significant: (i) patterns of diversification, (ii) portfolio planning, and (iii) risk return trade-offs.

> At the corporate level strategy, envrionment impacts on three areas: (i) Patterns of diversification, (ii) Portfolio Planning, and (iii) Risk return trade-off.

Patterns of Diversification: In diversifying, there are two models a company can follow: internal and external. Firms choosing the internal model stress the development of new products and services through research and development efforts within the organisations. Conversely, companies diversifying externally focus on making acquisitions.

Environment influences patterns of diversification in atleast three ways. First, firms differ in the synergies they try to exploit across their businesses. These synergies could be upset or enhanced by macroenvironmental changes. Second, different patterns of diversification manifest different vulnerabilities (see Table 39.1). Macroenvironmental changes may amplify these vulnerabilities. Third, macroenvironmental trends may open up or close out existing patterns of diversification. This is particularly so when the pattern of diversification is not conglomerate.[3]

Table 39.1 **Vulnerabilities in Diversitication Patterns**

Patterns of diversification	*Vulnerability*
Horizontal diversification	All businesses share the general economic environment
Vertical integration	Markets
Technology-related concentric diversification	Key technology synergy
Conglomerate diversification	Society and general economy

(**Source:** Fahey and Narayanan, *Op.Cit.*, p.197)

Portfolio Planning: With regard to portfolio planning (the type of businesses a corporate entity must have), two strategic issues are relevant. First, the composition of the firm's collection of businesses (or "portfolio") must be determined. This involves the question of whether the firm should follow a conglomerate, concentric, vertical, or mixed pattern of diversification (see Box 39.2). It also raises the question of what businesses to add to the portfolio.

The second key issue concerns how resources are to be allocated among the several businesses in the portfolio. An analytical framework called portfolio analysis has been developed to help corporate management address and structure the issue.

Prominent portfolio planning models available are the G.E.Model, BCG Model, McKinsey Model and the one developed by Arthur D.Little, Inc. Although all these differ in detail, they all basically follow a similar methodology. They all require the identification of strategic business units (SBUs), the positioning of SBUs on a matrix, and the application of a particular resource strategy for each SBU, depending on its placement on the matrix.

Macroenvironmental trends have important implications for portfolio planning. Typical portfolio planning focuses on competitive advantages within an existing industry, constrained by the internal financial resources of the firm.

Environmental analyses are also particularly important for planning potential future portfolios. The specific businesses to be targeted need to be considered in the light of macroenvironmental forecasts and predictions.

Rick-return Trade-offs: Political, economic, technological, and demographic shifts influence the returns and risks of existing and planned portfolios.

- In a conglomerate firm, the accepted macro-environmental trends suggested a persistent level of inflation in the economy. One of the consequent considerations was that additional investments in any business unit should be justified not only by competitive position but also by returns in excess of the forecasted rate of inflation.
- In a technology-related firm, a technology study suggested obsolescence of some key technologies within the next decade. As a result, the firm is searching for methods of converting technology so as to retain competitive advantage in their existing markets.[5]

It is important to consider environmental impacts on each of these characteristics of corporate-level strategy.

Box 39.2 **Ten Options for a Corporation**

In deciding on a corporate strategy, a company has basically ten options:

1. Concentration on a Single Business: The company concentrates on a single product, service, market, or technology. Indian Airlines, for example, operates aircraft for the benefit of domestic passengers and so is the case with Air India which files aircraft across the globle. Similarly, life Insurance Corporation concentrates in life business and so does the Indian Railways which operate railways.

2. Vertical Integration: This is the strategy of a company moving backward or forward, or both, along the channels of supply and distribution. The takeover of Parle by Coca-Cola is an example for vertical integration.

3. Concentric Diversification: Under this strategy, the company moves into new but related lines of business. There is a governing common thread that guides the company's acquisition and internal development policy. This thread may consist of technology, product similarity, or other valid reasons. The takeover of Tomco along with its subsidiaries by Levers is an example for concentric strategy. The subsidiaries are: Tata Vashishti Detergents (a joint venture with Maharastra Petrochemicals), Industrial Perfumes, International Fisheries, Kalyani Soap Industries (a joint venture with the West Bengal Government), and Tata Oil Clorox.

4. Conglomerate Diversification: This is unrelated diversification. Here, the constraints on the company's strategy are merely whether a business meets the minimum standard of expected profitability. J.K.group of companies belong to this category.

5. Joint Venture: Joint venture is a capital sharing arrangement between an MNC and a local company (or even a foreign government) or another MNC. Each partner holds shares in the subsidiary and shares the profits in relation to its ownership share. By following a joint venture route, MNCs can spread a given amount of investment across more locations and thereby minimise risks.

Most MNCs operating in our country have joint ventures with local outfits. Thus, we have Procter and Gamble having joint ventures with Godrej. Similarly, Maruti is jointly owned by Suzuki of Japan and the Government of India.

6. Retrenchment: This is a common short-run strategy that some companies adopt during periods of poor economic performance. At the corporate level, it can assume two variations. The first involves stringent across-the-board cost cutting to improve efficiency. Ceat Ltd., for example, has resorted to cost cutting and financial restructuring to restore healthy bottomline. The second demands the selective pruning or revamping of the weakest product or division. Hiving off Tomco by Tatas to Levers is a case to the point.

7. Divestiture: This is another limited strategy that involves either selling off parts of a company to another firm or "spinning off" financially and managerially independent companies. Such a policy is generally followed to reverse past mistakes. Sale of oral hygiene business by Ciba-Geigy is an example for the first variation of divestiture. For second is the example of Eicher group which has six independent units. They are Eicher Tractors Ltd., Eicher Motors Ltd., Royal Enfield Motors Ltd., Eicher International Ltd., Eicher Span Financial Services, and Eicher Consultancy Services.

8. Liquidation: This involves closing down the business for ever. Liquidation strategy is resorted to when all efforts to retrieve to a sick company have failed to yield results. During 1993 alone the BIFR recommended closure of as many as 262 sick companies.

9. Reorganisation under BIFR Scheme: Sick companies are referred to the Board for Industrial of Financial Reconstruction (BIFR) under the provisions of the Sick Industrial Companies (Special Provisions) Act, 1985. The Board prepares a scheme of rehabilitation if a sick unit is retrievable. Otherwise the Board recommends its closure. During 1993 alone as many as 415 schemes of rehabilitations were prepared and implemented by the Board.

10. Combination Strategies: The preceding Nine strategies are not mutually exclusive. They can be combined in almost any number of variations. Thus, conglomerates often shed their less profitable businesses. Single businesses diversify and large companies set up joint ventures. In today's competitive environment many companies are pursuing strategies that combine retrenchment and divestiture with concentric diversification.[4]

(**Source**: *World Development Report 1995,* p.3)

Business Level Strategy

Each division prepares its own strategy mainly translating the general statements of direction and intent, generated at the corporate level into concrete, functional objectives and strategies for individual business divisions or SBUs. In essence, business-level strategic managers (comprising principally of business and corporate managers) must determine the basis on which a company can compete in the selected product-market area. While doing so, they strive to identify and secure the most profitable and promising market segment. The strengths of market segment determine continuous viability of the corporation.

One well known model of business-level strategy was developed by Michael E.Porter of Harward Business School. In Porter's view, an organisation's ability to compete in a given market is determined by its technical and economic resources, as well as five environmental forces, each of which threatens the organisation's venture into a new market. The five forces are: threats top entry, bargaining power of consumers, the bargaining power of suppliers, the threat of substitute products and jockeying for position in a crowded market.

Environmental Impact on Business-Unit Strategy

The impact of environmental analysis on business unit strategy needs to be assessed with regard to (i) business definition, (ii) assumptions, and (iii) general strategic thrust.

The impact of environmental analysis on business-unit strategy must be assessed with regard to (1) business definition, (2) assumptions, and (3) general strategic thrust.

In broad terms, strategy formulation at the business or corporate level includes a definition of the business and positioning of the business in an industry. Definition and positioning are inevitably affected by industry structure; macroenvironmental trends, as they affect industry structure, open up opportunities and threats for business strategy. Each of the three elements of business definitions can be affected by environmental change: What customers does business serve? What customer needs are satisfied? What technologies are employed to satisfy these consumer needs?

Some *pivotal assumptions* always underline a firm's strategy-for example, industry assumptions such as actions of suppliers, competitive responses, the likelihood of new entrants, or the market penetration of substitute products. The success or failure of a strategy is often determined by the veracity of these assumptions. Assumptions about the macroenvironment, however, may also critically influence strategy success.

Finally, the general strategic thrust of the firm or its business units, such as share building or share maintaining, is built around assumptions about the industry. As we have noted, these assumptions are influenced by changes in the environment. Environmental analysis often signals the need for changes in strategic thrust by opening up pathways to gain market share or by rendering share maintaining strategies obsolete.[6]

Functional Level Strategy

Functional level strategy creates the framework for management of functions such as finance, research and development, and marketing-so that they support the business-level strategy. For example, if the business-unit strategy calls for the development of a new product, the R&D department will create plans on how to develop that product.

Functional strategies are more detailed than organisational strategies and have shorter time horizons. Their purpose is three-fold: (1) top communicate short-term objectives, (2) to describe the actions needed to achieve short-term objectives, and (3) to create an environment that encourages their achievement.[7] It is critical that lower level managers participate in the development of functional strategies so that they will better understand what needs to be done and feel more committed to the strategy.

Environmental Impact on Functional Level Strategy

Microenvironmental change has implications for the functional-level strategies of an organisation, over and beyond the business strategy. Any change in macroenvironment shall necessitate changes in how various functional strategies are performed. Traditionally, these functional changes are regarded as operating issues within the context of strategic management. Environmental changes offer opportunities for enhancing the operating capabilities of firms, as well as rendering some capabilities obsolete. Such enhancement of capabilities often accumulates over time, and these capabilities may become distinctive competencies that firms can wield to their advantage.[8]

Resource Analysis

Before formulating strategies the organisations' resources must be analysed. This analysis is necessary to identity the organisation's competitive advantages and disadvantages, its strengths and weaknesses relative to its present and likely future competitors. The question is not "what do we do well or poorly?" but rather "what are we doing better or worse than anyone else?"[9]

TYPES OF STRATEGIES

Be it corporate, unit or functional level, strategies can be any of four types: (i) Strengths and opportunities (SO), (ii) Weakness and opportunities strategies (WO), (iii) Strengths and threats strategies (ST) and; (iv) Weakness and threats strategies (WT). Table 39.2 illustrates the four types. It may be understood that the four types of strategies are derived from the TOWS matrix, a variant of SWOT matrix. In Table 39.2, the first, second, third and fourth are SO, WO, ST and WT strategies respectively.

SO strategies seek to use a firm's internal strengths to take advantage of external opportunities. Managers would like their companies to be in a position in which internal strengths can be leveraged to take advantage of external trends and events. Organisations generally pursue other strategies to get into a situation in which they can apply SO strategies., When a firm has major weaknesses, it strives to

Table 39.2 **Matching Key External and Internal Factors to Formulate Alternative Strategies**

Key Internal Factor		*Key External Factor*		*Resultant Strategy*
Excess working capacity (an internal strength)	+	20% annual growth in the cell phone industry (an external opportunity)	=	Acquire Cellfone, Inc.
Insufficient capacity (an internal weakness)	+	Exit of two major foreign competitors from the industry (an external opportunity)	=	Pursue horizontal integration by buying competitors' facilities
Strong R&D expertise (an internal strength)	+	Decreasing numbers of younger adults (an external threat)	=	Develop new products for older adults
Poor employee morale (an internal weakness)	+	Strong union activity (an external threat)	=	Develop a new employee benefits package

(**Source:** Fred R.David, *Strategic Management*, Pearson, 2003, p.200)

convert them into strengths. When there are major threats, the firm seeks to avoid them in order to concentrate on opportunities.

WO strategies aim at improving internal weaknesses by taking advantage of external opportunities. Often, internal weaknesses prevent a firm from seizing and exploiting opportunities existing in external environment. Technology may be one such weakness. Environment around the firm offers immense opportunities, but lack of technical expertise prevents it from explaining them.

ST strategies use a firm's strengths to ward off external threats. Texas Instruments, for example, used its legal department to collect nearly $700 million in damages and royalties from nine Japanese and Korean companies that infringed on patents for semiconductor memory chips.

WT strategies are defrusive tactics directed at reducing internal weakness and avoiding external threats. A firm faced with external threats and internal weaknesses tends to be in a precarious situation. In fact, such a company may have to fight for its survival, merge, retrench, declare bankruptcy, or choose liquidation.

Institutionalising the Strategy

Corporate level, business-level and functional level strategies provide important means of communicating what must be done to implement the overall strategy. By translating long-term intentions into short-term guides to action, they make the strategy operational. But the strategy must also be institutionalised, must permeate the very day-to-day life of the company if it is to be effectively implemented.

Three organisational elements provide the fundamental, long-term means for institutionalising the firm's strategy: (1) structure, (2) leadership, and (3) culture. Successful implementation requires effective management and integration of these three elements to ensure that strategy "takes hold" in the daily life of the firm.[10]

Strategy Implementation

Formulating a strategy is not enough. It must be implemented. Two things are relevant in this context. First, successful strategy implementation depends in part on the organisation's structure. Second, the strategy must be operationalised, or translated into specific policies, procedures, and rules that will guide planning and decision making by managers and employees.

Structure and Strategy: Effectiveness of strategy depends in part on how well it is implemented. Strategy implementation in turn depends on how the organisation's activities are divided, organised and coordinated - in short, on the structure of the organisation.

There exists close relationship between organisational effectiveness and structures as postulated by McKinsey & Co. in their famous Seven-S model (see Fig.39.6)

Figure 39.6 **The Seven-S Model**

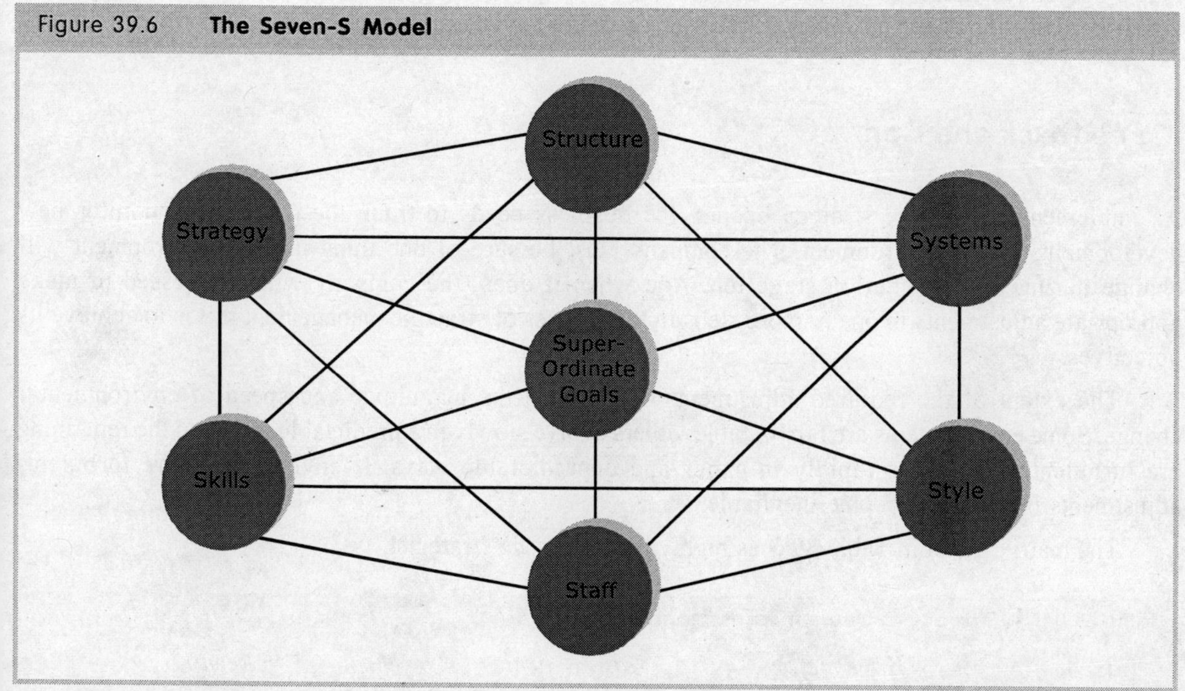

The firm of consultants found that neglecting any one of seven key factors could lead to doomed strategies. As the Fig.39.6 illustrates, each of these factors is equally important and interacts with all other factors. Any number of circumstances may dictate which of the factors will be the driving force in the execution of any particular strategy.

Operationalising Strategy: A strategy needs to be translated into the organisation's day-to-day operations. Operational plans fall into two general classes: single use plans and standing plans.

Single Use Plans: Single use plans are designed to be dissolved once they have achieved specific, non-recurring goals. Single-use plans are not likely to be repeated. The example for a single-use plan is a company which is expanding rapidly and which desires to set up a new warehouse. It needs a single-use plan for the warehouse.

The major single-use plans are programmes, projects, and budgets. A programmne is a single-use plan that covers a relatively large set of activities. It shows (1) the major steps required to reach an objective, (2) the organisation unit or member responsible for each step, and (3) the order and timing of each step. Projects are smaller, separate portions of programmes; they are limited in scope and contain distinct directives concerning assignments and time. If the programme is to transfer inventory from one warehouse to another, one related project might be to evaluate floor space at the proposed installation. Budgets are statements of financial resources set aside for specific activities in a given period of time; they are primarily devices to control an organisation's activities, and thus are important components of programmes and projects.

Standing Plans: Whenever organisational activities occur repeatedly, a single decision or set of decisions can effectively guide those activities. Once established, standing plans allow managers to conserve time because similar situations are handled in a predetermined, and consistent manner. For example, a bank manager can easily handle a loan request form depending on the criteria laid down for approvals.

Major types of standing plans are policies, procedures and rules. A policy is a general guideline for decision making. It sets up boundaries around decisions, telling managers which decisions can be made and which cannot. A procedure is a set of detailed guidelines to carry out a policy. It provides a detailed set of instructions for performing a sequence of actions that occurs often or regularly. Rules are statements that a specific action must or must not be taken in a given situation. They are the most explicit of standing plans; they are not guides to thinking or decision making, but substitute for them.

Feedback and Control

As implementation of the strategy occurs, the business needs to track the results and monitor new developments in the environment. The company must be sure of one thing that the environment will change during implementation stage too. And when it does, the company will be pressed to make appropriate adjustments in one or more steps in the process of strategic management if it is to achieve its objectives.

The extent of the required adjustments depends on the magnitude and speed of environmental change. Some environments are fairly stable, others evolve slowly in a predictable way, and the remaining are turbulent and change rapidly in major and unpredictable ways. If environments are turbulent, adjustments in strategy become inevitable.

The matrix given in Table 39.3 as highly helpful to the strategist.

Table 39.3 **A Strategy-Evaluation Assessment Matrix**

Have major changes occurred in the firm's internal environment?	*Have major changes occurred in the firm's external environment?*	*Has the firm progressed substantially towards achieving its stated objectives?*	*Result*
No	No	No	Take corrective actions
Yes	Yes	Yes	Take corrective actions
Yes	Yes	No	Take corrective actions
Yes	No	Yes	Take corrective actions
Yes	No	No	Take corrective actions
No	Yes	Yes	Take corrective actions
No	Yes	No	Take corrective actions
No	No	Yes	Continue present strategic course

(**Source:** Fred R.David, *Strategic Management*, p.305).

POLITICAL STRATEGY

Companies often use political strategies to support their corporate, business and functional strategies. Political strategy is understood as a set of actions designed to influence actors in the external arena of a company. Environmental changes have implications for political strategy. These implications may be discussed at two levels: (1) stakeholders and (2) political strategies.

Political strategy is a set of actions designed to influence actors in the external areas of a firm.

The company's stakeholders are those groups who can directly or indirectly place demands on the organisation. Environmental change, however, can affect the company's stakeholders and their demands and, thus, the organisation's requisite political strategy-in atleast two ways. First, it can give rise to new stakeholders, who frequently place new types of demands on the company, can cause the demands of existing stakeholders to change, or can increase the intensity of the existing demands. Second, differing degrees of connectedness exist among potential and current stakeholders. These often take the form of networks or coalitions. Environmental changes create new networks and coalitions which in turn will have their own impact on organisations.

Through its impact on stakeholders and their demands, environmental change affects the political tactics (i.e. actions and moves) used by companies. It influences the objectives (i.e. the focus of the tactics), the nature of the tactics (i.e., what tactics are employed), the intent of the tactics and the timing of the tactics.

QUESTIONS

1. What is integration of environmental segments? How is the integration achieved?
2. How does environmental analysis become part of strategic management?
3. What is strategic management? Explain the process of strategic management.
4. What impact does environment have on each phase of strategic management?

REFERENCES

1. John A.Pearce and Richard B.Robinson, *Strategic Management*, Richard D.Irwin, 1988, p.22.
2. Cited in *Management* by Stoner and Freeman, 1994, p.198.
3. Fahey and Narayanan, *Macroenvironmental Analysis for Strategic Management*, West Pub.Co., 1986, p.196.
4. E.R.Gray and L.R.Seltzer, *Management*, MacMillan, 1990, p.224.
5. Fahey and Narayanan, *op.cit*., p.197.
6. *Ibid*, p.195.
7. Stoner and Freeman, *op.cit*, p.206.
8. Fahey and Narayanan, *op.cit*., p.193.
9. Stoner and Freeman, *op.cit*., p.193.
10. Pearce and Robinson, *op.cit*., p.57.

Subject Index

A

Accommodation strategy 538
Acherman's model 535-539
Action stage 47
Actual sickness 341
Adjudication 336
Administrative survaillance 473
Adverse strategy 537
Agri exports 433
Agriculture 94
— Role of 431-434
— Extent of output 435
— Problems of 435-439
— Agenda for action 440
Agriculture and society 434
Ancillaries 452
Antidumping measures 96
Arbitration 335
Attitudes 515
Attracting foreign capital 79
— Measures to 79
— Implication for India 81
Audi Alteram partem 258
Authoritarianism 144
Authority 520

B

Badla charge 394
Balance Sheet for India 104
Balanced Regional Development 444
— Meaning of 444
— Critical for Backwardness 445
— Causes for Backwardness 445-46
— Measures to Remove Regional imbalances 449-452
— Failure of Regional Planning 453-454
— Suggestions to rename imbalances 454
Bank rate 411
Banking policy 453
BCG Model 652
Benefits of Stock Exchanges
— To Company 392
— To Investors 392
BIFR Scheme 654
Bigbull 390
Bioprofessional managers 126
BOPs 486
BOT 486
Budget 426
Bullish 394
Business
Nature of 1
— Scope of 2
— Characteristics 2-6
— Objectives 6-12
— Critics of 13-14
Business and Society
— Ecology and business 565-580
— Women and Business Opportunities 580-586
— Child Labour and Business 586-590
— Consumarisation 590-593
— Rural Development 593-594
— Mokets and people 594-596
— Physically Handicapped 596-597
— AIDS 597-600
Business culture 507
Business Ethics
— Nature of 603
— Sources of 603-605
— Importance of 605-606
— Are businessmen ethical 606-609
— Ethical Dilemmas 609-610
— Managing ethics 610-615
Business participation in Cultural affairs
— Cross-cultural literacy 528-529
— Managing Diversity 529-531
Buyer power 21

C

CAD/CAM 128
Call/Notice Money 419
Capital account 486
Capital Account Transaction 248
Capital budget 427
Capital receipt 427
Capitalism 191
Cash reserve ratio (CRR) 412
Categorization of industries 211
— Private 211
— Schedule A 211
— Schedule B 211
Causes of sickness 342-350
Cellular services 372

Central Boards 290
Certificate of Deposit (CDs) 420
Chain of networks 70
Check board organization 70
Claims and counter claims 202
Classification of Companies
— Public 253
— Private 253
— Foreign 253
— Government 253
— Company limited by guarantee 253
— Unlimited 254
— Holding and Subsidiary 254
Clearing House 406
Code of ethics 611-613
Coercive and Inductive control 170
Collective Bargaining 335
Collectivism 516
Combination Strategy 654
Commencement of business 255
Commercial Banks 422
Commercial Bills 419
Commercial Paper (CPs) 420-21
Communications 358
Communism 192
Company 251
Company Law Board 257
Companies Act
— Evaluation of 250
— Meaning of companies 250
— Definition of companies 250
— Classification of Companies 252-253
— Formation of Company 254
— Company Law 256
— Administration 256
— Some observations of 257
— Amendment bill 260
— Simplifying 263
Competition Act, 2002
— Objective 233
— Provisions 233
Competitive advantage 540
Competitive rivalry 21
Competitiveness 44
Concentric Diversification 653
Concepts of Wages
— Minimum wage 338
— Fair wage 338
— L:iving wage 338
Conciliations 336
Conglomerate Diversification 653
Constitution 157
Consumer protection act 590
Consumerism 590
Continuous process technology 129
Contraction of money 411
Control of Prices
— Demand management 457
— Supply management 457-459
Corporate accountability 547
Corporate Culture and Ethical Climate 615-616
— Improving 616-619
Corporate ethics 609
Corporate Governance
— Nature of 621
— The Context 622-623
— Factors influencing 623-625
— Mechanisms of 625-632
— The Present 632-633
— The Future 633
Corporate level strategy 651
Cosmocorp 31
Credit Control Measures 411
— General 411-412
— Bank rate 411
— Open market operations 411
— CRR 412
— SLR 412
— Refinance Policy 412
— Selective credit controls 413
— Minimum Margin 413
— Fixing ceiling 413
— Charging discrimination rates of interest 413
— Morel suasion 413
— Direct action 413
Cross boarder acquisition 59
CSR 533, 535
Cultural manifestations 512-513
Cultural resources 526-527
Culture 604
Culture and glabalisation 510-511
Cultures Environment
— Nature of 506-507
— Levels of 507-508
— Impact on business 508-528
Curative measures of sickness 348-351
Current account 486
Current Account Transaction 248

D

Decade Plus Years on Reforms
— Growth of the Economy 499
— Sustainability 499
— Economic Prospects 499-501
— State of Poverty 501
— Access to water and sanitation 501
— Status of Health 501
— Sound sector 502
— Emerging techniques 502
— New agricultural varities 502
Deforestation 566
Democracy 143
Democratic 159
Demutualisation 406
Deregulation 633
Desirable corporate governance 631
Developing economies 63
Developmental Banks 412
— Meaning of 377
— Institutions 377
— Operations and Trends 379-380
— Critical assessment 380-384
Developmental imports 469
DFHI 421-422
Direct and indirect control 170
Direct investment 58
Directive principles 161
Disintermediation 633
Disinvestment 296
Disinvestment Commission 304
Dispute Settlement Methods
— Collective Bargaining 335
— Code of dispute 335
— Grievance procedure 335
— Arbitration 335
— Conciliation 336
— Adjudication 336
Dispute Settlement Procedure 97
Diversification 651
Diversity advantage 530
Downsizing 59
Dry land forming 441-442
Dual prices 458

E

E – Business 132
E – Commerce 132
Ecology 564
Economic cost 593
Economic Environment
— Nature of 189
— Importance of 189
— Factors 190
Economic Factors
— Growth strategy 190
— Economic system 191
— Economic planning 195
— Industry 196
— Human resource 200
Economic planning 195
Economic system 191
Economics of scale 110
Education 518-519
Effect of sickness 344
Elements of Banking system 422
ELOB 404
Employment 270
Energy 358,361
— Includes 358
— Sources of 361-362
Entry stage 47
Entry strategies 55-56
— Exports and Imports 56
— Tourism and Transportation 57
— Performance Services 57
— Use of Assets 57
— Franchising 58
— Direct Investment 58
Entry Threats 18
Environment 16
— Forces of 16
— Internal 16
— Technological 16, 53, 113
— Economic 17, 53
— Political 17
— Global 17
— Social-Cultural 18, 53
— Analysis of 23
Environment analysis 23, 646-647
— Steps 23, 24
— Linkages 24
— Benefits of 24, 25
— Limitations of 25, 26
Environmental Factors 19
Equal – access voucher 295
Ethical climate 615
Ethical Dilemmas
— Face-to-face ethics 609

— Corporate policy ethics 609
— Functional areas of ethics 610
Ethical training programme 613
Ethics 522, 603
Ethics committee 613
European Union 63
Exchange rate management 486
Executive or Government
— Business responsibilities to 145
— Responsibilities to business 147
Exit policy 353
— Arguments for 353-55
— Arguments against 355-56
Expansion of money 410-411
Export earnings of PSEs 272
Exports 56
Exit Barriers 18
Extended hands 70
Extent of money 409-410
Extent of sickness 341
External sector 469
Externalities 169

F

Face-to-face ethics 609
Facilities to SSIs
— Policies and incentives 311
— Economic reforms 312
— Infrastructure 312
— Industrial centers 312
— Marketing 312
— Pollution control 313
— Women Entrepreneurs 313
— Central Government Network 313
— Credit dispensation 314
Factor conditions 540
Fair rate of return 463
Fair wage 338
Family 519-520
FDI 32, 58, 59, 62
— Reasons for the flow of 60
— Flow of 63
FEMA 81, 248
FEMA Act, 1999
— Scope of 248
— Provisions 248-249
FERA 235
— Objectives of 235
— Scope 235
— Provisions of 236-238
— Reflections of 238
— Amendment to 242
— FERA to FEMA 247
Final Act 93
Financial Institutions 377
Financial sector 377
Fine Forces Frame Work 20
Fiscal measures 457
Fiscal Policy 426
— Meaning of 426
— The Budget 426
— The Union Budget 426-427
— Trends in Expenditure 428-430
— Evolution of 430
— Agenda for Future 430
FMS 133
Forces driving CSR 539-541
Forecasting 24
Foreign Banks 425
Foreign company 253
Foreign investment 214
Foreign Technology Agreements 214
Foreign Trade
— Nature of 468
— Economic Development from 469-472
— Significance 472-475
— Export strategy 475-478
— Imports 478
— Regulation of 478
— Exim Policy 2002-2007 478-483
Form output 435
Formal and Informal Control 170
Fortiori 258
Franchising 58
Functions of Stock Exchange 391
Fundamental rights 160
Future shock 115

G

GATS 96
GATT 89
GATT to WTO 94
GE Model 652
Geocorp 31
Global corporation 35
Global Envrionment 110-111
— Scanning of 111
— Monitoring 111
— Forecasting 111
— Assessment 111

Global industry 52
Globalisation 28, 543
— Meaning of 28
— Dimensions as 29
— Drivers of 31
Good control system 175
Govt. company 253
Green field investment 59
Grievance procedure 335
Growth centers 452
Growth rate of public sector 270
Growth strategy 190
GSP 104

H

Handicraft sector 323
Health and safety measures 94
Heimsker 640
High control 515
Holding and subsidiary company 254

I

IDR Act, 1951 220
— Objectives 220
— Scope of 221
— Provisions 221
Imports 56
Incipient sickness 341
India's Global Trade 73
India's strengths and weaknesses 85
— Reverse FDI Flow 86
— Transference 90
— Reciprocity 90
Indian joint venture 58
Indian Railways 363-367
Individualism 516
Industrial Disputes
— Meaning of 330
— Causes for 331
— Settlement methods of 334
Industrial Labour
— Importance of 325
— Extent of 325
— Changes in 325
Industrial Licensing 219
— Objectives of 219
— Legislature Framework 220
— Criticisms of 222
Industrial Licensing Policy 213
Industrial Policy 208, 210
— Meaning 208
— Objectives 210
— Rationale of 209
— Resolution of 1948 209
Industrial policy 1956 210
Industrial Policy 1991
— Objectives 212
— Industrial licensing 213
— Foreign Investment 214
— Foreign Technology 214
— Public Sector Policy 215
— MRTP Act 216
— Merits of 217
— Limitations of 217
Industrial policy 1999 212
Industrial production 196
Industrial scapegoat 570
Industrial Sickness 340
— Definition of 340
— Extent of 341
— Causes for 342-344
— Effect of 344
— Remedies 345-350
Industrialisation and Economic Development 273
Industry 196
Infrastructure 148, 358
— Includes 358
— Growth of 358-360
Infrastructure facility 322
Innocenti plant 284
Institutionalization 633
Integration of Segments 645-646
— Objectives 645
— Steps involved in 645-646
International Business
— Players in 34
— Challenges of 44-50
International Theory 59
Internet services 372
Intuition 617
Investment Flows 74
— Reasons for Poor 76
Inward flows 75
Inward oriented strategy 471
IRDP 593
Iron of Fate 284
Irrigation 441
Islamic Law 150

Issues management 546
Isteem 150

J

Janakiraman Committee 301
Jobbers 394
Joint venture 58
Judicial Activism 154
Judicial powers 152
Judiciary
— Social Laws 149
— Powers 152
— Activism 154

K

Karve Committee 309
Khadi and village industries 323

L

Laissery faire 176
Learning strategy 538
Levels of Culture
— National 507
— Business 507
— Organisational 507
— Occupational 507
Levels of Strategy
— Corporate level 651-654
— Business level 654-655
— Functional level 655
Liberty 159
License 219
Limited liability 251
Liquidation 653
Living wage 338
Locational advantage 61
Low control 514

M

Maintenance imports 469
Major Innovations 114
Management Buyout 295
Management of Technology 133
Managing diversity 46, 48, 531
Managing Ethics
— Top management 610-611
— Code of ethics 611-613
— Ethics committees 613
— Ethics hotlines 613
— Ethics Training Programmes 613
— Ethics and Law 615
Mandiwala 394
Market potential 53
Marxism 192
Marxists 14
Mass production technology 129
McKinsy model 652
MEN 90
MFA 104
Michael E.Porter 654
Micro risk 54
Minimum wage 338
Mixed sector 209
MMMF 417
MNC 29, 31, 34, 35
— Indian MNCs 36
— Benefits of 36, 37, 38
— Problems brought by 37
Monetary measures 457
Monetary Policy 408
— Meaning of 408
— Nature of 409
— Extent of 409-410
— Expansion of Money 410
— Contraction of Money 411
— General controls 411-413
— Selective credit controls 413
— Evoluation of 413-414
— Structural adjustments 414-415
Money Market 415
— Meaning of 415
— Functions of 415-416
— Growth of 416-417
— Operations in 418-420
Moral idealism 617
MOU 287
MRTP Act 1969
— Objectives 226
— Regulation of trade practices 226
MTPs 227
— Meaning of 227
— Regulation of 228
— Examples of 227
Multiprofessional managers 126

N

Narasimhan Committee on DFIS
— Appreciation of 385

— Weaknesses of 386
— Recommendations of 386
National culture 507
National income 199
National Reward Fund (NRF)
— Establishment of 356
— Eligible units under 356
— Operation of 357
Natural Environment
— Nature of 636
— Impact on Business 637-642
— Analysis of 643
Natural pollution 565
New Economic Policy
— Background to the 490-491
— New Policy 491
— Evaluation of 491-497
New technology 135
Nirma 515
Normal trade relations 90
NPAs 316
NRF 356
Nucleus plant 452

O

Occupational culture 508
Omkar Goswami Committee on sickness 351
Open market operations 411
Operationalising Strategy 657
Opportunities 649
Opportunity cost 593
Orderly growth 148
Organisation Structure 66
— Factors Affecting 66
— International Division 67
— World Wide functional 67
— Geographic Area 67
— Product Organisation 68
— Mixed Structure 69
— Matrix Structure 69
Organisational commitment 538
Organizational culture 508
Outward oriented strategy 471
Ownership Pattern
— Ministry 290
— Departmental undertaking 290
— Statutory Corporation 290
— Central Boards 290
— Companies 290

P

PDS 458, 457-459
Per capita income 199
Performance Contracting 287
Political Environment Analysis 186
Political Institutions
— Legistature 145
— Executive 145
— Judiciary 145
Political Pholosoplies 143
— Democracy 143
— Totalitarianism 143
Political risk 54
Political Strategy 658
Political System 143
Pollution 135
Population trend 201
Portfolio planning 652
Pot – pourri 258
Preventive measures of sickness 345-348
Price Controls
— Objective of 456
— Control of 456-459
— PDS 459-465
— Problems of 462-463
Private company 253
Private Sector Banks 425
Private sector units 211
Privatisation 293
— Meaning of 293
— History of 293
— Nature and objectives of 294
— Role of 294
— Arguments against 297
— Rangarajan Committee on 304
Product life cycle theory 61
Production strategy 538
Productivity 121
Profit maximization 543
Promotional and Regulatory control 171
Public company 253
Public Distribution System (PDS)
— Rational of 459
— Goods to be included 459-460
— Supplies to 460
— Forms of 460
— Success of the 460-461
— Measures to Strengthen 461
— Revamped 462

— Measures to improve 464
— Who benefits from 465
Public goods 169
Public Sector Enterprises 265
— Definition of 265
— Objectives of 266
— Evolution of 266
— Rationale for 267
— Growth and Role of 267
— Performance 276
— Ownership pattern 290
— Industrial Policy Statement on 291
Pure Democracy 143

R

R & D 121
Rangarajan Committee 304
— Recommendations of 386
Reactionaries 14
Refinance policy 413
Religion 523-524
Remedies of sickness 345-350
Reorganisation 654
Republican 143
Resistance to change 130
Resistance strategy 538
Resource Analysis 655
Retrenchment 653
Reva SWOT analysis 648-649
Revenue budget 427
Revenue receipt 427
Reverse FDI FLOW 86
Road Transport 368-369
Routes of Privatisation
— Site to outsiders 294
— Management Buyout 295
— Equal-access voucher 295
— Spantaneous 295
RTPs 228
— Meaning of 228
— Regulations of 229
— Examples of 229
Rural credit 441

S

Safety valves 90
Sanctimonious 607
Scam 390
Schedule A Industries 211
Schedule B Industries 211
SCM 96
SCRA Act, 1956 395
Second generation reforms 497-498
Secular Totalitarianism 144
Securities law 626
Selective Credit controls 413
Separate Legal Entity 251
Seven signs of privatization 302
Seven-S Model 657
Shipping 370-371
Short selling 394
Sick unit 340
Signals of sickness 343-344
Single Use Plans 657
Small batch technology 128
Small firm effects 70
Small Scale Industry (SSI)
— Meaning 306
— Growth of 307
— Significance of 307
— Facilities for 311
— Problems and Remedials 315
Small sector industrial policy 320
SO Strategies
Social amalgam 326
Social audit 539, 546
Social change 119
Social cost 593
Social forecasting 546
Social Institutions 136
Social Responsibility 533
— Meaning of 533
— Models of 535-539
— Forces driving 539-541
— Arguments for 541-543
— Arguments against 543-544
— Prominence of CSR 545
— Barriers to CSR 545
— Implications of CSR 546
— Limits to 549
— Common characteristics of 549-550
— The evolving idea of 550-551
Social scanning 546
Social security 338
Socialism 192
Socialist 158
Socialist Law 154

Sources of Business Ethics
— Religion 604
— Cultural Experience 604
— The legal system 605
Sovereign 158
Speculation 394
— Nature of 394
— Types of 394
ST Strategies
Stakeholders 659
Standing Plans 657
Star status countries 84
State Intervention 168-183
— Reasons for 168
— Types of 170
— Extent of 171
Statutory audit 621
Statutory Corporations 290
Statutory Liquidity Ratio (SLR) 412
Stock Exchanges 390
— Nature of 390
— Functions of 391
— Benefits of 391
— Growth of 393
— Dealings of 393
— Organisation of 394
— Positive features of 399
— Negative features of 399-404
— Reforms in 404-406
Strategic Management 649
— Meaning of 650
— Process of 650
— Benefits of 650
— Level of strategy 651
— Impact of Environment 651-654
— Types of strategies 655-658
Strategy 12
Strategy formulation 650
Strengths 647
Structural adjustments 490
Structure and Strategies 658
Structure of WTO 93
Sukhamoy chakrvarthy committee 413
Supernational enterprise31
Supplier power 21
Supply management 457-459
Sustainable development 580
SWOT 320
SWOT analysis 647
Systems of Laws
— Islamic Law 150
— Common Law 151
— Civil Law 151

T

Tariffs and Quotes 149
Tax reforms 633
Technological discontinuity 123
Technological Environment 113
— Features of 115
— Impact of 116
— Technology Status 136
— Analysis of 140
— Science and Technology Policy 2003, 138
Technology 5, 113
Technology and Economy 121
Technology and plant 128
Technology and society 117
Technology transfer 149
Tejiwala 394
Telecommunications 372-375
Textiles and clothing 95
The Age of Discontinuity 293
The Essential Commodities Act, 1955
— Objectives of 465
— Scope of 465
— Definition of Essential Commodities 466
— Provisions of 466-467
The Preamble 157
— Souerign 158
— Socialist 158
— Secular 159
— Democratic 159
— Republic 159
— Liberty 159
— Fraternity 159
Theocracy 144
Theoretic Totalitarianism 144
Theory of authority 603
Theory of Moral unity 603
Threat of
— Substitute 21
— Entrants 21
Time for change 163
Tiny enterprises 320
Top 10 PSEs 272
Tortured childhood 587
Totalitarianism 143, 144

TQM 130
Trade barriers 109
Trade creation 108,109
Trade diversion 109
Trade in Services
— Includes 483
— Determinants of 483-484
— Promoting 484-485
Trade Union Movement 237
Trading Blocks 107
— Impact of 108
Transparency 90
Transport 358,363
— Includes 358
Treasury Bills 419
Treats 649
Trends in Trade Union 328
Tribal Totalitarianism 144
TRIMS 96
TRIPS, 89, 95
Tsunami 637
Types of Intervention
— Formal and Informal 170
— Coercive and Inductive 170
— Direct and Indirect 170
— Promotion and Regulatory 171
Types of Strategies
— SO strategies 655—656
— WO strategies 656
— ST strategies 656
— WT strategies 656

U

Unfair labour practices 332
Unfair Trade Practices (UTPs)
— Concept of 231
— Conditions of 231
— Examples 231
— Regulation of 231
Union budget 426
Union rivalry 332
Unlimited company 254
Utilitarianism 617
UTPs 231

V

Vertical Integration 653
Village industries 322
Vision 6

W

Wage Demands 332
Wage Policy 336
Weaknesses 647-648
Wholly owned subsidiary 59
WLL (M) 372
WO Strategies
Work ethic 515
World stage 47
WT Strategies
WTO 89
— Principles of 89
— Functions of 91
— Structure 92
— Misunderstanding about 92
— Arguments for Joining 101-012
— Arguments against membership 102
— Review of Performance 105

Company and Name Index

3G 21
ABB 33, 38
ACC 599
ACM 107
AFTA 108
AIG 35
AMU 107
ANCOM 107
ANZ CERT 108
Apeejay 560
ASEAN 108
ASSOCHAM 357
Bajaj 4, 559
Banker America 35, 108
Basham 177
Bata 38
Bharat Gold Mines 277
BHEL 268
BIFR 277
Birlas 555
BP 35
CACM 107
Cadbury 631
Cannon 30
CARE 421
CARICOM 107
CBDT 351
CEAO 108
CEE AC 107
CFTI 313
Chandaria Group 561
CII 75,314
City Group 35
Coke 39
CPC International 38
CRISIL 421
CWEI 314
Cycle Corporation of India 277
Daewoo 203
DEC 38
Deepak Nayyar 180
Desail 256
Deshmukh 256
DGS & D 311
DICs 313
Dr. Ambedkar 161
E&FC 488
EC 107
ECOWS 107
EFTA 107
Ericsson 21
Essar Group 556
EU 32
Exxon Mobil 35
FASB 259
FATT 32
FCI 274, 459
FICCI 314
Ford Motor 7, 35
Fuji Xerox 61
GATT 89
GCC 107
GE 31, 35
GICI 356
Gittelte 38
GM 34, 35, 36, 131
Godrej 557
Group Bull 38
Hair Group 34
Hero Honda 558
Hidaya Hulla 160
HLL 558
HP 615
HSBC 35
IBM 30, 38, 52, 131
ICRA 421
ICSI 314
IIMA 9
IMF 301, 486
Infosys 7
Intel 35
ISRO 149
ITC 560
ITT 37
KFC 55, 83, 619
L&T 557
LAIA 107
LERMS 487
LIC 3
LOC 268, 460
M&M 558
Mafatlal 560
McKinesy 4, 39
MERCO SUR 32, 107

Microsoft 35
Mistubishi 35
MNC 29, 31, 34, 35
MNE 34, 35
Morocco 89
Motorola 21
MRA 108
MRF 588
MRTP 196, 216
Muragappa Chettiar Group 561
Mysore Tobacco Co 152
NAFTA 32, 107
Nagaland Pulp & Paper Co 277
Nani Palkhivala 161
Narmada Dam 595-596
NCCF 460
Nehru 164
Nokia 21
Norton 26
NPC 313
NRF 288
NSCC 406
NSE 399
NTT 30
OECS 107
Oil & Natural Gas 268
ONGC 268
OTCEI 399
P&G 38, 42
Pizza Hut 55
PPDCs 313
Prizer 35
PTA 107
RAMCO 559
Rank Xerox 61
RCA 60
RDE 33
Reva 648
Royal Dutch 35
RTCs 313
RTZ-CRA 41
SACU 107
SAIL 1, 268
SaintGobin 26
SAPTA 108
SFCs 313
Shri Ram 562
SIDBI 313
SIDCs 313
SIDO 313
SIEMENS 34
SIICs 313
Singer Corporation 38
Singhania 556
SISIs 313
SSIDCs 313
Tata 4, 10, 12, 36, 147, 203
Tata Iron & Steel 274
Tatas 555
TCI Bhorukia Group 561
TCOs 313
Thapar Group 557
TISCO 1
TNC 34, 35
Toyota 7, 30, 62
TRIPS 89, 95
TVS 558
UERS 488
UNCTAD 75
UNICEFs 589
Union Carbide Corporation 48
Usha Martin 558
VDEAC 108
Videocon 556
Vodophone 21
Wal-Mart Stores 35
WDR 180
WTO 32, 46, 89
Xerox 11, 127
Yahoo 35